Personal Finance and Investments

'The reader should not expect to find unambiguous answers to all the many questions concerning personal finance and investments,' Keith Redhead argues in the preface to this new textbook, thus underlining the role personal judgement plays in personal finance and investments. Personal judgement should be informed by many perspectives; hence his interdisciplinary approach to the study of personal finance and investments. In this book, the author draws from finance, psychology, economics and other disciplines in business and the social sciences, recognising that personal finance and investments are subjects of study in their own right rather than merely branches of another discipline.

Considerable attention is given to some topics, which are either ignored or given very little attention in other texts. These include:

- the psychology of investment decision-making
- stock market bubbles and crashes
- property investment
- the use of derivatives in investment management
- regulation of investments business.

More traditional subject areas are also thoroughly covered, including:

- investment analysis
- portfolio management
- capital market theory
- market efficiency
- international investing
- bond markets
- institutional investments
- option pricing
- macroeconomics
- the interpretation of company accounts.

Packed with over one hundred exercises, examples and exhibits and a helpful glossary of key terms, this book will help the reader to grasp the relevant principles of money management. The book avoids non-essential mathematics and provides a new approach to the study of personal finance and investments. The book will be essential for students and researchers engaged with personal finance, investments, behavioural finance, financial derivatives, and financial economics.

Keith Redhead is Principal Lecturer in the Department of Economics, Finance and Accounting at Coventry University Business School. He is also the author of *Introducing Investments: A Personal Finance Approach* and *Financial Derivatives: An Introduction to Futures, Forwards, Options and Swaps*.

Personal Finance and Investments

A behavioural finance perspective

Keith Redhead

Routledge
Taylor & Francis Group

LONDON AND NEW YORK

First published 2008
by Routledge
2 Park Square, Milton Park, Abingdon, Oxon OX14 4RN

Simultaneously published in the USA and Canada
by Routledge
711 Third Avenue, New York, NY 10017

Routledge is an imprint of the Taylor & Francis Group, an informa business

© 2008 Keith Redhead

Typeset in Perpetua by
Keystroke 28 High Street, Tettenwhall, Wolverhampton
Printed and bound by CPI Group (UK) Ltd, Croydon, CR0 4YY

British Library Cataloguing in Publication Data
A catalogue record for this book is available from the British Library

Library of Congress Cataloging in Publication Data
Redhead, Keith, 1949-
Personal finance and investments : a behavioural finance perspective / Keith Redhead.
p. cm.
Includes bibliographical references and index.
ISBN 978-0-415-42859-0 (hb) — ISBN 978-0-415-42862-0 (pb) — ISBN 978-0-203-89563-4
(eb) 1. Investments. 2. Finance, Personal. 3. Investment analysis. 4. Portfolio management. I. Title.
HG4521.R3655 2008
332.6—dc22
2007048856

ISBN10: 0–415–42859–9 (hbk)
ISBN10: 0–415–42862–9 (pbk)
ISBN10: 0–203–89563–0 (ebk)

ISBN13: 978–0–415–42859–0 (hbk)
ISBN13: 978–0–415–42862–0 (pbk)
ISBN13: 978–0–203–89563–4 (ebk)

For Sue, with love and thanks.

Contents

Detailed Contents

EXHIBIT 2.1: Mis-selling or miscommunication? Apparent mis-selling of financial products may be the result of different perceptions of risk between advisers and clients

EXHIBIT 7.1: An example of an investment fund that aims to track the FTSE 100 index

 EXHIBIT 9.1: Example of an investment trust using share buy-backs (share repurchases)

 EXHIBIT 9.2: M&G Fund of Investment Trust Shares

EXHIBIT 16.1: M&G Index Tracker Fund

 EXHIBIT 16.2: Example of a Socially Responsible Investment Fund

 EXHIBIT 16.3: Example of a Socially Responsible Investment Fund based on religious principles

 EXHIBIT 16.4: Example of an emerging markets fund

Preface

This book approaches personal finance from an investments perspective, and investments from a personal finance perspective. Texts in the area of finance tend to be either on corporate finance or investments. However the appropriate dichotomy may be between corporate finance and personal finance. Texts on personal finance would cover investments, as the current one does. In the future texts may emerge covering other aspects of personal finance such as saving and debt. The present text pays some attention to saving and debt, but the emphasis is on investments. This emphasis stems largely from the fact that there is far more academic literature on investing than on saving and borrowing. There are a few texts available specifically on personal finance with coverage of savings and debt, but unfortunately they tend to be at a relatively elementary level of analysis with little reference to the academic literature.

The current text differs from other texts on investments in a number of ways:

1. It recognises that investing is a behaviour, which can be analysed from the perspectives of a number of disciplines. Many investment texts are based solely on financial economics. When they allow another discipline into the analysis it is typically by means of a separate chapter, or section of a chapter, on behavioural finance. This entails a consideration of the implications of cognitive psychology. The present text does not separate behavioural finance into a separate chapter, but integrates it into many aspects of investing. It also goes beyond cognitive psychology and introduces the significance of a number of other disciplines such as social psychology, sociology, accounting, macroeconomics, politics, demography, gerontology, media studies, and marketing.
2. It uses less mathematics than most other texts. Although mathematics can provide rigour, it can also be a barrier to communication. Many readers find mathematics impenetrable, and can lose sight of the fundamental principles by being distracted by mathematical methodology. Furthermore mathematics can limit discussion to the measurable dimensions, whereas many important aspects of personal finance and investing are not measurable.
3. There has been an attempt to integrate the most recent (at the time of writing) literature into the discussion so that readers become acquainted with the most recent ideas and evidence.
4. The text recognises that personal finance is about money management. Correspondingly the concepts and principles covered are related to the money management problems of individual investors.
5. Many of the investment theories are illustrated by numerical examples.
6. The text has a UK orientation. Whilst non-UK residents can use the text to learn about the principles and processes of personal finance and investments, the institutional examples (e.g. savings schemes, pension schemes, and the regulatory framework) are UK-based. However about 95% of the text has universal relevance.
7. There are chapters dealing with issues that are important but rarely given emphasis in other texts. Examples include the psychology of financial decision-making, stock market bubbles and crashes, the significance of institutional investors, the purposes and processes of regulation,

property investment and finance, and alternative investments such as structured products and hedge funds.

8. The text recognises that most investment at the personal level is carried out through institutional investors. Consequently there is much more emphasis on institutional investors than is typically the case with other texts.

THEORY AND PRACTICE

This book should be useful to practitioners in the fields of personal finance and investments as well as to students. Sometimes practitioners dismiss theory as irrelevant to their needs. However an understanding of relevant theory can be of great assistance to practitioners. It is worth quoting from Cordell *et al.* (2006:78):

> Although academic research is often obtuse and unrealistic, many articles have implications that have relevance to the real world inhabited by practitioners. Plowing through the mathematics and statistics of some articles may be a stretch for most practitioners, but the inferences drawn from articles are often worthy of the financial service professional's time and effort. Indeed, many of the financial concepts used daily by practitioners . . . were born in academic articles.

This book incorporates the contributions of more than 800 recent articles, which are of relevance to both practitioners and academics. The intention has been to make the concepts and implications of those articles readily accessible to those who lack the time to devote to reading the articles themselves. However, the articles are referenced so the reader is able to refer to the articles where this is desired.

THE ONLY THING THAT IS CERTAIN IS UNCERTAINTY

The reader should not expect to find unambiguous answers to all the many questions concerning personal finance and investments. One of the reasons for ambiguity is the existence of differences in opinion. There is, in particular, a dichotomy between two schools of thought. One school is known as the traditional or neoclassical tradition (but which could be referred to as the arbitrage–optimisation tradition). According to this school of thought most people act rationally (or nearly so) and financial markets allow them to do so. Markets are expected to be accessible and investors should have equal access to information. Arbitrage and optimisation are important concepts in this tradition. The returns from investments are expected to be no more, nor less, than fair compensation for delaying expenditure and accepting risk. This is probably the dominant school of thought amongst academics.

The main alternative school of thought is referred to as behavioural. According to this approach people are frequently irrational and financial markets do not always provide conditions that permit rational investors to fully achieve their objectives. Sentiment plays a large part in this tradition. Practitioners are often more comfortable with this school of thought.

The reader may find that there are different answers to the same questions. This is to be expected, particularly when there are radically different ways of thinking about problems. The debates continue. It should not be assumed that one perspective is correct for all times and in all markets.

According to the efficient market hypothesis all investments are correctly priced since they reflect all relevant information (or are sufficiently accurately priced to preclude the possibility of profiting from mispricing). The debate about the efficient market hypothesis may seem arcane but it is central to the debate between the two main schools of thought. Traditional finance theory is largely premised on market efficiency. If financial markets were not efficient, the case for traditional finance theory would be weakened. It may be expected that degrees of efficiency vary from time to time and from market to market.

There are many financial market adages. One is: 'The only thing that is certain is uncertainty'. This applies not only to financial markets but also to the analysis and understanding of those markets.

Chapter 1

Introduction

OBJECTIVE

The objective of this chapter is to provide an understanding of:

1. The functions and operation of financial systems.
2. The nature of personal financial planning.
3. The nature of investment risk.

People save and invest for various purposes: for holidays, home improvements, cars, deposits for house purchase, children's education, old age, and general security. Some of these are short-term objectives and others long term. The single biggest long-term objective is usually the provision of a retirement income. The time horizon of the investment will influence the nature of the investment. Savings for a holiday are unlikely to be put into a risky investment such as shares. Saving for a pension is unlikely to be in low return investments such as bank or building society accounts.

The largest investment item for many people is their pension fund. At an annuity rate of 8% per annum (p.a.), a pension of £20,000 a year requires a pension fund of £250,000. Whether a pension is being provided by an employer or being funded by the employee, a substantial sum of money needs to be accumulated. So successful investing is vital.

The need to invest for retirement is becoming increasingly important as governments progressively back away from promising adequate state pensions. In Europe and North America, as well as elsewhere in the world, the proportion of retired people in the population is rapidly increasing. This is often called the demographic time bomb. In the United Kingdom (UK), for children born in 1901, the average life expectancy was 45 for males and 49 for females (Harrison 2005). Those born in 2002 had average life expectancies of 76 for males and 81 for females. Life expectancy is steadily increasing, and with it the average period of life in retirement. The result is a rising ratio of pensioners to workers. It is often seen to be unrealistic to expect those of working age to pay the increasingly high taxes needed to pay good pensions to members of the retired population. One answer is to encourage people to provide for their own pensions by accumulating pension funds during their working lives (another approach is to raise the retirement age).

Table 1.1 *Percentage of the population that is 65 or older*

	1960	2000
Italy	9.0	17.1
Japan	5.7	17.3
Germany	10.8	17.2
France	11.6	16.1
UK	11.7	15.6
US	9.2	12.6
Canada	7.6	12.5

According to a World Bank publication (Palacios and Pallares-Miralles 2000) the percentages of the populations of the UK, Germany, and France over 60 in 2000 were 20.7%, 20.6%, and 20.2% respectively. The expected percentages for 2030 were 30.1%, 36.35%, and 30.0% respectively. According to the US Census Bureau (1999), in Western Europe (the members of the European Union as of 1999) the ratio of people of retirement age (65+) to those of working age (20–64) was about 0.15 in 1950. By 2000 it had nearly doubled to 0.29. It is projected to approximately double again, to about 0.64, by 2050. The ratio of pensioners to people of working age would have risen from about 1 to 6 in 1950, to around 4 to 6 in 2050. It is clearly unrealistic to expect those of working age to be able, and willing, to pay sufficient taxation to provide so many retirees with adequate pensions. Table 1.1 shows some Organisation for Economic Cooperation and Development (OECD) figures that illustrate the ageing populations in a number of countries (derived from OECD population pyramids).

There is also the issue of how to invest. Stock market investments, particularly shares, are seen by many people to be too risky. However, historically shares have massively outperformed other forms of investment such as bank deposits. The issue of relative risk needs to be seen in relation to an investor's time horizon. The picture from a 40-year perspective is very different from that of a one-month perspective. Investments in shares can benefit from time diversification; over a long time span good periods can balance out bad periods. Also from a long-term perspective, the accumulated income from investments becomes more important in determining the final sum accumulated. For example £1,000 invested at 4% over 40 years will grow to £4,801, whereas at 8% it would grow to £21,725. The income receipts from stock market investments may be more stable than the interest receipts on bank or building society deposits.

According to the Barclays Capital Equity Gilt Study (1999; the study is updated annually on the Barclays Capital website), £100 invested in a balanced portfolio of UK shares in 1918 would have grown to nearly £420,000 by 1998 (with dividends, net of basic rate tax, being reinvested). An investment of £100 in Treasury bills over the same period would have grown to less than £2,500 (the Treasury bill rate of return is roughly equivalent to premium bank or building society deposits). These represent rates of return of approximately 11% p.a. and 4% p.a. respectively. When allowance is made for the effects of inflation on the purchasing power of money, the average rate of return from bank and building society deposits has not been far above zero. The message seems to be that the accumulation of wealth over long time periods, such as the periods typically required for the accumulation of pension funds, requires investments to be made in stock markets.

FUNCTIONS OF FINANCIAL SYSTEMS

A financial system can be looked upon as a combination of financial markets, institutions, and regulations that aim to perform a set of economic functions. Most of those functions have a direct bearing on investment decisions and behaviour. The functions might be regarded as the provision of means of:

1. Settling payments.
2. Investing surplus funds.
3. Raising capital.
4. Transferring funds from surplus units (savers) to deficit units (borrowers).
5. Managing financial risk.
6. Pooling resources.
7. Dividing ownership.
8. Producing information.
9. Dealing with incentive problems.

1. *Settling payments.* This refers to the mechanisms for making payments. Mechanisms include cash, cheques, credit cards, and so forth. This relates to investment only in so far as there needs to be a mechanism of paying for investments.
2. *Investing surplus funds.* This is the investment process. Investors have varied needs and wishes concerning risk, return, liquidity, and other characteristics of investments. A financial system should provide a wide range of investment choices so that individuals can satisfy their investment objectives.
3. *Raising capital.* Some people or organisations have expenditure that exceeds their income. They would need to raise capital by borrowing or selling shares. A financial system should provide suitable financial instruments for obtaining funds. Such instruments would include bank loans, various forms of bond, and various types of share.
4. *Transferring funds from surplus units to deficit units.* This brings functions 2 and 3 together. Not only should there be suitable financial instruments for investors and those raising capital, but there should be markets or intermediaries for bringing them together. For example banks are intermediaries that transfer money from investors who deposit money to borrowers who receive loans. Stock markets transfer money from investors, who buy shares or bonds, to the firms that issue the shares and bonds.
5. *Managing financial risk.* Most people or organisations that invest or raise funds face risks from price movements. For example an investor in shares will lose in the event of a fall in share prices. Financial systems should provide instruments for managing such risks. Risk management instruments include derivatives such as forwards, futures, swaps, and options. There are also other risks that need to be managed, such as default risk. Financial systems generate credit rating agencies that inform investors of the levels of such risks.
6. *Pooling resources.* When businesses and governments borrow they want to raise large sums of money. Individuals normally have small sums to invest. By pooling the small sums of a large number of individuals, large sums are made available to businesses and governments. The pooling of large numbers of small amounts is carried out by intermediaries such as banks, pension funds, and unit trusts.

3

7. *Dividing ownership.* When an investor buys shares in a company, the investor becomes part owner of the company. Share issuance is a means of dividing the ownership of a company among a large number of investors. The transfer of ownership to investors entails the transfer of risks as well as prospective profits.

8. *Producing information.* The most common form of information produced by financial systems is information about prices. This would include prices of shares, bonds, and money (interest rates are prices of money). Information about prices allows investors to measure their wealth, and helps them to take decisions about how to allocate their wealth between different types of investment. Interest rates are likely to influence decisions about saving and borrowing.

9. *Dealing with incentive problems.* Incentive problems include principal-agent, moral hazard, and adverse selection problems. It is in relation to such matters that regulation can be particularly important.

Principal-agent problems can arise when investors allow others to take decisions for them, or follow the advice of others. For example an investor may allow a financial adviser to choose investments. There is a risk that the adviser chooses the investments that pay the highest commission to the adviser, rather than the investments that are best for the investor. This would be a case of the adviser exploiting the situation of having more information than the investor. The investor is referred to as the principal, the adviser as the agent, and the inequality of information as asymmetric information.

The principal-agent situation can lead to moral hazard. Moral hazard can arise when the agent takes the decisions but the principal bears the risks arising from those decisions. For example a fund manager may make investments that are riskier than the investors would like. This could be possible as a result of the fund manager (the agent) having more information (asymmetric information) than the investor (the principal).

Adverse selection can be another consequence of asymmetric information. Consider the case of annuities. Annuities are incomes for life sold by insurance companies. In exchange for a lump sum the insurance company guarantees a monthly income for the rest of the life of the person buying the annuity. Individuals know more about their health and prospective lifespans than insurance companies can know (asymmetric information). People with short life expectancy are less likely to buy annuities than those who expect to live for a long time (adverse selection). Those who expect long lives stand to benefit most from annuities. If insurance companies price annuities according to average lifespans, they will lose money because people buying them will tend to have longer than average lives. Women tend to live longer than men. If annuities are priced to match average life expectancy (average of men and women together), women will buy annuities to a greater extent than men.

INVESTORS AND BORROWERS

The financial system serves the function of transferring money from those who want to invest to those wishing to borrow (the term borrower is being used loosely here since firms that raise capital by issuing shares are, strictly speaking, not borrowing but selling equity in their enterprises). The cash flows are illustrated by Figure 1.1. Savers invest by depositing money in banks (or building societies), by buying bonds, or by buying shares. The borrowers may be individuals who obtain bank

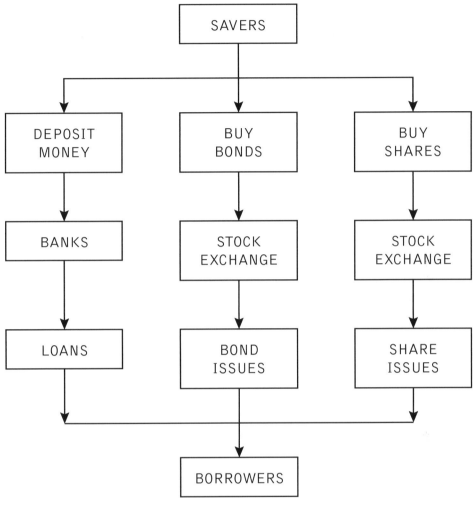

Figure 1.1

loans or mortgages, governments that sell bonds, or private companies that raise money by both of these means plus the sale of shares. The money passes from investors to borrowers through the intermediation of banks or stock exchanges.

Most stock market investment by individuals is through the medium of institutional investments such as pension funds, insurance funds, unit trusts, and investment trusts. The financial system cash flows where stock market investment is carried out through institutional investments is illustrated by Figure 1.2.

PERSONAL FINANCIAL PLANNING

Personal financial planning is the process of planning one's spending, financing, and investing so as to optimise one's financial situation. A personal financial plan specifies one's financial aims and objectives. It also describes the saving, financing, and investing that are used to achieve those goals.

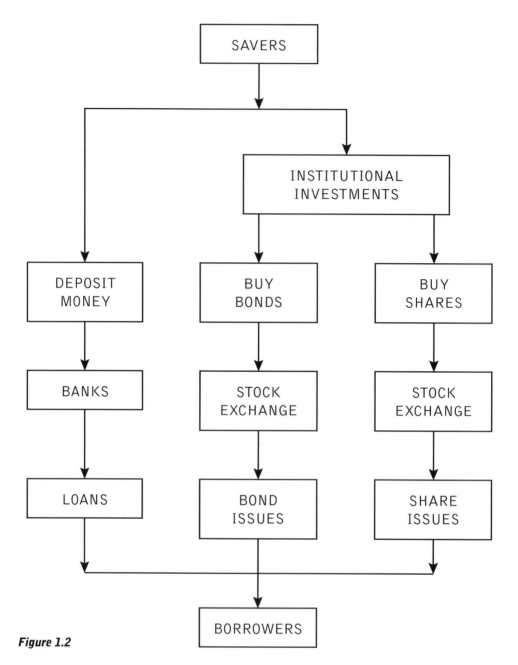

Figure 1.2

A financial plan should contain personal finance decisions related to the following components:

1. Budgeting.
2. Managing Liquidity.
3. Financing Large Purchases.
4. Long-term Investing.
5. Insurance.

Budgeting

The budgeting decision concerns the division of income between spending and saving. Saving will increase one's assets and/or reduce one's debts. If spending exceeds income (i.e. there is negative saving), assets will be reduced and/or liabilities increased. The excess of assets over liabilities is one's net worth. Saving increases net worth (negative saving reduces it).

Some saving might be very short term, for example keeping some of this month's salary to finance spending next month. Very short-term saving is part of the process of managing liquidity. Other saving is medium term: saving for a holiday, a car, or a deposit on a house are examples. Such saving is for the purpose of financing large purchases. Long-term saving can have an investment horizon of 40 years or more. The most important long-term saving for many people is saving for a pension to provide an income in retirement. Other purposes of long-term saving include the financing of children's education, and building up an estate to pass to one's heirs.

Long-term saving for a pension will feel much more important when the investor is 55 than when that investor is 25. However, early saving is far more productive than later saving. For example £1,000 invested for ten years at 8% p.a. will grow to £2,159, whereas the same sum invested at the same rate of return for 40 years will grow to £21,725.

Managing Liquidity

Liquidity is readily available cash, or other means of making purchases. Liquidity is needed for items such as day-to-day shopping and meeting unexpected expenses such as repair bills. Liquidity management involves decisions regarding how much money to hold in liquid form, and the precise forms in which the money is to be held. Generally the more liquid an asset is, the lower the return to be expected from it. The most liquid assets are banknotes and money in chequeable bank accounts. These assets provide little or no interest. Slightly less liquid assets, such as deposit accounts in banks or building societies, provide more interest but are slightly less accessible. It is normally inappropriate to hold all of one's wealth in liquid form since assets that are less liquid (such as bonds and shares) generally offer much higher expected rates of return.

The alternative to using one's own liquidity might be to borrow, for example by using a credit card. Credit management is concerned with decisions about how much credit to use, and what sources of credit to use. Whilst credit is a source of additional liquidity, it has the disadvantage that interest has to be paid; and often at a high rate.

Financing Large Purchases

The finance for large purchases may be generated by saving, or by borrowing. Savings need not be in highly liquid form (until the purchase is made) but should not be in a risky form. Such savings would be expected to yield more interest than liquid cash, but a lower return than should be available from risky assets such as shares and long-term bonds.

The accumulation of money for an expenditure in one, two, or three years might be in the form of bank deposits or other short maturity money market investments. Over such a timescale, the risk of capital loss from investment in shares or long-term bonds might be seen as excessive relative to the potential extra return from such investments. As a general rule, the value of stock market investments increases more than in proportion to time whilst risk increases less than proportionately to the passage of time. Such relationships make stock market investments unsuitable for short-term saving, but very suitable for the long-term accumulation of wealth.

The types of large expenditure for which saving or borrowing are likely to used include holidays, car purchase, higher education, and house purchase. Large expenditures, such as house purchase, are likely to be partly financed by borrowing (for example by means of mortgages). Short timescale expenditures such as holidays are more likely to be financed by saving. The credit management involved when borrowing requires consideration of factors such as the number of years required for repayment and the affordability of the monthly repayments. For a particular size of debt, reducing the monthly payments will entail increasing the number of years for which repayments will be made. Consideration should also be given to the potential variability of regular payments. For example mortgage borrowing typically carries the risk that interest rates, and hence monthly repayments, will rise.

Long-term Investing

Although there may be some other reasons for long-term saving, such as funding children's education or provision of a legacy to pass on to one's heirs, the most important is the provision of a retirement income. To appreciate the scale of what is involved for an individual, consider the case of someone expecting to fund 20 years of retirement income from 40 years of work. Suppose that the aim is to maintain the standard of living at the level achieved during the working life. In the absence of a prospective real rate of return on investments, one-third of the income received while working needs to be saved in order to provide the retirement income.

The need to save one-third of one's income is based on a zero real net rate of return on investments (the real net rate of return is the return after taking account of inflation and taxation). Historically the real net rates of return on bank and building society accounts have been only a little above zero, on average. The achievement of high real net rates of return has required investment in shares. So the attainment of good investment returns has necessitated acceptance of the risk associated with investment in shares. However that risk needs to be seen from a long-term perspective. Figures 1.3 and 1.4 illustrate the behaviour of expected asset value and risk in relation to the passage of time.

The shape of the curve in Figure 1.3 can be explained as being similar to the effect of compound interest. The shape of the curve in Figure 1.4 might be explained in terms of the effects of time

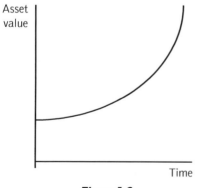

Figure 1.3

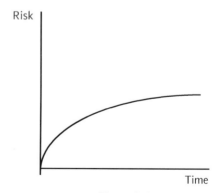

Figure 1.4

diversification; over a long time span good periods tend to offset bad periods. The two figures illustrate why stock market investments should be used for long-term rather than short-term savings. In the short term shares provide high risk relative to return, in the long term they tend to produce high return relative to risk. (Some academics have questioned the notion of time diversification. Fisher and Statman (1999) discuss the views of dissenters.)

The effects of time diversification have been illustrated by Fidelity, which is a major investment management company (Fidelity International 2005). Examining the period 1985 to 2005, they found that the UK stock market (as measured by the FTSE All-Share Index) produced a profit in 77% of one-year periods, where a one-year period is 12 consecutive months (e.g. June 1986 to May 1987, March 1992 to February 1993). There was a profit in 81% of five-year periods, where a five-year period is 60 consecutive months (e.g. September 1988 to August 1993). Every ten-year period (120 consecutive months) showed a profit. An international portfolio of stocks (as measured by the MSCI World Index) produced figures of 71%, 81%, and 100% respectively.

In the same publication, the sudden nature of stock market movements was highlighted. During the period 1990 to 2005 the UK stock market produced an average return of nearly 9% p.a., and the international portfolio showed an average return of around 7% p.a. However removing the best 40 days reduced the UK average annual return to slightly less than zero. Removal of the best 20 days reduced the average annual return on the international portfolio to about minus 2%.

Swank *et al.* (2002) argued that since many occupational pension plans have an unlimited future investment period (no foreseeable termination date), they should hold 100% of their assets in the form of shares. There seems to be virtually no risk that shares (alternatively referred to as equities) would underperform other investments over such a long investment horizon. They suggest that the failure to hold 100% in shares partly arises from short-term unpredictability of stock market performance, which could require the company (or other pension provider) to fund shortfalls in some years. There is also the career risk of investment managers, who could find that a few years of poor investment returns result in the loss of their jobs. The time horizons of providers and managers may be shorter than the investment horizon of the pension fund. Time diversification is elaborated further in Chapter 13 on portfolio diversification.

Insurance

Insurance entails making payments to an insurer for financial protection. There is property insurance which provides compensation in the event of damage to, or loss of, property such as houses and cars. Life assurance pays money to dependants in the event of one's death. A range of other eventualities can be insured against. For example it is possible to take out insurance to cover health care expenses or loss of income.

Sometimes insurance is combined with a savings scheme. This is the case with life assurance products such as endowment policies and whole-of-life policies. Someone considering such schemes should give thought to the question of whether it might be advantageous to keep insurance policies and savings schemes separate.

THE NATURE OF INVESTMENT RISK

When people think of risk they often focus on capital risk. Capital risk is the risk that the value of the investment might fall. Stock market investments, shares and bonds, are subject to capital risk since the prices of such investments can fall. However this may not be the most important source of risk for an investor. Two other risks, which are often overlooked, are inflation risk and income risk.

Inflation risk is the risk that the purchasing power value of assets can be eroded by inflation. To give an idea of the potential effect of inflation, consider the impact of 2.5% p.a. inflation over 40 years. The purchasing power of £1 would fall to 37p. At an inflation rate of 5% p.a., the real value of the £1 would fall to 14p. Over the last half-century, a period during which UK inflation rates have at times exceeded 20% p.a., inflation has inflicted severe damage on the wealth of people with investments in deposits and bonds. This is a major reason for the fact that real net interest rates from banks and building societies have averaged little more than zero. There have been periods when real net interest rates have been negative (investments in banks and building societies have declined in real value even after reinvestment of interest). For example if the interest rate is 3% p.a. and inflation is 5% p.a., there is a loss of purchasing power of about 2% p.a.

The apparent risk-free nature of bank and building society deposits is called further into doubt when income risk is considered. This is a particular problem for investors who want an immediate income from their investments. Income risk is the risk that income payments from an investment (interest or dividends) can fall. Interest rates on bank and building society deposits fluctuate with variations in the economy's short-term interest rates. For example during 2001 interest rates on premium accounts in the UK fell from around 6% p.a. to about 4% p.a., and in the US the fall was from about 6% p.a. to less than 2% p.a. Someone who depends on interest to provide an income would have found such falls to be very problematical.

Bank and building society accounts are not the only investments that suffer from inflation risk and income risk. Conventional annuities, which are guaranteed fixed incomes bought at retirement using money in pension funds, also suffer from such risks. Inflation reduces the purchasing power of fixed incomes, and the level of the fixed incomes depends on long-term interest rates at the time of retirement (for example the annual income bought for a particular sum in 2001 was about half the income bought with the same sum ten years earlier). As a result there is a move towards annuities that are based on investment in shares. Although investment in shares has high capital risk, it has relatively low inflation risk and income risk.

CORE PRINCIPLES OF PERSONAL FINANCIAL PLANNING

The assessment of personal financial needs, either by a financial adviser or someone evaluating their own needs, can be based on CORE: Circumstances, Objectives, Risk, Expenditure.

The circumstances of an individual would include factors such as age, income, existing assets and liabilities, and family responsibilities. Age is important since it determines both the time span over which regular savings can take place, and the level of risk that can be accepted. Someone who starts saving for a pension at the age of 25 may have a prospective 40 years over which to accumulate a pension fund, someone starting to save at 55 may have just 10 years. The monthly payments into a pension scheme by the 25 year old will be much smaller than the payments required from the 55 year old. Also the longer time span will allow the younger person to make higher risk investments since there is more scope for good future periods to offset bad periods.

Income, including prospective future income, has considerable significance. Not only does a high income allow for high savings, a high prospective future income might also be seen as permitting greater risk taking, as the potential for replacing poor investments is greater. Stability of prospective future income is also important; someone with a stable and predictable income is in a better position to accept risk from investments than someone with an unstable and uncertain future income.

Prospective future income is often seen as a form of wealth, referred to as human capital. In addition to human capital there is wealth in the form of real estate property and wealth in the form of financial assets. A person's existing wealth is a determinant of both the need to save, and the level of risk that can be accepted. Someone with £250,000 in a pension fund has less need for another £1,000 in the fund than someone with just £10,000. The person with the larger pension fund can afford to accept more risk on the additional £1,000 than the person with the small fund.

The form of existing wealth has implications for the nature of additional investments. If existing wealth is low risk, there may be a greater willingness to accept risk from new investments. There is also the desirability of diversification; that is the avoidance of 'putting all of one's eggs in the same basket'. If a person's wealth contains no shares, there may be a greater willingness to put new saving into shares than if shares already constitute a substantial part of the person's wealth. Likewise the principles of portfolio diversification would impact on the choice of shares, for example if the existing share portfolio is entirely in UK shares then additional share investment may be made in the shares of foreign countries.

Financial liabilities also impact on investment decisions. A person with a large mortgage commitment, or other form of debt, may be reluctant to allocate money to risky investments. Indeed the best strategy might be to use any available money to reduce the debt rather than make investments. Financial liabilities could also be in the form of family commitments. Someone with dependent children is in a very different position to a person who has no dependants. A person with no dependants can save more and take greater risks with the savings.

The financial objectives have significance for the amount to be saved, the investment horizon, and the acceptable level of risk. A 25-year-old person saving for a pension at 65 would invest differently from a 25-year-old person saving for a deposit on a house in two years from the present. The former has an investment horizon of 40 years, the latter one of 2 years. Long investment horizons allow for more risk taking than short horizons. Also for the accumulation of a specific target sum of money, long periods of accumulation require smaller monthly savings than short periods. Someone wishing to accumulate money to meet unforeseen emergencies has a high need for liquidity. By liquidity is meant the ability to turn the asset into cash quickly and without the risk of loss. Bank and building society deposits are very liquid.

People vary considerably in their attitudes to, and perceptions of, risk. Some are extremely risk-averse, even to the extent that large prospective gains are not seen as adequate compensation for the possibility of small losses. At the other extreme some people are excited by the prospect of potential gains to the extent that they are willing to accept the possibility of substantial losses. Some people do not perceive risk in that they have full confidence in their expectations; it has been suggested that a feature of stock market bubbles and crashes is that some people forget that markets are uncertain and behave as if the direction of share price movements is known with certainty. There are also people with narrow perceptions of risk; someone needing income from investments may choose a bank (or building society) rather than shares and bonds in order to avoid the risk of capital loss. Such a person may be insufficiently aware of the income risk from bank deposits. Interest rates are variable with the effect that the income from a bank or building society deposit fluctuates; possibly much more than the dividends from shares and definitely more than the coupons from bonds.

Expenditure on investments is affected by both the ability and the willingness to save. The former is affected by income, the latter by attitudes and circumstances. Many people are reluctant to save, preferring to ignore their future financial needs or assuming that others (e.g. future taxpayers) will provide for them. Others give saving to meet future needs a high priority in their use of income.

CONCLUSION

The population of the UK (and Western Europe and North America) is ageing. The ratio of pensioners to people of working age is increasing. The ability of governments to provide adequate pensions will diminish as the proportion of pensioners to taxpayers (who pay for state pensions) rises. Raising the age at which pensions start to be paid is one part of the solution; in the UK the pension age is being increased from 65 to 68. Increasing private pension provision is another dimension of the solution. The achievement of an adequate pension requires that people save. It also requires the investment of those savings in a form that produces a high rate of growth. History indicates that investment in shares provides much higher returns, on average, than investment in bank or building society accounts.

Financial systems provide means of investing for the purpose of accumulating wealth. Most people who accumulate wealth for the purpose of funding retirement income do so through institutional investments. In the UK pension funds are the largest institutional investments but insurance funds, unit trusts, OEICs (Open-Ended Investment Companies), and investment trusts are also important. Saving is essential to the provision of an adequate retirement income. If the necessary level of saving is not carried out by an employer which provides an occupational pension, people need to budget in order to save adequately. The average return on stock market investments (i.e. shares) is much higher over time than the interest paid on bank and building society accounts. Although from a short-term perspective shares may be seen as too risky, over long periods (such as those relevant to pension saving) the growth potential of investment in shares dominates considerations of risk.

The message thus far is that people need to save, and to invest much of that saving in the stock market. This will probably be through institutional investments. Later chapters will show that the charges on those institutional investments can heavily affect long-term wealth accumulation, so that low cost investments such as index tracker funds have advantages. It will also be seen that the process of investing requires people to be aware of, and compensate for, psychological biases. It will also be shown that financial derivatives (particularly futures and options), whilst risky on their own, can be useful for risk reduction. The availability of reduced-risk stock market investments should encourage those investors with a high aversion to risk to put their savings into stock market investments.

Chapter 2

The psychology of personal investment decisions

OBJECTIVE

The objective of this chapter is to provide an understanding of:

1. The purposes and constraints of personal financial decisions.
2. The characteristics of various investments, including their risks.
3. The management of risk.
4. The psychology of personal financial decisions.
5. Differences in attitudes to saving.

CHOICE UNDER CONSTRAINT

When making personal investment decisions investors seek to achieve objectives whilst taking account of their circumstances (which might be regarded as the constraints that they face). Objectives would include obtaining a high rate of return on their investments and the avoidance of substantial risk. Another objective might be the maintenance of adequate liquidity. Another could be the receipt of a high and stable income without resort to selling or cashing in investments.

Relevant circumstances (constraints) are many and varied. Table 2.1 lists some relevant circumstances. This chapter will consider these objectives and circumstances in turn. First, however, the impact of various personal characteristics and circumstances will be illustrated by Table 2.2 in which a '+' indicates a favourable disposition towards a particular characteristic of an investment and a '−' indicates an aversion to a feature of an investment instrument.

OBJECTIVES

The objective of a high rate of return is based on the view that it is better to have more money rather than less. A high rate of return means that, when the investment is eventually sold or cashed in, the sum of money received by the investor is relatively large. Return comprises both income yield and capital gains.

Table 2.1

Age (stage in the life cycle)

Investment horizon

Size of existing assets

Diversity of existing assets

Liabilities

Net worth

Current income

Stability of income

Earning potential

Family responsibilities

Tax bracket

Expected legacies

Intended legacies

The objective of liquidity relates to the speed and cost of turning an investment into cash. A liquid asset is one that can be transformed into cash quickly and at little cost. An illiquid asset is one that cannot be converted into cash quickly and which may require the investor to accept a low price in order to find a buyer for the asset.

Many investors depend on their investments to provide income. Although income could be obtained by selling investments (maybe to cash in capital gains), there may be reasons for not doing so. One reason may be the avoidance of the possibility that selling investments could jeopardise future income receipts. 'Never touch the capital' is a rule of thumb that aims to preserve the source of future income. Another reason might be that an investment is indivisible, for example the ownership of a house for the purpose of obtaining rental income – it is not possible to part sell the house to augment rental income.

TYPES OF RISK

Low risk is probably the most complex and multifaceted of the objectives. This is largely because risk has many dimensions. It has been suggested that there are more than 20 forms of risk that an investor may face. Some of the more important risks will be mentioned here.

Market risk is the risk that the value of an asset falls because of a generalised decline in asset prices. For example the price of a share may fall as part of a general decline in the stock market. Market risk is a form of capital risk. Capital risk is the risk of a reduction in the value of an investment. Market risk is alternatively known as systematic, or non-diversifiable, risk.

Non-systematic risk is the risk that the value of an investment may fall as a result of factors specific to that investment. For example the price of a company's shares may fall because a competitor begins to offer a superior product. Non-systematic risk is alternatively known as specific, or

Table 2.2

	Growth potential	Income yield	Capital risk	Income risk	Liquidity
High capital risk aversion			−		+
High income risk aversion		+		−	
Advanced age			−		+
Young age	+				
Long investment horizon	+				
Short investment horizon	+		−		+
Large existing assets	+				
Low existing assets	+		−		+
High diversity of existing assets	+				
Low diversity of existing assets	+		+		+
Large liabilities	+	+	−	−	+
Low liabilities	+				
High net worth	+				
Low net worth	+		−		+
High current income	+				
Low current income	+	+	−	−	+
Stable income	+				
Unstable income	+	+	−	−	+
High earning potential	+				
Low earning potential	+	+	−	−	+
High family responsibilities	+	+	−	−	+
Low family responsibilities	+				
Large expected legacies	+				
Low expected legacies	+		−		
Large intended legacies	+		−		
Low intended legacies	+				
High income tax bracket	+	−			
Low income tax bracket	+	+			

diversifiable, risk. It is called diversifiable risk because a well-diversified portfolio of shares should eliminate such risk (strong performances tending to offset weak ones).

An increase in interest rates tends to be accompanied by declines in asset prices. This relationship is particularly reliable in the case of long-dated bonds. A bond is an investment that typically pays the investor a constant sum (the interest or coupon) each year and then repays the original investment on a maturity date. If interest rates on other investments rise, bonds become relatively less attractive and their prices fall. The impact of interest rate changes increases with the maturity (strictly speaking the duration) of a bond. This is a form of *capital risk,* which is the risk that the value of an investment may fall.

Interest rate changes are also associated with *income risk.* Income risk is the risk that the income receipts from an investment will fall. A long-dated bond has little income risk since the coupon receipts are known with certainty until the maturity date of the bond. On the other hand a bank or building society deposit has high income risk. As short-term interest rates fluctuate so too will the interest payments to investors.

A source of both capital and income risk on bonds is *default risk.* This is the risk that the issuer of the bond fails to make coupon (interest) payments, or fails to repay the principal amount on the maturity date of the bond.

A related risk is *credit risk.* Bonds are given credit ratings by credit rating agencies. The ratings are intended to indicate the likelihood of default. If the credit rating of an issuer, or bond, is reduced the market price of the bond will fall.

A form of both capital and income risk is *inflation risk.* This is the risk that general price inflation erodes the purchasing power value of an investment and the income derived from that investment. This is alternatively known as purchasing power risk.

Currency, or exchange rate, risk relates to investments denominated in foreign currencies. If the currency in which the foreign investment is priced falls relative to the investor's own currency, the value of the investment and income from it will fall in terms of the investor's own currency.

Political risk is the risk that governmental decisions will adversely impact on the value of investments or the income from them. Since the income relevant to investors is after-tax income, changes in tax rates are a form of political risk.

World-event risk is the risk of events impacting negatively on investments. The terrorist attacks of 11 September 2001 provide an example of such risk.

Liquidity risk is the risk that it becomes difficult to liquidate an investment. If buyers for a particular investment become scarce it may become difficult to sell, at least without having to substantially lower the selling price.

So risk is varied in nature. The objective of achieving low risk may need to address a large number of different risks.

CONSTRAINTS

Some constraints arise from the attitudes of the investor. It is sometimes said that investors are motivated by greed and fear. Greed relates to the desired rate of return and fear is concerned with the level of risk. An investor who seeks a high rate of return and who is tolerant of risk will tend to choose investments that offer high potential returns albeit at the cost of high risk. Conversely an investor who is content with a modest rate of return whilst being intolerant of risk (i.e. highly risk-averse) would choose investments that offer limited returns and relative certainty.

A factor that should affect risk tolerance/aversion is the age of an investor. Someone saving in order to fund a retirement pension but with 40 years to retirement is in a position to accept risk. There is scope for periods of good investment performance to compensate for poor periods, furthermore there is time for the investor to retrieve investment failures by increasing the rate of saving in the future. Someone with just a few years to retirement does not have these advantages of a long investment horizon and needs to be more conservative in terms of investment strategy.

A number of individual circumstances interrelate. The factor of age is linked with the issues of investment horizon and stage in the life cycle. The investment horizon is the period to the moment at which investments will be liquidated to finance expenditure (for example expenditure on an annuity to provide a retirement income). Short investment horizons allow little scope for accepting risk. Retirement is not the only source of an investment horizon during a person's lifetime. The life cycle can produce other horizons such as the purchase of a house, for which a deposit may need to be saved, or the finance of children's education.

The amount, and nature, of existing assets should also influence investment decisions. An investor whose wealth is already substantial will be better able to tolerate risk than someone who has little existing wealth. The nature of the existing wealth also has significance. Someone who already has a large sum in a safe and liquid form is in a strong position to put new savings into relatively risky and illiquid investments. The value of existing wealth, relative to needs, will also have implications for the amount of saving that someone should aim for. If assets are already considerable, little further saving and investment may be necessary.

The nature of existing wealth has implications for new investment since investors should bear in mind the desirability of diversification. If one's existing wealth is primarily in residential property then one should consider investing new wealth in assets such as bonds and shares. Someone whose existing wealth is primarily in residential property should be aware that investing in more property, perhaps in pursuit of rental income, provides high exposure to any downturn in property prices. An investor should also give thought to whether new investments should be influenced by his/her income from employment. Employment income may already provide exposure to the fortunes of a business, investing in shares or bonds issued by that business would increase exposure to the risk of that firm performing badly. More broadly, someone employed in a cyclical industry might be well advised to invest outside that industry in order to avoid compounding the losses from a downturn in that industry.

It is not only the amount and nature of existing assets that should be considered when allocating savings. Liabilities should also be considered. Someone with large debts relative to wealth and income may not be in a strong position to accept risk. In fact the first priority for any surplus funds is often reduction of debt. This is particularly so if the interest payable on the debt is high relative to potential returns on investments.

Income should also influence investment decisions. It is not only the size of current income but also potential future income, and the prospective stability of income, that has implications for investment behaviour. Someone with low prospective income may use any investments as a means of augmenting income. Such an investor should be income risk-averse. There should be little tolerance for the risk of a falling investment income. The investor should therefore avoid investments that have income risk. This entails avoidance of investments such as bank or building society deposits since the interest from such investments is subject to considerable variation. The investor should prefer investment in long-term bonds and in shares with high and stable dividend payments. Similar considerations apply to people whose employment income is prospectively unstable since they might look to investments as a source of stable income.

If someone can confidently anticipate a rising future employment income that person could not only reduce current saving but could also be willing to accept a relatively high risk on current investments. High future income would allow the investor to compensate for current low saving by increased future saving, and would give scope to replenish investments in the event of any losses incurred as a result of accepting high risk.

Family responsibilities also impinge on financial decision-making. An unattached person is probably in a better position to take risks than someone with dependants. Legacies are also significant. Someone who is confident of inheriting a substantial sum of money before retirement has less need to save, and can take more risks with investment choices. Someone wishing to bequeath money has a greater need to save from current income.

Taxation can impact on investment decisions. For example people often have different tax rates for income and for capital gains. Someone in a high income tax bracket but subject to low capital gains tax would tend to prefer investments whose returns are in the form of capital gains rather than interest or dividend payments. Such an investor might be inclined to a growth-oriented unit trust rather than a building society account or bond fund.

It appears to be the case that interest rates contain a component to compensate for expected inflation. For example if inflation of 2.5% p.a. is expected and a bank account offers 3.5% p.a., the real interest rate is expected to be 1% p.a. because 2.5% of the interest simply compensates for the erosion of the value of money due to rising prices. However income tax is applied to the whole of the interest, not just the real interest. At an income tax rate of 40% the 3.5% p.a. is reduced to 2.1% p.a. A pre-tax positive real interest rate becomes a post-tax negative real interest rate (minus 0.4% p.a.). The procedure of taxing the whole of an interest return rather than just the real interest can cause investments to provide negative after-tax real returns. People with high income tax rates but low capital gains tax rates might prefer investments that provide returns in the form of capital gains, such as unit trusts that invest in shares, rather than investments that provide returns in the form of interest, such as bonds and building society accounts.

Some constraints are self-imposed. For example many people take an ethical view when investing. This may cause them to look for investment funds that adopt an ethical dimension. Such funds may avoid investments in firms involved in tobacco, alcohol, gambling, or armaments. Human rights and environmental records are also likely to be considered by funds that have an ethical dimension.

Many people may feel that they lack the expertise to make informed investment choices. An analogy could be drawn with medical treatment. Many people would prefer that a doctor decide on their appropriate treatment on the grounds that the doctor has much greater understanding of the medical condition, and its treatments, than they do. Although increased choice is usually seen as a good thing, it may not be if people lack the expertise to exercise the choice.

CHARACTERISTICS OF INVESTMENTS

It is worthwhile considering the characteristics of some forms of investment popular amongst individuals. The most popular is probably the bank or building society deposit. On the upside these are free of capital risk, offer an income yield, and are usually liquid. On the downside they lack substantial growth potential, are subject to a high level of income risk, and have inflation risk.

Rental, or buy-to-let, property has become popular in recent years. Such investment has growth potential and provides an income yield. On the downside it is illiquid and subject to both income and capital risk. The income risk relates to the possibility that rents fall, or that a property fails to attract tenants and remains unoccupied for long periods. The capital risk exists because property prices can fall.

A third investment alternative is provided by equity unit trusts, which invest in a broad portfolio of shares. These provide growth potential and are liquid. On the downside they are prone to both capital and income risk. The income risk is such that no income yield may be forthcoming during some periods.

A related investment possibility is provided by high income equity unit trusts. These differ from other equity unit trusts in persistently providing an income yield, and probably with less income risk.

A higher current level of income is normally available from bond unit trusts. These are liquid with relatively low levels of income and capital risk. However they do not usually offer much growth potential and are vulnerable to inflation risk.

HUMAN CAPITAL

One source of wealth that is often overlooked when considering personal finance is human capital. Human capital is the present value of future employment earnings. It is enhanced by investment in education and training.

An individual's wealth can be classified into four categories: an investment portfolio (including residential property as well as financial assets), the present value of future state and occupational pension receipts, the present value of expected legacies, and human capital. Especially for young people, human capital may be the largest element in total wealth. These four sources of wealth are employed to meet the individual's objectives. The objective may merely be to maximise lifetime consumption of goods and services, but there may be other objectives.

The preparation for retirement involves converting human capital into financial wealth. Proximity to retirement also influences the choice of the type of financial wealth. Bonds provide a constant stream of income with relatively little risk that the bond price will fall substantially or that the income will not be received. It is usually recommended that as retirement approaches the proportion of financial wealth held in the form of bonds should increase. There are three reasons for this.

First, a short period to retirement gives little opportunity to recover from the effects of a stock market crash. Switching towards bonds provides some immunity against a crash. Someone who has a long period to retirement can compensate for investment losses by saving more (possibly with the aid of working more) during the remaining period to retirement. Someone close to retirement does not have this facility to the same extent. (The facility of choosing to save more could be seen as an option that hedges, i.e. provides protection, against investment losses.)

Second, short of a stock market crash there is a risk of some decline in share prices. The value of equity (share) investments tends to increase more than proportionately to the passage of time (due to compound returns) whereas the risk (measured by the dispersion of possible values) increases less than proportionately to the passage of time. This renders shares more suitable as long-term investments and less suitable as a preparation for imminent retirement.

A third reason for switching towards bonds over time relates to the nature of human capital. For most people human capital behaves like bonds in that it provides a fairly constant and regular stream of income. Human capital declines as the remaining working life declines. The passage of time reduces a bond-like form of capital (human capital) and it appears to be appropriate to replace it with bonds on the grounds that they have similar characteristics.

Van Eaton and Conover (2002) drew the implication that, since human capital is relatively low risk, investors whose assets are predominantly in the form of human capital should hold 100% of their financial assets in the relatively high risk form of shares. Later in life as human capital has declined, and equity (share) holdings have increased, the risk level of the total portfolio will be higher. At that stage some switching from shares to bonds would be appropriate in order to keep portfolio risk within acceptable limits. This reasoning justifies the common advice that investors, as they grow older, should switch from equities to bonds.

Human capital is subject to mortality risk since death eliminates human capital. From the perspective of the family, the death of an income-earner is a financial loss as well as a personal loss. Human capital can be insured by the purchase of life assurance. In the event of death the loss of human capital is offset by the receipt of an insurance payment. Life assurance is not the only way of obtaining protection against the death of an income-earner. Chapter 13 on portfolio diversification develops the theme of holding a diversified portfolio of assets as a means of obtaining protection from the consequences of the loss of one asset. A portfolio of other assets (shares, bonds, mutual funds, investment properties, etc.) provides a source of income for the family in the event of the death of an income-earner. Portfolio construction and life assurance are alternative means of managing the mortality risk of human capital. Conventionally decisions relating to investment portfolios and life assurance are taken separately but Chen, Ibbotson *et al.* (2006) argue that portfolio decisions and life assurance decisions should be taken jointly since they are alternative means of managing the mortality risk of human capital.

RISK MANAGEMENT

All financial decisions are influenced by the risks faced and the approach taken to management of those risks. Individuals and households face a number of risks and effective decision-making requires that those risks be recognised.

Risk may be regarded as uncertainty that matters (an alternative definition of risk is uncertainty that can be measured). Our experience provides us with a vast number of uncertainties, but many of them do not matter to us. The result of a football match is uncertain but if it is of no interest to a person then it is not a risk for that person. House prices are uncertain and to a potential house buyer that uncertainty is important; it is therefore a source of risk.

Risks facing individuals and households can be divided into six types.

1. Sickness, disability, and death.
2. Unemployment.
3. Housing. Property is vulnerable to events such as fire and a decline in market value.
4. Consumer durable risk. For example cars are vulnerable to theft or accidental damage.

5.   Liability risk. This is the risk that others may have a financial claim against you because they suffer a loss for which you could be held responsible, e.g. causing injury in a road accident or being sued for negligence.
6.   Financial asset risk. The risk that the value of investments, or the income from them, may fall.

Many decisions, not just those that are specifically risk management decisions, will be influenced by these risks. However a person may fail to identify some of the risks and hence fail to take account of them. Approaches to decisions that specifically relate to risk management may be divided into four categories.

1.   Risk avoidance. For example one way to manage stock market risk is to refrain from investment in the stock market.
2.   Risk reduction. This is concerned with reducing the likelihood or severity of losses. For example if stock market investment is through a well-diversified portfolio (perhaps by means of a unit trust) the risk is reduced relative to an investment in a small number of stocks.
3.   Risk retention. This is a decision to accept risk and bear any losses that may arise.
4.   Risk transfer. This entails passing the risk to another person or organisation. For example a property owner may insure against fire. At the cost of the insurance premium, the risk of loss through fire is transferred to the insurance company.

In relation to investment (financial asset) risk, investors could see risk in relation to three possible benchmarks. One benchmark is zero; an investor may primarily be concerned with the possibility of a return below zero, a loss in absolute terms. Another possible benchmark relates to an alternative investment, for example performance relative to a stock index such as the FTSE 100; underperformance may be regarded as an opportunity loss. A third benchmark could be a predetermined personal goal; underperformance indicates that personal financial planning is not proceeding in line with expectations.

Risk means different things to different people. Investment decisions are often taken in consultation with a financial adviser. However what the adviser understands by risk may differ from what the client understands by risk. Diacon (2004) found that advisers were less fearful of losses (less loss-averse) than investors, and less likely to see financial services products as complicated. He also found that advisers were more willing to trust the providers of financial products and to trust regulators.

Experts tend to think of risk as objective and measurable, and to have a narrow definition of risk. Individual investors are more likely to have a subjective and multidimensional view of risk. The risk perceptions of individual investors may be widely shared as a result of social interaction. Non-experts may demand certainty of expectations, which experts know cannot be provided. Uncertainty of expectation could be frustrating for the clients of advisers. The differing perceptions of risk, between adviser and client, could be responsible for some of the mis-selling claims in the UK during the 1990s and 2000s. The adviser may not fully communicate the potential range of variability of investment outcomes, possibly because of a failure to understand the extent of a client's misunderstanding of risk. Diacon suggested that it might be useful to include consideration of risk perception and behavioural finance in the training of financial advisers (behavioural finance is the application of psychology to the understanding of financial decision-making).

Among non-experts risk is perceived as greater if the person lacks information about, or control over, outcomes. Lack of information and control in regard to investment outcomes leads to mistrust of providers of financial services and mistrust of financial advisers (Sjoberg 2001). The mistrust of financial advisers may be based on a perceived affiliation bias whereby advisers are seen as being too trusting of the providers of financial services. Also experts tend to think in terms of an average consumer, whereas individuals are concerned specifically with their own case.

Filbeck *et al.* (2005) examined the relationship between personality type and attitude to risk. Personality types were classified according to the Myers-Briggs Type Indicator, which uses four dimensions.

1. Extroversion versus introversion. Extroverts focus their attention on other people whereas introverts are inwardly focused.
2. Sensing versus intuition. Sensing people tend to focus on facts whereas the intuition group are more concerned with abstract ideas.
3. Thinking versus feeling. The thinking group attempt to be objective and logical in their decision-making. Feeling people are subjective decision-makers.
4. Judging versus perceiving. Judging individuals lead organised, and orderly, lives. Perceiving people lead flexible and spontaneous lives.

They found that extroversion versus introversion had no bearing on attitude to risk. Sensing individuals were more tolerant of risk than the intuition people. Thinking people were more tolerant of risk than feeling people. Individuals with a preference for judging were able to tolerate more risk than those with a preference for perceiving.

The management of risk is based on an investor's attitude to risk. An investor who is tolerant of risk would accept levels of risk that would be deemed unacceptable by someone with a strong aversion to risk. Attitudes towards risk vary considerably between people. Grable *et al.* (2004) found that men were more tolerant of risk than women. They also found that people with high incomes were more willing to accept risk than those on low incomes. Hallahan *et al.* (2004) found that risk tolerance is greater for men, young people, well-educated people, those on higher incomes, those with higher wealth, and single people.

It is common for financial advisers to measure attitude towards risk, typically using a set of questions, before providing advice to a client. However another factor identified by Grable *et al.* (2004) throws the usefulness of such risk measures into doubt. They found that recent stock market performance influenced attitudes to risk; a finding confirmed by Yao *et al.* (2004). A recent rise in share prices makes people more tolerant of risk whereas a recent fall causes them to be more averse to risk. The consequence is that attitudes to risk change over time and that measurement of attitude to risk at a single point in time may produce an unrepresentative result.

Exhibit 2.1 indicates possible differences between financial advisers and their clients in relation to the perception of risk. This draws on psychological factors discussed in this chapter, and in Chapter 24 on noise trading and behavioural finance. Differences in the perception of risk can cause communication failures between advisers and their clients. Advisers may give what they see as good advice, when the advice is viewed in the light of their own perceptions. The clients interpret what they hear in the light of their perceptions, and their interpretations could differ from those of the advisers. In consequence clients may feel that they were misled (mis-sold), whilst the advisers believe that their advice was good.

EXHIBIT 2.1   MIS-SELLING OR MISCOMMUNICATION?

Apparent mis-selling of financial products may be the result of different perceptions of risk between advisers and clients.

Table 2.A

Adviser	Client
Risk is objective	Risk is subjective
Unemotional about client's money	Emotional about own money
Objective benchmarks (e.g. stock index)	Personal benchmarks
Objective expectations	Hindsight biased expectations
Knows certainty is impossible	May expect certainty
Assumes constant risk-aversion	Risk-aversion variable
Focus on relevant risk (e.g. income risk)	Focus on irrelevant risk (e.g. capital risk)
Focus on appropriate horizon (e.g. 5 years)	Focus on inappropriate horizon (e.g. 1 month)
Focus on whole portfolio	Focus on individual investments
Financial products understood (familiar)	Financial products complicated (unfamiliar)
Providers trusted	Providers not trusted
Regulators trusted	Regulators not trusted
More information, therefore less uncertainty and less distrust	Less information, therefore more uncertainty and more distrust

THE PSYCHOLOGY OF PERSONAL FINANCE

Many retail investments are stock market related. These include pension funds, Individual Savings Accounts (ISAs), unit trusts, and investment bonds. It is desirable that decisions relating to stock market related investments should be made rationally.

Psychological research has indicated that there are biases in decision-making. These biases have implications for the decisions as to whether to invest in stock market related products, the extent of such investment, and the nature of the investments. The biases could cause investors to make poor decisions; or financial advisers to give poor advice. If investors understand the psychological biases to which they may be prone, they may be able to compensate for them when making investment decisions. If a financial adviser knows the psychological biases that affect clients, the adviser can try to offset those biases by appropriate information and advice. Whilst a financial adviser should discover and accept a client's preferences, the adviser should attempt to dispel misperceptions and misjudgements that arise from the client's psychological biases. Simultaneously advisers should guard against the biases to which they themselves may be prone.

Psychological research has found a number of systematic biases that affect investors. These include: overconfidence, hindsight bias, representativeness, conservatism, narrow framing, retrievability, and ambiguity-aversion. In addition social influences and moods (emotions) affect investment decisions. All of these biases interfere with the process of rational decision-making. Psychological factors can be divided into self-deception, heuristic simplification, social influence, and emotions (Hirshleifer 2001). Some psychological influences may belong to more than one of these categories.

Self-deception

Self-deception is the process whereby people exaggerate their abilities. People tend to think that they are better than they really are. One psychological bias is overconfidence. Overconfidence arises partly from self-attribution bias. This is a tendency on the part of investors to regard successes as arising from their expertise whilst failures are due to bad luck or the actions of others. This leads to excessive confidence in one's own powers of forecasting. It is capable of explaining a number of types of apparently irrational behaviour. For example it can explain why some investors hold poorly diversified portfolios. If investors are highly confident about their selection abilities, they will not feel the need to reduce risk by means of diversification. It could also explain why some investors trade very frequently, to the point where transaction costs cause their investment behaviour to be loss making. Overconfidence can explain why some investors churn their portfolios; that is persistently sell and buy. This behaviour entails a new set of initial charges each time with the effect that the investors lose. This churning may be recommended by overconfident financial advisers (who incidentally receive a new set of commission payments each time the churning occurs).

Odean (1998a) has shown that one of the effects of overconfidence is that turnover of investments tends to be high, that is people trade shares more as a result of overconfidence. Statman *et al.* (2006) found that trading volumes rose when stock prices had recently risen, which was seen as consistent with the overconfidence bias; overconfident investors trade more frequently following market gains since they mistakenly attribute their gains to their investment skills. Barber and Odean (2000) have shown that as turnover rises net profits tend to fall. Psychological research has found that men tend to be more overconfident than women. Barber and Odean (2001a) found that single men trade 67% more than single women. Correspondingly single men on average experienced investment returns 3.5% per year lower than single women.

The hindsight bias is similar to the overconfidence bias except that it relates to evaluations of the past rather than the future. Fischhoff (1982) explains that with the hindsight bias people consistently exaggerate what could have been anticipated. People tend to view what has happened as having been inevitable, and see it as having been predictable before it happened. People even misremember their own predictions; memory is fallible. Azar (2000) suggested that if people cannot remember their original judgement, they will reconstruct the recollection of the original judgement in the light of subsequent information. 'I knew that would happen' and 'I knew it all along' are statements that characterise the hindsight bias. The hindsight bias is the inability to correctly remember one's prior expectations after observing new information. The hindsight bias prevents people learning from their own mistakes, since they are unable to remember those mistakes. People are unable to recognise their own errors. There is self-denial about past errors. If someone has a self-image of being a clever investor, past errors in forecasting may be subject to distortions of memory aimed at maintaining the self-image. Memory is never a faithful recollection of the past; it is amended by the human mind.

Good decision-making in financial markets relies on learning from the past. Learning may entail the comparison of new information with previous expectations. This requires an accurate recall of previous expectations. The hindsight bias involves the contamination of recollections of expectations by new information. The recalled expectations of an outcome are biased towards information about the outcome. The person remembers forming an expectation that is close to what subsequently happened.

Another psychological bias, which is related to overconfidence, is referred to as optimism or as self-enhancement bias. Most people believe that they are above average. Researchers have found that this belief relates to choosing investments, academic performance, and driving ability.

To the extent that some investors attribute profits from rising markets to their own talents, rising markets could be self-perpetuating. Overconfident investors may be encouraged to invest further and thereby reinforce an upward movement in stock prices. Conversely a falling market reduces confidence and investing. This is consistent with the view that markets exhibit overreaction; they rise too high and fall too low (known as the overreaction hypothesis). It also helps to explain why small investors tend to buy following market rises, and sell following falls.

Another bias based on optimism is the outcome bias, which causes people to expect to get what they want. Decisions are made in the expectation that what is wanted to happen will happen; in other words, wishful thinking. An investor may expect a high return on an investment because a high return is what is wanted. This could generate overconfidence and an underestimation of risk. Overconfidence could be based on excessive belief in one's own talents or on the belief that events will turn out to be favourable. In both cases the investor may underestimate risk when making investment decisions.

Some other biases have similarities with the concept of overconfidence. As a result of the confirmation bias investors pay more attention to evidence that supports their opinions than to evidence that contradicts them. This can bolster overconfidence and cause investors to persist with inappropriate investment strategies. Another cognitive bias is the illusion of control. In some circumstances people behave as if they were able to exert control where this is impossible or unlikely. The illusion of control, together with overconfidence, may explain why so many investors choose actively managed funds when tracker funds outperform them and have lower charges. A study by the Financial Services Authority (FSA) has confirmed the findings of academic studies which found that the relative past performance of actively managed funds is no indicator of future relative performance. It may be that overconfidence in their own selection abilities, and the illusion of control provided by the facility of choosing between funds, cause investors (or their financial advisers) to select actively managed funds when tracker funds offer better potential value. (Of course financial advisers might be influenced by the fact that actively managed funds typically pay higher commissions.)

According to Langer (1975), people often find it difficult to accept that outcomes may be random. Langer distinguishes between chance events and skill events. Skill events entail a causal link between behaviour and the outcome. In the case of chance events, the outcome is random.

People often see chance events as skill events. When faced with randomness, people frequently behave as if the event were controllable. If people engage in skill behaviour, such as making choices, their belief in the controllability of a random event appears to become stronger. There is considerable evidence that investment managers are unable to consistently outperform stock markets. This suggests that the outcome of investment management is random. However since the investment managers engage in skill behaviour, analysis, and choice, they tend to see portfolio performance as controllable. Retail investors and financial advisers are also likely to see the performance of their investment choices as controllable; the act of choosing enhances the illusion of control.

Self-deception is increased by the distorting effects of memory. Memory is not a factual recording of past events. Memories are influenced by many personality and emotional factors. To some extent people remember what they want to remember. Inaccurate memories can lead to poor decisions. Goetzmann and Peles (1997) and Moore et al. (1999) investigated the recollections of investors. They found that investor memory of the past performance of their investments was better than the actual performance of those investments. People tend to have a self-image of being good investors and want to believe that their investment decisions have been good. The mind perceives the past in such a way as to be consistent with the self-image. The mind feels uncomfortable with information that contradicts the self-image. This is known as cognitive dissonance. The mind will adjust memory in order to reduce cognitive dissonance and maintain the positive self-image.

It is not just memory that adjusts in order to maintain a positive self-image. Planning might be adjusted. For example a young person with a self-image of being fit and attractive might avoid saving for a pension since the idea of retirement produces a self-image of being old in the future.

Heuristic Simplification

Heuristic simplification arises from the limitations of people's cognitive powers (such as memory and thought). It involves the process of using short cuts to deal with complex decisions. Rules-of-thumb are examples of heuristic simplification. Such short cuts can produce a tainted perception of the situation being thought about.

Representativeness helps to explain why many investors seem to extrapolate price movements. Many investors appear to believe that if prices have been rising in the past then they will continue to rise, and conversely with falling prices. The concept of representativeness suggests that this is because those investors see an investment with recent price increases as representative of longer-term successful investments, and conversely with price falls.

Another result of representativeness is a tendency to assume that good companies are good investments. Good firms are often seen as representing good investments. The issue of whether a share is a good investment depends upon whether it is over-, under-, or fairly priced. Shares of a good company may be overpriced, and hence would not represent a good investment. Shares of a weak company may be underpriced, and hence are attractive as an investment. An example of this error was the enthusiasm for the 'nifty-fifty' stocks (actually 76 stocks) in the United States in the early 1970s. The firms were seen as so good that their shares were considered to be a good buy at any price (Fesenmaier and Smith 2002). The demand pushed the stock prices up to unrealistic levels. Subsequently, as the mispricing was gradually corrected, the nifty-fifty stock prices showed relative declines and most of them underperformed the market over the following decades (Wal-Mart was an exception).

The findings of Cooper *et al.* (2001) can be interpreted as evidence of representativeness. They investigated companies that added '.com' or '.net' to their names between June 1998 and July 1999 (a period during which the Internet stock bubble was developing). They found that those companies provided an average return, between 15 days before the name change to 15 days after, that was 142% above that of similar companies. For the companies whose business had no relation to the Internet, the figure was 203%. It would appear that investors saw companies with .com or .net in their names as representative of potentially highly successful companies. Cooper *et al.* (2005) found that mutual funds (unit trusts) can increase the flow of investment funds from retail investors by changing their names to something that reflects recently successful investment styles.

The effects of representativeness on thinking and decision-making can be illustrated by the following example. A man has recently been convicted. You are told that he is aggressive, short-tempered, and has a history of violence. You are asked to guess whether his conviction was for murder or speeding. It is likely that many people would guess murder. This is because the description fits the popular image, or stereotype, of a murderer. The man is seen as representative of murderers. However, since speeding convictions vastly outnumber murder convictions, it is much more likely that the conviction was for speeding.

Next consider a coin being tossed five times. If there were five heads would you take the view that the coin is biased? Many people might take that view since a run of five heads would be seen as representative of biased coins. Five successive heads does not fit the image or stereotype of randomness. However there is a 3.125% chance that an unbiased coin would produce a run of five heads. Since the number of unbiased coins is vastly greater than the number of biased coins, it is much more likely that the coin is an unbiased one that has produced five heads purely by chance.

Next consider a unit trust that has beaten the average performance of similar trusts in five successive years. Do you consider the fund manager to have investment skills that are superior to the average? Bearing in mind the wealth of evidence that past performance is no guide to future performance, and that relative performance in successive years appears to be random, perhaps the appropriate conclusion is that the run of five successive good years has occurred by chance. However, many people are likely to conclude that the fund manager has superior investment skills. There is evidence that a run of successes tends to attract a lot of investors to a unit trust. A unit trust with a recent run of success is seen as representative of long-term strong performers.

The concept of conservatism suggests that investors are slow to change their views following the receipt of new information. This may help to explain why small investors often delay investing until the market has risen for a period of time. It has been observed that small investors often invest just before the market peaks, and sell just before it troughs.

A concept related to conservatism is anchoring. People are heavily influenced by past, or suggested, prices when forming judgements about appropriate prices. The past, or suggested, price acts as an anchor that becomes the basis for forming a judgement. This applies to various markets, not just stock markets. For example Northcraft and Neale (1987) have shown that anchoring operates in the housing market. They took two groups of estate agents to a house. One group were told that the asking price was $119,900 and the second group were told $149,900. When asked to give their own valuations the first group averaged $117,745 and the second averaged $130,981. This suggests that the best strategy when selling a property is to set the asking price at the top of the range of possibilities (and when buying a newly constructed property it is probably safe to assume that the house builder has done the same).

Professional analysts, such as stockbrokers, appear to be subject to anchoring. It might be thought that if an analyst suggests an appropriate price for a share and the share price subsequently moves away from that level, an investor would see a trading opportunity. For example a fall in the share price below the analyst's forecast should indicate a buying opportunity. Unfortunately for the private investor, the effect of the share price move seems to be that the analyst moves the forecast in the same direction as the share price. Cornell (2000) demonstrated this effect in relation to Intel. Those results were consistent with studies by Womack (1996) and Brav and Lehavy (2001) whose findings showed that adjustments subsequent to analysts' forecasts took the form of the forecasts being changed towards actual prices rather than actual share prices moving towards the forecasts.

Samuelson and Zeckhauser (1988) suggested the existence of a status quo bias (alternatively known as an endowment bias). People have a tendency to hold the investments they already have and exhibit some reluctance to change them. Status quo bias appears to increase as the number of investment options increases. The more complicated the investment decision, the greater the likelihood that the investor chooses to change nothing. Kempf and Ruenzi (2006) confirmed this finding. They found that when choosing a mutual fund (unit trust), individuals tended to choose one that they had chosen previously. This tendency to repeat choices was found to strengthen as the amount of choice increased.

Lin et al. (2006) found that the strength of the endowment effect (status quo bias) depended on the emotional state of the investor. They found that the endowment bias only occurred when people felt happy, and it was absent when they felt sad. Lerner et al. (2004) found that two negative emotions, sadness and disgust, had opposing effects on the endowment bias. Disgust enhanced the endowment effect, whereas sadness reduced it. These studies indicated that emotion and mood could affect cognitive biases and hence decisions.

Narrow framing refers to the tendency of investors to focus too narrowly. One aspect is focus on the constituents of a portfolio rather than the portfolio as a whole. Since individual investments tend to be more volatile than the investor's portfolio as a whole, such narrow framing causes investors to overestimate price volatility. This could cause people to invest too little.

Another dimension of narrow framing is the focus on the short term even when the investment horizon is long term. It is not rational for an investor accumulating assets for retirement 25 years hence to be concerned about the week-to-week performance of the portfolio. Yet long-term investors do focus on short-term volatility. Studies have shown that when, in experimental situations, people have been presented with monthly distributions of returns they are less likely to invest than when they are shown annual distributions (with the annualised volatility being the same in both cases). The implication is that focus on short-term volatility deters investment. It appears that people do not appreciate the effects of time diversification. By time diversification is meant the tendency for good periods to offset bad periods with the effect that the dispersion of investment returns does not increase proportionately with the period of the investment. Investors who focus too much on short-term fluctuations overestimate stock market risk and allocate too little of their money to stock market investment.

Another bias is retrievability (alternatively known as availability), which suggests that more attention is given to the most easily recalled information. Retrievability is consistent with the overreaction hypothesis, one dimension of which is the overemphasis on recent information and recent events when making investment decisions.

In terms of investments, one source of information is press coverage. If retrievability operates, stocks that receive (favourable) press coverage are relatively likely to be bought in large numbers and hence more likely to be overpriced. Gadarowski (2001) confirmed this by demonstrating that shares with extensive press coverage subsequently performed poorly (there was a relative decline from excessively high prices). Katona (1975) indicated that what the media reports could have considerable influence on social learning. The behaviour of large segments of population can change suddenly in response to news. Retrievability can also lead people to the belief that investment skills are more common than they actually are. Press coverage of successful fund managers such as Warren Buffett and George Soros greatly exceeds press coverage of poor managers. In consequence the retrievability of such coverage can result in the impression that many investment managers are capable of outperforming stock markets.

Ambiguity-aversion (alternatively known as familiarity bias) suggests that investors prefer to invest in companies that they feel they understand. Over 90% of the equity investments of investors in the United States, UK, and Japan is in companies in their own countries. This home bias exists despite the demonstrated benefits of international diversification. The preference for the familiar results in the holding of portfolios that are insufficiently diversified. In consequence investors bear more risk than is necessary.

Related to ambiguity-aversion (familiarity bias) are findings that investors may be affected by the image of a company or sector. For example pharmaceutical companies may have an image of 'health and beauty' whereas chemicals companies might have an image of 'dirty and polluting'. MacGregor *et al*. (2000) showed that image affected investment decision-making. They found that a positive image enhanced judgements of recent performance, expectations of future performance, and the willingness to invest.

Ambiguity-aversion suggests that increased knowledge (or the feeling of increased knowledge) about an asset renders investors more prepared to invest in it. Benartzi and Thaler (1999) found that people are more willing to invest in a stock when an explicit distribution of potential outcomes is provided. This could also be seen as an example of frame dependence, which means that decisions are affected by the way in which the choices are presented. Kahneman and Tversky (1979) found that an individual may reject an investment when it is presented in terms of risks surrounding gains but may accept when the presentation is in terms of risks relating to losses.

Frame dependence can be illustrated by a coin-tossing choice. One option is that there is a prize of £100 for tails. The other option is a gift of £100, which is contingent on a coin toss such that heads would entail the loss of the £100. In both cases tails provides £100 and heads provides nothing. However people are more likely to choose the second option. People are more willing to take a bet when it is expressed in terms of losses than when it is presented in terms of gains.

In relation to investment decisions, it has been found that the way information is framed will influence choices. For example different stock indices can change at different rates. At the time of writing, the FTSE All-Share Index has risen substantially more than the FTSE 100 Index over recent years. If the performance of a fund is presented in relation to the FTSE 100, it would appear to be much more impressive than if its performance is presented relative to that of the FTSE All-Share Index. As another example it has been found that if stock market returns averaged over 30 years are presented, people are more likely to invest than if 30 single year returns are presented. Many single year returns are negative, but no 30-year period has yielded negative returns.

Diacon and Hasseldine (2007) investigated framing effects and found that the presentation format of prior performance affected investment fund choice. They found that presenting past information in terms of fund values as opposed to percentage yields significantly affected investment choices. The alternatives were charts one of which showed the accumulated growth in the value of a fund over time relative to a base value, such as 100, and the other showed a series of vertical lines indicating the growth in each year. The charts of cumulative value growth evoked considerably more positive response than series of growth rates. The presentation of a series of vertical lines indicating annual growth rates produced perceptions of greater risk.

Choice bracketing could be defined as 'a series of local choices that each appear to be advantageous but which collectively lead to a bad global outcome' (Read *et al*. 1999: 172). People are seen as making appropriate decisions within narrow frames but, when these decisions are aggregated, the overall outcome is not the best possible. For example if each new investment is made without regard to the overall portfolio, whilst each investment seen in isolation may seem rational, the resulting portfolio may be unbalanced and poorly diversified. Another example relates to investment horizons. If an investor uses a short horizon, such as one month, for evaluating the risk-return characteristics of investments the resulting portfolio may not be the best from a longer-term perspective. Evaluating investments on a month-by-month basis may lead to the choice of bank deposits in order to avoid the high short-term volatility of stock market investments. However if the objective is to accumulate a pension fund over 35 years, bank deposits would be a poor choice since they provide a low long-term return compared to stock market investments. The investor should consider the risk-return characteristics of investments from a 35-year perspective, not from a one-month perspective.

Mental accounting is the process of separating financial decisions rather than seeing them in aggregate (Thaler 1985). Someone who simultaneously has a bank deposit with a low interest rate and a debt at a high interest rate exhibits mental accounting. Perhaps the bank deposit is regarded as saving for the deposit on a house, and the debt was incurred for the purchase of a car. By separating the two financial decisions the person is losing money. It would have been better to finance the car purchase by taking money (i.e. borrowing) from the house deposit money and then making repayments into that bank account. There would have been a net saving of interest.

Mental accounting can be similar to choice bracketing in its effects. Someone may have a portfolio of investments but allocate investments to various mental accounts. This leads to a focus on components of the portfolio rather than the whole portfolio. For example a person may have investments in a pension fund and simultaneously hold investments in ISAs. In order to achieve a well-diversified portfolio of investments, the person should take account of the nature of the pension fund investments when deciding upon the ISA investments. If the pension money is invested in a UK growth fund, it may be appropriate to invest the ISA money in a different fund. Diversification reduces dependence upon one fund, or type of fund, and hence reduces the potential effect of relative underperformance on the person's total wealth. The investor should see the investments in aggregate rather than allocate them to mental accounts, which are then considered in isolation.

This goes beyond financial portfolios. Three major forms of wealth are financial assets, residential property, and human capital (i.e. future earnings). These three should be seen in aggregate rather than allocated to three mental accounts. For example holding one's financial wealth in the form of shares of the company for which one works produces an excessive dependence upon the success of that company. When deciding on financial assets the nature of the other assets should be considered. Financial investing should not be seen in isolation from the other assets, that is it should not be put into a separate mental account. Since shares tend to have returns unrelated to those from property and human capital, they should have a place in a well-diversified portfolio. Shares may provide good returns at times when property and human capital are underperforming. In the context of the overall portfolio shares may reduce risk (see Chapter 13). The tendency of people to put them into a separate mental account leads to an exaggeration of their risk. This may help to explain why so many people are reluctant to invest in the stock market (Barberis *et al.* 2003).

Mental accounting helps to explain the preference for high dividend yield shares on the part of many investors (Statman 1997). Some investors take a 'never touch the capital' approach when investing for income. Capital growth could be converted into income by selling shares, but this is not allowed by the mindset. Although cashing in on capital growth by share sales is an alternative source of income to dividends, the investor feels that it would be reducing the capital. The only acceptable source of income comes from dividends. This separation of dividends and capital is a manifestation of mental accounting.

Mental accounting can be used to produce examples of frame dependence. Consider the offer of a bet in which £15 is received from a coin toss that is heads, against a loss of £10 with tails. Also consider the offer of a bet in which if heads results you keep all the money you have already plus £15, whereas with tails you keep all your money except £10. People tend to prefer the second bet despite the bets being identical. In the second bet the offer is framed in such a way that it removes mental accounting. The bet, seen in isolation, is less attractive than when it is seen in the context of the person's existing wealth.

Hedesstrom *et al.* (2004, 2007) studied the use of heuristics in the context of the Swedish Premium Pension Scheme, which is a compulsory pension scheme allowing subscribers to choose between a large number of funds. If a participant failed to express a preference, their funds were invested in a default fund. The study identified some heuristics and also investigated whether the amount of interest (involvement) shown by participants affected the use of heuristics. The heuristics found to be operating included a default bias, which is the tendency to choose the default fund. This could reflect a view that the default fund was the fund recommended by the pension plan managers. There was a tendency to avoid funds with either extremely high or extremely low risk; referred to as extremeness aversion. Another heuristic was a tendency to choose own-country funds (familiarity bias, ambiguity-aversion). Also there was a tendency to divide investments evenly between the chosen funds; known as the 1/N bias on the grounds that 1/N is allocated to each of the N chosen funds.

Hedesstrom *et al.* considered the possibility that the use of heuristics was related to the level of investor motivation. It could be the case that participants showing little or no interest (involvement) in the investment choice are more likely to demonstrate the use of heuristics than more motivated investors. Although those showing high involvement were less prone to the default bias, they were no less susceptible to other heuristics such as the familiarity bias and the 1/N heuristic.

31

The Catering Theory of Dividends

According to the catering theory of dividends (Baker and Wurgler 2004) investors have a desire for dividends, and that the resulting demand for dividends varies over time. In consequence there will be times when the prices of dividend paying shares will be bid up relative to the prices of non-dividend paying shares. Companies will adjust their dividend policies in response to this time-varying demand for dividends. Firms initiate (or withdraw from) payment of dividends when investors have a particularly strong (or weak) demand for dividends. Periods of high demand for dividends are accompanied by increased dividend payouts.

Gemmill (2006) provided support for the catering theory of dividends using evidence from split-capital investment trusts in the UK. He observed that over the period 1998–2001 split-capital funds traded at a 9% premium (were worth 9% more) relative to conventional investment trusts. He found that this arose from an increase in the demand for dividends on the part of retail investors. He also observed that there was a large increase in the number of such funds issued during that period. The increase in new issues was interpreted as a response to a demand for high dividend investments.

Unlike conventional investment trusts, split-capital investment trusts can provide high dividend investments by splitting themselves into different classes of share. One such class is the income (or dividend) share, which pays all the dividends earned by the fund but at the cost of foregoing potential capital gains from share price rises. Gemmill suggested that the rising stock market at the time had reduced the rate of dividend yield (the dividend yield is the dividend divided by the share price, so a rise in the share price reduces the dividend yield). In search of dividends some investors turned to split-capital investment trusts. Gemmill noted that at the time investment trust advertising emphasised yield.

It may be that the 'never touch the capital' attitude of some retail investors makes dividends a salient feature which is valued. This can lead to high prices for investments that offer high dividend payments.

The Social Dimension

In addition to personal biases there are biases that result from social influences. Schachter *et al.* (1986) related the degree to which a person is dependent on what others think and do to a number of factors. Social influence is strongest in conditions of uncertainty and when self-confidence is low. It is also strong when circumstances change substantially, and rises with the extent that previously held views are demonstrated to be incorrect. Asch (1952) conducted experiments that showed that people were inclined to follow others even when they felt that the others were wrong; he called this 'conformity'.

Hong *et al.* (2004) found that social households in the United States were more likely to invest in the stock market than non-social households. A social household is one in which the members interact with other people in the neighbourhood. Information is obtained and opinions are formed through talking with others. In consequence social people are more likely to become interested in, and learn about, investing than less socially active people. Shiller and Pound (1989) found that when an investor pays attention to a stock it is often (more than 50% of cases) because another person has mentioned the stock to the individual.

Subsequent to buying the stock, the investor is likely to speak about it to a number of other people.

Duflo and Saez (2002) investigated pension scheme participation in the United States. They suggested that the decision to participate was strongly influenced by the social norms of peer groups. People in a peer group tend to develop the same attitudes as other members of the group. The group studied was very homogeneous in most respects (they were university librarians). Despite a large degree of uniformity in respect of characteristics such as education and income, there was a wide variation in pension scheme participation rates between locations. Participation rates varied between 73% and 14%. Duflo and Saez took the view that the variation could be explained in terms of differences in social norms, or culture, between the different locations.

Influence of Emotion and Mood

Investment decisions can be affected by unrelated emotions (Loewenstein *et al*. 2001; Slovic *et al*. 2002). A favourable sports result or good news about a friend can engender a good feeling, and the good feeling can affect investment decisions. The effect of emotions increases with the complexity and uncertainty surrounding the decision. Decisions about complex and uncertain matters are particularly influenced by emotions (Forgas 1995).

Studies by psychologists have found that mood appears to affect predictions about the future. People in a good mood are more optimistic about the future than people in a bad mood (Wright and Bower 1992). The impact of mood on financial decisions has been referred to as the 'misattribution bias' (Nofsinger 2005). If a person is in a good mood, there will be a tendency to be optimistic when evaluating an investment. Good moods may cause people to be more likely to make risky investments (for example choosing shares rather than bonds).

Weather and the length of daylight are factors that can affect mood. The effects of such factors on investment decisions have been researched. Hirshleifer and Shumway (2003) investigated the effects of sunshine on stock market returns. When the sun is shining people feel good. This may increase optimism and affect investment decisions. It may be the case that investors are more likely to buy shares when the sun is shining. The purchases would cause stock prices to rise. Stock markets in 26 cities were examined. It was found that stock market returns (price increases) were higher on sunny days. When comparing the sunniest days with the worst days, it was found that there was an annualised difference of 24.6% on average.

Kamstra *et al*. (2003) looked at the relationship between hours of daylight and stock market returns. They found that stock markets performed relatively poorly during the autumn as the hours of daylight fell. This was most marked for the more northerly stock markets. Consistent with the theory was the observation that the effect occurred over October to December in the northern hemisphere, and over April to June in the southern hemisphere. This study is consistent with the view that sunlight affects mood and mood affects investment decisions. Sunlight enhances optimism about the future and the prospective future returns from investments.

According to the socionomic hypothesis (Prechter 1999; Nofsinger 2005), moods can be transmitted through social contact and a widely shared, or social, mood emerges. Contact between people conveys mood as well as information. Collectively shared moods influence individual decisions, with the effect that trends emerge. At times mood can dominate reason in the decision-making process. It has been found that people in depressed moods are less willing to take risks (Yuen

33

and Lee 2003) and a negative mood is associated with a desire for asset preservation and safety (Kavanagh *et al.* 2005). Positive mood renders people more trusting (Dunn and Schweitzer 2005), and for many people trust in the financial services industry is a big issue when considering investments. Positive social mood results in perceptions of trustworthiness, low risk, and high returns whilst negative social mood is associated with low trust, high perceived risk, and low anticipated returns (Olson 2006).

It has often been suggested that investors in institutional investments, such as unit trusts and OEICs, have a tendency to buy when the market has risen and to sell after the market has fallen. The tendency to buy when prices are high and to sell when they are low could be explained by social mood. As social mood reaches its peak the level of optimism in society draws more people into investment. The optimistic social mood causes normally very risk-averse investors to begin investing. They buy at the peak of social mood, which coincides with the peak of the stock market. Conversely the pessimism associated with low social mood leads to the selling of investments, just when the stock market is at its lowest. This helps to explain the tendency for many investors, particularly retail investors, to buy at high prices and sell at low prices. Buying at high prices and selling at low prices results in losses.

Alternatively the poor (buy high–sell low) investment strategy may be explained by the 'house money' and 'snake bite' effects (Thaler and Johnson 1990). After making a gain people are willing to take risks with the winnings since they do not fully regard the money gained as their own (it is the 'house money'). So people may be more willing to buy following a price rise. Conversely the 'snake bite' effect renders people more risk-averse following a loss. The pain of a loss (the snake bite) can cause people to avoid the risk of more loss by selling investments seen as risky. The 'house money' and 'snake bite' effects are contradicted by the predictions of prospect theory.

Prospect Theory

Prospect theory is arguably the most developed theory in behavioural finance (Kahneman and Tversky 1972, 1973, 1982). There are three key elements to prospect theory: (1) perceived probabilities are subject to bias; (2) investors are more concerned about gains and losses than levels of wealth; and (3) investors feel losses more than gains.

In relation to perceived probabilities, the biases are tendencies to exaggerate small and large probabilities and underweight medium ones. See Figure 2.1.

In Figure 2.1, subjective (perceived) probabilities are referred to as decision weightings. When plotted against actual probabilities the decision weights are too high at low and high probabilities and too low at medium probabilities. The exaggeration of low probabilities may help to explain the popularity of lotteries. The exaggeration of high probabilities suggests that highly likely (but not certain) events are treated as being certain.

Figure 2.2 is a value function. It depicts subjective values assigned to gains and losses relative to a reference point. The reference point is subjective and may, for example, be the purchase price of an investment. The reference point divides the region where someone feels that they are making gains from the region in which they feel that they are making losses.

It is to be noted that the slope of the function for losses is steeper than the slope for gains. This is because, on average, people find the pain of losses to be about 2.25 times as intense as the pleasure from gains. Given an evens chance of winning or losing, people on average require the prospect

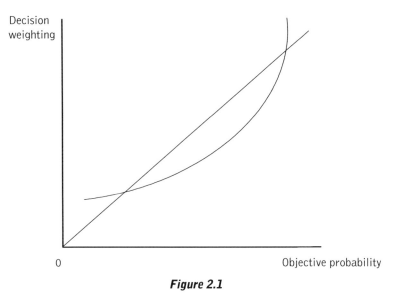

Figure 2.1

of a £225 win to balance the prospect of a £100 loss. This relatively large fear of loss, known as loss-aversion, will tend to deter retail investors from stock market related investments. Loss-aversion may explain the popularity of guaranteed equity funds, which guarantee that the original investment cannot be lost whilst providing gains from rises in share prices. Guaranteed equity funds are described in Chapter 34 on structured products.

Another feature of Figure 2.2 is the tendency for the slope of the value function to become less steep as gains or losses increase. This implies that as gains are made investors will become less inclined to take risks, since the addition to value of a higher gain is less than the reduction in value resulting from a lowered gain. It also implies that as losses increase investors become more willing

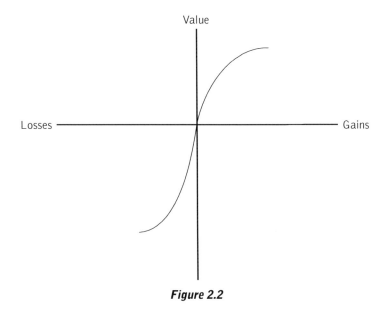

Figure 2.2

to accept risk. This is because the value of a loss reduction outweighs the value of a further loss. So, for example, in a losing situation an 'evens' bet looks attractive. An aspect of loss-aversion is that people will avoid the risk of making losses (by avoiding risks) when in a gaining situation but will accept risk in order to attempt to recover from a loss. Prospect theory sees investors as being loss-averse rather than risk-averse.

This behaviour in a loss-making situation is consistent with the idea of an escalation bias (Shefrin 2001). An escalation bias leads to 'averaging down' whereby as the price falls the investment is treated as being an increasingly good bargain. The thinking is that if a share was a good buy at £2, it is a fantastic bargain at £1 and more should be bought. It is psychologically difficult to consider the possibility that the initial purchase was at an excessively high price. The rational behaviour would be to consider the possibility that an item of bad news justifies the price fall. The investor's psychology makes it difficult to look for the bad news and its implications for the value of the share.

The psychological difficulty in considering the possibility that the initial purchase was at an excessively high price could be seen as an example of cognitive dissonance. Evidence that beliefs or decisions are wrong causes mental stress. This may result in the reluctance to admit an error. Holding a poorly performing investment too long is an aspect of the reluctance to admit that the investment was a mistake.

The reference point is subjective, but is likely to be influenced by one or more past values. Possibilities include the purchase price of the investment, the highest price seen, or an average of observed previous values. Heath *et al*. (1999) concluded, on the basis of evidence from the exercise of employee stock options, that the most likely reference point used is the highest price of the previous 12 months. It appears that people periodically update the reference point to reflect unrealised profits. However the study of the Boston housing market by Genesove and Mayer (2001) is consistent with the purchase price constituting the reference point.

Lin *et al*. (2006a), from a survey of investors, concluded that multiple reference points could be present simultaneously. The most important was the outcome from not investing at all. Two other significant reference points were the expected outcome, and the outcome from the best-performing alternative. The outcome from the worst-performing alternative was not a significant reference point; the observation that the outcome could have been worse did not appear to provide any comfort. Consistent with the curvature of Figure 2.2 was the finding that the direction of deviation from a reference point was more important than the size of deviation in the generation of feelings of regret or pleasure. Contrary to prospect theory, no asymmetry between upward and downward deviations was found. Upward and downward deviations from reference points appeared to have equivalent effects on feelings of regret and gratification.

Since reference points are subjective values they are susceptible to psychological biases. An important feature of reference points is that they appear to be influenced by the form in which information is presented, in other words according to how a situation is framed. For example telling an investor that a portfolio has risen in value by 5% might give the feeling that the reference point has been exceeded whereas saying that it has underperformed a benchmark by 5% could cause a perception of loss, whilst both statements may record the same outcome. The latter framing is likely to raise the reference level. A statement that share price gains have outweighed losses may cause a different reference level than a statement that some losses have held back the overall profit. The former statement, which is positive, is likely to engender a more positive perception of the outcome than the latter statement, which is negative.

It has been suggested that reference points may evolve over time with the result that loss-aversion is accompanied by disappointment aversion (Ang *et al*. 2005; Fielding and Stracca 2007). Under loss-aversion an investor has a fixed reference point, which might be the current level of stock prices or the current value of personal wealth. Gains and losses are evaluated against the reference point. The reference point could evolve according to the investment horizon. If reference points change over time there could be a disappointment aversion in addition to a loss-aversion. In the case of loss-aversion the pain of losses exceeds the pleasure of gains, when the gains and losses are of the same magnitude. In the case of disappointment aversion the pain or pleasure is brought about by deviations from expectations. The disappointment related to outcomes below expectations is stronger than the pleasure related to outcomes that exceed expectations. Although losses on investments may occur only in the short term, there may be disappointments in the long term. Although there may be gains in the long term, they would result in negative feelings if they fell below expectations. Whether loss-aversion and disappointment aversion are alternatives or coexist, the tendency for the pain of loss or disappointment to exceed the pleasure of exceeding reference points could deter investors from risky investments such as stocks.

Reference points can be influenced by self-imposed rules aimed at establishing self-control. People are prone to mental accounting, with different investments being allocated to different purposes (Kahneman and Tversky 1982). For example one portfolio may be for the purpose of funding retirement whilst another is for financing children through university. Mental accounting keeps these two portfolios separate so that neither is subsidised by the other. It may be that in aggregate the two portfolios are showing strong gains whilst one is showing a loss. The mental accounting will cause the perception of loss, in relation to a portfolio, despite the overall profit. One frequent rule for self-control is 'never touch the capital'; this means that dividends and interest should be used to finance spending but not the capital sum. A low dividend may lead to a forced withdrawal of capital. There may have been a strong capital appreciation, but the mental accounting that separates capital and dividends could result in feelings of failure and loss. Another example of how the framing of information influences perceptions is the line often used by financial advisers when attempting to sell regular savings schemes: a share price rise is good because you become richer but a fall is also good because your money buys more shares (these are both positive statements). A client is less likely to be told: a share price rise is bad because your money buys fewer shares but a fall is also bad because you become poorer (negative statements).

Shefrin and Statman (1984a) have argued that investors account for dividends, and capital gains/losses, separately at some times and together at other times. In the event of a small fall in share prices an investor may combine the capital loss with dividends in order to be able to see an overall gain. In the event of a large fall in share prices, the investor may separate them in order to be able to feel that there is a gain in relation to dividends. An implication of this ability to switch mental accounting is that investors prefer a combination of dividends and capital growth to receiving the whole benefit in the form of capital gains.

A report produced jointly by Distribution Technology and the Pensions Institute in the UK (Distribution Technology 2005) found that pension fund investment was consistent with prospect theory. In the context of pre-retirement financial planning, investors who are underfunded and anticipating a low retirement income tend to take a high level of investment risk in an attempt to remedy the underfunding. This is consistent with the observation that people in a loss-making position are more willing to accept risk than people in a profit-making position.

The report put investors into three categories. The first category, which accounted for more than a half of people, was distinguished by 'loss avoidance'. This category was characterised by a refusal to take any risk. In terms of prospect theory, this group exhibited 'total loss-aversion'. The second category (the smallest) was distinguished by 'extreme loss-aversion'. Whilst prepared to take some risk, the compensation required to take risk (in terms of expected additional return) was extremely high. The third category (the second largest) was distinguished by 'moderate loss-aversion'. It is among this group that realistic views of long-term investment were found. The third category tended to have relatively high levels of general education and to be relatively young.

The Disposition Effect

Prospect theory appears to be able to explain the disposition effect. The disposition effect is the willingness of investors to sell investments that show gains but not investments that show losses. Odean (2001) found that investors using a discount brokerage held losing stocks for an average of 124 days and winning stocks an average of 102 days. He also found that an average of 15% of gains were realised against only 10% of losses. Locke and Mann (1999) found that futures traders were also prone to the disposition effect. Further evidence for the disposition effect comes from Ferris *et al*. (1987) and from Schlarbaum *et al*. (1978).

Grinblatt and Keloharju (2001) found that a large positive return in one week increased the likelihood of a sale the following week. A large decrease reduced the likelihood of a subsequent sale. The effects were most pronounced for investment behaviour which occurred very soon after the price moves. The results were common to both individual investors and institutional investors (institutional investors include pension funds, insurance funds, and unit trusts). Statman *et al*. (2006) found that turnover in a particular stock was positively related to recent returns (price movements) on that stock. This is consistent with the disposition effect proposition that investors are more willing to sell following a price rise. They found the relationship to be stronger in the cases of small capitalisation stocks and earlier time periods, which they saw as evidence that individual investors may be more prone to the disposition effect than institutional investors. Barber *et al*. (2007) found a disposition effect in the Taiwan Stock Exchange, where investors appeared to be about twice as likely to sell a stock showing a gain than a stock showing a loss. However, institutional investors (specifically mutual funds) did not demonstrate the disposition effect.

Genesove and Mayer (2001) examined the disposition effect in the Boston housing market during the 1990s. They found that owners who faced selling at a loss tended to set their asking prices too high. To the expected selling price, they added 25–35% of the difference between the property's expected selling price and their original purchase price. As a result their houses were on the market for a relatively long time before being sold.

Shefrin and Statman (1984) interpreted the disposition effect in terms of the fear of regret and seeking pride. Selling a loss-making investment triggers feelings of regret. There is a realisation that the decision to buy it was bad. Selling an investment at a profit validates the decision to buy, and produces a feeling of pride. In consequence investors prefer to sell investments whose prices have risen rather than those whose prices have fallen. The disposition effect is reinforced by the tendency for many investors to treat 'paper losses' differently to realised losses. While the position is still held prices could rise; when it is sold the loss is confirmed.

The disposition effect appears to be absent when share price movements are general rather than specific to individual company shares. Nofsinger (2001) found that asset price rises and falls, resulting from news about the general economy, did not result in the disposition effect. This could be interpreted in terms of the significance of personal decision-making. Pride and regret arise when profits and losses can be seen as resulting from one's own decisions. Those feelings are less likely when profits and losses are seen as arising from events outside one's control (Clarke *et al.* 1994).

The question arises as to whether psychological biases reflect an investor's personality, whether the biases can be reduced by learning, and whether interaction with others can affect the biases. These matters have implications for financial advisers when dealing with clients who are subject to biases. Weber and Welfens (2006) have researched these issues in relation to the disposition effect. They tested for individual differences, stability of the bias, and the effects of learning. They found that there were substantial individual differences in proneness to the disposition effect. While most people appeared to exhibit the disposition effect, some behaved in the opposite manner. Loss realisation aversion (the reluctance to sell investments that were making losses) was found to be much more common than the tendency to sell investments that had risen in price. Investors exhibiting a strong tendency to sell profit-making investments were not necessarily the same as those reluctant to sell loss-making investments. The study suggested that the two sides of the disposition effect were unrelated.

Weber and Welfens (2006) found that investors who were prone to the disposition effect in one choice situation were also subject to the effect when making other choices. For example, an investor prone to the disposition effect when making stock market decisions tended to be prone to the effect when making housing market decisions. The strength of the effect was also stable over time. Someone with a strong disposition effect at one point in time would tend to have a relatively strong disposition effect at a later point in time. There appeared to be individual stability of the effect across different decisions and over time. These observations are consistent with the view that the disposition effect reflects stable personality traits. It was also found that interaction between investors reduced the individual stability of the effect. This suggests that social influences can affect the extent of individual psychological biases.

Weber and Welfens (2006) found that learning reduced the extent of the disposition effect. The tendency to be affected by the disposition effect was stable when considering the relative strength of the effect between individuals, but the absolute size of the effect was reduced by learning. This is consistent with the view that the effect is the result of a lack of knowledge of investment.

A feature of Figure 2.2 is the tendency for the slope of the value function to become less steep as gains or losses increase. This implies that as gains are made investors will become less inclined to take risks, since the addition to value of a higher gain is less than the reduction in value resulting from a lowered gain. This is consistent with the disposition effect since the sale of stocks would achieve a reduction in risk. Figure 2.2 also implies that as losses increase investors become more willing to accept risk. This is because the value of a loss reduction outweighs the value of a further loss. So, for example, in a losing situation an 'evens' bet looks attractive. Again this is consistent with the disposition effect since keeping stocks would avoid a reduction in risk.

The tendency for the slope of the value function to become less steep as gains or losses increase is also consistent with the hedonic editing hypothesis, which posits a preference for integrating losses and separating gains (Lim 2006). By selling a number of loss-making investments simultaneously, an investor can reduce the pain of loss since the pain from each additional sale is reduced as a result of the curvature of the value function (the diminishing sensitivity to loss). By selling profitable investments individually the pleasure is maximised since the diminishing pleasure implied by the curvature is avoided; each sale makes its maximum contribution to the feeling of pleasure. Lim found that there was a tendency for investors to sell losing stocks in bundles and gaining stocks separately.

Frederick (2005) has presented evidence that the accuracy of the perception of risk, and risk tolerance, are related to a personality characteristic referred to as 'cognitive reflection'. Cognitive reflection is the ability to resist the first impulse or intuition. It is the tendency to reflect and think about a problem rather than following initial inclinations. People who are high in cognitive reflection tend to be good at evaluating risky investment situations, and tend to be willing to take risks.

Avoidance of Psychological Biases

Montier (2003/2004) offered advice on how to counter some of the errors that arise from psychological biases. His points (somewhat paraphrased) included:

1. You know less than you think.
2. Be less certain in your views.
3. Listen to those who do not agree with you.
4. You did not know it all along; you just think you did.
5. Do not take information at face value; consider how it is presented.
6. Do not confuse good firms with good investments.
7. Easily recalled events are less likely than you think.
8. Be prepared to sell your losers and hold your winners.

It has been suggested that financial advisers should educate their clients not only about financial products, but also about the psychological biases that the clients may exhibit. Farrow (2006) suggested that financial advisers should recognise the role emotions play in the decision-making of their clients and should help them to manage those emotions. Attempts at eliminating negative behaviour on the part of clients can be an important part of an adviser's service. Farrow proposed that the recommendation of index tracker funds could be useful to such a process. However there is a danger that an adviser who attempts to correct psychological biases, and to remove emotion from decision-making, may find that clients go to another adviser who treats the biases as preferences to be accommodated.

SAVING AND SELF-CONTROL

Thaler and Shefrin (1981) describe the self-control problem as the interaction between a person's two selves: the planner and the doer. The doer wants to spend now rather than later, and delays unpleasant tasks. The planner is inclined to save for the future and get unpleasant tasks dealt with quickly. There is a conflict between desire and will power as a result of the influence of both short-term emotion and long-term rational concerns.

When making decisions involving the present there is a tendency to procrastinate. For example most people would rather receive £50 now than £100 in two years (foregoing a 41% p.a. return) whereas £100 in six years is preferred to £50 in four years. From a finance perspective the two choices are the same, except one is deferred (Ainsle 1991). People seem to view the present very differently to how they view the future. The attitude to the present appears to be characterised by strong desire and weak will power.

Choi *et al.* (2001) found that many low savers actually wanted to save more. They found that two-thirds of their sample recognised that they were saving too little. The problem was one of will power. They also found that whereas a third of the people surveyed intended to increase their savings rates in the near future, most of those well-intentioned people (86%) did not do so. Procrastination was present; the intended increase in saving was postponed.

Rabinovich and Webley (2007) focused their study on people who had expressed an intention to save. In this way they separated the implementation of an intention from the formation of the intention (arguably the two behavioural processes behind intentional saving). The factors that increase the likelihood that saving intentions are implemented may be different to the factors that lead to the formation of intentions to save. The study identified those who succeeded in implementing their saving intentions as the 'plan-and-do' group and those who failed to implement their saving intentions as the 'plan-in-vain' group. Time horizon and expenditure control techniques were found to be important factors in the successful implementation of saving intentions.

Time horizon, the inclination to think ahead, has a positive effect on both the intention to save and the implementation of the intention. Rabinovich and Webley found significant differences in time horizon between plan-and-do and plan-in-vain groups. The tendency to think ahead is associated with the successful implementation of saving intentions. The expenditure control techniques, which were found to help the successful implementation of saving plans, made the saving process automatic and partially independent of will power. Automatic deduction of saving from salary is an example of an automatic process. Use of mental accounting can also facilitate the implementation of saving intentions. If money to be saved were transferred to a separate account, psychology would give it a different status. The account containing savings is perceived differently to an account for expenditure, and the designation of a separate mental account for savings reduces the likelihood of spending from that account.

To help with will power people employ rules-of-thumb and environmental controls (Thaler and Shefrin 1981; Hoch and Loewenstein 1991; Nofsinger 2002). Environmental controls include automatic deductions from salary and monthly standing orders into savings or pension plans. Thaler (1994) found that most people who invested in a pension plan one year, contributed again the following year. They form a habit to help their will power. However, people tend to leave pension contributions until close to the last possible date (Shefrin and Thaler 1992); they seem to need a deadline in order to assert self-control. Thaler (1994) suggested that people find it easier to save from lump-sum payments than from regular income. Saving money from a monthly salary requires more self-control (Thaler and Shefrin 1981).

It has often been wondered why many investors prefer cash dividends in preference to selling shares as a means of turning capital gains into cash. Selling part of a shareholding as a means of turning a capital gain into cash may have tax advantages relative to receiving dividends. Nonetheless investors frequently prefer to receive cash dividends. This appears to be irrational from the perspective of maximising income. It may be explicable in terms of rules-of-thumb employed to help will power. One such rule-of-thumb is 'never touch the capital'. The capital, be it a sum of money in a bank deposit or a holding of shares, is treated as being untouchable. This piece of self-discipline ensures that the capital remains intact in order to provide income in the future.

Distribution Technology and the Pensions Institute (Distribution Technology 2005) found that most retirees with pension funds choose annuities (retirement incomes) that start at a high level, but without rises, in preference to annuities that start lower but rise over time to compensate for inflation. This is consistent with a preference for immediate expenditure.

Habitual Non-Savers

Scottish Widows, the UK financial services company, carries out an annual survey into pensions saving behaviour. The 2005 survey (Scottish Widows 2005) concluded that about 17% of people with sufficient income to save do not do so; this is consistent with the British Household Panel Survey, which suggests that about 18% of people are persistent non-savers (Department for Work and Pensions 2003). The Scottish Widows figure is possibly an underestimate since anyone in a defined-benefit pension scheme (i.e. an occupational pension that relates the pension to salary and years of service) is seen as saving, irrespective of whether they save outside the pension scheme, and it excludes people under 30. The non-savers are consistent and habitual non-savers. Differences in income levels do not seem to substantially affect this group; the proportion of non-savers remains fairly constant as income levels rise (considering the 30–50 age group the Scottish Widows survey found that 14% of those earning £30,000 to £40,000 were non-savers, and 12.5% of those earning over £40,000 were non-savers). However the proportion of non-savers declines past the age of 50.

The Scottish Widows survey identified a number of characteristics that appeared to distinguish habitual non-savers from savers. Non-savers are more likely to take a negative view of other people. Non-savers see themselves as relatively less happy, less healthy, less emotionally secure, and as having a worse romantic and social life. Non-savers are more likely to want a complete change in their lives. They are more likely to feel that they are unable to control, and cope with, their situation in life. They are less able to plan ahead. Non-savers are much more likely to be smokers. The main reason given for not saving is that they cannot afford it (even though many have high incomes), and many say that they could not reduce their spending without significantly affecting their lifestyles. Somewhat paradoxically, non-savers are more likely to believe that they will be able to live comfortably on a low income in retirement.

Non-savers are less likely to own their own homes, and those who do own their homes tend to have less valuable properties than savers (note that the survey was constructed so as to eliminate income and age as explanatory factors). Non-savers are more likely to have non-mortgage debts; they are less likely to see themselves as responsible in their borrowing and in their use of the borrowed money.

The Scottish Widows findings are broadly consistent with the results of the 'Family Resources Survey 2003-04', carried out by the Department for Work and Pensions (Department for Work and Pensions 2005), which found that 27% of households had accumulated absolutely no savings. It is not surprising that the Scottish Widows survey found that non-savers were less happy, less satisfied, and less able to cope with their situations in life. It has been found that debt has a negative effect on psychological well-being (Brown *et al.* 2005) and that people in (non-mortgage) debt are prone to stress, depression, and anxiety (Citizens Advice 2003). It would seem reasonable to presume that, if debt causes stress and psychological disorders, the existence of accumulated savings would improve psychological well-being. Possession of accumulated savings provides a buffer against adversity. Possession of money gives a degree of control over the effects of unforeseen adverse events, and reduces feelings of stress. Events that require expenditure to deal with problems, cause much more stress when the required money is not available. Accumulated savings provide a sense of independence, security, and control. However the study by Brown *et al.* (2005) indicated that it was regular saving, rather than accumulated wealth, that had a beneficial effect on psychological well-being.

Watson (2003) researched the relationship between materialism and saving behaviour. It was found that highly materialistic people were more likely to see themselves as spenders, and were more inclined to borrow. In particular they were favourably disposed towards borrowing for non-essential purposes and luxury items. People with low levels of materialism were more likely to save, and were more likely to own financial investments such as shares and mutual funds (unit trusts).

The complicated nature of the factors that affect the accumulation of debt (and possibly, by extension, saving behaviour) has been highlighted in a study conducted by Stone and Maury (2006). They developed a model capable of predicting indebtedness. The factors used in the prediction included demographic, financial, economic, psychological, and situational aspects.

Self-Control, Personality Traits, and Social Mood

The results of both the Scottish Widows survey and the Stone and Maury study suggested that saving behaviour could be related to aspects of personality. Olson (2006) reported that the most prominent classification of personality types is the Five-Factor Model. The five factors are extroversion versus introversion, agreeableness versus antagonism, conscientiousness versus heedlessness, emotional stability versus neuroticism, and openness-to-experience versus closed-to-experience. Some researchers have concluded that the five factors can be divided into two groups, thus making a two-factor model. Olson posited engagement and self-control as the two factors. Engagement encompasses extroversion and openness to experience, whereas self-control covers emotional stability, agreeableness, and conscientiousness. Low scores on the self-control traits have been found to be associated with stealing, drug and alcohol abuse, absenteeism from work, bad behaviour towards other people, and poor handling of stress. Research has found that deficiencies in self-control are linked to addiction, crime, domestic violence, bankruptcy, and academic failure; and negative emotions appear to impair self-control (Tice *et al.* 2001). The characteristics of low self-control people seem to be broadly consistent with the characteristics of non-savers identified in the Scottish Widows study.

Personality traits are not immutably fixed, and can be influenced by external factors. One such factor is social mood, which is mood that is pervasive within society. Prechter (1999) posited that during periods of negative social mood people are more likely to display the characteristics of low self-control. Negative social mood appears to be associated with distress, anxiety, antagonism, conflict, and reduced interest in work and achievement. For those who do save, social mood could influence the way in which the savings are invested. Negative social mood is likely to be associated with caution and risk-aversion, and hence the avoidance of stock market investments. Positive social mood is thought to engender engagement, including engagement with the high return, high risk investments associated with stock markets.

43

INFLUENCES ON RETIREMENT SAVING BEHAVIOUR

Jacobs-Lawson and Hershey (2005) investigated psychological determinants of retirement saving behaviour. They found that the existence, and extent, of saving for retirement was related to three psychological characteristics. One of those characteristics is 'future time perspective', which is a measure of the extent to which people focus on the future (it is alternatively known as 'future orientation'). A number of studies (Burtless 1999; Hershey and Mowen 2000; Lusardi 1999) found that future time perspective is positively related to the tendency to save for retirement.

Another characteristic that Jacobs-Lawson and Hershey (2005) found to be related to saving for retirement was knowledge of financial planning for retirement. A number of studies have indicated that financial knowledge is positively related to levels of retirement saving (Ekerdt *et al.* 2001; Grable and Lytton 1997; Hershey and Mowen 2000; Mitchell and Moore 1998; Yuh and DeVaney 1996). The third characteristic investigated by Jacobs-Lawson and Hershey was risk tolerance. Grable and Joo (1997) and Yuh and DeVaney (1996) found that risk tolerance was positively related to the level of retirement saving.

The findings of Jacobs-Lawson and Hershey were consistent with the results of previous studies in that higher levels of retirement saving were associated with greater degrees of future time perspective, knowledge of financial planning for retirement, and financial risk tolerance.

Harrison *et al.* (2006) investigated attitudes to retirement saving by the use of focus groups. One finding was that positive or negative feelings about ageing and retirement have effects on saving. Some people dislike the thought of growing old whereas others relish the prospect of being free of the need to work. It is possible that the fear of old age is dealt with by putting the future out of mind, and that is likely to put preparation for the future out of mind. Those looking forward to retirement may be more inclined to prepare for it. Three other factors found to deter saving for retirement were (1) the view that pension savings would be offset by reduced state benefits, (2) a mistrust of financial advisers, and (3) social pressures that encourage current spending.

Neukam and Hershey (2003) suggested that 'financial inhibition' and 'financial activation' were important determinants of retirement saving. Financial inhibition encompasses fear-based factors that deter saving. Such factors include the negative thoughts about growing old, as identified in the Harrison *et al.* (2006) study. If old age is associated with images of poor health and faded looks, people may be reluctant to prepare for it. Thoughts of old age evoke feelings of fear and anxiety. Little thought is given to retirement since such thought has unpleasant connotations. Financial activation relates to goal-based motives that encourage saving. If old age were associated with leisure and freedom to choose how to use time, there would be a greater incentive to save for retirement.

Financial inhibition is fear-based and financial activation is goal-based. They are two distinct characteristics rather than two ends of the same dimension. Neukam and Hershey (2003) found that the people who saved most were those with the strongest financial goals and the lowest level of fear. The goals and fears were not only related to visions of old age, but also to the planning process. The personal characteristics interact. For example a strong drive towards saving (planning) for retirement could be offset by a high level of fear about the planning process; a strong desire to accumulate wealth for retirement could be offset by a fear of stock market risk or a distrust of the financial services industry. This latter point is close to the Harrison *et al.* (2006) observation that mistrust of financial advisers can deter retirement saving. The importance of fears concerning the saving (retirement planning) process relates to the Jacobs-Lawson and Hershey (2005) findings that financial knowledge and risk tolerance are positively related to retirement saving.

Automatic Enrolment in Pension Schemes

Information overload can deter retirement saving (Turner 2006). If the choice between investment alternatives is too large and too complex, many employees take a default option. The default option may be to do nothing. One remedy is to provide default options other than non-participation. Automatic enrolment in pension schemes (with the right to withdraw) makes the default option one of participation. This is likely to bring into a pension scheme both those who wish to save but fail to take action, and those who give little or no thought to financial matters. Another dimension of positive default options is to have a default fund that would be suitable for the average employee. A suitable contribution rate might be provided as the default rate, perhaps with an element of automatic escalation over time. Alternatives to the default options could be provided for the employees who wish to exercise choice. Turner (2004) reported that in Sweden's mandatory scheme 82% of new entrants allowed their entire contributions to be paid into the default fund whilst more than 600 other funds were available. Mitchell and Utkus (2006) provide evidence that pension fund participants like to be at the average and like to avoid extremes when making choices. This is consistent with the observation that plan participants tend to accept default options, which may be seen as the average (middle-of-the-road) options.

Akerlof (1991) concluded that most people succumb to the desire of current expenditure during their peak earning years and delay saving for retirement. Pension plan administrators often find that the most difficult step is to get people to start contributing. People tend to procrastinate. In the UK, the government is considering a change in company pension regulations so that employees join pension schemes automatically. The decision of the employee is thus one of whether to leave the scheme rather than one of whether to join. Procrastination would leave employees in the pension scheme. Madrian and Shea (2000) concluded that automatic enrolment plans are successful in increasing participation rates. In studying a plan that was changed to automatic enrolment, they found an increase in the participation rate from 49% to 86%. However most participants chose the minimum contribution level; the analysis of Madrian and Shea indicated that many participants would have chosen a higher contribution rate if they had explicitly chosen to opt into the scheme. Choi et al. (2001) found that people who would otherwise have contributed more into a pension scheme accept the default contribution rate when enrolment is automatic. So whilst automatic enrolment increases the number of members, those who would have joined anyway contribute less than they would have done in the absence of automatic enrolment.

The temptation to spend immediately is also reflected in choices made at retirement. When there is an option to take a lump sum in the place of part (or all) of the pension, people tend to choose the lump sum. This would be reinforced by the fear of dying soon after retirement with the effect that the money spent on an annuity would be lost. An annuity is an income for life that is purchased with a pension fund. Annuities provide insurance against longevity risk, which is the risk that someone could outlive their money. Longevity risk is the risk that a person's money is fully spent before death so that the person has no money during the later years of life. An annuity could be the default option at retirement.

Save More Tomorrow:

Benartzi and Thaler (2004) used the principles of behavioural finance to develop a practical programme for increasing the level of saving into pension schemes. The programme is called Save

More Tomorrow (SMarT). The programme was designed to help employees who want to save more for retirement but find that their will power is lacking.

One feature of SMarT is that there is a time lag between commitment to the scheme and the date on which payments begin. This overcomes the problem that people tend to value immediate money very highly (sometimes called hyperbolic discounting). People find it easier to commit to a future investment than an immediate one.

A second feature is that increases in payments to the scheme coincide with pay rises. By using part of a pay rise, contributors do not feel that they are reducing their disposable income (take-home pay). This avoids the aversion to loss identified by prospect theory. It does not seem to matter whether the pay rise is a real one, or simply matches inflation, since people seem to suffer from money illusion. The real rise is the increase in the purchasing power of the wage; if prices are rising, the real rise is less than the rise in money terms. Money illusion causes people to see money rises as real ones. Evidence for money illusion has been found by Kahneman *et al.* (1986) and by Shafir *et al.* (1997).

A third feature is that the contributions to the pension scheme increase every time there is a pay rise, until a predetermined maximum proportion of income is reached. The status quo bias indicates that when faced with a choice people tend to do nothing (i.e. they maintain the status quo). This causes procrastination. If the decision has already been made to increase contributions to the scheme, maintenance of the status quo entails proceeding with the existing arrangement to increase contributions.

A fourth feature is that employees can opt out of the plan if they wish to. This makes commitment to the scheme less binding, and hence makes the commitment more likely. The status quo bias tends to keep people in the scheme.

Benartzi and Thaler applied SMarT in a company and found that it was successful in raising rates of saving into a pension fund. They found that the average saving rate for participants in the programme increased from 3.5% to 13.6% over 40 months. They also found that 78% of the employees joined the programme, and that 80% of the joiners were still in the scheme after 40 months.

Benartzi and Thaler estimated that implementation of SMarT throughout the United States could increase personal saving by $125 billion per year. Investment of such additional sums in stock and bond markets would put substantial upward pressure on share prices and bond prices. Successful plans to increase saving into pension funds could cause large rises in share (and bond) prices. After all, share prices are determined by demand and supply. A large increase in demand would be expected to result in a considerable rise in prices. The new savers would be rewarded with capital gains, and that might further encourage saving. There could be positive feedback investing whereby rising share prices lead to increased investment, which in turn raises share prices (and hence investment). Behavioural biases would tend to reinforce this upward trend (as described in Chapter 27 on stock market bubbles and crashes).

CLASSIFYING INVESTORS

Many of the predictions of behavioural finance are mutually inconsistent. Some behavioural biases predict overreaction whilst others predict under-reaction, some indicate underestimation of risk whereas others suggest overestimation, and some lead to excessive trading whilst others entail

Table 2.3

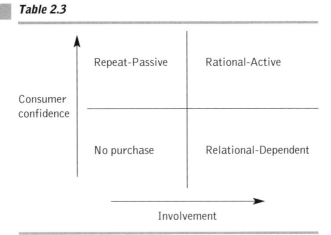

inertia. Other opposing predictions can be deduced from the principles of behavioural finance. Behavioural biases cannot apply equally to all investors. People differ in their susceptibility to particular psychological biases. Different biases impact different investors to varying extents. The question arises as to whether people can be categorised in terms of which behavioural biases are most influential in their decision-making.

Categorisations of savers and investors have been proposed by Beckett *et al.* (2000) and by Keller and Siegrist (2006). The Beckett *et al.* classification is shown in Table 2.3.

The term 'Consumer confidence' covers a number of attributes: uncertainty, perception of risk, complexity, and knowledge. The term 'Involvement' encompasses control, participation, and contact.

The 'No purchase' group makes no investment. This group is characterised by low confidence and low involvement. The group includes people who leave large sums of money on deposit rather than investing more profitably.

The 'Repeat-Passive' group takes little interest in the investment process (has low involvement) but has sufficient confidence to take some risk. This group persistently invests in the same shares or funds. Its members show loyalty to the particular shares or funds, which they repeatedly invest in.

The 'Rational-Active' group comes closest to the investors of conventional (non-behavioural) finance theory. This group demonstrates the inclination, and has sufficient confidence in its ability, to choose actively between investments. These investors are willing to accept risk and to exercise control over their own investments.

The 'Relational-Dependent' group contains the investors who seek professional advice. They take an interest in the investment process but do not have sufficient confidence, in their ability to understand investment choices, to make their own evaluations of the alternatives.

The Keller and Siegrist (2006) classification is shown in Table 2.4.

Keller and Siegrist make the (often overlooked) point that many people are not interested in saving, investing, and wealth accumulation. Money is not very important to members of the 'Money dummies' and 'Open books' clusters. Possessing money and increasing wealth are not important goals for them. They show low interest and involvement in matters of personal finance. However, 'Money dummies' are more favourably disposed towards stock market investing than 'Open books' (partly because 'Open books' tend to see stock market investing as immoral).

47

Table 2.4

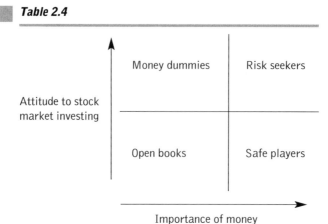

The investment of money is important to members of the 'Risk seekers' and 'Safe players' clusters. Possessing money and increasing wealth are important goals for them. They are more inclined to save than the 'Money dummies' and 'Open books'. They differ in their attitudes to stock market investing. 'Safe players' are more likely to keep their money on deposit rather than investing in stocks. 'Risk seekers' are more favourably disposed towards stock market investments and are relatively tolerant of risk. They are more confident about managing money than the other groups.

Tables 2.3 and 2.4 have been intentionally drawn to show parallels between the two classifications. Although the correspondence is far from perfect, there is a degree of correspondence between the quadrants in the two tables ('Repeat-Passive' with 'Money dummies'; 'No purchase' with 'Open books'; 'Rational-Active' with 'Risk seekers'; 'Relational-Dependent' with 'Safe players').

Possibly the weakest correspondence is between 'Relational-Dependent' and 'Safe players'. Both are concerned with saving and investing. However, with regard to stock market investments, the 'Relational-Dependent' group are probably more concerned with the complexity of the choices such that they seek professional advice. The 'Safe players' have a tendency to avoid stock market investment because it is seen as immoral. It is possible that this apparent difference between the groups arises from the Keller and Siegrist questionnaire, which asked about attitudes to the morality of stock market investing rather than its complexity or risk.

It is not difficult to assign behavioural biases to the four quadrants. Investors in the top left-hand quadrant are more likely to exhibit conservatism, status quo bias, and familiarity bias. The bottom left-hand quadrant would tend to contain the non-savers and procrastinators. The top right quadrant would be expected to contain the investors with a tendency towards overconfidence. The bottom right quadrant could contain a significant proportion of the investors for whom the complexity of choice is a problem.

The more loss-averse investors are probably in the bottom quadrants. Investors in the lower quadrants may be subject to biases that cause exaggerated perceptions of risk, such as the retrievability (availability) bias and the narrow framing that leads to excessive focus on short-term volatility.

An understanding of how different people think about saving and investment is important to policy-makers seeking to encourage saving for retirement and to financial institutions wanting to market their own investment products.

The Need for Targeted Marketing

Lee (2002) took the view that there should be different approaches to marketing financial services, dependent upon the characteristics of the consumer group being targeted. Using cluster analysis consumers of financial services were divided into four groups. The four groups were named 'open to direct means', 'cherry pickers', 'needs human touch', and 'undecided'. Their relative levels of affluence followed that order.

The 'open to direct means' cluster did not need contact with advisers when deciding upon the purchase of financial services. They preferred to arrange financial services via the Internet, telephone, or post. This group was the most affluent, the most highly educated, the youngest, and the most knowledgeable about financial services.

The 'cherry pickers' were prepared to use direct means to arrange some financial services, such as credit cards and insurance, but preferred human contact for other services, such as mortgages and investments. This was the second most affluent group, and tended to be middle-aged. They had a reasonably good level of education, but not as much as the 'open to direct means' cluster.

The 'needs human touch' group strongly preferred face-to-face interaction. They were relatively poorly organised with respect to financial management. The 'undecided' group expressed no preference between direct and human contact delivery of financial services. It was the least affluent cluster, and contained relatively older members. They were relatively poorly organised in respect to financial management, and often expressed budgeting difficulties.

It appears that it is not just the nature of financial products that needs to be varied according to the characteristics of the targeted groups, but the means of marketing and delivering the products also need to be varied. Some groups require more personal input than others. Human contact is a more expensive form of marketing and sales than direct means such as websites, telemarketing, and post. Unfortunately it seems that the consumers who require the most expensive delivery are the consumers whose relative lack of affluence makes them the least attractive to the providers of financial services.

There is evidence that marketing effort should be influenced by economic factors as well as by the characteristics of targeted groups. Tang *et al.* (2007) found that the effects of changes in economic and stock market conditions differed according to the socio-demographic characteristics of the consumers. A rise in unemployment is associated with reduced demand for financial products but the rich and the over 55s are less affected than other groups. Rises in inflation have a negative effect on purchases of savings products but affect older people less than younger people. Conversely the negative effect of stock market falls is greatest for the over 55s.

THE POSSIBILITY OF MISLEADING MARKETING

Investors should not only be aware of their psychological biases, but they should also be aware of how marketing can be misleading. Capon *et al.* (1996) found that the main factor in the decision of which fund to choose was the fund performance in the recent past. Zweig (2000) observed that fund managers took advantage of this by timing their advertising to coincide with relatively good performance of their funds. Investment companies typically operate a family of funds. The better performing funds from the family can be advertised, and the company as a whole thereby appears

49

in a favourable light. The time period over which the advertised performance is measured could also be chosen with a view to achieving the most favourable presentation of a fund.

Huhmann and Bhattacharyya (2005) found that most mutual fund (unit trust) advertisements did not provide the information necessary for informed choices. Advertisers were found to use techniques that increase the likelihood that the advertisements are noticed but decrease the likelihood that they are read. The advertisements were concerned with conveying perceptions of success regardless of the accuracy of those perceptions.

Although there are publications that show performance figures for all funds in a company's range over standard time periods (e.g. *Money Management* and *Money Observer* in the UK), there are still ways in which investment companies can legally manipulate information. One possibility is 'burying the dead'. This entails merging poorly performing funds into stronger ones. Suppose that a company has a 'UK Special Situations' fund that has performed poorly over a number of years. Also suppose that the company has a 'UK Growth' fund that has performed well. If the company merges the special situations fund into the growth fund, the poorly performing fund disappears from the performance figures leaving only the strong fund. Investors in the special situations fund would have suffered poor performance but no current performance figures would reveal that.

Jordan and Kaas (2002) investigated the potential of using behavioural finance biases in the construction of advertisements. They found that the anchoring bias could be used to influence expectations of fund returns. Including a high percentage in the advertisement, even if the percentage is not related to investment returns, will raise the consumers' expectations of fund return. They found that the representativeness bias could be used. Representativeness entails the use of stereotypes, and if the investment company is reputable and well known it conforms to a positive stereotype. Funds managed by the company are seen as representative of the company. Jordan and Kaas found that funds managed by reputable, well-known investment companies were seen as relatively less risky. They also investigated the affect heuristic, which is the effect of positive feelings towards a product. They found that if advertising could engender positive emotions associated with a fund, the fund would be seen as relatively less risky. It was found that advertising could be effective, in using the behavioural biases, on both knowledgeable and naive investors. The effects were greater in the case of naive investors.

MAXIMIN AND MINIMAX

The measurement of risk by means of the standard deviation of a normal distribution of possible outcomes assumes a symmetrical attitude to risk. A 50% probability of loss is seen as fully compensated by a 50% probability of gain. Prospect theory suggests that this is not so, and that the trauma of loss is greater than the pleasure of profit. In the presence of such loss-aversion, standard deviation may not be the most appropriate measure of risk. Maximin and minimax provide alternative measures of risk.

The maximin approach to decision-making seeks to obtain the highest minimum value ('maximin' comes from the 'maximum minimum' value). Someone using such a decision-making criterion may choose to measure risk in terms of the maximum loss.

The minimax regret criterion seeks to minimise opportunity cost and implies that risk should be measured as the maximum opportunity loss. Consider an investor who needs to choose between investing wholly in deposits, an equal combination of deposits and shares, and wholly in shares.

Table 2.5

	100% shares	50% shares	0% shares
20% rise	120 (0)	110 (10)	100 (20)
no change	100 (0)	100 (0)	100 (0)
20% fall	80 (20)	90 (10)	100 (0)

Suppose that there are three possible outcomes: a 20% rise in share prices, stable share prices, and a 20% fall in share prices. Table 2.5 depicts the outcomes from an investment of £100 for each of the three share price scenarios. The opportunity loss relative to the most successful strategy, for each share price scenario, is shown in brackets.

The minimax regret criterion suggests the investment strategy that has the lowest maximum opportunity loss. In the case of Table 2.5, it suggests an even split between shares and deposits. Risk is being measured as the maximum opportunity loss (10 in the case of the chosen strategy, 20 in the cases of the other two strategies). This approach is concerned with minimising regret ('minimax' regret comes from the 'minimum maximum' regret).

CONCLUSION

Personal investment decisions are choices made under constraint. An obvious constraint is the amount of money available for investment, which is affected by wealth, income, debts, and personal (including family) commitments. Another constraint is limited knowledge of the investment options. Investment objectives include growth, income, low risk, and liquidity (liquidity is the ability to turn the investment into cash quickly and cheaply). These objectives may entail trade-offs; for example high prospective growth may involve high risk.

Risk is not a simple characteristic. There are many types of risk. Some investments that are commonly seen as risk-free do carry risks. For example, building society and bank accounts are typically subject to the risk that interest rates might fall or that inflation would reduce the purchasing power of the invested money. Some risks are not obvious. For example there is the risk that an investment manager may perform relatively badly; this is known as management risk and provides a reason for choosing index tracker funds that simply aim to follow a stock market index (such as the FTSE 100) without attempting to outperform the stock market (see Chapter 9 on mutual funds).

People may choose to retain, avoid, reduce, or transfer risks. Diversification is a major way of reducing risk and entails holding a wide range of different investments in anticipation that losses on some would be offset by gains on others (see Chapter 13 on portfolio diversification). In this context investors should be aware that residential property, occupational pension rights, and human capital (earning power) are components of their wealth portfolios. Insurance transfers risks to an insurance company. Some institutional investments, such as stock market investments that guarantee that the capital cannot be lost, may use derivatives (particularly options) to insure the capital against loss (see Chapter 34 on structured products).

Investors should be aware of their psychological biases when choosing investments. They should also be aware of how marketing can seek to exploit their psychological biases. There are psychological biases that entail self-deception. No one is perfectly rational. Everyone has a tendency to see what they want to see, and remember what they want to remember. Self-image can affect perceptions of investment decisions, and the outcomes of those decisions, just as it affects perceptions of many aspects of people's lives.

People are bombarded with more information than the human mind can handle. This has implications for many decisions, including investment decisions. Mental short cuts (rules-of-thumb), known as heuristic simplifications, are used. Everyone uses heuristic simplifications, even when they are unaware of them. People are often reluctant to accept that events occur by chance, and attempt to think of reasons and causes. People are often slow to change their opinions in the light of new evidence.

A person's ideas and behaviour are affected by the ideas and behaviour of others. There is a tendency to conform to the standards and opinions of people with whom we interact. There can be forms of 'groupthink' where all members of a group think and behave in similar ways. These social influences affect investment decisions as well as other decisions. Likewise moods and emotions affect investment decisions. Personality characteristics affect the level of saving, the types of investment into which the savings are put, and the willingness to sell or change those investments. People vary in terms of whether they are primarily concerned with the level of their wealth, changes in the level of their wealth, or avoiding the regret of making bad decisions.

Further reading

Readers who would like to pursue further their studies of behavioural finance may find the following books interesting:

Montier, J. (2002). *Behavioural Finance.* Wiley.
Nofsinger, J. R. (2005). *The Psychology of Investing,* 2nd edn, Pearson Education/Prentice Hall.
Shefrin, H. (2000). *Beyond Fear and Greed: Understanding Behavioral Finance and the Psychology of Investing.* Harvard Business School Press.
Shiller, R. J. (2005). *Irrational Exuberance,* 2nd edn, Princeton University Press.

Part 1

Basics of Money, Bond, and Property Markets

Chapter 3

Interest rates and money market investments

OBJECTIVE

The objective of this chapter is to provide readers with the knowledge required to be able to:

1. Distinguish between simple interest and compound interest.
2. Calculate average compound rates of interest.
3. Understand the nature of variable and fixed interest rates.
4. Be familiar with the convention for quoting interest rates on an annualised basis.
5. Distinguish between nominal and real interest rates.
6. Calculate interest rates and discount rates.
7. Distinguish between interest yield and total return.
8. Identify, and evaluate, money market investments.
9. Understand the implications of holding foreign currency deposits.
10. Compare the prospective returns from money market investments and stock market investments.

Money market investments tend to be short term (maturities of a year or less) and low risk, in the sense that their values are not strongly subject to market fluctuations. The most common form of money market investment is the deposit, although there are other forms such as bills and commercial paper. The return on deposits is in the form of interest. There are a number of features of interest rates and interest payments of which investors should be aware.

SIMPLE INTEREST AND COMPOUND INTEREST

Suppose that £100 is invested for two years at an interest rate of 10% p.a. At the end of year 1, the £100 will have grown to £110 [£100 × 1.1].

The £110 is invested at 10% for year 2 and grows to £121 [£100 × 1.1 × 1.1]. The interest of £21 includes £20 interest on the original investment of £100. This is known as simple interest.

There is also £1, which is interest on the first £10 interest. This interest on interest is known as compound interest.

The value of £121 at the end of two years is known as the future value of the initial £100.

EXAMPLE 3.1

(1) Suppose that £1,000 is invested for 10 years at 5% p.a.

    (a) What is the future value of the £1,000?

    (b) What is the simple interest?

    (c) What is the compound interest?

Answers

[using the y^x or $\wedge$ function on a calculator]

    (a) £1,000 $\times$ $(1.05)^{10}$ = £1,628.89.

    (b) £1,000 $\times$ 0.05 $\times$ 10 = £500.

    (c) £1,628.89 $-$ £1,000 $-$ £500 = £128.89.

(2) What would the answers be if the £1,000 were invested for 45 years?

Answers

    (a) £1,000 $\times$ $(1.05)^{45}$ = £8,985.01.

    (b) £1,000 $\times$ 0.05 $\times$ 45 = £2,250.

    (c) £8,985.01 $-$ £1,000 $-$ £2,250 = £5,735.01.

(3) What would the answers be if the £1,000 were invested for 45 years at 10% p.a.?

Answers

    (a) £1,000 $\times$ $(1.1)^{45}$ = £72,890.48.

    (b) £1,000 $\times$ 0.1 $\times$ 45 = £4,500.

    (c) £72,890.48 $-$ £1,000 $-$ £4,500 = £67,390.48.

Compound interest becomes more important as time and interest rates increase.

When considering deposits with interest payable more frequently than once a year, the effective interest rate is higher than the simple rate. Increased frequency of compounding raises the effective rate. For example, an investment of £100 at an interest rate of 6% payable annually leads to the receipt of £106 at the end of the year. If the interest were payable six monthly, the value of the investment at the end of the year would be £100 $\times$ (1.03) $\times$ (1.03) = £106.09. There is interest on interest since the £3 interest from the first six months is reinvested for the second six months. If the interest were payable three monthly, the value of the investment at the end of the year would be £100 × (1.015) × (1.015) × (1.015) × (1.015) = £106.14. A high frequency of interest payment entails more interest on interest and hence a greater value at the end of the year. The effective interest rate is alternatively known as the Annual Equivalent Rate (AER). In the UK providers of savings products (retail deposits) are required to quote the AER so that savers can easily make comparisons between the alternatives available.

When considering deposits covering periods of more than one year, simple annual returns are based on dividing the returns over the period by the number of years in the period. For example if a deposit produces returns of 0%, 10%, and 20% in successive years, the average simple rate of interest would be (0% + 10% + 20%)/3 = 10%.

Such an approach ignores the reinvestment of interest returns during the period of investment. The compound rate of interest is based on receipts being reinvested and producing their own returns. The average compound rate of interest would be $(1.0 \times 1.1 \times 1.2)^{1/3} - 1 = 0.097$ i.e. 9.7% p.a. When compounding (interest on interest) is allowed for, the interest rate required for the realisation of a particular sum of money is lower (in this case 9.7% p.a. rather than 10% p.a.).

THE AVERAGE COMPOUND RATE OF INTEREST

The average compound rate of interest is the average rate of interest over a period of time taking account of compounding. It is the rate of interest which, if applied each year of an investment, would produce the same final outcome as the succession of interest rates actually experienced. It is a geometric average. A geometric average is calculated by multiplying together a series of values, and then finding the appropriate root (this is illustrated by Exercises 3.1, 3.2, 3.3, 3.4, and 3.5).

Alternatively the geometric average, the average compound rate of return, can be calculated as a root of the investment return over the full period. In this case the equation is:

$$R = (\text{Final Value of Investment/Initial Investment})^{1/n} - 1$$

where R is the average compound rate of return and n is the number of years for which the investment is made. Using the power of 1/n is equivalent to taking the nth root. For example if a deposit grows from £100 to £130 over five years the average compound rate of return would be calculated as:

$$R = (£130/£100)^{1/5} - 1 = 0.0539 \text{ as a decimal, or } 5.39\% \text{ p.a. as a percentage.}$$

The 1 is subtracted as a means of removing the value of the original investment since only the interest is being calculated.

EXERCISE 3.1

(a) A bank deposit pays interest at 3% one year and 6% the next. What is the average compound rate of interest?

(b) If the bank account paid interest rates of 3%, 6%, and 9% in successive years what would the average compound rate of interest be?

Answer

(a) $\sqrt{(1.03)(1.06)} - 1 = \sqrt{1.0918} - 1 = 1.0449 - 1 = 0.0449$ as a decimal, i.e. 4.49% p.a. as a percentage. (Note that $\sqrt{1.0918}$ could alternatively be expressed as $1.0918^{1/2}$.)

(b) $[(1.03)(1.06)(1.09)]^{1/3} - 1 = 1.1901^{1/3} - 1 = 1.0597 - 1 = 0.0597$ as a decimal, i.e. 5.97% p.a. as a percentage. (Note that $1.1901^{1/3}$ is the cube root of 1.1901.)

Further examples of the calculation of average compound rates of return are provided in exercises 3.2, 3.3, 3.4, and 3.5.

VARIABLE AND FIXED INTEREST RATES

A deposit at a variable interest rate is subject to interest rate variations as rates in the money markets change. Typically the bank can make the change at any time with little or no notice. Such deposits are subject to income risk. Income risk relates to the uncertainty as to the level of income that an investor derives from a deposit. A fall in interest rates entails a fall in income receipts.

A fixed rate deposit guarantees the interest rate for a specified period. For example a five-year fixed rate deposit will pay the specified interest rate for the full five years, irrespective of what happens to interest rates in the money markets.

Both of these types of deposit typically pay, or accumulate, interest on an annual basis. The compounding of interest is normally on a predetermined date, often the anniversary of the deposit.

An intermediate investment between these two is a deposit on which the interest is fixed for a period, after which it is revised. A typical example would be a six-month rollover deposit on which the interest rate is fixed for six months after which it is changed, in line with money market rates. There would be a succession of six-month periods, during each period the interest rate is fixed. At the end of each period the interest rate is reset and the new rate is fixed for the following six months. In such a case interest is payable, or accumulates, twice a year. Compounding would be six monthly.

CONVENTION FOR QUOTING INTEREST RATES

The wholesale money markets are the markets in which institutions such as banks, building societies, insurance companies, pension funds, investment companies, large corporations, and government bodies lend to, and borrow from, one another. In the wholesale money markets interest rates are always quoted on a per annum (p.a., i.e. per year) basis. The interest rate is quoted per annum whatever the period of the investment. If the investment period, or frequency of compounding, is less than a year the annual interest rate is multiplied by the fraction of the year. For example, a six-month deposit with an interest rate of 5% p.a. pays interest of half 5%, i.e. 2.5%, over the six months. If the period is three months and the quoted rate is 6% p.a., the interest paid each three months is a quarter of 6%, i.e. 1.5%. In such cases the effective annual rate is greater than the quoted rate because of compounding ($1.015 \times 1.015 \times 1.015 \times 1.015 = 1.0614$ which is 6.14% p.a.). In the case of retail deposits for personal savings it is the effective annual rate, i.e. the annual equivalent rate (AER), that must be quoted.

If the investment period is longer than a year, interest rates are regarded as compounded annually (unless a shorter period is specified). For example a three-year investment at 7% p.a. is treated as paying interest annually at 7%. So at the end of three years an investment of £100 would be worth $£100 \times 1.07 \times 1.07 \times 1.07 = £122.50$.

NOMINAL AND REAL RATES OF INTEREST

If inflation is expected, some interest is required simply to compensate for the expected rise in prices. The real interest is the yield net of compensation for inflation. The real interest rate measures the returns from an investment in terms of enhanced purchasing power.

For example if the rate of interest is 3% p.a., a deposit of £100 will grow to £103 over a year. If prices rise by 3% over the year, £103 at the end of the year will buy the same amount as £100 bought at the beginning of the year. The investor makes no real gain from the deposit. The real interest rate is zero.

The real interest rate is given by the expression:

$$R_r = (1 + R_n)/(1 + i) - 1$$

where R_r is the real interest rate, R_n is the nominal interest rate, and i is the rate of inflation. The nominal interest rate (alternatively known as the money interest rate) is the rate quoted by banks, building societies, and other deposit takers.

In the previous example the real rate of interest can be calculated as:

$$R_r = (1.03)/(1.03) - 1 = 0$$

i.e. the real rate of interest is zero. If the nominal rate of interest were 7% p.a., the real interest rate would be:

$$R_r = (1.07)/(1.03) - 1 = 0.039 \text{ i.e. } 3.9\% \text{ p.a.}$$

Note that in this case simply subtracting the rate of inflation from the nominal rate of interest gives a close approximation to the real rate of interest. It should also be remembered that, when evaluating prospective investments, it is the rate of inflation expected to occur during the period of the investment that should be used in the calculation of the real rate of interest.

EXERCISE 3.2

(a) A bank deposit pays 8% p.a. one year and 10% p.a. the next. Calculate the average compound rate of return on the basis of annual interest payments.

Answer

$\sqrt{(1.08)(1.1)} - 1 = \sqrt{1.188} - 1 = 1.09 - 1 = 0.09$ as a decimal, which is 9% p.a. as a percentage.

(b) If the interest in (a) were paid on a six-month basis what would be the effective average annual compound rate of return (assuming that the interest rate quotes are wholesale money market quotes)?

Answer

$\sqrt{(1.04)(1.04)(1.05)(1.05)} - 1 = \sqrt{1.1925} - 1 = 1.092 - 1 = 0.092$ as a decimal, which is 9.2% p.a. as a percentage.

(c) Suppose that the rates in (a) are nominal interest rates and that inflation in the two years was 5% and 8% respectively. Calculate the average compound real rate of return.

Answer

$\sqrt{(1.08/1.05)(1.1/1.08)} - 1 = \sqrt{(1.0286)(1.0185)} - 1 = \sqrt{1.0476} - 1 = 1.0235 - 1 = 0.0235$ as a decimal, which is 2.35% p.a. as a percentage.

(d) What would be the nominal and real values of an investment of £100 at the rates in (c) at the end of the two years.

Answer

The nominal value would be £100 $\times$ (1.08) $\times$ (1.1) = £118.80.
The real value would be £100 $\times$ (1.08/1.05) $\times$ (1.1/1.08) = £104.76.

EXERCISE 3.3

(a) If nominal one year interest rates over the next five years are expected to be 5% p.a., 6% p.a., 6% p.a., 5% p.a., and 4% p.a., what should a £100 investment grow to over the five years? What would be the average compound nominal rate of return?

(b) If £1 invested now is expected to be worth £1.50 in five years, what is the average compound nominal rate of return? If inflation were expected to be 2% p.a., what would the expected average compound real rate of return be?

(c) If £100 invested now is expected to be worth £140 in five years, what is the expected average compound nominal rate of return?

Answer

(a) $1.05 \times 1.06 \times 1.06 \times 1.05 \times 1.04 = 1.2883$

So £100 would grow to £128.83 over the five years.

The average compound nominal rate of return is:

$(^5\!\sqrt{1.2883}) - 1 = 1.052 - 1 = 0.052$ i.e. 5.2% p.a.

(b) $(^5\!\sqrt{1.50}) - 1 = 1.08447 - 1 = 0.08447$ i.e. 8.45% p.a. (to two decimal places).

The average compound nominal rate of return would be 8.45% p.a.

To keep pace with inflation the pound needs to rise to:

£ $1.02^5 = $ £1.10408 over the five years.

In real terms, after five years, £1.50 would be worth £1.50/1.10408 = £1.3586.

The average compound real rate of return would be:

$(^5\!\sqrt{1.3586}) - 1 = 1.06321 - 1 = 0.06321$ i.e. 6.32% p.a. (to two decimal places).

(c) £140/£100 = 1.40

$(^5\!\sqrt{1.40}) - 1 = 1.06961 - 1 = 0.06961$ i.e. 6.96% p.a. (to two decimal places).

EXERCISE 3.4

An investor, who pays income tax at 40%, has a bank deposit that pays 3%, 3.5%, 4%, 4%, and 4.5% p.a. before tax in five successive years. Inflation is 2%, 2.5%, 2.5%, 3%, and 3% p.a. respectively in the five years.

(a) What is the pre-tax average nominal rate of return?

(b) What is the pre-tax average real rate of return?

(c) What is the post-tax average real rate of return?

Answer

(a) $[(1.03)(1.035)(1.04)(1.04)(1.045)]^{0.2} - 1 = 0.038$ i.e. 3.8% p.a.

(b) Over the five years the price level rises at an average rate of:

$[(1.02)(1.025)(1.025)(1.03)(1.03)]^{0.2} - 1 = 0.026$ i.e. 2.6% p.a.

The average real rate of return is $(1.038/1.026) - 1 = 0.0117$ i.e. 1.17% p.a.

Alternatively:

$$[(1.03/1.02)(1.035/1.025)(1.04/1.025)(1.04/1.03)(1.045/1.03)]^{0.2} - 1$$
$$= [1.0098 \times 1.0098 \times 1.0146 \times 1.0097 \times 1.0146]^{0.2} - 1$$
$$= 0.0117 \text{ i.e. } 1.17\% \text{ p.a.}$$

(c) The after-tax rates of return are: 1.8%, 2.1%, 2.4%, 2.4%, and 2.7% p.a.

The average after-tax nominal rate of return is:

$$[(1.018)(1.021)(1.024)(1.024)(1.027)]^{0.2} - 1 = 0.0228 \text{ i.e. } 2.28\% \text{ p.a.}$$

The average after-tax real rate of return is: $(1.0228/1.026) - 1 = -0.0031$ i.e. -0.31% p.a. In real terms, after tax, the value of the investment falls.

EXERCISE 3.5

A building society account pays interest at 3%, 2%, 2%, 3%, and 2% p.a. in successive years. Inflation is 2.5%, 2%, 1.5%, 2%, and 1.5% p.a. during those years.

(a) What is the money value of a deposit of £1,000 by the end of the five years (with interest reinvested) for

    (i) someone who pays no tax,
    (ii) someone who pays tax at 20%, and
    (iii) someone who pays tax at 40%?

What is the average compound nominal rate of return in each case?

(b) What is the real value of the deposit at the end of the five years in each of the three cases? What are the average compound real rates of return?

Answer

(a) The money values of the deposits after five years are:

    (i) £1,000 $\times$ 1.03 $\times$ 1.02 $\times$ 1.02 $\times$ 1.03 $\times$ 1.02 = £1,125.84
    (ii) £1,000 $\times$ 1.024 $\times$ 1.016 $\times$ 1.016 $\times$ 1.024 $\times$ 1.016 = £1,099.72
    (iii) £1,000 $\times$ 1.018 $\times$ 1.012 $\times$ 1.012 $\times$ 1.018 $\times$ 1.012 = £1,074.08

The average compound nominal rates of return are:

    (i) $(1.12584)^{0.2} - 1 = 0.024$ i.e. 2.40% p.a.
    (ii) $(1.09972)^{0.2} - 1 = 0.0192$ i.e. 1.92% p.a.
    (iii) $(1.07408)^{0.2} - 1 = 0.0144$ i.e. 1.44% p.a.

(b) To keep pace with inflation, the £1,000 would need to increase to:

£1,000 $\times$ 1.025 $\times$ 1.02 $\times$ 1.015 $\times$ 1.02 $\times$ 1.015 = £1,098.64

The real values of the deposits after five years are:

(i) $1125.84/1098.64 = £1,024.76$
(ii) $1099.72/1098.64 = £1,000.98$
(iii) $1074.08/1098.64 = £977.65$

The average compound real rates of return are:

(i) $(1.02476)^{0.2} - 1 = 0.0049$ i.e. 0.49% p.a.
(ii) $(1.00098)^{0.2} - 1 = 0.0002$ i.e. 0.02% p.a.
(iii) $(0.97765)^{0.2} - 1 = -0.0045$ i.e. -0.45% p.a.

According to the Fisher Effect, nominal interest rates exceed real interest rates by the amount required to compensate for expected inflation. Laatsch and Klein (2003) found a relationship between changes in nominal interest rates and changes in inflation. Their evidence was consistent with a one-to-one relationship between changes in nominal interest rates and changes in inflation. They found the changes in nominal interest rates and changes in inflation to be simultaneous.

Measuring Inflation – RPI and CPI

In the UK two measures of inflation are frequently quoted; the Retail Price Index (RPI) and the Consumer Price Index (CPI). The RPI is used for indexing state benefits such as pensions, interest on national savings products such as index-linked savings certificates, and payments on index-linked gilts. The CPI is used as the target inflation rate for Bank of England monetary policy.

Both the RPI and CPI are based on hypothetical shopping baskets containing representative selections of the goods and services that people buy. Both indices are calculated monthly as measures of the movement in the price of the shopping basket. It should be noted that it is highly unlikely that any individual, or household, would buy exactly the same combination of goods and services as the hypothetical shopping basket contains. Since everyone has a unique pattern of expenditure, everyone will experience a different rate of inflation. Prices of goods and services do not all rise at the same percentage rate. Published inflation figures are averages. Individuals and households will experience inflation rates that differ from the averages in a way that depends upon which goods and services they buy, and in what proportions. For example at the time of writing there is concern that low-income pensioners have an inflation rate that exceeds the published rates since a high proportion of their expenditures is on electricity and gas, which have experienced relatively high rates of price increase.

There are differences between the two inflation measures in terms of which consumers, and which goods and services, are covered. The RPI excludes the top 4% of people, in terms of income, and pensioners dependent on state benefits. So about 14% of UK households are excluded in the sense that their expenditure patterns are not considered when determining which goods and services should be covered, and in what proportions. The CPI excludes some important housing costs, such as mortgage interest payments and council tax. According to statistics published by the Office for National Statistics, at the time of writing (early 2007) such housing costs explained about 1.21% p.a. of the 1.78% p.a. excess of the RPI over the CPI.

Another factor that helps to explain the difference between the rates is the method of averaging. The RPI uses arithmetic averages whereas the CPI uses geometric averages (Office for National Statistics 2006). The arithmetic averaging of the RPI makes no allowance for the possibility that consumers would switch between brands and products as their relative prices change. The geometric averaging of the CPI allows for the possibility that people will make some switches from goods whose prices rise rapidly to those whose prices rise more slowly. This reduces the CPI relative to the RPI and, in early 2007, was estimated to account for about 0.55% of the difference between the two measures of inflation. The difference in averaging techniques would normally tend to reduce the CPI relative to the RPI.

RATES OF INTEREST VERSUS RATES OF DISCOUNT

Some investments, such as Treasury bills, pay no interest. Capital gain is the only source of return. Bills promise the payment of a specific sum of money at maturity and provide a return to investors by selling at a lower price. The price difference is known as the discount. The percentage rate of discount on bills is expressed relative to the sum payable at maturity whereas the interest on deposits is expressed relative to the sum invested. As a result a particular rate of discount is worth more than the rate of interest of the same percentage.

As an illustration consider a discount rate of 10% and an interest rate of 10%. If the maturity value of the bill is £100, a discount rate of 10% implies a current price of £90. The 10% discount is applied to the £100 maturity value and is worth £10. An interest rate of 10% would be applied to the current price and is therefore worth £9. A discount rate of 10% is equivalent to an interest rate of $(£10/£90) \times 100 = 11.1\%$.

EXERCISE 3.6

If the current rate of discount on Treasury bills is 11% p.a., calculate the price of a £50,000 91-day bill with 60 days to redemption. What would its price be in four weeks' time if p.a. discount rates remain unchanged?

Answer

The 60-day rate of discount is

$(60/365) \times 11\% = 1.81\%$

So the price of the Treasury bill is:

$[(100 - 1.81)/100] \times £50,000 = £49,096$

After four weeks there would be $60 - 28 = 32$ days to redemption. The 32-day rate of discount is:

$(32/365) \times 11\% = 0.96\%$

So the price of the Treasury bill would be:

$$[(100 - 0.96)/100] \times £50,000 = £49,518$$

INTEREST YIELD AND TOTAL RETURN

When money is deposited in a bank account it leads to a flow of interest payments, and these payments are the only source of return on the deposit. Other investments have two sources of return: not only are there income flows such as interest payments but there are also capital gains or losses. In the case of deposits there are no capital gains or losses, but investments such as bonds are subject to price fluctuations and gains/losses resulting from them.

The interest yield (also known as the coupon yield) on a bond is calculated as the annual coupon divided by the current bond price. The coupon is the periodic payment to the investor where the period is typically either six months or a year. The total return on a bond is known as the redemption yield. The redemption yield incorporates both the coupon yield and the prospective capital gain.

Consider a bond that pays a coupon of £4 every six months (and hence £8 per year), is currently priced at £97, and matures in one year at which point the investor will be paid £100 by the issuer of the bond. The interest yield is:

$$£8/£97 = 0.0825 \text{ i.e. } 8.25\% \text{ p.a.}$$

In addition there will be a capital gain of £100 − £97 = £3. As a rate of return the capital gain is £3/£97 = 0.0309 i.e. 3.09% p.a. The redemption yield (total return) is 8.25% + 3.09% = 11.34% p.a.

SHORT MATURITY (MONEY MARKET) INVESTMENTS

A variation on the normal deposit is the certificate of deposit (CD). A bank receiving a deposit may issue a CD to the depositor stating that at maturity (which is frequently three months from issue) the deposit plus interest will be paid to the holder (bearer) of the CD. An advantage of a certificate of deposit to the investor, as compared to a normal time deposit, is that it can be sold and hence is more liquid. When making a three-month bank deposit, the investor loses access to the money for three months. When buying a three-month CD, the investor has an asset that can be sold to another investor if the money is needed before three months have elapsed. This enhanced liquidity leads investors to the acceptance of rates of interest below the rates for ordinary deposits of the same maturity. Banks are thus able to borrow at lower interest rates than would otherwise be applicable to the period of the deposit.

Certificates of deposit are used in the wholesale, rather than the retail, money markets. The wholesale money markets deal only in large sums, for example multiples of £1 million (whereas the retail money markets deal in any size of investment). As a result investors in CDs tend to be companies, banks, and other financial institutions. Retail investors would normally have access to such instruments through collective investment vehicles such as unit trusts or insurance funds.

65

Another form of short-term investment is the bill. Bills are instruments that can be sold in the money market prior to maturity. Unlike deposits bills do not have an interest yield. The return that a bill provides to its holder arises from the fact that it is bought at a discount. The issuer of a bill promises to pay a specified sum of money at its maturity date. An investor buying the bill will pay a smaller sum for it and thus obtains a return in the form of a capital gain.

Bills may be issued by central government, in which case they are often known as Treasury bills (e.g. in the UK and the United States), and typically have maturities of three or six months. Treasury bills are sold by auction (tender). There are two forms of auction used. In a bid price auction investors pay the price that they bid. In a striking price auction all successful bidders pay the same price. In both cases the bills are sold to the highest bidders. The bid price auction is probably the most frequent type.

Bills may also be issued by firms as a means of short-term borrowing, normally with maturities of 12 months or less. Such private sector bills include bills of exchange. Bills of exchange are used for trade credit. The buyer of the goods signs a bill drawn up by the seller. The buyer thereby promises to pay, the holder of the bill, for the goods at the end of a specified time period. If a bank guarantees payment (against default by the trade signatory), the bill is known as a bank bill and is seen as having a lower risk of default. Bills can be sold, at a discount, in the money markets. In this way the suppliers of goods can receive money immediately whilst the buyers defer payment.

Commercial paper is similar to a bill of exchange, except that it is issued by a corporate borrower or a bank for general borrowing rather than for financing a specific trade transaction. An issuer of commercial paper will set up a programme with a specified time period (for example five years) and a stated borrowing ceiling (for example £500 million). The firm would not normally borrow up to the ceiling immediately, but would issue commercial paper over time as the need arose. Periodically paper would be sold, or repaid, subject to the borrowing ceiling not being exceeded. A bank (or several banks) would be appointed to deal with issues. The bank dealers contact potential investors in order to place the commercial paper. The market is wholesale with minimum denominations that put it out of reach of most individual investors. Retail investors wishing to access this market would normally do so by means of institutional investments such as unit trust money market funds.

Money market investments have two roles in a portfolio. One role is as an investment. The other role is as a lubricant. Typically there are constant inflows and outflows of cash. However the inflows and outflows are not synchronised. Some periods have net inflows, and other periods experience net outflows. Money market investments (including conventional bank deposits) are a means of bridging the time interval between inflows and outflows, and thereby operate as a lubricant. Also some investments are not continuously available and money market investments may be held with a view to turning them into cash when opportunities arise. Such occasional investment opportunities include properties and venture capital.

For individual investors the dominant form of money market investment is the bank or building society deposit. Minhas and Jacobs (1996) found that the interest rate was not the only factor of importance to such investors; it was not even the most important. They found that the personal service obtained at their bank or building society branch was more important to investors than the interest rate received. Interest rates were found to be the second most important factor, and easy accessibility to cash was another significant factor.

Costanzo and Ashton (2006) found that there was reluctance, on the part of the suppliers of financial services, to be innovative in the provision of money market investments for retail investors. They found recognition, on the part of financial services suppliers, that the development of innovative products is expensive in terms of time and resources. The suppliers were also found to regard investors as conservative, and hence resistant to innovation. Investors were seen as being unable to understand innovative investment products. There appeared to have been no committed effort to develop new types of deposit. This lack of innovation may seem disappointing in the light of the development of interest rate derivatives markets, and the potential for innovation that they could provide (see Chapters 44 and 45 on interest rate futures and interest rate swaps, respectively).

Interest rates in the wholesale money market may be higher than those in the retail money market. One reason is lower administration costs arising from the fact that the wholesale money market deals only in large sums of money. For example it is cheaper to administer 100 deposits of £1 million than a million deposits of £100. One way in which retail investors can access wholesale money market investments is through money market institutional investments such as unit trusts. Exhibit 3.1 illustrates a money market unit trust.

EXHIBIT 3.1   LEGAL & GENERAL CASH TRUST

OBJECTIVE

The investment objective of this Trust is to secure a high yield from those deposits or short-term instruments in which investment is permissible for a money market fund.

The manager expects generally to invest in overnight and short-term deposits but may exercise such flexibility within the objective as deemed desirable.

Total expense ratio: 0.50% p.a.*

The total expense ratio is the ratio of the Trust's operating costs (excluding overdraft interest and transaction charges) to the average net assets of the Trust.

Table 3.A

Holdings at 05/02/07			Percentage of Total
Bayerische Landesbank	5.310%	12/02/2007	12.09
National Australia Bank	5.280%	06/02/2007	11.54
Britannia Building Society	5.320%	14/02/2007	9.67
Rabobank	5.310%	07/02/2007	9.67
Alliance & Leicester	5.170%	12/02/2007	7.26

* There was another class of units with a total expense ratio of 0.20% p.a.
Source: Legal & General (Unit Trust Managers) Limited.

(cont. on P.68)

Table 3.A *continued*

Holdings at 05/02/07			Percentage of Total
Coventry Building Society	5.310%	07/02/2007	7.26
Dexia	5.170%	27/02/2007	7.26
Dresdner Bank	5.170%	16/04/2007	7.26
Royal Bank of Scotland	5.235%	04/05/07	7.26
Northern Rock	5.185%	26/03/2007	4.84
Alliance & Leicester	5.64%	19/06/2007	3.63
Dresdner Bank	5.670%	27/07/2007	3.63
Northern Rock	5.365%	02/07/2007	3.63
Northern Rock	5.670%	29/07/2007	3.63

In Exhibit 3.1 some of the banks are based outside the UK. Nevertheless they take deposits in sterling, as well as many other currencies. For example National Australia Bank takes deposits not only in Australian dollars but also in many other currencies, including the pound sterling. However, UK investors can choose to make investments in foreign currencies.

FOREIGN CURRENCY DEPOSITS

An alternative to a deposit in an investor's national currency is a deposit in a foreign currency. This alternative may seem attractive if the foreign currency interest rate is high relative to the home currency interest rate. Investors should be wary of such an alternative for two reasons. The first reason is based on what is known as the 'International Fisher Effect'.

According to the International Fisher Effect, high foreign currency interest rates tend to be offset by a fall in the value of the foreign currency. Although the difference between domestic and foreign interest rates is unlikely to be exactly matched by exchange rate movements, deviations in one direction are as likely as deviations in the other. The expected interest rate, net of the effects of currency movements, should on average equal the rate available on domestic currency deposits.

The second reason for being wary of foreign currency deposits is the uncertainty of exchange rate movements. The net rate of return from a foreign currency deposit could turn out to be either above or below the rate on a domestic currency deposit, depending on how the exchange rate moves. Since it is impossible to predict exchange rate movements, there is risk involved. So foreign currency deposits provide risk without any expectation of a higher rate of return.

The same reasoning applies to borrowing in foreign currencies. This was highlighted in the 1980s when some UK residents took out mortgages in Swiss francs on the grounds that the Swiss franc interest rate was lower than the pound sterling interest rate. Unfortunately for those borrowers, the Swiss franc strengthened against the pound. The result was a dramatic increase in the value of the mortgage debts, when measured in terms of pounds.

68

It may seem tempting to try to control the exchange rate risk by taking out forward contracts to guarantee future exchange rates. Whilst this reduces the currency risk, it does not ensure the benefits of a higher foreign currency interest rate. Forward exchange rates embody the currency price changes suggested by the International Fisher Effect. An interest rate advantage would be precisely offset by a forward discount that precisely offsets the interest rate advantage. The forward exchange rate guarantees that the currency price movement offsets the interest rate difference with the effect that the interest rate on the foreign currency is rendered identical to the rate on the domestic currency. This is known as 'Interest Rate Parity' and is a relationship that holds very closely among the major currencies.

RELATIVE PERFORMANCE OF MONEY MARKET INVESTMENTS

The outcome of investing in money market investments (such as building society accounts) needs to be compared with other investments, such as stock market investments. Using the endowment equation (as shown in Chapter 5) it is possible to calculate the outcome of investing on a regular basis over a period of time. Table 3.1 shows the result of investing £1,000 a year at various interest rates over periods of 20 and 40 years.

Over 20 years to July 2006 the rates of return from stock market investment (as represented by the FTSE All-Share Index) and building society accounts (based on accounts paying relatively high interest rates) were as shown by Table 3.2. These rates are based on data from *Money Management* magazine, August 1996 and August 2006 issues. Table 3.2 also shows the results of investing £1,000 a year for 40 years (with net interest and dividends reinvested, assuming that the average rates of return over 40 years equal the averages over 20 years).

These numbers are money values. In other words they take no account of the tendency for inflation to reduce the purchasing power of money. When rates of return (rates of interest) are adjusted for the effects of inflation, the results are real rates of return. The Barclays Capital

Table 3.1 *Sums accumulated by investing £1,000 a year*

Interest Rate (% p.a.)	20 years (£)	40 years (£)
1	22,019	48,886
2	24,297	60,402
3	26,870	75,401
4	29,778	95,026
5	33,066	120,800
6	36,786	154,760
7	40,995	199,640
8	45,762	259,060
9	51,160	337,890
10	57,275	442,590

Table 3.2   *Rates of return and accumulated sums over 40 years*

FTSE All-Share	10.11% p.a.	(£456,037 after 40 years)
Building Society	5.31% p.a.	(£130,340 after 40 years)

Equity Gilt Study (2006) provides the real annual rates of return on equities (i.e. shares) and cash (i.e. money market investments) in the UK over periods of 20, 50, and 105 years to 2006, as shown in Table 3.3.

Investing £1,000 a year for 50 years in equities (with net dividends reinvested) would have produced £354,946 in real terms. Investing £1,000 a year in money market investments (with net interest reinvested) would have produced £64,463 in real terms. Money market investments, such as building society or bank accounts, may appear to be safe but history indicates that better returns are available from investing in shares.

The amount by which the return on shares exceeds the return on money market investments is referred to as the equity risk premium. It is named as such because the additional return on shares (equities) is seen as the reward for accepting the higher risk of investing in shares. The Barclays Capital figures in Table 3.3 suggest that over a recent 50-year period the equity risk premium was 6.6% − 2% = 4.6% p.a. This is lower than most estimates relating to other time periods. For example Dimson and Marsh (2001) estimated that over the period 1955–2000 the equity risk premiums for the UK, the United States, Germany, and Japan were all in the 6.2% to 7.0% p.a. range.

The comparison of performances should take account of risk as well as return. In relation to risk money market investments, such as bank and building society deposits, are superior to stock market investments. The value of £1,000 deposited in a bank cannot fall. The same amount invested in shares can fall in value. The time span of the investment is important when considering risk. Figures published in the *Daily Telegraph* (26 February 2005) and adapted by Rutterford (2007) consider the frequency of outperformance of equities in the UK, relative to deposits, over various investment horizons between 1899 and 2004.

The time periods (investment horizons) considered ranged from 2 years to 18 years. There were 104 two-year periods (1899–1901, 1900–2, 1901–3, etc.) and equities outperformed deposits during 66% of those periods. When considering ten-year time periods, there were 96 periods (1899–1909, 1900–10, 1901–11, etc.) and equities outperformed deposits in 93% of those periods. In the case of 18-year investment horizons (1899–1917, 1900–18, 1901–19, etc.), there were 88 periods and equities outperformed deposits during 87 of those 88 periods. Investing in shares is more risky than investing in deposits but that relative risk appears to diminish as the investment horizon gets longer.

Table 3.3

	20 years	50 years	105 years
Equities	7.4%	6.6%	5.2%
Cash	4.1%	2.0%	1.0%

CONCLUSION

Interest rates are varied in nature, and an investor who is presented with a rate of interest must be aware of its nature. There is a difference between simple interest and compound interest. When calculating an average rate of interest over a period of years, the effect of compounding needs to be taken into account. There is sometimes a choice between variable and fixed rates of interest. A distinction should be made between nominal and real interest rates. The return on some money market investments, in particular bills, is quoted as a rate of discount rather than as a rate of interest. The investor should also be aware that the interest yield on an investment is not necessarily the total return on that investment.

Money market investments have maturities of one year or less. They include CDs, bills, and commercial paper. Bank and building society deposits are usually money market investments, and may be in foreign currencies. Historically money market investments have provided much lower average returns than stock market investments.

Although money market investments are typically seen as low risk, it will be seen in later chapters that they bear substantial amounts of some forms of risk (particularly income risk and inflation risk). Most people limit their money market investments to bank and building society deposits. However other types of money market investment can be made by individuals, particularly through the medium of institutional money market investments such as money market unit trusts and pension funds. Although money market unit trusts, OEICs, and pension funds may obtain higher rates of interest than individuals can obtain directly, investors should assure themselves that the higher rates are not eliminated (or more than eliminated) by charges made by fund managers.

Investors in the money markets should beware of 'money illusion'. Money illusion is the failure to realise that inflation erodes the purchasing power of money. Someone who suffers from money illusion fails to see the distinction between nominal and real rates of interest.

Chapter 4

Investing in bonds

OBJECTIVE

The objective of this chapter is to provide:

1. An understanding of the nature of bonds.
2. An appreciation of the role of bond rating agencies.
3. A knowledge of the alternative forms of coupon payment.
4. An understanding of the various types of government bonds, as illustrated by UK gilts.
5. Knowledge of what is meant by bond strips, bond yields, and bond price volatility.
6. An appreciation of the nature of preference shares.
7. Information about the relative performance of bonds.

GOVERNMENT BONDS, CORPORATE BONDS, AND EUROBONDS

Bonds are used for long-term borrowing by the issuer. Central governments are major issuers of bonds (and in the UK government bonds are called gilt-edged securities, or gilts). Bonds are issued in a wide variety of forms. However, most government bonds conform to a conventional format. A conventional government bond pays a fixed sum of money, known as the coupon, at regular intervals such as every six months. It has a definite redemption date on which the government is obliged to pay the nominal, or par, value of the bond to its owner. Its market price is expressed in relation to its nominal or par value. For example pounds per £100 nominal (so a market price of £96 means that £96 must be paid for every £100 to be repaid at redemption).

Governments are not the only issuers of bonds. In particular, firms issue corporate bonds. Corporate bonds vary very considerably in terms of their risk. Some corporate bonds are secured against assets of the company that issued them, whereas other bonds are unsecured. In the UK, bonds secured on the assets of the issuing company are known as debentures. Property companies often issue debentures. Bonds that are not secured are referred to as loan stock. Banks are major issuers of loan stock. The fact that unsecured bonds do not provide their holders with a claim on the assets of the issuing firm in the event of default is normally compensated for by means of a higher rate of coupon payment.

There are two types of debenture. Mortgage (fixed charge) debentures entail a fixed charge; which means that there are specific assets that bondholders can sell (arrange to be sold by a receiver) in order to reclaim their money in the event of default. Floating charge debentures allow the company to change the assets used as security. The company can sell the relevant assets so long as it replaces them with equally satisfactory assets. (Note that this meaning of the term 'debenture' is UK specific.)

Sometimes there are bonds with differing priorities of payment in the event of the issuer becoming insolvent. Bonds with a high priority for repayment are often referred to as being senior debt, whilst those bonds that would be redeemed only after the senior debt (and only if sufficient funds remain) would be termed subordinated debt. The greater risk of non-redemption of subordinated debt is compensated for by a higher rate of coupon yield.

When new corporate bonds are issued, their yields are generally set with reference to government bonds. Corporate bonds offer a spread over the government bond yield in order to compensate for the greater risk of default. Companies, unlike the governments of developed countries, can find themselves in a position in which they cannot pay the money owing to the holders of their bonds.

Bond issues are typically credit rated. There are credit rating agencies (such as Moody's and Standard & Poor's) that give ratings to bond issues. A high credit rating indicates a low risk of default, whereas a low rating is suggestive of a high default risk. Low credit ratings are associated with high rates of yield. Bonds with very low credit ratings and hence subject to very high risk of default are often referred to as junk bonds.

Many corporate bonds have call features. This means that the issuer has the right to redeem the bonds before the maturity date. A bond is likely to be called if interest rates fall below the coupon rate, since the issuer could then redeem the bond with money borrowed at a lower coupon rate. This is to the disadvantage of investors since they can only reinvest the money at a lower rate of yield. This potential disadvantage would be compensated for by means of a higher coupon rate on callable bonds.

Some corporate bonds are putable. This means that the investor has the right to sell the bond to the issuer, at a predetermined price, before the maturity date. Investors might exercise this right when interest rates rise so that the proceeds can be reinvested at a higher rate of yield. The right to sell the bond at a predetermined price implies that the investor is protected against price falls. Since the right to sell provides potential advantages to investors, it would be offset by a lower coupon rate on the bond.

In the UK the corporate bond market is much smaller than the government bond (gilts) market. The value of corporate bonds in the market is less than 10% of the value of outstanding gilts. Frequently a gilt issue will have more than £5 billion of the issue in the market, corporate bond issues rarely exceed £0.5 billion. Bond liquidity is the ability to trade a bond easily without having to make price concessions (e.g. lowering the price in order to attract a buyer). The relatively small size of corporate bond issues can render them illiquid. While gilts are usually very liquid, many corporate bonds seldom trade. To compensate for the lack of liquidity, corporate bonds tend to have higher yields than government bonds.

Eurobonds are bonds denominated in a currency that is not the currency of the country in which the bonds are issued. So a bond denominated in sterling but sold in Paris would be a eurosterling bond. Eurobonds are often issued in several financial centres at the same time, for example a US dollar eurobond might be simultaneously issued in London, Paris, Sydney, Hong Kong, and Singapore (the prefix 'euro' has no geographical or currency significance). Eurobonds are often bearer bonds. This means that coupons and principal are payable to the holder (bearer) of a bond, and bonds are not registered in the names of investors. This allows investors to retain anonymity.

Eurobonds tap the large stateless pool of cash and are traded in a secondary market of screens and telephones. Eurobond markets are volatile and little regulated. They can become illiquid since there is no obligation on any body to make a market in eurobonds. In other words there is liquidity risk; in adverse market circumstances, holders of bonds may be unable to sell them because there is no one willing to buy.

Eurobonds are not the only form of international bond. Bonds may be issued in the country whose currency is being borrowed, by a borrower in another country. Those bonds are known as foreign bonds. So a German company might borrow Canadian dollars by issuing Canadian dollar bonds in Canada. Such bonds sometimes have names that symbolise the country whose currency is being borrowed. For example bonds issued in the United States are called Yankees, bonds issued in Britain are known as Bulldogs, and those issued in Japan are called Samurais.

DEFAULT RISK AND BOND RATING AGENCIES

A bond rating is an assessment of the default risk of a bond by an independent agency. The ratings reflect only default risk, which is the risk that the issuer of the bond will fail to meet coupon payments or the repayment of principal. The ratings do not reflect other types of risk such as interest rate risk (which includes the risk that interest rate changes will cause capital losses to holders of bonds). Ratings are specific to a bond issue, rather than to the issuer.

There are a number of bond rating agencies worldwide, but the global market is dominated by two agencies. These are S&P (Standard and Poor's) and Moody's. The rating agencies assign debt issues to risk categories and label those categories with letters. Table 4.1 shows the letter grades used by S&P and Moody's.

Debt rated BBB by S&P (or Baa, by Moody's) and above is classed as investment grade. Bonds rated BB (or Ba) and below are classed as speculative grade. Speculative grade bonds are alternatively referred to as high yield or junk bonds. The first two categories (AAA/Aaa and AA/Aa) indicate a very strong capacity to pay coupons and repay principal. The next four categories (A to B) indicate that the issuer is currently able to meet payments but has some susceptibility to adverse changes in economic conditions. The issues in the next two categories (CCC/Caa and CC) are prone to default unless there is a favourable change in economic conditions. The next category (C/Ca) indicates that a bankruptcy petition has been filed, but payments are still being made. The bottom category (D/C) indicates that the issuer has already failed to make coupon payments or principal repayments.

There is evidence that bond ratings provide a useful guide. For example Altman (1991) studied the default rates for US bonds over the period 1971–90. It was found that ratings were a good guide to subsequent default rates. For example bonds rated AAA had a default rate of 0.17% over ten years whereas 37.85% of bonds rated CCC defaulted during the ten years following the rating.

Exhibit 4.1 illustrates the use of bond ratings in the construction of an investment fund. It will be noted that the portfolio includes non-UK issuers. However non-UK issuers may issue bonds denominated in pounds sterling. Some of the investments are described by the letters FRN, which stand for Floating Rate Note. FRNs are bonds whose coupon rates are changed at regular intervals (see Chapter 45 on interest rate swaps).

Table 4.1

Standard and Poor's	Moody's	
AAA	Aaa	
AA	Aa	
		Investment grade
A	A	
BBB	Baa	
BB	Ba	
B	B	
CCC	Caa	
		Speculative grade
CC		
C	Ca	
D	C	

EXHIBIT 4.1   M&G CORPORATE BOND FUND

OBJECTIVE

The Fund invests in sterling denominated fixed and variable rate securities, including corporate bonds and debentures, with the aim of achieving a higher return from investment than would be obtainable in UK Government fixed interest securities (i.e. gilts) of similar maturities. The Fund may, however, hold gilts where it is deemed appropriate. The investment manager has the power to use futures traded or dealt on eligible derivatives markets (currently being the London International Financial Futures and Options Exchange) for the purpose of hedging the capital value of the Fund against the risks of adverse movements in long-term interest rates. More than 35% of the value of the property of the Fund may be invested in Government and other public securities issued or guaranteed by any of:

- the Government of the United Kingdom or of a member State other than the United Kingdom;
- the Government of Australia, Canada, Japan, New Zealand, Switzerland, USA;
- the African Development Bank, Asian Development Bank, Eurofima, European Economic Community, European Bank for Reconstruction and Development, European Coal and Steel Community, European Investment Bank, International Bank for Reconstruction and Development, International Financial Corporation.

Policy for achieving objective

The Fund invests in sterling denominated 'investment grade' debt (BBB and above), typically with an emphasis on A and BBB rated credits, although this may not always be the case. The Fund endeavours to limit the exposure to any individual credit to 3% of the total value of the portfolio.

Fund size: £1.18 billion (29 June 2007)
Initial charge: 3%
Annual charge: 1%

Table 4.A

Ten largest holdings on 30 June 2007 (as percentages of the total fund)

United Kingdom (Government of) 4.25%	5.20
Cash & Cash Equivalents	4.85
France Telecom FRN	2.53
British Telecommunications PLC	1.95
Barclays Bank 6%	1.69
United Kingdom (Government of) 4.25%	1.69
Land Securities FRN	1.56
BG Energy Capital 5.875%	1.55
United Kingdom (Government of) 5%	1.55
Holmes Financial No.10 FRN	1.42

Source: M&G Securities Limited.

High default risk should be associated with high yields. Part of the additional yield reflects the possibility of loss through default. If bonds with a particular risk rating are regarded as having a specific probability of default, weighting the potential loss against the probability of loss indicates the size of loss on the average bond of the risk class. If that loss is converted into an annual percentage of the current price of the bond, it could be concluded that the percentage should be added to the yield on the bond. For example a 20% chance of default over the next ten years might be compensated by a 2% p.a. addition to the bond yield. This addition is often expressed as a spread over the yield on a government bond of similar maturity (government bonds being regarded as free of default risk). It is expected that there should also be a risk premium that reflects the uncertainty about the statistical probability of default. The chances of default may be higher during economic recessions, and there is uncertainty about the future state of the economy. The excess (spread) of corporate bond yields over government bond yields would reflect both a default premium and a risk premium. The pattern of yields associated with bonds of varying default risks is known as the risk structure of bond yields.

In addition to default risk there is credit-migration risk. Default risk is the risk that an issuer of bonds will fail to pay the coupons or the redemption value at maturity. Credit-migration risk is the risk that the credit rating of a bond will fall (i.e. that default risk increases).

During the sub-prime mortgage crisis of the summer of 2007 the credit rating agencies were subject to considerable criticism. A conflict of interests was highlighted. The issuers of bonds pay the agencies, and the issuers of bonds want high credit ratings. If an issuer does not get a high rating from one agency it could transfer its business to another agency. Credit rating agencies are motivated to give excessively favourable credit ratings in order to attract and retain business. It became apparent during the sub-prime mortgage crisis that some portfolios of assets had received very high credit ratings despite containing some assets backed by sub-prime mortgages.

ALTERNATIVE FORMS OF COUPON PAYMENT

The conventional pattern of coupon payments is often deviated from, particularly by corporate bonds and eurobonds. Some bonds have floating coupon payments wherein the coupon is changed periodically to reflect the general level of interest rates. Typically each coupon payment will be different, with the difference reflecting changes in interest rates. Floating rate bonds show less price variation than conventional bonds since changes in the coupon tend to match changes in the discount rate (see Chapter 40 on bond prices and redemption yields). Floating rate bonds (alternatively known as floating rate notes – FRNs) can be a useful alternative to short-term bank deposits, or to other short-term money market investments such as certificates of deposit and bills. The investor receives short-term interest rates without the need to constantly reinvest (rollover) money when short-term investments mature. At each interest rate reassessment date the value of a floating rate note returns to its par value, thereby maintaining the value of the capital invested. Floating rate notes are equivalent to short-term money market investments in terms of both interest yield and low risk of capital loss.

There are deferred coupon bonds, which entail no coupon payments for a period of years, at the end of which coupon payments commence. Step up bonds pay a low coupon initially, but the coupon rises after a number of years. Zero coupon bonds pay no coupons; the return to the investor arises from the difference between the buying and selling prices. Serial bonds repay part of the principal (original sum invested), as well as the coupon, on the coupon payment dates.

GILTS (GILT-EDGED SECURITIES)

Gilts (gilt-edged stock) are bonds issued by the UK government as a means of borrowing money. Since they are backed by the government's ability to levy taxes, there is no risk of default (no risk that the issuer will fail to make payments to investors). This absence of default risk means that they are less risky than most other forms of long-term investment.

Issuing Gilts

Gilts are issued through the Debt Management Office, which is a department of the Treasury (the Treasury is part of the UK government). Until 1997 gilts were issued by the Bank of England on behalf of the government. Gilts are issued by tender, by auction, or as tap stock.

Sale by tender entails the Debt Management Office (DMO) offering a quantity of gilts and stating a minimum acceptable price. The price at which the gilts are sold is the highest price at which all the gilts can be sold, or the minimum price. For example £1 billion of gilts may be offered with a minimum price of £100. The total demanded by investors at prices at, and above, £102 may amount to the full £1 billion. In that case all investors pay £102.

If the amount tendered for at £100 or above is less than £1 billion, the gilts will be sold at £100. The unsold gilts will be treated as tap stock. This means that the DMO will gradually sell them over time when investors become ready to buy them.

In the auction process, professional investors (largely institutional investors) state the quantities that they want and the prices that they are prepared to pay. If the auction is oversubscribed only the highest bidders will receive the gilts. Successful bidders pay the price that they offered. Private investors, seeking small quantities of gilts, may apply for gilts on the basis of paying the average of the prices paid by the successful participants in the auction. Sale by auction involves no minimum price. The gilts are sold to the highest bidders. All the gilts would be sold and none would be left over as tap stock.

Tap sales involve the Debt Management Office selling newly issued gilts to market-makers. The market-makers subsequently sell them on to other investors. Market-makers undertake to be always ready to quote prices at which they are prepared to buy and sell. They hold gilts as principals which means that they invest in, and trade, gilts for their own profit.

The gilt-edged market is part of the London Stock Exchange and the market-makers, dealers, and brokers are members of the stock exchange. The Central Gilts Office provides a computerised service for payments and settlements between buyers and sellers.

Conventional Gilts

Most gilts issued by the UK Treasury are conventional in nature. Conventional gilts have two standard characteristics. These are the payment of fixed coupons every six months, and the repayment of the nominal value of the gilt on a specified maturity date. The coupon and maturity year are detailed in the descriptions of gilts published in the financial media.

Most UK gilts are described as Treasury, Conversion, or Exchequer. There is no significance for the investor in the name of the gilt. The name is followed by an interest rate and a year. These indicate the value of the coupon and the year in which the gilt is due to mature. The maturity date of a gilt is the date on which the final coupon and the nominal value are payable to the holder of the gilt.

If a gilt is described by the title Exchequer 8% 2015, this gilt pays £4 every six months (£8 a year) for each £100 of nominal value. The nominal value is the principal sum payable by the Treasury, to the investor holding the gilt, on the maturity date of the gilt. The year of maturity is shown in the title of the gilt. In the current example maturity will occur in 2015.

Double-dated Gilts

These gilts have two years in their title. This is because the Treasury can redeem them (pay the nominal value to bondholders) at any time between two dates. In effect the Treasury has a call option on the gilts (in the United States they are referred to as callable bonds). The Treasury has the right to buy back the gilts at the nominal value at any time between the two dates. If the current interest rate on other bonds is below the coupon rate of the gilt (the rate of interest on the nominal value), it is advantageous to the Treasury to redeem the gilts before the final maturity date. For example if the current interest rate is 6% p.a. and a gilt pays a dividend of £8 a year (per £100 nominal), the Treasury could redeem it with money borrowed by selling gilts paying £6 a year.

The Treasury must pay for this call option. The Treasury has to pay for the right to redeem the gilts before the final maturity date. This payment is made by means of a coupon rate (percentage dividend) that is greater than the rate on gilts that lack the right to redeem before the final maturity date.

Undated Gilts

Undated gilts have no maturity date. The Treasury is never obliged to redeem these gilts, it may simply continue to pay coupons into perpetuity (hence these gilts are alternatively known as perpetuities). It has been several decades since such gilts were last issued, but a quantity of them remains in the market. They are unlikely to be redeemed by the Treasury so long as current interest rates are above the coupon rates of the undated gilts. The undated gilts in existence tend to have very low coupon rates.

Index-linked Gilts

Index-linked gilts give investors automatic protection against inflation by continually raising the coupon payments, and the principal sum to be paid to the investor at maturity, in line with the Retail Prices Index (RPI). Specifically the RPI figure used is the one current eight months before the date that the coupon, or principal, is to be paid. The eight-month time lag is used so that the money value of the next coupon is always known.

An index-linked gilt will have an initial nominal coupon and an initial nominal redemption value. The sum actually payable is adjusted to reflect inflation from a point in time eight months prior to the issue of the gilts. The sum payable is the initial nominal amount multiplied by the ratio of the new RPI to the initial RPI (the ratio of the RPI eight months before the present to the RPI eight months before the gilt was issued). So, for example, a doubling of the level of retail prices causes a doubling of the money value of the coupons payable to the investor with the effect that the real value (purchasing power value) of the coupons remains unchanged. The real value of the principal payable to the investor at redemption (the redemption value) is also maintained by means of the inflation adjustment.

In the UK index-linked government bonds provide a tax advantage, relative to other gilts, for individual investors. Private investors pay income tax on gilt coupons but do not pay tax on capital gains from gilts (capital gains are the profits from price rises). A substantial proportion of the returns from index-linked gilts takes the form of capital gains arising from the index-linking. It might be thought that this tax advantage would increase the demand for index-linked gilts with the effect that their prices would rise. It might further be thought that the price rise would go to the point at which the prospective after-tax returns on index-linked gilts fell into line with the expected after-tax returns on other gilts (bearing in mind the inverse relationship between bond prices and their yields). However, since individuals constitute only a small proportion of the market for index-linked gilts, the increased demand may not be sufficient to remove the after-tax yield advantage of index-linked gilts for private investors.

Rump Stocks

A rump stock is a gilt of which little remains in the market. They are often the result of conversion offers. A conversion offer involves the Debt Management Office making an offer to exchange holdings of an existing gilt issue for a new issue of gilts. Investors may then choose to replace existing gilts with new ones without incurring transaction costs such as dealing charges. Not all investors respond to conversion offers. As a result some of the original gilt issue remains in the market. If only a small amount remains in investors' hands, liquidity may become very poor. Poor liquidity means that it is difficult to buy or sell the gilts since there are few potential buyers and sellers.

GILT STRIPS

A gilt strip market began in the UK in December 1997. Strips is the acronym for Separately Traded and Registered Interest and Principal Securities. Stripping a gilt involves breaking it down into its individual cash flows which can be traded separately. Each individual coupon payment date becomes a maturity date for a strip, and the coupon becomes the redemption value. These are alternatively known as zero coupon gilts since they provide the investor with just one cash flow, which is the redemption value of the strip payable at maturity. The nominal value of the original gilt can also be traded separately from the coupons, it becomes a strip with a redemption (maturity) date corresponding to the redemption date of the original gilt. For example a gilt with five years to maturity can be broken down into 11 strips, one for each remaining coupon and one for the redemption value (principal sum). These strips would have maturities of six months, one year, 18 months, two years, and so forth.

Coupons from different strippable bonds that are paid on the same day are fungible (interchangeable) when traded as strips. The maturity value of a strip could contain coupons from a number of different conventional gilts. One purpose of conversion issues has been the replacement of gilts that lack fungibility with gilts that are fungible with others (share coupon payment dates).

Gilts, inclusive of gilt strips, can be held either directly or through institutional investment funds such as unit trusts or OEICs. Exhibit 4.2 illustrates a gilt fund. The percentages that immediately follow the name of the bond are the coupon rates (e.g. UK Treasury 8% is a gilt, which pays coupons of £8 per year for each £100 of nominal value). The dates that follow are the dates on which the bonds mature. It should not be presumed that a bond issued by the European Investment Bank is denominated in Euros. That bank could issue bonds in many other currencies, including the pound sterling.

EXHIBIT 4.2 HENDERSON GLOBAL INVESTORS UK GILT FUND (AS AT 31 AUGUST 2007)

Objective

To provide a return by investing primarily in United Kingdom Government securities. The fund may invest in other transferable securities, money market instruments, derivatives and forward transactions, deposits and units in collective investment schemes.

Benchmark: FTA British Government All Stocks Index
Fund size: £329.63 million
Charges:* (without exit fees)   Initial: 4.00%
                                       Annual: 1.00%

                     (with exit fees)   Initial: 0%
                                       Annual: 1.5%

Table 4.B

Ten largest holdings (as percentages of the total fund)	
UK Treasury 8% 07/12/15	18.4
UK Treasury 5.25% 07/06/12	13.6
UK Treasury 4.25% 07/12/2027	10.2
European Investment Bank 4.75% 06/06/12	6.1
UK Treasury 4.75% 07/03/2020	5.8
UK Treasury 5% 07/03/2025	5.4
UK Treasury 4.25% 07/03/2036	5.4
UK Treasury 8% 07/06/2021	4.8
UK Treasury 4.25% 07/03/2011	4.4
UK Treasury 4.25% 07/12/2046	4.4

*Other charging structures were available.
Source: Henderson Global Investors.

GILT YIELDS

There are two frequently used measures of the yield of a gilt. One is known as coupon yield (alternatively known as interest, flat, or running yield). This is calculated as the annual coupon divided by the current market price of the gilt. The deficiency of this measure is that it ignores potential capital gains or losses. The return from an investment comprises both periodic payments (coupons or dividends) and capital gains or losses arising from changes in the market value of the investment.

The other popular measure of yield, known as redemption yield or yield to maturity, takes both forms of investment return into account. It includes prospective capital gains or losses as well as coupons. It is the compound average annual rate of yield based upon the presumption that the investor will hold the gilt until its redemption (maturity) date.

The redemption yield can be interpreted as the rate of discount that will equate the sum, of the present values of the future cash flows, to the current market value of the gilt. As such it is often treated as the rate of interest offered by the gilt (more accurately it approximates an average of interest rates relating to the various cash flows from the gilt).

The holding period return is similar to the redemption yield except that the bond is not held to its redemption date. A forecast is made of the future selling price. The holding period return is the rate of discount that equates the future cash flows, that is the future coupons plus expected selling price, to the current price of the bond. If the bond has already been sold, the holding period return is alternatively known as the realised compound yield.

When gilts are traded, the accumulated rights to the next coupon have to be paid for by the buyer. These rights are referred to as accrued interest. For example if a bond that pays a £4 coupon every six months is sold three months after the last coupon payment date, there will be £2 accrued interest. This accrued interest is added to the market price when the buyer pays the seller. During the seven working days prior to the payment of the coupon, the reverse occurs. The coupon is payable to the investor who holds the gilt seven working days before the coupon payment date. If the gilt is sold during this seven-day period the seller must compensate the buyer for the absence of coupon receipts during this period. The compensation is referred to as rebate interest. The gilt price exclusive of accrued or rebate interest is known as the clean price. The gilt price inclusive of such adjustments is the dirty price. Prices quoted in the financial media are clean prices.

EXERCISE 4.1

If a bond paid no coupon after six months but a coupon of £10 plus the redemption value of £100 after one year, what redemption yield is implied by a current price of £95? What is the interest yield?

Answers

The interest yield is £10/£95 = 0.1053 = 10.53% p.a.
The rate of capital gain is £5/£95 = 0.0526 = 5.26% p.a.

Interest yield plus rate of capital gain equals redemption yield, i.e. 10.53% + 5.26% = 15.79% p.a.

Alternatively:

Let r = redemption yield.
£95 = £110/(1+r)
£95(1+r) = £110
1+r = £110/£95 = 1.1579
r = 1.1579 −1 = 0.1579 i.e. 15.79% p.a.

EXERCISE 4.2

(a) A bond pays an annual coupon of £5 and is priced at £96. It matures in 364 days. Calculate its interest yield and redemption yield. If it was due to mature in one year 364 days would the redemption yield be higher or lower than in the first case?

(b) If a zero coupon bond is priced at £90 and matures in two years, what is its redemption yield?

Answers

(a) Interest yield = 5/96 = 0.0521 (5.21% p.a.)

Redemption yield = (5/96) + [(100-96)/96] = 0.0521 + 0.0417 = 0.0938 (9.38% p.a.)
If the bond was due to mature in two years rather than one the annual rate of capital gain would be halved and the redemption yield would be lower.

(b) £90 = £100 / $(1 + r)^2$
$(1 + r)^2$ = £100/£90 = 1.111
$1 + r = \sqrt{1.111} = 1.0541$
∴ r = 0.0541 (5.41% p.a.)

GILT PRICE VOLATILITY

Gilt prices vary because interest rates vary. A relatively high sensitivity to interest rate movements is observed amongst undated gilts. Suppose that an undated gilt pays coupons amounting to £4 a year. If rates on other long-term investments (long-term interest rates) are 4% p.a., the undated gilt would be priced at about £100. A coupon of £4 on an investment of £100 provides an interest rate of 4% p.a., which matches rates of return elsewhere. If interest rates on other long-term investments rose to 8% p.a., rational investors would not pay £100 for a gilt paying £4 a year. Investors would be prepared to pay around £50 for the gilt since £4 on £50 produces a rate of return of 8% p.a. Conversely a fall in interest rates on other investments to 2% p.a. would imply a price of £200 for the gilt. The coupon of £4 a year provides 2% p.a. when the gilt price is £200. It can be seen that the gilt price is inversely proportional to the long-term interest rate available elsewhere in the market. A doubling of the interest rate causes a halving of the gilt price, and vice versa. This degree of volatility is relatively extreme. There is always an inverse relationship between interest rates and gilt prices but rarely a proportionally inverse one. Usually the change in gilt price is less than proportionate to the interest rate change.

PREFERENCE SHARES

Preference shares, despite their name, are more like bonds than ordinary shares since most of them pay a fixed dividend each year. Unlike bonds they confer part ownership of a company, but like bonds they normally entail no voting rights. They further differ from bonds in that the firm is not obliged to make the dividend payments on preference shares if profits are not sufficient. Bonds are debts of the issuer and the issuer is legally obliged to pay the coupons and to repay the principal at maturity. Preference shares come in various forms, as follows:

- irredeemable
- redeemable
- cumulative
- non-cumulative
- participating
- convertible.

Apart from the irredeemable/redeemable and cumulative/non-cumulative distinctions these characteristics are not mutually exclusive. For example a preference share could be irredeemable, cumulative, participating, and convertible whereas another might be simply irredeemable and cumulative.

Whilst most preference shares are irredeemable, some are redeemable (redeemable means that the sum received from the issue of the shares would be repaid by a specified date). In the case of cumulative preference shares, the firm is required to pay any missed dividends when profits become adequate. Back payments of missed dividends must be made before any dividends on ordinary shares (common stock) can be paid. In the case of a non-cumulative preference share, there is no obligation on the issuer to pay any previously missed dividends. So a missed dividend may be lost forever.

Participating preference shares provide participation in unusually good profit levels. If the company's profits are exceptionally good, the payments to holders of participating preference shares will exceed the normal dividend level. Convertible preference shares are similar to convertible bonds in that the holder has rights to convert the preference shares into ordinary shares on predetermined terms.

THE RELATIVE PERFORMANCE OF BONDS

The investment performance of bonds is generally thought to lie between the performances of shares and money market investments, in terms of both return and risk. The Barclays Capital

Table 4.2

	10 years	50 years	105 years
Equities	5.0%	6.6%	5.2%
Gilts	5.6%	2.1%	1.2%
Corporate bonds	8.1%		
Cash (money market)	2.9%	2.0%	1.0%

Equity Gilt Study (2006) found the average annual real rates of return in the UK, up to the end of 2005, as shown in Table 4.2.

Although gilts outperformed equities (shares) in the ten years up to 2005, that outperformance was fairly unusual. Figures published in the *Daily Telegraph* (26 February 2005) and adapted by Rutterford (2007) looked at the number of times gilts outperformed equities during various time periods between 1899 and 2004. Over ten-year periods (1899–1909, 1900–10, 1901–11, etc.) gilts outperformed equities in only 17% of the periods.

It is to be expected that corporate bonds should provide higher returns than gilts because of the default risk of corporate bonds. Table 4.2 shows that corporate bonds outperformed gilts during the period 1995–2005. However convincing judgements about the performance of corporate bonds, relative to gilts and equities, requires data on more than a ten-year period.

CONCLUSION

There are many types of bond. The variety reflects the many different needs of borrowers and investors. The variety entails the need for information on the part of investors when faced with a plethora of choice. Credit rating agencies provide some of that information in that they help to reduce uncertainty about the likelihood of default. It is not just default risk that investors need to know about; they also need to be able to ascertain prospective returns and risks. There are alternative measures of yield and of risk. Investors should understand measures of yield, particularly redemption yield, and measures of risk, particularly duration (more detail is provided in Chapters 40 and 41). The variety of investment alternatives is added to by preference shares, which are often treated as virtually equivalent to bonds in many cases. It will be seen in later chapters that many bonds have derivative features, particularly option features, and that this vastly increases the variety of bonds.

In terms of both returns and risks, bonds lie between money market investments and shares. They tend to have higher returns, but also greater risk, when compared to money market investments. They tend to have lower average returns, and lower risk, when compared with equity investments (i.e. shares).

85

Individuals can buy bonds directly (government bonds can even be bought at post offices in the UK), and can also buy them indirectly by means of institutional investments. Buying through institutional investments, such as unit trusts, has the advantage of risk reduction by diversification but there is the possibility that the fund charges seriously reduce the income derived from the investment. Use of index-tracking bond funds could reduce this problem since their charges can be much lower than those of actively managed bond funds.

The vast variety of bonds available provides the investor with immense choice. Although the amount of choice allows investors to meet their investment needs closely, too much choice can be confusing. In the bond market investors are faced with much more information than they can typically handle. Substantial amounts of choice, and information, can cause procrastination. Investors need to be aware of this possibility. They should also be aware that huge amounts of choice and information could elicit the heuristic simplification biases described in Chapter 2 on the psychology of personal investment decisions.

Chapter 5

Property investment and mortgages

OBJECTIVE

The objective of this chapter is to provide knowledge of:

1. Investing in property.
2. Property pricing.
3. Various types of mortgage and their characteristics.
4. The debate about the desirability of fixed-rate mortgages.
5. The use of mortgage schemes to turn home ownership into an income.
6. The equations on which mortgage and endowment calculations are based.

BUYING YOUR OWN HOME

When considering housing a choice needs to be made between buying a home and renting. Each has its advantages and its disadvantages. The advantages of renting include mobility. When renting it is relatively easy to move home since no buying and selling is involved. Another advantage is the low initial cost. When buying a property a substantial deposit is usually required. In addition there are other initial costs such as stamp duty (a tax on home purchases in the UK). These initial costs are avoided when renting. A third advantage of renting is the absence of responsibility for repairs. The landlord must pay for the maintenance of the property.

The disadvantages of renting when compared with buying include the likelihood that the rent will increase over time, whereas the price at which you bought the property remains constant. Also irrespective of how much rent is paid, and for how long it is paid, the resident never owns the rented property. The buyer of a home does own it and, when the mortgage used to buy it is paid off, no regular payments are required for the privilege of living there. Meanwhile the renter continues to pay rent. The buyer of a home has an investment as well as a place to live. History shows that the investment tends to rise in value over time.

Homeowners bear some risks, which are avoided by those who rent. One risk is that property prices may fall. Although in the past property prices have tended to rise, that has not always been the case.

87

There have been periods during which prices in general have fallen, such as the early 1990s in the UK. Also prices in particular locations, or for particular types of property, may fall. For example if a major local employer closes down, house prices could fall as people sell. People may sell their homes because they move to a different area in order to obtain work.

Another risk facing homebuyers, when buyers finance purchases by borrowing, is that interest rates may rise. Most buyers borrow money by way of mortgages. Most mortgages in the UK are variable rate, which means that mortgage interest rates vary. A rise in mortgage interest rates raises the cost of buying a home, perhaps to the point that the buyer is forced to sell as a result of no longer being able to finance the mortgage payments. If this occurs at a time when property prices have fallen, the selling price may not be enough to pay off the outstanding mortgage debt. People are then left without a home, and in debt. The situation in which a person's home is worth less than the mortgage debt is known as negative equity. (A person's equity in a home is its value minus the outstanding mortgage debt.)

Opportunities for Gearing

By gearing is meant borrowing in order to finance an investment. When buying a home people frequently borrow most of the purchase price. It is not unusual for 90% of the purchase price to be financed by borrowing by means of a mortgage. This has implications for percentage gains (and losses) from property investment.

Suppose that someone pays £100,000 for a house using £10,000 of their own money plus a mortgage borrowing of £90,000. Initially their equity in the house is £10,000. If the value of the house subsequently rises to £120,000, the homeowner's equity rises to £30,000 (£120,000 minus £90,000). In consequence of a 20% rise in the value of the property, the house buyer's investment has risen in value by 200% (£10,000 to £30,000).

Borrowing to buy amplifies percentage profits (and losses). It is easy to finance a high proportion of the cost of property purchase by mortgage borrowing. It is much less easy to finance a high proportion of the cost of other forms of investment (such as stock market investment) by borrowing. The facility of making highly geared investments is a characteristic of property markets.

Lack of Diversification

One difficulty with home ownership, when considered as an investment, is the absence of diversification. When investing in the stock market it is usual to hold shares in a number of different companies (for example shareholdings in 50 different firms). This is known as diversification, and it helps to reduce risk. Poor performances from some shares might be offset by strong performances on others. Holding a diversified portfolio of shares entails less risk than holding the shares of just one company. The average price variation of a diversified portfolio, of say 50 different shares, should be less than the price volatility of an individual share.

Home ownership does not allow for such diversification. Typically the whole investment is in just one property. If a change in local circumstances reduces the value of a home, there are no offsetting price increases from other properties.

Lack of Liquidity

Liquidity is the speed and ease with which an investment can be turned into cash without the need to lower the price. Usually bank deposits can be cashed quickly, and stock market investments sold quickly. Property is typically much less liquid. It usually takes several months to sell a residential property. The property may be advertised for several months before a buyer is found. A protracted, and costly, legal process then follows. An offer to buy may be withdrawn at a late stage in the process with the result that the selling process starts all over again.

BUY-TO-LET

Many people do diversify their holdings of residential property by buying homes with the intention of renting them to tenants. The objective is to gain from both price increases and the receipt of rent. Often the rent receipts are used to make mortgage payments relating to the purchase of the properties.

Buy-to-let can seem to be a very attractive investment. The mortgage used to buy the property is financed from the rent receipts, and eventually the buyer has a property without a mortgage. However buying-to-let does have risks and drawbacks. One risk is that the property could stand empty for long periods; it may not always be possible to find tenants. Mortgage payments must continue to be paid even when there is no rent being received.

Another risk is that tenants could damage the property and/or fail to pay rent. It is possible that the general level of rents could fall, perhaps in consequence of a surplus of properties available to rent. It is possible for mortgage interest rates to rise. It is also possible for property prices to fall. The owner of the property has to deal with its maintenance, irrespective of whether the property is occupied. Maintaining a property in good repair, and collecting rent, can be irksome functions. If an agent is paid to carry out such roles, fees must be paid.

PROPERTY UNIT TRUSTS, REAL ESTATE INVESTMENT TRUSTS, AND PROPERTY COMPANIES

A route to property investment, without the work and worry of its management, is through indirect investment. This also provides a high level of diversification. Three indirect forms of property investment are property unit trusts (or property OEICs), Real Estate Investment Trusts (REITs), and the shares of property companies. Each of these holds a diversified portfolio of properties. Individuals can become part owners in those portfolios by buying the units, or shares, issued by these institutional investors. By combining the relatively small investments of individuals, these institutions can buy large portfolios of properties. Aggregating the investments from a large number of individuals provides the institutions with large sums of money to invest.

The types of property held by these institutional investors include:

retail outlets such as shops, shopping centres, and retail warehouses;
office space such as office blocks and business parks;
industrial premises including industrial estates and distribution warehouses;
leisure facilities such as hotels, cinemas, and pubs.

89

The diversification of a portfolio entails a variety of different types of property in a variety of locations. Poor returns for some types, and places, would tend to be offset by good yields elsewhere. For example if only one property is held and it has no tenants, there is zero rental return. If a hundred properties are held it is extremely unlikely that they would all lack tenants. The diversification provided by these institutional investments tends to be enhanced by the tendency to hold indirect property investments in addition to direct property holdings. For example a property unit trust is likely to hold REITs and property company shares in addition to a direct property portfolio. In this way the spread of property investments becomes wider.

The returns to the individual investors come from both increases in the values of the properties and the rent (and lease) payments from their tenants. The attractiveness of this type of investment is enhanced by the fact that returns from property do not vary in line with stock market returns. Since property market returns (profits) and stock market returns (profits) tend to vary independently of each other, property investments can be useful for diversifying an investment portfolio. In other words, by mixing property investments with stock market investments poor performance from one may be offset by strong performance on the other. Exhibit 5.1 shows an example of a property unit trust.

EXHIBIT 5.1   LEGAL & GENERAL UK PROPERTY TRUST (28 MAY 2007)

INVESTMENT OBJECTIVE AND POLICY (ABRIDGED)

The investment objective is to achieve income and capital growth through investing generally in real commercial property. The investment policy is to invest predominantly in commercial property in the UK. The scheme will aim to diversify risk by seeking exposure principally in three main sectors:

Retail (e.g. shopping centres, retail warehouses, standard shops, supermarkets, and department stores);
Offices (e.g. standard offices and business parks); and
Industrial (e.g. standard industrial estates and distribution warehousing).

In addition, the scheme may also gain exposure to other commercial property sectors, including the smaller leisure sector (e.g. leisure parks, restaurants, pubs, and hotels).

The scheme may also invest in other property-related assets (including property-related UK transferable securities and mainly UK property-related collective investment schemes), in money market instruments, deposits, money market-related collective investment schemes, and government and public securities.

Trust expense ratio:*   1.30% p.a.
Property expense ratio:*   0.19% p.a.

---

*Other classes of unit trust have lower expense ratios.
Source: *Legal & General (Unit Trust Managers) Limited*

The trust expense ratio shows the operating expenses that relate to the management of the Trust as a percentage of the average net assets of the Trust. The property expense ratio shows the operating costs that relate to the management of the property assets as a percentage of the average net assets of the Trust.

Table 5.A

Ten largest holdings
66–7 Newman Street, London
Station Retail Park, Carlisle
51 Lincoln's Inn Fields, London
Plot 5, Sherwood Park, Annesley
991 Doddington Road, Lincoln
Riverside Retail Park, Leven
19/20 Noel Street, London
Carpetright Unit, Hazelwick Avenue, Crawley
Unit E, Stafford Park 1, Telford
Tavistock Industrial Estate, Twyford, Berks

DETERMINANTS OF PROPERTY PRICES

Property prices are determined by the forces of demand and supply. So an analysis of the determination of property prices entails a consideration of the influences on demand and those on supply. In the case of residential property important factors affecting demand are thought to be household incomes and mortgage interest rates. A rise in incomes provides the finance for an increase in spending on residential property. A fall in mortgage interest rates makes mortgages, and hence property purchase, more affordable. In the UK these factors have been accompanied by a willingness, on the part of mortgage lenders, to lend increasing multiples of income (the maximum mortgage loan used to be about three times annual income, at the time of writing loans of around five times income were not uncommon).

Demographic factors also affect demand. If the population of a region or country were increasing, there would be an increase in the demand for residential property. In the UK increasing longevity (people living longer) and net immigration have added to the demand for housing. If there were an increase in the proportion of single occupants, for example due to increasing divorce rates, there would be increased demand for properties.

Demand for residential property is enhanced by the fact that it is seen as more than a source of accommodation. It is also seen as a form of investment and as a status symbol. These reasons for the purchase of property may lead to demand rising faster than incomes. It is interesting to note that in the UK the ratio of the average price of a house to average annual earnings rose from about

91

3 in 1995 to 5.8 in 2005 (Nationwide Building Society 2005). Property prices are subject to bubbles and crashes in a similar way to stock markets (see Chapter 27 on stock market bubbles and crashes). The rise in the ratio of property prices to incomes may be the result of positive feedback trading whereby increasing prices cause increases in demand because buyers extrapolate price rises (that is past price rises are seen as indicating future price rises).

There is evidence that professional valuers emphasise different aspects of a property than the buyers. Adair *et al.* (1996) found that buyers put more emphasis on house size and condition than valuers. Valuers put more emphasis on location, in terms of characteristics of the neighbourhood, than buyers. Adair *et al.* suggested that differences between valuers and buyers could produce a difference between valuations and sale prices of the order of 10%. They found that valuers and buyers both tended to use a larger number and range of characteristics when evaluating detached properties as opposed to terraced properties.

A major factor affecting the supply of residential property is the availability of building land. This is likely to be affected by planning permission from governmental bodies. In the UK one of the reasons suggested for the rise in property prices has been the failure of new home construction, resulting from low availability of building land, to match the increase in demand for homes.

In the case of commercial property, demand will be affected by the factors that determine other forms of business investment. These factors are the prospective productivity of the investment (the prospective rental income from the property) and the cost of financing the purchase of the property. The cost of financing the purchase of commercial property, the cost of capital, is related to interest rates. High interest rates would be associated with a high cost of capital. The demand for commercial property rises when prospective rental income rises, but falls when the cost of capital rises.

The supply of commercial property is affected by the availability of suitable building land. It is likely to be affected by planning constraints. It is also affected by the attitudes of property developers. If developers see construction as potentially profitable, the supply from them would increase.

THE ROLE OF ANCHORING IN PROPERTY VALUATION

Anchoring is a concept that has emerged from the literature on behavioural finance, notably from Tversky and Kahneman (1974). Anchoring entails people being influenced in their estimations of value by numbers provided, even when those numbers are irrelevant or inappropriate. Northcraft and Neale (1987) found that estate agents anchored to the asking price of a property and were heavily influenced by it. High asking prices tended to elicit high valuations. However Diaz (1997) found no evidence that professional valuers operating in markets familiar to them anchored on anonymous opinions, although Diaz and Hansz (1997) found that valuers operating in geographically unfamiliar markets were influenced by anonymous opinions. They found that the prices of comparable properties also became anchors. Gallimore (1994, 1996) concluded that property valuers were subject not only to anchoring but also exhibited a confirmation bias. The confirmation bias entails valuers making quick judgements, and then seeking evidence in support of the early valuations.

Property valuation appears to be prone to 'appraisal smoothing', that is the tendency for values based on expert estimates of price to fluctuate less than prices observed from the process of buying and selling. Diaz and Wolverton (1998) demonstrated that valuers anchor to their previous valuations and adjust their valuations insufficiently to take full account of changing circumstances.

The effect of anchoring to asking price in property negotiations has been explored (Black and Diaz 1996; Black 1997; Diaz *et al.* 1999). It was found that property professionals gave too much weight to asking price, even when the asking price was inconsistent with relevant information. It might be the case that market data is intellectually demanding whereas an asking price is a simple, and undemanding, piece of information (Diaz 1999).

MOMENTUM IN PROPERTY PRICE TRENDS

One observed feature of share price movements is that they tend to demonstrate short-term momentum and longer-term reversion. This means that, in the short term, strong performance tends to persist whereas there is subsequent reversion. Stocks that have performed well in the recent past will tend to show good performance in the near future. This strong performance is likely to show some reversal after a time. The chapters in Part 7 on market efficiency, particularly Chapter 23 on concepts and weak form evidence, indicate relevant evidence.

There have been a number of studies of property (real estate) markets, particularly commercial property markets, indicating the existence of momentum (Young and Graff 1996, 1997; Graff *et al.* 1999; Lee and Ward 2001; Marcato and Key 2005; Devaney *et al.* 2007). Marcato and Key found evidence of some subsequent reversal. Although the studies tended to focus on commercial property, the Young and Graff studies found momentum effects for residential property. Overall the various studies found that the persistence of price trends was greatest for the extremes. The top 25% of properties in one year tended to be high performers the following year, and the bottom 25% one year tended to be poor performers the following year.

One important difference between stock market prices and the property market prices used in the studies is that, whereas stock prices are determined by trading, valuations by real estate professionals were the source of the property prices. The observed serial persistence in property price changes was actually persistence in the direction and size of valuation changes. If valuers were conservative in revising values, those revisions might be smoothed over time rather than occurring at one point in time. Such smoothing, which could be the result of anchoring on previous valuations, would give the appearance of a momentum effect.

The question has been raised as to why, if serial persistence in returns from real estate exists, the effect is not eliminated by property investors buying and selling on the basis of previous price movements. If investors, particularly arbitragers who both buy and sell, act so as to fully exploit profitable opportunities those opportunities should cease to exist. Devaney *et al.* (2007) pointed out that the information on property valuations may not be widely disseminated and that there are significant transaction costs. Momentum appears to exist in stock markets where price changes are universally known and transaction costs are relatively low. So it is perhaps not surprising that real estate investors do not trade so as to eliminate trends in property prices.

In both stock and real estate markets, trading on the basis of recent price movements could serve to continue the trend rather than eliminate it. Such positive feedback trading could perpetuate profit opportunities rather than eliminate them. This raises issues relating to the efficient market hypothesis (see the chapters in Part 7 on market efficiency, particularly Chapter 23 on concepts and weak form evidence). Proponents of the efficient market hypothesis believe that traders eliminate any unjustified price moves by buying underpriced assets and selling overpriced assets. Opponents of the efficient market hypothesis believe that assets can continue to have unjustified prices for long periods, and that deviations from justified prices can increase. The evidence of momentum (serial persistence) is evidence against the efficient market hypothesis.

A COMPARISON OF PROPERTY AND STOCK MARKET INVESTMENTS

In the UK housing is often seen as the best long-term investment in terms of total return. At the same time the stock market is seen as the most risky. The perception of relative long-term returns is more readily explained by the principles of behavioural finance than by reality. The principle of retrievability (availability) says that perceptions are heavily influenced by 'information' that is readily recalled. It is possibly the case that the media tends to report stock market crashes more readily than rises, whilst tending to report heavily housing market price rises. A perception of housing as a profitable and safe investment, that is superior to stock market investment, seems to have formed.

It is informative to look at recent UK history. For example £100,000 spent on the average UK residential property at the beginning of 1988 would have grown to about £288,000 by the end of 2003 (based on the Halifax Property Index) whereas £100,000 invested in a portfolio of shares reflecting the FTSE All-Share Index would have grown to about £503,000 over the same period. So in terms of financial returns on the investment, stock market investment proved superior. However it does appear that stock market investment provides more risk. The figures shown in Table 5.1 indicate that both investments were subject to a substantial amount of risk. The figures show the returns in each of the years during the period. The stock market was more volatile. It also showed substantial losses in some years, whereas when the housing market produced losses they were more modest. The stock market more than compensated for its loss-making years by providing substantial gains in many years. However the perspective of behavioural finance is again useful here. According to prospect theory, people weight the pain from losses more than twice as heavily as the pleasure from gains. This is known as loss-aversion and would cause large stock market losses, such as those in 2001 and 2002, to feel very painful to many investors.

The two years following 2003 saw relative outperformance by the stock market. During 2004 the FTSE All-Share Index showed a return of 31.9% against a rise in the Halifax UK House Price Index of 17.9%. During 2005 the FTSE All-Share Index showed a yield of 15% against 9.6% for the Halifax House Price Index (*Money Management*, April 2006).

McRae (1995) pointed out that in real terms (i.e. after adjusting for inflation) the rise in the prices of detached houses in the UK averaged less than 2% p.a. over the period 1945 to 1993. Figures relating to house price increases are not the full story of investing in residential property. The property also provides accommodation if owner-occupied, or rental income if it is a buy-to-let property. The value of the accommodation or rent should be added to the capital gains from price increases when assessing the total return from housing. Against these items should be set certain costs such as maintenance, insurance, and property taxes (council tax).

It can be seen from Table 5.1 that share prices and house prices often move in opposite directions. This suggests that a combination of shares and property is good for portfolio diversification. Poor performances of one may be offset by good performances of the other, so an investment portfolio containing both will be relatively stable (see Chapter 13 on portfolio diversification).

Table 5.1

	Stock market	Housing market
1988	11.87%	34.29%
1989	36.07%	3.07%
1990	−9.52%	0.81%
1991	20.46%	−3.49%
1992	20.21%	−7.42%
1993	28.40%	1.50%
1994	−5.83%	−0.20%
1995	23.91%	−1.34%
1996	16.69%	8.52%
1997	23.89%	4.48%
1998	14.50%	4.55%
1999	24.66%	13.53%
2000	−5.66%	3.13%
2001	−13.05%	15.49%
2002	−22.43%	23.11%
2003	21.31%	17.07%

Source: The Halifax

MORTGAGES AND THE PURCHASE OF PROPERTY

Mortgages are debts secured by property. They are often used for the purchase of homes. The borrower borrows for a period such as 25 years. The borrower undertakes to make periodic, typically monthly, repayments to the lender. If the borrower fails to maintain the payments, the lender has the legal right to take the property by which the mortgage is secured. Lenders differ in the amount they will lend but three times annual earnings is a typical upper limit.

Mortgage lenders like to protect themselves if they lend a high proportion of the value of a property. They face the risk that a borrower might default after a fall in property prices. If the lender repossesses the property and sells it, the selling price may be less than the outstanding mortgage debt. Lenders often require borrowers who borrow a high proportion of the value of a property to take out mortgage indemnity insurance. Such insurance would reimburse the lender for any surplus of the debt over the selling price of the property. A situation in which the mortgage debt exceeds the value of the property is known as negative equity.

Mortgages in the United Kingdom can be financed on either a repayment, or an endowment, basis (other possibilities include pension mortgages and ISA mortgages). Repayment mortgages entail monthly payments that cover both interest and debt reduction. If the interest rate were constant for the full period of the mortgage, the monthly payments would also be constant. With variable-rate mortgages the monthly payment will change as interest rates change. In the UK most mortgages are variable rate.

95

Interest rates on variable-rate mortgages are determined by the demand and supply for funds. If there is an increase in borrowing, or a fall in saving, interest rates will rise. A fall in borrowing or rise in saving will reduce interest rates. Monetary policy of the central bank (the Bank of England in the UK, the European Central Bank in the Eurozone) will influence interest rates by operating through demand and supply. The interest cost of a mortgage to a borrower reflects what the lender (a bank or building society) has to pay for the funds. If demand and supply determines that the mortgage lender must pay more to its depositors, the variable-rate mortgage borrowers should expect the increased interest costs to be passed on to them. In the case of base rate tracker mortgages, the mortgage interest rate is guaranteed to be a specified amount above the Bank of England base rate (or other benchmark interest rate). It is to be expected that base rate tracker mortgages are financed by means of the bank or building society borrowing on a similar basis.

In the early years of a repayment mortgage most of the monthly payment would reflect interest on the debt, with relatively little being left over for reducing the size of the debt. In later years, when part of the debt has been repaid by means of these monthly sums and interest costs have thereby been reduced, more of the monthly payment is available for reducing the debt. Towards the end of the mortgage term, the outstanding debt will have been significantly reduced with the result that interest is a smaller portion of the payments. As a mortgage term nears its end, most of the monthly sum is used for debt reduction (capital repayment).

Endowment mortgages entail none of the debt being repaid until the mortgage matures. The borrower pays interest on the entire sum borrowed throughout the period of the mortgage. In addition the borrower makes monthly contributions to an endowment fund operated by an insurance company. The intention is that, at maturity, the accumulated endowment fund will be sufficient to pay off the mortgage debt. However there is a risk that the accumulated sum will not be sufficient (there is also the possibility that it will be more than sufficient with the effect that there is a lump sum available to the borrower in addition to the sum required to repay the mortgage).

Endowment mortgages are the most common form of interest-only mortgage. It is possible that the lender does not insist that the borrower makes provision for repayment at the end of the mortgage term. However it is usual for borrowers to be required, or at least encouraged, to establish a savings scheme that will be expected to repay the mortgage when it reaches the end of its term. Although endowment policies have been the most common savings schemes other methods have included pension funds, where the lump-sum component pays off the mortgage debt, and tax-advantaged savings schemes (PEPs and ISAs).

CHARACTERISTICS OF REPAYMENT MORTGAGES

The nature of repayment mortgages has implications for the pattern of interest and principal payments on the part of the borrower. The characteristics of the repayment process can be seen by demonstrating the effects of differing interest rates and terms to maturity on the monthly payments, the total interest paid, and the rate at which the mortgage debt is reduced.

Characteristic 1
The monthly repayments increase as the interest rate rises, but not proportionately. For example, at 5% p.a. a £100,000 15-year mortgage will cost £790 per month. At 10% p.a. the same mortgage would cost £1,075 per month. A doubling of the interest rate entails a 36% increase

in the monthly payment. The absence of proportionality can be explained in terms of the higher monthly payments reducing the mortgage debt more rapidly in the later years. In consequence less of the debt needs to be paid off in the early years. Also the total debt repayment is not affected by interest rates.

Characteristic 2

A reduction in the term of a mortgage increases the monthly payments, but not proportionately. For example, a £100,000 30-year mortgage at 5% p.a. entails a monthly payment of £536 whereas an equivalent 15-year mortgage involves payments of £790 a month. Halving the period of the mortgage causes a 47% increase in the monthly payments. The absence of proportionality can be explained in terms of the reduced cumulative interest payment resulting from the faster repayment of the mortgage debt.

Characteristic 3

The cumulative interest payments increase more than proportionately with the term of the mortgage. For example, with an interest rate of 5% p.a. a £100,000 15-year mortgage would entail cumulative interest payments of £42,342 whereas an equivalent 30-year mortgage involves total interest costs of £89,493. Raising the term of the mortgage by 100% increases the total interest payments by 111%. This can be explained in terms of the lower debt repayments in the early years, in the case of the 30-year mortgage, and the resulting higher annual interest costs together with the longer period over which interest is payable.

Characteristic 4

The cumulative interest payments are larger with higher interest rates and they rise more than proportionately. A 25-year £100,000 mortgage at 5% p.a. entails total interest payments of £75,377. An equivalent mortgage with a 10% p.a. interest rate would involve total interest payments of £172,610. This can be explained in terms of less of the capital being paid off in the early years when the interest rate is higher. Not only is the interest rate higher, so is the average size of the mortgage debt.

Characteristic 5

The time taken to the repayment of half the mortgage debt will here be referred to as the half-life of the mortgage. The relationship between interest rates and the half-life of a mortgage is that the half-life rises with increases in the interest rate, but the rise is less than proportional. At 5% p.a. a 25-year £100,000 mortgage has a half-life of 16 years 2 months (i.e. 194 months). At 10% p.a. the half-life is 18 years 10 months (i.e. 226 months). With the higher interest rate less of the debt is repaid in the early years.

Characteristic 6

The half-life of a mortgage rises with increases in the term of the mortgage and the increase in the half-life is more than proportional to the increase in the term of the mortgage. A 15-year £100,000 mortgage at 5% p.a. will have a half-life of 8 years 10 months (i.e. 106 months). An equivalent mortgage with a term of 30 years would have a half-life of 20 years 2 months (i.e. 242 months).

The Tilt

The tilt is the tendency for mortgages to exert cash flow pressures on borrowers in the early years of the mortgage. One source of the tilt is inflation, and the effects of expected inflation on interest rates. Interest rates tend to incorporate expectations of inflation. If the real interest rate is 3% p.a., and inflation is expected to be 2% p.a., nominal (money) interest rates are likely to be about 3% + 2% = 5% p.a. (see Chapter 3 on money market investments). High expected inflation is associated with high interest rates, and hence high monthly repayments on a mortgage. However inflation erodes the value of money. With an inflation rate of 2% p.a., at the end of 25 years it would require $(1.02)^{25}$ = £1.64 to buy what £1 would have bought at the beginning of the 25 years. This implies that £1 at the end of 25 years is equivalent to a current $1/1.64$ = 61p in terms of purchasing power. So over time inflation reduces the value of money and hence the value, in purchasing power terms, of monthly mortgage payments.

High expected inflation raises the real value of mortgage payments in the early years since interest rates would be high but inflation would not have had time to substantially reduce the real value of the monthly payments. By the end of the mortgage period, inflation would have substantially reduced the real value of the monthly mortgage payments. Table 5.2 illustrates the inflation tilt on a repayment mortgage for the cases of expected, and experienced, inflation of 0%, 2%, and 4% p.a. and corresponding nominal interest rates of 3%, 5%, and 7% p.a. It is assumed that the initial mortgage debt is £100,000 repayable over 25 years and that inflation rates and interest rates are constant (the validity of the basic principle does not depend upon the assumption of constancy).

In the absence of inflation the real monthly cost remains at £474 throughout. With 4% p.a. inflation the early real cost is high at £707 per month whereas by the end of the mortgage period the real cost is down to £265. Inflation causes the real cost of the mortgage payments to be tilted towards the early years.

One way to alleviate the tilt could be to have an interest-only period at the beginning. For example the first five years could be interest-only (there is no repayment of the debt, only the interest is paid). At the end of the first five years the mortgage becomes a 20-year repayment mortgage. Table 5.3 shows the monthly payments during the first five years and the subsequent 20 years.

It can be seen from Table 5.3 that, although the real value of the early payments is reduced, there is not necessarily a moderation of the extremes. For example in the '2% and 5%' case the highest real value is £598, which exceeds the highest real value (£585) in the absence of the interest-only period (in Table 5.2).

Table 5.2

	Inflation and interest rates		
	0% and 3%	2% and 5%	4% and 7%
Money value of monthly payments	£474	£585	£707
Real value of payments at beginning	£474	£585	£707
Real value of payments at end	£474	£357	£265

Table 5.3

| | Inflation and interest rates | | | | | |
| | 0% and 3% | | 2% and 5% | | 4% and 7% | |
	First 5	Last 20	First 5	Last 20	First 5	Last 20
Money value of monthly payments	£250	£555	£417	£660	£583	£775
Real value of payments at beginning	£250		£417		£583	
Real value of payments at end of 5 years	£250		£378		£479	
Real value of payments at start of year 6		£555		£598		£637
Real value of payments at end of 25 years		£555		£403		£291

Other sources of the tilt include the tendency for the real value of salaries and wages to be relatively low in a person's earlier working years, and for the purchase of a home to be associated with expenditure on fittings and furniture. The latter source of the tilt can be partially compensated by means of a cashback payment. A cashback entails increasing the mortgage borrowing above the amount needed for the purchase of the property. The additional amount borrowed is paid to the borrower as a lump sum at the time that the property is purchased. Effectively it is the provision of a loan, for unspecified purposes, on the same terms as the loan for financing the purchase of the property.

FIXED-RATE MORTGAGES

It is often possible to obtain mortgages on which the interest rate is fixed for a period of time, for example five years. Theories of the term structure of interest rates throw light on such products, including the advantages and disadvantages.

The starting point is the pure expectations theory of the term structure. This suggests that long-term interest rates are averages of expected future short-term interest rates. For example the interest rate for a five-year loan would be the average of the next five one-year rates. There would be no expected difference between (a) borrowing for five years and (b) borrowing for one year with a view to renewing the borrowing at the end of the year (and renewing on the next three anniversaries). The word *expected* is important here since future interest rates are uncertain.

On this view the advantage of the fixed-rate mortgage is that it provides certainty of interest rate costs over the period of the loan, not that it entails an advantageous interest rate. The interest rate payable matches the expected average rate to be paid on a variable-rate mortgage. At the end of the five years the fixed rate would have proven to be either higher or lower than the corresponding average variable rate. However at the beginning of the period there is no way of knowing which would be the case. The expected rate is in the middle of a range of possibilities.

The expected future interest rates are those that are anticipated by money market participants (for example banks). The likelihood of an individual borrower (or adviser) being able to produce a superior forecast of future interest rates is, at best, very remote. Interest rates are notoriously difficult to forecast, and the best advice is not to try. The choice between fixed- and variable-rate mortgages should not be made on the basis of whether the borrower believes that interest rates will be higher or lower than the fixed rate. The borrower should also be aware that making the choice on the basis of whether the fixed rate is higher or lower than the current variable rate involves an implicit forecast of interest rates. The implicit forecast is that interest rates will remain unchanged.

A decision to take out a fixed-rate mortgage should be based on the value of the certainty that the fixed rate provides. The borrower with a fixed rate avoids the risk that interest rates will rise to the extent that repayments cease to be affordable. The borrower must expect to pay for the reduction of risk. This relates to an extension of the pure expectations theory of the term structure of interest rates. The principle of expectations with risk premium says that long-term interest rates equal the average of the expected future short-term rates plus a risk premium. The risk premium is an addition to the interest rate to reflect the higher risk (and lower liquidity) faced by the lender.

This point can be elaborated by considering how the lender (bank or building society) obtains the money to be lent to the borrower. The bank might borrow money for five years by selling five-year bonds in the financial markets. The rate of interest payable on the bonds will determine the fixed rate that the bank will charge its customers. Investors in five-year bonds face more risk than investors in shorter-term assets; an increase in interest rates would reduce the market value of the bonds. To compensate for this extra risk the investors would require extra interest; that is a risk premium. So the bank has to pay a risk premium and this will be passed on to borrowers in the form of higher interest rates. So fixed-rate mortgage borrowers should expect to pay extra interest for the increased certainty about the interest rates payable. Fixed-rate mortgage borrowers should expect to pay the average of expected future variable interest rates plus a risk premium.

Consideration of how banks and building societies raise funds for the provision of fixed-rate mortgages also explains why early redemption penalties are often imposed. Often borrowers with fixed-rate mortgages want to change to a variable rate when interest rates fall. However the provider has borrowed on a fixed-rate basis and is committed to continue to pay the fixed rate. Early termination of the mortgage would leave the bank or building society paying the high rate of interest, and making a loss in doing so since the money must now be lent at the lower interest rate. The mortgage provider would therefore expect compensation for this loss from the borrower. A borrower needs to realise that the interest rate certainty provided by a fixed-rate mortgage involves a guarantee that precludes advantageous interest rate movements as well as adverse ones. A cost of avoiding rises is the loss of potential falls.

It has been suggested by the UK government (in 2003, by Gordon Brown, then Chancellor of the Exchequer) that the UK system of mortgage lending should move towards the system of long-term lending typical of the United States and mainland Europe. In the UK most mortgages are provided on a variable interest rate basis, and fixed rates have not normally been for more than five years. In the United States and mainland Europe interest rates are typically fixed for the duration of the mortgage term (e.g. 25 years). The reason for this preference, on the part of the UK government, for long-term fixed-rate mortgages is the view that the variability of short-term mortgage rates has contributed to price instability in the UK housing market and that long-term interest rates are more stable than short-term rates. It is certainly the case that short-term interest rates are more variable than long-term rates.

The experience of the US Savings and Loan Associations (the American equivalent of the UK building societies) during the 1980s indicates that there could be dangers in moving to the use of long-term fixed-rate mortgages. Loans were made at interest rates fixed for periods such as 25 years whilst those loans were financed by taking short-term deposits. Interest rates on deposits could rise but interest rates on loans were fixed. As interest rates rose the Savings and Loan Associations were pushed into loss-making situations. Their interest receipts were fixed but their interest costs rose.

American mortgage providers now reduce those interest rate risks by collaterising the mortgage loans. This involves bundling mortgages together into a form of bond and selling those bonds to investors (particularly institutional investors). As a result the assets of the mortgage providers cease to be long-term fixed-rate loans and become short-term variable-rate deposits. The mortgage providers thus avoid the risks arising from having fixed-rate assets and variable-rate liabilities. If long-term fixed-rate mortgages become commonplace in the UK, it can be expected that mortgage-backed bonds will become an important component of the range of available investments.

An important aspect of the long-term fixed-rate mortgages used in the United States is that borrowers can choose to repay mortgages before they reach their maturity dates, perhaps in order to replace a mortgage with a new one at a lower interest rate (in the event of interest rates falling). This is a form of option given to the mortgage borrower by the mortgage provider, and it provides the borrower with the potential for financial gain at the expense of the provider. Options must be paid for, and the payment would be in the form of an interest rate premium. Interest rates payable by borrowers will be increased by the amount of the interest rate premium. In consequence the interest rate payable by the fixed-rate borrower will exceed the average expected future short-term interest rate.

In the UK, fixed-rate mortgage borrowers face early redemption (repayment) penalties if they repay their mortgages before the end of the fixed-rate period. Such penalties are often so high as to make switching to a cheaper mortgage unprofitable. When the redemption penalty is added to the new mortgage cost, the borrower is often no better off after the transfer to the cheaper mortgage. Lenders impose redemption penalties because they typically finance fixed-rate mortgage lending by fixed-rate borrowing. If a borrower redeems (repays) a mortgage when interest rates fall, in order to switch to a mortgage with the new lower interest rate, the lender is left paying the high fixed rate whilst no longer receiving the high rate. This produces a loss for the lender, and the redemption penalty is compensation for the loss.

The Miles Report on the UK Mortgage Market

In December 2003 Professor David Miles produced his first report on the UK mortgage market. A particular focus of the report was on the reasons for the relative lack of long-term fixed-rate mortgages in the UK. In order to put the report into the context of finance theory, it is useful to begin by quoting from a *Financial Times* editorial on 10 December 2003.

> It is easy to describe the perfect mortgage market. Lenders would compete fiercely. Consumers would be well informed. Products on offer would be priced in relation to the cost of funds. Over the length of the loan, a variable-rate mortgage would generally be the cheapest. Borrowers would pay a little extra for the benefits of a loan with an up-front discount. The insurance benefits of a fixed-rate loan against interest rate volatility would

also attract a premium. And a long-term fixed-rate without redemption penalties would cost more still.

What this quote is describing is a mortgage market based on the expectations-with-risk-premium yield curve. The Miles report could be seen as an account of how, and why, the UK mortgage market differs from what would be expected on the basis of that theory.

The expectations-with-risk-premium theory of the yield curve suggests that long-term interest rates, which would be the basis for fixed-rate mortgages, are based on averages of current and expected short-term interest rates. There is an addition to the interest rate, a risk premium, to compensate investors for the additional (capital) risk of long-term as opposed to short-term investments.

In the absence of the risk premium, the expected costs of fixed-rate and variable-rate mortgages would be equal. This arises from the view that long-term interest rates (fixed mortgage rates) are averages of current and future short-term interest rates (variable mortgage rates). The risk premium will cause the fixed mortgage rate to be a little higher than the expected average variable mortgage rate. The risk premium can be seen as the price to be paid for the additional certainty provided by the fixed-rate.

In some instances fixed-rate mortgages allow the borrower to redeem the mortgage without penalty. In the event of a fall in long-term interest rates, the borrower can take out a new mortgage at the lower interest rate and use the proceeds to pay off the existing (high interest) mortgage. This facility, which is common in the United States, gives the borrower an option. The borrower has the choice between continuing to borrow at the existing interest rate and switching to a lower rate, if a lower rate becomes available. The borrower pays for this option by way of an interest rate premium; the interest rate should be higher than would be the case in the absence of the option.

The interest rates that banks and building societies charge their mortgage borrowers should reflect the rates at which the banks and building societies can themselves borrow. These are the interest rates determined in the money and capital markets. If a mortgage initially has a rate of interest below the market rate (discounted mortgage) it is to be expected that in later years there will be a higher rate of interest such that, over the life of the mortgage, the average interest rate paid by the house-buying borrower reflects the average interest rate paid by the bank or building society.

All of these characteristics of a 'model' mortgage market are based on certain assumptions. One assumption, which the Miles report believes to be met, is that mortgage providers compete for business. Another assumption, which is not fully met, is that borrowers are well informed and rational.

Some borrowers appear to be well informed about mortgage choices whilst others are not. The result is that banks and building societies compete actively for the business of the informed borrowers whilst exploiting the uninformed borrowers. The uninformed borrowers subsidise the informed borrowers. The uninformed borrowers typically pay a standard variable rate, which is high. Informed borrowers frequently borrow at discounted rates, which are artificially low as a result of cross-subsidy from the payers of the standard variable rate.

Borrowers might be divided into four groups: payers of the standard variable rate, borrowers who initially pay a discounted rate but move to the standard variable rate after the discount period, borrowers who move to another discounted rate after the initial discount period (possibly with a new lender), and borrowers who choose a long-term fixed-rate mortgage.

In the UK very few borrowers have long-term fixed-rate mortgages. Those borrowers who opt for a succession of discounted rate mortgages, taking out a new mortgage (probably with a new lender) each time the period of discount ends, have paid the least over time. These borrowers, sometimes known as 'rate tarts', have enjoyed a relatively low average rate of interest over the period during which they have had mortgage debts. The borrowers who have paid the standard variable rate have paid a higher average interest rate over the life of the mortgage. The Miles report concluded that those who pay the standard variable rate subsidise the rate tarts.

The report took the view that this cross-subsidy was a reason for the failure of long-term fixed-rate mortgages to become a significant part of the UK mortgage market. The prospect of a succession of discounted interest rates makes a long-term fixed rate look relatively expensive.

Another reason suggested for the reluctance to take long-term fixed-rate mortgages is the failure to appreciate the presence and nature of interest rate risk. The report ventured the opinion that people, typically, do not understand interest rate risk. They are often unaware of the possibility of substantial interest rate rises. This is related to another opinion of the report: that borrowers focus excessively on the immediate cost of a mortgage rather than taking a long-term view of prospective costs over the life of the mortgage. If borrowers fail to appreciate interest rate risk, they will not be prepared to pay the extra interest (interest rate premium) embodied in long-term fixed rates as the cost of protection against interest rate rises. So they are reluctant to take out, apparently expensive, long-term fixed-rate mortgages.

The report takes the view that the relative absence of long-term fixed-rate mortgages in the UK is a factor in the high house price volatility in the UK. Short-term interest rates, the rates upon which variable-rate mortgage interest rates are based, are more volatile than long-term interest rates, which are the rates that form the basis of long-term fixed-rate mortgages. If borrowers choose variable-rate mortgages, and respond to immediate mortgage costs rather than long-term prospects, there will be large increases in demand for houses when rates fall and declines in demand when interest rates rise. The result is house price surges and collapses.

It might be noted that this, apparently short-sighted, behaviour of mortgage borrowers is what would be expected on the basis of the principles of behavioural finance. Narrow framing, retrievability, and anchoring between them predict that people focus on the recent past (narrow framing), base their views about normal rates on what can be readily observed and recalled (retrievability), and come to regard such recent interest rates as the norm (anchoring).

The Potential Use of Bond Options

The second part of the Miles report was published in March 2004. One aspect of the second part was an examination of how mortgage lenders could manage the risk of early repayment of long-term fixed-rate loans. Lenders would raise money in the capital markets by selling long-term bonds. The interest rate payable on those bonds would determine the long-term fixed-rate interest rate charged to mortgage borrowers. In the event that a fall in market interest rates causes borrowers to repay their mortgages in order to remortgage at the lower rates, the lenders face losses. The new mortgage lending that replaces the old mortgage lending is at the lower interest rate. The lenders are committed to paying interest on the bonds at the high interest rate whilst their mortgage lending is at the low interest rate.

To mitigate against this loss, mortgage lenders could buy call options on bonds. This strategy is based on two relationships. First, there is an inverse relationship between bond prices and interest rates so that a fall in interest rates is associated with a rise in bond prices. Second, rising bond prices generate pay-offs from call options. The call options provide the right to buy bonds at the old price (the strike price). The bonds bought at the old (low) price can then be sold at the new (high) price. So the use of call options provides the mortgage lender with a cash flow that offsets the loss arising from borrowers who remortgage in order to replace their mortgages with new ones at a lower interest rate.

Miles also addressed the question as to who would provide the call options. It was suggested that issuers of bonds, including the UK government, would find it advantageous to write (i.e. sell) call options. Writing call options is a hedging strategy for issuers of bonds. The sale of the options entails the receipt of a sum of money corresponding to the price (premium) of the options. That receipt of money offsets any fall in the bond prices that may occur prior to the sale of the bonds.

The UK debate about the increased use of long-term fixed-rate mortgages needs to be seen against the backdrop of the US debate about the virtues of moving away from them. In the United States it is being argued that long-term fixed-rate mortgages have increased mortgage costs. This is partly due to the risk premium on long-term loans, which is required to compensate lenders for the higher risk of lending long term. It is also due to the cost of the call options bought by lenders seeking to hedge the risk of early repayment of mortgages (a cost which is passed on to borrowers in the form of higher interest rates).

CAPPED-RATE MORTGAGES

A mortgage that protects against interest rate rises whilst allowing rates to fall is known as a capped mortgage. Capped mortgages contain an interest rate option that must be paid for (in the same way that insurance policies have to be paid for).

A capped mortgage sets an upper limit to the variable interest rate to be paid without setting a lower limit. The borrower avoids very high interest rates but is not committed to a fixed rate. The bank or building society offering such a mortgage buys an interest rate option from an options dealer.

An interest rate option (or cap) will compensate for an interest rate rise above a particular level. The seller of the option undertakes to pay the interest difference if the rate goes above a particular level. The bank or building society thus has an upper limit to its interest payments, and is thus able to pass an upper limit on to its customers.

The seller of the option takes on a risk. If interest rates rise the bank or building society receives payments from the provider of the option, but if rates fall there are no payments to the option dealer. The seller of the option has potential losses but no prospective gains. The provider of the option will therefore require payment for the option. This payment will reflect the potential for loss.

So the bank or building society must pay for the option. It will pass the cost on to the ultimate beneficiary of the interest rate cap, that is the borrower. This cost will be reflected in an addition to the interest rate that the borrower pays. If the borrower makes an early withdrawal from the mortgage agreement, the lender may not have fully recouped the price of the option from the additional interest payments. The bank or building society may seek a cash payment from the borrower to compensate for the unpaid portion of the cost of the option. If a borrower insures against interest rate rises, the insurance has to be paid for irrespective of whether the insurance subsequently turns out to be required.

In the case of collar mortgages, the lender sets an upper and a lower limit to interest rates. The benefit of avoiding high interest rates is obtained by forgoing the possibility of low rates. In effect there are two options: one in the borrower's favour and one that is potentially unfavourable. Because the borrower has potential for both gain and loss from options, it may be that there is no net cost for the options and hence no premium to be added to the mortgage interest rate. The cost of the favourable option is met by the acceptance of the unfavourable option. The cost of protection from high interest rates is the inability to benefit from low rates.

OTHER FORMS OF MORTGAGE

Discounted-rate mortgages allow a percentage deduction from the standard variable interest rate during the first few years of the mortgage. This appears to be a marketing device aimed at attracting business to the mortgage provider. Although there is an automatic transfer to the standard variable rate when the period of discount ends, lenders will often offer a discounted rate for a further period if borrowers request it (in order to avoid losing borrowers who switch mortgages in search of a new discounted rate). Usually there are penalties for repaying mortgages before the end of the discount period. Such penalties make transfer of a mortgage to a new lender during the discount period (which entails repayment of the existing mortgage) unattractive. Sometimes mortgages offer cashbacks, where a lump sum is paid to the borrower. Such cashbacks have to be repaid in the event of the mortgage being terminated within a prescribed period.

A related product is the *graduated-payment mortgage*. This differs from the discounted-rate mortgage in that the low rates of the early years are combined with higher than normal rates in later years. When graduated-payment mortgages were introduced in the UK there were protests (supported by seLctions of the media) from mortgage holders who found that they had signed contracts that allowed them out of relatively high interest rates only at the cost of financial penalties.

Graduated-payment mortgages were effectively abandoned in the UK as a result of the adverse publicity surrounding them. The fact that some people could not understand them resulted in no one having access to them. This lack of borrower (and media) sophistication in the UK may be the reason why other types of mortgage popular in North America have not been introduced on a large scale in the UK.

Two of these other types are *balloon mortgages* and *shared-appreciation mortgages*. Balloon mortgages may allow interest-only payments for a few years, after which the balloon mortgage is repaid by taking out a conventional mortgage. Shared-appreciation mortgages entail the lender charging reduced interest rates in return for a share of any capital gains arising from increases in the value of the property. An attempt to introduce shared-appreciation mortgages in the UK resulted in borrower (and media) protests when property price rises led to borrowers losing from the schemes. Many borrowers were unwilling to accept that if house prices rise rapidly, the cost of shared-appreciation mortgages would be much higher than the cost of other mortgages. Again, there was a lack of financial sophistication on the part of many borrowers (and sections of the media).

One form of mortgage that has recently gained popularity in the UK is the *offset mortgage*. An offset mortgage sets positive bank (or building society) account balances against a mortgage with the effect that interest is paid only on the excess of the value of the mortgage over the value of the positive bank balance. Positive bank balances reduce mortgage interest payments rather than earning interest. Since interest on bank balances is taxable, this gives a net gain. The disadvantage of offset mortgages is that the mortgage interest rate is typically higher than rates obtainable on other types of mortgage.

A related scheme is the *current account mortgage*. Whereas the offset mortgage involves two accounts, the mortgage account and the savings account, the current account mortgage entails just one account. Expenditure increases the total debt and saving reduces it. Interest is payable on whatever balance is outstanding.

Islamic Mortgages

Islamic teaching prohibits the paying and receipt of interest. Interest, referred to as riba, is banned under Sharia (Islamic) law since it is regarded as usury. Conventional mortgages are therefore unacceptable under Sharia law.

Islamic, or Sharia, mortgages avoid the explicit exchange of interest. The bank buys the property and immediately sells it to the mortgagor at a higher price. The mortgagor pays for the property in instalments over the term of the mortgage. This arrangement is called murabaha. The difference between the price paid by the bank and the price at which the property is sold to the mortgagor is equivalent to the cumulative mortgage interest.

Ownership is shared between the mortgagor and the bank. This is known as musharaka. Over time, as instalments are paid, the bank's share of the ownership declines and the mortgagor's share of the ownership increases. By the end of the term of the mortgage, the mortgagor gains full ownership of the property.

EQUITY RELEASE MORTGAGES AND HOME REVERSION PLANS

An equity release mortgage is a means of obtaining an income from a person's home. A mortgage is taken out against the person's property and the proceeds can be used to buy an annuity, which provides an income for life. No payments are made in respect of the mortgage until the person dies (or goes into long-term care). The mortgage interest is compounded over time until the mortgage is repaid upon death.

The longer the person lives, the greater will be the mortgage debt to be repaid from the value of the property. If the person has a long life, little or nothing of the value of the property would be left to be passed on to the heirs. The mortgage interest rate tends to be relatively high; partly to compensate the mortgage lender for the possibility that in some cases the accumulated mortgage debt will exceed the value of the property.

Home reversion is another means of releasing equity from the value of a person's home. This entails exchanging a percentage of the value of the property for a lump sum or income for life (an annuity). The proportion of the property value exchanged will exceed the proportion received as cash or annuity value. For example, 50% of the value of the property may be given in exchange for a cash value of 25%. This difference provides an interest return for the provider of the cash or annuity. The person retains the right to live in the property for the rest of their life. The provider of the cash or annuity receives no money until the property is sold upon the death of the person.

THE MORTGAGE AND ENDOWMENT EQUATIONS

A repayment mortgage entails an initial sum (debt) which is paid off over a succession of ensuing time periods. The equation showing the periodic (e.g. monthly) payments to be made under a repayment mortgage agreement is:

$$p = \frac{M \times r}{1 - [1/(1+r)^T]}$$

where p = periodic payment

M = initial size of mortgage

r = periodic interest rate (annual interest rate/number of payments per year)

T = number of payments (e.g. number of months to maturity).

A factor that affects the application of the mortgage equation is the use of the annual rest. The annual rest entails the recalculation of the outstanding mortgage debt for interest purposes just once a year. So payments that reduce the value of the debt have no effect on interest costs until the following year. Interest continues to be charged on the debt in existence at the beginning of the year, rather than on the actual size of the debt. Not all mortgage lenders use the annual rest; many lenders now recalculate the debt on a monthly or daily basis so that capital repayments have a quick effect on interest costs.

With the annual rest the mortgage payments made during a year are accumulated by the lender, without interest, and the accumulated sum is used to retire part of the mortgage debt at the end of the year. When using the mortgage equation, use of the annual rest is equivalent to making payments annually rather than monthly. Table 5.4 compares monthly mortgage payments without (on the left) and with (on the right) the annual rest. Table 5.5 compares the accumulated total of payments over the life of the mortgage in the two cases. (In both cases a fixed interest rate is assumed. 100,000 is borrowed.)

It can be seen from Table 5.4 that the annual rest raises the monthly payments. It has its greatest impact when the mortgage term is short and interest rates are high. By multiplying the monthly

Table 5.4 *Monthly payments without and with the annual rest*

Mortgage term (years)	Interest rate (% p.a.)		Interest rate (% p.a.)	
	2	*10*	*2*	*10*
5	£1,753	£2,125	£1,768	£2,198
10	£920	£1,322	£928	£1,356
25	£424	£909	£427	£918

Table 5.5 *Total cumulative payments without and with the annual rest*

Mortgage term (years)	Interest rate (% p.a.) 2	10	Interest rate (% p.a.) 2	10
5	£105,180	£127,500	£106,080	£131,880
10	£110,400	£158,640	£111,360	£162,720
25	£127,200	£272,700	£128,100	£275,400

payments in Table 5.4 by the number of monthly payments over the term of the mortgage, the cumulative sum of payments is obtained. The resulting values are shown in Table 5.5.

The annual rest increases the total cumulative payments. The effect is most pronounced when the interest rate is high and the mortgage term is short.

In the case of loans, including mortgages, the Annual Percentage Rate (APR) has to be quoted to borrowers (in the UK). The APR takes into account not only the frequency of payment and the annual rest, but also charges and fees that affect the effective rate of interest paid. The APR reflects the 'total charge for credit', which includes payments such as fees and administration charges in addition to the interest payments.

Another factor affecting the application of the mortgage equation is the issue of whether the mortgage is a flexible mortgage. A flexible mortgage allows for overpayment so that the debt is reduced more quickly. In the case of some flexible mortgages there is even a facility to miss some payments.

An endowment is the reverse of a mortgage, it involves a series of payments into a fund that result in a sum at the end of the term. An endowment mortgage involves paying interest only on the mortgage debt, which is paid off at maturity from the proceeds of an endowment policy. The equation for an endowment is:

$$M = p[(1+y)^T - 1] / y$$

where M = sum to be accumulated

    p = periodic payment

    y = rate of return on the endowment fund (per period)

    T = number of periods (e.g. months).

The question as to whether an endowment policy will produce a sufficient sum to repay a mortgage rests on the rate of return on the endowment fund. If the rate of return on the endowment equals the rate of interest on the mortgage, the endowment and repayment mortgages will be identical in terms of the size of the periodic payments. This is illustrated by Exhibit 5.2. If the rate of return on the endowment is higher than the mortgage interest rate, the endowment mortgage will be the cheaper (or will provide more than enough to pay off the mortgage). If the rate of return on the endowment is lower than the mortgage interest rate, the endowment mortgage will entail the higher monthly payments (or will provide insufficient funds to redeem the mortgage at maturity). Since endowment policies are typically based on stock market investments the relative performance of the two types of mortgage depends upon whether stock market returns (net of the charges on an endowment policy) exceed, or fall short of, mortgage interest rates. History suggests that holders of endowment mortgages would normally be better off, but they bear more risk.

EXHIBIT 5.2

ENDOWMENT MORTGAGE

An endowment policy can be used to pay off a mortgage debt. For example if returns on an endowment are 10% p.a., an annual payment of £16,380 into an endowment will be worth £100,000 in five years. This can be used to repay a £100,000 debt. An endowment mortgage involves paying interest on the £100,000 debt each year. If interest rates are 10% p.a., this amounts to £10,000 p.a. So the total annual payment is £16,380 + £10,000 = £26,380.

REPAYMENT MORTGAGE

Repayment mortgages involve amortising the debt (gradually paying it off).

Mortgage repayment schedule on a £100,000 five-year debt with interest fixed at 10% p.a.

Table 5.B

Year	Interest on debt	Repayment of debt	Remaining debt
1	£10,000	£16,380	£83,620
2	£8,362	£18,018	£65,602
3	£6,560	£19,820	£45,782
4	£4,578	£21,802	£23,980
5	£2,398	£23,982	−£2

There is a constant payment (interest plus repayment) of £26,380 each year. The £2 surplus arises because of rounding to the nearest pound.

The annual payments on the two types of mortgage are the same (£26,380) because the rate of return on the endowment fund equals the mortgage interest rate.

EXERCISE 5.1

(a) A repayment mortgage of £100,000 is to be paid off in equal monthly instalments over 25 years. What are the monthly mortgage payments at a constant interest rate of 6% p.a.?

(b) Someone is planning to accumulate £250,000 over 40 years. What is the required annual contribution to the endowment fund if the rate of return on the fund is 5% p.a.?

Answers

(a) $p = (M \times r)/ \{1 - (1 + r)^{-T}\}$
$p = (100,000 \times 0.005)/ \{1 - (1.005)^{-300}\}$
$p = £644.30$

(b) $M = p[(1+y)^T - 1]/y$
$250,000 = p[(1.05)^{40} - 1]/0.05$
$250,000 = p \times 120.8$
$p = 250,000/120.8 = 2069.54$

The required annual contribution is £2,069.54.

EXERCISE 5.2

With a mortgage borrowing of £100,000, and a fixed interest rate of 6% p.a., what are the monthly mortgage payments and total (aggregated over the full period of the mortgage) interest payments for mortgages of (a) 10, (b) 20, and (c) 30 years?

Answers

(a) Over 10 years the monthly payment would be:

$(£100,000 \times 0.005)/ \{1 - [1/(1.005)^{120}]\} = £1,110.21$

The monthly interest rate of 0.5% (0.005) is derived by dividing the annual interest rate by 12. The number of payments is the number of years multiplied by 12.
  The total payment over 10 years is:

£1,110.21 $\times$ 120 = £133,225.20

The total interest payment is:

£133,225.20 − £100,000 = £33,225.20

(b) Over 20 years the monthly payment would be:

$(£100,000 \times 0.005)/ \{1 - [1/(1.005)^{240}]\} = £716.43$

The total payment over 20 years is:

£716.43 × 240 = £171,943.20

The total interest payment is:

£171,943.20 − £100,000 = £71,943.20

(c) Over 30 years the monthly payment would be:

(£100,000 × 0.005)/{1 − [1/(1.005)^{360}]} = £599.55

The total payment over 30 years would be:

£599.55 × 360 = £215,838

The total interest payment is:

£215,838 − £100,000 = £115,838

It is useful to show these results in table form.

Table 5.C

Term in years	Monthly payment	Total interest	Total payment
10	£1,110.21	£33,225.20	£133,225.20
20	£716.43	£71,943.20	£171,943.20
30	£599.55	£115,838	£215,838

Have Endowment Mortgages Been a Bad Choice?

Since the late 1990s endowment mortgages have fallen into disrepute in the UK because in many cases they failed to provide enough money at maturity to repay the mortgage debts. Correspondingly there have been accusations that endowment mortgages were mis-sold. However, Booth and Rodney (2002) made the point that the negative perception may be based on money illusion, which is the failure to distinguish between real and nominal (i.e. money) values (see Chapter 3 on interest rates and money market investments in relation to the distinction between nominal and real interest rates).

The period since the early 1990s has been one in which inflation has fallen. Correspondingly interest rates (nominal interest rates) have fallen. The returns on the investments in which endowment policies are invested fell in consequence of the general fall in interest rates (and associated fall in returns on investments such as bonds). As a result values of endowment policies, in money terms, rose less rapidly than had been expected. The mortgage debts to be repaid when the endowment policies matured were specified in money terms. The failure of the money values of endowment policies to grow sufficiently to match the money values of the mortgage debts left many people with shortfalls; their endowment policy values fell short of the mortgage debts to be repaid.

The failure of the money values of endowment policies to grow to the anticipated values does not mean that the policies failed to perform in real terms. The failure on the part of the policyholders (and their advisers) was to incorrectly forecast the course of inflation. Looking at the matter in real terms, the real values of the mortgage debts did not fall as rapidly as had been expected. Over the period of the mortgages inflation, by eroding the value of money, eroded the value of the mortgage debts. When the mortgages, and endowment policies, were commenced the anticipated repayment at maturity would have been based on the real value of the endowment policies rising whilst the real values of the mortgage debts fell. The problem can be seen as one in which the endowment policies performed as expected in real terms, but in which the real values of mortgage debts fell less rapidly than expected. In other words the fall in the rate of inflation reduced the rate at which money lost its real value and hence reduced the rate at which the real value of mortgage debts fell.

Thus far it appears that the people with endowment mortgages lost out, whether values are expressed in money terms or real terms. However, they gained from a fall in interest rates. Lower inflation is associated with lower nominal interest rates, which are interest rates in money terms. The lower rate of decline in the real value of the mortgage debts would have been (approximately) offset by lower nominal interest rates.

Nominal interest rates could be seen as real interest rates plus compensation for inflation (compensation for the fall in the value of money). The element of nominal interest rates that compensates for inflation fell because inflation was lower. The lower inflation caused slower erosion in the real value of the mortgage debts. Endowment mortgage holders experienced shortfalls because the fall in inflation rates reduced their total monthly payments (endowment policy premiums plus mortgage interest). They were losers at the time that mortgages and endowment policies matured, but had been gainers before the maturity dates.

COLLATERALISED LOANS AS OPTIONS

Mortgages are collateralised loans. A collateralised loan is a loan against which the borrower provides collateral as security for the lender. In the case of mortgages, the collateral is usually property; in most instances it is the property that is purchased with the proceeds of the loan.

Imagine that someone borrows £500,000 to buy a home, and that within a year local circumstances have changed so dramatically that the market value of the property has fallen to £25,000. Many people would choose to default on the loan.

A call option gives the right to buy something at a particular price, without the obligation to do so. A mortgage can be seen as giving the borrower the right to buy the property for the value of the mortgage (any deposit paid for the property is history and is no longer relevant to the decision-making). If the value of the property rises, or stays above or near the value of the loan, the borrower continues to make the mortgage payments. The borrower is said to exercise the right to buy the property. If the value of the property were to fall below the value of the loan (a situation known as negative equity) the borrower might choose to default on the loan. The borrower chooses not to exercise the option to buy. (Of course by doing so the borrower could effectively forfeit the chance of obtaining future loans.)

The mortgage lender is giving the borrower an option. The lender might expect some payment for the option in the form of a higher interest rate. Such an interest rate enhancement would depend upon the likelihood of default. A borrower who has paid a substantial deposit (down payment) on the property starts with the value of the loan being much less than the value of the property. Such a borrower is unlikely to default because a substantial property price fall is required to bring the value of the property down to below the value of the loan. Someone taking out a mortgage equal to the value of the property (a 100% mortgage) is more likely to default. Any fall in the value of the property induces negative equity and the incentive to default. So mortgage lenders are likely to charge higher interest rates for 100% mortgages, or to levy other charges (perhaps in the form of insurance premiums).

CONCLUSION

Residential property can be regarded as a form of investment. It can take the form of one's own home, or a property bought for the purpose of letting to tenants. One attraction of investing in property is that it can be done in a geared manner; in other words the property can be bought with borrowed money. Disadvantages include the inability to obtain a well-diversified portfolio of properties, and the lack of liquidity (property is expensive to sell and cannot be sold very quickly).

Commercial property can be bought indirectly through institutional investments such as unit trusts, investment trusts, property company shares, insurance bonds, and pension funds. However management charges can be relatively high, and there is no possibility of reducing management charges by buying an index tracker fund.

Property prices are determined by the forces of demand and supply. In consequence prices can fall as well as rise. There have been times when many people have forgotten that property prices can fall. As Coggan (2006a) states: 'When investors think any asset is "safe" and cannot fall in value, they bid its price up to a level at which their intuition no longer applies.' Not only can investors forget that investment in property has risks but also property investment decisions are subject to the same psychological biases as other investment decisions (see Chapter 2 on personal investment decisions). There is a common perception that investment in property has provided greater gains than stock market investment. The historical evidence does not clearly support this belief.

The gearing offered by property investment takes the form of mortgages. Mortgages come in a wide variety of forms: variable, fixed, discounted, capped, interest-only, and Islamic being some of the popular mortgages in the UK. Capped mortgages entail the use of options. An interest rate option is a form of derivative that provides insurance against adverse interest rate changes. A holder of a capped mortgage must expect to pay for the option by way of higher interest rate payments, just as other forms of insurance must be paid for.

An interest-only mortgage is usually combined with an endowment policy whose purpose is to eventually pay off the mortgage debt. An endowment policy is a form of institutional investment, which accumulates an investment sum over a period of years in the anticipation that the sum accumulated will be sufficient to repay the mortgage debt when the mortgage reaches its maturity date (see Chapter 10 on life assurance and assurance-related investments). Repayment mortgages gradually pay off the mortgage debt over time; slowly reducing the debt in the early years but more rapidly in the later years. There has been some concern, particularly at government level, about the economic implications of the UK preference for variable as opposed to fixed-interest rate mortgages.

There are also facilities to turn a property into an income. Equity release entails taking out a mortgage loan in order to buy an annuity for the purpose of providing a pension (see Chapter 11 on pensions).

Part 2

Basics of Stock Markets

Chapter 6

Stock exchanges

OBJECTIVE

The objective of this chapter is to provide knowledge of:

1. The purpose and functions of stock exchanges.
2. The distinction between primary and secondary markets.
3. Types of stock exchange.
4. Stock market trading systems.
5. Bid-offer spreads.
6. Types of purchase and sale order.
7. Processes by which shares are issued.
8. Different types of share.

THE FUNCTIONS OF A STOCK EXCHANGE

The main purpose of a stock exchange is the transfer of money from investors to those wishing to obtain capital. The investors buy shares and bonds from issuers and thereby transfer money to them in exchange for potential future cash flows.

In the absence of a financial intermediary such as a stock exchange, the direct transfer of money from investors to those wishing to obtain funds would be problematical for a number of reasons. First, there would be the difficulty of how investors and those seeking funds are to find each other. Second, companies and governments want to raise large amounts of capital whereas individual investors normally want to invest relatively small sums. Individual investors have limited sums to invest, and they usually prefer to spread their investments amongst a number of companies so as to avoid the risk of suffering heavily from the poor performance of one firm. A stock exchange provides size transformation: relatively small sums from a large number of investors are aggregated so as to provide a large sum for the firm or organisation raising capital.

Third, stock exchanges provide maturity transformation. Companies need to obtain funds for the long term, whereas investors typically want immediate access to their money. A stock exchange provides a means of reconciling these two objectives. A firm may sell securities with distant maturities (or, in the case of ordinary shares, with no maturity date) whilst the buyers of such securities can obtain quick access to their money by selling the securities (securities include shares and bonds).

Another function of a stock exchange, which is performed as a byproduct of the financial intermediation, is to communicate information about the companies whose securities are being traded. The prices of stocks and bonds reflect the evaluation of investors and dealers (some of whom carry out very detailed analyses of the firms) of the performance of the firms. Share prices, and their changes, can communicate information of value to those inside as well as those outside the companies whose shares are being traded.

PRIMARY AND SECONDARY MARKETS

When stocks and bonds are initially issued they are said to be sold in the primary market. Subsequent to their initial sale they are traded in the secondary markets. Primary trading involves buying and selling newly created securities, whereas secondary trading involves shares and bonds that are already in existence. The fact that financial investments can be sold in a secondary market renders them more liquid, and hence more attractive. This enhanced liquidity makes investors more willing to buy in the primary market, and causes them to be less demanding in terms of required rates of return. An active secondary market improves the operation of the primary market and allows companies to raise money easily and on favourable terms. Secondary-market trading volume far exceeds the level of primary-market dealing.

The secondary market is the market in which previously issued securities are traded. It is the means by which stocks or bonds bought in the primary market can be converted into cash. The knowledge that assets purchased in the primary market can easily and cheaply be resold in the secondary market makes investors more prepared to provide borrowers with funds by buying in the primary market. A successful primary market depends upon an effective secondary market.

If transaction costs are high in the secondary market the proceeds from the sale of securities will be reduced, and the incentive to buy in the primary market would be lower. Also high transaction costs in the secondary market might tend to reduce the volume of trading and thereby reduce the ease with which secondary market sales can be executed. It follows that high transaction costs in the secondary market could reduce that market's effectiveness in rendering primary market assets liquid. In consequence there would be adverse effects on the level of activity in the primary market and hence on the total level of investment in the economy.

Price volatility in the secondary market might also be detrimental to the operation of the primary market. High volatility means that buyers in the primary market stand a considerable risk of losing money by having to sell at a lower price in the secondary market. This can reduce the motivation to buy in the primary market. Two factors that affect the price volatility of securities in the secondary market are the depth and breadth of that market.

The depth of the market is based on the likely appearance of new orders stimulated by any movement in price. If a rise in price brings forth numerous sell orders, the price rise will be small. A decline in price that stimulates many buy orders would be a small decline. A deep market would be characterised by the appearance of orders that tend to dampen the extent of any movement in price. Greater depth is thus associated with lower volatility.

The breadth of the market reflects the number and diversity of the traders in the market. If there is a large number of market participants with differing motivations and expectations there is less likely to be substantial price changes than would be expected when there is a small number of traders, or when the traders have common views such that they buy or sell together. A broad market is a large heterogeneous market characterised by relative price stability.

STOCK EXCHANGE LISTING

If a company wants its shares to be traded on a stock exchange, the shares must be listed on that stock exchange. The ability to sell shares on the stock exchange makes people more willing to invest in the company. Consequently they would accept a lower return on the shares and hence the company can raise capital more cheaply. The stock exchange also provides a market price for the shares, and thereby allows a valuation of the company.

Listing requires a substantial amount of documentation from the company, especially in terms of published accounts. The substantial amount of documentation is costly for the company but is useful for investors who want detailed information before investing. The information helps to establish the correct share price. More certainty about the correctness of the share price encourages investors and reduces the return that they require. Hence the cost of capital to the company is reduced.

The information aids corporate governance, which entails monitoring the management of the company. This governance is conducted by investors (especially institutional investors) and by the media. A stock exchange listing makes takeover bids easier, since the predator company is able to buy shares on the stock market.

TYPES OF STOCK EXCHANGE

In many countries there are both national and regional stock exchanges. National exchanges tend to trade the stocks of large companies. National exchanges impose demanding listing conditions. If shares in a company are to trade on a stock exchange, they must be listed. The exchange may prescribe criteria for listing in terms of history of the company, its profits, its capital, the integrity of its management, and possibly other factors. Shares in a firm can be traded on a stock exchange only if the stock exchange authorities give approval: that is list the stock. Examples of national stock exchanges include the New York Stock Exchange, American Stock Exchange, London Stock Exchange, Tokyo Stock Exchange, and the Frankfurt Borse. A single stock exchange, the Euronext exchange, covers France, the Netherlands, Belgium, and Portugal.

Regional exchanges tend to cater for the stocks of smaller companies. Their listing requirements are normally less stringent than those of the national exchanges. The financial costs involved in obtaining a listing also tend to be lower. So it is easier for a company to get its shares traded on a regional exchange, but probably at the cost of being traded on a less liquid market (i.e. on a market in which there is a lower frequency, and smaller volume, of trading). Regional stock exchanges also cater for small stockbroking firms by offering cheaper membership than the national exchanges. Examples of regional stock exchanges include the Pacific and Midwest exchanges in the United States, Osaka and Nagoya in Japan, Munich and Hamburg in Germany.

In addition to formal stock exchanges there are over-the-counter (OTC) markets. At one extreme these markets are unorganised with trading taking place between individuals on an unregulated basis, typically there is no restriction on the ability of people to buy and sell outside of organised exchanges. At the other extreme over-the-counter markets may be highly organised and sophisticated. Examples of organised over-the-counter markets are the NASDAQ and upstairs markets in the United States.

The NASDAQ market specialises in the trading of high technology stocks. Trading takes place via telephone or computer contacts. Market-makers display the prices at which they are prepared to buy and sell on computer networks. Investors, normally via brokers, trade with the market-makers by means of telephone or computer links. The upstairs market is mainly used by institutional investors and handles large buy and sell orders (block trades). When an institution places an order with a broker, traders at the brokerage firm will contact other institutions in an attempt to find one willing to trade. In the absence of finding a trading counterparty, the dealers at the stockbroking firm will attempt to execute the order with market-makers.

Shares in a company may be listed on more than one stock exchange. This is referred to as multiple listing. Shares in a company may also be simultaneously traded on formal exchanges and over-the-counter markets. Stocks of very large multinational companies may be traded on more than one national stock exchange. For example the London Stock Exchange lists more than 600 foreign stocks. Trading in such stocks can effectively be global and may operate on a 24-hour basis (as one exchange closes, trading may continue on others). This is one dimension of the globalisation of financial markets: that is the tendency for financial markets in different countries to become integrated into a single market. A major factor leading to globalisation has been the development of telecommunications. Other factors have been the tendencies towards international diversification of portfolios, and deregulation of national financial markets.

STOCK MARKET TRADING SYSTEMS

Order-driven Systems

Order-driven systems operate by matching buy and sell orders. Investors are proactive in terms of both price and quantity. Orders to buy and sell determine stock prices. Stock prices move towards the level at which orders to buy are matched by orders to sell. This can be illustrated by demand and supply curves as shown in Figure 6.1.

In Figure 6.1, P_A is the ask (or offer) price which is the price at which investors buy. P_B is the bid price, at which investors sell. Investors offering P_A or more will buy at P_A. Sellers requiring P_B or less will sell at P_B. The quantity that buyers demand at P_A matches the quantity that sellers wish to supply at P_B. The excess of P_A over P_B is known as the bid-offer or bid-ask spread (the scale of Figure 6.1 greatly exaggerates the size of the spread).

In an order-driven system stock prices are determined directly by demand and supply. The agent or body facilitating the trading process (the stock exchange) holds no position in shares and is entirely reactive to those seeking to buy or sell.

Order-driven systems involve investors stating the quantities that they wish to buy or sell. The quantities may be linked with maximum buying, or minimum selling, prices. These are limit orders in which buyers state the highest price they are willing to pay and sellers state the lowest price they

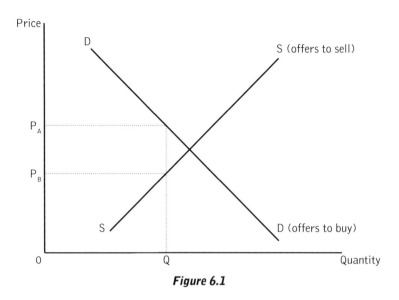

Figure 6.1

will accept. Alternatively an order could simply state a quantity, with an acceptance of the market price (these are known as market or 'at best' orders). The operation is illustrated by Table 6.1, which shows a hypothetical situation at the beginning of a trading day.

Table 6.1 illustrates the demand and supply schedules for a share. At a high share price, 105p, there are only 1 million shares demanded by potential buyers. At lower share prices more investors want to buy the shares. When the share price is low, at 95p, investors want to buy 6 million shares.

At a high share price, 105p, many investors want to sell shares. At 105p, 8.5 million shares are offered for sale. At lower share prices investors are less keen to sell. At a price of 95p only 1.5 million shares are offered for sale.

Table 6.1

Stock price	Buy orders (millions of shares)	Sell orders (millions of shares)
95	6	1.5
96	5.5	1.5
97	5.2	2
98	5	3
99	3.5	3.2
100	3	3.75
101	2.75	4
102	2.5	4.25
103	2	5
104	1.75	6.5
105	1	8.5

121

The buy orders might consist of 1 million market orders (investors willing to accept whatever the market price may be), with the remainder being limit orders (stipulating a maximum buying price). The quantities are cumulative, for example the orders at 103p comprise the market ('at best') orders plus the 103p limit orders plus orders with higher limit prices (i.e. the 2 million shares are the desired purchases by those investors willing to pay 103p or more).

The sell orders might consist of 1.5 million market ('at best') orders, with the remainder being limit orders. Again the quantities are cumulative. However, as opposed to the buy orders, the cumulative number of sell orders increases with increasing price. The fall in the cumulative number of buy orders and rise in the cumulative number of sell orders at progressively higher share prices is consistent with a downward sloping demand curve and upward sloping supply curve.

At the beginning of the trading day the stock price will be set at the level that results in the highest number of shares traded. The stock exchange would establish a price at which the largest possible number of investors can carry out their desired trades. That price is 99p per share. At 99p there are 3.2 million shares traded. All the sellers can trade and buyers can buy 3.2 out of their desired 3.5 million shares. At any other price fewer shares would be traded, and hence fewer investors would be satisfied. For example at a price of 98p only 3 million shares would change hands, and potential buyers would fail to acquire 2 million of the desired shares. At a price of 100p, there would be 3 million shares traded. In that case sellers would be unable to sell all that they want to (0.75 million shares would be unsold). At the share price of 99p the highest possible number of shares are traded; and the largest possible number of investors are able to carry out their desired transactions.

After the trades at 99p are executed the number of remaining orders at each price would be as shown in Table 6.2. Table 6.2 shows the situation immediately after 3.2 million shares have been traded at 99p per share. All the investors that were willing to sell at 99p or less have been able to sell, and so there are no investors wanting to sell at 99p or less. Most of the potential buyers who were willing to pay 99p or more have been able to buy. The unsatisfied demand is just 0.3 million shares (in Table 6.2 it is assumed that the highest price offered by the unsatisfied investors is 99p, although it is possible that some of the unsatisfied potential buyers are willing to pay more).

The buy and sell orders in Table 6.2 would be limit orders. Limit orders specify maximum buying prices or minimum selling prices. A limit order to buy stipulates the highest price that the buyer is prepared to pay. A seller using a limit order indicates the lowest price that would be acceptable.

A market order is an order to buy or sell at the best available price. If an investor makes a market order to buy in the situation of Table 6.2, the purchase would be at 100p (so long as the desired purchase is for 0.55 million shares or less). The price of 100p is the lowest price at which sellers are willing to sell. An investor who makes a market order to sell in the circumstances of Table 6.2 would sell at 99p (so long as the sale is of 0.3 million shares or less). The price of 99p is the highest price at which buyers are willing to buy. (It might be noted that this provides a bid-offer spread of 1p, i.e. 100p – 99p where 100p is the offer price and 99p is the bid price.)

New limit orders would either add to the existing number of orders, or would allow existing orders to be satisfied. For example a new limit order to buy at 98p or less would add to the unsatisfied demand at 98p. A new limit order to buy at 100p or less could be immediately satisfied by being matched with limit order sellers who are prepared to sell at 100p (so long as the purchase

Table 6.2

Stock price	Buy orders (millions of shares)	Sell orders (millions of shares)
95	2.8	0
96	2.3	0
97	2	0
98	1.8	0
99	0.3	0
100	0	0.55
101	0	0.8
102	0	1.05
103	0	1.8
104	0	3.3
105	0	5.3

is of 0.55 million shares or less). This would allow some limit order sales to be executed at 100p, thereby reducing the number of sell orders at 100p in Table 6.2 to less than 0.55 million.

A new limit order to sell at 101p or more would add to the size of the orders in Table 6.2. A new limit order to sell at 99p or more could be satisfied immediately at a price of 99p (so long as it is for 0.3 million shares or less). It would reduce the number of unsatisfied buy orders. For example a limit order to sell 0.1 million shares at 99p would reduce the outstanding buy orders at 99p from 0.3 million shares to 0.2 million shares.

Limit orders remain on the limit order book until they are withdrawn by the investors, or until they can be executed as a result of new orders arriving. The arrival of buy orders at 100p or above will allow execution of some of the sell orders in Table 6.2. If sell orders at 99p or less are submitted, some of the buy orders in Table 6.2 can be executed. In this way order matching can be continuous throughout the trading day. Typically these order-driven matching systems are computerised.

If some but not all orders at a price can be executed, the oldest orders get priority. Normally buyers and sellers are not shown the whole of the limit order book, only the highest buy price and the lowest sell price are shown (99p and 100p in Table 6.2).

Quote-driven Systems

In a quote-driven system, market-makers quote prices at which they are willing to sell (offer or ask prices) and prices at which they are willing to buy from investors (bid prices). Stockbrokers (on behalf of private investors), or institutional investors, transact with the market-makers on the basis of the quotes provided. Market-makers are proactive and investors reactive in terms of the prices. The firms that operate as market-makers are usually banks or stockbrokers.

Market-makers, or dealers as they are sometimes known, trade as principals. Trading as principals entails buying and selling for their own account and holding positions in the stocks for which they make a market. In terms of transactions, they are reactive rather than proactive. Their trading is in response to buy or sell orders from investors. If they wish to change their stock positions, they must move their price quotes.

If investors are net buyers, market-makers would find that their stockholdings decline. If they want to stop such a decline, they raise their quoted prices so as to deter buyers and encourage sellers. Conversely net sales by investors might raise the stockholdings of market-makers to undesirable levels. In response, market-makers would lower prices in order to encourage buyers and deter sellers. In these ways, the price quotes of market-makers respond to the pressures of demand and supply.

The excess of the offer price over the bid price is known as the bid-offer spread. It provides a source of profit for the market-maker as well as compensating for the risks inherent in the process of market-making. The market bid-offer spread is the excess of the lowest offer price over the highest bid price and is normally smaller than the spreads of individual market-makers.

Bid-offer Spreads

Bid-offer spreads (alternatively known as bid-ask spreads) are the spreads between the buying and selling prices of share dealers. A dealer, operating as a market-maker, quotes a price at which he/she is prepared to sell – the offer price – and a price at which he/she is willing to buy – the bid price. The offer price is always above the bid price. The difference between the offer and bid prices, the bid-offer spread, is the profit of the dealer. The question arises as to what factors affect the bid-offer spread.

From the perspective of investors, dealers (in their role as market-makers) provide two important services. The first is immediacy. The dealer sells from, and adds to, their own holdings of a stock in order to accommodate the trades of investors. As a result investors can immediately execute a trade without having to wait for a counterparty to emerge. For example a buyer need not wait for a seller to come forward since the dealer stands ready to sell.

A second service is the maintenance of price stability. For example buy orders, in the absence of corresponding sell orders, would tend to push up prices. Sell orders would push prices down. By being willing to trade from their own stockholdings, dealers reduce such price fluctuations.

The bid-offer spread of dealers can be seen as the price to be paid, by investors, for these services. The spread can also be seen, from the perspective of the dealer, as compensation for costs and risks. The costs would include the administrative costs of transferring shares. The risks arise from price fluctuations and information-based investors.

A dealer, who operates as a market-maker, holds shares. The dealer is at risk from a fall in share prices when shares are held (and from a price rise when the dealer has a short position). The bid-offer spread can be seen as a source of compensation for accepting such risks. For shares that are infrequently traded, such as shares in smaller companies, the risks are greater. This is because positions are held for longer between trades. If shares are held for a long time, the risk of losses from price falls is greater. As a result the bid-offer spreads for such shares tend to be relatively high.

Another form of risk arises from the possibility that some investors may possess information that the dealer does not. Such investors are able to make profits at the expense of the dealer. For example if an investor has information that suggests a share price fall, that investor could sell the shares to the dealer at a price that turns out to be high. It is the dealer who suffers the loss from a fall in the share price. The bid-offer spread can be viewed as providing the dealer with compensation for bearing the risk that such information-based trading may occur.

Markets in which the Trading Systems Operate

Order-driven systems are the most common. They predominate in Europe and the Far East. In the United States there is considerable use of quote-driven systems. NASDAQ, which has become the main market in North America for high technology stocks, is quote-driven. Market-makers display their quotes on computer screens. Investors (or brokers on their behalf) will buy or sell at the quoted prices by means of computer or telephone links.

Hybrid systems combine order-driven and quote-driven systems. The New York Stock Exchange (NYSE) is probably the best known example of a hybrid system. On the NYSE there are firms acting as 'specialists'. Each stock is allocated to a specialist. Specialists will operate by matching orders when there is a sufficient volume of trading. When trading volumes are low, such that matching buy and sell orders is not possible, specialists will act as market-makers (providing a quote-driven system). In other words, to the extent to which specialists are unable to match buy and sell orders they will trade on their own account. They buy from unmatched sellers, and sell to unmatched buyers. In this way they maintain the liquidity of the market.

It is to be noted that trades do not have to go through a specialist. There will be a 'crowd' of traders and brokers around each specialist. Members of this crowd are able to trade with each other. This is possibly an additional source of both order-driven and quote-driven trading.

On the New York Stock Exchange, specialists have the additional function of ensuring orderly markets. This function requires them to ensure that price changes between one deal and the next are small. To achieve this they must sell in rising markets and buy in falling markets. Whilst most of the time the specialists succeed in moderating price movements, the system broke down during the stock market crash of October 1987. At the height of the crash, many specialists stopped trading. They lacked the resources to cope with the huge volumes of sell orders with which they were presented.

The London Stock Exchange also uses a hybrid system. The major stocks (including the constituents of the FTSE 100 Index) are traded by order-driven matching. Smaller stocks are traded on a quote-driven (market-maker) basis. Up to 1996 all stocks were traded by means of a quote-driven system. The change to a hybrid system reflected the belief that for major stocks order-driven systems generate lower bid-offer spreads, whilst for smaller stocks market-makers are required in order to ensure liquid markets. There is also a market-maker system for small deals in the major stocks, but the prices have to reflect the prices in the order-driven market.

Most other exchanges in the world are purely order-driven. However market-makers are often very important to order-driven as well as to quote-driven systems. In particular the limit orders in order-driven systems often come from market-makers. Market-makers may be especially important in continuous-matching order-driven systems. They provide trades when other potential counter-parties are absent. In these ways market-makers provide liquidity to order-driven systems.

In the UK trading in gilts (government bonds) is quote-driven. Gilt-Edged Market-Makers (GEMMs) provide continuous two-way prices (bid-offer). They are obliged to trade at their quoted prices if approached by investors or their brokers. To facilitate this role they are able to borrow gilts from institutional investors via money-brokers. They are also able to borrow money through money-brokers. These borrowing facilities are essential for the maintenance of the ability to meet their obligations to buy and sell at their quoted prices.

TYPES OF ORDER

An investor who wants to buy shares on a stock exchange has a number of different types of order available. The simplest, and most common, is the market order. A market order stipulates that the shares should be traded at the most favourable price available. The most favourable price would be the lowest available price for a purchase, and the highest available price for a sale. The trade takes place at a price that is currently available in the market.

Other types of order specify particular prices. A buy limit order specifies that the purchase should take place only if the price is at, or below, a specified level. A sell limit order specifies a minimum selling price such that the trade should not take place unless that price, or more, can be obtained.

A market-if-touched order becomes a market order if the share price reaches a particular level. This differs from a limit order in that there is no upper limit to the buying price, or lower limit to the selling price. As soon as there has been a trade in the market at the specified price, the order becomes a market order. The specified price is not necessarily obtained.

A stop order is also an order that becomes a market order once there has been a trade in the market at a particular price. However it involves selling after the price has fallen to a specified level, or buying after the price has risen to a level. Stop orders are concerned with protecting profits, or limiting losses. They seek to ensure that a selling price is not too low, or that a buying price is not too high.

Another dimension to an order is the length of time for which it remains in force. A fill-or-kill order is to be cancelled if it cannot be executed immediately. An open order, otherwise known as a good-till-cancelled order, remains in force until it is specifically cancelled by the investor. Alternatively the investor can specify the period of time for which the order should remain open, e.g. a day, a week, or a month.

SELLING SHARES IN THE PRIMARY MARKET

The sale of shares in the primary market entails the sale of newly created shares. These may be the first issue of shares by a newly floated company. The other source of new shares is the issue of additional shares where an initial issue has already taken place.

The issue of shares by a company that has not previously sold shares could be through a number of routes. Three popular means of issue are public offers, tenders, and placements. Public offers invite investors, including private investors, to subscribe for shares. Often there would be application forms in newspapers. The share price would be set by the issuing company. Investors would choose the number of shares for which they apply. If the aggregate number applied for exceeds the number being issued, individual investors may receive fewer shares than the number for which they applied.

Tenders invite investors to quote prices. Those quoting the highest prices receive the shares for which they apply. Placements involve the investment bank, which is handling the share issue, selling the shares to institutional investors. Placements do not involve general invitations to apply for shares. Selected institutions are approached directly.

Introductions take place when there are already a number of shareholders, and the company is simply seeking permission for the shares to trade on the stock exchange. Introductions do not entail raising capital. They may be part of the process of moving from AIM (Alternative Investment Market) to the main market, or may allow a foreign company to have its shares traded in London as well as in its home country.

The issue of additional shares, when shares in the company are already in the market, is normally by means of rights issues. In many countries, any addition to the total number of shares must be offered first to existing shareholders. The offer would be in proportion to the number of shares already held. For example a one for two rights issue entails one new share being offered for every two already held.

To encourage the take up of the offer, the new shares are usually offered at a lower price than the existing shares. One effect of this discount is that the share price subsequent to the rights issue is lower than the share price before it. For example if the shares are initially 100p and there is a one for two rights issue at 70p, the share price might be expected to fall to 90p [(100p + 100p + 70p)/3 = 90p]. As an alternative to buying additional shares, investors can sell their rights to new shares. In the current example, the buyer of such rights obtains the ability to pay 70p for shares that are expected to be worth 90p.

Share issues are often underwritten by banks. A bank underwriting a share issue agrees, for a fee, to buy any shares not taken up by investors. This guarantees that the issuing company receives the money that it expects. In the case of rights issues, firms sometimes avoid paying a fee to underwriters by using the deep discount route. In a rights issue, failure to sell the new shares would result from the share price (prior to the issue) falling below the sale price of the new shares. The deep discount method prices the new shares at such a low level that the market price is extremely unlikely to fall so far.

EXHIBIT 6.1

RIGHTS ISSUES

A one for four rights issue entails one new share for every four held. A one for four rights issue may be at 160p when the current share price is 200p.

Table 6.A

4	shares	@	200p	=	800p
1	rights	@	160p	=	160p
5	shares cost				960p (192p each)

It is to be expected that the rights issue would cause the share price to fall by 200p − 192p = 8p.

Instead of exercising the right to buy at 160p, the investor could sell the right. The price receivable could be around 192p – 160p = 32p, since the buyer has the right to buy shares for 160p when they are prospectively worth 192p.

DEEP DISCOUNT

A one for one rights issue may be used.

Table 6.B

1	share	@	200p	=	200p
1	rights	@	40p	=	40p
2	shares cost				240p (120p each)

Instead of exercising the right to buy at the discounted price an investor could sell the rights. In the one for one case, the rights might be sold for 80p (120p−40p).

It might be noted that the one for four rights issue at 160p raises the same amount of money as the one for one rights issue at 40p (the latter involves selling four times the number of shares at a quarter of the price).

TYPES OF SHARE

The most common type of share is known as the ordinary share (alternatively referred to as common stock). Ordinary shares represent part ownership of the issuing company. They pay dividends at regular intervals (typically every six months). The sizes of the dividends are at the discretion of the issuing company, and are likely to be related to the level of profit made by the company. There is no legal obligation for the company to pay dividends. In the case of bankruptcy, holders of ordinary shares are the last to receive any proceeds from the winding up of the company, and typically will receive nothing. However the holders of ordinary shares are not liable for any outstanding debts of the company.

Shareholders (the holders of ordinary shares) are residual claimants on a company's profits and assets. Creditors have to be paid before shareholders. In bad times there may be no profits left for the shareholders after the creditors have been paid. In good times the creditors (who include bondholders) get the same amount as usual; the additional profits and asset values belong to the shareholders. Ordinary shares are therefore risky, but have the potential to be very profitable.

Another type of share is the preference (or preferred) share. In some ways preference shares are more similar to bonds than to ordinary shares. In particular, most pay a fixed dividend each year and typically do not confer voting rights on the holder. Unlike bonds, preference shares constitute part ownership of the issuing company and the company does not have a legal obligation to pay the dividends. The absence of the legal obligation to pay dividends is related to the fact that preference shares are seen as part of the equity of the company rather than the debt of the company (bonds are debts). However no dividends can be paid to the holders of ordinary shares if preference shareholders have not received their full dividend payments. In the event of bankruptcy the holders of preference shares have a prior right, relative to the holders of ordinary shares, to the receipt of remaining assets. However bondholders, and other creditors, have a prior right to the holders of preference shares.

There are many varieties of preference share. These varieties include:

- cumulative preference shares
- non-cumulative preference shares
- redeemable preference shares
- convertible preference shares
- participating preference shares
- stepped preference shares.

With the exception of the first two, these characteristics are not mutually exclusive. For example it is possible to issue non-cumulative, redeemable, convertible preference shares.

Cumulative preference shares entail the obligation on the part of the issuing company to pay any missed past dividends before any dividends are paid to the holders of ordinary shares. Non-cumulative preference shares entail no such obligation with the effect that missed dividends may be lost forever. A redeemable preference share has a maturity date on which the original sum invested is repaid, whereas most preference shares have no maturity date (the issuer may pay the dividends forever and never repay the principal sum). Some redeemable preference shares provide the issuer with the right to redeem at a predetermined price without the obligation to do so; in effect such preference shares provide the issuer with a call option, which would be paid for by means of a higher dividend for the investors. Convertible preference shares give the holder the right to convert preference shares into ordinary shares at a predetermined rate; the investor pays nothing to convert apart from surrendering the convertible preference shares. In some cases the right to convert arises only in the event of a failure to pay dividends. Participating preference shares allow the issuing company to increase the dividends if profits are particularly high; the preference share dividend can exceed the fixed level if the dividend on ordinary shares is greater than a specified amount. Stepped preference shares pay a dividend that increases in a predetermined way.

CONCLUSION

Stock exchanges exist to facilitate the transfer of funds from savers to organisations, which need to raise money. They also provide a means whereby existing investors can sell their investments. Stock exchanges may be order-driven, quote-driven, or a hybrid of these two systems. In all stock market trading systems, the forces of demand and supply determine share prices. In addition to market orders, which accept the ruling share price, it is possible to place limit orders which specify upper limits to buying prices or lower limits to selling prices. Newly issued shares are said to be sold in the primary market; they can be sold by public offer, tender, placement, or through a rights issue. In addition to ordinary shares there are various types of preference share.

Most individual investors buy shares indirectly through institutional investors such as insurance companies, pension funds, and unit trusts. As a result much of the trading on stock exchanges involves institutional investors. Some types of institutional investment, namely investment trusts and exchange-traded funds, are bought and sold on a stock exchange rather than being transacted with institutional investors (see Chapter 9 on mutual funds).

Stock markets operate most efficiently if they exhibit depth and breadth. A market that is deep has a large number of traders such that small price movements bring forward many new buy or sell orders. This helps to avoid excessive share price swings since price falls are met by new purchase orders, and price rises are met by new sales. As a result price falls and rises are moderated. A broad market contains traders with differing opinions such that some will be forecasting price rises whilst others expect falls. Such heterogeneity of views also helps to prevent large price swings. However, as will be seen in Chapter 27 on stock market bubbles and crashes, the heterogeneity of views can be replaced by homogeneity. When stock markets are characterised by uniformity of opinion, extreme share price movements can result. If the overwhelming majority of investors expect a rise, there would be many buyers and few sellers. Sharp price rises (a bubble) would result. If the majority expects a price fall, sales would dominate purchases and share prices could fall dramatically (and hence a stock market crash could occur).

Chapter 7

Stock indices

OBJECTIVE

The objective of this chapter is to provide knowledge of:

1. How stock indices differ in respect to the method of calculation.
2. Unweighted, price-weighted, and value-weighted approaches to the calculation of stock indices.
3. The use of arithmetic and geometric means in the calculation of stock indices.
4. The adjustment for changes in the constituent stocks of an index.
5. How to evaluate alternative stock indices.

TYPES OF INDEX

Stock indices are measures of the price performance of stock portfolios, which may be seen as representative of a stock market as a whole or of a segment of the market. The better known indices include the Dow Jones Industrial Average, the Standard & Poor's 500, and the NASDAQ in the United States; the FTSE 100 in the United Kingdom; the Nikkei 225 in Japan; the DAX in Germany; the CAC 40 in France; and the Hang Seng in Hong Kong. All countries with stock markets have at least one index, and some countries (in particular the United States) have numerous indices.

Indices are not only calculated for national stock markets, there are also regional and global market indices. For example FTSE, MSCI, S&P, and Dow Jones all produce stock indices for both the world as a whole, and Europe as a whole. There are often sub-indices, for example European indices exclusive of the UK.

Indices are also calculated for bonds. There are indices of bond yields as well as indices of bond prices. Each bond index relates to a particular type of issuer (e.g. government, AAA-rated corporate, etc.) and to a specific maturity band.

This chapter is primarily concerned with the mechanics of the calculation of indices. This is of importance since it determines the comparability of the movements of different indices, and the interpretation that can be put upon a change in a particular index. Indices can be categorised in a number of ways: (1) the number of stocks included; (2) the method of weighting the stock prices; and (3) the nature of the averaging.

The number of stocks can vary from a small number of large company stocks (for example the Dow Jones Industrial Average is based on just 30 stocks) to inclusion of every stock traded on a particular market (for example the New York Stock Exchange Composite Index). The indices based on a small number of stocks have the advantage of easy calculation, but the disadvantage of being imperfectly representative of the market as a whole.

Index Weighting

The contribution of individual stock prices to an index may be unweighted (as in the case of the Financial Times Ordinary Share Index), value weighted (for example the Financial Times Stock Exchange (FTSE) 100), or price weighted (such as the Dow Jones Industrial Average).

In the case of unweighted indices an average of daily rates of share price change is calculated each day; this is an average of stocks on one day. The product of such changes (that is multiplying them together, for example an average 10% rise one day followed by an average 20% rise the next gives a rise of 32% over the two days: $1.1 \times 1.2 = 1.32$) since a base date provides the index. The calculation involves two stages: one is averaging stock price changes on a single day; the other involves compounding the daily averages over time. The calculation gives all stocks equal influence irrespective of the sizes of the companies.

To illustrate the calculation of an unweighted index, suppose that it is to be based on just three stocks whose prices and numbers of shares issued are as shown in Table 7.1. The changes relate to just one day (so no compounding over time is involved). It is further supposed (a) that stock A rises in price by 15% during the day while the other two prices remain unchanged, and (b) that stock C undergoes a 15% price rise while the other two prices remain constant during the day. Before the price rise, the index equals 100.

In the event of a 15% rise in the price of A, the new index will be (using arithmetic means):

$$\frac{\text{New value}}{\text{Old value}} \times 100 = \frac{(1.15 + 1 + 1)}{(1 + 1 + 1)} \times 100 = 1.05 \times 100 = 105$$

If the price of C rises by 15%, the new index will be:

$$\frac{\text{New value}}{\text{Old value}} \times 100 = \frac{(1 + 1 + 1.15)}{(1 + 1 + 1)} \times 100 = 1.05 \times 100 = 105$$

Table 7.1

Stock	Price	Number of shares
A	50p	10 million
B	100p	10 million
C	200p	5 million

It can be seen that a 15% rise in either stock price has the same effect on the index despite the fact that C has a higher stock price and is issued by a larger company.

Price-weighted indices weight percentage price increases by the initial stock prices. The index at time T can be calculated as follows:

$$\frac{\text{Sum of stock prices at time T}}{\text{Sum of stock prices on the base date}} \times \text{Base value (Initial index)}$$

The calculations, using the data in Table 7.1 and 15% price rises for stocks A and C respectively but based on a price-weighted approach, produce the following indices:

(a) $\dfrac{\text{New value}}{\text{Old value}} \times 100 = \dfrac{(57.5\text{p} + 100\text{p} + 200\text{p})}{(50\text{p} + 100\text{p} + 200\text{p})} \times 100 = 1.0215 \times 100 = 102.15$

(b) $\dfrac{\text{New value}}{\text{Old value}} \times 100 = \dfrac{(50\text{p} + 100\text{p} + 230\text{p})}{(50\text{p} + 100\text{p} + 200\text{p})} \times 100 = 1.086 \times 100 = 108.6$

It can be seen that the impact on the index is four times as great when the price rise is in stock C rather than stock A. This reflects the fact that stock price C is initially four times stock price A. So stocks with high prices have the greatest influence on the index.

Using the same example but calculating a value-weighted index (weighting percentage increases by the market capitalisations of the companies: market capitalisation being stock price times number of shares issued) may be based on the formula:

$$\text{Index at time T} = \frac{\text{Sum of the market capitalisations at time T}}{\text{Sum of the market capitalisations on the base date}} \times \text{Base value (Initial index)}$$

Using the figures from the previous example, a 15% increase in the price of stock A raises the index from 100 to:

$$\frac{\text{New value}}{\text{Old value}} \times 100 = \frac{(\pounds5.75\text{m} + \pounds10\text{m} + \pounds10\text{m})}{(\pounds5\text{m} + \pounds10\text{m} + \pounds10\text{m})} \times 100 = 1.03 \times 100 = 103$$

whereas a 15% increase in the price of stock C raises the index to:

$$\frac{\text{New value}}{\text{Old value}} \times 100 = \frac{(\pounds5\text{m} + \pounds10\text{m} + \pounds11.5\text{m})}{(\pounds5\text{m} + \pounds10\text{m} + \pounds10\text{m})} \times 100 = 1.06 \times 100 = 106$$

The impact of the rise in stock price C is double that of the rise in stock price A. This reflects the fact that the initial market capitalisation of C (200p × 5 million) is twice that of A (50p × 10 million). When indices are value weighted, large companies have the greatest influence. Some indices, rather than using the full market capitalisation, use the value of shares available to investors in the free float. This alternative excludes shares held by the issuer and not available for purchase by investors (such shares are said to be 'closely held').

All the calculations thus far have used arithmetic means. It is interesting to repeat the calculations using geometric means. The computations and resulting indices are as follows:

Unweighted

(a) $\dfrac{\text{New value}}{\text{Old value}} \times 100 = \dfrac{\sqrt[3]{(1.15 \times 1 \times 1)}}{\sqrt[3]{(1 \times 1 \times 1)}} \times 100 = \sqrt[3]{1.15} \times 100 = 104.8$

(b) $\dfrac{\text{New value}}{\text{Old value}} \times 100 = \dfrac{\sqrt[3]{(1 \times 1 \times 1.15)}}{\sqrt[3]{(1 \times 1 \times 1)}} \times 100 = \sqrt[3]{1.15} \times 100 = 104.8$

Price weighted

(a) $\dfrac{\text{New value}}{\text{Old value}} \times 100 = \dfrac{\sqrt[3]{(57.5 \times 100 \times 200)}}{\sqrt[3]{(50 \times 100 \times 200)}} \times 100 = 104.8$

(b) $\dfrac{\text{New value}}{\text{Old value}} \times 100 = \dfrac{\sqrt[3]{(50 \times 100 \times 230)}}{\sqrt[3]{(50 \times 100 \times 200)}} \times 100 = 104.8$

Value weighted

(a) $\dfrac{\text{New value}}{\text{Old value}} \times 100 = \dfrac{\sqrt[3]{(5.75 \times 10 \times 10)}}{\sqrt[3]{(5 \times 10 \times 10)}} \times 100 = 104.8$

(b) $\dfrac{\text{New value}}{\text{Old value}} \times 100 = \dfrac{\sqrt[3]{(5 \times 10 \times 11.5)}}{\sqrt[3]{(5 \times 10 \times 10)}} \times 100 = 104.8$

The unweighted, price-weighted and value-weighted computations produce identical results. The results are the same irrespective of whether the 15% increase is in the price of stock A or in the price of stock B.

EXERCISE 7.1

A stock index portfolio consists of stocks A, B, and C.

Assess the effects of a 10% increase in the price of share A on stock indices that are: (a) unweighted, (b) price weighted, and (c) value weighted.

Consider the effects for stock indices that are based on arithmetic means, and for indices based on geometric means.

Table 7.A

Stock	Price	Number of shares issued
A	100p	10 million
B	400p	5 million
C	500p	1 million

Answers

Suppose that the indices initially stand at 100.

Arithmetic

(a) Unweighted

$$\frac{1.1 + 1 + 1}{1 + 1 + 1} = \frac{3.1}{3} = 1.033$$

$$1.033 \times 100 = 103.3$$

(b) Price weighted

$$\frac{110 + 400 + 500}{100 + 400 + 500} = \frac{1010}{1000} = 1.01$$

$$1.01 \times 100 = 101$$

(c) Value weighted

$$\frac{11 + 20 + 5}{10 + 20 + 5} = \frac{36}{35} = 1.029$$

$$1.029 \times 100 = 102.9$$

Geometric

$$\frac{\sqrt[3]{(1.1 \times 1 \times 1)}}{\sqrt[3]{(1 \times 1 \times 1)}} = 1.032$$

$$1.032 \times 100 = 103.2$$

EXERCISE 7.2

Two stock indices, one value weighted and one price weighted, are based on the same three stocks: A, B, and C. The numbers of shares in issue and the initial share prices are as follows:

Table 7.B

Stock	Number of shares	Share price
A	1,000,000	500p
B	5,000,000	200p
C	25,000,000	20p

The indices have an initial value of 1,000 (for both the value-weighted and price-weighted versions).

(a) What will be the values of the new indices following a 10% increase in the price of A which occurs at the same time as a 10% fall in the price of C?

(b) What would the new indices be if half of the shares in A are closely held and the indices are calculated on a free-float basis (again suppose that the indices are both initially 1,000)? (Base the calculations on arithmetic averages.)

Answers

(a) Initial value weighted:

$$\frac{(1,000,000 \times 500) + (5,000,000 \times 200) + (25,000,000 \times 20)}{(1,000,000 \times 500) + (5,000,000 \times 200) + (25,000,000 \times 20)} \times 1,000 = 1,000$$

Value weighted following price changes:

$$\frac{(1,000,000 \times 550) + (5,000,000 \times 200) + (25,000,000 \times 18)}{(1,000,000 \times 500) + (5,000,000 \times 200) + (25,000,000 \times 20)} \times 1,000$$

$$= \frac{2,000}{2,000} \times 1,000 = 1,000$$

Initial price weighted:

$$\frac{500 + 200 + 20}{500 + 200 + 20} \times 1,000 = 1,000$$

Price weighted following price changes:

$$\frac{550 + 200 + 18}{500 + 200 + 20} \times 1,000 = \frac{768}{720} \times 1,000 = 1,067 \text{ (to nearest whole number)}$$

(b) Initial value weighted:

$$\frac{(500,000 \times 500) + (5,000,000 \times 200) + (25,000,000 \times 20)}{(500,000 \times 500) + (5,000,000 \times 200) + (25,000,000 \times 20)} \times 1,000 = 1,000$$

Value-weighted following price changes:

$$\frac{(500,000 \times 550) + (5,000,000 \times 200) + (25,000,000 \times 18)}{(500,000 \times 500) + (5,000,000 \times 200) + (25,000,000 \times 20)} \times 1,000$$

$$= \frac{1,725}{1,750} \times 1,000 = 986 \text{ (to nearest whole number)}.$$

The price-weighted indices are the same as in part (a).

So the results are:

Value weighted = no change
Value weighted (free-float) = decrease
Price weighted = increase

ADJUSTING FOR CHANGES IN THE CONSTITUENT STOCKS OF AN INDEX

In most cases the constituent stocks in an index are changed as some firms grow and others experience relative decline. For example every three months some companies are removed from the FTSE 100 Index and replaced by others in order to ensure that the index remains close to covering the largest 100 firms by market capitalisation. Such changes in the composition of the index portfolio should not affect the value of the index, since they do not result from overall market movements. This requires adjustments to the formula used for calculating the index.

Suppose that a value-weighted index stands at 1120 and is based on the three stocks in Table 7.2.

Table 7.2

Stock	Market capitalisation
Shoddigoods plc	£100 million
Nore Turn Airlines plc	£50 million
Cowboy Construction plc	£40 million

When the periodic review date is reached, it is found that the constituents of the index portfolio are no longer the three largest companies. The index is still at 1120 and the market capitalisations are still as shown in Table 7.2. However the market capitalisation of a fourth company, Gonoff Foods plc, has grown to £45 million. As a result Gonoff Foods replace Cowboy Construction in the calculation of the index (so that the index continues to be based on the three largest firms).

The index had been calculated as:

$$\frac{\text{Sum of Market Capitalisations on the Current Date}}{\text{Sum of Market Capitalisations on the Base Date}} \times 1000$$

i.e. $$\frac{\text{£100m} + \text{£50m} + \text{£40m}}{\text{Sum of Market Capitalisations on the Base Date}} \times 1000 = 1120$$

Consequent upon the change in the constituent stocks, an adjustment needs to be made to the formula to ensure that the change in the composition of the index portfolio does not change the index. A change in the stocks used to calculate the index should not, in itself, cause a change in the index. The adjustment factor is shown as AF in the following equation.

$$\frac{\text{£100m} + \text{£50m} + \text{£45m}}{\text{Sum of Market Capitalisations on the Base Date}} \times 1000 \times AF = 1120$$

AF will take the value of $(100 + 50 + 40) / (100 + 50 + 45) = 190/195 = 0.974$.

EXERCISE 7.3

A value-weighted index is based on three stocks; A, B, and C. The current value of the index is 1000. The share prices and numbers of shares are:

Table 7.C

Share	Share price	Number of shares
A	100p	1,000,000
B	200p	1,000,000
C	40p	2,000,000

(a) If stock C were to be replaced by stock D, which is priced at 20p with 5,000,000 shares issued, calculate the adjustment factor required to ensure that the replacement does not affect the index.

(b) Subsequent to the replacement, the price of stock D rises to 25p. What will the new index be?

Answers

(a) The total market capitalisation before the replacement is:

($£1 \times 1,000,000$) + ($£2 \times 1,000,000$) + ($£0.4 \times 2,000,000$) = $£1,000,000$ + $£2,000,000$ + $£800,000$ = $£3,800,000$

The total market capitalisation after the replacement is:

($£1 \times 1,000,000$) + ($£2 \times 1,000,000$) + ($£0.2 \times 5,000,000$) = $£1,000,000$ + $£2,000,000$ + $£1,000,000$ = $£4,000,000$

The adjustment factor required is:

$£3,800,000/£4,000,000 = 0.95$

Use of this adjustment factor produces an index of:

$$\frac{£4,000,000}{£3,800,000} \times 1000 \times 0.95 = 1000$$

(b) If the price of stock D rises to 25p, the new market capitalisation will be:

($£1 \times 1,000,000$) + ($£2 \times 1,000,000$) + ($£0.25 \times 5,000,000$) = $£1,000,000$ + $£2,000,000$ + $£1,250,000$ = $£4,250,000$

So the new index should be:

$$\frac{£4,250,000}{£3,800,000} \times 1000 \times 0.95 = 1062.5$$

Alternatively:

$$\frac{£4,250,000}{£4,000,000} \times 1000 = 1062.5$$

EVALUATING ALTERNATIVE STOCK INDICES

When evaluating a stock index, it is necessary to consider it in relation to the functions that it is expected to perform. If an index fulfils its intended purposes then it will be evaluated positively.

Indices have a number of uses. First, they are used to measure and monitor market movements. Second, they should provide a means of ascertaining changes in aggregate wealth over time. Third, they have a role as barometers of the wider economy; in particular stock market movements tend to be leading indicators which means that they provide indications of likely future changes in the level of activity in the economy as a whole. Fourth, they provide a means of evaluating the performance of fund managers by providing benchmarks against which portfolio managers can be compared. Fifth, they provide the basis for derivative instruments such as futures and options. Sixth, they provide the framework for the creation of tracker funds whose aim is to reflect closely the performance of a stock market. Seventh, they are required by capital market models, in particular the capital asset pricing model, for a number of purposes: ascertaining discount rates for capital projects, estimating required rates of return on shares, and deriving fair rates of return for utilities.

Unweighted, price-weighted, and geometrically averaged indices are much less satisfactory than indices that are value weighted and arithmetically averaged. For the purpose of measuring stock market values, it is necessary to have an index that accurately reflects the total market capitalisation of the market. An arithmetically averaged value-weighted index does accurately measure the aggregate value of the stocks covered by the index, whereas other indices do not. A reliable measure of the total value of the market is also required for ascertaining changes in aggregate wealth over time and as a basis for derivative instruments. Arithmetically averaged value-weighted stock indices are the only indices that are macroconsistent, which means that it is possible for all investors to hold the index portfolio simultaneously (Enderle *et al.* 2003). An index portfolio is a portfolio of shares that matches a stock index in terms of the constituent shares and their relative proportions.

An index will also perform its functions more effectively if it covers a large number of stocks. Indices that provide a very broad coverage, and hence reliably reflect the whole market, include the Wilshire 5000 in the United States (which covers about 7,000 stocks) and the FTSE All-Share Index in the UK (which covers about 750 stocks). Such stock indices are referred to as broad-capitalisation indices. Enderle *et al.* (2003) suggested a number of factors that characterise a good broad-capitalisation index. One desirable characteristic is completeness, which is a measure of the comprehensiveness of the coverage of relevant stocks. Another desirable feature is investability; it should be possible for fund managers to buy all the shares in the index. Investability is particularly important for the managers of index tracker funds, but may require some sacrifice of completeness in order to eliminate illiquid stocks. Indices should also have investor acceptance. It is ironic that the world's most closely followed index, the Dow Jones Industrial Average, covers only 30 stocks and is price weighted. So the index which possibly exhibits the highest investor acceptance is characterised by very low completeness.

Although the FTSE All-Share Index is probably the most informative general stock index in the UK, since it is value weighted and based on a broad coverage of shares, it is not the most widely quoted. The most frequently quoted index in the UK is the FTSE 100. Whilst benefiting from being value weighted, the FTSE 100 is based on only 100 stocks. Roughly speaking, these are the shares of the largest 100 UK companies (although the stocks covered will tend to differ slightly from the top 100 due to technicalities of index construction). Since the performance of smaller-company shares can differ substantially from that of larger-company shares, the focus of the FTSE 100 on larger companies means that it does not fully reflect the behaviour of the stock market as a whole. The FTSE 100 is also dominated by a small number of sectors: oil, telecommunications, pharmaceuticals, and financial sector companies. This bias towards a few sectors reduces the ability of the FTSE 100 to reflect the whole market.

Other UK indices, which are also value weighted, are the:

FTSE 250 – the 250 companies below the FTSE 100 ranked by market capitalisation
FTSE 350 – the constituents of the FTSE 100 plus those of the FTSE 250
FTSE SmallCap – the FTSE All-Share stocks, excluding those in the FTSE 350.

At the time of writing the FTSE 100 companies represented about 80% of the total market capitalisation of the UK stock market, the FTSE 250 about 16%, and the FTSE SmallCap about 2%. The FTSE 100, FTSE 250, and FTSE SmallCap added together comprise the FTSE All-Share Index. The FTSE All-Share Index covers about 98% of the market capitalisation of UK stocks. The other 2% accounts for more than 1,000 very small companies whose shares are not eligible for inclusion in the FTSE All-Share Index. These percentages indicate the dominance of large companies. That dominance is further emphasised by the fact that the top ten companies accounted for nearly half of the FTSE 100 by market capitalisation, and hence nearly 40% of the total UK stock market.

EXHIBIT 7.1   AN EXAMPLE OF AN INVESTMENT FUND THAT AIMS TO TRACK THE FTSE 100 INDEX

HSBC FTSE 100 INDEX FUND (31 AUGUST 2007)

Profile

The fund aims to match the performance of the FTSE 100 Index. Investments are made in each stock held within the index, a technique known as full replication.

Fund size: £414,240,000

> ### Table 7.D
>
> *Ten largest holdings (as percentages of the total fund)*
>
> | | |
> |---|---|
> | Royal Dutch Shell Plc | 8.21 |
> | BP Plc | 7.07 |
> | HSBC Holdings Plc | 6.92 |
> | Vodafone Group Plc | 5.55 |
> | GlaxoSmithkline Plc | 4.85 |
> | Royal bank of Scotland Group Plc | 3.60 |
> | Barclays Plc | 2.64 |
> | Anglo American Plc | 2.54 |
> | AstraZeneca Group Plc | 2.42 |
> | Rio Tinto Plc | 2.26 |

The top ten holdings amounted to 46.06% of the total fund, which implies that the largest ten companies accounted for 46.06% of the FTSE 100 Index on 31 August 2007.

Source: HSBC Investments (UK) Limited.

Unfortunately most stock indices consider only stock price changes and fail to incorporate dividends. An index that incorporates dividends would be most appropriate if the aim is to have a benchmark against which to evaluate fund managers, a structure that tracker funds can try to replicate, and a measure of market return that can be used in models such as the capital asset pricing model. Clarke and Statman (2000) pointed out that the Dow Jones Industrial Average, which was initiated on 26 May 1896 at a value of 40.94, had reached 9,181.43 by 31 December 1998. They estimated that, with dividends included, it would have grown to 652,230.87. The inclusion of dividends increases the final outcome by more than 71 times. Taking account of inflation the figures would become 442.87 and 31,460.30. It is rare for a stock index to include an adjustment to take account of inflation.

In recent years there has been a change in the way that value-weighted indices are constructed. The move has been towards a free-float basis and away from a total-capitalisation basis. Free float includes only those shares that are seen as available for purchase, rather than all shares. The free-float basis excludes shares held by governments, founding families, and non-financial companies. The stock-index weighting is thus based on the total value of a company's shares available for purchase, and not on the full market capitalisation of the company. One reason for this change has been the growth of funds that seek to track stock indices. Such a fund may aim to buy shares in proportion to their weights in an index. If the weights are based on total capitalisation but only a

141

small proportion of the shares are available in the market, the purchases by index-tracking funds could distort the market by causing unjustified increases in the prices of such stocks.

Not only are there stock indices for individual countries, but also there are indices for the world as a whole and for regions of the world (e.g. Europe). There are alternative views as to the most appropriate weighting for multi-country stock indices. One approach is to weight each country by its contribution to global market capitalisation. However the ratio of stock market capitalisation to national income (GDP) varies considerably between countries. If the wish is that the weighting of an index should reflect the total asset base of a country, using national income (GDP) rather than market capitalisation might provide a better means of weighting. This approach would provide a more stable weighting since relative GDP is less volatile than relative market capitalisation.

Emerging market indices raise particular issues. Markets are classified as emerging markets either as a result of the country having a low national income per head, or because of a low stock market capitalisation relative to national income. Emerging market countries often have heavy restrictions on foreign ownership of shares. The market capitalisation available for foreign investors can be much less than that available for domestic investors. The restrictions on foreign ownership can arise from either national governments or from the companies themselves. Two types of emerging-market stock index are available. There are indices based on total market capitalisation and indices based on the shares available for foreign investors. The performances of the two different types of index can be dramatically different. Indices are available both for individual emerging markets, and for groups of emerging markets.

Institutional investors, such as unit trusts, use stock indices as benchmarks for performance measurement. Index tracker funds aim to replicate the performance of an index. European Union legislation prevents unit trusts (and OEICs) holding more than 10% of their portfolio in a single stock. Vodafone's takeover of Mannesmann in 2000 raised its market capitalisation to more than 10% of the FTSE 100. To enable institutional investors to benchmark against a relevant index, FTSE International (a major indexing organisation) has introduced capped versions of its FTSE 100 and All-Share indices. These capped indices limit the maximum weighting of a stock in the index to 10%.

One criticism of the use, by institutional investors, of value-weighted stock indices as performance benchmarks is that it encourages closet tracking. The portfolio managers keep their portfolios close to the composition of the stock index in order to avoid the risk of underperforming the index by a substantial amount. In consequence they tend to resemble index tracker funds (without the low cost advantages of index tracker funds). One consequence is that smaller companies tend to be omitted from portfolios because they play little, if any, part in a value-weighted stock index. Also a value-weighted stock index may be dominated by a few large companies or sectors; with the effect that it does not constitute a well-diversified portfolio. A portfolio manager who keeps close to the index would not be holding a well-diversified portfolio; the portfolio would be too dependent on a small number of companies or sectors.

It may be argued that, in order to avoid those consequences, an unweighted index should be used as the performance benchmark. An unweighted index might encourage more consideration of the shares of smaller companies, since the index would give them as much significance as the shares of large companies. An unweighted index would also remove the tendency to become dependent on a small number of large companies or sectors. The effect might be that a portfolio manager who operates as a closet tracker would have a well-diversified portfolio, which includes a significant holding of the shares of smaller companies.

Although most stock indices are based on arithmetic averages, there are some that use geometric averaging. A UK example is the FT Ordinary Share Index (the FT30), which is a geometrically averaged equal-weighted index based on 30 stocks. In the past this was the most quoted UK index, but has been overshadowed by the FTSE 100 and the FTSE All-Share Index since the 1980s. Geometric averaging has particular problems.

The geometric mean overestimates the effects of rises in the prices of smaller company stocks and underestimates the effects of changes in the stock prices of larger companies. Since large corporations are large because of rapid growth in the past, it follows that the use of geometric means gives too little weight to the stock prices of rapidly growing companies and too much weight to the stock prices of slow growth companies. So the use of geometric means underweights stocks whose prices rise rapidly and overweights stocks whose prices increase slowly. In consequence, over time, indices based on geometric means tend to understate the true rate of increase in stock prices. The same argument and conclusion applies to indices based on unweighted arithmetic means.

There is a more general way in which geometric averaging understates rises in a stock market. This arises because geometric averages are lower than arithmetic averages. Consider an index based on three shares which experience price increases of 25%, 50%, and 75%. The arithmetic average increase is 50%. The geometric average is:

$$(1.25 \times 1.5 \times 1.75)^{1/3} - 1 = 0.486 \text{ i.e. } 48.6\%$$

The mathematical properties of geometric averages cause understatement of average price increases. The cumulative effect of such understatement over time can substantially distort the calculated market rise.

CONCLUSION

Stock indices can be unweighted, price weighted, or value weighted. Either arithmetic or geometric means may be used when calculating indices. In the last few decades, new indices have normally been value-weighted indices using arithmetic means. This type of index is generally seen to provide the most accurate representation of movements in the overall stock market.

One popular use of stock indices is the provision of a basis for index tracker funds. These are institutional investments that aim to track the performance of an index rather than outperform the index (see Chapters 9 and 16 on mutual funds and styles of portfolio construction, respectively). Index tracker funds have the advantage of relatively low management costs, and in consequence fund charges can be low. In addition index tracker funds avoid the risk of underperformance by a fund manager (evidence shows that, on average, fund managers underperform stock indices; as detailed in the chapters in Part 7 on market efficiency and Chapter 17 on fund managers' performance evaluation).

Another major use of stock indices is the provision of a value that underlies financial derivatives such as futures, options, and swaps. These derivatives are used for risk management, either to reduce existing risk or to take on risk in the hope of making profits (see the chapters in Part 8 on stock index futures and Part 9 on stock options). Financial derivatives based on stock indices are widely used in fund management for the purpose of managing risk or increasing returns. Some institutional investments, such as stock market related funds that guarantee that the investment cannot fall below a particular value, use derivatives especially options (see Chapter 34 on structured products). Stock index futures are often used in the structuring of futures funds, which frequently are forms of index tracker fund (see Part 8 on stock index futures).

Chapter 8

The rationale and conduct of regulation

OBJECTIVE

The objective of this chapter is to provide knowledge of:

1. The reasons for regulation of investment business and markets.
2. The drawbacks of regulation.
3. Informal self-regulation
4. The system of regulation in the United Kingdom.
5. Quality assurance in investment services.
6. How systems of regulation differ between countries.
7. The role of the European Union in the regulation of investments business.
8. The lessons of the Enron and Worldcom experiences.

Investments can be mis-sold. There can be malpractice and misrepresentation. These could arise from inadequate training of advisers or from conflicts of interest. For example if advisers are paid by commission, they may be inclined to sell the products that pay the highest commission rather than the products most suitable for the needs of their clients. A major source of possible malpractice is asymmetric information; the supplier of an investment product knows much more about it than the consumer does. Full and accurate information could be withheld from the consumer.

The economic rationale for regulation can be described under three headings. The first is the need to correct market imperfections. The second relates to the existence of economies of scale in monitoring the suppliers of financial products. The third involves the establishment and maintenance of consumer confidence in the market by ensuring that the suppliers do not fall below a specified standard.

CORRECTION OF MARKET IMPERFECTIONS

There are numerous potential imperfections in the market for retail financial products. A perfect market requires all participants to have full information. Consumers of financial services typically lack full information. It is difficult to ascertain the quality of financial products at the point of purchase. The technicalities of many products render them difficult to assess by consumers. Many financial products are long term in nature, the realisation that a poor product has been bought does not occur until it is too late. There is a temptation for consumers to take a 'free-rider' approach whereby each consumer assumes that other consumers have investigated the soundness of products and their providers. There may be a temptation for commission-seeking sales personnel to distort the information provided to consumers. Many financial products are not purchased frequently (for example pensions and endowment policies) with the result that consumers do not develop knowledge of products and providers.

One purpose of regulation is thus the imposition of requirements upon providers in relation to the provision of information to consumers. This regulation should encompass not only the provision of adequate and accurate information to consumers, but also the ability of sales personnel to communicate such information. Financial advisers should not only provide high quality information, but should be able to understand the information that they give. It is possible for poor advice to be given as a result of the adviser failing to fully understand the product being offered.

ECONOMIES OF SCALE AND DELEGATED MONITORING

In the absence of regulation and supervision by an agency, consumers would need to investigate and monitor the providers of financial services. This would require time, effort, and money on the part of the consumers. This would entail considerable duplication, as all consumers would be carrying out the same process. There would also be the loss of the economies of scale derived through a specialist regulator acquiring expertise by means of carrying out investigation and monitoring on a frequent basis.

In the absence of such a regulatory agency many consumers would find the investigation and monitoring of firms beyond their level of expertise or resources. Consumers might be tempted to take a free-rider approach wherein each assumes that other consumers are carrying out the investigations and monitoring (with the possible result that no one performs these functions). Each individual consumer is unable to derive the full benefits of their own supervision, since the benefits would accrue to all consumers (many of whom may not contribute to the process of supervision). Meanwhile the costs of investigation and monitoring are likely to be disproportionately high for any individual consumer who chooses to carry out a supervisory function.

Since there are high costs involved in investigating and monitoring the providers of financial services, it is rational for consumers to delegate some of the supervisory role to a regulatory agency. The rationality of this is reinforced by the economies of scale in regulation, and by the desirability of spreading the costs of regulation amongst all those who benefit from it. This rationale is a variation on delegated monitoring theory.

CONFIDENCE IN MINIMUM STANDARDS

The theory relevant to this point is known as Akerlof's Lemons paradigm. If consumers know that there are good and bad products on the market, but do not have enough information to distinguish between them, they may decide not to buy in order to avoid the possibility of finding that they have bought a bad one. In this way the existence of substandard products can reduce the total level of demand in the market. When consumers know that there are low quality products in the market, good products may become tarnished by the generalised reputation of poor products. (The sub-prime mortgage crisis of the summer of 2007 provided an example of Akerlof's Lemons. Some banks and hedge funds had heavy exposure to the weak sub-prime mortgage assets, but nobody knew which had the heavy exposures. Banks became reluctant to lend to any organisation because they did not know whether the borrower was one of those with heavy exposure to the weak assets.)

One role of regulation is to set minimum standards and thereby remove substandard products from the market. Suppliers would also have an interest in regulation, which enhances consumer confidence by eliminating the possibility of low quality products. It is doubtful whether such confidence can be created without formal regulation. There would always be the risk that unscrupulous firms would attempt to exploit the confidence created by reputable firms. The chance that some providers of financial services will fail to abide by an informal (explicit or tacit) agreement about minimum standards would disincline the honest providers from abiding by the agreement. Indeed firms that abide by such an agreement, when other firms do not, may put themselves at a competitive disadvantage – particularly if the maintenance of a good standard entails additional costs, and hence higher prices.

In the UK, the House of Commons Treasury Committee (2004) highlighted sources of low consumer confidence:

> The bear market has exposed a catalogue of problems and scandals that has left a large body of savers feeling disillusioned with the long-term savings industry. These problems include:
>
> - about half of all with-profits policyholders, with savings worth around £160 billion, now find themselves in closed funds offering very limited long-term growth prospects;
> - endowment mortgage policyholders are suffering a collective shortfall of approaching £40 billion;
> - a £3 billion shortfall emerged at Equitable Life;
> - savers with precipice bonds have suffered capital losses estimated at £2.2 billion;
> - the FSA is pressing for £350 million to compensate investors for losses on split capital investment trusts.

HAZARDS OF REGULATION

Regulation has a number of potential hazards. Regulators may be subject to institutional capture, which means that those being regulated gain control of the regulatory process. Regulation involves costs, which are likely (at least in part) to be borne by the consumers that the regulation aims to protect. Regulation can reduce competition between firms supplying financial services. Regulators may pursue their own agenda with objectives other than the protection of consumers. Moral hazard can emerge, which means that consumers cease to take care in the mistaken belief that the regulator eliminates all risks.

Related to the point about institutional capture is the issue of whether self-regulation or statutory regulation is the most appropriate structure. More accurately the issue concerns the appropriate point on the spectrum between these two extremes. Self-regulation is regulation of the financial services industry by the financial services industry. Self-regulation, with no governmental dimension, is unlikely to command full public confidence. Statutory regulation (regulation by central government) can be bureaucratic and inflexible.

Self-regulation can, in large part, be identified with practitioner input into the regulatory process. Practitioner input has advantages but also poses potential dangers. On the plus side, practitioner input utilises the expertise of the firms being regulated. This helps to avoid the situation in which the regulated firms are able to hide or obscure deficiencies by exploiting the relative ignorance of non-practitioner regulators. Second, practitioners are likely to have a professional interest in ensuring that standards and public confidence are maintained. Third, those being regulated may be more prepared to cooperate if the regulators have experience within the industry. Fourth, practitioners would have an interest in ensuring that the potentially less scrupulous firms do not gain a free-rider advantage (exploiting an enhanced public image of the industry) arising from the responsible behaviour of the more scrupulous suppliers.

On the downside, self-regulation could be more susceptible to regulatory capture. This involves the financial services industry gaining control over the regulatory agency and using it for the industry's purposes. Related to this is the potential for using regulatory requirements as a means of hindering the entry of new firms to the industry. The imposition of such barriers to entry would reduce competition and thereby operate against the interests of consumers. Another drawback is that a regulatory agency without statutory powers may be unable to fully enforce its decisions. This would result in reduced credibility and low public confidence.

Costs of Regulation

A regulatory authority supplies regulatory services to both consumers and providers of financial services. The costs of this regulation are likely to be borne partly by consumers, and partly by the firms supplying financial services. The consumer pays through higher prices and the industry pays to the extent that it does not fully pass on its own costs to consumers. One problem is that there is not a market for regulation. So the beneficiaries of regulation are unable to express their preferences in terms of the amount of regulation and the price they are prepared to pay for it. Regulation and its costs are excessive if the regulator supplies more regulation than the beneficiaries would choose to pay for under a market mechanism. Since it is impossible for the recipients of regulation to express their preferences as to quantity and price through a market mechanism it is impossible to know whether the extent of regulation exceeds, or falls short of, the level that the beneficiaries would demand.

Moral Hazard

Moral hazard leads to people taking too much risk since they believe that they are protected against loss. Consumers may cease to take care in the mistaken belief that the regulator eliminates all risks.

Investors may be unclear about the scope and level of protection that can be expected from a regulatory body. Consumers cannot expect to be protected against all possibility of losing money. It is possible that consumers perceive an implicit contract between themselves and a regulator. An implicit contract can create the impression that the consumer need not take care when buying financial services.

Moral hazard can create a situation in which regulation renders adverse events more likely to occur. For example if regulation guarantees that investments are safe, investors would be tempted to put their money into high risk (and hence high prospective yield) investments knowing that they are protected from the risk of capital loss. In this way protection against loss makes the loss more likely.

Moral hazard may affect not only the consumers of financial products but also the providers and advisers. This was pointed out by the House of Commons Treasury Committee (2004):

> Across the industry there is a danger that companies and trade bodies are abrogating their responsibilities in relying so heavily on the FSA to police and deliver good standards of behaviour. External regulation by a body such as the FSA should not be seen as a substitute for effective self-regulation within the industry via codes which react quickly and flexibly to problems as they arise. All the major trade bodies in the long-term savings industry should have clear codes of practice which take the standards of behaviour laid down by the FSA as a minimum but aim to improve on the FSA's requirements in those areas where the industry feels that better standards will do most to help its customer base.

The sub-prime mortgage crisis of summer 2007 provided possible examples of moral hazard. Mortgage lenders were packaging portfolios of mortgages and selling those packages to banks and other financial institutions. It was suggested that the facility of selling the mortgages caused the mortgage lenders to make excessively risky loans, since the mortgage lenders would not have to bear the consequences of default by borrowers. Another source of moral hazard identified during the crisis arose from the readiness of monetary authorities (particularly the US Federal Reserve and the European Central Bank) to support the financial system during the crisis. It was argued that the support protected the institutions, which had made risky loans, from the full consequences of their actions. Correspondingly it could be seen as encouraging risky lending in the future.

Regulation cannot be expected to be perfect; there is always a risk that unscrupulous operators will slip through the regulatory net. Furthermore there are risks that regulation does not seek to reduce. For example regulators do not seek to protect investors from the risk that the investments underlying the financial products may fall in value. The possibility that stock markets could fall and thereby reduce the value of a pension fund or endowment policy is not a risk that a regulator could try to reduce. Regulators cannot protect consumers against all possibility of loss. A regulatory system cannot be expected to relieve the consumer of responsibility for exercising judgement and care.

INFORMAL SELF-REGULATION

It should not be forgotten that there is always informal, as well as formal, regulation. Abolafia (1996) has argued that to understand the operation of financial markets it is important to understand their social structures especially the social rules which influence and constrain behaviour within them. Markets cannot operate without some restraint on individual opportunism, particularly since there needs to be a degree of trust between market participants. The effective operation of markets requires broadly shared ideas of what constitutes appropriate behaviour, such as shared conventions and social norms.

Abolafia (1996) observes that individual traders conduct themselves within a set of rules (formal and informal) and social arrangements. Trading transactions are carried out within a context of norms of exchange and the wish to maintain personal reputations. Traders who contravene rules or norms may be sanctioned by other traders and could be excluded from trading opportunities.

Baker (1984) studied trading on an options exchange and found that the effectiveness of informal policing of social norms of trading behaviour depended on the size of the market. In larger markets the contravention of norms of behaviour was less easily constrained by informal sanctions. He saw this as an explanation for the observation that the larger markets were more volatile despite their greater depth and breadth. However, particularly in the case of derivatives, it may be that high volatility is the cause of the large size of a market rather than the large size of the market being the cause of the high volatility.

Fenton-O'Creevy et al. (2005) point out that the informal social pressures have their limits. They found, in the City of London, that the tacit norms about the extent to which it is acceptable to exploit the information asymmetry between traders and private individuals varied significantly between firms.

REGULATION OF INVESTMENT BUSINESS IN THE UK

The Financial Services Authority

Regulation of investment business in the UK is conducted by the Financial Services Authority (FSA), and is a form of statutory regulation. The FSA recognises that it is impossible to remove all risk and failure from the financial system. It therefore seeks to prioritise in seeking to achieve its four statutory objectives set out in the Financial Services and Markets Act (2000). Those objectives are to (1) maintain market confidence, (2) promote public understanding of the financial system, (3) secure appropriate consumer protection, and (4) reduce financial crime.

Securing appropriate consumer protection includes ensuring that consumers receive accurate advice and information. Communications with consumers should be clear, fair, and accurate. It is accepted that consumers should take some responsibility for their decisions, but the information upon which the decisions are based should be of a good standard.

The financial crime that the FSA seeks to reduce includes money laundering, fraud and dishonesty, and criminal market conduct. Criminal market conduct comprises insider dealing and market manipulation. Insider dealing is the use of privileged information for personal gain. For example the finance director of a firm may have information about company profits before anyone else, and may trade shares on the basis of that privileged information. Market manipulation may entail issuing false or misleading information with the intention of influencing share prices for personal gain.

The FSA has identified a set of generic risks to its objectives. For example risks to the consumer protection objective could be classified under: failure of companies; crime and market abuse; misconduct or mismanagement; market malfunction; and inadequate understanding of products or services. Prudential risk is the risk that a firm collapses because of poor management. Bad faith risk is the risk of dishonest behaviour such as fraud, misrepresentation, and mis-selling. Complexity (or unsuitability) risk is the risk that customers fail to understand products. The FSA aims to reduce prudential, bad faith, and complexity risk. However the FSA does not deal with performance risk, which is the risk that investments fail to provide expected returns.

After identifying risks to objectives, it is necessary to prioritise. The FSA assesses the likelihood of a risk being realised, and evaluates the impact of such a realisation. The risks focused upon would be those with high likelihood of resulting in problems, and with substantial significance for the attainment of one of the four objectives.

Rather than carrying out routine compliance visits to all financial services companies, the FSA focuses on companies that pose the greatest risk. Each company is allocated to one of four categories, ranging from high risk to low risk. High risk companies receive close attention whereas low risk firms are monitored less closely. In addition the FSA pursues themes that are common to large numbers of firms, for example the provision of comparative information about financial products to consumers so that consumers can make informed choices.

The FSA is empowered to undertake general investigations into the business of persons or firms. It may also conduct specific investigations if there is suspicion of a particular unacceptable activity. The FSA has the power to require questions to be answered, information to be provided, and documents to be submitted. The FSA is able to apply for a search warrant to enter a property and seize documents. The FSA can remove permission to pursue particular activities from firms and individuals. It can also take disciplinary action in the form of issuing private warnings, publishing statements of misconduct, and imposing financial penalties.

Financial Advisers and their Clients

UK financial advice firms, and individual advisers, are characterised by depolarisation. This means that they fall into three categories. Independent financial advisers offer financial products from the whole market. Multi-tied advisers offer products from a limited range of providers. Tied advisers offer the products of just one financial services provider. Advisers are required to inform their clients as to which of the three categories they belong.

A financial adviser must not give investment advice unless the client's personal and financial circumstances have been fully ascertained. These circumstances include information about employment, assets, liabilities, expenditure, attitudes, and objectives. Of particular importance is the client's attitude to risk. The adviser must ascertain the client's attitude to risk and also try to ensure that the client understands the risks that accompany relevant financial products.

Financial advisers paid by commission have a conflict of interest. The products that are best for the client are not necessarily those that pay the highest commission. It might be argued that advisers should have sufficient integrity to consider only the interests of their clients, but even the highest integrity does not eliminate bias. Research into the behaviour of auditors has indicated that the psychological processes involved in conflicts of interest can occur without any conscious intention to indulge in corruption (Moore *et al.* 2006). Confirmation bias, which entails a focus on supporting information and rejection of opposing information, is not a conscious process. Montier (2007) has referred to the notion that people are able to exclude self-interest in decision-making as the 'illusion of objectivity'. Biases from motivated reasoning are widespread; evidence exists for their presence amongst medics and judges. The human mind is not a disinterested computer; its operation is affected by moods, emotions, motives, attitudes, and self-interest.

151

The Financial Ombudsman

The Financial Ombudsman Service helps to settle disputes between consumers and financial firms. The existence of the ombudsman service is intended to increase public confidence in financial services and thereby to encourage people to invest. It is also intended to help to redress the effects of asymmetric information wherein consumers have much less knowledge about investments than the firms that provide them.

The ombudsman can consider complaints about a wide range of financial services and there is no cost to consumers. The decisions of the ombudsman are binding on firms but not on consumers. Consumers are expected to first complain to the firm with which they have a grievance, and then turn to the ombudsman if they are not satisfied. If consumers are not content with the rulings of the ombudsman they are able to pursue their complaints further through the courts. The ombudsman can order that a firm pays compensation to a consumer but, unlike the Financial Services Authority, cannot impose fines on firms. The ombudsman cannot intervene if the firm against which the complaint is made is not authorised by the Financial Services Authority.

The Pensions Regulator, the Pension Protection Fund, and the Pensions Ombudsman

In the UK the regulation of occupational pension schemes is separate from the regulation of private pensions and other financial services. The Pensions Regulator oversees all work-based pension schemes. Work-based schemes include not only occupational pensions but also stakeholder and personal pension schemes where employees have arrangements for deduction from wages and salaries. The Pensions Regulator takes a proactive approach in aiming to identify and prevent potential problems, such as underfunding of pension schemes.

The Pension Protection Fund aims to protect members of defined-benefit (final-salary) occupational pension schemes where the employer becomes insolvent leaving insufficient in the pension fund. It also compensates members of occupational pension schemes (defined contribution as well as defined benefit) in cases of fraud or misappropriation. The Pension Protection Fund is largely financed by a levy on all private sector defined-benefit pension schemes, where the levy on a scheme rises with the degree of underfunding of that scheme.

The Pensions Ombudsman deals with complaints relating to occupational pension schemes, and some aspects of personal pension schemes. The Pensions Ombudsman decides about complaints and disputes relating to the operation of pension schemes, but not those relating to sales and marketing (which are dealt with by the Financial Ombudsman Service). A decision from the Pensions Ombudsman is binding on all parties.

QUALITY ASSURANCE IN INVESTMENT SERVICES

Many people take the view that competition has failed consistently to ensure good quality for retail consumers of financial products and services. This has been evidenced by the mis-selling of unsuitable pensions; the tendency for many consumers to cancel policies before they mature, which suggests that the products were unsuitable; and many endowment policies have failed to satisfy customers since they have not met the consumer expectation that they would be sufficient to redeem mortgage debts at maturity.

Quality could be seen as the satisfaction of the retail investor with the service provided. This is dependent upon whether the expectations of the investor are met. One problem in the investment service industry is that the outcomes of investment decisions are largely beyond the control of investment advisers and investment managers. The behaviour of financial markets is the main determinant of whether expectations, in the sense of desired investment returns, are met. The quality assurance role of the investment professionals may be limited to ensuring that the investments of their clients perform at least as well as the average.

Karapetrovic and Willborn (1999) suggest that quality could be defined in terms of the perception of the retail investor about achieving satisfactory returns under acceptable risks within a planned time. However investment professionals can only be responsible for returns relative to benchmarks determined by market performance. The quality assurance role of investment advisers may entail managing customer expectations. In particular investment advisers may need to ensure that the expectations of clients are clear and realistic (Ojasalo 2001). Investment advisers may need to explain the nature of market risk to their clients. The need for professional integrity is considerable since some clients may withdraw when they understand the risks. Advisers need to be willing to explain risks even though it could cause them to lose clients.

Quality assurance involves providing confidence to clients that their requirements for quality are met. In quality assurance the word 'quality' is used in the sense of conformity, or compliance, of product (or service) specification to a standard. Product, or service, specification can be defined in terms of the function of the product or service, in terms of its structure, or in terms of the manner of production or provision (Groocock 1998).

For function to be used for the specification, it is necessary for the product to have a specific outcome. For example a bank deposit offering a fixed rate of interest over a specified number of years would promise a specific future sum of money. If the investor receives that sum of money, the function of the investment would have been performed and the investor's expectations met. The possibility that the bank will fail to pay the investor is a remaining weakness in the quality assurance. To complete the quality assurance the investor would need to define the product specification in terms of the manner of production, perhaps by choosing a large, well-capitalised bank.

Specification of function cannot be used for products for which it is not possible to specify the future sum of money to be received by the investor. In such a case specification of structure may be appropriate. For example the specification of structure might, for a unit trust, include details of the investment strategy (e.g. diversified portfolio of UK shares); the investment managers (e.g. Acme Portfolio Management plc); the charges (initial, annual, and terminal); and the dates and nature of periodic reports. It would be easy for a regulator to check that these features had been complied with. This may appear to be assurance of form rather than content but, when dealing with financial markets characterised by uncertainty, it is not possible to assure content in the sense of a specific future monetary value.

Product, or service, specification defined in terms of the manner of production or provision tends to entail a much larger set of prescriptions in the form of long rule books. Such a rule book would cover aspects such as: the training and assessment of investment professionals; requirements for independence and unbiased 'best' advice; and requirements for financial advisers to know their clients and to conduct fact-finds for that purpose. Ascertaining the investment goals and financial circumstances of the client is crucial for an adviser. This is necessary to ensure that the goals are appropriate and achievable. The adviser should determine the client's net worth, income, and expenditure. Projections of future income (both level and stability) and expenditure are also necessary.

Accountability could be a component of quality assurance, and of regulation. If financial advisers have to document their reasons for their recommendations, inappropriate criteria such as commission rates may be used less. Hilton (2001) suggested that giving explanations could force decision-makers to make assumptions explicit and to examine other options more closely. Hilton pointed out that experimental research had shown that if people know that they will have to justify their decisions, they would use more information and be less subject to confirmation bias. Confirmation bias is the behavioural finance bias that takes the form of ignoring information that contradicts a person's existing views. Reduction of confirmation bias entails the consideration of a wider range of alternatives. There are risks to such accountability requirements; advisers may make recommendations on the basis of what is most easily defended, which may not necessarily be the ideal advice for the client. Accountability could produce excessive conformity and conservatism.

COMPARATIVE REGULATORY SYSTEMS

An important issue arises as to how the regulation of asset managers can improve investor protection without limiting competition. Inadequate investor protection can cause investors to be reluctant to invest. Good companies can be tainted by the reputation of bad companies. Conversely excessive regulation may increase the costs of entry to the industry and hence reduce competition. For example consumer protection may be improved by demanding high capital requirements, but if new entrants to the market need to have large amounts of capital many potential financial services firms will be unable to enter the market; the result would be less competition and reduced innovation. More generally excessive regulation can deter both companies and consumers by imposing substantial costs on them.

The organisation of the financial services industry can significantly affect investors' exposure to loss. Large groups have greater financial resources than small independent companies. Also large groups may wish to compensate investors for any losses in order to maintain their own reputations. Large groups thus have both the resources and the motive for protecting investors. Large groups dominate European markets with the exceptions of the UK and France which have many smaller independent firms (the United States also has many independent investment companies). Arguably markets in which retail investment operations are predominantly within large financial conglomerates require less regulation by authorities.

Forms of regulation include (1) capital requirements, (2) conduct of business rules, (3) requirements concerning the separation of clients' assets, (4) disclosure requirements, (5) auditing, and (6) investor compensation schemes. The relative importance of each of these reflects the organisational structure of the respective national markets. For example countries in which investment services operations are part of large financial conglomerates tend to have less need of consumer compensation schemes than those in which there are many small independent investment companies.

European regulation tends to rely on monitoring by public agencies, such as the Financial Services Authority in the UK. The US system puts more emphasis on private contracting in which more responsibility falls on investors and investment firms. In the United States there is an emphasis on ensuring that investors have good information (through disclosure requirements) so that they can make informed decisions.

The Enforcement Theory of Regulation

The distinction between the European and US systems could be seen in terms of a spectrum of imperfect approaches to regulation described by Shleifer (2005) as the enforcement theory of regulation. At one extreme of the spectrum is the approach of no external intervention on the basis that the market mechanism would produce optimum solutions. The next approach is to allow private litigation wherein aggrieved participants can take an offending counterparty to court. Next along the spectrum is regulation, which entails intervention by a regulatory agency with a view to preventing abuse. The other extreme along the spectrum is public ownership such that the government owns the relevant organisations (e.g. state ownership of banks).

The enforcement theory of regulation recognises a trade-off between two social costs: disorder and dictatorship. Disorder is an ability of private agents to disadvantage others through overcharging, cheating, defrauding, imposing arbitrary costs, and so forth. Dictatorship is an ability of the government, and government officials, to disadvantage people in the same ways. Movement along the spectrum of regulation, from a purely free market to government ownership, is paralleled by movement from disorder to dictatorship.

None of the methods of regulation is perfect. A perfectly free market could entail, for example, providers of financial services using information asymmetries to take advantage of private individuals. The opportunity for litigation is not perfect since there are legal costs. Arguably investors would prefer that abuse is prevented rather than needing to undergo the costs, inconvenience, and uncertainty involved in court proceedings. Furthermore the – relatively wealthy – providers of services could afford superior legal representation.

An intermediate system between litigation and regulation is litigation based on public rules. The government could create a set of rules and then leave the enforcement of those rules to private parties using the courts. For example the government may lay down requirements for the disclosure of information and conduct of business. Private parties could then take legal action against an offending organisation if those requirements are not met. That type of legal action could be easier, cheaper, and less susceptible to relative legal talent than action based on vague and imprecise criteria.

Regulation has the advantage that the regulators can accumulate expertise and could be backed by specific laws, but there are risks that the processes and officials could fail to be even-handed. The regulator could be subject to political influence, open to bribery, or vulnerable to capture. Capture entails the organisations being regulated gaining influence over the regulator with the effect that regulation comes to be used to the advantage of those organisations rather than to the advantage of consumers such as individual investors.

From the perspective of the enforcement theory of regulation, the European approach is close to regulation whereas the US approach is closer to a market mechanism subject to the use of litigation. Both make some use of the intermediate approach of litigation based on public rules laid down by government.

155

THE EUROPEAN UNION AND THE REGULATION OF INVESTMENTS BUSINESS

The 1957 Treaty of Rome, which established the European Economic Community, set as a target the free movement of goods and services among member countries. This included financial services and required, ultimately, the abolition of all restrictions on the freedom to supply financial services across national frontiers. A major barrier to the achievement of this aim related to the regulation of financial services. A single financial market across the European Union appeared to require the harmonisation of the regulatory systems of the different countries, in other words agreement on a common set of rules.

Member countries proved reluctant to make concessions regarding their own regulations. The issue then arose as to which regulations should apply to a firm that sold services across borders or established branches in other countries. Should the regulations be those of the home country (the country in which the firm is based) or those of the host country (the country in which the sales are taking place)? For a period it was taken that the regulations of the host country should apply. One justification for this was the view that if home-country regulation applied then firms from countries with lax regulatory requirements (and hence low costs of compliance with regulations) would have a competitive advantage. A related argument concerned competitive laxity. There would be an incentive for financial services firms to locate their head offices in the member countries with the most relaxed regulations, and for national governments to relax regulation in order to attract financial services firms. By relaxing its regulatory regime a country could give its financial services firms a competitive advantage.

However a European Court case in 1979 eased the problem of different national regulations. The outcome of the case implied that the Treaty of Rome merely required the mutual recognition of national laws. This meant that harmonisation of national laws was not necessary for the movement to a single market. Mutual recognition of national laws is much easier than harmonisation. The Cockfield report of 1985 proposed that, in cases of mutual recognition, regulation should be based on home-country requirements. The regulations of the country in which the financial institution was registered or licensed would apply no matter where it was doing business. This accepted the principles of freedom of establishment and the cross-border provision of services within the European Union since an institution authorised in one country would be deemed to be authorised in all other member states.

The principles of mutual recognition and home-country regulation were applied in two directives on the marketing of unit trusts (and OEICs) in 1985 and 1988. These allowed a unit trust (or OEIC) that had been approved in one member country to be sold anywhere in the European Union without further authorisation, provided it met investor protection requirements in force in the host country.

The UK example of the creation of a single national regulator (the FSA), as opposed to regulation being divided between a number of bodies, has been followed by other European Union member states (Sweden, Denmark, Germany, and Austria). It has also been suggested that there should be a single pan-European financial regulator. The idea of a pan-European regulator was taken up by the Economic and Monetary Affairs Committee of the European Parliament. Currently the approach being pursued is towards a single regulator in each country rather than a single pan-European regulator. It has been pointed out that a pan-European regulator would need cross-border enforcement powers, which would be difficult without harmonised civil and criminal law (Roberts 2004).

ENRON, WORLDCOM, AND LEMONS

George Akerlof, a Nobel prize-winning economist, wrote an article entitled 'The Market for "Lemons": Quality, Uncertainty and the Market Mechanism' (Akerlof 1970) in which he discussed asymmetric information and its implications. Asymmetric information is the term referring to the fact that the managers of a corporation know more about its operation than investors know. Investors cannot be sure about which corporations are good (the peaches) and which are bad (the lemons). However the managers do know whether their firm is a peach or a lemon.

Shares as Lemons

The accounting scandals surrounding Enron and Worldcom have been used as explanations of stock market falls in the period subsequent to the revelations. This sequence of events can be interpreted as a problem of asymmetric information.

Since investors cannot easily distinguish between peaches and lemons, the price that they are willing to pay for shares will fall between the high value of a peach and the low value of a lemon. The price of the stock would be depressed by the knowledge that lemons are more likely than peaches to issue shares. Lemons are happy to sell shares since the price obtainable exceeds their value (the price being between the values for peaches and lemons). Peaches are less prepared to sell their shares because they are priced too low. So lemons are more likely to sell shares with the result that investors are more likely to be offered shares in lemons than in peaches. This is known as adverse selection.

Another consequence of asymmetric information is moral hazard. Moral hazard is the temptation for the managers to take excessive risks, or engage in activities that are not in the interests of shareholders.

A form of moral hazard is the principal–agent problem. Shareholders are the principals and managers are their agents. The agents may act in their own interests rather than in the interests of the principals.

Asymmetric information can interfere with the effective operation of stock markets. If good firms are unwilling to sell shares because the price is too low, and if investors are unwilling to buy shares since the corporations that sell them may be lemons, there will be an insufficient volume of trading in shares. It is thus desirable to increase the amount of information about corporations available to potential investors.

Information could be generated privately. Investors could engage in the search for information, or employ others to do so. Unfortunately this encounters the free-rider problem. Some investors will stand back and allow others to bear all the effort and cost of information acquisition whilst sharing in the benefits. This discourages the active investors since they will not draw all the benefits arising from their information-generating activities. The result is that the amount of information produced privately will fall below the most desirable level.

One way in which the free-rider problem may be reduced is by the use of collective investments (such as unit trusts, investment trusts, investment bonds, and pension funds) to channel the wealth of individuals into stocks. The managers of such collective (institutional) investments might engage in information-seeking activities on behalf of the individual investors. The fact that the cost of the information generation is spread amongst a large number of individuals moderates the free-rider problem. However, there is a risk that the principal–agent problem might be present. The managers of the collective investments may reward themselves to such a degree that the benefits of the information acquired are used to enrich those managers rather than the individuals who provided the money for the collective investments.

An alternative would be for the government, or other regulatory authority, to intervene with a view to ensuring the provision of an adequate amount of information about firms. This normally entails a requirement, placed upon corporations, to produce accounts that meet prescribed standards and for those accounts to be verified by independent auditors. For this to be effective as a means of reassuring investors that they can distinguish between peaches and lemons, the audited accounts need to be regarded as reliable sources of information.

The revelations of accounting irregularities at Enron and Worldcom have undermined confidence in audited accounts. Investors found themselves unsure about which corporations were peaches, and which were lemons. Corporations that had appeared to be good could no longer be regarded as such with confidence. The perceived likelihood of a firm turning out to be a lemon had increased. To the extent that share prices reflect an average of the values of peaches and lemons, the increased probability that firms are lemons reduces that average and hence the share prices.

Bonds as Lemons

It is useful to consider the implications of asymmetric information from the point of view of bondholders as well as from the perspective of shareholders. In relation to profit uncertainties, such as those arising from the revelation of accounting irregularities, bondholders suffer less than shareholders. Bondholders receive fixed coupon (interest) payments to which the corporation is legally committed. Bondholders will suffer only if the profit/loss position is so weak that the corporation is unable to meet its legal obligations to bondholders.

From a different perspective, bondholders are more vulnerable than shareholders. Borrowers may have an incentive to take on investment projects that are riskier than lenders (which include bondholders) would like. Risky investments may be very profitable, but entail the possibility that everything will be lost. In the event of high profits, bondholders do not share in the increased payouts. The gains accrue to shareholders, who may include the managers. The benefits to managers would be enhanced if they are incentivised by share option schemes. Bondholders receive the same coupon payments whatever the level of profit. If the investment fails, bondholders, as well as shareholders, may lose everything. Shareholders have an incentive to take risks whilst bondholders would prefer a low risk approach.

This moral hazard increases as share prices fall. At low share prices, the shareholders have less to lose from taking risks. The incentive to take risks is therefore greater. Since falling share prices increase moral hazard, investors will become more reluctant to buy a firm's bonds when its share price falls.

Adverse selection occurs when those most likely to benefit from a transaction are the ones who most actively seek out the transaction and are thus most likely to be selected. In the case of bonds, adverse selection implies that borrowers who are bad credit risks are the ones that most actively sell bonds (selling bonds is a form of borrowing).

Bonds may be subject to legally binding restrictive covenants aimed at reducing moral hazard. Such restrictive covenants are of four types: covenants to discourage undesirable behaviour, covenants to encourage desirable behaviour, covenants to keep collateral valuable, and covenants to provide information.

Restrictive covenants need to be monitored and enforced. Bondholders need to check on whether the covenants are being adhered to, and take legal action if they are not. The free-rider problem arises again. Not all bondholders will participate in policing restrictive covenants. Many will assume that others are doing it. Those that do participate may be discouraged from doing so by the fact that others are taking the benefits without incurring the costs. The free-rider problem is likely to cause the degree of monitoring and enforcement to fall below desirable levels.

Institutional investors, such as pension funds and insurance companies, may be more willing to monitor and enforce restrictive covenants since the benefits would accrue to a large number of individual investors in their funds. Such institutional investors may hold a significant quantity of the bonds. However the principal–agent problem remains. The institutional fund managers are agents operating on behalf of individual investors, who are the principals. The agents may be more concerned with their own interests than with those of the principals.

CONCLUSION

Regulation is justified on the grounds of correcting market imperfections, the exploitation of economies of scale in monitoring suppliers of financial services, and the maintenance of consumer confidence. Regulation has its problems; these include the costs of regulation, the emergence of moral hazard, and regulatory capture.

In the UK the Financial Services Authority (FSA) is the regulator for investment business. Objectives of the FSA are the maintenance of market confidence, promotion of financial education, consumer protection, and the reduction of financial crime. Approaches to regulation differ between countries, partly because of the different structures of the financial services industries. The European approach to regulation differs significantly from the American approach, but recent history indicates that regulatory systems on both sides of the Atlantic have been unable to prevent all errors and abuses. No means of regulation is perfect, and the consumer must remain wary of possible failures and abuses.

The rise of institutional investments has made the regulation of such investments central to the maintenance of consumer confidence. There are types of risk that regulation does not attempt to remove, such as the risk of loss from stock market movements. The regulator may seek to ensure that consumers and advisers understand those risks, but does not prevent consumers taking such risks. If investors do not want the risk of equity investment, they may choose lower risk (and lower prospective return) bond or money market investments. Ensuring that consumers understand the risks is part of the educational aim of the FSA. However it is not just the consumers that may need financial education; the financial advisers and investment managers may also need it. The following quote is of interest:

> The recent fall in equity markets has exposed the fact that some of those manufacturing or selling long-term savings products often have a poor understanding of the underlying risks inherent in them. Too often, therefore, savers have bought long-term savings products without any satisfactory explanation of the inherent risks.
>
> (House of Commons Treasury Committee 2004)

The quote also highlights another risk that is only indirectly addressed by regulation. This is management risk, which is the risk that the manager of a fund performs poorly relative to the market. Consumers can avoid this risk by investing in index tracker funds, which aim to track the stock market rather than trying to outperform it (see Chapter 9 on mutual funds). They thus avoid the possibility that fund managers, in attempting to outperform the market, actually underperform the market. The regulatory role is limited to attempting to ensure that fund managers are competent. Chapters 9 on mutual funds, Part 7 on market efficiency, and Chapter 17 on the evaluation of the performance of fund managers cite considerable evidence to the effect that, on average, investment managers underperform stock markets.

Moral hazard is a major problem. Investors may believe that regulation is more pervasive than it actually is and, in consequence, they fail to take proper precautions. Investors, and their advisers, should not only be fully aware of the risks inherent in investments; they should also be aware of the risks inherent in themselves. The risks inherent in themselves include the psychological biases identified by behavioural finance. Investors should be aware of the psychological and social influences on their investment decisions, as described in Chapters 24 and 2 dealing with behavioural finance and the psychology of personal finance, respectively. Investors should be prepared to regulate themselves.

Part 3

Institutional Investments

Chapter 9

Mutual funds (unit trusts, OEICs, investment trusts)

OBJECTIVE

The objective of this chapter is to provide knowledge of:

1. The purposes of mutual funds.
2. Unit trusts, OEICs, and investment trusts.
3. Index (tracker) funds.
4. The effects of charges and taxation on investment returns.
5. Tax-advantaged investment schemes.
6. Pound cost averaging.
7. Evidence on the performance of mutual funds.

BENEFITS OF MUTUAL FUNDS

A major form of institutional investment is the mutual fund. Mutual funds come in many varieties. In the United Kingdom there are three broad types. These are investment trusts, unit trusts, and OEICs (Open-Ended Investment Companies – pronounced 'oiks'). Some people prefer to restrict the term 'mutual funds' to unit trusts and OEICs, but this is just a matter of semantics. Similar instruments exist in other countries, but often with different names. These forms of collective investment have both similarities and differences.

All forms of mutual fund allow investors to have a spread of investments for a small money outlay. For example £1,000 can buy part of a fund, which contains more than 100 different shareholdings. In this way small investors can enjoy the risk-reduction benefits of a well-diversified portfolio. Stockbroker commission costs would render the acquisition of a large number of different shareholdings impractical for small investors. The returns from mutual funds come in two forms: one is the dividend (or interest) income from the investments and the other is the increase in the prices of the investments. There is a risk that prices fall but diversification reduces this risk since, to some extent, losses on some investments will be offset by gains on others.

Mutual funds provide other advantages to investors. They provide administration of the investments on behalf of investors. For example dividends could be automatically reinvested on behalf of the investors. They remove the need for investors to ascertain which shares or bonds to buy; the choice is made by professional fund managers. However these services have to be paid for by annual fees taken from the dividends (or from the capital of the fund), and it is controversial as to whether the investment choices of professional fund managers are, on average, superior to random stock selections.

Mutual funds permit a choice of investment strategy. There are general, high income, and growth funds. There are funds that focus on asset classes, for example funds that invest exclusively in bonds. Many funds allow for particular geographical orientations (Europe funds, North America funds, Far East funds, etc.).

DIFFERENCES BETWEEN UNIT TRUSTS, INVESTMENT TRUSTS, AND OEICs

A unit trust is a fund managed by a bank, insurance company, or investment company. Individual investors buy units in the fund. An investment trust is a company whose purpose is to invest in other companies. Individual investors buy shares in the investment trust company. An OEIC (Open-Ended Investment Company) is a company whose purpose is to invest in other companies (like an investment trust). Individual investors buy shares in funds operated by the OEICs, but these shares are similar to the units sold by unit trusts.

An investment trust has a board of directors, which decides on broad investment strategy and objectives. The implementation of the strategy and objectives is normally carried out by an investment management company. A unit trust is constituted by a trust deed. The unit trust manager is responsible for the day-to-day operation of the fund (the manager is normally an insurance company, bank, or investment company). Each unit trust fund has a trustee, which must be independent of the manager. The role of trustee is normally taken by a bank or insurance company. The trustee is custodian of the assets (e.g. it holds the share certificates), maintains a register of unit holders, and generally oversees the management of the trust fund. The trustee has the role of protecting the interests of unitholders and ensuring that the managers do not stray from their stated objectives. The managers are able to advertise and market unit trusts directly to the public. The funds are exempt from capital gains tax; instead such taxes are payable by unitholders whose individual capital gains exceed the personal exemption limit (investment trusts and their investors receive similar treatment in relation to capital gains tax). UK authorised unit trusts investing in equities can hold no more than 10% of the fund in any one company, and no more than 10% of the issued capital of a company can be held.

Unit trusts are open-ended. The purchase or sale of units by individual investors causes the fund to expand or contract. Likewise the number of units increases or decreases. The transactions are carried out with the investment manager. OEICs are similar to unit trusts in these respects. Investment trusts are closed funds. The purchase or sale of shares by individual investors has no effect on the size of the fund. An unchanged number of shares change hands. Transactions are carried out with other investors through the medium of a stock exchange. In the case of investment trusts day-to-day fluctuations in demand are reflected in moving share prices. By contrast, unit trust (and OEIC) managers regularly issue new units (or shares) or buy back existing ones in order to accommodate fluctuations in demand.

Since sales of shares in investment trusts do not require the fund manager to sell any of the assets, the manager need not be concerned about the liquidity of the assets. This facilitates investments in illiquid markets such as private equity (venture capital), other small firms, and emerging markets. The sale of unit trusts and OEICs involves the liquidation of part of the fund. Assets need to be sold in order that the investment manager can redeem units. For this reason the managers of unit trusts and OEICs need to hold part of the fund in liquid assets. In particular part of the fund might be held on deposit in banks so as to avoid the sale of securities (shares, bonds) in the event of units being redeemed. This is likely to reduce the expected rate of return on the fund. If there is a substantial volume of sales by investors, the fund manager will be forced to sell securities. If the markets for those securities are not liquid, the sales could be at unfavourable prices. The problem is compounded by the possibility that redemptions will peak during times of market uncertainty with the result that asset sales occur when the markets are least liquid. The inflows and outflows of funds generated by retail investors can cause unit trusts and OEICs to be active buyers and sellers. As a result they can have a significant effect on stock market prices.

In the case of unit trusts, the value of a unit is directly based on the value of the investments in the fund. The total value of the units equals the total value of the investments in the fund. OEICs are similar to unit trusts in this respect. Unit trusts and OEICs must be valued on a daily basis, and to facilitate this they tend to restrict their investments to those whose prices are quoted every day (such as shares that are listed on a stock exchange). In the case of investment trusts, the total value of the investment trust shares normally differs from the total value of the investments held by the fund. The prices of investment trust shares are determined by demand and supply, and these forces can pull the value of an investment trust company away from the value of the investments that it holds. Net asset value (NAV) is the market value of all the assets held by the investment trust (net of liabilities) divided by the number of investment trust shares issued. If the price of the investment trust shares is less than the net asset value, those shares are said to trade at a discount to net asset value. If the price of the shares exceeds the net asset value, they are said to trade at a premium. In other words, if the total value of the investment trust shares is less than the value of the investments (net of any debts) held by the trust, the price of the investment trust shares is said to be at a discount to net asset value; in the opposite situation the shares are said to be trading at a premium to net asset value.

EXERCISE 9.1

Acme Investment Trust holds £100 million of shares, in a total of 200 companies, in its fund. There are 50 million Acme Investment Trust shares in issue. The Acme Investment Trust share price is 160p. What is the net asset value (NAV), and the percentage discount?

Answer

The net asset value is:

£100,000,000/50,000,000 = £2

The money value of the discount is 200p − 160p = 40p per share. The discount is 40p/200p = 0.2, which as a percentage is 20%. Acme Investment Trust shares trade at a discount of 20% to net asset value.

Unit trusts typically involve a difference between the buying (offer) price and the selling (bid) price. Frequently buying prices are 5–7% higher than selling prices (buying from the unit trust manager and selling back to the manager). Investment trusts and OEICs have a single price, although the buyer of an OEIC may have to pay an initial charge or the seller of an OEIC may have to pay an exit (withdrawal) charge. In the case of investment trusts, transaction costs are incurred through commission payments to brokers rather than via a spread between buying and selling prices (although, as with other shares, there will be a small bid-offer spread).

Unit trusts and OEICs are bought from the investment manager, and are redeemed by being sold back to the investment manager. In the case of investment trusts, shares are bought and sold through the stock market. One feature that distinguishes OEICs from unit and investment trusts is the fact that they are umbrella funds. There are several different funds within an OEIC.

OEICs came into existence in 1997 as a result of European legislation to create a single European market for investment products (Roberts 2004). Unlike unit trusts, OEICs are not based on trust law. They are based on specially framed company law. In common with European practice, OEIC shares have a single price rather than the separate buying (offer) and selling (bid) prices of unit trusts. OEICs seem to be gradually replacing unit trusts.

Another difference between investment trusts, on one hand, and unit trusts and OEICs, on the other, concerns the ability to borrow. Investment trusts have very extensive borrowing powers and can thereby increase their exposure to stocks by using borrowed money to buy shares. This is known as gearing or leverage. This increase in market exposure can render investment trust prices more volatile than those of unit trusts and OEICs, which are able to borrow only up to 10% of the fund. Another factor that can cause investment trust prices to be more volatile than those of unit trusts and OEICs is the existence of discounts and premiums. Investment trust prices can change as a result of variations in discounts and premiums, whereas unit trusts and OEICs do not have this source of price volatility. The increased risk arising from gearing has been suggested as an explanation for the discount on many investment trusts.

EXERCISE 9.2

An investment trust has 100% gearing (the principal investment has been matched by borrowing so as to double the size of the shareholding). If the money is borrowed at 6% p.a., what would be the return on the principal investment in the event of stock returns of (a) 0%, (b) 3%, (c) 8%, and (d) 15% p.a.?

In the event of a sudden (e) halving, and (f) doubling, of the value of the shares held by the investment trust, what would happen to the value (NAV) of the investment trust?

Answers

(a) If the portfolio return is 0% p.a. but 6% must be paid on a sum equal to the principal investment, the rate of return on the principal investment would be −6% p.a.

(b) If the total portfolio return is 3% p.a., this is equivalent to 6% p.a. on the principal investment since the total portfolio is double the principal investment. There is 6% p.a. interest on a sum equal to the principal investment. So the net return is 6% − 6% = 0% p.a.

(c) If the total portfolio return is 8% p.a., this is equivalent to 16% p.a. on the principal investment since the total portfolio is double the principal investment. There is a 6% p.a. rate of interest on a sum equal to the principal investment. So the net return is $16\% - 6\% = 10\%$ p.a.

(d) If the total portfolio return is 15% p.a., this is equivalent to 30% p.a. on the principal investment. So the net return is $30\% - 6\% = 24\%$ p.a.

(e) If the value of the shares held by the investment trust suddenly halved in value, there would be a loss equal to the principal investment (the value of the total portfolio was double the value of the principal investment). The assets would now be matched by liabilities (investments matched by debts) meaning that the investors have lost all their money but the debt can be repaid.

(f) If the value of the shares had suddenly doubled, the value of the shareholding would be four times the original principal investment. Net of the debt, the investment trust (its NAV) would be three times the value of the original principal investment. Investors would have tripled their wealth as a result of the doubling of share prices (ignoring any changes in discounts/premiums).

Some investment trusts are split-capital trusts. Split-capital trusts are split into income shares and capital shares. The holders of the income shares receive all the dividends from the investment trust plus a predetermined return of capital. Since the holders receive the dividends from the investments in capital shares as well as the dividends on their own investments, the holders of income shares may have a very high yield (high income yield) investment. The holders of the capital shares receive all the capital gains. The holders of the capital shares have a highly geared investment. They receive all the capital gains (from both their own investments and those of the holders of income shares) but would suffer the whole of any capital losses. Split-capital investment trusts have a winding up date on which the assets are sold and the proceeds distributed to the holders of the investment trust shares.

Some split-capital investment trusts issue zero dividend preference shares, alternatively known as zeros. Zero dividend preference shares pay nothing to the investor until the share matures. The return to the investor arises from the fact that the shares are bought at a discount to (a lower price than) the sum to be paid at maturity.

Unit investment trusts also have maturity dates. Unit investment trusts use passive fund management in the form of the buy-and-hold strategy. Assets are bought and held until the unit investment trust matures. The investments purchased are not changed during the life of the fund. The fund accepts initial capital from investors, and that capital is invested. There are no further cash flows into the fund from investors. The initial investments are held until the fund matures, and income from those investments is distributed to the investors. On the maturity date of the fund the investments are sold and the capital returned to the investors. Unit investment trusts frequently invest in bonds.

In the cases of unit trusts and OEICs the ultimate investor is taxed in almost exactly the same way as if he or she held the underlying assets directly. It is the unitholder or shareholder who is liable to tax, not the fund. In order to be exempt from capital gains tax, an investment trust must satisfy the following conditions. The company's income is derived at least 70% from securities. No single holding can exceed 15% of the fund. The investment trust's shares are quoted on the London Stock Exchange. The company must not distribute realised capital gains as dividends. It does not retain more than 15% of the income it receives from investment in securities. If an investment trust meets these conditions, liability for capital gains tax falls upon the investor rather than the investment trust (and many investors would have capital gains that fall below the annual exemption limit).

Unit trusts and OEICs are often available as either income or accumulation units (or shares). Income units pay the dividends to the investors whereas accumulation units reinvest the dividends (so as to enhance the rate of price increase). Investment trusts do not have such a division. Investment trusts distribute most of the dividends to their shareholders, but may retain some to reinvest within the fund.

Investment Trust Share Buy-Backs

In some cases the managers of investment trusts attempt to reduce the size of the discounts. One method entails the investment trust buying its own shares in order to increase demand and hence the share price. The bought-in shares can either be cancelled or held in treasury. Shares held in treasury can be reissued at a later date. If the repurchase of shares maintains a limit to the size of the discount, and if investors come to believe that the discount will be limited to that size, arbitrage could maintain the limit without the investment trust managers repurchasing shares. Arbitragers would buy shares, if the discount exceeded the limit, in the belief that the investment trust manager would maintain the limit. The arbitragers would buy the investment trust shares at the high discount, and hence low price, in the knowledge that they will be able to sell the shares at a lower discount (and hence higher price) to the investment trust manager. By buying the shares, the arbitragers raise the share price and thereby maintain the limit. In consequence the investment trust manager may not need to buy back shares.

The repurchase of shares by the investment trust manager is likely to enhance the return to shareholders. This is partly because the buy-back reduces the discount and hence raises the share price. It is partly because repurchasing at a discount entails buying into the investment trust portfolio at an advantageous price. The latter effect is illustrated by the following example.

The shares of an investment trust are priced at 320p and the net asset value (NAV) per share is 400p. This implies a 20% discount. The investment trust has issued 100 million shares. The investment trust holds investments of £400 million (400p × 100 million). The market capitalisation of the investment trust is £320 million (320p × 100 million).

Suppose that the investment trust buys back 15 million shares (15% of the outstanding issue is the maximum allowed in one financial year). The cost of the buy-back would be 320p × 15 million = £48 million (assuming that the buy-back does not immediately raise the share price). The money used for the buy-back is taken from the assets held by the investment trust. The NAV falls to £352 million (£400 million − £48 million). The number of shares has fallen to 85 million (100 million − 15 million) with the result that the NAV per share has risen to £352,000,000/85,000,000 = £4.14 (414p). This is a 3.5% increase in NAV per share. If the discount remains at 20%, there would also be an increase in the share price of 3.5% (since the ratio between NAV per share and the share price would be unchanged).

This effect on the share price arises from the fact that buying at a discount entails buying the shares, held by the investment trust, cheaply. Investors who sell the investment trust shares receive £48 million but give up a claim on £60 million of investments within the trust. The remaining shareholders profit by £12 million (£60 million − £48 million). The effect would be lessened if the share price rose during the buy-back. However such a share price rise would directly benefit existing shareholders (it would reduce the discount). (This example is based on one given in the Witan Investment Trust PLC Report and Accounts for 2005.)

EXERCISE 9.3

An investment trust trades at a 20% discount to net asset value, which amounts to £100 million. The investment trust manager spends £10 million on buying back shares.

(a) If the discount remains at 20%, what happens to the share price?

(b) If the discount immediately falls to 10%, and remains at that level, what happens to the share price?

Answers

The market capitalisation (share price × number of shares) is £100 million × 0.8 = £80 million.

(a) For every £100 of previous net asset value, £90 now remains since £10 has been used to repurchase shares. For every £80 of previous market capitalisation, £70 now remains since £10 worth of shares has been repurchased.

The implied discount rate is: 1 − (market capitalisation/net asset value).

The implied discount is: 1 − (70/90) = 0.2222, i.e. 22.22%.

In order for the discount to return to 20%, the market capitalisation must rise to £90 million × 0.8 = £72 million. The required rise in the share price is (72/70) − 1 = 0.0286, i.e. 2.86%.
 The share price rise is brought about by the purchase of a portion of the portfolio at a discounted price.

(b) For every £100 of previous net asset value, £90 now remains since £10 has been used to repurchase shares.

The market capitalisation first moves to £90 million to reflect the 10% discount.
It then falls to £80 million because of the share buy-back.

 The implied discount is: 1 − (80/90) = 0.1111, i.e. 11.11%.

A further change is required to restore the 10% discount. The market capitalisation should rise to £81 million.
 For every 100 shares previously in issue, there are now (80/90) × 100 = 88.88 shares. For every £80 of previous market capitalisation, there is now £81. This implies a share price rise of [(100/88.88) × (81/80)] − 1 = 0.1391, i.e. 13.91%. (If the market capitalisation were

unchanged a fall in the number of shares from 100 to 88.88 would need to be offset by a share price rise of 100/88.88. If the market capitalisation increases, the share price rise would need to be correspondingly greater.)

The share price rise is brought about by two factors. One factor is the effect of buying a portion of the portfolio at a discounted price. This factor can be repeated in subsequent periods. The other factor is a narrowing of the discount. There is likely to be a limit to the effect of this factor such that it cannot be repeated for many periods.

The narrowing of the discount provides a return of $(90/80) - 1 = 0.125$, i.e. 12.5%. This implies that the effect of buying at the discounted price is an addition to return of $13.91 - 12.5 = 1.41\%$. It might be noted that this figure is very close to half the return arising from buying into the portfolio at a discount of 20%.

Another approach to reducing discounts is to allow, at frequent intervals, investors to sell their shares to the investment trust manager at a small, predetermined discount. The belief is that this facility will support the share price and prevent large discounts from occurring since the emergence of a large discount would entice share purchases by investors who know that they can resell the shares to the manager at a low discount. The danger of a regular buy-back programme is that the investment trust could shrink until it is too small to be viable. It also removes the advantage that investment trusts have in being able to buy illiquid investments knowing that they cannot be forced to sell them to meet investor redemptions.

Share buy-back programmes also compromise the closed-ended nature of investment trusts. The closed-ended nature of investment trusts is also reduced by the new (since 2003) facility to hold shares in treasury. Shares held in treasury can be reissued so that increases in demand may be accommodated by the reissue of shares. The effects are that both reductions in demand, and increases in demand, can be met by changes in the number of shares in issue rather than by movements in the share price.

EXHIBIT 9.1   EXAMPLE OF AN INVESTMENT TRUST USING SHARE BUY-BACKS (SHARE REPURCHASES)

JPMORGAN FLEMING MERCANTILE INVESTMENT TRUST PLC (31 JULY 2007)

Objective

Long-term capital growth from a portfolio of UK medium and smaller companies.

Investment Policy

- To emphasise growth from medium and smaller companies. Long-term dividend growth at least in line with inflation.

- To use long-term gearing to increase potential returns to shareholders. The Company's gearing policy is to operate within a range of 90% to 120% invested.
- To invest no more than 15% of gross assets in other UK-listed investment companies (including investment trusts).

Benchmark

The FTSE All-Share Index excluding constituents of the FTSE 100 Index and investment trusts.

TABLE 9.A

Financial data (abridged)

Shareholders' funds	£1,519,269,000
Number of shares in issue	107,659,958
Net asset value per ordinary share with debt at fair value	1,404.3p
Share price	1,242.0p
Discount of share price to net asset value with debt at fair value	11.6%

Share Repurchases

The Board has maintained its active approach towards share repurchases in order to enhance the net asset value and minimise the absolute level and volatility of the discount on the Company's shares. In the six months to 31 July 2007, 17,398,801 shares were repurchased for cancellation at a total cost of £233.6m. Those purchases added approximately 22.6p to the net asset value per share. The discount, with debt at fair value, has ranged between 7.6% and 12.3% in the period from 1 February to 21 September 2007, with the average discount during the period 9.9%.

TABLE 9.B

Ten largest investments (as percentages of total net assets)

Taylor Wimpey	3.0
GKN	2.0
Ladbrokes	2.0
Burberry	1.8
Investec	1.8
Kesa Electricals	1.8
Berkeley	1.7
EMI	1.6
Travis Perkins	1.6
Mondi	1.5

TABLE 9.C

UK listed equity market capitalisation (as percentages of total net assets)

UK FTSE Mid 250 Companies	75.6
UK Smaller Companies	18.6
UK FTSE 100	1.4
UK Unquoted	0.1
Net Current Assets	4.2

Source: JPMorgan Asset Management.

Explanations for Investment Trust Discounts and Premiums

It is not well understood why many investment trusts trade at a discount to net asset value. One explanation is that the discount reflects the management charges that are paid out of the fund. If the share price is seen as the present value of expected future dividends, and dividends are net of fund management charges, the share price will be depressed by the effect of charges on net dividend receipts. Gemmill and Thomas (2006) found that charges tend to be high when there is a large board of directors, and when the members of the board largely come from the fund management company running the investment trust. However high fees were found to be associated with low ownership of the investment trust shares by the management company whereas discounts were large when the fund management company owned a large stake. This seems to suggest that large discounts are associated with low charges.

Another explanation runs in terms of poor investment performance causing share sales, which push down the prices of investment trust shares, thereby creating (or increasing) discounts. (Conversely strong investment performance could produce premiums to net asset value.) Fund charges and the perceived quality of fund management, as explanations for discounts and premiums, have been discussed by Ross (2002). A third explanation points to the fact that investment trusts often hold assets that are not easily valued. Such assets include unquoted shares and the infrequently traded shares of very small companies. Uncertainty as to net asset value may be partially responsible for discounts. Pontiff (1996) demonstrated that deviations of price from net asset value were related to (non-systematic) risk; high risk was associated with large deviations. The analysis of the discounts (and occasionally premiums) continues to be a subject of research (for example Ferguson and Leistikow 2001; Barclay *et al.* 1993; Lee *et al.* 1991).

Much of the debate concerning the explanation of discounts and premiums centres around the issue of investor rationality. Lee *et al.* (1991) propose that fluctuations in discounts are driven by changes in investor sentiment, and changes in sentiment are seen as reflecting irrational behaviour. Discounts are high when investors are pessimistic about future returns, and low when investors are optimistic. This is a general market sentiment that affects all investment trusts and other investments. The reason why investment trusts, on average, exhibit discounts is explained in terms of the additional risk imparted by the effects of unpredictable changes in sentiment.

Ferguson and Leistikow (2004) take the view that discounts and premiums can be explained without supposing that investors behave in an irrational manner. They explain discounts and premiums in terms of expected investment performance. One piece of evidence cited in favour of their view is the mean reversion of discounts following changes in fund managers. When the managers of a fund change the discount reverts towards the average investment trust discount. This is consistent with the view that the previous discount reflected the expected performance of the previous fund managers, and is not easily explained in terms of market-wide changes in investor sentiment. Conversely it is difficult to invoke a rational explanation for the tendency of investors to buy newly created investment trusts at a premium when past experience indicates that initial premiums soon turn into discounts, thereby providing early losses for the investors. It is notable that both approaches explain discounts in terms of expected fund performance; the difference appears to lie in how those expectations are formed.

EXERCISE 9.4

An investor has £100,000 to invest. The investor does not want to manage the investment over time. Assuming an average dividend yield of 4% p.a. on shares, compare the net dividend yield from:

(a) direct investment in a portfolio of shares,

(b) purchase of shares in an investment trust which has annual charges of 1% on NAV and whose shares sell at a 25% discount.

(c) What implications might be drawn about the explanation of the discount?

(d) How might the implications change if the discount were 20%?

Answers

(a) The dividend yield is 4% p.a., i.e. £4,000 p.a.

(b) If the investment trust sells at a 25% discount, the share price is $0.75 \times$ NAV. So

NAV = share price$/0.75 = 1.33 \times$ share price.

There is a dividend yield of 4% p.a. on NAV, and charges of 1% p.a. on NAV, leaving a net dividend yield of 3% p.a. The net dividend yield for a holder of the investment trust is $3\% \times 1.33 = 4\%$ p.a., i.e. £4,000 p.a.

The value of the dividends on NAV is 4% of £133,333, that is £5,333. From this, a charge of 1% of £133,333 (i.e. £1,333) is deducted. The dividend payable to the investor amounts to £5,333 − £1,333 = £4,000.

(c) The dividend yields from (a) and (b) are equal. The effect of the discount offsets the charges when considering the rate of yield on the investment trust. This might be seen as implying that

173

charges can explain the discount. The price of the investment trust falls to the extent required to raise the rate of yield sufficiently to offset the cost of the charges.

(d) If the discount were 20%, the share price would be $0.8 \times$ NAV. So

NAV = share price/0.8 = $1.25 \times$ share price.

The dividend yield on NAV, after charges, is 3% p.a. The dividend yield on the investment trust shares is $3\% \times 1.25 = 3.75\%$ p.a. This is below the 4% p.a. from direct investment in shares. The perceived quality of investment management, or the convenience of the management being carried out on the investors' behalf, could explain why the discount is less than 25%. Investors are willing to forgo 0.25% p.a. in order to benefit from professional investment management.

INDEX (TRACKER) FUNDS

An index fund, alternatively known as a tracker fund, aims to replicate the performance of a stock index. The emergence of index funds arose from the observation that actively managed funds fail, on average, to outperform stock indices. This is related to the issue of market efficiency. Active fund management is predicated on the view that portfolio managers can forecast market movements and the performance of individual stocks relative to the market with the effect that they can consistently outperform stock indices. If the efficient market hypothesis is correct, it is not possible to consistently forecast either overall market movements or the relative performance of individual stocks. If this is the case, investors should avoid the transaction and management costs associated with actively managed funds by investing in index funds whose aim is merely to move in line with the stock market (as measured by a stock index).

One advantage of index funds, to the individual investor in collective investments, is that they avoid management risk. The performance of actively managed funds can, during any period of time, vary considerably. Some will outperform a stock index and others will underperform it. The difference between the best and the worst can be considerable. If the direction and size of the deviations from the index occur by chance, as empirical evidence seems to suggest (see Part 7 on market efficiency and Chapter 17 on the evaluation of fund managers), the individual investor faces a management risk. Individual investors run the risk that their chosen funds are relatively poor performers. By investing in index funds they avoid this management risk (which is also known as active risk).

Another advantage of index funds, relative to actively managed funds, is that they ensure that the portfolio remains diversified. Actively managed funds, in their attempts to outperform the market, may hold poorly diversified portfolios. For example they may tilt the portfolio towards particular sectors. To the extent that actively managed funds hold inadequately diversified portfolios, they sacrifice part of the risk-reduction benefit of diversification. However some stock indices, and hence some index tracker funds, can be concentrated on a few sectors.

Probably the greatest advantage of index funds is that they are much cheaper to run than actively managed funds. For example many actively managed UK unit trusts and OEICs have a 6% initial charge, an annual 1.5% management charge, and transaction costs around 1% per year. This compares with index tracker funds which typically have a zero initial charge, a 0.5% annual charge, and minimal transaction costs.

In 2002 the Sandler report noted that the average actively managed UK unit trust under-performed the stock market by about 2.5% p.a., largely because of charges. However more than 90% of retail investors choose actively managed unit trusts rather than index trackers. The Sandler report suggested that this predominance of actively managed fund purchases was probably because they pay more commission to financial advisers. Since tracker funds pay lower commission to financial advisers, the advisers are less likely to recommend them to their clients.

A drawback of index funds is that they tend to omit the shares of very small firms. Even broad indices have a cut-off in terms of company size. For example, in the UK the FT All-Share Index covers about 800 stocks. This eliminates more than 1,000 firms whose market capitalisations are not sufficient. Actively managed funds are able to include any stocks, including those with very small market capitalisations.

TRACKING ERROR

Portfolios constructed to replicate an index rarely succeed in precisely tracking the index. The tracking error is the difference between the total return on the replicating portfolio held by the index fund, and the total return on the index. The total return consists of both dividends and capital gains (or losses).

An index fund may hold all the stocks in the index, with weights corresponding to those of the index. This involves little tracking error but can involve significant transaction costs. Alternatively a subset of the index might be used. This approach reduces transaction costs but increases tracking error.

Even if the replicating portfolio contains all the stocks in the index, appropriately weighted, there are sources of tracking error. The constituent stocks of an index are subject to change. Replacing stocks involves transaction costs. Furthermore the replacement is not instantaneous. Tracking is imperfect during the time taken to replace stocks.

Changes in the composition of an index can also affect stock prices. If index funds are widely used, stocks leaving the index will be sold in large numbers by index funds. As a result their prices fall and the funds receive unfavourable prices. Conversely stocks entering the index will be bought by index funds with the effect that their prices rise. The funds thus buy these stocks at raised prices. So the marginal stocks, those prone to move in and out of an index, are sold at low prices and bought at high prices. This weakens the performance of index tracker funds.

EXERCISE 9.5

An investor has £100,000 to invest. The investor does not want to manage the investment over time. Assuming an average dividend yield of 4% p.a. on shares, compare the net dividend yield from:

(a) direct investment in a portfolio of shares,

(b) investment in an actively managed OEIC with an annual management charge of 1.5% and annual trading costs of 0.5%,

(c) investment in an index tracker OEIC with an annual management charge of 0.3% and annual trading costs of 0.2%,

(d) purchase of shares in an actively managed investment trust with an annual management charge of 0.5% and annual trading costs of 0.5%. Suppose that the investment trust sells at a 20% discount to NAV.

(e) What other considerations would influence the choice between the investment alternatives?

Answers

(a) The yield is 4% p.a., i.e. £4,000 p.a.

(b) The net dividend yield on the actively managed OEIC is $4\% - 1.5\% - 0.5\% = 2\%$ p.a., i.e. £2,000 p.a.

(c) The net dividend yield on the index tracker OEIC is $4\% - 0.3\% - 0.2\% = 3.5\%$ p.a., i.e. £3,500 p.a.

(d) If the investment trust discount were 20%, the share price would be $0.8 \times$ NAV.

So NAV $=$ share price$/0.8 = 1.25 \times$ share price.

The dividend yield on NAV, after costs, is $4\% - 0.5\% - 0.5\% = 3\%$ p.a. The dividend yield on the investment trust shares is $3\% \times 1.25 = 3.75\%$ p.a.

The value of the dividends on NAV is 4% of £125,000, that is £5,000. From this, costs of 1% of £125,000 (i.e. £1,250) are deducted. The dividend payable to the investor amounts to $£5,000 - £1,250 = £3,750$. This is 3.75% of the £100,000 invested.

This is below the 4% p.a. (£4,000 p.a.) from direct investment in shares but better than the net dividend yields from the OEICs.

(e) The advantage of the OEICs and investment trust relative to direct investment is the convenience of professionals managing the investment on the investors' behalf.

The index tracker fund avoids management risk, which is the risk that the investment managers perform badly. This risk is present in actively managed funds. Investment trusts also suffer from the risk that the discount might increase and thereby reduce the market value of the investment.

EXCHANGE-TRADED FUNDS

Exchange-traded funds (ETFs) are a recent innovation on stock exchanges. An institutional investor creates an exchange-traded fund by depositing a block of shares with the ETF. In return the institution receives ETF shares, which may then be sold on a stock exchange. ETFs are shares that replicate stock indices such as the FTSE 100. In other words they are index tracker funds. They are not unit trusts, investment trusts, or OEICs. Relative to unit trusts and OEICs, exchange-traded funds have the advantage of being tradable at prices that continuously reflect the current value of the relevant index. Unit trusts and OEICs are bought and sold at prices that are established just once a day.

Relative to investment trusts, ETFs have the advantage of not being subject to discounts and premiums to net asset value. This is because ETFs are open-ended (like unit trusts and OEICs). Large blocks of ETF shares can be exchanged for portfolios of the underlying shares. The fact that trades can be settled using the underlying shares rather than cash serves to prevent the emergence of discounts and premiums. If discounts were to emerge they should be removed by arbitrage. Institutions could buy large blocks of ETFs at the low price and immediately exchange them for shares at a profit. So discounts should lead to large purchases that push prices up so as to eliminate the discounts. Premiums should lead to sales of ETFs as the underlying shares could be purchased at a lower price. Shares in exchange-traded funds can be bought and sold through stockbrokers in the same way as any other shares. It might be noted that ETFs are open-ended with respect to large trades (and with respect to redemptions rather than the creation of ETF shares) but are closed-ended for small investors since small investors would not be in a position to exchange large blocks of ETF shares for the underlying portfolios. Traded index securities (TRAINS) are similar to exchange-traded funds.

ETFs have two disadvantages for small investors. The first is that there may be poor liquidity; it could be difficult to find buyers and sellers (although this has not proven to be a general problem). The other is that ETFs are not useful for regular savings plans. Since each purchase entails stockbroker commissions, the cost of regular monthly purchases would be prohibitive. On the plus side, ETFs tend to have low fund management costs.

EFFECTS OF FUND CHARGES

Investment managers charge fees. These fees cover the costs of investment analysis, portfolio management, marketing, and administration. Sometimes the annual management charge is related to fund performance, but this is the exception rather than the norm. The payment of such charges reduces the returns to investors. The charges levied by fund managers vary considerably. In relation to unit trusts the cheapest tend to be index tracker funds (which aim to parallel a stock index). Tracker funds (index funds) typically have no front-end or exit charge and annual management charges of as little as 0.25% or 0.5%. Conversely actively managed funds tend to have initial charges of 5 to 7% and annual management charges of up to (and sometimes exceeding) 1.5% p.a. These differences in charges can have considerable effects on investment returns over time. (Comparison of management charges actually understates the difference in total annual costs since actively managed funds tend to trade shares more frequently and hence incur greater brokerage fees than index tracker funds.)

In addition to management charges there are stockbroker commissions. Each time that shares are bought or sold commission is paid to stockbrokers. For many funds such commissions can add well over 1% per year to the costs of operating the fund. This is particularly true for funds with high portfolio turnover (high churning). A portfolio turnover of 100% means that, on average, shares are bought and sold once a year. Some shares would be kept for several years whilst others are held for a fraction of a year, but the average holding period is one year. The average holding period is given by:

$$\text{Average Holding Period} = \frac{12 \text{ Months}}{\text{Portfolio Turnover}/100}$$

So an annual turnover of 100% gives an average holding period of 12 months and an annual turnover of 200% implies that shares, on average, are held for six months. High rates of turnover, and low average holding periods, entail high brokerage costs. As with other costs, unless there is an offsetting improved investment performance, the costs will reduce the rate of return obtained by investors in the funds. Index tracker funds have relatively low rates of portfolio turnover, and hence low brokerage costs, compared with actively managed funds.

There are three figures commonly used for the purpose of making cost comparisons between funds. First, there is the annual management charge (AMC). Second, there is the total expense ratio (TER), which is the annual management charge plus other fees such as audit and custody fees. However, TER does not necessarily include brokerage and other share dealing costs. Nor does the TER take account of initial charges. The reduction in yield (RIY) shows the effect of the TER costs, plus any initial or exit charges, on the percentage yield from the investment. The calculated RIY is very sensitive to the assumed period of investment. The normal practice is to assume a ten-year investment. Shorter investments have higher RIYs since the initial (and/or exit) charge would be spread over a smaller number of years. Conversely longer investments have lower RIYs. If published RIYs are based on ten-year investments, they can be misleading for investors with different investment horizons.

Consider the investment of £1,000 in each of fund A and fund B. Suppose that the investments in both funds grow at an average of 7% p.a. in real terms (that is in excess of what is needed to compensate for inflation). This growth rate is in line with historical experience of equity funds and incorporates both capital gains and net dividend income. The figure of 7% p.a. does not take account of management charges.

Suppose that A is an index tracker fund with no front-end charge and an annual management fee of 0.5%. All of the investors' money is invested and the charge reduces the average annual return to 6.5%. Suppose that B is an actively managed fund with a front-end charge of 6% and an annual management fee of 1.5%. Such a fund would also experience transaction costs from share dealing. If half the fund is traded each year at an average bid-offer spread of 1%, annual costs would increase by a further 0.5% to a total of 2%. An investor in B would find that only £940 is invested and that average annual returns, net of costs, are 5%. Table 9.1 shows the expected value of the two funds over various time periods. (The transaction costs of the actively managed fund are likely to be even higher than 0.5% p.a. since brokerage fees and taxes (stamp duty) need to be added.)

TABLE 9.1

Investment horizon (years)	A	B
5	£1,370	£1,200
10	£1,877	£1,531
15	£2,572	£1,954
20	£3,524	£2,494
25	£4,828	£3,183
30	£6,614	£4,063

Another way of looking at the effects of fund charges is to consider the situation of an investor who is holding an investment for the purpose of providing an income (for example to supplement a pension). Consider the holder of a fixed-income (i.e. bond) unit trust. If the bond portfolio held by the unit trust yields 5% p.a. and fund charges are 1.25% p.a., the investor loses a quarter of the income to fund charges. It would be worth considering the possibility of holding bonds directly. This possibility may be attractive in the light of the lower risk-reduction benefits of diversification in the case of bonds (particularly government bonds) when compared to shares. Besides government bonds can be bought in relatively small quantities quite cheaply through post offices (in the UK).

Reichenstein (1999) examined bond fund returns in the United States for the period 1994–98 and found a strong inverse relationship between expenses and net returns. Low cost funds consistently ranked among the best over the five-year period. The negative relationship between expenses and net returns was virtually one-to-one, suggesting that investors obtained no benefits from the payment of high charges. Any increment in expenses was at the cost of reduced net returns for investors.

EXERCISE 9.6

A fund has a prospective average growth rate of 8% p.a. over the next 35 years. Estimate the fund value, at the end of the 35 years, arising from a £10,000 investment in the fund with (a) no initial charge and a 0.5% annual charge, (b) no initial charge and a 1.5% annual charge, and (c) a 5% initial charge and a 1.5% annual charge.

Answers

(a) £10,000 × (1.075)^{35} = £125,689

(The figure of 1.075 is used because the net rate of return is expected to be 8% − 0.5% = 7.5% p.a. The value of (1.075)^{35} can be calculated using the power function of a pocket calculator.)

(b) £10,000 × (1.065)^{35} = £90,623

(c) £9,500 × (1.065)^{35} = £86,091

EXERCISE 9.7

You are considering an investment of £10,000 in a mutual fund for the purpose of adding to your retirement income. You expect to retire 40 years from now. You are choosing between an index tracker fund and an actively managed fund. The index tracker fund has no initial charge, an annual management charge of 0.3% of the value of the fund, and average annual share dealing costs of 0.2%. The actively managed fund has an initial charge of 5% of the value of the investment, an annual management charge of 1.5% of the value of the fund, and average annual share dealing costs of 1%. You have read that over the long term the average real rate of return on a balanced portfolio of shares has been 6% p.a. You expect that performance to continue for the next 40 years. On the assumption that the funds match the general market performance:

(a) What do you expect the value of the index tracker fund to be after 40 years?

(b) What do you expect the value of the actively managed fund to be after 40 years?

Answers

(a) The expected real rate of return on the index tracker fund, net of management charges and share dealing costs, is $6\% - 0.3\% - 0.2\% = 5.5\%$ p.a. The expected value of a £10,000 investment after 40 years is:

$£10,000 \times (1.055)^{40} = £85,133.09$

(b) The expected real rate of return on the actively managed fund, net of management charges and share dealing costs, is $6\% - 1.5\% - 1\% = 3.5\%$ p.a. Net of the initial charge the investment amounts to £9,500 (95% of £10,000). The expected value of the investment after 40 years is:

$£9,500 \times (1.035)^{40} = £37,612.97$

EXERCISE 9.8

You are considering an investment of £10,000 in a mutual fund for the purpose of adding to your retirement income. You expect to retire 40 years from now. You are choosing between an index tracker fund and an actively managed fund. The index tracker fund has no initial charge, an annual management charge of 0.5% of the value of the fund, and other costs (including brokerage fees) amount to 0.3% p.a. The actively managed fund has an initial charge of 5% of the value of the investment, an annual management charge of 1.5% of the value of the fund, and other costs (including brokerage fees) amount to 1.1% p.a. of the value of the fund. You have read that over the long term the average real rate of return on a balanced portfolio of shares has been 6% p.a. You expect that performance to continue for the next ten years. On the assumption that the funds match the general market performance:

(a) What is the annual total expense ratio (inclusive of brokerage fees) in each case?

(b) What do you expect the value of the index tracker fund to be after 10 years?

(c) What are the effects of expenses on the expected average annual return of the tracker fund?

(d) What do you expect the value of the actively managed fund to be after 10 years?

(e) What are the effects of expenses on the average annual return of the actively managed fund?

(f) What would be the effects of charges on the expected average annual returns of each fund if the investment horizon were five years rather than ten years?

Answers

(a) The annual total expense ratio for the tracker fund is $0.5\% + 0.3\% = 0.8\%$. For the actively managed fund it is $1.5\% + 1.1\% = 2.6\%$.

(b) The expected real rate of return on the index tracker fund, net of expenses, is $6\% - 0.8\% = 5.2\%$ p.a. The expected value of a £10,000 investment after ten years is:

$$£10,000 \times (1.052)^{10} = £16,601.89$$

(c) Expenses reduce the expected annual return on the tracker fund from 6% to 5.2%. There is a reduction in yield (RIY) of $6\% - 5.2\% = 0.8\%$ p.a.

(d) The expected real rate of return on the actively managed fund, net of management charges and share dealing costs, is $6\% - 2.6\% = 3.4\%$ p.a. Net of the initial charge the investment amounts to £9,500 (95% of £10,000). The expected value of the investment after ten years is:

$$£9,500 \times (1.034)^{10} = £13,271.78$$

(e) The expected average annual return on the actively managed fund is:

$$(13,271.78/10,000)^{0.1} - 1 = 0.0287 \text{ i.e. } 2.87\%$$

The effect of expenses is to reduce the expected average annual return from 6% to 2.87%. The reduction in yield (RIY) is $6\% - 2.87\% = 3.13\%$ p.a.

(f) If the investment horizon were five years, the expected average annual return from the index tracker fund would still be 5.2%.

The expected value of the actively managed fund after five years would be:

$$£9,500 \times (1.034)^{5} = £11,228.62$$

The average annual rate of return would be:

$$(£11,228.62/£10,000)^{0.2} - 1 = 0.0234 \text{ i.e. } 2.34\%$$

The effect of expenses is to reduce the expected average annual return from 6% to 2.34%. The reduction in yield (RIY) is $6\% - 2.34\% = 3.66\%$ p.a. The reduction is greater than in the case of the ten-year investment horizon because the initial charge of 5% is spread over a smaller number of years.

$\underline{\text{NB}}$ The RIY figures quoted by fund managers do not take account of share dealing costs such as brokerage fees and taxes. It is possible for brokerage costs to exceed 1% of the value of the fund per year. In the UK there is a 0.5% tax (known as stamp duty) on share purchases. This tax raises share dealing costs.

EXERCISE 9.9

Suppose that it is observed that the long-term real rate of return on the stock market, net of tax, has been 6% p.a. and an investor believes that the return will be the same in the future. If the investor invests £1,000 in an OEIC fund with a view to leaving the money invested for 40 years, allowing net dividends to be reinvested, what would be the expected future value of the investment if it were invested:

(a) In an actively managed fund with an initial charge of 5%, an annual management fee of 1.5% of the value of the fund, other annual charges of 0.2%, and annual stockbroking fees of 1%.

(b) In an index tracker fund with no initial charge, an annual management fee of 0.1% of the value of the fund, other annual charges of 0.2%, and annual stockbroking fees of 0.1%.
Assume that the expected annual return, before charges, is the same for both funds.

(c) Is this a reasonable assumption?

(d) A fund of funds is a portfolio of OEICs/unit trusts. The fund manager buys and sells OEICs/unit trusts in an attempt to be invested in the most successful funds at any time. An additional management fee is charged by the manager of the fund of funds. If the manager of the fund of funds charges 1.5% p.a., and the charges of the component funds are as indicated in (a) above, what would be the expected future value of £1,000 invested for 40 years if the manager of the fund of funds does not, on average, identify the most successful funds? (Assume that the initial charge is paid only when the first investment is made, and is not repeated each time that funds are switched.)

Answers

(a) The initial charge of 5% would reduce the sum invested to $£1,000 \times (1 - 0.05) = £950$. The total annual cost of operating the fund is $1.5 + 0.2 + 1 = 2.7\%$ of the value of the fund. This reduces the expected real return to $6 - 2.7 = 3.3\%$ p.a. The expected future value of the investment would thus be:

$$£950 \times (1.033)^{40} = £3,481.26$$

(b) The full £1,000 would be invested. The total annual cost of operating the fund is $0.1 + 0.2 + 0.1 = 0.4\%$ of the value of the fund. This reduces the expected real return to $6 - 0.4 = 5.6\%$ p.a. The expected future value of the investment would be:

$$£1,000 \times (1.056)^{40} = £8,842.13$$

(c) The assumption that the expected annual return, before charges, is the same for both funds is reasonable if it were the case that the actively managed fund fails to produce consistent outperformance of the stock market. If the active fund management were to succeed in enhancing returns by more than an average of $2.7 - 0.4 = 2.3\%$ p.a., the actively managed fund would prove to be superior to the index tracker fund. The efficient market hypothesis suggests that actively managed funds will not consistently beat the stock market, even before charges are considered. The empirical evidence suggests that any average outperformance from actively managed funds is unlikely to exceed the effect of fund charges.

(d) The expected real return in (a) is further reduced to $3.3 - 1.5 = 1.8\%$ p.a. The expected future value of the investment would thus be:

$$£950 \times (1.018)^{40} = £1,939.25$$

A fund of funds is a unit trust, OEIC, or investment trust that invests in other collective investments, for example a unit trust that invests in other unit trusts and OEICs. It should be borne in mind that whilst the investor in a fund of funds gains from two layers of fund management if the fund management is successful, underperformance could be compounded if the fund management were poor. Two layers of charges would be payable. Charges are payable to the manager of the fund of funds and to the managers of the funds held within the fund of funds. So the total amount of charges may be high. Exhibit 9.2 provides an example of a fund of funds.

EXHIBIT 9.2   M&G FUND OF INVESTMENT TRUST SHARES

It is possible to hold investment trust shares within a unit trust or OEIC. This exhibit provides an example.

Fund Objective

The portfolio is normally limited to shares of investment trust companies. These shares provide a wide spread of investment in the UK and overseas stockmarkets and are often available at substantial discounts in relation to underlying asset values. Income is not a major factor, and the yield can be expected to be slightly less than the average for investment trust companies.

Fund size: £37.74 million (28 September 2007)
Initial charge: 4%
Annual charge: 1%

TABLE 9.D

Ten largest holdings (as percentages of the total fund (30 June 2007))	
Merrill Lynch World Mining Trust	5.54
Advance Developing Markets Trust	4.85
Scottish Mortgage Investment Trust	4.19
Dolphin Capital Investors Ltd	3.96
Real Estate Opportunities Ltd	3.87
Fidelity European Values	3.57
The Monks Investment Trust	3.04
Aberdeen Asian Income Fund Ltd	2.64
TR Property Investment Trust	2.62
Hansa Trust	2.52

Source: M&G Securities Limited.

183

Charges, Commission, and Factory Gate Pricing

One factor that increases the level of charges is the payment of commission to the financial adviser who recommends the investment product to a customer. The adviser would receive a percentage of the money invested; in the case of a unit trust this might be 3%. This percentage is part of the initial charge on purchases. There is often a trail commission, which is a sum paid to the adviser each year that the investment is held by the customer. This might be 0.5% of the value of the investment, and is part of the annual charge on the fund. Paying advisers by means of commission is very controversial, and leads to the suspicion that advisers often recommend investments that pay high commissions rather than investments that are best for the customer.

The controversial nature of commission-based advice was highlighted by the House of Commons Treasury Committee (2004):

> In the Committee's view it seems likely that as long as most of the selling activity in the long-term savings industry is rewarded on a commission basis, many savers may remain suspicious that they are being sold a product for the wrong reasons. Shifting away from the current commission-based sales system common in much of the industry is likely to be a key component of any strategy to rebuild consumer confidence in the industry after the long catalogue of mis-selling scandals in recent years.
>
> For IFAs to receive trail commission whether or not they are providing any real on-going advice to the client is unacceptable. The persistence of this practice is a clear sign that the market for financial advice is not working in the best interests of consumers.

An alternative to paying for financial advice indirectly via fund charges (and thereby commission) is for the customer to pay the adviser directly by means of a fee. An irony is that commission-based advisers often advertise their advice as being 'free', despite the fact that indirect payment by the customer via fund charges is often more expensive than paying a fee to the adviser.

Harris (2007) cited an opinion poll, which indicated that only one-third of consumers of financial products believed personal financial advisers to be trustworthy. This was accompanied by a report of the view that the fact that producers of financial products (financial institutions) pay financial advisers to sell those products (via commission) creates problems concerning the way consumers (clients) view financial advisers. Harris suggested a 'factory gate pricing' approach to the payment of advisers (the suggestion was made in relation to investment bonds, but is applicable to other financial products such as unit trusts and OEICs). Factory gate pricing by the producer would entail an annual management charge (and possibly an initial charge) but would not incorporate any element of cost to cover payments to advisers. Payment would be directly from consumer to adviser, and not from producer to adviser. Payments would be agreed between the adviser and the consumer.

The payment could take one or more of a number of forms such as a percentage of the sum invested being paid to the financial adviser (equivalent to initial commission), an annual charge payable to the adviser (equivalent to trail commission), or a single payment specified in money terms (which may be related to the number of hours of work carried out by the adviser). This factory gate pricing approach should make the charging structure more transparent to the consumers of financial products. It might also make advisers more likely to recommend products that do not pay commission, such as investment trusts and money market investments. Such a broadening of the range of constituent investments could result in the recommended portfolio being more closely tailored to the needs of the consumer. However so long as commission-based advisers continue to promote their services as free, the less sophisticated consumers are likely to choose them in preference to advisers who are transparent about their charges.

Are Investors Deterred by High Charges?

For most goods and services consumers prefer to pay low prices. The question arises as to whether this is also the case for mutual funds. Do retail investors prefer to invest in funds with low charges? It may be the case that retail investors do not appreciate the impact of charges on the long-term performance of mutual funds.

Barber *et al.* (2005) investigated this issue in the United States. They found that investors were deterred by initial charges (front-end loads) but not by high annual charges. They found that initial charges were associated with lower demand, particularly from experienced investors. However investors, even experienced investors, appeared to be unaffected by the level of annual charges. This implies that mutual fund managers are able to raise annual charges without adversely affecting the sales of their funds.

This may help to explain the increase in annual charges over time. Bogle (2005) reported that, in the United States, the six decades after 1945 experienced nearly a doubling of charges as a proportion of the value of funds. This is despite strong economies of scale in mutual fund management as found by Latzko (1999).

Latzko took the view that mutual fund charges could be divided into three major categories. There are fees paid to investment managers. These fees normally rise less than proportionately to the increase in fund size. The second category is administrative expense, which can also be expected to rise less than proportionately to the size of the fund. The third category is the cost of marketing, which need not rise in proportion to the size of funds under management. Latzko found that the cost of operating mutual funds rose at a slower rate than the size of the funds.

The implication seems to be that retail investors do not appreciate the impact of fund charges on investment performance. In consequence retail investors are prepared to pay high charges, and the mutual fund industry has taken advantage by raising charges. Barber *et al.* (2005) took the view that investors undergo a learning process. Although many have learned to avoid initial charges, few have learned to avoid high annual charges (which can be avoided by investing in low cost index tracker funds).

EFFECTS OF TAXATION ON INVESTMENT RETURNS

Taxation has a considerable effect on the returns to an investment. Table 9.2 illustrates the outcome of a lump-sum investment of £1,000 over investment horizons of 10 years, 20 years, and 30 years. It is assumed that the value of the investment grows at an average of 8% p.a.

The first row shows the outcome of an investment that is tax deductible and accumulates tax-free. If the investment is tax deductible then the sum actually invested, as the result of an outlay of £1,000, is £1,000/0.6 = £1,667. (If an investment of £1,667 could be deducted from income for tax purposes, a 40% taxpayer would enjoy a £667 reduction in income tax liability. So the

TABLE 9.2

	Period of investment		
	10 years	20 years	30 years
Tax deductible investment (at 40% tax)plus tax-free accumulation	£3,598 (13.66%)	£ 7,768 (10.79%)	£16,771 (9.85%)
Tax-free accumulation	£2,159 (8%)	£4,661 (8%)	£10,063 (8%)
Deferred tax at 24%	£1,880 (6.52%)	£3,782 (6.88%)	£7,888 (7.13%)
Deferred tax at 40%	£1,695 (5.42%)	£3,197 (5.98%)	£6,438 (6.4%)
Annual taxation at 40%	£1,598 (4.8%)	£2,554 (4.8%)	£4,082 (4.8%)

investment, net of tax relief, would cost £1,000.) The sums of money shown are the values of the investment at the end of the respective periods. The percentages in parentheses show the (average compound per annum) rates of return.

The second row shows the outcome of an investment that is not tax deductible but which is allowed to accumulate free of tax. The third row shows the results of an investment that is free of tax during the life of the investment but which is subject to tax at 24% on investment returns when the investment is liquidated. The fourth row is similar to the third row except that the tax rate is 40%. The fifth row shows the outcomes when the investment returns are taxed each year.

It can be seen that the tax treatment makes a considerable difference. For example the 30-year outcome with the most favourable tax treatment is more than four times the outcome with the least favourable treatment. In the UK pension funds are highly favoured investments, in terms of tax treatment. Pension contributions are tax deductible, pension funds are free of capital gains tax, interest and bond coupon receipts are tax free, and dividends from shares receive favourable tax treatment (from the perspective of payers of the 40% tax rate).

Individual Savings Accounts (ISAs) and Personal Equity Plans (PEPs), whilst not being tax deductible, do receive favourable tax treatment. Such investments are free of capital gains tax, interest and bond coupons are tax-free, and dividends from shares receive favourable tax treatment (from the perspective of payers of the 40% tax rate).

In the UK capital gains tax is payable only when investments are sold, in other words the tax is deferred. Furthermore the rate of capital gains tax is lower than the rate of income tax (24% as against 40% if the investment is held for ten years or more). So investments that provide returns in the form of capital gains are more favourably treated than investments whose returns are in the form of periodic payments such as interest, coupons, or dividends. This means that shares are treated more favourably than bonds and bank (and building society) deposits since shares produce more of their return in the form of capital gains.

These conclusions are applicable to payers of the standard rate of tax as well as to those who pay the higher (40%) rate. The relative advantage of shares is further reinforced by the fact that the first £9,200 (the figure at the time of writing) of capital gains in any financial year is free of tax.

EXERCISE 9.10

A unit trust fund has a prospective average annual return of 7.5% over the next 25 years. Estimate the value of a £1,000 investment after 25 years when the returns are (a) tax-free, (b) subject to a deferred tax (i.e. taxed at the end of the 25 years) of 20%, and (c) subject to an annual tax of 20%.

Answers

(a) $£1,000 \times (1.075)^{25} = £6,098$

(b) $\{(£6,098 - £1,000) \times 0.8\} + £1,000 = £5,078$

(The investor retains 80% of the accumulated return plus the initial investment of £1,000.)

(c) $£1,000 \times (1.06)^{25} = £4,292$

(The annual tax of 20% turns a 7.5% p.a. return into a 6% p.a. return since $0.8 \times 7.5 = 6$, and 0.8 is the portion that the investor retains after tax.)

EXERCISE 9.11

Suppose that an investor anticipates an (annual) income tax rate of 40%, and a (deferred) capital gains tax rate of 20%. What would be the final value of an investment of £1,000 for ten years under the following circumstances?

(a) The investment yields an average of 6% p.a. entirely in dividends.

(b) The investment yields an average of 6% p.a. entirely in price rises.

Answers

(a) The yield after income tax is $6 \times (1 - 0.4)\% = 3.6\%$ p.a.

$(1.036)^{10} = 1.42429$
$1.42429 \times £1,000 = £1,424.29$

(b) The value of the investment, after ten years, before tax is deducted is:

$(1.06)^{10} \times £1,000 = 1.79085 \times £1,000 = £1,790.85$

The capital gains tax to be paid is:

$£790.85 \times 0.2 = £158.17$

The investment, after capital gains tax, amounts to:

$£1,790.85 - £158.17 = £1,632.68$

It is to be noted that although the investment of part (b) yields the same pre-tax total return as that of part (a), it provides the higher post-tax value at the end of ten years. That is because the return in the case of (b) is in the form of capital gains, which are relatively lightly taxed.

EXERCISE 9.12

You have £5,000 to invest for a period of 40 years. The chosen investment fund has a prospective yield of 6% p.a., of which 3% p.a. is from dividends and 3% p.a. from capital gains. If the government introduces a tax-advantaged investment scheme with 20% income tax and no capital gains tax, what would you expect the value of the fund to be after 40 years?

Answer

After income tax at 20%, the rate of dividend yield is $3 \times (1 - 0.2) = 2.4\%$ p.a. The total rate of return is therefore $3 + 2.4 = 5.4\%$ p.a. The value of the investment after 40 years is:

$$£5,000 \times (1.054)^{40} = £5,000 \times 8.196424 = £40,982.12$$

INDIVIDUAL SAVINGS ACCOUNTS

ISAs were introduced in the 1999 Finance Act and are due to have unlimited lives. They provide tax-advantaged investments. As of 6 April 2008, up to £3,600 per year could be invested in a cash ISA with a bank, building society, or other deposit taker. The interest on the cash is tax-free and the money can be withdrawn at any time without loss of the tax relief (although if the money is withdrawn subsequent to the financial year in which the investment was made, it cannot be reinvested in that year's ISA).

Up to £7,200 (minus any amount invested in a cash ISA) could be invested in a stocks and shares ISA. The investment could be in the form of collective investments such as unit trusts, investment trusts, open-ended investment companies (OEICs), and life assurance funds. Alternatively (or additionally) the investment could be in direct holdings of shares or bonds.

Stocks and shares ISA investments are free of capital gains tax and bond coupons are free of income tax. Investors receive a tax credit on bond coupons. At the time of writing UK investors in bonds are treated as having paid a 20% tax on bond coupons and this implied tax is reclaimable, by the ISA manager, from the Inland Revenue. The reclaimed tax is paid to the ISA investors in the form of tax credits added to their ISA accounts. In the case of equity investments (either direct shareholdings or collective investments in shares) no tax is payable on dividends but there is no tax credit to be reclaimed. Higher-rate taxpayers avoid the additional tax on dividends that arises from being higher-rate taxpayers, but there is no income tax advantage for basic-rate taxpayers.

Cash ISAs, and stocks and shares ISAs, can either be with two different providers (the providers include banks, building societies, insurance companies, and investment companies) or with the same provider. There is a facility to switch from a cash ISA to a stocks and shares ISA, but not in the opposite direction. Investments can be withdrawn at any time without loss of the tax advantages. An investor may choose different providers for ISAs in successive years.

CAT-marking

'CAT' stands for Charges, Access, and Terms. CAT standard investments must have low charges, provide easy access, and be subject to fair terms. ISAs that bear the CAT label must abide by a set of rules. In the case of stocks and shares ISAs there should be a maximum annual management charge of 1% (in the case of life assurance funds this is 3%), regular saving must be possible at £50 per month (£25 for life assurance funds), and lump-sum investments of £500 allowed (£250 for life assurance funds). In the case of cash ISAs, the CAT label implies easy withdrawal of small sums at short notice.

Interest rates on cash ISAs are also required to follow changes in market interest rates without significant delay. Stakeholder savings plans and Child Trust Funds can be held in an ISA and they replicate CAT standards (although management charges can be up to 1.5% p.a.).

Self-select ISAs

Self-select ISAs offer high flexibility. Instead of choosing between funds offered by a single investment manager, the holder of a self-select ISA can hold funds from several different investment managers. Self-select ISAs also provide the facility of investing directly in shares and bonds. Self-select ISAs are sold by stockbrokers and by firms of financial advisers. There will be charges to be paid to the plan operator (charges that are additional to those of the funds held within the ISA) whereas holding ISAs operated by individual investment managers (packaged ISAs) usually avoids the additional layer of charges.

It is possible to take out a self-select ISA with a discretionary service. With a discretionary service the stockbroker (or financial adviser) takes the investment decisions. With an advisory service the investor receives advice from the stockbroker but the investor takes the decisions. With an execution-only service the investor takes the decisions and the stockbroker merely follows the investor's instructions.

Fund Supermarkets

Fund supermarkets allow an investor to invest across a range of investment managers within a single ISA. It is also possible to operate through a fund supermarket when investing in collective investments outside an ISA. A fund supermarket is a form of wrap account.

Wrap accounts are online platforms that allow investors to see their full range of investments in one place. They also provide valuations of the investment totals. Liabilities may also be included. A fund supermarket can be seen as a wrap account that is limited to collective investments. Those collective investments could be inside ISAs, inside pension plans, or outside both and could include unit trusts, OEICs, investment trusts, life assurance funds (investment bonds), and exchange-traded funds.

VENTURE CAPITAL TRUSTS AND ENTERPRISE INVESTMENT SCHEMES

VCTs and EISs are UK schemes that encourage investment in small companies. The encouragement is through the provision of tax breaks. At the time of writing, venture capital trusts (VCTs) had been the more successful in attracting investors.

Venture capital trusts are similar to investment trusts. A VCT holds a portfolio of shares of unquoted companies and/or companies listed on the Alternative Investment Market (AIM), which is the junior stock exchange in the UK. These companies are new and/or small enterprises that are too new and/or too small to have their shares listed on the main stock exchange (that is to have their shares traded on the main stock exchange). Since April 2006 the maximum size of a company that qualifies for VCT funding has been £7 million of gross assets (previously it was £15 million). The VCT has a stock exchange listing and is professionally managed by a fund manager.

Like investment trusts, the market value of a VCT usually differs from the sum of the values of its investments in companies. VCTs often trade at a discount to their net asset values. Since the market for VCTs tends to be illiquid, sales of VCTs are likely to involve large discounts to underlying value. The fact that the tax breaks apply only to investment in new issues, and not to the purchase of existing VCTs, also makes large discounts likely.

Investments in a VCT attract tax relief at 20% up to the investment ceiling of £100,000 per year. Investments are also free of income tax and capital gains tax. All dividends from a VCT are free from income tax. No capital gains tax is payable on gains made on the sale of VCT shares. VCTs can distribute realised capital gains tax-free as enhanced dividends. These tax breaks are subject to minimum holding periods (which can be as low as three years). A further tax concession relates to the facility of sheltering capital gains from other sources. Capital gains from other sources are sheltered from tax if they are invested in a VCT. The capital gains tax is not payable until the VCT investment is sold.

The tax advantages of VCTs tend to be variable. For example for a two-year period, 2004–6, the tax rules were changed. The tax relief was raised to 40% for most investors. The investment ceiling for these tax breaks was raised from £100,000 to £200,000 per year. However the facility of sheltering capital gains from other sources was removed. For the 2006–7 tax year the maximum tax relief was lowered to 30%, but otherwise the tax rules were the same as those for the 2004–6 period.

Venture capital investment in a company is usually for a limited period, typically five to ten years. The investment is often accompanied by the provision of some managerial expertise. The company (VCT) that provides the capital looks towards making a capital gain from selling its stake in the enterprise to another investor (possibly through a takeover) or from selling shares following a stock market flotation. Venture capitalists also fund MBOs (Management Buy-Outs). MBOs entail the purchase of a company by its existing management.

Enterprise investment schemes (EISs) involve the investment being made in a single unquoted company rather than a portfolio of companies. Unlike VCTs, EIS investments do not have an upper limit to the annual investment. However only the first £200,000 per year attracts the tax concessions of 20% relief plus freedom from capital gains tax. The whole of the investment can be used to shelter capital gains from other sources. Capital gains from other sources are not taxable until the EIS investment is sold. The EIS tax concessions may also be applicable to investments in AIM (Alternative Investment Market) quoted companies, where shares are being issued to raise capital for investment. EIS investments are likely to be less liquid than VCTs since EISs are not stock exchange listed and hence cannot be sold through a stock exchange.

POUND COST AVERAGING

Pound cost averaging refers to an advantage of buying unit trusts (or other institutional investments) on a regular basis. More units are bought at low prices than at high prices so that the average purchase price is less than the average price of units.

Suppose that a monthly investment of £150 is made for three months during which the price per unit is 75p for one month, 100p for one month, and 125p for one month. (So the average price is [75 + 100 + 125]/3 = 100p.)

When the price is 75p, 150/0.75 = 200 units are bought. At 100p, 150/1 = 150 units are acquired. At 125p, 120 are received. The total is 470 units.

If the whole £450 were spent on units at the average price of 100p, 450 units would be acquired. Monthly investing led to 20 more units.

An additional advantage of investing on a periodic basis, rather than investing the whole sum at a single point in time, is that there is some time diversification. When investing at a single point in time there is a risk that the shares or units would be bought at their highest price. Although it may be that the purchase occurs at the lowest price, it is impossible to know when prices are low until after the event. Single lump-sum investments bear the risk that purchases are made at high prices. By investing on a periodic basis, ups and downs are smoothed out with the result that the average purchase price avoids the extreme values. In other words, risk is reduced by time diversification (in the sense of diversification of the timing of investments).

When compared with investing an initial lump sum, the gain from pound cost averaging has to be weighed against the returns from the unit trust over the relevant period. Monthly investment involves a delay in investing that entails foregoing some of the returns from the units. However lump-sum investing bears the risk that the investment is made when prices are high. The chapters dealing with behavioural finance, in particular 2 and 24, indicate that investors often buy after the market has risen. Emotional factors and psychological biases tend to cause people to invest when prices are high. Pound cost averaging takes the emotion and adverse psychology out of the investment process.

EXERCISE 9.13

The prices of a unit trust at the end of each of 12 successive months are:

50p, 40p, 50p, 60p, 50p, 70p, 65p, 80p, 75p, 60p, 80p, and 100p.

How does a regular monthly investment of £100 compare with investing the whole £1,200 at the average unit price (in terms of the value of the investment at the end of the twelve months)?

Answer

The average unit price is 65p. Spending £1,200 at 65p buys 1200/0.65 = 1846.15 units, which are worth £1846.15 at the end of the year.

Spending £100 per month acquires:

100/0.5 + 100/0.4 + 100/0.5 + 100/0.6 + 100/0.5 + 100/0.7 + 100/0.65 + 100/0.8 + 100/0.75 + 100/0.6 + 100/0.8 + 100/1.0

= 200 + 250 + 200 + 166.67 + 200 + 142.86 + 153.85 + 125 + 133.33 + 166.67 + 125 + 100

= 1963.38 units, which are worth £1,963.38 at the end of the year.

EXERCISE 9.14

The prices of shares in an OEIC at the end of six successive months were:

125p, 100p, 150p, 75p, 125p, and 175p

(a) What was the average (end of month) price of the shares?

(b) How many shares could be bought with £1,500 at the average price?

(c) What would the resulting shareholding be worth at the end of the six-month period?

Suppose that an investor spread the £1,500 investment evenly over the six months in order to benefit from pound cost averaging (investing £250 at the end of each month):

(d) How many shares were bought?

(e) What was the average price of the shares bought?

(f) What was the value of the resulting shareholding at the end of the six-month period?

(g) Comment on the results.

Answers

(a) $(125 + 100 + 150 + 75 + 125 + 175) / 6 = 125p$

(b) £1,500 / £1.25 = 1200 shares.

(c) $1200 \times £1.75 = £2,100$.

(d) £250/£1.25 + £250/£1 + £250/£1.50 + £250/£0.75 + £250/£1.25 + £250/£1.75
$= 200 + 250 + 166.67 + 333.33 + 200 + 142.86 = 1292.86$ shares.

(e) The average price of the shares bought through monthly investment is £1,500/1292.86 = 116p.

(f) $1292.86 \times £1.75 = £2,262.51$.

(g) As a result of the pound cost averaging, more shares are bought at low prices than at high prices. In consequence the average purchase price of the shares is less than the average (end of month) price: 116p as opposed to 125p. Correspondingly the number of shares bought through monthly investment is greater than the number that could have been bought at the average price: 1292.86 as opposed to 1200.

Investing all the money at the lowest price would be ideal, but it is not possible to know the lowest price until the end of the investment period (by which time the opportunity to buy at the lowest price has gone).

An advantage of spreading the investment over time is that there would be a tendency for low prices to offset high prices thereby removing the risk that the whole investment is made at a high price (this is time diversification).

DILUTION LEVIES, DILUTION ADJUSTMENTS, AND FAIR VALUE PRICING

Open-Ended Investment Companies (OEICs) have a single published price. In principle buyers and sellers face the same price (unlike unit trusts in which the buying price is higher than the selling price). However the underlying securities (typically company shares) do not have single prices. The price of the OEIC is based on the mid-prices of the shares held in the fund. The mid-prices lie halfway between the offer and bid prices, which are the prices at which shares are bought and sold respectively. The effect of the single pricing of OEICs is that buyers of OEICs pay less than the true cost of the shares, and sellers of OEICs receive more than the actual receipts from the sale of shares held by the fund. This benefits investors who buy and sell frequently (holding the OEICs for short periods) at the expense of long-term investors.

The subsidy for short-term investors becomes greater when other transaction costs are considered. Buying and selling the shares held by the fund entails brokerage fees. These fees increase the effective cost of buying, and reduce the receipts from selling. If OEIC investors face a single price for buying and selling, they do not pay the brokerage costs. Those who buy and sell frequently receive free brokerage at the expense of the value of the fund, and hence at the expense of long-term investors. The effect is increased where taxes are payable on share transactions (such as the 0.5% stamp duty payable on share purchases in the UK).

The negative effect of single pricing on the value of the fund (arising from bid-offer spreads, brokerage costs, and taxation) is known as dilution. To overcome the cross-subsidy, between long-term and short-term investors, management companies may impose dilution levies or dilution adjustments. A dilution levy is a charge imposed on a buyer or seller of an OEIC for the purpose of covering the difference between the price of the OEIC and the actual net value of the transactions in the shares traded by the fund. A dilution adjustment is similar to a dilution levy, with the difference that the price of the OEIC is adjusted. If purchases of OEICs by investors exceed sales (redemptions), the price may be adjusted upwards to reflect the true net cost of buying shares for the fund. If sales of OEICs by investors exceed purchases, the price may be adjusted downwards in order to reflect the real net receipts from the sale of shares by the fund. This is sometimes known as swinging single pricing. A typical dilution adjustment may be $+/-0.30\%$. However in the cases of OEICs that deal in investments with high bid-offer spreads the adjustment may be much higher. For example a smaller companies fund could experience a dilution adjustment of $+/-1\%$. One result is that OEIC prices can fluctuate even when stock prices are stable.

Chapman (2006a) points out that dilution levies and dilution adjustments are little used by OEIC managers in the UK. It is frequently the case that several months, and in some cases more than a year, pass between occasions on which a levy or adjustment is imposed. The application of levies or adjustments is typically reserved for days on which net sales or purchases are particularly large, or when an exceptionally large single transaction is made. However dealing costs are incurred continuously; and those costs are borne by long-term investors. Chapman cites the Financial Services Authority as suggesting that the average annual dilution cost is 0.19% of fund value but he expresses the view that dilution could be much greater, and estimates that in some cases annual dilution costs could exceed 0.6%. Over long periods of time these dilution costs would have a substantial impact on the values of the investments of long-term investors. Forcing long-term investors to pay the trading costs of short-term investors can be very detrimental to the former.

It would also be disadvantageous to the marketing efforts of the fund manager to the extent that marketing makes use of experienced long-term returns.

One way of dealing with the issue is to use dual pricing, so that there is a higher price for buying the OEIC than for selling. The difference could incorporate the transaction costs. In that way investors who frequently move into, and out of, OEICs pay the transaction costs instead of those costs falling on investors who remain invested for long periods. Another possibility is to use a futures fund (stock index futures combined with bank deposits; see Part 8 on stock index futures) as part of the total fund. As short-term investors buy and sell OEICs, the resulting cash flows are matched by purchases and sales of futures contracts. The transaction costs of dealing in futures are much lower than the costs of dealing in shares.

Fair value pricing may be applied to both OEICs and unit trusts. It becomes necessary when market prices are stale (out of date). Published share prices are the prices at which the shares were last traded. In the cases of the shares of small companies there may be long periods between share deals. It may be several hours, days, or even weeks since the shares in a particular company were last traded. In consequence the published share price may be very different from the price at which the shares would trade in the present. When valuing OEICs (or unit trusts) it may be inappropriate to use published share prices when those prices are stale. Investors in OEICs and unit trusts would be paying and receiving prices that are poorly related to the true values of the shares held by the funds. When the companies whose shares are held by the fund experience infrequent trading in their shares, investment management companies may adjust the prices of the shares held in an attempt to more accurately reflect the prices at which the shares would trade currently. The share prices used as a basis for valuing OEICs and unit trusts are the prices that the fund managers believe would prevail in the light of current market conditions.

MUTUAL FUNDS AND THE PROVISION OF LIQUIDITY

Mutual funds provide investors with liquidity since it is easy to acquire, and dispose of, portfolios of shares by means of buying and selling mutual funds. If investors were to create or liquidate portfolios directly, they would be involved in high costs in terms of time, effort, and money. By using mutual funds they avoid the expenditure of time and effort. In the case of index tracking funds, where initial charges are usually zero, they also avoid the financial costs. In the case of investment trusts, the financial costs are greatly reduced since only one purchase or sale transaction is involved.

However there are costs to the mutual funds of providing such liquidity. These costs arise from fund managers being forced to trade in shares when their retail investors choose to buy or sell, rather than when the fund managers would choose to trade. Since investment trusts (closed-ended funds) are not affected by retail trades in this way they do not bear these costs.

Retail investors tend to buy into mutual funds (e.g. buying units in a unit trust) when markets are rising and sell when markets are falling. The immediate effect of retail investment is an addition to the cash held in the fund, and the immediate effect of retail sales is a reduction of the cash held. A result of this is that mutual fund managers have a relatively large proportion of their funds in cash during rising markets (just when the funds should have a relatively large proportion in shares) and a low proportion in cash during falling markets (when a high proportion in cash would be preferable). Even during stable markets the transactions of retail investors will force fund managers into trades that they would otherwise not choose to make.

In these ways the provision of liquidity, by mutual funds, to retail investors can adversely impact on the performance of the funds. This would suggest a case for initial and/or exit (withdrawal) charges that are payable into the fund. In this way frequent transactors in unit trust units, or OEIC shares, would compensate long-term investors for their negative impact on fund performance. This could be seen as payment, by frequent transactors, for the liquidity provided by the funds.

EXERCISE 9.15

An OEIC keeps 5% of its fund in bank deposits in order to meet potential redemptions. If the real rate of return on the stock market as a whole is 7% p.a. whilst the real interest rate on bank deposits is 2% p.a., what is the effect of this liquidity provision on the rate of return of the fund?

Answer

The expected real rate of return on the fund is reduced from 7% p.a. to:

$(0.95 \times 7\%) + (0.05 \times 2\%) = 6.75\%$ p.a.

The provision of liquidity has reduced average real return from 7% p.a. to 6.75% p.a.

EXERCISE 9.16

An OEIC keeps an average of 5% of its fund in bank deposits in order to meet redemptions of shares (i.e. to provide liquidity for investors). When the market rises, increased demand for its shares leads to a net cash inflow and the bank deposits held increase to 10% of the fund. When the stock market falls, net sales of shares reduce the holding of bank deposits to 0% of the fund. During periods of market rise the real return on the (non-cash) portfolio is 17% p.a. During periods of market weakness the real return is -3% p.a. Bank deposits yield a real return of 2% p.a. Periods of market strength, and periods of weakness, occupy equal lengths of time. What is the effect of holding part of the fund in bank deposits on the average real return of the fund?

Answer

In the absence of bank deposits (no provision for the redemption of shares) the average real return is:

$(0.5 \times 17\%) + (0.5 \times -3\%) = 7\%$ p.a.

In the presence of bank deposits the real return during market strength is:

$(0.9 \times 17\%) + (0.1 \times 2\%) = 15.3\% + 0.2\% = 15.5\%$ p.a.

During market weakness the real return is -3% p.a. (there are no bank deposits).

So in the presence of bank deposits (during periods of market strength) the average real return is:

$$(0.5 \times 15.5\%) + (0.5 \times -3\%) = 6.25\% \text{ p.a.}$$

The provision of liquidity in a volatile market reduces the average real return from 7% p.a. to 6.25% p.a.

It might be noted that index tracker funds maintain 100% exposure to the stock market rather than holding part of the fund in deposits. Index tracker funds thereby avoid the reduction in returns arising from the holding of bank deposits (or other money market investments).

EVIDENCE ON THE PERFORMANCE OF MUTUAL FUNDS

There have been numerous studies of the performance of mutual funds. Performance is measured in terms of total return, that is dividend yield plus capital gains. Generally these studies have found that (1) on average funds underperform stock indices, (2) past relative performance is not a good guide to future relative performance, and (3) funds with low charges and low portfolio turnover tend to outperform those with high charges and high turnovers.

A number of studies have found that mutual funds produce higher returns than indices before charges and costs are considered, but underperform indices after allowance is made for such expenses (for example Shukla 2004; Wermers 2000; Daniel *et al.* 1997). Although on average mutual funds appear not to outperform stock indices, some funds will provide better returns than indices. The question arises as to whether some funds persistently provide superior returns. Although a few studies have suggested some persistence in relative performance in the short term (up to three years) there is probably a consensus that there is no long-term persistence in performance (for example Hendricks *et al.* 1993; Kahn and Rudd 1995; Jain and Wu 2000). It appears that past performance is not a useful guide for choosing between mutual funds. Although the evidence of research studies indicates an absence of long-term persistence in the relative performance of funds, many investors believe that particular fund managers are persistently good or bad (and switch funds to follow favoured fund managers when those preferred managers move on to other funds). There is little research evidence on the effectiveness of this strategy, but Gallo and Lockwood (1999) found that when poorly performing funds change manager the result is on average an improvement in performance.

The majority of studies suggest that funds with high expenses tend to provide investors with lower returns (for example Reichenstein 1999; Indro *et al.* 1999; Bogle 1998; Carhart 1997). However, some studies point the other way (for example Shukla 2004). There is also evidence that high portfolio turnover (and hence high brokerage costs) is associated with lower net returns (Carhart 1997). Bogle (2002) compared the performance of high cost US mutual funds (top quartile for annual costs, 1.8%) against the performance of low cost mutual funds (bottom quartile, 0.6% p.a.) over 1991–2001 and found that the low cost funds outperformed the high cost funds by more than the cost differential (by 2.2% p.a.). The low cost funds also exhibited lower risk than the high cost funds. The strongly performing low cost funds included index tracker funds. The relative advantage of index tracker funds was further enhanced by the consideration that they tended not to have front-end fees (loads) and by the fact that many of the worst performing actively managed funds had been withdrawn or merged into other funds with the effect that the weakest funds were removed from the data when the average performance was calculated.

The question arises as to why investors predominantly buy actively managed funds if the evidence tends to suggest that index tracking funds are likely to perform better. One explanation comes from behavioural finance. Investors incorrectly perceive their ability to select funds that will perform well. Goetzmann and Peles (1997) measured the recollections of investors in relation to the recent performance of their mutual funds. They investigated two groups of private investors and found that both groups overestimated the absolute performance, and performance relative to the market. These overestimates were substantial: both groups overestimated performance relative to the market by around 5% p.a. It was suggested that memory adjusts in such a way as to improve the recalled performance. Cognitive dissonance has been suggested as an explanation (Baker and Nofsinger 2002). If people like to see themselves as wise investors, their memories of investment performance adjust to confirm their self-image. If reality conflicts with self-image, the memory of reality changes in order to be consistent with the self-image.

Another explanation arises from the influence of financial journalism on investors. Winnett and Lewis (2000) pointed out that financial journalists often promote the idea that it is possible to identify prospective future outperformers. A theme that runs through much financial journalism is that it is possible to spot winners and to beat the market. There is often a focus on identifying 'stars' and 'dogs' from league tables of funds. Financial journalism often implies that relative returns can be forecast from selective samples of past performance. However, Winnett and Lewis acknowledged that some deviation from typical financial journalism has emerged from presentations and discussions of index tracker funds. As a result some financial journalists are now willing to discuss the idea that the market cannot be beaten.

An alternative explanation may lie in the fact that many mutual fund investors know little about the relative performance of actively managed funds. If a financial adviser recommends an actively managed fund, the investor is likely to follow that advice. If financial advisers were paid by means of commission, relative commission levels could affect their memories of relative performance. If actively managed funds pay more commission to the adviser than index tracker funds, the adviser's perception and memory of relative performance may be influenced. If one's livelihood is at stake, one's perception and recollection of the evidence is likely to be affected by self-interest. It will be seen from the chapters that deal with behavioural finance (social and psychological biases in investment decision-making), in particular Chapters 2 and 24, that no one is immune from bias. The human mind is not a disinterested computer, and memory is not a mechanical recording of the past.

Financial advisers may have a conflict of interests. The investments most suitable for their clients may not be those that pay the highest commission to the advisers. Fund managers may also face conflicts of interest. Maximising returns for investors in their funds, whilst avoiding unacceptable risk, might be seen as the only objective. However the fund managers also have a loyalty to the investment management companies that employ them. Gaspar *et al.* (2006) investigated the possibility that loyalty to the employing company could dominate loyalty to the fund investors. In particular they investigated the possibility of cross-subsidisation between funds managed by the same company.

There is some evidence of a 'smart money effect' in that returns on new cash flows to mutual funds are higher than the average return for all mutual fund investors. This appears to be evidence supporting the view that investors can identify superior fund managers. However, Sapp and Tiwari (2005) concluded that the relative outperformance of new money arose from a momentum effect. There is evidence that over a three- to twelve-month period there is some persistence in the performance of shares in that good performances continue for a few months, as do bad performances (see Chapter 23 on weak form market efficiency). Sapp and Tiwari concluded that mutual fund investors invest in funds with recent good performance, and that the momentum effect causes the relatively good performance to persist for a few months following the investment of new cash. So the superior returns to new investments were seen to be a result of momentum rather than the result of identifying good fund managers.

Weigand *et al.* (2004) presented evidence that mutual fund managers tended to be momentum traders. It appeared that mutual fund managers often chose stocks on the grounds that those stocks had recently performed well. Weigand *et al.* found that this had adverse effects on mutual fund performance since the momentum effect (continuation of past price rises) soon ceased or reversed. They recommended that individual investors should not be guided in their choices of stocks by the choices of mutual fund managers.

Walter and Weber (2006) also found that mutual fund managers had a tendency towards momentum trading. They also concluded that mutual fund managers were prone to herding, which entails making the same trading decisions as other managers. To the extent that mutual fund managers share a tendency towards momentum trading they would all buy following price rises, and sell following price falls, with the effect that they make the same trading decisions. There may be other factors that lead to herding, such as the desire to avoid substantial underperformance relative to other fund managers. One source of risk for the retail investor is the possibility that their fund manager underperforms relative to the average fund manager; this is known as active risk or management risk. Copying other fund managers reduces such active risk.

Walter and Weber (2006) found evidence consistent with the view that herding is most pronounced among successful fund managers. This may be because successful managers want to preserve earlier relatively strong performance in order to guarantee their bonuses, whereas unsuccessful ones gamble by deviating from the consensus in the hope of achieving relative outperformance. It is also consistent with prospect theory, which predicts that gainers act conservatively (and preserve their gains) whereas losers take risks, which could reverse the losses. Another factor explaining herding among mutual fund managers may be window dressing. Managers may fill their portfolios with recently successful stocks at times when they are due to report their portfolios in order to give the impression that they had selected successful stocks.

It is often the case that an investment management company will have a range (or family) of different unit trusts or OEICs. For example a family of funds might include UK equity general, UK equity growth, UK equity income, UK smaller companies, and UK special opportunities funds together with a range of other funds covering overseas investments and other asset classes. Gaspar *et al.* (2006) suggested that the investment management company might regard some funds as high value. High value funds would include those charging high fees. Also since retail investors are disproportionately attracted to funds exhibiting recent high performance, particularly when those funds are new, such funds are likely to be regarded as high value funds by the company. Gaspar *et al.* found evidence that investment management companies reallocate performance among funds within a family so as to favour high value funds. One mechanism appears to entail the trading of shares between funds at prices favourable to the high value funds.

Dowen and Mann (2004) found that the existence of a large family of funds was advantageous to the average performance of funds within the family. There appeared to be cost savings when the same investment management company managed a large number of funds. They also found economies of scale such that large totals of assets under management were associated with lower average percentage management costs. The implication is that, on average, individual investors are better off in large funds, which are members of large fund families.

Star Performers and the Role of Chance

Financial journalists often make play of the idea of star funds that have performed exceptionally well over a past period. However the laws of probability suggest that a few funds will show consistently good performance, but purely as a matter of chance. If there is a 50% chance of beating the average in any year, it is to be expected that a fund has a $(0.5)^{10} = 0.1\%$ chance of outperforming the average every year for ten years. So out of 1,000 funds, one can be expected to outperform every year for ten years, purely as a matter of chance. The corresponding figure over five years is 31 funds $[(0.5)^5 \times 1000]$. Since there are thousands of funds available to investors, it is not surprising that a few will appear to be star funds with consistently high returns.

When ranking funds on a risk-adjusted basis some will appear to be outstanding performers. The question arises as to whether such funds should be seen as having superior investment management. If they do exhibit high-quality fund management, they would be candidates for purchase. However some funds would show exceptional performance simply as a matter of chance. Marcus (1990) looked at the performance of the Magellan fund in the United States. That fund had outperformed the S&P 500 index in 11 out of the 13 years up to 1989, and appeared to be a star performer. Using computer simulations Marcus found that, in a sample of 500 funds, the expectation was that there is a 99.8% chance that the best performing fund would beat a stock index in 11 years or more.

Evidence consistent with the existence of star performers comes from Kosowski et al. (2006). They employed a distribution of returns that provided a better representation of experienced returns than the normal distribution. They concluded that there were more top-performing fund managers than would be expected on the basis of chance. They found that in a sample of 1,788 US domestic equity mutual funds, 29 met their criterion of superior performance as opposed to the 9 that would have been expected on the basis of pure chance. However they found that the superior returns apparently resulting from skill mostly occurred before 1990, and were limited to growth funds (as opposed to income funds). They also found that these apparently superior skills showed persistence over time, a result also found by Harlow and Brown (2006). Harlow and Brown found that by identifying causes of persistence in relative performance, it was possible to successfully identify future high performers with nearly 60% accuracy.

Fund managers have a vested interest in promoting the funds that have shown such high returns, since the information will attract many new clients. Journalists will also report on such funds since they provide a degree of sensationalism. A cynic might be tempted to suggest that newspapers may be more inclined to report on such funds if the fund managers pay for advertisements in those newspapers.

Arguably publicised strong performance is a very effective form of advertising. Atkinson and Sturm (2003) examined the selection of 'all-stars' by a major US mutual fund advisory service.

199

Describing a mutual fund as an 'all-star' appeared to have a positive effect on the flow of money into the fund; so it proved to be effective advertising. The authors reported no convincing evidence of post-selection performance that was superior to the market.

CONCLUSION

Mutual funds comprise unit trusts, OEICs, and investment trusts. They are all collective investments in that they aggregate the investments of a large number of individuals. The sums thus accumulated are used to buy a portfolio of assets, which has more diversification than can normally be achieved by an individual.

Financial journalists often describe particular mutual funds as stars or dogs. Stars are the top performers, and dogs are at the bottom (this is easy reporting for the journalists since their investigations need go no further than published performance tables). This categorisation is always based on past performance and is typically taken to imply something about the quality of investment management (and hence prospective future performance). However, investment performance will vary simply as a matter of chance. It is far from clear that the stars and the dogs reach their relative positions as a result of anything other than pure chance. In Chapter 17 on evaluating the performance of fund managers and in Part 7 on market efficiency, it will be seen that the evidence indicates that past performance is a very poor guide to future performance.

In the chapters – 2 and 24 in particular – that deal with behavioural finance (the social and psychological biases that influence investors), it is contended that people are reluctant to accept that some outcomes are the result of chance. People tend to look for causes, and for patterns in events, and are prone to see causes and patterns that do not exist. Investors should seek to overcome this psychological bias, along with the other biases that are common amongst investors.

If it is accepted that good performance is a matter of luck, rather than investment management skill, the individual investor may be advised to buy an index tracker fund that simply aims to follow a stock market index. Index tracker funds avoid the costs of active fund management (and hence have lower charges) and they avoid management risk, which is the risk that a particular fund will perform relatively badly. Over long periods of time, even small differences in fund charges can make a large difference to the final value of an investment. Taxation can also have a substantial impact on the long-term outcome of an investment.

The evidence on mutual fund performance tends to be unfavourable to active fund management, and hence favourable to index tracker funds (the evidence is presented in this chapter and in Part 7 on market efficiency and Chapter 17 on evaluating the performance of fund managers). However, as indicated in Chapters 7 and 13 on stock indices and portfolio diversification, respectively, index tracker funds may not provide the best possible diversification. Portfolio diversification reduces portfolio risk since the weak performance of some shares would tend to be offset by strong performance from others. However stock indices may not represent well-diversified portfolios. For example in the UK the largest ten companies represent nearly half the total value of the stock market, and those companies are concentrated in a small range of sectors.

Mutual funds often use financial derivatives (futures, options, and swaps). Although when used on their own derivatives can be very risky, when used in conjunction with a portfolio of investments they can reduce risk (as shown in Parts 8, 9, and 10 on futures, options, and swaps). Not only can derivatives reduce risk, but also they can be used to enhance returns. Chapter 34 on structured products shows how whole new classes of mutual funds can be constructed by using financial derivatives.

Chapter 10

Life assurance and assurance-related investments

OBJECTIVE

The objective of this chapter is to provide knowledge of:

1. Life assurance without an investment component.
2. Life assurance with an investment component.
3. With-profits policies.

Human capital is the present value of prospective future earnings. For many people, particularly young people, human capital is their most valuable asset. It is an asset that can be enhanced by undertaking education and training. It is an asset that can be reduced by illness, and lost through death. Insurance policies can be taken out to protect against the effects of illness on earning power (often known as Permanent Health Insurance). Insurance policies can protect a person's dependants against the financial effects of the person's death; this is life assurance. Human capital combined with insurance is much less risky than human capital alone.

Life assurance policies pay out a sum of money upon the death of the insured person. They divide into term assurance, whole-of-life policies, and endowment policies.

TERM ASSURANCE

Term assurance provides a payout in the event of death occurring before the expiry date of the policy. The term involved may range from a few weeks to cover a foreign trip to 25 years to cover a mortgage. Normally the client would pay a regular monthly sum (the premium) for the duration of the policy. The sum assured could be constant, increasing, or decreasing. The payment in the event of death may be a lump sum or a stream of income payments (the income alternative is known as family income benefit).

Renewable term assurance allows the client to extend the term assurance when, or before, the original policy reaches its expiry date. Convertible term assurance policies allow the client to convert to a permanent life assurance within the term of the original policy. These options to renew or convert guarantee future insurability for an additional cost of about 10% of the premium payments.

The insurance company holds two portfolios. There is a portfolio of liabilities in the form of prospective payments to policy beneficiaries. There is also a portfolio of assets, financed by client premiums. Both portfolios are subject to uncertainty. The uncertainty relating to the liabilities arises because it is not possible to predict precisely the number and timing of claims. However, due to the law of large numbers, there is a reasonably high predictability. Actuarial tables provide good predictions of average life expectancy, and if an insurance company has a large number of clients it can reasonably expect that claims would reflect the averages. The uncertainty of the portfolio of assets arises from asset price changes, and changes in the rates of return on reinvested investment income. The insurance company is involved in asset-liability management. This entails attempts to offset the risks of the two portfolios against each other. In the case of the portfolio of assets the law of large numbers cannot be relied upon since there are risk factors common to many financial assets (these are known as systematic risks).

A portfolio of bonds is often used since bonds are long term (as are the liabilities) and provide relatively predictable cash flows if they are held to maturity. Another factor that favours investment in bonds is that the cash flows (coupons and repayment of principal) from most bonds are predetermined in nominal (i.e. money) terms. Life assurance liabilities are also specified in nominal terms. However equity investments (shares) are also held because, over long periods, shares tend to provide much higher returns than bonds. Also the long-term nature of the investment allows for returns in bad periods to be offset by those of good periods with the effect that the risks of equity investment do not rise in proportion to the period of the investment. Insurance companies frequently have surpluses of assets, which are funds in excess of what is required to match expected liabilities. It is possible to use such surpluses for relatively risky investments, such as shares and property.

WHOLE-OF-LIFE POLICIES

An important form of institutional investment is the insurance fund (or life assurance fund). These funds typically aim to provide a sum of money at a point of time in the future (or at death if that occurs earlier). They incorporate an element of life insurance. Commonly they require the investor to make a constant stream of contributions to the fund over the period covered by the policy. However some allow for lump-sum contributions or for variable periodic payments. Life assurance investments divide into whole-of-life policies, endowment policies, and investment bonds.

Whole-of-life assurance policies are permanent; they pay out upon death. Since payouts are inevitable, whole-of-life policies are more expensive than term assurance policies. (In some cases such policies have a termination age, for example 70. In such cases policyholders must cancel the policy and take a surrender value when they reach the termination age.) The life office's need to build an investment reserve to pay benefits on policies means that the policies acquire a surrender value. The policyholder may cancel the policy and take its cash value. However the cost of the life assurance renders such policies unsuitable for someone whose concern is simply with accumulating savings.

Without-profit policies invest solely in fixed income securities such as bonds. With-profits policies invest in shares and property as well as fixed income securities. In consequence, with-profits policies entail more potential for growth in the value of the investment. Unit-linked whole-of-life policies (which are usually invested in unit trusts) provide even greater growth potential, but at the cost of greater risk. Unit-linked policies often allow the client to vary the relative levels of insurance cover and investment over time. For example when family commitments are high the life assurance cover may be raised at the expense of the rate of accumulation of units in the investment funds. In some cases the monthly premium to be paid may be varied at the discretion of the policyholder.

Without-profit policies may ensure a fixed rate of interest for the life of the policy. In such cases the insurance company may permit policyholders to borrow against the accumulated value of the fund. A policy taken out when interest rates are low will provide a low return, but could allow the policyholder to borrow at a correspondingly low rate of interest. Policyholders thus have the facility of borrowing against their policies at a low rate of interest and investing the proceeds at a higher rate when interest rates rise.

ENDOWMENT POLICIES

Endowment policies can be likened to savings plans with attached life assurance. They typically specify a period of time, such as 10 or 25 years, during which regular monthly payments are made. These monthly premiums finance the cost of insurance cover and contributions to an investment fund. At the end of the policy term, the accumulated value of the investment fund is paid to the policyholder. If the holder dies before the end of the term, the policy beneficiaries receive the higher of the value of the investment fund or the guaranteed sum assured. The guaranteed sum assured is the amount for which the person's life is insured. The investment funds are usually either with-profits or unit-linked. With-profits funds are discussed later in this chapter. Unit-linked funds are similar to unit trusts and frequently entail stock market investment. There is thus a risk that the value of a policy could fall sharply just before maturity if the stock market slumps at that time. However the sum assured will be paid to the policyholder if that sum is greater than the value of the units on the maturity date.

An endowment policy can be used to pay off a mortgage debt. Throughout the term of the mortgage, interest is paid on the debt. In addition regular payments are made into an endowment fund. At the end of the mortgage term the sum of money accumulated in the endowment fund is used to pay off the mortgage debt. For example if returns on an endowment are 10% p.a., an annual payment of £16,380 into an endowment will be worth £100,000 in five years. This can be used to repay a £100,000 debt. An endowment mortgage involves paying interest on the £100,000 debt each year. If interest rates are 10% p.a., this amounts to £10,000 p.a. So the total annual payment is £16,380 + £10,000 = £26,380.

The main alternative to an endowment mortgage is a repayment mortgage. Repayment mortgages involve amortising the debt (gradually paying it off). A repayment mortgage is illustrated in Table 10.1.

The repayment mortgage entails a constant payment of £26,380 each year, which is identical to the annual sum paid in the above case of an endowment mortgage. This identity of payments arises because the assumed annual return on the endowment fund equals the assumed rate of interest.

However endowment funds are normally largely invested in equities (shares). Over long periods, such as the typical term of a mortgage, equity investments have provided average returns that exceed interest rates. This excess return means that the endowment fund not only pays off the

Table 10.1 *Mortgage repayment schedule on a £100,000 five-year debt with interest fixed at 10% p.a.*

Year	Interest	Repayment	Remaining debt
1	£10,000	£16,380	£83,620
2	£8,362	£18,018	£65,602
3	£6,561	£19,819	£45,783
4	£4,579	£21,801	£23,981
5	£2,399	£23,981	£0

mortgage but also produces a lump sum for the policyholder. Alternatively the prospective excess return allows for reduced payments into the endowment fund, but with the risk that equity returns turn out to be less than anticipated so that there is insufficient to pay off the mortgage. In the event of the policyholder dying before the policy matures, the insurance component of the endowment policy will provide a sum of money to pay off the mortgage debt.

Endowment policies are portable, which means that an endowment policy taken out to repay the mortgage associated with the purchase of one property can be transferred to a new mortgage taken out for the purchase of another property. This is usually much better than terminating a policy and starting another. This is partly because the charges of the endowment policy (particularly the charges that pay commission to the financial adviser who sold the policy) tend to be concentrated in the first year or two of the policy, with the effect that little or nothing is returned to the investor if the policy is terminated in the early years. It can be many years before investment returns cover these early costs. Not only do early costs impair the surrender value of an endowment policy, but also the insurance company may not pay the true value of the policy upon surrender. It may be better to sell a policy than surrender it. Some institutional investors will buy second-hand endowment policies. The institution pays less than the full value of the policy, but still pays more than could be obtained by surrendering the policy. Indeed there are mutual funds that invest in portfolios of second-hand endowment policies.

FRIENDLY SOCIETY POLICIES

Friendly society policies are a form of endowment policy. They are savings schemes with a small amount of life assurance attached. They differ from other endowment policies in that the fund is exempt from income and capital gains taxes. At the time of writing contributions are limited to £25 per month (£300 per year). The tax concessions are dependent upon a policy running for at least ten years.

INVESTMENT BONDS

Investment bonds, alternatively known as single premium bonds, are investment products with a nominal amount of life assurance cover. Typically life cover is 1% of the value of the original investment. If the investor dies the life assurance company would pay the beneficiaries either 101%

of the original investment, or the current value of the investment, whichever is the greater. Investment bonds may be unit-linked or with-profits.

An investor in a unit-linked bond normally has a choice of funds. These include managed, general, fixed interest, and specialist funds. Managed funds are invested in a spread of shares, bonds, property, and deposits. General funds invest in a diversified portfolio of shares, which may or may not include shares in foreign companies. General funds might aim to meet the investment objective of capital growth, or high income, or a balance of the two. General funds can take the form of index tracker funds that seek to parallel the performance of a stock index such as the FTSE All-Share Index. Fixed interest funds invest primarily in bonds, often with a high proportion of government bonds. Some insurance companies offer guaranteed equity bonds that are based on a stock market but which use options to guarantee that the value of the fund will not fall below a minimum level.

Specialist funds can have various types of specialisation. The specialisation might be geographic, for example focusing on Europe, North America, or Japan. There may be an industry focus, such as high technology or financials. The specialisation could be related to firm size or situation, for example smaller company or recovery funds.

Other funds often made available to investors include property, money market, and with-profits funds. Property funds invest in industrial and commercial property. Money market funds invest in bank deposits and other money market instruments such as Treasury bills and commercial paper. With-profits funds are often unitised; investors acquire units in a with-profits fund.

Specialist funds are the most risky, particularly since they involve non-systematic (specific) risk as well as systematic (market) risk. General equity funds are next in order of riskiness, although they avoid much of the non-systematic risk if they are well diversified. Managed funds and with-profits funds are less risky than pure equity funds since they mix shares with less risky assets such as bonds and deposits. Money market funds are the least risky in the sense of uncertainty of capital value. Historically the average annual returns are related to the proportion of shares in the fund; the higher this proportion, the higher the returns over the long term.

Investment bonds usually allow the bondholder to switch between investment funds at any time. However there may be a charge for a switch. Investment bonds are often segmented into a number of separate policies, perhaps five or ten. The policies within the bond are usually identical. An advantage of the segmentation is that each policy can be surrendered (i.e. encashed) at a different point in time.

One disadvantage of investment bonds relative to unit trusts, investment trusts, and OEICs arises from the tax treatment of capital gains. In the cases of unit trusts, investment trusts, and OEICs a capital gains tax liability arises only if the individual investor has gains above the exemption limit (and only when the investment is sold). In contrast investment bonds pay tax on capital gains within the fund with the effect that investors suffer the effects of tax on capital gains irrespective of whether they, as individuals, fall below or above the threshold at which capital gains tax becomes payable. Since the taxation of investment bonds treats capital gains as income, the taxation occurs as gains are realised. Although it is the fund rather than the investor that is taxed, the effect is the same from the perspective of the investor.

Another relative disadvantage of investment bonds is that that they tend to have relatively high initial charges (it is not unusual for as much of 7% of the initial investment to be lost in payment of up-front charges). Part of the high initial charge is used to pay relatively generous commission

TABLE 10.2

Fund	Unit trust	Investment bond
Fidelity Special Situations	£73,886	£51,024
Framlington Equity Income	£38,244	£29,803
Henderson Preference and Bond	£39,526	£29,787
Invesco Perpetual High Income	£81,407	£54,940

to the financial adviser; in consequence financial advisers could recommend investment bonds even though they may not be the most suitable investment for their clients.

The *Financial Times* on 16 July 2005 (Knight 2005, based on figures provided by Hargreaves Lansdown) compared direct investment in unit trusts with investment in the same funds within a single premium investment bond (provided by Skandia). Table 10.2 shows the results of £10,000 invested in a unit trust, and in an investment bond, over a period of 15 years.

Many investment bonds require the investment to be held for a minimum period such as ten years; this contrasts with unit trusts and OEICs, which can be sold back to the managers at any time. It also contrasts with investment trusts, which can be sold on the stock market at any time.

An attraction for higher-rate taxpayers who want current income is the facility of top slicing. It is possible to take 5% of the initial investment as tax-free income each year, for up to twenty years (in effect this amounts to a return of the sum invested). No tax is payable until the investment bond matures, and the tax on the gains from the bond are then taxed at the taxpayer's marginal rate of tax in the year of maturity. This has advantages for a higher-rate taxpayer who will have retired by the time the bond matures. If the marginal rate of tax after retirement is the basic rate, the whole of the gains from the bond over its entire life could be taxed at the basic rate. The total gain, from an investment bond held for twenty years, would be divided by twenty and the resulting sum added to the investor's total income at maturity. If the gains (divided by twenty), when added to the person's income at maturity, fail to take the total income into the higher-rate tax band there will be no higher-rate tax payable.

As an example, consider an investor who has a pension of £25,000 and a maturing investment bond. If the gains on the bond over twenty years amount to £200,000, the sum of £200,000/20 = £10,000 is added to the £25,000 pension in order to ascertain tax liability. If the resulting sum of £25,000 + £10,000 = £35,000 falls below the higher-rate tax threshold, basic rate tax is applied to the whole £200,000. Since the Inland Revenue deems basic rate tax to have been paid, no tax liability arises. The result is that the higher-rate taxpayer has taken an income from the investment bond over twenty years, and has received a maturity value, without having incurred a higher-rate tax liability on the returns from the investment bond. This advantage of top slicing needs to be weighed against the disadvantage of incurring capital gains tax paid by the fund in which the bond is invested. If the investor normally pays capital gains tax, this disadvantage does not apply. Investment bonds are likely to be useful for higher-rate taxpayers, who have ongoing capital gains tax liabilities and who anticipate a substantial fall in income at retirement. (They can also have advantages for inheritance tax planning when held in trust.)

Maximum investment plans (MIPs) are similar to investment bonds, but entail the investment of regular monthly or annual premiums. They run for specified periods, frequently ten years. At the end of the period the investor can either cash in the bond or leave it to accumulate without necessarily investing any more money in it.

WITH-PROFITS FUNDS

Like unit trusts and investment trusts, with-profits funds offer the means of pooling the investments of thousands of small investors into a large fund that can hold a diversified portfolio of investments without incurring disproportionate transaction costs. Compared with unit and investment trusts, with-profits funds provide a reduced risk means of participating in stock market investment. Such a fund might be the basis of a pension plan, investment bond, or an endowment policy. If an investor puts a lump sum into a with-profits investment bond, for example, the value of that investment cannot fall below its initial value irrespective of what happens in stock markets. Furthermore the scheme provider (typically an insurance company) will add a sum of money to the plan holder's personal fund each year. This sum is known as an annual or reversionary bonus and once added cannot be taken away. The money value of the investor's personal fund can only grow; it cannot fall. The scheme provider will normally add a further bonus, known as the terminal bonus, on the date that the investor's investment matures.

The term 'with-profits' arises from the participation in the profits (or losses) of other parts of the insurance company's business. 'With-profits' policyholders share in the profits and losses of the company's other lines of business, such as term assurance and annuities. In the case of a proprietary insurance company (one that has shareholders), profits from the other lines of business are shared between 'with-profits' policyholders and shareholders. A mutual insurance company is owned by its 'with-profits' policyholders, who receive all the profits (and bear all the losses).

In the case of a with-profits endowment policy the insurance company, in exchange for a commitment by the policyholder to pay monthly premiums over an agreed number of years, guarantees the payment of a lump sum at the end of the period. The reversionary (annual) bonuses are added to that guaranteed lump sum. For example a reversionary bonus of 5% increases a guaranteed lump sum of £10,000 to £10,500. In the case of an endowment policy, reversionary bonuses are dependent upon the policy being held for the full term agreed when starting the policy. A terminal bonus will be added on the maturity date of the endowment policy. Both reversionary and terminal bonuses are subject to change from year to year.

So a with-profits investment provides a high degree of security. It further reduces risk through the smoothing of investment returns over time. The insurance company (or other provider) will manage a fund that will typically consist of shares, bonds, property, and bank deposits (and other money market investments). Investments into a with-profits scheme will go into this fund and the returns on the fund will pay for the bonuses. The provider of the with-profits scheme will put some of these returns into a reserve in years in which the fund performs particularly well and will take money out of the reserve in order to pay bonuses in years that show relatively poor investment performance. Good and bad years are averaged out so that the private investor in the with-profits scheme is protected against the extremes of stock market fluctuations.

The operation of a with-profits scheme can be illustrated by means of Table 10.3. It shows the returns from £1,000 invested in 1989.

TABLE 10.3

	Investment		Allocated		Guaranteed	
	% Return	Cumulative total	% Added	Cumulative total	% Added	Cumulative total
1989	24.1	1,241	10.0	1,100	8.0	1,080
1990	−8.3	1,138	3.0	1,133	2.0	1,101
1991	13.5	1,292	9.0	1,235	6.0	1,167
1992	17.1	1,512	12.0	1,383	8.0	1,260
1993	28.8	1,948	21.0	1,673	14.0	1,436
1994	−4.2	1,866	4.0	1,740	3.0	1,479
1995	16.6	2,176	12.0	1,949	9.0	1,612
1996	10.7	2,409	10.0	2,144	8.0	1,741
1997	17.2	2,823	13.0	2,423	9.0	1,898
1998	13.3	3,198	12.0	2,714	9.0	2,069

In Table 10.3 the second column shows the percentage returns on the with-profits fund net of charges. The third column indicates the value of the individual's investment on the basis of having a proportionate share of the assets of the fund (proportionate to the initial investment); this is sometimes referred to as the 'asset share'. The fourth column shows the percentage addition to the fund value allocated to the individual investor. This is often referred to as the smoothed allocation since it reflects the principle of reallocating investment returns between time periods. For example in 1993 only 21% of the 28.8% return was allocated to investors whereas in the following year the allocation was 8.2% higher than the returns on the fund.

This is not the only possible means of smoothing. Another approach is revealed by the following abstract.

HOW WE APPLY SMOOTHING

We work out the value of the unsmoothed asset shares underlying three sample plans which are identical to yours in all respects except that one will have started one year earlier than yours, and one two years earlier. We then take the average of these three values, which gives what we call the smoothed asset share value of the sample plan that started at the same time as yours.

(Tunbridge Wells Equitable 2006)

The fifth column shows the cumulative total of allocations made to the individual investor. The sixth column contains the percentage allocations that are guaranteed, and hence cannot be lost by the investor. These guaranteed returns correspond to the reversionary bonuses. They may be based on the present cumulative total of allocations, or on a projection of the cumulative total by the maturity date of the policy. The final column shows the cumulative guaranteed total which consists of the initial investment plus the sum of the annual reversionary bonuses. The values in this column constitute the lowest level that the investment could reach irrespective of what happens in stock markets.

At maturity of the pension or endowment plan (or at death if earlier) a terminal bonus is added to the guaranteed total. The terminal bonus is the difference between the total guaranteed and the total allocated. At maturity the investor receives the sum in the fifth column, made up of the guaranteed total (initial investment plus annual bonuses) and a terminal bonus. The difference between the sums in the third and fifth columns remains with the scheme provider as reserves. These reserves, sometimes known as orphan funds, are available for the payment of bonuses in future years in which investment returns are poor.

From the perspective of the scheme provider the value of the private individuals' policies constitutes a liability, whereas the underlying portfolio of investments is an asset. The surplus (or excess) is the amount by which the value of the investments held by the underlying fund exceeds the aggregate value of the liabilities (the total value of all the individual with-profits policies). Companies providing the schemes are required to maintain a surplus as reserves, and this surplus must be at least equal to a specified minimum value. This minimum surplus used to be known as the solvency margin, but since 2004 the minimum amount of solvency capital that must be shown in the balance sheet has been known as the 'risk capital margin'.

The surplus remaining above the required minimum solvency margin (risk capital margin) will be divided between the current payment of bonuses to the scheme members, the reserves (available for bonus payments in future years), and dividends for shareholders (this is not applicable if the company is a mutual and hence owned by its with-profits policyholders – a mutual has no shareholders).

It is sometimes argued that the annual (reversionary) bonuses reflect the current income on investments (dividends, interest, etc.) whilst the terminal bonuses arise from capital gains on the investments. This cannot be precisely true since in many years annual bonus rates deviate substantially from the rates of income yield on investments. Nevertheless there may be a kernel of truth in the idea, although it seems likely that some part of expected capital gain would be incorporated into the annual bonus if the annual bonus were based on prospective long-term returns. In the case of the Prudential (2006): 'Rates of regular bonus are determined for each type of policy primarily by targeting them at a prudent proportion of the long-term expected future investment return on the underlying assets.' (Here the annual or reversionary bonus is called the regular bonus.)

One question concerns the cost of the risk reduction provided by the guaranteed sums. Some argue that the risk reduction is more apparent than real. Instead of fluctuations in the current value of the policy, there is uncertainty as to the size of the terminal bonus. However with profits policies do provide a form of disaster insurance; in the event of an extreme collapse of share prices the policyholder is protected. It is likely that the provider covers its guarantees to policyholders by investing a sufficient proportion of the fund in low risk securities such as government bonds, Treasury bills, and high-grade bank deposits. A cost of the risk reduction is the lowering of prospective investment returns arising from investment in low risk (and hence low return) assets.

Some providers of with-profits policies seek further risk reduction, as an individual's policy approaches maturity, by switching the mix of investments allocated to the particular policyholder. A gradual switch from higher risk to lower risk investments aims at ensuring increasing stability of the asset share relating to that policy, and seeks to ensure that the fund value does not fall below the sum required to meet the guaranteed bonuses.

Unitised with-profits policies were introduced in response to the emergence of unit-linked policies based on unit trusts. Unitised with-profits policies were introduced in order to facilitate switches with other units within unit-linked policies. Investors could now sell units in one type of fund in order to buy units in another. In some cases the value of the with-profits units will never fall (so long as the policy is not terminated before the maturity date). In other cases the protection against a fall only applies towards the end of the policy term. The cost of the protection may be covered by the type of smoothing illustrated by Table 10.3, or by means of a more mechanical procedure such as deducting 0.5% from the annual return on units. The final return to the investor will be the value of the units plus any terminal bonus. Whether the policy is conventional or unitised, the maturity value should be similar. As with conventional with-profits policies, termination of a unitised with-profits policy before its maturity date could involve a reduction in value in the form of an exit penalty or 'market value adjustment' (which may also be applied in the event of switching from with-profits units to units in other funds).

Companies justify 'market value adjustments' by pointing out that when policyholders prematurely terminate their policies at a time of low stock market prices, the declared value of holdings may be greater than the true values. If the declared values were paid, the fund – and hence other investors – would lose. The market value adjustment is intended to ensure that the money paid to those investors who prematurely terminate reflects the true value of their investments as measured by the 'asset share'. The asset share represents the policyholder's fair share of the fund taking account of premiums paid, returns on the fund, deductions for fund charges and expenses, and profits (or losses) from other lines of business. If the declared values of holdings exceed asset shares, bonuses need to be reduced in order to remove the discrepancy.

The Significance of Financial Strength

Financial strength refers to the amount of money that a life office has in its financial reserve. It is a measure of a life company's ability to meet its liabilities and provides an indication of how likely the company is to pay future bonuses. A company with large reserves has more investment freedom, allowing greater exposure to equities (more emphasis on shares). Large reserves also allow bonus rates to be maintained when markets fall.

Only those with sufficient financial strength can invest in the relatively volatile asset classes of equities and property and continue to deliver consistent returns. Weaker companies are forced to maintain a higher proportion of their investments in bonds and deposits. Bonds and deposits tend to offer less growth potential than equities.

One way of determining a company's financial strength is to look at its 'free asset ratio'. This is a measure of the free assets that a company holds expressed as a percentage of total assets. Free assets are assets remaining after liabilities have been accounted for. However the information provided by the free asset ratio is not unambiguous; free assets may be large because the company tends to be mean with its bonus payments.

Since 2004, in order to improve the transparency of with-profits funds, the Financial Services Authority has required fund providers to use a 'realistic balance sheet' measure of financial strength. This is intended to replace the 'free asset ratio', which failed to take account of all balance sheet risks. This new measure is based on a more realistic calculation of free assets (assets that are genuinely in excess of all current and potential future liabilities, allowing for all possible eventualities). The new measure is sometimes referred to as 'excess realistic assets'.

Under the new system the minimum amount of solvency capital that must be shown in the balance sheet is known as the 'risk capital margin'. The size of the 'risk capital margin' depends on the level of investment risk; so a fund provider with a high proportion of the fund in shares (equity) will have a higher 'risk capital margin' than one invested mainly in bonds. The 'risk capital margin' must be put aside out of what would otherwise be free assets.

The free assets, or reserves, of a with-profits fund are often called the inherited estate. Typically asset shares are not credited with any part of the investment return earned on the inherited estate. However the inherited estate would be used to provide resources for smoothing and the provision of guarantees (Prudential 2006). Inherited estates are alternatively known as orphan estates, or orphan funds. Not all of the money in such estates may be required for meeting risk capital margins, for paying bonuses to policyholders, or for smoothing. Such estates could be accumulated over many decades and would be enhanced by the fact that some policyholders fail to claim the value of their policies at maturity (sometimes because of death, or possibly because the policy is forgotten). Inherited estates may arise partly through past bonus payments being too low. Companies (typically life assurance companies) may distribute orphan funds amongst current policyholders and shareholders but approval from the Financial Services Authority is required for such a move. Previous policyholders (who may have received low bonuses) would have no rights to a share of such a distribution. So existing policyholders would receive money that was accumulated as a result of the with-profits policies of past policyholders.

Criticisms

One criticism made of with-profits policies is that the term 'with profits' is in reality a misnomer. Originally this term was used on the grounds that with-profits policyholders shared in the profits made from the company's other operations (non with-profits business). In reality with-profits funds typically do not receive income from sources other than the with-profits fund itself.

Another criticism sometimes made is that most companies give policyholders little information. Most companies give no information about investment returns, asset shares, or the smoothing. It has been suggested that this lack of information allows companies to manipulate payouts so that transfer values (the sums transferred when switching to other providers) are reduced in order to boost maturity values (which are the values used in sales and marketing). It may also be possible that transfer values are trimmed for the purpose of replenishing reserves.

If a policyholder terminates a policy before maturity a transfer value is payable. This transfer value should equal the cumulative value of the allocated returns (inclusive of the initial investment). If this value exceeds the asset share (the accumulated assets resulting from the initial investment plus investment returns) then the transfer value should equal the asset share. The use of the asset share rather than the cumulative smoothed allocation is referred to as a 'market value adjustment'.

Many observers suspect that, under the cover of incomplete information, some companies set transfer values below both the asset share and the smoothed allocation. The surplus might be used to enhance maturity values. Potential new clients may be made aware of maturity values but not experienced transfer values. It is possible for companies to boost their sales of new policies by boosting maturity values at the expense of transfer values.

CONCLUSION

Life assurance provides a lump sum, or an income, for dependants in the event of the death of the insured person. It is possible to take out life assurance on its own, or in combination with an investment. Whole-of-life policies, endowment policies, and investment bonds combine life assurance with investments. These are collective investment schemes that have much in common with mutual funds such as unit trusts. In particular they provide means of investing in a diversified portfolio of assets such as shares, bonds, and property.

A disadvantage of life assurance linked investments is that in the UK they are taxed unfavourably relative to other collective investments (such as unit trusts, OEICs, investment trusts, and pension funds). In addition to the tax disadvantages, they tend to be subject to higher charges than other collective investments. It was shown in Chapter 9 on mutual funds how taxation and charges could severely reduce investment values, especially when investments are long term. These disadvantages render life assurance linked investments unsuitable for most individuals, when compared to the alternatives. However they continue to be recommended by many financial advisers, presumably because they provide relatively high commission payments for the advisers.

With-profits funds have the feature that the sum invested, plus subsequent annual bonuses, cannot be lost. This protection against loss should have appeal for loss-averse investors. Prospect theory (see Chapter 2 on personal investment decisions, and Chapter 24 on noise trading and behavioural finance) indicates that the pain of a loss is greater than the pleasure from a gain of the same size. This renders people fearful of losses. In consequence the protection against loss, provided by with-profits funds, should appeal to many people.

Another collective investment that provides protection against loss is a guaranteed equity bond (see Chapter 34 on structured products). One difference between these types of fund is that with-profits funds invest in a wide range of assets (including shares, bonds, property, and cash) whereas guaranteed equity bonds are normally based solely on shares. This difference should render the returns on with-profits funds less volatile, but at the expense of a lower long-run return.

Another difference lies in the means of providing the protection against losses. In the case of with-profits funds, a part of the returns from investments is allocated to a reserve. Money is taken from the reserve and allocated to investors in the event of a fall in asset prices. In the case of guaranteed equity funds, the protection is provided by the purchase of options by the fund managers (see Chapters 31 and 34 on stock options and structured products, respectively). In both cases the protection comes at a cost to the investor, so that the reduced risk is accompanied by lower expected returns.

Chapter 11

Pensions

OBJECTIVE

The objective of this chapter is to provide knowledge of:

1. Types of pension schemes and pension funds.
2. Annuities.
3. The life-cycle analysis of pension funding.

In most developed countries the pension system has three components. First, there is a state pension that aims to provide a basic retirement income for everyone. State pensions are financed from current tax receipts. Pensions financed from current revenues are referred to as pay-as-you-go pensions. In the UK there is a basic state pension plus an earnings-related state pension known as the state second pension. In the UK there is a pensions tax credit whose function is to guarantee a minimum level of income, which exceeds the basic state pension. The pensions tax credit adds to the basic state pension on a means-tested basis. If a retiree has pension rights in addition to the basic state pension (e.g. state second pension, occupational pension, private pension), the pensions tax credit is reduced by 40p for every pound of additional pension. If the additional pension exceeds a particular level, no pensions tax credit is payable. There is concern that the pensions tax credit may deter people from saving for a pension since the private pension receipts would reduce entitlement to the pensions tax credit. Unlike private sector pensions, state pensions are backed by the ability of the government to tax and borrow (this guarantee extends to other state-funded pensions such as those of civil servants, the armed forces, and teachers).

Second, there are pensions arranged by employers. Such pensions are usually called occupational pensions. Occupational pensions may be operated on a pay-as-you-go basis or may be funded. Funded schemes entail the accumulation of investments with which to finance the pensions. Third, there may be a layer of pension financed on a voluntary basis. UK examples would be additional voluntary contributions (AVCs), personal pension plans, and stakeholder pensions. Employees can supplement their occupational pensions by paying into an AVC fund, a personal pension plan, or a stakeholder pension. So an employee can retire with a state pension, plus an occupational pension, plus a supplementary pension. For many people either the occupational pension or the supplementary pension is absent, and frequently both are absent. Many people do not have an occupational pension available, in which case the non-state part of the pension provision is a personal pension plan or a stakeholder pension.

In many countries, pension funds are the dominant form of institutional investment. These funds are built up during the working life of the investor and then used to finance an income during retirement. They may be operated by the company for which the person works. The company invests over time to build up a fund that is used to provide a retirement income for its employees. Alternatively the employees invest in a fund of their choosing with a view to building up a sum of money that can be used to buy an annuity (guaranteed stream of income) at retirement. The most important assets within the portfolios of pension funds tend to be stock market investments in the form of shares and bonds. However other assets are frequently held, particularly deposits and property. Some funds have even been known to hold alternative investments such as works of art.

The importance of funded pensions varies considerably between countries. For example IFSL (International Financial Services, London) estimated that in 2004 the UK accounted for $1,464 billion in pension funds whereas Germany had just $268 billion and France $164 billion. However the importance of pension funds in Germany and France seemed to be increasing rapidly since pension funds in both had more than doubled in the previous three years (the 2001 figures being $125 billion for Germany and $65 billion for France).

It seems likely that many people see the different forms of pension as substitutes for each other. For example the provision of an occupational pension by an employer may make it less likely that people personally save for their retirements. There is evidence that there is perceived substitutability between state pensions and personal provision. Attanasio and Rohwedder (2004) investigated the behaviour of pension investors in the UK. They found a negative relationship between state pension provision and private retirement saving. They found that the extent of perceived substitutability increases with age, up to the point where each additional £1 of state pension provision reduces personal provision by £0.75. Fraser *et al.* (2000) found that the provision of state pensions in the United States affected the form of personal pension saving. State pensions increased the proportion of personal pension savings held in equity-related investments. This is presumably because state pensions are seen as low risk and hence allow the acceptance of high risk investments such as equities (shares) in personal pension schemes.

EXHIBIT 11.1 THE FRENCH STATE PENSIONS RESERVE FUND

Since 2004 the French government has been investing in a portfolio whose function is to support the state pension scheme in future years.

It was estimated that by 2040 state pensions would be costing 2.8% of national income.

It has been estimated that, if the French government contributes the legal minimum amount each year until 2020, the fund would meet 22% of the cost of the state pension scheme.

In 2007 the fund comprised 26% in bonds, 62% in equities (shares), and 12% in cash.

The fund is largely financed from taxation and the sale of state-owned assets (such as privatisations and the sale of licences).

215

> The fund is intended to provide a better distribution between generations. The fund aims to avoid passing an unacceptably high proportion of the pensions burden on to future generations. By financing the fund the generation, which will soon retire, is partially financing its own prospective pension needs. Otherwise the full cost would be borne by future generations.
>
> *Source: Newlands (2007).*

TYPES OF PENSION SCHEMES

Pension schemes can be divided into defined-benefit and defined-contribution schemes. Defined-benefit schemes are virtually always pensions provided by employers for their employees. They stipulate a particular level of income in retirement, normally based on final salary and length of service. Defined-contribution pension schemes do not involve a prescribed income in retirement, instead they prescribe levels of contribution to the fund prior to retirement. The retirement income obtained through a defined-contribution scheme depends upon the growth rate of the fund and the annuity rates available at the time of retirement. In the UK both employer and employee contributions to pension schemes are tax-deductible. However the pension is taxable.

Pensions may be personal or occupational. Personal pensions are arranged by individuals in order to provide incomes for their retirement. Occupational pensions are arranged by their employers. Occupational pensions may be final salary or money purchase. Occupational schemes will either involve contributions to the pension fund by the employer only (non-contributory schemes), or by both employer and employee.

Final-salary pension schemes link the size of the pension income to the employee's salary at retirement, and to the number of years worked for the employer. Such schemes are defined-benefit schemes. The pension benefits are specified, in part by Inland Revenue rules, rather than the means of financing them being specified. For example a pension may be set at 1/80th of final salary for every year worked for the employer (so 40 years service provides a pension of $40 \times 1/80 = 40/80$th, i.e. $1/2$, of final salary). Members of defined-benefit occupational pension schemes usually have to wait until the 'normal retirement age' of the scheme (typically either 60 or 65) before drawing the pension. If a member wishes to draw a pension earlier, there would usually be an actuarial reduction of around 5% per year of early retirement. For example retirement at 55, when the normal retirement age is 60, would entail a reduction in the annual pension of about 25%.

In the case of defined-benefit pensions there is a difference between the pension plan and the pension fund. The plan is a contractual obligation on the part of the employer to provide specified pension benefits. The pension fund is a pool of investments, which is intended to finance the pension payments stipulated by the pension plan. It is not unusual for the value of the investments in the pension fund to fall short of the present value of the payments promised by the pension plan; in other words pension plans are often underfunded.

Although there are actuarial reductions for retirement before the normal retirement age, there are not usually actuarial enhancements for retirement after the normal retirement age. Arguably this asymmetry is an anomaly in occupational pension schemes. If the annual payment is reduced when the expected number of years of payment rises, the annual payment should be increased when the expected number of years of payment is reduced. It is notable that in the UK there are enhancements to the basic state pension if the pension claim is deferred.

An alternative form of defined-benefit scheme is the CARE scheme (career average revalued earnings). In the case of CARE schemes the link is not with final-salary, but with the employee's average salary during their career with the employer. Each year's salary is revalued in line with inflation up to the retirement date when assessing the size of the pension. Those who enjoy rapid promotion will gain more from a final-salary scheme than from an average salary scheme. However some employees may find that their earnings peak at the beginning, or in the middle, of their careers rather than at the end. Those employees may gain from an average salary scheme. When average earnings are revalued in line with price inflation, rather than wage inflation, average salary schemes will tend to provide less than final-salary schemes if wage inflation exceeds price inflation (as it normally does).

Money-purchase schemes entail payments into a pension fund. At retirement the pension fund is usually used to buy an annuity. Taking money out of a pension fund and using it to buy an annuity is known as 'vesting'. A retirement annuity is an income guaranteed for the life of the recipient. The retirement income depends upon the performance of the pension fund up to the retirement date, and upon the annuity rates available at the retirement date. Money-purchase schemes are also known as defined-contribution schemes since the size of the contributions to the scheme are prescribed by rules. There is no upper limit to the level of income that a defined-contribution scheme can provide at retirement (whereas UK Inland Revenue rules put an upper limit on the pension income from a defined-benefit scheme).

Personal pensions are always of the money-purchase type. Personal pension plans and stakeholder pensions are variants of personal pensions. Stakeholder pensions are distinguished by relatively low charges and liberal conditions. Not only can working people who do not have an occupational pension use stakeholder pensions, but also people without employment incomes and people who are members of occupational schemes can use stakeholder pensions. They are restricted to people whose incomes fall below a specified level. Employers may use stakeholder pensions for their employees. Employers could also use group personal pensions, which are effectively groups of individual personal pension plans. Additional voluntary contributions (AVCs) are a form of personal pension that aims to top up occupational schemes. They may be contributions into a pension fund arranged by the employer, or into an independently operated fund in which case they are known as free-standing additional voluntary contributions (FSAVCs).

Most of the money in pension funds is invested in stock markets. In consequence there is a high degree of uncertainty concerning the future value of a pension fund. In the case of money-purchase schemes, it is the recipient of the pension who bears this risk. The recipient also bears the risk that annuity rates, and hence the retirement income that can be purchased, will be low at retirement. Since annuities are based on government bonds (gilts), this risk relates to the possibility that rates of yield on government bonds will be low at the time of retirement.

In the case of final-salary schemes, the employer bears the risks. A combination of poor investment performance, low bond yields, and high rates of salary growth can result in pension funds being insufficient to meet the pension commitments. In such a case the employer must replenish the pension fund out of that employer's business revenues.

In the UK up to 25% of a pension fund can be taken as a tax-free lump sum rather than being used to buy an annuity. In the case of money-purchase (defined-contribution) schemes, the tax-free lump sum can be taken at a different time than the annuity purchase. In the case of final-salary schemes there may also be a choice of taking part of the pension rights as a tax-free lump sum (this is known as commutation). However this may not be on favourable terms. The lump sum available is often less than the value of the income that is given up.

The Teachers' Pension Scheme in the UK may be used as an example. In this case the pensioner has no choice, part of the pension rights must be taken as a lump sum. The lump sum is three times the annual pension and is regarded as constituting 20% of the total pension rights. The Teachers' Pension Scheme pays 1/80 of final salary for each year of full-time employment. So for a teacher with 40 years of service the annual pension is 50% (40/80) of final salary. The lump sum is considered to be equivalent to a further 12.5%. In other words the lump sum is regarded as equivalent to 25% of the annual pension. However at the annuity rates available at the time of writing such a lump sum would buy an annuity of about 15% of the annual pension. (The annuity rate is the annual income purchased as a percentage of the sum paid for it.) For the lump sum to be equivalent to 25% of the annual pension, the lump sum should be about five times the annual pension.

EXHIBIT 11.2   TEACHERS' PENSION SCHEME (ENGLAND AND WALES)

The teachers' pension scheme in which the lump sum is compulsory is the scheme applicable to teachers in service before 31 December 2006. There is a new scheme for teachers entering service from 1 January 2007 onwards.

Old scheme (for teachers in post by 31 December 2006)

The normal pension age is 60. Pension of 1/80th of final salary for each year served, plus lump sum of three times annual pension. The pensions are index-linked to the Retail Prices Index (RPI).

New scheme (for teachers joining from 1 January 2007)

The normal pension age is 65. The pension is 1/60th of final salary for each year served. Option of taking up to 25% as a lump sum on the basis of the lump sum being twelve times the annual pension foregone. Pensions index-linked to the RPI.

To see the effect of taking 25% of the pension rights as a lump sum consider a teacher with 40 years service retiring with a final salary of £36,000. The pension without taking the lump sum would be:

(£36,000/60) × 40 = £24,000 p.a.

The pension when the lump sum is taken would be:

£24,000 × 0.75 = £18,000 p.a.

And the lump sum would be:

(£24,000 − £18,000) × 12 = £6,000 × 12 = £72,000

Under the old scheme a teacher retiring after 40 years service with a final salary of £36,000 would receive a pension of:

(£36,000/80) × 40 = £18,000 p.a.

And a lump sum of £18,000 × 3 = £54,000

In the case of the UK Teachers' Pension Scheme employees have no choice; they must take the lump-sum component. In most private sector final-salary pension schemes there is a choice. The employee should look carefully at whether the lump sum is a true equivalent of the pension income foregone (the relationship between the pension income foregone and the lump sum is often called the commutation factor). Typically the maximum lump sum after 40 years service is 1.5 times final salary. At the time of writing annuity rates would generate an income from such a lump sum that is well short of the pension income given up.

It might be noted that commutation of part of the pension effectively turns a 1/60th scheme (which is typical of UK private sector occupational pension schemes) into a 1/80th scheme. Someone taking a full pension after 40 years in a 1/60th scheme receives 40/60th of final salary as annual pension. Commutation of 25% into a lump sum reduces this to 30/60th, which is the same as 40/80th. So commutation turns a 40/60 pension into a 40/80 pension plus a lump sum of 1.5 times final salary (three times annual pension). This is the same as public sector pensions such as the Teachers' Pension Scheme. However public sector pensions are normally fully indexed to inflation whereas private sector final-salary schemes are not compelled to match price increases above 2.5% p.a.

OCCUPATIONAL PENSION SCHEMES IN THE UK

Since the early 1900s large UK companies have operated staff pension schemes, which are managed by the companies themselves rather than by outside organisations such as insurance companies. They are known as 'self-administered' pension schemes. They are based on the concept of the legal trust, which is a legal entity that separates the control of assets from the right to benefit from them. A board of trustees administers the pension scheme on behalf of the beneficiaries. Investments are put into a ring-fenced fund separated from the employer's finances. An alternative form of occupational pension arrangement, used by many employers, is the insurance company-administered group pension scheme. Insurance company group schemes have been attractive to small and medium-sized firms. The attraction for such firms arises from the reduced risks, and administration costs, made possible by the pooling of funds (the insurance company operates a fund in which a number of firms can invest their pension payments).

There are examples of multi-employer pension schemes where a group of employers jointly operate a scheme. The Universities Superannuation Scheme is an example, which covers UK universities (those designated as universities before 1992; post-1992 universities are covered by the Teachers' Pension Scheme which is not a funded scheme). Another UK example of a multi-employer pension scheme is the Building and Civil Engineers' Benefits Scheme, which covers about 7,000 employers and over 200,000 employees.

Investment managers within the company that operates the scheme may manage the investments in a 'self-administered' pension fund, but this is rare. Frequently the investment management is put into the hands of financial institutions. Alternatively the investments can be put into tax-exempt unit trusts managed by financial institutions; often insurance companies.

Pension scheme trustees are often not investment specialists. They tend to engage pension fund consultants for assistance with the selection and monitoring of institutions that undertake investment management. The companies that operate as pension fund consultants are often firms of actuaries. They draw up shortlists of investment management organisations, from which the trustees choose.

If the trustees operate on a 'balanced' basis they assign the asset allocation decision to the appointed investment manager. The asset allocation decision relates to the allocation of funds between asset classes, where asset classes are categories such as UK shares, overseas shares, bonds, property, and money market investments. If the trustees operate on a 'specialist' basis, they themselves decide on asset allocation (with advice from pension consultants) and then award mandates to investment management organisations. The management of each asset class may be awarded to a different investment manager (or managers). The specialist approach often uses a core-satellite style, which entails a core fund being managed as an index tracker (or group of index trackers) and the remainder being managed by a number of specialised active fund managers.

How a pension fund is managed is influenced by the age of the fund. Younger funds (with relatively young members) can take more risk and are likely to be tilted towards equities (shares) in order to enhance long-term growth prospects. Older funds (with older members) are likely to emphasise bonds in order to achieve security and predictability.

Personal pension funds are sometimes managed in a similar manner, but with regard to the age of the individual member rather than the average age of a group of members. This is referred to as lifestyling. The lifestyling strategy gradually switches the person's pension fund out of shares and property and into bonds and cash (money market investments) during the last few years before retirement. The intention is to protect the person from any sharp fall in share or property prices that might occur shortly before retirement. More sophisticated versions of the lifestyle approach not only relate the switch to period to retirement but also to market performance. In such versions the switch out of shares is greater following strong stock market performance than after weak performance. The better the performance the quicker the move from shares to bonds; the weaker the performance the slower the move. In this way there is less likelihood of switching from shares to bonds when share prices are particularly low. In some cases the automated asset allocation strategy may be based entirely on market performance rather than time to retirement.

Until 1999 most company pension schemes were defined-benefit schemes (pension based on salary and years of service). Since 1999 many companies have been closing defined-benefit schemes to new employees and replacing them with defined-contribution schemes (pension based on an accumulated pension fund). This has been partly due to the risks that defined-benefit schemes impose on employers. These risks take several forms. There is the risk of stock markets performing poorly with the effect that the employer has to make large additional contributions to the pension fund. Another major form of risk arises from changes in longevity; if pensioners live longer they draw more from the pension fund. Falling bond yields and unexpectedly fast salary increases can exacerbate these risks. The Pensions Act 1995 imposed requirements to top-up pension funds when they appear to be insufficient to meet projected liabilities (pension payments). In addition to the risks Accounting Standard FRS17, issued in 2001, meant that changes in pension fund assets would impact on company accounts. This potentially increases the problems, for companies, of falls in stock market prices.

In the UK the law requires the employer to guarantee the pensions of defined-benefit scheme members. Employers have the right to wind up a scheme. When a scheme is wound up, the pension fund is sold and the proceeds are used to buy annuities. The annuities immediately pay an income to retired members, and provide for future incomes for those who have not yet retired. However before June 2003 it was legal for an employer to wind up a pension scheme that was underfunded. Winding up a pension scheme in such a situation was a particular problem for active members (those who had not yet retired) since the law required that existing pensioners should get first priority in the allocation of funds. In June 2003 the UK government introduced emergency measures that prevented a solvent company choosing to abandon its pension commitments. A problem remained where an employer became insolvent when the pension fund was underfunded.

The Pensions Act 2004 established a Pension Protection Fund, which will pay pensions up to £25,000 p.a. in circumstances where an employer becomes insolvent when the pension scheme is underfunded. This is in addition to the Pension Compensation Scheme, which provides compensation when an employer steals assets from the pension fund. The Pension Protection Fund is funded by a levy on occupational pension schemes.

Before the Pensions Act 2004 the law required that a fund being wound up should be used to secure the full cost of pensions in payment (i.e. pensions to those who had already retired). Those still working received a share of what was left over. Someone recently retired received the whole pension whilst someone about to retire received a (perhaps substantially) reduced pension. The Pensions Act 2004 sought a fairer distribution of funds.

National Pension Savings Scheme

One of the recommendations of the UK Pensions Commission report of 2005 was the establishment of a National Pension Savings Scheme for workers not covered by occupational pension schemes. Workers would be automatically enrolled in the scheme although they would have the right to opt out. It appears that the UK government is likely to introduce the scheme (Department for Work and Pensions 2006).

The proposed National Pensions Savings Scheme deals with some of the behavioural finance issues concerning pension participation (see Chapter 2 on the psychology of personal investment decisions; and Ambachtsheer 2007). One issue is that of procrastination, which entails people persistently delaying participation in a scheme with the effect that membership occurs late in a person's working life if at all. Automatic enrolment deals with this problem.

Another behavioural problem is bad decision-making in relation to investment choices. Although there is evidence that many people choose a default option, many people make inappropriate investment decisions. For example myopic risk-aversion (concern with short-term risk when an investment is long term) could cause participants to choose 'low risk' bank or building society deposits, which yield very low returns. More balanced portfolios, inclusive of 'risky' stock market investments, offer much higher rates of return (see Chapter 3 on interest rates and money market investments for an indication of the prospective differences in rates of return). Other investors could move between investment alternatives in counterproductive ways. For example there is evidence that many people move between investment alternatives too frequently, thereby incurring high transaction costs. Furthermore individual investors have a tendency to buy when prices are high (after a period of rising prices) and sell when prices are low (following a period of falling prices). It appears likely that the scheme managers would make investment choices for participants, thereby preventing scheme members from making behavioural errors (Chapter 2 on the psychology of personal investment decisions details many of the thought patterns that lead to investment errors).

EXHIBIT 11.3   PENSIONS COMMISSION (TURNER COMMISSION)

KEY CONCLUSIONS OF THE FIRST REPORT – 'PENSIONS: CHALLENGES AND CHOICES' (2004)

Chapter 1: The demographic challenge and unavoidable choices

Life expectancy is increasing rapidly and will continue to do so. This is good news. But combined with a forecast low birth rate this will produce a near doubling in the percentage of the population aged 65 years and over between now and 2050, with further increase thereafter. The baby boom has delayed the effect of underlying long-term trends, but will now produce 30 years of very rapid increase in the dependency ratio. We must now make adjustments to public policy and/or individual behaviour which ideally should have been started in the last 20–30 years.

Faced with the increasing proportion of the population aged over 65, society and individuals must choose between four options. Either:

(i)   pensioners will become poorer relative to the rest of society; or

(ii) taxes/National Insurance contributions devoted to pensions must rise; or

(iii) savings must rise; or

(iv) average retirement ages must rise.

But the first option (poorer pensioners) appears unattractive; and there are significant barriers to solving the problem through any one of the other three options alone. Some mix of higher taxes/National Insurance contributions, higher savings, and later average retirement is required.

Source: Pensions Commission 2004.

PENSION TRANSFERS AND PENSION UNLOCKING

Employees with occupational pensions have three possibilities when leaving the employer. First, the pension could be left where it is. This is known as a preserved or deferred pension. The individual can then draw the pension at pension age. In the UK the law requires that the value of a deferred pension should rise in line with inflation (as measured by the Retail Prices Index) up to 2.5% p.a. This is known as limited price indexation.

A second possibility is to transfer the pension to another company scheme. This would be the scheme operated by the individual's new employer. A third alternative would be to take a transfer to a personal pension. A problem with these two possibilities is that the transfer value of the pension rights may not reflect their full value.

Pension unlocking involves the transfer of (normally deferred) defined-benefit pension rights to a personal pension. The individual then immediately draws the pension, inclusive of the cash lump sum. Pension unlocking has been criticised by regulators (the Financial Services Authority). Taking a pension early can substantially reduce the size of the annual pension. The reduction is even greater if the firm arranging the pension unlocking takes a large commission payment (as is usually the case).

PENSION FUNDS

One means of accumulating assets whilst enjoying tax breaks is to invest in a pension fund. In the UK, contributions to a pension fund are deductible against income tax. The investments in a pension fund accumulate free of capital gains tax. The income from bonds, cash, and property within a pension fund is free of tax. Dividends from shares within the fund do not attract any tax liability beyond the basic rate, which is assumed to have been paid (a firm's payment of corporation tax is deemed to preclude shareholders from the requirement to pay tax at the basic rate).

Before April 2006 there were limitations as to how much could be paid into a pension plan each financial year. In the case of personal pension plans the limit varied between 17.5% and 40% of earned income; the percentage rising with age. There was also an upper limit to the income that could be used as a basis for contributions into a personal pension fund (this upper limit was about 4.5 times average earnings). From April 2006 the whole of a person's earned income in a year was eligible for tax-deductible pension contributions (i.e. the entire income could be invested in a pension fund) but with annual and lifetime limits. The initial annual ceiling on tax-deductible contributions was £215,000. The initial lifetime limit was £1,500,000. If the pension fund at retirement were to exceed the lifetime ceiling, there would be tax penalties. It is intended that the limits will rise over time, for example the lifetime limit is due to rise to £1,800,000 by the 2010–11 tax year.

Before April 2006, the maximum that an employee could pay into an employer's pension scheme was 15% of income (salary plus bonus). If the employee paid less than 15%, that employee was able to make payments into an AVC (additional voluntary contribution) fund so long as the total of the two payments did not exceed 15% of income. The AVC payments could be paid into the pension fund arranged by the employer, or into a fund operated by another provider (such as an insurance company). Employees whose pensions were not payable from the proceeds of investment funds (for example civil servants, teachers, and armed forces personnel have their pensions paid from general taxation) could also pay into AVCs, so long as their total pension contributions were not more than 15% of income. AVC payments are tax deductible (they are subtracted from income when tax is assessed) and AVC funds attract the same tax advantages as other pension funds. As a result of the Pensions Act 2004, from April 2006 the sum of occupational pension contributions and AVC payments (and any other pension contributions) was subject to the same

Table 11.1 *Pension funds accumulated from £1,000 per year without management charges*

	3%	6%	9%
10	£11,464	£13,181	£15,193
20	£26,870	£36,785	£51,159
30	£47,575	£79,057	£136,305
40	£75,400	£154,758	£337,872

limits as all other pension schemes. From that date all UK private pension schemes became subject to the same rules.

Personal pensions are usually tax-advantaged wrappers in which institutional investments, such as unit trusts, are held. The pension plan is a legal and administrative arrangement for holding an investment fund, which is usually managed by an institutional investor such as an insurance company. In the UK there is an alternative to institutional investments. The alternative is the Self-Invested Personal Pension (SIPP). SIPPs allow policyholders to manage their own funds. SIPPs may contain both institutional investments and directly held shares and bonds. Property may also be held within a SIPP. Rent and capital gains from the property would be tax-free within the SIPP fund.

ACCUMULATION OF PENSION FUNDS

Tables 11.1 and 11.2 illustrate the result of investing £1,000 a year in a pension fund. They show how pension funds accumulate over differing periods and at varying rates of growth of the pension fund. The number of years is shown vertically and the average rates of investment growth, as percentages per annum, are shown horizontally. It can be seen that the effects of increased periods, and increased rates of growth, are dramatic. The combination of a long period with a high rate of growth is particularly striking. The tables also demonstrate the effects of management charges. A charge by the fund manager of 2% p.a. may not sound much, but it has a huge effect on the final value of the fund. The effect of the management charge becomes increasingly dramatic with long periods and high rates of growth.

The sensitivity of the final outcome to the period of time, over which pension contributions are paid, indicates the desirability of starting pension contributions early in life. For example in Table 11.1 it can be seen that with 6% growth, someone starting contributions 20 years late (e.g.

Table 11.2 *Pension funds accumulated from £1,000 per year with management charges of 2% p.a.*

	3%	6%	9%
10	£10,462	£12,006	£13,816
20	£22,019	£29,778	£40,995
30	£34,784	£56,084	£94,459
40	£48,885	£95,024	£199,630

at 45 rather than 25) will need to pay in £4,207.10 a year in order to achieve the same pension as could be obtained from £1,000 per year over 40 years ([£154,758/£36,785] × £1,000 = £4,207.10).

The sensitivity of the final pension fund to differences in growth rates shows the level of uncertainty involved. It also indicates the risk taken by companies offering final-salary schemes. A lower than expected rate of growth can leave the company with a substantial shortfall to make up. This helps to explain why so many employers are closing final-salary pension schemes to new employees, and replacing them with money-purchase (defined-contribution) pension schemes. With money-purchase pension schemes, it is the employee rather than the employer who runs the risk of low investment returns.

EVIDENCE ON THE RATE OF GROWTH OF PENSION FUNDS

There has been research on the performance of pension funds, with a particular focus on whether actively managed or index tracker funds provide the highest prospective returns for the equity component of pension funds. Much of the relevant evidence comes from research on mutual funds. For example Wermers (2000) found that although gross returns from actively managed equity funds outperform a broad stock market index by 1.3% p.a., the net fund returns underperformed by 1% p.a. The 2.3% difference arose because actively managed funds had high management costs, high share-trading costs, and held part of the fund in (low-yielding) cash and bonds. Drew and Stanford (2001) found that the average actively managed equity pension fund underperformed a benchmark by about 0.5–1.0% p.a. Malkiel and Radisich (2001) found that the average actively managed fund produced rates of return 1–2% p.a. less than index tracker funds, partly because of fund management fees and partly because of trading costs.

Although actively managed funds, on average, may underperform the question remains as to whether some funds persistently perform strongly so that investors (or their advisers) can choose the funds that will perform well in the future. There is evidence from studies of mutual funds to indicate that there is some persistence in the relative performance of actively managed funds (Bal and Leger 1996; Elton *et al.* 1996a; Stewart 1998; Carpenter and Lynch 1999). However these studies indicate only a short-run persistence in relative performance of one to three years. Other studies (Carhart 1997; Cheng *et al.* 1999) found that there was no persistence of relative fund performance. Drew *et al.* (2002) found that choosing the pension funds that had performed best in the past was of no use for the purpose of obtaining high relative performance in the future. They found that the market index tended to outperform actively managed pension funds. They concluded that a fund's track record was not a useful guide to fund selection and investors would be best advised to invest in index tracker funds. Bogle (1992) and Malkiel (1995) had also concluded that the best strategy for investors was to choose index tracker funds.

ANNUITIES

Annuities are guaranteed incomes. They may be for specific periods, for example ten years. More frequently the income is guaranteed for the life of the holder. They are often used for pension purposes. Upon retirement a person would buy an annuity and thereby guarantee a retirement income payable until death. Once the annuity is taken out it cannot be changed. The buyer of the annuity also needs to be aware that the money used to buy the annuity is not usually refundable. If someone dies immediately after buying an annuity, the money used to buy the annuity is normally lost. However it is possible to buy a guarantee, which ensures that the annuity is paid for a minimum period such as five or ten years from the date of purchase. This ensures that the annuity is not wholly lost if death occurs within the period of the guarantee, but there is a cost in the form of a reduced annuity rate. Since April 2006 value protection annuities have been available. Value protection annuities guarantee a lifetime income but also pay a lump sum if death occurs before the age of 75. This potential lump-sum payment comes at the cost of a lower lifetime income (lower annuity rate).

Annuities can be looked upon as a form of insurance. Annuities that pay an income for the rest of a person's life insure the individual against the possibility of outliving the money set aside for retirement. As with other forms of insurance, risk is pooled so that there are both gainers and losers. The pooling mechanism uses the funds of those who die early to subsidise the income of those who live longer than average. There is a 'mortality cross-subsidy' whereby those who die young subsidise those who live long lives.

When an annuity is taken out, an annuity rate is stipulated. For example an annuity rate of 7% p.a. means that a payment of £100,000 secures an annual income of £7,000 per year. Annuity rates vary with age, sex, and sometimes also the health of the individual. The annuity rate will improve as the age at which the annuity is undertaken increases. Since an older person has a shorter life expectancy, the annuity provider would expect to pay the income over fewer years. The prospective shorter period allows for increased annual payouts. Since women have longer life expectancies than men, annuity rates tend to be lower for women than for men. Existing health problems that could shorten life might entail higher annuity rates. The same is true for lifestyle factors such as smoking.

When calculating the annuity rate, the insurance company will estimate the number of years that the person will live. For this purpose an average life expectancy is estimated, and each individual is treated as if they will die at the expected age. The insurance company assumes that it will return the individual's capital over the number of years it expects the person to live. In addition there would be some interest on the capital, typically based on the yield of government bonds (annuity funds are typically invested in government bonds). The interest will decline over time because the capital is progressively returned to the individual.

Where a person has a lower than average life expectancy, it may be possible to obtain an 'enhanced rate annuity' or an 'impaired life annuity'. Enhanced rate annuities are available for people with moderately reduced life expectancies (e.g. reduced by an average of five years in the case of smokers). Such people would include smokers, the obese, and diabetics. In such cases the annual annuity income may be enhanced by, perhaps, 10% or 20%. Impaired life annuities are available for people with very serious conditions. Impaired life annuities can provide very large enhancements, for example inoperable cancer may be associated with a six-fold increase in the annual annuity income.

Wealth also affects longevity (life expectancy); rich people live longer than poor people. So insurance companies give richer people lower annuity rates. Insurance companies tend to look at the size of the pension fund in order to ascertain relative wealth (Budden 2006). Large pension funds will attract lower annuity rates. An insurance company may have several trigger points at which annuity rates are reduced. As the size of the pension fund increases beyond a trigger point the annuity rate is reduced. Longevity is also affected by the region in which the annuitant lives. Life expectancy is greater in some parts of the country when compared to others. Higher annuity rates could be paid in regions with relatively low life expectancies.

Annuities as Pensions

When used as a pension, an annuity is a regular payment made by an insurance company for the rest of the pensioner's life in return for a pension fund. The pension fund would have been built up over the working life of the pensioner. The annuity payments will depend upon the size of the pension fund available for the purchase of the annuity. The annuity payments will also depend upon the rates of yield available from government bonds at the time that the annuity is purchased.

Annuities normally invest in government bonds (gilts). The annuity payments to the pensioner arise partly from the yield on the government bonds, and partly from the repayment of the initial purchase price of the annuity. The purchase price of the annuity is returned to the pensioner over time at a rate that would return the entire sum by the (actuarially) expected date of death. Insurance company statisticians (actuaries) determine the expected date of death.

Conventional annuities pay the same sum of money each year until death (they are called level annuities). The real value of the income (value in terms of purchasing power) will fall over time as prices rise. It is possible to buy annuities that are inflation-proofed (index-linked). In that case the insurance company would fund the annuity using index-linked gilts. Alternatively an escalating annuity might be chosen such that the annuity income rises by a set percentage each year, for example 3% p.a. An index-linked annuity, or a 3% escalating annuity, might reduce the initial annuity income by about one-third.

To the extent that the annuity payments depend on the yields on government bonds, potential pensioners face a high degree of uncertainty. Yields on government bonds can vary considerably over time. In consequence annuity rates can change substantially from year to year. If a person retires in a year in which annuity rates are relatively low, that person suffers a low pension for the rest of his or her life. The system of obtaining a pension by buying an annuity at retirement involves a considerable amount of risk. The size of the pension depends upon when this occurs. Retirement at a time when government bond yields are low results in a low pension.

Booth and Wood (2000) made the point that a historically low annuity rate does not necessarily mean that the annuitant is disadvantaged. It depends upon why the bond yields, which determine the annuity rates, are low. Interest rates, and bond yields, can be divided into real rates and compensation for expected inflation (see Chapter 3 on interest rates and money market investments for the distinction between nominal and real interest rates). If bond yields are low because expected inflation is low, and if the expectation of low inflation subsequently proves to be accurate, the apparently low annuity rates are low only in money terms. The difference between historically high and historically low annuity rates would be one of the distribution of future real payments over time rather than average levels.

Booth and Wood (2000) provided a numerical example, which contrasted a situation of 3% p.a. real yield and 6% p.a. expected inflation (producing 9.2% p.a. nominal yield) with a situation of 3% p.a. real yield and 2.5% p.a. expected inflation (a 5.6% p.a. nominal yield). In the first circumstance the sum of £98,205 bought a level annuity of £10,000 p.a. whereas in the second case the annuity was £7,832 p.a. However inflation of 6% p.a. erodes the real (purchasing power) value of the £10,000 annuity faster than inflation of 2.5% p.a. reduces the real value of the £7,832 annuity. Whereas initially the real value of the £10,000 annuity was the higher of the two, Booth and Wood showed that within eight years the real value of the £7,832 annuity was the greater one. Thereafter the difference in favour of the £7,832 annuity became progressively greater.

Arguably the risk is not so much whether there will be a low or high annuity rate on the retirement date as whether the expected rate of inflation reflected by the annuity rate will be realised. A subsequent inflation rate lower than the rate reflected in the annuity rate would be good for the annuitant whereas if inflation turns out to be higher the annuitant would lose.

There is no obligation to buy an annuity from the manager of the pension fund. The 'open market option' allows the policyholder to take the proceeds of the pension fund away from the fund manager and to buy an annuity from another provider. This is an important facility since the difference between the best and worst annuity rates can be as much as 25% (e.g. 6% p.a. against 7.5% p.a.). However there could be a penalty charged by the pension fund manager if the money is transferred to another provider. In the case of occupational money-purchase (defined-contribution) pension schemes, the trustees of the scheme usually buy the annuities.

People are often reluctant to buy an annuity upon retirement. One reason might be an underestimation of life expectancy. People will be reluctant to pay for an income for life if they expect that life to be relatively short. O'Brien et al. (2005) found that, in the UK, on average men underestimated life expectancy by 4.6 years and women underestimated their life expectancies by 6 years. As well as underestimating longevity people may also underestimate longevity risk, which is the risk that their own lifespans will differ significantly from the average (Drinkwater and Sondergeld 2004). Longevity risk makes the insurance dimension of annuities, the annuity cross-subsidy, important as a means of ensuring that retirees do not outlive their assets.

Concepts from behavioural finance may also help to explain the reluctance to buy annuities (Mitchell and Utkus 2006). Hyperbolic discounting is the tendency to heavily overweight the present relative to the future. People prone to hyperbolic discounting dislike any delay in enjoying their money such that even short postponements of the receipt of income entail heavy discounting of the future receipt. A 'live for today' attitude is a manifestation of hyperbolic discounting. The possibility that death could occur soon after buying an annuity poses the possibility of loss. Prospect theory suggests that there is a high loss-aversion, and hence may indicate that retirees might avoid the possibility of loss by not buying an annuity. However since the loss would be accompanied by death, the loss would not be painful (loss-aversion is based on the pain of losing money). If the concern is with passing on wealth to heirs, the purchase of an annuity normally prevents that inheritance so that the timing of death is not a concern from the perspective of inheritance.

ALTERNATIVE TYPES OF ANNUITY

Alternatives available to the buyer of an annuity include the level annuity, escalating annuity, index-linked annuity, with-profits annuity, and unit-linked annuity. A related possibility is an income drawdown scheme.

A level (or conventional) annuity pays a fixed amount each year for the rest of the person's life. An escalating annuity increases the payments by a predetermined percentage each year. The cost of these annual increases is a lower initial payment relative to a level annuity. Index-linked (inflation-linked) annuities guarantee that the payment rises each year to keep pace with inflation, again at the cost of a lower initial payment compared with a level annuity. Someone who is prepared to delay the receipt of an annuity (or part of it) may do so. The effect of the delay is to enhance the size of annuity to be received in later years.

Investment-linked annuities allow the person to benefit from investment returns within a tax-favoured fund. As with other annuities, the mortality cross-subsidy applies and the fund normally reverts to the insurance company when the annuitant dies. Some investment-linked annuities allow the annuitant to convert to a conventional annuity.

A with-profits annuity links the payments to the with-profits fund of an insurance company. When taking out the annuity, the holder specifies a growth rate for the with-profits fund (an anticipated bonus rate). A high specified growth rate implies a relatively large fund over time, and hence a high level of income that can be drawn from the fund. However if the fund fails to grow at the specified rate (the actual annual bonus falls short of the anticipated rate) those withdrawals will prove to be excessive. The consequence is a smaller fund and a lower income in subsequent years.

If the specified growth rate is less than the rate actually achieved, the fund size increases as does the income that can be drawn in future years. A low specified rate implies an assumption that the fund will be relatively small in future. This entails a low initial income. If the actual growth rate turns out to be higher than the specified rate, the low initial income is less than could have been paid with the result that the fund becomes larger. This means that future income payments will exceed the initial payment.

If the specified growth rate matches the actual annual bonus rate, the fund size and income would be stable. In addition with-profits annuities may produce terminal bonuses. Typically the entitlements to terminal bonuses are paid out as they arise. An annuity holder will receive any entitlement to a terminal bonus, which arises in a year, as an addition to that year's income.

> The regular bonus declared each year has a permanent effect on the income received. This income will increase if the bonus declared is higher than the anticipated bonus rate selected by the policyholder or (subject to the minimum income guarantee) decrease if the bonus declared is lower than the anticipated rate.
>
> An additional bonus may be declared each year which increases the income received for 12 months only.
>
> (Prudential 2006)

The annual (or regular) bonus rate does not determine the current year's income from the annuity. That income is determined by an annuity rate in the same way as other annuities. The annual bonus rate determines the future growth rate of the annuity fund, and thereby the future growth rate of the income paid to the policyholder. A with-profits annuity cannot be surrendered (i.e. exchanged for a cash sum) but typically can be converted to a conventional annuity.

Unit-linked annuities operate in a similar way to with-profits annuities, but are linked to unit trusts. This entails an additional risk. Unit trust prices can go down as well as up (as opposed to an investment in a with-profits fund). A consequence is that the income payments can fall as a decline in unit trust prices pulls down the value of the fund (and hence the potential flow of income that it can support). Conversely there is a potential for increased income resulting from rising unit prices. As is normal for investments, the relatively high risk is associated with relatively high expected returns and hence income levels. There are few unit-linked annuities available. With-profits annuities tend to be the preferred form of investment-linked annuity because of the smoothing mechanism that provides some protection against stock market fluctuations.

Investment-linked annuities, either with-profits or unit-linked, will provide a better pension than conventional annuities if the investment funds produce better returns than gilts. Although funds that invest in the stock market typically tend to outperform gilts, there is a risk that they may fail to do so during some periods.

INCOME DRAWDOWN (UNSECURED PENSIONS) AND PHASED RETIREMENT SCHEMES

With-profits and unit-linked annuities may be attractive to pensioners who face low annuity rates at retirement due to low yields on government bonds. Another alternative for such pensioners is to use income drawdown (alternatively known as an unsecured pension). This enables people to defer buying an annuity whilst drawing an income from their pension fund.

The pensioner leaves the pension fund invested but takes part of the fund each year as an income. The amount that is taken each year is subject to upper and lower limits. Between 0% and 130% of an income benchmark can be withdrawn each year. The income benchmark is approximately equal to the annual annuity that could have been purchased with the money.

The pensioner can choose to use the fund to buy an annuity when annuity rates are judged to be satisfactory. A fall in the value of the investments held by the pension fund would reduce the income available from exercising the drawdown. Also an implication of the absence of the mortality cross-subsidy is that there is a risk that the fund will be exhausted before death.

Income drawdown is useful for people who would like their pension fund to pass to their heirs upon death. Prior to the purchase of an annuity, there is no loss through funds being retained by the insurance company at death in order to finance the mortality cross-subsidy. Income drawdown avoids the risk that the pension fund might be lost as a result of death shortly after retirement. In the event of death the remainder of the pension fund becomes part of the person's estate (subject to a tax deduction). Another means of avoiding the loss of the whole pension fund upon death is the use of phased retirement.

Under phased retirement a person vests only part of the pension fund each year. Many personal pension funds are segmented (clustered) with the effect that it is possible to use some of the segments to buy annuities whilst leaving the remainder in the pension fund. For each segment vested, 25% can be taken as tax-free cash. The tax-free cash received each year upon vesting some segments becomes part of the income stream generated by phased retirement. Any segments of the pension fund that remain unvested at the time of death are part of the estate that is inherited by the heirs. Phased retirement is subject to the risk that the unvested segments of the pension fund would fall in value in the event of a stock market downturn. Such a fall would reduce the income generated through the phased retirement. However it could be seen as less risky than using the whole pension fund to buy an annuity at a single point in time since that point in time may prove to be one at which pension funds and/or annuity rates are low. Phasing the purchase of annuities avoids the risk that the chosen single point in time may prove to be particularly unfavourable.

Before 6 April 2006 retirees who used income drawdown or phased retirement had to use their pension funds to buy an annuity by the age of 75. Since 6 April 2006 it has been possible to use an ASP (Alternatively Secured Pension). This is similar to income drawdown without age limit. The portion of the pension fund that remains upon death is available to be passed to heirs, but there are restrictive limits to the amount of income that can be drawn each year. The maximum that can be withdrawn each year is 70% of an income benchmark (which reflects the income available from buying a level annuity). At the time of writing the UK government was looking at ways of restricting the availability of Alternatively Secured Pensions.

Unsecured pensions (income drawdown schemes) and Alternatively Secured Pensions pose questions concerning the appropriate form of investment. Low growth investments (such as bank deposits) combined with drawdown near to the maximum could lead to a depletion of the fund over time. Riskier investments could entail an abrupt fall in the value of the pension fund and the income from it.

APPLYING THE PRINCIPLE OF DIVERSIFICATION

Someone with a very large pension fund could use a mixture of annuities and arrangements. Every annuity and arrangement has its advantages and drawbacks. An individual may find that a combination is most suitable. For example a mixture of conventional and inflation-linked annuities may be used to provide a core income with some protection against inflation. This could be combined with an investment-linked annuity to provide some scope for real income growth. Part of the fund could be used for drawdown and/or phased retirement in order to provide something for heirs. A combination would constitute a portfolio of retirement incomes and portfolios tend to reduce risk. Every annuity and arrangement has risks (even inflation-linked annuities bear the risk that the income will fail to keep pace with rising standards of living, whereas investment-linked annuities might help the income to do so). A portfolio would tend to dampen the effects of particular types of risk. Retirees with occupational pensions plus AVCs could consider the diversification dimension when deciding how to use the AVC funds. Using the AVC to buy an annuity that is of the same type as that provided by the employer may not be the best strategy.

CALCULATING A LEVEL ANNUITY

The calculation of an annuity rate can be illustrated by the following example. Someone has a pension fund of £100,000. The actuarial expectation is that the person will live for another ten years. If the ten-year interest rate (yield on government bonds) is 8.5% p.a., how much can be paid to the pensioner each year? The first payment is to take place one year from the present.

The annuity equation is:

$$p = M / [\{1 - (1+r)^{-T}\} / r]$$

where p is the annual income, M is the size of the pension fund, r is the relevant rate of (redemption) yield on government bonds, and T is the period for which the annuity is expected to be paid.

$$p = 100,000 / [\{1 - (1.085)^{-10}\} / 0.085]$$
$$p = £15,240.77$$

An annual income of £15,240.77 can be paid to the pensioner.

It can be noted that a mortgage is equivalent to a negative annuity. An annuity entails the initial payment of a lump sum, and a subsequent series of cash receipts. A mortgage involves the initial receipt of a lump sum (which is typically used to buy a property), and a subsequent series of cash payments. This equivalence of annuities and mortgages implies that the annuity equation can be used for the purpose of calculating mortgage payments.

There is a related equation for the calculation of the final sum to be expected from a series of cash payments. The accumulation of a pension fund may entail periodic payments into an investment scheme. The equation for the expected final value of the pension fund to be generated by those payments is:

$$M = p.[(1 + r)^T - 1]/r$$

where M is the expected final sum of money, p is the periodic payment into the fund, r is the average rate of return on the fund, and T is the length of time for which the payments are made.

EXERCISE 11.1

(a) You are advising a client with savings of £100,000. The client wants to fund constant annual expenditure for ten years with a zero savings balance at the end. If the ten year interest rate is 8.5% p.a., how much can be withdrawn each year? The first withdrawal is to take place one year from the present.

(b) A mortgage of £100,000 is to be paid off in equal monthly instalments over 25 years. What are the monthly mortgage payments at a constant interest rate of 6% p.a.?

c) Someone is planning to retire in 40 years' time with a pension fund of £250,000. What is the required annual contribution to the pension fund if the expected rate of return on the fund is 5% p.a.?

Answers

(a) $p = M / [\{1 - (1+r)^{-T}\} / r]$
$p = 100,000 / [\{1 - (1.085)^{-10}\} / 0.085]$
$p = £15,240.77$

(b) $p = M / [\{1 - (1+r)^{-T}\} / r]$
$p = 100,000/ [\{1 - (1.005)^{-300}\} / 0.005]$
(Annual interest of 6% implies a monthly $6/12 = 0.5\%$)
$p = £644.30$

(c) $M = p. [(1+r)^T - 1] / r$
$250,000 = p. [(1.05)^{40} - 1] / 0.05$
$250,000 = p \times 120.8$
$p = 250,000 / 120.8 = 2069.54$

The required annual contribution is £2,069.54.

EXERCISE 11.2

A person has an annual income of £20,000, of which £2,500 each year is invested in a pension fund. The contributions to the fund are made over 40 years, and the average rate of return on the fund is 5% p.a. in real terms (i.e. allowing for inflation). The expected life expectancy at retirement is 20 years. The real rate of return on government bonds at the time of retirement is 2.5% p.a. What annual pension should the person receive?

Answer

The first step is to calculate the expected value of the pension fund at the end of the 40 years during which contributions are made.

$$M = p.[(1 + r)^T - 1]/r$$
$$M = £2,500 [(1.05)^{40} - 1] / 0.05$$
$$M = £302,000$$

The next step is to calculate the annuity payments to be expected from that sum of money.

$$p = M/ [\{1 - (1+r)^{-T}\} / r]$$
$$p = £302,000/[\{1 - (1.025)^{-20}\}/0.025]$$
$$p = £19,372$$

The annual pension is £19,372.

COMPANY PENSION SCHEME BALANCE SHEETS

Final-salary (defined-benefit) pension schemes pay a pension based on the salary at retirement and the number of years worked for the employer. Since the year 2000 many UK companies have withdrawn final-salary pension schemes, at least for new employees. To understand why that has happened it is useful to look at the composition of company pension scheme balance sheets. Table 11.3 depicts a hypothetical balance sheet.

As for liabilities the 'current liability' is the present value of prospective future payments based on current, or final, salaries and number of years served to date. The pension beneficiaries include existing pensioners, existing employees, and past employees with paid-up pension rights. The calculation of the current liability is based on final salary (or, in the case of existing employees, current salary), years of service (up to the present), predicted lifespans (based on actuarial statistics), and the rate of discount chosen to convert future values into a present value.

Since existing employees may experience salary increases prior to retirement, their pension rights can be expected to rise in consequence. The item 'liability in respect of future salary increases' is the present value of the additional pension arising as a result of future salary increases. Added together, 'current liability' and 'liability in respect of future salary increases' amount to 'accrued

233

Table 11.3

Assets		Liabilities	
Pension fund	£100m	Current liability	£80m
Unfunded liability	£10m	Liability in respect of future salary increases	£30m
		Accrued liability for past service	£110m
PV (contributions for future service)	£50m	Future service liability	£50m
Total assets	£160m	Total liabilities	£160m

liability for past service'. The 'current liability' is alternatively known as the 'accumulated benefit obligation' and 'accrued liability for past service' is alternatively known as the 'projected benefit obligation'. Inclusion of 'liability in respect of future salary increases' is controversial because these additional pension costs will be realised only if the employees continue to work for the employer.

Pension rights will also increase as a result of the number of years served rising with the passage of time. The item 'future service liability' is the present value of the expected increase in pension payments brought about by prospective increases in the number of years of employment.

On the asset side of the balance sheet, the 'pension fund' is a portfolio of investments; it is likely to include bonds, shares, cash, and property. The investments may be valued at market prices but could be given valuations that aim to smooth out market fluctuations. Any such smoothing is referred to as actuarial smoothing. For example instead of the full value of an increase in share prices being accredited to the pension fund in the year of the rise, only 20% might be allocated in that year with four further 20% tranches being credited in each of the following four years. If the pension fund is less than 'accrued liability for past service', there is an 'unfunded liability'. It is the purpose of the pension fund to meet the 'accrued liability for past service'.

The other item on the asset side of the balance sheet is the present value of contributions for future service. These are contributions, to which the company is committed, to meet the 'future service liability'. Since it is a commitment, it is treated as an asset despite the fact that the actual payments have not yet been made. (For the same reason 'unfunded liability' appears as an asset. The employer has a commitment to pay this sum and effectively owes it to the pension fund.)

Pension funds have tended to invest heavily in shares and property. This is partly because of the long-run return potential of shares, and the fact that long-term investing allows some amelioration of risk due to periods of good performance offsetting periods of poor investment returns. It is also because defined-benefit schemes are usually linked to salary or price levels (salary levels up to retirement and price levels after retirement). Such linking provides inflation protection to the beneficiaries of defined-benefit schemes. The pension fund managers thus invest in assets that provide protection against inflation: shares and property. Asset-liability management requires assets that match the risks produced by liabilities that are measured in real terms, as opposed to nominal (money) terms. Since the cash flows from bonds are usually specified in nominal terms, bonds are not ideal for matching liabilities that are determined in real terms.

During the stock market downturn of 2000–3, many company pension schemes became underfunded. The fall in share prices reduced the value of pension funds and created unfunded liabilities. In some cases the risk of becoming underfunded caused pension fund trustees to switch from shares to bonds in order to guarantee the pension funds' ability to meet the 'accrued liability for past service'. Another reason for the emergence of underfunding was the fall in the rates of yield on bonds. Bonds are important for the financing of pension liabilities once employees have retired. If bond yields fall more bond investment is needed and the difference in size between the pension fund accumulated, and the pension fund required, is increased. Unfunded liabilities imposed increased pension contribution commitments on companies. They were black holes in pension schemes, and needed to be filled from company profits. In order to reduce the risk that underfunding would occur in the future, many companies closed their final-salary pension schemes to new employees. Over time this is likely to bring about a further switch from shares to bonds, in defined-benefit schemes, as pension schemes mature. The maturity of a pension scheme is measured by the ratio of retired to active members. If a scheme is closed to new members it will steadily mature as active members retire. As schemes mature fund managers tend to rebalance portfolios from shares towards bonds.

In the UK the Pensions Act 1995 required a minimum funding requirement (MFR) to be met. If assets were less than 90% of liabilities, the shortfall must be made up within one year. If assets were less than 100% of liabilities, the shortfall must be made up within five years. If assets were not well in excess of liabilities, the MFR encouraged funds to move towards less risky investments (typically from shares to bonds). The employer normally underwrites the liabilities of a final-salary occupational pension scheme. The employer makes good any deficiency by topping up the fund. MFR did not work well and the Pensions Act 2004 replaced it with a 'scheme-specific funding requirement'.

In addition to meeting any unfunded liabilities, companies are faced with 'normal costs'. 'Normal costs' are the costs to be paid by the company in respect of additional pension liabilities that emerge with the passage of time. Actuaries use several methods to estimate 'normal cost'. One approach is to estimate how much would need to be invested now to provide for any benefits that have been earned during the year. If the employees are young relatively little needs to be invested since there is a long time for the investments to grow in value, but if employees are close to retirement larger sums must be invested because of the short time available for investment growth. This means that the 'normal costs' tend to rise over time. Often actuaries prefer to even out the flow of contributions by way of constant annual money payments, or paying a constant percentage of the wage bill.

The values that appear in a pension scheme balance sheet are subject to a large amount of judgement. One figure that is very dependent on judgement, and which can make a considerable difference to balance sheet values, is the discount rate used to ascertain the present value of the projected pension payments. Another number that requires a substantial input of judgement is the expected rate of increase in salaries.

In the UK the funds of a pension scheme are kept separate from those of the employer by being placed in a trust. A trust is a legal relationship whereby assets are placed under the control of trustees. The trustees have to ensure that the pension fund is managed in accordance with the terms of a trust deed.

LIFE CYCLE ANALYSIS OF PENSION FUNDING

Computer software models exist for estimating the level of saving (as a percentage of earnings) required for a pension. The relevant variables (determining factors) are:

The required pension as a percentage of pre-retirement income.

Whether the required pension is measured in money or real terms.

The expected period of retirement (based on the expected retirement age and actuarial projections of longevity).

The period over which pension fund contributions will be paid.

The expected real rate of return on investments prior to retirement.

The expected rate of return on the investments that fund the annuity payments.

The amount of the pension requirement provided by state benefits.

The amount of the pension requirement provided by existing personal and occupational pension rights.

Two approaches to determining the desirable level of retirement income are: (1) using a proportion of pre-retirement income, for example planning for a pension that is two-thirds of pre-retirement income, and (2) planning for a pension that maintains the pre-retirement standard of living. The method of calculation differs between the two approaches.

Fixing a Proportion of Pre-retirement Income

The calculations in this case involve two stages. First, the size of the pension fund required for the retirement income is calculated using the annuity equation. Second, the level of annual saving required to produce that pension fund is calculated using the endowment equation.

The annuity equation is:

$$p = M / [\{1 - (1+r)^{-T}\} / r]$$

where p is the annual income, M is the size of the pension fund, r is the relevant rate of (redemption) yield on government bonds, and T is the period for which the annuity is expected to be paid.

The equation for an endowment is:

$$p = (M \times y)/[(1 + y)^t - 1]$$

where p is the annual investment, M is the sum to be accumulated, y is the expected rate of return on the endowment fund, and t is the number of years until retirement.

It is to be noted that the expected retirement lifespan is an actuarial average. The individual is assumed to live for the average period. Some people live for longer, and others for shorter, retirement periods. Since a life assurance company provides annuities (pensions) for a large number of people, it can assume that those living shorter lives balance those living longer lives. In effect those that die before the average retirement period subsidise those that live longer lives. This allows the life assurance company to calculate each person's pension fund requirement on the basis of an average retirement lifespan.

EXAMPLE 11.1

Suppose that someone expects to earn £30,000 a year for the next 40 years and anticipates 20 years of retirement. Further assume that the person expects zero real interest (interest net of inflation). How much should be saved for retirement on two-thirds income?

Answer
The person needs £400,000 at retirement in order to fund £20,000 a year for 20 years. In order to accumulate £400,000 the person must save £10,000 a year for the 40 years of work.

It can be noted that the level of expenditure (consumption) in this case is the same before, and after, retirement. In other words this rate of saving achieves not only the desired proportion of income but also the maintenance of a constant level of consumption (a constant standard of living). There is a permanent income of £20,000 p.a.

EXAMPLE 11.2

Consider the case in Example 11.1 but with an expected real rate of interest of 5% p.a.

The annuity equation:

$$£20,000 = M/[\{1 - (1.05)^{-20}\}/0.05]$$

should be solved for M.

$$£20,000 \times [\{1 - (1.05)^{-20}\}/0.05] = M$$
$$M = £249,244$$

The sum of £249,244 needs to be accumulated.
The next step is to find the rate of saving that would achieve that sum.
The endowment equation needs to be solved for p.

$$p = [£249,244 \times 0.05]/[(1.05)^{40} - 1]$$
$$p = £2,063$$

It can be seen from these two examples that a rate of return on the invested funds makes a considerable difference to the amount that must be saved. With zero real interest £10,000 a year needs to be saved, with 5% p.a. real interest the required annual saving is just £2,063.

Fixing a Constant Consumption Stream

If the aim is to have the same standard of living in retirement as before, the calculations should seek to ensure that the level of expenditure (consumption) could be maintained into retirement. The calculation involves equating the present value of expected income with the present value of planned expenditure. The constant level of expenditure (consumption) calculated in this way is sometimes referred to as 'permanent income' (Friedman 1957). The equation is:

$$\Sigma C/(1 + r)^t = \Sigma Y_t/(1 + r)^t \qquad (1)$$

C is the constant expenditure per annum (permanent income) throughout the lifetime of the individual. Y_t is the level of (after tax) income in period t. Y_t is not necessarily the same in every period. The rate at which the cash flows are discounted to the present is shown by r.

EXERCISE 11.3

Suppose that someone expects to earn £30,000 a year for 40 years, and then to have 20 years of retirement.

What would be that person's permanent income if interest rates were expected to be 5% p.a.?

Answer

$$\Sigma C/(1 + r)^t = \Sigma Y_t/(1 + r)^t$$

These can be treated as two annuities, and the annuity equation can be rewritten as:

$$M = p \times [\{1 - (1 + r)^{-T}\}/r]$$

where M is the present value of the annuity.
With an interest rate of 5% p.a., equating the present values of the two annuities gives:

$$C[\{1 - (1.05)^{-60}\}/0.05] = £30,000[\{1 - (1.05)^{-40}\}/0.05]$$

Solving for C gives:

$$C = £30,000 \ \frac{\{1 - (1.05)^{-40}\}/0.05}{\{1 - (1.05)^{-60}\}/0.05}$$

$$C = £30,000 \ \frac{\{1 - 0.1420456\}}{\{1 - 0.0535355\}}$$

$$C = £30,000 \times \frac{0.8579543}{0.9464645} = £30,000 \times 0.9064833 = £27,194.5$$

The person has a permanent income of £27,194.5; in other words the income of £30,000 a year for 40 years can finance consumption at £27,194.5 a year for 60 years. By saving

£30,000 − £27,194.5 = £2,805.5 a year whilst working, the level of expenditure enjoyed during the person's working life can be maintained during retirement. The annual level of consumption of £27,194.5 is achieved both during the working life and in retirement.

This permanent income approach is challenged by evidence that many people fail to maintain their consumption levels into retirement. Banks *et al.* (1998) found that many people experienced a drop in consumption at retirement. This evidence suggests that it is often the case that people do not save enough to smooth consumption levels over their lifetimes, with the effect that their living standards fall when they retire.

Variations on the Basic Equation

The basic equation can be varied in order to encompass real life circumstances. For example suppose that an individual expects a state pension in addition to his/her own provision. Equation 1 would be amended as follows:

$$\Sigma\, C/(1 + r)^t = \Sigma Y_t/(1 + r)^t + \Sigma\, P_t/(1 + r)^t$$

P_t is the expected state pension in year t (P_t will be zero prior to the state retirement age).

ESTIMATED EFFECTS OF DELAYING PENSION FUND CONTRIBUTIONS

Byrne *et al.* (2006) estimated the effects of delaying the start date for contributions to a defined-contribution pension scheme in the UK. Realistic assumptions were made about the pattern of earnings during a person's lifetime, about the prospective growth rates of pension funds, and of annuity rates available at retirement. The outcomes were measured in terms of replacement rates, defined as level annuities as a proportion of income immediately prior to retirement. It was assumed that retirement occurs at age 65 and that 10% of income is contributed to the pension fund (which is about average). Table 11.4 selects some figures, for men, from the study. Two of the investment

Table 11.4

Age at start	Fund strategy	Replacement rate
25	100% equity	39%
	Life-cycle	35%
35	100% equity	33%
	Life-cycle	30%
45	100% equity	23%
	Life-cycle	21%
55	100% equity	11%
	Life-cycle	10%

Table 11.5

Contribution period	Fund strategy	Replacement rate
25–65	100% equity	38%
	Life-cycle	35%
25–30; 40–65	100% equity	30%
	Life-cycle	27%

alternatives used in the study were 100% equities (shares) and a life-cycle fund, which invests 1 − age (1 minus the person's current age) in equities and the remainder in bonds. Table 11.5 provides figures for women who take a career break.

A few points need to be noted. The pensions are level annuities, which are not index-linked and hence are susceptible to erosion by inflation. The replacement ratios are averages (medians) of distributions of possible outcomes. The dispersions of those distributions are greater for the 100% equity funds than for the life-cycle funds.

CONCLUSION

As in other developed countries, the population of the UK is ageing. The ratio of retired people to those of working age is increasing. Future governments, and taxpayers, are unlikely to be able and willing to finance generous state pensions. Employers are also showing increased reluctance to provide substantial pensions. Pension provision is increasingly the responsibility of the individual.

Pension funds are institutional (collective) investments but differ from other institutional investments, such as unit trusts, in important ways. First they are very long term. A UK resident starting work at the age of 21, for example, faces the prospect of retiring at the age of 68 or later. Payments into pension funds could occur over 47 years or more. The length of the investment period has implications for the type of asset within the pension fund. It also implies that it is particularly important to avoid high fund charges. It was seen in Chapter 9 on mutual funds that high fund charges have a devastating effect on the long-term accumulation of capital.

A second distinguishing feature is that pension fund accumulation is a necessity. The accumulation of money through unit trusts could strongly enhance future purchasing power, and is thus very desirable. However the accumulation of funds for retirement is essential; it is required for the avoidance of poverty in old age. This has implications for the form of pension fund investment. Pension fund investments, particularly as a person approaches retirement, should avoid excessive risk. The pension fund investor should ensure that an adequate retirement income is guaranteed. The risk of an inadequate pension should be avoided.

The avoidance of high charges would lead an investor towards index tracker funds since such funds typically benefit from low charges. However most index tracker funds are invested in shares, and only in shares. This is risky. It is important, especially as retirement is being approached, to hold a balanced portfolio that provides diversification of risk (see Chapter 13 on portfolio diversification). Such a fund would hold bonds, property, and cash as well as shares. Even in relation to the component of a pension fund invested in shares, index tracker funds may not provide optimum diversification. For example, in the UK, the largest ten companies account for approximately half the total value of the stock market. So a small number of companies dominate stock indices, and the index funds that track the stock indices.

An implication is that, although index tracker funds have cost advantages over actively managed funds (and also have slightly higher expected returns on average – as indicated in Chapters 9 and 17 on mutual funds and on the evaluation of fund management, respectively, and Part 7 on market efficiency), there is still an important role for fund managers and financial advisers. Index tracker funds do not answer the question of how a fund should be allocated between asset classes (i.e. between shares, bonds, property, cash, etc.). There is also a decision to be made in respect to which index, or indices, should be tracked. For example in the UK a financial adviser, or pension trustee, may choose not to invest in a fund that tracks the FTSE All-Share Index on the grounds that the index is dominated by a small number of companies and hence may not provide the best diversification. Investing part of the money in a fund that tracks the FTSE 250, and part in a FTSE All-Share tracker, might be a solution. The FTSE 250 covers the 250 companies that are next in size below the FTSE 100 (which covers the 100 largest UK companies). By putting some of the equity (share) investment into a fund that tracks the FTSE 250, the pension fund manager reduces the unbalancing effect of the dominance of very large companies.

Studies in behavioural finance have found that people tend to procrastinate when thinking about pension investment, with the effect that the start of pension investment can be excessively delayed. In fact studies in neurofinance have suggested that the human brain finds it unnatural to plan so far ahead. Saving for such a distant goal requires more self-control than many people can manage. Schemes, based on the principles of behavioural finance, have been developed to increase the rate of investment in pension funds. One such scheme is 'Save More Tomorrow' (see Chapter 2 on personal investment decisions). In the UK distrust of pension advisers and providers, resulting from pensions mis-selling scandals and the problems of Equitable Life, has probably added to the reluctance to start pension plans.

Chapter 12

The importance and significance of institutional investors

OBJECTIVE

The objective of this chapter is to provide knowledge of:

1. The importance of institutional investors in financial markets.
2. The liquidity theory of asset prices.
3. The issue of whether institutional investors take a short-term view.
4. The importance of institutional investors to corporate governance.
5. The Sandler report on institutional investments in the UK.

RISE OF THE INSTITUTIONAL INVESTOR

In most developed economies the dominant form of investment is indirect. Indirect investment involves individuals putting money in a fund, which then uses that money to buy shares or other securities. Typically most of the shares issued within an economy are held indirectly through various types of fund. These funds are known as institutional, or collective, investments. Pension funds, insurance funds, and mutual funds (such as unit trusts and OEICs) are major institutional investors. Direct shareholding by individuals accounts for a minority of the total number of shares held.

Institutional investors have come to dominate securities markets. For example it has been estimated that around 75% of UK shares are held through institutional investments (UK and overseas institutions), as opposed to being held directly by individuals. In 1963 UK individual investors held 54% of UK company shares. According to Hill and Duffield (2000), by the end of 1998 UK private investors held only 16.7% of UK shares. This fall continued and by the end of 2006 the figure was down to 12.8% (Office for National Statistics 2006). A significant trend in share ownership has arisen from the international diversification of portfolios. By the end of 2006 the proportion of UK shares held by overseas investors had risen to 40% (Office for National Statistics). Another significant trend has been a steady increase in the relative importance of institutional investments over time, for example it has been estimated that in 1957 less than 20% of UK shares were held by institutional investors; by the end of 2006 institutional investors held about 75% of the UK shares held by UK investors.

Randall *et al*. (2003) reported that in the United States net cash flows into equity mutual funds grew from $13 billion in 1990 to $310 billion in 2000. In the same period the number of investor accounts rose from 22 million to 162 million, and the value of US mutual fund assets increased from $239 billion to $3,962 billion. Best (2005) suggested that the rise in institutional investors has led to the emergence of an investment culture wherein investment has become part of the lifestyle of many people. This is evidenced by the growing importance of newspaper 'money' sections, which help to turn investment into entertainment (Shiller 2000). The media coverage of stock market issues helps to further the investment culture, and the expenditure by institutional investors on newspaper advertising encourages newspaper coverage of investment issues. The expansion of media (print, broadcast, and Internet) coverage of stock market and other investment issues has been paralleled by an increase in investment-related advertising. Just as the advertising of consumer goods has helped to create a consumer culture as well as increasing demand for the specific goods advertised, the advertising of specific investments by institutional investors would have helped to create an investment culture.

According to IFSL (International Financial Services, London) worldwide funds in pension, insurance, and mutual funds reached $45.9 trillion ($45,900,000,000,000) by the end of 2004. This was approximately evenly split between pension, insurance, and mutual funds. This contrasts with $30.8 trillion in private wealth. According to IFSL, fund management accounts for about 0.5% of national income (GDP) in the UK. In 2004 it employed over 40,000 people in the UK and generated net exports of £1.42 billion. The revenues of the fund management industry totalled £7.7 billion.

One social implication of the growth in the relative importance of institutional investments is the disappearance of the distinction between workers and owners. In aggregate workers (in large part) own the companies for which they work. The term 'in aggregate' is important here since it is not a direct ownership of the specific companies for which they work. Each worker through rights in pension funds, life assurance policies, and other institutional investments owns a slice of the aggregate of firms that have issued shares.

The trend towards increased importance of institutional investors is likely to continue, particularly with regard to pension funds. A major factor behind this expectation is the phenomenon often referred to as the demographic time bomb. The ratio of pensioners to workers is relentlessly rising. It has been estimated that by 2020 a ratio of just three workers for every pensioner is likely to be typical in developed countries (compared, for example, to more than five workers per pensioner in 1990). It is projected that the ratio will continue to fall as life expectancy increases. The question arises as to whether members of the workforce will be able (and willing) to pay the taxes required to support such a large number of pensioners. It is likely that the current (and future) workforce will need to accumulate substantial pension fund investments in order to avoid poverty in retirement or the need to continue working beyond present retirement ages (an often suggested partial solution to the problem is an increase in the age at which state pensions become payable).

Many governments allow savings schemes that provide tax advantages for people. Much of this saving goes into institutional investments. One purpose of such schemes is to encourage people to save and make their own provision for retirement. UK tax-advantaged schemes motivated

243

by this objective include personal pension plans, additional voluntary contributions (AVCs), stakeholder pensions, Individual Savings Accounts (ISAs), and friendly society policies. Another purpose of encouraging financial investment is the provision of a flow of capital to businesses, which seek to raise money by issuing shares or bonds. One implication of a decline in the ratio of workers to pensioners is that pension funds could move from a position of being net buyers of shares and bonds to being net sellers. An ageing population could create a situation in which payments from pension schemes exceed contributions to the schemes. Among other consequences, this would reduce the flow of capital to businesses.

The main purpose of some schemes is to encourage investment in enterprises that might otherwise have difficulty raising finance. In the UK, venture capital trusts (VCTs) and enterprise investment schemes (EISs) provide tax concessions for investments in companies that are too small to raise capital by means of issuing shares via a listing on a stock exchange. A venture capital trust is a form of investment trust that holds the shares of companies that are too small, or too young, to be able to have their shares traded on a stock exchange.

INSTITUTIONAL INVESTORS AND PRIVATE EQUITY

Institutional investors can have a role in providing finance for young businesses beyond the provision of collective investments such as venture capital trusts. Institutional investors may own private equity firms, which are firms that buy the shares of new or small businesses even though the shares are not tradable on a stock exchange. Money invested in such companies is often described as private equity. In the UK and Europe the terms private equity and venture capital tend to be used synonymously. Private equity firms become co-owners of the companies in which they invest and take an active managerial role in the companies. The expectation may be that the shares will eventually be sold to another private equity firm, to another firm that makes a takeover bid, or through a stock exchange when the shares are accepted for a stock exchange listing.

Institutional investors, particularly pension funds and insurance companies, are important providers of funds to private equity firms whether or not they own the private equity firms. Private equity firms put together funds for their purchases, and institutional investors are major suppliers of such funds. Often considerable debt is incurred when a private equity firm makes acquisitions. The acquired firms are usually bought with borrowed money. The amount borrowed will normally substantially exceed the capital provided by the private equity firm for the acquisition. One way in which private equity firms take their profits is through refinancing. When improvements in an acquired company become clear the private equity firm may borrow more from banks on the basis that the acquired company is now more valuable (and provides more collateral for the loans). The private equity firm takes the newly borrowed money as profit.

Private equity firms not only provide finance for new and expanding privately owned businesses, but also for reorganised privately owned businesses. Although some of the finance goes to start-up and early stage companies, in recent years much of the funds have been used to help finance the purchases of existing enterprises by the managers of those enterprises – known as management buyouts (Roberts 2004). It is not only privately owned businesses that are acquired. Public companies (i.e. companies whose shares are traded on a stock exchange) may be bought and turned into private companies (i.e. companies whose shares are not traded on a stock exchange). Subsidiaries of other companies may be bought and then operated as private companies.

244

In 2006 the European Private Equity and Venture Capital Association released figures relating to sources of European private equity in 2005 (Valdez 2007). Pension funds provided 24.8% of the finance, banks 17.6%, funds of funds (such as venture capital trusts) contributed 13.1%, insurance companies provided 11.1%, and individual investors 6%. Individual investors are deterred by the large minimum sums, and low liquidity. Individuals wishing to invest in private equity would normally do so through venture capital trusts (or other collective schemes).

Private equity is important to the economy. It has been estimated that companies financed by private equity employ around 2.7 million people in the UK, which is around 18% of the private sector workforce (Valdez 2007). Private equity deals entail large sums of money; it is common for deals to be for much more than £100 million, and they are sometimes for more than £1 billion. The timescale of the investment is typically three to five years. Private equity firms aim to buy businesses that have potential for development. Private equity firms aim to improve the businesses acquired, and to sell them at a profit.

THE LIQUIDITY THEORY OF ASSET PRICES

Pepper and Oliver (2006) proposed the liquidity theory of asset prices. Their suggestion is that a major driver of stock markets is the amount of liquidity available for investment. In other words, if people have more money to invest, they will invest more and thereby push up share prices. Pepper and Oliver illustrate the point by considering a takeover financed by bank borrowing (this is not the only possible source of increased liquidity). Money is created when loans are made. So the act of financing a takeover with borrowed money increases the money supply (liquidity). The purchase of the shares of the target company pushes the share price up. The sellers of the shares then have money available for investment, and may use the money for the purchase of other shares thereby pushing share prices up. The people who sell those shares will receive money, some of which will be used for share purchases. This process can continue through a number of rounds, and at each round share prices are pushed up. The cumulative increase in expenditure on shares can be estimated by means of a multiplier equation:

$$I = E \times [1 / (1 - k)]$$

where I is the cumulative increase in spending on shares, E is the initial expenditure on the shares of the target of the takeover bid, and k is the proportion of receipts from sales of shares that is invested in other shares. A high rate of reinvestment (a high level of k) produces a large multiplier effect and a large cumulative expenditure on shares (a large I). In the event of a substantial number of takeovers in a time period, this liquidity impact on the stock market could be considerable. There would be strong upward pressure on share prices.

Institutional investors are potentially significant for this process since the proportion of shares held by institutions has significance for the value of k. Whereas individual investors may use part of the receipts from share sales for purposes other than purchase of other shares, institutional investors are likely to use a high proportion (in many cases 100%) on the purchase of other shares. So if institutional investors hold a high proportion of the shares traded on stock markets, the value of k will be high and so will the value of I. As the importance of institutional investors increases, so too would the effect of liquidity changes on the level of stock indices.

245

It should be borne in mind that decreases in liquidity can occur with consequent downward multiplier effects. The presence of institutional investors could serve to magnify both upward and downward movements in stock indices.

EXERCISE 12.1

The takeover of a company is financed by borrowing £10 billion from banks. The sellers of shares in the company that is taken over spend 95% of their receipts on other shares. The sellers of these shares in turn spend 95% of the receipts on other shares. Each time shares are sold 95% of the proceeds are spent on other shares. What is the cumulative increase in spending on shares?

Answer

The cumulative increase in spending on shares, I, is given by the multiplier equation:

$$I = E \times [1/(1-k)]$$

where E = £10 billion and k = 0.95 (95%).

$$I = 10 \times [1/(1-0.95)] = 10 \times [1/0.05] = 10 \times 20 = 200$$

The cumulative increase in spending on shares is £200 billion.

The liquidity multiplier described above explains a process that drives the stock market either up or down. It indicates the cumulative increase in spending on assets but does not indicate the size of the resulting rise or fall in the average price of the assets. Congdon (2006) has suggested that the extent of the market movement can be estimated by considering the demand for liquidity on the part of institutional investors. He demonstrated that institutional investors (life assurance and pensions) have a fairly stable demand for liquidity in the sense of the ratio of liquid assets to other assets.

If the institutional investors experience a change in liquidity that moves the liquidity ratio away from the desired level, they will attempt to restore the desired ratio. For example the central bank (Bank of England) may buy government bonds from the institutions. The money used to pay for the bonds adds to the liquidity of the institutions. The institutions attempt to restore their liquidity ratios to the desired values by spending the surplus liquidity on assets such as shares, bonds, and commercial property. This will drive up asset prices. Share, bond, and property prices will rise. So long as the holding of liquidity exceeds the desired amount investment spending will continue. To the extent that each institution's expenditure is another institution's receipt of money, the attempt by each institution to reduce its holding of liquidity does not reduce the aggregate holding of liquidity by institutions. Although each institution attempts to reduce its liquidity holding to the desired level, the institutions in aggregate fail to do so.

Some of the additional money will be lost to the institutions, for example to individual shareholders who sell to institutions, but much will remain with the institutions. If the institutions hold a high proportion of total investment assets, most of the additional money may remain with the institutions. The desired ratio of liquidity to other assets is restored by a rise in share, bond, and property prices.

Suppose that institutional investors, in aggregate, hold non-liquid assets of £1,000 billion. Also suppose that, on average, the institutions desire to hold liquid assets equal to 4% of non-liquid assets. Together they require £40 billion of liquid assets. If the Bank of England buys £30 billion of gilts from them, they would have a liquid assets ratio of about 7%. In aggregate they would not rid themselves of the surplus £30 billion, since the institutions would tend to pass the money between themselves as shares and bonds (and commercial property) are bought from each other. Some of the money, say £10 million, would be lost to the institutions. This would reduce the aggregate holding of liquidity to 6% of the original value of non-liquid assets. The institutions would still have £60 billion of liquid assets.

The desired ratio of liquid assets to non-liquid assets is restored by a rise in asset prices. Share, bond, and property prices would rise until the desired ratio is restored. So long as the actual ratio exceeds the desired ratio, spending on shares and bonds (and commercial property) would continue, as would the resulting rise in prices. Prices would rise until the total value of non-liquid assets reached £1,500 billion. The liquidity ratio of 4% would then have been restored (£60 billion of liquid assets against £1,500 billion of non-liquid assets). A £20 billion increase in the money held by the institutions leads to a £500 billion increase in the aggregate value of shares and bonds (and commercial property) held by the institutions. This £500 billion increase results from rising share and bond (and commercial property) prices. An initial reduction in liquidity would generate falling prices.

The amount of liquidity lost to the institutions in this process will be low if the institutions hold a high proportion of the available non-liquid assets. A low loss would entail a high rise in asset prices. For example if all of the £30 billion increase in the money supply remained with institutional investors, the aggregate value of non-liquid assets would need to rise to £1,750 billion. The institutions would have liquidity amounting to £70 billion (the original £40 billion plus the new £30 billion) and the restoration of a 4% liquidity ratio would require prices to rise until the total value of non-liquid assets reached £1,750 billion.

The major source of liquidity to the institutions comes from net investment by individual investors. There is evidence that the flow of money into equity funds has an impact on stock market movements. Evidence for a positive relationship between fund flows and subsequent stock market returns comes from Edelen and Warner (2001), Neal and Wheatley (1998), Randall *et al.* (2003), and Warther (1995). The question arises as to what influences the net investment by retail investors into institutional funds. Indro (2004) suggests that market sentiment (an aspect of crowd psychology) plays an important role. Indro found that poll-based measures of market sentiment were related to the size of net inflows into equity funds. It appears that improved sentiment (optimism) generates investment into institutional funds, which in turn brings about a rise in stock market prices (and vice versa for increased pessimism).

SHORT-TERMISM

The proponents of the short-termism view believe that stock markets systematically misprice shares. It is claimed that this results in a misallocation of investment funds such that long-term investment by companies falls below the level consistent with economic efficiency. Institutional investors are seen as often being short-termist. They are frequently evaluated on the basis of recent short-term performance and this could incline them to take a short-term view of the investments they make.

During the 1950s, 1960s, and 1970s American and British rates of investment, and rates of economic growth, lagged behind those of Japan and West Germany. One theory put forward to explain this relates to the structure and behaviour of financial markets. In the United States and the United Kingdom stock markets have been important sources of corporate finance. In Japan and Germany banks have been the dominant source of funds for firms seeking to finance investment. (It might be noted that since the 1980s the relative economic performance of these countries has reversed.)

Adherents of the short-termist view say that stock market investors have been too concerned with immediate, rather than long-term, profits and dividends. They claim that stock prices are determined primarily by short-term profit and dividend prospects, with long-term profitability receiving too little attention. This has resulted in companies overemphasising short-term profits. It is argued that companies have reduced investment in order to boost short-term profits. Firms that fail to focus on the short term, and which invest for the long term, find that the market undervalues their shares. The low share price renders these companies vulnerable to takeover by other firms. In order to protect themselves from takeover, firms avoid investment projects whose pay-offs are long term.

This short-termism theory is popular among some politicians (usually of the left) and journalists, and hence has been widely publicised. Research undertaken by economists tends to refute the theory. Economists who have looked for evidence relating to short-termism have concluded that the facts do not support the view that American and British stock markets are short-termist.

If stock markets place too much weight on current dividends, low-yielding stocks would be relatively undervalued. However evidence from both the United States and the UK indicates that the opposite is the case: low-yielding stocks are overvalued relative to higher yielding stocks. Empirical evidence concerning the relationship between price-earnings ratios and relative mispricing is also inconsistent with the notion of short-termism. It is widely believed that the major factor underlying variations in price-earnings ratios relates to differences in growth prospects. A high ratio of stock price to profits per share is thought to reflect potential for future growth in profits. If participants in financial markets were short-termist there would be a tendency to shun such stocks, which would thereby become undervalued. However research evidence suggests that high price-earnings ratio stocks tend to be overvalued. Also the evidence from studies of the effects of announcements relating to investment projects indicates that announcements of investment spending result in stock price increases. This is opposite to what would be expected from short-termist financial markets. (The empirical evidence, relating to the relationship of dividend yields and price-earnings ratios to relative mispricing, is discussed in Chapter 25 on market anomalies.)

Investment analysts often appear to focus strongly on current profits and dividends. However this is not evidence of short-termism. Current profits and dividends convey information about the future. The proportion of profits that firms choose to pay out as dividends can provide clues about the knowledge and thinking of senior executives within the company, with regard to its future prospects.

Fund managers are also often seen as being short-termist. This is believed to arise from the fund managers being subject to appraisal on a short-term, often quarterly, basis. Many would deny that the main appraisers take such a short-term view. Even if they did, the achievement of short-term performance might depend upon taking a long-term view. A rise in the price of a stock, relative to the market, in the short term is likely to be based on a re-evaluation of the firm's long-term prospects. By taking a long-term view of a company's prospects a fund manager can assess whether the stock is correctly valued. If the fund manager turns out to be right in deciding that a stock is mispriced, and trades accordingly, the resulting profit could arise in the short term as other market participants subsequently revise their views of the firm's future prospects (and trade accordingly). The stock price change that generates short-term profits occurs as a result of a re-evaluation of the company's long-term prospects. The fund manager makes a short-term profit by taking a long-term view.

Some support for the short-termist view of fund managers comes from behavioural finance. The chapters – 2 and 24 in particular – dealing with behavioural finance indicate that the psychological biases that affect investors include heuristics that cause an excessive focus on the short term. Narrow framing entails an excessive focus on short-term performance and the recency bias causes a focus on the recent, rather than longer-term, past. A fund manager may have a preference for a long-term perspective but if clients, such as trustees or retail investors, judge a manager's performance in terms of short-term returns then the manager may feel compelled to adopt a short-term perspective.

Noise trading is trading based on sentiment rather than market fundamentals, and such trading can cause stock prices to deviate from fundamental values for long periods of time (see Chapter 24 on noise trading and behavioural finance). Stock prices may be overpriced but still continue to rise. A fund manager who sells overpriced shares before prices stop rising could be judged to have failed. Stock prices may be cheap but continue to fall. A fund manager who buys underpriced shares whose prices then fall may be judged to have failed. Such pressures might cause a fund manager to focus on predicting the behaviour of noise traders rather than ascertaining the long-term fundamental values of stocks. This may explain the frequent use of technical analysis by fund managers. Technical analysis could be regarded as a means of forecasting market psychology and its effects (see Chapter 22 on technical analysis).

If it becomes commonplace for fund managers, or their clients, to focus on the short term it becomes very difficult for individual fund managers to stand out from the crowd. Investing is subject to substantial uncertainty and there is a high risk of being wrong. A fund manager who makes a wrong judgement is likely to be called upon for an explanation. If the fund manager had followed the practice of other fund managers there is likely to be less criticism than if the fund manager had been unconventional. To fail when everyone else fails is safe; to fail when others succeed is dangerous. Fund managers may feel impelled to follow the behaviour of other fund managers as a means of self-protection, in the same way as many animals herd for self-protection. Self-protection could also lead them to adopt strategies expected by their clients, even when the fund manager believes that they are wrong. If it is the case that (psychologically biased and financially naive) clients expect a focus on short-term past and future performance, fund managers may feel obliged to adopt such a strategy. Following a strategy understood by clients makes it easier to explain failures. Guyatt (2005) referred to this as 'gravitation towards the defensible' and in a study of institutional fund managers found that this tendency, plus a pull to short-termism and a tendency to herd, influenced active fund managers whereas managers of index tracker funds were free of such influences.

It is sometimes claimed that institutional investors put pressure on companies to make large dividend payments. These large dividends are seen as reducing the funds available to finance investment. The problem with this line of argument is that it assumes that firms face a choice between dividend payouts and investment. There is no such choice since firms are able to finance investment by means other than undistributed profits. Investment can be financed by borrowing or by issuing shares. Furthermore, the reinvestment of profits is only beneficial if there are good investment opportunities.

The payment of dividends that investors may choose to use for the purchase of bonds or shares has advantages for the economy. Investors are likely to fund the companies with the most promising prospects. In this way the market works to ensure that money is directed towards its most productive uses. Profits retained by firms, and used to finance internal investments, might be used more profitably by other companies with better investment opportunities.

Another factor that concerns adherents of the short-termism theory is the effect of hostile takeover bids. The belief is that the threat of takeover encourages managers to maximise short-term profits and dividends in order to boost the share price and deter predators. This is seen as involving the curtailment of long-term investment. However, as has been pointed out above, such a response would not be expected to result in an increase in the share price. There is no evidence that companies that invest heavily are more likely to be taken over.

High inflation in the United States and the UK, relative to that in Japan and Germany, could also provide a rationale for the suggestion that firms have been short-termist in their approach to investment. High levels of inflation tend to bias the repayment of debt, in real terms, towards the early part of the repayment period. High inflation tends to be reflected in high interest rates. It also erodes the real value of debt. The effect of the high interest rates is immediate, whereas the process of eroding the real value of money (and hence of debt) takes time to have its cumulative effect. In consequence the real interest cost is biased towards the early years of the debt. This may incline management away from investment projects whose returns are not generated relatively quickly. It is interesting to note that the relatively poor performance of the US and UK economies during the 1960s and 1970s tended to coincide with the period during which their inflation rates were relatively high. The improved economic performance of the United States and the UK since the 1980s has coincided with reduced rates of inflation.

INFLUENCE OF INSTITUTIONAL INVESTORS ON COMPANIES AND ANALYSTS

The growing importance of institutional investors, in terms of their holding an increasing proportion of the total number of shares issued, has implications for corporate governance. Corporate governance concerns the way in which companies are controlled. Until the 1970s 'managerial capitalism' was dominant. A feature of managerial capitalism was that shareholding was fragmented. A company's shares were held by thousands of different shareholders. As a result shareholders could not easily coordinate to influence the management of companies. In consequence the managers of firms often operated them for their own benefit rather than for the benefit of shareholders.

The concentration of shareholdings in the hands of a relatively small number of institutions has made it possible for those shareholders to exert influence over the management of companies. Shareholders have voting rights at the annual general meetings, and those voting rights include elections for the board of directors. Institutional shareholders can now force the managements to give priority to 'shareholder value', in other words the interests of shareholders can now take precedence over the interests of managers. In the last resort institutional investors can replace directors. However that possibility may be enough to ensure compliance by managers. There are other methods available, for example putting investors on the board of directors as non-executive directors. Also share option schemes may be introduced in order to give the managers a personal interest in the value of the shares.

Most individual shareholders do not own enough stock in a company to be able to influence its management. Most individual shareholders do not believe that it is worth their time and effort to try, particularly since they would bear the costs whilst the benefits are shared with shareholders who do nothing. Selling shares is easier than trying to influence managements.

The situation is different for large institutional shareholders. Since such shareholders often have large numbers of shares in a firm, they may be able to influence the firm's managers. The large shareholdings also allow a substantial proportion of the benefits to accrue to their funds.

The question of whether institutional shareholder activism has been effective is controversial. M.P. Smith (1996) investigated the effects of activism by the Californian public sector pension fund CalPERS. He found that CalPERS activism in relation to 34 firms from 1987 to 1993 gained the fund $19 million at a cost of $3.5 million. Other studies have found no evidence of the effectiveness of activism. Song *et al.* (2003) examined the effects of activism by the Council of Institutional Investors (a coalition of US pension funds). They found very little evidence of the efficacy of the activism. Karpoff *et al.* (1996) concluded that shareholder proposal submissions did not lead to any obvious improvement in firm performance, even when the proposals had passed.

The US evidence suggests that, whereas some public sector pension funds are activist, few if any company pension funds are. This may be because company managements choose who runs their pension funds, and company managements do not like activism. Investor activists are likely to be seen as nuisances by corporate managers.

The need for diversification of a fund tends to reduce the level of shareholdings in any one company. This diversification is often enforced by regulations. To the extent that this reduces the holdings of shares in a particular firm, it reduces both the ability to influence managements and the rewards from doing so. The alternative of selling shares in a poorly performing company may often be preferred to activism. One type of fund, the index tracker, does not have the alternative of selling. It may be that the only way in which an index tracker fund can improve its performance is by taking an activist approach. The larger institutional investors may also be drawn towards activism on the grounds that the relatively large size of their stockholdings renders those holdings illiquid.

Evidence in support of the effectiveness of institutional investor activism comes from Gillan and Starks (2000) who found that corporate governance proposals from institutional investors received more votes than those sponsored by individuals or religious organisations. Hartzell and Starks (2003) found an inverse relationship between institutional ownership and executive pay.

251

Chung *et al.* (2002) concluded that large institutional shareholdings deterred the use of creative accounting to distort profit figures. Cornett *et al.* (2007) found a positive relationship between institutional investor shareholding and operating cash flow returns. They found that both the percentage of stock held by institutional investors, and the number of institutions holding the stock, were positively related to performance.

There is some evidence that, even when choosing to sell rather than intervene, institutions can be influential. Parrino *et al.* (2003) found that some institutional sales are motivated by poor investment returns, and that institutional sales may play a role in bringing about changes in company management. In particular institutional sales can lead to the replacement of a chief executive officer and increase the likelihood of an outsider being appointed.

Cremers and Nair (2005) classified corporate governance mechanisms as internal and external. The internal mechanism entails monitoring of the company by block holders. Block holders are investors who hold large blocks of shares, and institutional investors are major block holders. The external mechanism entails the threat of takeover by other companies. External corporate governance is often measured in terms of the level of shareholders' rights. A high level of shareholders' rights renders takeovers easier. Research has shown that a high level of shareholders' rights is associated with high rates of return for shareholders. Cremers and Nair demonstrated that those high rates of return for shareholders depend upon high levels of internal corporate governance, which means relatively high levels of block holding. This complementary relationship between internal and external corporate governance was found to be particularly strong for small companies.

Institutional investors may not only influence the companies in which they invest but also the investment analysts who make recommendations about the shares of the companies. Chapter 21 on ratios and Chapter 26 on further evidence on market efficiency, indicate that investment analysts have a tendency to be too optimistic about the prospects of particular stocks. This appears to be the case when their investment bank does (or prospectively does) business with the company whose shares are being analysed. There is a conflict of interest wherein pressure from within their investment bank influences the recommendations of analysts. Good recommendations are favoured in order to please corporate clients (or prospective clients). If an analyst makes a negative recommendation on the stock of a company, that company could transfer its business to another investment bank.

There is evidence that institutional investors exert a counteracting influence, which acts to push analysts towards making more accurate and balanced recommendations. Ljungqvist *et al.* (2007) made the point that analysts are dependent on institutional investors for performance ratings and trading commissions. When institutional investors were major shareholders, analyst recommendations were found to be more accurate. This tendency for the presence of institutional investors to moderate internal pressures towards excess optimism is consistent with research indicating that institutional investors are able to recognise biases in analysts' forecasts and recommendations. Malmendier and Shanthikumar (2007) provided evidence consistent with the view that institutional investors perceive the biases of investment analysts whereas private investors do not. The influence from institutional investors over the output of investment analysts could serve to make stock markets more informationally efficient (see Part 7 on market efficiency).

THE SANDLER REPORT

The Sandler report into the long-term savings industry in the United Kingdom was published on 9 July 2002 (HM Treasury 2002). The main points of the Sandler report included:

1. Individuals face a choice that is too large, too complex, and with too much obscure jargon.
2. Consumers do not understand savings products.
3. There should be simple low cost stakeholder investments that could be sold without financial advisers.
4. Pensions taxation and rules should be simplified.
5. Consumers often pay high fees for poor performance.
6. There is no relationship between fund charges and performance.
7. Competition does not operate to keep charges down.
8. There is a wide disparity in charges.
9. Sales of tracker funds should rise relative to sales of actively managed funds.
10. Financial advisers should be paid by means of fees rather than commission.
11. Life companies should not be able to take part of the profits of with-profits funds.
12. Investors should receive information about the smoothing of with-profits funds.
13. Tax breaks on with-profits bonds should be ended.

The suggestion that the choice facing retail investors is too large and too complex, and that there should be simple (stakeholder) options available, receives support from one of the principles of behavioural finance. The 'status quo bias' predicts that, when faced with complex choices, people tend to do nothing (Samuelson and Zeckhauser 1988). In their theory of 'choice under conflict' Tversky and Shafir (1992) suggested that the decision to take no action, or to postpone an action, increases when there are many options. When faced with many choices, the task of taking a decision can be overwhelming. The result can be inaction. This may help to explain why so many people fail to take saving and investing decisions, and hence fail to save and invest.

Kempf and Ruenzi (2006) found that evidence from the US mutual fund (unit trust) market provided support for the status quo bias. The status quo bias suggests that when faced with a complex choice people make no change to their existing position. If their existing position is one of having no investment, they will continue to have no investment; in other words they do nothing. If they have investments, they will continue with the same investments. Kempf and Ruenzi looked at the relationship between previous inflows into particular mutual funds and subsequent rates of investment into those funds. They found that the funds with high previous inflows tended to be the funds with subsequent high inflows. This indicates that investors tend to invest in the same funds as they already hold. Of particular interest was the observation that this tendency was especially strong when the choice of funds was very large. For example they found that the status quo bias was three times stronger when there were more than 100 alternative funds in a sector than when there were 25 funds to choose from.

Agnew and Szykman (2004) suggested that there could be a problem of information overload. As a result of information overload investors have too much information to comprehend, and consequently take no investment decisions. Iyengar and Lepper (2000) showed that having too much choice hampers investors' ability to identify the most suitable options. Other researchers have found that information overload can lead to decisions being based on emotion rather than reason (Shiv and Fedorikhin 1999; Dreman 2004).

Two contributions to Mitchell and Utkus (2004) support the view that increased choice can result in reduced saving. Sethi-Iyengar *et al.* (2004) found that if US pension plans offered more funds, employee participation fell. When employees became overwhelmed with the complexity of the decision they reduced their pension plan participation. Faced with complex investment choices, some employees simplified the decision by choosing the default option of doing nothing. Scott and Stein (2004) also found an inverse relationship between the number of options available and the extent of participation. People may feel overwhelmed by too much choice, and abandon interest. However it is not to be presumed that zero choice achieves maximum pension plan participation. Papke (2003) found that workers with pension plans that offered some choice of investments, as opposed to no choice, were more likely to join the pension scheme.

The view that if investors do not understand savings products they will not invest receives support from the behavioural finance concept of the illusion of truth (Reber and Schwartz 1999). According to this idea people are more ready to believe what they find easy to understand rather than what they find difficult to understand. It is a short step to extend the idea to personal finance. People are less likely to invest if they are unable to understand the investment.

The suggestion that there should be simple investment products, such as stakeholder products, which could be sold without financial advice, has received criticism from Diacon (2004). Diacon compared perceptions of risk between financial advisers and investors. He found that perceptions of risk differed between them, and that the risk perceptions of investors tended to be the higher. Without the financial advice, which could modify perceptions of risk, investors may be too risk-averse in their investment decisions. In particular they may avoid stock market investments, and hence avoid the equity investments that should provide the highest potential returns. The view of Diacon accords with that of Benartzi and Thaler (1999).

One area of attention in the Sandler report was the issue of actively managed versus index tracker funds. Actively managed funds attempt to outperform stock markets by stock selection and market timing. Index tracker funds aim to move in line with stock markets. Sandler pointed out that, when allowance is made for charges, actively managed funds on average underperform stock indices. Yet the vast majority of retail sales (93%) was of actively managed funds as opposed to funds that track a stock index. This is possibly because actively managed funds tend to pay financial advisers more commission. Index trackers are also less risky since they avoid management risk (active risk), which is the risk that an actively managed fund may perform badly relative to a stock index.

The average underperformance of actively managed funds is what would be expected on the basis of the efficient market hypothesis. According to the efficient market hypothesis, if the stock market is informationally efficient it is not possible for fund managers to consistently outperform the market. This is consistent with the wealth of empirical research that indicates that there is little, if any, persistence in fund performance (e.g. Rhodes 2000). The evidence indicates that there is no reason to believe that funds that have performed well in the past will continue to do so in the future. In fact the winner–loser phenomenon, for which evidence exists, suggests that today's good performers will be tomorrow's bad performers, and vice versa (DeBondt and Thaler 1985; Bremer and Sweeney 1991). Ambachtsheer *et al.* (1998) found two characteristics of pension funds that were positively related to fund performance. Those characteristics were fund size and the proportion of the fund invested in index tracker funds. Large size provides economies of scale and hence lower percentage costs. Many of the costs of managing and administering funds do not rise in proportion to the size of the fund. The authors suggested that the positive association between performance and use of index tracking arose since use of index tracking was a sign of fund management competence. An alternative explanation might be the relatively low cost of operating index tracker funds.

Sandler did not suggest that there is no place for active fund management. However he said that most customers, and advisers, lack the expertise to choose between active fund managers in order to find the potentially successful ones.

Informational efficiency is conventionally divided into the weak, semi-strong, and strong forms. The weak form of the efficient market hypothesis suggests that all historical market information (past prices, past trading volumes) is fully taken into account in current market prices. An implication of the weak form of the hypothesis is that there is no scope for making profits from analysis of historical share prices and trading volumes. So technical analysis, particularly chartism, is expected to be of no value. Attempts to forecast stock prices using charts based on previous stock prices will fail since all the information available from past price data is already reflected in stock prices.

A semi-strong form efficient market is one in which security (share and bond) prices fully take account of all publicly available information. In addition to market information on past prices and trading volumes publicly available information includes macroeconomic data (such as interest rates, inflation rates, economic growth rates), company data (such as dividends, profits, sales), and non-economic events (such as political events, technological developments, discoveries of natural resources). The implication is that asset prices immediately move to reflect any new information so that no one can make profits by means of purchases or sales based on analysing the new information.

The fairly high level of informational efficiency in stock markets is to be contrasted with the low level in the market for retail investments. The retail investor is often very ignorant of institutional investments such as unit trusts and investment bonds. There is therefore asymmetric information between the client and the financial adviser, and between the fund manager and the individual investor. Individual investors have less information than the professionals with whom they deal. The asymmetric information can lead to adverse selection where advisers seek to sell the products that pay them the highest commission, rather than the products that offer the best value to their clients.

The report suggested that fees should replace commission-based remuneration. This should remove commission bias where advisers recommend the investments that pay the highest commissions. It should also lead to competition based on charges that results in lower, and more uniform, charges. Sandler pointed out that there is little consistency in charges with large variations in charges for essentially identical products. This is symptomatic of low informational efficiency and ineffective competition. The report also points out that there is a lack of correlation between charges and performance.

Ambachtsheer (2005) highlighted both information asymmetry and the principal-agent problem as reasons for many retail investors paying too much for too little. The principal-agent problem arises from agents (financial advisers and fund managers), who should be acting on behalf of the

255

principals (individual investors), acting in their own best interests rather than the interests of the investors. Advisers and fund managers could exploit the relative ignorance of retail investors by imposing excessive charges on investment products such as unit trusts, OEICs, pensions, and life assurance related investments.

Cocco and Volpin (2007) found principal-agent problems in the operation of company pension schemes. They found that the proportion of company executive directors among the pension scheme trustees affected the operation of the schemes. A large proportion of company insiders was associated with lower company contributions to the schemes and higher risk taking in the fund management. This evidence was seen as supporting the view that insider trustees acted on behalf of their companies rather than on behalf of the pension scheme members. Trustees (the agents) should act on behalf of the members of the pension scheme (the principals).

George Akerlof, a Nobel prize-winning economist, wrote an article entitled 'The Market for "Lemons": Quality, Uncertainty and the Market Mechanism' (1970) in which he discussed asymmetric information and its implications. Asymmetric information, as mentioned in Chapter 8, is the term referring to the fact that the managers of a corporation know more about its operation than investors know. Investors cannot be sure about which corporations are good (the peaches) and which are bad (the lemons). However the managers do know whether their firm is a peach or a lemon. Likewise financial advisers may be peaches or lemons, but retail investors do not know which are the lemons. The same may be true of funds and their managers. Individual investors may be aware that some financial advisers do not offer good advice, and that many fund managers do not perform well. Since investors cannot easily distinguish between peaches and lemons, they are less willing to invest for fear of buying a lemon.

Another consequence of asymmetric information is moral hazard. One form of moral hazard is the temptation for fund managers to take excessive risks, or engage in activities that are not in the interests of investors. An aspect of moral hazard is the principal-agent problem. Investors are the principals and managers are their agents. The agents may act in their own interests rather than in the interests of the principals. Likewise financial advisers may recommend investments that pay high commissions at the expense of the investors. This is a form of adverse selection and moral hazard. Many people believe that financial advisers provide free and unbiased advice. They do not realise that the adviser is paid according to the amount, and type, of sales.

Simple stakeholder products and more information about with-profits policies (both recommended by Sandler) would help to overcome problems of asymmetric information, adverse selection, and moral hazard. The Sandler report called for the introduction of simple stakeholder investments that would have no initial charge, annual charges capped at 1% (subsequently amended to 1.5%), and carefully designed investment policies. They could be sold without the need for a financial adviser.

With-profits policies were criticised for being opaque with respect to performance and charges. Sandler suggested that investors should be provided with more information about with-profits funds. Investors would have to be given information on smoothing, the process by which managers hold money back in good years in order to top up policies in bad years. Customers should be given four figures each year: the redemption value of the policy, the proceeds available on death, projections of the payout at maturity, and the value of the unsmoothed assets.

CONCLUSION

The main institutional investors are pension funds, insurance companies, and mutual funds such as unit trusts, OEICs, and investment trusts. In recent years another group of institutional investors, hedge funds, have gained considerable importance (see Chapter 16 on styles of portfolio construction).

Most investment by individuals is carried out through institutional investors. In the UK, institutional investors account for around 75% of stock market investment. The investment behaviour of the institutions therefore has considerable significance for the behaviour of the stock market. It might be thought that this dominance of the institutions would introduce considerable rationality to the stock market. However evidence presented in Chapter 24 on noise trading and behavioural finance, and in Chapter 27 on stock market bubbles and crashes, suggests that institutional investors are prone to the same psychological and social influences as individual investors. In particular institutional investors appear to have a tendency towards herding. There is little evidence to support the view that institutional investors tend to be short-termist in their investment behaviour.

It might be thought that, since institutional investment managers are professionals, institutional investors should be able to outperform the stock market by their management of funds. However, on average, they fail to do so. Furthermore the empirical evidence suggests that no institutional fund manager is capable of consistently outperforming the stock market, except by chance. Evidence on such matters is presented in Chapters 9, on mutual funds, and 17, on evaluating the performance of fund managers, and in Part 7 on market efficiency. The evidence suggests that individual investors should avoid the expense of actively managed institutional funds, and should invest in institutional funds that aim to track stock indices (and that charge individual investors much less). The Sandler report on the savings products provided by institutional investors in the UK suggested that more use should be made of index tracking funds.

There is one way in which the managers of index tracker funds can enhance their fund returns. This entails investor activism. Investor activism involves the participation, by investors, in the decision-making processes of companies. Institutional investors may seek to get their representatives elected on to the board of directors of a company as non-executive directors. The institutional investors may do this if they feel that they can improve the management of the company. Alternatively, institutional investors could block the election of board members who are seen as detrimental to the company or its shareholders. The rise in the importance of institutional investors has allowed such investor activism. Since the institutions hold large blocks of shares they can cooperate on activism in a way that thousands of small investors could not.

One way in which the relative expertise of institutional investors has impacted on their strategies has been through their use of derivatives (see Chapters 28 and 31 on stock index futures and on stock options, respectively). In particular funds that guarantee that the original capital cannot be lost, or that pay high yields, have been structured and sold to individual investors (see Chapter 34 on structured products). Some hedge funds have used more complex derivatives strategies. Derivatives can be used either to reduce portfolio risk, or to increase risk in the hope of increased returns.

Some economists have argued that changes in the money supply are major driving forces for share prices. It is further argued that institutional investors form an important element in the transmission mechanism whereby money supply changes impact on stock markets. In particular attempts by institutions to maintain their preferred ratios of money to shareholdings may result in the ratios being maintained through the medium of share price movements.

Part 4

Capital Market Theory

Chapter 13

Portfolio diversification

OBJECTIVE

The objective of this chapter is to provide knowledge of:

1. The principle of Markowitz diversification.
2. Efficiency frontiers.
3. The use of the Markowitz equations to calculate the expected return and risk of a portfolio.
4. The merits of international diversification.
5. The role of property in portfolios.
6. The advantages of adding a risk-free asset to the investment alternatives.
7. Asset allocation lines.
8. The significance of asymmetric correlation and leptokurtosis.
9. Behavioural portfolios.
10. Value-at-risk.
11. Post-modern portfolio theory.
12. Time diversification.
13. The importance of financial advice and financial education.

The idea that investment portfolios should be diversified is well established. The saying 'Don't put all your eggs in one basket' expresses a basic principle of diversification. Spreading one's assets among a large number of investments lessens the risk of losing everything as a result of adverse developments relating to one investment. Share portfolios are often in the form of 50 or more different stocks since poor performances on some of the investments tend to be offset by strong performances on others. The observation that industries vary in their performances over time leads to the shareholdings being spread across a number of different industries. So a portfolio may have shares in firms involved in engineering, chemicals, banking, electricals, transport, brewing, insurance, food processing, retailing, oil, computing, water, and pharmaceuticals. Spreading investments across industries, as well as across individual firms, allows for poor performances in some industry sectors to be offset by strong performances elsewhere. A more complete

261

TABLE 13.1

Return	Probability
2%	25%
6%	50%
10%	25%

diversification would involve a spread of investments across asset classes. The main asset classes are equities (shares), bonds, deposits, and property (real estate).

Spreading one's wealth amongst asset classes, and within those classes among different sectors, will tend to provide most of the benefits of diversification. This approach is sometimes referred to as naive diversification. A more sophisticated approach has been suggested by Harry Markowitz (Markowitz 1952, 1959). This involves basing the choice of investments upon their correlations (or upon their covariances) in order to maximise the expected degree of offset between them. What follows will focus on this latter form of diversification, often known as Markowitz diversification. The exposition will initially be concerned with diversification between asset classes; particularly equities, bonds, and deposits. A more complete approach would extend to the choice of individual securities, for example the specific shares to be bought and the relative contribution of each stock to the portfolio.

EXPECTED RETURN AND RISK

In finance the term 'expectation' does not suggest that a specific single outcome is anticipated. Instead the word 'expectation' is used in the statistical sense, which is the average of a range of possible outcomes. Consider Table 13.1.

There are three possible returns on an investment, and each of those returns has the probability (likelihood) indicated in Table 13.1. The expected return is the weighted average of the three possible returns, with the weighting being based on the probability of occurrence. The expected return is therefore:

$$(2\% \times 0.25) + (6\% \times 0.5) + (10\% \times 0.25) = 6\%$$

EXERCISE 13.1

The most frequently used measure of risk is standard deviation. The equations for standard deviation are:

$$V = (\Sigma f d^2)/(N-1)$$
$$\sigma = \sqrt{V}$$

where V is variance, f is frequency, d is deviation from the mean, N is the number of observations, and σ is standard deviation.

Suppose that the following monthly returns have been observed over the past year: 5% p.a., 6% p.a., 2% p.a., 8% p.a., 5% p.a., 3% p.a., 4% p.a., 5% p.a., 6% p.a., 7% p.a., 4% p.a., 5% p.a.

Estimate the expected return and standard deviation of returns.

Answer

The first step is to calculate the expected return, which is:

$$[(2 \times 1) + (3 \times 1) + (4 \times 2) + (5 \times 4) + (6 \times 2) + (7 \times 1) + (8 \times 1)]/12 = 60/12 = 5$$

The expected return is 5% p.a., and is the mean (average) of the observed returns.
The next step is to calculate the value of Σfd^2.

Table 13.A

d	d^2	f	fd^2
2–5	9	1	9
3–5	4	1	4
4–5	1	2	2
5–5	0	4	0
6–5	1	2	2
7–5	4	1	4
8–5	9	1	9
			$\Sigma fd^2 = 30$

$$V = (\Sigma fd^2)/(N-1) = 30/11 = 2.727$$
$$\sigma = \sqrt{V} = \sqrt{2.727} = 1.65$$

The standard deviation of returns is 1.65% p.a.

EXERCISE 13.2

From the table what are (a) the average deviation, and (b) the standard deviation, of returns?

TABLE 13.B

Return	Probability
−2%	25%
6%	50%
14%	25%

Answers

(a) The average deviation of returns is:

$$0.25 \, (6 - [-2]) + 0.5 \, (6 - 6) + 0.25 \, (14 - 6) = 2 + 0 + 2 = 4\%$$

(b) The standard deviation of returns can be calculated as:

$\sigma = \sqrt{\Sigma Pd^2}$ where P is the probability of an outcome.

$$\sigma = \sqrt{\{\, 0.25 \, ([-2] - 6)^2 + 0.5 \, (6 - 6)^2 + 0.25 \, (14 - 6)^2 \,\}}$$
$$= \sqrt{\{0.25 \, (-8)^2 + 0 + 0.25 \, (8^2)\}} = \sqrt{\{\, 16 + 0 + 16\,\}} = \sqrt{32} = 5.66\%$$

In the table here the returns are more spread out than in the table in Exercise 13.1, the deviations are more extreme which means that volatility is greater. This is reflected in higher values for the average and standard deviations.

It is to be noted that standard deviation can be calculated using either frequencies or probabilities.

THE PRINCIPLE OF DIVERSIFICATION

The role of correlation in the determination of portfolio risk can be seen from the following example in which the combination of risky assets produces a risk-free portfolio.

There are two securities in this example, A and B. There are three possible eventualities (circumstances). Examples of eventualities might be economic boom, equilibrium, and recession. Table 13.2 shows the returns from the securities in each of the three different circumstances. Table 13.3 shows the returns from a portfolio comprising 0.8A and 0.2B. In eventuality 1 the contribution to total return from holding 0.8A is $0.8 \times 7.5 = 6\%$, the contribution from the 0.2B is $0.2 \times 20 = 4\%$, giving a total return of $6 + 4 = 10\%$. In the second circumstance A provides $0.8 \times 10 = 8\%$, B contributes $0.2 \times 10 = 2\%$, so that the total portfolio return is $8\% + 2\% = 10\%$. In eventuality 3 security A contributes $0.8 \times 12.5 = 10\%$, and B contributes $0.2 \times 0 = 0\%$, with the result that the total portfolio return is 10%.

The portfolio of 0.8A plus 0.2B is a risk-free portfolio. Under all three of the possible eventualities the return is 10%. Since there is no uncertainty about the return, there is no risk. The expected return is 10% and the standard deviation of returns is 0%. So by combining two risky investments in an optimal ratio, risk has been eliminated. The optimal proportions of 0.8 and 0.2 (4 to 1) arise from the ratio of deviations from the expected return; B has a deviation four times

TABLE 13.2

Eventuality	Return on A	Return on B
1	7.5%	20%
2	10%	10%
3	12.5%	0%

TABLE 13.3

Eventuality	Portfolio return (0.8A + 0.2B)
1	6 + 4 = 10%
2	8 + 2 = 10%
3	10 + 0 = 10%

that of A (10% compared with 2.5%). The other factor involved in ascertaining the optimal proportions in a portfolio is the correlation of returns, although this factor was not relevant to ascertaining the proportions in the example above since only one correlation was involved (between A and B).

EXERCISE 13.3

An investor wants to combine two shares, A and B, into a portfolio. There are four possible eventualities, based on the growth rate of the economy. The probabilities of the four eventualities and the rates of return on the two shares in the four situations are as shown in the table.

Table 13.C

Eventuality	Probability (%)	Return on share A (% p.a.)	Return on share B (% p.a.)
1	20	8	−4
2	30	6	2
3	30	4	8
4	20	2	14

(a) What are the expected returns for the two shares?

(b) How can the shares be combined into a portfolio whose risk is zero? What is the expected return of that portfolio?

(c) Why is it not normally possible to find a portfolio of two shares that has zero risk?

Answers

(a) The expected return on share A is:

$(8 \times 0.2) + (6 \times 0.3) + (4 \times 0.3) + (2 \times 0.2) = 5\%$ p.a.

The expected return on share B is:

$(-4 \times 0.2) + (2 \times 0.3) + (8 \times 0.3) + (14 \times 0.2) = 5\%$ p.a.

(b) The average deviation of returns for share A is:

$[(8 - 5) \times 0.2] + [(6 - 5) \times 0.3] + [(5 - 4) \times 0.3] + [(5 - 2) \times 0.2] = 1.8\%$ p.a.

The average deviation of returns for share B is:

$[(5 - \{-4\}) \times 0.2] + [(5 - 2) \times 0.3] + [(8 - 5) \times 0.3] + [(14 - 5) \times 0.2] = 5.4\%$ p.a.

Since the ratio of average deviations is 3 to 1 (5.4/1.8) the ratio in the portfolio should be 3 to 1, i.e. 0.75% A and 0.25% B. The expected portfolio return in each of the four situations is shown in the table.

Table 13.D

Eventuality	Portfolio return
1	$(8 \times 0.75) + (-4 \times 0.25) = 6 - 1 = 5\%$ p.a.
2	$(6 \times 0.75) + (2 \times 0.25) = 4.5 + 0.5 = 5\%$ p.a.
3	$(4 \times 0.75) + (8 \times 0.25) = 3 + 2 = 5\%$ p.a.
4	$(2 \times 0.75) + (14 \times 0.25) = 1.5 + 3.5 = 5\%$ p.a.

Since the expected return is the same in all four cases, the risk is zero.

(c) The construction of a portfolio with zero risk requires the combination of shares with perfectly negative correlation. It is highly unlikely that a perfectly negative correlation exists between a pair of stocks.

The Markowitz approach seeks to incorporate securities with low correlations of returns. By minimising correlations, the chance of poor performances by some investments being offset by strong returns on others is increased. In the examples above the coefficient of correlation was -1, with the result that it was possible to completely eliminate risk. Although negative correlations rarely exist, there is still scope for reducing risk by using the criterion of low correlation. It can be seen from equation (2) in the Markowitz equations below, that lower correlations will tend to result in lower variances. An important insight of the Markowitz approach is the observation that the risk-reduction effects of diversification can be maximised by choosing investments with relatively low correlations with each other.

Risk is often divided into systematic and non-systematic risk. Systematic risk is the risk arising from movements in the market as a whole. Systematic risk cannot be removed by diversifying a portfolio (hence it is also known as non-diversifiable risk). Non-systematic risk is the risk that is specific to a particular firm or industry sector. Non-systematic risk can be removed by diversifying a portfolio (and is therefore alternatively known as diversifiable risk). Non-systematic risk tends to decline as the number of different stocks in the portfolio increases. The presence of systematic risk tends to cause correlations to be positive. The presence of non-systematic risk causes the positive correlation to be less than perfect, and provides scope for risk reduction by means of diversification. Figure 13.1 shows that as the number of different stocks in the portfolio increases total risk decreases. Greater diversification reduces non-systematic risk but not systematic risk.

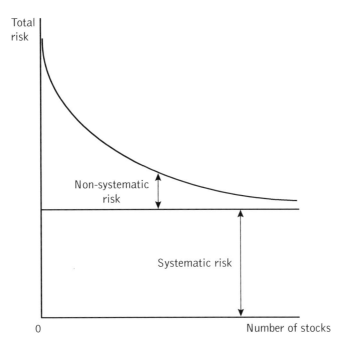

Figure 13.1   *Diversification and risk*

THE EFFICIENCY FRONTIER

Another conclusion of the Markowitz analysis is that it is possible to construct a set of points, in risk-return space, that cannot be improved upon. Such a set of points is depicted in Figure 13.2.

The curve in Figure 13.2 is known as the efficiency frontier. Portfolios that produce points on the efficiency frontier provide the highest expected returns for each level of risk, and the lowest level of risk for each expected rate of return. Once on the efficiency frontier it is not possible to increase expected returns without increasing risk, nor is it possible to reduce risk

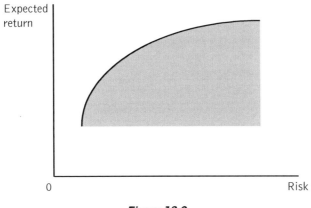

Figure 13.2

267

without reducing expected returns. Points on the efficiency frontier are said to dominate points in the shaded area below it. Any point below the efficiency frontier can be improved on, in terms of increasing expected returns and/or reducing risk, by changing to a portfolio on the efficiency frontier. Rational investors would be expected to hold portfolios on the efficiency frontier.

THE MARKOWITZ EQUATIONS

There is an equation for the expected return on a portfolio (in the sense of statistical expectation) and an equation for the expected variance (risk) of the portfolio. The equations used here will be based on the choices between the three asset classes of equities, bonds, and deposits.

The equation for the expected rate of return can be written as:

$$E(R_p) = (W_e)E(R_e) + (W_b) E(R_b) + (W_d) E(R_d) \tag{1}$$

where $E(R_p)$ is the expected return on the portfolio; (W_e), (W_b), and (W_d) are the portfolio weightings in equities, bonds, and deposits respectively (the weightings sum to 1); $E(R_e)$, $E(R_b)$, and $E(R_d)$ are the expected returns on equities, bonds, and deposits respectively.

The equation for the expected portfolio variance can be written as:

$$V_p = (W_e)^2 \sigma_e^2 + (W_b)^2 \sigma_b^2 + (W_d)^2 \sigma_d^2 + 2(W_e)(W_b)\sigma_e \sigma_b \rho_{eb} + 2(W_e)(W_d)\sigma_e$$
$$\sigma_d \rho_{ed} + 2(W_b)(W_d)\sigma_b \sigma_d \rho_{bd} \tag{2}$$

Where V_p is the variance of the portfolio; σ_e, σ_b, and σ_d are the expected standard deviations of returns on equities, bonds, and deposits respectively; ρ_{eb} is the expected correlation between the returns on equities and the returns on bonds, ρ_{ed} and ρ_{bd} have corresponding interpretations. The portfolio standard deviation is the square root of the portfolio variance, i.e. $\sigma_p = \sqrt{V_p}$.

By using equations (1) and (2) it is possible to find the highest expected return for any level of expected risk, and the lowest risk for each level of return. This optimisation procedure is based on the use of the coefficients of correlation and standard deviations of returns. This use of correlation coefficients and standard deviations distinguishes Markowitz diversification from naive diversification. Markowitz diversification achieves the best (optimal) level of diversification possible, whereas naive diversification cannot aspire to such optimality.

Combining assets in a portfolio achieves an expected return that is a weighted average of the expected returns of the individual assets. However the risk is less than the average of the individual risks, unless the coefficients of correlation all equal $+1$. Consider equations 3 and 4, which are generalised versions of equations 1 and 2 (generalised to allow for any number of assets in a portfolio).

$$E(R_p) = \sum_{j=1}^{n} W_j E(R_j) \tag{3}$$

$$V_p = \sum_{j=1}^{n} W_j^2 \sigma_j^2 + \sum_{j=1}^{n} \sum_{k=1}^{n} W_j W_k \sigma_j \sigma_k \rho_{jk} \tag{4}$$
$$j \neq k$$

The expected return of a portfolio, $E(R_p)$, is the weighted average of the expected returns from the individual securities. The weighting of security j (the proportion of the portfolio in security j) is represented by W_j and the expected return on security j shown as $E(R_j)$.

In equation 4, V_p is the variance of the portfolio returns (therefore $\sqrt{V_p}$ is the standard deviation of returns). The standard deviations of securities j and k are represented by σ_j and σ_k respectively. The coefficient of correlation between the returns of j and k is shown as ρ_{jk}.

If all the coefficients of correlation equal $+1$, the portfolio standard deviation would be a weighted average of the standard deviations of the individual securities. This averaging of the standard deviations is illustrated by Example 13.1.

EXAMPLE 13.1

Suppose that a portfolio comprises equal values of two securities with standard deviations of return of 0.2 (20% p.a.) and 0.4 (40% p.a.). If the correlation between returns is $+1$ then:

$$V_p = (0.5)^2(0.2)^2 + (0.5)^2(0.4)^2 + 2(0.5)(0.5)(0.2)(0.4)(1)$$
$$= (0.25)(0.04) + (0.25)(0.16) + 0.04$$
$$= 0.01 + 0.04 + 0.04 = 0.09$$
$$\therefore \sigma_p = \sqrt{0.09} = 0.3$$

The standard deviation (risk) of the portfolio, shown as σ_p, is 0.3 (i.e. 30%). This is the average of the risks of the individual securities (20% and 40%).

If the coefficients of correlation are less than $+1$, the portfolio risk would be less than the average of the risks of the individual securities. This is illustrated by Example 13.2.

EXAMPLE 13.2

If the correlation is 0.4, but other values are the same as in Example 13.1, the portfolio risk would be calculated as follows:

$$V_p = (0.5)^2(0.2)^2 + (0.5)^2(0.4)^2 + 2(0.5)(0.5)(0.2)(0.4)(0.4)$$
$$= (0.25)(0.04) + (0.25)(0.16) + (0.04)(0.4)$$
$$= 0.01 + 0.04 + 0.016 = 0.066$$
$$\sigma_p = \sqrt{0.066} = 0.257$$

The standard deviation (risk) of the portfolio is less than the average of the standard deviations (risks) of the two securities.

It can be seen that as the correlation falls below $+1$, the risk of the portfolio falls below the average of the risks of the individual securities that comprise the portfolio. As the correlation falls, the risk of the portfolio declines. Portfolio risk is at its lowest when the correlation is -1. When the correlation is -1 it is possible to find a proportion, for the two securities, that reduces risk to zero.

EXAMPLE 13.3

Suppose that a portfolio comprises equal values of two shares with standard deviations of return of 0.2 (20% p.a.) and 0.4 (40% p.a.). If the correlation between returns is -1 then:

$$V_p = (0.5)^2(0.2)^2 + (0.5)^2(0.4)^2 + 2(0.5)(0.5)(0.2)(0.4)(-1)$$
$$= (0.25)(0.04) + (0.25)(0.16) - 0.04$$
$$= 0.01 + 0.04 - 0.04 = 0.01$$
$$\therefore \sigma_p = \sqrt{0.01} = 0.1$$

The standard deviation (risk) of the portfolio is 0.1 (i.e. 10%). Since there is a perfectly negative correlation it is possible to find weights that reduce risk to zero.

$$V_p = W_1{}^2 \sigma_1{}^2 + W_2{}^2 \sigma_2{}^2 + 2W_1 W_2 \sigma_1 \sigma_2 \rho$$
$$V_p = W_1{}^2 \sigma_1{}^2 + W_2{}^2 \sigma_2{}^2 + 2W_1 W_2 \sigma_1 \sigma_2 (-1)$$
$$V_p = W_1{}^2 \sigma_1{}^2 + W_2{}^2 \sigma_2{}^2 - 2W_1 W_2 \sigma_1 \sigma_2$$
$$V_p = (W_1 \sigma_1 - W_2 \sigma_2)^2$$
$$\sigma_p = \sqrt{V_p} = W_1 \sigma_1 - W_2 \sigma_2$$

A zero risk portfolio has a standard deviation of zero.

$$0 = W_1 \sigma_1 - W_2 \sigma_2$$
$$W_2 \sigma_2 = W_1 \sigma_1$$
$$W_2 = W_1 \sigma_1 / \sigma_2$$

In the present example:

$$W_2 = W_1 (0.2/0.4) = 0.5W_1$$

If the share with a standard deviation of 0.4 has half the weighting (1/3) of the share with a standard deviation of 0.2 (a weighting of 2/3), the portfolio will have a standard deviation of zero.

$V_p = (2/3)^2(0.2)^2 + (1/3)^2(0.4)^2 + 2(2/3)(1/3)(0.2)(0.4)(-1)$

$= 0.0178 + 0.0178 - 0.0356 = 0$

$\sigma_p = 0$

It is to be noted that the share with the lower standard deviation has the higher weighting. A relatively large amount of the low standard deviation share is required to offset a relatively small amount of the high standard deviation share.

Figure 13.3 illustrates some possible expected return/risk combinations for securities X and Y. If the correlation of returns between X and Y were -1, it would be possible to find a portfolio of X and Y that reduces risk to zero. It would be possible to achieve a point such as A. If the correlation were $+1$, a portfolio of X and Y would be on the straight line XY; the risk of the portfolio would be an average of the risks of the two securities.

Between these extremes lie the more realistic correlations. Correlations would usually be between 0 and $+1$. In such cases portfolio risk would be greater than zero but lower than an average of the risks of the two securities. The possible combinations of expected return and risk would lie on a curve such as XY. The curve XY is an efficiency frontier for portfolios comprising X and Y. Along this curve the expected return is an average of the expected returns of X and Y, but the portfolio risk (standard deviation) is less than an average of the two risks.

The importance of correlations in the estimation of portfolio risk is illustrated by Exercises 13.4, 13.5, and 13.6.

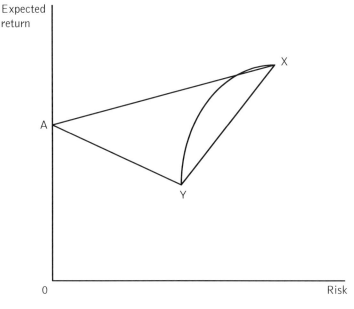

Figure 13.3

EXERCISE 13.4

A portfolio consists of stocks A, B, and C in equal proportions. Each has an expected return of 10% p.a. and an annual standard deviation of returns of 8%. The coefficient of correlation between the returns of A and B is 0.9, whilst the correlations between A and C and between B and C are both 0.

(a) Calculate the expected return and risk of the portfolio.

(b) Show how risk can be reduced by changing the proportions of A, B, and C. Why has the risk reduction occurred?

Answers

(a) Let $E(R_p)$ = expected return on the portfolio.

$E(R_p)$ = (1/3)10% + (1/3)10% + (1/3)10% = 10% p.a.

Let V = variance of the portfolio.

$V = (1/3)^2 \, 8^2 + (1/3)^2 \, 8^2 + (1/3)^2 \, 8^2 + 2(1/3)^2 \, 8^2(0.9) + 2(1/3)^2 \, 8^2 \, (0) + 2(1/3)^2 \, 8^2 \, (0)$

$V = (0.11)64 + (0.11)64 + (0.11)64 + 2(0.11)64(0.9)$

$V = 7.11 + 7.11 + 7.11 + 2(7.11)(0.9)$

$V = 21.33 + 12.8 = 34.13$

Standard deviation $= \sqrt{V} = \sqrt{34.13} = 5.84$

(b) One possibility is to increase the proportion held in C to 40% and reduce the proportions held in A and B to 30% each.

$V = (0.3)^2 \, 8^2 + (0.3)^2 \, 8^2 + (0.4)^2 \, 8^2 + 2(0.3)^2 \, 8^2(0.9)$

$V = 5.76 + 5.76 + 10.24 + 10.37 = 32.13$

Standard deviation $= \sqrt{V} = \sqrt{32.13} = 5.67$

Portfolio risk has been reduced because there is now a higher proportion in the stock whose correlations, with both of the other stocks, are low.

EXERCISE 13.5

An investor has a portfolio of three stocks. Their expected returns are A 7%, B 8%, and C 9% p.a. The expected standard deviations of returns are A 12%, B 14%, and C 16% p.a. The correlations between returns are AB 0.3, AC 0.8, and BC 0.2.

(a) Calculate the portfolio expected return and risk if each of the stocks constitutes one-third of the portfolio.

(b) Suggest weightings for A, B, and C that would produce a portfolio with lower risk. Explain why risk is reduced.

Answers

(a) Expected return is: $([1/3] \times 7) + ([1/3] \times 8) + ([1/3] \times 9) = 8\%$ p.a.

Portfolio variance, V_p, is:

$$V_p = (1/3)^2(0.12)^2 + (1/3)^2(0.14)^2 + (1/3)^2(0.16)^2 + 2(1/3)(1/3)(0.12)(0.14)$$
$$(0.3) + 2(1/3)(1/3)(0.12)(0.16)(0.8) + 2(1/3)(1/3)(0.14)(0.16)(0.2)$$

$$V_p = 0.0016 + 0.00218 + 0.00284 + 0.00112 + 0.00341 + 0.001$$

$$V_p = 0.01215$$

Standard deviation $= \sqrt{0.01215} = 0.1102$ i.e. 11.02% p.a.

(Note that either the percentage or the decimal expression of standard deviation can be used. For example a calculation could measure standard deviation as 12% or 0.12. Equivalent answers are obtained.)

(b) Risk might be reduced by increasing the weighting of the relatively low risk share, A, and increasing the weighting of the share with low correlations, B. For example 40% A, 40% B, and 20% C.

$$V_p = (0.4)^2(0.12)^2 + (0.4)^2(0.14)^2 + (0.2)^2(0.16)^2 + 2(0.4)(0.4)(0.12)(0.14)(0.3) +$$
$$2(0.4)(0.2)(0.12)(0.16)(0.8) + 2(0.4)(0.2)(0.14)(0.16)(0.2)$$

$$V_p = 0.0023 + 0.00314 + 0.00102 + 0.00161 + 0.00246 + 0.00072$$

$$V_p = 0.01125$$

Standard deviation $= \sqrt{0.01125} = 0.1061$ i.e. 10.61% p.a.

EXERCISE 13.6

Shares A, B, and C have expected rates of return of 6% p.a. and standard deviations of returns of 10% p.a. The coefficients of correlation between the returns are:

A and B 0.9

A and C 0.2

B and C 0.2

(a) Calculate the risk of a portfolio of 40% A, 40% B, and 20% C.

(b) Suggest a portfolio with lower risk.

(c) What practical difficulties would an investment manager face when calculating the risk of a portfolio of shares?

Answers

(a) $V = (0.4)^2(0.1)^2 + (0.4)^2(0.1)^2 + (0.2)^2(0.1)^2$
$$+ 2.(0.4)^2(0.1)^2(0.9) + 2(0.4)(0.2)(0.1)^2(0.2)$$
$$+ 2.(0.4)(0.2)(0.1)^2(0.2)$$

$$= 0.0016 + 0.0016 + 0.0004 + 0.00288 + 0.00032 + 0.00032$$

$V = 0.00712$

$\therefore$ Standard deviation of portfolio returns $= \sqrt{0.00712} = 0.0844$, i.e. 8.44% p.a.

(b) Since C has a low correlation with both A and B, a higher proportion of C might reduce risk. One possibility is 30% A, 30% B, and 40% C. In this case the risk would be calculated as:

$V = (0.3)^2(0.1)^2 + (0.3)^2(0.1)^2 + (0.4)^2(0.1)^2$
$$+ 2(0.3)^2(0.1)^2(0.9) + 2(0.3)(0.4)(0.1)^2(0.2)$$
$$+ 2(0.3)(0.4)(0.1)^2(0.2)$$

$V = 0.00598$

$\therefore$ Standard deviation of portfolio returns $= \sqrt{0.00598} = 0.0773$, i.e. 7.73% p.a.

(c) The calculations in (a) and (b) have involved just three shares. In reality there are thousands of shares that might be incorporated into a portfolio and calculating correlation coefficients between each possible pair of shares would be problematic. Even a portfolio of 50 different shares (not an unusual number) would involve 1,225 correlation coefficients. Correlating each share with a stock index would be a little less accurate but would reduce the number of correlations required to 50.

Another practical difficulty is that past statistical data may not be a reliable guide to future values. Returns, risks, and correlations can change over time so that the past is not always a reliable guide to the future.

It is often stated that the main insight of the Markowitz equations is the observation that low correlation is crucial to risk reduction. In the extreme, if perfectly negative correlations can be found then it is possible to construct entirely risk-free portfolios. However (near) zero risk could be achieved in the absence of correlations of -1. This can be seen from another feature of the Markowitz equations, namely that an increase in the number of different shares tends to reduce risk.

Consider a case in which all correlations are zero, and in which all shares have a standard deviation of returns of 20% p.a. (i.e. 0.2). Where there are two shares held in the portfolio, in equal proportions, the portfolio variance (σ^2) and standard deviation (σ) will be:

$$\sigma^2 = W_1{}^2 \sigma_1{}^2 + W_2{}^2 \sigma_2{}^2 = (0.5)^2(0.2)^2 + (0.5)^2(0.2)^2 = 0.01 + 0.01 = 0.02$$

$$\sigma = \sqrt{0.02} = 0.1414, \text{ i.e. } 14.14\% \text{ p.a.}$$

Where there are three shares held in the portfolio, in equal proportions, the portfolio variance and standard deviation will be:

$$\sigma^2 = W_1{}^2 \sigma_1{}^2 + W_2{}^2 \sigma_2{}^2 + W_3{}^2 \sigma_3{}^3 = (0.333)^2(0.2)^2 + (0.333)^2(0.2)^2 + (0.333)^2(0.2)^2$$

$$= 0.00444 + 0.00444 + 0.00444 = 0.01332$$

$$\sigma = \sqrt{0.01332} = 0.1154, \text{ i.e. } 11.54\% \text{ p.a.}$$

Where there are four shares held in the portfolio, in equal proportions, the portfolio variance and standard deviation will be:

$$\sigma^2 = W_1{}^2 \sigma_1{}^2 + W_2{}^2 \sigma_2{}^2 + W_3{}^2 \sigma_3{}^3 + W_4{}^2 \sigma_4{}^2 = (0.25)^2(0.2)^2 + (0.25)^2(0.2)^2 + (0.25)^2(0.2)^2 + (0.25)^2(0.2)^2$$

$$= 0.0025 + 0.0025 + 0.0025 + 0.0025 = 0.01$$

$$\sigma = \sqrt{0.01} = 0.1, \text{ i.e. } 10\% \text{ p.a.}$$

It can be seen that increasing the number of different shareholdings will reduce portfolio risk. By increasing the number of shares held sufficiently, portfolio risk can be reduced to (close to) zero.

However positive correlations would mean that risk cannot be reduced to zero (although increasing the number of shareholdings still reduces risk).

The risk-reduction effect would be greatly reduced if some shares have high weightings in portfolios. For this reason index tracker portfolios may not provide maximum risk reduction. Index tracker portfolios aim to reflect the composition of a stock index such as the FTSE 100. The larger companies tend to account for substantial proportions of the index, e.g. BP has accounted for about 10% of the FTSE 100.

Consider the three-share example above but with the weighting of one company being twice that of the other two.

$$\sigma^2 = W_1{}^2\sigma_1{}^2 + W_2{}^2\sigma_2{}^2 + W_3{}^2\sigma_3{}^3 = (0.5)^2(0.2)^2 + (0.25)^2(0.2)^2 + (0.25)^2(0.2)^2$$

$$= 0.01 + 0.0025 + 0.0025 = 0.015$$

$$\sigma = \sqrt{0.015} = 0.1225, \text{i.e. } 12.25\% \text{ p.a.}$$

The increased concentration of the portfolio increases risk from 11.54% to 12.25% p.a.

Another reason why index tracker funds do not minimise risk is that the shareholdings do not take account of correlations. Stock indices are often dominated by a few sectors, for example more than 50% of the FTSE 100 is comprised of shares from the oil, financial, telecommunications, and pharmaceutical sectors. Shares from the same sector are likely to exhibit relatively high correlations. It seems likely that a 1/N portfolio (i.e. a portfolio holding shares in equal proportions) that holds a very large number of different shares, including shares of companies that are too small to be included in most stock indices, would provide lower risk than an index tracker portfolio.

The downside of a 1/N portfolio is that transaction costs are incurred when the portfolio is rebalanced to maintain the equal proportions. The rebalancing entails selling shares whose prices have risen and buying those whose prices have fallen. In other words, rebalancing enforces a contrarian investment strategy.

FOREIGN INVESTMENTS AND PORTFOLIO RISK

Investing in the securities of foreign countries has two opposing effects on the risk of a portfolio. Risk is reduced since the foreign investments increase the degree of diversification of the portfolio. On the other hand there is an additional source of risk to the extent that foreign investments are priced in foreign currencies. The consensus view is that the risk-reducing effects are greater than the risk-enhancement effects.

Both of these effects can be interpreted in terms of the Markowitz equation for the measurement of portfolio risk. The risk-reduction effect of increased diversification is enhanced by choosing investments in those countries whose stock markets show the lowest correlations with the domestic market (and with one another). The effects of international diversification on portfolio risk can be illustrated by means of Figure 13.4.

Figure 13.4 shows how the risk of a portfolio tends to decline as the number of different stocks in the portfolio increases. The decline is most rapid when the correlation of returns between the stocks is low. The correlation is likely to be lower between a domestic and a foreign stock than between two domestic stocks. As a result the risk of the international portfolio (comprising both domestic and foreign stocks) tends to decline faster than the risk of the portfolio containing only domestic stocks. Furthermore since the returns on the domestic and foreign stock markets will not be perfectly correlated, the lowest achievable risk will be lower for the international portfolio than for the domestic portfolio. Systematic (non-diversifiable) risk for internationally diversified

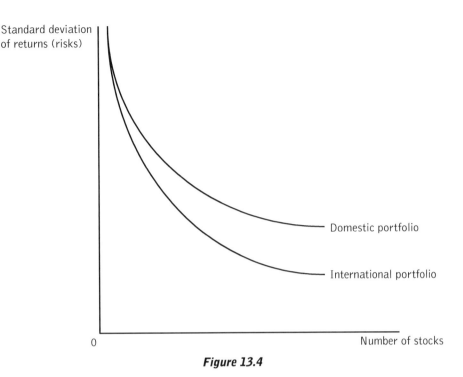

Figure 13.4

portfolios is lower than systematic risk for domestic portfolios.

Whereas the increased diversification provided by foreign investments reduces risk, the acquisition of currency exposure increases it. For the most part foreign stocks are priced in foreign currencies. If a foreign currency loses value relative to the domestic currency, the domestic currency value of the foreign investment will fall. A security may provide high returns in terms of its own currency, but a relative fall in that currency would offset those returns for foreign investors. Exchange rate movements can turn strong profits into heavy losses (or vice versa). A US dollar investment might produce a 10% return in dollar terms, but if the dollar falls 20% against the Euro the result for a European investor is a 10% loss.

This can be expressed in terms of the Markowitz formula. The risk of a foreign security, held as an investor's only asset, is represented by σ_F in equation 5.

$$\sigma_F{}^2 = \sigma_D{}^2 + \sigma_C{}^2 + 2\,\rho_{DC}\,\sigma_D\,\sigma_C \tag{5}$$

In equation 5, σ_D represents the risk (standard deviation of returns) of the security from the point of view of an investor in the foreign country. The currency risk is shown as σ_C. The correlation between the returns on the security (to an investor in the foreign country) and the exchange rate movements is represented by ρ_{DC}. It might be noted that the weighting for both the security risk and the currency risk is 1; this is because they both relate to the full value of the investment.

A numerical example can illustrate some of the implications of equation 5. Suppose that the risk (standard deviation of returns) for an investor in the foreign country is 20% p.a. and that a UK investor faces a 15% p.a. exchange rate risk. If this relates to a UK investor buying a US

277

security, the risk for a US investor is 20% whereas the UK investor faces that risk plus a 15% p.a. currency risk. Suppose further that there is zero correlation between the returns on the security for a US investor and the currency movements. Introducing these values into equation 5 gives:

$$20^2 + 15^2 + 2(20 \times 15 \times 0) = 400 + 225 = 625$$

$$\sigma_F{}^2 = 625$$

$$\therefore \sigma_F = 25$$

The combination of a security risk of 20% p.a. and a currency risk of 15% p.a. produces a foreign security risk of 25% p.a.

From the perspective of a well-diversified international portfolio, the contribution of currency risk to total risk depends upon the correlations between the various foreign currencies. If such correlations are low, as appears to be the case, much of the currency risk is removed as a result of diversifying among currencies.

It could be argued that not all of the currency risk should be included in the calculation of total risk. For example the investor's annual expenditure might be partly spent on imported goods. This may give a currency risk, which is opposite to that on foreign investments. A rise in the US dollar against the Euro will make imports from the United States more expensive for Europeans, but that currency movement enhances investment returns on US securities held by Europeans. One currency exposure offsets the other. To the extent that this happens, the exchange rate exposure of foreign investments can be seen as reducing risk rather than increasing it.

In most countries investors, even institutional investors, invest primarily in their own country. The UK stock (equity) market is less than 10% of the world market by value, and the UK bond market is about 3% of the world market. However most UK pension, insurance fund, and unit trust investments are in UK shares and bonds. This has been referred to as home bias, and the behavioural finance concept of familiarity has been used as a possible explanation. It is suggested that investors prefer familiar investments, such as those of their own country, and perceive those familiar investments as both yielding higher prospective returns and providing lower risk. Strong and Xu (2003) reported a Merrill Lynch survey in which fund managers from continental Europe predicted that their stock returns would outperform UK, US, and Japanese stock returns. Simultaneously UK fund managers were forecasting that UK stocks would perform better than the others. Fund managers were optimistic about their domestic stocks, relative to foreign stocks, in terms of both return and risk. When investors do buy foreign stocks, they buy them in companies that are familiar. These tend to be large, and export-oriented, companies (Kang and Stulz 1997). The home bias hinders the achievement of the full degree of international diversification required to obtain the greatest possible benefits from international diversification.

EXERCISE 13.7

Suppose that the UK, US, and Eurozone stock markets each have an expected return of 8% p.a. and that, from a sterling perspective, the expected standard deviations are UK 20%, US 25%, and Eurozone 25% p.a. (inclusive of expected currency risk). Suppose also that the expected correlations between stock markets are 0.5 in each case. What are the expected returns and risks of:

(a) A portfolio wholly invested in UK shares.

(b) A portfolio evenly divided between UK and US shares.

(c) A portfolio evenly divided between UK, US, and Eurozone shares.

Comment on the results.

Answers

(a) The expected return is 8% p.a. and the expected risk (standard deviation of returns) is 20% p.a.

(b) The expected return is 8% and the expected risk is estimated as follows:

$$V = 0.5^2 0.2^2 + 0.5^2 0.25^2 + 2(0.5)(0.5)(0.2)(0.25)(0.5) = 0.01 + 0.015625 + 0.0125$$
$$= 0.038125$$

$$\sigma = \sqrt{0.038125} = 0.1953, \text{ i.e. } 19.53\% \text{ p.a.}$$

(c) The expected return is 8% and the expected risk is estimated as follows:

$$V = 0.33^2 0.2^2 + 0.33^2 0.25^2 + 0.33^2 0.25^2 + 2(0.33)(0.33)(0.2)(0.25)(0.5) +$$
$$2(0.33)(0.33)(0.2)(0.25)(0.5) + 2(0.33)(0.33)(0.25)(0.25)(0.5)$$

$$V = 0.004444 + 0.006944 + 0.006944 + 0.005556 + 0.005556 + 0.006944 = 0.036388$$

$$\sigma = \sqrt{0.036388} = 0.1908, \text{ i.e. } 19.08\% \text{ p.a.}$$

These calculations illustrate that diversifying a portfolio internationally can reduce risk. The risk reduction appears to increase as the number of countries (or regions) is increased. The addition of currency risk partially offsets the risk-reduction effects of diversification. The risk-reduction from international diversification would be enhanced by lower currency risk and lower correlations between stock markets. Including both the US and the Eurozone helps to diversify currency risk when compared with including just one of them. Raising the proportion of UK investment slightly would reduce risk because the UK has the lowest risk, but the UK proportion should not be raised very much otherwise the benefits of diversification would be reduced.

EXHIBIT 13.1   EXAMPLE OF AN INTERNATIONAL FUND

HENDERSON GLOBAL INVESTORS INTERNATIONAL FUND (AS OF 31 AUGUST 2007)

Objective

To aim to provide capital growth by investing in companies in any economic sector and any area of the world.

Benchmark: MSCI World Index
Fund size: £49.25 million
Charges:* (without exit fees) Initial 5%
                                     Annual 1.5%
                (with exit fees) Initial 0%
                                       Annual 2%

Table 13.E

Ten largest holdings (as percentages of the total fund)	
Nintendo Company	2.4
Nestle SA	1.8
Siemens AG	1.6
Man Group	1.6
Koninklijke Numico	1.6
American Express Company	1.5
Altria Group Inc	1.5
Procter & Gamble	1.5
Merck & Co Inc	1.5
Mizuho Financial Group NPV	1.4

Table 13.F

Country breakdown	(%)
United States	50.7
Japan	9.9
Germany	5.6
United Kingdom	5.6
Switzerland	5.0
Singapore	3.8
Canada	3.2
Italy	3.1
Greece	2.3
Other	10.8

*Other charging structures were available.
Source: Henderson Global Investors.

ASYMMETRIC CORRELATION AND LEPTOKURTOSIS

Problems arise for the use of Markowitz diversification when two of its assumptions are violated. One of these assumptions is that correlation coefficients are the same irrespective of whether prices are rising or falling (the assumption of symmetric correlation). The other is that the distribution of asset returns can be described by a normal distribution.

There is evidence that correlations are much higher during market falls than during rises. Erb *et al.* (1994) found that correlations among the stock markets of the US, Japan, UK, and Germany were higher when both of the correlated markets were falling than when both were rising. This is known as asymmetric correlation and implies that the benefits of diversification fall just when they are most needed.

The finding that correlations are higher in falling markets than in rising markets has been confirmed by other studies using both international and single economy correlations, e.g. Longin and Solnik (1995, 2001), Ang and Chen (2001), Jacquier and Marcus (2001), Meric *et al.* (2002). A study by Roll (1988) of the stock market crash of October 1987 found that all 23 of the countries studied suffered the crash.

However there is evidence that international diversification can substantially reduce risk during periods of weak market performance. Asness (2005) provided some figures that were indicative of the prospective benefits of international diversification during stock market weakness. The figures related to the benefits of holding internationally diversified portfolios for investors in France, Germany, Japan, the United Kingdom, and the United States. Using data from 1950 to 2004, the worst ten-year periods from a home-country portfolio were compared with the worst ten-year periods from a global portfolio (formed by equally weighting each country's contribution to the portfolio). The worst case returns, in real terms, were as shown in Table 13.4. In each case the global portfolio proved to show a lower downside risk in the sense of the highest ten-year loss.

Correlations between national stock markets not only vary as a result of market direction, but also vary between country pairs. Bessler and Yang (2003) investigated the interdependence between national stock markets. They found that the Japanese market was relatively isolated from the other markets studied, in that it was not strongly influenced by the other markets and had little influence over those others. The French and Canadian stock markets showed a high degree of correlation with movements in other markets. These findings suggest that Japan is useful for diversification, whilst France and Canada are less so. The US market was found to have a consistently strong influence over other markets. The Meric *et al.* (2002) study found that during a falling market the US market had considerable influence over other (France, Germany, Japan, UK) stock markets whilst the other markets had no influence over the US market, or over each other.

The Markowitz equation for the measurement of risk uses a single number for correlation. This coefficient of correlation may be based on a period containing rising, falling, and relatively stable markets. Such a value is likely to understate the correlation when both assets (or markets) are

Table 13.4

Country	Home-country portfolio (%)	Global portfolio (%)
France	−57.9	−21.2
Germany	−44.6	−35.5
Japan	−53.8	−42.9
United Kingdom	−61.3	−21.9
United States	−39.9	−11.3

falling. In consequence the true risk of the portfolio would also be underestimated. Most of the research on correlation between national markets seems to have focused on equity markets. Hunter and Simon (2005) considered the government bond markets and found that the benefits of diversification across major government bond markets did not decrease following sharp market falls, or during periods of high volatility.

Leptokurtosis is alternatively called fat tails. The ends of the distribution of returns decline less rapidly than in the case of a normal distribution. In other words, extreme values are more likely than a normal distribution would predict. In the presence of leptokurtosis, normal distributions understate the true level of risk. The use of risk measures (standard deviations) based on normal distributions when using the Markowitz equation to estimate risk will tend to cause the level of risk to be underestimated. The distributions of returns on shares appear to exhibit leptokurtosis.

In the presence of asymmetric correlation and leptokurtosis, the Markowitz equation for estimating risk could have a downward bias. The equation might understate the level of risk of a portfolio.

If finding low correlations (symmetric or otherwise) is a problem, a portfolio manager might carry out research to find investments with low correlations. Daniel and Blank (2002) looked for asset classes that showed negative correlation with equities. They also applied criteria that required the assets to be suitable for institutional portfolio managers. Such criteria included adequate size of trades, liquidity of markets, and acceptable transaction costs. Assets identified included gold, copper, crude oil, farmland, and forestry. Other researchers have concluded that real estate can provide good diversification for an equity, or broader, portfolio.

CONSISTENCY AND THE ROLE OF DIRECT PROPERTY INVESTMENT IN PORTFOLIOS

The Markowitz equations are applied using computer software. Values for expected asset returns, risk, and correlations are the inputs and expectations of portfolio return and risk are the outputs. The application can be conducted for varying investment horizons (investment holding periods). If a particular asset appears in the resulting portfolios for all investment horizons, that asset is said to have consistency. Direct property investment is the purchase of the property itself rather than shares in property companies or property-based institutional investments. If direct property were to be included in an investment portfolio, and if there were uncertainty concerning the length of time for which properties would be held, it would be desirable that property has consistency. Direct property investments need to have a place in an optimum portfolio for all relevant investment horizons.

Lee and Stevenson (2006) found that property possesses the attribute of consistency. Property appears to be particularly useful for risk reduction. Portfolios with investment horizons ranging from 5 to 25 years were investigated. Not only did they check for consistency but also they compared optimum portfolios inclusive and exclusive of direct property. They found that the inclusion of property both increases returns and reduces risk, particularly towards the low return/low risk end of the efficiency frontier. It was found that the inclusion of property tended to reduce bond holdings rather more than it reduced share and cash holdings.

Lee and Stevenson (2006) found that the consistency of direct property investment was robust in the sense that the Markowitz-based software indicated that property had a place in optimal portfolios for all investment horizons from 5 to 25 years, and for most levels of portfolio return. This result held irrespective of whether property was used for return enhancement or risk reduction. The research results indicated that the risk reduction effects were greater than the return-enhancement effects. The benefits of including property tended to rise as the investment horizon extended.

Fraser *et al.* (2002) confirmed the particular advantage of property in long-term portfolios. They found no long-run correlation between property returns and returns on either shares or bonds. Stevenson (2004) confirmed that property real estate has diversification benefits but indicated that it was likely to reduce expected return as well as risk. It was suggested that this could be because property is low risk compared with both shares and bonds. McGreal *et al.* (2006) concluded that the income streams from property portfolios had little risk, but there was higher risk associated with the price change element of property returns.

DIRECT PROPERTY INVESTMENT IN INSTITUTIONAL AND PRIVATE PORTFOLIOS

Montezuma (2004) made the point that there are important differences between institutions and individuals in relation to direct residential property investment. One important difference is that, for investing institutions, property is an investment and serves no other function. For an individual household property is likely to have a consumption role, as a place to live, as well as an investment function. The optimum amount of housing from a consumption perspective will differ from the optimum contribution to an investment portfolio. For example the optimum from an investment view may be a one-bedroom flat, but the family may be unhappy with that amount of accommodation.

Another important difference is that an institutional investor would be able to hold a diversified portfolio of residential properties. Most individual property owners have just one property. Institutional investors benefit from the risk-reduction effects of diversification whereas most individual households do not. Institutional investors may have systematic risk only. The properties of individuals will bear both systematic and non-systematic risk. The greater risk of property investment, for most households, would tend to reduce the optimum amount of property from an investment perspective.

Institutions have more flexibility as to the amount of property to be held. If an institutional fund manager decides to reduce the weighting of residential property in the portfolio by 10%, the manager could reduce the weighting by selling properties. The individual household is not able to sell 10% of its home.

There are common features between institutions and households in relation to investment in residential property. There are low correlations with other asset classes such as bonds and shares. The low correlations make housing attractive as a means of diversifying portfolios. Transaction costs are high relative to other assets, and transaction times are also high (it takes time to sell a property). These transaction features make residential properties unsuitable as short-term investments, inhibit frequent portfolio adjustments, and prevent quick response to changing conditions.

MARKOWITZ DIVERSIFICATION VERSUS THE 1/N STRATEGY

One popular form of naive diversification amongst retail investors is the 1/N strategy. The 1/N strategy entails equal division of investment money between the available funds. For example when given a choice of five funds for pension investments people will often divide their pension contributions equally between the funds. Siebenmorgen and Weber (2003) found that financial advisers were also prone to recommending 1/N strategies, and to ignoring correlations between investments when estimating portfolio risk. The 1/N strategy is often seen as irrational behaviour since it involves the loss of the benefits of Markowitz diversification.

However if the range of available funds reasonably reflects the distribution of asset classes, the improvement available from Markowitz diversification may be marginal. The ranges of funds that allow reasonable diversification from the 1/N strategy might include the following: a UK equity fund (i.e. a fund of UK shares), an international equity fund, a commercial property fund, a bond fund, and a cash (or money market) fund. Conversely if the available funds comprised four bond funds and one equity fund, the 1/N strategy would not provide good diversification.

Exercise 13.8 illustrates how it might be difficult to unambiguously improve on the 1/N strategy by a simple application of the principle of Markowitz diversification. At a more sophisticated level, DeMiguel *et al.* (2006) have demonstrated that a 1/N strategy may be superior to Markowitz diversification when account is taken of the fact that estimated values of expected returns, standard deviations, and correlations are subject to statistical error. The fact that the estimated values of these parameters, which are used in the Markowitz model, are subject to uncertainty adds to the risk of a portfolio based on Markowitz diversification. This addition to risk may exceed the benefits of Markowitz diversification relative to the 1/N strategy.

EXERCISE 13.8

(a) A financial adviser suggests that a client should divide an investment equally between five OEIC funds: a UK equity fund, a European equity fund, a property fund, a bond fund, and a cash fund. (Equal division between funds is known as a 1/N strategy.)

(b) The financial adviser considers an adjustment to the asset allocation that involves increasing the weightings of the UK equity fund and the bond fund to 25% each, and lowering the cash fund to 10%. The change is based on the observation that the UK equity fund and the bond fund both have higher prospective yields than the cash fund, and on the observation that the UK equity fund and the bond fund have a low correlation. Would the financial adviser improve on the 1/N strategy by achieving both higher expected returns and lower risk (as measured by standard deviation)?

Table 13.G

	Expected return (% p.a.)	Standard Deviation (% p.a.)
UK equity fund	8	14
European equity fund	10	18
Property fund	6	10
Bond fund	5	9
Cash fund	3	1

Table 13.H Correlations between returns

	UK equity	European equity	Property	Bond	Cash
UK equity		0.7	−0.1	−0.3	0
European equity			0	−0.1	0
Property				0.3	0
Bond					0

Using the tables what are the expected (forcast) return and risk of the portfolio?

Answers

(a) Using the Markowitz equations, the expected return on the 1/N portfolio is:

$$E(R_p) = 0.2(8) + 0.2(10) + 0.2(6) + 0.2(5) + 0.2(3) = 1.6 + 2 + 1.2 + 1 + 0.6 = 6.4\% \text{ p.a.}$$

The expected variance of returns is:

$$V_p = (0.2^2 \times 14^2) + (0.2^2 \times 18^2) + (0.2^2 \times 10^2) + (0.2^2 \times 9^2) + (0.2^2 \times 1^2)$$
$$+ 2(0.2 \times 0.2 \times 14 \times 18 \times 0.7) + 2(0.2 \times 0.2 \times 14 \times 10 \times [-0.1]) + 2(0.2 \times 0.2 \times 14 \times 9 \times [-0.3]) + 2(0.2 \times 0.2 \times 18 \times 9 \times [-0.1]) + 2(0.2 \times 0.2 \times 10 \times 9 \times 0.3)$$

$$= 7.84 + 12.96 + 4 + 3.24 + 0.04 + 14.112 - 1.12 - 3.024 - 1.296 + 2.16 = 38.912$$

The standard deviation is the square root of the variance, hence:

$$\sigma_p = \sqrt{38.912} = 6.24 \text{ (to two decimal places).}$$

Note that in the calculation the terms that include a correlation of zero have been omitted on the grounds that their values would be zero.

(b) The expected return on the alternative portfolio would be:

$$E(R_p) = 0.25(8) + 0.2(10) + 0.2(6) + 0.25(5) + 0.1(3) = 2 + 2 + 1.2 + 1.25 + 0.3$$
$$= 6.75\% \text{ p.a.}$$

So the objective of raising the expected rate of return is achieved.
The expected variance of the alternative portfolio would be:

$$V_p = (0.25^2 \times 14^2) + (0.2^2 \times 18^2) + (0.2^2 \times 10^2) + (0.25^2 \times 9^2) + (0.1^2 \times 1^2)$$
$$+ 2(0.25 \times 0.2 \times 14 \times 18 \times 0.7) + 2(0.25 \times 0.2 \times 14 \times 10 \times [-0.1]) + 2(0.25 \times 0.25 \times 14 \times 9 \times [-0.3]) + 2(0.2 \times 0.25 \times 18 \times 9 \times [-0.1]) + 2(0.2 \times 0.25 \times 10 \times 9 \times 0.3)$$

$$= 12.25 + 12.96 + 4 + 5.0625 + 0.01 + 17.64 - 1.4 - 4.725 - 1.62 + 2.7 = 46.8775$$

The standard deviation is the square root of the variance, hence:

$\sigma_p = \sqrt{46.8775} = 6.85$ (to two decimal places).

Risk is higher than in the case of the 1/N strategy. Despite attempting to follow the principles of Markowitz diversification by choosing to emphasise a low correlation combination of funds, the adviser has not succeeded in raising returns without increasing risk. Even if the correlation between the UK equity and bond fund had been as low as −1, the alternative strategy would not have succeeded in reducing risk relative to the 1/N strategy. Despite the benefits of low correlation, switching from a low risk fund to high risk funds raises portfolio risk. The movement of money from the very low risk cash fund to the higher risk funds increases the overall risk.

THE SIGNIFICANCE OF INCLUDING A RISK-FREE ASSET AMONGST THE INVESTMENT ALTERNATIVES

If a risk-free asset (treasury bill or bank deposit) is available to them, investors may hold combinations of the risk-free asset and a portfolio of risky assets. Rational investors would choose a portfolio of risky assets on the efficiency frontier. More specifically they would choose the portfolio depicted by point A in Figure 13.5. This is known as the market portfolio.

The rate of return on the risk-free asset is shown as R_f. Rational investors would hold combinations of the risk-free asset and the portfolio at A. Point A indicates the expected return/ risk combination of the portfolio that produces the highest capital market line. The capital market line is the set of points that represent combinations of the risk-free asset and the market portfolio.

To the left of point A investors are combining positive amounts of the risk-free asset with the portfolio at A. To the right of point A investors combine negative amounts of the risk-free asset with the portfolio. In other words, to the right of point A investors borrow money in order to hold an amount of the market portfolio that exceeds their wealth.

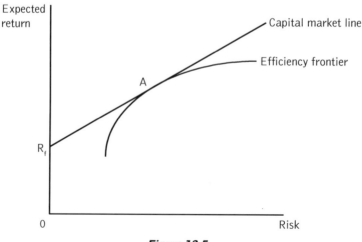

Figure 13.5

The expected rate of return for a portfolio that lies on the capital market line is given by:

$$E(R_p) = (1 - w)R_f + wE(R_m) \tag{6}$$

which can be rearranged to:

$$E(R_p) = R_f + w[E(R_m) - R_f] \tag{7}$$

where $E(R_p)$ is the expected return on the investor's portfolio, w is the proportion of the investor's portfolio that is held in the market portfolio (hence the proportion held in the risk-free asset is $1 - w$), R_f is the rate of return (rate of interest) on the risk-free asset, $E(R_m)$ is the expected rate of return on the market portfolio.

EXERCISE 13.9

A fund manager intends to construct a portfolio of shares, bonds, and deposits. The expected returns on these asset classes are 10% p.a., 5% p.a., and 3% p.a. respectively. The expected standard deviations of returns are 20% p.a., 15% p.a., and 0% p.a. respectively. The coefficients of correlation between returns are:

shares/bonds 0.5
shares/deposits 0
bonds/deposits 0

(a) Calculate the expected return and standard deviation of a portfolio comprising 60% shares, 30% bonds, and 10% deposits.

(b) How could the fund manager construct a portfolio with half the risk of the portfolio of part (a)?

Answers

(a) The expected return would be:

$(10 \times 0.6) + (5 \times 0.3) + (3 \times 0.1) = 7.8\%$ p.a.

The expected variance would be:

$V = (0.6)^2(0.2)^2 + (0.3)^2(0.15)^2 + (0.1)^2(0)^2 + 2(0.6)(0.3)(0.2)(0.15)(0.5) + 2(0.6)(0.1)(0.2)(0)(0) + 2(0.3)(0.1)(0.15)(0)(0)$

$V = 0.0144 + 0.002025 + 0 + 0.0054 + 0 + 0 = 0.021825$

The expected standard deviation is:

$\sigma = \sqrt{V} = \sqrt{0.021825} = 0.1477$ i.e. 14.77% p.a. (to two decimal places).

(b) One approach would be to halve the weightings of the risky assets so that the portfolio becomes: 30% shares, 15% bonds, 55% deposits.

The expected variance would now be:

$V = (0.3)^2(0.2)^2 + (0.15)^2(0.15)^2 + (0.55)^2(0)^2 + 2(0.3)(0.15)(0.2)(0.15)(0.5) +$
  $2(0.3)(0.55)(0.2)(0)(0) + 2(0.15)(0.55)(0.15)(0)(0)$

$V = 0.0036 + 0.00050625 + 0 + 0.00135 + 0 + 0 = 0.0054562$

The expected standard deviation is:

$\sigma = \sqrt{V} = \sqrt{0.0054562} = 0.073866$ i.e. 7.39% p.a. (to two decimal places).

EXERCISE 13.10

There are two risky assets available, a share and a bond. The share has an expected return of 8% p.a. and an expected standard deviation of returns of 16% p.a. The bond has an expected return of 4% p.a. and an expected standard deviation of returns of 10% p.a. There is also a risk-free asset available, a bank deposit paying 2% p.a. The expected coefficient of correlation between the returns on the share and the returns on the bond is 0.3. The coefficient of correlation between the bank deposit and the share is 0, as is the correlation between the bank deposit and the bond.

(a) Calculate the expected return, and the expected standard deviation of returns, of a portfolio comprising 50% of the share and 50% of the bond.

(b) Calculate the expected return, and the expected standard deviation of returns, of a portfolio comprising 25% of the share, 25% of the bond, and 50% of the deposit.

(c) How could an investor raise the expected return to 10% p.a.? What level of risk might be involved?

Answers

(a) $E(R_p) = (0.5)8 + (0.5)4 = 6\%$ p.a.

  $V_p = (0.5)^2(0.16)^2 + (0.5)^2(0.1)^2 + 2(0.5)(0.5)(0.16)(0.1)(0.3)$
    $= 0.0064 + 0.0025 + 0.0024 = 0.0113$

  $\sigma_p = \sqrt{V_p} = \sqrt{0.0113} = 0.1063$ i.e. 10.63% p.a.

(b) $E(R_p) = (0.25)8 + (0.25)4 + (0.5)2 = 4\%$ p.a.

  $V_p = (0.25)^2(0.16)^2 + (0.25)^2(0.1)^2 + (0.5)^2(0)^2 + 2(0.25)(0.25)(0.16)(0.1)(0.3)$
    $+ 2(0.25)(0.5)(0.16)(0)(0) + 2(0.25)(0.5)(0.1)(0)(0)$

  $V_p = 0.0016 + 0.000625 + 0 + 0.0006 + 0 + 0 = 0.002825$

  $\sigma_p = \sqrt{V_p} = \sqrt{0.002825} = 0.05315$ i.e. 5.315% p.a.

Note that this is exactly half the risk as that provided by the portfolio in part (a). This is to be expected since the portfolio of part (b) comprises 50% of the portfolio of part (a) and 50% the risk-free asset.

(c) The investor could borrow a sum equal to his or her wealth. The whole of the investor's wealth, plus the sum borrowed, would be invested in the portfolio of part (a).

The expected return would be 10% p.a.

$$E(R_p) = (1.0)8 + (1.0)4 - (1.0)2$$
$$10 = 8 + 4 - 2$$

The expected standard deviation of returns would be:

$$2 \times 10.63 = 21.26\% \text{ p.a.}$$

(the risky assets amount to double the portfolio of part (a)).

It is often argued that when the investment horizon is very long term, as may be the case with a pension fund, the best portfolio would be one invested 100% in equities (i.e. shares, stocks) on the grounds that the probability of shares underperforming deposits or bonds over the very long run is extremely low. However Asness (2005) makes the point that a better portfolio might be a combination of equities and bonds, which is leveraged by means of borrowing to increase the sum invested. An examination of the US markets found that a portfolio of 60% stocks plus 40% bonds, when leveraged to the risk level of a 100% stocks portfolio, provided higher long-run returns than an unleveraged portfolio invested 100% in equities. In terms of Figure 13.5, the optimal portfolio at point A was 60% equities and 40% bonds. By borrowing to add sufficiently to the portfolio to bring the risk level up to that of 100% equities, the resulting portfolio provided a higher return than a 100% equities portfolio. By borrowing money an investor was able to leverage the portfolio to a point on the capital market line to the right of point A and obtain a return in excess of what an unleveraged portfolio invested solely in stocks could provide.

ASSET ALLOCATION LINES

Farrar (1962) found that US mutual funds (unit trusts) were, typically, not on the efficiency frontier. This finding has been supported by subsequent studies by other researchers. Individual investors can nevertheless create investment opportunities that correspond to the capital market line by combining holdings of risk-free assets (e.g. bank or building society deposits) with holdings of a unit trust. The resulting opportunities will be on what is termed an asset allocation line. Such an asset allocation line is illustrated in Figure 13.6.

The point marked by X describes the risk-return characteristics of a unit trust. An investor can attain a point along the asset allocation line by combining a holding of the unit trust with a bank deposit (or debt if the chosen position is to the right of point X).

The investor could get closer to the capital market line by holding a portfolio of unit trusts (which will further reduce non-systematic risk and move point X towards the efficiency frontier).

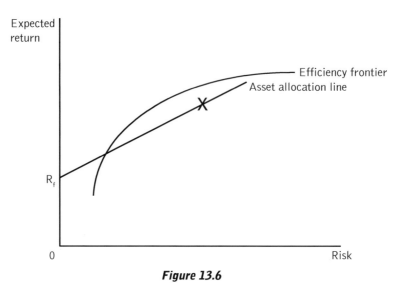

Figure 13.6

Alternatively the investor might choose a unit trust that tracks a broad stock index, for example the FT All-Share Index. In this way an investor can get close to the capital market line (however even index tracker funds based on broad indices do not fully correspond to the market portfolio at A in Figure 13.5, since the market portfolio contains all possible investments – domestic stocks, foreign stocks, bonds, property, etc.).

BEHAVIOURAL PORTFOLIOS

The Markowitz model of portfolio construction suggests an optimal, or ideal, approach to portfolio building. However people do not typically think in terms of the Markowitz model. In particular, people are prone to mental accounting (Thaler 1985; Prelec and Loewenstein 1998). Investors tend to place each investment into a separate mental account. This means that each investment is treated separately and interactions are overlooked. People tend to ignore correlations when gauging the risk contributed by an investment to a portfolio.

Investors tend to ignore the interactions between mental accounts and between investment assets. For example an investor may have two pension funds, four Individual Savings Accounts (ISAs), a unit trust savings scheme, and an endowment policy. Mental accounting implies that the investor is concerned about the risk and return of each of these separately rather than seeing them as components of a total portfolio. An implication is that an additional investment, for example a new ISA, is evaluated in isolation from the other investments without regard to its correlation with the other investments. This tendency to ignore correlations between components of the total portfolio leads to a sub-optimal portfolio construction from the perspective of Markowitz portfolio theory.

A person may keep retirement savings in one mental account whilst keeping savings for a new car in another mental account. Separating funds according to their goals is a mechanism that helps with self-control, and with the ability to monitor progress towards goals. Shefrin and Statman (2000) showed how the psychological biases of investors cause them to think of their portfolios as a pyramid of assets. Each layer in the pyramid represents assets intended to meet a particular goal, and each layer forms a mental account. People are seen as having separate mental accounts for each investment goal, and as being willing to take different levels of risk for each goal. Investments are chosen for each mental account in order to meet the desired risk and return characteristics of that mental account. There may be a goal of safety and a mental account is established to meet that goal with investments in risk-free assets. There may be a goal of income generation, which is met by the establishment of a mental account containing investments with a high income yield. There may be a goal of capital growth with a mental account containing growth-oriented investments. The result of the various goals and mental accounts is that the investor ends up with a group of mini-portfolios. There is a pyramid of mini-portfolios, each focused on a different goal. As a result the overall portfolio fails to be efficient in the sense of Markowitz diversification.

A study applying acquisition pattern analysis to financial products appears to be consistent with the Shefrin and Statman pyramid. Paas *et al.* (2007) found a common order of acquisition of financial products reflecting risk levels of the products. The first product to be acquired is normally a savings account, followed by a pension fund, then mutual funds and finally shares. This is consistent with the idea of building a pyramid of assets beginning with the least risky assets as the base of the pyramid followed by layers comprising assets of increasing levels of risk. Paas *et al.* also found that, when disposing of investments, the more risky assets tended to be the first to go and the least risky were the last to be discarded.

Other aspects of investment behaviour that undermine the achievement of Markowitz optimality have been identified by Benartzi and Thaler (2001) in a study of employee pension funds in the United States. One aspect is the tendency to use a '1/N rule'. When offered a choice of N funds into which to invest, many employees choose to put 1/N of the money into each of the funds. In other words the money is divided equally between the funds irrespective of whether that produces an optimal diversification from the perspective of Markowitz theory. Even more perverse is the tendency to invest a large proportion of the money (Benartzi and Thaler found it to be 42%) in the shares of the employing company. Not only does this result in a poorly diversified financial portfolio but, when human capital is considered, the diversification is even worse. Employees are making both their current and their retirement incomes dependent upon the fortunes of a single company.

Another psychological bias that affects portfolio construction is the familiarity bias (alternatively known as ambiguity-aversion). Investors appear to prefer investments that seem familiar to them. Huberman (2001) found that investors tend to buy the shares of local companies. Coval and Moskowitz (1999) found that professional investment managers were also subject to this familiarity bias. French and Poterba (1991) identified a home bias, which deters investors from international diversification.

VALUE-AT-RISK

The concept of value-at-risk (VaR) uses the principles of portfolio diversification in risk management. Risk management is the process of identifying, measuring, and controlling risk. This does not necessarily mean attempting to eliminate or reduce risk. Some amount of risk may be seen as desirable, particularly if higher risk is seen as being associated with higher prospective returns. Risk management aims to ensure that the risk-taking aspects of investing are carried out in an understood and controlled manner. Risk management is a continuous process since there are continuous changes in the composition of an investor's portfolio, the risk characteristics of the assets in the portfolio, and the attitudes and circumstances of the investor.

Value-at-risk is the maximum loss that a portfolio is likely to suffer during a specified period and with a specified probability. If there is a 5% probability that the value of a portfolio will fall by more than £1 million during a month, the value-at-risk for one month and 95% confidence is £1 million. The figure for the value-at-risk might be interpreted as the loss, which has a chance of 5% of being exceeded (when the confidence level is 95%) or a chance of 1% of being exceeded (if the confidence level is 99%).

Figure 13.7 illustrates value-at-risk with confidence levels of 95% (5% chance that there will be a loss greater than the value-at-risk) and 99% (1% chance that there will be a loss greater than the value-at-risk). In these cases value-at-risk is expressed as a number of standard deviations from the mean. This value is determined by the chosen confidence level; on the basis that the distribution of returns follows the standard normal distribution. A confidence level of 95% will always have a value-at-risk of -1.645 standard deviations, and a confidence level of 99% will always have a value-at-risk of -2.326 standard deviations. Turning these numbers into money values requires multiplication by the money value of the standard deviation. If a portfolio is estimated to have a monthly standard deviation of returns of £100,000, the value-at-risk at a confidence level of 95% is £164,500 and the value-at-risk at a confidence level of 99% is £232,600.

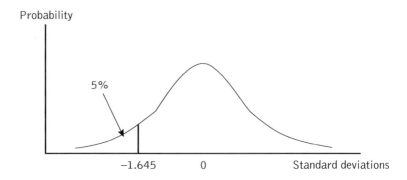

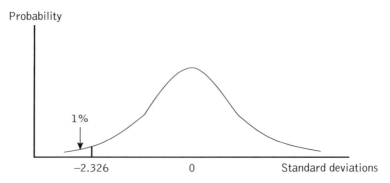

Figure 13.7   *Normal distributions with mean of zero*

A big advantage of value-at-risk is that it measures risk as a single number. However it does have drawbacks. One problem is that while it tells the user about the maximum loss on, say, 99% of time periods it says nothing about the size of the loss on the remaining 1% of occasions. Another problem is that it can be difficult to estimate value-at-risk in practice. Different estimation methods can produce very different results.

It is necessary to estimate the future return distribution of a portfolio from data on the historical returns of the assets in the portfolio. A simple approach would be to use a recently observed distribution, for example the percentage gains and losses on the last 100 trading days. If a 99% confidence level were to be used, the value-at-risk would be the largest daily percentage loss during the last 100 trading days. Using a 95% confidence level the value-at-risk would be the fifth largest percentage loss during the last 100 trading days. Once the value-at-risk as a percentage of the portfolio is ascertained, the money value of value-at-risk can be derived from the value of the portfolio. A more sophisticated approach to determining value-at-risk is to use the Markowitz equations described earlier in this chapter (equations 3 and 4).

EXERCISE 13.11

A pension fund holds £20 million in a portfolio of shares and £30 million in a portfolio of bonds. The daily volatility (standard deviation) of the portfolio of shares is 2% and the daily volatility of the portfolio of bonds is 1%. The coefficient of correlation between the returns of the two portfolios is zero. What is the value-at-risk on the total portfolio for a confidence level of 99%?

Answer

Using the Markowitz equations for estimating portfolio risk:

$$V = W_1{}^2 \sigma_1{}^2 + W_2{}^2 \sigma_2{}^2 + 2W_1 W_2 \sigma_1 \sigma_2 \rho$$

$$\sigma_p = \sqrt{V}$$

$$V = (0.4^2 2^2) + (0.6^2 1^2) + (2 \times 0.4 \times 0.6 \times 2 \times 1 \times 0)$$

$$\therefore V = (0.16 \times 4) + (0.36 \times 1) + 0 = 0.64 + 0.36 = 1$$

$$\sigma_p = \sqrt{1} = 1$$

The volatility (standard deviation) of the total portfolio is 1%.

In money terms the standard deviation is $0.01 \times (£20m + £30m) = £0.5m$. At a confidence level of 99% the value-at-risk is 2.326 standard deviations. So the value-at-risk is $2.326 \times £0.5m = £1.163$ million.

One problem with the measurement of value-at-risk using the Markowitz model is that the model assumes a normal distribution of returns. However there is considerable evidence that investment returns do not follow the normal distribution. In particular they are characterised by fat tails. In other words extreme values have higher probabilities than suggested by normal distributions. This is a particular problem for a measure that focuses on a tail of the distribution of returns. The significance of this deficiency can be checked by back-testing. This may entail checking the proportion of times value-at-risk has been exceeded in the past against the proportion predicted by the normal distribution (and chosen confidence level).

Using Value-at-Risk to Ascertain Investor Risk Preferences

Nevins (as described by Veres 2006) has suggested that a value similar to value-at-risk could be used to ascertain the risk-aversion of the clients of financial advisers. If the value-at-risk were presented as a 'worst case scenario', the client could then see both an expected value (mean of the distribution) and the worst case scenario. This combination of values could be presented for a number of investment strategies. It is likely that the client would find that a low expected value is associated with a relatively high worst case scenario, and vice versa. The client's attitude to the risk-return trade-off would be revealed by the choice made. Risk-averse clients would choose low expected return and high worst case strategies. Risk-tolerant clients would choose high expected return and low worst case strategies.

The presentation of pairs of numbers is a simpler procedure than the usual practice of administering a questionnaire to the client as a means of ascertaining attitude to risk. It becomes possible to separate out portfolios designed for different purposes, and hence having varying investment horizons. For example saving for a car has a much shorter investment horizon than saving for retirement. Each investment horizon would have its own investment strategy, and its own risk preference. Presentation of combinations of values in relation to each investment horizon would be practical whereas use of a questionnaire for each investment horizon would probably not be feasible.

This is consistent with ideas presented by Valentine (and reported by Ramachandran 2006). Valentine argues that there are different time horizons for different investment purposes (saving for a holiday, saving for a home extension, saving for children's education, saving for retirement, etc.), and that a single questionnaire cannot ascertain the risk-return preferences applicable to all the investment horizons. Each investment horizon would have a different risk-return preference. Arguably portfolios for long investment horizons (such as pension fund investment) should accept more risk and expect more return than portfolios developed for shorter-term objectives (such as financing home improvements).

POST-MODERN PORTFOLIO THEORY

Markowitz diversification (often referred to as modern portfolio theory) treats risk as being measurable in terms of the standard deviation of returns, as illustrated by Figure 13.8.

The use of the normal distribution is questionable from the perspectives of both behavioural finance and statistics. Prospect theory (see Chapters 2 and 24 on the psychology of personal investment decisions and noise trading and behavioural finance, respectively) suggests that investors have an asymmetric attitude to risk: that the pain of losses is stronger than the pleasure of gains. The symmetric normal distribution does not reflect this loss-aversion, since the normal distribution gives equal weight to upside and downside deviations from the mean. The normal distribution

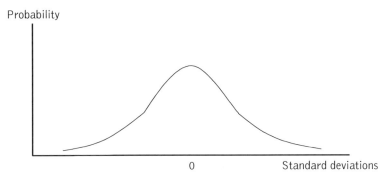

Probability

0   Standard deviations

Figure 13.8   *Normal distribution with mean of zero*

is a distribution around the mean of the distribution, whereas an investor may have a different reference point. An investor may have a Minimum Acceptable Return (MAR) against which prospective deviations are measured, rather than measuring deviations relative to the mean of the distribution.

There are also statistical issues concerning the nature of the distribution. A distribution may be skewed. It is useful to see skewness in relation to the mode of the distribution. The mode corresponds to the highest probability. In the case of a normal distribution, the mode coincides with the mean and the dispersion of prospective returns is the same in both the upside and downside directions. A skewed distribution is characterised by a larger dispersion in one direction than in the other. A negatively skewed distribution has a wider dispersal on the downside, so that there is enhanced probability of very poor outcomes. For a loss-averse investor this possibility of very large losses may cause a perception of high risk. This would be magnified if kurtosis is present, in other words if there is a fat-tailed distribution indicating relatively high probabilities of extreme values. If returns exhibit high downside semi-variance, then returns that fall below the mean tend to be a long way below. High downside semi-variance would be associated with perceptions of high risk.

Post-modern portfolio theory (Swisher and Kasten 2005) seeks to reformulate Markowitz diversification in terms of downside risk rather than total risk. The risk-return trade-off is between downside risk and return. Not only does prospect theory suggest that downside deviations impact most strongly on risk perceptions, but also it is questionable as to whether upside dispersion constitutes risk at all. Some would argue that investors are concerned only with deviations below their minimum acceptable returns when judging risk, and that uncertainty about the prospective deviations above the minimum acceptable returns does not impact on perceptions of risk.

Downside risk is measured in terms of deviations below the minimum acceptable return. Swisher and Kasten (2005) report that F. Sortino provided a formula for measuring downside risk that combined three elements:

1. Downside frequency, which is the proportion of returns falling below the minimum acceptable return.
2. Average downside deviation, which is the average size of the deviations below the minimum acceptable return.
3. Downside magnitude, which is the 'worst case scenario' deviation. It may be measured as the deviation below which just 1% of returns would fall.

295

The resulting single number is expressed as a percentage rate of return (just as standard deviation is expressed as a percentage rate of return). Unfortunately the measure of downside risk cannot simply be inserted into the Markowitz equations.

TIME DIVERSIFICATION

If diversification across different investments reduces risk by way of bad performances from some investments being offset by good performances from others, it might be expected that over time bad periods could be offset by good periods. The idea of time diversification is that over time there are periods when returns are low and other periods when investment returns are high. If an investor holds assets for a long time span, it might be expected that good periods would offset bad periods so that long-term risk is moderated.

The shape of the curve in Figure 13.9 can be explained as being the result of compounding returns. The shape of the curve in Figure 13.10 might be explained in terms of the effects of time diversification; over a long time span good periods tend to offset bad periods. The two figures illustrate why stock market investments should be used for long-term rather than short-term savings. In the short term shares provide high risk relative to return, in the long term they tend to produce high return relative to risk.

In Figure 13.10, risk is measured as standard deviation of returns. Variance of returns is seen as being proportional to the length of time that an investment is held. This is what would happen if prices changed randomly from day to day (known as a random walk). Standard deviation is the square root of variance; so standard deviation is proportional to the square root of time. For example extending the length of time from one year to four years entails a doubling of the risk ($\sqrt{4} / \sqrt{1} = 2/1 = 2$), and an extension from four to nine years increases risk by a further 50% ($\sqrt{9} / \sqrt{4} = 3/2 = 1.5$). Whereas risk, as measured by standard deviation, increases with time, it does so at a decreasing rate as depicted in Figure 13.10. The decelerating rate of increase of standard deviation could be explained in terms of a tendency for movements towards extremes to be offset by opposite movements; random movements mean that there is a tendency for deviations towards extreme values to be offset by subsequent changes in the opposite direction.

The evolution of portfolio value over time could be envisaged in terms of Figure 13.9 adjusted for risk. The curve in Figure 13.9 shows the means (mid-points) of possible outcomes at different points in time. The width of the distributions of possible values around the means is indicated by

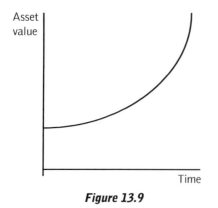

Figure 13.9

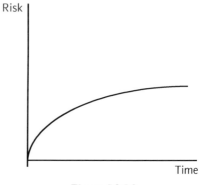

Figure 13.10

the curve in Figure 13.10. As the length of the investment period increases the dispersion of possible values around the mean becomes greater. Whereas the means increase at an accelerating rate, the dispersions increase at a declining rate. One consequence is that the chance of a very poor outcome, such as an overall loss, declines over time.

Swank *et al.* (2002) argued that even the curve of Figure 13.10 may exaggerate the rise in the risk from holding stocks for increasing periods of time. They provided evidence that returns on stocks had some tendency towards mean reversion, which means that there is some tendency for price movements to subsequently reverse. It is slightly more likely that a good period will be followed by a bad period, and vice versa. The curve of Figure 13.10 is based on the price change in each period being unrelated to that of previous periods. A tendency towards mean reversion increases the time diversification effect such that risk (standard deviation) rises more slowly than Figure 13.10 shows.

The effects of time diversification have been illustrated by Fidelity, which is a major investment management company (Fidelity International 2005), as mentioned in Chapter 1. Examining the period 1985 to 2005, they found that the UK stock market (as measured by the FTSE All-Share Index) produced a profit in 77% of one-year periods, where a one-year period is 12 consecutive months (e.g. June 1986 to May 1987, March 1992 to February 1993). There was a profit in 81% of five-year periods, where a five-year period is 60 consecutive months (e.g. September 1988 to August 1993). Every ten-year period (120 consecutive months) showed a profit. An international portfolio of stocks (as measured by the MSCI World Index) produced figures of 71%, 81%, and 100% respectively.

Swank *et al.* argued that since many occupational pension plans have an unlimited future investment period (no foreseeable termination date), they should hold 100% of their assets in the form of shares. There seems to be virtually no risk that shares (equities) would underperform other investments over such a long investment horizon. They suggest that the failure to hold 100% in shares partly arises from short-term unpredictability of stock market performance, which could require the company (or other pension provider) to fund shortfalls in some years. There is also the career risk of investment managers, who could find that a few years of poor investment returns result in the loss of their jobs. The time horizons of providers and managers may be shorter than the investment horizon of the pension fund.

Figure 13.10 uses the conventional (amongst finance academics) approach to defining risk, which is as standard deviation of returns. However some researchers (Payne 1973; Olsen 1997; Fortuna 2000) report that most investors define risk as the chance of losing money. When risk is defined in this way, equity risk (stock market risk) declines with the length of the investment horizon. This is partly because of the rise in the expected values of investments over time and partly because of the behaviour of standard deviation, which reflects the effects of time diversification (Mukherji 2002).

Historically the real net rates of return on bank and building society accounts have been only a little above zero, on average. The achievement of high real net rates of return has required investment in stocks. So the attainment of good investment returns has necessitated acceptance of the risk associated with investment in stocks. However that risk needs to be seen from a long-term perspective. If risk is defined in terms of the likelihood of making a loss, or underperforming a low yield investment, then risk declines to low levels as the investment horizon lengthens.

Consideration of time diversification leads to the standard recommendation of financial advisers; bank deposits for short-term investments and shares for long-term investments. By extending the analysis to bonds, whose returns and risks are generally believed to fall between those of deposits and equities, the recommendation becomes: deposits for the short term, bonds for the medium term, and stocks for the long term. An increase in the investment horizon reduces the probability of making losses from equity investments; in other words it reduces the likelihood of shares underperforming an investment with zero return. Likewise a long investment horizon reduces the probability of equities underperforming other investments with lower returns than stocks, such as deposits and bonds (although the probability of underperformance is greater than in the case of a zero-return investment). Correspondingly an increase in the length of the investment horizon reduces the chance of a medium-return and medium-risk investment, such as bonds, underperforming a low return and low risk investment such as bank deposits.

Mukherji (2002) pointed out that individual investors need to bear horizon risk in mind. A 25 year old may have a retirement horizon of 40 years and anticipates investing over that period. However personal circumstances can change and could shorten investment horizons. So even if it is accepted that equities are appropriate for a 40-year investment, horizon risk could lead to the holding of some deposits and bonds in a portfolio.

THE ROLES OF FINANCIAL ADVICE AND FINANCIAL EDUCATION

Most people have little expertise in personal finance matters, and many have little interest in financial decision-making. The question arises as to whether people should seek professional personal finance advice. There is also an issue of the need for increased education in matters of personal finance.

In the UK experiences of financial advice have been mixed, and there is widespread distrust of financial advisers. The regulator, the Financial Services Authority, and the financial services industry are attempting to increase levels of trust. One aspect of this is the elevation of education, training, and qualifications requirements of financial advisers with a view that in future all advisers should have chartered status, which reflects levels of training and qualification on a par with other professionals such as accountants and solicitors. Many UK consumers of financial products have unpleasant memories of the 1980s and 1990s when unqualified financial advisers sold, on a commission basis, financial products without full understanding of either the products or the needs of their customers. One result was a spate of mis-selling scandals, and another was widespread distrust of financial advisers and of the financial services industry. This distrust is now holding back the general level of participation in financial services, such as pensions, with the result that many people have inadequate provision.

The United States appears to be ahead of the UK in terms of levels of both adviser expertise and consumer confidence. The development of financial services training and qualification for advisers in recent years is reflected in a generation gap amongst US consumers. Elmerick *et al.* (2002) examined the use of financial planners (advisers) by US households. They found that people under 35 were more likely to consult financial planners than those over 35. The use of professional financial advisers was also found to be higher amongst consumers with higher levels of education and income. A distinction is made between specialist financial advice and comprehensive advice. Specialist advice is concerned with just one aspect of personal finance; some advisers would be concerned only with mortgage advice, others only with investments, and others only with insurance. Comprehensive advice covers the full range of financial services. The findings of Elmerick *et al.* (2002) with respect to the influence of factors such as age and income relate primarily to the use of comprehensive financial advice.

Black *et al.* (2002) highlight the need for a theoretical basis for personal financial planning. Comprehensive financial advice allows for the application of portfolio theory, such as Markowitz diversification, to the management of personal finances. Comprehensive financial planning also gives considerable scope for the management of the psychological biases identified by behavioural finance. In particular, comprehensive financial planning can avoid the mental accounting tendency to put different aspects of personal finance into separate compartments whose interrelationships are ignored.

Byrne (2007) examined the behaviour of members of a UK defined-contribution pension scheme. It was found that those members who had received professional advice about their pension were more likely to be aware of their saving needs, to have more investment knowledge, and to take more interest in their investments. An interesting finding was that UK pension scheme members avoided the common US error of including a substantial amount of their own company's shares in their pension funds. This error is commonly assigned to a familiarity bias, which leads people to invest in what they feel they understand. However there appeared to be a bias towards property investment amongst the UK pension scheme members. This may also be due to a familiarity bias, and can result in an overweighting of property in investors' portfolios. To the extent that advice can offset the biases identified by behavioural finance, such as familiarity biases, its importance is enhanced.

Dolvin and Templeton (2006) demonstrated the benefits of financial education to pension scheme members in the United States. They found that those who attended seminars on financial education subsequently rebalanced their pension fund portfolios in a manner that rendered those portfolios more efficient, when compared to the portfolios of those who did not attend. In particular portfolio diversification was improved.

CONCLUSION

Diversification is a key element in portfolio construction. By including a diverse variety of investments in a portfolio, risk can be reduced. There would be a tendency for poor performances of some investments to be offset by good performances from others. Institutional investments such as pension funds and mutual funds (which include unit trusts and OEICs) offer individual investors diversified portfolios. Individuals with limited investment funds would not be able to directly build a well-diversified portfolio since the transaction costs of acquiring many small shareholdings would be prohibitive. Institutional investments can hold diversified portfolios so that investors in those institutional investments indirectly acquire diversified portfolios.

The process of diversification goes beyond shareholdings from the investors' own country. International diversification further reduces portfolio risk since stock markets around the world can provide differing performances. A poor return from investments on one stock market could be offset by stronger performance from another stock market. Nor need diversification be limited to shares.

Risk reduction can be enhanced by the inclusion of other asset classes such as property, bonds, and cash. If a portfolio manager feels uncertain about how to select assets in some markets, futures contracts could be used. Stock index futures could be used as a means of incorporating exposure to a broad coverage of shares in a foreign stock market. Likewise bond futures could be used to provide effective inclusion of overseas bonds. Currency futures could be used to remove the currency risk of foreign investments. The use of futures in portfolio management is discussed further in Parts 8 and 10 dealing with stock index and currency futures, respectively, and bond futures in Chapter 43.

In principle optimum diversification is achieved by the application of the Markowitz equations. However this requires a huge amount of data input since it entails estimating expected returns and standard deviations for all assets, and correlation coefficients between each pair of assets. The estimates of expected returns, standard deviations, and correlation coefficients are subject to statistical error. These problems have led some to suggest that 1/N approaches, which hold assets in equal proportions, may be as good as the use of the Markowitz equations.

There are further problems with the measures of standard deviation and correlation. The standard deviation measure of risk treats upside deviations, as well as downside deviations, as undesirable. However investors do not dislike unexpected gains; they only dislike losses. A problem with both standard deviation and correlation is that their estimated values are based on the past, which is not necessarily a good guide to the future. In particular correlation coefficients may be affected by the direction and speed of stock market movements. A dramatic fall in markets may be accompanied by rising correlations. In other words the benefits of diversification are reduced when they are needed most.

For the private investor, who considers institutional investments, achieving diversification may appear to be simple. The manager of the institutional fund might be expected to achieve the full benefits of diversification. However managers of actively managed funds could intentionally unbalance their portfolios in an attempt to outperform the stock market. Even index tracker funds, which mirror the whole stock market, may not provide optimum diversification since a few large companies might dominate the stock market. A fund that mirrors such a stock market would hold a disproportionate amount of the shares of a few large companies. However a combination of such an index tracker fund with one that tracks an index of smaller company shares would help to overcome this problem.

Behavioural finance suggests that people do not fully diversify their portfolios since they do not see their portfolios as single entities. Mental accounting causes people mentally to divide their portfolios into a number of separate portfolios. From the perspective of Markowitz diversification this appears to be irrational since it prevents full diversification (for example the same asset may appear in several of the sub-portfolios). However if mental accounting is accepted as a useful tool for the management of personal finances it is not necessarily irrational. Mental accounting might better be seen as an investor preference than as a form of irrational behaviour.

Chapter 14

Capital market theory:
The capital asset pricing model

OBJECTIVE

The objective of this chapter is to provide knowledge of:

1. The meaning of beta.
2. The single index model.
3. The use of the security market line to estimate the required rate of return of a stock or a portfolio.
4. The use of the security market line to identify mispriced stocks.
5. Multifactor forms of the capital asset pricing model.

THE MEANING OF BETA

The beta of the capital asset pricing model (CAPM) can be interpreted in several ways. One is as the relationship between expected percentage changes in the stock price and percentage changes in a stock index. A beta of 1 indicates that a 1% rise in a stock index would be expected to be associated with a 1% rise in the stock price. Likewise a stock with a beta of 2 would be expected to experience a 2% price rise. A stock with a beta of 0.5 has an expected price rise (fall) of 0.5% when the stock index rises (falls) by 1%. This view of beta sees it as a measure of market risk (systematic risk – the risk to a share price of movements in the stock market as a whole). High beta stocks tend to show high price volatility.

A second interpretation of beta views it in terms of the characteristic line. The characteristic line relates the excess return of the individual stock (the excess of the stock return over the risk-free interest rate) to the excess return of the stock index portfolio. A graph is drawn based on a set of points that have excess return on the stock on the vertical axis, and the excess return on the market index on the horizontal axis. These points are based on a series of observations from past time periods (a time series). Figure 14.1 shows a hypothetical example of a characteristic line.

The points marked by an $\times$ are observed combinations of the excess return on the individual stock ($r_i - r_f$) and the excess return on the stock index portfolio ($r_m - r_f$), where the stock index portfolio is used as a proxy for the market portfolio. The characteristic line is the straight line that

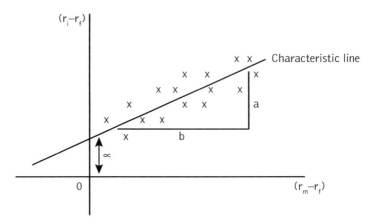

Figure 14.1

provides the best fit to the set of observed points. The beta of the stock is the gradient of the characteristic line (a/b). The intercept of the characteristic line with the vertical axis is the alpha ($\propto$) of the stock. The vertical distances between the characteristic line and the observed points reflect non-systematic risk (risk specific to a particular stock as opposed to systematic risk which is the market risk to which all stocks are subject), whilst movements along the characteristic line reflect systematic risk (the effects of changes in market return; beta is the measure of the magnitude of those effects).

The alpha of a stock is its risk-adjusted excess return, in other words the amount by which the excess return is above the level justified by beta. In equilibrium alpha will be zero. Arbitrage will tend to move alpha towards zero (through purchases of positive alpha stocks and sales of negative alpha stocks).

A third interpretation of beta is in terms of covariances and variances or, equivalently, in terms of correlations and variances.

$$\text{Beta} = \sigma_{im} / \sigma_m^2 \qquad \text{alternatively} \quad \text{beta} = \rho.\sigma_i / \sigma_m$$

σ_{im} is the covariance between the returns on the individual stock and those on the market (or stock index) portfolio, σ_m^2 is the variance of the market (stock index) portfolio, ρ is the coefficient of correlation between the returns on the individual stock and the returns on the market (stock index) portfolio, σ_i is the standard deviation of returns on the individual stock, and σ_m is the standard deviation of returns on the market (stock index) portfolio.

These three interpretations of beta are different ways of looking at the same thing. They are alternative perspectives on the same measure of systematic (market) risk.

The third way of expressing beta (β) can be extended to illustrate the decomposition of the variance of a share (or a portfolio of shares) into systematic (general market) risk and non-systematic (sector- or firm-specific) risk. This decomposition is shown by the equation:

$$\sigma_i^2 = \beta_i^2 \sigma_m^2 + \sigma_{ei}^2$$

The variance of the share or portfolio (σ_i^2) equals the systematic risk ($\beta_i^2 \sigma_m^2$) plus the non-systematic risk (σ_{ei}^2). The systematic risk is the risk arising from the tendency for the return on a share to be affected by changes in the return on the market as a whole. The variance of the market is measured by $\sigma_m^{\ 2}$ and the extent to which that affects the individual investment is measured by $\beta_i^{\ 2}$. When a stock index is used to represent the market, this is known as the single index model.

When dealing with portfolios of shares, the non-systematic risk term $\sigma_{ei}^{\ 2}$ can be replaced by $\Sigma W_i^2 \sigma_{ei}^{\ 2}$. In this case σ_{ei} is the standard deviation of share i within the portfolio, and W_i is the weight (by value) of share i in the portfolio. The effect, of an expansion in the number of stocks, on the portfolio non-systematic risk can be understood by considering the case of equal weighting. If the number of different stocks is N, the weighting of each stock is $1/N$ and W_i^2 is equal to $1/N^2$. As N increases, $1/N^2$ diminishes rapidly causing non-systematic risk to decline.

In the case of actively managed portfolios, such as the majority of mutual funds, another source of risk enters the equation. This is management risk. Management risk is the risk that the portfolio manager produces a relatively poor performance with the effect that the portfolio provides a low (risk-adjusted) rate of return. Exercise 14.1 illustrates the effect of management risk on the total risk of a portfolio.

EXERCISE 14.1

A mutual fund has a beta of 0.9. The market risk (standard deviation of returns of the market portfolio) is 20% p.a., there is specific (non-systematic) risk of 10% p.a., and there is a management risk of 15% p.a.

(a) On the assumption that the three sources of risk are uncorrelated, what is the total risk of the fund?

(b) What would be the total risk if there were correlations of 0.25 between the sources of management risk and the sources of market risk, and 0.25 between the sources of management risk and the sources of specific risk (and zero between market and specific risk)?

(c) How much has management risk added to total risk in cases (a) and (b)?

Answers

(a) The Markowitz equation for estimating variance is:

$$\text{Variance } (\sigma_p^{\ 2}) = \sum_{j=1}^{n} W_j^2 \, \sigma_j^{\ 2} + \sum_{j=1}^{n} \sum_{k=1}^{n} W_j W_k \sigma_j \, \sigma_k \rho_{jk}$$

$$j \neq k$$

Using the Markowitz equation, the total risk is estimated to be:

$$\text{Variance } (\sigma_p^{\ 2}) = (1^2 \times 0.9^2 \times 0.2^2) + (1^2 \times 0.1^2) + (1^2 \times 0.15^2) + 2(1 \times 1 \times 0.9 \times 0.2 \times 0.1 \times 0) + 2(1 \times 1 \times 0.9 \times 0.2 \times 0.15 \times 0) + 2(1 \times 1 \times 0.1 \times 0.15 \times 0)$$

$$= 0.0324 + 0.01 + 0.0225 = 0.0649$$

The standard deviation (σ_p) is: $\sqrt{0.0649} = 0.2548$ i.e. 25.48% p.a.
(Note that the weightings are all equal to 1 since all risks apply to the whole portfolio.)

(b)

$$\text{Variance } (\sigma_p{}^2) = (1^2 \times 0.9^2 \times 0.2^2) + (1^2 \times 0.1^2) + (1^2 \times 0.15^2) + 2(1 \times 1 \times 0.9 \times 0.2 \times 0.1 \times 0) + 2(1 \times 1 \times 0.9 \times 0.2 \times 0.15 \times 0.25) + 2(1 \times 1 \times 0.1 \times 0.15 \times 0.25)$$

$$= 0.0324 + 0.01 + 0.0225 + 0 + 0.0135 + 0.0075 = 0.0859$$

The standard deviation (σ_p) is: $\sqrt{0.0859} = 0.2931$ i.e. 29.31% p.a.

(c) In case (a) the total risk, in the absence of management risk, would be estimated from:

$$\text{Variance } (\sigma_p{}^2) = (1^2 \times 0.9^2 \times 0.2^2) + (1^2 \times 0.1^2) + 2(1 \times 1 \times 0.9 \times 0.2 \times 0.1 \times 0) = 0.0324 + 0.01 = 0.0424$$

So the standard deviation (σ_p) is $\sqrt{0.0424} = 0.2059$ i.e. 20.59% p.a.

Management risk has added $25.48 - 20.59 = 4.89\%$ p.a.

In case (b) the total risk, in the absence of management risk, would be estimated from:

$$\text{Variance } (\sigma_p{}^2) = (1^2 \times 0.9^2 \times 0.2^2) + (1^2 \times 0.1^2) + 2(1 \times 1 \times 0.9 \times 0.2 \times 0.1 \times 0) = 0.0324 + 0.01 = 0.0424$$

So the standard deviation (σ_p) is $\sqrt{0.0424} = 0.2059$ i.e. 20.59% p.a.

Management risk has added $29.31 - 20.59 = 8.72\%$ p.a.

There are reasons for supposing that the sources of management risk are correlated with the sources of both systematic risk and non-systematic risk. The sources of management risk can be divided into market timing (tactical asset allocation) and stock selection. It seems reasonable to presume that the effects of market timing are related to the size of the systematic risk (market volatility). It also seems reasonable to presume that the sizes of the effects of stock selection are related to the extent of non-systematic risk (firm-specific factors).

ESTIMATING FUTURE VALUES OF BETA

It is to be emphasised that stock index portfolios are used as proxies for the market portfolio, which cannot be measured. It is therefore to be expected that the resulting measure of beta is imperfect. Some researchers have noted that other sources of risk premiums are positively correlated, and hence might be incorporated into a measure of beta. These sources include firm size, price-earnings ratio, and the price/book-value ratio. A beta that takes account of the fundamental characteristics of the firm, as well as its covariance with the market portfolio, is known as a fundamental beta. Evidence suggests that fundamental beta produces a better estimate of future beta than does historical beta alone, where historical beta is the beta estimated from the characteristic line or from covariances and variances (Rosenberg and Guy 1976).

Another refinement used in forecasting beta is to adjust historical beta to reflect the observation that portfolio betas tend to regress towards 1 over time (Blume 1971). Some users of individual stock betas take the view that beta tends to revert to the mean where the mean is the market beta, i.e. 1. When estimating future beta, this mean-reversion is taken into account by calculating a weighted average of historical beta and the value 1. A weighting of 2/3 for the historical beta and 1/3 for 1 may be typical. So a beta estimated from the past to be 1.3 would become $(1.3 \times 2/3) + (1 \times 1/3) = 1.2$.

Such an adjusted estimate of beta is sometimes called a shrinkage estimate. Regression towards 1 is not the only possible justification for using shrinkage estimates of beta. Bayesian mathematics provides another rationale (Pastor 2001). Bayesian estimates reflect not only sample data but also prior knowledge. For example when considering an individual share, say Tesco, it is known that it is a stock and that on average stocks have a beta of 1. This prior knowledge provides an estimate of the Tesco beta (estimated to equal 1). The Bayesian estimate is then a weighted average of the beta estimated from past data and the value 1. It is also known that Tesco is a supermarket company. If supermarket companies on average have a beta of 0.8, this value provides a third estimate of the Tesco beta. The Bayesian estimate would now be a weighted average of three estimates.

It has been widely observed that betas for individual stocks are unstable over time whereas portfolio betas exhibit much greater stability. This is consistent with the view that beta encompasses a number of different sources of systematic risk (such as interest rates, exchange rates, and commodity prices). An individual stock beta may be unstable as a result of the stock returns reacting to changes in some of the sources of systematic risk underlying beta but not to others. The market as a whole reacts to all sources of systematic risk but an individual stock responds to only some of them. So the individual stock will appear to have a high beta at some times and a low one at others, dependent upon which source of systematic risk is changing at the time. Portfolios are likely to contain stocks which, taken together, react to a wide variety of sources of systematic risk.

THE SINGLE INDEX MODEL

The estimation of portfolio risk using the Markowitz equation requires a huge input of data. The standard deviation of returns is required for every security. In addition the coefficient of correlation of returns between each pair of securities is required. Since the available securities are numbered in thousands, the number of correlations to be estimated is massive. Although the development of computer technology has rendered the task feasible, there is an alternative approach that requires less information. This alternative is the single index model, which has proven to be effective in portfolio analysis.

To estimate the systematic risk of a portfolio, the single index model requires just the beta of each stock and the standard deviation of the market portfolio. The standard deviation of returns of the market portfolio is usually proxied by the standard deviation of a market index portfolio, such as the portfolio that the FTSE 100 or the S&P 500 is based on.

The systematic risk of each stock equals its beta multiplied by the standard deviation of the market portfolio. The beta of a portfolio is the weighted average of the betas of the individual shares in that portfolio. The systematic risk of the portfolio is the portfolio beta multiplied by the standard deviation of returns of the market portfolio. For a well-diversified portfolio, systematic risk approximates total risk.

THE SECURITY MARKET LINE

Risk on the capital market line is total risk (see Chapter 13 on portfolio diversification). Total risk is the sum of systematic (non-diversifiable) risk and non-systematic (diversifiable) risk. However, all rational investors would be expected to hold the market portfolio. The market portfolio would contain all investment assets. It follows that the market portfolio is perfectly diversified and has only systematic (non-diversifiable) risk. If the market portfolio has only systematic risk, the variable on the horizontal axis could be beta.

Investments along the capital market line are available to all investors. The risk of any investment along that line (any combination of the risk-free asset and the market portfolio) will be limited to systematic risk. Therefore when considering investments on the capital market line, beta can be the measure of risk on the horizontal axis.

The derived relationship between required rates of return and betas is known as the security market line (SML). For any security, or portfolio of securities, there is a required (expected) rate of return related to the beta of the investment. Increases in beta (systematic risk) are associated with increases in the expected rate of return. Systematic risk is compensated for by enhanced expected return. The acceptance of non-systematic risk does not result in higher expected returns. Since non-systematic risk can be eliminated by diversification, and since rational investors are assumed to eliminate it in this way, the acceptance of non-systematic risk is not rewarded by increased expected returns.

The security market line (often referred to as the capital asset pricing model) can be described by means of equation 1. In equation 1, $E(R_i)$ represents the expected (required) rate of return on security i. R_f is the return on the risk-free asset, β is the beta of the security, and $E(R_m)$ is the expected return on the market portfolio.

$$E(R_i) = R_f + \beta[\,E(R_m) - R_f\,] \tag{1}$$

The expected (required) rate of return on security i consists of two components. The first component is the risk-free rate of return, R_f. The second component is the risk premium, shown as $\beta[E(R_m) - R_f]$. The risk premium is the reward for accepting systematic risk, which is measured by beta.

The market portfolio is treated as having a beta of 1. So the risk premium of the market portfolio is $[E(R_m) - R_f]$ and the expected return is:

$$R_f + E(R_m) - R_f = E(R_m)$$

It might also be noted that if beta is zero, indicating an absence of systematic risk, the expected return is the risk-free rate R_f.

The risk premium of a share (security), $\beta[E(R_m) - R_f]$, is the addition to the expected (required) rate of return on the share arising from the systematic risk of the share. That addition to return must reflect the risk preference of investors. If investors are highly risk-averse, the risk premium should be high. If investors were risk tolerant, the risk premium would be lower. This suggests that $E(R_m)$ should be interpreted as the required rate of return on the market portfolio. It is the rate of return required to compensate for accepting the systematic risk of the market portfolio. However if markets are in equilibrium, $E(R_m)$ can also be interpreted as the forecast rate of return on the market portfolio. In equilibrium the forecast, or anticipated, rate of return equals the required rate of return. Likewise in equilibrium $E(R_i)$ can be interpreted as both the required rate of return, and the forecast rate of return, on an individual security.

The application of the security market line is illustrated by Exercise 14.2.

EXERCISE 14.2

The rate of return on Treasury bills (a risk-free asset) is 5% p.a. over the next three months. The expected rate of return on the FT All-Share Index portfolio over the same period is 8% p.a. An investment trust portfolio has a beta of 1.2 and an expected rate of dividend yield of 4% p.a. What might be the expected rate of capital growth of the investment trust portfolio?

Answer

The security market line (the capital asset pricing model) states that:

$E(R_p) = R_f + \beta(E[R_m] - r_f)$

i.e. $E(R_p) = 0.05 + 1.2\,(0.08 - 0.05) = 0.086$

i.e. 8.6% p.a.

So the expected rate of return on the investment trust portfolio is 8.6% p.a., of which 4% p.a. is in the form of dividend yield. So the expected rate of capital gain on the investment trust portfolio is 8.6% − 4% = 4.6% p.a. Since the period under consideration is three months (1/4 of a year) the per annum percentage needs to be divided by four. So the expected rate of capital growth over three months is 4.6/4 = 1.15%.

TRADING RULES BASED ON THE SECURITY MARKET LINE (CAPITAL ASSET PRICING MODEL)

The security market line provides a required rate of return. In equilibrium the required rate of return would equal the anticipated rate of return. However the market for a particular security may not be in equilibrium. If the market is out of equilibrium, trading opportunities would be available. A trading opportunity is the ability to achieve an anticipated rate of return in excess of the required rate of return (or to avoid an anticipated rate of return lower than the required rate). Such opportunities are illustrated by Figure 14.2.

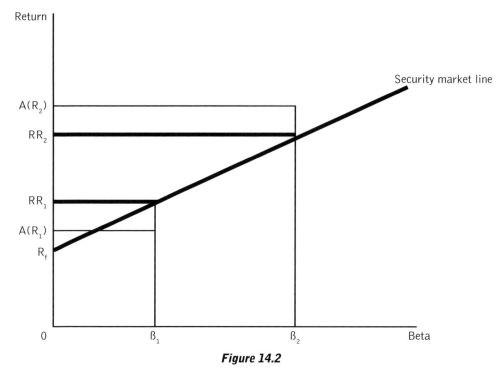

Figure 14.2

β_1 $\qquad\qquad$ = beta of share 1
RR_1 $\qquad\qquad$ = required (expected) rate of return on share 1
$A(R_1)$ $\qquad\quad$ = anticipated (forecast) rate of return on share 1
$A(R_1) - RR_1$ = alpha of share 1
β_2 $\qquad\qquad$ = beta of share 2
RR_2 $\qquad\qquad$ = required rate of return on share 2
$A(R_2)$ $\qquad\quad$ = anticipated rate of return on share 2
$A(R_2) - RR_2$ = alpha of share 2

Share 1 has a negative excess rate of return and should be avoided (or sold if already held). Share 2 has a positive excess rate of return and should be considered as a possible purchase.

EXERCISE 14.3

The rate of return on Treasury bills (a risk-free asset) is 4% p.a. The expected return on the FT All-Share Index portfolio is 9% p.a. Stocks A and B both have anticipated (forecast) returns of 10% p.a. and a price of 100p. Stock A has a beta of 0.8 and stock B has a beta of 1.7.

Are these shares mispriced? If so, should they be bought or sold?

Answer

The required rate of return for A should be, according to the security market line:

$4 + 0.8(9 - 4) = 8\%$ p.a.

308

The anticipated return of 10% p.a. indicates that A should be bought (i.e. A is underpriced). For stock B the required rate of return is:

$$4 + 1.7(9 - 4) = 12.5\% \text{ p.a.}$$

The anticipated return of 10% indicates that B should be sold (i.e. B is overpriced).

Estimating Anticipated Returns

There are many potential ways of estimating the future returns from holding a share. One approach is based on the Gordon growth model. The Gordon growth model is a model for estimating the fair (i.e. theoretical) price of a share. The equation is:

$$P = D/(r - g) \tag{2}$$

where P is the fair price of the share, D is the expected next dividend, r is the required rate of return, and g is the expected growth rate of dividends.

The equation can be rearranged to give:

$$r = (D/P) + g \tag{3}$$

where r is the anticipated rate of return on the share, D the expected next dividend, P the current share price, and g the expected growth rate of the share price. Equation 3 equates the anticipated rate of return to the expected dividend yield (D/P) plus the expected rate of capital gain on the share (g).

The question arises as to how g may be estimated. One approach is to use equation 4.

$$g = ROE \times (1 - d) \tag{4}$$

where g is the growth rate of the firm's equity (net worth), ROE is the return on equity, and d is the dividend payout rate (i.e. the proportion of profits paid to shareholders). An analogy can be drawn with a bank account; g can be looked upon as the rate of growth of the bank balance, ROE is analogous to the rate of interest, and d is the proportion of the interest that is withdrawn.

If ROE is assumed to be constant, the rate of growth of profit (i.e. equity $\times$ ROE) equals the rate of growth of the firm's equity. Thus g is both the rate of growth of equity and the rate of growth of profit.

If the dividend payout rate is constant, the rate of growth of dividends equals the rate of growth of profits. Thus g is the rate of growth of equity, the rate of growth of profits, and the rate of growth of dividends.

Returning to the Gordon growth model (equation 2), it can be seen that (with a constant r and g) the growth rate of the share price equals the growth rate of the dividends. So the expected growth rate of the share price (i.e. the expected rate of capital gain) is equal to g, which is estimated from equation 4.

EXERCISE 14.4

The share price of a company is 200p. Its expected next dividend is 5p. The dividend (and share price) growth rate is expected to be 4% p.a. The risk-free interest rate is 4.5% p.a. The share has a beta of 1.2 and the expected rate of return on the stock market as a whole is 8.5% p.a.

(a) Estimate the expected (forecast) rate of return on the share.

(b) Estimate the required rate of return.

(c) Consider whether the share is suitable for purchase.

Answers

(a) Rearranging the Gordon growth model gives an expression for expected (forecast) returns.

The Gordon growth equation:

$$P = D/(r - g)$$

(where P = share price, D = expected next dividend, r = required rate of return, and g is the expected growth rate of dividends) can be rearranged to give:

$$R = (D/P) + g$$

(where R = forecast rate of return, and g = expected growth rate of dividends = expected growth rate of the share price.* (D/P) is the expected rate of dividend yield and g the expected rate of capital gain).

Thus

$$R = (5/200) + 0.04 = 0.065$$

The forecast rate of return is 6.5% p.a.

(b) The security market line can be expressed as:

$$r = r_f + \beta[E(r_m) - r_f]$$

(where r = required rate of return, r_f = risk-free rate of return, β = beta of the share, and $E(r_m)$ = expected return on the market).

Thus

$$r = 0.045 + 1.2[0.085 - 0.045] = 0.045 + 0.048 = 0.093 \qquad \text{i.e. } 9.3\% \text{ p.a.}$$

(c) The forecast rate of return, 6.5% p.a., is below the required rate of return, 9.3% p.a. This share is not a good buy. In other words it is overpriced.

---

* The equality between the expected growth rate of dividends and the expected growth rate of the share price can be seen from the Gordon growth model.

$$P = D/(r - g)$$
$$P(1+g) = D(1+g)/(r - g)$$

A growth in dividends of g produces a growth in the share price of g.

There are limitations to the usefulness of the security market line. Estimates of beta are subject to statistical error; this is partly due to non-systematic risk. Betas can change over time, and hence an estimate based on the past may not be a good guide to the future beta. The security market line uses just one source of risk (market beta); other sources of risk may affect expected returns. The expected return on the market portfolio is usually proxied by the expected return on a stock index (since the market portfolio and its return are not measurable). The chosen stock index may not be a good proxy for the market portfolio. The expected return on a stock index (portfolio) is very uncertain since historical returns may not be a reliable guide to the future.

In the equation for the security market line (equation 1), $E(R_i)$ is appropriately interpreted as the required rate of return on the stock and $E(R_m)$ as the required rate of return on the market portfolio. $E(R_m)$ reflects risk-aversion. High risk-aversion is associated with high required rates of return; more return is required to compensate for risk. The required rate of return on a stock is compared with the forecast rate of return on that stock, with a view to selecting stocks whose forecast returns exceed their required returns. Likewise the required rate of return on stocks in aggregate may be compared with the forecast rate of return when deciding upon whether part of an investor's wealth (or how much of that wealth) should be invested in shares.

Evidence from psychological research indicates that risk-aversion (and perception) is inversely related to forecast returns. Alhakami and Slovic (1994) found that judgements of risk and benefit were inversely related. People in a positive mood perceive choices as less risky, and the prospective outcomes as more favourable (Isen 1997; Nygren *et al.* 1996). Social mood is collectively shared mood that is widespread in society. The socionomic hypothesis (Prechter 1999; Nofsinger 2005; Olson 2006) sees risk-aversion declining and forecast returns increasing with improvements in social mood (conversely with declining social mood); an inverse relationship between risk-aversion and anticipated return. So circumstances that induce a more positive approach to risk taking also enhance forecasts of return. A change in mood, either individual or collectively shared, influences investment decisions in two ways that reinforce each other.

In terms of Figure 14.2, a decline in risk-aversion (or perception of risk) reduces the gradient of the security market line. This is consistent with the requirement for less return to compensate for risk. Simultaneously anticipated (forecast) return increases. Both changes enhance the attractiveness of the investment; they reinforce each other. The converse would be the case for adverse mood changes.

Supply and Demand

If the anticipated rate of return on a share differs from that derived from the security market line (the required rate) the market is out of equilibrium. Since each investor has their own anticipations, investors are likely to differ in their opinions as to whether the market for a security is in equilibrium. Investors would also tend to differ in their views as to whether alpha is positive or negative. In other words investors would differ in their views as to whether a share is overpriced or underpriced.

This is consistent with a downward sloping demand curve for the asset. Investors who believe that there is an anticipated return in excess of the required rate would see the market price as being too low, and could be prepared to buy at a higher price than the current market price. Investors with the opposite view regard the share as overpriced and would require a lower price before they

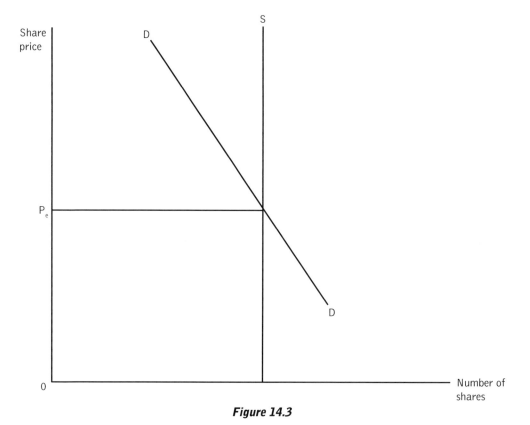

Figure 14.3

considered buying. As the stock price falls an increasing number of investors will see it as underpriced (offering an anticipated return in excess of the required return). Hence as the stock price falls the number of investors willing to buy increases. The demand, supply, and equilibrium price for the share are shown by Figure 14.3.

The line DD shows the number of shares demanded (by investors in aggregate) at each price. The vertical line S indicates the number of shares issued. P_e is the equilibrium share price and the actual share price should tend to equal the equilibrium share price. The price that each investor is prepared to pay could be based on that investor's use of a dividend discount model (with the required rate of return obtained from the security market line) and/or the price-earnings ratio (see Chapters 19 and 21 on dividend discount models and on ratio analysis, respectively).

OTHER INVESTMENT MANAGEMENT APPLICATIONS

Beta and the security market line have other applications in investment management. An investment manager who attempts to time market movements might switch into high beta shares when market rises are expected and into low beta stocks when prices are expected to fall. In this way gains from a rising market are enhanced and losses from a falling market are reduced.

The slope of the security market line can be looked upon as the price of risk. A shallow slope might incline an investment manager to hold low beta shares on the grounds that the reward, in terms of expected extra return, is insufficient to compensate for the risk of holding high beta stocks. Conversely a steep gradient would favour the choice of high beta stocks since the expected addition to return would be substantial.

The level of the security market line, relative to the yield on zero-beta investments such as bonds, will influence the choice between shares and other investments. If the security market line were high relative to bond yields, shares would offer relatively attractive returns. In such a situation a portfolio would be weighted towards shares and away from bonds. If the security market line is low relative to bond yields, portfolios are likely to have a lower proportion invested in shares. (This highlights the point that, although the security market line uses the return on short-term risk-free assets such as Treasury bills or high-grade bank deposits, arguably the relevant comparison for share investments is the return on government bonds since both shares and bonds are long-term investments.)

USING THE SINGLE INDEX MODEL TO MAKE THE CAPITAL ASSET PRICING MODEL OPERATIONAL

With respect to applying the capital asset pricing model (CAPM), there are two particular difficulties to overcome. First the model uses a market portfolio that cannot be observed or measured. The market portfolio contains every investment asset, financial and physical, from throughout the world. Even if it could be identified, many of its constituent assets are not traded and hence could not be incorporated into portfolios. The other difficulty is that the CAPM is expressed in terms of expectations of future values whereas observable data relates to the past.

The single index model is a variation on the ideas of the CAPM. The single index model uses a broad stock index (such as the FTSE All-Share Index or the S&P 500) in place of the market portfolio. It is based on observations of the past rather than expectations of the future.

The CAPM is expressed in terms of the security market line:

$$E(R_s) = R_f + \beta[E(R_m) - R_f] \qquad (5)$$

where $E(R_s)$ is the required (expected) rate of return on a share, R_f is the risk-free rate of return, β is the beta of the share, and $E(R_m)$ is the expected rate of return on the market portfolio. The equation can be rewritten in excess return form as:

$$E(R_s) - R_f = \beta[E(R_m) - R_f] \qquad (6)$$

The single index model is written as:

$$R_{St} - R_{Ft} = \alpha + \beta(R_{It} - R_{Ft}) + e_t \qquad (7)$$

where R_{St} is the observed return on a share during a period, R_{Ft} is the risk-free interest rate during that period, α is the average return (on the share) in excess of what would be expected on the basis of the return on the index, β is the beta of the share, R_{It} is the observed return on the stock index, and e_t is the deviation (during a period) of the excess return on the share from the excess return that would be expected on the basis of α, β, R_{It}, and R_{Ft}. In terms of Figure 14.1, e_t is the vertical distance between the characteristic line and the observed point for a period.

The term e_t does not appear in the equation of the security market line because the expected value of e_t, in a period, is zero. The security market line reflects the CAPM, which is based on expectations.

The risk of a share, as measured by standard deviation of returns, is estimated as:

$$(\beta^2\sigma_I^2 + \sigma_e^2)^{0.5} \tag{8}$$

The term $\beta^2\sigma_I^2$ measures systematic risk, which is the risk from movements in the index (σ_I is the standard deviation of returns on the index portfolio). The term σ_e^2 measures the non-systematic risk, which is the risk specific to a particular share (σ_e is the standard deviation of the error terms, e_t).

If certain assumptions are made about the values of e_t, the parameters (α, β, σ_e) of the single index model (equation 7) can be estimated by a statistical technique known as regression. In particular the value of e_t in a period should be unrelated to its value in other periods, and should also be independent of past and present values of R_{It} and R_{Ft}.

Regression analysis provides estimates of α, β, and σ_e rather than their true values. Departure of the estimates from true values can arise because of the random nature of the deviations e_t. The random deviations produce 'noise' (irrelevant information). The noise distorts the statistical estimates. The deviations, e_t, are assumed to average zero but in reality rarely do so. Randomly chosen numbers may have a (statistical) expectation of a zero mean but the actual mean from a sample is unlikely to be zero. The actual (non-zero) mean of the deviations will influence the regression estimates of α, β, and σ_e.

The estimated value of beta will be affected by a number of factors such as the time period from which data is taken, the frequency of the data (daily, weekly, monthly), and the stock index chosen. Taking monthly observations from the most recent five-year period of a broad market index is a frequently used approach. The estimated beta should be stable over time (that is exhibit stationarity). A beta value that does not exhibit stationarity is unreliable.

MULTIFACTOR FORMS OF THE CAPITAL ASSET PRICING MODEL

Fama and French (1993, 1996) proposed a three-factor form of the capital asset pricing model. In addition to the market excess return of the standard (i.e. one-factor) model, the three-factor model adds factors relating to firm size and the value/growth distinction. The factor SMB is the return on the shares of small firms minus the return on the shares of big firms. The factor HML (high minus low book/market) is the return on value stocks minus the return on growth stocks.

The three-factor model can be written as:

$$R_{St} - R_{Ft} = \alpha + \beta_1(R_{Mt} - R_{Ft}) + \beta_2(SMB_t) + \beta_3(HML_t) + e_t \tag{9}$$

where R_{St} is the return on a share in period t, R_{Ft} is the risk-free interest rate, R_{Mt} is the market return, and $\beta_1, \beta_2, \beta_3$ are the betas relating to the three factors.

An additional factor that has been investigated is liquidity. Liquidity can be seen as the ability to trade shares quickly, at low cost, and without significantly moving the share price. Liquidity is seen as desirable by investors and its absence may be a reason for enhanced return on an investment;

that is a premium. Pastor and Stambaugh (2001) set out to discover if liquidity risk is reflected in share prices and returns. Using the Fama and French three-factor model, they found that α was a function of sensitivity to liquidity. Stocks with high sensitivity to liquidity (i.e. with high liquidity betas) exhibited higher returns. Liu (2006) also found a liquidity premium, which was additional to the Fama–French three-factor premiums.

One implication of liquidity being a determinant of the required rate of return is that stock market trading systems can have significance for share prices. Trading systems that enhance liquidity will reduce the liquidity premium within required returns. The reduction in required rates of return will, according to dividend discount models, increase share prices. To the extent that high trading volumes are associated with high liquidity, high volumes of stock trading could be expected to help in lowering liquidity premiums.

Momentum is another factor that has been used in capital asset pricing models. Momentum is the tendency for recent high returns (stock price increases) to persist for a time. So a stock that has exhibited a recent high rate of return may be expected to have a higher return in the (near) future. Adding a momentum term to the Fama–French three-factor model gives equation 10.

$$R_{St} - R_{Ft} = \alpha + \beta_1(R_{Mt} - R_{Ft}) + \beta_2(SMB_t) + \beta_3(HML_t) + \beta_4(UMD_t) + e_t \qquad (10)$$

The momentum factor, UMD (up-minus-down), measures the recent return on a portfolio of the best performing stocks minus the recent return on a portfolio of the worst performing stocks. Arguably adding the momentum factor incorporates a behavioural finance dimension to the capital asset pricing model, since momentum is thought to arise from behavioural factors such as representativeness, herding, and social mood (Hirschey and Nofsinger 2008).

Sapp and Tiwari (2006) suggested that retail investors tend to follow a strategy of selecting mutual funds that have exhibited high recent returns. In consequence retail investors often initially show apparent talent in the selection of mutual funds (this is sometimes called 'the smart money effect'). The momentum effect tends to confirm the wisdom of their choices, in the period immediately following the investments, as the stocks held by the chosen mutual funds continue to perform relatively well. The behavioural finance concepts of overconfidence and illusion of control could turn such initial success into exaggerated expectations of returns.

An alternative form of the capital asset pricing model (CAPM) is the Consumption-based capital asset pricing model (CCAPM). According to the CCAPM the required return from a stock is related to the extent that its returns protect consumption during economic downturns. When the economy goes into recession incomes fall and it becomes difficult to maintain consumption. If investment yields also fall the impact on consumption is greater. Stocks that threaten reduced dividends during economic downturns would be required to offer higher average returns in compensation. So betas should reflect the sensitivity of stock yields to macroeconomic conditions. If small company shares and value stocks pay dividends that fall during economic downturns, the enhanced returns from such stocks are explained by the CCAPM. So the CCAPM may be capable of explaining the usefulness of the Fama–French three-factor model (Jagannathan and Wang 2007). Jagannathan and Wang pointed out that empirical evidence is not generally supportive of the CCAPM and, in particular, the evidence does not indicate that the CCAPM could replace the Fama–French three-factor version of the CAPM.

CONDITIONAL AND UNCONDITIONAL FORMS OF THE CAPITAL ASSET PRICING MODEL

In equations such as 1, 9, and 10 the betas (β_1, β_2, β_3, etc.) are treated as being constant. Forms of the capital asset pricing model with constant betas are known as unconditional forms. Conditional forms allow the values of the betas to vary. Variation in beta over time is referred to as time-varying risk. It can be argued that the proliferation of risk factors, as shown in equation 10, is the result of using unconditional forms when a conditional form of the capital asset pricing model should be used (Scheicher 2000). Even if the evidence is seen as rejecting unconditional forms of the capital asset pricing model, it does not necessarily refute conditional forms. It could be the case that a one-factor conditional form is superior to multi-factor unconditional forms.

Not only might betas be time varying but also the aggregate risk premiums ($R_{Mt} - R_{Ft}$; SMB_t; HML_t; UMD_t) could be time varying. A model is conditional if either betas and/or risk premiums are time varying (Merton 1980). There is some evidence that aggregate risk premiums are related to business cycles (see Chapter 18 on the economic environment). For example some studies (such as Fama 1990; Lovatt and Parikh 2000) have found that market returns could be predicted by the dividend yield on shares, the default spread on bonds (the difference between yields on government and corporate bonds), and the term spread (the latter being the difference between yields on short maturity and long maturity bonds). The studies found all three to be positively related to expected (required) rates of return, and hence to aggregate risk premiums. The default and term spreads were seen as having a business-cycle pattern; so the associations between those spreads and required returns provided evidence for an association between the business cycle and required returns (and hence risk premiums).

The evidence on the usefulness of conditional models is mixed. For example Lewellen and Nagel (2006) concluded that variations in beta and the risk premium would have to be implausibly large. The results of a study by Fletcher and Kihanda (2006) indicated that conditional models performed better than unconditional models, although their results were not unambiguous.

CONCLUSION

The capital asset pricing model is one of the pillars of finance theory. Unfortunately it appears to be a wobbly pillar.

The capital asset pricing model (CAPM) is used in investment analysis since the security market line provides a required rate of return for a stock. This required rate of return is compared with anticipated returns or used to discount expected dividends (see Chapter 19 on dividend discount models). CAPM is used in the evaluation of portfolio performance, including the performance of institutional fund managers, since it provides a means of risk adjustment (see Chapter 17 on evaluating the performance of fund managers). CAPM, as a means of risk adjustment of returns, has been central to empirical tests of the efficient market hypothesis (see Part 7 on market efficiency). Beta is used as a means of ascertaining hedge ratios when using stock index futures (see

Chapter 30 on hedging with stock index futures). CAPM, and the single index model, could be regarded as providing a theoretical justification for index tracker funds. The risk premium component of the security market line provides a justification for the excess of stock market returns over returns from risk-free investments (as compensation for accepting risk).

Doubts about the capital asset pricing model arise from its assumptions, some of which are clearly unrealistic. It assumes that all investors have the same expected holding period for investments, that all investors have unlimited lending and borrowing facilities at the risk-free interest rate, that all investors use the Markowitz model, and that all investors have identical expectations about returns, risk, and correlations in relation to shares and other securities.

It could be argued that the validity of assumptions is not important so long as the model provides good predictions. It has been argued that the capital asset pricing model is incapable of making predictions because the market portfolio cannot be identified and measured. Attempts to test predictions of CAPM give ambiguous results because failures may be due to failures of informational efficiency rather than failures of the model (see Part 7 on market efficiency). It will be seen in the next chapter that the empirical evidence on CAPM has often failed to support it. Further, some researchers have found that the model needs to be amended in order to give good predictions. If there is uncertainty as to which variation of CAPM should be used, there is uncertainty as to what CAPM predictions are.

Chapter 15

Capital market theory: Alternatives and criticisms

OBJECTIVE

The objective of this chapter is to provide knowledge of:

1. The assumptions of the capital asset pricing model.
2. The arbitrage pricing model.
3. The application of the factor approach to bonds.
4. Critical evaluation of capital market theory.
5. The zero-beta capital asset pricing model.
6. Evidence from empirical research.

ASSUMPTIONS OF THE CAPITAL ASSET PRICING MODEL

The capital asset pricing model (CAPM) is developed on the basis of a number of assumptions.

1. Investors are able to hold a portfolio of all investment assets, the market portfolio. All investment assets are divisible, so that fractions of assets can be held.
2. Investors maximise returns for any level of risk (and minimise risk for any level of return). Investors are risk-averse and measure risk in terms of standard deviations of returns.
3. All investors have the same investment horizon. All investment decisions are made at the beginning and no changes are made during the period of the investment horizon.
4. All investors have the same expectations about risk and return on investment assets. Information is freely available to all investors.
5. There is a single borrowing and lending rate.
6. There are no taxes and no transaction costs. All investors are allowed to sell short.

A central idea of the standard CAPM is that there is only one risk that affects the long-term average return on an investment. That risk is market risk, which is the tendency of a stock to move in response to movements in the market as a whole. Market risk is measured by beta. Beta is often approximated as the expected percentage change in a share price divided by the percentage change in a stock index. High beta stocks embody greater market risk; their price volatilities tend to be high relative to that of the market as a whole. (The multi-factor version of the CAPM proposed by Fama and French (1993) moves the model away from its reliance on a single risk factor.)

The capital asset pricing model is reflected in the security market line (SML). The equation for the security market line is:

$$E(R_i) = R_f + \beta(E[R_m] - R_f) \tag{1}$$

where $E(R_i)$ is the expected (or required) rate of return on security i, R_f is the risk-free rate of return (e.g. the return on Treasury bills), β is the beta of the share, and $E(R_m)$ is the expected return on the market portfolio (where the market portfolio is often approximated by a stock index portfolio). The term $\beta(E[R_m] - R_f)$ is referred to as the risk premium.

THE ARBITRAGE PRICING MODEL

Arbitrage pricing theory (APT) has been proposed as an alternative to the capital asset pricing model. APT makes fewer assumptions than CAPM, particularly in regard to the market portfolio (Ross 1976). A core idea of arbitrage pricing theory is that several systematic influences (rather than just one) affect the long-term average returns of securities. As in the CAPM, risks other than the systematic influences are regarded as diversifiable and hence are not compensated for by way of increased expected returns. The several sources of systematic risk are dealt with by means of using several betas. Each beta captures the sensitivity of the stock to the corresponding systematic factor. Examples of systematic factors could include unexpected interest rate changes, unexpected exchange rate movements, unexpected changes in the rate of inflation, and unexpected changes in the level of industrial production (Chen *et al.* 1986).

Arbitrage pricing theory suggests that the security market line should be replaced by the following equation (which uses the example of three systematic influences):

$$E(R_i) = R_f + \beta_1(RPF1) + \beta_2(RPF2) + \beta_3(RPF3) \tag{2}$$

where $E(R_i)$ is the expected (or required) rate of return on the security and R_f is the return on a risk-free asset. The three beta values applicable to the three risk factors are shown as β_1, β_2, and β_3. The three risk premiums are shown as RPF1 (Risk Premium of Factor 1), RPF2, and RPF3. The theory stipulates neither the number, nor the nature, of the risk factors. This information has to be obtained by empirical investigation.

The Role of Arbitrage

In the case of the capital asset pricing model, equilibrium exists when all stocks lie on the security market line. If stocks exhibit risk/return combinations that deviate from the security market line, arbitrage opportunities will arise. Those stocks that exhibit returns below the line can be sold (sold short if necessary) and the proceeds used to buy stocks with expected returns above the line.

Such an arbitrage procedure allows an investor to increase expected returns without committing more capital (in the case of short selling no capital is used). This arbitrage will involve selling overpriced stocks and buying underpriced stocks. This will tend to move stocks on to the security market line and hence restore market equilibrium.

There is a corresponding equilibrium relationship in the arbitrage pricing model. Instead of the one-dimensional relationship of the CAPM (i.e. the security market line which uses only one risk factor), APT has an n-dimensional relationship (n being the number of risk factors). In the case of the CAPM, equilibrium requires all stocks to be on the security market line. This equilibrium condition could alternatively be expressed as an absence of arbitrage opportunities. The equilibrium relationship of arbitrage pricing theory can also be expressed as an absence of arbitrage opportunities. However the arbitrage of APT needs to take account of all n risk factors.

If the arbitrage entails short selling (borrowing shares and selling them), the short positions provide negative betas. The arbitrage transactions would be in a proportion that involves the positive betas of purchased stocks exactly cancelling the negative betas of the short positions in stocks. There would be net zero betas. The difference between the market values of the short and long positions would be matched by investing, or borrowing, at the risk-free rate.

The stocks sold would tend to fall in price, and hence their expected rates of return would rise towards the equilibrium rates. The stocks purchased would rise in price with the effect that the expected rates of return fall towards the equilibrium rates. The pursuit of arbitrage profits thus tends to move stocks towards equilibrium.

According to the arbitrage pricing model, all investments (portfolios) with identical risk characteristics should exhibit the same expected rate of return. If this is not the case, it is possible to short sell stocks (portfolios of stocks) with low expected returns and buy those with high expected returns. The purchases and sales should be such as to render all the net betas equal to zero. In other words, the resulting portfolio is risk-free. The difference in the costs of the two portfolios (short sold and bought) is matched by investing or borrowing at the risk-free rate. The result is an arbitrage that produces a profit without risk. Pursuit of such arbitrage profits will tend to move stock prices towards their equilibrium values. Equilibrium exists when all stocks, and portfolios, with identical risk characteristics provide the same expected rate of return.

An Example of Arbitrage

This example will use a one-factor version of the arbitrage pricing model for the sake of clarity of exposition, but the principle extends to multi-factor versions of the model. Suppose it is possible to construct a portfolio of stocks that provides a return that exceeds the return implied by the risk of the portfolio. In equation 3 this is represented by a positive alpha (α).

$$E(R_1) - R_f = \alpha + \beta_1(E[R] - R_f) \tag{3}$$

$E(R_1)$ is the anticipated return on portfolio 1, R_f is the risk-free return, β_1 is the beta of portfolio 1, and $E[R]$ is the expected return from the single risk factor (the return required to compensate for the risk of that factor). By diversifying the portfolio all non-systematic risk is eliminated. The positive alpha can be exploited in an arbitrage trade by taking a long position in (i.e. buying) portfolio 1 and taking a short position in (short selling) a portfolio with an alpha of zero (portfolio 2). Portfolio 2 provides the expected return $E(R_2)$ in equation 4.

$$E(R_2) - R_f = \beta_2(E[R] - R_f) \tag{4}$$

The two portfolios should be combined with the following weights:

$$W_1 = \frac{\beta_2}{\beta_2 - \beta_1} \qquad\qquad W_2 = \frac{-\beta_1}{\beta_2 - \beta_1}$$

It is to be noted that the two weights add up to 1. If it were the case that portfolio 1 has a beta of 0.8 and portfolio 2 has a beta of 1.2 (i.e. $\beta_1 = 0.8$ and $\beta_2 = 1.2$), the weights would be:

$$W_1 = \frac{1.2}{0.4} = 3 \qquad\qquad W_2 = \frac{-0.8}{0.4} = -2$$

This provides a net beta of zero:

$$W_1 \times \beta_1 = 3 \times 0.8 = 2.4 \qquad W_2 \times \beta_2 = -2 \times 1.2 = -2.4$$

$$2.4 - 2.4 = 0$$

The alpha of the arbitrage portfolio is (based on the weighting of portfolio 1):

$$3 \times \alpha$$

So if α were 2% p.a., the arbitrage portfolio would produce a return of 6% p.a. The monetary amount by which the long portfolio exceeds the short portfolio is financed by borrowing. The interest paid on the borrowed money is matched by the risk-free component (the component that excludes alpha) of the return on the arbitrage portfolio (the risk-free return component arises from the fact that there is a net long position with zero beta).

Arbitrage should move alpha towards zero. The purchase of the positive alpha portfolio would raise its price and hence reduce its return. The tendency of arbitrage to move alpha to zero ensures that the return on a portfolio comprises the risk-free rate plus a component that compensates for systematic risk.

The arbitrage of the arbitrage pricing theory would not take place unless it was risk-free. This requires an absence of non-systematic risk. So the arbitrage process, and the resulting equilibrium relationship between systematic risks and return, will only apply to well-diversified portfolios. Arbitrage pricing theory does not generate a risk-return relationship for individual stocks.

The capital asset pricing model does produce a risk-return relationship (the security market line) that applies to individual stocks as well as to portfolios. However the CAPM depends upon the use of the market portfolio which is impossible to fully identify, measure, or trade. Arbitrage pricing theory does not require the market portfolio to generate its results. The CAPM assumes that all investors are rational and well informed. The APT merely requires that a small number of arbitragers are rational and well informed. The CAPM assumes that all investors hold the same portfolio (the market portfolio) whereas the APT does not. So APT requires fewer assumptions than CAPM; in particular it does not need the assumptions relating to the market portfolio.

321

The Nature of Risk Factors

The risk factor used in the basic form of the CAPM is the excess return on the market portfolio, $(E[R_m] - R_f)$. The amount of exposure of an investment to that risk factor is measured by its beta. Correspondingly the risk premium required by investors is proportional to the beta of the investment. The risk premium, $\beta(E[R_m] - R_f)$, is the compensation required by investors for accepting exposure to market risk.

The risk factors of the APT can also be described as excess rates of return. In each case the risk factor is the addition to return required to compensate for accepting that particular risk (with a beta of 1). The risk factor can, at least in principle, be measured by isolating the risk factor in question. For each risk factor a portfolio (involving both long and short positions) is constructed such that all other risk factors are zero (net betas are zero) and only one source of risk remains. The resulting portfolio is known as a factor portfolio. The excess return on the factor portfolio (portfolio return minus risk-free interest rate) is used as the risk factor within a multi-factor version of the arbitrage pricing model. This definition of a risk factor might also be regarded as the risk premium of that factor. The required return on a portfolio is the risk-free interest rate plus the sum of factor risk premiums weighted by the factor betas.

EMPIRICAL EVIDENCE

Three UK studies (Clare *et al.* 1997a; Garrett and Priestley 1997; Antoniou *et al.* 1998) have found four or five risk factors when investigating arbitrage pricing models. For example Clare *et al.* found the return on the market portfolio, a price index (the RPI), bank lending, corporate bond yields, and spreads between corporate bond yields and government bond yields to be risk factors. There was some (but not perfect) consistency between the studies.

RETURNS ON BONDS

The factor approach to ascertaining the required rate of return on bonds parallels the approaches of the capital asset pricing model and arbitrage pricing theory. Whereas the CAPM uses just one factor (the excess return on the market portfolio) and APT uses a number of factors which can vary according to the user, the factors employed when analysing bond returns tend to be related to the yield curve. The yield curve is the relationship between bond yields on a per annum basis (vertical axis) and bond maturity in years (horizontal axis). The two most important factors relate to the level and slope of the yield curve. In particular an intermediate rate of interest (e.g. the redemption yield on bonds with ten years to maturity) may be used to proxy the level of the yield curve and the spread between short- and long-term interest rates (i.e. the difference between them) may be used to proxy the slope of the yield curve. The equation for the required rate of return can be presented as equation 5.

$$R_b = R_f + (b_1 \times F_1) + (b_2 \times F_2) \tag{5}$$

R_b = required rate of return on bond
R_f = risk-free rate of return
b_1 = exposure to intermediate rate

F_1 = risk premium per unit exposure to intermediate rate
b_2 = exposure to spread
F_2 = risk premium per unit exposure to spread.

CRITICISMS OF CAPITAL MARKET THEORY

There are three main criticisms of the capital asset pricing model. There is the argument that it is impossible to identify, and measure, the market portfolio. There is the point that it is not possible for individual investors to borrow at the risk-free rate of interest. Third, there is the observation that not all empirical studies have established a direct link between beta and average annual returns.

The argument that it is not possible to identify the market portfolio is often referred to as the Roll critique (Roll 1977; Roll and Ross 1980). Since every investor is assumed to hold the same portfolio, that portfolio must contain all available investments. All available investments includes not only shares and bonds but also a wide range of other investments. Those other investments include property, land, works of art, human capital, and other tangible and intangible assets. Furthermore, those assets would be drawn from throughout the world. To approximate the market portfolio with a national stock index would involve limiting the measure to one type of asset (shares) in one country. Even an international stock index would exclude a wide variety of financial and non-financial wealth. The Roll critique suggests that the capital asset pricing model can be neither tested nor used since it rests on a wealth aggregate that cannot be measured, or even fully identified.

The arbitrage pricing model avoids this critique because it does not require the use of the market portfolio. The risk factors to be used are not predetermined by theoretical considerations; they are to be established by empirical research.

The point about risk-free borrowing is as troublesome to arbitrage pricing theory as it is to the capital asset pricing model. Individual investors are able to acquire risk-free assets, for example Treasury bills issued by national governments or deposits in banks with high credit ratings. However individuals are not free of default risk, consequently they cannot expect to be able to borrow at a risk-free rate. The lenders would require a risk premium to compensate for the risk of default by individual investors. One consequence of this is that the capital market line takes the shape shown in Figure 15.1.

In Figure 15.1, R_d is the rate of interest at which money can be deposited or invested (the risk-free rate). The rate of interest at which money can be borrowed is shown as R_b. The range of investment alternatives is no longer shown as a straight line tangent to the efficiency frontier. The range is shown as R_d-A-B-C. Significantly this new range includes part of the efficiency frontier, A-B. An implication of this is that investors will not all hold exactly the same portfolio of risky assets. Any portfolio between A and B could be held by rational investors.

Another implication of an inability to borrow and lend at the same rate concerns the choice of techniques for acquiring high beta portfolios. If an investor wants a high beta portfolio, there are two alternatives. The investor could buy a portfolio of high beta stocks, or the investor could borrow in order to hold a larger portfolio of lower beta stocks. If borrowing rates are relatively high investors are more likely to choose the first method. The demand for high beta stocks would be higher than the CAPM predicts. In consequence high beta stocks would be relatively overpriced and their returns lower than would be predicted on the basis of their betas. High beta stocks

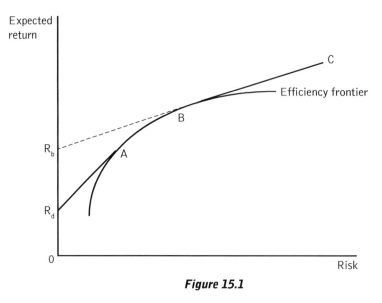

Figure 15.1

would not provide full compensation, by higher expected returns, for their relatively high systematic risks.

THE ZERO-BETA CAPITAL ASSET PRICING MODEL

Referring back to Figure 15.1, when investors have a choice of efficient portfolios the chosen portfolio could be on the curved efficiency frontier between points A and B. In Figure 15.2 such a point is indicated as D.

Taking a tangent at point D gives the broken line that intercepts the vertical axis at R_0. The rate R_0 can be transferred into the figure for the security market line, as shown in Figure 15.3. The result

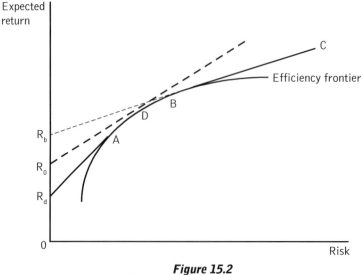

Figure 15.2

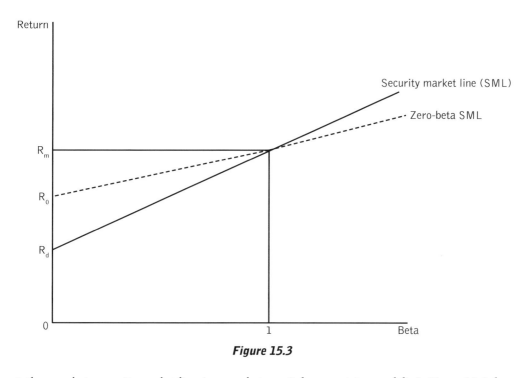

Figure 15.3

is the zero-beta security market line (or zero-beta capital asset pricing model). In Figure 15.3 the market portfolio (the chosen portfolio on the efficiency frontier, point D) has a beta of 1 and an expected return of R_m (the market return). The zero-beta security market line has a slope that is less steep than that of the normal security market line.

EMPIRICAL EVIDENCE

The third source of criticism of the CAPM arises from the empirical evidence on the relationship between beta and average annual returns. Not only is the evidence mixed, but also it is bedevilled by the difficulty of separating tests of the capital asset pricing model from tests of the efficient market hypothesis. A failure to find a relationship between beta and returns could be due to an inadequacy of either, or both, of the theories. There have been fewer tests of the APT than of the CAPM, and hence it remains to be seen whether the APT is a better predictor of investment returns than the CAPM.

Two early empirical studies of the capital asset pricing model supported the zero-beta version. These studies were by Black *et al.* (1972) and Fama and MacBeth (1973). Not only did they find that the security market line intersected the vertical axis above the risk-free interest rate, but they also found that the vertical intersect and gradient of the line varied between periods. In particular it appeared that there were periods during which the gradient was downward sloping, in other words there were times when higher beta entailed lower returns.

A body of evidence has supported the positive relationship between beta and returns; some studies were based on individual stocks and some on portfolios of shares. Kothari *et al.* (1995) and Clare *et al.* (1998) found positive relationships between beta and return for individual stocks.

Sharpe and Cooper (1972), Chan and Lakonishok (1993), and Grundy and Malkiel (1996) demonstrated that high beta portfolios have higher returns than low beta portfolios.

However other studies have either refuted the usefulness of beta as a predictor of relative returns, or suggested that beta is not the only risk factor that is related to returns. Such studies include Basu (1977), Banz (1981), Fama and French (1992, 2006), Chan and Chui (1996), Miles and Timmermann (1996), Strong and Xu (1997), and Liu (2006). Factors that appeared to explain returns (either in addition to, or instead of, beta) included book-to-market ratios, price-earnings ratios, firm size, momentum, and liquidity. Book-to-market ratios (the ratio of the book value per share to the share price) often appeared to be significant. Some studies suggested that non-systematic (i.e. diversifiable) risk was related to returns. Such studies included Friend *et al.* (1978), Gooding (1978), Lakonishok and Shapiro (1984), Fuller and Wong (1988), and Corhay *et al.* (1988). Goyal and Santa-Clara (2003) found that non-systematic risk was related to returns whereas systematic risk was not; the converse of what the capital asset pricing model suggests.

A form of the capital asset pricing model that treats beta as constant over time is referred to as an unconditional capital asset pricing model. Some research, which has been carried out on the one-factor (market-risk premium) version of the model, has allowed beta to vary over the business cycle. The form of the model that entails such a time-varying beta is referred to as the conditional capital asset pricing model. The evidence on the usefulness of the conditional model is mixed (Lewellen and Nagel 2006).

MUTUAL FUNDS AND THE DEATH OF BETA

Erosion of confidence in the strength, or existence, of a positive relationship between beta and returns has been referred to as the death of beta. Karceski (2002) suggested that the weakness of the relationship could be explained in terms of the importance of mutual funds, and the response of mutual fund managers to the behaviour of retail investors.

Karceski observed that people invested in mutual funds about eight times as much during bull (rising) markets as during bear (falling) markets. Since mutual fund managers tend to be paid in relation to the size of funds under management, they would want to maximise cash inflows during bull markets. Retail investors favour mutual funds showing relatively strong recent performance. Achievement of strong performance in bull markets, relative to other funds, might be obtained by holding a portfolio of high beta stocks. The eight-to-one investment ratio between bull and bear markets implies that the relative gain from high beta stocks during bull markets outweighs the relative loss during bear markets, with respect to maximising cash inflows from retail investors over stock market cycles. Karceski found that, on average, the shares held by mutual funds had betas higher than one. Bathala *et al.* (2005) also found that institutional investors, such as mutual funds, had a preference for higher beta stocks. Antunovich and Laster (2003) provided another reason why mutual fund managers might prefer high beta stocks. Top performers among mutual fund managers are rewarded disproportionately to managers whose performance is average (Brown *et al.* 1996). This reward structure increases the motivation to outperform, and to accept increased risk in the pursuit of outperformance.

If mutual fund managers favour high beta shares there would be a disproportionate demand for such shares, which would cause a rise in their prices relative to lower beta shares. The rise in the prices of higher beta stocks would bring about a fall in their percentage rates of return (since the money value of returns would be divided by higher prices). The result would be a weakening of the relationship between beta and returns. The mutual fund bias against lower beta shares would lower those share prices and hence raise returns, further reducing any positive relationship between beta and returns. The conclusion is that the rise in the relative importance of institutional investors, such as mutual funds, in stock markets may be a factor in reducing (or eliminating) the relationship between beta and returns. In other words the increase in the importance of mutual funds has been a causal factor in the death of beta.

CONCLUSION

Arbitrage is central to much of finance theory, particularly in relation to establishing equilibrium prices. So it is not surprising that a capital market theory based on arbitrage has emerged: the arbitrage pricing model.

The arbitrage pricing model avoids some of the doubtful assumptions of the capital asset pricing model. In particular it does not need to assume the ability to identify a market portfolio containing all investment assets. However it does assume the effectiveness of arbitrage; and it requires very sophisticated arbitrage.

In Chapter 23 on the concepts and weak form evidence of market efficiency, it will be seen that very simple arbitrage often fails. Effective arbitrage requires arbitragers to process considerable amounts of information. It also requires that arbitragers are able to borrow without limit. The limitless borrowing potential not only relates to money but also to borrowing investment assets such as shares and bonds. This assumption does not hold. In fact many investors are not even allowed to borrow shares and bonds.

The real test might be whether the arbitrage pricing model produces good predictions, or at least better predictions than the capital asset pricing model. Thus far there is a limited amount of evidence on this. One problem for researchers is that the model does not indicate the nature of the risk factors to be used.

Part 5

Portfolio Management

Chapter 16

Styles of portfolio construction

OBJECTIVE

The objective of this chapter is to provide knowledge of:

1. Active and passive fund management.
2. Index (tracker) funds.
3. Stages of portfolio construction.
4. Goals-based investing.
5. Value stocks and growth stocks.
6. Style investing and style rotation.
7. Hedge funds.
8. Ethical investing.
9. Emerging market funds.

A portfolio manager faces a number of choices in relation to portfolio construction. In particular there is the choice between active and passive management. This choice may be made in relation to each of a number of stages of portfolio construction.

ACTIVE AND PASSIVE MANAGEMENT

Active portfolio management attempts to outperform the market by choosing investments that are likely to show high returns. The market is often proxied by a broad-based stock index, such as the S&P 500 or the FTSE All-Share Index. Active portfolio managers believe that they have the ability to identify the individual securities (shares and bonds), sectors, or asset classes (shares and bonds are the main asset classes) that will perform relatively well. In effect this involves the belief that the fund manager has superior knowledge or understanding that provides a forecasting ability that is better than that of other market participants. Asset prices reflect the market consensus forecasts, active portfolio managers believe that they have the ability to produce forecasts that are better than the market consensus. Active portfolio managers take the view that they can identify situations in which the consensus of other investors is incorrect as to what the price of a security should be. Active fund managers may alternatively (or additionally) take the view that they can successfully time markets. Market timing is the attempt to identify points where the market is about to rise or about to fall. The fund manager would aim to sell before falls and buy before rises. Market timing is alternatively known as tactical asset allocation.

Portfolio managers who employ a passive style do not seek to outperform the market. They operate as if either assets are fairly priced or it is not possible to make profits from any mispricing. Passive management can take one of three forms: a buy-and-hold strategy, responsive portfolio changes, and index tracking.

PASSIVE MANAGEMENT

In the buy-and-hold strategy of passive management, the fund manager buys a portfolio of securities and holds them for the duration of the investment horizon (the investment horizon is the period for which the investment will be held). While the portfolio is held no attempt is made to change its composition. There may be a dimension of active management in the original construction of the portfolio, but thereafter the portfolio is left unaltered.

A second form of passive management involves portfolio changes, but not changes that result from the fund manager taking views that differ from the market consensus. This type of passive management entails adjusting the composition of the portfolio in response to three types of change. The three factors whose variations can lead to alterations in the portfolio are the risk-free interest rate, the consensus view on the risk and return characteristics of the market portfolio, and the degree of risk-aversion exhibited by the investors on whose behalf the fund is managed. This form of passive fund management entails holding a combination of a risk-free investment (such as a bank deposit) and a portfolio of risky securities (which is likely to be the portfolio corresponding to a stock index). A rise in the risk-free interest rate would cause an increase in the proportion of the fund held on deposit. A rise in the (market consensus) expected return on the portfolio of securities, or a fall in the consensus expectation of risk, would cause the fund manager to switch money from deposits into the portfolio of securities. Increased risk-aversion on the part of the investors in the fund would lead to the manager increasing deposits as a proportion of the fund. The relative proportions of risk-free and risky investments (e.g. bank deposits relative to shares) within the fund are subject to frequent change, but not as a result of the portfolio manager trying to outperform the market by forecasting asset price movements.

INDEX TRACKING

A third type of passive management entails the attempt to track the performance of a stock index. Such funds are known as index funds or tracker funds. Index funds give up the possibility of outperforming an index for the security of not underperforming.

An index (tracker) fund aims to replicate the performance of a stock index. The emergence of index funds arose from the observation that actively managed funds fail, on average, to outperform stock indices. This is related to the issue of market efficiency. Active fund management is predicated on the view that portfolio managers can forecast market movements and the performance of individual stocks relative to the market. If the efficient market hypothesis is correct, it is not possible to consistently forecast either overall market movements or the relative performance of individual stocks. If this is the case, investors should avoid the transaction and management costs associated with actively managed funds by investing in index funds whose aim is merely to move in line with the stock market.

The first issue to resolve is the question of which index to track. This largely depends upon the objectives of the fund manager. For a fund that aims to track the UK market, a fund manager wishing to focus on the shares of large companies may choose the FTSE 100 whereas a fund manager looking for a broader portfolio may choose the FTSE All-Share Index.

The choice of index would be influenced by the fact that many fund managers are prevented from buying particular shares. Some countries have regulations that prevent certain shares being acquired by foreign investors. Overseas managers of index funds would choose indices that exclude those shares. Some share issues are not fully marketed; for example parts of some privatisation issues may continue to remain in the hands of the government. There are stock indices that include only the marketed component of share issues when weighting shares in the index. Those indices are likely to be the ones preferred by the managers of index funds, who wish to avoid any liquidity problems arising from share issues that are only partially available for investors.

One advantage of index funds over a buy-and-hold strategy of passive investment is that the index fund may provide an optimal level of diversification whereas a buy-and-hold strategy is less likely to do so. The market portfolio of the capital asset pricing model is the ultimate perfectly diversified portfolio. When using a broad stock index as the benchmark to track, an index fund could be seen as seeking to approximate the market portfolio of the capital asset pricing model. To the extent that this is the case, the capital asset pricing model might be seen as providing a theoretical justification for index funds.

One advantage of index funds, relative to actively managed funds, is that they are more likely to ensure that the portfolio remains well diversified. Actively managed funds, in their attempts to outperform the market, may hold poorly diversified portfolios. For example they may tilt the portfolio towards particular industries. To the extent that actively managed funds hold inadequately diversified portfolios, they sacrifice part of the risk-reduction benefit of diversification.

However these arguments rest on the use of a suitable stock index. Some stock indices fail to provide optimal diversification. For example in October 2005 the top ten UK companies accounted for 54% of the FTSE 100 Index, and that top ten was concentrated in just four sectors (oil, banks, pharmaceuticals, and telecoms). Even the FTSE All-Share Index, which is broader, was concentrated in four sectors: oil & gas (18%), banks (17%), pharmaceuticals (8%), telecoms (8%). Even if a stock index provides a reasonable degree of diversification at a point in time, changes in relative share prices can cause the index to become unbalanced. Kat (2004) cited the example of the S&P 500, in which technology and financial services stocks together accounted for about 18% of the index in 1990. By 2000 the combined weighting of those two sectors had risen to about 44%.

Another advantage of index tracker funds, to the individual investor in collective investments, is that they avoid management risk (alternatively known as active risk). The performance of actively managed funds can, during any period of time, vary considerably. Some will outperform the index and others will underperform it. The variation between the best and the worst can be considerable. For example over the ten-year period to 1 October 2005 the best performing unit trust/OEIC in the UK equity sector provided total returns of 346% whereas the worst performer lost 4%. Over the same period three index tracker funds gained 97%, 97%, and 98%, the FTSE All-Share Index produced 111%, and the average (median) unit trust/OEIC provided 92% (*Money Management*,

October 2005). If the direction and size of the deviations from the index occur by chance, as empirical evidence seems to suggest, the individual investor faces a management risk. Individual investors bear the risk that their chosen funds will be relatively poor performers. By investing in index tracker funds they avoid this management risk.

Probably the greatest advantage of index funds is that they are much cheaper to run than actively managed funds. For example many actively managed UK unit trusts and OEICs have a 6% initial charge, an annual 1.5% management charge, and transaction costs around 1% per year. This contrasts with index tracker funds which typically have a zero initial charge, a 0.5% annual management charge, and minimal transaction costs. At the time of writing the cheapest UK index tracker fund had a zero initial charge and a 0.1% annual management charge.

A drawback of index funds is that they tend to omit the shares of very small firms. Even broad indices have a cut-off in terms of company size. For example in the UK the FTSE All-Share Index covers about 750 stocks. This eliminates more than 1,000 firms whose capitalisation is not sufficient. Actively managed funds are able to include any stocks, including those with very small capitalisations.

Another drawback is that an index tracker fund will hold disproportionately high amounts of overpriced shares, and disproportionately low amounts of underpriced shares. Even if it is accepted that it is not possible to identify mispriced shares, or to make profits from identified mispricing, it may still be the case that many shares are mispriced. Stock indices, on which index tracking funds are based, are normally value-weighted indices. The proportions of stocks in the indices, and hence in index tracking funds, reflect the relative market capitalisations of the respective companies. Since market capitalisation is equal to the number of shares in issue multiplied by the share price, overpriced shares will have excessively high capitalisations and underpriced shares will have disproportionately low capitalisations. Index tracking funds will therefore have excessive holdings of overpriced shares and too few underpriced shares. This will be bad for fund performance. This is a problem for the whole of the fund management industry, not just for index tracking funds. If indices are biased towards overpriced shares it is because the stock market is similarly biased. In turn the average portfolio will have an overweight holding of overpriced shares (and be underweight in underpriced shares).

One suggested solution for tracker funds is to use measures other than market capitalisation on which to base the size weighting. Possible alternative measures of size include profits, dividends, sales, and book value. For the fund management to remain passive the size criterion must be permanently adhered to. However the initial choice of size criterion would impart an active aspect to the fund management. Funds that use such approaches to weighting are sometimes called fundamental trackers. An example of a situation in which they would have been superior to conventional index trackers was the bubble in high technology stocks in the late 1990s. The extraordinary rise in the prices of high technology stocks massively increased their market capitalisations and hence raised their weightings in index tracker funds. When the bubble burst, the tracker funds lost money. Holding high technology stocks in proportion to their profits, dividends, or book value would have kept them at a tiny weighting within the tracker funds and the large losses would have been avoided.

One problem with fundamental trackers is that rebalancing of shareholdings would be required as relative profits, dividends, sales, or book value changed. Rebalancing entails transaction costs and may involve buying when prices have risen and selling when they have fallen. For example if a fundamental tracker weights holdings in proportion to profits, the shares of a company whose profits have risen may need to be bought. If the rise in profits (or the anticipation of the rise) were accompanied by a rise in the share price, the fund may be buying the shares after their price has risen. A conventional index tracker would unambiguously gain from the price rise. A conventional index tracker would also avoid transaction costs in that rebalancing automatically follows the market; if the market capitalisation of a company rises because of an increase in its share price, its weighting in the tracker portfolio would automatically rise as a result of the higher share price.

A further difficulty faced by open-ended mutual funds (unit trusts and OEICs) that track indices arises when redemptions exceed new investment. Actively managed funds tend to keep a small proportion of the fund in cash with a view to using that cash to finance withdrawals. If an index tracker fund holds cash, the part of the fund held in cash will not track the index. This would be a source of tracking error. If 100% of the fund is held in shares, the portfolio could be unbalanced by the sale of shares in order to finance redemptions by investors. One way round this problem would be to match cash holdings with stock index futures, particularly since futures can be traded quickly and cheaply. Cash can be held and exposure to the index maintained by using stock index futures. Futures, matched by cash, may provide a means of avoiding the potentially unbalancing effects of small inflows and outflows. Inflows and outflows of cash can be accompanied by purchases and sales of stock index futures with the effect that a balanced exposure to the stock index is maintained.

METHODS OF INDEX TRACKING

There are four main methods of indexation: full replication; stratified sampling; optimisation; and synthetic funds.

Full Replication

This may be achieved by holding all the stocks in the index in the proportions in which they occur in the index. Whereas this could be feasible for indices covering a small number of individual stocks, more broadly based indices are difficult to replicate in this way. Tracking a narrow index by full replication will be reasonably accurate and will involve few portfolio changes (which will occur only when the composition of the index changes). However a narrow index may not provide a well-diversified portfolio.

The management of even a narrow index has its problems. For example dividends would need to be reinvested in the index proportions, and this may entail some small transactions that are disproportionately expensive. Indices do not have management and brokerage costs whereas index funds do incur such costs. Such costs make it unlikely that perfect tracking will be achieved (there will be some tracking error). When attempting to fully replicate a broad index the problems increase. In particular a broad index may include stocks that are small and illiquid. The trading of small illiquid stocks can be disproportionately expensive, and may in some instances not be possible.

Stratified Sampling

The tracking of a broad index involves constructing a portfolio with characteristics similar to those of the index portfolio. Tracking a broad index will involve more frequent portfolio changes and less accuracy (there will be more tracking error) since perfect replication of the index is unlikely.

335

On the positive side a broad index is likely to provide a more balanced portfolio, and one that more faithfully represents the overall market.

Stratified sampling is one approach to the construction of a fund that tracks a broad index. Instead of holding all the stocks in an index, stratified sampling holds only a sample of the stocks. It is likely that the shares of all companies above a particular size are held. For example if a UK index fund is based on the (more than) 750 shares in the FTSE All-Share Index, it may be that all of the top 100 stocks are held (in the same proportions as in the index). A representative sample of the remaining shares is then purchased. There are many ways in which the sampling could be undertaken.

A sampling technique should try to ensure that the portfolio held reflects the index being tracked. It may be that the portfolio held invests in sectors proportionately to the sector distribution of the index. This may be further refined in order to have a similar distribution between large, medium, and small companies. There could even be further refinements in terms of other characteristics of the companies and their shares.

Generally the tracking error from stratified sampling can be expected to be a little greater than from full replication. However holding a sample, rather than all of the shares in the index, is likely to reduce brokerage costs. There is a trade-off; more precise tracking may entail increased costs. It should be borne in mind that, since transaction costs produce some downside tracking error, it could even be the case that the stratified sampling approach reduces tracking error.

Optimisation

Optimisation is a sample method based on the view that stock returns are determined by a set of attributes such as size, price-earnings ratio, volatility, liquidity, etc. (Rudd 1980). Optimisation attempts to ensure that the shares in the portfolio reflect the attributes of the shares covered by the stock index. Shares for the portfolio are chosen in an attempt to mirror the attributes of the shares in the index.

One problem with optimisation is that it relies on the past being a good guide to the future. In particular it relies on historical risk-return relationships continuing into the future, which may not happen. Also as the attributes–of the market and of individual stocks–change, portfolio rebalancing will be needed. This raises transaction costs and allows tracking error if there are any delays. It should also be remembered that statistical relationships are never precise; statistical estimates are subject to errors that could undermine the reliability of the sampling.

EXHIBIT 16.1

This exhibit shows an example of a UK index tracker fund, which uses replication, and an example of a fund tracking a European stock index by using other tracking methods.

M&G INDEX TRACKER FUND (AS OF 30 JUNE 2007)

Fund objective

The fund is designed to track the FTSE All-Share Index.

Policy for achieving objective

The fund is a mainstream UK fund that replicates the FTSE All-Share Index. The fund holds nearly all companies in the index at exactly the weight they represent in the FTSE All-Share Index.

Initial charge: 0%
Annual charge: 0.3%

Table 16.A

Top ten holdings (as percentages of the total fund)	
BP	6.08
HSBC Holdings	5.61
Vodafone Group	4.60
GlaxoSmithKline PLC	3.93
Royal Dutch Shell A	3.93
Royal Bank of Scotland Group	3.10
Royal Dutch Shell B	3.01
Barclays	2.37
Anglo American	2.25
AstraZeneca	2.08

Source: M&G Securities Limited.

LEGAL & GENERAL EUROPEAN INDEX TRUST

Objective

The investment objective of this trust is to track the capital performance of the European equity markets, as represented by the FTSE World Europe (excluding UK) Index, by investing in a representative sample of stocks selected from all economic sectors.

Securities in the FTSE World Europe (excluding UK) Index will be held with weightings generally proportionate to their company's market capitalisation.

Use may be made of optimisation techniques to construct and maintain a portfolio, the underlying value of which exhibits the performance characteristics of the Index.

Total expense ratio:* 0.80% p.a.

Table 16.B

Ten largest holdings on 31 January 2007 (as percentages of the fund)

Total	2.54
Nestlé	2.21
Novartis	2.10
Roche (NES)	2.06
UBS	2.04
Banco Santander Central Hispano	1.85
Telefonica	1.68
BNP Paribas	1.59
Siemens	1.55
ING Groep	1.51

*There was another class with a lower total expense ratio.
Source: Legal & General (Unit Trust Managers) Limited.

Synthetic Index Funds (Futures Funds)

Synthetic index funds involve the use of stock index futures, and will be discussed further in Part 8 on stock index futures. A stock index futures contract is a notional agreement to buy a portfolio of shares (the portfolio reflected by the stock index) on a future date at a price (index level) agreed in the present. Stock index futures reflect the actual (spot) stock index and tend to show parallel price movements. Buying futures contracts does not entail an expenditure of money; a relatively small (returnable) deposit called initial margin is all that is required.

Futures funds keep most of the investment in bank deposits (or cash equivalent investments such as Treasury bills) and use a small portion to meet the initial margin requirements of futures contracts. The futures contracts provide exposure to movements in the stock index. The result is an investment that is the equivalent of a full replication index tracker fund.

Futures funds have a number of advantages when compared with other approaches to constructing index tracker funds (Bruce and Eisenberg 1992). One advantage is simplicity in that only one instrument is bought, the futures contract, rather than a large number of individual stocks. Also the potentially complex decision-making of sampling and optimisation is avoided. Futures also tend to have lower transaction costs: lower commissions, smaller bid-offer spreads, and typically no taxes. Liquidity is normally not a problem with futures whereas it could be a problem with many stocks. When money flows into, and out of, a fund on a continuous basis the adjustments to a futures fund are much easier than in the case of a share-based fund.

Futures funds have some disadvantages relative to other index tracker funds. One disadvantage is that futures are not available for all stock indices. For example they are available for the FTSE 100 but not the FTSE All-Share Index whereas most UK index tracking funds are based on the FTSE All-Share Index. There is also a risk that the futures will be mispriced at the time of purchase, and that they are bought when overpriced. Since futures tend to have short maturities (especially the liquid contracts) they need to be rolled over (replaced with new contracts) at frequent intervals. The risk of mispricing will occur at each rollover date.

TRACKING ERROR

Portfolios constructed to replicate an index rarely succeed in precisely tracking the index. Tracking error is the amount by which an index tracker fund deviates from its benchmark index. The tracking error is the difference between the total return on the index tracker fund and the total return on the index. The total return consists of both dividends and capital gains (or losses).

The portfolio may hold all the stocks in the index, with weights corresponding to those of the index. This involves little tracking error but can involve significant transaction costs. Alternatively a subset of the index might be used. This approach reduces transaction costs but increases tracking error. However it should be remembered that transaction costs impart a (downward) tracking error.

Even if the portfolio contains all the stocks in the index, appropriately weighted, there are sources of tracking error. The constituent stocks of an index are subject to change. Replacing stocks involves transaction costs. Furthermore the replacement is not instantaneous. Tracking is imperfect during the time taken to replace stocks.

Changes in the composition of an index can affect stock prices. If index tracker funds are widely used, stocks leaving the index will be sold in large numbers by index tracker funds. As a result their prices fall and the funds receive unfavourable prices. Conversely stocks entering the index will be bought by index tracker funds with the effect that their prices rise. The funds thus buy these stocks at raised prices. So the marginal stocks, those prone to move in and out of an index, are sold at low prices and bought at high prices. This weakens the performance of index tracking portfolios.

It is not just the sales and purchases of the funds that will affect the prices of the marginal stocks. Other traders (arbitragers), in anticipation of the reconstitution of stock indices, would seek to take advantage by selling the stocks to be removed and buying the stocks to be added. When the sales by index tracker funds reduce the prices of deleted stocks arbitragers would buy back at the lower price (having sold at a higher price). Likewise arbitragers, having initially bought stocks to be added, would subsequently sell the added stocks when the purchases by index funds have driven their prices up. Stocks expected to be removed will fall in price before the reconstitution date, and the prices of prospective additions will rise. By the reconstitution date prospective deletions would have fallen in price, and prospective additions would have experienced price rises. Deleted stocks may subsequently rise in price, and additions fall in price, when arbitragers subsequently reverse their positions. The result is that index tracker funds experience losses on stocks to be deleted, prior to the reconstitution date, and losses on added stocks subsequent to the reconstitution date.

Whilst there seems to be no doubt that stock prices move around the time of the reconstitution date, there is some controversy concerning whether they subsequently fully return to their previous prices. In other words, there is a question as to whether some or all of the initial price movement is permanent. The view that initial price changes are fully reversed is known as the Price Pressure Hypothesis and the view that they are permanent is the Imperfect Substitution Hypothesis. According to the price pressure hypothesis, prices revert as arbitragers unwind their arbitrage positions or as other investors switch to other stocks. If prices have risen, other investors may sell the expensive stocks and buy cheaper stocks; conversely when prices have fallen. According to the imperfect substitution hypothesis there are impediments to arbitrage and other investors do not switch because other stocks are not good substitutes in their portfolios. Studies of these hypotheses include those of Lynch and Mendenhall (1997) on the S&P 500 and Vespro (2006) on the FTSE 100, CAC 40 and SBF 120. Both studies indicated that there was partial reversion of prices, with the Vespro results being the closer to complete price reversion. It appears that index tracker funds tend to change their portfolios close to index reconstitution dates despite the price disadvantages incurred.

Madhavan and Ming (2003) report a study by Blitzer according to which additions to the S&P 500 index tended to gain 8.5% between the announcement and reconstitution dates, whilst stocks removed fell by an average of 11.7%. The price changes reversed subsequent to the reconstitution dates. There are reasons to believe that indices such as the FTSE All-Share Index (the index most commonly tracked by UK index funds) are less susceptible to such effects. In the case of the FTSE All-Share Index, additions and subtractions are likely to be a very small proportion of the value of a fund. In the case of the S&P 500, the additions and subtractions could be a significant proportion of the total fund value since S&P 500 additions and subtractions are decided by committee rather than by criteria such as relative size (for example additions and subtractions in the FTSE 100 are based on replacing declining firms with growing firms so that the index continues to represent the largest UK companies). Another problem with the S&P 500 system is that there is a chance that the additions and subtractions could be of substantially different sizes with the effect that rebalancing may be necessary throughout the portfolio (replacement of a relatively small capitalisation stock with a large one requires increased investment in that stock at the expense of all the other stocks in the index).

Chen, Noronha *et al.* (2006) found that the problem was greatest for funds that tracked indices of small company shares since the index changes are usually large relative to the market capitalisation of the index. They found the effect on the Russell 2000 index (a small-cap index) to be around 1.5% p.a. Large capitalisation indices are less affected since the changes are small relative to the total market capitalisation of the index. They found the effect on the S&P 500 (a large-cap index) to be about 0.1% p.a.

It is to be noted that these negative effects are effects on the index; they do not reflect a failure to accurately track the index. In fact if investors were to accept some imperfection in tracking the worst of these effects could be avoided. By reconstituting an index tracker fund some time before, or after, the index reconstitution date much of the detrimental effect on the fund could be avoided. By accepting a little more tracking error the index tracker investors could enjoy a higher rate of return. It might also be noted that there is a reduction in the ability of stock indices accurately to measure aggregate stock market movements since a downward bias is imparted. In other words the existence of index tracker funds leads to a situation in which stock indices underestimate market rises over time. It is also a factor that should favour actively managed funds since such funds should be able to avoid the detrimental effects.

One issue concerns the importance of the tracking error. If the objective of index tracking is the avoidance of dramatic underperformance, a small tracking error is not necessarily important. Since the reduction of tracking error is likely to involve increased costs of share trading, as the portfolio is frequently and precisely rebalanced, imperfect tracking may be seen as worth tolerating. However if the tracking error is not random, or appears to be increasing, the fund manager may decide that some portfolio rebalancing is required.

PASSIVE CORE (CORE-SATELLITE) FUNDS

A hybrid strategy is known as the passive core (or core-satellite) approach. In this case the fund manager manages part of the portfolio passively, and the remainder actively. If the passively managed component seeks to track an index, the resulting portfolio might be seen as a closet tracker. A passive core strategy that uses index tracking for the passive core of the portfolio allows the fund manager to exercise judgement whilst ensuring that the performance of the portfolio does not fall substantially below that of the index, and hence the average of funds. A variation on this theme is the 'enhanced' index fund, which is primarily an index tracker but with a tilt in a direction that is seen as potentially providing outperformance.

STAGES OF PORTFOLIO CONSTRUCTION

The construction of a portfolio may involve one stage, two stages, three stages, or possibly even more. The fund manager must decide on the number of stages and their nature. There is also a choice between active and passive management at each stage (and if passive, which type of passive management).

A one-stage process involves the portfolio manager seeking the optimum portfolio from the entire range of securities available (or under consideration). This could be achieved by employing the Markowitz equations or Sharpe's single index model. Alternatively a stock index portfolio might be used. In reality many fund managers would employ less formal procedures. If the optimum portfolio is amended in the light of the manager's market forecasts, or is affected by such forecasts, the strategy would be an active one. The strategy would be an active one if the manager takes bets on individual securities (or sectors or asset classes). A passive strategy would be uninfluenced by any forecasts that the fund manager may make.

A two-stage process might involve the optimisation process being divided into separate stock selection (and bond selection) and asset allocation stages. In the first stage a stock portfolio is decided upon, and simultaneously a bond portfolio is established. These two separate portfolios can be derived using the types of approach indicated for the one-stage process (Markowitz diversification, index portfolios, etc.). In the second (asset allocation) stage the fund manager seeks an optimum combination of the stock and bond portfolios. This could be based on Markowitz optimisation, or a less formal procedure. The operation could additionally involve portfolios of investments in asset classes other than stocks and bonds, for example real estate and money market instruments. The fund manager has the choice between active and passive styles at each of the two stages.

A three-stage process might introduce a sector allocation (sector rotation) decision between the stock selection and asset allocation stages. Stocks may be divided into sectors such as oils, banks, insurance, pharmaceuticals, utilities, construction, retailers, and so on. Bonds may be divided according to types of issuer, maturity, and credit rating. The fund manager might seek an optimum portfolio for each sector or division. An optimum portfolio of the sector portfolios would then constitute the stock portfolio. Likewise a portfolio of various bond portfolios (one for each chosen category of bond) would be constructed. The stock and bond portfolios would then be combined to form the portfolio of risky assets. The fund manager might then choose to combine this with a holding of risk-free assets (such as deposits or Treasury bills). An active manager would then deviate from such a base portfolio by increasing the proportion held in some assets, and decreasing the weighting in others, according to the manager's forecasts of relative performance.

If the fund manager includes foreign securities in the portfolio there would be more stages. Separate portfolios might be created for each country. There would then be a portfolio of country portfolios.

An approach that involves determining first the asset allocation, then the sector allocation, and finally the stock selection is referred to as a top-down strategy. An approach that seeks undervalued investments, irrespective of sector or asset class, is known as bottom-up. In the top-down strategy, a passive approach at the asset allocation and sector allocation stages may involve determining percentage allocations for each asset or sector (perhaps allowing the fund manager a limited amount of discretion to vary the percentages on the basis of market views, in which case the strategy is a hybrid between passive and active).

As prices change the original percentages are disturbed. For example an increase in share prices relative to bond prices raises the proportion of the portfolio in shares relative to the proportion in bonds. The fund manager then faces a choice between two alternative passive strategies. One strategy, a form of buy-and-hold, would be to accept the new proportions and not carry out any buying and selling transactions. Another strategy would be to sell shares and buy bonds in order to restore the original percentage allocations.

Country Diversification versus Sector (Industry) Diversification

If an investment manager faces a choice between diversification across countries or diversification between industrial sectors, or needs to decide on the order of country and sector allocation in a multi-stage process, the relative scope for diversification benefits could influence the choice.

However the empirical evidence on relative diversification benefits does not give unambiguous guidance. The consensus seems to be that in the past country diversification has been the more effective in portfolio risk reduction (improving the risk-return profile) but that more recently sector diversification has improved its relative merits, particularly in relation to portfolios invested in European markets.

Estrada *et al.* (2005) pointed out that there were differences in opinion such that some argue that country diversification is the more effective means of risk reduction, and should therefore be the first stage in the portfolio optimisation process, whereas others suggest that industry diversification is more effective and should take precedence. They compared country and industry effects in Europe over the period 1989 to 2003 and found that they offered approximately equal diversification opportunities. The result held even when TMT (technology, media, telecommunications) stocks were excluded. TMT stocks might be thought to have distorted the results since their bubble and crash could have reduced the correlation of TMT with other industry sectors. When the sample period was divided into two, 1989–96 and 1997–2003, it was found that in the earlier period country diversification was the more effective whereas in the latter period industry diversification came to the fore. These results held even after the exclusion of TMT stocks.

Hauser and Vermeersch (2002) investigated the relative merits of country and industrial sector diversification based on international portfolios invested in developed capital markets (US, Japan, UK, France, Germany, Switzerland, Italy and Canada). Their sample period was 1980 to 2001. Until 1994 country diversification surpassed industrial sector diversification, but by a decreasing margin. In the post-1994 period the two diversification effects were approximately equal. However it should be borne in mind that the international diversification of the study was limited to a group of countries, which were homogeneous in the sense of having well-developed capital markets.

The apparent change in the relative effectiveness of country and industry diversification may be explained in terms of increasing correlation between countries and falling correlation between industrial sectors. Barnes *et al.* (2001) found that, in the second half of the 1990s, industrial sector correlations fell and cross-country correlations rose. The rise in cross-country correlations, and decline in potential for country diversification, was most marked in the European Union.

STRATEGIC AND TACTICAL ASSET ALLOCATION

A portfolio manager may determine a strategic asset allocation and allow some tactical asset allocation. The strategic asset allocation may entail weighting asset classes at the levels applicable in the absence of any views about short-term market movements. Table 16.1 illustrates such a strategic asset allocation.

Tactical asset allocation would be allowed by stipulating ranges around the central percentages of Table 16.1. Movements within the ranges would be made in the light of short-term expectations of market movements. Table 16.2 illustrates possible ranges.

GOALS-BASED INVESTING

Goals-based investing is a structure for personal investment management that draws on both traditional investment principles and behavioural finance (Nevins 2004). It has been suggested that it is a useful framework for financial advisers to use when dealing with clients. The central

Table 16.1

UK shares	40%
Overseas shares	20%
UK bonds	20%
Overseas bonds	10%
UK money market	10%

behavioural finance principle involved is mental accounting. The proponents of mental accounting suggest that many people do not see their wealth as forming a single portfolio. Instead finances are divided into separate accounts; the separation may take the form of distinct, observably separate, pools of assets or the separation may merely be in the mind of the investor. Each account has its own portfolio and is related to its own specific goal. It is likely that each account has its own investment horizon.

Nevins (2004) suggests measures of risk that differ from the conventional one of standard deviation. He points out that prospect theory sees people as loss-averse rather than risk-averse; that is people are primarily concerned with losses. Correspondingly risk should be measured in terms of the likelihood and severity of loss. The conventional standard deviation measure is concerned with a single time period and ignores price movements within the period and the potential cumulative effect of losses in successive periods. Conventional measures of return and risk are concerned with annualised measures whereas measurement that relates to the whole investment horizon may be more appropriate.

If risks are measured in terms of the violation of investor goals, the prospective achievement of goals could override attitudes to risk. A risk-tolerant investor need not hold a risky portfolio if a low risk portfolio would meet a goal. Conversely if a conservative portfolio could not meet a goal, a higher yielding risky portfolio must be accepted even by a highly loss-averse investor. For example portfolios whose goal is the provision of a pension would normally need to hold risky assets.

Conventionally investment advice begins with ascertaining the client's attitude to risk, using verbal questioning and/or a questionnaire, in order to obtain a single measurement of risk-aversion/tolerance. In the case of goals-based investing, several measurements of risk are required: one for each mental account. Each measurement of risk would be related to a specific goal, and would be measured against a reference value expressed in terms of the goal. For example when saving for retirement the goal may be in terms of retirement income and risk would then be measured in terms of deviations from the desired level of retirement income.

Table 16.2

UK shares	35–45%
Overseas shares	15–25%
UK bonds	15–25%
Overseas bonds	5–15%
UK money market	5–15%

One problem is that verbal questioning requires very good communication with the client. If clients have a poor understanding of risk, and are unclear about their own feelings towards risk, the process of measuring their attitudes to risk can be difficult. There is considerable scope for a failure of communication (Callan and Johnson 2002). The alternative of using questionnaires is also open to difficulties. There is the problem of whether a questionnaire accurately measures attitude towards risk. Yook and Everett (2003) found that different questionnaires produced very different results; so at least some of the questionnaires were inaccurate. Confidence in the questionnaires was also undermined by the observation that the relationships between questionnaire responses and investment decisions appeared to be weak.

The approach of conventional portfolio management is to treat the investor's portfolio as a single entity, and to measure attitude to risk in relation to the whole portfolio. The behavioural finance alternative is to allow for multiple investment strategies, each relating to a separate mental account (Shefrin and Statman 2000; Brunel 2003). Each strategy is linked to the goal encompassed by a mental account, on the basis that there would be a separate mental account for each goal. Arguably mental accounting should be seen as a preference rather than as a bias, such that the adviser should accommodate to the preference rather than treating it as an aberration that should be eliminated. Mental accounting may be a useful technique for organising personal finances, and for achieving self-control in financial matters.

Goals-based investing may not be suitable for investors who do not have precise goals, but where goals are clear to the investor it may be an appropriate approach. There are alternative ways of describing goals. One approach is to link them to life-cycle factors such as saving for a deposit on a home, saving for children's education, and saving for a retirement pension. Shefrin and Statman (2000) suggest that mental accounts might be differentiated in terms of risk; for example between low risk funds that are intended to ensure that poverty is avoided through to funds that can be risked in the hope of very large gains. Chhabra (2005) took the view that investors divide their portfolios according to three types of risk: specifically a personal risk concerned with the avoidance of loss, the market risk of conventional theory, and aspirational risk concerned with the prospect of falling behind other people in terms of wealth. Correspondingly there may be a holding of risk-free assets to satisfy safety risk, a balanced portfolio for the market risk, and an aggressive portfolio aimed at high growth to satisfy aspirational risk. Chhabra suggests that risk allocation precedes asset allocation. Brunel (2003) suggested that there are four fundamental goals: liquidity, income, capital preservation, and growth. It could be the case that an individual separates mental accounts in terms of their investment horizons; for example long-term, medium-term, and short-term pools of assets.

It may be that an investor would feel more comfortable with a goals-based investment strategy than with a single-portfolio strategy. One problem in the financial services industry has been the tendency for many people to terminate savings plans early (such as pension plans and endowment policies). If goals-based investing makes them feel more comfortable with their savings plans, they may be more likely to persist with them. For an asset allocation to be useful, the investor must adhere to it even in falling markets. Feelings of regret may cause an investor to abandon a strategy in adverse conditions. Brunel refers to this as 'decision risk'.

The goals-based investing proposed by Brunel would entail a separate sub-portfolio to meet each of the four fundamental goals. For example, liquidity may be achieved with a bank deposit; income by a mixture of value stocks and corporate bonds; capital preservation by government bonds; and growth by a portfolio of value and growth stocks. The proportions of the four sub-portfolios in the total portfolio would reflect the goals and risk attitude of the investor. Brunel's argument implies that a portfolio comprising such a set of sub-portfolios could be more resilient and robust to decision risk in the face of adverse developments. The investor might remain more committed to it than to a traditional portfolio, which does not have goals-based sub-portfolios.

A problem with goals-based investing is its complexity. From the perspective of a financial adviser, several measures of risk may need to be made and several investment strategies devised and implemented. The task could be simplified by the creation of a variety of institutional investment products suited to different goals (see Part 3 on mutual funds, pensions, and assurance-related investments). Structured products can be created to meet investment goals that cannot be otherwise achieved (see Chapter 34 on structured products and the other chapters in Parts 8 and 9 on futures and options). The adviser can then customise an investment portfolio for an individual by choosing the institutional investments that best match the investment goals of the individual.

VALUE STOCKS AND GROWTH STOCKS

There is a widespread belief that there are groups of shares that have common features in terms of characteristics and behaviour. The most favoured grouping appears to be between value stocks and growth stocks. Value stocks are shares that appear to be relatively underpriced in terms of criteria such as price-earnings ratios, price-to-book ratios, and the fair prices determined by dividend discount models (see Chapters 19 and 21 on dividend discount models and on ratio analysis, respectively). Value stocks tend to have relatively high dividend yields. Growth stocks are identified by an expectation of rapid growth in earnings (company profits) and hence in share price.

Probably the most frequently used measure, to classify shares into the value and growth categories, is the price-to-book ratio. The book value of a firm is its net value (assets minus liabilities) as shown on its balance sheet. Division of this book value by the number of shares in issue gives the book value per share. The price-to-book ratio is the share price divided by the book value per share. (The price-to-book ratio is alternatively known as the market-to-book ratio.)

Stocks of companies with a low price-to-book ratio are generally classified as value stocks, whereas a high ratio indicates a growth stock. The total number of stocks under consideration is referred to as the universe of stocks. Sometimes this universe of stocks is divided into value and growth stocks such that half the total market capitalisation is classified as value and the other half as growth. Allocating the whole universe in this way creates style jitter. Style jitter is the term given to the tendency for stocks to move from one category to the other. An alternative procedure, that reduces style jitter, is to divide the universe of stocks three ways. One-third of the market capitalisation is seen as consisting of value stocks, one-third as growth, and one-third as not readily classifiable as either.

Style investing involves the concentration of a portfolio on either value or growth stocks. Passive style investing keeps the portfolio to one of the two styles (or keeps the emphasis on one). Active style investment entails switching between styles in the light of forecasts of the relative performance of the two styles. Active style investment might take the form of moving the whole portfolio from one style to the other, or of changing the relative emphasis from one to the other.

Often the value-growth classification is further refined by allocating stocks along other dimensions. A popular additional dimension is the size of firms as measured by market capitalisation. The simplest of these divides companies into large and small, so that half of the market capitalisation falls into each of the two groups. The addition of this refinement produces four styles: large value, small value, large growth, small growth.

Lakonishok *et al.* (1994) defined growth stocks as the shares of firms with high growth rates, and value stocks as those of firms with low growth rates. Investigating US stocks over the period 1963 to 1990, they found that over five-year periods growth stocks averaged a total return of 81.8% whereas the return from value stocks averaged 143.4%. (The growth stocks were shares of the top 10% of companies in terms of growth, and value stocks were from the bottom 10% of firms.)

Ahmed and Nanda (2001) expressed the view that investors are best served by combining value and growth features when selecting shares. They defined value stocks as those with low price-earnings ratios, and growth stocks as those with relatively high growth rates of earnings per share. High returns were available from both the lowest (bottom quintile) of stocks in terms of price-earnings ratios and the highest (top quintile) of stocks in terms of the growth rate of earnings per share. They found that the best performance was obtained from portfolios containing shares that were in the highest categories (quintiles) in terms of both the value and the growth characteristics; that is shares that had both the lowest price-earnings ratios and the highest growth rates of earnings per share. A conclusion was that value and growth investment styles are not mutually exclusive.

IMPLICATIONS OF STYLE INVESTING

Barberis and Shleifer (2001) developed a model of style investing. According to this model investor behaviour is driven by relative returns. The model makes two key assumptions. First, money moves towards styles that have done relatively well in the past. Second, these flows of money affect the relative prices of the investments. A style could be any categorisation that investors judge to be relevant, e.g. value/growth, passive/active, large company/small company.

Investors do seem to be attracted to styles that have performed well in the recent past. Sirri and Tufano (1998) found that retail investors (i.e. private individuals) appear to base their unit trust choices on prior performance. This was supported by Odean (2001) who found that nearly half of new investment went into the top 10% of funds, ranked in terms of recent performance.

According to the Barberis and Shleifer (2001) model, the prices of favoured styles are driven up to levels that are probably not warranted by the fundamental merits of the investments. Funds flow from styles that are out of favour to those in favour. The model divides investors into two groups: fundamentalists and switchers. The fundamentalists look at the underlying quality of investments, whereas switchers chase the market by buying into the style that has recently performed well (the switchers might be described as momentum or positive feedback traders). The switchers may be influenced by the representativeness bias (a behavioural finance psychological bias) and see an investment with recent good results as representative of investments with good long-term returns. There may also be agency factors, for example the trustees of a pension fund may choose a style that has performed well recently on the grounds that it is easier to justify such a choice when they have to account for their decision.

An investment style can go through a life cycle. The style arises as the result of good fundamental factors, which attract those investors who focus on fundamental factors. The investment by the fundamentalists causes prices to rise and the rising prices attract switchers. Switchers then invest and thereby push prices up further. When the fundamental value of the investments covered by

347

the style turns downward, the process is reversed. The success of a style may arise because of good fundamentals relating to its investments, or to bad fundamentals relating to the opposite style.

Style investing could produce co-movement of returns, even when the investments are otherwise unrelated. The returns from an investment may be influenced by the success of a style with which it is associated. In consequence a factor other than general market risk (systematic risk) will influence returns. It can also produce some apparent anomalies. For example Royal Dutch and Shell are the same company, so they should trade at the same price. Froot and Dabora (1999) found that Royal Dutch moves with the US market whilst Shell moves with the UK market. Royal Dutch is a constituent of the US S&P 500 index and hence is a constituent of the S&P 500 style. Shell is a constituent of the UK FTSE 100 and hence is subject to the behaviour of investors for whom the FTSE 100 is a style (e.g. FTSE 100 index trackers and funds for which the FTSE 100 is the benchmark).

STYLE ROTATION

The principles of behavioural finance have been used to produce models that suggest rotation between momentum and contrarian styles of investing. The momentum style entails positive feedback trading: rising share prices lead to purchases and falling prices are seen as a signal to sell. The contrarian style involves selling after rises and buying after falls; it is based on the premise that markets will reverse direction. Swaminathan and Lee (2000) produced a diagrammatic representation of style rotation. This is shown in Figure 16.1.

In Figure 16.1, glamour stocks have high price-to-book ratios, high trading volumes, and a long history of earnings being better than expected. Value stocks have low price-to-book ratios, low trading volumes, and long-term negative earnings surprises.

Swaminathan and Lee (2000) refer to the process shown in Figure 16.1 as the momentum life cycle. According to the momentum life-cycle hypothesis, stocks are subject to bouts of under-

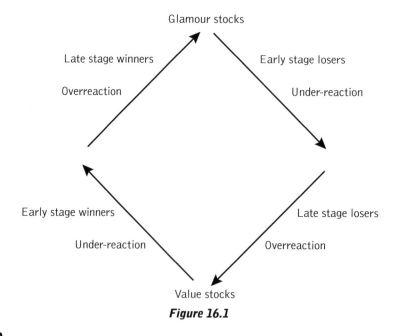

Figure 16.1

reaction and overreaction, and of popularity and neglect. A stock that experiences good news moves up the left-hand side. When the stock begins to disappoint investors in terms of earnings, it will begin to decline – initially slowly but subsequently more rapidly. As the stock moves down the right-hand side, the pace of price fall increases. Eventually the rate of price decline becomes subject to overreaction as investors extrapolate recent price movements too far into the future.

The momentum life cycle suggests that early stage winners and losers exhibit return continuation so that momentum trading should be profitable. An investor should buy recent risers and sell recent fallers. Late stage winners and losers tend to exhibit reversals, so contrarian strategies should be profitable. An investor should buy recent fallers and sell recent risers.

Behavioural finance has been criticised for predicting both momentum and contrarian effects. Style rotation models have been developed to reconcile these opposing predictions. Barberis *et al.* (1998) base initial under-reaction and subsequent overreaction on conservatism, anchoring, and representativeness. Following a long history of good news about earnings and share price rises, bad news items are initially given little weight. This is the effect of conservatism and anchoring affecting the thinking of investors. A consequence is that there is little price decline in the face of bad news. There is under-reaction to the bad news. This is the situation in the top right-hand quadrant of Figure 16.1. The opposite situation occurs in the bottom left-hand quadrant for the same reasons. The psychological biases of conservatism and anchoring cause under-reaction to a change in news.

The top left and bottom right quadrants reflect the effects of representativeness on the thinking of investors. Stocks with good recent histories are seen as being representative of long-term strong performers. This leads investors to extrapolate the past into the future and to become over-optimistic about the potential success of the respective stocks. Conversely poor recent histories can lead to excessive pessimism. These stages exhibit overreaction on the part of investors.

Daniel *et al.* (1999) used the overconfidence and confirmation biases of behavioural finance. In their model, an investor estimates the value of an investment and also assesses the precision of the estimate. Confirmation bias causes the investor to overweight information consistent with the estimate and underweight information that contradicts the view taken. In consequence, confidence in the accuracy of the estimate increases. The increased confidence then leads to overreaction.

PASSIVE STRATEGIES, ACTIVE STRATEGIES, AND PARRONDO'S PARADOX

There is considerable evidence that active trading can reduce investment returns (e.g. Barber and Odean 2000; and Odean 1999). It has been supposed that this is because of the transaction costs incurred by active investors. Although transaction costs are part of the explanation, they may not be the whole explanation. Parrondo's paradox may contribute to the explanation (Spurgin and Tamarkin 2005). Parrondo's paradox was first discovered in physics, but seems to have applicability in many other disciplines (Spurgin and Tamarkin illustrate its applicability to investments). The operation of the paradox can be illustrated by a coin-tossing game (this illustration is based on Harmer and Abbott 1999).

In game A the player tosses a biased coin and bets on each throw. The player is aware of the bias and therefore expects a positive outcome over time. In game B the player tosses one of two coins and bets on each throw; one coin is biased and the other unbiased. Coin 1 is tossed if the player holds a sum of money which is a multiple of three (the number three has no particular significance,

349

any number could be used), otherwise coin 2 is tossed. Since the player knows the bias of coin 1, the game has a prospective positive return over time.

Either game played alone is expected to yield a positive return, but alternating between the games (either randomly or in a pattern) generates losses. This is an illustration of the paradox. The reason for the paradox remains a mystery but there are numerous examples of its operation in many different applications. The operation of the paradox depends upon there being some connection between the two games (the role of the number three links the wealth from game A to the playing of game B). It is believed that the explanation lies in a ratchet effect whereby losses are not easily reversed.

The implication for investment strategy is that switching between profitable investments could result in losses. For example remaining invested in value stocks prospectively yields a positive return, and remaining invested in growth stocks also has an expectation of positive return, but a strategy of switching between the two investment styles could yield negative returns. The reason for Parrondo's paradox is not yet understood, but its existence strengthens the case for passive portfolio strategies.

HEDGE FUNDS

Although hedge funds have existed since 1949, it is only since the mid-1980s that they have achieved a significant role amongst investment vehicles. Hedge funds are typically private partnerships with the management team being general partners, and accepting unlimited liability for losses, and other investors being limited partners (with liability limited to the sums invested). The partnership structure tends to dictate that there should be a small number of partners, and hence that each partner should contribute a large amount of capital.

There is no generally accepted definition of hedge funds. However a typical characteristic is that they attempt to profit in all market conditions: rising, falling, and stable. Hedge funds are often absolute return investments, which seek positive returns irrespective of the direction of markets; in contrast to mutual funds whose returns tend to move in the same direction as markets as a result of their holding only long positions. The performance of hedge funds may therefore be linked more closely to the investment skills of the managers than to market performance. An investor in a hedge fund could be seen as investing in the investment skills of the fund managers.

Hedge funds are characterised by their flexibility of investment style and strategy. Hedge fund managers have the flexibility to make substantial changes to security selection, asset allocation, and trading strategy. They often use short selling, leverage, and derivatives. Although early hedge funds were hedged in the sense that they held offsetting long and short positions, nowadays many hedge funds do not follow such a strategy. Arguably the term 'hedge fund' is a misnomer for those funds that do not adopt the style of offsetting long and short positions.

By short selling is meant the practice of borrowing shares and selling the borrowed shares. This means that stock is owed and needs to be returned to the lender in the future. Such a short position in stock benefits from a falling price. If stock prices fall it costs less to buy the shares for the purpose of returning them to the lender. A fund that has a long position in (that is owns) some stocks and a short position in others is hedged against general market movements. The fund manager short sells overpriced stocks and buys underpriced stocks, with a view to profiting when the prices move to their appropriate values, whilst being immune from movements in the stock market as a whole. To the extent that it is possible to identify mispriced shares, hedge funds that employ such a long-short equity strategy are able to profit from both under and overpricing whereas conventional (long only) funds are limited to making profits from underpriced shares. Hedge funds that seek complete offsetting of long and short positions take no net position on the stock market; such funds are said to follow absolute return strategies.

This is risk arbitrage rather than pure arbitrage. The fund is exposed to the specific (non-systematic) risks of the individual securities that arise from firm- or sector-specific events. In the case of shares there is the risk that the fund manager has not correctly discerned which are overpriced and which are underpriced. There is no certainty as to how long it will take for relative mispricing between shares to be corrected. It is also unlikely that exposure to overall market movements is completely avoided (particularly since stock betas cannot be precisely ascertained and are liable to change).

Sometimes a hedge fund will be hedged in one dimension whilst being speculative in another. For example during the period 2004–5 some hedge funds used Collateralised Debt Obligations (CDOs). A CDO is a portfolio of bonds divided into tranches according to default risk such that the buyers of the tranche with the highest default risk are the first to lose money in the event of a bond defaulting. Those who buy the riskiest tranche suffer immediately if one of the bonds defaults. Some hedge funds took a long position in the more risky tranches and short sold less risky tranches. There was a gain in that the yields on the more risky tranches were higher than those on the less risky with the effect that income receipts exceeded payments. As far as interest rate risk is concerned this position is largely hedged. An unexpected rise in interest rates would cause losses in the long position but offsetting profits in the short position; an unexpected fall in interest rates causes losses in the short position offset by profits in the long position (recall that there is an inverse relationship between interest rates and bond prices). However as far as default risk is concerned the hedge funds are being speculative. They are betting that the yield difference between the tranches is more than is required to compensate for the difference in default risk. In the event of an unexpectedly high level of defaults, or credit rating downgrades, the hedge funds stood to lose (and in many cases did lose).

The process of short selling entails additional risk in that the borrower of stock must pay a deposit, known as margin, and more must be paid if the stock price rises. It is possible that the mispricing worsens before it improves, in particular the price of the short sold stock could rise before it falls. There could come a point where the fund is unable to meet the calls for additional margin payments and is forced to close out the short position by buying shares at a high price, which would result in losses.

Other characteristics of hedge funds are that they are largely exempt from regulation, typically prevent investors from withdrawing their money early, and levy fees that are related to fund performance. The avoidance of regulatory control over investment strategy is achieved by organising funds as limited partnerships. Although this provides flexibility of investment strategy, it reduces the liquidity of hedge fund investments. Investors may lose access to their funds for several years; hence investments in hedge funds may be very illiquid. A small number of hedge funds are listed on stock exchanges. This improves their liquidity but subjects them to a greater degree of scrutiny. Many hedge fund managers desire not only flexibility and independence with respect to their investment strategies, but also secrecy.

The flexibility allows hedge funds to borrow heavily. An implication of this leverage is that profits and losses for investors are magnified. If a £100 million investment is financed by £20 million from investors and by borrowing £80 million, and if the fund grows to £120 million, the investors would make a profit of 100% on their investment (£120 million minus £80 million debt repayment leaves £40 million – ignoring interest payments). If the investment falls to £80 million, the debt can be repaid but the investors are left with nothing. Hedge funds often borrow several times the sums provided by investors. This high leverage substantially increases the risks of investing in hedge funds.

One attraction of hedge funds to other fund managers is that their returns show low correlations with the returns on other investments, such as shares and bonds. So the inclusion of hedge fund investments in a portfolio is useful for the purpose of reducing portfolio risk by diversification. This arises from the wide variety of investments and strategies available to hedge fund managers. A downside of the flexibility is that such a high degree of discretion by hedge fund managers means that there is a considerable risk of mistakes on the part of managers. In other words there is a high level of management risk. This is not helped by the high degree of secrecy employed by many hedge fund managers concerning their investments and strategies. Hedge funds are often small, and reliant on just one or two fund managers. Hitherto they have shown a high failure rate, although there is disagreement about the size of failure rates with Roberts (2004) suggesting that around 20% of funds fail each year whereas Baquero et al. (2005) found an annual failure rate of 8.6% between 1994 and 2000.

Managers of hedge funds are often rewarded in relation to performance in addition to receiving a fixed proportion of the fund value each year. This aligns the interests of managers and investors. This alignment of interests is often reinforced by the hedge fund managers having substantial personal investments in the fund. However there are disadvantages for the investors. Whilst the managers receive large performance-related rewards in the good years, at the expense of investors, there are no cash flows from the managers to the investors in bad years. Second, this reward structure may encourage the managers to take excessive risks. Since managers receive a proportion of profits but do not make payments in the event of losses, the incentive is to take high risks. The managers gain if the risks pay off, but they do not lose if the risks result in losses. Third, a succession of poor performances may cause the managers to abandon the funds. This may explain why such a high proportion of hedge funds terminate.

Hedge funds can be categorised according to their investment strategy. A broad division is between directional and non-directional funds. Directional funds take a position on the direction of movement of a market; the market could be a stock market, a bond market, a currency market, or a commodity market. Non-directional funds aim to make arbitrage profits. The arbitrage profits would be sought from buying underpriced assets and taking short positions in (short selling) overpriced assets. The long and short positions tend to hedge each other, thus removing exposure to general market movements.

Hedge funds following directional strategies can be divided into a number of categories according to the type of strategy. Those that follow macro strategies seek to make profits from economic changes at the country or regional level. Some funds take the strategy of focusing on emerging markets, such as those of countries with new or small stock markets. Another strategy is to take long positions in equities, that is buying shares. Other hedge funds concentrate on the opposite strategy, that is short selling securities, which they consider to be overpriced.

Hedge funds pursuing non-directional strategies can also be divided into more specific categories. There are funds that use fixed-income arbitrage, which entails long and short positions in bonds. Event-driven hedge funds seek to take positions in stocks so as to profit from events such as mergers, takeovers, or restructuring. Equity hedge is an investment style that uses long and short positions in equities, buying underpriced and short selling overpriced shares. Distressed securities hedge funds focus on companies that are in financial difficulties. Hedge funds that specialise in convertible arbitrage buy and sell securities of the same company thereby profiting from relative mispricing, for example between convertible bonds on the one hand and combinations of shares and non-convertible bonds on the other.

Non-directional strategies may be at the macro level, for example long in European equities and short in US equities to take advantage of an expected relative outperformance in Europe. It does not matter if there are global market movements, since the combination of long and short positions hedges the fund against stock market movements that are common to Europe and the United States. What matters to the fund is the relative performance in Europe and the United States. It is likely that such a fund uses stock index futures (see Part 8 on stock index futures). Stock index futures profit (or lose) from movements in stock indices without the need to directly invest in shares. Not only does the use of futures avoid the costs of selecting and trading individual stocks, but also it can remove the risk of adverse movements in exchange rates between the US dollar and European currencies. The only initial cash flow when acquiring a futures position is the provision of a (returnable) deposit, which represents a small percentage of the value of the underlying stocks (e.g. 5% of the value of the shares covered by the futures contracts). The use of stock index futures thus provides a means of achieving leverage, since the value of shares covered by the futures is far greater than the value of the deposit (a 5% deposit means that exposure to a £1-million's worth of shares is obtained from a cash outlay of just £50,000; a twenty-fold leverage).

Merger arbitrage hedge funds may buy the securities of a company that is being acquired and short sell the securities of the acquiring company. Alternatively they may seek to profit from superior assessments of the likelihood of success of takeover bids. For example suppose that £3 is bid for the shares of the target company whereas the share price was previously £2. If the share price rises to £2.60, the market is taking the view that the takeover bid has a 60% probability of success $[(2.60 - 2)/(3 - 2) = 0.6$, i.e. 60%]. A hedge fund manager who believes that success is more than 60% probable would buy the shares, whereas a view that the probability of success is less than 60% would lead to short selling.

Shleifer and Vishny (1997) pointed out that there is a principal-agent (asymmetric information) problem in the operation of hedge funds. Those who invest in hedge funds are often ignorant of the strategies and markets used by the hedge fund managers. Being ignorant of the investment processes, the investors are likely to judge hedge funds on their past performance. The behavioural finance principles of retrievability and narrow framing suggest that the investors would tend to focus on recent performance.

An implication of these features is that funding could be at its weakest just when arbitrage opportunities are at their strongest. When prices and fundamental values show greatest divergence, the potential profits from arbitrage are at their highest. The fund managers know this, but the investors do not. It is possible that the wide discrepancy between actual and fundamental prices has resulted from a recent widening of the difference between them. Such a widening is likely to

353

have caused losses on a fund that is using an arbitrage strategy. The investors have seen losses in the recent past and are reluctant to invest more money, and may even be inclined to withdraw funds. Dunbar (2000) tells of the difficulty that Long-Term Capital Management faced when it tried to raise more capital following losses. Hedge fund managers face the possibility of involuntary liquidation of positions because of the withdrawal of funds. That involuntary liquidation could occur when the arbitrage positions are making losses. Long-Term Capital Management experienced increased divergence in its arbitrage positions, and hence losses, following the default on Russian bonds in 1998.

Many hedge funds have lock-up periods during which investors cannot withdraw their funds. Such lock-up periods can be as much as five years. Investments in such hedge funds are illiquid. Most individuals who invest in the hedge fund sector do so through a fund of funds. A fund of funds invests in a portfolio of hedge funds. A disadvantage to the individual investor is that there are two sets of charges. The hedge fund managers make charges, and so does the manager of the fund of funds. There are advantages from investing through a fund of funds. First they provide risk reduction by diversification. Since hedge funds vary considerably in their strategies, correlations can be expected to be low and hence the benefits of diversification are likely to be high. Another advantage is that funds of funds are typically much more liquid than the hedge funds. An investor can sell holdings in a fund of funds immediately, or in a relatively short period of time. The manager of the fund of funds bears the liquidity risk. If large numbers of individual investors redeem their fund of funds holdings, the fund of funds managers can have problems. They have to return money to investors but may be unable to turn their holdings of hedge funds into cash. The charges made by the managers of funds of funds may in part be seen as compensation for accepting liquidity risk.

The International Monetary Fund (IMF) estimated that by the end of 2004 there were 9,000 hedge funds managing a total of $1,000 billion. HedgeFund Intelligence estimated that by early 2006 a total of more than $1,500 billion was being managed by hedge funds. The investors in hedge funds are very wealthy individuals and institutional investors such as pension funds and insurance companies. Most individuals are limited to investing through funds of funds operated by institutions since minimum sums for direct investment in hedge funds are very high. An individual hedge fund may manage a sum in the region of $100 million to $1,000 million but a hedge fund company may manage many funds, sometimes more than a hundred.

At the time of writing (2006) there are moves to introduce some regulation of hedge funds. This is partly driven by anxiety about the high degrees of leverage among funds. If a large number of funds default on their debts to banks, the international banking system may be unable to absorb the losses. Also hedge funds have the potential to distort markets, for example it has been estimated that 20% of the oil price increase during 2005 was the result of purchases by hedge funds. The impact of hedge funds on markets is not necessarily negative. It has been argued that they benefit markets by adding depth and liquidity; the fact that hedge funds trade securities such as shares, bonds, and derivatives makes it easier for others to find counterparties with whom to trade. They may also help to move assets to their correct prices. For example buying underpriced shares and simultaneously selling overpriced shares would tend to move both towards their correct prices. A situation in which securities trade at their correct prices is referred to as informational efficiency (see Part 7 on market efficiency).

354

Hedge Fund Performance

The question of whether hedge funds are good investments remains unresolved. They often claim to offer double-digit rates of return irrespective of whether stock markets are rising or falling. However there is considerable evidence that conventional funds, on average, fail to outperform stock markets (see Chapters 9, 11, and 17 on mutual funds, pensions, and portfolio performance evaluation, respectively, and Part 7 on market efficiency). If conventional fund managers cannot consistently pick successful shares or time changes in the direction of markets, why should we expect better from hedge fund managers? Even if the first few hedge funds could find profitable opportunities, the massive increase in their numbers and size must raise doubts about whether there are enough profitable opportunities for them all to succeed. Their potential is undermined by their tendency to incur high trading costs; it has been estimated that they trade about eight times as much as conventional funds. This entails enormous transaction costs such as brokerage commissions, bid-offer spreads, and taxes. At the time of writing (November 2006) the FTSE Hedge Fund Index had shown a return of 4.5% over the previous twelve months whereas the FTSE All-Share Index had shown a return in excess of 18%. This is a very crude comparison, but more sophisticated research has suggested that hedge fund returns are far from exciting (Kat and Amin 2001; Kat and Palaro 2006). It appears that hedge funds could be useful for portfolio diversification, although not through funds of funds because of the second layer of charges. Even the portfolio diversification benefits of hedge funds have to be qualified. Whereas they may reduce portfolio risk when risk is measured solely in terms of standard deviation, they may increase risk when kurtosis is considered (Kat 2003). Kurtosis measures the likelihood of extreme falls in value.

The evaluation of hedge fund performance is difficult for a number of reasons. One of those reasons is that data on hedge funds is far from perfect, in particular data is frequently provided by the fund managers without any independent verification. Amenc *et al.* (2004) reported that more than 40% of hedge funds covered by two major databases were not effectively audited, which reduced the reliability of the reported data. Another reason for the difficulty of evaluating hedge fund performance is survivorship bias. If the analysis of returns considers only those hedge funds that survive for the whole period being examined, the performance figures would be enhanced by the absence of the hedge funds that failed during the period. Although this is a problem with all fund performance measurement, it is a particular problem for the measurement of hedge fund performance since hedge funds have a high failure rate. In other words hedge funds, on average, have short lives.

Gregoriou (2002) carried out a survival analysis of hedge funds. Survival analysis estimates the probable life of an entity and seeks to ascertain what factors affect the length of its life. Gregoriou found that the median life of a hedge fund was 5.5 years (based on data from the period 1990 to 2001). It was also found that factors associated with relatively long life were large size, high returns, low leverage, and low minimum purchase requirements. It appeared that poor performance was the main reason for funds becoming defunct and that the early years were the most dangerous for funds. Funds of hedge funds had a median survival time of 7.5 years. Baquero *et al.* (2005) also found that mature, large hedge funds with high returns were less likely to liquidate. Amin and Kat (2003) found that the attrition rate of hedge funds was lower for the larger and better performing funds but, contrary to other studies, found that newer funds suffered less attrition than older funds.

355

Publicised figures for hedge fund returns often suggest that their average annual rates of return are much higher than those available on other types of fund. However performance may be exaggerated by survivorship bias. The exclusion of the poorer performing hedge funds, which are discontinued because of the poor performance, from calculations of average rates of return leads to an overstatement of average hedge fund returns (i.e. a survivorship bias). Baquero *et al.* (2005) concluded that survivorship bias accounted for 2.11 percentage points of the average annual return on hedge funds. Amin and Kat (2003) estimated that the survivorship bias was about 2 percentage points per annum on average, and also concluded that survivorship bias caused an understatement of risk. Taking dead funds into account leads to higher measures of risk as well as lower measures of return. Amin and Kat found results for funds of hedge funds that were similar to those for individual hedge funds, but more modest; for example their estimated survivorship bias for funds of hedge funds was 0.63% p.a. Research by Fung *et al.* (2004) indicated that, when allowance was made for survivorship bias, hedge fund returns showed no outperformance on average. In other words they found no evidence of investment management skill. Amin and Kat (2003a) took the view that, on average, hedge fund returns fell between the averages for shares and bonds (i.e. less than shares but more than bonds).

Evaluation of investments requires attention to risk as well as return. Amin and and Kat (2003a) observed that the risk of hedge funds, as measured by their standard deviations, fell between the risks of shares and bonds. They also pointed out that, since the returns on hedge funds are not highly correlated with the returns on shares and bonds, hedge funds appear to offer good risk reduction through diversification. However standard deviation alone is not an adequate measure of risk when considering hedge funds. In particular kurtosis and skewness are important as additional measures of risk.

Hedge funds appear to be subject to greater kurtosis than other investments, which means that extreme returns are more likely. If the high kurtosis is accompanied by negative skewness, the probability of very large losses is enhanced. Amin and Kat (2003, 2003a) show that the introduction of hedge funds into a portfolio will increase the kurtosis and distort the skewness of the portfolio. So although the diversification effect of hedge funds may reduce risk as measured by standard deviation, the introduction of hedge funds into a portfolio would increase risk as measured by kurtosis and skewness.

Even the reduction of standard deviation may be limited, dependent upon the hedge fund strategy. Amenc *et al.* (2003) measured the correlations of hedge fund returns with stock returns during declining stock markets. Some, such as convertible arbitrage and event-driven hedge funds, were found to have rising correlations with stocks. So an investment manager seeking to diversify with hedge funds should be selective about which hedge fund strategies are appropriate. In the extreme, hedge funds that use a short-selling strategy may be unlikely to improve risk-return trade-offs since their risk-reduction effects would be at the cost of lower expected portfolio returns. Stock market rises would be offset by losses on the hedge funds.

Kat (2005) found that forming portfolios of hedge funds, known as funds of hedge funds, reduces standard deviation but worsens skewness and kurtosis. Furthermore it was found that correlations with portfolios of shares increased when hedge funds were combined into portfolios; so the diversification benefits were reduced. Using funds of hedge funds, rather than individual hedge funds, as an addition to other portfolios reduces risk to the extent that the fund of hedge funds has a lower standard deviation than individual hedge funds. However it entails higher risk by way of skewness, kurtosis, and higher correlation with other components of the total portfolio.

Lhabitant and Learned (2002) also found that whilst reducing some measures of risk, the combination of hedge funds into funds of hedge funds worsened skewness and kurtosis. They found that between five and ten funds was enough to achieve the risk-reduction benefits whereas increasing the number of funds further worsened skewness and kurtosis. Additionally, increasing the number of hedge funds raises the correlation of the hedge fund portfolio with portfolios of shares, thereby reducing the diversification benefits. Too much diversification in the hedge fund portfolio reduces that portfolio's value as a diversifier of the total fund.

Amenc *et al.* (2004) examined the extent to which managers of funds of hedge funds in Europe took account of the peculiar risk and diversification characteristics of hedge funds. They found that funds of hedge funds tended to contain an excessive number of funds. This ignores research findings on the relationship between the number of hedge funds in the portfolio and the effects on the portfolio into which the fund of hedge funds is placed. Many managers of funds of hedge funds fail to consider the adverse effects of kurtosis, skewness, and correlation with other portfolio assets.

Investors may consider high liquidity, as well as high return and low risk, to be a desirable characteristic of investments. Hedge funds perform poorly in this regard since they tend to be illiquid.

Long-Term Capital Management

Long-Term Capital Management (LTCM) is one of the most famous hedge funds. One reason for its fame is the eminence of its founders who included Nobel Prize winning finance professors and star traders. In the first three years the fund generated very high returns and by 1998 the value of the fund was about $125 billion (of which about $120 billion was financed by borrowing; so the fund was highly geared).

The strategy of the fund was to pursue arbitrage opportunities. When similar assets traded at different prices the more expensive one would be sold short, and the cheaper one would be bought. The strategy depended on the prices of the two assets converging within a time scale over which the fund could afford to maintain the trading position. Another feature of the fund strategy was its high degree of diversification. The positions that were taken covered a wide range of uncorrelated markets.

An example of an early success was the purchase of $2 billion of 29.5-year US Treasury bonds and the simultaneous short sale of $2 billion of 30-year Treasury bonds on the grounds that the spread between the prices was incorrect. Since two similar bonds were held, the position was hedged against general market movements. The fund made a $25 million profit on this position very quickly (Levy and Post 2005). When a trading position aims to profit from a narrowing of a wide difference between two values it is often referred to as a 'convergence trade'.

In 1998 LTCM bought a large quantity of Russian bonds and simultaneously short sold a large quantity of US Treasury bonds. LTCM took the view that Russian bond prices were too low relative to US Treasury bonds and that the difference between the prices should reduce. Russian bond

357

prices were expected to rise relative to US Treasury bond prices. However the spread widened rather than narrowing.

In August 1998 the Russian government defaulted on its bonds. This led to panic in the markets and a 'flight to quality' as investors tried to sell risky bonds and buy safer ones. Russian bond prices fell relative to US Treasury bond prices. Long-Term Capital Management (LTCM) tried to sell some of its bonds but found that it was difficult to do so. There were two major reasons for the difficulty encountered.

First, there was a sharp decline in market liquidity. Buyers were few and the bonds could not be sold without substantial price reductions. Banking regulations compounded this problem. One way in which banks make money is by providing liquidity. When other investors want to sell assets the banks may buy. The buying price gives the banks a profit margin, and the other investors forego this margin in order to be able to sell. In other words the banks make money by providing liquidity. So in August 1998 banks should have bought the bonds that other investors wanted to sell. However banking regulations required banks to increase their capital reserves when market volatility increased. In order to increase their capital the banks sold assets. Rather than being buyers the banks were sellers. Instead of providing liquidity the banks required liquidity. Instead of stabilising markets the banks added to the market instability.

Second, the assets held by the fund had become highly correlated (Stulz 2001). In theory the well-diversified investments should have had low correlations. However Long-Term Capital Management became a victim of herd behaviour. Observing its success, and the calibre of its management, other investors were copying its trades. The assets held by the fund had become correlated because they had a common set of owners. The prices of investments held by LTCM had become a function of market expectations of the trading decisions of the fund's managers. As the fund tried to sell its investments, so did those who were copying its trading behaviour. This increased the difficulty encountered by LTCM when attempting to make its sales. There was a problem of reflexivity in that LTCM was not simply reacting to market conditions; it was creating market conditions.

Having a risky position combined with a high degree of gearing can be very dangerous. LTCM nearly became bankrupt. By late 1998 investors in LTCM had suffered losses of over 90%. LTCM had to be rescued by a group of major banks organised by the US Federal Reserve. LTCM suffered from aspects of markets that are explicable in terms of behavioural finance rather than traditional economic analysis. One aspect was the tendency for 'irrational' trading behaviour to persist for a long time. The 'irrational' sentiment behind a price anomaly could persist for a long time, and due to herding it could be shared by a large number of investors. In such a situation betting against the herd can be dangerous. A trader taking such a bet can make substantial losses if the anomaly is slow to be corrected, and if it becomes larger before it becomes smaller. In principle arbitrage should correct price anomalies, but arbitragers may be overwhelmed by 'irrational' traders for long periods. One is reminded of J. M. Keynes's adage that markets can remain irrational for longer than you can remain solvent. Even when hedge funds do hedge, the hedging is not complete. Some dimensions may be hedged, for example exposure to general bond market movements, whilst other dimensions remain exposed (dimensions such as factors that affect relative price movements). A significant amount of risk may be borne. Long-Term Capital Management was dissolved in December 1999.

358

SOCIALLY RESPONSIBLE INVESTING

There is an investment style, or family of styles, that considers more than the return and risk characteristics of portfolios. These styles also encompass an ethical dimension. The funds following a Socially Responsible Investing (SRI) approach would avoid investments in companies that fail certain ethical criteria.

SRI funds vary as to what type of investment is avoided. Investments that are commonly avoided by such funds include the securities of companies involved in armaments, alcoholic drinks, tobacco products, and gambling. SRI funds might also avoid investments in companies that are seen as having poor records in terms of environmental pollution, exploitation of labour, or cruelty to animals. There are some investments that are regarded as desirable by some SRI funds and undesirable by others. For example nuclear power may be seen as desirable by some funds since it avoids the emission of greenhouse gases, whereas other funds could see it as undesirable because of the risk of accidents and contamination. The relative aversion to particular industries can vary over time. For example Statman (2005) pointed out that in 1999 gambling was the second most likely industry to be screened out by SRI funds whereas by 2003 it had fallen to fifth.

It might be thought that investors would have SRI real estate funds available, as well as SRI equity funds, since different building designs and locations can have considerable significance for the environment. Property funds holding only environment friendly real estate might be expected to appeal to environmentally conscious property fund investors. Rapson *et al.* (2007) reported that there were few SRI property funds available. They also found that the institutional investors, which were active in the provision of SRI funds for financial assets, did not necessarily show an SRI approach in their real estate investments. Also companies showing environmental concerns with regard to property were not necessarily very active in the provision of SRI equity funds.

Statman (2005) suggested that SRI funds vary in terms of how strictly they adhere to the principles of social responsibility. If the adherence is so strict that investment returns could be reduced, the number of investors in a fund might be reduced. Statman cited evidence that most investors would avoid SRI funds if they believed that investment returns would be adversely affected by the SRI approach. There may be a trade-off in that some relaxation of the adherence to SRI principles could be required in order to attract enough investors to render a fund viable.

Some funds use a positive ethical screening approach. Such funds would choose to invest in companies whose objectives are seen as ethically desirable. Examples might include companies that recycle waste or supply organically produced food. More typical is the fund that adopts negative ethical screening. Negative ethical screening eliminates ethically undesirable companies. Some funds go a step further and attempt to influence company policy by means of investor activism or engagement with companies (Hudson 2006). For example the fund managers may propose motions at the annual general meetings of companies, or even attempt to get their representatives onto boards of directors as non-executive directors.

The ethics upon which a fund may be based could be derived from religious beliefs. Muslims often seek investments that conform to Shariah (Islamic) law. In this case companies eliminated by the screening process would include those involved in alcohol, gambling, pork, and pornography. Although Shariah law forbids the payment or receipt of interest, share dividends and other forms of profit sharing are acceptable. FTSE International, a major producer of stock indices, has created a Global Islamic Index that tracks the performance of stocks regarded as consistent with Shariah law.

Ethical screening poses practical problems. There is the issue of whether a company is seen as ethical. For example avoidance of companies involved in alcohol would obviously preclude breweries and distilleries. Does the preclusion extend to pub chains, which sell food and soft drinks as well as alcohol? Does it extend to restaurant chains that offer alcohol to be consumed with meals? Does it extend to hotel groups, which make alcohol available to residents? Does it extend to chocolate manufacturers who include liqueurs within their range of products? Judging companies as ethical or unethical involves deciding upon where to draw the line between the two types of company.

Another practical issue concerns the difficulty of obtaining relevant information about companies. It is not necessarily easy to find out everything that a company does, and how it does it. If a company is engaged in unethical operations, it may be reluctant to provide information about them. Fortunately the investor's task is eased by organisations that specialise in ascertaining whether companies meet ethical criteria. In the UK the Ethical Investment Research Service (EIRIS) maintains a database of ethical funds and individual companies.

Ethical screening could remove many companies from consideration for investment portfolios. Up to 60% of the FTSE 100 companies could be eliminated (Harrison 2005). Large companies are prone to disqualification because they are involved in a vast number of operations, and somewhere among the operations ethical criteria are likely to be contravened. One result is that ethical funds are likely to be disproportionately weighted towards small and medium-sized companies. There is a danger that ethical screening leaves a fund dependent upon a small number of sectors. To help with the evaluation of the performance of ethical funds, stock indices based on ethically acceptable stocks have been constructed. These include the FTSE4Good stock indices.

It might be thought that SRI funds would, on average, underperform other funds since they are more restricted in their investment choices. Funds able to choose any investment might be expected to outperform those with a more restricted range from which to select. Also SRI funds might be expected to be relatively poor in terms of portfolio returns (and risks) because they have multiple objectives; a situation which renders their task more difficult than that of funds whose objectives are defined solely in terms of return and risk. Furthermore the companies in which they invest may pursue multiple objectives rather than simply profit-maximisation. For example the Global Reporting Institute seeks a 'triple bottom line' reporting framework, wherein accounting profit is not the only measure of company performance. The satisfaction of ethical criteria must, according to this framework, also be treated as objectives.

The research evidence appears not to support the view that SRI funds underperform other funds in terms of investment returns and risk. Guerard (1997) and Diltz (1995) concluded that there was no statistically significant difference between ethically screened and unscreened equity portfolios in terms of performance. Van de Velde et al. (2005) also found no statistically significant difference between the returns on SRI funds and other funds. D'Antonio et al. (1997) obtained similar results for the case of bond investments. There is some evidence that SRI funds have enjoyed higher returns than the average (Heal 2001). This is reflected in the relative performance of stock indices that are based on the types of stock used in SRI funds. The Goodmoney Industrial Average is a stock index designed to cover the same industries as the stocks used to calculate the Dow Jones Industrial Average but screened according to ethical criteria. The Goodmoney has outperformed the Dow Jones over some periods. Likewise another index of ethically acceptable stocks, the Dow Jones Sustainability Index, has outperformed its corresponding general index, the Standard & Poor's 500. Hussein and Omran (2005) presented evidence that stock indices based on stocks chosen to be consistent with Islamic principles outperformed general stock indices over a period from 1996 to 2003. This period included a bull market and a bear market. Islamic indices showed relative outperformance during the bull phase but underperformed during the bear market (with a net outperformance over the whole period).

Of the explanations for the relatively good performance of ethically acceptable stocks, one concerns management and another relates to consumer behaviour. The management-based argument suggests that attention to ethical dimensions and strong profitability are two aspects of high quality management. Managers who succeed in the ethical dimension are seen as being generally aware and capable, and their abilities also show through in the achievement of high profits. The consumer-based argument suggests that the companies shunned by SRI funds are also boycotted by socially concerned consumers. Such consumer boycotts undermine the profitability of companies that fail SRI criteria, and cause the relative underperformance of their stocks.

To the extent that investors in SRI funds believe that their investment behaviour affects the ethical behaviour of companies, their motivation for such investment appears to contradict standard investment theory. Standard theory suggests that people investing on the basis of ethical criteria would push up the prices of their chosen stocks, and thereby reduce the anticipated returns. Investors unconcerned by ethical considerations then sell such overpriced stocks, and in doing so negate the effects of the ethical investors. Winnett and Lewis (2000) argue that financial journalists promote the idea that SRI investing will have effects on the behaviour of corporations. This could be seen as a dimension of the 'illusion of control' identified by behavioural finance. Ethical investors and financial journalists could be seen as suffering from the illusion that investment behaviour affects corporate behaviour.

Webley *et al.* (2001) found that ethical investors demonstrated a strong commitment to ethical investment. They were prepared to persist with ethical investments even if the funds performed badly. In fact some investors were found to increase their ethical investments when those investments performed badly, whereas poor performance by other funds led to reduced investment. The ethical nature of a fund is seen as a desirable characteristic alongside high expected return and low risk; to many investors it may be the most important characteristic. For some investors ethical investment is based on ideology and identity, and they may regard their investments as making a statement about their identity. Ethical investments are seen as contributors to their self-image. Such investors might be committed to ethical investments even if ethical investing had no effect on the behaviour of businesses. Some ethical investors hold both ethical and ordinary funds. This could be explained in terms of the behavioural finance concept of mental accounting, whereby investors are seen as separating their wealth into a number of different portfolios. The separate portfolios are then managed according to differing criteria. Ethical criteria may be used for some of the portfolios, but not all.

EXHIBIT 16.2 EXAMPLE OF A SOCIALLY RESPONSIBLE INVESTMENT FUND

NORWICH UNION SUSTAINABLE FUTURE UK GROWTH FUND (AS AT 30 JUNE 2007)

Fund size: £109.85 million
Annual charge: 1.5%
Benchmark: FTSE All-Share Index

Aim

To provide long-term capital growth through investment in UK shares. Limited investment in UK bond markets may be made from time to time. All investments will be expected to conform to our social and environmental criteria.

Table 16.C

Top ten holdings (as percentages of the total fund)	
Vodafone Group	5.7
BG Group plc	4.3
BT Group	4.1
GlaxoSmithkline	3.8
Royal Bank of Scotland	2.5
Pearson	2.4
Legal & General	2.4
Lonmin	2.4
Informa Group	2.3
WSP Group	2.2

Source: Norwich Union.

EXHIBIT 16.3 EXAMPLE OF A SOCIALLY RESPONSIBLE INVESTMENT FUND BASED ON RELIGIOUS PRINCIPLES

SWIP ISLAMIC GLOBAL EQUITY FUND

The SWIP Islamic Global Equity Fund aims to provide investors with long-term capital growth by investing in global equities. The portfolio contains shares from around 75 companies whose activities are compliant with Islamic Shariah principles. This means we aim to avoid investing in companies whose activities include:

- gambling
- tobacco
- the production or sale of pork products
- the production of intoxicating liquor
- arms manufacturing
- non-Islamically structured banking, finance, investment or life insurance business, or any other interest-related activity.

The benchmark index of the fund is the FTSE Global Islamic index, which contains around 1,500 stocks. We will normally hold stocks contained within the index. We may also invest in a company not on the index if we think it will benefit long-term performance. To ensure such companies are appropriate under Islamic law, we have employed a specialist screening provider to research their suitability. The Shariah Advisory Board will then ultimately approve the stock.

Source: Scottish Widows Investment Partnership Limited.

EMERGING MARKET FUNDS

The term 'emerging markets' tends to be used for stock markets in countries with low national income per person, or for markets where the total capitalisation of the stock market is low relative to national income. Emerging markets, especially those in the first group, tend to be particularly risky. There are certain forms of risk to which they are particularly prone.

Political risk can be very high. A number of commercial services, such as Political Risk Services, assess political risk. Political risk exists in all markets, but is probably greatest in emerging markets. Diamonte *et al.* (1996) found that changes in political risk had a greater impact on emerging markets than on developed markets. Emerging market countries are sometimes prone to abrupt changes in government. Mei and Guo (2004) found an association between political uncertainty and financial crises. Their study revealed that most financial crises had happened during periods of elections and political transition. There was increased market volatility in election and transition periods. Corruption is often endemic in emerging economies. Sometimes major shareholders are also members of the government of the country. External shareholders could be at a disadvantage in such cases. New taxes may be imposed on investment income payable to non-residents, foreign investors may face restrictions on the nature of their investments, and investments may even be expropriated. Regulations relating to the repatriation of capital can be a concern for foreign investors. The prospect of such regulations being introduced or tightened can be a significant deterrent to investment in the affected country, and such regulations severely affect the liquidity of existing investments.

Liquidity is often a problem in emerging markets. Finding trading counterparties can be a problem. Large price concessions may be necessary to find buyers or sellers. Ownership is sometimes concentrated in a few hands. In such cases large investors may have market power that can be used to an investor's disadvantage.

There is also information risk in that accounting standards, and financial analysis, are often poor in emerging markets. This may be combined with poor market regulation, inadequate corporate governance, and little legal protection for investors. When such factors are combined with a culture of corruption, plus family and social networks that intertwine between markets and governments, the outside investor is at risk of being severely disadvantaged relative to the insiders.

La Porta *et al.* (2000) pointed out that countries with well-functioning legal systems and legal protection of investors have more developed capital (stock and bond) markets. The type of legal system affects the level of investor protection; the common law system, which tends to be used in British Commonwealth countries, gives relatively good protection since it allows the application of the principle of fairness. They also found a negative relationship between investor protection and concentration of ownership, particularly where the concentration entailed family control of companies. Concentration of ownership, within a family, of a company may be associated with poor protection for the other investors. Such concentration of ownership is a feature of many emerging markets.

One attraction of emerging market investments, as components of diversified portfolios, is their low correlations with investments in developed markets. This gives scope for reducing portfolio risk. However Barry *et al.* (1998) found evidence of an increase in correlations. They also found that emerging markets, considered individually, tend to display much more risk without providing more return than developed markets.

Bruner *et al.* (2003) provided an overview of issues relating to investments in emerging markets. Their definition of an emerging market entailed criteria that indicated that the market was in transition to becoming developed (so many of the underdeveloped markets were not considered to be emerging markets). They pointed out that many emerging markets were not completely open to foreign investors. They also suggested that the availability and reliability of information are significant features in the distinction between emerging and developed markets, as is the transparency of the market. The information concerned encompasses both market-wide and company-specific data. The quantity and quality of information, together with the speed and accuracy with which the market processes information, tend to be inferior in emerging markets compared with developed markets. They also confirmed that, whereas relatively low correlations with developed markets continues to make emerging markets attractive from the perspective of risk reduction by diversification, the correlations are tending to increase as the emerging markets become increasingly integrated with global markets. In consequence the diversification advantages are being reduced. They also confirmed that, individually, emerging markets tend to have relatively high volatility without necessarily offering higher prospective returns.

EXHIBITS 16.4   EXAMPLE OF AN EMERGING MARKETS FUND

HENDERSON GLOBAL INVESTORS EMERGING MARKETS FUND (31 AUGUST 2007)

Objective

To aim to provide capital growth by investing in emerging market companies. These companies will either be incorporated in emerging markets or, if incorporated elsewhere, derive a majority of their revenue from, or from activities related to, emerging markets. For the avoidance of doubt the Fund may also invest in securities of other investment vehicles whose objectives are compatible with that of the Fund.

Summary

The Fund's investment process is designed to provide exposure to the growth potential of the world's emerging markets by delivering performance comparable to that of the MSCI Emerging Markets Index. The Fund is managed primarily on a passive basis to replicate the performance of its benchmark by using risk control techniques such as optimisation and stratified sampling. Where the fund manager can identify good potential for excess returns on a risk-adjusted basis, she may seek to add value through Henderson's proprietary Multi-Strategy Enhanced Index process.

Fund size: £119.09 million

Charges*: (without exit fees)   initial 5%

annual 1.5%

(with exit fees)   initial 0%

annual 2%

Table 16.D

Ten largest holdings (as percentages of total fund)	
Ishares MSCI Taiwan	3.9
Samsung Electronics	3.1
China Mobile (HK)	2.6
Vale Rio Doce (CIA) PRF Series 'A'	2.4
Petroleo Brasileiro	2.2
Posco	1.9
Gazprom ADR	1.7
America Movil	1.6
China Construction	1.6
Teva Pharmaceutical Industries ADR	1.4

(Ishares are a form of exchange-traded fund, and ADR stands for American Depositary Receipt.)

Table 16.E

Country breakdown (as percentages of total fund)

South Korea	14.8
Taiwan	11.3
Brazil	9.9
China	8.8
Russia	8.5
South Africa	6.7
India	5.1
Mexico	4.9
Hong Kong	4.9
Other	25.1

* Other charging structures were available.

Source: Henderson Global Investors.

CONCLUSION

Chapter 13 on portfolio diversification described the principles of portfolio construction based on the Markowitz equations; an approach known as mean-variance optimisation. Investors were seen as choosing between combinations of risky assets and a risk-free asset, along the capital market line.

In practice, fund management deviates from mean-variance optimisation. Many investors like to make forecasts about the relative performance of shares (and other securities), and to bias their portfolios towards the prospective strong performers to the extent that they deviate from mean-variance optimisation. This is referred to as active fund management.

Other investors take passive approaches to fund management, which entail deviation from mean-variance optimisation. One form of passive management is the buy-and-hold strategy, which involves buying a portfolio of investments and holding that same portfolio irrespective of any subsequent changes in views about prospective returns, risks, and correlations. So even if the portfolio is initially mean-variance efficient, it would deviate from mean-variance efficiency over time. Another form of passive fund management is index tracking. This is the attempt to mirror the performance of a stock index. Stock indices are unlikely to be mean-variance efficient.

The Markowitz equations may be applied to the entire portfolio. This is referred to as one-stage portfolio construction. Multi-stage portfolio construction entails the construction of sub-portfolios, and the combination of the sub-portfolios into a total portfolio. Each sub-portfolio may be constructed using the Markowitz equations, or may use a different approach. The construction of a portfolio of sub-portfolios may be based on the Markowitz equations, or may entail a different approach. When a multi-stage portfolio strategy is used, it may utilise a variety of different techniques of portfolio construction.

Prospective returns, risks, and correlations may not be the only criteria used for the selection of investments for a portfolio. Many investors are concerned about the ethical dimension of their investments. Such investors may wish to avoid investments in companies involved in armaments, gambling, tobacco, and alcohol. They may also take account of companies' attitudes to environmental or human rights issues when deciding upon where to invest.

Psychological biases can affect investment choices. For example the familiarity bias causes people to invest in companies that they feel that they know and understand. Mental accounting leads people to create a set of separate portfolios, perhaps each being related to a particular goal. The use of a set of distinct portfolios may help people to organise their financial affairs. Although mental accounting leads investors away from mean-variance optimisation, it may nonetheless be useful. However it may be the case that people ignore correlations between assets to an excessive extent, and could benefit from the Markowitz insights concerning the desirability of low correlations for risk reduction.

One group of institutional investors, hedge funds, use a very wide variety of portfolio constructions. Some emphasise arbitrage, some use high levels of gearing, some take heavy bets on the direction of price movements, and many make substantial use of derivatives. Those using derivatives sometimes construct very complex structured products. The variety of styles of portfolio construction used by hedge funds is vast. Hedge funds are primarily aimed at other institutional investors and high net worth individuals. However retail investors can invest in them through funds of hedge funds.

Chapter 17

Evaluating the performance of fund managers

OBJECTIVE

The objective of this chapter is to provide knowledge of:

1. The measurement of money-weighted and time-weighted rates of return.
2. The evaluation of risk.
3. The assessment of portfolio performance using reward per unit of risk.
4. The assessment of portfolio performance using differential return.
5. The inadequacies of the alternative measures of portfolio performance.
6. The attribution of fund performance between asset allocation and stock selection.
7. The assessment of market-timing skills.
8. Evidence relating to the persistence of fund performance.

Frequently portfolio performance is evaluated by means of comparison with general stock indices, such as the FTSE 100 or FTSE All-Share Index. However this may not be appropriate if the evaluated fund follows a particular style. For example a smaller companies fund should be compared with a smaller companies index rather than a general stock index. Also portfolios have management and transaction costs, whereas indices do not. For this reason it may be more appropriate to evaluate the performance of a fund against that of other funds. For this purpose a comparison universe of other funds may be used.

The evaluation of portfolio performance is often made on the basis of returns alone. Since maximising the rate of return is seldom the sole objective of a fund manager, the evaluation of performance should address itself to more than one criterion of success. Furthermore merely measuring realised performance is insufficient; attention should also be paid to the sources of over- or underperformance.

Portfolio return is the most obvious criterion of success, but it is not obvious how return is to be measured. In addition to the question of the start and end dates to be used (a decision that can make a huge difference to apparent performance) there is the choice between money- and time-weighted measures. These alternatives will be detailed in the first section.

Risk is the second most frequently cited measure of performance. The second section will look at alternative measures of risk. This will be followed by a consideration of risk-return relationships and the various measures that aim to provide a single number that simultaneously evaluates return and risk. Related to this is the matter of the benchmarks against which values can be judged.

Although return and risk will be the criteria to receive most attention in what follows it is important to bear in mind that they are not the only criteria. Other criteria will relate to specific fund objectives. For example a high income fund might be judged to have failed if its rate of dividend yield is less than that on the average general fund, or an ethical fund could be viewed negatively if it is found to be holding shares in a tobacco company. Management, administration, and trading costs may be another criterion for evaluation. Although it may be argued that if return is measured net of costs then the figure for return takes costs into account, some people might contend that relative returns are partly due to luck and hence cannot be relied on to be repeated in the future whereas costs are less prone to variation.

MONEY- AND TIME-WEIGHTED MEASURES OF RETURN

The distinction between money- and time-weighted measures of return arises when there are cash inflows to, or outflows from, the portfolio during the period of assessment. The money-weighted measure uses the rate of discount that equates the present values of the inflows and outflows. Suppose that a share is bought for £1 and one year later another is purchased at the new price of £1.06. The price at the end of the second year is also £1.06. A dividend of £0.04 per share is received at the end of each year. The money-weighted rate of return is given by r in the following expression:

$$£1 + £1.06/(1+r) = £0.04/(1+r) + £0.08/(1+r)^2 + £2.12/(1+r)^2$$

This gives a rate of return of about 5.8% p.a.

The time-weighted approach calculates a rate for each period separately and finds the average. Thus:

Period 1 $(£0.04 + £0.06)/£1 = 0.1$ i.e. 10%

Period 2 $£0.08/£2.12 = 0.0377$ i.e. 3.77%

This implies a compound average rate of:

$$\sqrt{(1.1)(1.0377)} - 1 = 0.0684 = 6.84\% \text{ p.a.}$$

The time periods used will depend on the frequency of cash flows. The time-weighted measure of return should be based on periods during which no cash flows take place.

Although it is not the case that one measure is always more appropriate than the other, the time-weighted approach seems to be more favoured than the money-weighted method when evaluating the performance of fund managers. This preference arises because portfolio managers typically do not control the cash inflows and outflows to which their funds are subjected. Additions to, and withdrawals from, a fund will affect the money-weighted rate of return. Two fund managers may choose identical portfolios but differ in their money-weighted rates of return because of different patterns of additions and withdrawals on the part of clients. Money-weighted rates of return should not be compared with rates on a benchmark portfolio since the two portfolios are unlikely to have the same pattern of cash inflows and outflows, and the pattern of such cash flows will affect the money-weighted rate of return.

A third approach is to take the arithmetic mean of a succession of periodic returns. For most purposes this is unsatisfactory. To illustrate its unsatisfactory nature, consider an outcome in which an investment doubles in value during one period and halves the next period. Obviously the investment has the same value after the two periods as it had at the beginning. The two-period return is zero. Using an arithmetic average, the two-period return is calculated as:

$$(100\% - 50\%)/ 2 = 25\%$$

which is clearly incorrect. In this case the time-weighted approach provides the correct answer, since it uses a geometric rather than an arithmetic average.

$$2 \times 0.5 = 1$$
$$\sqrt{1} - 1 = 0$$

There is one possible use of the arithmetic average. It could be seen as indicating the typical periodic return. Consider the following series of returns:

10% 15% 20% 10% 15% 20%

Arguably the typical rate of return is 15%. This figure is provided by the arithmetic average, but not by the geometric average. If the investor asks the question 'What rate of return can I expect this period?' the answer is provided by the arithmetic average. The arithmetic average has its worth when the focus is on the return of a single period. It is not satisfactory when the concern is with the average rate of return over a number of periods.

THE EVALUATION OF RISK

Much of the academic work on portfolio performance evaluation has been concerned with whether the returns are more than, or below, what would be expected on the basis of the level of risk incurred. Substantial attention will be paid to such risk-adjusted measures of portfolio return in what follows. Prior to that, two general points relating to risk should be mentioned.

If the fund objectives include maintenance of a particular risk profile, then deviation from the corresponding risk level would be regarded negatively. A fund with the objective of below average risk should not exhibit risk levels above those of otherwise similar funds.

There is a widespread acceptance that some risk cannot be diversified away, whereas other forms of risk can. It is reasonable to expect that a fund manager will diversify the portfolio to the extent required to remove unnecessary risk. Although some funds, for example high technology funds, may have objectives that render full diversification impossible, portfolio managers should still be expected to avoid risk that can be removed by means of the level of diversification permitted by the fund policy. While some risk will always remain, fund managers should be judged negatively if they fail to employ diversification to the full extent consistent with fund objectives.

REWARD PER UNIT OF RISK

A crude approach to risk adjustment is to rank the performance of a fund relative to a class of funds. For example if a fund were classified as an international growth fund, its performance would be ranked against other international growth funds. However this is an unsatisfactory form of risk adjustment since international growth funds would have varying levels of risk and there may be sub-groups of funds, which may be more relevant as benchmarks (for example international technology, or international smaller companies).

More sophisticated risk-adjusted measures of return fall into two types. One type is concerned with the returns relative to the risk undertaken, and involves a division of returns by the level of risk incurred in order to obtain those returns. This is often referred to as 'reward per unit of risk'. This section will elaborate that approach. The following section will be concerned with an alternative approach, which ascertains the difference between the returns on the managed portfolio and those on a benchmark portfolio, often referred to as the 'differential return' measure.

The Sharpe and Treynor Measures

Two portfolio performance measures that use reward per unit of risk are the 'Sharpe' and 'Treynor' measures. Both use excess return in the sense of the excess of the portfolio return over the return on a risk-free investment such as a Treasury bill or a short-term bank deposit. This excess return is then divided by a measure of risk so as to ascertain the amount of excess return for each unit of risk undertaken. The Sharpe measure uses the standard deviation of returns of the portfolio to measure risk whereas the Treynor measure uses the portfolio beta as the numerical indicator of risk.

Algebraically these can be described as:

Sharpe measure $\quad (R_p - R_f)/\sigma_p$

Treynor measure $\quad (R_p - R_f)/\beta_p$

R_p is the rate of return on the portfolio, R_f is the rate of return on a risk-free investment, σ_p is the standard deviation of returns on the portfolio, and β_p is the portfolio beta.

The Treynor measure tends to be favoured when the portfolio being assessed is one of a number of portfolios being held such that any non-systematic (firm-specific) risk can be expected to be removed by diversification. In such a case only the non-diversifiable (systematic) risk is relevant. Beta is a measure of non-diversifiable risk.

The Sharpe measure is appropriate when the portfolio stands alone rather than being part of a portfolio of portfolios. In that case all risk should be included. So the portfolio standard deviation, which encompasses both diversifiable and non-diversifiable risk, should be used.

M Squared

A variation of the Sharpe measure is known as the M^2 (or Modigliani squared) measure (Modigliani and Modigliani 1997; Graham and Harvey 1997). The M^2 measure uses the standard deviations of the portfolios being compared but instead of obtaining figures for reward per unit of risk, it obtains measures of return for the purposes of the comparison. The M^2 measure brings the standard deviations of the portfolios into equality with the standard deviation of a stock index, such as the FTSE All-Share Index, by (hypothetically) investing in risk-free assets or borrowing. For example if a portfolio has a standard deviation which is twice that of the stock index, the portfolio would be adjusted so that it is 50% invested in the original portfolio and 50% invested in risk-free assets (such as Treasury bills or bank deposits). Conversely a portfolio that has a standard deviation which is two-thirds that of the stock index would be geared by borrowing a sum equivalent to half the value of the original portfolio. The borrowed money would be invested in a portfolio with the same composition as the original portfolio with the effect that the new adjusted portfolio would have a standard deviation equal to that of the stock index.

Since all the adjusted portfolios have a standard deviation equal to that of the stock index there is no need for any further risk adjustment. The portfolios can be evaluated simply by comparing the returns of the adjusted portfolios. The M^2 measure of the performance of a portfolio is the return on the adjusted portfolio minus the return on the stock index.

Information Ratios

Another variation on the Sharpe measure is the information ratio. The information ratio typically uses the return on a stock index portfolio in the place of the return on a risk-free investment (Chapman 2006). Since performance measures are seen as indicators of investment management skill, comparison of returns with a passive strategy seems appropriate. This is approximated by comparing portfolio returns with the returns from a stock index (which may have been the index used in an index tracking strategy).

The divisor would also be based on the returns from a stock index portfolio. Instead of using the standard deviation of returns of the evaluated portfolio (or the standard deviation of the excess returns over a risk-free rate) information ratios often use the standard deviation of returns relative to those on the portfolio of shares that reflects a stock index (the standard deviation of the excess returns over the returns from a stock index portfolio). On this measure it is the investment manager who keeps the variations in portfolio returns close to those of the stock index portfolio who is judged to be low risk. Information ratios use non-systematic risk, rather than total risk, when measuring excess return per unit of risk. This non-systematic risk tends to arise from active investment management decisions, and hence could be referred to as management risk or active risk. If an investment manager comes close to tracking the stock index, the standard deviation would be very low. If the manager simultaneously succeeds in outperforming the index, the information ratio would be high.

An information ratio might be expressed as:

$$(N - S) / \sigma_{(N-S)}$$

where N is the return on the portfolio being evaluated, S is the return on a stock index portfolio, and $\sigma_{(N-S)}$ is the standard deviation of the difference between N and S. The information ratio could be seen as the return from taking non-systematic risk divided by the amount of non-systematic risk taken, or as the return from active portfolio management divided by the management (active) risk incurred.

A Generalised Sharpe Ratio

Dowd (2000) pointed out that, when considering an addition to an existing portfolio, the evaluation of the additional investment should take account of its correlation with the existing portfolio. The additional investment could be either an individual security or a portfolio. For example a relatively poor Sharpe ratio may be acceptable if it is associated with negative correlation between the additional investment and the existing portfolio (so that the additional investment reduces portfolio risk). In other words the benchmark against which returns are measured should not be the risk-free interest rate, or the returns on a stock index, but a benchmark reflecting the correlation with the existing portfolio. Dowd suggested that the required (i.e. benchmark) return on the additional investment should be the expected return on the existing portfolio adjusted by a risk premium. The risk premium depends on the ratio between the standard deviation of the existing portfolio and the standard deviation of the prospective new portfolio, which incorporates the additional investment.

To be acceptable, an additional investment that increases portfolio risk must enhance the portfolio rate of return. The Sharpe ratio of the prospective new portfolio (the portfolio following the incorporation of the additional investment) should be at least equal to the Sharpe ratio of the existing portfolio. Evaluation of whether an additional investment meets this criterion requires use of the generalised Sharpe measure. Whereas the conventional Sharpe measure uses the risk-free interest rate as the benchmark, and the information ratio uses a stock index as the benchmark, the generalised Sharpe ratio uses the return on the existing portfolio adjusted for a premium reflecting correlation.

The generalised Sharpe measure might be expressed as:

$$(N - B) \, / \, \sigma_{(N-B)}$$

where N is the expected return on the additional investment, B is the benchmark return (expected return on the existing portfolio adjusted by a premium), and $\sigma_{(N-B)}$ is the standard deviation of the difference between N and B.

DIFFERENTIAL RETURN

The differential-return method of evaluating fund performance involves comparing the return on the fund with the return on a benchmark portfolio. The benchmark could be a stock index portfolio, such as the FTSE 100, or could be an average of funds with similar objectives to the fund being assessed. Using a stock index fails to take account of differences in risk between the stock index portfolio and the fund being evaluated. Comparison with the average performance of similar funds comes closer to comparing like with like, in particular it involves a benchmark with broadly

373

equivalent risk. However the risk adjustment is crude, and it could be the case that funds on average underperform some absolute benchmark (one advantage of using a stock index portfolio is that it can be interpreted as an absolute benchmark).

An alternative benchmark could be the returns on a hypothetical portfolio whose risk matches that of the fund being evaluated. This provides a relatively precise risk adjustment together with provision of an absolute benchmark (but begs the question as to whether it represents an attainable portfolio; only portfolio characteristics that can be attained with an actual portfolio can reasonably be used to assess the performance of real portfolios).

Jensen's Alpha

One technique that utilises hypothetical fund characteristics is the 'Jensen' measure. This derives a benchmark rate of return using the securities market line from the capital asset pricing model. The securities market line provides a theoretical rate of return comprising two components. The first component is a risk-free rate of return (such as the return on Treasury bills or deposits in major banks), the second component is a reward for accepting risk.

The component of expected return that is seen as the reward for accepting risk is the product of the portfolio beta (the beta of the portfolio being evaluated) and the market excess return. The market excess return is the difference between the return on a balanced portfolio, consisting of a mix of all available investments (often approximated by a stock index portfolio), and the return on risk-free assets. Algebraically:

$$R_b = R_f + \beta_p (R_m - R_f) \tag{1}$$

where R_b is the expected or theoretical rate of return on the assessed portfolio, R_m is the return on the market portfolio, R_f is the risk-free rate of return, and β_p is the beta of the portfolio being assessed. By using the beta of the portfolio under assessment, the comparison of the observed and expected returns provides a risk-adjusted evaluation. The systematic risk of the hypothetical portfolio is rendered equal to that of the evaluated portfolio so that returns can be compared without any further need for risk adjustment.

The differential return is expressed as $R_p - R_b$. If this is positive the realised return on the fund being evaluated exceeds the benchmark rate of return and the fund is viewed as over-performing. Conversely a negative value indicates underperformance. $R_p - R_b$ is often referred to as Jensen's alpha. It is estimated simultaneously with beta by regressing portfolio excess returns (portfolio returns minus the risk-free rate of interest) against market excess returns. Both positive and negative alphas often fail to be (statistically) significantly different from zero.

The use of beta as the measure of portfolio risk is appropriate when diversifiable risk can be ignored. Such would be the case if the portfolio being evaluated is extremely well diversified or is part of a larger portfolio such that the larger portfolio contains no diversifiable (firm-specific) risk. If neither of these conditions holds then the standard deviation of returns becomes the relevant measure of risk.

Jensen's alpha uses the security market line of the single-factor capital asset pricing model to obtain an index of portfolio performance. Corresponding performance indices can be generated using multi-factor models. The single-factor model treats market risk (measured by beta) as the only risk factor that determines the benchmark return (required rate of return) of a portfolio. Multi-factor forms of the capital asset pricing model and the arbitrage pricing model allow for other risk factors (such as company size and macroeconomic variables) to have an influence on the benchmark rate of return. Multi-factor models entail multiple betas and, like the single-factor model, ignore non-systematic risk which is assumed to be removed by diversification.

Appraisal Ratios

The appraisal ratio extends the Jensen alpha to provide a measure of abnormal return per unit of non-systematic risk. Jensen's alpha represents the average of the deviations from the security market line. Non-systematic risk could be measured as the standard deviation of the observed deviations from the security market line. The appraisal ratio is obtained by dividing Jensen's alpha by this standard deviation. If the evaluated portfolio is well diversified, or is part of a broader portfolio that removes non-systematic risk by diversification, the appraisal ratio has no significance. Appraisal ratios are similar to information ratios, with the difference that a benchmark return based on the security market line is used instead of the return on a stock index portfolio.

Use of the Capital Market Line

Parallel to the use of beta and the securities market line by the Jensen measure it is possible to produce a benchmark rate of return using the portfolio standard deviation within the capital market line of the capital asset pricing model. The algebraic formulation would be:

$$R_b = R_f + (R_m - R_f)S_p/S_m \tag{2}$$

which differs from the Jensen measure in using the ratio of the standard deviation of the evaluated portfolio (measuring the total risk, diversifiable as well as non-diversifiable) to the standard deviation of the market portfolio. This ratio is used in the place of beta, which measures non-diversifiable risk only.

EXERCISE 17.1

The interest rate on a risk-free bank deposit is 5% p.a. The return on the FTSE All-Share Index portfolio has been 10% p.a. with an annual standard deviation of 8%. Portfolio A has had a beta of 0.5, an annual standard deviation of 5%, and has provided a return of 8% p.a. Portfolio B has had a beta of 1.5, an annual standard deviation of returns of 15%, and has provided a return of 12% p.a.

Evaluate the performances of portfolios A and B relative to each other and relative to the FTSE All-Share Index.

Answer

<u>Sharpe measure</u>

Portfolio A $(8-5)/5 = 0.6$
Portfolio B $(12-5)/15 = 0.47$
Market (FT All-Share Index) portfolio $(10-5)/8 = 0.625$

Portfolio A is superior to portfolio B but inferior to the All-Share Index (market) portfolio. Portfolio B is inferior to portfolio A and to the All-Share Index (market) portfolio.

<u>Treynor measure</u>

Portfolio A $(8-5)/0.5 = 6$
Portfolio B $(12-5)/1.5 = 4.67$
Market portfolio $(10-5)/1 = 5$

(The beta of a market index is normally treated as being equal to 1.)
Portfolio A is superior to portfolio B and to the All-Share Index (market) portfolio. Portfolio B is inferior to portfolio A and to the All-Share Index (market) portfolio.

<u>Capital market line measure</u>

Portfolio A

$R_b = 5 + (10-5)5/8 = 8.125\%$ p.a.
$8\% - 8.125\% = -0.125\%$ p.a.

Portfolio B

$R_b = 5 + (10-5)15/8 = 14.375\%$ p.a.
$12\% - 14.375\% = -2.375\%$ p.a.

(Note that the index has an R_b equal to the actual return: $R_b = 5 + (10-5)8/8 = 10$. So $R - R_b = 0$.)
A is superior to B but inferior to the All-Share Index (market) portfolio.
B is inferior to A and inferior to the All-Share Index (market) portfolio.

<u>Jensen measure</u>

Portfolio A

$R_b = 5 + 0.5(10-5) = 7.5\%$ p.a.
$8\% - 7.5\% = 0.5\%$ p.a.

Portfolio B

$R_b = 5 + 1.5(10-5) = 12.5\%$ p.a.
$12\% - 12.5\% = -0.5\%$ p.a.

(The stock index will have an R_b equal to the actual return. $R_b = 5 + 1(10-5) = 10$. So $10 - R_b = 0$.)
A is superior to B and to the All-Share Index (market) portfolio.
B is inferior to A and to the All-Share Index (market) portfolio.

PROBLEMS WITH PORTFOLIO PERFORMANCE EVALUATION

In relation to the performance measures that use beta a problem arises because of the unreliability of estimates of beta. Betas are calculated from historical price data. The values of beta derived from the statistical analysis will vary according to the time intervals used (e.g. upon whether weekly, monthly, or quarterly data is employed). They will also vary with differences in the time spans from which the data is taken (e.g. upon whether observed values are taken from the last year, last five years, or last ten years). Betas can also vary when different stock indices are used as proxies for the market portfolio (which in principle contains all assets). The rankings of portfolios, relative to one another, will thus be dependent upon the database used for the estimation of beta.

It should also be remembered that beta values are estimates. Statistical analysis of historical data produces an estimate of the true beta. The estimate is unlikely to equal precisely the true beta. The estimate is subject to a margin of error (standard error). Portfolio performance evaluation that uses beta is vulnerable to the possibility that the estimate of beta used may be substantially different from the true value that should be used. The difficulties are compounded by the likelihood that the true value of the portfolio beta varied over the time period being considered. This is partly because of changes in individual stock betas and partly due to changes in the composition of the portfolio. Fama and French (2004) go so far as to suggest that, because of the failures of the capital asset pricing model when tested empirically, beta should not be used in portfolio performance evaluation.

Measures of performance using standard deviations of return face problems of interpretation when a fund manager deliberately changes the beta of the portfolio during the period of assessment. Such variations in beta are likely to reflect market views taken by the portfolio manager; a bullish view leads to an increased beta, vice versa for a bearish view. Changes in beta are associated with changes in expected portfolio returns. In effect the fund manager is engineering variations in portfolio returns. These controlled fluctuations in returns should not be regarded as resulting from uncertainty, and should not be deemed to be due to portfolio risk. Unfortunately the standard deviation of returns incorporates such variations and hence treats them as reflecting risk.

In addition, over- or underperformance may be the result of luck rather than the relative skills of the fund managers. Over- or underperformance needs to be shown to persist for a number of years before conclusions can be drawn about fund managers' investment skills.

When ranking funds on a risk-adjusted basis some will appear to be outstanding performers. The question arises as to whether such funds should be seen as having superior investment management. If they do exhibit high-quality fund management, they would be candidates for purchase. However some funds would show exceptional performance simply as a matter of chance. Marcus (1990) looked at the performance of the Magellan fund in the United States. That fund had outperformed the S&P 500 index in 11 out of the 13 years up to 1989, and appeared to be a star performer. Using computer simulations Marcus found that, in a sample of 500 funds, the expectation was that there is a 99.8% chance that the best performing fund would beat a stock index in 11 years or more.

Weidig *et al.* (2005) pointed out that when evaluating private equity funds (which include venture capital trusts) data problems are significant. The absence of continuous fund pricing based on actual transactions, and the frequent absence of dividend distributions, render the measurement of performance difficult. The problems of evaluating funds also apply to the evaluation of funds of funds, which are portfolios of private equity funds. Although these problems may prevent the evaluation of individual funds of funds, it may be possible to evaluate funds of funds as an asset class. Weidig *et al.* constructed hypothetical funds of funds and found a number of features. Using a technique known as Monte Carlo simulation they randomly constructed 50,000 historically possible funds of funds, and recorded measures of return and risk. They found that the diversification provided by funds of funds reduces risk, both in terms of standard deviation and in terms of skewness. Sharpe ratios were found to be three to five times higher for funds-of-funds than for individual funds.

Comparison Portfolios

When seeking a basis for comparison of a fund manager's performance, there are two possibilities. There is comparison against an average of other fund managers, and comparison against an index. The reward-per-unit-of-risk approaches above tend to compare a fund's performance against that of other investment managers, whereas the differential-return measures use benchmarks based on market indices.

When making a comparison against an average of managers it is important that it should be an average of the managers who started the comparison period rather than an average of the managers who finished it. If a manager loses the management of a fund during the period of comparison, that fund should be considered when calculating average performance. Typically if a manager loses the management of a fund, it is because of poor performance. A failure to consider such funds when calculating averages imparts an upward bias to the average. This bias is known as 'survivorship bias' and it should be avoided.

Value-at-Risk and the Omega Measure

Instead of measuring portfolio performance in terms of reward per unit of risk or differential return, value-at-risk provides an evaluation in terms of the size of prospective losses. Behavioural finance (in particular prospect theory) suggests that investors exhibit loss-aversion. Investors are seen as being particularly concerned about the possibility of loss. Measures based on reward per unit of risk take account of risk-aversion but not loss-aversion. Risk-aversion treats upside deviations and downside deviations as equally bad, whereas prospect theory indicates that downside deviations (in particular losses) are the more important dimension of risk to investors. Value-at-risk provides a measure that indicates the prospective size of losses, and hence may be of relevance to loss-averse investors.

Value-at-risk is the maximum loss that a portfolio is likely to suffer, during a specified period and with a specified probability. If there is a 5% probability that the value of a portfolio will fall by more than £1 million during a month, the value-at-risk for one month and 95% confidence is £1 million. The figure for the value-at-risk might be interpreted as the loss, which has a chance of 5% of being exceeded (when the confidence level is 95%) or a chance of 1% of being exceeded (if the confidence level is 99%).

Figure 17.1 illustrates value-at-risk with confidence levels of 95% (5% chance that there will be a loss greater than the value-at-risk) and 99% (1% chance that there will be a loss greater than the value-at-risk). In these cases, as shown in Chapter 13, value-at-risk is expressed as a number

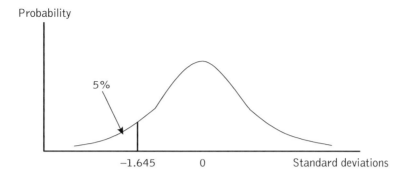

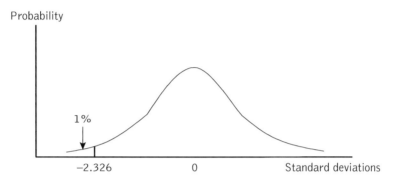

Figure 17.1 *Normal distributions with mean of zero*

of standard deviations from the mean. This value is determined by the chosen confidence level; on the basis that the distribution of returns follows the standard normal distribution. A confidence level of 95% will always have a value-at-risk of -1.645 standard deviations, and a confidence level of 99% will always have a value-at-risk of -2.326 standard deviations. Turning these numbers into money values requires multiplication by the money value of the standard deviation. If a portfolio is estimated to have a monthly standard deviation of returns of £100,000, the value-at-risk at a confidence level of 95% is £164,500 and the value-at-risk at a confidence level of 99% is £232,600.

Shadwick and Keating (2002) and Murphy (2002) have proposed a measure of portfolio performance, which they term omega. This measure entails the specification of a threshold portfolio value, or a threshold rate of return. Omega is the ratio of the area, under the distribution curve, on the right of the threshold to the area on the left of the threshold. In Figure 17.1, omega for a threshold of -1.645 standard deviations would be 95/5 and omega for a threshold of -2.326 standard deviations would be 99/1. The threshold may be chosen to correspond to a return of zero, so as to provide a performance measure of use to loss-averse investors.

An advantage of omega is that, unlike measures such as the Sharpe ratio, it does not assume that the distribution of returns is normally distributed. The normal distribution illustrated in Figure 17.1 is not the typical distribution of returns from investments. More typically distributions of returns are characterised by kurtosis, which means that the probability of extreme values is greater

379

than indicated by normal distributions (this is often referred to as 'fat tails' since the ends of the distribution are higher than those of the normal distribution). Distributions are also commonly characterised by skewness, which means that the peak (known as the mode) of the distribution is not in the middle. For example the mode may be tilted to the left indicating a concentration of possible returns towards the low end. A combination of returns skewed towards the bottom, and a high probability of extreme returns, would be unwelcome to loss-averse investors since it indicates a significant chance of extreme losses. The standard deviation, as used in performance measures such as the Sharpe ratio, does not reflect kurtosis and skewness whereas those two characteristics of distributions are important dimensions of risk. Loss-averse investors are likely to be concerned about kurtosis and skewness. Omega does not assume a normal distribution and it takes account of the effects of kurtosis and skewness.

ATTRIBUTION

The performance of a fund manager depends partly on the allocation of the portfolio between asset classes (for example between equities, bonds, and deposits) and partly upon selection within classes (which stocks to buy). If a portfolio contains foreign currency investments there is a currency dimension to the returns: profits or losses arising from exchange rate movements. It is possible to measure the contribution of each of these different decisions (asset allocation, stock selection, and currency choice) to the overall performance of the portfolio.

To separate the effects of asset allocation from those of stock selection, it is necessary to compute an average return for all investments (weighted by the total market value of each asset class) for the investment period being considered e.g. the past year. Then an average rate of return of each asset class is calculated. The results may (hypothetically) be those illustrated by Table 17.1. It can be seen that equities over-perform by 1.8% p.a., bonds underperform by 2.2% p.a., and deposits underperform by 4.2% p.a. relative to the average rate of return for the aggregate of all investments.

The next step is to compare the portfolio that is being evaluated with the average portfolio. The average portfolio reflects the total values of the different asset classes available to be held. Table 17.2 compares hypothetical figures for a portfolio being evaluated and an average portfolio.

It can be seen that the portfolio being evaluated is 15% overweight in equities, 10% underweight in bonds, and 5% underweight in deposits. The portfolio return (relative to the average portfolio) arising from the asset allocation decision is based on the extent to which it is overweight in the

Table 17.1

Asset class	Rate of return (% p.a.)
Equities	10
Bonds	6
Deposits	4
All investments	8.2

Table 17.2

Asset class	Weightings of average portfolio (%)	Weightings of evaluated portfolio (%)
Equities	60	75
Bonds	30	20
Deposits	10	5

over-performing asset class and underweight in the underperforming asset classes. The asset allocation contribution to portfolio performance is thus calculated as shown in Table 17.3.

It can be seen that the total contribution of the asset allocation decision to fund performance is:

$$0.27\% + 0.22\% + 0.21\% = 0.7\% \text{ p.a.}$$

The portfolio being evaluated has a rate of return of 9% p.a., whereas the average portfolio has a rate of return of 8.2% p.a. Thus there is an additional return of 0.8% p.a. of which 0.7% is due to asset allocation. It follows that the return arising from stock and bond selection is 0.1% p.a. The contribution of stock and bond selection can be further broken down into sector allocation and selection within sectors using a procedure similar to that illustrated by Table 17.3.

In order to determine the currency contribution to portfolio return when foreign investments are included, one approach is to compare a fully hedged version of the fund with a version that is completely unhedged against currency movements. The profit or loss on the forward or futures position that is needed to hedge the portfolio equals the loss or profit on the currency exposure. The currency contribution to portfolio return is the negative of the profit or loss on the forward or futures position that would be needed to hedge the fund against currency movements.

Another approach, which aims to ascertain the contribution of currency selection, is to use the analysis of Tables 17.1, 17.2, and 17.3 but with different currencies rather than different asset classes. The weightings of the average portfolio of currencies might be based on the relative stock market capitalisations of the respective countries.

The contribution of country selection to portfolio performance could be ascertained in a similar way; again possibly using a weighting system based on relative stock market capitalisations. In this

Table 17.3

Asset class	Over-weighting (1)	Over-performance (2) (%)	Contribution to relative performance: (1) x (2) (%)
Equities	0.15	1.8	0.27
Bonds	−0.10	−2.2	0.22
Deposits	−0.05	−4.2	0.21

case the returns on broad stock indices could be used in order to separate the effects of country choice from the effects of stock selection.

Style Analysis

Sharpe (1992) developed a technique for ascertaining the asset allocation of a portfolio together with the extent to which asset allocation explains portfolio returns. The importance of these ideas is underlined by studies that suggest that more than 90% of portfolio returns can be explained by asset allocation (e.g. Brinson *et al.* 1991).

Sharpe considered twelve asset classes (styles). The asset classes were:

- bills
- intermediate bonds
- long-term bonds
- corporate bonds
- mortgages
- value stocks
- growth stocks
- medium-cap stocks
- small stocks
- foreign stocks
- European stocks
- Japanese stocks.

Sharpe regressed fund returns on indices representing the asset classes. The regression coefficient on each index measures the allocation to that asset class. The R-square of the regression indicates the proportion of returns explained by the asset allocation. The proportion of return variability not explained by asset allocation is attributed to security selection within asset classes. The contribution of security selection to returns was found to average nearly zero (-0.074% per month) and to be normally distributed around the mean (based on 636 mutual funds).

It is common for institutional portfolios, particularly unit trusts and OEICs, to be evaluated by means of comparison with funds that follow a similar style. Not only does style provide the relevant peer group of funds against which the performance of a portfolio is to be compared but it also provides a criterion for evaluation. Investment managers may be evaluated in terms of how well they remain within the bounds of a style, as well as being evaluated in terms of criteria such as risk-adjusted return. So, for example, a UK fund that has the stated objective of following a high income style would be evaluated negatively if its dividend yield were below that of the FTSE All-Share Index.

An alternative to comparing a fund with a peer group of other funds is to use a style benchmark. A style benchmark is a portfolio of style indices. Style indices are stock indices designed to reflect the performances of securities belonging to particular styles. Style benchmarks are particularly useful for evaluating portfolios that exhibit a mixture of styles rather than a single style. For example a fund might be judged to have a style that is 50% large capitalisation value stocks and 50% small-capitalisation growth stocks. The benchmark against which its performance is judged would comprise an index of large capitalisation value stocks and an index of small capitalisation growth stocks, in equal proportions. The comparison against the style benchmark could be on either a raw basis or a risk-adjusted basis.

When evaluating a portfolio that has a mixture of styles, it is necessary to ascertain the combination of styles possessed by the portfolio. Two approaches to the discovery of the combination of styles are 'holdings-based style analysis' and 'returns-based style analysis'. Holdings-based style analysis determines investment style by examining the individual securities (investments) that comprise the portfolio. Each security is classified as belonging to a particular style and the combination of securities in the portfolio provides a corresponding combination of styles. For example if 40% of the portfolio value is accounted for by shares classified as large capitalisation growth stocks, the portfolio is seen as being 40% large capitalisation growth. There would be percentages relating to other styles. For example the remaining 60% might be composed of 20% small capitalisation growth and 40% high-grade corporate bonds.

One problem with holdings-based style analysis is that fund managers do not continuously provide updated information about the composition of their portfolios. Information about portfolio composition is provided at discrete intervals, such as every six months. There is a risk that the portfolio being analysed and evaluated is out of date. Other problems relate to the difficulty of determining the styles of individual securities, and the large number of securities whose styles may need to be determined. Returns-based style analysis determines the style (or combination of styles) of a portfolio by analysing the relationship between its returns and the returns of a portfolio of style indices. Returns-based style analysis attempts to identify the style(s) of a portfolio by finding the combination of style indices that would have most closely replicated the observed performance of the portfolio over a recent period.

Returns-based style analysis estimates the parameters (β) of an equation that takes the following form:

$$R_p = \beta_0 + \beta_1 I_1 + \beta_2 I_2 + \beta_3 I_3 \tag{3}$$

where R_p is the return on the portfolio being analysed. I_1, I_2, I_3 are the returns on style indices 1, 2, and 3 (there could be any number of style indices). $\beta_1, \beta_2, \beta_3$ represent the exposures of the portfolio to the style indices (the βs sum to 1). β_0 is the component of portfolio return that is not explained in terms of exposure to style indices, and which may be ascribed to stock selection.

Equation 3 states that the portfolio behaves as if it comprises three style indices (index portfolios) in the proportions indicated by the β values. There is a risk that the regression result is spurious. The portfolio may appear to behave as if it comprises style indices 1, 2, and 3 whilst in reality it might be comprised of styles 4 and 5.

ASSESSING MARKET-TIMING SKILLS

Market timing entails forecasting market movements with a view to adjusting a portfolio to take advantage of the expected movements. If a fund manager were capable of timing the market, that manager would raise the portfolio beta before the market rises and lower it before a fall. The characteristic line for a successful market timer would be concave to the vertical axis as illustrated

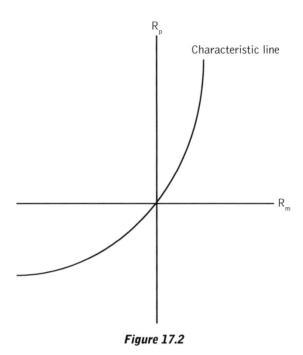

Figure 17.2

in Figure 17.2. The concave characteristic line shows that excess returns on the portfolio being managed rise more than proportionately to those on the market portfolio; and fall less than proportionately (excess returns in the sense of excess over the risk-free rate). In Figure 17.2, R_p represents the excess return on the portfolio being managed and R_m represents the excess return on the market portfolio.

Treynor and Mazuy (1966) tested US mutual funds (unit trusts) to find whether the fund managers exhibited market-timing ability. The research involved testing whether an equation of the form shown by equation (4) had a positive β_2.

$$R_p = \alpha + \beta_1 R_m + \beta_2 R_m^2 \tag{4}$$

A positive β_2 would show that the portfolio excess return rises more than in proportion to (and falls less than proportionately to) the excess return of the market portfolio. They found that β_2 was not significantly different from zero and therefore concluded that their sample of mutual fund managers did not exhibit market-timing ability.

Similar research by Henriksson (1984) also cast doubt on the effectiveness of market timing. Studies of US mutual funds by Daniel *et al.* (1997) and by Wermers (2000) found no timing ability. Kon (1983), Chang and Lewellen (1984), and Coggin *et al.* (1993) found that fund managers had negative market-timing skills.

Tactical asset allocation applies market timing to a set of asset classes, rather than just equities (versus bank deposits). Typically both stock (equity) and bond markets would be timed. Weigel (1991) produced a model in which an investment manager with perfect market timing would obtain a return, during a period, equal to:

$$R = r_f + \max[(R_e - r_f), (R_b - r_f), 0] \tag{5}$$

where R is the portfolio return, r_f is the rate of return on risk-free investments (such as bank deposits), R_e is the rate of return on equities, and R_b is the rate of return on bonds. The equation states that the portfolio return would be the highest of the returns on equities (shares), bonds, and risk-free investments.

Weigel estimated the parameters of the equation:

$$R = \alpha + \beta_e(R_e - r_f) + \beta_b(R_b - r_f) + \gamma\{\max[(R_e - r_f), (R_b - r_f), 0]\} \qquad (6)$$

where γ indicates the extent to which market-timing skill is present. Weigel found that the group of investment managers investigated showed a statistically significant value of γ, indicating that there was some market-timing ability (albeit far from perfect market timing). However α was negative, which suggests that the positive market timing was offset by negative performance in other aspects of investment management.

Volkman (1999) investigated the ability of US mutual fund managers to select underpriced securities, and to time the market, during the 1980s. It was found that, on average, there was no apparent ability to identify underpriced shares (or other securities). Attempts to time the market were found to have, on average, negative effects on performance. In a number of cases there appeared to be a trade-off whereby the apparent ability to identify underpriced shares (and other securities) was associated with a tendency to lose money through attempts to time the market.

Blake and Timmermann (2005) examined the performance of UK-based international-equity pension funds over the period 1991–1997 by decomposing performance into stock selection and market-timing elements. They found that both elements usually made negative contributions to performance. The losses from poor stock selection were seen as possibly resulting from information asymmetries between UK and overseas investment managers whereby investors have an information advantage when investing in their own country. Correspondingly there is a relative disadvantage when investing in a country other than one's own. The negative effects of market timing indicated that UK pension fund managers were not able to determine good asset allocations between overseas stock markets in terms of enhancing returns.

HOLDINGS-BASED PERFORMANCE MEASUREMENT

Grinblatt and Titman (1993) developed a measure of investment management performance that gives information about the quality of stock selection. By observing the changes in the composition of a portfolio over time it may be possible to ascertain which stock selection decisions made positive, or negative, contributions to performance. The performance measure is provided by the equation:

$$H_t = \Sigma(W_{jt} - W_{jt-1})\,R_{jt}$$

where H_t is the holdings-based measure of performance, W_{jt} is the portfolio weighting of asset j at time t, W_{jt-1} is the weighting at time $t - 1$, and R_{jt} is the return on asset j between dates $t-1$ and t.

For each share or bond (j) the equation multiplies the return on that asset during a period, R_{jt}, by the change in its portfolio weighting during that period, $W_{jt} - W_{jt-1}$. The results for all N assets in the portfolio (j $= 1$ to N) are added together in order to ascertain H_t.

If the investment manager increases the weights of securities with positive returns, there will be a positive contribution to H_t. If the manager decreases the weighting of assets that have negative returns, there will be a positive contribution to H_t. Increasing the weights of assets with relatively strong performance, whilst reducing the weightings of assets with relatively poor performance, would result in a high value for H_t. The values of H_t over a number of successive time periods could be averaged in order to obtain a measure of the stock selection ability of the investment manager.

One advantage of this holdings-based measure is that it allows a detailed analysis of how each investment decision contributes to overall performance. One disadvantage is that it detects only the immediate effects of investment choices. If the weighting of a share is increased but the relative outperformance of that share does not occur until a later period, the beneficial effects of the investment choice are not shown by this holdings-based measure.

PERSISTENCE OF PERFORMANCE

A fund shows persistence of performance if its relative performance is consistently good, or consistently bad, from year to year. The market consists (in large part) of investment professionals trying to outperform the market. Since in aggregate professionals are (most of) the market, their attempts to outperform the market amounts to professionals attempting to outperform each other. They cannot all be successful. The question arises as to whether any of them are persistently successful, and whether any success is due to skill rather than to luck. Arguably if there is no persistence of relative performance, there is no point in conducting portfolio performance evaluation. If past performance is not a guide to future performance, knowing how well fund managers have performed in the past is of no use for investment choice.

Studies of UK pension funds have been conducted by Brown *et al.* (1997); Blake *et al.* (1999), and by Gregory and Tonks (2006). Overall their findings were that there was some persistence of performance but that it was small and short-lived. In the United States, studies by Lakonishok *et al.* (1992) and Malkiel (1995) on mutual funds found some evidence of persistence. However this persistence did not apply to all periods and in some cases was susceptible to alternative explanations. When looking at the strategy of using the most consistent outperformers from the past in order to choose funds, Malkiel found that the strategy was not useful for long-term investing. Malkiel suggested that most investors should buy low cost index tracker funds rather than try to find outperforming funds.

Kahn and Rudd (1995) found persistence of return for bond funds (but not equity funds). However such persistence was outweighed by the average underperformance of bond funds due to management and trading costs. A study of US mutual funds by Carhart (1997) found evidence of persistence of relative performance over the four years following ranking. The problem with such a time span is that it may take nearly four years to identify potential strong performers, by which time the relatively strong performance may be waning (reminiscent of the Monty Python sketch in which the expert says 'it is too early to know but too late to do anything about it'). Gains from knowledge of four-year outperformance may not offset the costs of moving from fund to fund as the strong performers change. Rhodes (2000) in producing a report for the UK Financial Services Authority based on both a review of existing literature and original research concluded that:

The literature on the performance of UK funds has failed to find evidence that information on past investment performance can be used to good effect by retail investors in choosing funds. The general pattern is one in which investment performance does not persist. Small groups of funds may show some repeat performance over a short period of time, particularly poorly performing funds. However the size of this effect and the fact that it is only very short lived means that there is no investment strategy for retail investors that could usefully be employed. The results from the US literature are similar.

The results concurred with the earlier analyses in finding that there was no persistency in the performance of managed funds after 1987. There was evidence of repeat performance before this point but it would be misleading to suggest that retail investors could use this finding in the present day.

The weight of evidence is that information on past performance cannot be exploited usefully by retail investors.

Some evidence of persistence in US mutual fund performance has been presented by Jan and Hung (2004). They estimated fund alphas over three-year periods. The alphas were used to forecast relative fund performance after a short lag and after a long lag (immediately after the end of a three-year period, and two years after the end of a three-year period). They found that a positive short-lag alpha was predictive of good relative performance, and that this effect was stronger when combined with a long-lag positive alpha. Recent past winners had some tendency to be future winners, and funds that were both recent and more distant past winners were the most likely to be future winners.

Using Transition Matrices to Measure Persistence of Performance

Tables 17.4 and 17.5 illustrate transition matrices (Chapman 2006, based on research by the WM Company). Table 17.4 relates to pension funds investing in UK equities (shares) and Table 17.5 relates to pension funds investing in European equities (exclusive of UK equities). The first period was 1997/99 and the second period was 2000/02. The left-hand column divides the funds into quartiles based on first period performance (the first quartile is the top 25%, through to the fourth quartile being the bottom 25%). Performance was measured by information ratios. The other four columns show performance, in the second period, divided into quartiles. So, for example, Table 17.4 shows that of the top quartile performers from the first period only one was in the top quartile

Table 17.4

First period quartile	Second period quartile			
	1	2	3	4
1	1	6	13	18
2	7	12	11	8
3	13	14	7	4
4	16	6	7	8

Table 17.5

First period quartile	Second period quartile			
	1	2	3	4
1	0	6	18	13
2	0	8	10	19
3	21	11	3	1
4	16	11	6	4

in the second period whereas 18 had dropped to the fourth quartile whilst 16 of the bottom quartile performers from the first period had risen to the first quartile during the second period.

If there were persistence in performance, funds in the top quartile in the first period would be in the top quartile in the second period and funds in the bottom quartile in the first period would be in the bottom quartile in the second period. Tables 17.4 and 17.5 indicate that the opposite was the case. For example in Table 17.4 of the 38 funds in the top quartile in the first period, 31 were in the lowest two quartiles in the second period. Of the 37 bottom quartile funds from the first period, 16 were in the top quartile in the second period. Rather than showing persistence in performance, the tables indicate reversal. It is probably not a coincidence that the first period experienced a bull market whereas the second period covered a bear market. It appears that fund performance tables are turned upside down when markets change direction (Chapman 2006).

CONCLUSION

There are various ways of judging the relative performance of an investment fund. A simple approach is to compare its performance with that of similar funds. However this does not fully take account of differences in risk between funds. Return is one dimension of portfolio performance, and risk is another. When comparing funds some risk adjustment is necessary so that both dimensions of performance are taken into account. If a fund achieves higher returns by incurring more risk, it cannot unambiguously be said that the fund has superior performance.

Risk-adjusted measures of performance may aim to rank the performances of funds, possibly including stock indices as hypothetical funds amongst the funds being ranked. It would be informative to include index tracker funds, including trackers that use futures funds, among the funds being ranked. Alternatively a benchmark rate of return for a portfolio may be derived from a formula that takes account of the risk of the portfolio.

Portfolio performance evaluation also looks for the reasons for variations in performance. For example attribution analysis seeks to ascertain whether outperformance, or underperformance, arises from stock selection or asset allocation.

The results of empirical research suggest that, on average, institutional fund managers do not persistently perform well. Not only do they (slightly) underperform stock indices, on average, but there is little tendency for the strong performers in one period to be strong performers in subsequent periods. For individual investors there seems to be little, if any, scope for successfully picking prospective winners amongst institutional funds such as mutual funds and pension funds. Some researchers have concluded that the best strategy for retail investors is to buy low cost index tracker funds, on the grounds that if the future winners amongst actively managed funds cannot be identified investors should avoid paying their high charges and avoid the risk that their chosen funds turn out to be very poor performers.

However the chapters dealing with behavioural finance, in particular Chapters 2 and 24, indicate that retail investors will continue to believe that they can identify prospective winners. The psychological biases of overconfidence and illusion of control engender the belief that selection can be successful. The representativeness bias will provide part of the explanation for the choices, and the hindsight bias plus cognitive dissonance will convince the investors that they chose well.

Part 6

Investment Analysis

Chapter 18

The economic environment

OBJECTIVE

The objective of this chapter is to provide knowledge of:

1. The relationship between economic cycles and stock market cycles.
2. The determinants of macroeconomic values, including interest rates.
3. The money supply transmission mechanism and its implications for share prices.
4. The importance of politics and demography for share prices.
5. Theories of exchange rate determination.

The difficulties of investment analysis are summarised by Coggan (2006):

> The most obvious problem is the sheer amount of information that needs to be analysed. When deciding to buy a particular share, investors need to assess the probity of the management, the appeal of the group's products, the threat from competitors in the sector and the economic conditions before even beginning to calculate the correct value of the shares, using a host of different measures. Not only do they need to understand conditions now, but predict how they will develop over the next five years or so.
>
> But even a very well-informed investor can struggle. That is because predicting financial markets is not like predicting the weather, an area where, over the years, short-term forecasting has improved because of better collection of data and sophisticated computer models.
>
> The key is that the weather does not change because of our forecasts. But a stock market is made up of humans interacting; their perceptions (and the way they act upon them) changes the conditions.

In the current text, the discussion of investment analysis begins with the economic environment.

BUSINESS CYCLES AND STOCK MARKETS

There are periodic fluctuations in economic activity. Economies move through cycles of expansion and recession. Fluctuations in the level of economic activity are accompanied by fluctuations in corporate profits, interest rates, inflation rates, and other economic variables. Stock market prices also appear to have cycles, and those cycles are thought to be related to the cycles of the economy. If there is some regularity to the business cycle (economic cycle), and if stock market cycles are related to the business cycle, forecasting business cycles could be used as a means of forecasting stock market movements.

It should be made clear that the present discussion is concerned with fluctuations in the economy rather than the long-term growth of the economy. The long-term growth could be seen as providing a trend, and the fluctuations (cycles) as deviations around that trend. Sometimes the economy will be above the long-term trend, and sometimes below it. Somewhat surprisingly strong long-term economic growth does not appear to be associated with strong long-term stock market performance. For example Ritter (2005) investigated 16 countries over the 1900–2002 period and found a negative relationship between national income growth per head and stock market returns. However this has no bearing on the relationship between stock market cycles and economic cycles, which is the concern of the present discussion.

Share prices depend upon prospective profits and the dividends paid out of those profits. An important determinant of the profitability of a company is the profitability of the industry to which it belongs. In turn the profitability of the industry is strongly affected by the state of the economy. It is easier for a firm to be profitable when the economy is strong, and expenditure on goods and services is growing rapidly, than when growth is weak.

Fluctuations in stock markets will be affected by fluctuations in economic activity. Stock market cycles are related to economic cycles (alternatively known as business cycles). However industries are affected to differing extents. Some industries such as food and pharmaceuticals barely have cycles since they produce necessities that are little influenced by consumer incomes. Other industries such as consumer durables (e.g. cars) and capital goods (e.g. industrial machinery) are heavily affected by business cycles.

Industries that are relatively unaffected by economic fluctuations are referred to as defensive in stock market terms. The shares tend to have low betas. Industries that are heavily affected by business cycles are referred to as cyclical. The shares have high betas.

One factor that affects sensitivity to the business cycle is the influence of economic activity on sales. In some industries consumers cannot easily reduce or delay purchases when actual or prospective income falls; examples are food, pharmaceuticals, and water. In other industries reduction or delay is easier. For example the replacement of a car could be delayed until income prospects improve.

Two other significant factors that affect sensitivity to business cycles are operational and financial leverage. Operational leverage is the extent to which the company has fixed costs. Fixed costs cannot be reduced when demand for a firm's products falls. Since costs cannot be reduced in line with revenues, profits fall more than proportionately to a decline in sales. This tendency is strengthened if the firm has financial leverage. Financial leverage is the use of borrowing for obtaining finance. Interest on debt must be paid irrespective of the level of sales.

Suppose a firm has fixed costs of £2 million per year, sells its products at £5 each and incurs variable costs of £1 per unit of output. Sales of 1 million units provide a profit of £2 million (sales revenue of £5 million minus costs of £3 million). Sales of 0.5 million provides zero profit (sales revenue of £2.5 million minus costs of £2.5 million). A 50% fall in sales completely removes the profit.

Suppose that the firm also has debt financing (interest) costs of £1 million per year. Sales of 1 million units provide a profit of £1 million (sales revenue of £5 million minus costs of £3 million minus interest of £1 million). A fall in sales to 0.75 million would eliminate profits (sales revenue of £3.75 million minus costs of £2.75 million minus interest of £1 million). A 25% fall in sales completely removes the profit.

Arguably the first stage in investment analysis is to forecast movements in the economy as a whole. This will affect both the extent of one's investment in shares, and the particular shares chosen.

However forecasts need to be not only accurate, but also early. An accurate forecast, which is made after other analysts have reached the same conclusion and acted upon it, is unlikely to lead to profits. The trades of the early investors would tend to move prices so as to remove profit opportunities for those that act later. Forecasts may suggest share price increases would provide profits for those who buy before prices rise, but the purchases would push up prices and thereby remove further profit opportunities. Investors who are late with their investment decisions will tend to miss opportunities to make profits.

DeStefano (2004) found that stock markets rose during the early stages of economic expansion but that the stock price rises fell towards zero as the expansionary phase of the business cycle approached its end. Stock markets cease to rise while the economy is still growing; the stock market peaks before the economy peaks. During the early stages of economic contraction (recession) the stock market tends to fall, but in the later stages of the contraction stock markets rise strongly. The stock market rises while the economy is still contracting, so the stock market reaches its lowest point before the economy does. As a crude approximation it might be said that stock markets rise when the rate of economic growth is rising (becoming more positive or less negative) and stock markets fall when the rate of economic growth falls (becoming less positive or more negative). DeStefano suggested that changes in expectations about future company profits largely explained the stock market cycle.

Moore and Cullity (1988) have established an average sequence of business cycle and financial market leads and lags in the United States for the period 1920–82 as follows:

Stock price peak to business cycle peak	7 months
Stock price trough to business cycle trough	5 months

Siegel (1991, 1998, 2001) has examined US data for the period 1802–1997. He too has found a tendency for stock market turning points to precede turning points in economic activity. His analysis suggests an average lag between stock market peaks and peaks in economic activity of 5.6 months, with a standard deviation of 4.4 months. However, particularly since 1945, there have been a number of stock market falls that were not followed by economic downturns. He found that the average lag between stock market troughs and troughs in economic activity was 5.1 months with a standard deviation of 1.73 months. Not only was there a smaller variation in the length of the lag between stock market and economic upturns (than in the case of downturns) but also stock market upturns were more reliable indicators of economic upturns.

The ability to forecast upturns was more profitable than the ability to forecast downturns. The average percentage rise in stock prices between stock market and economic troughs was 23.86% whereas the average fall between the peaks was 6.49%. Siegel found that the best timing was to switch out of stocks four months before peaks in economic activity and into stocks four months before the troughs.

There are a number of causal factors that help to explain the pattern of observed cycles. In particular, interest rates tend to follow corresponding cycles. When the economy is in recession, interest rates tend to be low. If economic activity is low, there is reduced demand for loans and low demand to borrow is associated with low interest rates. Recession also leads to central banks, such as the Bank of England, reducing interest rates. Interest rates are reduced by central banks because low economic activity tends to entail low inflation. If inflation falls below target, the central bank will lower interest rates. Conversely during periods of economic expansion interest rates tend to be relatively high.

One problem with using business cycle anticipation as an investment timing strategy is the variability of the lags between stock market and economic peaks and troughs. The seven-month and five-month lags mentioned above are averages, and there is a wide dispersion around the averages. In consequence there is considerable uncertainty concerning the length of the lags. As indicated above, Siegel also found considerable variation in lags, especially between the peaks.

Since stock prices lead the economy, what investors need are factors that lead both stock markets and the economy. There is a need for indicators that lead the stock market and hence provide a means of forecasting the stock market. One possibility is that stock price movements in some industries might precede general stock price movements. Hong et al. (2007) found that movements in the stock prices of mining and metals companies preceded general stock market movements by about two months.

Zweig (1986) used a combination of monetary and momentum indicators to forecast the direction of US stock markets. The method gave good results for the period between the early 1950s and mid-1980s. However Vergin (1996) found that over the period 1984–95 the method failed to be useful.

A study by Boehm and Moore (1991) attempted to allocate between stocks, bills, and bonds in five countries by using leading indicators. The results did not suggest a consistently useful means of forecasting stock market movements.

Siegel (1991, 1998, 2001) has cited numerous examples of failures by market professionals in their attempts to forecast turning points in economic activity. Despite the huge potential rewards from successful forecasting, and the substantial sums spent on economic forecasting, the general result of forecasting efforts has been one of failure.

Fama and French (1989) examined the periods 1927–87 and 1941–87 for the United States. They found that both the dividend yield on stocks and the default spread (the difference in yield between corporate and government bonds) were related to returns (and prices) of both stocks and bonds. The dividend yield and default spread were highly correlated. The significance of dividend yield and default spread increased from high-grade to low-grade bonds and from bonds to stocks. This is consistent with dividend yield and default spread being indicative of risk premiums.

When the dividend yield and the default spread are high, investors are requiring a high return from their investments. This occurs when the economic environment is poor. Investors perceive a higher risk from investing in such periods. This suggests a time-varying-risk explanation of market swings. Adverse economic conditions provide more risk, and in consequence investors require higher returns to compensate for the increased risk. The increase in investment yield entails a fall in stock and bond prices so that dividends and coupons represent higher percentage returns on investments.

Further studies (Fama 1990; Lovatt and Parikh 2000) found that market returns could be predicted by the dividend yield, the default spread, and the term spread (the latter being the difference between yields on short maturity and long maturity bonds). The studies found all three to be positively related to expected (required) rates of return. The default and term spreads were seen as having a business cycle pattern; so the associations between those spreads and required returns provided evidence for an association between the business cycle and required returns. Since required returns have an inverse relationship with stock market prices, the evidence is consistent with a relationship between the business cycle and stock market prices (returns).

It is not only the level of real economic activity that influences stock market prices. Inflation also has an impact. Ibbotson and Brinson (1993) and Boudoukh and Richardson (1993) have found that high inflation (above 4% p.a.) adversely affects stock market prices. Flannery and Protopapadakis (2002) found that announcements about changes in inflation rates affected stock markets. Higher-than-expected inflation rates were found to depress stock markets (vice versa for lower-than-expected inflation rates). They found that announcements of higher-than-expected money supply growth also negatively affected stock markets (conversely for lower-than-expected).

It may be the case that announcements of higher-than-expected rates of inflation or monetary expansion dampen stock markets by raising the fear of interest rate increases. Bernanke and Kuttner (2005) found that when interest rate changes by the US Federal Reserve were separated into expected and unexpected components, the unexpected component had a significant inverse relationship to stock market prices. They also found that reversals in the direction of change of interest rates resulted in extreme stock market reactions. For example a fall in interest rates, which follows a series of rises, brings about a sharp rise in share prices.

Social mood has been proposed as an explanation for the tendency for stock market movements to lead movements in the economy (Prechter 1999; Nofsinger 2005). Social mood is related to the general level of optimism or pessimism within society. Such positive or negative feelings are transmitted between people with the result that there is a widely shared emotional state. It is not limited to financial and economic aspects of people's lives, but those aspects are affected.

The responses of financial markets to changes in social mood are much faster than the responses of other markets. Jansen and Nahius (2003), in a study of 11 European countries, found that the stock market and consumer confidence moved simultaneously rather than with a lag. This is consistent with both being responses to changes in social mood. The response of consumer confidence, and business confidence, to change in social mood takes time to have an impact on the economy. Increased stock market investment can be carried out almost instantly whereas expenditures, particularly business spending, can take time to plan and execute. So stock markets respond faster to a change in social mood than the rest of the economy, and hence stock markets lead the business cycle.

397

Increases in consumer and business spending may be financed largely by borrowing. Since borrowing from the banking system increases the money supply, another consequence of an improvement in social mood would be monetary expansion. Conversely, declining social mood is characterised by a falling stock market and subsequent reductions in expenditure and money creation.

Saving Ratios and the Economy

Money for investment is generated by saving. If people save more, there is more money available to be invested. In the UK the saving ratio, the proportion of disposable income that people save, has been very variable. For example during the 1990s it varied between 11.6% in 1992 and 4.9% in 1999 (Halifax Financial Services 2005).

It has been suggested that the household saving ratio is related to macroeconomics (see, for example, Rutterford 2007). One observation is that the saving ratio tends to be higher when inflation is high, possibly because people save more in order to offset the erosion in the real value of their existing savings caused by rising prices. There also appears to be a relationship between house prices and saving. The saving ratio appears to fall when house prices are rising rapidly. This could be due to a wealth effect whereby rising house prices make people feel richer, and hence causes them to feel that they do not have to save much. Also many people borrow against the increased value of their homes, and spending borrowed money is negative saving.

There appears to be a relationship between economic growth rates and saving ratios. When the economy is growing rapidly, and unemployment is low, saving tends to be low. During periods of low growth or recession saving ratios are higher. This has been explained in terms of high growth causing high consumer confidence and a perceived reduced need to save. An alternative explanation of the relationship is that high saving is accompanied by reduced consumer spending, which slows economic growth. This may help to explain why stock markets tend to fall when inflation rises; higher inflation causes higher saving and lower spending. Another worrying feature of higher inflation, for stock markets, is that it tends to be associated with higher interest rates.

AN OVERVIEW OF MACROECONOMIC ANALYSIS

IS-LM Analysis

Macroeconomists frequently employ an IS-LM framework to analyse aggregate demand in the economy. This framework is illustrated by Figure 18.1.

The IS curve reflects expenditure on goods and services and slopes downwards on the grounds that expenditure, particularly investment in plant and equipment, increases as the cost of borrowing to finance that expenditure declines. Changes in expenditure (demand) arising from factors such as increased government spending or higher exports (i.e. increases unrelated to interest rate or national income changes) will shift the IS curve to the right. This is illustrated in Figure 18.1 by the shift from IS_1 to IS_2. It can be seen that the result is an increase in aggregate demand and in interest rates. Autonomous reductions in expenditure would have the opposite effects.

The LM curve reflects conditions in the money markets. It is based on the view that increased economic activity is associated with rising interest rates. If the central bank (e.g. Bank of England, European Central Bank, or US Federal Reserve) increases the money supply the LM curve will

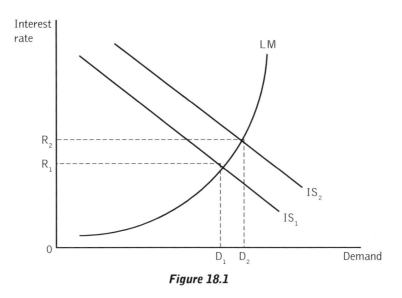

Figure 18.1

shift to the right. This is illustrated as a shift from LM_1 to LM_2 in Figure 18.2. The shift is associated with a lower interest rate and higher level of demand in the economy. In terms of monetary policy higher money supply and lower interest rates tend to be two sides of the same coin. Irrespective of whether the money supply change causes the interest rate change, or vice versa, the two tend to be linked. The opposite, a tightening of monetary policy, would be shown as a leftward shift of the LM curve.

From the perspective of stock, bond, and property markets (i.e. asset markets) the money supply and interest rates have a direct bearing. Increased money supply and lower interest rates tend to be supportive of asset price increases. A higher money supply means that there is more cash available for investment in shares, bonds, and property. Lower interest rates render the alternative

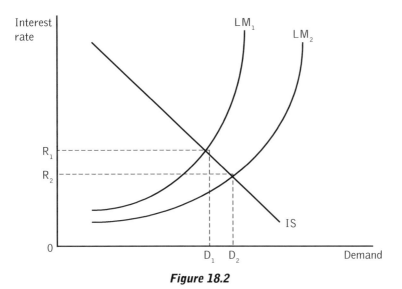

Figure 18.2

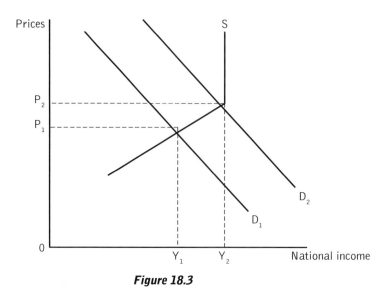

Figure 18.3

of keeping money in bank (or building society) deposits less attractive, and make borrowing to invest less costly.

Aggregate Demand and Supply

The IS-LM framework is commonly used as the basis for analysing the determination of aggregate demand (expenditure) in the economy. However, economic analysis requires that supply is also taken into account. Figure 18.3 illustrates aggregate demand and supply schedules.

D_1 and D_2 are aggregate demand curves derived from IS-LM analysis. One reason for the downward slope is the reduction in the real money supply, and hence leftward shift of the LM curve, resulting from an increase in the general price level. The intersection of the aggregate demand and supply curves is shown as determining the general price level and national income. The vertical section of the aggregate supply curve depicts full employment, which puts an upper limit on national income. The rightward shift of the aggregate demand curve from D_1 to D_2 may result from expansionary economic policy (e.g. higher government spending and/or an increase in the money supply) and in this case can be seen to restore full employment at the cost of an increase in the general level of prices.

Inflation and the Phillips Curve

The rise in the general price level as full employment is achieved is unlikely to be a one-off increase. It is more likely to be a persistent tendency towards inflation. This can be explained with the help of Figure 18.4, which depicts an expectations-augmented Phillips curve.

The Phillips curve shows the relationship between unemployment and the rate at which wages rise (i.e. wage inflation). The basic relationship is one in which lower unemployment is associated with a higher rate of wage inflation. The rate of wage inflation is affected not only by the level of unemployment but also by expectations of price inflation. Wage demands are seen as incorporating compensation for expected price inflation. Expected price inflation shifts the Phillips curve

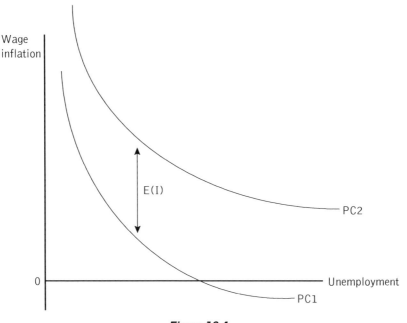

Figure 18.4

upwards, for example from PC1 to PC2 in Figure 18.4. PC1 is the Phillips curve without expectations of price inflation and PC2 is the Phillips curve inclusive of expected price inflation of E(I). The Phillips curve rises by the amount of the expected inflation.

It is widely believed that the trade-off between unemployment and wage inflation is not permanent and that in time unemployment returns to a natural rate. The natural rate of unemployment (alternatively known as the non-accelerating inflation rate of unemployment) is the rate corresponding to equality of demand and supply in the labour market, and at which the unemployed are in the process of moving between jobs rather than being permanently unemployed.

Expectations of inflation have implications for interest rates. The nominal interest rate is the real interest plus an addition to compensate for inflation. For example, if 3% inflation is expected a 3% interest rate would be required merely to compensate for rising prices. That 3% would be added to the rate of interest that would otherwise be paid (the real rate of interest). Thus:

$$r_n = r_r + E(I)$$

where r_n is the nominal interest rate, r_r is the real interest rate, and E(I) is the expected rate of inflation.

If there were uncertainty about the rate of inflation, a risk premium may be required. If inflation were expected to be 3% p.a. but could range between 0% and 6%, investors may require a risk premium to compensate for the possibility of a high inflation rate since a high inflation rate would seriously reduce the real rate of interest received. The uncertainty about the rate of inflation is referred to as inflation risk. Thus:

$$r_n = r_r + E(I) + RP$$

where RP is the risk premium (Pilbeam 2005). To the extent that higher inflation carries higher inflation risk, and hence a higher risk premium, this may help to explain why stock markets often fall when inflation unexpectedly rises.

Interest Rates

A macroeconomic variable that is particularly important from the perspective of investment analysis is the rate of interest. In reality there are many different interest rates at any one time (depending upon the maturity and risk of the investment) but it is convenient to summarise them into a single rate for the purpose of analysing the factors that determine interest rates.

Two approaches to explaining interest rates entail (1) the demand and supply of loanable funds, and (2) the demand and supply of money. Figure 18.5 shows the demand and supply of loanable funds.

The demand for loanable funds (DD) comes from businesses wanting to finance investment, governments funding budget deficits, and individuals financing expenditure (e.g. purchasing housing). The supply of loanable funds (SS) comes from the savings of individuals and businesses, and government budget surpluses. A change in the money supply by a central bank (e.g. Bank of England, European Central Bank) would also affect the supply of loanable funds.

Figure 18.5 depicts a rightward shift of the supply curve, for example due to an increase in savings by individuals or an increase in the money supply by a central bank. It can be seen that the result is a decline in the interest rate from I_1 to I_2 and an increase in lending from L_1 to L_2.

Factors that lie behind the loanable funds approach can be broken down into the productivity of capital and the time preferences of people. Capital includes land, buildings, machinery, vehicles, software, knowledge, and anything else whose purchase can increase the potential to produce goods and services. The productivity of capital can be expressed as a percentage per year, referred to as the rate of return on capital. This return on capital is the source of the dividends, coupons, and interest paid on shares, bonds, and loans. It is largely the expected rate of return on capital that determines the position of the demand curve for loanable funds. A high

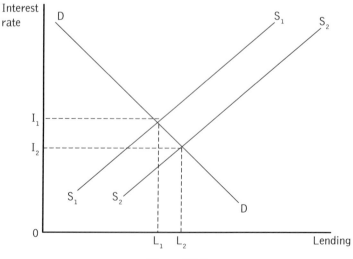

Figure 18.5

productivity of capital causes the demand curve to be high, with a high interest rate at each level of borrowing.

A factor that determines the position of the supply curve of loanable funds is the time preference of people. Generally people require some compensation for delaying consumption. If they are to save in the present with a view to spending in the future, the prospective future spending should exceed the current spending foregone. The achievement of this excess of future value over current value requires a rate of interest on the saving. An increased level of saving requires an increased interest rate.

For the demand to come together with the supply to determine the rate of interest by their interaction requires that the interest rate (rate of return) of the demand curve is compatible with that of the supply curve. In particular the supply curve may be based on risk-free interest rates (i.e. known for certain) whereas the productivity of capital is very uncertain. A risk premium should be subtracted from the productivity of capital in order to provide the risk-free component of return. It is the risk-free component that is compatible with the interest rate of the supply curve. The risk premium to be subtracted depends upon the degree of uncertainty surrounding the productivity of capital, and upon the degree of distaste for uncertainty (risk-aversion) exhibited by the people who supply the loanable funds.

Another way of looking at the determination of interest rates is in terms of the demand and supply of money. It should be borne in mind that notes and coin constitute only a small portion of the money supply. Most money is in the form of bank deposits. Figure 18.6 illustrates this view of interest rate determination.

It can be seen that an increase in the money supply by a central bank from M_1 to M_2 will reduce the interest rate from I_1 to I_2. This is consistent with the prediction from the loanable funds model.

The process whereby an increase in the money supply becomes associated with a fall in the interest rate can be looked upon from different perspectives. One process entails open market operations. Open market operations involve the central bank buying or selling government securities such as bonds and Treasury bills. The purchases, by the central bank, put money into the

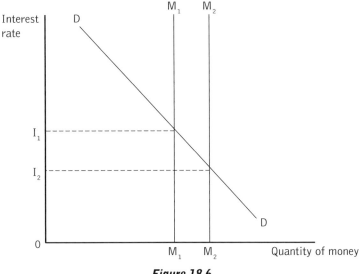

Figure 18.6

403

hands of the sellers and thereby increase the money supply (the money would be newly created by the central bank). Simultaneously the purchase of bonds and bills would push up their prices and thereby lower their yields. The higher money supply is associated with lower yields, on bills and bonds, and hence lower interest rates.

There is a chain of causation that runs from the interest rate to the money supply. Bank credit is a form of money. When someone borrows from a bank newly created money is added to their bank balance. To the extent that lower interest rates cause increased borrowing they will simultaneously generate an expansion of the money supply.

By announcing a base rate, or repo rate, the central bank (e.g. the Bank of England) signals to the money markets the level of interest rates that it would like to see. Money market interest rates then move to the desired levels with the assistance of open market operations by the central bank. The announcement of a new interest rate may be enough without the need for significant open market operations. For example if an interest rate fall is announced traders will realise that this implies a rise in Treasury bill prices. In anticipation of a rise in prices traders will buy Treasury bills, thereby causing the price rise. The higher price of Treasury bills reduces their rate of yield into line with the newly announced interest rate. There is a transfer of funds from Treasury bills to other money market investments in search of higher rates of yield. The increased supply of funds into those other investments lowers their rates of interest. In this way an announcement by the central bank of a change in interest rates moves interest rates in the money markets to the desired level, with little need for further action by the central bank.

Central banks and the money market forces of demand and supply can both play a part in the determination of interest rates. For example during the sub-prime mortgage crisis of 2007 interest rates in the London inter-bank market rose by more than 1 percentage point as a result of a reduced supply of loans rather than in consequence of Bank of England action. The relative importance of central bank decisions and money market forces could vary over time. Many take the view that short-term interest rates are normally determined by the central bank rather than by the forces of supply and demand (Pepper and Oliver 2006). If the interest rate does not move to bring the demand for, and supply of, money into equality some other mechanism must be present. Surplus money may be used to buy goods and services, or to buy investment assets such as shares, bonds, and property. An excess demand for money (insufficient supply) could be remedied by reduced expenditure or the sale of investments. The process of adjusting to a discrepancy between demand and supply of money is known as the money supply transmission mechanism.

STOCK MARKETS AND THE MONEY SUPPLY TRANSMISSION MECHANISM

The chain of causation that runs from money supply changes to interest rate changes, and thereby to the demand for goods and services, has been referred to as the Keynesian transmission mechanism. An alternative view of the transmission mechanism, referred to as the monetarist transmission mechanism, entails the money supply having a direct effect on the demand for goods and services as well as operating through interest rates. From the perspective of investment analysis, the monetarist transmission mechanism seems to suggest that increases in the money supply would have a direct impact on stock markets. An increase in the money supply is associated with increased expenditure on goods and services, and on all forms of investment. This effect of money supply changes on investment markets is probably also consistent with Keynesian theory (Leijonhufvud 1968; Redhead 1981).

The transmission mechanism of how money supply changes are transmitted to the real economy (the economy of goods, services, and workers) is an issue that has concerned macroeconomists. The early Keynesian view was that money supply changes operated through interest rate movements. An increase in the money supply was seen as lowering interest rates and thereby increasing borrowing for the purpose of financing investment in productive capacity. This investment in goods and services increased the incomes of the producers of investment goods, who increased their expenditure as a result thereby providing another round of increased incomes. This process leads to a multiple increase in incomes and expenditure. The monetarist transmission mechanism accepted this effect via interest rates, but added that there would be a direct effect. An increase in the money supply would directly cause an increase in expenditure on goods and services (both investment and consumer) as people sought to exchange their additional holdings of money for goods and services.

These transmission mechanisms did not always explicitly allow for effects that operated via shares. Leijonhufvud in his reinterpretation of Keynes's general theory broadened the Keynesian transmission mechanism (Leijonhufvud 1968; Redhead 1981). More recently, and more explicitly, Pepper and Oliver (2006) have proposed a liquidity theory of asset prices. According to this theory, changes in the money supply are a major driver of share prices. An increase in the money supply, relative to the demand for money, causes an increase in expenditure on shares as people attempt to reduce their surplus holdings of money. In this way an increase in the money supply can cause an increase in share prices. So the transmission mechanism is broadened such that an increase in the supply of money has impacts on the real economy via interest rates, share prices, and direct expenditure on goods and services.

Congdon (2006) has also proposed a transmission mechanism that includes changes in share prices. He demonstrated that institutional investors (life assurance and pensions) have a fairly stable demand for liquidity in the sense of the ratio of liquid assets to other assets. If the institutional investors experience a change in liquidity that moves the liquidity ratio away from the desired level, they will attempt to restore the desired ratio. Money is a component of liquidity. An increase in the money supply could disturb the liquidity ratio of institutional investors. The institutions attempt to restore their liquidity ratios to the desired values by spending the surplus liquidity on assets such as shares and bonds. This would drive up share and bond prices. So long as the holding of liquidity exceeds the desired amount, investment spending will continue. To the extent that each institution's expenditure is another institution's receipt of money, the attempt by each institution to reduce its holding of liquidity does not reduce the aggregate holding of liquidity by institutions.

Some of the additional money will be lost to the institutions, for example to individual shareholders who sell to institutions, but much will remain with the institutions. The desired ratio of liquidity to other assets is restored by a rise in share and bond prices. Suppose that institutional investors, in aggregate, hold £1,000 billion of shares and bonds. Also suppose that, on average, the institutions desire to hold liquid assets equal to 4% of non-liquid assets. Together they require £40 billion of liquid assets to match the share and bond holdings.

Suppose that the central bank (Bank of England) buys government bonds from the institutions. The money used to pay for the bonds adds to the liquidity of the institutions. If they receive additional money of £30 billion, they would have a liquid assets ratio of about 7%. In aggregate they would not rid themselves of the entire surplus of £30 billion, since the institutions would tend to pass the money between themselves as shares and bonds are bought from each other. Some of the money, say £10 million, would be lost to the institutions. This would reduce the aggregate holding of liquidity to 6% of the original value of shares and bonds. The institutions would still have £60 billion of liquid assets.

The desired ratio of liquid assets to share and bond holdings is restored by a rise in share and bond prices. Prices would rise until the desired ratio is restored. So long as the actual ratio exceeds the desired ratio, spending on shares and bonds would continue, as would the resulting rise in prices. Prices would rise until the total value of shares and bonds reached £1,500 billion. The liquidity ratio of 4% would then have been restored (£60 billion of liquid assets against £1,500 billion of shares and bonds). An initial £30 billion increase in the money held by the institutions leads to a £500 billion increase in the aggregate value of shares and bonds held by the institutions. This £500 billion increase results from an average rise in asset prices of about 50%. Conversely, an initial reduction in liquidity would generate falling prices.

The empirical evidence of the effects of money supply changes on stock market prices seems generally to indicate that money supply movements affect share prices, with money supply increases appearing to cause share price rises (Dhakal *et al.* 1993; Hashemazadeh and Taylor 1988; Mookerjee 1987). However not all studies have found such a causal relationship (Singh 1993).

Congdon (2005) criticised macroeconomists, and macroeconomics texts, for ignoring the role of share prices (and property prices) in the transmission mechanism. He illustrated the potential power of the role of share prices in the transmission mechanism by describing three recent episodes in UK financial history. The early 1970s, mid-1980s, and late 1990s were all characterised by rapid money supply growth accompanied by sharp share price rises. In these cases the money supply growth was particularly marked in the financial sector. There appeared to be a strong relationship between growth in the money holdings of institutional investors (particularly life assurance companies and pension funds) and rises in share prices as measured by stock indices.

Giuliodori (2005) found that the housing market formed part of the monetary transmission mechanism. It was found that house prices were significantly affected by interest rate changes. In particular house price movements may enhance the effects of interest rate changes on consumer expenditure in countries where housing and mortgage markets are relatively developed and competitive.

POLITICAL AND DEMOGRAPHIC EFFECTS ON SHARE PRICES

The discussion of the liquidity theory of asset prices highlights the point that share prices are determined by the forces of demand and supply. Prices rise when there are net purchases of shares and fall when there are net sales.

Political and demographic developments can impact on the demand for shares. There is a worldwide trend to shift the emphasis from state provision of pensions to private provision. This arises from an ageing population and the tax implications of maintaining generous state pensions. Private pension schemes are largely invested on stock markets. So an increase in the amount of investment in private pensions leads to expenditure on shares and a consequent rise in share prices.

This trend is likely to be strengthened by the 'baby-boomer' generation. During the period 1945 to 1963 there was an exceptionally high birth rate in Western Europe and North America.

The resulting population bulge (the baby-boomers) is now approaching retirement. It might be expected that they will increase their saving, and hence stock market investment, as the need to fund their retirement becomes increasingly apparent. This suggests rising share prices brought about by the increased demand for shares.

There are aspects of the details of government policy towards private pension provision that will have an effect on the demand for shares. For example the introduction of a system of additional voluntary contributions by the UK government will have added to the demand for shares, as would the removal of restrictive limits to pension fund contributions in 2006.

Mosebach and Najand (1999) presented evidence consistent with the life-cycle investment hypothesis, which suggests that the demand for shares rises as the average age of the population increases. Their findings indicated that, in the United States, investing for retirement had produced a relatively stable inflow of funds to the stock market. Their research also found that net inflows of funds to the stock market led to stock price rises.

There are some factors that may be acting to reduce the demand for shares. The switch by some pension funds away from shares and towards bonds would have dampened the demand for shares, and resulted in sales of shares. The fall in popularity of endowment mortgages would have had a similar effect. Endowment policies add to the demand for shares, and their decline reduces this effect. Furthermore as endowment policies mature they are encashed with the result that shares are sold.

Both pension fund switches from shares to bonds and the decline in the popularity of endowment mortgages were largely caused by poor stock market performance during the period 2000–3. A vicious circle emerged. Falling share prices led to these effects on pension funds and endowment policies, and these effects in turn put further downward pressure on share prices.

EXCHANGE RATES

When investing overseas, exchange rate movements can make substantial differences to returns. An overseas investment is simultaneously an investment in a foreign stock (or bond) market, and an investment in a foreign currency. Strong positive returns on the foreign stock market can be turned into losses if the value of the foreign currency (relative to the investor's home currency) experiences a substantial fall. Conversely appreciation of the foreign currency, relative to the investor's home currency, can turn an investment loss into a profit. The analysis of overseas investments involves an analysis of currency exchange rates.

The economic analysis of exchange rates can involve analysis of:

1. The balance of payments.
2. Purchasing power parity.
3. Monetary policy.
4. International portfolio balance.

These four factors have strong interrelationships. One common factor appears to be that they are much more useful for predicting long-term (horizons of several years) than short-term (horizons of days, weeks, or months) currency movements.

The analysis of exchange rate movements from the perspective of the balance of payments is premised on the view that exchange rates (the prices of currencies in terms of one another) are determined by the forces of demand and supply. If the demand for a currency increases, its price in terms of other currencies will rise. If the supply of a currency increases, its price will fall. The balance of payments on current account is the balance between exports and imports of goods and services. Exports entail demand for the home currency since foreign buyers will need the home currency to pay for their purchases. Imports entail supply of the home currency; the home currency would be sold for the purpose of buying the foreign currencies required for the purchase of the imports. An excess of exports over imports suggests that demand for the home currency is greater than the supply with the effect that its price rises in terms of other currencies. An excess of imports over exports suggests an excess supply and a fall in price. So if the balance of payments on current account is in surplus (exports greater than imports) the home currency should appreciate in value, whereas if the balance is in deficit (imports greater than exports) the home currency should depreciate in terms of other currencies.

The balance of payments on current account is not the whole balance of payments. There is also the balance of payments on capital account. The balance of payments on capital account is the balance of investment flows into, and out of, a country. It is the aggregate of the balance of payments on current account and the balance of payments on capital account that provides the demand/supply relationship for a currency. For example the huge US current account deficits of recent years (and decades) have been balanced by net inflows on capital account as the residents of other countries (particularly Japan) have invested heavily in US government bonds. Arguably the balance of payments on current account is more permanent than the balance on capital account, which could change very quickly if investors' preferences change. So countries with persistent current account deficits, such as the UK and the United States, are vulnerable to sharp falls in their currencies if international investment flows cease to support their currencies. Conversely surplus countries and regions, such as Japan and the Eurozone, are vulnerable to currency appreciations.

Purchasing Power Parity (PPP) relates to relative prices between countries. The theory comes in two forms: absolute PPP and relative PPP. According to absolute PPP, tradable goods should cost the same in every country after adjusting for exchange rates. According to relative PPP, exchange rate movements should parallel differences in inflation rates. So, for example, according to relative PPP, if the UK has an inflation rate 1% p.a. higher than in the Eurozone then the pound should fall by 1% p.a. against the Euro. Froot and Rogoff (1995) estimated that, when disturbed, relative PPP takes an average of eight years to become re-established.

This view is closely related to a monetary policy analysis of exchange rates, according to which exchange rate movements should reflect relative rates of money supply growth. If the UK has a rate of money supply growth that is 1% more than in the Eurozone, the pound would be expected to fall at 1% p.a. against the Euro. This is related to the view that there is a close relationship between money supply growth and inflation.

Another possible link between monetary policy and exchange rates operates through interest rates. A rise in interest rates on a currency renders that currency more attractive, and hence increases demand for it. In this way higher interest rates on a currency are likely to be associated with an increase in the price of that currency in terms of other currencies. This is consistent with the portfolio balance approach to explaining exchange rate movements. According to this view exchange rate movements occur as a result of international investors adjusting the distribution of their portfolios between currencies.

CONCLUSION

Stock markets do not exist in isolation from the economies and societies in which they operate. Changes in the economy affect the factors that influence share prices, such as profits, company growth prospects, and interest rates. Changes in society also have impacts. As the average age of a population increases, the ability of the state to provide good pensions declines. It becomes increasingly important for people to make their own provision for retirement. This is typically carried out through the medium of institutional investments, especially pension funds.

One particular economic variable, highlighted by some economists, is change in the money supply. Economists have long observed that money supply growth impacts on the prices of assets, such as shares, bonds, and property; a portion of the extra money is spent on such assets. Changes in the money holdings of institutional investors may be particularly significant, particularly if they have preferences in relation to the proportion of their funds to be held in cash. An increase in the money supply that leaves institutional investors with more money than they want to hold is likely to result in share (and bond) price rises as the institutions spend their surplus cash on such investment assets. The resulting rise in asset prices could be an important part of the mechanism that restores the desired ratio of cash to other assets.

Exchange rates are important for investments, particularly international investments. A strong performance from a foreign stock market can be negated by weakness in that country's currency. This exchange rate risk can be dealt with, particularly by large investors such as institutional investors, by the use of derivatives. Currency derivatives can be used to hedge exchange rate risk (see Chapter 39 on currency forwards, futures, swaps, and options). Stock index and bond futures can be used to structure futures funds with low exchange rate risk (see Part 8 on stock index futures and Chapter 43 on bond futures). Futures funds using futures on foreign stock indices effectively create index tracker funds based on those foreign stock markets.

Not only does the economic environment have significance, but also the social environment is important to stock (and other asset) markets. Attitudes towards saving and investing are crucial for stock market behaviour. Levels of saving, and hence investing, are greatly influenced by the attitudes prevalent in society. For example if there were social pressure towards conspicuous consumption, the result would be more spending and hence less saving. With less money being spent on investments, the growth in asset prices would be reduced. Conversely high levels of spending on goods and services could be beneficial for company profits, and thereby beneficial for dividends and share prices. If investing becomes a subject of general interest, and successful investing a source of social status, the result could be enhanced levels of investment and consequent asset price increases.

Chapter 27 on stock market bubbles and crashes discusses how the spread of ideas in society can have consequences for stock market behaviour. People are greatly influenced by social pressures, which can result in the spread of ideas. These include ideas concerning investments. Investors can show herding behaviour, in which common beliefs lead to common actions resulting in stock market bubbles and crashes.

Chapter 19

Dividend discount models

OBJECTIVE

The objective of this chapter is to provide knowledge of:

1. Discounting future cash flows to obtain a present value.
2. The use of dividend discount models to obtain the fair prices of shares.
3. Variations on the dividend discount model, such as the Gordon growth model, stochastic dividend discount models, and multi-period models.
4. The estimation of the growth rate of dividends.
5. The effects of investment opportunities on share prices.
6. Problems with the use of dividend discount models.

Investment analysts need to produce estimates of what stock prices should be. Stock selection requires views as to which shares are underpriced or overpriced in the market. There are several approaches. One involves discounting prospective future dividends in order to arrive at their present value, which is regarded as the fair price of the share. Another approach obtains estimates of the price-earnings ratio and of prospective earnings and uses those estimates to ascertain the appropriate, or fair, price of the stock.

DISCOUNTING CASH FLOWS

A sum of money received (or paid) in the present is worth more than the same sum in the future. One explanation for this runs in terms of the fact that money can earn interest. A unit of money received now is worth more than the same unit received one year from now because it can earn interest over the year. If the interest rate were 10% p.a., then receipts in the present are worth 10% more than identical receipts one year hence.

To render a future cash flow comparable with a current one, the future sum is discounted. This involves dividing the future sum by one plus the decimalised rate of interest. In the case of a receipt of S one year hence, when the interest rate is 10% p.a., the present value (PV) is given by:

$$PV = S/1.1$$

More generally:

$$PV = S/(1 + r)$$

where r is the decimalised rate of interest.

If the cash flow is to occur two years from now, then (assuming a rate of interest of 10% p.a.) because of compound interest an identical sum in the present is worth 21% more (21% being the total interest received over two years). The present value of the future sum would be:

$$PV = S/(1.1)^2 = S/1.21$$

(Note that S/1.21 invested for two years at 10% p.a. would be worth [S/1.21]×1.21 = S.)
More generally:

$$PV = S/(1 + r)^2$$

Correspondingly the present value of a sum three years hence is $S/(1 + r)^3$, four years hence $S/(1 + r)^4$, and so on. It follows that the present value of a future stream of cash flows of S per year is:

$$PV = S/(1 + r) + S/(1 + r)^2 + S/(1 + r)^3 + \ldots + S/(1 + r)^n$$

where the final receipt (or payment) occurs n years from the present. This can be more formally expressed as:

$$PV = \sum_{k=1}^{n} S/(1 + r)^k$$

which states that the present value equals the sum of the discounted cash flows (the cash flow being S at the end of each year) relating to the next n years.

EXAMPLE 19.1

The present value of £100, to be received at the end of each of the next three years, with a discount rate (i.e. interest rate) of 10% p.a. would be:

$$PV = \sum_{k=1}^{3} 100/(1.1)^k$$

i.e. PV = £100/1.1 + £100/(1.1)^2 + £100/(1.1)^3

= £100/1.1 + £100/1.21 + £100/1.331

= £90.91 + £82.64 + £75.13

= £248.68

The time period is not necessarily a year. If it is not, an adjustment needs to be made to the interest rate. For example for six-monthly cash flows, an interest rate of 10% p.a. would be expressed as a rate of 5% per six-month period. (Interest rates are always expressed on a per annum — p.a. — basis; a six-month rate of 10% p.a. means 5% over six months. Likewise a three-month rate of 10% p.a. means 2.5% over three months.)

The cash flow may not be the same at the end of each time period, in which case the equation becomes:

$$PV = S_1/(1 + r) + S_2/(1 + r)^2 + S_3/(1 + r)^3 + \ldots + S_n/(1+r)^n$$

$$\text{or } PV = \sum_{k=1}^{n} S_k/(1 + r)^k$$

where $S_1, S_2, S_3, \ldots, S_n$ are the cash flows at the ends of periods 1, 2, 3, . . ., n respectively. There may also be a different interest rate (discount rate) for each time period.

DISCOUNTING EXPECTED FUTURE DIVIDENDS

This approach to share price valuation uses variations on the discounted cash flow model. The simplest variant is based on an unchanging annual dividend payment on the shares.

$$P = D/(1 + r) + D/(1 + r)^2 + D/(1 + r)^3 + \ldots + D/(1 + r)^n \tag{1}$$

P is the fair price of the share, D is the annual dividend on the share, r is the discount rate, and n is the number of years for which the firm is expected to exist. The rate of discount, r, is also known as the required rate of return. The required rate of return is the rate required by investors in the light of what is available on other investments. The required rate of return can be looked upon as composed of the rate of yield on long-term government bonds plus a risk premium to reflect the fact that shares are riskier than government bonds. The required rate of return is often calculated by means of the security market line, which is derived from the capital asset pricing model.

If the firm is assumed to last forever, that is n is treated as infinite, equation (1) can be simplified to equation (2):

$$P = D/r \tag{2}$$

Fama and French (2004) take the view that the failures of the standard capital asset pricing model, when tested empirically, make it unsuitable as a means of estimating the required rate of return.

THE GORDON GROWTH MODEL

The assumption of an unchanging annual dividend is unrealistic for most stocks. The Gordon growth model takes a step towards greater realism by allowing for a growth in annual dividends. Dividends are assumed to grow at a constant annual rate. This growth rate of dividends is shown as g in equation (3).

$$P = D(1 + g)/(1 + r) + D(1 + g)^2/(1 + r)^2 + D(1 + g)^3/(1 + r)^3 + \ldots + D(1 + g)^n/(1 + r)^n \tag{3}$$

D is the most recent dividend, so D(1 + g) is the next dividend. Equation (3) assumes that the next dividend is payable one year from the present. If the company is expected to continue forever (n approaches infinity), equation (3) can be simplified to equation (4):

$$P = D(1 + g)/(r - g) \tag{4}$$

EXERCISE 19.1

Lotek plc has just paid its annual dividend of 10p per share. The required rate of return is 12.5% p.a.

(a) If that level of dividend payment is expected to be constant into the future what is the fair price of the shares?

(b) If the next dividend payment is expected to be 7.5% higher than the last and if that rate of dividend growth is expected to be maintained throughout the future, what then is the fair price of the shares?

Answers

(a) P = D/r where P is the fair price of the shares, D is the expected constant dividend and r is the required rate of return. So:

P = 10/0.125 = 80p

(b) Using the Gordon growth model, P = D(1 + g)/(r−g) where g is the expected dividend growth rate, D is the most recent dividend and D(1 + g) is the expected next dividend. So:

P = 10(1.075)/(0.125−0.075) = 215p

ESTIMATING THE GROWTH RATE OF DIVIDENDS

An investment analyst using the Gordon growth model would need to forecast the rate of dividend growth. This can be done by using equation (5):

$$g = ROE \times (1-d) \tag{5}$$

In equation 5, g is the growth rate of profits, ROE (return on equity) is the rate of return that the company can obtain from reinvested profits, and d is the dividend payout rate (the proportion of profits paid as dividends to shareholders). With a constant dividend payout rate, the growth rate of dividends will equal the growth rate of profits.

For example, if the firm pays out 60% of profits as dividends (whilst reinvesting 40%) and the new investment yields 20% p.a. then:

$$g = 0.2 \times (1 - 0.6) = 0.08$$

Dividends (and profits) are expected to grow at 8% p.a. Out of each pound of profit 40p is reinvested to yield $40p \times 0.2 = 8p$ more profit per year. For every £1 profit this year, there will be £1.08 profit next year.

From equation 4 it would appear that a reduction in the dividend payout rate would reduce the share price by reducing dividends. From equation 5 it would appear that a reduction in the dividend payout rate would increase the share price by increasing the expected growth rate of dividends. Miller and Modigliani (1961) showed that, under certain conditions, changes in the dividend payout rate have no effect on the share price. This is known as the Dividend Irrelevance Theorem.

EXERCISE 19.2

The share price of a company is 100p. Its expected next dividend is 3p. The dividend (and share price*) growth rate is expected to be 4% p.a. The risk-free interest rate is 5% p.a. The share has a beta of 0.8 and the expected yield on the stock market as a whole is 8% p.a.

Use the Gordon growth model and the security market line to form an opinion as to whether the share is correctly priced.

Answer

Rearranging the Gordon growth model gives an expression for expected returns.

The Gordon growth equation: $P = D(1 + g)/(r - g)$

(where P = share price, D(1 + g) = expected next dividend, r = required rate of return, and g is the expected growth rate of dividends) can be rearranged to give:

$$R = [D(1 + g)/P] + g$$

where R = forecast rate of return, and g = expected growth rate of dividends = expected growth rate of the share price.* [D(1 + g)/P] is the expected rate of dividend yield and g the expected rate of capital gain. Thus:

$$R = (3/100) + 0.04 = 0.07$$

The forecast rate of return is 7% p.a.

The security market line can be expressed as:

$$r = r_f + \beta[E(r_m) - r_f]$$

where r = required rate of return, r_f = risk-free rate of return, β = beta of the share, and $E(r_m)$ = expected return on the market. Thus:

$$r = 0.05 + 0.8[0.08 - 0.05] = 0.05 + 0.024 = 0.074 \text{ i.e. } 7.4\% \text{ p.a.}$$

The forecast rate of return, 7% p.a., is below the required rate of return, 7.4% p.a. This share is not a good buy. In other words it is overpriced.

The equality between the expected growth rate of dividends and the expected growth rate of the share price can be seen from the Gordon growth model.

$$P = D(1 + g)/(r - g)$$

$$P(1+g) = D(1+g)^2/(r - g)$$

A growth in dividends of g produces a growth in the share price of g. In other words a growth in dividends by a factor of (1 + g) entails an increase in the share price by a factor of (1 + g).

STOCHASTIC DIVIDEND DISCOUNT MODELS

Stochastic dividend discount models allow for the possibility that dividends do not increase every year. A stochastic form of the Gordon growth model is shown by equation (6):

$$P = D(1 + pg)/(r - pg) \tag{6}$$

In equation (6), p is the probability that the dividend will increase in a period (e.g. a year). For example if p is 0.5, there is a 50% chance of a dividend increase in a particular year.

Stochastic dividend discount models provide a distribution of possible future stock prices rather than a single price. The equation indicates the average (mean) of a distribution of possible prices but actual prices could differ from that average. Stochastic models can be refined to allow for the possibility of dividend reductions.

MULTI-PERIOD MODELS

A further step towards greater realism is provided by multi-period dividend discount models. The simplest of these is the two-period model. The two-period model assumes dividend growth at an untypical rate for a number of years after which growth proceeds at a normal rate. The first step, when using a two-period model, is to estimate the share price that will prevail at the future point in time at which the growth rate will change. If the untypical growth rate is G, the normal growth rate g, and the untypical growth is expected to continue for N years, the estimate of what the share price will be N years from now (using the Gordon growth model) is given by equation (7).

$$P_N = D(1 + G)^N(1 + g)/(r - g) \tag{7}$$

The term $D(1 + G)^N(1 + g)$ represents the dividend expected at the end of period $N + 1$. Application of the Gordon growth model then estimates the share price N years from the present. This expected future share price is represented by P_N. The current fair price of the stock is given by discounting the expected future price and the dividends expected during the period of untypical dividend growth. The current fair price is given by equation (8), which assumes that the untypical dividend growth continues for three years.

$$
\begin{aligned}
P = {} & D(1 + G)/(1 + r) + D(1 + G)^2/(1 + r)^2 \\
& + D(1 + G)^3/(1 + r)^3 + P_N/(1 + r)^3
\end{aligned}
\tag{8}
$$

Some investment analysts use three-period models in which the period of untypical growth is followed by a period during which growth changes from the untypical to the typical rate. At the end of this transition period the third period, during which growth proceeds at a normal rate, begins. The Gordon growth model, used in multi-period dividend discount models, could be either stochastic or non-stochastic.

EXERCISE 19.3

AB plc has a new product and is enjoying rapid growth. The company has just paid an annual dividend of £2 and expects dividends to grow at an annual rate of 20% over the next three years. The growth rate of dividends is expected to be 10% p.a. after three years. Calculate the fair price of the share if the required rate of return is 12% p.a.

Answer

The first step is to calculate the share price expected for a point in time three years from the present. The dividend expected to be paid four years from now is $£2(1.2)^3((1.1) = £3.80$. The expected share price, for the point in time three years hence, is:

$$P_3 = D_4/[r - g] = £3.80/[0.12 - 0.1] = £3.80/[0.02] = £190$$

The present fair value of the share is:

$$P = D_1/[1+r] + D_2/[1+r]^2 + D_3/[1+r]^3 + P_3/[1+r]^3$$

$$P = £2[1.2]/[1.12] + £2[1.2]^2/[1.12]^2 + £2[1.2]^3/[1.12]^3 + £190/[1.12]^3$$

$$P = £2.14 + £2.30 + £2.46 + £135.24 = £142.14$$

EXERCISE 19.4

(a) The most recent dividend paid on shares in WMB plc was 10p per share. WMB dividends are expected to grow at 5% p.a. The required rate of return is 8% p.a. What is the fair price of the shares?

(b) What would be the fair price of the shares if dividend growth were expected to fall to 4% p.a. after three years?

(c) If the rate of dividend growth were to remain at 5% p.a. but with a 20% chance that there will be no dividend growth in a year, what would be the fair price of the shares?

Answers

(a) Using the Gordon growth model:

$$P = D(1+g)/(r-g) = (10 \times 1.05)/(0.08 - 0.05) = 10.5/(0.03) = 350p$$

(b) The first step is to estimate what the share price will be in three years' time, this can be done by means of the Gordon growth model. The dividend expected in four years is:

$$10p \times (1.05)^3 \times 1.04 = 12.04p$$

Using the Gordon growth model, the expected future share price (for three years from the present) is:

$$P_3 = 12.04/(0.08 - 0.04) = 12.04/0.04 = 301p$$

This expected share price is discounted to the present together with the next three dividends in order to estimate the current fair price of the share.

$$P = 10(1.05)/1.08 + 10(1.05)^2/(1.08)^2 + 10(1.05)^3/(1.08)^3 + 301/(1.08)^3$$

$$P = 9.72 + 9.45 + 9.19 + 238.94$$

$$P = 267p \text{ (to nearest whole number)}$$

(c) The equation for the stochastic version of the Gordon growth model is:

$$P = D(1 + pg)/(r - pg)$$

So $$P = 10(1 + 0.8[0.05])/(0.08 - 0.8[0.05])$$

$$P = 10(1.04)/(0.08 - 0.04) = 10.4/0.04 = 260p$$

EXERCISE 19.5

A high technology stock is expected to pay no dividends during the first five years. It is expected to pay a dividend of 50p at the end of year 6. Dividends are expected to grow at 14% p.a. after year 6. The required rate of return is 16% p.a. Estimate the fair price of the shares.

Answer

The first step is to forecast what the share price will be at the end of year 6. The Gordon growth model can be used for this purpose.

$P_6 = 50(1.14)/(0.16-0.14)$

$P_6 = 57/0.02$

$P_6 = 2850$

This predicted price, and the year 6 dividend, are then discounted to the present.

$P = 50/(1.16)^6 + 2850/(1.16)^6$

$P = 1190p$

So the fair price of the shares is 1190p, i.e. £11.90.

(Alternatively: $P_5 = 50/(0.16 - 0.14) = 50/0.02 = 2500$

$P = 2500/(1.16)^5 = 1190p)$

DISCOUNTING CAPITAL GAINS

The future returns to be discounted in ascertaining the fair prices of shares need not be only dividends. Relevant returns include capital gains. Indeed for a share that pays no dividends, the prospective capital gains are the basis for estimating the current fair value. In such a case the current fair price is the discounted value of an expected future price (future prices contain accumulated capital gains).

This became apparent when considering the two-period version of the dividend discount model. In that case the current fair price was the sum of the discounted expected future value and the discounted values of the interim dividends. The model still holds if the expected interim dividends are zero.

Expected future prices indicate prospective capital gains, and capital gains are as much part of the return on shares as dividends. The expected future price, which is discounted, may be based on a dividend discount model or some other means of forecasting the future share price.

EFFECTS OF INVESTMENT OPPORTUNITIES ON THE SHARE PRICE

The Gordon growth model has implications for the relationship between the dividend policy of a firm and its share price. This can be illustrated by the case of a firm that has to choose between (a) distributing all of its profits, and (b) distributing half its profits. In these two cases the rate of reinvestment would be zero and 50% respectively. Suppose that expected next period profits are 20p per share and that the required rate of return is 10% p.a. In the first case the expected rate of growth is zero (ignoring the possibility of growth unrelated to investment). So in case (a) the fair price of the share, using the Gordon growth model, is given by:

$$P = 20/(0.1-0) = 200p.$$

In the second case 50% of profits are reinvested. Suppose that profits can be reinvested to earn 16% p.a. The growth rate of profits (and dividends) would be:

$$0.16 \times 0.5 = 0.08 \text{ (i.e. 8\% p.a.)}.$$

With profits of 20p, there is reinvestment of 10p at 16% yielding 1.6p. Hence profits grow at the rate of $1.6/20 = 0.08$. A constant dividend payout rate implies a growth rate of dividends of 0.08.

Using the Gordon growth model (noting that the next period dividend is expected to be $20p \times 0.5 = 10p$):

$$P = 10/(0.1 - 0.08) = 10/(0.02) = 500p.$$

It can be seen that the decision to reinvest half the profits raises the fair price of the share from 200p to 500p.

The conclusion that lowering the dividend payout rate increases the share price rests on the fact that the profits can be reinvested to earn a rate of return that exceeds the required rate of return. It can be shown that if the best investment opportunity available to the firm offers a rate of return lower than the required rate, reinvestment of profits will tend to reduce the share price. For example if reinvested profits were expected to earn 4% p.a., the expected growth rate of dividends would be:

$$0.04 \times 0.5 = 0.02 \text{ (i.e. 2\% p.a.)}.$$

The fair price of the share would be:

$$P = 10/(0.1 - 0.02) = 10/0.08 = 125p.$$

In this case the reduction of the dividend payout rate (and increase in the reinvestment rate) reduces the fair price of the share from 200p to 125p. When the firm lacks strong investment opportunities, reinvestment of profits will tend to reduce the value of the firm.

Another Perspective on Share Pricing

The analysis of the effects of investment of profits on share prices presents another way of looking at the determination of share prices.

$$P = (E_1/r) + \text{value added by investing profits}$$

where P is the current fair price of the share, E_1 the expected next period's earnings (profits), and r the required rate of return.

The value added by investing profits is the difference between the share price estimated on the basis of all profits being paid as dividends, and the share price estimated on the basis of part of the profits being invested to expand the firm. Consider a case in which the required rate of return is 12.5% p.a. and profits can be invested to earn 20% p.a. The growth rate of earnings (profits) would be:

g = dividend payout rate × return on investment.

In the case in which all profits are paid as dividends, g = 0. As a result the estimated share price would be (using the Gordon growth model and expected earnings of 100p):

P = 100/(0.125 − 0) = 800p (which equals E_1/r).

In a case in which half of the profits are invested, g = 0.5 × 0.2 = 0.1. In consequence the estimated share price would be (using the Gordon growth model):

P = 50/(0.125 − 0.1) = 2000p.

In this case the value added by investing profits is 2000p − 800p = 1200p.
The equation:

P = (E_1/r) + value added by investing profits

helps to explain price-earnings ratios. A high price-earnings ratio may be the result of a low required rate of return, r, or a high value added by investing profits. Stocks whose price-earnings ratios are high as a result of high value added by investing profits are often referred to as growth stocks.

PROBLEMS WITH DIVIDEND DISCOUNT MODELS

A number of difficulties arise when attempting to apply dividend discount models to stock price valuation. One is the issue as to which form of dividend discount model to use. One approach to that problem is to use several forms and use a weighted average of the results with the weighting based on the relative likelihood of a form being the most appropriate. According to a survey carried out by Dukes et al. (2006), the constant dividend version of the model is rarely used by market professionals. Even the more sophisticated versions, such as multi-period models, are used only by a minority. This is despite the tendency for practitioners to use several valuation approaches simultaneously. However a survey by Glaum and Friedrich (2006) indicated that discounted cash flow was considered to be the most important valuation technique. The Glaum and Friedrich survey found that analysts changed the relative importance of different techniques over time. In particular they found evidence that, at a point in time, the favoured technique was the one providing price estimates in line with currently observed prices.

Another issue is the reliability of the estimates of variables such as the required rate of return and the growth rate of dividends. Estimates of the fair price of a share are highly sensitive to small changes in such variables, particularly when the required rate of return and the growth rate of dividends are very close.

Suppose that the most recent dividend was 10p, the expected rate of dividend growth is 9% p.a., and the required rate of return is 10% p.a. The Gordon growth model would estimate the fair price of the share as:

$$P = 10(1.09)/(0.1 - 0.09) = 10.9/0.01 = 1090p.$$

If the expected rate of dividend growth were 8% p.a., the fair price of the share would be estimated as:

$$P = 10(1.08)/(0.1 - 0.08) = 10.8/0.02 = 540p.$$

Small variations in the expected rate of dividend growth or the required rate of return can result in large changes in the estimated fair prices of shares.

Dividends do not normally grow at a constant rate. Estimating the future growth rate of dividends is very difficult and subject to considerable uncertainty. For example Dimson and Marsh (2001) found a very high level of independence of annual dividend growth from one year to the next, thus making annual dividend growth largely unpredictable. The required rate of return is very uncertain because it will differ dependent upon the capital market model used (single-factor capital asset pricing model, multi-factor capital asset pricing model, arbitrage pricing models, etc.). The required rate of return will also vary with the values of beta and expected market return used, and these are subject to considerable uncertainty. For example estimates of beta, and expected market return, will vary with the choice of stock index used to proxy the market portfolio. They will also vary with the time period from which data is taken.

Dividend discount models are inappropriate for companies that pay no dividends, or pay shareholders in other ways. In some cases firms pay money to shareholders by means of repurchasing shares in addition to, or instead of, paying dividends.

The Gordon growth model fails to give meaningful results when the expected growth rate of dividends exceeds the required rate of return. In such cases the estimated share price is negative, and negative share prices are impossible.

Changes in interest rates cause changes in the discount rates used in dividend discount models. A fall in interest rates lowers discount rates and raises the estimated stock prices. It is important to distinguish between interest rate movements caused by changes in real interest rates, and movements caused by changes in expectations of inflation (see Chapter 3 on interest rates and money market investments). A fall in nominal interest rates caused by a fall in real interest rates justifiably indicates a rise in the fair prices of shares. A fall in nominal interest rates resulting from lowered expectations of inflation does not imply a change in fair prices. In such a case the fall in nominal interest rates would tend to be offset by a fall in expected dividend growth. The expected rate of dividend growth, in money terms, comprises an element of real growth and an element of inflation. Failure to make the distinction between real and nominal interest rates, and to take account of the effects of variations in inflation on nominal dividend growth, is referred to as inflation illusion (or money illusion). Campbell and Vuolteenaho (2004a), Feinman (2005), and Modigliani and Cohn (1979) suggested that investment analysts have been susceptible to such inflation bias. The bias implies that stock prices have been too low in periods of high inflation, and too high in periods of low inflation.

In the chapters dealing with behavioural finance, in particular Chapters 2 and 24, it is shown that social and psychological factors distort decision-making. These distorting factors affect investment analysts as well as other participants in investment markets. It seems likely that social influences, cognitive biases, mood, and sentiment affect users of dividend discount models. For example, expectations of dividend growth rates may be influenced by such factors.

Psychological research has indicated that people in a positive mood may underestimate risk and overestimate prospective returns, and vice versa for negative moods (Isen 1997; Nygren *et al.* 1996). Consider the Gordon growth model (equation 4):

$$P = D(1 + g)/(r - g) \tag{4}$$

A favourable mood might increase the estimated dividend growth rate, g. In addition a reduction in perceived risk, or in risk-aversion, would reduce the required rate of return, r. Both of these effects would raise the estimated fair price of the stock, P. To the extent that moods are widely shared, the market as a whole could produce distorted prices. According to the socionomic hypothesis moods are transmitted between people and spread throughout society to bring about widely shared social moods (Prechter 1999; Nofsinger 2005; Olson 2006). So society as a whole can be in either a positive or a negative mood, and stock prices can correspondingly be biased upwards or downwards.

EXERCISE 19.6

(a) Shares in ABC plc have a beta of 1.2, the risk-free interest rate is 4% p.a., and the expected return on the FT All-Share Index is 7% p.a. Use the security market line to estimate the required rate of return on the stock.

(b) The most recent dividend paid by ABC plc is 10p per share, and dividends are forecast to grow at 5% p.a. Use the Gordon growth model to estimate the fair price of the shares.

(c) Why might you be unsure about the accuracy of your estimate of the fair price of the share?

Answers

(a) The equation for the security market line is:

$$r = r_f + \beta[E(R_m) - r_f]$$

The required rate of return on shares in ABC plc is:

$$r = 0.04 + 1.2[0.07 - 0.04] = 0.076 \qquad \text{i.e. } 7.6\% \text{ p.a.}$$

(b) The equation for the Gordon growth model is:

$P = D(1 + g)/(r - g)$

The estimated fair price of the share is:

$P = 10(1.05)/(0.076 - 0.05) = 10.5/0.026 = 404p$ (to the nearest whole number).

(c) Uncertainties as to the reliability of an estimate of the fair price of the share arise from the possibility that (i) the models used are wrong, (ii) the way the models are used is wrong, and (iii) the data used in the application of the models is wrong.

  (i) The capital asset pricing model, from which the security market line is derived, may not be the best asset pricing model. Another model, such as the arbitrage pricing model, might be more suitable. Also the Gordon growth model may not be the most relevant variation on the dividend discount model; and the dividend discount approach to share pricing might not be the most suitable approach.

 (ii) The market portfolio of the capital asset pricing model should include all forms of asset: stocks, bonds, property, human capital. It should also include all such assets from every country. To approximate the market portfolio with a stock index from a single country (as is typically done in applications of the security market line) may provide a very inaccurate figure.

(iii) The data used in the models is based on history and judgement. Even if history reliably repeats itself, it is impossible to know precisely what history tells us. Statistical techniques that aim to estimate values such as beta, based on past values, do not provide single unique numbers but merely provide a distribution of possibilities (it is the average, or mean, of the distribution that is used). Furthermore there may be changes in circumstances that render the past unreliable as a guide to the future. Such factors render variables such as beta, expected market return, and expected dividend growth rates difficult to estimate. As a result the values actually used may not be accurate. To the extent that judgement plays a part in estimating variables, the uncertainty is increased.

ALTERNATIVES TO EXPECTED DIVIDENDS

Expected dividends are seen as appropriate cash flows to discount on the grounds that people invest for the purpose of receiving future cash flows. Dividends are the cash flows that are provided by shares. However where shares do not pay dividends alternative cash flows need to be considered.

One cash flow that can be used is the sum of money available for distribution to shareholders, even though it may not actually be paid to them. This sum of money might be termed Free Cash Flow to Equity (FCFE) and could be measured as:

Net Earnings + Depreciation Expense + New Borrowing

 − Capital Spending − Increase in Working Capital − Debt Repayments

FCFE can then be used in equations that mirror those used by dividend discount models. For example the parallel to the Gordon growth model would be:

$$P = FCFE_1/(r - g)$$

where P is the fair price of the share, $FCFE_1$ is the expected next period FCFE, r is the required rate of return, and g is the expected growth rate of FCFE.

FUSION INVESTING

Arguably one defect of dividend discount models is that they ignore psychological factors in the determination of share prices. Shiller (1984) proposed a model in which a dividend discount model is combined with a term that indicates investor sentiment. The combination of dividend discount models and investor sentiment in the valuation of shares has been referred to as 'fusion investing' (Lee 2003).

In Shiller's model the market price of a share is the discounted value of expected dividends plus a sentiment term. The sentiment term indicates the demand from noise traders who reflect investor sentiment. Noise traders are unsophisticated investors with no particular expertise. When noise traders are bullish prices will exceed their fair (fundamental) values. Conversely when noise traders are bearish prices will be below fundamental values. Sometimes noise traders are largely inactive and prices reflect the fair values indicated by dividend discount models. At other times noise trader sentiment can have a major impact on prices.

Fisher and Statman (2000) measured the investment sentiment of large, medium, and small investors by means of published survey data. They found a negative relationship between sentiment and subsequent equity returns. This suggests that positive sentiment causes stock prices to be too high, with subsequent low returns as prices move down towards their fair levels (fundamental values). Conversely negative sentiment is associated with excessively low prices, and subsequent high returns as share prices move up towards their fundamental values.

Brown and Cliff (2005) also used survey data to measure investor sentiment, and found that investor sentiment affected stock prices. They found that investor optimism led to overvaluation, and subsequent low returns as prices moved back towards their fundamental values. The relationship appeared to be strongest amongst large capitalisation shares with high price-to-book ratios (i.e. large-cap growth stocks). Sentiment was more important in causing overvaluation than undervaluation. This asymmetry could result from the relative difficulty of short selling, so that sales of shares in response to perceived overpricing is difficult with the result that overpricing could be substantial. Underpricing would be more readily corrected since there are no restraints on buying stock.

Baker and Wurgler (2006) measured investor sentiment by means of proxies such as closed-end fund (investment trust) discounts and share turnover. They also found that sentiment affected stock prices such that positive sentiment caused overpricing and subsequent low returns, and negative sentiment was associated with underpricing and subsequent strong returns. They concluded that sentiment was most important in the cases of stocks that were not easily valued by means of dividend discount models. They suggested that the companies whose share prices were most affected by sentiment were those which did not pay dividends or were characterised by being new, small, high growth, unprofitable, or distressed. The valuation of such stocks was seen as being very subjective and hence susceptible to sentiment. On the other hand shares yielding stable dividends were seen as amenable to objective evaluation and their prices were less affected by investor sentiment. Baker and Wurgler concluded that the valuation of shares should incorporate investor sentiment.

In a survey of analysts, Glaum and Friedrich (2006), found that discounted cash flow was the most favoured technique for estimating the fair prices of shares. They also found that analysts paid considerable attention to market sentiment when estimating fair prices. These findings suggest that stock analysts use a form of fusion investing.

CONCLUSION

Active fund management requires investment analysis. An active fund manager may seek to ascertain which shares are underpriced, and which overpriced. Underpriced shares would be candidates for purchase whereas overpriced shares should be avoided. There are a number of approaches to investment analysis. Chapter 14 on the capital asset pricing model described one approach. The current chapter has described another approach, or group of approaches, based on discounting expected future cash receipts. Later chapters will consider the use of accounting information, financial ratios, and technical analysis. In practice investment analysts and fund managers use a number of different methods for estimating the fair prices of shares. The managers of tracker funds do not bear the costs of investment analysis, and the efficient market hypothesis suggests that investment analysis is pointless (see Part 7 on market efficiency).

Dividend discount models are based on the view that investors buy shares because of the income (dividends) to be received from them. The models can be refined in many ways such as allowing for dividend growth, variations in the growth rate, and interruptions to the process of dividend growth. Even very sophisticated models have their problems. Can the analyst be sure that the most appropriate version of the model is being used? Are the values of variables used good estimates?

The accuracy of the variables input into a model is crucial. However good the model is, it will fail if the inputs are poor. Unfortunately the values of variables such as required rates of return and dividend growth rates are subject to considerable uncertainty. Furthermore, even small variations in the values of such inputs can cause large variations in the estimated fair price of a share. Estimation of required rates of return entails the use of capital market theory such as the capital asset pricing model. There is considerable uncertainty about the validity of such models, and the estimates derived from them are subject to statistical error (see Part 4 on capital market theory). Estimates of prospective rates of dividend growth are vulnerable to psychological biases. For example the estimates of dividend growth could be affected by optimism bias and the moods of investment analysts. Even market professionals, such as investment analysts and fund managers employed by institutional investors, are subject to such behavioural biases.

What superficially appears to be a potentially objective means of estimating what share prices should be is, in reality, very subjective. The same could be said of the other approaches to investment analysis. Personal judgement lies at the heart of investment analysis.

Chapter 20

Company accounts and economic value added

OBJECTIVE

The objective of this chapter is to provide knowledge of:

1. The structure of company balance sheets.
2. Profit and loss accounts.
3. Cash flow statements.
4. The analysis and interpretation of company accounts.
5. Tobin's q.
6. Economic value added and other abnormal earnings share pricing models.

Company accounts are important for analysing investments because they provide information about the amount, and sources, of profit. Items in the accounts also provide the data for ratio analysis. The accounts comprise the balance sheet, the profit and loss account, and the cash flow statement.

THE BALANCE SHEET

Table 20.1 shows the balance sheet for a hypothetical company (all values are in £million; numbers in brackets are liabilities).

The balance sheet shows the financial position at a point in time, and is alternatively known as the position statement. The balance sheet could be looked upon as an accounting equation.

Sources of funds = Uses of funds
Shareholders' funds £156m + Creditors £120m = Assets £276m

The more permanent assets are termed fixed assets while the less permanent are referred to as current assets. Intangible assets include items such as patents and goodwill. Goodwill arises from acquiring another company and paying more for it than the value of its assets (more generally,

Table 20.1

Fixed assets	
Intangible assets	30
Tangible assets	<u>234</u>
	264
Current assets	
Stocks	50
Debtors	58
Investments and short-term deposits	6
Cash at bank and in hand	<u>18</u>
	132
Creditors amounts falling due within one year	(120)
Net current assets	12
Total assets less current liabilities	276
Creditors amounts falling due after more than one year	<u>(120)</u>
Net assets	<u>156</u>
Capital and reserves	
Called-up share capital	4
Reserves	<u>152</u>
Shareholders' funds	156

goodwill can be looked upon as the difference between the book value and the market value of a company). Tangible fixed assets include land, buildings, machinery, equipment, and vehicles. The values of tangible fixed assets are stated at their net book value. The net book value of an item is its original (historic) cost minus an estimate of the extent to which it has depreciated in value with use and time.

Current assets are the less permanent items, typically having prospective lives of less than a year. Trade creditors and bank overdrafts, where the debt is to be settled within one year, are subtracted from the current assets to give the net current assets figure. Net current assets are alternatively known as working capital. The sum described as shareholders' funds is the amount that balances the accounts. The money allocated to the category of shareholders' funds is the sum that equates sources of funds with uses of funds. It could be looked upon as the difference between what the company owns and what it owes.

Shareholders' funds are alternatively referred to as the book value of the company. This is not necessarily what the company is worth to the shareholders. The book value is based on Generally Accepted Accounting Principles (GAAP). One of those principles is that assets are usually valued at their historic cost (what the company paid for them). From the historic cost a sum is deducted to reflect the depreciation arising from use and the passage of time. In the case of debtors a provision may be made for bad debts (debtors likely to default), alternatively known as non-performing debts. The value of the investors' shareholdings is determined by the market value of the shares, and is equal to the number of shares issued times the share price. This value is alternatively known as the market capitalisation of the company. The value of shareholders' funds that appears in the accounts is not the same as the value of the shareholdings as determined by the stock market.

The ratio between the market value and the book value is known as the market-to-book ratio, or the price-book value ratio. In the present example, if the share price were 200p and there were 150 million shares in issue the market value of shareholders' investments would be £300 million. This implies a market-to-book ratio of $300/156 = 1.92$. The difference between the market and book values might be looked upon as value added by the management of the company.

THE PROFIT AND LOSS ACCOUNT

The profit and loss account is alternatively referred to as the income statement. It indicates how well the company has performed over a period of time, typically a year. Table 20.2 shows a hypothetical profit and loss account (values in £million; values in brackets are outflows).

The profit and loss account shows the sales income minus the costs of trading (the costs of production and distribution). The sum available for distribution to shareholders is the profit after tax. In Table 20.2 it can be seen that profit after tax is £28 million, of which £14 million is paid to shareholders as dividends and £14 million is retained for investment in the business.

Another useful value is the operating profit, alternatively known as earnings before interest and taxes (EBIT).

EBIT = total revenues − operating costs (including depreciation)

In the present example operating profit (EBIT) is £44 million.

Table 20.2

Turnover – continuing operations	400
Cost of sales (including depreciation of £54m)	(314)
Gross profit	86
Administration expenses	(42)
Operating profit (earnings before interest and taxes)	44
Interest payable	(4)
Profit before taxation	40
Tax on profit	(12)
Profit after tax attributable to shareholders	28
Dividends	(14)
Retained profit for year	14

Earnings before interest, taxes, depreciation, and amortisation (EBITDA) is calculated by adding back depreciation and amortisation to EBIT. Depreciation and amortisation (amortisation is the depreciation of intangible assets) are costs that do not involve immediate cash outlays. EBITDA could be looked upon as the amount of cash created by the company. In the present example:

$$\text{EBITDA} = \text{EBIT} + \text{depreciation} = £44m + £54m = £98m.$$

One justification for the use of EBITDA is that depreciation and amortisation expenses are not cash flows, and they represent the allocations of historic costs rather than expectations of future capital expenditure. In consequence they may not be particularly useful for assessing the ongoing profitability of a company. The current cost of acquiring fixed assets (capital expenditure rather than depreciation) is of greater relevance for this purpose.

Another justification for the use of EBITDA is that it indicates a company's flexibility to respond to changing circumstances. Since depreciation and amortisation are not cash flows, EBITDA is a better measure than operating profit of the cash flow available for new investment. An alternative to EBITDA in this context is operating cash flow.

Earnings per share (EPS) are derived from the profit and loss account, such that:

$$\text{EPS} = \frac{\text{Profit after tax attributable to shareholders}}{\text{Number of ordinary shares}}$$

The EPS can be influenced by exceptional and extraordinary items that impact on profits temporarily. For example the sale of a building will add to profits in a year, but would not be repeated and hence that part of profit does not arise from ongoing business. Investment analysts will often adjust the EPS figure in order to remove the effects of exceptional and extraordinary items. This normalised EPS is referred to as headline EPS.

THE CASH FLOW STATEMENT

The third financial statement in a published set of company accounts is the cash flow statement. This statement shows sources of cash and how the cash has been used. Table 20.3 shows a hypothetical cash flow statement for a period (which is usually a year). The uses of funds (outflows) are shown in brackets.

The item 'Financing' refers to additional finance, for example borrowing more money. The item 'Servicing of finance' refers to repaying debt and paying interest on debt. The uses of funds are alternatively known as applications of funds. It can be seen from Table 20.3 that the largest application of funds was on capital expenditure (i.e. investment in the business).

Cash flow statements can be seen as dealing with three types of activity: operating activities, investing activities, and financing activities. Operating activities provide sales revenue and incur costs of production. Investing activities include purchases and sales of plant, property, and financial assets. Financing activity refers to issuing or redeeming shares and debt, and the payment of dividends. Profits and losses from operating activities must be matched by offsetting net flows from the combination of investing and financing activities.

429

Table 20.3

Net cash inflow from operations	72
Servicing of finance	(4)
Taxation	(12)
Capital expenditure	(114)
Dividends paid	(14)
Financing	<u>74</u>
Increase in cash in the year	26

ANALYSIS OF ACCOUNTS

Accounts may be subjected to cross-section analysis and time-series analysis. One form of cross-section analysis entails common-size statements. In order to facilitate comparison between companies of differing sizes balance sheet items may be expressed as percentages of net assets or total capital employed. Common-size profit and loss accounts could express components as percentages of turnover. Financial ratios can also be used for cross-section analysis, that is for comparing firms.

Time-series analysis may use the techniques of trend statements, ratio analysis, and variability analysis. Trend statements can be used for components of profit and loss accounts. A base date is chosen and the component of the accounts is given a base value of 100. Subsequent years' values are then expressed relative to the base value. A rise of 10% leads to a value of 110 being recorded. The results over a number of years are examined for any patterns or trends. Financial ratios can also be subjected to time-series analysis in order to identify any trends.

Variability analysis aims to measure the dispersion of financial ratios and trend-statement values over time. One approach might be to subtract the lowest observed value from the highest and divide the result by the average. Another approach would entail the division of the standard deviation of observed values by the average value.

A number of changes over time can render time-series analysis difficult. Changes in accounting standards, accounting policies, and accounting practices over time can make the interpretation of apparent patterns difficult. Changes in the composition of a firm's business over time can also pose problems for the interpretation of a time-series. A particular source of change that creates problems of interpretation is price change, in other words inflation (Redhead 1976).

The inflation problem arises because most items in accounts are valued at historic cost, which are the prices originally paid. However historic costs are likely to differ from current prices. As a result historic cost accounting can cause published accounts to be misleading. A highly simplified example can illustrate this.

Suppose that a firm buys 50 units of raw material each year and sells 50 units of finished output. Further suppose that inflation is running at 100% p.a. (i.e. prices double each year). The simplified

Table 20.4

Turnover	£150	(£3 × 50)
Cost of sales	£100	(£2 × 50)
Profit	£50	

Table 20.5

Turnover	£150	(£3 × 50)
Cost of sales	£200	(£4 × 50)
Loss	£50	

profit and loss account for a year in which the raw material costs £2 per unit and the output sells at £3 per unit might look like that of Table 20.4.

The profit and loss account shows a profit of £50. However to maintain the same level of production into the next year requires expenditure of £200 (£4 × 50) on raw materials. The receipt of £150 from sales is not enough to meet the new raw material costs; an extra £50 is needed. Looked at from this perspective there is a loss of £50 rather than a profit of £50. The adjustment of accounts to incorporate the effects of inflation is known as inflation accounting. In the example of Table 20.4, inflation accounting would involve using replacement costs (the costs of replacing the raw materials) rather than historic costs when valuing cost of sales. Using replacement costs rather than historic costs would produce the accounts of Table 20.5.

The use of historic costs is known as FIFO (first in first out) and the use of replacement costs is LIFO (last in first out).

CREATIVE ACCOUNTING AND THE INTERPRETATION OF ACCOUNTS

When interpreting a set of accounts the user should be aware of how accounts can be rendered misleading. The process of attempting to mislead users of accounts is often referred to as 'creative accounting'. The following list indicates some creative accounting techniques.

1. Revenue may be recorded too early. In particular revenue from sales may be recorded in the accounts before the sale is agreed.
2. Bogus revenues may be recorded. For example refunds from suppliers might be recorded as revenues.
3. Income from recurring business may be artificially boosted by the inclusion of one-off gains. There could be a failure to fully separate non-recurring gains from recurring income. Also losses from recurring business might be described as non-recurring.
4. Current expenses could be allocated to a later period. This could take the form of depreciating or amortising too slowly or failing to write off worthless assets immediately.

5. Future expenses may be shifted to a current period. For example depreciation or amortisation may be too rapid.
6. There may be a failure to record all liabilities.
7. Current income may be allocated to a later period.
8. Unrealistic valuations might be given to inventories.
9. Unrealistic bad debt provisions could be made.
10. Items may be held 'off-balance sheet'.

Indications of the range of creative accounting techniques can be found in Schilit (1993), Griffiths (1995), and T.Smith (1996).

From an investor's perspective creative accounting is only important if investment analysts fail to see through it. Breton and Taffler (1995) found that many analysts were unable to spot creative accounting. Foster (1979) found that public revelations of creative accounting caused falls in share prices, which suggests that analysts had not previously been aware of its use by the respective corporations. The deficiency of accounting skills on the part of investment analysts would not matter too much if most firms sought to be fair and accurate in their accounts. Naser and Pendelbury (1992) found that UK auditors believed that creative accounting was widely used. However Aboody et al. (1999) investigated one particular source of creative accounting, namely revaluations of fixed assets, and concluded that upward revaluations were generally not creative fabrications. (Fixed assets could be revalued upwards in order to lower debt to asset ratios and thereby reduce apparent gearing, which could result in being able to borrow on improved terms.)

Chung et al. (2002) investigated whether the extent of institutional ownership of a company's shares influenced the tendency of the company management to manipulate accounts. They found that high institutional ownership was associated with mitigation of the manipulation of accounts. Institutional ownership was found to deter manipulation of accounts in companies with poor returns on their shares (or with low values for Tobin's q), but not in those with good returns (or with high values of Tobin's q). The conclusion of the study was that institutional shareholders appeared to be able to reduce earnings management, which suggests that such shareholders were aware of actual or potential manipulation of accounts (earnings management).

TOBIN'S q

It is possible to give an economic interpretation to a concept related to the price-book value ratio (market-to-book ratio) if assets are valued at replacement cost. The replacement cost is the amount that a company would have to pay to replace its assets.

Where assets are valued at their replacement costs, the price-book value ratio is known as Tobin's q. By dividing shareholder value and replacement cost of assets by the number of shares issued, a ratio of share price to replacement cost per share is obtained.

$$\text{Tobin's q} = \frac{\text{shareholder value}}{\text{replacement cost of assets}} = \frac{\text{share price}}{\text{replacement cost per share}}$$

The constant dividend version of the dividend discount model states that the fair price of a share is given by P in the equation:

$$P = D/r$$

where D is the constant dividend and r is the required rate of return. This can be expressed in terms of market capitalisation where N is the number of shares issued, and hence $P \times N$ is the market capitalisation.

$$P \times N = (D \times N)/r$$

If the rate of return on the replacement cost of assets is R (and bearing in mind that a constant dividend is consistent with all earnings being paid as dividends, i.e. zero reinvestment), this equation can be rewritten as:

$$P \times N = (R \times \text{replacement cost of assets})/r$$

That is:

shareholder value $= (R \times \text{replacement cost of assets})/r$

and   shareholder value/replacement cost of assets $= R/r$

So:

Tobin's $q = R/r$

It can thus be seen that when book value is interpreted as replacement cost, the price-book value ratio can be interpreted as:

$$R/r$$

The benefit of valuation at replacement cost is that book value represents the current cost of investing in the business. What holds in this case does not necessarily hold for the price-book value ratio in general. Valuation in the accounts is generally not at replacement cost.

Sometimes q is used as a guide to investment. When applied to the stock market as a whole it may be expressed as:

$$q = \frac{\text{value of stock market}}{\text{corporate net worth}}$$

It has been suggested that when q is relatively high investors should switch out of shares since companies are likely to sell shares for the purpose of investing in their businesses (since shares are highly valued relative to investment assets). The sale of shares would tend to depress their prices.

Conversely a low q is seen as a buy signal. When q is low it is cheaper for firms to expand by takeovers than by internal growth. The purchase of shares during takeover bids would raise share prices.

THE ABNORMAL EARNINGS SHARE PRICING MODEL

This approach to estimating the fair price of a share decomposes the share price into two components. One component is the book value, and the other is the present value of expected abnormal earnings. Abnormal earnings are defined as the excess of earnings over the required return on the book value. These relationships are described by equations 1 and 2.

$$P_0 = B_0 + A_1/(1+r) + A_2/(1+r)^2 + A_3/(1+r)^3 + \ldots + A_\infty/(1+r)^\infty \qquad (1)$$

where P_0 is the fair price of the share, B_0 is the current book value per share, r is the required rate of return, and A_1, A_2, etc. are the expected abnormal earnings per share in years 1, 2, etc.

$$A_1 = E_1 - (B_0 \times r) \qquad (2)$$

where E_1 is expected earnings per share in year 1. There would be corresponding equations for subsequent expected values of A [e.g. $A_2 = E_2 - (B_1 \times r)$].

The share price estimates produced by the abnormal earnings model are not dependent upon accounting practices. They are not affected by decisions as to how to allocate depreciation over time. This can be demonstrated by means of a (highly) simplified set of accounts.

Suppose that shareholders invest £100 in a company and that the company immediately spends the £100 on capital equipment. The company has net cash flows of £110 in each of two years, and then ceases business at the end of the second year. There are no payments to shareholders until the end of year 2, at which point all assets are paid to shareholders as a dividend. The company has a required rate of return (cost of capital) of 10% p.a. The accounts are shown as Tables 20.6 and 20.7.

Table 20.6

	Year 1	Year 2
Opening book value	100	110
Net cash flow	110	110
Depreciation charge	100	0
Earnings	10	110
Discounted earnings	9.09	90.91
Abnormal earnings	0	99
Discounted abnormal earnings	0	81.82
Dividends	0	220
Discounted dividends	0	181.82

Table 20.7

	Year 1	Year 2
Opening book value	100	160
Net cash flow	110	110
Depreciation charge	50	50
Earnings	60	60
Discounted earnings	54.55	49.59
Abnormal earnings	50	44
Discounted abnormal earnings	45.45	36.36
Dividends	0	220
Discounted dividends	0	181.82

In Table 20.6, all of the depreciation is assigned to year 1. In Table 20.7, the depreciation is equally divided between years 1 and 2.

From Table 20.6 it can be seen that adding together book value (at the beginning of year 1) and discounted abnormal earnings gives £181.82 as the estimated share price (at the beginning of year 1). It can be seen that this equals the discounted value of the expected dividends.

In Table 20.7, the initial capital expenditure is depreciated over two years; £50 in each of the years. Adding together the initial book value and the discounted abnormal earnings gives £181.81 as the fair price of the share. This is the same as the sum from Table 20.6 and the discounted dividends (except for £0.01 due to rounding). It can thus be seen that accounting practice, in terms of the allocation of depreciation charges between years, has no effect on the estimated share price when the abnormal earnings model is used.

As a digression, these observations highlight the difficulty of giving an economic interpretation to accounting values. Comparing Tables 20.6 and 20.7 shows differences in the pattern of earnings and book values. However they have identical cash flows, dividends, and estimated share prices. Both of the accounting practices are acceptable in terms of accounting principles (deferring depreciation beyond the year in which the capital was acquired is referred to as accruals accounting). It thus appears that accounting measures of earnings (profit) and book value do not necessarily have a clear economic interpretation.

Ohlson's Model

Ohlson's (Ohlson 1995) variation of the abnormal earnings model simplifies the abnormal earnings component of the valuation using the approach of the Gordon growth model. A persistence parameter is used to model the pattern of future abnormal earnings. The persistence parameter, denoted by ω, defines the relationship between successive values of abnormal earnings such that:

$$A_{t+1} = \omega A_t$$

The abnormal earnings of one year are ω times the abnormal earnings of the previous year. Ohlson proposed that ω should take values between 0 and 1.

Within equation 1, the term:

$$A_1/(1+r) + A_2/(1+r)^2 + A_3/(1+r)^3 + \ldots + A_\infty/(1+r)^\infty$$

becomes:

$$A_0\omega/(1+r) + A_0\omega^2/(1+r)^2 + A_0\omega^3/(1+r)^3 + \ldots + A_0\omega^\infty/(1+r)^\infty$$

which can be simplified to $A_0\omega/(r + 1 - \omega)$. It might be noted that $\omega - 1$ corresponds to g in the Gordon growth model; they both represent the growth rate of a cash flow.

Thus the abnormal earnings model estimates the fair price of the share to be:

$$P_0 = B_0 + A_0\omega/(r + 1 - \omega) \tag{3}$$

According to the abnormal earnings model, the difference between the share price and book value per share equals the present value of expected abnormal returns. If the share price exceeds the book value, the firm is adding to shareholder value by prospectively making abnormal returns. A share price below book value suggests that the firm's operations reduce shareholder value.

ECONOMIC VALUE ADDED

Economic Value Added (developed by Stern, Stewart, & Co.) is a special case of the abnormal earnings model. The distinguishing feature of Economic Value Added is that it imposes a specific method of accounting. Different methods of accounting produce different measures of book value and earnings (profits) for a year. The method of accounting used with Economic Value Added attempts to give increased economic meaning to measures of book value and earnings. The results should provide a good measure of value added during a year.

One aspect of Economic Value Added is that intangible assets such as research and development, training, advertising, and software development should be treated in the same way as other forms of investment when compiling company accounts. This moves the book value of invested capital closer to a true measure of how much has been invested. However a high degree of subjectivity remains when drawing up accounts (Barker 2001). Judgement is required in deciding which items of expenditure should be treated as investments (i.e. capitalised in the balance sheet). There is also subjectivity involved in decisions such as the choice of the number of years over which such intangible investments should be amortised (depreciated).

To a large extent Economic Value Added is similar to the concept of residual income in that it subtracts the cost of equity capital from profits. Normal accounting profit makes no allowance for the fact that equity capital has an opportunity cost (which is its earnings in the best alternative use). Residual income is obtained by subtracting the opportunity cost of equity capital from accounting profit. The result indicates whether the firm is creating or destroying economic value. Economic value is created if accounting profit exceeds the opportunity cost of equity capital. If accounting profit falls short of the cost of equity capital, the firm is destroying economic value.

Value-added measures evaluate recent management performance based on the ability of management to add value to a company. They are used by investment analysts as indicators of future equity returns, on the premise that past performance is indicative of future performance that should affect the returns on the shares of the company. The question arises as to whether accounting profit or Economic Value Added is the more useful for investment analysis. Biddle *et al.* (1997, 1999) found that accounting profit was more highly associated, than Economic Value Added, with returns on shares. Kyriazis and Anastassis (2007) provided evidence in support of those findings. The results of a survey of stock analysts by Glaum and Friedrich (2006) indicated that abnormal earnings models (residual earnings models) were little used by stock analysts.

CONCLUSION

Thorough investment analysis requires attention to the accounts of the company whose share price is being analysed. The profitability and financial strength of a company are important considerations. An analyst should also be aware of the techniques used by some accountants to present misleading representations of companies. Analysts should be able to see through creative accounting techniques in order to see a true picture of the company.

The consideration of company accounts leads to other groups of investment analysis techniques. Some are based on price-to-book ratios. Tobin's q is a well-known variant of this approach. Others are related to dividend discount models (see Chapter 19 on dividend discount models) but the cash flows to be discounted are expected abnormal earnings. Economic Value Added (developed by Stern, Stewart, & Co.) is a well-known variant.

The interpretation of accounts can be subject to many of the psychological biases identified in the chapters (particularly 2 and 24) dealing with behavioural finance. Many of those biases relate to inaccurate perceptions. There is the possibility that analysts and investors will see what they want to see. Accounts are sufficiently complex and multifaceted to allow for considerable ambiguity and scope for subjective interpretation. Accounting is not a purely objective process. There is considerable scope for opinion, both in the construction and in the interpretation of accounts.

Chapter 21

Ratio analysis

OBJECTIVE

The objective of this chapter is to provide knowledge of:

1. Price-earnings ratios as means of valuing shares.
2. Other market ratios.
3. Financial adequacy ratios.
4. Z scores
5. Ratios as indicators of general market movements.
6. Yield gaps, yield ratios, and 'The Fed Model'.
7. Problems with ratio analysis.
8. The usefulness of following professional investment analysts.

An investment analyst needs to combine all the information provided by ratios and accounts. This may involve a search for trends in these financial indicators together with comparisons with other companies. A thorough analysis of a company would go beyond the ratios and accounts, but this financial data provides an essential component for an analysis of the prospects of a company from the perspective of an investor.

PRICE-EARNINGS RATIOS

Price-earnings ratios provide a means of ascertaining the appropriate price of a stock. The price-earnings ratio is the ratio of the share price to the earnings (profits) per share. This can be expressed by equation 1.

$$PE = P/eps \tag{1}$$

PE is the price-earnings ratio, P is the current share price, and eps is the earnings (i.e. profits) per share.

The price-earnings ratio can be either backward looking or forward looking. In the backward-looking version, eps could be interpreted as the most recent earnings per share. In the forward-looking version, eps is an estimate of earnings per share during the next period. Published price-earnings ratios (in the financial media or company reports) are normally backward looking. For the purposes of investment analysis, it may be necessary to have a forward-looking ratio. (Alternatively the past earnings per share could be used in conjunction with a justified price-earnings ratio relating to the present. The justified price-earnings ratio would be the ratio that the investment analyst believes should prevail in the present. If this justified ratio differs from the published ratio, it follows that the fair price of the share differs from the actual price. The fair price is the price that the investment analyst believes is justified by current information.)

According to a survey of US market professionals carried out by Dukes *et al.* (2006) the use of price-earnings ratios for stock price valuation is widespread. Forward-looking versions are the most popular, but many use current ratios and past earnings. Sometimes the past earnings are averages from a number of previous years. Such trailing earnings averages could be based on figures up to ten years into the past (Harney and Tower 2003). Block (1999) also found a tendency for stock analysts to make considerable use of multiples, such as price-earnings ratios, and found that multiples were more used than discounted cash flow techniques. However Glaum and Friedrich (2006) found discounted cash flow to be more popular and that multiples tended to be used as checks to ascertain that the discounted cash flow results were broadly consistent with the multiples. Glaum and Friedrich found that the relative popularity of valuation techniques changed over time, and that the favoured technique tended to be the one that gave price estimates close to observed current prices.

Estimation of a forward-looking price-earnings ratio, and the simultaneous forecast of earnings per share for the corresponding future period (normally the next period), allows for the estimation of a fair price for the share. This is shown by equation 2.

$$P = PE \times eps \tag{2}$$

Multiplication of the price-earnings ratio (PE) by the earnings per share (eps) provides an estimate of the fair price of the share (P). The fair price of the share is the price that the analyst believes that it should be. If the fair price differs from the actual price, there may be a perceived profit opportunity from trading in the share.

The use of equation (2) requires that PE is estimated separately from eps. The estimation of PE can be carried out in at least four distinct ways. First an average of past price-earnings ratios for the company (whose share price is being analysed) can be used. Second, an average of price-earnings ratios for similar firms can be used. The similarity may be based upon sector, for example the appropriate price-earnings ratio for a firm in the airline sector could be estimated from other companies in the same sector.

A third approach is based on the Gordon growth model. The Gordon growth model can be written as shown in equation 3.

$$P = D/(r-g) \tag{3}$$

439

P represents the fair price of the share, D the expected next dividend, r the required rate of return (comprising a risk-free interest rate plus a risk premium), and g is the expected growth rate of dividends. Dividing both sides of equation 3 by eps gives equation 4.

$$P/eps = (D/eps)/(r-g) \tag{4}$$

P/eps is the price-earnings ratio (PE). The term D/eps is the dividend payout rate; that is the proportion of earnings (profits) paid as dividends to shareholders.

From equation 4, it can be seen that the price-earnings ratio rises with increases in the dividend payout rate and the expected growth rate of dividends. However it should be noted that these two variables are not independent, a higher dividend payout rate involves lower reinvestment of profits and hence might be expected to reduce the growth rate (but there is evidence that higher dividend payout ratios are associated with higher subsequent growth rates; Arnott and Asness 2003; Asness 2005). Equation 4 also shows that the price-earnings ratio is inversely related to the required rate of return. This implies that a rise in interest rates or an increase in the perceived riskiness of the share (which raises the risk premium) would cause a fall in the price-earnings ratio.

Suppose that the dividend payout rate is 0.5, the required rate of return is 12% p.a., and the expected growth rate of dividends is 2% p.a., then putting these figures into equation 4 gives:

$$PE = 0.5/(0.12 - 0.02) = 5$$

If the expected next period earnings per share are £3, use of equation 2 gives:

$$P = 5 \times £3 = £15$$

The fair price of the share is £15. If the market price is below £15, this stock should be considered for purchase.

Regression analysis constitutes a fourth means of estimating the price-earnings ratio. Regression analysis is a technique for ascertaining the statistical relationship between one variable and one or more other variables. Equation 5 illustrates a hypothetical example of the result of a regression analysis.

$$PE = 3 + 2g + 0.5 \ (D/eps) \tag{5}$$

This hypothetical regression equation estimates the price-earnings ratio to be equal to three plus twice the growth rate of company earnings plus half the dividend payout rate. Putting forecasts of the growth rate of earnings, and of the dividend payout rate, into equation 5 yields a number which is the estimated price-earnings ratio.

Whitbeck and Kisor (1963) used a sample of 135 US stocks and produced the following regression equation:

$$PE = 8.2 + (1.5 \times \text{earnings growth}) + (6.7 \times \text{dividend payout rate}) - (0.2 \times \text{standard deviation of earnings})$$

440

[8.2 is referred to as the constant and 1.5, 6.7, and 0.2 as the coefficients]. Whitbeck and Kisor claimed that the equation was useful for selecting stocks (buying when the actual PE is below the PE estimated by the equation on the grounds that the actual stock price was too low – vice versa when the actual PE is above the estimate).

Malkiel and Cragg (1970) regressed the price-earnings ratio on analysts' forecasts of earnings growth rates, estimates of normal earnings, forecasts of future earnings, and expectations of the future variability of earnings. They concluded that such regression equations were not useful for selecting stocks. This was because:

1. The constant and the coefficients varied from year to year (i.e. they were unstable).
2. Analysts' forecasts were not accurate.
3. The equations exclude important firm-specific factors.

EXERCISE 21.1

A company has a dividend payout rate of 0.4, the required rate of return on its shares is 12% p.a., there is a 2% p.a. expected growth rate of dividends, and earnings per share are forecast to be 50p during the next year. Estimate a fair price for the share.

Answer

Using the formula for the price-earnings ratio that states:

$$\frac{P}{eps} = \frac{D/eps}{r - g}$$

$$P/eps = 0.4/(0.12 - 0.02) = 0.4/0.1 = 4$$

With a price-earnings ratio of 4, and earnings per share forecast at 50p, the fair price of the share is estimated to be:

$$P = (P/eps) \times eps = 4 \times 50p = 200p$$

EXERCISE 21.2

Shares in LM plc are currently £40. LM's latest 12-month earnings were £4 per share, of which £2 was paid as dividends (reflecting a constant dividend payout rate of 0.5).

(a) What is the current price-earnings ratio?

(b) If earnings are expected to grow at 8% p.a. and the required rate of return is 12% p.a., what is the justified price-earnings ratio?

(c) Would you buy this share?

Answers

(a) The current price-earnings ratio is £40/£4 = 10

(b) The justified PE = [D/eps]/[r − g] = [£2/£4]/[0.12 − 0.08] = 0.5/0.04 = 12.5

(c) On the basis of a price-earnings ratio of 12.5, the fair price of the share is PE × eps = 12.5 × £4.32 = £54 [£4.32 is used in preference to £4 for earnings on the view that it is the future earnings per share that determines the current share price: £4.32 = £4 × 1.08]. At £40 the share appears to be underpriced and hence should be regarded as a potential purchase.

EXERCISE 21.3

XYZ plc has a constant dividend payout rate of 0.5. The required rate of return is 10% p.a. and the expected rate of dividend growth is 4% p.a. Earnings during the next year are expected to be 20p per share. (a) Estimate the fair price of the share. (b) Is it possible to be sure that an estimate of the fair price is accurate?

Answers

(a) The price-earnings ratio may be estimated as:

PE = 0.5/(0.1 − 0.04) = 0.5/0.06 = 8.33

The fair price of the share is then estimated as:

8.33 × 20p = 167p (to the nearest whole number).

(b) There are a number of sources of uncertainty about the accuracy of the estimate.

(i) Only one method of estimating the price-earnings ratio was used, the method based on the Gordon growth model. Other methods such as sector average, historical average, or regression analysis may have given different answers.

(ii) All of the variables used are subject to uncertainty in their estimation. The dividend payout rate, the required rate of return, the growth rate of dividends, and the future level of earnings cannot be known with certainty. They are estimated on the basis of past values and judgement. Personal judgement is fallible and the past may not be a reliable guide to the future. Besides, the statistical methods for estimating future values from past values provide distributions of possible values rather than specific numbers. The required rate of return is derived from a model such as the capital asset pricing model, which may not be a very reliable model on which to base estimates.

EARNINGS PER SHARE

The earnings-per-share ratio can be broken down into two other ratios. These are return on equity and book-value-per-share. Thus:

Earnings-per-Share = Distributable Earnings/Number of Shares

= (Distributable Earnings/Stockholder's Equity) × (Stockholder's Equity/Number of Shares)

The ratio Distributable Earnings/Stockholder's Equity is the return on equity (ROE). Distributable earnings are the earnings (profits) available for distribution to shareholders. The second ratio, Stockholder's Equity/Number of Shares, is the book-value-per-share. The number of shares typically means the number of ordinary shares.

The return on equity ratio can be broken down into two other ratios. These are the return on assets (ROA) and the asset/equity ratio. The return on assets ratio is:

Distributable Earnings/Total Assets

The Asset/Equity ratio is:

Total Assets/Stockholder's Equity.

The return on equity is thus calculated as:

ROE = ROA × (Asset/Equity).

The return on assets (ROA) can be seen as the product of two further ratios, these being the profit margin and the turnover-of-assets.

ROA = Profit Margin × Turnover of Assets

where

Profit Margin = Distributable Earnings/Sales

and

Turnover of Assets = Sales/Total Assets.

DIVIDEND YIELD, EARNINGS YIELD, AND ROCE

Dividend yield is the dividend per share divided by the share price. The dividend yield shows the income (cash flow) obtained by the investor but ignores the capital gain that accrues as a result of a rise (or fall) in the share price.

Earnings yield is earnings (profits) divided by market capitalisation (which is the share price times the number of shares). It is alternatively measured as earnings per share divided by the share price. Earnings yield reflects the potential for capital gains as well as dividends. If a firm pays a small proportion of its earnings as dividends but invests a high proportion to expand the firm, the result may be faster growth and a consequent rise in the share price.

ROCE (return on capital employed) is earnings divided by the total capital. Total capital includes both market capitalisation (value of shares issued) and long-term debt (value of bonds issued). ROCE is a measure of the percentage return on the total capital used by a firm. An investor could compare this return with the yield on alternative investments such as government bonds. When interpreting earnings yield and ROCE, an investor should take note as to whether the earnings figures being used are pre-tax or after-tax.

OTHER MARKET RATIOS

Ratios that entail the share price or market capitalisation may be referred to as market ratios. The price-earnings ratio is a market ratio. Market ratios that can be used in addition to the price-earnings ratio are the price/cash-flow ratio and the EV/ebitda ratio. To calculate the price/cash-flow ratio it is necessary to ascertain free cash-flow.

To obtain a figure for free cash-flow, depreciation and amortisation charges (and any other charges that are book entries rather than cash expenses) are added to profits after interest and tax paid. From this figure, maintenance capital spending (spending needed to maintain capital) should be subtracted. The figure needs to be adjusted to recognise that profits resulting from changes in unpaid invoices or stock levels do not provide cash-flow. Division of free cash-flow by the number of shares issued gives free cash-flow per share. Division of the share price by the free cash-flow per share produces the price/cash-flow ratio.

EV is an abbreviation for enterprise value, which is market capitalisation plus debt minus cash. Ebitda stands for earnings before interest, tax, depreciation, and amortisation. It is calculated by adding back interest, depreciation, and amortisation (amortisation is the depreciation of intangible assets) to pre-tax profit.

Three other ratios that may be used by investment analysts are the price-to-book, price-to-liquidation, and price-to-sales ratios.

The price-to-book ratio is:
$$\text{Share price}/\text{Book-value-per-share}$$
where book-value-per-share is:
$$\text{Shareholders' funds}/\text{Number of shares}$$

Shareholders' funds amount to the firm's assets minus its liabilities. Book value is alternatively known as net asset value. (The book-to-market ratio is the inverse of the price-to-book ratio, i.e. book-value-per-share/share price.)

The price-to-liquidation ratio is:
$$\text{Share price}/\text{Liquidation value per share}$$
where liquidation value per share is:
$$\text{Liquidation value}/\text{Number of shares}$$

The liquidation value is the sum expected from selling the firm's assets and repaying its debts. The liquidation value per share is based on the firm going out of business and may be regarded as the minimum value of the share.

The price-to-sales ratio is:

$$\text{Share price}/\text{Sales per share}$$

The price-to-sales ratio may be used where a firm has no earnings. It could be used as an alternative to the price-earnings ratio for new firms that have yet to generate any profits, or for firms that are performing too badly to be profitable.

FINANCIAL ADEQUACY RATIOS

Three sets of ratios are used as indicators of the ability of a firm to meet its financial obligations. First, financial leverage ratios show the extent to which the firm is financed by debt. Second, coverage ratios assess the ability of the firm to meet the obligations arising from its debts. Third, short-term solvency ratios indicate the ability of the firm to repay debts becoming due over the coming year.

Financial Leverage (Gearing) Ratios

Debt provides risk for a company since servicing of the debt must be undertaken whatever the operational profitability of that company. There is a possibility that operational profits are insufficient to meet debt interest and repayments with the result that the firm becomes bankrupt. This risk rises with increased importance of debt in the financing of the firm; that is with increased leverage. (Debt arises from bank loans and the sale of bonds. The sale of shares does not constitute debt; the firm has no legally binding commitment to make payments to shareholders.)

There are many forms of financial leverage ratio. Two possibilities are as follows:

Long-Term Debt to Equity $=$ Long-term debt/Shareholders' equity and

Total Debt to Equity $=$ (Long-term debt $+$ Current liabilities)/Shareholders' equity

Long-term debt is debt that is repayable more than a year into the future and current liabilities constitute debt that matures in a year or less. Long-term debt includes bonds issued by the firm. For the purposes of the ratios, bonds are usually valued at book value. Book value is the price at which the bonds were originally sold. Shareholder's equity is the total value of all the shares held by shareholders. Often each ratio is calculated twice, once using the original issue price of the shares and once using the current market price of the shares. High ratios indicate high leverage and hence risk. Ratios may alternatively divide debt by shareholders' equity plus debt.

Coverage Ratios

Coverage ratios are concerned with the assessment of the ability of a firm to meet interest and other inescapable payments. They relate the resources available for the payments to the level of payments due. The interest coverage (or debt coverage) ratio is:

(Earnings $+$ Interest charges paid)/Interest charges paid

Since earnings are quoted net of interest payments, it is necessary to add the interest payments back in order to ascertain the total sum available for the payment of interest.

A more comprehensive coverage ratio that takes lease payments into account is the fixed-charge coverage ratio which is:

$$\frac{\text{Earnings} + \text{Interest charges paid} + \text{Lease payments}}{\text{Interest charges paid} + \text{Lease payments}}$$

Short-Term Solvency Ratios

Before buying a stock an investor might wish to feel sure that liquidity problems are not likely to appear. Four of the ratios that may be calculated in order to assess the adequacy of a firm's working capital are the current ratio, the acid-test ratio, the inventory-turnover ratio, and the accounts-receivable-turnover ratio.

The current ratio is shown as:

Current ratio = Current assets/Current liabilities

Current assets are assets either in the form of cash, or due to be converted into cash during the coming year (i.e. liquid assets). Current liabilities are either payable already, or due to be payable in the coming year. The current ratio thus provides an assessment of the company's ability to meet its immediate liabilities.

Current assets include inventories, and in some circumstances there may be difficulty in converting inventories into cash. The acid-test ratio (alternatively known as the quick ratio or liquid asset ratio) recognises this by removing inventories from current assets.

Acid-Test Ratio = (Current assets − Inventories)/Current liabilities

The inventory-turnover ratio indicates the speed with which inventories can be converted into cash. The accounts-receivable-turnover ratio shows how quickly the firm's customers pay their bills. These factors also affect the ability of the firm to meet its commitments.

Z SCORES

Altman (1968) generated a Z score, which uses financial ratios to produce a number which is purported to provide a method of gauging whether a company is likely to fail in the short or medium term. Ratio 1 is the ratio of working capital to total assets. Ratio 2 is the ratio of accumulated retained earnings to total assets. The third ratio is that of ebit (earnings before interest and taxes) to total assets. Ratio 4 is market capitalisation to total liabilities. Ratio 5 is sales to total assets.

For publicly listed companies (i.e. companies whose shares are traded on a stock exchange):

Z = (1.2 × Ratio 1) + (1.4 × Ratio 2) + (3.3 × Ratio 3) + (0.6 × Ratio 4) + (1.0 × Ratio 5)

A healthy company should have a Z score of 2.99 or more; an unhealthy one a score of 1.81 or less. Some would take the view that the direction of change in the Z score is more important than the current value.

Other analysts have used different ratios and weightings. For example Marais (1982) developed a Z score for UK companies. Four ratios were used. Ratio 1 was the ratio of pre-tax profit plus depreciation to current liabilities. Ratio 2 was that of current assets less stocks to current liabilities. The third ratio was that of total borrowing to total capital employed less intangibles. Ratio 4 was stocks to sales.

There are drawbacks to the use of Z scores. One drawback is that the method is not suitable for some types of company, namely utilities, property companies, and companies in the banking, insurance, and financial sectors. A second drawback is that Z scores tend to favour long-established companies relative to new ones. A third problem is that some of the accounting values are capable of manipulation by management; at the least differences in accounting practices will influence ratios.

There is empirical evidence that Z scores are useful for predicting bankruptcies, and for helping investors to choose shares that will perform well (and avoid those that will perform badly). Such evidence comes from Altman (1968), Altman *et al.* (1977), Taffler (1983, 1997), Clark and Weinstein (1983), Aharony *et al.* (1980), and Katz *et al.* (1985). However there is no economic or accounting theory underlying the models, which can be accused of data mining. There are those who doubt the usefulness of the models, for example Pratt (1993) and Zavgren *et al.* (1988).

RATIOS AS INDICATORS OF GENERAL MARKET MOVEMENTS

Ratios can be used not only for analysing individual stocks but also for forecasting movements in the stock market as a whole. Bleiberg (1989) sorted quarterly US price-earnings ratios for the period 1938–87 into quintiles (top 20%, second 20%, etc.). He found that periods of low price-earnings ratios were followed, on average, by strong market performance whilst periods with high ratios tended to be followed by poor performance. For example periods when the ratio was in the bottom 20% were followed, on average, by market rises of 29.79% over the following two years. Periods when the ratio was in the top 20% were followed, on average, by falls of 0.68% over the subsequent two years.

Bierman (2002) suggested that the price-earnings ratio would have more explanatory power if it were adjusted for liabilities and cash holdings. If companies have debts, buyers of shares accept responsibility for those debts. The value of a debt, per share, should be added to the share price to obtain an effective purchase price. The share price used in the price-earnings ratio should be the market price plus the value of the debt, which the buyer of the share is committed to paying. Conversely the presence of cash holdings effectively reduces the share price since part of the purchase price of the share could be returned to the shareholder.

The appropriate measure for earnings per share is also controversial. It is often suggested that the earnings in a single year are not appropriate since they reflect temporary factors such as the position in the business cycle, and that a cyclically adjusted measure of earnings per share should be used. Harney and Tower (2003) found that, for the purpose of predicting stock market performance, earnings averaged over long periods were more useful than the most recent earnings figures.

Asness (2005) used the average real earnings over the previous ten years to produce price-earnings ratios for the S&P 500 over the period 1927–2004. For each rolling ten-year period (1927–36, 1928–37, 1929–38, etc.) the initial price-earnings ratio was compared with the real return over the following ten years. It was found that subsequent returns were inversely related to the initial price-earnings ratios. With initial price-earnings ratios of less than 10.1 the average (median) annual return was 10.9%, whereas for initial price-earnings ratios above 19.9 the subsequent average annual return was −0.1%.

Market yield (the ratio of dividends to share prices) also appears to bear some relationship to subsequent market performance. Campbell and Shiller (1998) found that in the US market yields were indicative of market movements over the following ten years. A period with a high dividend yield tended to be followed by a strong market performance over the following ten years. They found a similar relationship in a number of other countries.

The use of the stock market's dividend yield as an indicator of subsequent market performance suffers from problems. One of these problems is that some companies repurchase shares instead of paying dividends. The repurchase of shares is an alternative to dividends as a means of transferring money to shareholders. Another problem is that some companies do not pay dividends, choosing to reinvest profits instead. A change in the proportion of companies following such a practice can impact on the market dividend yield although the dividend yield of other companies may remain unchanged.

THE YIELD GAP, THE YIELD RATIO, AND 'THE FED MODEL'

The yield gap is a long-standing approach to rating equities (shares) relative to bonds. It is expressed either as:

Yield gap = dividend yield − gilt yield or as:
Yield gap = gilt yield − dividend yield

The gilt yield is usually measured as the redemption yield on long-dated gilts (UK government bonds) and the dividend yield is measured as the stock market's dividend payments divided by the aggregate value of shares.

One problem with this approach is that, whereas the gilt redemption yield is the whole return on gilts, the dividend yield is not the whole return from equities. To obtain the whole return on equities, in money terms, it is necessary to add the real rate of capital growth and the rate of inflation (the product of these amounts to the capital growth in money terms) to the rate of dividend yield. Whilst the real rate of capital growth varies little over time, inflation can vary substantially. In consequence changes in the yield gap are more indicative of variations in inflation rates than of relative real returns. The gilt yield incorporates the expected rate of inflation whereas the dividend yield does not. Investment rules may suggest that investors should switch from shares to bonds if the gilt yield rises relative to the dividend yield. However such a guide to investment is not valid if the relative rise in the gilt yield merely reflects higher expected inflation.

The same argument concerning inflation relates to the yield ratio. This is the ratio of the redemption yield on gilts to the dividend yield on shares. Whilst a high ratio is seen as indicative of a strong performance from gilts relative to shares, and hence as a sign to favour gilts against shares, it may simply reflect expected inflation rates. Despite this reservation some studies have found that the yield ratio does have some value as an indicator of future relative investment performance between equities and gilts (Wadhwani and Shah 1993; Clare *et al.* 1994; Levin and Wright 1998).

The yield gap, and yield ratio, can alternatively be expressed in relation to index-linked gilts. This eliminates the distortions introduced by inflation. The gilt yield and dividend yield would now both be expressed in real terms. The only remaining lack of comparability would come from the fact that capital growth should be added to dividend yield in order to obtain the total real return from equities, whilst the redemption yield on index-linked gilts constitutes their entire real return.

Another possibility is to compare the redemption yield on gilts with the inverse of the price-earnings ratio of the aggregate stock market. This approach is popular in the United States where it is referred to as 'The Fed Model', despite the absence of evidence that the Federal Reserve uses it. The earnings yield (the reciprocal of the price-earnings ratio) is compared with the redemption yield on government bonds. Either the difference between them, or their ratio, can be used. If the difference or ratio is at variance from the expected value, it may be concluded that the general level of the stock market is incorrect. The analyst may then ascertain the change in the level of stock prices required to move the earnings yield into the appropriate relationship with the redemption yield on government bonds. However this is based on the assumption that the mispricing is in the stock market rather than the government bond market. It is also subject to the criticism that the redemption yield on government bonds comprises compensation for inflation as well as a real rate of return, whereas the earnings yield is purely a real yield. A change in the government bond yield caused by a change in expectations of inflation should not imply a change in the earnings yield since stocks would compensate for inflation by way of increased price appreciation.

Consider equation 4 again:

$$P/eps = (D/eps)/(r-g) \tag{4}$$

where P is the stock price, eps is earnings per share, D/eps is the dividend payout rate, r is the required rate of return, and g is the expected growth rate of dividends. An increase in the yield on government bonds raises r and lowers P/eps, but if the rise in government bond yields (and hence r) is the result of higher expected inflation there should be an offsetting rise in g. The increase in the discount rate could be matched by a rise in the expected growth rate of dividends (and hence growth rate of stock prices). The failure to recognise the need to adjust g is referred to as inflation illusion and can lead to mispricing of equities in the aggregate (Asness 2003; Campbell and Vuolteenaho 2004a; Feinman 2005).

PROBLEMS WITH RATIO ANALYSIS

Care needs to be taken when using ratios for investment analysis. One source of difficulty is that companies use differing accounting methods in the measurement of earnings and other values.

Reported values would be affected by accounting practices. Variations in ratios between companies may reflect differences in accounting methods rather than more fundamental differences. Also differences in reporting dates can reduce the usefulness of ratios for comparing companies. The aggregation of accounts across a group of companies can hide the problems of some subsidiaries within the group.

The effects of differences in accounting practices would be particularly extreme where creative accounting is used. Creative accounting involves the deliberate abuse of the subjectivity inherent in accounting to select accounting policies or make assumptions in order to bias the figures in the direction chosen by management. At a less extreme level figures could be distorted by window dressing, for example advancing or delaying transactions so that they are included in, or excluded from, the end of year accounts.

Looked at from the viewpoint of some financial ratios a firm may be seen as healthy while other ratios may indicate that it is not healthy. There is no established means of weighting the relative importance of different ratios. There will therefore be ambiguity with regard to the evaluation of the company. Also some analysts believe that it is the direction of change in the ratios, rather than the current values of the ratios, that reveals most about a company. Such analysts take the view that trends in ratios over a number of years are more important than their values in a particular year.

There is a risk that the focus on ratios distracts the analyst from the multitude of other factors that are pertinent to the potential success of a company. It should also be borne in mind that the past is not necessarily a reliable guide to the future. A company may be successful because it responds to poor financial ratios by reorganising its structure and procedures.

It is important not to confuse a good company with a good investment. Firms with strong ratios, robust earnings growth, good sales potential, and quality management are good companies. If all these positive attributes are fully (or more than fully) reflected in the share price, the share is not necessarily a good investment. Good investments are shares that increase in price more than other shares (Solt and Statman 1989). A good investment is a share whose price inadequately reflects its value. Such an undervalued share may be from a good company or a weak one. An undervalued share provides gains when its value becomes fully realised. Counter-intuitively good companies may be the worse investments if it is the case that many investors confuse good firms with good investments and hence buy the shares of good firms, thereby driving up their prices too far.

FOLLOWING PROFESSIONAL INVESTMENT ANALYSTS

As an alternative to carrying out investment analysis themselves, individual investors may choose to follow the recommendations of professional analysts. Analysts typically possess better information, about a company, than private investors. Their assessments of companies, and of the prospective earnings of those companies, might be expected to be superior to that of non-professionals. The analyses that are made public are those of stockbrokers and investment banks. A purpose of making them public is to attract business from investors. Stockbroker and investment bank analysts are known as sell-side analysts. Institutional investors also use investment analysts, who are referred to as buy-side analysts. The opinions of buy-side analysts are not made public.

Analysts will make earnings predictions, which may be useful to investors who use price-earnings ratios when making investment decisions. Analysts also make trading recommendations as to whether particular shares should be bought or sold. Private investors may choose to base their decisions on the recommendations of analysts. One problem that arises is that it may be difficult to interpret and compare the recommendations of different analysts. There is a lack of consistency in the terminology used. There are also sources of ambiguity. To what investment horizon does a recommendation relate? What expected percentage outperformance is a buy recommendation based on?

Another difficulty faced by individual investors relates to the timeliness of recommendations. Analysis is not static. Analysts constantly review their opinions as new information becomes available. Their big clients may be phoned or e-mailed to inform them of updates to recommendations. The general public is not likely to receive such updates. Private investors who follow analysts' recommendations may be using out-of-date recommendations.

Another source of uncertainty faced by individual investors concerns the accuracy of the predictions and recommendations of professional analysts. In terms of predictions of earnings, analysts are often thought to be a little conservative (e.g. Degeorge *et al.* 1999). This is because company managements like to beat the earnings estimates, and this is more readily achieved if the estimates are low. Analysts like to please company managements on the grounds that access to information would be more readily provided.

It is unclear whether professional analysts are any good at stock selection. The studies referred to in Part 7 on market efficiency tend to suggest that either there is no ability to pick winners, or that the gains from picking winners are eliminated by transaction costs. For example Barber *et al.* (2001) found that if an investor without transaction costs bought stocks recommended as a 'strong buy' during 1985 to 1996 and held them until the rating was downgraded, the investor would have outperformed the market. However when transaction costs are considered, the investor would have underperformed the market.

Francis *et al.* (2004) found that analysts' forecasts of earnings were more accurate than forecasts produced by the mechanical application of earnings models. However they reported that the earnings forecasts of analysts tended to be too optimistic in that their forecasts overestimated earnings. They also reported a common cognitive bias, which appeared to reduce the ability of analysts to fully incorporate new information when revising earnings forecasts with the result that there was underreaction to new information. This cognitive bias is consistent with the conservatism and anchoring biases identified by behavioural finance.

Cornell (2001), in a study of Intel, threw doubt on the usefulness of the recommendations and forecasts of investment analysts. It was observed that a negative announcement regarding revenue caused a fall in the stock price of about 30%. Cornell concluded that this was an overreaction such that the stock could not have been accurately priced both before, and after, the announcement. Following Intel's announcement of lower expected revenue growth a number of analysts lowered their buy/sell recommendations, which seems perverse if the stock price was either too high before the announcement or too low after it. A change from sell to buy recommendations might have been expected. No analyst raised their recommendation. Cornell examined a number of analysts' reports on Intel and found that none contained sufficient detail to determine what the analysis was based on.

One source of doubt about the accuracy of analysts' recommendations is the relative absence of recommendations to sell. Overwhelmingly recommendations are positive or neutral; they are rarely negative. Yet one might expect recommendations to be approximately evenly spread between buy, neutral, and sell. It seems likely that this imbalance arises from conflicts of interest. One conflict of interest arises from the need for access to information from the management of a firm whose shares are being analysed. Analysts may be reluctant to give negative recommendations for fear that an annoyed management will cease to be accommodating in relation to the provision of information. Francis *et al.* (2004) cite anecdotal evidence indicating that analysts who produce unfavourable forecasts of earnings experience reprisals by way of blocked or withheld communications with corporate managers.

Analysts at investment banks have another source of conflicts of interest. The companies whose shares are being analysed may be clients (or potential clients) of the investment banking arm of the bank. A poor stock recommendation by an analyst could result in the loss of the company as a client for investment banking services. The investment banking people may put pressure on analysts with a view to encouraging positive recommendations. Evidence consistent with such a conflict of interest is provided by Michaely and Womack (1999) and by Francis *et al.*

Investment bankers are not the only source of pressure. Gibson (2004) suggests that analysts in both stockbroking and investment banking firms face pressure from equity clients and traders. If a stockbroker (or investment bank) has clients with large holdings of a particular share, those clients would be unhappy to find that an analyst working for the stockbroker downgrades the recommendation on the share. A recommendation downgrade is likely to result in a fall in the share price. For similar reasons traders working for the stockbroker or investment bank might be upset by a downgrade. Some institutional investors, particularly hedge funds, pay their fund managers on a performance-linked basis. Such managers may see pressure on analysts to improve recommendations as a means of raising the performance of shares held in their funds. Analysts are likely to come under pressure from clients and traders to maintain a positive recommendation on a share.

Investors following the recommendations of analysts should also appreciate the motivations of those analysts. A significant portion of an analyst's pay is based on reputation (Kim and Nofsinger 2004; Gibson 2004). For example institutional investors conduct annual surveys in which they evaluate analysts. There is a risk that analysts focus more on promoting themselves than on working on their analyses.

Investment analysts can be expected to exhibit a wide variety of opinions about the fair prices of shares. There are many techniques and models for valuing shares (various dividend discount models, abnormal earnings models, financial ratios, and so forth). There are also many sources of data. At numerous points judgement is required as to which techniques or models to use, which data to use, how to interpret the data, how to analyse the data, and so forth. The results of statistical analysis are affected by the choice of time periods and observation intervals. The results of analysis are also affected by the choice of capital market theory to be used (the one-factor capital asset pricing model, multi-factor capital asset pricing models, arbitrage pricing theory, and so forth). With so much judgement involved it is to be expected that there would be a wide variety of opinions amongst investment analysts about what share prices should be. It is also clear that there is plenty of scope for manipulating the results of investment analysis for the purpose of achieving desired forecasts and recommendations. The chapters in Part 7 dealing with evidence relating to market efficiency discuss other studies concerning the usefulness of analysts' recommendations.

CONCLUSION

Financial ratios have been one of the most favoured tools of investment analysis for a long time. They provide a means of interpreting company accounts, and constitute a step towards an objective analysis of accounting information. They can shed light on a number of characteristics of a company, such as its profitability, its financial strength, and its ability to provide a flow of dividends to shareholders. They can also indicate whether the stock market as a whole is fairly priced, particularly relative to other investment assets such as bonds.

Ratio analysis does not provide an entirely objective and reliable means of investment analysis. Ratios are derived from company accounts. The figures used in the construction of ratios are likely to be influenced by the accounting procedures adopted by the company. To the extent that subjective judgement is used in the production of accounts, that subjectivity will affect ratios derived from the accounts. There is no established way of ranking the importance of different ratios, so if they give contradictory messages the analyst must make subjective judgements. Although individual ratios may seem to give unambiguous messages, the aggregate of ratios can give very ambiguous information. In the presence of ambiguity, the psychological biases described in the chapters on behavioural finance (especially Chapters 2 and 24) can strongly influence the reasoning of investment analysts.

The psychological biases can affect professional analysts, irrespective of their techniques of analysis. The individual investor may decide to look at the recommendations of the professionals on the grounds that the professionals have more expertise, resources, and time for investment analysis. However professionals could be influenced not only by psychological biases but also by conflicts of interest. They are also likely to be influenced by each other. People are normally influenced by the opinions of others. In the same way analysts are likely to move their forecasts into line with those of other analysts. There may be a rational reason for this on the grounds that the other analysts may have based their forecasts on information that is not generally available. Conformity might, alternatively, be the result of herding behaviour. If you were wrong when everyone else was wrong, your error may be forgiven. If you were wrong when others were right, your job may not be secure.

Chapter 22

Technical analysis

OBJECTIVE

The objective of this chapter is to provide knowledge of:

1. The nature of technical analysis.
2. Behavioural finance as a theory of technical analysis.
3. Chart patterns.
4. Dow theory.
5. Elliot wave theory.
6. Other technical indicators.
7. Criticisms of technical analysis.
8. Research evidence.

THE NATURE OF TECHNICAL ANALYSIS

Technical analysts believe that stock markets have a dynamic of their own, independent of outside economic forces. Technical analysis is the study of internal stock market information. Any relevant outside information is seen as being embodied in stock market data so that there is no need to look for information outside the market. Technical analysts study the market itself, not the external factors that might be reflected in the market prices and volumes. The information produced by the stock market, particularly in relation to prices and trading volumes, is what technical analysis is concerned with. Whereas fundamental analysis (such as dividend discount models and ratio analysis) uses economic data that is usually obtained from sources other than the stock market, technical analysis uses data from the stock market itself.

Technical analysts base trading decisions on prior price and volume data in order to determine past market trends and patterns from which predictions of future market behaviour are derived. Technical analysts usually attempt to forecast short-term price movements. The methodology rests on the belief that stock market history tends to repeat itself. If a certain pattern of prices and volumes has previously been followed by particular price movements, it is suggested that a repetition of that pattern will be followed by similar price movements. Technical analysts assert

■ **454**

that the study of past patterns of variables such as prices and trading volumes allows investors to identify times when particular stocks (or sectors, or the overall market) are likely to fall or rise in price. The focus tends to be on the timing of purchases and sales. Most technical analysts use charts of stock prices (and frequently also data on volumes of buying and selling).

Levy (1966) suggested that technical analysis is based on the following assumptions:

1. The market price of securities (such as shares and bonds) is determined by supply and demand.
2. Supply and demand are determined by numerous rational and irrational factors. These include both objective and subjective factors.
3. Apart from minor fluctuations the prices of individual securities, and the level of the market as a whole, tend to move in trends which persist for significant periods of time.
4. Trends change in reaction to shifts in supply and demand. These shifts in supply and demand can be detected in the action of the market itself.

Assumptions 3 and 4 are controversial. Supporters of the efficient market hypothesis (EMH) take the view that new information is very quickly reflected in security prices. If information is very quickly reflected in prices, trends do not have an opportunity to emerge. Technical analysts believe that new information does not arrive in the market at a single point in time; they take the view that new information comes to the market over a period of time. For example new information may be available first to insiders, second to professionals, and lastly to the public. As the information gradually becomes more widely available, the share price gradually moves to its new equilibrium price. Technical analysts look for the beginning of a movement from one equilibrium price to another without attempting to predict the new equilibrium price. They attempt to profit from forecasting the direction of movement; that is they try to identify trends and profit from them.

Whatever the reason for a change in price, if the share price responds sufficiently slowly, a trend emerges. A slow response of prices to shifts in supply and demand provides the potential to profit from technical analysis.

BEHAVIOURAL FINANCE AND TECHNICAL ANALYSIS

An alternative underpinning for the technical analysts' belief in trends comes from the theories of behavioural finance. Batchelor and Ramyar (2006) point to psychologists' findings on the illusion of control. People find it difficult to accept that events are random, and will imagine the existence of patterns among random events. The illusion of control is particularly likely in circumstances wherein people are expected to maintain an appearance of competence, for example amongst traders in financial markets. Fenton-O'Creevy et al. (2003) reported an experiment in which professional traders were given the task of using a computer mouse to control the position of a dot on a computer screen. Changes in the position of the dot were random, the mouse was not even connected to the computer, but the traders believed that they were influencing the position of the dot.

Behavioural finance suggests that people have a conservatism bias, which causes them to be slow to update their beliefs in response to new information. They might initially under-react to news so that prices will fully reflect new information only gradually. As a result there is momentum in stock market movements; in other words trends appear. The disposition effect can also slow adjustment to new information and thereby allow trends to emerge as gradual adjustment takes place. The disposition effect causes investors to be reluctant to sell losing positions. Since stocks that show loses are sold reluctantly and slowly, the downward price movement is gradual. Gradual price movement produces a trend.

Other behavioural finance theories that can explain some types of pattern examined by technical analysts are 'sample size neglect' and representativeness. It appears that many people treat a small sample as being just as indicative as a large one. They may trade on the basis of a short succession of pieces of news. For example a short run of good company earnings news might cause share purchases that result in price increases when the length of the run of earnings news is insufficient to produce statistically significant conclusions. A company with a recent short run of good earnings news may be seen as representative of companies with strong long-run potential. The upward movement is reversed when the run of good news stops (Chopra *et al.* 1992). So a pattern of momentum (trends) and reversals emerges.

Representativeness might be seen as judgement based on stereotypes. The mind makes the assumption that situations sharing similar characteristics are alike. A long-term upward price movement starts as a short-term upward price movement. Representativeness causes investors to assume that a short-term upward move is indicative of a forthcoming long-term upward trend (conversely for falls). Many investors buy shares that have recently experienced price rises. Investors like to buy recent winners since they believe that a past price trend is representative of a future price trend. Dhar and Kumar (2001) found that private investors tended to buy stocks that had risen in price during the three months prior to purchase. DeBondt (1993) found that the market forecasts of private investors reflected the recent performance of the market.

There is research indicating that recent stock market performance affects attitude to risk, and hence the willingness to invest (Shefrin 2000; MacKillop 2003; Grable *et al.* 2004). A recent rise in share prices makes investors more risk tolerant, and hence more prepared to invest. A recent fall raises risk-aversion, and hence creates an inclination to sell. These changes in attitude to risk reinforce existing market movements, and thereby perpetuate trends. Price rises lead to share purchases and hence to further price rises; price falls result in sales which further depress prices. Momentum, the tendency for a market to continue to move in the current direction, is reinforced by changes in attitude to risk.

The sample size neglect bias (alternatively known as the law of small numbers) is associated with the 'gambler's fallacy'. The gambler's fallacy is the belief that if numbers appear at random, there is some mechanism that ensures that each number appears on the same number of occasions (Nofsinger 2002a). There is a belief that a self-correcting mechanism exists to ensure this. For example people affected by the gambler's fallacy might expect that since the number 17 has not been drawn in a lottery for several weeks, it is likely to be drawn next time. Of course the likelihood of it being drawn continues to be based on a random process; the past frequency has no significance for future occurrences. The gambler's fallacy may help to explain the reversal patterns that technical analysts look for. It may be the case that investors who are subject to the gambler's fallacy feel that a succession of rises must soon be followed by falls, or vice versa. If the gambler's fallacy leads to the belief that rises and falls are approximately equal in number, investors subject to this bias will tend to sell after a few rises (or buy after a few falls). Their trades may then cause the price reversals they expect.

Representativeness may help to explain the trends that technical analysts attempt to exploit. Technical analysts might be regarded as seeking to profit from the psychological biases, such as representativeness, of other investors. However technical analysts could also be subject to psychological biases. If representativeness is based on the assumption that situations sharing similar characteristics are alike, technical analysts who look for standard chart patterns that indicate future share price changes may be influenced by the representativeness bias. Looking for chart patterns that are repetitions of previous patterns might be looking for stereotypes on which to base judgements.

The proposition that markets exhibit trends may be interpreted as a view that markets have memory. Today's price behaves as if the market remembers previous price movements. This might be justified by observing that investors and traders have memories; and the market comprises investors and traders. Fenton-O'Creevy *et al.* (2005) point out that a residue of emotion and reasoning is carried forward from one investment decision to the next. If a feeling of optimism or pessimism has been engendered by investments, the feeling will impact on subsequent investment decisions.

Benartzi and Thaler (1995) suggest that the reference price is the share price that an investor compares to the current share price. Investors anchor on their reference prices in that they measure profits and losses in relation to the reference price. It may be the case that a large number of investors, in a share, anchor on the same reference price; for example the highest price reached over the previous 12 months. This imparts memory to the market, which effectively remembers the reference price. This could help to explain the concept of trading ranges, which are much used by technical analysts. A trading range entails a price fluctuating around a central value, and within limits (the limits are known as support and resistance levels). The central value of a trading range may correspond to the reference price.

Zielonka (2004) gave support to the view that behavioural finance can provide a rationale for technical analysis. A sample of technical analysts was presented with a number of technical analysis rules. The rules were of three types. Some were rules already used by technical analysts (and which could be explained in terms of behavioural finance principles). The second set of rules was invented by the researcher, and the rules were based on behavioural finance principles. The third set of rules was invented by the researcher, and was not based on principles of behavioural finance. The technical analysts saw the first two sets of rules as having high predictive power. The third set of rules was seen as having low predictive power. In other words the technical analysis rules based upon, and explicable in terms of, behavioural finance were seen as having strong predictive value whereas the rules not based on behavioural finance were not.

Behavioural finance can be used to explain the use of volume data by technical analysts. The evidence on overconfidence indicates that overconfidence is associated with high volumes of trading, and that overconfidence is also associated with rising stock prices.

PRICE CHARTS

The following exposition aims to describe some of the more frequently used charts.

Figure 22.1 shows a bar chart. For each day, or other chosen time interval, there is a vertical line. The top of the vertical line indicates the highest price reached during the day and the bottom shows the lowest price. There is a short horizontal line on each vertical line. This horizontal line indicates the closing price on the day. Japanese candlestick charts also indicate the opening price. Marshall

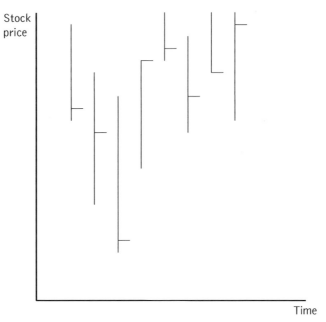

Figure 22.1

et al. (2006) examined the profitability of Japanese candlestick technical analysis using the stocks that comprised the Dow Jones Industrial Average over the period 1992–2002. They found that the candlestick trading strategies were not profitable; the candlestick analysis lacked predictive power.

Figure 22.2 illustrates a line chart. It involves daily closing prices joined by straight lines to make a graph.

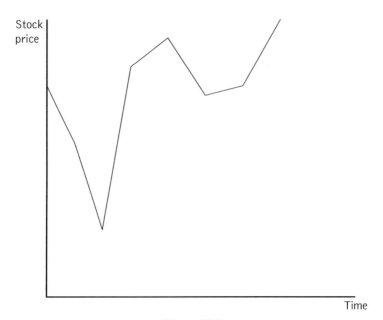

Figure 22.2

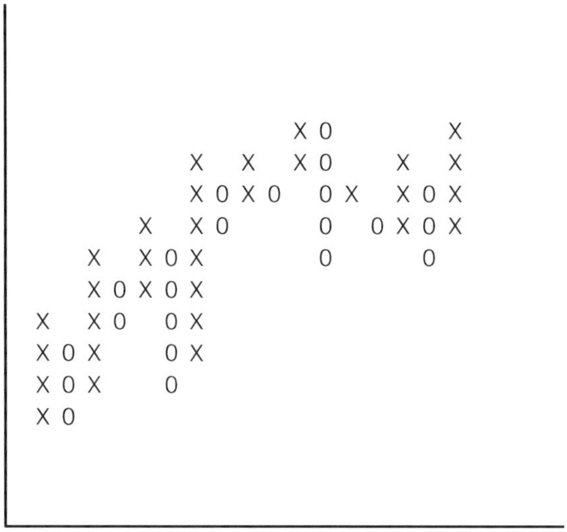

Figure 22.3

Figure 22.3 illustrates a point-and-figure chart. A price interval is decided upon, for example 10p. For every successive one-interval increase in price, an X is entered in the same column (going upwards). If the stock price falls by 10p from a previous high, an O is entered in the next column. Each successive 10p price decline is then indicated by a O (going downwards) in the same column. When the price rises by 10p above the lowest price, an X is entered in the next column. An unusual aspect of point-and-figure charts is that although the horizontal axis plots time, it is not in regular intervals of time.

One aim is to find areas where price reversals are frequent since this is seen as presaging a substantial price movement (break out from a trading range). This would appear as a horizontal stretching out of the chart.

CHART PATTERNS

There are a vast number of chart patterns employed by technical analysts. What follows is merely indicative of some of the patterns. Line charts will be used for the examples.

Price Channels (Trend Channels)

Figure 22.4 illustrates a rising trend channel. The share price remains within the channel shown by the upward sloping parallel lines until point A. At point A, it breaks out of the channel in a downward direction. The chartist may interpret this as a signal to sell the stock since it is seen as forecasting a fall in the stock price. Trend channels could also be horizontal or downward sloping. In these cases a breakout in the upward direction could be seen as indicative of a price rise, and would therefore be a buy signal. Horizontal trend channels with parallel bounds are sometimes referred to as trading ranges.

Behavioural finance provides reasons for thinking that trends are possible. Conservatism suggests that investors do not respond quickly to new information, since they take time to change their opinions in the light of new evidence. In consequence price adjustments to new information may

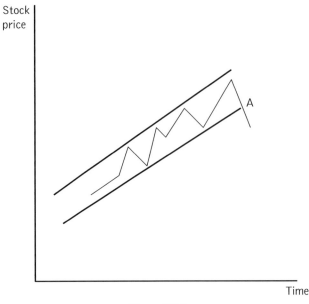

Figure 22.4

be gradual, and gradual adjustments provide trends. Confirmation bias, the tendency to give too little weight to evidence that contradicts an existing opinion, reinforces conservatism. Another source of an emerging trend may be the disposition effect, this is the preference for selling an investment that is showing a profit rather than one that is making a loss. This could hamper upward price adjustments and delay downward price movements. Price adjustments are thus slowed with the result that trends appear (Grinblatt and Han 2001).

Once a trend has started representativeness and overconfidence could render it persistent. Representativeness can lead investors to believe that recent price movements are indicative of the future direction of price movements; it thus induces buying in a rising market and selling in a falling one. The result is positive feedback trading (buying because prices have risen and selling because they have fallen) which reinforces price trends. Overconfidence causes investors to forget that markets are uncertain and to believe too firmly in their forecasting powers. An overconfident investor may be inclined to invest (or disinvest) heavily on the basis of a view arising from representativeness.

The lines constituting the bounds of a trading range are not necessarily parallel. Figure 22.5 illustrates a triangle. In this case converging lines bound the series of stock prices. The upward breakout at point A might be interpreted as an indication of subsequent price rises.

Price channels are often interpreted in terms of the bounds providing limits to the extent of variation of share prices, such that share prices tend to remain within the bounds. The rationale may be in terms of investors seeing share prices as being too high when they rise above the higher bound (so shares are sold and as a result prices fall) and too low when they fall below the lower bound (so that investors buy and thereby push prices back up into the channel). It may be that investors who regret not having sold before the previous price fall regard a rise to the upper bound as providing a good selling opportunity, and investors who regret not having bought prior to the price rise see a price fall as providing a good buying opportunity. Such an interpretation would

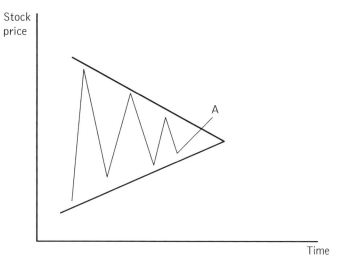

Figure 22.5

see the upper bound as a resistance level and the lower bound as a support level. These patterns may be based on horizontal price channels (trading ranges). Figure 22.6 illustrates such a channel.

However sometimes the lower bound is seen as the resistance level, and the upper bound as the support level. Such support and resistance patterns may be based on the premise that people remember past share prices and may regret lost opportunities. Users of this approach suggest that for a period of time stock prices trade within the range bounded by the support and resistance levels. If the share price breaks out of the range in an upward direction people who had not previously bought regret not having done so. As a result they would buy if the price re-enters the trading range. There would be buying at the top of the trading range, the support level. This buying will tend to prevent the share price falling below the support level.

If the stock price falls below the bottom of the trading range, the investor regrets not having sold. Investors decide to sell if they can do so within the trading range. If the stock price returns to the trading range, many investors will sell. The bottom of the trading range becomes an upper limit to the share price. This is the resistance level. If the share price rises above the resistance level, many investors will sell with the result that prices fall.

It could be the case that the upper price is seen as the resistance level and the lower price as the support level, until the price makes a significant move out of the trading range. When that happens, the upper price level becomes the support or the lower price level becomes the resistance. Support and resistance levels reflect a market memory, which allows past price history to influence current price prospects.

If sufficient traders took the same view about the resistance and support levels of prices, the resistance and support levels could become self-fulfilling prophecies. Resistance and support levels

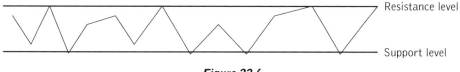

Figure 22.6

emerge because traders believe in their existence and trade accordingly. The shared opinion might arise from the social influences identified by behavioural finance. People in a group have a tendency to conform to each others' opinions. Traders constitute a group of people who interact with one another and form shared opinions. Those shared opinions may include resistance and support levels.

Resistance and support levels could also be explained in terms of the behavioural finance concept of anchoring. Faced with uncertainty, which is frequently the case in financial markets, people will tend to anchor on numbers presented to them. Those numbers become benchmarks against which prices are compared. If a trader is presented with resistance and support price levels, anchoring could cause that trader to treat those levels as benchmarks. Trading is then conducted in relation to those benchmarks.

Another possible explanation comes from the observation of price-end biases. There is evidence that investors favour price quotes ending in 0 or 5, most particularly 0. In the absence of a bias, each of the ten end numbers would experience approximately 10% of quotes. Varki *et al.* (2006) found that more than 25% of price quotes ended in 0. One explanation lies in the reduction of the 'cost of thinking' (Shugan 1980). Investors trade off the benefits of accuracy against the mental cost of achieving that accuracy. Estelami (1999) found that cognitive difficulty is a function of price ends, with price ends of 0 requiring the least computational effort. Despite their greater use of sophisticated investment analysis techniques, the professional investors managing institutional investments are prone to the price-end bias as well as private investors.

The microstructure of stock markets provides a means of introducing the price-end bias into share prices. In particular many orders to buy or sell are limit orders. Limit orders to buy specify purchase at a stated price, or a lower price if possible. Limit orders to sell specify sale at a stated price, or a higher price. An investor making a market order (an order that does not specify a price) to buy would be matched against the best limit order to sell. A market order to sell is matched against the most favourable limit order to buy. Many trades entail triggering limit orders. If the limit orders tend to have price endings of 0, many trades will be at prices ending in 0.

If the price-end bias results in limit orders that specify prices ending in 0, there may be a tendency for prices to oscillate between prices ending in 0. Market orders to buy would push prices up until the limit orders to sell at a price ending in 0 are triggered. Market orders to sell push prices down until the market orders are matched against limit orders to buy at a price ending in 0. Share prices would move between two prices, each ending in 0, with limit orders serving to prevent prices moving outside those upper (resistance) and lower (support) limits. Limit orders to sell would satisfy market orders to buy, thereby stemming further upward price movement. Limit orders to buy would satisfy market orders to sell, thereby preventing further price falls. The result is the type of trading range used by technical analysts, with resistance and support prices at share prices ending in 0.

Evidence consistent with the existence of resistance and support levels comes from a study by Cyree *et al.* (1999). They investigated whether psychological barriers exist in the values of stock indices, specifically at index levels ending in 00. They researched stock indices in several different countries and found statistically significant barriers for most of the stock indices studied.

Reversal Patterns

Chartists frequently believe that when the direction of a share price (or market index) changes, characteristic chart patterns may develop as the turn occurs. The head-and-shoulders configuration

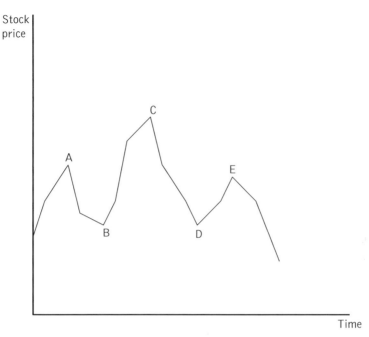

Figure 22.7

illustrated by Figure 22.7 is one of those reversal patterns. The peak at C is the head, and the lower peaks at A and E are the shoulders. When the share price falls from E to a level below D, further price falls are forecast. In other words, such an eventuality constitutes a sell signal.

The volume (quantity) of trading in shares may also play a role in the interpretation of a head-and-shoulders pattern. It is suggested that the shoulder at A follows a substantial rise in the market and is based on a heavy volume of trading. The surge in prices to the head at C is expected to be accompanied by a lighter volume of trading. Following another correction (i.e. fall) the price rises again, to E, but on a much lighter volume of trading.

One explanation of the head-and-shoulders pattern is based on behavioural finance. Investors, under the influence of psychological biases such as representativeness and overconfidence, participate in positive feedback trading. That is, they invest on the basis that the recent direction of price movement will continue. Recent share price rises are seen as indicating future rises with the effect that investors buy more shares. These share purchases cause further increases in stock prices; the forecasts become self-fulfilling. The result is an upward trend in share prices. Some investors, less influenced by the psychological biases, take profits periodically by selling shares. As a result there are dips in the share price. These dips are followed by a resumption of the upward trend as the psychological biases reassert their influence. Each new share price peak is higher than the previous one, and each new trough is higher than the previous trough.

A partial explanation of the process comes from the behavioural finance concept of anchoring. Mussweiler and Schneller (2003) examined the effects of charts with salient highs and salient lows. The peaks of a head-and-shoulders pattern are examples of salient highs. Mussweiler and Schneller found that both private and professional investors anchored on the salient highs and lows. Salient highs and lows became comparison standards to which price expectations were assimilated. They also found that the process of assimilation was based on a selective accessibility mechanism similar to the operation of a confirmation bias. Subsequent to a salient high investors would look for, and give emphasis to, information that justified the expectation of a price rise. The converse followed a salient low. Investors anchor on peaks and expect them to be repeated; what goes up will go up again. Vice versa for troughs.

A chartist may see the head-and-shoulders pattern as indicating that the psychological biases, causing the positive feedback trading, are losing their strength. The first sign is the failure of a trough to be higher than the previous one (point D, sometimes referred to as the neckline). The second sign is a peak below the previous peak (point E, a shoulder). The third sign is a fall in the share price below the previous trough (below D). The chartist may then conclude that the positive feedback trading, caused by psychological biases, has run its course and that there is no longer an upward impetus to the market. A peak below a previous peak could be seen as indicating that the anchoring effect is weakening, or that it is being dominated by an underlying downward trend. On the grounds that the psychological biases would have led to an unjustifiably high stock price, the trading message drawn by a chartist would be that shares should be sold since they are due for a fall in price. Converse reasoning would explain the use of a reverse head-and-shoulders, which indicates that stock prices will rise and that therefore shares should be bought. Osler (1998) tested the head-and-shoulders pattern on the Dow Jones Industrial Average and concluded that the pattern was not a useful predictor.

Figures 22.8 to 22.11 illustrate some other reversal patterns looked for by chartists. In each case the dotted line indicates the general pattern that the actual charts (unbroken lines) are interpreted as revealing.

Moving Averages

Technical analysts use not only prices relating to individual dates, but also moving averages. A moving average is an average of a series of previous prices, for example the average of the last 200

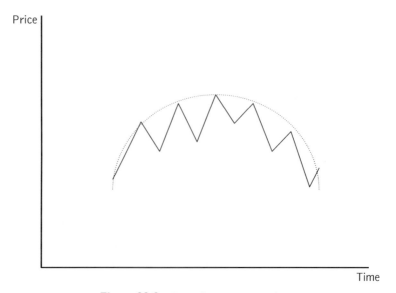

Figure 22.8   *Rounding top reversal*

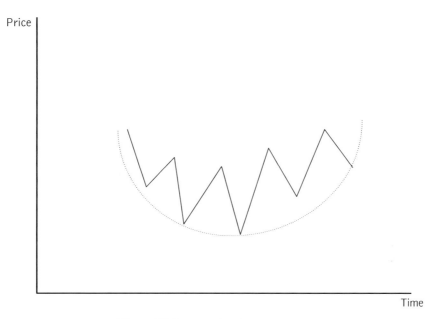

Figure 22.9 *Rounding bottom reversal*

daily prices. (Each day the oldest price is removed from the calculation of the average and the most recent price introduced). Chart patterns can be based on moving averages as well as daily prices.

One popular technique is to use moving averages and daily prices on the same chart. If the current price is a predetermined percentage above or below the moving average, a buy or sell

Figure 22.10 *Double top reversal*

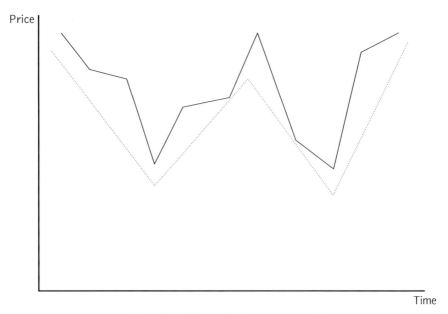

Figure 22.11 *Double bottom reversal*

signal may be indicated. For the market as a whole, the proportion of stocks currently above their moving average is seen as an indicator of general market sentiment. Points at which a chart of daily prices crosses a chart of moving averages are seen as significant. For example, a daily price chart that crosses a moving average chart from below might be seen as providing a buy signal. The signal may be dependent upon whether the moving average is rising or falling at the time. Each investor will have his or her individual trading rules.

A study by Brock *et al.* (1992) suggested that moving average strategies could be successful. They found that stock returns following buy signals from a moving average rule were higher than those following sell signals. However Ready (2002) found that the moving average rule would not, in practice, be profitable because of transaction costs and the fact that stock prices would have already moved by the time the trader could act upon the signal. Bessembinder and Chan (1998) concluded that, although moving averages have some forecasting power, they could not produce profitable trading strategies when transaction costs are taken into account. Sullivan *et al.* (1999) found that the most profitable trading rule tended to change over time. In a UK study Hudson *et al.* (1996) also found that moving average technical trading rules had predictive value, but that when transaction costs were considered the trades would not have been profitable. They found that the predictive value was stronger for sell signals than for buy signals, and that the predictive value appears to have declined over time. Mills (1997) also found the decline in the predictive value over time in the UK. Taylor (2001) used techniques similar to those of Brock *et al.* and concluded that, net of transaction costs, it was unlikely that trading profits were available for the tradable assets studied. Taylor also found that simple autocorrelation (serial correlation) between consecutive returns had greater predictive power than the strategies used by Brock *et al.*

DOW THEORY

One of the oldest technical tools is the Dow theory. Its main purpose is to forecast the future direction of the overall stock market. The Dow theory is based on the belief that market movements are analogous to movements of the sea. It sees three simultaneous movements in the market. Daily or weekly fluctuations correspond to ripples. Secondary movements (which last a few months) are the waves. Primary trends of a year or more are analogous to tides. It is the primary trend that is referred to as either a bull or a bear market. The daily or weekly movements are seen as having little or no predictive value. However secondary movements in stock indices are used to forecast changes in the direction of the primary trend.

A bull market is characterised by both high and low points of successive secondary movements moving in an upward trend, especially if this were accompanied by rising volumes of stocks traded. Each new peak is above the previous peak, and each new trough is above the previous trough. Trading volume should increase with moves made in the direction of the primary trend; for a rising primary trend, volume should be heavier for advances than for falls. The market is sustained by rising support levels and would break through successively higher resistance levels. When the market eventually falls through a support level and then is unable to bounce back beyond a previous resistance level, the beginning of a bear market is signalled.

A bullish primary trend is seen as being initiated by informed investors, who anticipate a recovery. Subsequently uninformed investors start buying, thereby reinforcing the upward trend. While the uninformed investors continue to buy, the informed investors start to sell. Sales by informed investors cause the temporary downturns (the waves). This is consistent with theories of the emergence of stock market bubbles (Kindleberger 1989). Support for the Dow theory has been provided by Glickstein and Wubbels (1983).

ELLIOT WAVE THEORY

Elliot wave theory sees markets as moving in cycles. There are very long-run cycles that last many decades. Superimposed on these are cycles of shorter duration. In turn there are cycles of even shorter duration superimposed upon the latter cycles. This pattern of cycles within cycles continues down to cycles of very short duration.

Analysis of the Elliot cycles is based on waves. Each cycle has eight waves. Five waves carry the market up and three waves carry it down. At the end of the cycle the market is higher than at the beginning. This is illustrated by Figure 22.12. It can be seen that the first five waves include three up-waves and two down-waves. The peak is then followed by three waves, two of which are down-waves.

The pattern of waves entails a succession of support and resistance levels, in a similar way to Dow theory. Elliot wave theory assumes that markets are driven by investor psychology. After a fall in prices investor optimism is seen as growing slowly at first but later the optimism becomes excessive and leads to a bubble at which prices peak. The bubble bursts and the market is then carried lower in the wave pattern.

Elliot wave theory is sometimes supplemented by the use of Fibonacci numbers. Fibonacci numbers seem to fit the pattern of development of a range of natural phenomena from the reproduction of petals on a flower to the formation of galaxies. Some people believe that they can

467

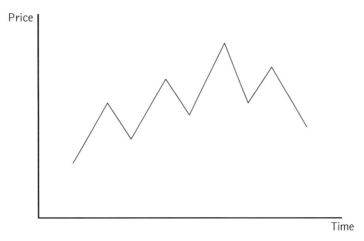

Figure 22.12

also explain stock market developments. Fibonacci numbers are taken from a sequence in which each number is found by adding together the previous two in the series. The sequence runs 1, 1, 2, 3, 5, 8, 13, 21, 34, and so forth. Users of the theory employ various combinations and ratios of Fibonacci numbers to predict market tops and bottoms, along with support and resistance levels. Elliot wave theory seems to lend itself to the use of Fibonacci numbers since it sees cycles as comprising eight waves, five on the upswing and three on the downswing. These are Fibonacci numbers. Batchelor and Ramyar (2006) found no evidence that Fibonacci numbers worked in US stock markets over the period 1914–2002.

Although Batchelor and Ramyar (2006) found no empirical support for technical trading based on Fibonacci numbers, they suggested that the principles of behavioural finance could explain the use of those numbers. The relevant principle is that of anchoring. They refer to Chapman and Johnson (2002) in pointing out that if traders are presented with numbers, albeit irrelevant numbers, before making a judgement then those numbers could become starting points when thinking about prospective prices. (However it could be argued that if a sufficient number of traders take them seriously, the numbers could become relevant as a result.)

Tversky and Kahneman (1974) presented subjects with a number determined at random by a wheel of fortune, and asked whether the percentage of African nations belonging to the United Nations was above or below that number. The subjects were also asked to estimate the actual percentage. There was a high correlation between the number from the wheel and the estimates of the percentage membership. The subjects had anchored on the irrelevant number from the wheel when making their estimates of the percentage membership.

OTHER TECHNICAL INDICATORS

The forecasting techniques of technical analysts are not limited to charts. Technical analysts also use filter rules, relative strength, and short interest ratios amongst many other indicators.

A filter rule states that an investor should buy when a stock price (or market index) has risen by a predetermined percentage above a previous low point. Conversely the investor should sell when the price or index falls by a particular percentage below a previous high. The percentages are at the discretion of the investor, but should be established prior to the market movements.

Relative strength is measured by the ratio of a stock price to a market index. Changes in the ratio are taken to indicate buying or selling opportunities. A momentum trader would take a rise in the ratio as a signal to buy the stock (and a fall as a signal to sell). A contrarian would interpret a rise in the ratio as a sell signal (and a fall as a buy signal).

The short interest ratio is the ratio of short sales (selling borrowed stock) to total trading. A rise in the ratio has two opposing interpretations. Some technical analysts see a rise in the ratio as indicative of bearish sentiment, and hence as constituting a sell signal. Others interpret a rise as a buy signal on the grounds that the short positions will have to be covered by stock purchases. These stock purchases would tend to push up stock prices.

The trin statistic is the ratio of the average trading volume in declining stocks to average volume in rising stocks. Ratios above 1 are considered bearish on the grounds that a relatively high volume of trades in declining stocks is indicative of net selling pressure. Conversely ratios below 1 are seen as bullish. Apart from the trin statistic, generally trading volume is seen as indicative of the strength of a trend. A price movement accompanied by a relatively high quantity of trades is seen as more significant than one in a low volume market.

To a technical analyst the breadth of the market is the extent to which movement in a market index is reflected widely in the price movements of individual stocks. The most common measure of breadth is the difference between the number of stocks that rise and the number that fall. If the difference is large, the market movement is seen as strong since it is widespread. For example a market rise is regarded as stronger if a large majority of stocks are rising as opposed to the rise being the result of price increases for a few large capitalisation stocks.

Some technical analysts watch mutual fund cash holdings. If mutual funds (unit trusts and OEICs) have large cash holdings, technical analysts might forecast a market rise on the grounds that the cash will be used to buy shares. This demand for shares would tend to push prices up. Conversely low mutual fund cash holdings are seen as a bearish signal. There is little scope for purchases by mutual funds to support the market. Edelen and Warner (2001), Neal and Wheatley (1998) and Warther (1995) found that an increased flow of money into equity funds was followed by rises in share prices.

Another measure used by technical analysts is the put-call ratio. Put options give the right to sell shares at a specified price, and are bought by investors who expect share prices to fall. Call options give the right to buy shares at a specified price, and are bought by investors who expect share prices to rise. The ratio of puts bought to calls bought is used as an indicator of the expectations of investors. However technical analysts differ as to their interpretation of the ratio. Some see a high put-call ratio as bearish on the grounds that it indicates that investors (on balance) expect price falls. Other technical analysts take a contrarian view and see a high put-call ratio as a buy signal. Contrarian analysts base their analysis on the belief that investors are usually wrong.

Simon and Wiggins (2001) investigated a trin indicator, the put-call ratio, and an index of volatility (VIX, which is based on the volatility implied by prices of options) as technical indicators of market sentiment. They found that these technical indicators had predictive power for stock index futures prices. In particular they concluded that traders could make profits from contrarian strategies based on these indicators. The view taken is that when market sentiment is very negative, favourable news may lead to large cash inflows and hence price rises. Contrarian investors may invest when sentiment is poor in order to make profits when the cash inflows occur. The researchers suggested that the findings for stock index futures markets could be generalised to stock markets.

Since there are many technical trading techniques, most technical analysts use a number of techniques (both chart and non-chart). It is typical for technical charts to contain several indicators. Technicians often include as many price and volume indicators as are reasonable on one chart. It is unlikely that all the techniques point to the same conclusion. In the absence of consistency between the different indicators, a technical analyst is likely to use judgement to seek a consensus of the signals.

SOME CAVEATS

The foregoing should be seen as merely indicative of the wide range of technical analysis techniques employed. However what might appear as mechanical trading rules are in reality subject to a high degree of subjective interpretation. Technical analysts differ as to which charts, or other indicators, they use. They also differ as to the interpretation and significance to be assigned to a particular chart pattern or indicator. They even differ as to whether a particular chart pattern is present at all. It has been suggested that the recommendations of technical analysts can be so heavily qualified that they could be seen as consistent with any outcome (Batchelor and Ramyar 2006). Rules are often both vague and complex.

If technical analysis is seen as subjective and ambiguous, it may be the case that technical analysts are the victims of the psychological biases identified by behavioural finance. For example the representativeness bias causes people to see patterns where there are none. The confirmation bias leads to events being interpreted as supportive of one's views. The hindsight bias distorts memory, which becomes selective in only remembering what a person wants to remember with the effect that past analysis is recalled as successful.

When using trading rules an investor should be wary of 'data mining'. Observation of large numbers of figures from the past will always throw up some patterns and rules that would have been profitable in the past. Purely as a matter of chance some rules would have been profitable; since there are an infinite number of potential rules the laws of chance would suggest that some would have been profitable. The acid test is whether such patterns and rules will turn out to be consistently profitable in the future (a valid test of a pattern or rule cannot be on the facts from which it was hypothesised; it has to be tested on new data).

It is possible for a trading rule to continue working simply because it has become a self-fulfilling prophecy. If a number of technical analysts believe that a pattern signals a price rise, they will buy. Their purchases push up the price and hence bring about the forecast price movement. Patterns could cease to repeat themselves because of changes in the market. It is not unusual for a trading rule to be abandoned because it no longer works.

Chart patterns may be self-destructing, which means that if a successful pattern becomes widely used it will cease to be successful. If a pattern indicates an upward trend, and if the pattern is known by many investors, that pattern could induce trading by many investors as soon as it becomes apparent. The result could be that the price immediately moves to its 'correct' level with the effect that the trend does not emerge. A pattern, which in the past has successfully predicted a gradual upward price trend, could induce many purchases with the effect that the stock price immediately increases to its new level. The widespread anticipation of the trend eliminates the trend. There may be a continual search for new profitable trading rules, followed by destruction of successful rules through overuse. The profits available from successful rules would accrue only to the first investors to use them. An implication is that well-known rules are unlikely to be useful.

The idea of resistance and support levels raises a paradox. Suppose that 200p is seen as a resistance level for a particular share. No one would buy at 199p since there is apparently no scope for a rise of more than 1p, but plenty of scope for a price fall. If no one is prepared to buy at 199p, then 199p becomes the resistance level. Hence no one would be prepared to buy at 198p. So the conundrum develops implying lower and lower prices. If investors are to buy (or hold) at 199p, they must believe that the price can rise above 200p.

GAMES PEOPLE PLAY

If one takes the view that the fundamentals that should determine share prices are factors such as the level of savings available for stock market investment, the profitability of businesses, and the rates of return available on other investments (e.g. interest rates) then technical analysis may be seen as focusing on irrelevant factors. Technical analysts could be seen as playing games with each other, probably with professionals tending to outplay amateurs. Much of technical analysis is concerned with forecasting the behaviour of other technical analysts. Those who are the first to identify (and act upon) the trend or indicator that everyone else is looking for will be able to profit when the others act upon it. Double guessing the behaviour of other investors is more important to a technical analyst than assessing the true values of shares based on factors such as the expected profitability of companies.

Such points were identified by J. M. Keynes (1936) in *The General Theory of Employment, Interest and Money*. A few quotes from the book may be of interest.

> The actual, private object of the most skilled investment to-day is 'to beat the gun', as the Americans so well express it, to outwit the crowd, and to pass the bad, or depreciating, half-crown to the other fellow. (p. 155)
>
> For it is, so to speak, a game of Snap, of Old Maid, of Musical Chairs - a pastime in which he is victor who says *Snap* neither too soon nor too late, who passes the old maid to his neighbour before the game is over, who secures a chair for himself when the music stops. (pp. 155–6)
>
> We have reached the third degree where we devote our intelligences to anticipating what average opinion expects the average opinion to be. (p. 156)

Technical analysis is often much derided. Its usefulness is often dismissed because of the absence of statistical evidence supportive of its effectiveness, the absence of convincing explanations as to why it should work, and the body of evidence that supports the weak form of the efficient market hypothesis (according to which past price movements cannot be used to forecast future price movements).

However the fact that many investors use technical analysis provides a justification for learning about it. To the extent that successful investing requires an understanding of how other investors think (their investment behaviour influences price movements), it is useful to have an appreciation of the technical analysis that some of them would be using.

Also technical analysis could, at times, produce self-fulfilling prophecies. If many users of technical analysis believe that prices will go up, and buy as a result, their behaviour will cause the expected price rise. Conversely if technical analysis charts overwhelmingly suggest falling prices, and their users are induced to sell, the sales would cause the predicted price falls. So in some circumstances technical analysis may be valid simply because many investors believe in its validity.

IMPLICATIONS OF CROWD PSYCHOLOGY

From the perspective of fundamental analysis, technical analysis appears to be very narrow in its focus. Fundamental analysis considers a multitude of pieces of information about the economy and about individual companies. Fundamental analysis also uses many models, such as dividend discount models and earnings multipliers (price-earnings ratios). In contrast technical analysis largely focuses on just one variable, namely the share price (or the level of a stock index).

Pepper and Oliver (2006) suggest that the narrow focus of technical analysis can be justified in terms of the nature of crowd psychology. When people behave as a crowd, their behaviour is different from what would be observed if they operated as individuals. Fundamental analysis (and much of finance theory) sees investors as operating as rational individuals. The behaviour of the investment community is seen as the aggregate of the actions of millions of individuals each rationally operating in their individual self-interests. However when people start behaving as a crowd, different patterns of behaviour emerge. A crowd does not use sophisticated models to conduct a detailed analysis of a complex set of pieces of information. A crowd reacts to things that are simple and easily observed. In the context of stock markets, crowds may react to share prices (and stock index values) to the exclusion of all other information. If technical analysis is seen as a means of forecasting the behaviour of investors when behaving as a crowd, technical analysis may be justified in its focus on prices.

Flanegin and Rudd (2005) suggest a cyclical pattern of crowd psychology, which generates a cyclical movement in stock markets. They also propose that technical trading rules can detect the presence of such cycles. They say that bulls and bears have opposed views about the future of the market. The bulls and bears are two crowds whose sizes are in a constant state of change (it is suggested that Internet investing has assisted in the development of a crowd mentality). For one of the crowds to grow, investors must switch from the other crowd. As fewer investors remain in the other crowd, it becomes increasingly difficult to recruit from that crowd. As the relative size of the larger crowd increases, its growth rate falls. To the extent that stock market movements arise from the trading of investors who switch from being buyers to being sellers, or vice versa, the share price movements reflect the movement of investors between the two groups. When movement between the groups stops, share prices stop moving. This could create the conditions for a reversal in the direction of share prices. This implies that when the vast majority of investors are thinking and doing the same thing, the wise investor should do the opposite.

Fundamental analysis (such as dividend discount models, company accounts, and ratio analysis) is based on the view that stocks have fair (or fundamental) prices, which are the correct prices that accurately reflect all relevant information. Any deviation of stock prices from such fundamental values, perhaps resulting from crowd psychology, would be subsequently corrected by well-informed rational investors. In other words, prices revert to the mean. Technical analysis does not suggest that there is a fundamental, or correct, price. Technical analysis is concerned with the direction in which prices move. There is no assumption of a reversion to fundamental value (i.e. there is no mean reversion). The implication is that prices could persistently rise, or fall, without constraint. Prechter and Parker (2007) suggested that socionomic analysis provides the same possibility. High degrees of uncertainty about valuations, together with herding and fluctuations in social mood, produce markets that do not move towards fundamental values (i.e. do not mean revert). The implication seems to be that prices could rise or fall without apparent limits. This is a frightening thought in the light of the importance of stock market investments; for example for the accumulation of pension funds.

FURTHER EVIDENCE FROM EMPIRICAL RESEARCH

Park and Irwin (2004) reviewed the academic research on the profitability of technical analysis. They divided the research into 'early' and 'modern' studies. The modern studies were distinguished by the increased sophistication of the research methodology. They concluded that the early studies predominantly failed to find evidence to support the usefulness of technical analysis in stock markets but that many of the modern studies produced results favourable to technical analysis. They surveyed 92 modern studies: 58 found that technical analysis could be profitable, 24 reported negative results, and the remaining 10 indicated mixed results. However the modern studies indicated that technical trading ceased to be profitable in US stock markets after the late 1980s. Studies of emerging stock markets indicated continuing scope for profits from technical analysis.

Testing the profitability of technical trading is difficult for a number of reasons. One problem arises from the risk of data snooping. Data snooping (which is similar to data mining) entails investigating the data to see which rules might work before testing the rules. Technical trading rules that fit the past are created and then tested. If the rules are derived from the data on which they are tested, positive outcomes are to be expected. The researcher may test rules currently used in markets, and those rules may be ones that are used because they would have been profitable in the past. Data snooping may also involve the selection of markets and time periods favourable to the discovery of affirmative results. To avoid the effects of data snooping, the tests might be carried out on a completely fresh set of data. It may take a number of years for the new data to become available since the new period to be studied should not overlap with the original period (otherwise it would contain data from the original period).

For profitability to be unambiguous it must exceed any required compensation for additional risk. If apparent profits are gained through accepting increased market risk, they cannot genuinely be attributed to technical analysis. Merely gearing up a stockholding (increasing a stockholding with borrowed money) would be expected to increase profits at the cost of higher market risk. For technical trading to add value it should raise profits to an extent that exceeds the addition to profits expected from accepting more risk. However the measurement of market risk, and hence the measurement of the enhancement to profits required to compensate for risk, is problematical. The difficulties involved are shown in Chapter 15 on the criticisms of capital market theory, and Part 7 on market efficiency.

Another problem entails obtaining good estimates of transaction costs. For technical trading to be profitable it must cover transaction costs. Profits that are absorbed by transaction costs are not real profits. Estimating transaction costs, particularly bid-offer spreads, is difficult. Non-synchronous trading also poses problems for the researcher. Available price information relates to the price at which a stock was last traded. The researcher could, in consequence, base conclusions on prices that are not those at which actual traders could transact. The researcher would be using out-of-date prices whereas investors would trade at new prices. Transaction costs and non-synchronous trading are referred to as aspects of market microstructure. Earlier in this chapter it was mentioned that Brock *et al.* (1992) found that technical trading rules, based on moving averages, had predictive power. Day and Wang (2002) found that adjustment for transaction costs, and for the effect of non-synchronous prices on the closing levels of the Dow Jones Industrial Average, eliminated the profits reported in the Brock *et al.* study.

COMPLEX, ILL-STRUCTURED TASKS

Olsen (1998) suggested that investment analysis was an example of a 'complex, ill-structured task'. Such tasks are characterised by a lack of a generally agreed set of characteristics that clearly define the methodology and information required for analysis. In this chapter it has been shown that there is a large variety of rules, techniques, and data sources used by different technical analysts. In previous chapters in this part it was shown that there are many other approaches to investment analysis. There were various dividend discount models, many types of financial ratio, capital market models such as the capital asset pricing model, and so on. The list of investment analysis techniques covered in the present text is not exhaustive; there are many other techniques. The decision process differs widely between analysts. Differences in data interpretation, data selection, weighting, manipulation, and analysis prevail. Complex, ill-structured tasks are common in the social sciences and are characterised by the frequent failure of experts to outperform simple strategies. This is illustrated in investment analysis by the tendency of analysts and portfolio managers to underperform stock market indices (see Chapters 9, on mutual funds, and 17, on the evaluation of the performance of fund managers, and Part 7 on market efficiency). In contrast many analysts appear to be convinced that their views are correct. Perhaps it is appropriate to remember the maxim that 'the only thing that is certain is uncertainty'.

CONCLUSION

Technical analysis has tended to divide academics from investment professionals. Whilst market practitioners often regard it as an essential tool of investment analysis, finance academics have felt uncomfortable with it. The criticisms made by academics tend to focus on the absence of a coherent body of theory to explain technical analysis, and on the difficulty of using statistical tests to ascertain its effectiveness.

In the past when technical analysts have proposed theories those theories have tended to be ad hoc and inconsistent. There has been no coherent rationale as to why technical analysis should work. However the recent development of behavioural finance could contribute to the emergence of theoretical justifications of technical analysis. If social and psychological forces influence stock market behaviour in consistent ways, technical analysis could be seen as a technique for identifying those forces and forecasting their effects. Behavioural finance could also be applied at another level in that it might be used to explain the behaviour of technical analysts. Technical analysts may be influenced by the same social and psychological biases as other market participants. Those biases would tend to influence technical analysts' interpretations of their charts and other data. The forecasts of technical analysts could be affected by the same biases as the analysts may be seeking to identify among others.

Academics are often frustrated by the imprecise nature of the forecasts made by technical analysts. The lack of precision makes statistical testing difficult. Furthermore attempts by academics to do their own technical analysis, and test its predictions, can be open to the charge of being too mechanical and simplistic. One possible solution is to examine whether users of technical analysis make profits. Institutional investors tend to use technical analysis alongside other methods of investment analysis. The research evidence on the ability of institutional investors to outperform stock market indices indicates that, at best, such outperformance is marginal (see Chapters 9 and 17 on mutual funds and on evaluating the performance of fund managers, respectively, and Part 7 on market efficiency). This evidence throws doubt on the effectiveness of investment analysis, including technical analysis. However since the stock market in aggregate is equal to the sum of investment portfolios, such findings might be expected. Investment analysis may be a zero-sum game in that those making profits make them at the expense of other analysts.

Part 7

Market Efficiency

Chapter 23

Market efficiency: Concepts and weak form evidence

OBJECTIVE

The objective of this chapter is to provide knowledge of:

1. The concepts of weak, semi-strong, and strong form informational efficiency.
2. Evidence of arbitrage failures.
3. Empirical evidence on the weak form of the efficient market hypothesis.
4. Evidence on overshooting and mean reversion.
5. Evidence on momentum and contrarian strategies.
6. The implications of market efficiency for investment analysis.

TYPES OF EFFICIENCY

Market efficiency can be divided into three types: allocative efficiency, operational efficiency, and informational efficiency. Allocative efficiency is concerned with whether funds are directed to their most productive uses. This is mainly a primary market issue; the primary market being the market in which borrowers issue securities and receive payment from the initial investors (the word 'borrowers' here includes companies that raise money by issuing shares although, strictly speaking, share issuance is not borrowing). Allocative efficiency is concerned with the issue of which borrowers receive the finance. An allocatively efficient market is one in which the available funds go to the borrowers who will make the most productive use of them. Allocative efficiency is not the main concern here. However, it is important to be aware that allocative efficiency is dependent on operational and informational efficiency.

Allocative efficiency is dependent upon securities (shares and bonds) being accurately priced. Accurate pricing requires informational efficiency. If securities are not accurately priced, investors could direct their money to uses that are not the most productive. For example during 1999 and early 2000 shares in Internet-related companies were seriously overpriced. For those people establishing Internet-related companies, the proceeds from share sales heavily exceeded the costs of establishing the companies. So there was a great incentive to set up Internet-related companies.

Too many Internet-related companies were created and most of them subsequently failed. The overpricing of shares issued by Internet-related companies had caused too much money to be invested in such companies. Much of this money could have been invested more productively elsewhere.

Operational efficiency relates to the costs and risks involved in the process of carrying out transactions in financial markets. One dimension relates to transaction costs such as bid-offer spreads, brokers' commissions, and taxes. The primary market is the market in which newly issued shares and bonds are sold. High transaction costs in the primary market would raise the cost of funds for companies and lower returns for investors (i.e. the costs would tend to be borne by both issuers and investors). The result would be a reduction in the total level of investment in the economy since issuers and investors would be deterred.

The secondary market is the market in which previously issued securities are traded. It is the means by which shares or bonds bought in the primary market can be converted into cash. The knowledge that assets purchased in the primary market can easily and cheaply be resold in the secondary market makes investors more prepared to provide companies with funds by buying in the primary market. A successful primary market depends upon an effective secondary market. High transaction costs in the secondary market would adversely impact on the primary market and hence on the total volume of investment.

If transaction costs are high in the secondary market the proceeds from the sale of securities will be reduced, and the incentive to buy in the primary market would be lower. Also high transaction costs in the secondary market would tend to reduce the volume of trading and thereby reduce the ease with which secondary market sales can be executed. It follows that high transaction costs in the secondary market would reduce that market's effectiveness in rendering primary market assets liquid. In consequence there would be adverse effects on the level of activity in the primary market and hence on the total level of investment in the economy.

Price volatility is the extent to which share and bond prices fluctuate, such that high volatility of prices entails frequent large price movements. High volatility of prices in the secondary market may be detrimental to the operation of the primary market. High volatility means that buyers in the primary market stand a considerable risk of losing money by having to sell at much lower prices in the secondary market. This could reduce the motivation to buy in the primary market. Two factors that affect the price volatility of securities in the secondary market are the depth and breadth of that market.

The depth of the market is based on the likely appearance of new orders stimulated by any movement in price. If a rise in price brings forth numerous sell orders the price rise will be small. A decline in price that stimulates many buy orders would be a small decline. Market depth would be enhanced by a relatively large number of market participants. A deep market would be characterised by the appearance of orders that tend to dampen the extent of any movement in price. Greater depth is thus associated with lower volatility.

The breadth of the market reflects the diversity of the traders in the market. If there are a large number of market participants with differing price expectations, substantial price changes would be less likely than would be expected when the traders have common views such that they buy or sell together. A broad market is a heterogeneous market characterised by relative price stability.

Operational efficiency is important for informational efficiency. An informationally efficient market is one in which security prices reflect all relevant information. By buying underpriced securities and selling overpriced securities, traders will tend to move prices to the levels that correspond with the available information. High transaction costs will reduce (or even eliminate) the potential profits from buying low or selling high (with a view to reversing the transaction when the pricing error has been corrected). Since such transactions move prices to the levels consistent with the available information, transaction costs that deter them will lessen the informational efficiency of the market.

Informational efficiency of the secondary market is important for the operation of the primary market. This is partly because issuers of shares or bonds in the primary market are likely to look at prices in the secondary market when determining the prices of new issues. For example the issue price of new shares may be based on the prices of shares of companies in the same sector. If the secondary market were informationally inefficient the guidance provided would be poor. The primary market, and its allocative efficiency, is thus dependent upon the informational efficiency of the secondary market.

THE MEANING OF INFORMATIONAL EFFICIENCY

Informational efficiency is conventionally divided into the weak, semi-strong, and strong forms (a classification originally suggested by Fama (1965)). The weak form of the efficient market hypothesis suggests that all historical market information (past prices, past trading volumes, short selling) is fully taken into account in the current market price.

An implication of the weak form hypothesis is that there is no scope for making profits from analysis of historical market prices and volumes. So technical analysis, particularly chartism, is expected to be of no value. Attempts to forecast share price movements using charts based on previous share prices will fail since all the information available from past price data is already reflected in the share price.

Suppose it was discovered that a particular chart pattern was successful in forecasting share prices. One day it may be found that the chart pattern suggests that a particular share will rise in price from 100p to 200p over the next month. Everyone familiar with the prediction of the chart pattern will try to buy shares, and no holder of the shares would be prepared to sell at less than 200p. This buying pressure will bring about a rapid rise in the share price to 200p. The share price rises immediately to the level predicted by the chart pattern. In other words the information contained in the chart pattern is immediately incorporated into the share price. Since nobody was prepared to sell at less than 200p, no one was able to profit from knowledge of the chart pattern by buying shares.

If prices move instantly to their new correct (fair) levels following the receipt of new information, it follows that new information is the only possible reason for a price movement. New information is unpredictable; if it were predictable it would not be new. Share prices that move in response to new information, and only to new information, must be unpredictable. This suggests that share prices should follow a random walk.

A random walk involves each day's price movement being independent of every previous day's price movement. Upward and downward movements are regarded as having equal likelihood on a day, irrespective of the previous direction of movement. Price movements reflect news coming into the market, and news is random both in timing and in nature (good and bad news have equal likelihood). However the efficient market hypothesis deviates from a pure random walk since it allows for upward price movements to dominate downward movements so that over the long term share prices tend to move upwards (there are random fluctuations around a rising trend).

A semi-strong form efficient market is one in which security prices take account of all publicly available information. In addition to market information on past prices and trading volumes, publicly available information includes macroeconomic data (such as changes in interest rates, growth rates, inflation rates), company data (such as profits, sales, quality of management and workforce, balance sheets), and non-economic events (such as political events, technological developments, and discoveries of natural resources). The implication is that asset prices immediately move to reflect any new information so that no one can make profits by means of purchases or sales based on analysing the new information.

Both types of market efficiency require prices to fully reflect any new information without any time lag. Incomplete or slow price movements will allow traders successfully to forecast price movements, and possibly to make profits from those movements. Although allowance is made for the possibility that a security price will not attain its true level until time has been taken to carry out the relevant analyses, it is proposed that any initial deviation from the true level is equally likely to constitute an over- or undervaluation. Temporary deviations from fair prices are equally likely to be positive or negative.

It is the 'news' element of information that is important, and to which the market is expected to react. For example if a company announces a 25% increase in profits whilst a 10% increase had been expected, the 'news' element is the 15% that had not been expected. The share price prior to the announcement should already reflect the expected 10% increase. If the increase in profits were 10%, there would be no news and the share price should not react. If the increase in profits had been 5%, the news would be negative despite the fact of the profits rise; in this case the share price should fall.

There remains the question of how asset prices move to their new levels if no one is able to profit from trading in the assets following the emergence of new information. In principle prospective buyers and sellers could adjust their buying and selling prices so that the equilibrium price moves without any shares being traded. However it seems likely that trading activity would play a part in moving prices. The buying of underpriced shares would push their prices up, and the selling of overpriced shares would push their prices down. One might expect that those traders who respond most quickly to new information will be able to make profits from the use of that information. A paradox is that the market efficiency that results from their trading depends upon those traders believing that markets are not efficient. If a trader believed that markets were efficient, that trader would not trade unless he or she had information that is not available to anyone else.

To make profits (specifically abnormal returns, which are returns in excess of what is normally available from an investment with a particular level of systematic risk) an investor may need information that is not available to other investors. Such additional information may be data or a different technique for analysing the data. It is not sufficient to identify good firms. If other analysts have also concluded that a firm is good, its share price will already be high. A good company is not a good investment (in the sense of earning abnormal returns) unless other investors have failed to fully recognise its quality. Conversely a weak firm may be a good investment if other investors have exaggerated its weakness, in which case its share price will be too low. A share price that is too low offers profitable investment opportunities.

Strong form efficiency allows no information to be used profitably, not even insider information. It suggests that security prices reflect all available information even if some of that information is held by only one person. The puzzle of how the information becomes reflected in the asset prices, without profitable trading by the possessor of the information, is even greater in this case.

The efficient market hypothesis has two separate (but related) interpretations. One interpretation is that all relevant information is reflected in existing prices. The second interpretation is that it is not possible to reliably profit from the identification of incorrect prices. The second interpretation does not necessarily require that all relevant information be reflected in share prices. It requires either that shares (or securities generally) are correctly priced, or that there is no reliable way of profiting from incorrect pricing.

Thousands of talented and highly trained analysts working for banks and brokers and employing state-of-the-art technology are constantly looking for profitable trading opportunities. Managers of large funds may be prepared to pay large sums to achieve marginal improvements in performance. For example the manager of a £10-billion fund would gain £10-million from a 0.1% improvement in performance. In the presence of such activity, it seems likely that few profitable opportunities remain and that investment assets are close to their correct (fair) prices.

It should be realised that although the efficient market hypothesis suggests that investment analysis may not be profitable, it does not imply that portfolio management is pointless. Portfolio management remains important even in perfectly efficient markets. It is still necessary to ensure that portfolio risk is consistent with the investor's attitude to risk, and that unnecessary risk (non-systematic risk) is eliminated. Portfolio management may also be necessary to achieve other objectives such as high yield, tax efficiency, and consistency with ethical principles. In an efficient market the role of a portfolio manager is to tailor the portfolio to the investor's needs rather than to try to outperform the stock market by stock selection or market timing.

ASSUMPTIONS OF THE EFFICIENT MARKET HYPOTHESIS

The efficient market hypothesis makes five important assumptions. One assumption is that investors are rational. This does not require all investors to be rational, but it does require that the rational investors outweigh the irrational ones.

A second assumption is that rational investors have adequate funds. If rational investors are going to dominate the markets, they must have the funds necessary to take advantage of all investment opportunities. It is only by being able to trade shares, which requires resources, that they are able to incorporate information into share prices. The adequacy of funds could arise either from having money or from being able to borrow money. A related point is that rational investors should be able to sell shares short. Selling short means borrowing shares and selling those borrowed shares. The ability to sell is as important as the ability to buy in relation to ensuring that share prices reflect all relevant information. Rational market participants should be able to sell overpriced securities (shares and bonds) as well as being able to buy underpriced ones.

A third assumption is that information is available instantaneously to many investors and that rational investors immediately use the information to make good assessments of share prices. If some investors were able to make good assessments more quickly than others, they would be able to make profits from the information received. Although this assumption will not hold in its absolute form, a high degree of market efficiency would be achieved if a substantial number of rational investors analyse the information, and trade on it, within one day of the information being available.

A fourth assumption is that rational investors do not believe that markets are efficient. This is a paradox. The existence of market efficiency depends upon rational investors not realising that it exists. If rational investors believed that markets are efficient, they would not carry out investment analysis and trade on the basis of that analysis. Investment analysis is based on the belief that shares may be mispriced so that profit can be made by estimating the correct price and buying or selling accordingly. It is through investment analysis and trades based on that analysis that share prices come to reflect new information.

A fifth assumption is that transaction costs, market impact effects, and required compensation for risk are not large enough to deter trading at prices close to fundamental value. Transaction costs include brokers' commissions, bid-offer spreads, and taxes such as stamp duty. Market impact effects are the effects of an investor's own purchases and sales on the share price. An investor may require some additional expected profit to compensate for the possibility that their own analysis may provide an inaccurate forecast. These factors could lead to investors not trading unless their estimate of fundamental value is substantially different from the actual share price. Investors would react only to very important pieces of new information. In consequence smaller deviations of share prices from their fundamental values are not corrected. Less important news would not be acted upon. Share prices would remain at levels that do not reflect all relevant information. Shares would not be efficiently priced.

PRICE ANOMALIES (ARBITRAGE FAILURES)

The law of one price suggests that identical assets should have the same price in different markets. If prices differed between markets, arbitragers would buy in the cheaper market and sell in the expensive one. This would generate a profit, and would also tend to move the prices into equality. The extra demand in the low-price market would tend to raise the price there, and the additional supply in the high-price market would tend to reduce the price in that market. The efficient market hypothesis implies that the price of an asset should be the same in all markets.

A related idea is that similar financial assets should trade at similar prices. If they did not, there would be an arbitrage profit available from buying the cheaper and simultaneously selling the more expensive one. Such arbitrage would tend to bring the prices into equality. The efficient market hypothesis suggests that similar assets should trade at similar prices. Effective arbitrage is useful (probably essential) for the maintenance of market efficiency.

There are reasons why arbitrage may fail to maintain equality between the prices of similar (or identical) assets. First, arbitragers may need a mechanism for selling short. They may need to be able to borrow securities (shares or bonds) in order to sell them with a view to taking advantage of overpricing. Such a mechanism may not be available for many potential arbitragers. Second, the correction of the relative mispricing should occur quickly. If arbitragers have to wait years to collect their arbitrage profits, they are unlikely to conduct arbitrage trades. Third, there is not always an identical, or similar, asset against which to arbitrage. For example it may be possible to arbitrage one UK share against a similar UK share (e.g. one large bank against another large bank) but there is nothing against which the UK stock market as a whole can be arbitraged. One implication is that arbitrage may establish correct relative prices, but cannot ensure correct absolute prices. Fourth, arbitragers must have sufficient money and/or borrowing facilities. Without such adequate financial resources, arbitragers would not be able to conduct the requisite trading.

Froot and Dabora (1999) found that the law of one price was violated in stock markets. Twin securities and dual-listed shares involve identical investments trading simultaneously on more than one stock exchange. For example, Royal Dutch/Shell was traded on nine different stock exchanges around the world and Unilever was traded on eight. Rather strangely the prices (when making appropriate exchange rate adjustments) differed considerably between exchanges, in some instances by as much as 50%. The fact that shares in the same company had different prices on different stock exchanges contradicted the efficient market hypothesis.

The fact that arbitragers do not exploit, and thereby correct, these price discrepancies might be explained by the concept of noise trader risk. With this type of arbitrage there is no guarantee that the price discrepancy will ever be corrected; there is no date by which it is guaranteed to be corrected. Indeed the discrepancy may become larger before it becomes smaller. Noise traders (irrational traders) can keep prices away from equality for prolonged periods.

An equity carve out occurs when a firm floats part of itself. Thaler and Lamont (2000) examined equity carve outs in the US high-tech sector between 1995 and 2000 (the latter part of that period coincided with the emergence of the high-tech bubble). A particular case was that of 3Com and Palm. In February 2000, 3Com sold 5% of its stake in Palm via a public offering. The remaining 95% of the shares were to be issued by the end of the year by giving existing shareholders in 3Com about 1.5 shares in Palm for every 3Com share held. It follows that the price of 3Com should have been at least equal to 1.5 times the price of Palm. After the first day of trading, Palm closed at $95.06 implying a minimum price for 3Com of $142.59. However 3Com closed at $81.81. This violation of the law of one price persisted for over two months. Although the 3Com/Palm case was probably the most dramatic, there were several other examples of carve out mispricing revealed by Thaler and Lamont (and also by Cornell and Liu 2001).

Apparent price anomalies are not restricted to equity markets. A callable bond allows the issuer to buy the bond back at a predetermined price. As a result an investor could lose profits since a substantial rise in the price of the bond might be lost if the issuer chooses to repurchase the bond at the predetermined price. It would be expected that a callable bond has less value than an otherwise identical non-callable bond to an investor. A callable bond should trade at a lower price than an equivalent non-callable bond. Longstaff (1992) found that some callable bonds were more expensive than their non-callable equivalents.

Lamont and Thaler (2003) pointed out that if the market fails to arbitrage away glaring discrepancies, there must be a strong suspicion that there is a widespread failure of arbitrage. Arbitrage failures are cases in which the market is failing to incorporate information into market prices. If information were being incorporated into prices efficiently, arbitrage opportunities would not persist. Each pair of similar assets should trade at similar prices if traders were considering all relevant information. The price of one member of a pair of similar assets is information that is relevant to the pricing of the other member of the pair. The persistence of arbitrage opportunities indicates that not all of the relevant information is being used. If relevant information is failing to determine prices when the price relationships are obvious, there must be doubt about less obvious cases. If the market gets simple cases wrong, it seems likely that it is getting much else wrong.

485

For many (probably most) investment assets there are no close substitutes against which to arbitrage. It is unlikely that there is a close substitute for the shares of a particular company. There is no close substitute for the whole stock market. There are no unambiguous 'correct' prices since different investors take different views using different pricing models (dividend discount, price-earnings ratios, technical trading rules, etc.). If investors do not pay attention to relevant information when deciding on fair prices, the uncertainty about the accuracy of market prices becomes greater. Market prices are consensus estimates of fair prices, but consensus does not necessarily imply truth or substance (Trumble and Cavazotte 2000). Behavioural finance research has shown that social pressures strongly influence opinions, and hence the consensus (see Chapter 27 on stock market bubbles and crashes). There is evidence that professional analysts are influenced by each other when determining price forecasts (see Chapter 21 on ratio analysis). The resulting consistency of views between analysts can give a spurious perception of accuracy and certainty, in the belief that if most experts agree on something then they are likely to be right.

EMPIRICAL EVIDENCE ON THE WEAK FORM OF THE EFFICIENT MARKET HYPOTHESIS

Kendall (1953) attempted to identify cycles in stock indices. He could not find any. One day's level appeared to be equal to the previous day's plus or minus a random amount. Roberts (1959) showed that a series of cumulative random numbers looked like a series of share prices such that observers believed that they could identify price patterns. Osborne (1959) found that share price movements conformed to the Brownian motion of physics in that successive movements appeared to be random and the standard deviation of cumulative changes was proportional to the square root of time. Moore (1964) looked for correlations between share price changes and previous price changes (serial correlation). The average coefficient of correlation was not significantly different from zero (statistically). He concluded that past price changes cannot be used to forecast future price changes.

Fama (1965) confirmed the absence of serial correlation. He also employed runs tests, which sought to ascertain whether runs of successive upward or downward price movements were longer or shorter than would be expected on the basis of random price movements. He concluded that lengths of runs were consistent with a random series of price movements. So there was no observable tendency for prices to trend upwards or downwards. However Niederhoffer and Osborne (1966) found slight evidence of serial correlation and runs using intra-day rather than weekly or daily data. Intra-day serial correlation appeared to be slightly negative.

Conrad and Kaul (1988) and Lo and MacKinlay (1988) found positive serial correlations over short periods using weekly returns of New York Stock Exchange stocks, but the correlation coefficients were small. Campbell *et al.* (1997) and Lovatt *et al.* (2007) found that daily stock returns contained a strong element of predictability. In an investigation of intermediate horizon (3- to 12-month periods) stock price movements, Jegadeesh and Titman (1993) found that stocks exhibit a momentum in which good or bad recent performance continues. They concluded that while the performance of individual stocks is insufficiently predictable, portfolios of the best performing stocks from the recent past appear to outperform other stocks with enough reliability to provide opportunities for profit.

The question arises as to whether any correlation between current and previous returns provides the possibility of earning excess returns (trading profits) net of transaction costs. Transaction costs could exceed any potential gains. Efficient markets should be characterised by transaction costs setting upper limits to correlation coefficients, with higher transaction costs allowing greater serial correlation. Jennergren and Korsvold (1975) observed higher correlation coefficients in markets with higher transaction costs when examining Norwegian stocks.

Another approach to testing for weak form efficiency is to ascertain whether trading rules, such as those used by chartists, have any predictive value. One trading rule that has been investigated is the filter rule. A typical filter rule might involve buying when a stock price rises 5% above its previous low point and selling when the stock price falls 5% from its previous high. Alexander (1964) and Fama and Blume (1966) concluded that it was not possible to make profits by using filter rules to forecast price movements. However Sweeney (1988, 1990) suggested that filter rules can produce statistically significant risk-adjusted excess returns after adjusting for the types of transaction costs faced by professional traders.

Chartists argue that tests of simple and mechanical trading rules cannot be used to draw conclusions about the complex and subtle techniques actually employed. There is also the point that it is impossible to test the whole infinite variety of trading rules, and hence it is always possible that effective trading rules exist among those that have not been tested. Furthermore technical analysts would not publicise effective techniques for fear that widespread knowledge of the techniques would reduce the profits available to themselves. Perhaps it is only the ineffective trading rules that become widely known, and hence subject to testing.

Contrary to much of the other evidence, one study has suggested that some widely known chartist techniques have predictive power. Lo *et al.* (2000) found that some technical analysis patterns occurred far more frequently than would be expected on the basis of chance. The most common patterns were double tops (and bottoms), followed by head and shoulders (and inverted head and shoulders). Although the researchers ascertained that the charts provided information about future share prices, they did not investigate whether the information could be used to make trading profits. Niarchos and Alexakis (2003) found that on the Athens stock exchange there was a possibility of profitable intra-day (i.e. within a trading day) trading based on stock price patterns.

There are counterviews and debates about the evidence. Shiller (1984, 1988) has suggested that there may be fads and fashions in investment. If such fashions spread slowly, share price trends could emerge as a result. Fashion is not the only possible driving force. Since the late 1990s some people have argued that demographic trends are having a similar effect. In North America and Europe the post-war bulge generation (people born in the baby boom of the late 1940s to the early 1960s) is moving into the last decade or so before retirement. They are reaching the stage at which family responsibilities are lessening as their grown-up children leave home, their mortgages are being paid off, and the necessity of saving for retirement is becoming increasingly apparent. They thus become more able and willing to save. The additional saving would involve increased financial investment. This may have an upward pull on stock market prices that continues for a long period of time. If this line of reasoning is accurate, a strong and long-lasting upward price trend may be expected.

A study by Peters (1991), which analysed S&P 500 price changes from 1928 to 1989, showed that securities markets are highly leptokurtotic. Leptokurtotic markets exhibit fat tails in their returns distributions. The probabilities of very high and very low values are greater than would be predicted by normal distributions. This is consistent with markets trending in a particular direction, i.e. consistent with price movements being related to previous price movements. Peters suggested that as few as three variables can accurately predict market movements. However since these three variables frequently change, there may be no practical way of making profits from predicting market movements. Also leptokurtosis may have alternative explanations, such as the observed distribution being an amalgam of several different normal distributions (it is likely that over a prolonged period a stock index would have been subject to numerous different distributions of returns).

Overshooting (Overreaction) and Mean Reversion

Summers (1986) simulated a series of share prices, which overreacted to new information. Overreaction means that prices rise too high and fall too low. He went on to show that the techniques used in the early tests of serial correlation were not able to discriminate between an overreacting series and a random series. The tests could not identify the presence of overreaction. Such tests cannot therefore be used to refute the proposition that markets are prone to overreaction.

It has often been suggested that the observed volatility of stock markets is greater than might be expected from the efficient market hypothesis. The stock market crash of October 1987 is an example of volatility that is difficult to explain in terms of new information coming into the market. Share prices are seen as being the present values of expected future dividend receipts, but dividends show much less fluctuation than share prices.

Shiller (1981) tested the hypothesis that stock price volatility exceeds what is justified on the basis of variations in dividends. The basic premise of these studies is that stock prices should be more stable than dividends since stock prices reflect expectations of dividends. Consider an analogy with tossing a coin. If a coin is tossed 100 times the expectation is that there will be 50 heads. Each time the coin is tossed 100 times the forecast would be of 50 heads. The forecast does not vary; it has zero volatility. However on most occasions that the coin is tossed 100 times the actual number of heads will differ from 50. The observed numbers of heads will tend to form a normal distribution with a mean of 50. The observed number of heads is more volatile than the forecast number of heads. The implication of this reasoning for share prices is that they should exhibit greater stability than dividends. Share prices are based on expected dividends, which should be more stable than actual dividends. The volatility of share prices should be less than the volatility of dividends. Shiller's research found that stock prices were much more volatile than dividends.

These studies have their critics. It has been suggested that the price fluctuations arise from variations in the required rate of return by which expected dividend streams are discounted, perhaps due to changes in the risk premiums (Cochrane 1991). It has also been suggested that the apparent serial correlation arises from small sample bias, the tests being based on a small number of observations (Cecchetti *et al.* 1990).

Although studies of short-term serial correlation tended to find that there was no significant correlation coefficient, investigations of longer time periods have suggested that markets overreact to new information. Tests covering periods of several years (Poterba and Summers 1988; Fama and French 1988) have found a tendency for prices to deviate from their fair values and then revert towards them (mean reversion). In other words significant negative serial correlation has been found over multi-year time horizons. This is consistent with Shiller's (1984, 1988) view that fads appear to exist in securities markets. Episodes of apparent overshooting followed by corrections give the appearance of asset prices fluctuating around their fair values. Market prices seem to exhibit excess volatility.

Research by Brown and Cliff (2005) is consistent with the view that fads, or sentiment, influence stock prices. Brown and Cliff used a measure of sentiment based on the balance between bullish and bearish investment newsletters. Their results were consistent with the view that share prices initially overreact and then mean revert with the effect that, following positive sentiment, there are relatively low returns for a period as prices mean revert. Prices initially show unjustified rises, but subsequently experience falls as the unjustified rises are corrected. Conversely periods of negative sentiment are followed by relatively high returns as the underpricing, caused by the negative sentiment, is subsequently corrected.

DeBondt and Thaler (1985, 1987) have put forward an overreaction hypothesis. The overreaction hypothesis suggests that when investors react to unanticipated news, which will benefit a company's stock, the price rise will initially be greater than it should be. There will be a subsequent price decline to the level justified by the new information. Conversely the price fall arising from adverse news will initially be exaggerated, requiring a subsequent correction.

DeBondt and Thaler proposed a directional effect and a magnitude effect. The directional effect is the tendency for an initial overreaction to be followed by a moderating movement in the opposite direction. The magnitude effect is the tendency for the size of the correction to be related to the extent of the initial overreaction. A relatively large initial overreaction will be followed by a relatively large compensating correction. Brown and Harlow (1988) added the intensity effect, which states that the shorter the duration of the initial price change, the more extreme the subsequent response will be. Brown and Harlow found that overreaction (all three effects) was most marked in the case of short-term responses to negative news.

A related observation by DeBondt and Thaler (1985, 1987) is sometimes referred to as the winner-loser problem. Stocks that have been relatively good performers over the last three to five years will tend to underperform during the next three to five years, conversely past underperformers become future outperformers. Jegadeesh and Titman (1993) found evidence consistent with this observation.

Momentum and Contrarian Strategies

Investment strategies based on the view that the recent direction of share price movement will continue are known as momentum strategies. Contrarian strategies are based on the view that the direction of movement will reverse. There is evidence that technical trading rules based on momentum and contrarian strategies might produce opportunities for profit. A number of studies have divided stocks into 'winner' and 'loser' portfolios. The winner portfolios contain those stocks that have performed well in the recent past; the loser portfolios contain those that have shown poor recent returns. The studies have then investigated whether there is a significant difference in their subsequent performances. If markets are weak form efficient there should be no significant difference between the returns (price movements) of the two portfolios.

Research has shown there to be significant differences between the returns to winner and loser portfolios. Some studies have found that winner and loser portfolios chosen on the basis of the returns (price changes) during one week exhibit contrarian behaviour in the following week. A relatively good performance one week tends to be followed by a relatively bad performance the next week, and vice versa (Lehmann 1990). Similar findings have arisen from consideration of returns over one month and the following month (Jegadeesh 1990). However when the period used has been six months or a year momentum strategies appear to have been successful; winner portfolios continue to significantly outperform loser portfolios (Jegadeesh 1990; Jegadeesh and Titman 1993; Fama and French 1996). Paradoxically tests using three- and five-year periods have found contrarian strategies to work; the losers from one period become the winners in the next period, and vice versa (De Bondt and Thaler 1985, 1987; Chopra *et al.* 1992).

Hong *et al.* (2000) provide evidence to indicate that momentum in share prices is the result of gradual diffusion of information about a company, and that stocks with slower information diffusion provide more potential for momentum profits. They point out that over investment horizons of three to twelve months, there appear to be opportunities to profit from trading strategies based on momentum in that winners continue to perform well and laggards continue to perform poorly. They propose that slow diffusion of information is particularly characteristic of poorly performing small companies whose shares are neglected by analysts. Company managements do not enthusiastically publicise bad news, and few investors seek information about neglected small companies. In consequence share prices adjust very gradually to new information and exhibit momentum during the adjustment process.

Doukas and McKnight (2005) used a sample of 13 European stock markets over the period 1988–2001 to test the hypothesis that momentum was caused by slow diffusion of information. They also tested an alternative explanation of momentum, which is that it results from investor conservatism. Investor conservatism is a cognitive bias identified in behavioural finance. Conservatism causes investors to be slow to change their opinions. So even if information were provided quickly, investors would be slow to respond to it. The slow response results in a slow adjustment of stock prices to the new information. The information-induced trades that move prices to their new levels occur gradually over time, rather than immediately after the release of the information. Doukas and McKnight concluded that both hypotheses contributed to the explanation of the momentum effect.

Further evidence on momentum and contrarian strategies comes from Chan *et al.* (1999) who used measures of price momentum and earnings momentum. The earnings momentum measures considered the impact of unexpected earnings (profits) announcements on the behaviour of share prices, and the impact of changes in analysts' earnings forecasts. Unexpectedly good earnings and upward revisions of analysts' forecasts tend to cause share price rises; conversely for bad earnings and downward revisions. It was found that investing on the basis of price momentum and the two forms of earnings momentum could produce profits over six-month and one-year periods. No evidence of reversals, and hence no evidence of profitable contrarian strategies, was found. It was suggested that the evidence was consistent with the view that information is gradually incorporated into share prices. An explanation proposed for the gradual incorporation of information was the procrastination of analysts in the adjustment of their forecasts. Downward revisions of forecasts may be particularly slow since analysts do not want to antagonise the companies whose shares are being evaluated.

Chan *et al.* (2000) found that momentum strategies could work in international investing. In particular they found that increasing portfolio weights in countries whose stock markets had recently performed well, and reducing weights in relatively poorly performing markets, could improve portfolio performance. Schiereck *et al.* (1999) used German data to test for momentum and reversion. The momentum effect was found to be strong for six months. Based on periods of two to five years they found reversal effects, which would allow profits from contrarian strategies.

Forner and Marhuenda (2003) found momentum and contrarian effects in the Spanish stock market. They concluded that momentum strategies could be profitable on a 12-month basis and that contrarian strategies offered profitable opportunities over 60-month periods. Antoniou *et al.* (2005) found overreaction and contrarian effects on the Athens stock exchange.

Levy and Post (2005) have pointed out that there are practical considerations that reduce the likelihood of successful momentum strategies. First, momentum strategies are likely to require high turnover of shareholdings with the effect that transaction costs are high. Second, the momentum effect is strongest among small capitalisation stocks. Small capitalisation stocks tend to be illiquid, which makes high turnover impossible. Third, most of the return available from momentum strategies comes from taking short positions in poorly performing shares. For many investors short positions (borrowing shares which are then sold) are not possible. However Kothari and Shanken (2002) found that portfolio performance could be improved by tilting the portfolio towards high momentum stocks.

Some studies have concluded that prospective profits from momentum trading are illusory (Lesmond *et al.* 2004; Agyei-Ampomah 2007). Agyei-Ampomah found that for periods up to six months transaction costs eliminated profits from momentum trading, but did not fully offset profits when longer periods were considered. However it was also found that most of the apparent momentum trading profits arose from short selling poorly performing stocks. The process of borrowing shares can be expensive, difficult, and subject to risk. Agyei-Ampomah suggested that the costs and difficulties of taking short positions in stocks were capable of preventing the exploitation of the apparent profit opportunities.

Research on relative strength has also produced conflicting findings. Proponents of relative strength strategies look at the ratio between a stock price and the level of a stock index. A change in this ratio may signal a trade. Momentum traders see an increase in the ratio as indicative of a buying opportunity (and a decline as a sell signal). Levy (1966) produced findings that suggested that a strategy based on relative strength could outperform a buy-and-hold strategy (a strategy of simply buying stocks and holding them without indulging in any further transactions). Arnott (1979) found that a stock that had been strong in the past would tend to be weak in the future. Brush (1986) found that relative strength models could not be used to predict which stocks would achieve superior performance after adjusting for risk and transaction costs. Ryan and Overmeyer (2004) found that momentum trades on the basis of relative strength in the German stock market were profitable, even after allowing for transaction costs. Profits from the strategy appeared to be available for about 12 months. Of interest was the apparent absence of any subsequent reversal during the following two years; in other words there was no sign of overreaction and consequent profits from a contrarian strategy. They interpreted the evidence as being consistent with delayed reaction to firm-specific news.

Serial Correlation in Volatility

ARCH (autoregressive conditional heteroskedasticity) and GARCH (generalised ARCH) models allow price changes to be serially uncorrelated but not independent. Predictability comes not through being able to forecast price changes but by being able to forecast the variance of the changes. Although the best forecast of a price change may be zero, the variance of possible price changes will depend upon past volatility. Al-Loughani and Chappell (1997) found that the FTSE

100 Index between 1983 and 1989 did not follow a random walk but demonstrated significant heteroscedasticity (variances were serially correlated). Their results provided evidence against the random walk hypothesis. The results did not necessarily provide evidence against the weak form of the efficient market hypothesis since they did not test whether the predictability of volatility provided the opportunity to earn excess profits. However, it has been suggested that the serial correlation in variance arises from the inappropriateness of the asset pricing model used rather than from market inefficiency (e.g. Schwaiger 1995).

THE MAGNITUDE AND SELECTION BIAS ISSUES

Investment analysis is concerned with improving portfolio returns (without increasing risk). For a fund manager an improvement of 0.1% p.a. would be worthwhile. For example in the case of a £10-billion fund an increase of 0.1% amounts to £10 million. The fund manager would regard the strategy that provides the 0.1% increase as successful. However a researcher looking for success, or otherwise, in investment analysis is unlikely to detect an improvement of 0.1% p.a. Given the typical volatility of stock markets, statistical techniques would not identify such a small increase. A small increase would be swamped by typical annual volatility with the effect that it becomes invisible to the statistician. So the researcher would conclude that there is no evidence for successful investment analysis, despite the fact that the analysis was successful. This has been referred to as the magnitude issue. It might also be noted that the fund manager cannot be sure that the investment analysis has been successful; an increase of 0.1% p.a. could easily occur by chance.

The selection bias issue is concerned with the choice of techniques to be investigated. A researcher is limited to investigating publicly known techniques. This may preclude the successful techniques. If an analyst has a technique that is successful, that analyst would not reveal it. The analyst would use it to make money. So researchers do not investigate successful techniques. The techniques available for investigation are the ones that analysts are willing to make public; in other words the ones that are unsuccessful. So a volume of research that suggests the failure of investment analysis may merely reflect the absence of research on successful analysis.

CONCLUSION

Finance academics and investment practitioners have not always been in agreement. Perhaps the biggest source of division has been the efficient market hypothesis (EMH). Although the academic world is less committed to the hypothesis than it used to be, the EMH remains one of the pillars of capital market theory. However the strength of that pillar is questionable.

If the weak form of the EMH is correct, technical analysis is futile. The weak form of the EMH suggests that it is not possible to use market data, particularly past prices, to make profits from investment analysis. According to the weak form of the EMH, popular techniques such as chartism (predicting share price movements from charts) are no more useful than reading tea leaves.

Many investors, including institutional investors, use technical analysis. The EMH implies that retail investors would do well to shun funds that waste money on such analysis, and to invest in low cost index tracker funds instead.

Some of the early empirical studies indicated that past price data did not provide a means of predicting future price movements. It was also observed that people tended to see patterns and trends in randomly generated series of prices. This receives support from behavioural finance, which indicates that people are uncomfortable with the idea of randomness and see patterns and causes where there are none.

Later empirical research has produced more ambiguous results. In particular the EMH appears to be contradicted by blatant failures of arbitrage. If it is easy to make profits from obvious failures of arbitrage to maintain the law of one price, it seems likely that profit opportunities will be available where price discrepancies are less obvious. If the price of a share in one market fails to take full account of the price of the same share in another market, it seems likely that other market data is also incompletely reflected in prices.

Behavioural finance suggests that investors are less than perfectly rational. In particular the concept of representativeness suggests that there is a tendency for investors to extrapolate price movements (see the chapters – in particular 2 and 24 – dealing with behavioural finance and investor psychology). If prices have been moving in a direction, many investors believe that they will continue to move in that direction. There is a body of empirical research that finds a tendency for markets to overreact; both rises and falls are exaggerated. The existence of stock market bubbles and crashes could be seen as evidence in support of this idea (see Chapter 27 on stock market bubbles and crashes).

Further reading

Further insights into market efficiency can be obtained by reading:

Haugen, R. A. (2002). *The Inefficient Stock Market: What Pays Off and Why,* 2nd edn, Pearson.
Malkiel, B. G. (2004). *A Random Walk Down Wall Street,* 8th edn, Norton.
Shleifer, A. (2000). *Inefficient Markets: An Introduction to Behavioral Finance,* Oxford University Press.

Chapter 24

Noise trading and behavioural finance

OBJECTIVE

The objective of this chapter is to provide knowledge of the implications of noise trading and behavioural finance for market efficiency, particularly in regard to:

1. The role of rumours in financial markets.
2. Underreaction to news.
3. Overreaction to news.
4. Inaccurate perceptions of risk.
5. Moods and emotions.

One of the assumptions of the efficient market hypothesis is that, in aggregate, market participants behave in a rational manner. There are lines of reasoning that suggest that irrational behaviour can have significant impacts on financial markets. The concepts of noise trading and behavioural finance suggest that individual market participants do not consistently behave rationally.

NOISE TRADING AND RUMOURS

Fisher and Statman (2004) distinguish between information traders and noise traders. Information trading is driven by the fundamental values of stocks (and other securities) whereas noise trading is driven by sentiment (Shefrin and Statman 1994). In an efficient market there are only information traders and value alone determines prices. Noise traders can move prices away from fundamental value and render markets inefficient. According to Fisher and Statman stock markets are in a bubble when bullish sentiment moves prices above fundamental value and in a negative bubble when bearish sentiment pushes prices below fundamental value.

Roll (1988a) found that value-related news explained only 35% of the variation in monthly stock returns and Fair (2002) found that many large price changes occurred in the absence of value-related news. Noise traders appear to have a substantial impact on price movements. Bullish noise trading can drive prices higher as fundamental value falls, and bearish noise trading can push prices down even when fundamental value rises. When a market movement occurs in the absence of value-related news, the market movement becomes the news. Investors may react to such price changes on the grounds that they reveal how other investors are thinking. In particular it may be assumed that other investors know something, or understand something, that justifies the market movement and an informational cascade ensues with investors copying each other. Fama and French (2004a) showed that unless noise traders (stupid or misinformed investors) exactly cancel each other out there would be a noise trader effect on prices. Unless there is a mistaken overpricing to offset every mistaken underpricing, the mistakes affect prices.

A noise trader uses irrelevant, or inaccurate, information when making investment decisions. One type of unreliable information, on which noise traders may base their trades, is rumour. However rumours may affect even professional traders. If trading on rumour is regarded as noise trading, then market professionals are sometimes noise traders. Even respected financial newspapers and magazines participate in the spreading of rumours, and websites are an abundant source of rumours.

For financial market traders to profit from new information, they must act on the news before other traders. There is pressure to respond quickly. There may not be time to check on the accuracy of a rumour before acting on it. As a result even competent professionals may engage in noise trading. Pressure to act quickly is likely to engender anxiety and stress, which renders people more susceptible to accepting rumours. It is not always possible to know whether a piece of information is good or bad. One of the behavioural finance heuristics is the dilution heuristic according to which use of poor information can dilute the use of good information, and hence noise trades can crowd out information trades.

Kimmel (2004) points out that rumours emerge in conditions of uncertainty, which are frequent in financial markets. Rumours are particularly prone to emerge when emotions, especially feelings of fear, are high. In a situation of change people may be unable to understand the changes. The resulting uncertainty generates fear and the need for information relevant to the future. Uncertainty about the future creates stress, and interacts with stress, to produce a need for information which can be used to guide actions.

Rumours are more likely to circulate if they are credible. Rumours received from trusted sources are more likely to be believed. In addition to the plausibility and source of a rumour, its frequency of repetition affects its acceptability. The more often a rumour is heard, the more likely it is to be believed. Repetition fosters belief.

It appears that in financial markets the most prevalent rumours concern short-term events; it is the immediate future that is of greatest concern. Kimmel and Audrain (2002) found that the number of rumours was related to the importance of their content, to the accuracy of previous rumours, and to levels of anxiety. They also found that rumours that subsequently turned out to be true, became more precise over time. In contrast, false rumours became increasingly distorted.

Rumours, true or false, have an impact on market prices. For example DiFonzo and Bordia (1997) showed that rumours affect investment decisions, even when the rumours come from sources that lack credibility. They found that price changes resulting from rumours tend to follow trends that exhibit persistence. Apart from their specific 'information' content, rumours can have a further effect on markets by influencing market sentiment. Rumours can generate feelings of optimism or pessimism.

495

Some researchers have considered the role of the media in the provision of stock market information, and in particular whether the media provide good information or noise. Tetlock (2007) found that media optimism/pessimism could influence market prices but that the effects were subsequently eliminated, which was interpreted as suggesting that the information conveyed was noise. Noise was seen as having a merely temporary effect on prices. Media pessimism was followed by price falls, which were subsequently reversed. The falls were larger, and lasted longer, in the case of the stocks of smaller companies. This latter point was interpreted as indicating that small investors were most strongly affected by the media. This view was based on the grounds that the stocks of smaller companies tend to be held by private individuals.

Liden (2006) investigated the value of stock recommendations from newspapers and magazines. It was found that, although the overall value of the information was about zero, there was a difference between buy and sell recommendations. Sell recommendations tended to be useful indicators; they contained good information. Buy recommendations were actually misleading in the sense that recommended stocks tended to fall in price.

Another source of noise appears to be advertising of the products of the company whose shares are being considered. Fehle *et al.* (2005) found that when a company advertises its products, it simultaneously advertises its shares. When a company advertises its products, its stock price tends to rise. From the perspective of stock trading, the advertising could be seen as noise. It was observed that the increase in share purchases took the form of small purchases, which indicates that small investors are the ones influenced by the product advertising when making their investment decisions.

Rational investors might be expected to correct the errant price movements caused by noise traders. Unjustified falls would be countered by purchases on the part of rational investors, conversely unwarranted rises would tend to cause rational investors to sell and thereby eliminate the inappropriate price movement. Trading that tends to maintain prices at stable, equilibrium levels is referred to as negative feedback trading. The efficient market hypothesis assumes that negative feedback trading dominates financial markets.

Shleifer and Summers (1990) suggested that rational investors face two forms of uncertainty that could result in them not correcting the effects of noise traders. First, their rational valuations may be wrong. This possibility could make them reluctant to pursue the more modest profit opportunities, so that small deviations from fair value may remain uncorrected. Second, rational investors face uncertainty as to how long the stock prices will stay away from their fundamental values. The effects of uncertainty on the trading behaviour of rational investors allow noise traders to move prices away from the values that would accurately reflect the available information.

Shleifer and Vishny (1997) also pointed out limits to the correction of mispricing including the particular difficulty of exploiting overpricing. To profit from overpricing an investor needs to short sell; that is, borrow shares and then sell them. The resulting short position provides a profit from a fall in the share price since the shares could be bought at a price lower than the selling price when being returned to the lender. The extent of such trades is limited by the fact that many investors are not allowed to short sell. The possibility that the return of the shares to the lender could be demanded at any time renders the time horizon of the short sale uncertain, and thereby causes the short sale to be riskier and less desirable.

A constraint on the rationality of investment behaviour is the limit to the amount of information that investors can process. Bounded rationality is the limited rationality that arises when, in the face of a deluge of information, investors fail to analyse it all and as a result do not behave in a totally rational manner. In addition, behavioural finance suggests that there are systematic psychological biases that distort decision-making and prevent rational behaviour. The limitations on the price-correcting trades of rational investors makes it less likely that they would correct mispricing arising from the psychological biases identified by behavioural finance.

Noise traders are sometimes referred to as uninformed traders. Jordan and Kaas (2002) found that whilst both informed and uninformed investors are subject to behavioural finance biases, uninformed investors are more strongly affected by the biases. In other words, noise traders are particularly prone to psychological biases in their trading behaviour.

BEHAVIOURAL FINANCE

Behavioural finance applies the findings of psychological research on decision-making to investment decisions. Apparent irrationalities in decision-making are seen as arising from two sources. First, there are errors in the processing of information. This partly arises from self-deception. Second, there are biases and errors in the decision-making based on the processed information. This is partly due to heuristic simplification. In other words people perceive situations inaccurately, and then make decisions that are inconsistent with perceptions. There are two layers of errors.

There is evidence from psychological studies that there are systematic biases in the way people think. Research has found a number of systematic biases that affect investors. These include overconfidence, illusion of control, hindsight bias, confirmation bias, cognitive dissonance, representativeness, retrievability, narrow framing, mental accounting, conservatism, status quo bias, anchoring, ambiguity-aversion, loss-aversion, regret, emotion, group-think, and herding (see Chapter 2 on the psychology of personal investment decisions). All of these biases interfere with the process of rational decision-making that is assumed by the efficient market hypothesis.

However Ko and Huang (2007) have suggested that overconfidence could be beneficial, rather than detrimental, to market efficiency. There is a view that since it is costly to acquire information in terms of time and money, it is rational to limit the amount of information acquired. This is referred to as rational inattention (Huang and Liu 2007). According to Ko and Huang overconfident investors would devote more resources to the acquisition of information than more rational investors. Since overconfident investors believe that they can use information profitably, they will seek relatively large amounts of information. An effect of this behaviour of overconfident investors is that more information is put into the market. In consequence stock prices reflect a larger amount of information and hence get closer to their fundamental, or true, values. In other words overconfident investors make markets more efficient.

UNDERREACTION

Figure 24.1 illustrates the share price movements when there is overreaction or underreaction. At time T there is an item of news to which the share price should move, from P_1 to P_2, as indicated by the unbroken line. If the market overreacts, the price rises to P_3 before moving to P_2. If there is underreaction, the initial price movement is insufficient. Initially the share price moves only to P_4, the remaining price movement occurring subsequently.

497

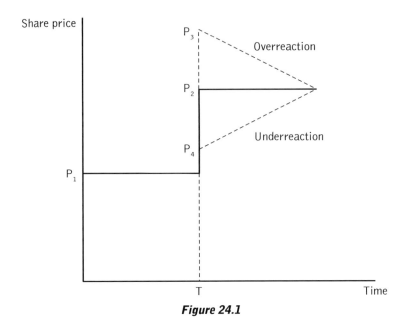

Figure 24.1

If there were a consistent tendency to under- or overreaction to new information, investors could profit from the information. Underreaction would imply that investors could profit from buying subsequent to the news. Overreaction would provide profits from selling after the news. The opportunity to make such profits is inconsistent with the efficient market hypothesis.

The concept of conservatism suggests that investors are slow to change their views following the receipt of new information. This is consistent with the research findings that following unexpected earnings announcements it can take several weeks for the resulting stock price movements to be completed. Investors take time to change their views about a stock, following news of unexpectedly high or low company profits.

The idea of cognitive dissonance relates to the desire to avoid dissonance. Dissonance occurs when new information contradicts existing beliefs. The extent of the dissonance depends on the level of commitment to the beliefs. Commitment develops when the individual has a choice to make. The level of commitment to that choice (and the commitment to the beliefs associated with it) increases with the amount of money, time, and effort invested in that choice or set of beliefs. The level of commitment is stronger where the choice or belief deviates from the norm. Group-think is a name given to the tendency for members of a group to share beliefs and to mutually reinforce those beliefs (Hilton 2001). If an individual takes a view that deviates from the group-think norm, the degree of commitment to that view will be high.

A phenomenon similar to conservatism is anchoring. People often start from a particular value, the anchor, and then adjust their evaluation from this point. The anchor might, for example, be the purchase price of a share or the highest price that it has reached. It has been suggested that most people adjust too conservatively and hence give too much weight to the anchor value when evaluating the appropriate value for an investment. This can cause investors to underestimate possible deviations from their original estimates (Shefrin 2000; Tversky and Kahneman 1982, 1982c).

In an experiment Tversky and Kahneman (1974) asked people to answer such questions as 'What is the percentage of African nations in the UN?' A wheel of fortune was spun in front of the subjects who were then asked whether their answer was above or below the number provided by the wheel. They were then asked to give their answers. The subjects were found to be heavily influenced by the wheel of fortune. For example the average estimate was 25 and 45 for groups that received 10 and 65 respectively from the wheel.

Professional analysts, such as stockbrokers, appear to be subject to anchoring. It might be thought that if an analyst suggests an appropriate price for a share and the share price subsequently moves away from that level, an investor would see a trading opportunity. For example a fall in the share price below the analyst's forecast should indicate a buying opportunity. Unfortunately for the private investor, the effect of the share price move seems to be that the analyst moves the forecast in the same direction as the share price. Cornell (2000) demonstrated this effect in relation to Intel. Those results were consistent with studies by Womack (1996), and Brav and Lehavy (2001) whose findings showed that adjustments subsequent to analysts' forecasts took the form of the forecasts being changed towards actual prices rather than actual share prices moving towards the forecasts. This throws doubt on the idea that investment analysts move share prices towards the levels consistent with relevant information, and hence throws doubt on the idea that markets are efficient.

The appropriate prices of shares are uncertain and past prices are likely to be anchors for current prices. Stock markets tend to underreact to information such as earnings reports (e.g. Liu *et al.* 2001); and investors may expect a company's earnings to be in line with an apparent historical trend (and underreact to a deviation from that apparent trend). This is consistent with past prices acting as anchors for future prices. Anchoring may also explain the expectation, held by many investors including technical analysts, of a share price trading within a range of values for a period of time. All of these effects of anchoring can hinder the process of incorporating new information into a share price, with the effect that it takes time for the price to reflect all relevant information.

The fear of regret is another explanation for underreaction. If an investment decision proves to be incorrect there would be the pain of regret at having made a bad decision. One defence against the risk of regret is the avoidance of decisions. Fear of regret could slow the process of incorporating new information into share prices through transactions in the shares.

Ambiguity-aversion (alternatively known as familiarity bias) suggests that investors prefer to invest in companies that they feel that they understand. Over 90% of the equity investments of investors in the United States, UK, and Japan is in companies in their own countries. This home bias exists despite the demonstrated benefits of international diversification. Likewise there are biases towards the investor's local region and the firm that employs them. This preference for the familiar results in the holding of portfolios that are insufficiently diversified. In consequence investors bear more risk than is necessary. The bias also hinders the flow of money to some areas or sectors. In consequence asset prices are slow to adjust to new information. The unfamiliar remains underpriced and the familiar remains overpriced.

OVERREACTION

Overconfidence causes people to overestimate their abilities and to overestimate the accuracy of their forecasts. Overconfidence arises partly from self-attribution bias. This is a tendency on the part of investors to regard successes as arising from their expertise whilst failures are due to bad luck or the actions of others. This leads to excessive confidence in one's own powers of forecasting. Overconfidence appears to be greater when feedback on decisions is deferred or ambiguous (Fischhoff *et al.* 1977). Financial markets are characterised by delayed feedback, since anticipated price adjustments can take a considerable amount of time. The feedback is also ambiguous (are outcomes to be judged in absolute terms, or relative to a benchmark – and what benchmark is appropriate?). Noise trading in financial markets can cause feedback to be inconclusive (might apparently successful forecasting merely be the accidental result of noise?).

Overconfidence is capable of explaining a number of types of apparently irrational behaviour. For example it can explain why some investors hold undiversified portfolios. If investors are highly confident about their stock selection abilities, they will not feel the need to reduce risk by means of diversification. It could also explain why some investors trade very frequently, to the point where transaction costs cause their investment behaviour to be loss making (Barber and Odean 2000, 2001a).

To the extent that some investors attribute their profits from rising markets to their own talents, rising markets could be self-perpetuating. Overconfident investors may be encouraged to invest further and thereby reinforce an upward movement in stock prices. Conversely a falling market reduces confidence and investing. This is consistent with the view that markets exhibit overreaction.

In one study of overconfidence Lichenstein and Fischoff (1977) gave people market reports on 12 stocks and asked them to forecast the direction in which their prices would move. Whereas only 47% of the predictions were correct, on average people were 65% confident that their forecasts would be correct.

Odean (1998a) has shown that one of the effects of overconfidence is that turnover of investments tends to be high, that is people trade shares more as a result of overconfidence. Barber and Odean (2000) have shown that as turnover rises net profits tend to fall. Psychological research has found that men tend to be more overconfident than women. Barber and Odean (2001a) found that single men trade 67% more than single women. Correspondingly single men on average experienced investment returns 3.5% per year lower than single women.

Some other biases tend to reinforce overconfidence. According to the confirmation bias, investors pay more attention to evidence that supports their opinions than to evidence that contradicts them. This can cause investors to persist with unsuccessful investment strategies. Another cognitive bias is the illusion of control. In some circumstances people behave as if they were able to exert control, or able to forecast events, where this is impossible or unlikely. The illusion of control is associated with the underestimation of risk. Also related to the concept of overconfidence is optimism bias. Optimism bias is the tendency for people to regard themselves as better than average (Hilton 2001).

The hindsight bias is the inability to correctly remember one's prior expectations after observing new information. The hindsight bias prevents people learning from their own mistakes, since they are unable to remember those mistakes. People are unable to recognise their own errors. There is self-denial about past errors. If someone has a self-image of being a clever investor, past errors in forecasting may be subject to distortions of memory aimed at maintaining the self-image. Memory is never a faithful recollection of the past; it is amended by the human mind.

Good decision-making in financial markets relies on learning from the past. Learning may entail the comparison of new information with previous expectations. This requires an accurate recall of previous expectations. The hindsight bias involves the contamination of recollections of expectations by new information. The recalled expectations of an outcome are biased towards information about the outcome. The person remembers forming an expectation that is close to what subsequently happened.

The hindsight bias can lead to overreaction by investors. People may form expectations by averaging outcomes with their previous expectations of those outcomes. For example expectations of future returns could be formed by averaging realised investment returns with previously expected returns. Hindsight-biased investors, when forming such averages, incorrectly remember their prior expectations. They amend their memories in the light of realised returns. New information about returns thus becomes overweighted, and hence has excessive influence on the formation of expectations. Expectations change too much. The result is overreaction to the new information. Hindsight bias is not limited to naive investors; Biais and Weber (2006) found that market professionals were prone to hindsight bias.

Representativeness helps to explain why many investors seem to extrapolate price movements. Many investors appear to believe that if prices have been rising in the past then they will continue to rise, and conversely with falling prices. The concept of representativeness suggests that this is because those investors see an investment with recent price increases as representative of longer-term successful investments, conversely with price falls. DeBondt and Thaler (1985) argued that because investors are subject to the representativeness bias, they could become too optimistic about past winners and too pessimistic about past losers. Trading that is influenced by the representativeness bias can move share prices away from the levels that accurately reflect all relevant information.

Everyone uses heuristics. Heuristics are rules of thumb that help people to make sense of the deluge of information with which they are bombarded. Social psychology has established that we tend to judge people by appearances. If someone, who is newly encountered, resembles a person one has known then it is assumed that the new acquaintance has a similar personality to the older acquaintance. Representativeness refers to the tendency to evaluate something with reference to something else, which it resembles. A share price pattern that was followed by a price rise in the past may be seen as indicating a price rise in the future.

One aspect of representativeness is often referred to as the law of small numbers. It is a belief that random samples will resemble each other more closely than the principles of statistical sampling theory would predict. People tend to have an image of what a random sample should look like, and take the view that samples that differ from the image are not random. Consider the following two sequences of coin tossing:

THTHHT

and

TTTHHH

Both sequences are equally likely but when asked which is more likely most people will say the first. The first series fits the image of a random sequence whereas the second does not.

This may help to explain the popularity of chartism; people do not always see random sequences as being random, and tend to attribute patterns to the sequences. People are biased towards believing that a causal factor is the reason for a sequence of events and find it difficult to accept that events can occur by chance; they are reluctant to accept that an apparent pattern can emerge purely by chance. Investors tend to over-interpret patterns that arise from coincidence. A pattern arising from coincidence may be interpreted as indicative, or representative, of a genuine pattern of events. A result could be overreaction to a random sequence of events even when the number of events is small or the length of the sequence is short (Kahneman and Riepe 1998).

Cooper *et al.* (2001) provided an interesting example of representativeness. They studied firms that changed their names to incorporate some mention of dot.com between June 1998 and July 1999, a period which coincided with the dot.com share price bubble. Some of the firms that made the change did not significantly operate in the Internet business. It was found that those non-Internet firms, on average, experienced a 140% increase in share price during the 60 days following the name change. The name changes conveyed no information about the operations of the firms. Some investors appear to have seen the letters 'dot.com' in a name as representative of potential strong performers.

Retrievability bias causes too much attention to be given to the most easily recalled information (it is alternatively known as the availability or memory bias). In consequence there is a tendency to give too much emphasis to the most recent information. Retrievability is consistent with the overreaction hypothesis, one dimension of which is the overemphasis on recent information and recent events when making investment decisions. According to the overreaction hypothesis share prices are prone to rise too high and fall too low. Experiments by Kahneman and Tversky (1972, 1973) indicated that people not only give too much weight to recent experience when making forecasts but also make forecasts that are too extreme. Another aspect of the retrievability bias is the overemphasis on one's own experience. Some people appear to learn only from their own mistakes, rather than being able to learn from the experiences of others. The retrievability bias limits the amount of information used in investment decision-making, and hence limits the amount of information reflected in asset prices as a result of trading.

It has been observed that the shares of companies with low price-earnings ratios tend to outperform those of companies with high price-earnings ratios. This has been called the price-earnings ratio effect. DeBondt and Thaler (1990) argued that this price-earnings ratio effect could be explained in terms of extreme expectations of future earnings growth. The extreme forecasts of earnings growth lead to excessively high share prices and hence price-earnings ratios that are too high, and which subsequently fall when the error is realised. Thus the shares of firms with high price-earnings ratios tend to perform less well than the shares of firms with low price-earnings ratios, since some price decline is required in order to correct the exaggerated price-earnings ratio.

Francis *et al.* (2004) cited evidence that professional investment analysts' earnings forecasts tend to be overoptimistic with the degree of exaggeration increasing as the forecast horizon becomes longer. Cornell (2001), when examining the case of Intel, concluded that many analysts' recommendations were based on factors other than divergences between market price and fundamental value. Possible factors mentioned were rating the company, as well as the stock, and reacting to the recent price movement of the stock (the momentum effect of extrapolation). Francis *et al.* cited evidence that professional investment analysts exhibited herding behaviour such that they were influenced by each other's forecasts and hence produced similar forecasts. Any of these possible factors could exaggerate market swings in response to announcements of changes in company performance, and hence generate overreaction.

INACCURATE PERCEPTIONS OF RISK

Narrow framing refers to the tendency of investors to focus too narrowly. One aspect is focus on the constituents of a portfolio rather than the portfolio as a whole. Another dimension of narrow framing is the focus on the short term even when the investment horizon is long term. It is not rational for an investor accumulating assets for retirement 25 years hence to be concerned about the week-by-week performance of the portfolio. Yet long-term investors do focus on short-term volatility. Studies have shown that when, in experimental situations, people have been presented with monthly distributions of returns they are less likely to invest than when they are shown annual distributions (with the annualised volatility being the same in both cases). The implication is that focus on short-term volatility deters investment. It appears that people do not appreciate the effects of time diversification. By time diversification is meant the tendency for good periods to offset bad periods with the effect that the dispersion of investment returns does not increase proportionately with the period of the investment. Investors who focus too much on short-term fluctuations overestimate stock market risk and allocate too little of their money to investment in shares.

This has been suggested as a possible explanation of what is called 'The Equity Premium Puzzle'. The puzzle is why the excess of equity returns over returns on bonds and deposits is so high (when averaged over long periods of time). Although additional return is appropriate in order to compensate for the extra risk, it is generally thought that the additional return actually received is much more than is justified by the extra risk. However if investors focus too strongly on the short term they may overestimate equity risk and hence require an excessive premium on the expected rate of return in order to induce them to invest in shares. Focus on individual stocks, rather than the portfolio as a whole, would also cause investors to overestimate stock market risk since the risk of individual shares exceeds the risk of portfolios. In terms of explaining the equity premium puzzle, these factors may be reinforced by loss-aversion. The idea of loss-aversion comes from prospect theory and suggests that people are much more sensitive to losses than to gains. Investors may not only overestimate the likelihood of large losses, they also feel a disproportionate amount of pain as a result of losses (Benartzi and Thaler 1995).

The idea of mental accounts has similarities with narrow framing. The principle of mental accounts sees people as separating aspects of their finances into separate accounts rather than seeing their financial situation as an integrated whole. For example income and wealth may be segregated such that only current income is used for current spending, and wealth is treated as something to be preserved. In consequence changes in the level of wealth have little effect on spending.

The concept of mental accounts has been proposed as an explanation of the apparent preference, on the part of many investors, for stocks that pay high dividends (Statman 1997). Such investors may be prepared to use dividends to finance spending since dividends are seen as income, whereas they would not sell some of their shares to fund expenditure even when the real value of the shares has increased. Dividends are treated as available for spending but capital gains are not.

Mental accounting can cause investors to overestimate risk by failing to take the risk-reduction effects of diversification into consideration. Chapter 13 on portfolio diversification shows how combining assets into a portfolio reduces risk since poor performances from some investments may be offset by good performances from others. If an investor separates investments into different mental accounts, the potential risk reduction of such offsetting is ignored. In consequence total risk is overestimated.

503

Hindsight-biased investors may underestimate volatility. This is because they amend their recollected expectations into line with observed outcomes. A rational investor, upon observing a return that is substantially different from the previously expected return, would raise the expectation of volatility. A hindsight-biased investor would not be aware of the substantial discrepancy, and would therefore underestimate volatility. Hindsight-biased investors form distorted expectations of future returns and risk, and as a result construct inefficient investment portfolios. Hindsight bias, by distorting expectations of return and risk, can prevent share prices from reflecting relevant information.

The illusion of control is the tendency to believe that chance events are amenable to personal control (Langer 1975). The illusion of control can cause an underestimation of risk. If events are seen as controllable, they will be seen as less risky (Gollwitzer and Kinney 1989). DeBondt (1998) suggested that one manifestation of the illusion of control was the belief of many investors that they would be sufficiently astute to sell before a large fall in prices. This belief that they would be able to avoid losses by selling in time causes such investors to underestimate the risks of their investments. The degree of illusion of control can be affected by the individual's environment (Taylor and Armor 1996). Competitive and stressful environments can produce illusion of control (Friedland et al. 1992). Fenton-O'Creevy et al. (2005) found that traders in financial markets were subject to the illusion of control. They also found that the illusion of control was associated with poorer performance.

The illusion of knowledge is the tendency for people to believe that additional information always increases the accuracy of their forecasts. It is the belief that more information increases the person's knowledge and hence improves decisions (Peterson and Pitz 1988). For example people often believe that knowledge of previous drawings of lottery numbers improves their ability to predict future lottery numbers. Some information is irrelevant, or may be beyond a person's ability to interpret, but the person may still regard the information as improving their ability to forecast. Tumarkin and Whitelaw (2001) found that, despite providing no useful information, website message board postings increased trading volume in the respective shares. Despite the absence of useful information from the messages, as indicated by subsequent price movements, it appeared that some investors believed that it added to their knowledge and expertise (and traded as a result). The illusion of knowledge causes investors to be overconfident and to misinterpret the amount of risk from an investment. Investors, who overestimate the accuracy of their forecasts, underestimate the risks taken.

Fenton-O'Creevy et al. (2005) found that professional traders also failed to appreciate the significance of sample size for risk. In the case of an illiquid stock there would be few trades, in other words a small sample size. In the case of liquid stocks there would be a high volume of trading, and hence a large sample of trades. A particular percentage deviation from a previous price is more likely to be a chance event when trades are infrequent than when they are frequent. A 10% price change in an infrequently traded share is more likely to be the result of random variation than the same percentage change in the price of a heavily traded share.

According to the familiarity bias, people tend to prefer things that seem familiar to them. Correspondingly investors prefer investments with which they feel familiar. Familiarity appears to reduce the perceived risk. Arguably the most familiar investments are those in the company for which the investor works. A study by John Hancock Financial Services (Driscoll et al. 1995) found that a majority of employees believed that shares in their own company were less risky than a diversified portfolio. Benartzi (2001) reported the findings of a survey which indicated that only 16.4% of respondents believed that shares in their own company were more risky than the stock market as a whole. Kilka and Weber (2000) found that Americans believed the US stock market would perform better than the German stock market whereas Germans believed that their stock market would be the stronger performer. Generally the evidence indicates that people view familiar stocks favourably, expecting them to deliver both higher returns and a lower level of risk. The result is that portfolios are biased towards investments that seem familiar. Tourani-Rad and Kirkby (2005) confirmed the familiarity bias in New Zealand, in that they found that the portfolios of New Zealand investors contained a disproportionate amount of New Zealand stocks but they did not confirm that it was the result of higher optimism with regard to the future performance of New Zealand stocks.

Finance professionals typically measure risk as the expected standard deviation of returns on an investment. The standard deviation of returns is a measure of volatility. It is assumed by conventional finance models, such as the Markowitz portfolio diversification model, that volatility and perceived risk are closely related. However research has found that there can be substantial differences between volatility and perceived risk. Choices appear to be better explained by perceived risk than by volatility (Jia *et al.* 1999). Perceived risk, in contrast to volatility, incorporates affective (emotional) reactions to uncertainty (Loewenstein *et al.* 2001). The distinction between volatility and perceived risk was reinforced by Weber *et al.* (2005). They found that presentational factors that affected expected volatility had no effect on perceived risk, and that perceived risk had more effect on investment choice than expected volatility. The familiarity of asset names, which may be expected to elicit emotional responses, had strong effects on risk perception and investment choice. This is consistent with the other evidence relating to the familiarity bias.

Vividness appears to be a factor in the incorporation of emotion into the perception of risk. Vividness refers to the emotional interest or excitement engendered by an event (Plous 1993). Stock market bubbles and crashes are examples of vivid events. The effects of vividness on attitudes and behaviour are not necessarily reasonable but are not permanent (Grable *et al.* 2006).

Prospect Theory

There are three key elements to prospect theory: (1) perceived probabilities are subject to bias, (2) investors are more concerned about gains and losses than levels of wealth, and (3) investors feel losses more than gains (Kahneman and Tversky 1972, 1973, 1982).

In relation to perceived probabilities, the biases are tendencies to exaggerate small and large probabilities and underweight medium ones. See Figure 24.2.

In this figure, subjective (perceived) probabilities are referred to as decision weightings. When plotted against actual probabilities the decision weights are too high at low and high probabilities and too low at medium probabilities. The exaggeration of high probabilities suggests that highly likely (but not certain) events are treated as being certain. This is consistent with the idea of overconfidence. Investors can become overconfident about their forecasts to the extent that they forget that markets are uncertain.

Figure 24.3 is a value function. It depicts subjective values assigned to gains and losses relative to a reference point. The reference point is subjective and may, for example, be the purchase price of an investment. The reference point divides the region where someone feels that they are making gains from the region in which they feel that they are making losses.

505

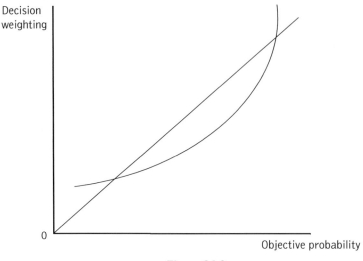

Figure 24.2

It is to be noted that the slope of the function for losses is steeper than the slope for gains. This is because, on average, people find the pain of losses to be about 2.25 times as intense as the pleasure from gains. Given an evens chance of winning or losing, people on average require the prospect of a £225 win to balance the prospect of a £100 loss. This relatively large fear of loss, known as loss-aversion, will tend to deter retail investors from stock market related investments. When combined with narrow framing and mental accounting, this asymmetric perception of risk increases the total perceived risk and thereby distorts decision-making. Risk premiums are too high, and hence asset prices are too low.

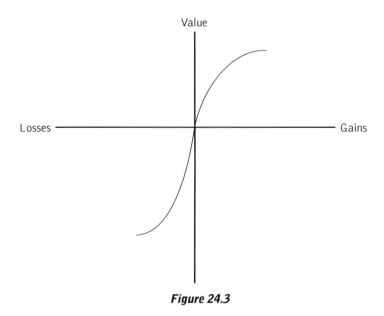

Figure 24.3

This is consistent with the 'endowment effect' (Thaler 1980). People often require much more to sell something than they were originally prepared to pay for it (Kahneman *et al.* 1990, 1991). This is seen as being associated with the pain of giving something up.

Another feature of Figure 24.3 is the tendency for the slope of the value function to become less steep as gains or losses increase. This implies that as gains are made investors will become less inclined to take risks, since the addition to value of a higher gain is less than the reduction in value resulting from a lowered gain. It also implies that as losses increase investors become more willing to accept risk. This is because the value of a loss reduction outweighs the value of a further loss. So, for example, in a losing situation an 'evens' bet looks attractive. An aspect of loss-aversion is that people will avoid the risk of making losses (by avoiding risks) when in a gaining situation but will accept risk in order to attempt to recover from a loss. Prospect theory sees investors as being loss-averse rather than risk-averse.

This behaviour in a loss-making situation is consistent with the idea of an escalation bias (Shefrin 2001). An Escalation Bias leads to 'averaging down' whereby as the price falls the investment is treated as being an increasingly good bargain. The thinking is that if a share was a good buy at £2, it is a fantastic bargain at £1 and more should be bought. It is psychologically difficult to consider the possibility that the initial purchase was at an excessively high price.

According to prospect theory, people in a position of gain become increasingly risk-averse and unwilling to accept gambles. When people are in a position of loss they become more inclined to accept risk. This may help to explain the disposition effect. The disposition effect is the inclination, when selling part of a portfolio, to sell assets that have risen in price relative to their purchase prices rather than assets that have fallen in price. The disposition effect can move share prices away from their fair values. Prices rise too slowly because of sales, and fall too slowly because of lack of sales. Prices thus fail to reflect all relevant information.

The disposition effect can be explained in terms of the avoidance of regret and the pursuit of pride. People want to feel good about themselves and hence take decisions that provide pride and avoid regret. Shefrin and Statman (1984) showed that these factors influence investment decisions. The sale of an investment that has risen in price produces the pleasant feeling that the investment decision was a good one. The sale of an investment that has fallen in price produces the unpleasant feeling that the original investment choice was a bad one. By realising successes through selling successful investments, and not realising failures, an investor can preserve the self-image of being a good investor. In consequence investors are more likely to sell investments showing gains than investments showing losses.

There is empirical research evidence in support of the disposition effect. For example Odean (1998) found that, on average, investors are approximately 50% more likely to sell a winner than a loser. Grinblatt and Keloharju (2001) found that if a share outperforms the market by 10%, the likelihood of sales increases by 26%, whereas an underperformance of 10% decreases the likelihood of sales by 14%. It is not just private individuals; professional investors such as institutional fund managers are also prone to the disposition effect (Frazzini 2006). Investors seem to prefer to sell winners rather than losers.

Narrow framing and mental accounting also help to explain the disposition effect. The disposition effect would not operate unless investors mentally separated components of portfolios.

There is evidence from mutual funds supportive of the prospect theory proposition that risk taking increases following losses, and declines following gains. Elton *et al.* (2003) studied mutual fund managers who were paid incentive fees; in other words whose fees were related to the performance of the funds managed by them. They observed that mutual fund managers when paid incentive fees were more likely to increase risk after periods of poor performance and to decrease risk following periods of strong performance. Incentive fees mean that the fund manager has a personal financial interest in fund performance and the findings of Elton *et al.* may be dependent upon the presence of incentive fees. This dependence is suggested by a study from Ammann and Verhofen (2007) who found that the behaviour of mutual fund managers seemed to contradict prospect theory. They found that strong prior performance led to increased risk taking (for example increased beta and more small capitalisation stocks) whereas poor performance tended to lead to the adoption of passive strategies, which exhibit lower risk.

INVESTORS HAVE FEELINGS

The size effect is the apparent tendency for the shares of small firms to outperform the shares of large firms. The book-to-market effect is the apparent tendency for the shares of companies with high book values relative to share prices to outperform the shares of companies with relatively low book values. DeBondt and Thaler (1987) argue that regret theory is consistent with both the size and book-to-market effects. Psychologists have found that individuals who make decisions that turn out badly have more regret (blame themselves more) when that decision was relatively unconventional. Losses on shares in a major blue-chip firm cause less regret than losses on a small, little-known firm. The former loss may be regarded as bad luck whereas the latter loss may be attributed to poor judgement. Higher book-to-market firms tend to have lower stock prices, perhaps because they are unfashionable, or in difficulties. Investments in firms that are small, unfashionable, or in difficulties are more unconventional. There is a high risk of feeling regret. Such investments are not the choices of the majority and require more courage and risk taking on the part of investors. Investors are betting on the accuracy of their own judgement. More courage is required to make investments in the shares of small, unfashionable, or problematic firms and as a result the shares of such firms tend to be shunned by many investors. In consequence those shares tend to have current prices that are low relative to the objective characteristics of the firms. Such relative underpricing provides potential for future outperformance in terms of the total returns on the shares.

In addition to cognitive biases, moods and emotions may have a role in investment decision-making. Hirshleifer and Shumway (2003) found that sunshine is strongly correlated with stock returns. Presumably sunshine causes investors to be happy and makes them feel more favourable towards investments. The relationship, between mood (emotions) and decision-making, has also been established by other researchers (Loewenstein *et al.* 2001; Slovic *et al.* 2002; Forgas 1995; Wright and Bower 1992; Kamstra *et al.* 2003). Even quantitative share pricing models involve an element of judgement that is affected by mood and emotion. For example dividend discount models, such as the Gordon growth model, involve estimates of future dividend growth rates. It may be that optimism arising from a good mood leads to a high estimate for the growth rate of dividends. That high estimate would result in the expected (fair) price of the share being relatively high. The rational investor of the efficient market hypothesis is an unemotional decision-maker. Emotions and moods may be irrelevant pieces of information that become reflected in share prices.

Users of pricing models are likely to be professionals. Shiller (1984) pointed out that most non-professional investors do not have knowledge of pricing models and investment analysis. They are likely to be noise traders affected by rumour and social mood. Social mood is a collectively shared state of mind (Prechter 1999; Nofsinger 2005; Olson 2006). Investors with no knowledge of analysis are particularly likely to be influenced by social mood when making investment decisions. DeLong et al. (1990) posited a class of investors whose expectations were not justified by fundamentals; they referred to them as noise traders. Unjustified expectations are referred to as investor sentiment. When sentiment is shared amongst investors, stock prices can deviate from fundamental values for long periods.

Evidence for the impact of social mood on stock prices is provided in Chapter 2 on the psychology of personal investment decisions and in Chapter 27 on stock market bubbles and crashes. Further evidence for the influence of social mood on share prices comes from Edmans et al. (2007) who measured social mood using the results of international football (soccer) matches. Stock markets were found to decline following defeats. The effects were related to the importance of the matches, and to the importance of football to the country (very important in Europe and Latin America, unimportant in North America). The effects were most pronounced amongst smaller company stocks; which is consistent with the observation that smaller company stocks are predominantly held by investors in the company's own country rather than in international portfolios. It is also consistent with other studies, which have found that the shares of small companies are the most affected by investor sentiment. The effect was found to be present in relation to other sports, but not as strongly as in the case of football. There was no apparent tendency for stock markets to rise following wins.

The findings of Edmans et al. (2007) are consistent with the results of other studies relevant to the relationship between football results and social mood. For example Schwarz et al. (1987) found that the results of international football matches affected feelings of well-being and views on national issues. Carroll et al. (2002) found a 25% increase in heart attacks in England following England's defeat by Argentina in the 1998 World Cup. Other studies have found that murder and suicide rates increase following sports defeats. There appear to be no corresponding improvements in social mood following wins. Edmans et al. relate the asymmetry of responses to losses and wins to prospect theory. According to prospect theory the pain of a loss is more than twice the pleasure of a win. Also prospect theory measures gains and losses against a reference point. If allegiance bias causes supporters to expect their team to win, the outcome of a match is evaluated relative to that expectation. So a win merely confirms the expectation whereas a loss represents a downward deviation from the expected outcome.

Lee et al. (1991) found that investment trust (US closed-end fund) discounts were not affected by macroeconomic factors. Those findings imply that the discounts are not affected by economic fundamentals. The researchers observed that investment trusts were particularly popular among small investors, as were smaller company stocks and new issues (initial public offerings). They found that movements in investment trust discounts, small company share prices, and the volume of new issues were correlated. They interpreted this as evidence for the influence of sentiment among small investors.

Emotions can be particularly important when there is 'ego-involvement', which entails investors identifying with their investment choices (Dweck and Leggett 1988). There is evidence that such people may hold on to particular investments too long (Sandelands et al. 1988). Ego-involvement is also likely to magnify the effects of stress (Riess and Taylor 1984) and thereby reduce the quality of investment decision-making.

Baker and Nofsinger (2002) suggest an attachment bias, whereby investors become emotionally attached to particular investments. Emotional attachment can cause investors to focus on good features and ignore bad ones. Bad news may be ignored. This could hinder the incorporation of information into a share price. If investors ignore bad news, the share price may fail to fully reflect that bad news. Baker and Nofsinger suggest that one way to avoid the effects of emotion, and perhaps other psychological biases, is to invest in index tracker funds. Arguably investors are relatively unlikely to become emotionally attached to index tracker funds.

Investors not only have feelings, they are also prone to superstitions. Kahneman and Tversky (1983) have suggested the existence of a 'conjunction fallacy'. The conjunction fallacy is the belief that contiguous events have a causal relationship. Unrelated, but simultaneous, events in two markets might be seen as causally linked whereas they are actually unrelated. Also events in successive time periods may be seen as forming a pattern when in reality they are independent events. From this perspective technical analysis might be seen as a complex set of superstitions.

Evidence on the possibility of negative effects of emotions and moods on investment decision-making comes from research on expert systems. Expert systems are computer programmes that use relationships, provided by experts, to make decisions. Camerer (1981) found that expert systems frequently outperformed the experts whose knowledge had been used in their creation. This phenomenon is known as bootstrapping. It may be the case that the superior performance of the computer arises from the absence of the effects of emotions and moods.

CRITICISMS OF BEHAVIOURAL FINANCE

There has been a tendency to establish psychological biases in laboratory conditions, and then to assume that they operate in the real world. In the real world investors have data and models for the generation of expectations. In the real world money is at stake. It may be that when money is involved people make a greater effort to behave rationally. Competition between investment professionals might be expected to remove errors of judgement resulting from psychological biases. If rational investors seek profits from arbitraging against irrational investors, the result could be that the market as a whole behaves rationally even though some investors do not. This argument is dependent upon arbitrage being effective.

Some behavioural finance theories predict that markets overreact to new information, whilst others predict underreaction. This may lead to an inability to make forecasts and testable predictions. Further, Fama (1998) has argued that apparent overreaction to information is about as common as underreaction, and that this is consistent with the efficient market hypothesis. There are other conflicting predictions from behavioural finance. For example the endowment effect and status quo effect predict that investors hold what they have, or do nothing, whereas the overconfidence bias predicts that investors trade too much. The herding tendency to follow the investment behaviour of others also appears to conflict with biases, such as overconfidence, that cause investors to overestimate their abilities to choose potentially successful investments.

The ideas of noise trading and behavioural finance have been used as criticisms of the efficient market hypothesis. However the impact of these criticisms may depend upon how efficiency is defined. Damodaran (2001) defines market efficiency in terms of market prices being unbiased estimates of true value. According to this interpretation of informational efficiency the market price of a share is not necessarily correct at a point in time, it is merely unbiased. An unbiased price is one that randomly deviates from the true value, and the deviations are not related to other variables. If market efficiency is defined in terms of prices being unbiased estimates of true value, rather than as fully reflecting all relevant information, it may be consistent with noise trading and behavioural finance. Such consistency would depend upon deviations from true value being totally random. This would imply an inability to consistently exploit the deviations in order to make profits from inaccurate pricing.

CONCLUSION

The efficient market hypothesis assumes that investors behave rationally in the sense that they use all relevant information and analyse it in the most effective way with a view of achieving the best possible outcomes (maximising expected utility) for themselves. However many investors appear to behave in irrational ways; irrelevant information such as rumour is used and the analysis may be subject to misperceptions, emotions, and other psychological biases.

The behaviour of such irrational, or noise, traders may nonetheless be consistent with the market being rational in two circumstances. One circumstance would be offsetting behaviour among irrational investors, and the other would be market dominance of rational investors over irrational investors. If the behaviour of irrational investors were random, their irrational actions would tend to cancel out. Irrationally motivated purchases by some would tend to be offset by irrational sales by others with little effect on the market as a whole, so that the investors who behave rationally would determine market movements. Even if there were some uniformity of behaviour among irrational investors, a sufficient preponderance of rational investors could neutralise the effects of the irrationality. For example if irrational behaviour caused an unwarranted fall in the price of a share, rational investors would take advantage of the underpricing by buying the shares. Those purchases would move the share price back up to its appropriate level. In this way the rational investors would ensure that the market, as a whole, remained rational.

There are reasons to expect that irrational trades would not be mutually offsetting. Behaviours such as herding and positive feedback trading will tend to point the market in a particular direction (see Chapter 27 on stock market bubbles and crashes). For rational investors to offset the resulting distortions they should be sufficient in number, adequately capitalised, and unrestricted. It might be expected that market professionals, such as the managers of institutional investment funds, would be rational. However there is evidence that market professionals are prone to the same social and psychological influences as other investors. Furthermore the fact that obvious arbitrage opportunities can remain unexploited (see Chapter 23 on weak form market efficiency) suggests that the professionals are either inadequately funded or otherwise constrained from investment behaviour that would remove the effects of irrational trading.

From the perspective of the individual retail investor it may seem that irrational institutional investment managers could be avoided by investing in funds that aim to track stock indices.

Unfortunately this does not completely avoid irrationality. If irrational investing increases the price of a stock, index tracker funds will hold a higher proportion of that stock since the price rise increases its market capitalisation. So index tracker funds hold disproportionately large amounts of overpriced shares. Conversely shares that become underpriced would have low weightings in tracker funds because of their low capitalisations. Index tracker funds would hold disproportionately large amounts of overpriced shares, and disproportionately low quantities of underpriced shares.

Further reading

Readers who would like to pursue further their studies of behavioural finance may find the following books interesting:

Montier, J. (2002). *Behavioural Finance,* Wiley.

Montier, J. (2007). *Behavioural Investing: A Practitioner's Guide to Applying Behavioural Finance,* Wiley.

Nofsinger, J. R. (2005). *The Psychology of Investing,* 2nd edn, Pearson Education/Prentice Hall.

Shefrin, H. (2000). *Beyond Fear and Greed: Understanding Behavioral Finance and the Psychology of Investing,* Harvard Business School Press.

Shiller, R. J. (2005). *Irrational Exuberance,* 2nd edn, Princeton University Press.

Chapter 25

Market anomalies

OBJECTIVE

The objective of this chapter is to provide knowledge of the implications of market anomalies for market efficiency, particularly in regard to:

1. Earnings surprises.
2. The size effect.
3. Value investing.
4. Calendar effects.

And also to provide knowledge of the difficulties encountered when interpreting evidence about the efficient market hypothesis.

A market is semi-strong form efficient if either (1) security (share and bond) prices reflect all relevant publicly available information, or (2) it is not possible to make profits from the identification of mispricing.

An anomaly is an exception to a rule; in this case an observation that appears to contradict the view that markets are informationally efficient. The observation of anomalies provides evidence against the semi-strong form of the efficient market hypothesis.

EARNINGS SURPRISES

One anomaly relates to the market response to earnings announcements. Although some early studies of price reactions to earnings announcements concluded that the price changes were completed very quickly, later research has suggested that part of the price response is subject to a significant time lag. If a lag occurs, investors would have the opportunity to make profits from knowledge of the earnings announcement. They would have time to undertake trades that take advantage of the resulting price trends. For example if it takes two months for a share price to complete a rise, an investor could buy after the earnings announcement and achieve profits for two months.

Latane and Jones (1979) developed the concept of standardised unexpected earnings, which could be defined as:

(actual earnings − predicted earnings)/(standard deviation of earnings).

The division by the standard deviation of earnings (or standard error of the estimate) reflects the fact that the element of surprise or news in a particular difference between actual and predicted earnings depends upon its relationship to previous differences. The surprise element in a particular difference is greater for a firm whose earnings are normally stable.

Jones *et al.* (1984) found that a substantial part of the price adjustment to unexpected earnings occurred after the day of the earnings announcement. Indeed price adjustments were still occurring more than 60 days after the announcement. In an efficient market, prices should adjust very quickly to earnings announcements, rather than with a lag. Other researchers, using different samples and different methods, have found similar results. For example Kanto *et al.* (1998) found that on the Helsinki stock exchange the adjustment of share prices to unexpected reported earnings was delayed by a statistically significant period. Liu *et al.* (2003), when investigating UK data, also found a post earnings announcement drift in share prices and hence concluded that the UK stock market was inefficient with respect to publicly available information about corporate earnings.

Doyle *et al.* (2006), whilst confirming the earnings surprise effect, made observations about the stocks with the greatest earnings surprises. They tended to have lower analyst coverage, small market capitalisation, low institutional ownership, high book-to-market ratios, low trading volumes, high trading costs, and high variation of analyst forecasts. So the stocks offering the greatest apparent profits tended to be the most difficult and costly to trade, with the largest risk of being mispriced. However the authors concluded that there was still value from following investment strategies based on earnings surprise, even if the most extreme surprises are excluded from the strategy.

THE SIZE EFFECT

Another anomaly has been referred to as the size effect. Banz (1981) found that small firms, in terms of market capitalisation, had provided much greater investment returns than large firms. Other researchers have confirmed the size effect. Fortune (1991) calculated the cumulative value of investments made in January 1926, one being in an S&P 500 portfolio and the other in a portfolio of small firms' stocks. He found that the latter significantly outperformed the former. Heston *et al.* (1999) found a size effect for a group of 12 European countries. Jensen *et al.* (1997) found that US small firms generated a statistically significant premium only when monetary policy is expansionary. Reinganum (1999) found that small company shares only outperformed when markets rose. Hulbert (1993) confirmed the outperformance of small capitalisation stocks, but concluded that there was no relative advantage from small company stocks when account is taken of commissions. Dimson *et al.* (2004) questioned the continued existence of the size effect by citing evidence that the small firm advantage reversed during the 1980s.

The shares of small companies are often traded infrequently. The absence of trades could mean that their prices do not move while the market as a whole is moving. In consequence their betas are underestimated. Also small firms would include those that have recently encountered difficulties, and borrowed heavily as a result. The increased gearing might have raised their betas so that the betas based on past data are underestimates. If the estimated betas are too low then expected returns would be too low. The observed high returns on small company stocks, relative to expected returns, could be the result of low expectations rather than high returns.

Banz (1981) suggested that the higher returns could be due to higher betas (greater systematic risk) and that the apparent excess of returns over what was expected on the basis of betas arose from underestimating beta. More generally Banz suggested that the apparent size effect could be due to inadequacies of the capital asset pricing model (CAPM). The expected rate of return is calculated by means of the CAPM. A deviation between the observed and expected rates of return could be due to the CAPM providing incorrect estimates. Tests of market efficiency tend simultaneously to be tests of the CAPM and the efficient market hypothesis. Differences between expected and observed rates of return could be the result of market inefficiency or defects of the CAPM (or both). Evidence indicating that the size effect arises from problems with the CAPM rather than from market inefficiency is provided by Chan et al. (1985). They showed that when another pricing model (the arbitrage pricing model) was used to measure expected return, the size effect disappeared.

Chen (1988) sought to explain the size effect in terms of arbitrage pricing theory. The small firm premium was seen as a reward for risk; small firms suffer disproportionately during recessions and provide higher expected returns to compensate for this risk. Chan and Chen (1991) argued that many small firms have problems that render them more risky, and suggested that their relatively high returns reflect increased risk. Berk (1995, 1997) pointed out that market capitalisation is not the only measure of size. If two firms are equal in size with respect to assets and cash flows but one has more risk than the other, the riskier firm will have a lower market capitalisation. So small firms, measured by market capitalisation, tend to be relatively risky. The high returns to small firms are compensation for high risk. Carvell and Strebel (1987) took the view that the small firm effect was a proxy for the neglected firm effect. Small firms are neglected by analysts, and in consequence there is more uncertainty about the market prices of small firms. Since little analysis is carried out on small firms there is considerable risk of mispricing – either upwards or downwards. The chance that an investor may be overpaying for a stock is a factor that increases the risk of the stock to the investor. From this perspective, return premiums on small firms can be regarded as compensation for bearing risk.

Another explanation of the size effect comes from behavioural finance. The familiarity bias implies that people prefer investments that seem familiar. Familiar shares may feel less risky than unfamiliar ones. Investors will normally have heard much more about large companies than small ones. The resulting familiarity may lead to increased purchases of the shares of large companies. In consequence those share prices are bid up, and hence the prospective rates of return fall. So the size effect may derive more from the low yields of large (familiar) firms than from the high returns of small firms. The current author is not aware of any studies that have investigated this explanation of the size effect. However there are several studies that have found the familiarity bias in other investment contexts (Huberman 2001; French and Poterba 1991; Coval and Moskowitz 1999).

The issue of whether the apparent abnormally high returns from smaller company stocks is explicable in terms of market inefficiency, problems with the capital asset pricing model, or compensation for risk remains unresolved. However the size effect appears to be related to two other anomalies: the price-earnings ratio effect and the January effect.

515

VALUE INVESTING (RATIO EFFECTS)

The main ratios that have been researched and used in stock selection are (1) the price/earnings ratio, (2) the dividend/price ratio (i.e. dividend yield), and (3) the book-price ratio (alternatively known as the book-to-market ratio). Shares exhibiting one or more of a low price-earnings ratio, a high dividend yield, and high book-to-market (low price-to-book) ratio are often referred to as value stocks. Value investing is an investment style that weights portfolios towards such shares.

The price-earnings ratio effect has been investigated by Basu (1977) and Reinganum (1981) among others. They both found that the shares of firms with low price-earnings ratios tended to yield abnormally high returns. However Reinganum concluded that the price-earnings ratio effect is a proxy for the size effect, whereas Basu took the view that the size effect was a proxy for the price-earnings ratio effect. Since companies with low price-earnings ratios tend to be small, it is difficult to judge whether the high returns are the result of size or the price-earnings ratio. Levy and Lerman (1985) found that after adjusting for the transaction costs necessary to rebalance a portfolio in order to maintain the low price-earnings ratio as prices and earnings change over time, the superior performance of portfolios of low price-earnings ratio stocks no longer held.

Jaffe et al. (1989) investigated US stocks over the period 1951–86. They ranked firms by earnings-price ratios (the reciprocal of the price-earnings ratio) and placed them in six groups. The first group had negative earnings (losses) and the other five groups contained stocks with successively greater earnings-price ratios. The stocks in each earnings-price group were then ranked according to size, with five size-based sub-groups within each earnings-price group. This procedure produced 30 stock portfolios. They found that returns rose with increasing earnings-price ratios (decreasing price-earnings ratios). They also found that returns were inversely related to firm size (i.e. firms with smaller market capitalisations had the higher returns). However the high earnings-price ratio firms tended to be small firms, so the question arose as to whether there were two different effects. When attempting to separate the two effects they concluded that they were separate and that each effect produced an increase in return of more than 3% p.a. when moving between the bottom and top groups in each case.

Roll (1995) reported that low price-earnings ratio stocks in the US (1985–94) produced the highest risk-adjusted returns, whether the risk adjustment was based on the capital asset pricing model or arbitrage pricing theory. Lakonishok et al. (1994) studied US stocks for the period 1968–90 and found that low price-earnings ratio stocks substantially outperformed high price-earnings ratio stocks. They established that this was distinct from a size effect on returns. However Fama and French (1992) found no price-earnings ratio effect that was distinguishable from the effects of firm size and price-to-book ratios. As for UK studies, Levis (1989) found that shares of low price-earnings ratio firms provided higher returns than shares of high price-earnings ratio firms. Levis found that this effect was most pronounced amongst small firms. However UK studies by Miles and Timmermann (1996) and by Strong and Xu (1997) did not find statistically significant relationships between low price-earnings ratios and returns.

Fama and French (1988) showed that the return on the aggregate stock market tended to be higher when the dividend-price ratio, the dividend yield, is high. This might be interpreted as a violation of the efficient market hypothesis since a piece of public information, the dividend yield, appears to be capable of being used to predict returns on the aggregate stock market. However the relationship between dividend yield and subsequent returns could be the result of changes in the risk premium. A high risk premium results in low stock prices, and hence a high ratio of dividends to price. The high risk premium entails a high expected (required) rate of return. The finding, by Fama and French (1989), that the yield spread between high- and low-grade bonds has predictive power for stock returns seems to support the risk premium interpretation. If this interpretation is accepted, the dividend yield, whilst being useful for predicting market returns, cannot be used to obtain returns in excess of a normal risk-adjusted rate. In the UK, Chan and Chui (1996) found that high dividend yields were related to high returns over the 1973–90 period, whereas Miles and Timmermann (1996) found no relationship over the 1979–91 period. Levis (1989) found that high dividend yield and high return were related during the 1961–85 period. Levis also found that risk, as measured by beta, had no effect on return. In the United States, Naranjo et al. (1998) found that, even when adjusting for risk, returns increased with increasing dividend yield during the 1963–94 period.

Owners' equity is the excess of the assets of a firm over its liabilities. The price-to-book value ratio is the stock price divided by owners' equity. There is evidence that shares of firms with low ratios tend to outperform those of firms with high ratios. Rosenberg et al. (1985) found that stocks with low price-to-book ratios significantly outperformed the average stock. Fama and French (1992) found that two variables, firm size and the price-to-book ratio, between them captured the cross-sectional variation in average stock returns during the period 1963–90. Furthermore, the price-to-book ratio had a consistently stronger role. Roll (1995) also found that a low price-to-book strategy was profitable. Kothari et al. (1995) suggested that the price-to-book effect was much reduced when survivor bias was controlled for (some firms with low price-to-book ratios may have folded and been removed from the data set with the effect that their dampening effects on returns did not appear in the data). Capaul et al. (1993) studied France, Germany, Switzerland, the UK, and Japan for the 1981–92 period. They concluded that low price-to-book ratio shares provided superior risk-adjusted performance to high price-to-book ratio shares. Miles and Timmermann (1996), Chan and Chui (1996), and also Strong and Xu (1997) found such a price-to-book effect for the UK. Loughran (1997) suggested that fund managers who follow a value investing approach (low price-to-book) in the United States do not show outperformance. He proposed that this is because the price-to-book effect does not exist for the largest firms, whereas most fund managers invest primarily in large firms – after all the large firms constitute most of the stock market (by market capitalisation).

Cohen et al. (2003) confirmed the price-to-book effect. Kothari and Shanken (2002) found that tilting portfolios towards low price-to-book stocks improved portfolio performance. The question arises as to why such a well-known anomaly should persist. In principle anomalies, which present opportunities for enhancement of profit without additional risk, should be removed by arbitrage. Arbitragers would be expected to buy low price-to-book shares and simultaneously short sell high price-to-book shares. Pursuit of profits by such a strategy should lower returns on low price-to-book stocks by raising their prices. At the same time returns on high price-to-book stocks would be raised because sales would reduce their prices. Ali et al. (2003) suggest that there are reasons to expect that such arbitrage will not take place. One reason relates to timescale. The price-to-book effect offers profits over a three- to five-year time period whereas arbitragers have shorter timescales. Notably Ali et al. found that the price-to-book effect declined as institutional ownership increased. Institutional investors may have longer investment horizons than arbitragers, and may seek to exploit the price-to-book effect by buying low price-to-book stocks (i.e. by value investing). Their purchases of such value stocks would tend to raise share prices and thereby reduce the relative returns.

Campbell and Vuolteenaho (2004) proposed a division of beta into 'bad beta' and 'good beta'. The beta of the capital asset pricing model measures the sensitivity of the returns on a stock to changes in the returns on the stock market as a whole. From a discounted cash flow perspective (see Chapter 19 on dividend discount models, and Chapter 20 on company accounts and economic value added) variations in the general level of share prices arise either from changes in expected cash flows or changes in the rates at which they are discounted. Likewise the prices of individual stocks can change as a result of either of these factors. 'Bad beta' measures the sensitivity of individual stock prices to general market movements caused by shifts in expectations concerning future cash flows. 'Good beta' measures share price sensitivity based on variations in discount rates, or variations in market sentiment.

Campbell and Vuolteenaho (2004) found that the betas of value stocks (low price-to-book) have a greater 'bad beta' component, whereas growth stocks (high price-to-book) have the higher 'good beta'. 'Bad beta' earns a high risk premium since changes in expectations of cash flow are seen as being associated with permanent (long-term) losses. 'Good beta' earns a relatively low risk premium since its fluctuations are seen as temporary (short-term). 'Good beta' losses are reversed when discount rates or sentiment reverse. From this perspective it is to be expected that value stocks should earn a higher risk premium, and hence higher return, than growth stocks.

This division of beta into 'bad beta' and 'good beta' may also help to resolve some other controversial issues. First, the risk premium that shares appear to have over bonds (their historical excess returns over bonds) might be explained in terms of shares having both 'bad beta' and 'good beta' whereas bonds have only 'good beta'. Second, the issue of time diversification might be addressed in terms of 'good beta'. Since the discount rate and sentiment factors that cause 'good beta' share price movements are temporary and reversible, market rises and falls resulting from such forces could be expected to even out over time. In other words down-periods and up-periods would diversify each other just as poor-performing and successful stocks diversify each other.

MISPRICING AS AN EXPLANATION OF ANOMALIES

Even if it is accepted that it is not possible to identify mispriced shares, or to make profits from identified mispricing, it may still be the case that many shares are mispriced. Since market capitalisation is equal to the number of shares in issue multiplied by the share price, overpriced shares will have excessively high capitalisations and underpriced shares will have disproportionately low capitalisations. If mispricing is corrected over time, there should be relatively low subsequent returns on overpriced shares and relatively high returns on underpriced shares. Correspondingly (on average) the shares of large capitalisation firms would be expected to underperform relative to the shares of low capitalisation firms.

Low price-earnings ratio shares are likely to be (on average) mispriced downwards since they tend to be low price shares. Conversely high price-earnings ratio shares are likely to be overpriced. So low price-earnings ratio shares may be expected to outperform high price-earnings ratio shares as the mispricing is corrected. The capital gains from the initially underpriced shares would exceed those of the overpriced shares.

Similarly high dividend yield shares are likely to be underpriced (a high dividend yield is obtained by dividing the dividend by a low share price) and low dividend yield shares overpriced. As mispricing is corrected over time the high yield shares should outperform the low yield shares. The size effect, the price-earnings ratio effect, and the dividend yield effect might be explicable in terms of mispricing.

Conversely DeBondt and Thaler (1985) have argued that stocks that have performed poorly in recent years are likely to be underpriced, whereas those with strong performance in the recent past are prone to be overvalued. Underpriced shares would be relatively likely to fall into the categories of small size, low price-earnings ratio, and high book-to-market ratio. The subsequent high returns to small, low price-earnings, and high book-to-market firms might be explained in terms of them being initially underpriced. The under- and overpricing could be explained in terms of particular shares (or types of share) being subject to swings in fashion amongst investors. De Bondt and Thaler provided empirical evidence in support of their proposition. Of note is their finding that the extra returns available from investing in stocks that had recently performed poorly, occurred mainly in January. Bremer and Sweeney (1991) found similar results in that stocks were mean reverting. Loser portfolios (whose prices had performed poorly in the past) tend to become winners whilst the winners in the past become losers. A trading strategy based on selling winner portfolios (portfolios of stocks that have performed relatively well) and buying loser portfolios could have earned profits in excess of risk-adjusted expectations.

Lakonishok *et al.* (1994) argued that anomalies were evidence of market inefficiency. Specifically they argued that anomalies were evidence of systematic errors in the forecasts of stock market analysts. They presented evidence that analysts extrapolate recent past performance too far into the future, and hence exaggerate the significance of such past performance for the fair prices of stocks. Their evidence suggests that professional analysts may be subject to the decision-making biases identified by behavioural finance, such as representativeness. La Porta (1996) provided support for these views by finding that analysts seem too pessimistic about firms with low growth prospects and too optimistic about firms with high growth prospects.

ANOMALIES OR RISK PREMIUMS?

Some commentators take the view that the evidence relating to anomalies implies that the efficient market hypothesis should be rejected (e.g. Fortune 1991). Others take the view that rather than the anomalies providing evidence against market efficiency they provide evidence of the inability of the capital asset pricing model to adequately incorporate risk (e.g. Clare *et al.* 1997). Williams (1994) posed the question as to whether a systematically higher return from certain stocks or at certain times simply compensates for greater risk or less information or the need to make more complex or more time-consuming decisions.

Fama and French (1993) argued that some of the anomalies could be explained in terms of risk premiums. They developed a three-factor model in which risk was measured by the sensitivity of a stock to (1) the returns on the market portfolio, (2) the relative returns from small versus large firms, and (3) the relative returns from high versus low book-to-market ratio firms. They found the model to be effective in explaining stock returns. Whilst size and book-to-market may not be risk factors themselves, they could be proxies for more fundamental risk factors. Fama and French concluded that some of the anomalies were not inconsistent with market efficiency when the appropriate risk adjustment was made. Daniel and Titman (1995) found that the factors of size and book-to-market themselves, not the betas on these factors, explained returns. In other words Daniel and Titman concluded that high returns could not be explained as risk premiums.

CALENDAR EFFECTS

The January effect was demonstrated by Rozeff and Kinney (1976) who found that average stock market returns in January tended to be much higher than in other months. Gultekin and Gultekin (1983) studied stock markets in 15 different countries and discovered a January effect in all of them. This implies that the January effect is not explicable in terms of the specific tax (or other institutional) arrangements in a country. Keim (1983) found that about half of the size effect occurred in January. In fact about a quarter of the size effect for the year was typically accomplished during the first five trading days in January.

Kato and Shallheim (1985) studied the Tokyo stock exchange and found excess returns for January and a strong relationship between size and returns (small firms substantially outperforming large firms). Fama (1991) reported results from the United States for the period 1941–81. Stocks of small firms averaged returns of 8.06% in January, whereas the stocks of large firms averaged January returns of 1.342% (in both cases the January returns exceeded the average return in the other months). For the period 1982–91 the January returns were 5.32% and 3.2% for the stocks of small and large firms respectively.

One possible explanation of the January effect is window dressing by fund managers. They are often required to publish the details of the portfolios that they hold at the end of the year. It has been suggested that they prefer to show large, well-known companies in their published portfolios. So they sell small company shares and buy large company shares in December, and then do the opposite in January. So the prices of small company shares rise in January. Although this may explain the relative outperformance of smaller company shares in January, it does not explain the general January effect (unless the window dressing entails a relative move to bonds and cash in December).

Cooper et al. (2006) discovered another January-related anomaly. They found that stock market returns in January were predictive of returns during the next 11 months. Strong January returns were indicative of strong returns during the rest of the year. The effect was referred to as the 'other January effect'.

Cross (1973), French (1980) and others have documented a weekend effect. They found that the average returns to stocks were negative between the close of trading on Friday and the close of trading on Monday. Gibbons and Hess (1983) examined a 17-year period between 1962 and 1978 and found that on average Monday returns were negative on an annualised basis (-33.5% p.a.). Keim and Stambaugh (1984) investigated the daily returns on the S&P 500 from 1928 to 1982 and found that, on average, Monday returns were negative. Kohers and Kohers (1995) also found a weekend effect, suggesting that there would be an advantage from buying on Mondays and selling on Fridays.

Calendar effects, such as the January effect and the weeekend effect, have been brought into doubt by Sullivan et al. (1999). They claim to have shown that the calendar effects can be completely explained by what they refer to as data snooping. They found that the same data that was used to identify a calendar effect was also used to test for the existence of the effect. They also demonstrated that, although the small number of calendar effects that have been reported are statistically significant, there are about 9,500 conceivable calendar effects. From 9,500 some can be expected to be statistically significant through chance.

Malkiel (2003) concluded that anomalies do not persist in the long run since they lose their predictive power when they are discovered. As an example he stated that as soon as evidence of the January effect was made public investors acted on the information and the effect disappeared. Gu (2003, 2004) provided evidence consistent with Malkiel's view by showing a decline in the January effect and a reversal of the weekend effect.

Some calendar anomalies may persist since it is difficult for arbitragers, and other traders, to make profits from them. One could be 'Sell in May and go away'. This is an old stock market adage, which was researched by Keppler and Xue (2003). They studied the 18 most developed national stock markets over the period 1970 to 2001. It was found that during the months November to April the average rate of stock price rise was 8.36%. The average rate of price rise during the months May to October was −0.37%. Not only were returns higher between November and April, but also risk was lower. Keppler and Xue suggested a number of explanations including the observation that bonuses tend to be paid around the end, or the beginning, of the year. Research on saving behaviour has found that people find it easier to save and invest from a lump sum than from regular earnings. Investment of such lump sums would tend to increase demand for stocks, and hence their prices, during the period in which the bonuses are invested.

OTHER ANOMALIES

The efficient market hypothesis implies that publicly available information in the form of analyses published by investment advisory firms should not provide means of obtaining rates of return in excess of what would normally be expected on the basis of the risk of the investments. However stock rankings provided by *The Value Line Investment Survey* appear to provide information that could be used to enhance investors' returns (Huberman and Kandel 1990). However there is evidence that the market adjusts to this information within two trading days (Stickel 1985). Similarly Antunovich and Laster (2003) and Anderson and Smith (2006) found that companies identified by *Fortune* magazine as the most admired subsequently performed better than a stock index (the S&P 500). The Antunovich and Laster study indicated that stock price reaction to the information is subject to drift in that it takes a significant amount of time to occur hence permitting investors to profit from the information. Conversely Shefrin and Statman (1997) obtained the opposite result when analysing annual surveys of firm reputation published by *Fortune* magazine. They found that, on average, the shares of firms with good reputations turned out to be relatively poor investments whereas the shares of companies with poor reputations subsequently performed well.

A positive relationship between the reputations of companies, as measured in a publicly available source, and returns on the shares of those companies contradicts the efficient market hypothesis since it implies that published information could be used to enhance investment returns. However it also contradicts some of the theories that have been used to criticise the efficient market hypothesis. One of the psychological biases proposed by behavioural finance theorists is the representativeness bias. Investors may assume that the shares of a good company are a good investment. The shares of firms with good reputations might be heavily bought such that their prices reach excessive levels. In consequence the subsequent returns on those shares would be low.

521

This behavioural prediction is contradicted by the results of the Antunovich/Laster (2003) and Anderson/Smith (2006) studies.

Agency problems could also cause the stock prices of firms with good reputations to reach excessive levels. Agency problems arise when people acting on behalf of investors behave in their own interests rather than in the interests of the investors. For example a fund manager (the agent) may operate in a self-interested way. One manifestation could be the investment of clients' money in the shares of companies with good reputations. This protects the fund manager from criticism in the event of poor investment performance since the fund manager could point to the reputations of the companies as a justification for the investments. To the extent that this increases the demand for the stocks of well-regarded firms, the prices of those stocks could rise above fair values. The result would be subsequent poor returns. The Antunovich/Laster (2003) and Anderson/Smith (2006) findings provide evidence against such predictions.

Another apparent anomaly is the deviation between the prices of investment trust shares and the net asset values. It is not clear why a portfolio of shares within an investment trust should have a different price to the same portfolio outside the investment trust. A suggested explanation is that the differences arise from the relationship between fund charges and the perceived quality of investment management. If the potential contribution of fund managers to returns is seen as less than the charges, there would be a discount to net asset value. In terms of dividend discount models, in the absence of any expected enhancement to returns from fund management, the future management charges are a deduction from future dividend receipts and the present value of the expected future net receipts is correspondingly reduced.

Lee *et al.* (1991) suggest that the existence of investment trusts (closed-end funds) is an anomaly because rational investors would not be expected to buy new issues. The tendency for investment trusts to fall to a discount subsequent to issue appears to offer an early loss. Rational investors should not make an investment that is expected to result in an almost immediate loss.

An anomaly that is consistent with the belief that markets in the shares of large firms are more likely to be efficient than the markets for small company shares is the neglected firm effect. Neglect means that few analysts follow the stock, or that few institutional investors hold it. So fewer market participants put new information into the market. Neglected stocks are more likely to be mispriced, and hence are more prone to offer profit opportunities. Arbel and Strebel (1983) found that an investment strategy based on changes in the level of attention devoted by security analysts to different stocks could lead to positive excess returns. Allen (2005) observed that, in aggregate, institutional investment funds specialising in small capitalisation companies in the United States outperformed the Russell 2000 (a stock index for small companies) whereas the institutions underperformed stock indices when managing funds of large capitalisation stocks. Allen suggested that the outperformance in the small capitalisation sector was partly due to an 'instant history bias' wherein performance figures are not reported unless there is a history of good performance prior to records being reported for the first time. However the view was taken that the outperformance was primarily because small company stocks were often neglected and that the resulting mispricing offered fund managers profitable opportunities.

Merton (1987) showed that neglected firms might be expected to earn high returns as compensation for the risk associated with limited information. The information deficiency resulting from the limited amount of analysis renders neglected firms riskier as investments. The relative absence of investment analysis makes it less likely that all relevant information is reflected in the share price. There is greater likelihood that the share is mispriced, and the mispricing could entail the share being overpriced. Investors may require compensation for the risk that the share is purchased at an overvalued price. This view sees the neglected firm premium as a form of risk premium rather than as a contradiction of the efficient market hypothesis. Investors require the higher returns as compensation for the additional risk, and the higher required rates of return entail lower prices. On a risk-adjusted basis neglected firms do not provide returns above a normal level.

Doukas *et al.* (2005) observed that not only were the stocks of neglected firms likely to trade at relatively low prices but also the shares of firms receiving excessive attention from analysts may trade at abnormally high prices. It was suggested that when an investment bank anticipates investment-banking business with a company, the coverage of that company by the bank's investment analysts increases. If it were accepted that investment analysts tend to be overly optimistic about the stocks of firms which are prospective clients of their banks, the result of increased attention from analysts could be rises in the prices of such stocks. If a number of investment banks seek business with a firm, the result could be excessive attention from analysts and a resultant overpricing of its shares.

Related to the small firm and neglected firm effects is the effect of liquidity on returns. Amihud and Mendelson (1991) argued that investors demand a premium to invest in illiquid stocks that entail high transaction costs. They found that such stocks did provide relatively high rates of return. Since the shares of small and neglected firms tend to be relatively illiquid, the liquidity effect may constitute part of the explanation of their high returns. However the lack of liquidity, and high transaction costs, may remove the potential to profit from the liquidity effect on stock returns.

The semi-strong form of the efficient market hypothesis has been brought into doubt by econometric studies which suggest that it is possible to forecast stock market movements to some extent. Pesaran and Timmermann (1994) looked at excess returns on the S&P 500 and the Dow Jones measured over one year, one quarter, and one month for the period 1954–71. For annual excess returns a small set of variables including dividend yield, inflation, interest rate changes, and the term premium explain about 60% of the variation in excess returns. For quarterly and monthly data, similar variables explain about 18% and 10% of excess returns respectively.

A number of studies have found that combinations of accounting ratios can be used to select shares that outperform. These studies include those of Ou and Penman (1989), Setiono and Strong (1998), Lev and Thiagarajan (1993), Abarbanell and Bushee (1997, 1998), and Al-Debie and Walker (1999). These studies have looked for combinations of accounting ratios (sometimes combined with macroeconomic variables) which appear to provide useful information for forecasting returns on shares. Whilst they were successful in finding such combinations they could be criticised for data mining, particularly since there seems to be no economic or accounting theory underlying the choices of ratios. (The data mining critique is based on the view that, since there is an infinite number of combinations of ratios and variables, the law of probabilities suggests that some combinations will be successful purely by chance. It is necessary to test an observed relationship on sets of data that are independent of the data set used to hypothesise the relationship. Such independent verification would indicate that there is a causal relationship rather than a statistical aberration.)

Some of the anomalies that apply to stocks within countries also seem to apply to national stock markets. Selecting countries for overseas investment on the basis of the anomalies appears to have potential. Asness *et al.* (1997) noted that within the United States the relative performance of stocks was positively related to high book-to-market ratios, small size, and high past year returns (momentum). For a 20-year period ending in 1994 they found that countries satisfying those three characteristics outperformed countries that did not. Richards (1997) investigated 16 national markets over the period 1970–95 and found that the type of winner–loser reversals found for US stocks also applied to countries. In particular he found that for periods up to a year relatively strong performance persisted (momentum) whereas over longer periods past relative outperformers (winners) became underperformers (losers) and vice versa (reversal). Emanuelli and Pearson (1994) studied 24 national markets and separated them on the basis of relative earnings revisions. They found that a portfolio of stocks from the countries with the greatest relative experience of positive earnings revisions outperformed an average of the 24 countries. A portfolio from the countries with the lowest positive (highest negative) earnings revisions underperformed.

A recently identified anomaly is the apparent failure of share prices to fully reflect underfunding of a company's pension scheme (Franzoni and Marin 2006). In an efficient market the valuation of the shares of a company should take account of the future costs arising from the need to remedy pension scheme underfunding. It appears that the market overvalues companies with severely underfunded pension plans.

THE CAPITAL ASSET PRICING MODEL AND PROBLEMS WITH TESTING THE EFFICIENT MARKET HYPOTHESIS

Tests of the efficient market hypothesis tend to compare experienced returns with expected returns. The expected returns are typically based on the capital asset pricing model (CAPM). The security market line, shown by equation 1, summarises the CAPM.

$$E(R_i) = r_f + \beta \left[E(R_m) - r_f \right] \tag{1}$$

$E(R_i)$ is the expected return on security i, r_f is the risk-free rate of return (normally proxied by the Treasury bill rate), β is the beta of the security, and $E(R_m)$ is the expected return on the market portfolio (normally proxied by a stock index). Informational efficiency is tested by ascertaining whether $E(R_i)$ can be consistently bettered. If it can then excess returns can be made and the market is not informationally efficient.

Such tests are dependent upon the capital asset pricing model (CAPM) providing a reliable estimate of the expected (required) return on the share. However the usefulness of the security market line in providing such a benchmark has been questioned. For example Fama and French (1992) found that long-term equity returns do not depend on beta. Roll (1977) has argued that the market portfolio should contain every available asset, and that it is impossible to measure the expected return on such a broadly based portfolio. Fama (1998) suggested that even small errors in choosing a benchmark against which to compare returns could accumulate large apparent anomalies over the long-term. Many of the results in studies of anomalies are sensitive to small benchmarking errors. If these lines of reasoning are correct, many of the tests of the efficient market hypothesis may be seen as invalid.

DATA MINING

Some studies, particularly studies of market anomalies, may be guilty of data mining. There are an infinite number of possible relationships between variables. For example UK stock market performance could be related to interest rate changes, corporate profitability, goals scored by Arsenal, migrations of African wildebeest – the list is endless. The first two in the list can be justified by finance theory, the others cannot. Any relationship between the latter two variables and UK stock market behaviour would be spurious since they are irrelevant variables. However if a researcher investigated UK stock market performance against every irrelevant variable some would show a relationship, purely by chance. Such a research procedure is called data mining. Relationships produced by such an approach should be treated with scepticism.

Errors of data mining should be revealed if a relationship is tested against out-of-sample data. Out-of-sample data is data that is different from the original set, from which the relationship was deduced. Out-of-sample data might be from a different time period or a different country. If the only testing is carried out on the same data that was used to deduce the relationship, there must be doubt about the adequacy of the tests.

The available empirical evidence on market efficiency is predominantly the evidence reported in academic journals. There is a bias from this source of information. There is a tendency for the journals only to publish statistically significant findings; indeed researchers may decide to submit only research findings that are statistically significant (on the grounds that they are the only papers likely to be published). All the research that finds no statistically significant relationships is consequently ignored. If it is the case that investigations of techniques of analysis tend to be statistically significant when they refute the efficient market hypothesis, and fail statistical significance when they support it, the literature has a bias against supporting the efficient market hypothesis.

SURVIVOR(SHIP) BIAS

Survivor bias is concerned with the possibility of dropouts from data sets. For example when examining a group of shares, or set of companies, it is important to ensure that the final group is identical to the initial group. Some published data sources remove some members of the group. If a company closes down and its shares become valueless, that company and its shares might be removed from published data. The set of companies or shares at the end of the period being studied would be different from the group at the beginning. The worst performers are removed from the data. Use of the published data in research studies imparts an upward bias. Removal of the worst performers improves the observed average. The performance of the group appears to be better than it really is. This may explain size and value effects. Small firms are more likely than large firms to cease trading and disappear from the reported data. If failed firms could be added back into the data sets, the relatively strong performance of small firms might disappear. Likewise firms with low share prices relative to fundamentals such as earnings, dividends, and book value may have low share prices because they are experiencing problems. Such firms are relatively likely to fail. If those that fail are removed from the sample under study, the reported average return is biased upwards (Kothari *et al.* 1995).

TESTING IMPOSSIBLE STRATEGIES

There is a possibility that prospective trades investigated by researchers would be impossible in practice. One possible source of error in research arises from non-synchronous trading. Published security (shares, bonds) price data is based on the last trade. In the case of the shares of large companies, or large government bond issues, the last trade is likely to have been only minutes ago. In the case of small company shares, or illiquid corporate bonds, the last trade may have been days ago. In the latter case the published prices are out of date and may be a poor guide to the price at which an investor could actually buy or sell in the present. Studies that use published price data could therefore be using irrelevant prices.

Another possible source of distortion is sometimes called 'look-ahead bias'. A researcher, using historical information, may find a relationship between two variables. For example a relationship might be found between money supply growth in a month and stock market performance in the same month. However money supply figures for a month are not published until a later month. Both the practical usefulness and some possible explanations of the relationship could be compromised by this bias. It must be remembered that markets can only be efficient with respect to knowable information.

Many studies of the efficient market hypothesis have assumed short selling. Short selling entails borrowing securities and then selling them; so the trader may owe shares without holding shares – a short position. In particular many studies have been based on hedged positions; the purchase of shares is financed by short selling other shares. However in many countries (including the UK) most investors are not allowed to short sell. Even where short selling is possible, not all of the money raised can be used for share purchase. A study may find that an investment strategy based on short selling (and perhaps investing all the proceeds) is profitable, and may conclude that the availability of such profit opportunities refutes market efficiency. However if the profit opportunities cannot practically be exploited, they cannot be regarded as refuting market efficiency.

CONCLUSION

Contradictions of the efficient market hypothesis tend to be called anomalies. Some people regard behavioural finance as an anomaly, or group of anomalies. Apart from behavioural finance there are apparent contradictions of the efficient market hypothesis.

Two well-researched anomalies are the size effect and the value effect. The size effect is based on observations that the shares of small firms tend to outperform those of large firms. The value effect is based on the observation that shares with low price-earnings, or low price-book, ratios tend to outperform those with high ratios. Tests of the efficient market hypothesis have been complicated by the fact that they are simultaneously tests of the capital asset pricing model. The size and value effects may indicate deficiencies of the capital asset pricing model rather than deficiencies of the efficient market hypothesis. In particular adding size and value as additional risk factors in the capital asset pricing model could remove these anomalies. The additional return from small and low ratio shares could be compensation for risk associated with these characteristics.

The size and value effects could also result from mispricing of shares. If shares were frequently mispriced, underpriced shares would be the more likely to exhibit low market capitalisations (small size), low price-earnings ratios, and low price-book ratios. However if it is not possible to identify the underpriced shares, it is not possible to make abnormal profits from them.

There are other apparent anomalies such as calendar effects, the neglected firm effect, and techniques that appear to produce abnormal profits. It has been suggested that there are dangers of data mining and data snooping. Since there is a vast amount of data available to researchers, it is not surprising that some of the data appears to be inconsistent with market efficiency purely by chance. If researchers look long enough (mine deep enough) they will find apparent anomalies. Rather than testing theory with the data, researchers may look at the data (snoop on it) to see which theories might be supported before embarking on the tests. Since research appearing to support an anomaly is more likely to be published than research that finds no relationships (and since promotion in academia rests upon publication), mining and snooping probably have assured futures. For academics they are pursuits that appear to offer abnormal profits.

If anomalies exist, and if they were means to attain abnormal profits, professional investors (who are presumably aware of the anomalies) should be able to outperform stock indices. Chapters 9, 11, 17, and 26 on mutual funds, pensions, the evaluation of fund managers, and the strong form of the efficient market hypothesis, respectively, present evidence that market professionals (institutional investors) do not on average outperform stock indices. This suggests that even if the efficient market hypothesis, in the sense that security prices reflect all relevant information, fails it remains possible that the efficient market hypothesis, in the sense that there are no opportunities to make abnormal profits from publicly available information, may nonetheless be reliable.

Chapter 26

Further evidence on market efficiency

OBJECTIVE

The objective of this chapter is to provide knowledge of:

1. Evidence relating to the semi-strong form of the efficient market hypothesis.
2. Evidence relating to the strong form of the efficient market hypothesis.
3. The adaptive and fractal market hypotheses.

A purpose of using investment analysis to estimate the fair prices of shares is to assist in investment decisions. If the market price of a share is below its fair price, it is cheap and therefore a potential buy. If the fair price is below the market price, the share is overpriced and should not be bought.

The efficient market hypothesis suggests that such investment analysis is futile. This is because either (1) share prices already reflect all relevant known information with the effect that they are already at their fair prices, or (2) it is not possible to make profits from any mispricing.

A semi-strong form efficient market is one in which security prices take account of all publicly available information. In addition to market information on past prices and trading volumes, publicly available information includes macroeconomic data (such as interest rates and inflation rates), company data (such as profits, sales, quality of management and workforce, balance sheets), and non-economic events (such as political events, technological developments, and discoveries of natural resources). The implication is that asset prices immediately move to reflect any new information or that no one can make profits by means of purchases or sales based on analysing the new information.

EVIDENCE SUPPORTING SEMI-STRONG FORM EFFICIENCY

The evidence indicating the existence of anomalies is evidence against the semi-strong form of the efficient market hypothesis. Much of the evidence supporting the semi-strong form of the efficient market hypothesis comes from event studies. These studies aim to establish whether it is possible to make profits from a publicly available item of news, particularly financial news relating to a specific company. If stock prices adjust very quickly to news, the market is efficient and there is no scope for trading profits following the news. If stock prices adjust slowly there is an opportunity for ascertaining, and trading upon, the direction of price change. Slow price changes indicate market inefficiency.

Ball and Brown (1968) investigated the usefulness of earnings published in company accounts from the point of view of making trading profits. Their sample of companies was divided into two groups, one with earnings that exceeded expectations and the other with disappointing earnings. In both cases most of the share price adjustment occurred during the 12 months leading up to the earnings announcement as information became gradually available through interim reports, brokers' analyses, and newspaper articles. The information not previously known was found to be incorporated into the share price almost immediately after the earnings announcement.

Excess returns on stocks, which are subject to revisions in the consensus of analysts' estimates of earnings, have been found to be available for up to 12 months. The market appears not to immediately react to changes in the consensus forecast. Furthermore studies have shown that revisions in the consensus of analysts' estimates of earnings tend to have momentum; that is an increase in the consensus forecast one month is often followed by another increase in the next month (Givoly and Lakonishok 1979).

Fama *et al.* (1969) investigated the potential for making profits from news about stock splits (for example replacing one old share with two new shares). A stock split adds nothing to the value of a company, and should have no effect on the total value of shares outstanding. However the split might convey information about future cash flows. The study hypothesised that announcements of forthcoming stock splits generated expectations of higher future dividends. After the split the firms that raised dividends experienced stock price rises whereas those that failed to meet the expectation of higher dividends underwent share price falls. The interpretation was that stock prices adjusted to the expectation of higher dividends very quickly after the announcements of the stock splits, and the price rise was subsequently added to or removed dependent upon whether the dividend expectations were realised.

Takeover and merger announcements can raise stock prices substantially, especially where premiums are being paid to the shareholders of an acquired firm. Dodd (1980) found no evidence of abnormal price changes subsequent to the immediate reaction. Firth (1975) studied the effects of a firm having 10% of its shares bought by a single entity (which may be seen as an indicator of a pending takeover bid) and found that most of the increase in share value occurred between the last trade before the announcement and the next trade. Only those with inside information (prior knowledge) could earn excess returns net of transaction costs.

Sunder (1973) investigated the effects on the stock market values of firms arising from a change to LIFO (last in first out) stock valuation. The benefit from the reduced tax liability showed up in higher share prices prior to (due to the change being anticipated) or immediately after the announcement of the change. Once the information about the change was public there was no scope for making trading profits from knowledge of the change. It also seems likely that the stock price rises resulted from the changes in the net of tax cash flows rather than the accounting changes as such. Research on the effects of alterations to accounting practices such as the treatment of depreciation has indicated that share prices do not react to changes that have no impact on expected net of tax cash flows (Kaplan and Roll 1972). The reaction of the market to dividend announcements has also been investigated. Pettit (1972) found that the information content of dividend announcements was immediately reflected in share prices.

Initial public offerings of shares are often made at prices below fair value in order to ensure that the offering is fully subscribed. This tends to provide the initial buyers with a capital.gain. The profits appear to be limited to those investors who are allocated shares in the initial sale. Purchases in the secondary market, soon after issue, do not provide profits. It seems that prices reach their fair values very quickly. All relevant information is quickly incorporated into prices (Ibbotson *et al.* 1988, 1994). Results from Miller and Reilly (1987), Chalk and Peavy (1987), and Hanley (1993) show that the price adjustment takes place within one day of the offering. Research into the effects of sales of large blocks of shares in the secondary market has found that any resulting price change is corrected within a day so that after the day of the sale there is no scope for making profits from knowledge of the disposal (Kraus and Stoll 1972).

A study of announcements relating to economic news (such as news concerning money supply, inflation, and interest rates) found no resulting trend in stock prices beyond the day of the announcement (Pearce and Roley 1985). One study has even found that stock price reactions to economic news are completed within an hour (Jain 1988).

EVIDENCE RELATING TO THE STRONG FORM OF THE EFFICIENT MARKET HYPOTHESIS

According to the strong form of the EMH even non-public information is quickly reflected in asset prices; so the small number of investors who have that information are unable to profit from it. Non-public information can be divided into two categories. There is the information held by corporate insiders on matters such as forthcoming earnings announcements, or takeover bids. The other arises from stock analyses that have not been made public (arguably this should include only analyses that use research methods that are not public, since publicly known techniques of security analysis could be regarded as publicly available information). If actively managed mutual funds are able consistently to outperform the market, that outperformance provides evidence that their private analyses can be used profitably. If the recommendations of investment analysts can be used to earn profits (in excess of normal or average returns), there is evidence against the efficient market hypothesis. Either the semi-strong or strong form of the hypothesis is challenged according to whether the analyst recommendations are made public or kept private.

The Trades of Insiders

Corporate insiders include directors and senior executives of the company. Insiders have access to privileged information and could use the information to profit from trading in securities markets before the information becomes public. Several studies of corporate insiders found that they consistently obtained abnormally high rates of return on their stock transactions (Jaffe 1974; Finnerty 1976, 1976a; Nunn *et al.* 1983; Nejat and Seyhun 1986). A later study by Peers (1992) confirmed these results but indicated that the opportunities for trading profits were limited to the most senior insiders. A UK study by Gregory *et al.* (1994) suggested that insider purchases were profitable but that there was no evidence of benefits from insider sales. Kiymaz (2002), in a study of the Turkish stock market, found that abnormal returns were available in the days preceding publication of price-sensitive information. The share price movements prior to publication suggested that insiders were trading profitably during the period preceding publication. Niederhoffer and Osborne (1966) found that specialists on the New York Stock Exchange, who have privileged knowledge of advance buy and sell orders (limit orders), can consistently obtain abnormally high rates of return.

A related issue concerns the potential for earning enhanced returns by following the trading behaviour of insiders. Studies by Lee and Solt (1986), Rozeff and Zaman (1988), Seyhun (1988, 1992), and Chowdhury et al. (1993) showed that it was not possible to earn excess returns in this way. Pope et al. (1990) estimated returns from following directors' trades, as reported by the London Stock Exchange, during the period 1977–84. Generally they found little evidence for benefits from following purchases but more evidence for the advantages of following sales.

The enormous illegal profits made by insider traders such as Ivan Boesky are suggestive that the market is not strong form efficient. Since a strong form efficient market is one in which profits could not be made on the basis of privileged information, prosecutions of insider traders who have made fortunes from using inside knowledge are evidence against strong form efficiency.

Using Non-Public Analysis: Mutual Fund Performance

There have been a number of studies of the ability to profit from non-public security analyses. Friend et al. (1962) studied the performance of US mutual funds (unit trusts) and found that, on average, they did not outperform stock indices. Jensen (1968) concluded that mutual funds earned, on average, about 1% p.a. less than would be expected on the basis of their betas (systematic risk). In aggregate they were not able to predict stock price movements well enough to outperform a buy-and-hold strategy. Also past performance of funds could not be used to predict future performance, suggesting that not even star fund managers possessed knowledge or expertise that would enable them to consistently outperform the market. Firth (1978) studied the performance of UK unit trusts. He found that, on a risk-adjusted basis, their performance tended to match that of the market as a whole. Also the past performance of individual trusts gave no guide to future performance. Cowles (1933) failed to find any evidence that professional investors achieved a performance that was superior to the results of a market tracking strategy. A study undertaken by Malkiel (1988) showed that during the 20 years to 1987, over 70% of pension fund managers were outperformed by the S&P 500 index.

Sharpe (1966) found that US mutual funds failed to outperform the Dow Jones Industrial Average. Ippolito (1989) concluded that US mutual funds outperformed the market, but not by enough to offset charges. Elton et al. (1993) concluded that mutual funds underperform the market and that funds with high fees and turnover do worse than those with low fees and turnover. Malkiel (1995) found that mutual funds underperform the market even before fund charges are considered. Daniel et al. (1997) and Wermers (2000) found that there was outperformance before fund charges were considered, but not net of fund charges. Blake et al. (1993) found that US bond funds underperformed bond indices and that the degree of underperformance was directly related to the fund charges. The majority of the evidence on the performance of professional fund managers is that returns, net of costs, are at best average.

Malkiel (1995) and Elton et al. (1996) suggest that many studies of market efficiency have overstated the true performance of mutual funds because of survivorship bias. Most data sets used have included records of all existing mutual funds. Mutual funds that were taken off the market due to poor performance (or were merged with other funds in order to bury their poor records) do not appear among the existing funds. The removal of such weak funds artificially boosts the apparent success of funds as a whole.

Grossman and Stiglitz (1980) and Cornell and Roll (1981) suggested that market equilibrium should provide some incentive for analysis. Those who acquire and process information should receive superior gross returns, but only average returns net of costs (which include the costs of the analysis). If no analysts were operating, the market would be inefficient and large profits would be available for the first analysts. As more analysts, attracted by the profits, enter the market efficiency improves and profits fall. Eventually the number of analysts expands to the point where the market efficiency is such that returns from analysis merely match the costs of analysis. At that point no more analysts enter the market. Equilibrium would have been reached where returns from analysis equal the costs of analysis so that there is no further incentive for new analysts to enter the market.

If some fund managers possessed investment management skills that enabled them to consistently outperform the market, it would be expected that those fund managers should persistently outperform the fund managers who lack the requisite skills. Hendricks *et al.* (1993) found the strongest consistency to be among the weakest performers. Carhart (1997) found that there was some persistence of relative performance across fund managers, but that it was largely due to charges and costs rather than investment returns. There was consistent inferior performance resulting from high management charges and high trading costs (as would result from high portfolio turnover). This is consistent with the efficient market hypothesis since persistence in relative performance resulting from differing management charges and trading costs does not imply any ability to outperform the market. The apparent absence of relative outperformance arising from investment management skills is consistent with the efficient market hypothesis, which predicts an absence of profits from stock selection and market timing.

Rhodes (2000) in producing a report for the UK Financial Services Authority based on both a review of existing literature and original research concluded that:

> The literature on the performance of UK funds has failed to find evidence that information on past investment performance can be used to good effect by retail investors in choosing funds. The general pattern is one in which investment performance does not persist. Small groups of funds may show some repeat performance over a short period of time, particularly poorly performing funds. However the size of this effect and the fact that it is only very short lived means that there is no investment strategy for retail investors that could usefully be employed. The results from the US literature are similar.
>
> The results concurred with the earlier analyses in finding that there was no persistency in the performance of managed funds after 1987. There was evidence of repeat performance before this point but it would be misleading to suggest that retail investors could use this finding in the present day.
>
> The weight of evidence is that information on past performance cannot be exploited usefully by retail investors.

Against all this evidence is the observation that a few individuals seem to have track records of persistently good investment performance. Such names include Warren Buffet, George Soros,

Peter Lynch, John Templeton, John Neff, Anthony Bolton, and Neil Woodford. They present an unresolved anomaly from the perspective of the efficient market hypothesis.

Gregory and Tonks (2006) found some persistency in relative performance amongst pension schemes in the UK. They estimated risk-adjusted performances where the risk-adjustment was based on the single-factor capital asset pricing model and on forms of the Fama–French multi-factor variations of the model. They investigated the subsequent relative performance of the top quintile, from a period, against the bottom quintile from the same period. The top quintile tended to outperform during the following period. The effect was strongest when comparing successive six-month periods and successive 12-month periods (the relative outperformance being in the range 1.6% to 1.9% p.a.). The relative outperformance was lower for three-year periods (0.2% to 0.8% p.a.), and tended to be negative for one-month and three-month periods.

Implications for Rational Retail Investors

One issue facing retail investors who are looking to buy an institutional investment such as a mutual fund is whether to invest in an actively managed fund or in an index tracker fund. If markets were efficient the answer would appear to be unambiguous; actively managed funds cannot be expected to consistently outperform the market and so it is pointless to pay their management fees. If markets were efficient, individual investors should invest in low cost index tracker funds. However the evidence from behavioural finance and studies of market anomalies throw doubt on the efficient market hypothesis. If markets are not informationally efficient, should investors choose to invest in actively managed funds on the grounds that it is possible to outperform the market?

Malkiel (2003a) argued that even if market efficiency is not accepted, retail investors should still choose index tracker funds. One point is that investment outperformance and underperformance is a zero-sum game. If some investment managers outperform the market, others must underperform the market. Obviously, in aggregate, the market performs in line with the market. Index tracker funds perform in line with the market. The aggregate market minus index tracker funds must therefore perform in line with the market. Actively managed funds are the aggregate market minus index trackers. So actively managed portfolios, in aggregate, must perform in line with the market. If some actively managed portfolios outperform others must underperform. This suggests that, on average, actively managed funds perform in line with the market before their costs are considered. When costs are taken into account actively managed funds, on average, could be expected to underperform the market. The conclusion seems to be that individual investors should invest in index tracker funds rather than waste money on management fees whilst taking the risk that their particular managers are relatively poor performers. However the existence of noise traders may allow professional fund managers, in aggregate, to outperform at the expense of those noise traders (assuming that the professionals are not noise traders themselves).

Evidence from empirical research cited in this chapter (and in Chapters 9 and 17 on mutual funds and on evaluating the performance of fund managers, respectively) tends to confirm the expectation that actively managed funds, on average, underperform stock markets after costs are considered. However questions still remain since some funds do outperform the market. Is such outperformance due purely to chance, since chance would generate outperformers as well as underperformers, or is investment management skill involved? If skill were involved, it would be expected that there would be some persistence in relative performance; in particular more funds would show continued outperformance than would be expected on the basis of chance. The evidence referred to in this text tends to indicate that there is probably no statistically significant persistence in performance, and if there is any such persistence it is limited to a very small number of investment managers. If relative performance of actively managed funds arises from chance rather than skill, the implication remains that retail investors should choose index tracker funds. (Malkiel provides additional evidence in support of the findings that funds, on average, underperform after costs and that there appears to be no persistence of relative performance.)

If any persistence in outperformance were the result of investment management skill, one more condition should be met before individual investors choose actively managed funds. There should be means of ascertaining which investment managers demonstrate the skill that leads to persistent outperformance. Furthermore the techniques for ascertaining which managers have skill should be reasonably easy to use, and should give reasonably precise and unambiguous results (it is of little use to an individual investor if the technique merely changes a 50:50 chance of correctly choosing to a 55:45 chance of correctly choosing). There is also the risk that if everyone identifies the outperformers, so much money would be switched to the outperformers that they are unable to continue the outperformance. The balance of evidence appears to be that it is probably not possible to forecast relative performance, and that if accurate forecasts are possible they are not sufficiently reliable for retail investors.

For it to be rational for retail investors to choose actively managed funds a number of conditions must be met, as indicated above, and those conditions do not appear to be met. It is not sufficient for markets to be informationally inefficient in the sense that stock prices fail to accurately reflect all relevant information. It must also be the case that markets are informationally inefficient in the sense that it is possible to consistently make profits from inefficiencies. Furthermore retail investors should be able to readily identify the fund managers capable of consistently making such profits.

Is it possible to conclude that investors in actively managed funds are irrational and that investors in index tracker funds are rational? Not necessarily. For example a rational investor might prefer an index tracker but also require a high dividend yield. In the absence of a low cost tracker fund based on an index of high income shares, the investor may choose a high income actively managed fund. Outside the United States the markets for retail investments tend to be incomplete in that they do not cater for all needs (whilst providing a plethora of choice for some types of fund).

Nor can it be concluded that investors in index tracker funds are all, or even typically, rational. Elton *et al.* (2004) found that a high proportion of investors in index tracker funds chose funds whose charges were similar to those of actively managed funds. In the UK annual management charges on index tracker funds range between 0.1% and 1.5%. It is surely irrational to invest in a fund charging 1.5% p.a. when exactly the same (pre-costs) performance could be obtained for 0.1% p.a. The low cost funds offer a virtually guaranteed advantage of 1.4% p.a. Elton *et al.* suggested that one explanation for high levels of investment in high cost tracker funds is the compensation structure for financial advisers. If a financial adviser were paid by means of commission, and if the level of commission were related to the level of fund charges, the financial adviser could be inclined to recommend high cost funds. Where charges are very low there is little cash flow from which fund managers can pay commission to financial advisers.

Using Non-Public Analysis: Analysts' Forecasts

Ambachtsheer (1974) found a correlation of 0.16 between forecast and actual outcomes. Even the low forecasting ability, indicated by this correlation coefficient, is useful in achieving better than average returns. Dimson and Marsh (1984) examined the ability of analysts to forecast returns on the shares of over 200 of the largest UK quoted companies. They found a coefficient of correlation of 0.08 between forecasts and outcomes. Although the correlation was extremely small, transactions carried out in the light of the forecasts appeared to result in a 2.2% outperformance of the market over the following year. Over half of the informational content of the forecasts was reflected in share prices within one month of the forecast.

Studies on American, British, and Canadian analysts have shown that excess returns are available to investors who follow the published recommendations of analysts employed by stockbrokers. These studies have shown that analysts' stock recommendations have a positive Information Coefficient (IC), where information coefficient is defined as the correlation between predicted and actual stock returns. The mean analyst IC appears to be about 0.1. Relevant studies include Davies and Canes (1978); Stanley *et al.* (1981); Bjerring *et al.* (1983); Dimson and Marsh (1984); and Elton *et al.* (1986).

Dimson and Marsh (1984) and Elton *et al.* (1986) found that there was little advantage from acting on the advice of a single firm of stockbrokers. However they suggest that by combining the advice of a number of brokerage firms the resulting information can lead to excess returns. Womack (1996) concluded that analysts seem to have good ability in both market timing and stock selection. Barber *et al.* (2001) found that there was a significant difference in returns between the previously most highly, and least favourably, rated stocks but the difference offered no profit opportunities when transaction costs were considered. Jha *et al.* (2003) concluded that analysts' recommendations were useful when combined with other information particularly when uncertainty is particularly high, such as in the cases of small company stocks and technology stocks. The direction of change in a recommendation may be more useful than the level of recommendation. The findings of Woolridge (2004) indicated that there was no advantage to be gained from following the stock recommendations of brokerage firms.

Some studies have concluded that there are no differences between analysts in their ability to forecast stock returns (Coggin and Hunter 1983; Dimson and Marsh 1984). Another study found that there was no evidence that one US brokerage firm was consistently better than another in recommending stocks (Elton *et al.* 1986). These results might be interpreted as evidence that the informational value of analysts' reports arises from the usefulness of commonly used analytical techniques rather than individual talent. Desai *et al.* (2000) investigated the recommendations of the analysts, identified by the *Wall Street Journal* as the top three for each industry, and found that they were successful in specifying the best buys amongst stocks. There is the possibility that the success of analysts' forecasts arises from self-fulfilling prophecies. If investors buy, when forecasts suggest price rises, their purchases would tend to bring about the rises. Conversely forecasts of falls would induce sales, thereby causing the falls that were forecast. Mikhail *et al.* (2004) found

535

that there was some persistence in analysts' abilities to select stocks in that superior (and inferior) ability tended to continue. Investors react to the recommendations of the superior analysts, with the reactions continuing for up to three months. However it was found that, net of transaction costs, knowledge of such persistence provided no opportunities for profit.

Herzberg and Wang (2002) developed a technique for identifying the best analysts. One criterion was whether the analyst was a leader or a follower. Leading analysts are prepared to produce recommendations that move away from the consensus view, whereas recommendation changes by followers are towards the consensus. A record of leading is seen as indicative of superior analysis, and this indication is seen as stronger when the movements away from the consensus are large. Another desirable attribute is accuracy of forecasts. Respect from other analysts, as measured by the extent to which those other analysts revise their recommendations towards the revised recommendations of lead analysts, is another characteristic of a superior analyst. Whether, and to what extent, revisions of recommendations by an analyst affect stock prices is another factor. An analyst who has a relatively substantial affect on stock prices is presumably highly regarded by market participants. Herzberg and Wang investigated whether the analysts identified as best, according to their criteria, provided recommendations that could be profitably followed. It was found that when such analysts made revisions to recommendations, investors could make profitable use of those revisions: particularly when they were leading revisions. The conclusion was that by cherry-picking the best analysts from brokerage firms it is possible to obtain better information than either the consensus or any individual brokerage firm provides, especially when lead revisions from those superior analysts are used.

Prediction Markets (Decision Markets)

Ray (2006) has argued that prediction markets exhibit strong form efficiency (and hence also weak and semi-strong form efficiency). Prediction markets are betting markets that exist beyond national frontiers, and beyond regulatory authorities. There is nothing to prevent people from using privileged (inside) information when placing bets. The markets thus draw out information from informed bettors who want to profit from their knowledge. The markets are able to elicit inside and expert information. The resulting prices may therefore exhibit a degree of informational efficiency that exceeds that of any regulated market. Regulated markets typically prohibit the use of privileged information, so that it is less easy for inside information to influence trading and thereby become incorporated into market prices. Prediction markets can be based on anything whose future value is uncertain, including financial values. Ray cites a number of studies, which indicate that prediction markets have been unusually accurate in their forecasts.

Prediction market bets relate to whether a particular event will occur. For example bets could relate to whether the FTSE All-Share Index will exceed 10,000 points on a particular date. If the index exceeds 10,000 on the specified date, someone betting that it would exceed 10,000 receives a sum of money. That sum of money might be £1,000 and people placing bets for and against the event occurring would determine the price of the bets. For example the price could be £200. Buyers would pay £200 for the prospect of winning £1,000. If the stock index does exceed 10,000 points, the buyer would receive £1,000 from a seller thereby making a profit of £800. If the index does not exceed 10,000 points, the seller receives the £200. The price of £200 implies a 20% probability that the index will exceed 10,000 points. In other words the prediction market forecasts a 20% probability that the FTSE All-Share Index will exceed 10,000 points on the designated date.

DEGREES OF EFFICIENCY AND THE ADAPTIVE MARKETS HYPOTHESIS

Arguably the issue is not whether a market is, or is not, efficient. The issue is how efficient a particular market is. Market efficiency could be seen to parallel the perfectly competitive market of economic theory. They are rarely, if ever, achieved in reality. Nonetheless they both constitute a useful benchmark against which to compare actual markets. They also serve to provide models that are useful for the interpretation and understanding of the real world.

Simon (1955) argued that investors exhibited 'bounded rationality', which means that they have limited capacities to absorb and analyse information. They are not able to make the precise calculations, which would provide the optimum solutions to their investment problems. Correspondingly market prices do not reach their precisely correct levels. Instead investors satisfice, which means they attain acceptable approximations to their optimum positions. Satisficing portfolios could be achieved by trial-and-error processes based on the use of behavioural heuristics. When market participants have achieved such satisfactory portfolios, the market will approximate informational efficiency.

Lo (2004) argued that, from time to time, circumstances would change. Changes in circumstances require new portfolios and new equilibrium prices. Market participants move towards the new satisficing portfolios using heuristics in a trial-and-error process. According to this view, behavioural heuristics are not incompatible with the efficient markets hypothesis. Behavioural heuristics are an aspect of the process whereby markets move from one approximation to efficiency to another. Lo called this the 'adaptive markets hypothesis'. Markets could be seen as following evolutionary paths wherein they adapt to changed circumstances by behavioural iterative processes that mirror the survival of the fittest process of natural selection. Successive solutions to the problem of determining optimal portfolios are tried using heuristics, and the solutions that approximate most closely to the optimum are the ones that survive. The heuristics of behavioural finance are the means of adjusting from one approximation to market efficiency to the next. Behavioural finance is complementary to, rather than a contradiction of, the efficient markets hypothesis.

An implication of the adaptive markets hypothesis is that the degree of market efficiency is not constant. Lo (2004) presented evidence showing that market efficiency, as measured by serial correlation, fluctuates over time. It is tempting to think that a market becomes steadily more efficient over time as the market participants become more sophisticated, but that does not appear to be the case. Degrees of efficiency show periods of decline as well as periods of advance. This is consistent with the view that changes in circumstances disrupt (approximate) efficiency and that markets take time to reach a new (approximate) efficiency.

Lo (2004) also explains how the new equilibrium positions can be path dependent. A new set of stock prices are path dependent if they are affected by the process by which the new equilibrium is achieved. A stock market crash could permanently deter some investors from the market. In consequence the market will have fewer investors. The absence of those investors will also affect the risk preference of the market, and hence the equilibrium stock prices (Part 4 on capital market theory shows how risk preferences, through models such as the capital asset pricing model, affect equilibrium prices by way of affecting risk premiums). A stock market crash does not simply cause

537

a temporary deviation of stock prices from their 'correct' levels; it also changes the 'correct' levels towards which the market eventually tends to move.

It is interesting to reflect on some views expressed by Fisher Black (1986). He argued that traders could be divided into information traders, who are rational traders using relevant information, and noise traders. Noise is irrelevant or meaningless information. Noise trading puts noise into market prices, causing them to depart from their true values. The deviations caused by noise trading can be cumulative. As a stock price diverges further from its true value, the scope for profits from information trading becomes greater. Although information trading tends to pull prices towards their true values, it can be difficult to distinguish noise from relevant and accurate information. Black argued that a market could be efficient even if a share price differs from its fundamental value by a factor of as much as two. This view appears to allow a market to be regarded as efficient even if the degree of efficiency varies over time.

THE FRACTAL MARKET HYPOTHESIS

Peters (1994) suggested that the efficient market hypothesis (EMH) should be replaced by a fractal market hypothesis (FMH). One feature of fractal analysis is that it allows for a multiplicity of investment horizons. This contrasts with the capital asset pricing model, which assumes that all investors have the same investment horizon.

Peters (1994) offered some basic assumptions of the FMH, including:

1. The market consists of many individuals covering a large number of investment horizons. At one extreme is the day trader who changes the investment portfolio on a daily basis, whereas at the other extreme may be a pension fund that changes its portfolio slowly and has a long investment horizon. However both types of investor trade in the market, and they both provide liquidity for the other.
2. Reaction to information depends upon the investment horizon. Short-horizon investors and long-horizon investors react to different types of information. Correspondingly they may use different types of analysis; perhaps technical analysis in the case of short-horizon investors and fundamental analysis in the case of long-horizon investors.
3. The stability of the market depends on liquidity, and a large number of investors with many different investment horizons create liquidity in the market. A market crash, as perceived by a short-horizon investor, may be a buying opportunity when seen by a long-horizon investor. The sales of the former provide the purchases of the latter, and stability ensues. If long-horizon investors shorten their investment horizons, perhaps due to increased uncertainty, the liquidity and stability from the variety of horizons is reduced. When horizons become uniform a market bubble, or market crash, could ensue as all investors react to the same news in the same way.
4. Prices reflect a combination of short-term technical trading and long-term fundamental valuation. The long-term trend in the market reflects changes in expected earnings, which are likely to be related to economic cycles. Short-term trends are more likely to reflect crowd psychology. Economic cycles are less volatile than trading activity, which makes long-term stock market returns less volatile than short-term movements (Rachev *et al.* 1999).

538

CONCLUSION

There is a body of research evidence from event studies that supports semi-strong form efficiency, but the support is not unambiguous. Strong form efficiency appears to be contradicted by the observation of insider trading profits, although studies of such trading are complicated by the fact that in many countries insider trading is illegal.

The private investment analysis of institutional investors is a form of inside information. This inside information does not appear consistently to provide profits. On average institutional investors fail to outperform the market, as represented by stock indices. Although some institutional investors have long runs of above-average performance, it is to be expected that a few would do so purely as a matter of chance.

The publicly available opinions of investment analysts, in aggregate, appear to have some value for making abnormal profits. Although such analysis seems to provide information of use to investors (albeit a modest amount) institutional investors do not seem to be able to make profits from it. The evidence on the inability of institutional investors consistently to outperform stock indices provides a persistent argument in support of the efficient market hypothesis (evidence on this is also provided in Chapters 9, 11, and 17 on mutual funds, pensions, and the evaluation of fund managers, respectively, and Part 7 on market efficiency).

Market efficiency has two alternative meanings. One is that security prices fully reflect all relevant information. The other is that there is no possibility of making abnormal profits (e.g. consistently outperforming stock indices). The mixed evidence on the first meaning leads to a conclusion that it is a matter of degrees of efficiency, rather than the existence or otherwise of full efficiency. However the evidence on the latter meaning seems to provide strong support for market efficiency. Efficiency in the second sense leads to suggestions that retail investors are better off with low cost index tracker funds than with actively managed funds. Why pay fund managers to outperform the market when they appear to be unable to do so?

Chapter 27

Stock market bubbles and crashes

OBJECTIVE

The objective of this chapter is to provide knowledge of:

1. Characteristics and causes of bubbles and crashes.
2. The implications of behavioural finance for the understanding of bubbles and crashes.
3. The role of investor overreaction.
4. The roles of borrowing and liquidity.
5. Portfolio insurance and its potential role.
6. Research using experimental markets.
7. Complexity theory as an explanation of bubbles and crashes.
8. Catastrophe theory as an explanation of crashes and surges
9. How crashes can generate banking crises.

The occurrence of stock market bubbles and crashes is often cited as evidence against the efficient market hypothesis. It is argued that new information is rarely, if ever, capable of explaining the sudden and dramatic share price movements observed during bubbles and crashes. Samuelson (1998) distinguished between micro efficiency and macro efficiency. Samuelson took the view that major stock markets are micro efficient in the sense that stocks are (nearly) correctly priced relative to each other, whereas the stock markets are macro inefficient. Macro inefficiency means that prices, at the aggregate level, can deviate from fair values over time. Jung and Shiller (2002) concurred with Samuelson's view and suggested that waves of over- and undervaluation occur for the aggregate market over time. Stock markets are seen as having some predictability in the aggregate and over the long run.

CHARACTERISTICS OF BUBBLES AND CRASHES

Bubbles and crashes have a history that goes back at least to the seventeenth century (MacKay 1852). Some writers have suggested that bubbles show common characteristics. Band (1989) said that market tops exhibited the following features:

1. Prices have risen dramatically.
2. Widespread rejection of the conventional methods of share valuation, and the emergence of new 'theories' to explain why share prices should be much higher than the conventional methods would indicate.
3. Proliferation of investment schemes offering very high returns very quickly.
4. Intense, and temporarily successful, speculation by uninformed investors.
5. Popular enthusiasm for leveraged (geared) investments.
6. Selling by corporate insiders, and other long-term investors.
7. Extremely high trading volume in shares.

Kindleberger (1989) and Kindleberger and Aliber (2005) argued that most bubbles and crashes have common characteristics. Bubbles feature large and rapid price increases, which result in share prices rising to unrealistically high levels. Bubbles typically begin with a justifiable rise in stock prices. The justification may be a technological advance, or a general rise in prosperity. Examples of technological advance stimulating share price rises might include the development of the automobile and radio in the 1920s and the emergence of the Internet in the late 1990s. Examples of increasing prosperity leading to price rises could be the United States, Western Europe, and Japan in the 1980s. Cassidy (2002) suggested that this initial stage is characterised by a new idea or product causing changes in expectations about the future. Early investors in companies involved with the innovation make very high returns, which attract the attention of others.

The rise in share prices, if substantial and prolonged, leads to members of the public believing that prices will continue to rise. People who do not normally invest begin to buy shares in the belief that prices will continue to rise. More and more people, typically people who have no knowledge of financial markets, buy shares. This pushes up prices even further. There is euphoria and manic buying. This causes further price rises. There is a self-fulfilling prophecy wherein the belief that prices will rise brings about the rise, since it leads to buying. People with no knowledge of investment often believe that if share prices have risen recently, those prices will continue to rise in the future. Cassidy (2002) divides this process into a boom stage and a euphoria stage. In the boom stage share price rises generate media interest, which spreads the excitement across a wider audience. Even the professionals working for institutional investors become involved. In the euphoria stage investment principles, and even common sense, are discarded. Conventional wisdom is rejected in favour of the view that it is 'all different this time'. Prices lose touch with reality.

One assumption of the efficient market hypothesis is that investors are rational. This does not require all investors to be rational, but it does require that the rational investors outweigh the irrational ones. However there are times when irrational investors are dominant. A possible cause of market overreaction is the tendency of some investors (often small investors) to follow the market. Such investors believe that recent stock price movements are indicators of future price movements. In other words they extrapolate price movements. They buy when prices have been rising and thereby tend to push prices to unrealistically high levels. They sell when prices have been falling and thereby drive prices to excessively low levels. There are times when such naive investors outweigh those that invest on the basis of fundamental analysis of the intrinsic value of the shares. Such irrational investors help to generate bubbles and crashes in stock markets.

Some professional investors may also participate on the basis of the greater fool theory. The greater fool theory states that it does not matter if the price paid is higher than the fundamental value, so long as someone (the greater fool) will be prepared to pay an even higher price. The theory of rational bubbles suggests that investors weigh the probability of further rises against the probability of falls. So it may be rational for an investor to buy shares, knowing that they are overvalued, if the probability-weighted expectation of gain exceeds the probability-weighted expectation of loss.

Montier (2002) offers Keynes's (1936) beauty contest as an explanation of stock market bubbles. The first level of the contest is to choose the stocks that you believe to offer the best prospects. The second level is to choose stocks that you believe others will see as offering the best prospects. A third level is to choose the stocks that you believe that others will expect the average investor to select. A fourth stage might involve choosing stocks that you believe that others will expect the average investor to see as most popular amongst investors. In other words, the beauty contest view sees investors as indulging in levels of second-guessing other investors. Even if every investor believes that a stock market crash is coming they may not sell stocks. They may even continue to buy. They may plan to sell just before others sell. In this way they expect to maximise their profits from the rising market. The result is that markets continue to rise beyond what the vast majority of investors would consider to be the values consistent with economic fundamentals. It is interesting to note that Shiller's survey following the 1987 crash (Shiller 1987) found that 84% of institutional investors and 72% of private investors said that they had believed that the market was overpriced just before the crash. Shiller suggested that people did not realise how many others shared their views that the market was overpriced.

SOCIAL AND PSYCHOLOGICAL FACTORS

As Hirshleifer (2001) points out, people have a tendency to conform to the judgements and behaviours of others. People may follow others without any apparent reason. Such behaviour results in a form of herding, which helps to explain the development of bubbles and crashes. If there is a uniformity of view concerning the direction of a market, the result is likely to be a movement of the market in that direction. Furthermore, the herd may stampede. Shiller (2000) said that the meaning of herd behaviour is that investors tend to do as other investors do. They imitate the behaviour of others and disregard their own information.

Brown (1999) examined the effect of noise traders (non-professionals with no special information) on the volatility of the prices of closed-end funds (investment trusts). A shift in sentiment entailed these investors moving together and an increase in price volatility resulted. Walter and Weber (2006) found herding to be present among managers of mutual funds.

Walter and Weber (2006) distinguished between intentional and unintentional herding. Intentional herding was seen as arising from attempts to copy others. Unintentional herding emerges as a result of investors analysing the same information in the same way. Intentional herding could develop as a consequence of poor availability of information. Investors might copy the behaviour of others in the belief that those others have traded on the basis of information. When copying others in the belief that they are acting on information becomes widespread, there is an informational cascade.

Another possible cause of intentional herding arises as a consequence of career risk. If a fund manager loses money whilst others make money, that fund manager's job may be in jeopardy. If a fund manager loses money whilst others lose money, there is more job security. So it can be in the fund manager's interests to do as others do (this is sometimes referred to as the reputational reason for herding). Since fund managers are often evaluated in relation to benchmarks based on the average performance of fund managers, or based on stock indices, there could be an incentive to copy others since that would prevent substantial underperformance relative to the benchmark.

Walter and Weber (2006) found positive feedback trading by mutual fund managers. In other words the managers bought stocks following price rises and sold following falls. If such momentum trading is common, it could be a cause of unintentional herding. Investors do the same thing because they are following the same strategy. It can be difficult to know whether observed herding is intentional or unintentional.

Hwang and Salmon (2006) investigated herding in the sense that investors, following the performance of the market as a whole, buy or sell simultaneously. Investigating in the United States, the UK, and South Korea they found that herding increases with market sentiment. They found that herding occurs to a greater extent when investor expectations are relatively homogeneous. Herding is strongest when there is confidence about the direction in which the market is heading. Herding appeared to be persistent and slow moving. This is consistent with the observation that some bubbles have taken years to develop.

Kirman (1991) suggests that investors may not necessarily base decisions on their own views about investments but upon what they see as the majority view. The majority being followed are not necessarily well-informed rational investors. The investors that are followed may be uninformed and subject to psychological biases that render their behaviour irrational (from the perspective of economists). Rational investors may even focus on predicting the behaviour of irrational investors rather than trying to ascertain fundamental value (this may explain the popularity of technical analysis among market professionals).

There are theories of the diffusion of information based on models of epidemics. In such models there are 'carriers' who meet 'susceptibles' (Shiller 1989). Stock market (and property market) bubbles and crashes are likened to the spread of epidemics. There is evidence that ideas can remain dormant for long periods and then be triggered by an apparently trivial event. Face-to-face communication appears to be dominant, but the media also plays a role. Cassidy (2002) suggested that people want to become players in an ongoing drama in which ownership of stocks gives them a sense of being part of a social movement. People invest because they do not want to be left out of the exciting developments.

The media are an integral part of market events because they want to attract viewers and readers. Generally, significant market events occur only if there is similar thinking among large groups of people, and the news media are vehicles for the spreading of ideas. The news media are attracted to financial markets because there is a persistent flow of news in the form of daily price changes and company reports. The media seek interesting news. The media can be fundamental propagators of speculative price movements through their efforts to make news interesting (Shiller 2000). They may try to enhance interest by attaching news stories to stock price movements, thereby focusing greater attention on the movements. The media are also prone to focus attention on particular stories for long periods. Shiller refers to this as an 'attention cascade'. Attention cascades can contribute to stock market bubbles and crashes.

Davis (2006) confirmed the role of the media in the development of extreme market movements. The media were found to exaggerate market responses to news, and to magnify irrational market expectations. At times of market crisis the media can push trading activity to extremes. The media can trigger and reinforce opinions.

543

It has been suggested that memes may play a part in the process by which ideas spread (Lynch 2001). Memes are contagious ideas. It has been suggested that the success of a meme depends upon three critical factors: transmissivity, receptivity, and longevity. Transmissivity is the amount of dissemination from those with the idea. Receptivity concerns how believable, or acceptable, the idea is. Longevity relates to how long investors keep the idea in mind.

Smith (1991) put forward the view that bubbles and crashes seem to have their origin in social influences. Social influence may mean following a leader, reacting simultaneously and identically with other investors in response to new information, or imitation of others who are either directly observed or observed indirectly through the media. Social influence appears to be strongest when an individual feels uncertain and finds no directly applicable earlier personal experience.

Deutsch and Gerard (1955) distinguish between 'normative social influence' and 'informational social influence'. Normative social influence does not involve a change in perceptions or beliefs, merely conformity for the benefits of conformity. An example of normative social influence would be that of professional investment managers who copy each other on the grounds that being wrong when everyone else is wrong does not jeopardise one's career, but being wrong when the majority get it right can result in job loss. This is a form of regret avoidance. If a bad decision were made, a result would be the pain of regret. By following the decisions of others, the risk of regret is reduced. This is safety in numbers. There is less fear of regret when others are making the same decisions.

Informational social influence entails acceptance of a group's beliefs as providing information. For example share purchases by others delivers information that they believe that prices will rise in future. This is accepted as useful information about the stock market and leads others to buy also. This is an informational cascade; people see the actions of others as providing information and act on that information. Investors buy because they know that others are buying, and in buying provide information to other investors who buy in their turn. Informational cascades can cause large, and economically unjustified, swings in stock market levels. Investors cease to make their own judgements based on factual information, and use the apparent information conveyed by the actions of others instead. Investment decisions based on relevant information cease, and hence the process whereby stock prices come to reflect relevant information comes to an end. Share price movements come to be disconnected from relevant information.

Both of the types of social influence identified by Deutsch and Gerard (1955) can lead to positive feedback trading. Positive feedback trading involves buying because prices have been rising and selling when prices have been falling, since price movements are seen as providing information about the views of other investors. Buying pushes prices yet higher (and thereby stimulates more buying) and selling pushes prices lower (and hence encourages more selling). Such trading behaviour contributes to stock market bubbles and crashes.

People in a peer group tend to develop the same tastes, interests, and opinions (Ellison and Fudenberg 1993). Social norms emerge in relation to shared beliefs. These social norms include beliefs about investing. The social environment of an investor influences investment decisions. This applies not only to individual investors, but also to market professionals. Fund managers are a peer group; fundamental analysts are a peer group; technical analysts are a peer group. Indeed market professionals in aggregate form a peer group. It is likely that there are times when these peer groups develop common beliefs about the direction of the stock market. Common beliefs tend to engender stock market bubbles and crashes.

Welch (2000) investigated herding among investment analysts. Herding was seen as occurring when analysts appeared to mimic the recommendations of other analysts. It was found that there was herding towards the prevailing consensus, and towards recent revisions of the forecasts of other analysts. A conclusion of the research was that in bull markets the rise in share prices would be reinforced by herding.

Research on investor psychology has indicated certain features about the behaviour of uninformed investors, who are often referred to as noise traders in the academic literature. Tversky and Kahneman (1982) found that they have a tendency to overreact to news. DeBondt (1993) found that they extrapolate trends, in other words they tend to believe that the recent direction of movement of share prices will continue. Shleifer and Summers (1990) found evidence that they become overconfident in their forecasts. This latter point is consistent with the view that bubbles and crashes are characterised by some investors forgetting that financial markets are uncertain, and coming to believe that the direction of movement of share prices can be forecast with certainty. Barberis et al. (1998) suggested that noise traders, as a result of misinterpretation of information, see patterns where there are none. Lee (1998) mentioned that a sudden and drastic trend reversal may mean that earlier cues of a change in trend had been neglected. Clarke and Statman (1998) found that noise traders tend to follow newsletters, which in turn are prone to herding.

It seems that many investors not only extrapolate price trends but also extrapolate streams of good or bad news, for example a succession of pieces of good news leads to the expectation that future news will also be good. Barberis et al. (1998) showed that shares that had experienced a succession of positive items of news tended to become overpriced. This indicates that stock prices overreact to consistent patterns of good or bad news. Lakonishok et al. (1994) concluded that investors appeared to extrapolate the past too far into the future.

There is evidence that the flow of money into institutional investment funds (such as unit trusts) has an impact on stock market movements. Evidence for a positive relationship between fund flows and subsequent stock market returns comes from Edelen and Warner (2001), Neal and Wheatley (1998), Randall et al. (2003), and Warther (1995). It has been suggested by Indro (2004) that market sentiment (an aspect of crowd psychology) plays an important role. Indro found that poll-based measures of market sentiment were related to the size of net inflows into equity funds. It appears that improved sentiment (optimism) generates investment into institutional funds, which in turn brings about a rise in stock market prices (and vice versa for increased pessimism). If stock market rises render market sentiment more optimistic, a circular process occurs in which rising prices and improving sentiment reinforce each other.

It has often been suggested that small investors have a tendency to buy when the market has risen and to sell when the market falls. Karceski (2002) reported that between 1984 and 1996 average monthly inflows into US equity mutual funds were about eight times higher in bull markets than in bear markets. The largest inflows were found to occur after the market had moved higher and the smallest inflows followed falls. Mosebach and Najand (1999) found interrelationships between stock market rises and flows of funds into the market. Rises in the market were related to its own previous rises, indicating a momentum effect, and to previous cash inflows to the market. Cash inflows also showed momentum, and were related to previous market rises. A high net inflow of funds increased stock market prices, and price rises increased the net inflow of funds. In other words, positive feedback trading was identified.

This buy high/sell low investment strategy may be predicted by the 'house money' and 'snake bite' effects (Thaler and Johnson 1990). After making a gain people are willing to take risks with the winnings since they do not fully regard the money gained as their own (it is the 'house money'). So people may be more willing to buy following a price rise. Conversely the 'snake bite' effect renders people more risk-averse following a loss. The pain of a loss (the snake bite) can cause people to avoid the risk of more loss by selling investments seen as risky. When many investors are affected by these biases, the market as a whole may be affected. The house money effect can contribute to the emergence of a stock market bubble. The snake bite effect can contribute to a crash.

The tendency to buy following a stock market rise, and to sell following a fall, can also be explained in terms of changes in attitude towards risk. Clarke and Statman (1998) reported that risk tolerance fell dramatically just after the stock market crash of 1987. In consequence investors became less willing to invest in the stock market after the crash. MacKillop (2003) and Yao et al. (2004) found a relationship between market prices and risk tolerance. The findings were that investors became more tolerant of risk following market rises, and less risk tolerant following falls. The implication is that people are more inclined to buy shares when markets have been rising and more inclined to sell when they have been falling; behaviour which reinforces the direction of market movement. Shefrin (2000) found similar effects among financial advisers and institutional investors. Grable et al. (2004) found a positive relationship between stock market closing prices and risk tolerance. As the previous week's closing price increased, risk tolerance increased. When the market dropped, the following week's risk tolerance also dropped. Since risk tolerance affects the willingness of investors to buy risky assets such as shares, the relationship between market movements and risk tolerance tends to reinforce the direction of market movement. During market rises people become more inclined to buy shares, thus pushing share prices up further. After market falls investors are more likely to sell, thereby pushing the market down further.

Projection bias is high sensitivity to momentary information and feelings such that current attitudes and preferences are expected to continue into the future (Loewenstein et al. 2003). Mehra and Sah (2002) found that risk tolerance varied over time and that people behaved as if their current risk preference would persist into the future. In other words the current level of risk tolerance was subject to a projection bias such that it was expected to continue into the future. Grable et al. (2006) pointed out that this interacts with the effects of market movements on risk tolerance. A rise in the market enhances risk tolerance, projection bias leads to a belief that current risk tolerance will persist, people buy more shares, share purchases cause price rises, price rises increase risk tolerance, and so forth. A virtuous circle of rising prices and rising risk tolerance could emerge. Conversely there could be a vicious circle entailing falling prices and rising risk-aversion.

The Role of Social Mood

People transmit moods to one another when interacting socially. People not only receive information and opinions in the process of social interaction, they also receive moods and emotions. Moods and emotions interact with cognitive processes when people make decisions. There are times when such feelings can be particularly important, such as in periods of uncertainty and when the decision is very complex. The moods and emotions may be unrelated to a decision, but nonetheless affect the decision. The general level of optimism or pessimism in society will influence individuals and their decisions, including their financial decisions.

There is a distinction between emotions and moods. Emotions are often short term and tend to be related to a particular person, object, or situation. Moods are free-floating and not attached to something specific. A mood is a general state of mind and can persist for long periods. Mood may have no particular causal stimulus and have no particular target.

Positive mood is accompanied by emotions such as optimism, happiness, and hope. These feelings can become extreme and result in euphoria. Negative mood is associated with emotions such as fear, pessimism, and antagonism. Nofsinger (2005a) suggested that social mood is quickly reflected in the stock market, such that the stock market becomes an indicator of social mood. Prechter (1999, 2001), in proposing a socionomics hypothesis, argued that moods cause financial market trends and contribute to a tendency for investors to act in a concerted manner and to exhibit herding behaviour.

Many psychologists would argue that actions are driven by what people think, which is heavily influenced by how they feel. How people feel is partly determined by their interactions with others. Prechter's socionomic hypothesis suggests that human interactions spread moods and emotions. When moods and emotions become widely shared, the resulting feelings of optimism or pessimism cause uniformity in financial decision-making. This amounts to herding and has impacts on financial markets at the aggregate level.

Slovic *et al.* (2002) proposed an affect heuristic. Affect refers to feelings, which are subtle and of which people may be unaware. Impressions and feelings based on affect are often easier bases for decision-making than an objective evaluation, particularly when the decision is complex. Since the use of affect in decision-making is a form of short cut, it could be regarded as a heuristic. Loewenstein *et al.* (2001) showed how emotions interact with cognitive thought processes and how at times the emotional process can dominate cognitive processes. Forgas (1995) took the view that the role of emotions increased as the complexity and uncertainty facing the decision-maker increased.

Information can spread through society in a number of ways: books, magazines, newspapers, television, radio, the Internet, and personal contact. Nofsinger suggests that personal contact is particularly important since it readily conveys mood and emotion as well as information. Interpersonal contact is important to the propagation of social mood. Such contact results in shared mood as well as shared information.

Prechter suggested that economic expansions and equity bull markets are associated with positive feelings such as optimism and enthusiasm whereas economic recessions and bear markets correspond to an increase in negative emotions like pessimism, fear, and anger. During a stock market uptrend society and investors are characterised by feelings of calmness and contentment, at the market top they are happy and enthusiastic, during the market downturn the feelings are ones of sadness and insecurity, whilst the market bottom is associated with feelings of anger, hostility, and tension.

Dreman (2001) suggested that at the peaks and troughs of social mood, characterised by manias and panics, psychological influences play the biggest role in the decisions of investment analysts and fund managers. Forecasts will be the most positive at the peak of social mood and most negative at the troughs. Psychological influences can contaminate rational decision-making, and may be dominant at the extreme highs and lows of social mood. At the extremes of social mood the traditional techniques of investment analysis might be rejected by many as being no longer applicable in the new era.

547

Shiller (1984) took the view that stock prices are likely to be particularly vulnerable to social mood because there is no generally accepted approach to stock pricing; different analysts use different models in different ways. The potential influence of social mood is even greater among non-professionals who have little, or no, understanding of pricing models and financial analysis. Nofsinger (2005a) saw the link to be so strong that stock market prices could be used as a measure of social mood.

Peaks and troughs of social mood are characterised by emotional decision-making rather than rational evaluation. Cognitive evaluations indicating that stocks are overpriced are dominated by a mood of optimism. Support for one's downplaying of rational evaluation receives support from the fact that others downplay rational evaluation. The optimism of others validates one's own optimism. It is often argued that the normal methods of evaluation are no longer applicable in the new era. Fisher and Statman (2002) surveyed investors during the high-tech bubble of the late 1990s and found that although many investors believed stocks to be overpriced, they expected prices to continue rising.

Eventually social mood passes its peak and cognitive rationality comes to dominate social mood. Investors sell and prices fall. If social mood continues to fall, the result could be a crash in which stock prices fall too far. The situation is then characterised by an unjustified level of pessimism, and investors sell shares even when they are already underpriced. Investors' sales drive prices down further and increase the degree of underpricing. Fisher and Statman (2000) provided evidence that stock market movements affect sentiment. A vicious circle could develop in which falling sentiment causes prices to fall and declining prices lower sentiment.

A PSYCHOANALYTIC PERSPECTIVE

Taffler and Tuckett (2002) provided a psychoanalytic perspective on the technology stock bubble and crash of the late 1990s and early 2000s, and in so doing gave a description of investor behaviour totally at odds with the efficient markets view of rational decision-making based on all relevant information. They made it clear that people do not share a common perception of reality; instead everyone has their own psychic reality. These psychic realities will have varying degrees of connection with objective reality. Decisions are driven by psychic reality, which is a realm of feelings and emotions. Reason may be secondary to feeling. Feeling affects the perception of reality. People are seen as engaging in wish-fulfilment wherein they perceive reality so that it accommodates to what they want. People see what they want to see. Unpleasant aspects of reality may be subject to denial, which is the pretence that unpleasant events and situations have not happened. Denial reduces the ability to learn from unpleasant experiences, since unpleasant experiences are removed from conscious awareness.

The unconscious mind operates as a censor that keeps out unpleasant information. People are constantly bombarded by far more information than the human mind can handle. The unconscious mind reduces incoming information to a quantity that can be dealt with. Although much of this rejected information is peripheral to needs, some information may be rejected because it is unpleasant. The conscious mind, the mind of which we are aware, does not receive complete information. The efficient market view of rational investors who base decisions on all relevant information does not sit comfortably with this psychoanalytic view of mental processes.

548

In relation to stock market bubbles, the psychoanalytic view of Taffler and Tuckett (2002) sees stocks as taking on a significance for the unconscious mind, which reflects experiences of infancy. The unconscious mind has considerable influence over thinking and decision-making. Since people are not aware of their unconscious minds, they are not aware of the influence of the unconscious mind over decision-making. The unconscious mind may exclude uncomfortable aspects of reality from awareness. When the bubble bursts, and prices fall, it becomes impossible to completely exclude unpleasant aspects of objective reality from awareness. Feelings of anxiety, loss, panic, and shame emerge. Selling the shares as quickly as possible could then become part of the process of denial.

In the view of Bargh and Chartrand (1999) people's goals, as well as their behaviours, are affected by factors outside conscious awareness. Investment behaviour is likely to be affected by emotions, which are outside conscious awareness.

THE IMPLICATIONS OF BEHAVIOURAL FINANCE FOR UNDERSTANDING BUBBLES AND CRASHES

Behavioural finance applies the psychology of decision-making to investment behaviour. Psychological research has indicated that there are a number of systematic distortions that cause investors to deviate from the model of rationality typically assumed by financial economists. Some of these biases help to explain how stock markets can experience bubbles and crashes.

Representativeness and Narrow Framing

It is not difficult to see how behavioural finance concepts can be used in the explanation of stock market bubbles and crashes. For example the concept of representativeness helps to explain the apparent tendency for investors to chase the market. Many people seem to believe that recent price rises will continue into the future, likewise recent price falls. As a result they buy when they see that prices have been rising, causing prices to rise further, and sell when they see that prices have been falling, accentuating the price falls. DeBondt (1993) reported a study of 38,000 forecasts of stock prices and exchange rates. He found that non-experts expected the continuation of apparent past trends in prices. They were optimistic in bull markets and pessimistic in bear markets.

One interpretation of representativeness is that investments that have shown recent price rises are representative of longer term successes (and conversely for those showing recent price falls). Another way of looking at representativeness views it as suggesting that people see patterns and trends where they do not exist. Recent upward price movements are interpreted as an upward trend that will continue into the future (conversely with price falls).

Thus representativeness explains how opinions about price trends can emerge, and through affecting trading those opinions become self-fulfilling. The persistence of such opinions, and hence the resulting bubbles or crashes, may be explained by the concepts of conservatism and confirmation bias. Conservatism renders people unwilling to change their opinions in the light of new information, so they may adhere to a view about the direction of prices even when those prices have moved too far. Confirmation bias is the tendency for people to pay attention to information that supports their opinions, and to ignore contrary evidence. Again this causes them to persist with market views, and trading behaviour, even when evidence suggests that those views may be incorrect.

Narrow framing suggests that investors focus too much on the short term. In consequence the very recent behaviour of share prices is focused upon and the longer term past is ignored. This reinforces the tendency of representativeness to lead to unjustified long-term expectations on the basis of short-term price movements.

These ideas are consistent with the emergence of stock price bubbles and crashes. Recent price increases cause expectations of future increases and investors buy shares. This pushes prices up further, and hence generates expectations of more increases and leads to yet more buying. There is an upward spiral often referred to as positive feedback trading or as 'chasing the market'. There is a corresponding, but opposite, pattern as the market falls.

Overconfidence

Psychological research has indicated that there is a self-attribution bias in decision-making. When an investment is successful, the investor believes that it is due to his or her skill. An unsuccessful investment is seen to fail as a result of bad luck or the actions of others. This self-attribution bias leads to overconfidence. Overconfidence is also reinforced by the hindsight bias, which is the false belief held by people who know the outcome of an event, that they would have predicted the outcome. Overconfidence may be particularly characteristic of inexperienced investors who find that their initial investments are profitable. Their belief in their own skill leads them to invest more. So a bull market can generate overconfidence, which causes more investing thereby reinforcing the upward price movement. There is a Wall Street adage, which says: 'Don't confuse brains with a bull market.'

However there are those who interpret their gains in a bull market as arising from their own skills. They see certainty where there is uncertainty. This can lead them to invest beyond a rational level, and painful losses result when the market falls.

Overconfidence can arise from excessive confidence in the quality of one's information and an exaggerated view of one's ability to interpret that information. This leads to an unwarranted degree of certainty about the accuracy of one's forecasts and a corresponding underestimation of risk (Barber and Odean 1999). In consequence overconfident investors are prone to invest to a greater extent than would be the case if they properly understood the quality of their forecasts. Barber and Odean have found that overconfident investors tend to take more risk than less confident investors.

During the late 1990s there was a bull market, particularly in technology stocks. During the bull market, individual investors increased their levels of trading. Investors allocated higher proportions of their portfolios to shares, invested in riskier (often technology) companies, and many investors borrowed money in order to increase their shareholdings (Barber and Odean 2001). It is likely that, during the bull market, individual investors attributed too much of their success to their own expertise and became overconfident as a result.

A psychological bias that helps to produce overconfidence is the illusion of control. People often behave as if they have influence over uncontrollable events (Presson and Benassi 1996). A number of attributes have been identified as fostering the illusion of control. One of these is the outcome sequence. Positive outcomes early give a person more illusion of control than negative outcomes early. This is akin to the tendency for some people to become addicted to gambling if their first few bets are successful. In a rising stock market people investing for the first time will experience gains. This is likely to engender the illusion of control, overconfidence, and the inclination to invest more. If significant numbers of people invest more, prices will continue to rise thereby reinforcing these psychological biases.

Another attribute that fosters the illusion of control is the acquisition of information. Increased information increases the illusion of control and the degree of overconfidence. This has been called the illusion of knowledge (Nofsinger 2005; Peterson and Pitz 1988). The information may or may not be relevant to the investments. Particularly for investors with little knowledge of investment, information does not give them as much understanding as they think because they lack the expertise to interpret it. They may be unable to distinguish relevant and reliable information from irrelevant and unreliable information. However to the extent that stock market gains lead investors to seek information, the information obtained is likely to increase the illusion of control and the extent of investing. The resulting investment will help to perpetuate the share price rises and thereby the psychological biases.

In addition to the outcome sequence, Presson and Benassi (1996) showed that choice, task familiarity, information, and active involvement foster the illusion of control. Barber and Odean (2002) pointed out that online investors tend to experience these attributes. In particular they make choices, become familiar with the process of trading, and have access to large amounts of information. The implication is that the development of online trading is likely to enhance the illusion of control, and hence any market instability to which the illusion of control might contribute.

At the time of writing, the most recent bubble was in technology stocks. During 1999 and up to March 2000 such stocks rose dramatically in price. Novice investors piled in either through direct share purchases or via unit trusts specialising in technology stocks. Many people came to believe that they could make a living out of trading shares (as 'day traders'). It seemed that some people even believed that their profits were due to their investment skills (typically people with no prior knowledge of investment or financial markets).

Familiarity and Celebrity Stocks

Best (2005) investigated the Internet stock bubble, which occurred in the late 1990s and burst in 2000. One conclusion was that Internet stocks acquired a form of celebrity status. Their prices exceeded fundamental value just as the earnings of celebrities appear to surpass the talent of the individuals concerned. Just as the perception of celebrities has an emotional dimension, investors in Internet stocks were seen as having an emotional attachment to them. Just as the media promotes celebrities, and the cult of celebrity, the media promoted Internet investing and a culture of Internet investing.

Part of the reasoning of the analysis provided by Best is similar to the familiarity bias of behavioural finance. The familiarity bias leads people to prefer to invest in things they think they know and understand. At the time of the Internet stock bubble large numbers of people were beginning to use the Internet, which therefore felt familiar to them. The Internet was new, exciting and appeared to offer huge potential. It is possible that Internet stocks, by association with the Internet itself, came to be seen as exciting investments with huge potential.

Arguably an Internet culture was emerging, wherein the Internet came to be seen as symbolic of a new age: the information age. A social mood emerged amongst Internet enthusiasts. People who identified with the information age saw use of the Internet as an expression of their personalities; they saw themselves as part of the new era. Investment in Internet stocks was an extension of their personal attachment to the internet. This parallels celebrity cults. The celebrities with whom a person identifies become part of that person's perception of self. To a fan, a celebrity is more than an actor or singer. To many buyers of internet stocks, the shares were more than financial investments. Another comparison might be with supporters of a football team; supporters identify with the team and have an emotional attachment such that association with the team helps to describe them as individuals. Behavioural finance has identified both familiarity and emotional involvement with particular investments as influences on financial decision-making. It seems likely that these factors were influential during the internet stock bubble of the late 1990s.

Best (2005) emphasised the role of the media in talking up the prices of internet stocks, and the creation of celebrity status for such stocks. Shiller (2000) argued that the media had become more involved in reporting stock market news, and in generating an investment culture. In doing so the media has made the subject of investment more entertaining and exciting to many people. An investment culture has been promoted, with investment being seen as part of a lifestyle option. Within this context it is not surprising that the media focused attention on internet stocks since such stocks offered excitement and glamour. The media became part of the process of generating the internet stock price bubble (Lovink 2002). The media played an important role in the creation of the celebrity status of internet stocks, just as the media plays an important role in the creation of celebrity status for people.

INVESTOR OVERREACTION

Empirical evidence on investor overreaction over some time periods is consistent with these ideas from behavioural finance. DeBondt and Thaler (1985) found that stocks with very poor returns over a three-year period subsequently outperformed those with the highest returns. A portfolio comprising the 35 biggest losers earned a cumulative return 25% higher than the portfolio of the 35 biggest winners over the subsequent three years. This may be the result of investor overreaction during the first three years.

This may be because of an extrapolation of news. Suppose that a company announces good news over the initial three years, such as profits that are repeatedly above expectations. It may be that investors come to expect more good news in the future and become excessively optimistic about the company's prospects. The stock price is driven up and the stock becomes a winner. However good news in the past is not an indicator of good news in the future, and as the expectations about the future prospects of the company shed the rosy bias of the extrapolation the stock price will move back down towards a more realistic level. The converse could be true of the effects of a run of bad news.

This phenomenon could take hold at the general market level. By early 2003 world stock markets had fallen over the previous three years. This may in part have been the result of an extrapolation of bad news. A sequence of negative news had occurred: the dot.com bubble burst; the global economy went into recession; corporate profits fell; terrorism escalated on September 11th, 2001; corporate scandals emerged from Enron, Worldcom, and Arthur Anderson; the likelihood of another Gulf war appeared; and the consequent general fall in share prices was another form of bad news. Investors' reactions may have been to expect the flow of bad news to continue. If the extrapolation of bad news was an incorrect reaction, stock prices at the beginning of 2003 were reflecting too much negative news and should have shown an upward movement if the flow of negative news ceased. It is also to be noted that not all of the recent news had been negative, for example interest rates had fallen substantially over the previous two years. Confirmation bias may have caused investors to ignore, or at least give too little weight to, such positive news.

Another explanation of overreaction is in terms of the retrievability (availability/recency) bias. People have a tendency to overweight recent information. When new information relevant to the price of an asset becomes available investors give disproportionate weight to this recent news relative to existing information. So they overreact to the new information. Subsequently, as the news becomes older, the weight attached to it declines. In consequence prices tend to move back to some extent. DeBondt and Thaler (1990) found that this psychological bias, and the resultant overreaction, occurs amongst professional security analysts (and institutional investors) as well as individual investors.

Mood affects investment behaviour (Baker and Nofsinger 2002; Nofsinger 2002). It has been suggested that good moods make people less critical. Good moods can lead to decisions that lack detailed analysis. Determinants of mood include weather, and the number of hours of daylight. Research by Hirshleifer and Shumway (2003) and by Kamstra et al. (2003) has indicated that these factors affect investment behaviour. Good weather, and long hours of sunlight, appears to encourage net buying and market rises. Nofsinger (2002b) has suggested an optimism bias. Optimism reduces critical analysis during the investment process, and it causes investors to ignore negative information.

One factor that can affect mood, and the level of optimism, is the recent performance of stock markets. A market rise is likely to improve the mood of investors, and their degree of optimism. A positive feedback cycle could emerge. Price rises improve mood and increase optimism. In consequence there are net purchases, so prices rise. These price rises positively affect mood and optimism. Such a positive feedback cycle could contribute to the development of a bubble. Conversely a downward vicious circle could arise with falling prices, worsening moods, and declining optimism.

THE CRASH

The bubble phase leads to share prices reaching unrealistic levels. These are share price levels far in excess of what can be justified by fundamental analyses using dividend discount models or price-earnings ratios (see Chapters 19 and 21 on dividend discount models and ratio analysis, respectively). Indeed one feature of bubbles, identified by Kindleberger (1989), is the emergence of 'new age' theories. New age theories are ad hoc theories that seek to justify why prices should be far in excess of what conventional share valuation models suggest.

There may then be an occurrence that causes prices to fall rapidly. One such occurrence might be the emergence of new companies. The new companies compete with existing ones and push down their profits. Also when the new companies float on the stock market, the additional supply of shares will help to depress share prices. Towards the end of the 1999–2000 technology stock bubble many new companies were issuing shares. This increased supply of shares overtook the growth in demand for shares. The result was that the prices of shares in the technology sector began to fall.

Rising interest rates could be another occurrence that leads to falling share prices. Bubbles often involve people borrowing money in order to buy shares. High interest rates could cause investors to sell shares in order to pay the interest. Such sales could set off a crash. In Japan in 1990 interest rates rose sharply. This was followed by collapses in the prices of both shares and property.

553

Rising interest rates can also reduce the demand for shares by making alternatives such as bank deposits more attractive. Higher interest rates also reduce expenditure on goods and services and thereby lower corporate profits. Lower expected profits can cause a fall in share prices.

Other factors that can precipitate share price collapses include share sales resulting from negative statements by people who are looked upon as experts. These may be genuine experts such as governors of central banks, or self-appointed experts such as newspaper gurus. Also prospective investors may stop buying because they deplete their sources of money. The flow of new investors on to the market will eventually stop. These factors can start a crash by increasing sales of shares and decreasing purchases. Cassidy (2002) suggested that a crash could be precipitated by a random event, or have no apparent catalyst, if stock prices have reached sufficiently unrealistic levels.

To the extent that shares are bought with borrowed money (leveraged buying), stock market crashes can cause banking crises. If investors are unable to repay their debts, banks may become bankrupt. This could result in depositors losing their money. The effects of leveraged buying worsened the 1929 stock market crash in the United States. That crash was also followed by a banking crisis in which banks failed and depositors lost money. Figure 27.1 illustrates the vicious circle that can emerge when shares are used as collateral against borrowing.

POST-KEYNESIAN PERSPECTIVES ON STOCK MARKET BUBBLES AND CRASHES

There has been a tendency for central banks to inject large amounts of money (usually referred to as liquidity) into the financial system following a crash. This may be to avert a banking crisis and may be for the purpose of stabilising the stock market. Some of that additional liquidity would be used for the purchase of shares, and would therefore slow or reverse the downward movement of share prices. Since this is equivalent to giving the stock market a put option, which gives protection against price falls, it has sometimes been called the Greenspan put (named after a past head of the US Federal Reserve, Alan Greenspan).

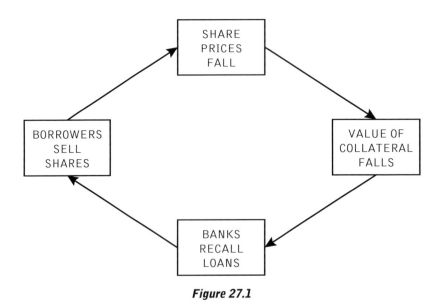

Figure 27.1

Raines *et al.* (2007) highlighted the asymmetry involved. They pointed out that central banks take action to soften crashes but take no action to weaken bubbles. The monetary authorities behave as if they believe that markets are efficient during bubbles but inefficient during crashes. Raines *et al.* supported this interpretation of central bank behaviour by making a number of references to the writings and speeches of Alan Greenspan. Such actions by monetary authorities lessen stock market risk, and could therefore serve to give an upward bias to stock prices.

The discussion of stock market bubbles and crashes in terms of social and psychological factors seems to be broadly consistent with the post-Keynesian interpretation, which is particularly associated with Galbraith (for example Galbraith 1988). Galbraith has focused on social mood and excessive optimism, with the latter often manifesting itself as a belief that the stock market offers a means to 'get rich quick'. Stock market speculation is seen as most likely to occur after a period of prosperity, which has allowed the accumulation of a substantial amount of savings. Those savings are available for investment. The facility of borrowing in order to enhance the level of stockholding also strengthens the conditions for the development of a bubble. The role of the accumulation of money (liquidity) available for investment is a factor emphasised in both the post-Keynesian and monetarist traditions. The monetarist view gives the money supply the central role in the explanation of bubbles and crashes. The liquidity theory of asset prices could be seen as being in the monetarist tradition.

BUYING ON MARGIN AND THE LIQUIDITY THEORY OF ASSET PRICES

A feature of bubbles is that share purchases are often financed with borrowed money. This is sometimes referred to as buying on margin, or leveraged buying. Shares are used as collateral for loans taken out for their purchase. There can be a circular process that entails rising share prices. This circular process is illustrated by Figure 27.2.

Pepper and Oliver (2006) have proposed the liquidity theory of asset prices. Their suggestion is that a major driver of stock markets is the amount of liquidity available for investment. In other words if people have more money to invest they will invest more and thereby push up share prices. Money is created when loans are made. So the act of financing share purchases with borrowed money increases the money supply (liquidity). The sellers of the shares then have money available for investment, and may use the money for the purchase of other shares thereby pushing share prices up. The people who sell those shares will receive money, some of which will be used for share purchases. This process can continue through a number of rounds, and at each round share prices are pushed up. The cumulative increase in expenditure on shares can be estimated by means of a multiplier equation:

$$I = E \times [1/(1 - k)]$$

where I is the cumulative increase in spending on shares, E is the initial expenditure on shares, and k is the proportion of receipts from sales of shares that is invested in other shares. A high rate of reinvestment (a high level of k) produces a large multiplier effect and a large cumulative expenditure on shares (a large I). There would be strong upward pressure on share prices. It should be borne in mind that decreases in liquidity can occur with consequent downward multiplier effects.

Congdon (2006) demonstrated that institutional investors (life assurance and pensions) have a fairly stable demand for liquidity in the sense of the ratio of liquid assets to other assets. If the institutional investors experience a change in liquidity that moves the liquidity ratio away from the

555

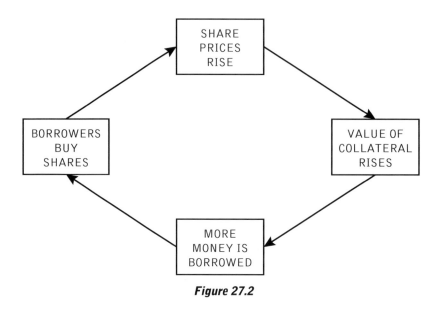

Figure 27.2

desired level, they will attempt to restore the desired ratio. Money is a form of liquidity. An increase in the money supply could disturb the liquidity ratio of institutional investors. The institutions attempt to restore their liquidity ratios to the desired values by spending the surplus liquidity on assets such as shares. This would drive share prices up. So long as the holding of liquidity exceeds the desired amount investment spending will continue. To the extent that each institution's expenditure is another institution's receipt of money, the attempt by each institution to reduce its holding of liquidity does not reduce the aggregate holding of liquidity by institutions.

Some of the additional money will be lost to the institutions, for example to individual shareholders who sell to institutions, but much will remain with the institutions. If the institutions hold a high proportion of the total value of shares, most of the additional money may remain with the institutions. The desired ratio of liquidity to other assets is restored by a rise in share prices.

Suppose that institutional investors, in aggregate, hold £1,000 billion of shares. Also suppose that, on average, the institutions desire to hold liquid assets equal to 4% of non-liquid assets. Together they require £40 billion of liquid assets to match the shareholdings. If they receive additional money of £30 billion, they would have a liquid assets ratio of 7%. In aggregate they would not rid themselves of the surplus £30 billion, since the institutions would tend to pass the money between themselves as shares are bought from each other. Some of the money, say £10 million, would be lost to the institutions. This would reduce the aggregate holding of liquidity to 6% of the original value of shares. The institutions would still have £60 billion of liquid assets.

The desired ratio of liquid assets to shareholdings is restored by a rise in share prices. Share prices would rise until the desired ratio is restored. So long as the actual ratio exceeds the desired ratio spending on shares would continue, as would the resulting rise in share prices. Prices would rise until the total value of shares reached £1,500 billion. The liquidity ratio of 4% would then have been restored (£60 billion of liquid assets against £1,500 billion of shares). An initial £30 billion increase in the money held by the institutions leads to a £500 billion increase in the aggregate value of shares held by the institutions. This £500 billion increase results from a 50% rise in share prices. An initial reduction in liquidity would generate falling prices.

The amount of liquidity lost to the institutions in this process would be low if the institutions held a high proportion of the available shares. A low loss would entail a high rise in share prices. For example if all of the £30 billion increase in the money supply remained with institutional investors, the aggregate value of shares would need to rise to £1,750 billion. The institutions would have liquidity amounting to £70 billion (the original £40 billion plus the new £30 billion) and the restoration of a 4% liquidity ratio would require share prices to rise until the total value of shares reached £1,750 billion. Share prices would rise by 75%.

TYPES OF TRADE

Pepper and Oliver (2006) have suggested that stock market trades can be divided into portfolio trades and liquidity trades. They subdivide portfolio trades into information trades and price trades.

Portfolio trades are concerned with improving the prospective risk/return characteristics of a portfolio. They may entail selling some shares and buying others, or switching between asset classes such as between cash and shares or between bonds and shares. Information trades are responses to news that has implications for share prices. Price trades are responses to price movements that are not justified by new information. Portfolio trades tend to ensure that share prices are efficient in the sense of accurately reflecting all relevant information.

Liquidity trades occur because investors have money to invest, or need to sell investments in order to raise money. Pepper and Oliver (2006) suggest that a major reason for liquidity trades is monetary imbalance in the sense of inequality between the demand for, and supply of, money. If people find that they are holding more money than they want, they may spend part of the surplus money on investments (shares, bonds, property). If they have less money than they need, investments may be sold in order to restore money holdings to the desired level. In these ways changes in the rate of increase of the money supply can affect share prices. Liquidity and portfolio trades are depicted in Figure 27.3.

Pepper and Oliver (2006) suggest that liquidity trades move the prices of shares (and other assets) away from their efficient levels so that prices no longer accurately reflect all available information. Price trades move prices back towards their efficient levels. Underpriced assets are bought, thereby pushing up their prices. Overpriced assets are sold, thereby pushing their prices down. Pepper and Oliver suggest that the volume of price trades is normally sufficient to restore prices to their efficient levels following disturbances arising from monetary imbalance.

Figure 27.3

Figure 27.4

Arguably this division of types of trade is incomplete. One omission is noise trading. This is trading based on irrationality, including trading based on irrelevant information or psychological biases. Figure 27.4 includes noise trading.

Noise trades might be regarded as irrational trades on an individual basis. Individuals may be affected by psychological biases such as the biases that lead to self-deception. Noise trading causes deviations of share prices from the efficient prices. Sometimes prices are above, sometimes below, dependent upon whether noise traders are net buyers or net sellers. The resulting movement of share prices around their efficient levels is noise. It may be that the prospective volume of price trades is sufficient to keep the level of noise to a low level. In other words price trading may be sufficient to prevent deviations from efficient prices becoming large.

Irrational trading is not always at an individual level. If investors operate as a crowd, herding can result. There can be synchronisation of investment behaviour. The irrational investors might be overwhelmingly buyers or overwhelmingly sellers. The result is powerful upward or downward pressures on markets. Price trades may be insufficient to offset the effects of herding with the result that there is a bubble or crash in share (or bond, or property) prices. Figure 27.5 adds herd trading to the diagram.

There may be another division to be made. Monetary imbalance is not the only source of liquidity trades. People save money and some of that saved money is invested. Savings provide a source of expenditure on investments. Net saving in an economy would tend to push up share prices. If the issue of new shares fails to keep pace with savings available for investment in shares, the result would be an increase in share prices. It is questionable whether price trades would offset a long-term accumulation of savings. Figure 27.6 includes net saving as a source of liquidity trades.

Figure 27.5

Figure 27.6

The portfolio trades tend to maintain market efficiency whereas the liquidity and irrational trades tend to disturb market efficiency. The maintenance of efficiency depends upon the relative power of these forces. In the case of long-term saving, a long-term upward trend in share prices and property prices (and fall in bond yields) might be expected if the cumulative level of net saving exceeds the cumulative issue of shares and bonds plus the cumulative construction of property.

MONETARY IMBALANCE AND EXTRAPOLATIVE EXPECTATIONS

Pepper and Oliver (2006) suggest that, if monetary imbalance persists in one direction for a long period, extrapolative expectations can result. By extrapolative expectations is meant the tendency to expect that price changes will continue in the direction recently observed. Extrapolative expectations lead to momentum (positive feedback) trading with the effect that a price movement continues in a particular direction. The psychological bias of representativeness helps to explain the emergence of extrapolative expectations. If extrapolative expectations are widespread the result is herd trading, and herd trading can overwhelm any tendency for price trades to restore 'efficient' prices.

Price traders could become part of the momentum trading process. Maximising returns entails following prices upwards until they peak. Selling too soon causes a loss of potential profits. This is the idea of rational bubbles, or the greater fool theory. It makes sense to buy overpriced investments if you expect that a greater fool will later buy at an even higher price. Rather than moderating price rises, price traders may accentuate the rises.

According to Pepper and Oliver (2006), a long period of rising prices is associated with an accumulation of investors who need to sell (since their holdings of money are less than the desired levels). Such investors may delay asset sales while prices continue to rise. A continuing rise in prices is likely to attract speculative investors who do not plan to hold the investments for the long term; Pepper and Oliver refer to their investments as being loosely held. A long period of rising prices would lead to many investors needing to sell shares in order to raise money for other purposes, and to many speculators with loosely held shares. When the expectation of price rises disappears, both groups of investors will sell. Share prices fall sharply.

A BEHAVIOURAL MODEL OF THE DOT.COM BUBBLE AND CRASH

Exhibit 27.1 draws together ideas from this chapter, and from Chapter 2 on the psychology of personal investment decisions, to suggest a description of the forces underlying the bubble and crash of the late 1990s and early 2000s.

EXHIBIT 27.1   A BEHAVIOURAL MODEL OF THE DOT.COM BUBBLE AND CRASH

The flow chart indicates how behavioural finance concepts could be used in an explanation of the dot.com bubble and crash of the late 1990s and early 2000s.

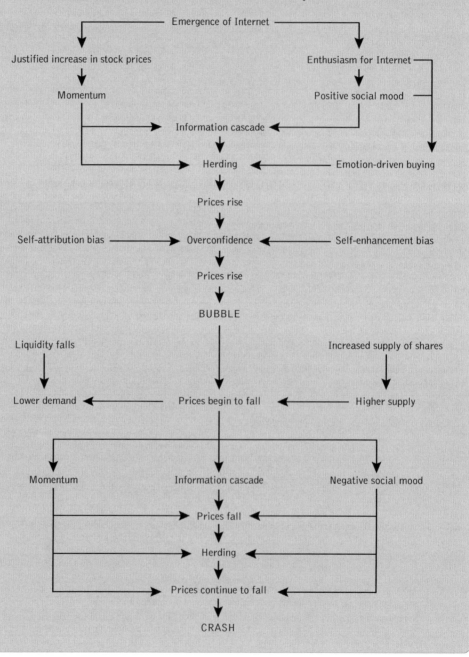

The role of momentum in the development of the bubble was particularly significant according to Boswijk *et al.* (2007). They divided investors into two groups. One group comprised fundamentalists who believed in the mean reversion of stock prices towards a true (fundamental) value such that deviations from true values would be corrected. The other group consisted of trend followers who believed that a direction of price movement would continue. The proportions of investors in the two groups vary over time. The researchers found that in the late 1990s almost all investors were trend following, and that the dominance of trend followers persisted for several years. This is consistent with strong momentum in the formation of the bubble. The studies by Best (2005) and by Muga and Santamaria (2007) indicated that high-technology (including dot.com) stocks were particularly susceptible to momentum trading (trend following).

PORTFOLIO INSURANCE

Portfolio insurance refers to the attempt to hedge a portfolio by simulating a put option. The purchase of a put option will provide the holder of the option with profits when stock prices fall. The decline in the value of a portfolio of stocks would be (at least partially) offset by profits from the option. The nature of a put option is such that the compensation for incremental falls becomes greater as the cumulative decline increases. Initially only a small part of the loss is covered, but after substantial falls the majority of any further falls are matched by gains on the option. Effectively the put option progressively reduces the exposure of the portfolio to the market as stock prices fall.

The same effect can be achieved by gradually selling stocks in response to falling stock prices with the effect that the exposure to the stock market is progressively reduced. This process is known as portfolio insurance, or dynamic hedging.

One effect of portfolio insurance is that falls in stock prices lead to sales of shares. Those sales cause further falls in the market and hence more sales. A vicious circle can develop. Price falls stimulate sales, which cause further price falls. This process can increase the intensity of a market decline, and possibly cause a crash.

In the presence of portfolio insurance, market rises can be reinforced. Price rises stimulate share purchases and hence further price rises. A virtuous circle can develop. Rising prices encourage purchases, which further increase prices and hence yet more purchases. This process can contribute to the development of a stock price bubble.

RESEARCH USING EXPERIMENTAL MARKETS

Laboratory experiments have been used to throw light on the development of bubbles and crashes, and in particular on whether they are based on 'rational' fundamental factors or 'irrational' behavioural factors. One problem with attempts to resolve this issue is that fundamental values (for example based on dividend discount models) are not observable in real market environments. Laboratory markets have the advantage of providing unambiguous fundamental values. The results of laboratory experiments, in which fundamental values are observable, might provide insights into analogous real-world markets.

Caginalp *et al.* (2000) surveyed results from laboratory experiments on stock trading. One study, whose results were typical, provided participants with a share whose fair (i.e. true) price was very easy to calculate on the basis of a dividend discount model. Participants were then asked to trade the shares over two hours, which were divided into a total of 15 periods. Demand and supply were matched in each period.

Although the share had an unambiguous value in each period, based on future cash flows, the price at which it traded deviated substantially from that value. Bubbles and crashes emerged from the trading. For example the trading of a group of business executives produced prices that varied between 20% of fair value and 630% of that value. It appears from such experiments that deviations of actual prices from fair, or fundamental, value can be long-lasting.

Dufwenberg et al. (2005) reported that laboratory experiments had shown that bubbles tend to occur with inexperienced traders but not with experienced traders. The extent to which this provides insights into the operation of real markets depends upon whether real markets are dominated by experienced or inexperienced investors. Dufwenberg et al. conducted experiments with mixtures of experienced and inexperienced traders. They found that bubbles were eliminated if at least one-third of participants were experienced. Since experienced investors probably dominate real markets, the implication is that bubbles are likely to be rare and unlikely to be caused by the relatively small proportion of inexperienced investors. They observed that bubbles and crashes in real markets were unusual (for example US stock markets had experienced just three clear cases in the twentieth century). They suggested that markets might be understood as being based on fundamentals for most of the time, with occasional lapses.

In general, the evidence from experimental trading (Caginalp et al. 2000) has indicated that speculative bubbles are more likely to emerge where:

1. The proportion of inexperienced traders is high.
2. The uncertainty about true (fair or fundamental) value is high.
3. The investment promises a small chance of profit, but that profit would be very high.
4. It is possible to finance purchases by borrowing money.
5. Short selling is difficult (i.e. it is difficult to borrow shares for the purpose of selling them).

It is interesting to note how well these characteristics describe the market in high-tech shares in the few years up to 2000.

COMPLEXITY THEORY AS AN EXPLANATION OF BUBBLES AND CRASHES

Complexity theory comes from physics and seems to be able to explain a wide variety of natural events. Montier (2002: 138–9) quotes Langton's description of complexity:

> From the interaction of the individual components . . . emerges some kind of global property . . . something you couldn't have predicted from what you know of the component parts. And the global property, this emergent behaviour, feeds back to influence the behaviour of the individuals . . . that produced it.

Complexity theory predicts two features of systems (referred to as complex adaptive systems). The first is that a power law captures the distribution of the probability of an event. A power law may be represented by the equation:

$$N = 1/s^\tau$$

In the case of stock markets N might represent the number of stock market crashes of a particular size and s might represent the size of the crash. It will be noted that an implication of the power law is that small crashes are relatively frequent whilst large crashes are rare.

The other feature that is predicted by complexity theory is that a crash is preceded and followed by periods of high volatility involving oscillations of increasing frequency and falling duration. It is suggested that this reflects increasing synchronisation of investor behaviour and that the crash results from nearly complete synchronisation (i.e. nearly all investors think and behave in the same way). When the market is distant from the crash investors are not synchronised with the effect that buyers and sellers tend to balance out. As the crash approaches there is increasing synchronisation of views concerning the direction of the market. When nearly everyone takes the view that the market will fall sellers overwhelm buyers with the result that prices fall dramatically.

Vandewaller *et al.* (1999) demonstrated that in the context of stock markets there is a tendency for volatility to cluster around stock market crashes. Volatility tends to be high just before, and just after, a crash. Johansen and Sornette (1999, 2001) found that the pattern of (increasingly frequent) oscillations is characteristic of market bottoms as well as market peaks.

Others take the opposite view about volatility. For example Olsen (1998) and Schwartz (1988) suggested that it is divergence of opinion that leads to share price volatility. This increase in divergence of opinion would emerge during periods characterised by increased differences in decision-making processes. Differences in data perception, selection, weighting, and analysis lead to variations in opinion among investors. Panchenko (2007) provided evidence that heterogeneity in views is associated with increased volatility (also Shalen 1993). Panchenko described periods in which investment analysts issue heterogeneous recommendations as 'analysts' wars' and found that volatility was about twice as high during such periods than in 'peace' periods.

Olsen (1998) suggests that standard finance theory has difficulty in explaining divergences of opinion; for example the efficient market hypothesis sees rational investors using all relevant information to establish stock prices that reflect all relevant information. There seems to be little scope for differences in opinion unless some investors have less information than others; in other words asymmetric information might be the only explanation for differences in opinion offered by standard finance theory. Behavioural finance suggests that differences in opinion are to be expected.

If all investors were provided with exactly the same information there would be differences in opinion about the direction of stock prices because of differences in the perception and interpretation of the information, differences in views about the relative importance of pieces of information, and differences concerning the appropriate way to analyse the information.

Olsen (1998) took the view that investment analysis is an example of 'complex, ill-structured tasks', which are common in the social sciences. Complex, ill-structured tasks are characterised by a lack of agreement concerning what is relevant information and how it should be analysed. The wide variety of approaches to investment analysis is symptomatic of a complex, ill-structured task. Experts do little better than novices when dealing with such tasks. Chapters 9, 11, 17, and 26, which provide evidence on the performance of investment analysts and fund managers, indicate that professional analysts and managers show little, if any, tendency to outperform passive strategies such as index tracking.

Investment analysis, as a complex, ill-structured task, gives rise to considerable variety in opinions, partly because of the wide variety of techniques of investment analysis. Such tasks are

563

also likely to be subject to the psychological biases, emotional and social influences described in the chapters dealing with behavioural finance and the psychology of decision-making, especially Chapters 2 and 24. Those chapters also indicate that such psychological and social factors can be particularly important in times of great uncertainty.

Complexity theory extends observations made in the natural sciences to the explanation of the behaviour of financial markets. Increasing synchronisation may be an appropriate explanation of increasing volatility in the study of inanimate matter, but the view that increasing volatility in financial markets arises from increasing differences rather than increasing synchronisation has intuitive appeal. High price volatility suggests alternate episodes of net buying and net selling, which seems more consistent with differences in opinion than with a developing uniformity of opinion.

CATASTROPHE THEORY AS AN EXPLANATION OF CRASHES AND SURGES

Catastrophe theory has used the possibility of a backward-sloping demand curve for shares as an explanation of stock market crashes. Figure 27.7 shows the form of demand-and-supply model used. The curves 1, 2, 3, 4, and 5 are demand curves with both downward and backward sloping sections. Good news moves the demand curve to the right, and bad news moves it to the left. The general level of the market is represented by 'Price', which might be looked upon as the value of a stock index.

Starting from demand curve 1 and price P_1 (determined by the intersection of demand curve 1 with the fixed supply) bad news will move the demand curve to the left. When it has moved to

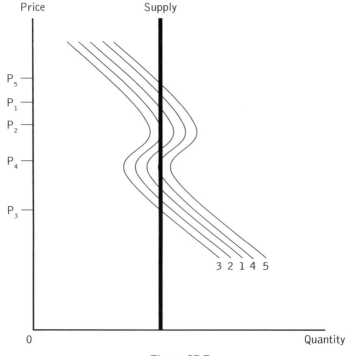

Figure 27.7

the position of demand curve 2 the new price, P_2, is determined at the point of tangency of demand curve 2 and the supply function. Further bad news could produce demand curve 3 and a dramatic fall in price to P_3. The fall from P_1 to P_2 is gradual (continuous). When the demand curve moves to the left of curve 2 the fall in price to the new intersection of demand and supply functions is sudden (discontinuous). The jump in price from P_2 to P_3 constitutes a crash.

If the news then improves, the demand curve will move to the right. However a full recovery in share prices is not achieved from a move back to demand curve 2, or even demand curve 1. Since the crash is not easily reversible, it is referred to as a catastrophe. It is called a catastrophe because the size of improvement of the news needed to reverse the fall is much greater than the size of deterioration that caused the fall. Correspondingly the model is an application of catastrophe theory.

If the news continues to improve, demand curve 4 and price P_4 might be achieved. There would be a point of tangency between the demand and supply functions. A further improvement in the news would cause demand to exceed supply until the price has risen substantially. If the news produces a move to demand curve 5, the result would be a sudden jump in price to P_5. There is thus a surge in share prices. The rise in price from P_3 to P_4 is continuous (gradual), whereas the rise from P_4 to P_5 is discontinuous (there is a jump in price).

So allowing for a section of the demand curve to be backward sloping leads to the prediction that there will be sudden (discontinuous) jumps in the general level of share prices. The question arises as to why a section of the demand curve should be backward sloping.

Leland (1987) developed a model similar to the one described here. Leland suggested that the backward-sloping section of the demand curve might be due to dynamic hedging (portfolio insurance). Dynamic hedging involves investors reducing their shareholdings in response to falling share prices (perhaps in an attempt to simulate a protective put option). So price falls lead to reduced demand for shares. Conversely price rises cause the hedge to be unwound, which entails buying shares.

Behavioural finance may provide explanations. The backward-sloping demand curve could be the result of investors extrapolating recent price movements, perhaps as a result of the representativeness bias. Recent falls are seen as indicating future falls, so investors sell in response to falling prices. Conversely price increases raise demand for shares since they are seen as indicative of further increases in price. These behaviour patterns are likely to be reinforced by other psychological biases such as overconfidence, conservatism, and confirmation bias.

Other explanations may run in terms of the use of technical analysis. Falling prices may trigger a sell signal. If a majority of charts point to a fall in the market, there will be selling of shares. So price falls may be the cause of a fall in demand for shares. Conversely rising prices could provide a buy signal with the result that a price rise stimulates additional demand.

PRICE BUBBLES AND BANKING CRISES

Crashes not only hurt investors, they can also damage banks. Slumps in stock prices can be detrimental to banks, particularly if banks have bought shares as well as lending to other buyers. The American stock market crash of 1929, and the Japanese stock market slump of the 1990s, involved stock price falls impacting on banks. However stock market crashes do not always severely damage banks.

Property price slumps nearly always damage the banks. This is because property speculation is primarily financed with money borrowed from banks. Bubbles in property prices are typically based on borrowing from banks. Property developers and speculators finance their purchases by borrowing. The purchased property is used as collateral for the loans.

So long as property prices continue to rise interest payments can be made, and loans repaid. When prices stop rising, problems appear. If interest is paid out of the profits from price rises (or from increased borrowing based on the enhanced collateral), a pause in the rises means that interest cannot be paid. Banks may then require loans to be repaid.

The developers and speculators may then sell property in order to pay off the loans. The property sales cause prices to fall. The fall in property prices reduces the value of the collateral. As a result banks demand repayment of loans. More property is sold, prices fall further, collateral declines further, and the banks demand more repayment. There is a downward spiral leading to bankruptcy of property developers and speculators. The values of their properties fall below the values of their debts. Such bankruptcies mean that bank loans are not fully repaid. The banks lose money. The Japanese property market slump and banking crisis of the early 1990s involved banks being severely weakened by such a process.

Banks lend money to each other. If one bank became bankrupt, the banks from which it had borrowed would lose money. There could be a domino effect wherein the collapse of some banks causes others to fail. This systemic effect could lead to a collapse of the whole banking system.

The prospect of banks failing might cause depositors to panic and attempt to withdraw their money. If depositors rushed to withdraw their money, banks could run out of cash and hence be unable to pay out the money. This is especially so since bank loans normally are not repayable on demand, and so banks cannot get their money back quickly. Failure to pay depositors would increase the sense of panic and encourage more attempts to withdraw cash. Such a run on the banks by depositors wanting to withdraw cash would hasten the collapse of the banks. Such behaviour by depositors was a feature of the American banking crisis that followed the Wall Street crash of 1929.

The possibility of a run on the banks is one reason why central banks, such as the Bank of England, act as lenders of last resort. This means that they will lend to banks in an emergency so that banks can pay their customers. Governments also often guarantee that bank deposits will be repaid in order to avoid the panic that leads to runs on the banks.

Even if banks do not collapse (and normally they do not), the effect of losses on their capital can cause a credit crunch. A credit crunch is a situation in which banks stop making new loans (or at least reduce the amount of new lending). A credit crunch may also entail the refusal to renew many loans, with the effect that the borrowers must repay the loans when those loans reach their maturity dates. Investors may become forced sellers if they need to sell assets in order to repay loans. If a fund has financed investments by means of borrowing from a bank, the refusal of the bank to renew the lending could force the fund to sell assets. Such forced selling puts downward pressure on asset prices and would exacerbate a crash. A credit crunch can bring about contagion between asset markets. For example in the summer of 2007 banks reduced lending, and refused to renew some maturing loans, because they feared that the borrowers held assets backed by sub-prime mortgages. Many borrowers became forced sellers since they needed to sell assets in order to repay the borrowed money. The forced selling extended to stocks and the sales of shares contributed to sharp falls in stock markets.

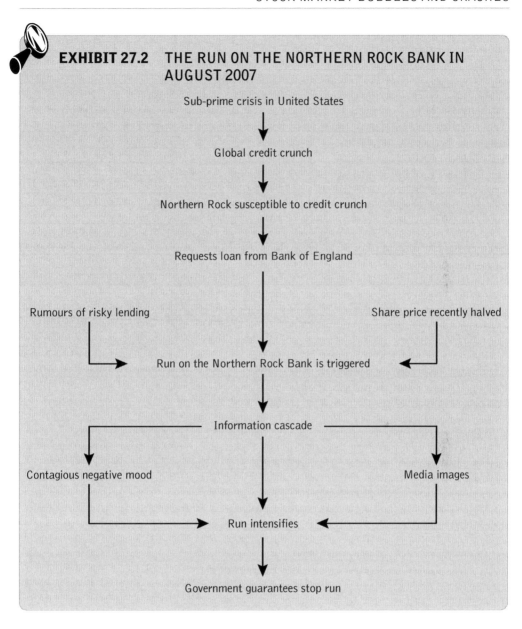

EXHIBIT 27.2   THE RUN ON THE NORTHERN ROCK BANK IN AUGUST 2007

Sub-prime crisis in United States

↓

Global credit crunch

↓

Northern Rock susceptible to credit crunch

↓

Requests loan from Bank of England

↓

Rumours of risky lending ———→ Run on the Northern Rock Bank is triggered ←——— Share price recently halved

↓

Information cascade

Contagious negative mood   Media images

Run intensifies

↓

Government guarantees stop run

CONCLUSION

Arguably the strongest evidence against the efficient market hypothesis is the existence of stock market bubbles and crashes. Whilst there is a wide variety of views about what causes, and what drives, bubbles and crashes, few observers suggest that they are caused by new information coming into the market. Such is the width of explanations for bubbles and crashes that some explanations come from physics (phynance) and some from biology using models of disease contagion. Models of contagion seem to fit comfortably with the concepts of information cascades and herding as explanations of investor behaviour during bubbles and crashes.

The concept of 'rational bubbles' suggests that the emergence of stock market bubbles is consistent with rational behaviour. It may be rational for investors to buy shares that they believe to be overpriced, so long as they expect to sell them at an even higher price. Weighing the expectation of profit against the possible loss in the event of price falls could lead to the conclusion that prospective profits outweigh possible losses (when both are weighted by probability of occurrence). It could be rational to buy in an overpriced market.

Another mechanism that does not depend on irrational behaviour is portfolio insurance. During the 1987 stock market crash some institutional investors simulated the purchase of put options. This simulation involved selling stock as the market fell, thereby reinforcing the downward movement in prices.

Behavioural finance suggests that the occurrence of stock market bubbles and crashes stems from irrational behaviour on the part of investors. The concept of positive feedback trading, reinforced by the representativeness bias, seems to provide a driving force that causes stock market prices to overreact. Laboratory experiments have shown that bubbles and crashes tend to emerge from trading behaviour, particularly in the presence of relatively naive investors.

Another possible driving force comes from money supply changes. A bubble could be generated by a rapid growth in money supply. The additional money is partially spent on assets such as shares and property, thereby producing asset price inflation in stock and property markets. The effect of money supply changes could then interact with positive feedback trading (based on extrapolative expectations) reinforced by representativeness.

A catastrophe is an event which whilst caused by a minor occurrence is not remedied by a reversal of the minor occurrence. The application of catastrophe theory to the explanation of stock market bubbles and crashes requires the demand curve for shares to have a backward-bending section. A backward-bending section could be explained in terms of either portfolio insurance or behavioural finance.

Further reading

Readers who would like to pursue further their studies of behavioural finance may find the following books interesting:

Montier, J. (2002). *Behavioural Finance,* Wiley.
Nofsinger, J. R. (2005). *The Psychology of Investing,* 2nd edn, Pearson Education/Prentice Hall.
Shefrin, H. (2000). *Beyond Fear and Greed: Understanding Behavioral Finance and the Psychology of Investing,* Harvard Business School Press.
Shiller, R. J. (2005). *Irrational Exuberance,* 2nd edn, Princeton University Press.

Part 8

Stock Index Futures

Chapter 28

Stock index futures

OBJECTIVE

The objective of this chapter is to provide knowledge of:

1. Financial futures.
2. Hedging, speculation, and arbitrage with futures.
3. The margin system and closing out.
4. Futures funds.
5. The relative merits of using futures and stocks for achieving investment objectives.
6. Contracts for Difference (CFDs).
7. Equity swaps.

FINANCIAL FUTURES

A financial future is a notional commitment to buy or sell, on a specified future date, a standard quantity of a financial instrument at a price determined in the present (the futures price). It is rare for a futures contract to be used for the exchange of financial instruments. Indeed many contracts, including stock index futures, have no facility for the exchange of the financial instrument. Instead, financial futures markets are independent of the underlying cash markets, albeit operating parallel to those markets.

The main economic function of futures is to provide a means of hedging. A hedger seeks to reduce an already existing risk. This risk reduction could be achieved by taking a futures position that would tend to show a profit in the event of a loss on the underlying position (and a loss in the case of a profit on the underlying position).

Positions in futures markets can be taken much more quickly and much more cheaply (in terms of transaction costs) than positions in the underlying spot markets. For example a position in stock index futures can be established within a few minutes (from the time of the decision) at little cost in terms of commissions and bid-ask spreads. The construction of a balanced portfolio of stocks would take much longer and would be more costly in terms of commissions and spreads. For these reasons, futures markets tend to be more efficient than the underlying spot markets; futures prices respond to new information more quickly. Hence futures have a second economic function, which might be termed price discovery. Futures prices may be indicative of what prices should be in the markets for the underlying instruments. This price discovery function is particularly important where the underlying spot market is poorly developed or illiquid, as in countries with poorly developed financial systems or for instruments that are not frequently traded.

Example of Hedging with Futures

The FTSE 100 Index stands at 6,000 on 14 February and a fund manager expects to receive £900,000 on 15 March. The intention is to invest that money immediately in a balanced portfolio of shares. The fund manager fears that share prices will rise by 15 March, meaning that fewer shares can be bought with the £900,000. Since the risk is that share prices will increase, the requisite futures position is one that would profit from a rise in share prices. Stock index futures are bought. A FTSE 100 futures contract relates to a value of stock equal to the futures index multiplied by £10. So, if the futures index were 6,000, each futures contract would relate to 6,000 $\times$ £10 = £60,000 worth of shares. Hedging a purchase of £900,000 of stock (at 14 February prices) requires the purchase of 15 FTSE 100 futures contracts.

Suppose that the index rises by 600 points by 15 March. The quantity of stock that could have been bought for £900,000 on 14 February now costs £990,000. This could be regarded as a loss of £90,000. However, if the futures FTSE 100 Index also were to rise by 600 points, there would be a futures profit of £90,000.

600 index points $\times$ £10 per point $\times$ 15 contracts = £90,000

The futures profit, when added to the £900,000, provides the £990,000 required to buy the quantity of stock that £900,000 would have bought on 14 February.

SPECULATION AND ARBITRAGE

In addition to hedgers, financial markets also have speculators and arbitragers. Speculators are traders who buy and sell in order to make profits from positions held for short periods of time. Speculators buy and sell futures simply to make profit, not to reduce risk. They believe that they have better information than other market participants concerning the appropriate price. Futures are very attractive to speculators because of the gearing provided. Traders need only make margin payments and hence can take positions for a cash outlay that is only a small fraction of the value of the positions.

If a speculator believes that something is overpriced the decision will be to sell, whereas perceived underpricing will result in buying. Speculators operate on the basis that the market will quickly correct any mispricing. The aim is to take positions earlier than other market participants with a view to making profits when the others trade. The trades of the others would push prices towards their new levels. If the new price is consistent with the speculator's expectation, a profit is realised. A variety of views will lead to two-way trading by speculators with the result that market liquidity is enhanced. Frequently, speculative trades heavily outnumber hedging trades.

Speculators are vital to futures markets. They facilitate hedging, provide liquidity, tend to ensure accurate pricing, and can help to maintain price stability. It is unlikely that hedgers wishing to buy futures will precisely match hedgers selling futures in terms of numbers of contracts. If hedgers are net sellers, there will be a tendency for futures prices to fall and that may generate profit opportunities for speculators. Speculators will buy the underpriced futures (the situation in which hedgers are net sellers and hence futures are underpriced is sometimes referred to as 'normal backwardation'). The purchases by speculators will allow the net sales on the part of the hedgers. In effect, speculators fill the gap between sales and purchases by hedgers. In so doing, they tend to maintain price stability since they will buy into a falling market, and sell into a rising one (in the event of hedgers being net buyers). If hedgers are net buyers, with the result that futures are overpriced, the situation is sometimes called 'contango'. Contango entails speculators selling futures.

A liquid market is one in which there is considerable buying and selling on a continuous basis. In a liquid market, hedgers can make their transactions with ease and with little effect on prices. Speculative transactions add to market liquidity. In the absence of speculators, hedgers may have difficulty in finding counterparties with whom to trade and they may need to move prices in order to entice counterparties.

Speculators also help to make a market informationally efficient. A market is informationally efficient when prices fully reflect all available relevant information. Speculators are likely to consider all relevant information when deciding upon the appropriate price of a futures contract. If actual prices differ from those judged appropriate, they will be brought into line with the estimated prices by speculative trades; underpriced futures will be bought (and so their prices will tend to rise), while overpriced futures will be sold until their prices have fallen to the level considered correct.

Some have taken the view that since futures provide a means of low cost speculation, a resulting increase in speculation would increase stock market volatility. Others point to the role of futures in conveying new information to markets, and in transferring speculation from the stock market to the futures market. These latter points are used to suggest that futures trading is more likely to reduce, rather than increase, stock market volatility. A number of researchers have investigated the impact of the introduction of futures on stock market volatility. Rahman (2001) investigated the effect of the introduction of futures based on the Dow Jones Industrial Average, looking at the three-month periods immediately preceding and following the introduction of those futures in 1997. It was found that the introduction of the futures had no effect on the price volatility of the stocks covered by the index. McKenzie et al. (2001) examined the impact of the introduction of individual share futures in Australia on the price volatility of the underlying shares. They found that in most cases the introduction of the futures resulted in a reduction of price volatility.

In addition to hedgers and speculators, there is a third category of trader known as arbitragers. Arbitragers also help to make markets liquid, ensure accurate pricing and enhance price stability. Arbitrage involves making profits from relative mispricing. Futures prices should bear a consistent relationship to stock prices. If this relationship is violated, an arbitrage opportunity may arise. If the futures price were too high relative to the stock prices, arbitragers could make a profit by simultaneously buying stocks and selling futures. Such trades will tend to restore the appropriate relationship between stock prices and futures prices (by raising stock prices and reducing futures prices).

573

THE MARGIN SYSTEM

The margin system is central to futures markets. There are three types of margin: initial margin, maintenance margin, and variation margin. The initial margin is a sum of money to be provided by both the buyer and the seller of a futures contract when they make their transaction; it is a deposit that is returned when the contract expires or is closed out. This margin is a small percentage of the face value of the contract (perhaps 5%). The initial margin is subject to variation (by a clearing house) and will depend on the volatility of the stock market. One function of initial margin is the provision of market discipline. The payment of initial margin may deter poorly capitalised speculators from entering the market.

Whereas initial margin is the sum to be initially deposited (with a clearing house), the maintenance margin is the sum that must remain deposited while the futures position is held. Initial and maintenance margins are frequently identical in value. Initial and maintenance margins could be in the form of money (which may earn interest) or other securities (which continue to provide a yield to the holder of the futures position). The margin will be drawn upon (by the clearing house) in the event of the holder of a futures position failing to make a variation margin payment.

Variation margin is payable and receivable on a daily basis. It reflects the profit or loss made from a futures contract during the course of a day. If the futures price moves to the holder's advantage, the holder will receive variation margin; if the futures price moves adversely, a payment must be made. This process of realising profits and losses on a daily basis is known as marking to market. If a contract holder fails to make a variation margin payment, the contract will be automatically closed out and the outstanding sum deducted from the maintenance margin (which is set at a level that is expected to exceed any likely variation margin call).

When a futures deal is agreed between a buyer and a seller, a clearing house takes over the role of counterparty to both buyer and seller. So, although buyer A bought from seller B, once the deal is registered the clearing house becomes the seller to buyer A and the buyer from seller B. An implication of this is that there is no need to investigate the creditworthiness of the person or entity with whom a deal is made (the need for such investigation could slow up futures dealing and undermine market efficiency). All default risk is taken by the clearing house. The clearing house protects itself from counterparty default risk by means of the variation and maintenance margins. Marking to market (the daily settlement of profits and losses) prevents the accumulation of counterparty debt and the maintenance margin is a source from which one day's outstanding variation margin payment can be drawn. If a trader fails to pay variation margin on a day, their futures contracts are closed out by the exchange and the variation margin payment taken from their maintenance margin. The remainder of the maintenance margin is then returned to the trader. Another implication of the margin system is that futures are highly geared investments. For example an initial margin of 5% of the value of the underlying stock means that the exposure acquired is 20 times the initial money outlay.

CLOSING OUT

The majority of futures contracts are closed out before they mature. There are typically only four maturity dates each year, and it is unlikely that the needs of futures users will coincide with one of those four dates (for many futures contracts there are maturity dates in March, June, September, and December). Closing out involves taking a futures position opposite to the original position. If a trader opened a position by buying a contract with a March maturity date, the trader could close out the position by selling a March futures contract; likewise, a trader with a short position (futures sold) could close it out by buying futures with the same maturity date. When futures contracts are closed out, the trader is left with no futures position; the purchases and sales cancel each other.

The closing transaction will typically not be with the same counterparty as the opening transaction; but, none the less, the transactions will cancel out, leaving the trader with no remaining futures position. This is because of the counterparty role of the clearing house. As soon as a futures trade is agreed, the clearing house becomes the counterparty to both buyer and seller. It is as if the buyer has bought from the clearing house and the seller sold to the clearing house. So when a closing out transaction occurs, the trader is left with identical long (bought) and short (sold) positions with the clearing house and the clearing house deems these to cancel each other out.

FUTURES FUNDS

Futures funds are structured investments that operate by means of keeping most of their assets in a liquid form such as short-term bank deposits, while the remainder is used to finance the margin requirements of futures trading. Profits and losses from stock market movements come from futures rather than from holding shares. The futures may relate to a sum of securities equal to the value of the fund, but not necessarily. Futures provide the flexibility to gain exposure to a quantity of assets in excess of the value of the fund, or to take a short position in the underlying investment. The gearing offered by futures provides an opportunity for futures funds to be highly geared. The market exposure of a futures fund might be several times the value of the fund. Obviously, such highly geared funds are very risky.

Futures funds are not always limited to stock index futures. They may contain a wide variety of futures contracts. Multi-sector funds would contain not only a range of financial futures, but also commodity futures. Furthermore, the contracts could derive from exchanges in a number of different countries. Such diversification helps to reduce the risk of the futures funds. Commodity futures may be particularly attractive to fund managers since they are likely to exhibit little or no correlation with the assets (such as stocks and bonds) that constitute the major part of investment portfolios. An asset that has low correlation with the other elements of a portfolio will tend to reduce the risk of the portfolio. Losses on some types of asset may be offset by profits on assets from other markets.

Trading on market movements can normally be achieved more quickly and cheaply by using futures than by using spot instruments such as shares and bonds. Futures bid-offer spreads and commissions are often much lower than in the spot markets and time need not be spent on deciding between specific securities. It follows that a fund that is likely to shift frequently between asset classes (e.g. between shares and bonds) would benefit from the use of futures rather than spot market instruments.

Futures allow quick and cheap movement not only between classes of asset, such as between shares and bonds, but also between national markets. The time and expense of researching foreign stocks can be avoided by using stock index futures relating to the foreign stock markets.

Furthermore, only margin payments are subject to currency exposure (exchange rate risk); the bulk of the fund can remain in the home currency.

EXERCISE 28.1

The manager of a futures fund has £1,000,000. The fund manager buys FTSE 100 futures relating to £1,000,000 of shares when the FTSE 100 stands at 5,000. The futures mature in one year.

(a) How many futures contracts are bought?

(b) Does any of the £1,000,000 need to be used in the purchase of the futures?

(c) What is the approximate capital gain on the fund over a year if the FTSE 100 rises by 10%?

(d) What must be added to the capital gain in order to find the total return on the fund?

Answer

(a) £1,000,000/(5,000 × £10) = 20 contracts.

(b) Initial margin must be provided.

(c) 10% (minus the net cost of carry).

(d) Interest on the money on deposit plus interest on maintenance margin (i.e. interest on approximately £1,000,000).

CONTRACTS FOR DIFFERENCE AND 130/30 FUNDS

An instrument that has similarities with a futures contract is a contract for difference (CFD). Frequently it relates to a particular stock (in the UK a CFD contract relates to 1,000 shares), but could relate to any marketable asset (or even non-marketable instruments such as stock indices). CFD contracts do not have fixed expiry dates and can be closed at any time. A CFD is a deal between an investor and a broker. The investor is expected to pay a deposit (typically 10% of the value of the shareholding to which the CFD relates). If losses are made the broker takes cash from the deposit (margin) and the investor is required to provide more cash in order to maintain the value of the deposit at 10%. If the position makes a profit, the investor receives cash.

An investor who takes a long position in a CFD relating to a share would profit from a share price rise, and lose in the event of a share price fall. The profits or losses would be calculated by reference to a specified share price (typically slightly above the share price when the contract was entered into; the offer price of the share might be used). If the share price were above the specified price, there would be a profit equal to the difference between the current price and the specified price. Conversely there would be a loss equal to the extent to which the current price is below the specified price. An investor with a long CFD is treated as if the shares are bought with borrowed money (which is what the broker might do in the absence of offsetting short positions). The investor pays interest and receives dividends.

An investor who takes a short position in a CFD profits from price falls and loses from price rises. The extent of profit or loss is based on the difference between the current share price and (typically) a share price slightly below the share price at the time that the contract was entered into (the bid price of the share might be used). An investor with a short CFD is treated as if the shares are sold short and the receipts are put on deposit (which is what the broker might do in the absence of offsetting long positions). The investor receives interest and pays sums equal to the share dividends.

Bid/offer prices might be quoted, for example, as 119p–121p. The buyer of a CFD would make a profit if the share price rises above 121p.

At a share price of 136p there would be a profit of $(136-121) \times 1,000 = 15,000p$, i.e. £150.
A share price of 110p would provide a loss of $(121-110) \times 1,000 = 11,000p$, i.e. £110.
At a share price of 110p, the seller of a CFD would profit by $(119-110) \times 1,000 = 9,000p$, i.e. £90.
At a share price of 136p the seller of the CFD would lose $(136-119) \times 1,000 = 17,000p$, i.e. £170.

Potential losses are very large in the event of prices moving heavily against an investor. A stop-loss arrangement entails automatic closure of a position in the event of a price movement beyond a particular level. However there is a risk that the price movement is so rapid that closure occurs only after the price has moved well beyond the chosen stop-loss price; such an occurrence is sometimes known as gapping.

A broker providing CFDs could take corresponding positions in the share. However if a broker has investors on both the long and short sides, the need to take positions in the share is reduced since the cash flows of long and short investors would match each other. Some concern has been expressed that if investors use CFDs as a substitute for share purchases, liquidity is taken from the stock market. Although brokers take offsetting positions in the stock market, liquidity is reduced to the extent that there is matching between long and short positions.

By using CFDs investors can obtain geared investments in, or short positions on, a share (or other instrument). An almost identical alternative is spread betting.

EXHIBIT 28.1 130/30 FUNDS

130/30 funds take a 100% long position in equities (shares). In addition they take a further market-neutral position by adding a further long position matched by a short position in other equities. In this way they take a short position in those shares about which they have a bearish view, balanced by a long position in stocks about which they are bullish. The name 130/30 implies that the market-neutral addition represents 30% of the basic long position (i.e. 30% of the net value of the fund). However the chosen percentage may differ from 30%.

As a result of the European Ucits III rules, the short positions are attained by using contracts for difference (CFDs) rather than by selling borrowed shares.

The question arises as to how a 130/30 fund differs from a hedge fund, which chooses a strategy of a long position plus a market-neutral (hedge/arbitrage) addition. Some might regard 130/30 funds as a form of halfway house between long-only funds and hedge funds. However they differ from hedge funds in that (1) they are relative value (e.g. relative to a stock index) rather than absolute return funds, (2) there is less secrecy about their strategy and operation, (3) they are more liquid in that they do not lock up investors' money for long periods, (4) they do not charge the very high fees often charged by hedge fund managers, and (5) their choice of strategy is more restricted than in the case of hedge funds.

The advantage of 130/30 funds, compared to long-only funds that simply buy stocks without taking short positions, rests on the success of the fund managers in identifying prospective outperforming and underperforming stocks. If the managers were wrong in their judgements, the 130/30 funds would underperform long-only funds. 130/30 funds entail more active risk (management risk), which is the risk of underperformance resulting from errors in fund management.

Source: Senior (2007).

EQUITY SWAPS

Equity swaps provide an alternative to futures funds as means of creating derivatives-based investment funds. An equity swap involves an agreement to exchange the returns on a stock index portfolio for a flow of interest payments. Such swaps could be arranged for any of the major stock indices, e.g. the S&P 500, FTSE 100, Nikkei 225, CAC 40, and DAX. Figure 28.1 illustrates an equity swap for the CAC 40 (the main French stock index).

Investor A has a balanced portfolio of French stocks but is bearish about the French stock market. As an alternative to selling the portfolio, the investor could enter an equity swap. The swap illustrated by Figure 28.1 would be suitable if the investor were bullish on the US dollar and US dollar interest rates.

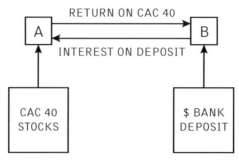

Figure 28.1

Investor B might be an American fund manager who wants an exposure to the French stock market but does not have the expertise to evaluate French stocks. By entering the equity swap of Figure 28.1 the American fund manager simulates a balanced investment in French stocks without getting involved in the analysis of individual French stocks. (Note that stock returns include capital gains or losses as well as dividends.)

Investor A has a portfolio of French shares and wishes to swap the returns for the interest on a US dollar bank deposit, thereby eliminating exposure to the French stock market without selling shares. Investor B obtains exposure to the French stock market without buying shares.

CONCLUSION

Stock index futures are significant tools for fund management. They allow fund managers to vary the level of market risk of their portfolios. Hedgers seek to reduce risk, speculators accept increased risk, and arbitragers pursue risk-free profits.

Stock index futures have advantages over shares. It is much easier to take a short position in futures than in shares. Transactions in futures can be carried out more quickly and more cheaply than transactions in shares. Stock index futures provide a very flexible tool for portfolio management.

It is even possible to create equity funds without buying shares. Futures funds entail combinations of risk-free investments, in the form of money market investments (see Chapter 3 on money market investments), and futures contracts. The use of futures enables fund managers to go beyond equity investments and to include bond, currency, and commodity futures (see Chapters 43 and 39 on bond futures and on currency forwards, futures, swaps, and options, respectively). In this way risk reduction by diversification can be increased (see Chapter 13 on portfolio diversification). Hedge funds often make considerable use of futures contracts of various types (see Chapter 16 on styles of portfolio construction).

One limitation of futures funds is that the shares of smaller companies are not covered since the indices on which futures are based tend to exclude the shares of smaller companies. In the UK there are futures contracts that cover the FTSE 100 and the FTSE 250 shares, but companies whose market capitalisations fall below the top 350 are not covered.

This chapter has provided hypothetical examples of the construction of futures funds, and more examples are presented in Chapter 29 on stock index futures prices. Futures funds are a form of structured product (see Chapter 34 on structured products). Futures funds based on stock indices are, when the notional value of the futures matches the value of the fund, a form of index tracker fund (see Chapters 9 and 16 on mutual funds and styles of portfolio construction, respectively). Futures funds could allow institutional fund managers to offer retail investors index tracker funds, which give better diversification than that provided by an index such as the FTSE 100 or the FTSE All-Share Index. These indices are dominated by the top ten companies and hence may not provide optimally diversified portfolios (see Chapters 7 and 13 on stock indices and portfolio diversification, respectively). For example a balanced combination of FTSE 100 and FTSE 250

579

futures would reduce the dominance of the very large companies, and would also give a broader coverage of industrial sectors.

Funds that use stock index futures rather than shares are still affected by, and impact on, the stock market. The link between the futures and stock markets is provided by cash and carry arbitrage (see Chapter 29 on stock index futures prices). Cash and carry arbitrage ensures that stock market movements are reflected by futures prices, and that futures price movements are reflected by the stock market.

Chapter 29

Stock index futures prices

OBJECTIVE

The objective of this chapter is to provide knowledge of:

1. The role of arbitrage in the determination of stock index futures prices.
2. Arbitrage strategies to make profits from observed mispricing.
3. The roles of hedgers and speculators in the determination of futures prices.
4. The role of risk in the pricing process.
5. The relationship between futures prices and expected future spot prices.

ARBITRAGE PRICING

The pricing of stock index futures can be looked upon as being based on cash-and-carry arbitrage. The futures price should be such that there is no arbitrage profit from simultaneously buying stock (with borrowed money) and selling futures. Likewise there should be no profit opportunity from selling stock (short) and simultaneously buying futures.

The excess of the financing cost (interest on the borrowed money) of holding the stock over the dividend receipts constitutes the net cost of carry. The selling price guaranteed by the futures should match the initial cost of the stock plus the net cost of carry. In other words, the futures price should provide a guaranteed capital gain that exactly compensates for the excess of the interest payments over the (expected) dividend receipts. Such a futures price is referred to as the fair futures price.

The fair value premium is the excess of the fair futures price over the spot (i.e. actual) stock index. The formula for the fair value premium is:

$$FP = I \times [\{(r-y)/100\} \times \{d/365\}]$$

FP is the fair value premium, I is the spot FTSE 100 Index, r is the interest rate, y is the expected percentage dividend yield on the index portfolio, and d is the number of days to maturity of the futures contract.

For example, let I = 6,000, r = 7% p.a., y = 2% p.a., and d = 91 days. Then:

FP = 6,000 × [{(7−2)/100} × {91/365}] = 75 index points
(So the fair futures price is 6,000 + 75 = 6,075.)

Short cash and carry involves selling (borrowed) stock and buying futures. In this case the excess of interest over dividends is a net inflow and this gain should be matched by having a guaranteed future purchase price that exceeds the spot sale price by the amount of this net inflow. The money from the stock sale is put on deposit. In the case of short selling, the borrower of the stock must pay sums equivalent to the dividends to the lender of the stock. The excess of interest over dividends is a net inflow that should be matched by a capital loss guaranteed by the futures price.

EXERCISE 29.1

If the rate of interest on risk-free bank deposits were 7.5% p.a., and if money could be borrowed at the same rate of interest, estimate the price of a FTSE 100 futures contract which matures in four months on the basis of a spot index of 4,000 and a zero expected rate of dividend yield on the FTSE 100 portfolio. How would the answer change if the expected rate of dividend yield were 4.5% p.a. (while the other values were as before)?

Answers

Using the formula:

$$FP = I \times \frac{(r - y)}{100} \times d/365$$

and treating four months as exactly one-third of a year gives (with zero expected dividend yield):

$$FP = 4,000 \times \frac{(7.5 - 0)}{100} \times \frac{1}{3}$$

$$FP = 4,000 \times 0.025 = 100$$

If the fair value premium is 100, the fair futures price is 4,000 + 100 = 4,100.
With an expected rate of dividend yield of 4.5% p.a. the calculation becomes:

$$FP = 4,000 \times \frac{(7.5 - 4.5)}{100} \times \frac{1}{3}$$

$$FP = 4,000 \times 0.01 = 40$$

If the fair value premium is 40, the fair futures price is 4,000 + 40 = 4,040

EXERCISE 29.2

A fund manager has £1,000,000 for a futures fund. The fund has an investment horizon of one year. The FTSE 100 stands at 5,000. The one-year interest rate is 5% and the expected rate of dividend yield on the FTSE 100 over the coming year is 3%. The fund manager puts £1,000,000 in a bank deposit and obtains market exposure by buying FTSE 100 futures.

(a) How many futures contracts, with a one-year maturity, are required for a fund that has a £1,000,000 exposure to the FTSE 100?

(b) What is the fair futures price?

(c) What is the rate of capital gain on the fund if the FTSE 100 rises by 20% over the year, and the futures price is initially at its fair level?

(d) What is the total return on the fund if the FTSE 100 rises by 20% over the year?

(e) How would the answers to (a),(c), and (d) change if the futures contracts were to provide a market exposure of £2,000,000 (while the sum of money on deposit remains at £1,000,000)?

(f) Is it the case that the whole of the £1,000,000 can be kept in a bank deposit?

Answers

(a) £1,000,000/(5,000 × £10) = 20 contracts.

(b) The fair futures price is 5,000 + 5,000(0.05−0.03) = 5,100.

(c) (6,000−5,100)/5,000 = 18%. (The futures price rises from 5,100 to 6,000.)

(d) 18% + 5% = 23%. (Capital gain on futures plus interest on deposit. Note that this is equal to the capital gain on the shares plus the dividends on the shares.)

(e) The number of contracts required would be 40. The futures profit would double to 1,800, so the rate of capital gain doubles to 36%. The total rate of return is then 36% + 5% = 41%.

EXERCISE 29.3

(a) If the FTSE 100 stands at 5,000, how can a futures fund with £5,000,000 be constructed so as to provide (i) £5,000,000 and (ii) £10,000,000 exposure to the market?

(b) The interest rate is 5% p.a., the expected dividend yield on the FTSE 100 is 3% p.a., and the futures mature in one year. What is (i) the capital gain, and (ii) the total return, on the two funds if the FTSE 100 rises by 30% over the year?

Answer

(a) (i) At £10 per index point each FTSE 100 futures contract relates to £50,000 of stock. The purchase of 100 contracts would provide exposure of £5,000,000 (most of the £5,000,000 is put on deposit but part may be used for paying initial margin).
(ii) £10,000,000 exposure would entail the purchase of 200 futures contracts.

(b) The net cost of carry is 5% − 3% = 2% p.a. The fair futures price is 5,000 × 1.02 = 5,100. If the FTSE 100 rises by 30%, it will increase to 6,500.

  (i) A 30% rise in the FTSE 100 would increase it to 6,500. The futures price converges on to (i.e. moves into equality with) the spot price by the futures maturity date. If the futures are fairly priced, the capital gain for the £5,000,000 exposure fund will be 6,500 − 5,100 = 1,400 index points (1,400 × £10 × 100 = £1,400,000). The capital gain for the £10,000,000 exposure would be 2,800 (£2,800,000).

  (ii) The total return includes the 5% interest on the £5,000,000 (£5,000,000 × 0.05 = £250,000) in addition to the capital gains.

The actual futures price may differ from the fair futures price. This is due to transaction costs such as commissions and bid-offer spreads. An arbitrager must make a gain that covers transaction costs before showing a net profit. The actual futures price can deviate from the fair futures price by as much as the transaction costs without arbitrage taking place. Arbitrage becomes profitable only when the actual futures price deviates from the fair futures price by an amount that exceeds the transaction costs.

In the absence of transaction costs, cash-and-carry arbitrage would tend to keep the actual futures price equal to the fair futures price because undervalued futures would be bought by arbitragers (pushing up the futures price) and overvalued futures would be sold (pushing the futures price down towards its fair value). In the presence of transaction costs, the cash-and-carry arbitrage merely keeps the futures price within a range of values known as the no-arbitrage band. The no-arbitrage band is between the fair futures price plus transaction costs and the fair futures price minus transaction costs. When the futures price is within the no-arbitrage band, there will be no further buying or selling by arbitragers to move the futures price towards the fair futures price (i.e. towards the middle of the no-arbitrage band). Within the no-arbitrage band, the gains from arbitrage are not sufficient to offset transaction costs. Figure 29.1 illustrates a no-arbitrage band.

If the futures price falls below the bottom of the no-arbitrage band, arbitragers would buy futures until the futures price reaches the bottom of the band, at which point arbitrage would stop. A futures price above the top of the no-arbitrage band would induce long cash-and-carry arbitrage, which involves selling futures. The sale of futures would move the futures price to the top of the no-arbitrage band, but no further. Once the futures price is within the band, arbitrage opportunities cease.

So the arbitrage pressure that tends to prevent deviations of actual futures prices from fair futures prices merely serves to keep the actual futures prices within a range (the no-arbitrage band) rather than ensuring equality with the fair futures price. Arbitrage occurs only when the actual futures price moves outside the no-arbitrage band (i.e. away from the fair futures price by more than the sum of the transaction costs). This is illustrated by the following exercises.

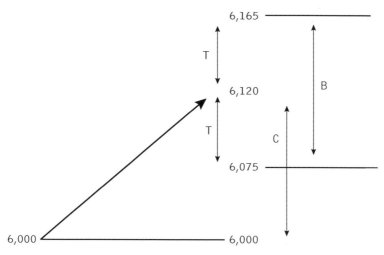

Figure 29.1 The no-arbitrage band

Spot index = 6,000
Net cost of carry (C) = 120
Fair futures price = 6,000+120 =6,120
Transaction costs (T) = 45
The no-arbitrage band (B) is 6,075 to 6,165 i.e. (6,120−45) to (6,120+45)
NB All values (spot and futures) relate to the same point in time.

EXERCISE 29.4

The FTSE 100 is 6,000. The three-month interest rate is 8% p.a. and the expected rate of dividend yield over the next three months is 4% p.a. What is the fair futures price for a futures contract maturing in three months' time?

How might an arbitrage profit be made if the actual futures price were (a) 6,100 and (b) 6,000 and there were no transaction costs. If the total transaction costs (commission, bid-offer spreads, stamp duty) amounted to £500 per £60,000 of stock would there still be arbitrage profits available?

Answers

The fair futures premium is:

$$6{,}000 \times \frac{(8-4)}{100} \times \frac{1}{4} = 60$$

So the fair futures price is: 6,000 + 60 = 6,060.

(a) If the actual futures price were 6,100, the futures would be overvalued. In the absence of transaction costs a profit is available from a long cash-and-carry arbitrage which entails buying stock and selling futures. There is a guaranteed profit from the stock and futures of 100 index points (amounting to 100 × £10 = £1,000 per £60,000 of stock and 1 futures contract). The corresponding net cost of carry is 60 index points (£600). So there is a net profit of 40 index points (£400).

(b) If the actual futures price were 6,000, the futures would be undervalued. So stock should be sold and futures bought (short cash-and-carry). There is neither profit nor loss from the stock and futures position. The net cost of carry accrues as profit and is 60 index points (60 × £10 = £600). The net cost of carry accrues as profit since interest is received at 8% p.a. (it is interest on the proceeds of selling borrowed stock) whilst dividends are paid to the lender of the stock at 4% p.a.

If the total of transaction costs were £500, there would be no net profit remaining in case (a) and only £600 − £500 = £100 in case (b). The futures price has to deviate by 50 index points from its fair value before any arbitrage profits become available.

In this case there is a no-arbitrage band of 50 index points either side of the fair futures price (6,010 − 6,110). Futures prices within this band do not induce arbitrage since they offer no net arbitrage profit.

In the absence of transaction costs, cash-and-carry arbitrage would tend to keep the actual futures price equal to the fair futures price because undervalued futures would be bought by arbitragers (pushing up the futures price) and overvalued futures would be sold (pushing the futures price down towards its fair value). In the presence of transaction costs, the cash-and-carry arbitrage merely keeps the futures price within the no-arbitrage band. When the futures price is within the no-arbitrage band, there will be no further buying or selling by arbitragers to move the futures price towards the fair futures price (that is towards the middle of the no-arbitrage band).

If the futures price falls below the bottom of the no-arbitrage band arbitragers would buy futures until the futures price reaches the bottom of the band, at which point arbitrage would stop. A futures price above the top of the no-arbitrage band would induce long cash-and-carry arbitrage, which involves selling futures. The sale of futures would move the futures price to the top of the no-arbitrage band, but no further. Once the futures price is within the band, arbitrage opportunities cease.

EXERCISE 29.5

The FTSE 100 is currently 5,000, the three-month interest rate is 7% p.a., and the expected dividend yield on the FTSE 100 portfolio is 3% p.a.

(a) What is the fair price of a FTSE 100 futures contract due to mature in three months?

(b) If each stock transaction incurs costs of 0.6% of the value of the stock, within what range of values should the actual futures price lie? (Ignore transaction costs on futures contracts.)

(c) If the actual futures price were 5,200, how could an arbitrager make a profit? What might be the effects of arbitragers pursuing such a profit?

Answers

(a) The futures premium over spot, FP, is given by :

  $FP = I \times [(r-y)/100] \times [d/365]$

  Treating $d/365$ as 0.25 (a quarter of the year) gives:

   $FP = 5,000 \times [(7-3)/100] \times 0.25 = 50$

  So the fair futures price is $5,000 + 50 = 5,050$

(b) Both long and short cash-and-carry arbitrages involve the purchase and sale of stock. So each arbitrage incurs transaction costs amounting to 1.2% of the value of the stock. Based on an index of 5,000 this amounts to 60 index points. So the no-arbitrage band would be 5,050 $+/-$ 60, i.e. 4,990 to 5,110.

(c) A futures price of 5,200 would be above the no-arbitrage band. Arbitragers could sell the overpriced futures and simultaneously buy stock (long cash-and-carry arbitrage). These transactions would tend to reduce the futures price and raise the spot index (and hence the fair futures price and the no-arbitrage band). The futures price would fall, and the no-arbitrage band would rise, until the futures price equalled the top of the no-arbitrage band. At that point arbitrage would cease, since it would no longer be profitable.

Since cash-and-carry arbitrage merely determines a band of possible futures prices around the fair futures price, there may be opportunities for enhancing profits by buying futures when the futures price is towards the bottom of the range of possible values (i.e. below the fair futures price). A rise in the actual futures price relative to the fair futures price would add to the profits arising from movements in the fair futures price. Buying when the actual futures price is below the fair futures price enhances the probability of a rise in the actual futures price relative to the no-arbitrage band of possible values. This is known as basis trading, and can be used to enhance the profits of hedgers and investors.

 If the futures contracts are held to maturity, such an addition to profit is assured since the actual futures price and the fair futures price converge as maturity is approached (on the futures maturity date the spot stock index, the fair futures price, and the actual futures price are equal).

 No-arbitrage bands provide both problems and opportunities for the managers of futures funds. The problems arise because movements of the actual futures price within the no-arbitrage band can produce tracking error. If the futures fund is used as a form of index tracker fund, such tracking error reduces the accuracy with which the futures fund tracks the index. This can be seen as basis risk. However there is an opportunity for basis trading. By buying futures when the actual futures price is below the fair futures price, the fund manager can add to returns. This adds an element of active fund management to a futures fund, which is used as a form of index tracker fund.

THE ROLE OF HEDGERS AND SPECULATORS

Arbitrage determines that the futures price will fall within a range of values, the no-arbitrage band. However it does not determine where, within that range, the futures price will lie.

This provides a role for hedgers and speculators to influence futures prices. Net buying by hedgers and speculators would move the futures price towards the top of the no-arbitrage band, while selling would induce a price movement towards the bottom of the band. Since net purchases would result from bullish views and net sales from bearish views, it follows that market expectations will play a part in determining the position of the futures price within the band.

Not only might such expectations affect the position of the futures price within the no-arbitrage band, but also they have the potential for moving stock prices, and hence the position of the band. To understand the processes involved, consider the situation in which hedgers and/or speculators buy futures to the extent that the futures price rises above the top of the no-arbitrage band. When the futures price rises above the top of the band, the opportunity for long cash-and-carry arbitrage arises. Arbitragers buy stock and sell the (overpriced) futures. This tends to put upward pressure on stock prices (and hence on the fair futures price and on the no-arbitrage band) as well as downward pressure on futures prices.

Conversely if futures prices were to fall below the bottom of the no-arbitrage band, the potential for profits from short cash-and-carry arbitrage would emerge. In that case futures would be underpriced, and so arbitragers would buy the cheap futures and simultaneously sell shares. Share prices would be pushed down and futures prices would be pushed up. However the process of short cash-and-carry arbitrage could be more difficult than long cash-and-carry arbitrage because short selling might be difficult. For arbitragers to sell shares they need to acquire the shares to sell. The shares would be borrowed, typically from institutional investors, and then sold. Such short selling could be restricted, expensive, and subject to uncertainties. Not everyone can borrow stock, fees must be paid to the lenders, and the lenders can demand return of the shares at any time (and in particular before the arbitrage profit has been obtained).

The findings of research carried out by Fung (2007) are consistent with the type of process just described. Fung identified net buying pressure in the stock market by a predominance of trades at offer (ask) prices, which are the buying prices of shares. A predominance of trades at bid prices, the prices at which shares are sold, indicated net selling pressure. Futures prices above no-arbitrage bands were associated with net buying pressure in the stock market, as would be expected from long cash-and-carry arbitrage. When the futures prices were below the bottom of the no-arbitrage band there was net selling pressure in the stock market, as would be expected from short cash-and-carry arbitrage. The response times to short cash-and-carry opportunities were longer than for long cash-and-carry opportunities, as would be expected from the difficulty of short selling.

EXERCISE 29.6

The FTSE 100 is 6,000, the three-month interest rate is 6% p.a., and the expected rate of dividend yield on the FTSE 100 over the next three months is 3% p.a.

(a) What is the fair price of a futures contract due to mature in three months?

(b) If financial institutions face transaction costs of 0.3% on both purchases and sales of stock, plus 0.5% tax on purchases, what is the no-arbitrage band of futures prices?

(c) If speculators adopt the view that that the FTSE 100 will be 6,200 in three months from the present, what would you expect to happen in the futures and spot markets?

Answers

(a) The fair futures premium is:

$$6{,}000 \times \frac{(6-3)}{100} \times \frac{1}{4} = 45$$

The fair futures price is:

$$6{,}000 + 45 = 6{,}045$$

(b) The no-arbitrage band will be 1.1% each side of the fair futures price. The 1.1% is based on buying costs of 0.3% plus 0.5% tax, and selling costs of 0.3%. These costs are incurred in the case of both long and short cash-and-carry arbitrage.

Based on the initial index of 6,000, the 1.1% is equivalent to 66 index points. So the no-arbitrage band should be:

$$6{,}045 + 66 = 6{,}111$$

to $6{,}045 - 66 = 5{,}979$

(c) If speculators believe that the FTSE 100 will be 6,200, they would buy futures at any price below 6,200 with a view to selling when the price rises to 6,200 (on the futures maturity date spot and futures prices are equal). These purchases would tend to pull the futures price out of the no-arbitrage band. As the futures price rises above the no-arbitrage band, arbitrage opportunities emerge. Arbitragers would sell the relatively overpriced futures and buy the relatively underpriced stock. This would put downward pressure on the futures price and upward pressure on the FTSE 100 (and hence the no-arbitrage band). If both speculators and arbitragers have adequate funds, the no-arbitrage band should rise until the value of 6,200 falls within the band. Speculation will cease when the FTSE 100 futures price reaches 6,200 and arbitrage will stop when the no-arbitrage band encompasses the value of 6,200.

THE ROLE OF RISK AND NOISE TRADERS

The arbitrage process is not entirely risk-free. Stock prices might move against the arbitrager during the time taken to assemble the portfolio. Indeed an arbitrager's own trading in pursuit of arbitrage profits could move prices such as to remove profit opportunities. Furthermore, future dividends cannot be known with certainty. In consequence, some risk remains and arbitragers may require compensation for such risk. Any compensation for risk tends to widen the no-arbitrage band but by amounts that differ between arbitragers and vary over time. So the boundaries of a no-arbitrage band should be seen not as definite values, but as imprecise borders.

These risk factors that arbitragers face are compounded by other uncertainties relating to arbitrage. One of these other uncertainties concerns non-synchronous trading. The prices quoted at a point in time are those of the last trade. For some stocks the most recent trade might have been one minute ago, for others an hour or more ago, whilst other shares might not have traded for a day or more. The result is that listed prices relate to different points in time and are therefore not comparable. The relevant prices are those that would pertain to the present moment, but not all prices do so. Since prices move over time, listed prices may be misleading. If an up-to-date price were available, it might differ from the published price. In consequence apparent arbitrage opportunities may not be real ones.

Arbitrage that involves short selling shares faces additional uncertainties. Not only might it be difficult to find a shareholder willing to lend stock, but also that shareholder could demand the return of the shares at an unfavourable point in time. The arbitrager could be forced to liquidate the arbitrage transactions before profits have been made, or whilst prices have moved so as to render the trade loss making.

Another set of risks might be described as noise trader risks. Noise traders are irrational traders (see Chapter 24 on noise trading and behavioural finance). Such traders can move markets in unpredictable directions. In particular they can increase mispricing for periods of time. Futures contracts have maturity dates on which spot (i.e. actual) and futures stock indices will be equal, with the consequence that the effects of noise traders would not be permanent. However futures contracts with distant maturities can experience prolonged price discrepancies. Not only does this delay the receipt of the arbitrage profits, but it can also create cash flow problems. When futures prices move against a trader, that trader must pay variation margin. If futures prices move against an arbitrager (before moving favourably), the arbitrager would need to finance variation margin payments. There is a risk that an arbitrager may be forced to terminate an arbitrage trade when it is loss making because of an inability to fund further calls for variation margin payments.

Holmes and Tomsett (2004) and McMillan and Speight (2006) conducted research on the significance of noise traders for FTSE 100 futures, with conflicting results. Holmes and Tomsett found that trading was predominantly informed trading rather than noise trading. This suggests that arbitragers are not faced with high degrees of price overreaction arising from psychological biases of noise traders.

McMillan and Speight (2006) concluded that mispricing arising from noise trading can persist and that the discrepancy between observed and fair prices can widen. They referred to the findings from behavioural finance to the effect that noise traders engage in momentum (positive feedback) trading reinforced by overconfidence and resulting in overreaction to news. Arbitragers face uncertainty as to whether pricing discrepancies will widen before they narrow. Do they take a small profit or wait for an uncertain larger one? Do they take the risk that further movement of futures prices away from fair prices will drain their resources available for financing variation margin payments?

EXERCISE 29.7

(a) If the FTSE 100 Index stands at 4,000 points, how can a futures fund with £10,000,000 be structured so as to provide (i) £10,000,000 and (ii) £20,000,000 exposure to the stock market?

(b) The interest rate is 4% p.a., the expected dividend yield on the FTSE 100 is 3% p.a., and the futures mature in one year. What is (i) the capital gain, and (ii) the total return, on the two funds if the FTSE 100 rises by 20% over the year and futures are fairly priced?

(c) How could a fund be structured to take advantage of an expected fall in the stock market? What would happen to the value of such a fund in the event of a 20% rise in the FTSE 100 over a year (with a 4% p.a. interest rate and a 3% p.a. expected dividend yield)?

(d) Why might a futures fund fail to perfectly track a stock index?

Answers

(a) (i) At £10 per index point each futures contract relates to £40,000 of stock. The purchase of 250 (£10,000,000/£40,000 = 250) contracts would provide exposure of £10,000,000 (most of the £10,000,000 is put on deposit in a bank but part may be used for paying initial margin, which also earns interest).

  (ii) £20,000,000 exposure would entail the purchase of 500 (£20,000,000/£40,000 = 500) futures contracts.

(b) The net cost of carry is 4% − 3% = 1% p.a. The fair futures price is 4,000 × 1.01 = 4,040 (the fair futures premium is 0.01 × 4,000 = 40). If the FTSE 100 rises by 20%, it would increase to 4,800 by the end of the year. Due to convergence the futures price will also be 4,800 when the futures mature at the end of the year.

  (i) If the futures are fairly priced, the capital gain for the £10,000,000 exposure fund would be 4,800 − 4,040 = 760 index points (760 × £10 × 250 = £1,900,000). The capital gain for the £20,000,000 exposure fund would be 760 × £10 × 500 = £3,800,000.

  (ii) The total return includes the 4% interest on the £10,000,000 (£10,000,000 × 0.04 = £400,000) in addition to the capital gains.

  In percentage terms, the rate of return on the £10,000,000 exposure fund is (£1,900,000 + £400,000)/£10,000,000 = 23%. The rate of return on the £20,000,000 exposure fund is (£3,800,000 + £400,000)/£10,000,000 = 42%. This demonstrates the benefits of gearing in a rising market.

(c) Instead of buying futures contracts, they are sold. For example 250 contracts might be sold. The change in the futures price would produce a loss. In this case there would be a loss of 760 index points, which amounts to £1,900,000. Taking account of the £400,000 interest reduces the loss to £1,500,000, i.e. 15% of the investment.

(d) A futures fund would fail to precisely track an index if basis changes (basis is the difference between the values of the spot and futures indices). The extent of potential basis change will depend upon the width of the no-arbitrage band, which in turn depends upon factors such as transaction costs and risks faced by arbitragers. Basis may also change as a result of liquidity problems, or as a result of arbitrage failing to keep futures prices within the no-arbitrage band. Changes in interest rates or expected dividend yield could change basis by changing the fair futures price. Small funds might find that the indivisibility of futures contracts prevents full replication of the index, and hence causes tracking to be imperfect. The index that the fund aims to track could be one on which no futures contracts are based, for example the FTSE All-Share Index. Replication of such an index with futures on another index, such as the FTSE 100, would be subject to the imperfections associated with cross-hedging. The two indices do not move precisely in line with each other.

EXERCISE 29.8

An actively managed OEIC keeps, on average, 5% of its fund in bank deposits in order to meet potential redemptions. If the real rate of return on the stock market as a whole is 7% p.a. whilst the real interest rate on bank deposits is 2% p.a., what is the effect of this liquidity provision on the rate of return of the fund?

If the liquidity provision were matched by stock index futures, what would be the effect on the rate of return of the fund (assuming that the total rate of return on the fund portfolio matches the total rate of return on the portfolio on which the stock index is based)?

Answers

The expected real rate of return on the fund is reduced from 7% p.a. to:

$$(0.95 \times 7\%) + (0.05 \times 2\%) = 6.75\% \text{ p.a.}$$

The provision of liquidity has reduced average real return from 7% p.a. to 6.75% p.a.

If futures are fairly priced, the return on futures plus bank deposits equals the total return on the share portfolio (capital gains plus dividends). The futures plus deposit is equivalent to an index tracker fund. Matching the bank deposit with futures should restore the expected real return on the fund to 7% p.a. (See Exercise 29.2 part (d) for an illustration of the equality, of total return, between a futures fund and an index tracker portfolio.)

FUTURES PRICES AND EXPECTED FUTURE SPOT PRICES

The activity of speculators might be expected to keep the futures index close to the expected future index. If the futures index is low relative to the expected spot value, speculators would buy in order to profit from a price rise as the futures index converges on to the expected index. If the futures index is above the expected index, speculators would sell futures in order to profit when the futures index falls towards the expected index. The purchases and sales of speculators would tend to push the futures price towards the expected future spot price. The normal situation would appear to be equality between the futures price and the expected future spot price.

However, according to the capital asset pricing model, the holder of a futures contract bears risk for which there should be compensation in the form of expected return. This expected return requires that the futures index should be below the expected future spot index. In such a situation the futures index should rise towards the expected index steadily over time in order to provide the expected return. So the convergence of the futures index onto the expected index would be gradual rather than rapid. The normal situation would be inequality between the futures price and the expected future spot price.

CONCLUSION

Stock index futures have a significant role in the management of investment portfolios, including those of institutional investors. Investment managers who use futures need to know about influences on futures prices. Some knowledge of whether futures are overpriced or underpriced could influence the timing of trades. An investor who needs to buy futures may look for a moment when the futures price is below the fair price. Likewise a prospective seller may attempt to time the sale to coincide with the futures price being above fair value. To achieve favourable timing it is necessary to understand what determines the fair price, and what determines deviations from the fair price. Whether stock index futures are used for managing portfolios of shares, or whether they are used as a class of investment in their own right (e.g. in futures funds), obtaining favourable deviations from fair price can add to investment returns. For example if a futures fund is used as a form of index tracker fund, trading futures when their prices show favourable deviations could enhance the return on the fund (this would add a dimension of active management to the index tracking strategy).

Although arbitrage may constrain the extent of deviations from fair value, it cannot prevent such deviations. The behaviour of hedgers and speculators will influence the direction and extent of deviation. In so far as hedgers and speculators are influenced by sentiment and other behavioural biases, an understanding of the principles of behavioural finance should be useful when using stock index futures.

Chapter 30

Hedging with stock index futures

OBJECTIVE

The objective of this chapter is to provide knowledge of:

1. Hedging with stock index futures.
2. Hedge ratios.
3. Sources of hedge imperfection.
4. Adjustment for futures premiums.

Stock index futures are contracts for notional purchases or sales of portfolios of shares on future dates at predetermined prices. The word 'notional' is significant because stock index futures provide no facility for delivery and receipt of stock via exercise of the contract. Stock prices to be paid or received in the future are guaranteed to be close to predetermined prices because stock price movements are (approximately) matched by compensatory cash flows from the futures.

Futures contracts are available on many stock indices. Stock indices on which futures are traded include the S&P 100, S&P 500, Nikkei 225, FTSE 100, DAX, CAC 40, and the Hang Seng. There are contracts relating to all the major stock markets. Contract sizes are based on sums of money per index point. So if an S&P 500 contract is based on $500 per index point and the index (in the futures market) stands at 1,200, then each futures contract relates to 1,200 × $500 = $600,000 of stock. Similarly, at £10 per index point, a FTSE 100 futures price of 6,000 indicates that each futures contract relates to 6,000 × £10 = £60,000 worth of shares.

THE NATURE OF HEDGING

Hedging is the reduction of an existing risk. When using stock index futures to reduce stock market risk, the anticipation is that any losses arising from movements in stock prices are offset by gains from parallel movements in futures prices. An investor might be anxious about the possibility that the prices of his or her stocks might fall. He or she could reduce the risk of a reduction in the value of the portfolio by taking a position in the futures market that would provide a gain in the event of a fall in stock prices. In such a case the investor would take a short position in stock index futures contracts. By taking a short position, he or she guarantees a notional selling price of a quantity of stock for a specific date in the future. Should stock prices fall and stock index futures behave in a corresponding fashion, the notional buying price for that date would be less than the predetermined notional selling price. The investor could close out his or her position in futures by taking a long position in the same number of contracts (i.e. by buying futures). The excess of the selling price over the buying price is paid to the investor in cash in the form of variation margin. This gain on the futures contracts is received on a daily basis as the futures price moves (the daily settlement is known as marking to market). Had the prices of stocks risen, the investor would have gained from his or her portfolio of equities, but lost on futures dealings. In either case, the investor has succeeded in reducing the extent to which the value of the portfolio fluctuates.

The use of futures to hedge the risk of a fall in stock prices does not require any alteration of the original portfolio. It is thus preferable to any form of hedging that involves changing the composition of the portfolio, such as liquidating part of the portfolio. The transaction costs of hedging with futures are also much lower than those of selling, and subsequently buying back, shares. There may be poor liquidity in many shares, particularly those of small companies. It could be difficult to sell illiquid shares, and the price may need to be reduced in order to entice buyers. If only the liquid, large company, shares are sold the portfolio becomes unbalanced.

EXAMPLE 30.1

A portfolio holder fears a generalised fall in equity prices and wishes to avoid a fall in the value of his or her portfolio.

5 April
The investor holds a balanced portfolio of shares valued at £1,000,000, but fears a fall in its value. The current FTSE 100 Index is 5,000.

The investor hedges by selling 20 June FTSE 100 futures contracts at a price of 5,000 each. The investor is thus committed to the notional sale of £1,000,000 of stock on the June futures expiry date at the level of equity prices implied by the futures price on 5 April. (£1,000,000 = 20 × 5,000 × £10, where each of the 20 futures contracts relates to stock worth £10 per index point, i.e. 5,000 × £10.)

10 May
The FTSE 100 Index has fallen to 4,500. Correspondingly, the value of the portfolio has declined to £900,000.

The investor closes out the futures position by buying 20 June FTSE 100 futures contracts at a price of 4,500. The notional buying price of each contract is thus 500 index points below the notional selling price.

Loss on the portfolio

$\quad$ = £100,000

Gain from futures trading

$\quad$ = £100,000 (20 × 500 × £10)

This is a perfect hedge since the futures profit precisely offsets the loss on the portfolio.

This strategy is one that reduces variations in the value of the portfolio holder's assets. If the FTSE 100 Index had risen, there would have been a cash market gain offset by a futures market loss.

EXAMPLE 30.2

Example 30.2 shows how a long position in futures can be used as a hedge. In this case, a fund manager anticipates receipt of £1 million on 10 January and intends to use it to buy a balanced portfolio of UK equities. The fund manager fears, one month earlier, that stock prices will rise before the money is received (with the consequence that fewer shares can be bought with the £1 million).

10 December
An investor anticipates the receipt of £1 million on 10 January. The current FTSE 100 Index is 5,500. The investor fears a rise in the index.

The investor buys 18 March FTSE futures contracts at a price of 5,500. The investor is thereby notionally committed to paying £990,000 (18 × 5,500 × £10) for stock on the futures maturity date.

10 January
The new FTSE 100 Index is 5,750.

The investor closes out by selling 18 March FTSE 100 futures contracts at a price of 5,700. The investor notionally guarantees a receipt of £1,026,000 (18 × 5,700 × £10) upon maturity of the futures contracts.

The investor requires an additional £45,455 in order to buy the quantity of stock that £1 million would have bought on 10 December (£1,000,000 × [5,750/5,500] = £1,045,455).

There is a profit from the futures of £36,000 [18 × (5,700 − 5,500) × 10].

SOURCES OF HEDGE IMPERFECTION

In Example 30.2 futures prices did not move precisely in line with the FTSE 100 Index and, as a result, the hedge was imperfect. Basis is the difference between the spot and futures indices. A change in basis will render a hedge imperfect. In Example 30.2, basis changes from 0 to 50 index points. The possibility of a change in basis is known as basis risk.

One risk faced by hedgers is the possibility that futures are mispriced at the time they are traded. Mispricing could arise as a result of the fair price being based on inaccurate estimates of future dividends. Another source of mispricing is the deviation of the actual futures price from the fair futures price within the no-arbitrage band. If a hedger buys when futures are overpriced, or sells when they are underpriced, there is a strong risk that an adverse change in basis reduces the effectiveness of the hedge. Futures with distant maturities often exhibit poor liquidity. Trading in illiquid markets may require large price concessions in order to attract trading counterparties. Buyers have to offer high prices and sellers must accept low prices. Large price concessions move futures prices, and hence basis, against the hedger.

Even if basis did not change, and the futures index rose to 5,750 in line with the spot index, the hedge would still be incomplete. The futures profit would be £45,000 whereas £45,455 is required. This hedge imperfection arises from the indivisibility of contracts. Indivisibility of contracts means that it is not possible to trade fractions of contracts, only whole contracts can be bought and sold. In consequence it is not possible to hedge the £1,000,000 precisely. The nearest whole number of contracts covers just £990,000. So £10,000 is left unhedged, and the hedge is thus incomplete.

Another source of hedge imperfection might be differences in the percentage price changes between the hedged portfolio and the FTSE 100 Index arising from the portfolio having a beta different from that of the index. This latter source of hedge imperfection can be dealt with by the use of hedge ratios.

HEDGE RATIOS

Hedge ratios become necessary when the price behaviour of the futures contract is likely to differ from that of the portfolio to be hedged. If the portfolio to be hedged shows relatively large variations, then it is appropriate to use more futures contracts than in the case of a more stable portfolio. It is unlikely that a portfolio of stocks, for which hedging is required, precisely corresponds to the composition of a stock index. It is thus probable that it will show more or less volatility than the index.

The beta factor of a stock is a measure of the extent to which it moves in line with stock prices in general. A balanced portfolio is likely to have a beta of about 1. A stock with only half the movement of the market as a whole would have a beta of 0.5, while one with double the degree of change has a beta of 2. The beta of a portfolio of stocks is the weighted average of the betas of the stocks that constitute the portfolio.

If a calculation indicates a beta of 1.2, the portfolio tends to change by 20% more than the stock index. Hedging the portfolio would require the value of the stock index futures contracts to exceed the portfolio value by 20%. The relatively large losses (or profits) arising from the high

Table 30.1   *Hypothetical stock betas and the corresponding market exposures*

Stock	Value of shares ($)	Stock beta	Market exposure($)
Aetna Life	531,250	1.1	584,375
American Express	600,000	1.2	720,000
Bethlehem Steel	432,500	1.0	432,500
Boeing	451,250	0.8	361,000
			2,097,875

volatility require correspondingly large offsetting profits (or losses) from futures contracts, and this necessitates a relatively large number of futures contracts.

The calculation of the appropriate number of futures contracts to trade will involve ascertaining the market exposure of the stock portfolio. The market exposure of the stock portfolio is not the same as its market value. Market value needs to be adjusted by the stock betas. Table 30.1 shows hypothetical stock betas and the corresponding market exposures, which are calculated by multiplying the market values of the stocks by the betas.

Having ascertained that the market exposure of the portfolio is $2,097,875, it is necessary to find the market exposure of a stock index futures contract. If the S&P 500 futures are to be used, if the contract size is $500 per index point, and if the S&P 500 index stands at 1,350, then each futures contract would relate to $1,350 \times \$500 = \$675,000$ of stock. The requisite number of futures contracts would be $\$2,097,875/\$675,000 = 3.1$ contracts (the beta of a stock index futures contract is being assumed to equal 1). This rounds down to three contracts. Although this technique of selling stock index futures in order to neutralise the general market exposure of a specific stock portfolio is not perfect (due to the imperfect reliability of betas and the inability to trade fractions of futures contracts), it can remove most of the market exposure of a portfolio and thereby allow an investor to take positions on the performance of individual stocks or sectors relative to the market as a whole.

The successful use of hedge ratios depends upon the estimates of beta being reasonably reliable. Estimates of beta, based on historical evidence, are subject to error and are therefore not perfectly reliable. This is due to the fact that the methods of statistical analysis do not provide a precise estimate of beta, instead a distribution (range) of possible values is provided.

Furthermore history is not always a reliable indicator of the future. If the characteristics of a company change, the beta of its shares may also change. Future betas, rather than past betas, are required for hedge ratios.

It should also be borne in mind that stock index futures hedge only systematic (market) risk. This is the risk to individual stocks from movements in the stock market as a whole. Stock index futures do not reduce non-systematic (stock-specific) risk. Unexpected changes in a company cause share price movements that are not hedged by stock index futures. (Portfolio diversification is required for the reduction of non-systematic risk.)

Investment managers may exploit this characteristic. If an investment manager wants to trade on the relative movements of equities (stock selection) rather than movements in the market as a whole, hedging with stock index futures can remove the general market exposure. Conversely an investor who wishes to trade on general market movements rather than individual stocks can do so by trading in futures rather than in shares.

EXERCISE 30.1

A fund manager anticipates the receipt of £3 million in two months. The intention is to invest the money equally between the three stocks X, Y, and Z. These stocks have betas of 0.9, 1.1, and 1.4 respectively. The FTSE 100 stands at 6,800. How can the fund manager hedge against a rise in stock prices using futures?

Answer

The market exposure of the proposed portfolio shown in the table is the sum of:

Table 30.A

X £1,000,000 × 0.9 = £900,000

Y £1,000,000 × 1.1 = £1,100,000

Z £1,000,000 × 1.4 = £1,400,000

Market exposure = £900,000 + £1,100,000 + £1,400,000 = £3,400,000

At £10 per index point, the market exposure of a futures contract is approximately 6,800 × £10 = £68,000. Hedging a prospective portfolio with a market exposure of £3,400,000 requires the purchase of:

£3,400,000 / £68,000 = 50 futures contracts.

EXERCISE 30.2

An investor holds the portfolio shown in the table.

Table 30.B

	Number of shares	Share price	Share beta
Bank of Coventry	20,000	300p	0.9
Coventry Motors	30,000	100p	1.5
Nuneaton Manufacturing	10,000	600p	1.3
Kenilworth Stores	25,000	300p	0.8

599

It is 15 November and the FTSE 100 Index is 4,700. How can the investor hedge the portfolio with futures? What factors could reduce the effectiveness of the hedge?

Answers

Calculate the market exposure of the portfolio by adding up the market exposures of the individual stocks (market exposure = number of shares × share price × beta).

Table 30.C

20,000	×	300p	×	0.9 =	5.4m
30,000	×	100p	×	1.5 =	4.5m
10,000	×	600p	×	1.3 =	7.8m
25,000	×	300p	×	0.8 =	6.0m
					23.7m

The total market exposure is 23,700,000p, i.e. £237,000. The market exposure provided by one futures contract is:

4,700 × £10 = £47,000 (assuming that the futures have a beta of 1)

Hedging the portfolio with futures would involve selling:

£237,000/£47,000 = 5.04 contracts.

Since it is not possible to trade fractions of contracts the investor would sell five futures contracts.

Factors that could reduce hedge effectiveness include changes in basis, the indivisibility of contracts (the inability to trade fractions of futures contracts), statistical error in the estimation of beta, instability of beta (beta can change over time), and non-systematic risk.

Hedges that have the objective of minimising risk are known as minimum variance hedges. Hedges can have other objectives, but minimising risk is probably the most usual. The optimum minimum variance hedge ratio is the ratio of the value of futures contracts to the value of the portfolio being hedged, which minimises risk. There have been a number of studies of optimum hedge ratios and hedging effectiveness including one by Chen et al. (2004). They examined futures on a number of underlying instruments, including stock indices and currencies, and hedges for periods ranging from one day to eight weeks. They found that for short-term hedges the optimum hedge ratios were less than one, and that optimum ratios rose towards one as the length of the hedging period increased. The hedge ratio of one was referred to as the naive hedge ratio. Also the effectiveness of hedging was found to be greater for the longer hedging periods, but effectiveness never reached 100%.

The tendency for the hedge ratio to approach one as the hedging period increases suggests that investment managers should not try to estimate hedge ratios (such as the beta-based ratios described above) but simply match the value of the futures to the value of the portfolio being hedged. The apparent rejection of beta as a useful hedge ratio is perhaps not too surprising in the light of the criticisms of beta (see Part 4 on capital market theory).

WHAT INDEX LEVEL IS 'GUARANTEED' BY FUTURES?

On the day that futures contracts reach maturity, the futures stock index will equal the spot (actual) stock index. The futures and spot indices will tend to converge as the futures maturity date approaches. The difference between the two indices is based on the expected difference between financing costs and dividend yields, and the cash flow significance of this difference falls as the time to maturity shortens.

A hedger can expect to guarantee the spot index only if intending to close out immediately after taking out futures contracts. If the intention is to hold futures contracts until their maturity date, the index guaranteed is the futures index (the futures index at the time of acquiring the futures contracts). Otherwise the locked-in index will fall between the initial spot and initial futures indices. This is illustrated by Figure 30.1, which makes the simplifying assumption of a constant spot index (this simplifying assumption does not negate the generality of the conclusion).

Consider a hedger attempting to guarantee the value of a portfolio that is being held. The objective is to make a futures profit (or loss) that matches the loss (or profit) on the portfolio. The hedger will sell futures to achieve this aim. In Figure 30.1, the futures index starts at a premium to the spot index and declines over time towards the spot index. (It converges onto the spot index.) If the futures were closed out at maturity, there would be a futures profit equal to the initial

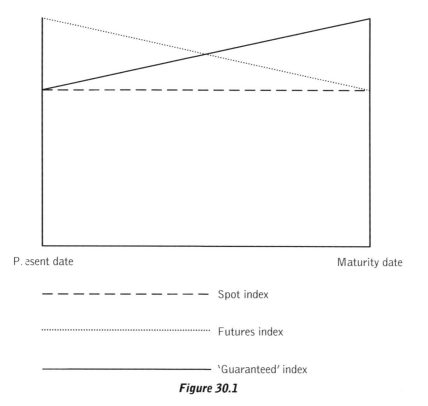

Present date   Maturity date

— — — — — — — — — — — — Spot index

··· Futures index

———————————————— 'Guaranteed' index

Figure 30.1

difference between the spot and futures indices. This means that the total portfolio value, inclusive of the futures profit, would correspond to the initial futures index. On the futures maturity date the original portfolio will be at its original value because the index has not changed (assuming that the portfolio maintains its relationship with the index), but will be enhanced by the futures profit.

If the futures were closed out immediately after being sold the futures index would not have had time to change. There would be no profit from the futures contracts and the value of the portfolio would correspond to the initial spot index. If the futures were closed out halfway to maturity, the portfolio value should fall midway between the values implied by the initial spot and initial futures indices. The 'guaranteed' portfolio value is a function of the period to closing out the futures contracts.

This conclusion is not invalidated if the spot index fails to remain constant. Movements of the spot index would tend to be accompanied by equivalent movements in the futures index so that futures profits/losses tend to offset losses/profits on the portfolio being hedged. In consequence, whatever happens to the spot index, early closing out guarantees the initial spot index and closing out on the futures maturity date guarantees the initial futures index. The futures provide a hedge against movements in the spot index.

Previously basis risk was defined as the possibility of a change in the relationship between the value of the portfolio being hedged and the futures index. Part of the basis is the difference between the futures index and the spot index. Convergence implies that some change in basis can be expected because the difference between the futures and spot indices will move from its initial value towards zero. Consequently basis risk could be alternatively defined as an unexpected change in basis.

There is no certainty that the 'guaranteed' portfolio value will be achieved. This is largely because of basis risk in the sense of the possibility of unexpected changes in basis. Part of basis is the difference between the spot and futures indices. Prior to maturity, this component of basis will rarely equal zero. However, at the maturity of the futures contract the futures index will equal the spot index. So at maturity this component of basis will equal zero. Prior to the futures maturity the relationship between the spot and futures indices may not change precisely as expected (e.g. due to changes in interest rates or changes in expectations of dividends). Unexpected changes in basis render hedges imperfect. In terms of Figure 30.1, the futures index may deviate from the dotted line with the effects that the futures profit differs from the expected level and the 'guaranteed' index shown by the unbroken line is not achieved.

Unexpected changes in basis can have a number of causes, particularly if basis is defined in terms of a relationship between the futures index and the value of the portfolio being hedged. Changes in interest rates or expected dividends will cause unexpected alterations in the relationship between the fair futures index and the spot index. Any change in the relationship between the actual futures and fair futures index (such as might arise from a change in market sentiment about the stocks covered by the index) would further disturb basis in an unpredictable way. In addition, the relationship between the hedged portfolio and the spot index may unexpectedly change. This is particularly likely if the portfolio is not completely diversified and hence demonstrates non-systematic risk. Even if well diversified a portfolio could experience an unpredictable change in its beta, with the result that the existing hedge ratio becomes inappropriate and hedge imperfection ensues.

The effect of the relationship between the futures and spot indices should be considered when calculating hedge ratios. Typically futures trade at a premium to the spot index. This means that futures price movements tend to exceed spot price movements since they are magnified by the premium. To offset this effect it may be appropriate to divide the market exposure by the futures index (or an average of spot and futures indices) rather than by the spot index. Specifically if the intention is to close out quickly the futures index should be used. The magnification effect of the futures premium is offset by a corresponding reduction in the number of futures contracts used. Division by the futures index entails division by the futures premium with the effect that the magnification factor is offset by a reduction in the number of futures contracts. If the intention is to close out at the futures maturity, the spot index might be used; convergence eliminates the futures premium by the futures maturity date. More generally, an average of spot and futures indices should be used depending upon the expected date of closing out (Redhead 1994, 1995, 1997).

CONCLUSION

There are times when investment managers want to reduce their stock market risk. Derivatives, such as stock index futures, can be used for risk reduction. The reduction of risk by taking an offsetting position in derivatives is known as hedging. The objective is to make a gain from the derivatives that compensates for a loss on the existing investment.

Perfectly predictable outcomes are not to be expected. There are a number of ways in which hedging with stock index futures may fail to be perfect. Some sources of hedge imperfection can be anticipated, and adjustments made. In particular hedge ratios could be employed to compensate for differences in volatility between the futures and the stock portfolio being hedged.

One approach to a hedge ratio is to use betas, specifically the beta of the futures relative to the beta of the portfolio. The beta of the stock index futures is sometimes assumed to be one, but this assumption may be questioned. Betas are based on the capital asset pricing model, which has been the subject of much criticism (see Part 4 on capital market theory). The effectiveness of beta as a source of hedge ratios is ultimately an empirical issue. An investment manager in search of a hedge ratio should compare the usefulness of beta-based hedge ratios with other approaches to the formulation of hedge ratios.

Part 9

Stock Options

Chapter 31

Stock options

OBJECTIVE

The objective of this chapter is to provide knowledge of:

1. The profit and loss potential of call and put options.
2. The factors that affect option prices.
3. The risks and potential pay-offs from selling (writing) options.
4. Boundary conditions.

A stock option is the right to buy or sell a specified number of shares at a pre-arranged price on, or before, a particular date. A right to buy is referred to as a call option, and the right to sell a put option. There are two other important distinctions. First, between European-style and American-style options. European-style options can be exercised (the right to buy or sell can be used) only on the maturity date of the option, which is known as the expiry date. An American-style option can be exercised at any time up to, and including, the expiry date. It is to be noted that the distinction has nothing to do with geography. Both types of option are traded throughout the world.

The second distinction is between over-the-counter (OTC) options and exchange-traded options. OTC options are the result of private negotiations between two parties (typically, a bank and a client). They may relate to any amount of any stock at any agreed price and have any expiry date. In other words, they can be tailor-made to the specific requirements of the client buying the option. Exchange-traded options are bought and sold on an organised exchange. They are standardised as to the amount and price of the stock, and the available expiry dates. Contracts would provide a limited range of strike prices and expiry dates. (Strike prices are the prices at which stocks can be bought or sold, and expiry dates are the dates on which the options cease to exist.) There is also a limitation as to which stocks are available. Most exchange-traded options are American-style.

CALL OPTIONS

A call option gives the buyer of that option the right, but not the obligation, to buy shares at a particular price. That price is known as the exercise or strike price. At the time of buying the

Table 31.1

Strike price	Calls			Puts		
	April	July	October	April	July	October
550p	27p	49p	64p	7p	27.5p	36p
600p	5p	26.5p	41p	35p	55p	63p

The BP share price is 568p.

option, there will be at least two strike prices available to choose from. For example, when the price of BP shares was 568p, the option strike prices available were 550p and 600p. If the holder of a call option decides to exercise it, he or she would buy a specific number of shares at the strike price chosen when buying the option. The number of shares covered by one option contract varies from country to country; examples are United States 100, UK 1,000, Germany 50.

It could be profitable to exercise a call option if the market price of the stock turns out to be higher than the strike price. In the event of the market price being lower than the strike price, the option holder is not obliged to exercise, and presumably will not, since exercising would realise a loss. The buyer of an option thus has potential for profit without the risk of a loss. For this favourable situation, the buyer of an option pays a premium. Continuing the previous example, the premiums for BP call options might be as shown in Table 31.1. January, April, and July are expiry months. The expiry month of an option is the month in which it ceases to be exercisable. Option premiums (i.e. prices) are expressed in the same currency units as the shares, e.g. pence in the UK, dollars in the United States. Premiums are payable at the time the option is bought.

Sometimes the word 'premium' is reserved for the price originally paid for the option by an investor whilst the term 'price' can relate to the market value of the option at any time. In the current text this distinction will not be made so that 'premium' and 'price' are treated as being synonymous. Even so the reader must bear in mind three different prices: the stock (share) price, the strike price of the option, and the price of the option (the latter being the price at which the option trades in the market).

EXAMPLE 31.1

An investor buys a 550p call option on BP shares at a premium of 27p per share when the share price is 568p (550p refers to the strike price, the price at which shares are bought if the option is exercised). Since each option contract on LIFFE relates to 1,000 shares, the cash outflow is £270. (LIFFE is the acronym for the London International Financial Futures and Options Exchange – LIFFE is pronounced 'life'.) Subsequently, the share price rises to 650p. The investor can then exercise the right to buy at 550p. There is a 100p pay-off (£1,000 per option contract). This 100p pay-off is the intrinsic value of the option. The net profit must take account of the 27p premium paid for the option. The net profit is thus 100p − 27p = 73p (£730 per option contract). The investor has guaranteed that the effective price to be paid for the shares will not exceed 577p; this comprises the strike price plus the premium paid for the option.

The Profit/Loss Profile at Expiry

Since an option buyer is not obliged to exercise an option, he or she has the right simply to disregard it. In such an event the premium paid is lost, but there would be no further loss. The premium paid is the maximum loss that can be incurred. On the other hand, the profit potential is subject to no limits. In principle, there is no upper limit to the stock price and hence no upper limit to the potential profit from the call option. Figure 31.1 shows the profit/loss profile of a call option at expiry (i.e. on the date at which it expires).

The option used for the illustration is the 550p BP call whose premium is 27p. If the buyer holds the option to the expiry date and the share price turns out to be 550p or less, there will be no point in exercising the option. There is no benefit from exercising an option to buy shares at 550p when those shares can be bought at a lower price in the market. In such a situation, the option buyer makes a net loss because of the payment of the 27p premium, which is non-returnable. This is shown in Figure 31.1, which depicts a loss of 27p at all stock prices up to 550p.

If the price of the share turns out to be greater than 550p, it could be worthwhile to exercise the option. The option holder could choose to exercise the right to buy at 550p and then immediately sell the shares at the higher price, thereby realising a gain. At a share price of 577p, this gross profit would exactly offset the premium paid. Hence, 577p is the break-even price at which net profit is zero. At prices above 577p, the gross profit exceeds the premium paid so that there is a net profit. (These figures would need some adjustment if bid-ask spreads and commission costs were to be taken into account.)

The gross profit referred to is alternatively known as the intrinsic value of the option. Intrinsic value can be defined as the pay-off to be obtained by immediately exercising the option (disregarding the premium paid) and is equal to the difference between the strike price and the market price of the stock when the option is in-the-money.

An in-the-money call option is one whose strike price is less than the market price of the stock, and which therefore offers an immediate gross profit. An at-the-money option is one whose strike price is equal to the market price. An out-of-the-money call option is one whose strike price is greater than the market price of the stock. Only in-the-money options have intrinsic value.

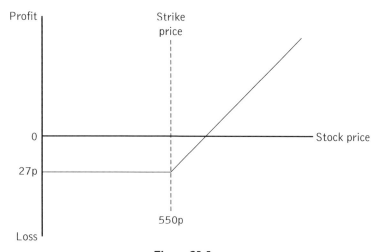

Figure 31.1

609

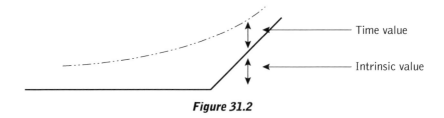

Time value

Intrinsic value

Figure 31.2

The Profit/Loss Profile Prior to Expiry

At the time that a traded option expires, its price (premium) will be equal to its intrinsic value. Prior to expiry the price of the option would normally exceed the intrinsic value. This excess of the price of the option over the intrinsic value is known as the time value. When an option is exercised, only the intrinsic value is realised. The seller of an option would obtain a price that incorporates time value as well as the intrinsic value; see Figure 31.2.

Time value is at its highest when the option is at-the-money. Time value declines as the option moves either in or out of the money and will approach zero as the market price of the stock diverges substantially from the strike price.

Time value is zero at the time that an option expires. So Figure 31.1, which shows the profit/loss profile at expiry, shows no time value. However prior to expiry an option would normally have some time value. When account is taken of the time value, the profit/loss profile of an option differs from the at-expiry profile depicted in Figure 31.1. A prior-to-expiry profile is shown by the broken curve in Figure 31.3.

The broken curve indicates the market price of the option minus the initial premium paid (27p in this case). The net profit shown by this prior-to-expiry profile is the price that the trader could sell the option for, minus the price (premium) that was paid for it. At stock prices below the option strike price, the option price consists of time value only. Above the strike price, the option price consists of both time and intrinsic values.

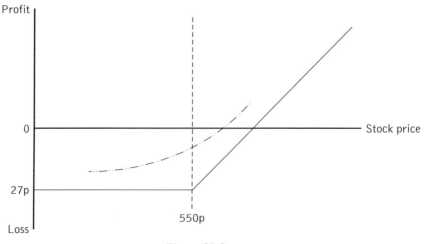

Figure 31.3

DETERMINANTS OF THE OPTION PRICE (PREMIUM)

The explanation of an option price divides into ascertaining intrinsic value and assessing the influences on time value. The intrinsic value of a call option is equal to the stock price minus the strike price of the option, with zero being the minimum intrinsic value. In principle, the option price cannot fall below the intrinsic value. If the option price were below the intrinsic value, there would be a guaranteed profit from buying the option and immediately exercising it (and selling the shares acquired). It would be irrational for anyone to sell an option for a price that is less than its intrinsic value, since more could be obtained from exercising it. These points are elaborated in the Boundary Conditions section at the end of this chapter.

The determination of time value is more complex. Major influences on time value include the expected volatility of the stock price, the length of the period remaining to the expiry date, and the extent to which the option is in or out of the money.

Time value can be looked upon as the price to be paid for (or the value of) the possibility of a future increase in intrinsic value. The higher the expected share price volatility, the greater will be the option price. An option on a volatile stock has a strong chance of acquiring intrinsic value at some stage prior to expiry. Similarly, the probability of an option acquiring intrinsic value prior to expiry rises with the length of time remaining to its expiry date. It can be seen from Table 31.1 that the options with the more distant expiry dates have the higher prices.

Time value is at its peak when the option is at-the-money and declines as the option moves either in or out of the money. Out-of-the-money options have less time value than at-the-money options because the share price has further to move before intrinsic value is acquired. In-the-money options have less time value than at-the-money options since their prices contain intrinsic value, which is vulnerable to a fall in the stock price, whereas at-the-money option prices contain no intrinsic value. The risk that existing intrinsic value might be lost reduces the attractiveness of the option and lowers its price.

PUT OPTIONS

A put option gives its holder the right, but not the obligation, to sell shares at a specified price prior to, or on, the expiry date of the option. The holder of an option can exercise it, sell it, or allow it to expire. It is worthwhile exercising an option – that is, exercising the right to sell shares at the strike (exercise) price – only if the market price of the stock turns out to be lower than the strike price. If the strike price is greater than the stock price, the option is said to have intrinsic value. The intrinsic value would be equal to the excess of the strike price over the stock price. An option without intrinsic value might simply be allowed to expire since its holder is not obliged to exercise it, and presumably would not if the strike price were below the market price of the stock (it would be better to sell the stock in the market).

Table 31.1 shows prices of BP put options. The price of BP shares was 568p. The months referred to in Table 31.1 are expiry months. At any one time the buyer of a BP put option would have three expiry dates from which to choose. When the April expiry date is reached, options with a January expiry date would be introduced. Substantial movements of the stock price would invoke the introduction of additional strike prices, so that there are strike prices either side of the stock price. As a result the number of available strike prices would exceed two.

611

EXAMPLE 31.2

An investor buys a 550p put option on BP shares at a price of 7p per share when the share price is 568p. Since each option contract relates to 1,000 shares, the cash outflow is £70.

Subsequently, the share price falls to 400p. The investor can exercise the right to sell at 550p. There is a gross profit from the option of 150p (£1,500 per option contract). This gross profit of 150p is the intrinsic value of the option. The net profit from the option must take account of the 7p premium paid for the option. The net profit is thus 150p − 7p = 143p (£1,430 per option contract). The investor has guaranteed that the effective selling price of the shares cannot fall below 543p, this sum being the sale receipts of 550p minus the 7p premium paid for the option.

The Profit/Loss Profile at Expiry

In the case of traded stock options, the premium is usually payable in full on the day following the purchase of the option. However, since the buyer is not obliged to exercise the option, and presumably will not do so if it involves selling at less than the market price of the share, the premium paid is the maximum loss the buyer of the option can incur. So, for example, a buyer of BP April 550p puts faces a maximum loss of 7p per share, which amounts to £70 per contract, since each put option contract is for the sale of 1,000 shares.

The maximum profit is limited only by the fact that stock prices cannot fall below zero. Since a stock price can fall to zero, the net gain from a put option can be as much as the strike price minus the premium paid. The buyer of April 550p BP puts stands to gain as much as 550p − 7p per share. This amounts to £5,430 per option contract.

Figure 31.4 shows the profit/loss profile of BP April 550p puts at expiry (i.e. on the day in April upon which the option ceases to be capable of being exercised). If the stock price is 550p, or higher, when the option expires the holder of the option records a net loss of 7p per share (£70

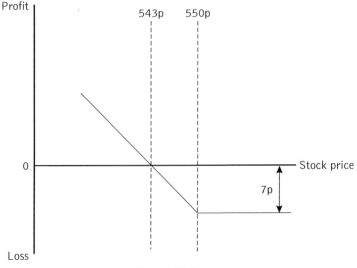

Figure 31.4

per option contract). If the stock price turns out to be less than 550p, there is a gross profit to be made by exercising the option. Exercising the option will allow the option holder to sell shares at 550p, while buying them at a lower price. This gross profit from exercising the option minus the premium paid for the option is the net profit. If the stock price lies between 543p and 550p there is a net loss, whereas below the break-even stock price of 543p there is a net profit. (It can be worthwhile exercising the option at stock prices between 543p and 549p since exercise would realise some intrinsic value to set against the premium paid for the option. In other words, exercise of the option would reduce the loss.)

The Profit/Loss Profile Prior to Expiry

Intrinsic value is the gross profit to be made from exercising the option. At expiry an option would have only intrinsic value, which could be equal to zero. Prior to expiry the option would have time value as well as intrinsic value. The profit/loss profile of Figure 31.4 is based on intrinsic value only. Since intrinsic value is the gross profit to be made from exercising the option it will be zero at stock prices at or above the strike price of 550p, whereas below 550p it will be equal to the difference between the stock price and the strike price. The net profit or loss at expiry is equal to the intrinsic value minus the premium paid.

Prior to expiry the price of an option will exceed its intrinsic value. The difference is the time value and is shown by the vertical distance between the prior-to-expiry profile and the at-expiry profile in Figure 31.5. The price of an option is the sum of the intrinsic and time values. When an option is exercised only the intrinsic value is obtained. When an option is sold both the intrinsic and time values are obtained.

The prior-to-expiry profile indicates the current market price of the option minus the price that the present holder paid for it. As time passes, the prior-to-expiry profile will tend to converge on to the at-expiry profile, with the convergence becoming complete as expiry is reached.

This convergence reflects the tendency for the time value of an option to decline with the

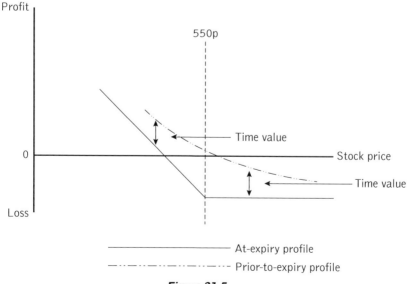

Figure 31.5

passage of time. This erosion of time value can be explained in terms of the likelihood of a substantial increase in intrinsic value falling as the time available for the requisite stock price movement declines. A second factor affecting time value is the expected volatility of the stock price. With high volatility there is a relatively high chance of substantial gains in intrinsic value at some stage prior to expiry. So, the greater is the expected volatility of a stock price, the greater will be the time value of an option on that stock.

A third factor affecting time value is the relationship between the stock price and the strike price of the option. Time value is at its highest when the stock price is equal to the strike price. When the stock price is equal to the strike price, the option is said to be at-the-money. As the stock price and strike price diverge, in either direction, time value declines.

When the stock price exceeds the strike price, the put option is said to be out-of-the-money. A better price can be obtained by selling the shares in the market than by exercising the option. Time value declines as the option moves further out of the money (in other words, as the stock price rises), reflecting the decreasing likelihood of the stock price declining sufficiently to cause exercise of the option to become profitable.

When the stock price is lower than the strike price, the put option is said to be in-the-money. A better price can be obtained by exercising the option than by selling the shares in the market. The option has intrinsic value since there would be a pay-off from immediate exercise of the option.

Time value declines as the option becomes deeper in the money (i.e. as the stock price falls). This can be understood in terms of there being an increasing amount of intrinsic value that is at risk of being lost. The price of an in-the-money option contains the intrinsic value of that option. The buyer of an in-the-money option bears the risk that a stock price rise will reduce intrinsic value, whereas the buyer of an at-the-money option does not. The risk borne rises as the option becomes deeper in the money. This risk is reflected in the time value. When there is more intrinsic value at risk, the time value will be lower. The buyer of an at-the-money option pays a higher price for time value than the buyer of an in-the-money option, with the price paid for time value declining as the option becomes deeper in the money.

WRITING OPTIONS

For every buyer of an option there must be a seller. The seller of an option is often referred to as the writer. The buyer of an option is said to have a long option position, whereas the writer of the option is said to have a short position. The profit/loss profile of a short (written) option is the mirror image of that of the long (bought) option. Profits of the buyer must equal losses of the seller, and vice versa. Figures 31.6 and 31.7 compare long and short positions for call and put options respectively.

The premium paid by the buyer obviously equals the premium received by the writer. The profit (loss) of the buyer will always equal the loss (profit) of the writer. It should be noted that the buyer of a call option has loss potential limited to the premium paid, but unlimited profit potential. Conversely, the writer of a call has a maximum profit equal to the premium received, but unlimited loss potential. In the case of put options, the buyer has a maximum loss equal to the premium, which constitutes the maximum profit of the writer. With put options the maximum profit of the buyer (maximum loss of the writer) occurs at a stock price of zero.

In the case of exchange-traded options, a long option position can be closed out by selling an identical option; leaving no option position remaining. Likewise, a trader can close out a written option by buying an identical option. Long and short positions in identical options cancel each other.

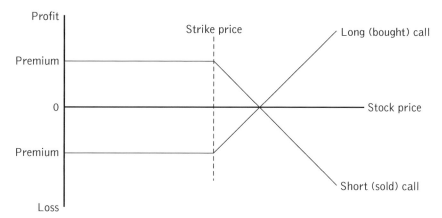

Figure 31.6

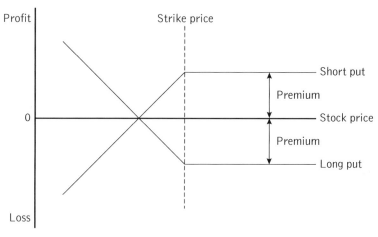

Figure 31.7

EXAMPLE 31.3

An investor writes a 550p call option on BP shares at a premium of 27p per share when the share price is 568p. Since each option contract on LIFFE relates to 1,000 shares, the premium receipts amount to £270. Subsequently, the share price rises to 650p. An option buyer might then exercise the right to buy shares at 550p. If the option writer is assigned to the option buyer (assignment of writers to meet the requirements of buyers who exercise is usually carried out on a random basis), the writer must sell shares for 550p to the option buyer. The option writer may need to buy shares at 650p in order to sell them at 550p. This entails a gross loss of 100p (the intrinsic value of the option). Taking account of the option premium received indicates a net loss of 73p (£730 per option contract). The loss of the option writer is equal to the profit of the option buyer.

EXERCISE 31.1

It is 6 January. The Lonrho share price is 662p. Lonrho March expiry option prices are:

Table 31.A

Strike price	Calls	Puts
650	55	43

(a) Calculate the intrinsic and the time value for both of the options.

(b) Suggest two alternative option strategies for profiting from a price rise. In each case what would be the profit, or loss, in the event of the share price reaching (i) 700p, and (ii) 800p, by the expiry date of the option?

Answers

(a) Calls: intrinsic value $662 - 650 = 12p$, time value $55 - 12 = 43p$.

Puts: intrinsic value 0, time value 43p.

(b) Buy a call: at 700p there would be a net cash flow of $700p - 650p - 55p = -5p$, i.e. a loss of 5p.

at 800p there would be a net cash flow of $800p - 650p - 55p = 95p$, i.e. a profit of 95p.

Write a put: at 700p there would be a net cash flow of 43p, i.e. a profit of 43p.

at 800p there would be a net cash flow of 43p, i.e. a profit of 43p.

MARKET PRACTICES AND TERMS

All the call options on a particular underlying stock together constitute a class of options. Similarly, all the puts on the same underlying stock would together comprise another class. Within each class there will be a number of series. An option series is specific to a particular strike price and a particular expiry month, as well as to a particular stock and call/put categorisation. So, for example, 50p December calls and 60p March calls on the stock of ABC are two different series within the same class (the class being ABC call options). There are often position limits to the number of option contracts in any one class that can be held or written by any one individual or organisation.

An option can be bought either to establish a new option position, or to close out an existing (opposite) option position. An opening purchase is a transaction whereby the buyer of an option becomes its holder; a closing purchase is a transaction in which a writer of an option buys an option identical to the one previously written, whereupon the two positions are deemed to cancel each other out. An opening sale is a transaction in which the seller of an option becomes its writer; a closing sale involves the cancellation of a previously purchased option.

Premiums in respect of exchange-traded options are normally payable via the broker to the clearing house on the morning following the day of the trade. Payment to the writer of the option would come from the clearing house, which usually acts as a registrar for all open contracts. If the holder of an option exercises it, the clearing house, using a random selection process, chooses a writer who is then assigned to sell shares (in the case of calls) or buy shares (in the case of puts) to or from the holder of the option at the strike price.

EXERCISE 31.2

The shares of Big Con plc stand at 110p. Put options with a strike price of 120p are priced at 14p.

(a) What is the intrinsic value of the options?

(b) What is the time value of the options?

(c) If the share price fell to 50p by the expiry date, what would be the profit/loss for a holder and for a writer of the option?

(d) What is the maximum loss for the writer of the option?

Answers

(a) 10p (120p − 110p, strike price minus stock price).

(b) 4p (14p − 10p, option price minus intrinsic value).

(c) The holder makes a profit of 56p, which equals the loss of the writer (70p − 14p, the new price of the option minus the premium paid; the new price is the intrinsic value of 120p − 50p = 70p).

(d) 106p (120p − 14p, the loss if the stock price falls to zero which amounts to the intrinsic value minus the premium received).

EXERCISE 31.3

It is 10 June and shares in Covuni Plc are 98p. Option prices are shown in the table.

Table 31.B

Strike price	Calls		Puts	
	September	December	September	December
90p	9p	$9^1/_2$p	1p	$1^1/_2$p
100p	2p	3p	4p	5p
110p	1p	$1^1/_2$p	13p	$13^1/_2$p

(a) Why are the 100p put options more expensive than the 100p call options?

(b) How might a speculator make a profit from a 2p rise in the share price?

(c) If the September 90p options are held to expiry and the share price remains at 98p, what would you expect the option prices to be at expiry?

Answers

(a) The put options have an intrinsic value of 100p-98p=2p. The call options have no intrinsic value; they are out-of-the-money.

(b) Write a 100p put option.

(c) The 90p call would have an intrinsic value of 98p-90p=8p. At expiry time value is zero. So the option price should be 8p. The 90p put would have expired out-of-the-money and hence would have zero value at expiry.

BOUNDARY CONDITIONS

Arbitrage possibilities impose minimum and maximum values for options; these values are often referred to as option price boundaries. For practical purposes, only the minimum values are of significance and hence the following account will focus exclusively on them.

It is useful to begin by considering American-style options, which are options that can be exercised at any stage prior to expiry. The prices of such options should not fall below their intrinsic values, otherwise the options could be purchased for less than their intrinsic values and immediately exercised to realise the intrinsic values. The possibility of such arbitrage will tend to prevent option prices being below the intrinsic values by inducing arbitrage-based purchases whenever option prices fall below such levels.

EXAMPLE 31.4

A share is priced at 100p and its 120p strike price put option is priced at 18p. The option price is below its intrinsic value, which is 120p − 100p = 20p. An arbitrage profit can be made by simultaneously buying the share and the put option for a total expenditure of 100p + 18p = 118p and immediately exercising the put. Upon exercise the share is sold for the strike price of 120p. Receipts exceed expenditures by 2p, which constitutes the arbitrage profit.

Any put option price below 20p provides an arbitrage opportunity, which involves buying the option. The additional demand for the option will tend to pull up its price until it reaches 20p, at which point arbitrage opportunities will cease.

Although the intrinsic value constitutes the minimum value in the case of American-style put options, the minimum values of American-style call options tend to be higher than their intrinsic values. This latter point can be appreciated by considering the case of European-style call options.

European-style options can be exercised on only one date: the expiry day. So a European-style option, prior to its expiry date, cannot be exercised to realise the intrinsic value. So it is not possible simply to buy the option and immediately exercise it for an arbitrage profit. Instead, the arbitrage is more complex in that the arbitrage transactions cannot all be completed in the present for an instant profit. Positions need to be held until the option expiry date.

EXAMPLE 31.5

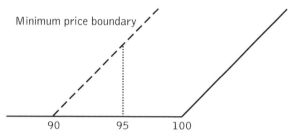

If the call option strike price is 100p and the present value of 100p is 90p, a stock price of 95p would imply a minimum option price of 5p. For example if the option price is 3p, it is possible to make a profit of at least 2p by short selling the stock (i.e. borrowing the shares and selling them) for 95p while putting 90p on deposit and buying the options for 3p. There is a cash inflow of 95p (share sale) and an outflow of 93p (90p deposit plus 3p option price). There is a net cash inflow of 2p.

If the option is in-the-money on the expiry date (share price above 100p), the option is exercised and the stock returned to the lender. There is a zero net cash flow at expiry since the deposit pays the 100p required for the share purchase resulting from exercise of the option. There is a profit because of the original net cash inflow of 2p.

If the option expires out-of-the-money (share price below 100p), the stock can be bought for less than 100p at expiry. In this case the profit will exceed the original 2p net cash inflow. The deposit produces 100p but less than 100p is required for the purchase of the share (that has to be returned to the stock lender). The difference between the share price and 100p accrues as additional profit.

Since the arbitrage involves buying the underpriced option, it would tend to push the option price up towards its minimum value. At the minimum value (5p), there would be no further arbitrage opportunities.

619

If the original option price were 5p, there would not be a guaranteed profit from arbitrage. There would be an initial zero net cash flow: an inflow of 95p from the sale of the share and an outflow of 90p + 5p = 95p for the deposit and purchase of the option. In the event of the option being in-the-money on the expiry date, there would be an inflow of 100p from the deposit and an outflow of 100p for the share purchase (by means of exercising the option).

In the case of a call option on a non-dividend paying stock, the arbitrage would involve selling the stock short (borrowing stock and selling it), using most of the proceeds to put money on deposit and buy a call option, and then waiting until the expiry date to exercise the option and return the stock to the lender. The arbitrage profit would be the excess of the initial proceeds of the stock sale over the combined amount of the sum on deposit and the cost of the option. Since the sum on deposit can earn interest up to the option expiry date, only the present value of the option strike price needs to be deposited. So an absence of arbitrage opportunities requires that the option price plus the present value of the strike price exceeds (or equals) the initial stock price. So the minimum value of the option should be the stock price minus the present value of the strike price (rather than the American-style case of stock price minus strike price), but if this is negative, the minimum value is zero (options cannot have negative prices). Arbitrage tends to prevent option prices falling below their minimum values, as demonstrated by Example 31.5. In the event of an option price falling below its minimum value, arbitrage-induced purchases of options would tend to push the option price towards the minimum value.

The excess of the stock price over the present value of the strike price is greater than the intrinsic value of the option (defined as stock price minus strike price). An American-style option should not have a price lower than that of a European-style option since the American-style provides everything offered by the European-style plus the facility of exercise before the expiry date. Consequently, the minimum value of an American-style call option should not be lower than the minimum value of a European-style call option. It follows that the minimum value of an American-style call option is the excess of the stock price over the present value of the strike price (i.e. the same as the minimum value of the European and greater than the intrinsic value). Again, if this value is negative the minimum option price is zero. See Figure 31.8, in which K is the strike price of the option, r is the risk-free interest rate, and T is the time to expiry of the option.

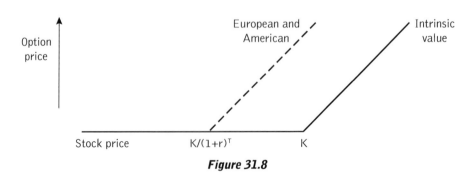

Figure 31.8

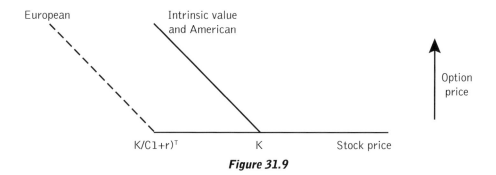

Figure 31.9

In the case of put options on non-dividend paying stocks, arbitrage possibilities determine a minimum value of a European-style option below the intrinsic value (and hence below the minimum value of the corresponding American-style option). The minimum value of the European-style put option equals the present value of the strike price minus the stock price, and that boundary is below the minimum value of the corresponding American-style put option (the strike price minus the stock price). See Figure 31.9.

These analyses of boundary conditions can be readily amended to allow for dividends.

CONCLUSION

Another important form of derivative for investment managers is the stock option. Stock options provide their holders with rights, but not obligations, to buy (call options) or to sell (put options) shares at a specified price. Stock index options give notional rights to buy or sell stock index portfolios at specified index values. Hedging by buying options is similar to buying insurance; protection against adverse events is obtained. Adverse price (or stock index) movements are offset by the options whilst advantageous movements are not offset by losses from options since there is no obligation to exercise options. Options can also be used as means of enhancing income receipts from portfolios since selling (writing) options entails the receipt of premiums; the premiums received add to the dividend receipts from portfolios.

Investment managers, including institutional investors, may use options in conjunction with portfolios of shares. Options could also be used as an investment class. Buying call options in conjunction with holding money in bank deposits (or other money market investments) structures options funds, which provide gains from rises in share prices whilst avoiding losses from price falls.

Chapter 32

Speculation with stock options

OBJECTIVE

The objective of this chapter is to provide knowledge of:

1. The gearing effects of call options.
2. Volatility trading.

THE EFFECTS OF GEARING

An option can be bought for a fraction of the price of the stock to which the option relates. This is the gearing provided by an option. Options can be looked upon as either low risk or high risk investments. In both cases the interpretation of risk is based upon the gearing effect offered by options. The maximum loss from buying stock is the price of that stock, whereas the maximum loss from buying a call option on that stock is the option premium. So buying a call option on 1,000 shares of stock can be seen as less risky than buying 1,000 shares of stock.

However, if the choice is between investing £1,000 in stock and spending £1,000 on stock options, then the options are the more risky. Again, this arises from the gearing offered by the options. Since the price of the option is a fraction of the price of the stock, percentage changes in the option price are prone to be much greater than percentage changes in the stock price. Suppose that XYZ stock is priced at 100p and a call option to buy at 100p is priced at 5p. A rise in the stock price to 110p might plausibly cause a rise in the option price to 13p. The stock price rises by 10%, whereas the option price rises by 160%. This arises from the gearing offered by the option. However, the possibility of high percentage profits is accompanied by potential large percentage losses. A fall in the stock price to 90p might cause a fall in the option price to 3p. The 10% fall in the stock price is accompanied by a 40% drop in the option price (and hence a 40% loss on the option). It may be that a more substantial fall in the stock price, say to 65p, virtually eliminates the value of the option so that a 35% fall in the stock price brings about a 100% fall in the option price. So if the choice is between £1,000 invested in stock and £1,000 in options, the latter is the more risky.

The foregoing example involved an at-the-money option gaining just 8p in value as a result of the stock price rising by 10p. One might think that the right to buy at 100p should rise in price by

10p as a result of a rise in the stock price from 100p to 110p. However, although there is an additional 10p in intrinsic value, the other component of the option premium, time value, falls as the stock price moves away from the option strike price (the initial option price of 5p was entirely time value; at the stock price of 110p the time value of the option is 3p). The change in the option price as a proportion of the change in the stock price is known as the delta of the option (in the present example the delta is $(13 - 5)/10 = 0.8$).

EXERCISE 32.1

It is 24 November. The Barclays Bank share price is 498p. Call options that are due to expire at the end of December have the prices as shown in the table.

Table 32.A

Strike price	Option price
460p	41p
500p	11p

(a) If the share price rises to 550p and the option prices rise to those shown in the second table, what are the percentage rates of return on (i) the shares, (ii) the 460p strike price options, and (iii) the 500p strike price options?

Table 32.B

Strike price	Option price
460p	90p
500p	51p

(b) In the event of a fall in the share price to 480p by the expiry date of the options, what are the percentage rates of return on (i) the shares, (ii) the 460p strike price options, and (iii) the 500p strike price options?

Answers

(a) (i) $550/498 = 1.1044$
$1.1044 - 1 = 0.1044$, i.e. 10.44%

(ii) $90/41 = 2.1951$
$2.1951 - 1 = 1.1951$, i.e. 119.51%

(iii) $51/11 = 4.6364$
$4.6364 - 1 = 3.6364$, i.e. 363.64%

(b)   (i) $480/498 = 0.9639$

   $0.9639 - 1 = -0.0361$, i.e. -3.61%

   (ii)   If the share price is 480p on the expiry date of the options, the 460p strike price call options would be worth $480p - 460p = 20p$. There is a fall of $41p - 20p = 21p$ in the price of the options.

   $21/41 = 0.5122$

   There is a loss of 51.22% on the option.

   (iii)   If the share price is 480p on the expiry date of the options, the 500p strike price call options would have no value. All of the investment would have been lost. The return would be -100%.

EXERCISE 32.2

It is 25 November. The Barclays Bank share price is 500p. At-the-money call options that are due to expire at the end of December are trading at 12.5p.

(a)   If the share price rises to 550p and the option price rises to 50p:

   (i)   What would be the return from £5,000 invested in shares?
   (ii)   What would be the return from £5,000 invested in options?
   (iii)   What would be the return from using options to gain exposure to £5,000 worth of shares whilst keeping the rest of the £5,000 uninvested?

(b)   If by the expiry date of the options the share price had fallen to 450p, what would be the outcome from the three investment strategies of part (a)?

Answers

(a)   (i) $550/500 = 1.1$

   $1.1 - 1 = 0.1$, i.e. 10% (£500)

   (ii) $50/12.5 = 4.$

   $4 - 1 = 3$, i.e. 300% (£15,000)

   (iii)   £5,000 worth of shares is 1,000 shares. Since each option contract relates to 1,000 shares, one option contract is bought. The cost of a contract would be $12.5p \times 1,000 = £125$. Its value rises to £500 as a result of the increase in the option price. There is a gain of £375. The return on the £5,000 is thus:

   $£5,375/£5,000 = 1.075$

   $1.075 - 1 = 0.075$, i.e. 7.5%

(b)   (i) $450/500 = 0.9$

   $0.9 - 1 = -0.1$, i.e. -10% $(-50/500)$

(ii) If the share price were 450p on the expiry date of the options, the options would be worthless. The whole of the £5,000 invested in options would be lost. The return would be −100%.

(iii) The £125 spent on the option contract would have been lost, but the uninvested £4,875 remains. The return is:

£4,875/£5,000 = 0.975
0.975 − 1 = −0.025, i.e. −2.5% (−12.5/500)

It can be seen that strategy (ii) has the highest risk and strategy (iii) the lowest risk. Options can be seen as either high risk or low risk investments according to whether the objective is to use options to match the expenditure on shares, or to match the number of shares to which the investor is exposed.

The gearing effect of options relates to the high percentage profits and losses, relative to shares, that arise because options cost much less than shares. The results above show that this gearing means that investing a specific sum of money in options, rather than shares, produces much greater risk (higher potential profits and losses). However using options to gain an exposure equivalent to that of a share holding may entail lower risk, relative to the shares. The most that can be lost using options are the premiums paid, whereas the entire value of a shareholding could be lost.

VOLATILITY TRADING AND THE COLLAPSE OF BARINGS BANK

Speculation with options may be based on forecasts of the direction of share price movements, and could take advantage of the gearing provided by options. Speculation can also be based on views about future share price volatility. Profiting from such views involves volatility trading. A simple volatility trading strategy is the straddle.

A long straddle is the simultaneous purchase of a call and a put on the same stock, at the same strike price and for the same expiry month (see Figure 32.1). A short straddle is the simultaneous sale of two such options (see Figure 32.2). A trader buying a straddle is taking the view that volatility will be high in the future, whereas the seller of a straddle takes the view that volatility will be low.

Suppose that 100p call options are 2p, while 100p put options are 3p. A long straddle could be constructed by simultaneously buying a 100p call and a 100p put so as to produce the profit/loss profile illustrated by Figure 32.3. The holder of the long straddle depicted in the figure would make net profits if the stock price moved outside the range 95p–105p. The maximum loss would be the sum of the premiums paid, 5p. This loss would be incurred if the stock price moved to, and stayed at, 100p.

A short straddle could be structured by means of writing a 100p call and simultaneously writing a 100p put. The resulting profit/loss profile is illustrated in Figure 32.4. The seller of the short straddle shown in the figure will make a profit if the stock price remains within the range 95p–105p. The maximum profit of 5p, equal to the sum of the premiums received, would be made in the event of the stock price moving to, and stabilising at, 100p.

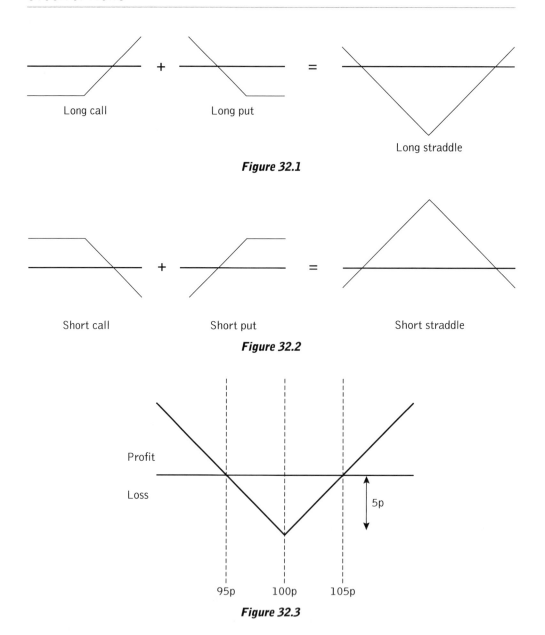

Figure 32.1

Figure 32.2

Figure 32.3

Thus the holder of a long straddle hopes for high volatility, whereas the holder of a short straddle desires low volatility.

The use of short straddles played a part in the collapse of Barings Bank in 1995. Baring's derivatives trader in Singapore, Nick Leeson (the 'Rogue Trader' upon whom the film of that name was based), took large unauthorised derivatives positions, which he concealed from the managers of the bank. These included substantial long positions in Nikkei 225 stock index futures, short positions in Japanese government bond futures, short Nikkei 225 call options, and short Nikkei 225 put options. The options positions amounted to short straddles. The long stock index futures stood to profit from rises in the Japanese stock market, and lose from falls. The short straddle

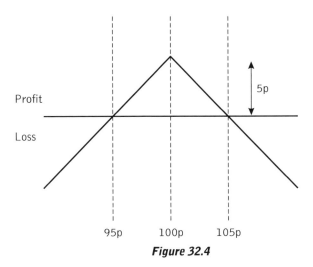

Figure 32.4

stood to profit from a stable market, and to lose from movements in either direction. Unfortunately for Leeson and Barings Bank, the Nikkei 225 fell heavily. There were losses on the stock index futures and the short put options. The accumulated losses exceeded the capital of Barings Bank, which was rendered insolvent. Barings Bank was subsequently sold to ING for the sum of £1.

OTHER VOLATILITY TRADING STRATEGIES

Use of volatility trading strategies such as the straddle is not necessarily based on making profits from stock price movements. It may be based on anticipated changes in market expectations of volatility. In Figure 32.5 the broken curve represents the profits/losses on the straddle prior to expiry. The vertical distance between the broken curve and the unbroken lines (which depict the profit/loss at expiry) is the sum of the time values of the two options. The time value is sensitive to changes in market expectations of stock price volatility. An increase in expected volatility would raise the time value and move the broken line up (vice versa for a decrease). The long straddle of Figure 32.5 may be constructed with a view to profiting from a rise in market expectations of volatility, which would cause the broken curve to rise.

The change in the price of an option (or combination of options), resulting from a change in the market expectation of stock price volatility, is referred to as the vega (or kappa) of the option.

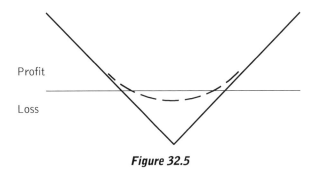

Figure 32.5

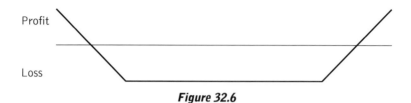

Figure 32.6

Another sensitivity of importance is the delta of the option (or combination of options). The delta of an option (or combination of options) is the change in the price of the option (or combination of options) resulting from a 1p change in the stock price. In the case of stock index options, it would be the option price change resulting from one index point change in the stock index.

Volatility trading strategies are often structured to have deltas as close as possible to zero. This is to ensure that the exposure is to changes in market expectations of volatility rather than to changes in the stock price. Long call options have positive deltas (the option price rises with stock price increases) and long put options have negative deltas (the option price falls with increases in the stock price). As a result the deltas tend to offset each other. For at-the-money options the call delta is about $+0.5$ and the put delta is about -0.5. So combining call and put options, which are both close to being at-the-money, brings the net delta to about zero. A zero delta entails no net option price change as a result of a small movement of the stock price.

The straddle is not the only strategy for trading (speculating) on expectations of stock price volatility. There are many other strategies, two of which are strangles and butterflies. A long strangle is constructed by buying a low strike price put option together with a high strike price call option. A short strangle entails writing the options. Figure 32.6 illustrates a long strangle.

A short butterfly can be structured by writing a low strike price call option, buying two middle strike price call options, and writing a high strike price call option. Alternatively it can be constructed by means of buying and selling put options in the same order. Figure 32.7 illustrates a short butterfly.

The long straddle exhibits the highest maximum loss, since the options are close to being at-the-money (therefore they have high time value).

The long strangle has a lower maximum loss, since the options are out-of-the-money (therefore they have relatively low time value). However the range of stock prices over which losses occur is greater than in the case of the straddle.

The short butterfly has lower loss potential than the long straddle or long strangle, but has restricted profit potential.

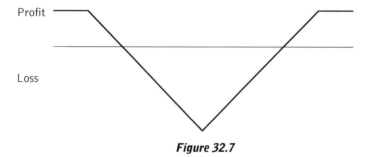

Figure 32.7

EXERCISE 32.3

It is 14 November 2005. FTSE 100 Index Options, which expire on 28 November, have the prices shown in the table.

Table 32.C

Strike price	Calls	Puts
5,425	68	7.5
5,475	31	18
5,525	9.5	46

The current FTSE 100 stands at 5,480. Using the data from the table, and with a view to keeping the delta of the strategy as close as possible to zero, construct (a) a short straddle, (b) a short strangle, and (c) a long butterfly. What are the maximum profits and losses? What are the break-even index values? (d) Compare the three strategies.

Answers

(a) In order to keep delta as close as possible to zero, the options that are closest to being at-the-money should be used for the straddle. So 5,475 strike price calls and puts are written.

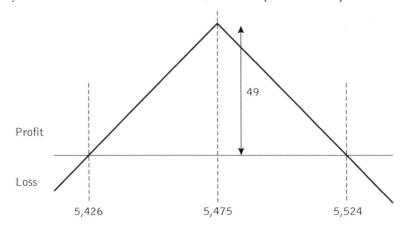

The maximum profit is 49 index points (£490 per pair of option contracts), which is realised if the index is 5,475 when the options expire. The maximum loss on the downside is 5,426 index points (£54,260 per pair of option contracts), which would be realised if the index fell to a value of zero. There is no maximum loss on the upside since there is no upper limit to the index. The break-even values of the index are 5,426 and 5,524 (5,475 + / −49).

(b) In order to ensure that the delta of the strangle is as close as possible to zero, the option strike prices should be approximately equal distance from the current index. A 5,425 strike put option, and a 5,525 strike call option, are written.

629

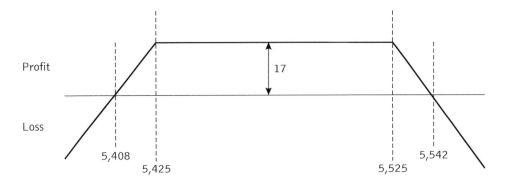

The maximum profit is 17 index points (£170 per combination of option contracts). This maximum profit would be received if the options were to expire at an index between 5,425 and 5,525. The maximum loss on the downside is 5,408 index points (£54,080), which would be incurred in the event of the value of the index falling to zero. The maximum loss on the upside is unlimited. The break-even index levels are 5,408 (5,425 − 17) and 5,542 (5,525 + 17).

(c) Construction of a long butterfly entails buying a 5,425 call, writing two 5,475 calls, and buying a 5,525 call. Alternatively a 5,425 put is bought, two 5,475 puts are written, and a 5,525 put is bought. The net expenditure using the calls is 15.5 (68 − 31 − 31 + 9.5), whereas the net expenditure using the puts is 17.5 (7.5 − 18 − 18 + 46). The butterfly is structured using call options because the lower cost enhances profits.

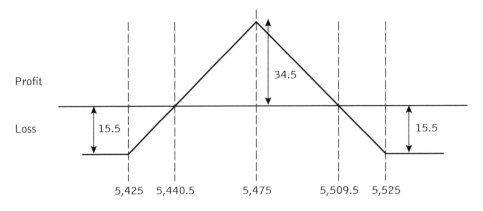

The maximum profit is 34.5 index points, which is obtained at an index level of 5,475. The maximum loss is 15.5 index points, obtained below 5,425 and above 5,525. The break-even index levels are 5,440.5 and 5,509.5.

(d) The straddle provides the highest maximum profit, the strangle entails the highest likelihood of profit, and the butterfly limits the size of prospective losses.

630

CONCLUSION

Although the main economic function of financial derivatives is probably hedging, most trades may be for the purpose of speculation. Speculators accept risk in the anticipation of making profit. The risk accepted by speculators is the risk that hedgers want to insure against. In aggregate hedgers transfer their risk to speculators. So speculators are vital to the successful operation of derivatives markets.

Whereas there is considerable speculative trading in both futures and options markets, speculators in options markets have more dimensions available for speculation. In particular, in options markets changes in stock price volatility can be traded as well as the direction of stock price change. An options speculator can take a position not only on the direction of stock price movement but also on whether market expectations of volatility will rise or fall.

This additional dimension of trading is important for another function of derivatives markets, which is discovery. Both futures and options markets can be used for price discovery. The price that is discovered is the future price expected by market participants, and from this a corresponding spot price can be inferred. Options also allow the discovery of market expectations of stock price volatility. An options price reflects the market participants' expectation of stock price volatility, which is known as implied volatility. Chapters 36, 37, and 38 on option pricing show how fair prices of options can be deduced from pricing models, wherein the expectation of stock price volatility is one of the values to be put into the model. Such models can be reversed so that instead of expectations of volatility being used to ascertain fair option prices, the actual option prices are used to deduce the market expectation of stock price volatility.

Chapter 33

Hedging with options

OBJECTIVE

The objective of this chapter is to provide knowledge of:

1. Hedging the value of a shareholding with options.
2. The relative merits of long and short option positions for hedging.
3. Hedging anticipated purchases of stock.
4. Vertical spreads.
5. Option cylinders.

Call options provide the right to buy shares at a particular price (the strike price), and put options give the right to sell at a strike price. Someone who is at risk from a price change can use options to offset that risk. A call option can be seen as a means of establishing an upper limit to the purchase price of a share (if the market price exceeds the strike price, then the option may be exercised in order to buy at the strike price). A put option provides a minimum selling price (exercise of the right to sell, at the strike price, might occur in the event of the market price being below the strike price).

So options can be regarded as means of insurance against adverse price movements. Call options provide insurance against share price rises since the price to be paid cannot exceed the strike price. Put options provide insurance against share price falls since the lowest price that could be received is the strike price.

HEDGING THE VALUE OF A SHAREHOLDING

Consider a holder of shares who seeks protection from a fall in the share price. The protection can be obtained by buying a put option. Profits from the option offset losses on the stock. However, profits from the rise in the stock price are not offset by losses from the option (apart from the premium paid for the option). So gains are made from a rise in the stock price.

A put option provides a lower limit to the selling price for a block of 1,000 shares. Table 33.1 shows the prices of BP put options when the price of BP shares was 568p. A holder of 1,000 BP

Table 33.1

Strike price	Calls			Puts		
	April	July	October	April	July	October
550p	27p	49p	64p	7p	27.5p	36p
600p	5p	26.5p	41p	35p	55p	63p

The BP share price was 568p.

shares would be able to ensure that the value of the stockholding could not fall below £5,500 (1,000 × £5.50) by buying a 550p put option. The option would provide the right to sell 1,000 BP shares at 550p. If the investor chooses an option that expires in April, the cost of providing such protection until the April expiry date would be £70 (1,000 × 7p). Of course, should the stock price remain in excess of 550p, the shareholder would not exercise the right to sell at 550p. In such a situation a better share price is obtained by selling in the stock market.

Although the shareholder has the right to exercise a put option and thereby sell shares at 550p, he or she is more likely to sell rather than exercise the option if the share price falls below 550p. This can be understood by considering the elements that make up an option price. The price of an option can be divided into its intrinsic value and its time value. The intrinsic value represents the pay-off that could be obtained by immediately exercising the option. For example, an April 600p put option has an intrinsic value of 32p when the stock price is 568p since, by exercising the option, shares can be sold at 32p more than the price at which they can be bought. The difference between the option price and the intrinsic value is termed time value, which is 3p in the case of the April 600p put options. Time value can be regarded as a payment for the possibility that intrinsic value will increase prior to the date on which the option expires, i.e. the date beyond which it cannot be exercised. If a stockholder exercises an option, only the intrinsic value is received, whereas if the option is sold, both the intrinsic and time values are obtained. It thus makes sense to sell an option in preference to exercising it.

In Table 33.1 the 550p puts have a strike price below the market price of the stock. Therefore, they offer no pay-off upon exercise and have zero intrinsic value. Their prices consist entirely of time value. Put options with strike prices below the market price of the stock are said to be out-of-the-money. When the stock price is equal to the strike price, the option is said to be at-the-money. Put options with strike prices above the stock price (the only ones with intrinsic value) are termed in-the-money.

Long Versus Short Option Positions

Hedging against a price fall can be carried out by means of buying a put option, and protection against a price rise can be obtained from the purchase of a call option. Alternatively, a call option might be written (sold) as a means of protection from a price fall or a put option written as a means of hedging against a price rise. Writing options is the better approach if the price change is relatively modest, whereas buying options is the more effective strategy in the event of a substantial

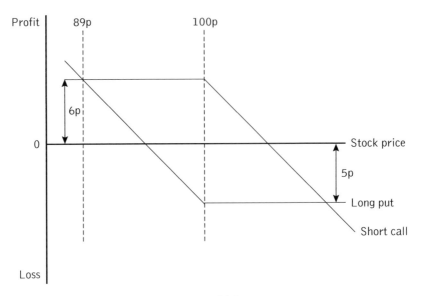

Figure 33.1

movement in the price of the stock. Figure 33.1 compares the purchase of a put option with the sale of a call option. The purchase of a put option constitutes a long put, and the sale of a call option provides a short call position.

In the example illustrated by Figure 33.1, the two options have the same strike price of 100p. The put is priced at 5p and the call at 6p. The long put provides protection against a fall in the stock price below 100p but, considering the premium (option price paid) of 5p, the put option does not confer a net advantage over an unhedged position until the stock price has fallen below 95p. So the long put is beneficial only in the event of a substantial price fall.

By writing the call for 6p, the option price (premium) is received and that receipt can be seen as providing downside protection. A stock price fall from 100p to 94p would leave the hedger no worse off since the loss of 6p on the stock would be offset by the proceeds of selling the option. However, the downside protection is constant in money terms and stock prices below 94p would entail a net loss. Of course, stock prices above 94p would entail a net profit. So the short call is advantageous in the case of a modest stock price fall.

The short call is superior to the long put down to a stock price of 89p. This is demonstrated in Figure 33.1. The net profit from the put option does not exceed that of the call option until the stock price has fallen sufficiently to generate an intrinsic value for the put option of 5p (to offset the put premium) plus 6p (to match the call premium). So the short option position is superior to the long option position until the stock price has moved by the sum of the two option premiums. In this case, a hedger seeking protection from a price fall but anticipating a fall of less than 11p would prefer the short call, whereas a hedger fearing a greater fall would buy a put option.

Writing call options whilst holding the respective shares can alternatively be seen as a means of enhancing portfolio returns. Lofthouse (2001: 418) expresses this point as a potential sales pitch to an investor:

Are there any stocks in your portfolio that you think are fairly valued? If there are, you must be indifferent between holding them or selling them. Imagine a strategy that, if the price of a stock remains much the same or falls, gives you an extra income by way of premium — it's effectively another dividend. If the stock rises and you are forced to sell the stock to meet a call, and you said you were indifferent whether you held it or not, the premium effectively gets you a higher selling price.

The drawback is the limited ability to gain from a rise in the share price.

EXERCISE 33.1

It is 14 November 2005. FTSE 100 Index Options have the prices shown in the table.

Table 33.A

Strike price	Calls	Puts
5,475	31	18

The FTSE 100 stands at 5,480.

(a) How can long and short option positions be used to hedge a portfolio of shares against a market fall (with a view to holding the option contracts to their expiry date)? What would affect the choice between the long and short option positions?

(b) What are the implications of having expectations of volatility that differ from the implied volatilities?

(c) Assuming that the portfolio of shares moves in line with the FTSE 100 (and that the number of option contracts matches the size of the portfolio) what would be the effect of a 20% fall in the FTSE 100, by the option expiry date, on the hedged portfolio?

(d) What would be the effect of a 20% rise in the FTSE 100?

(e) Comment on the results.

(f) What would be the effect of a 20-point fall in the FTSE 100, by the option expiry date, on the hedged portfolio?

(g) What would be the effect of a 20-point rise in the FTSE 100?

(h) Comment on the results.

Answers

(a) Option positions that would provide gains in the event of a market fall are required. Put options could be bought or call options sold. If necessary, the numbers of option contracts would be weighted by the beta of the portfolio. As to the choice between the long put and the

635

short call, the decision is likely to be based on the prospective size of the market decline. The short call is better for relatively small market falls of up to $31 + 18 = 49$ index points (the sum of the option premiums). The long put would be better as a hedge against declines greater than 49 index points.

(b) If the investor believes that the expectations of market volatility implied by an option price is too high, the investor would regard the option as being overpriced. This would deter the investor from buying the option, but would encourage a sale. If the implied volatility were seen as too low, the option would be regarded as underpriced. This would favour a purchase but discourage a sale. So considerations of expected market volatility could influence the choice between long and short option positions.

(c) A 20% fall in the market would reduce the FTSE 100 to 4,384. The long put would provide a pay-off of $5,475 - 4,384 = 1,091$, and a profit of $1,091 - 18 = 1,073$. Adding this profit to the new index gives $4,384 + 1,073 = 5,457$. Hedging by means of buying the put option limits the loss to $5,480 - 5,457 = 23$ index points. There would be a loss of 1,096 from the fall in the market offset by a profit of 1,073 on the option, resulting in a net loss of $1,096 - 1,073 = 23$ index points.

Writing the call option would have yielded a premium receipt of 31 index points. When added to the new index the result is $4,384 + 31 = 4,415$. Hedging by writing the call option has limited the loss to $5,480 - 4,415 = 1,065$ index points. There would be a loss of 1,096 from the fall in the market offset by a profit of 31 from the option resulting in a net loss of $1,096 - 31 = 1,065$ index points.

(d) A 20% rise in the FTSE 100 would take it to 6,576; a rise of 1,096 index points. If the long put had been used as the hedge, a premium of 18 index points would have been paid with the result that the effective rise in the index would have been limited to $6,576 - 5,480 - 18 = 1,078$ index points. There would be a gain of 1,096 index points from the rise in the market offset by a loss of 18 index points from the option leaving a net gain of $1,096 - 18 = 1,078$ index points.

If the short call had been used, there would have been a loss of $6,576 - 5,475 - 31 = 1,070$ from the option. So the gain would have been limited to $6,576 - 5,480 - 1,070 = 26$ index points. There would be a gain of 1,096 index points from the rise in the market offset by a loss of 1,070 from the option resulting in a net gain of $1,096 - 1,070 = 26$ index points.

(e) Since large movements in the market occurred, the long put was superior to the short call both when the market fell and when it rose.

(f) A 20-point fall in the market would reduce the FTSE 100 to 5,460. The long put would provide a pay-off of $5,475 - 5,460 = 15$, and a loss of $18 - 15 = 3$. Subtracting this loss from the new index gives $5,460 - 3 = 5,457$. Hedging by means of buying the put option entails a loss of $5,480 - 5,457 = 23$ index points. There would be a loss from the option (3) in addition to the loss from the fall in the market (20).

Writing the call option would have yielded a receipt of 31 index points. When added to the new index the result is $5,460 + 31 = 5,491$. Hedging by writing the call option has provided a profit of $5,491 - 5,480 = 11$ index points. The premium received from writing the option (31) would exceed the loss from the fall in the market (20) by 11 index points.

(g) A 20-point rise in the FTSE 100 would take it to 5,500. If the long put had been used as the hedge, a premium of 18 index points would have been paid with the result that the effective rise in the index would have been limited to $5,500 - 5,480 - 18 = 2$ index points. The 20 index point gain from the market rise would be offset by an 18 index point loss on the option.

If the short call had been used, there would have been a loss on the option of $5,500 - 5,475 = 25$ index points from the rise in the index offset by the 31 index points received from writing the call giving a net profit from the option of 6 index points. So the rise in the index would have been enhanced by 6 index points to 5,506 index points. The effective rise in the index is 26 index points. There would be a profit from the option (6) in addition to the rise in the market (20).

(h) Since small movements in the market occurred, the short call was superior to the long put both when the market fell and when it rose.

HEDGING ANTICIPATED PURCHASES

Options can be used to hedge intended purchases of stocks. Suppose it is 30 March and that a portfolio manager intends to buy BP shares with funds expected to become available in early April. The current price of BP shares is 568p and the portfolio manager wishes to avoid the risk of having to pay a much higher price. The prices of BP call options are shown in Table 33.1.

The portfolio manager could buy April 600p call options at 5p. Each option contract provides the right, but not the obligation, to buy 1,000 BP shares at a price of 600p per share. The price of the option is 5p per share, which amounts to £50 ($5p \times 1,000$) per option contract.

If when the stock was purchased in April the price were 650p, the portfolio manager could exercise the options and thereby buy stock at 600p. This represents a saving of 50p per share at a premium cost of 5p per share: a net benefit of 45p per share. The effective purchase price would be 605p (strike price plus premium paid).

By exercising an option the hedger obtains its intrinsic value, which is the difference between the stock price and the option's strike price. However the price of an option includes time value in addition to the intrinsic value. If the hedger sold the option, the time value as well as the intrinsic value would be received. The time value might be 2p and hence the sale price of the option would be 52p. The portfolio manager would have bought options for 5p and sold them for 52p. There would have been a profit of 47p per share rather than the 45p profit (intrinsic value minus premium) obtained from exercising the options. The effective price of the shares becomes 603p ($650p - 47p$). The shares are bought in the stock market for 650p (rather than being acquired by exercising the options) and are partially financed by the 47p profit from the options with the result that the net cost is $650p - 47p = 603p$ per share.

If the stock price were 600p or less at the time the stock was purchased, the options held would have no intrinsic value and therefore could not be profitably exercised. However, they would still have time value. For example if the share price were still 568p, the April 600p call options might be selling at 2p. The options would have been bought for 5p and could be sold for 2p. The net cost of 3p (i.e. £30 per contract covering 1,000 shares) compares favourably with the net cost of 5p (£50) incurred if the options were allowed to expire.

EXERCISE 33.2

A fund manager has a portfolio worth £100 million. The portfolio beta is 1.2. Both the FTSE 100 and the FTSE 100 futures are currently 5,000. FTSE 100 futures and options are based on £10 per index point. FTSE 100 at-the-money call options are priced at 20, and at-the-money put options cost 18.

(a) If the fund manager wants to hedge half the portfolio using futures, how many contracts should be used? Should they be bought or sold?

(b) If the futures index subsequently falls by 300 points, what is the profit or loss on the futures?

(c) What could cause the futures hedge to be imperfect?

(d) How could the hedge be carried out with options?

(e) If the FTSE 100 stands at 4,700 when the options expire, what is the profit or loss on the options?

(f) What are the merits of options, relative to futures, as instruments for hedging portfolios of shares?

Answers

(a) The market exposure of the portfolio is $1.2 \times £100$ million $= £120$ million. Half of this value is to be hedged by futures.

£60,000,000/(5,000 × £10) = 1,200 futures contracts.

To hedge against a stock price fall, futures contracts should be sold.

(b) The profit per futures contract is 300 × £10 = £3,000. The profit on 1,200 contracts is £3,000 × 1,200 = £3,600,000.

(c) Basis risk, the indivisibility of contracts, the instability of beta, and the existence of non-systematic risk.

(d) Either stock index put options are bought, or stock index call options are written.

(e) An at-the-money put option would have an intrinsic value of 300 points. The profit per contract would be 300 − 18 = 282 points, i.e. £2,820 per contract (£2,820 × 1,200 = £3,384,000). The profit on the written calls equals the premium received, i.e. 20 points or £200 per contract (£200 × 1,200 = £240,000 on 1,200 contracts).

638

(f)   An advantage of buying options is that profit opportunities are preserved; in this example the fund manager continues to be able to profit from rising share prices if the hedging is carried out by buying put options. A disadvantage of buying options is that a premium (price) must be paid for the options.

An advantage of writing options is that a premium is received. A disadvantage of hedging by writing options is that protection is only partial; writing options is suitable as a hedge against small index falls but not large falls since the protection is limited to the premium received. In the present example, writing calls protects the portfolio against a fall in the index of up to 20 points (i.e. down to 4980), but does not provide an offset against any further falls in the index.

SWITCHING BETWEEN STOCKS WITHOUT TRADING IN STOCKS

There may be occasions when a switch between shares is intended to be very temporary, needs to be carried out extremely quickly, or without affecting expected dividend receipts. In such circumstances there may be advantages in using an options strategy either as a replacement for, or as a means of changing the timing of, the switch. The options strategy would entail constructing a synthetic short position in the stock to be sold and simultaneously establishing a synthetic long position in the stock to be purchased. The synthetic short position eliminates the exposure to the stock that is currently held, whilst the synthetic long position creates an exposure to the stock that the fund manager wants to own.

A synthetic short position is created by buying put options and writing (selling) an equal number of call options with the same strike price and expiry date. The construction of a synthetic short position (short synthetic) is illustrated by Figure 33.2.

The synthetic short position could be looked upon as guaranteeing the sale of shares at the strike price. Consider the case of European-style options (i.e. options that can be exercised only on the expiry date). If the share price at expiry is less than the strike price, the put option is

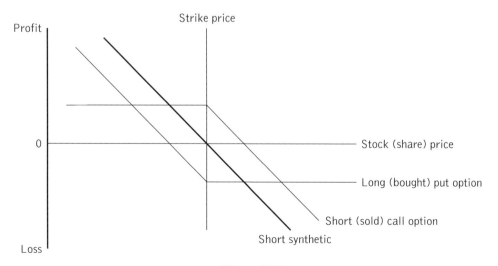

Figure 33.2

exercised and the shares are thereby sold at the strike price. If the share price at expiry exceeds the strike price the holder of the call option would exercise the right to buy shares at the strike price, and hence the writer of the call option (the holder of the short synthetic) sells at the strike price. In either case shares are sold at the strike price. Conversely a synthetic long position could be seen as ensuring the purchase of shares at the strike price.

A synthetic long position is constructed by means of buying call options and writing (selling) an equal number of put options with the same strike price and expiry date. In terms of market exposure the synthetic long position can be regarded as equivalent to buying the stock. The construction of a synthetic long position (long synthetic) is illustrated by Figure 33.3.

If the stock price on the option expiry date were above the option strike price, the call option would be exercised to buy shares at the strike price. If the stock price were below the strike price, the holder of the put option would exercise the right to sell shares with the result that the option writer (the holder of the synthetic long position) buys shares at the strike price. So the structure is equivalent to a forward purchase of shares at the strike price. Whatever happens to the share price, shares are bought at the strike price on the option expiry date. The construction of a synthetic is not dependent upon holding the options until the expiry date. The synthetic position exists even if the intention is to close out the options before the expiry date.

The possibility of constructing synthetic positions in stocks using options is potentially a source of considerable flexibility for fund managers. Switches between stocks can be achieved very quickly. The synthetics may subsequently be unwound as actual stock trades are undertaken, or as the need for a short-term switch disappears. The achievement of a switch without affecting dividend receipts in the near future would be another potential motivation for using the synthetics strategy. The construction of a short synthetic position in a stock also allows a trader to profit from a decline in the stock price, and the construction of a long synthetic can be a means of acquiring a highly leveraged exposure to a stock.

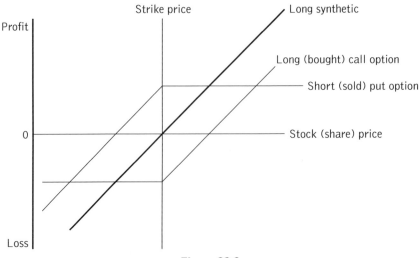

Figure 33.3

EXAMPLE 33.1

Suppose that a fund manager wants to switch from Sainsbury's shares to Tesco shares when Sainsbury's shares stand at 521p and Tesco shares at 563p. The Sainsbury's option prices for the nearby month (earliest expiry date) are as shown in the table.

 Table 33.B

Strike price	Calls	Puts
550	17	46.5

The Tesco option prices for the earliest expiry date are as shown in the second table.

 Table 33.C

Strike price	Calls	Puts
550	21	6

The price of a synthetic position in shares is equal to:

(PV) Strike price + Call price − Put price.

The present value of the strike price [(PV) Strike price] is given by

$K/(1 + rt)$

where K is the strike price, r the interest rate, and t the time to expiry of the option as a fraction of a year. Interest rates at the time were 7.5%. Sainsbury's options had 58 days to expiry; Tesco options had 13 days to expiry.

The synthetic price of Sainsbury's shares was:

$[550/(1 + \{0.075 \times 0.159\})] + 17 - 46.5 = 514$ p.

The synthetic price of Tesco shares was:

$[550/(1 + \{0.075 \times 0.036\})] + 21 - 6 = 563.5$ p.

The fund manager could construct a synthetic short position in Sainsbury's shares, thereby removing the exposure to Sainsbury's shares. Simultaneously a synthetic long position in Tesco shares is created, thereby obtaining an exposure to Tesco shares.

Whilst the price of the Tesco synthetic is close to the actual share price (563.5p as against 563p), the price of the Sainsbury's synthetic is significantly lower than the actual share price (514p as against 521p). This could be explained in terms of a dividend on Sainsbury's shares, prior to the option expiry date, being expected. Indeed this could provide the reason for using the synthetics rather than immediately trading in shares. Switching exposure by means of the synthetic enables the fund manager to retain the right to the forthcoming Sainsbury's dividend. Subsequent to the receipt of the dividend Sainsbury's shares might be sold, Tesco shares purchased, and the synthetics unwound. The synthetics would have been used to achieve the switch between the stocks whilst retaining the right to the forthcoming dividend.

EXERCISE 33.3

It is 14 November 2005. FTSE 100 Index Options, which expire on 28 November, have prices as shown in the table.

Table 33.D

Strike price	Calls	Puts
5,475	31	18

The FTSE 100 stands at 5,480.

(a) How can a synthetic short futures position be used to hedge a portfolio of shares against a market fall?

(b) Assuming that the portfolio of shares moves in line with the FTSE 100 (and that the numbers of option contracts match the size of the portfolio), what would be the effect of a 20% fall in the FTSE 100, by the option expiry date, on the hedged portfolio?

(c) What would be the effect of a 20% rise in the FTSE 100?

(d) Comment on the results.

Answers

(a) Option positions that would provide gains in the event of a market fall are required. Put options would be bought, and call options sold, to produce a synthetic short futures position. If necessary, the numbers of option contracts would be weighted by the beta of the portfolio.

(b) A 20% fall in the market would reduce the FTSE 100 to 4,384. The long put would provide a pay-off of $5,475 - 4,384 = 1,091$. Buying the put and simultaneously writing the call provides the pay-off of 1,091 from the long put and there would have been a net premium receipt of $31 - 18 = 13$ index points. So the outcome would be $4,384 + 1,091 + 13 =$

5,488 index points. There is no loss from the market fall; there is a net gain of 5,488 − 5,480 = 8 index points.

(c) A 20% rise in the FTSE 100 would take it to 6,576, a rise of 1,096 index points. There would have been a loss of 6,576 − 5,475 − 31 = 1,070 index points from the written call option. If the long put and short call had been used together, the loss of 1,070 on the call option would have been incurred. Additionally a premium of 18 index points would have been paid for the put option. So the net rise in the index would have been limited to 6,576 − 5,480 − 1,070 − 18= 8 index points.

(d) Use of the long put and short call together (the synthetic short futures position) virtually eliminated any movement of the FTSE 100. The short synthetic guarantees an index value of 5,488, which represents an 8-point gain relative to the original index level of 5,480.

VERTICAL SPREADS

Vertical spreads provide a strategy for hedging with options at a reduced cost. The cost reduction is achieved by the sale of options alongside purchases. The sales receipts offset the costs of purchase. Vertical spreads involve the simultaneous buying and selling of options on the same underlying share or stock index for the same expiry month but with different strike prices. Figure 33.4 illustrates a bull call spread: bull because it profits from a price rise; a call spread because it is constructed from call options. For clarity of exposition the situation on the expiry date of the options will be considered; in that way the complexity added by time value can be ignored.

The FTSE 100 Index is 4,700.
The FTSE 100 4,725 call is bought at a price of 60 index points.
The FTSE 100 4,825 call is written at a price of 20 index points.
The net price is 60 − 20 = 40 index points (at £10 per index point this amounts to £400).

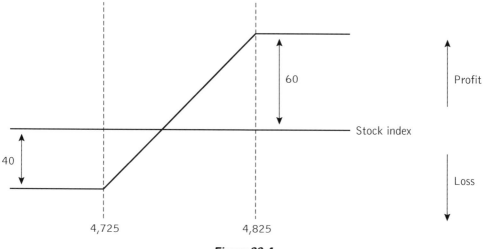

Figure 33.4

Below 4,725 neither option is exercised: the loss is the net premium of 40 index points. The maximum profit occurs above 4,825. The profit from exercising the 4,725 option, minus the loss from exercise of the 4,825 option and minus the initial net premium of 40, equals 60 index points. (If both options are exercised, the intrinsic value of the long call minus the intrinsic value of the short call is $4,825 - 4,725 = 100$.)

Above 4,825 the additional profits from the long 4,725 call are offset by losses from the short 4,825 call. The net profit remains at 60 index points since further gains from the long option, produced by rises in the index, are offset by increased losses from the written option.

Figure 33.5 illustrates a bear put spread: bear because it profits from a price fall and put because it is constructed using put options.

> The FTSE 100 Index is 4,700.
> The FTSE 100 4,725 put is bought at a price of 65 index points.
> A FTSE 100 4,625 put is written at a price of 25 index points.

At stock indices above 4,725 neither option would be exercised and the investor makes a net loss equal to the balance of the premiums: $65 - 25 = 40$ index points. As the stock index falls below 4,725, there is a pay-off from exercising the purchased 4,725 put option (the pay-off equals the intrinsic value). This pay-off increases until it reaches 100 index points, when the stock index is 4,625. The net gain at 4,625, taking account of the net premium, is $100 - 40 = 60$ index points.

If the FTSE 100 falls below 4,625, the 4,625 put will be exercised. Thus as the stock index falls below 4,625, the additional gains from exercising the 4,725 put are cancelled by losses on the 4,625 put leaving the net profit at a constant 60 index points. Below 4,625 both options are exercised. The pay-off from the 4,725 option, minus the intrinsic value of the 4,625 option and minus the net premium paid (40), equals the net profit of 60 index points.

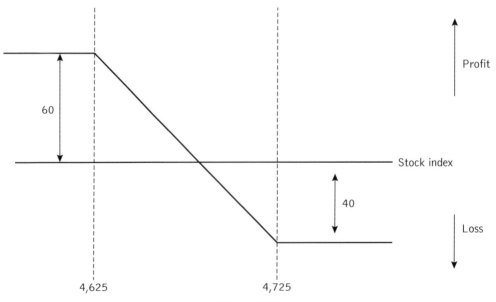

Figure 33.5

6,525   6,725

Figure 33.6

In addition to the bull call spreads and bear put spreads, there are bull put spreads and bear call spreads. Writing a put option with a high strike price (and high premium) and buying a put option with a low strike price (and consequent low premium) creates a bull put spread. A bear call spread involves selling a call option with a low strike price (and high premium) and buying a call option with a high strike price (and low premium).

Vertical spreads provide a relatively low cost means of hedging, but the extent of the hedge is limited. Protection is provided only within a price range. For example in Figure 33.4 there is no upside protection beyond an index level of 4825, and in Figure 33.5 there is no downside protection below 4,625.

OPTION CYLINDERS

Option cylinders provide protection outside a range of prices. They provide insurance against adverse price movements at the cost of foregoing the benefits of advantageous price movements. Figure 33.6 illustrates a short cylinder.

The purchase of a 6,525 put option might be financed by the sale of a 6,725 call option. The result is a zero-cost option, which provides protection against a fall in the index below 6,525 at the cost of foregoing gains from a rise in the index above 6,725.

A long cylinder could be structured by buying a 6,725 call option financed by writing a 6,525 put option, and would provide insurance against index rises above 6,725 at the cost of foregoing gains from falls below 6,525. Of course, when using traded options it is very unlikely that the option premiums would precisely offset each other. Figure 33.7 illustrates a long cylinder.

CRASH OPTIONS

Crash options are designed to give protection against sudden large market falls. Crash options are put options whose pay-offs are typically based on the fall in a stock index on a single day during the life of the option. For example a crash option may have a life of one year and pay the holder a sum of money based on the largest one-day market fall during the year. Longin (2001) pointed out that in 1987, in the United States, such an option would have paid out 20.5% of the notional value of the contract since the market fell 20.5% on 19 October. A standard one-year put option for the year of 1987 would have expired worthless because the market at the end of the year was higher than at the beginning of the year.

Figure 33.7

Crash options are normally cheaper than standard put options since the pay-off is not cumulative over time; it is limited to the size of the market fall on just one day. The value of a crash option comprises a sure value and a time value. At the end of the day of the first market fall, the option acquires some sure value. The sure value can increase only if there is a larger fall on a subsequent day. Crash options normally have daily settlement of the sure value. The sure value is payable to the option holder immediately after the market decline has occurred.

CONCLUSION

Options, as tools of investment management, can achieve outcomes that would otherwise be impossible. Provision of insurance against adverse price changes, whilst retaining the ability to benefit from favourable changes, is one such outcome. There is considerable flexibility available in the achievement of the outcome. The protection against adverse price movements can be relative to a particular price, as is the case when a single option position is taken. Alternatively the protection could be within a range of prices (when an options spread is used), or outside a range of prices (when an options cylinder is used). When using spreads or cylinders, the net cost of the options position can be reduced.

The flexibility goes further in that there is the choice between protection against any adverse price movement and protection only against extreme price movements. The investment manager could choose between hedging the whole value of a portfolio, and hedging part of it. There is also a choice between fixed hedging and delta hedging. The current chapter has considered fixed hedging, which entails holding options to their expiry dates. Chapter 39 on currency derivatives considers delta (dynamic) hedging, which entails using gains from option price movements prior to the option expiry date.

Chapter 34

Structured products

OBJECTIVE

The objective of this chapter is to provide knowledge of:

1. Options funds (guaranteed investment funds).
2. High yield funds (precipice bonds).
3. Bonds with variable principals (structured notes).

Behavioural finance predicts that investors may want investment products that do not match the characteristics of shares, bonds, or deposits. Prospect theory indicates that the pain from losses exceeds the pleasure from gains; this is known as loss-aversion. Loss-aversion suggests that investments, which allow for gains whilst providing protection from losses, would appeal to many investors. Options funds are able to meet this need since they are funds which guarantee that the investment value cannot fall below a specified level (for example the initial sum invested) whilst allowing for gains arising from rises in the stock market.

Another behavioural finance 'bias' is mental accounting. Mental accounting entails the separation of the components of a person's finances into a number of distinct accounts, as opposed to treating the finances as a unified whole. One result of mental accounting can be the separation of investments between their principal values and the incomes from them. The rule of thumb of 'never touch the principal' is an outcome of mental accounting. The possibility of drawing income by selling shares or bonds is rejected on the grounds that the sale of investments reduces the source of future income. This leads to a preference for shares and bonds with high dividend yields when high income is desired. High yield funds go a step further in meeting the desire for high income without selling any of the investment. Such funds enhance yields by selling options and adding the option premiums received to the dividends payable to investors.

Loss-aversion and mental accounting are often seen as preferences rather than as biases. Preferences should be accommodated rather than corrected. Structured products, such as option funds and high yield funds, provide means of accommodating the preferences of investors.

OPTIONS FUNDS (GUARANTEED EQUITY FUNDS)

The Nature of Options Funds

Options funds, or guaranteed equity funds, are a means of providing some of the potential profits from stock market investment whilst guaranteeing the return of the investors' capital. Such funds are marketed under a variety of different names such as guaranteed investment bonds, guaranteed equity bonds, guaranteed investment accounts, and guaranteed capital bonds. They are investments for fixed terms, often five years. These funds typically guarantee the return of at least the initial investment plus a proportion, such as 70%, of any increase in a stock market index.

The opportunity cost, when compared with a bank deposit, is the interest foregone. The opportunity cost, when compared with buying shares, is the proportion of the stock market return that fails to accrue to the investors (typically some of the capital gain and all of the dividends).

Generally the guarantees only apply if the investments are held for the full fixed term. Another potential problem concerns taxation. Many of the funds are subject to income tax rather than capital gains tax. This is a disadvantage for many investors, since it is often the case that an individual is above the threshold for paying income tax but below the threshold for paying capital gains tax.

The Fiduciary Call Approach

An options fund is characterised by upside exposure to a stock index together with a lower limit to the value of the fund. This profile of returns can be achieved in two main ways. One is the fiduciary call, which involves investment in risk-free assets (such as fixed-rate bank deposits, gilt strips, or high-grade zero coupon bonds) and call options. The risk-free assets provide the guaranteed minimum value, while the call options provide the exposure to the stock market.

The fiduciary call approach involves calculating the present value of the guaranteed sum and investing it in fixed-rate bank deposits (or other risk-free assets). This generates the guaranteed sum upon maturity of the fund. The remainder of the fund is used to buy call options. The cost of the downside protection is reduced profit on the upside. Potential returns from a rising stock market are less than would be obtained if the entire fund were to be invested in shares.

Whether options funds perform better than the alternatives, of a bank deposit or investment in shares, depends upon the performance of the stock market. This is illustrated by Exercise 34.1.

EXERCISE 34.1

(a) A fund manager has £1,000,000 and invests £952,381 in a bank deposit for one year at 5% p.a. The remaining £47,619 is used to buy a FTSE 100 at-the-money call option on £900,000 of stock when the FTSE 100 stands at 5,000. The option expires in one year. What is the value of the fund at the end of one year if the FTSE 100 is (i) 4,000, (ii) 5,000, (iii) 6,000, and (iv) 7,000?

(b) How does the investment strategy in (a) compare with (1) investing the £1,000,000 in a bank deposit, and (2) investing the £1,000,000 in a balanced portfolio of FTSE 100 shares?

Answers

(a) (i) £1,000,000, (ii) £1,000,000, (iii) £1,180,000 (the guaranteed £1,000,000 plus 0.9 of the 20% stock price rise), (iv) £1,360,000 (the guaranteed £1,000,000 plus 0.9 of the 40% stock price rise).

(b)

(1) In cases (i) and (ii) the investment strategy in (a) is inferior to the deposit by £50,000 (5% interest on £1,000,000). In cases (iii) and (iv) the strategy in (a) is superior to the deposit by £130,000 and £310,000 respectively (since the deposit of £1,000,000 would grow to £1,050,000).

(2) In case (i) the strategy in (a) is superior to the investment in shares (which would have provided £800,000 plus dividends). In case (ii) the strategy in (a) is inferior to the investment in shares by the amount of the dividend yield on the shares. In case (iii) the investment in shares would have provided £1,200,000 plus dividends, and in case (iv) the share investment would have produced £1,400,000 plus dividends. So in cases (iii) and (iv) the investment in shares would have outperformed the strategy in (a).

The Protective Put Approach

The other main approach to the structuring of options funds is the protective put. This entails holding a portfolio of shares together with put options that guarantee a minimum value of that shareholding. Protective put strategies (sometimes referred to as portfolio insurance) also involve some investment in risk-free assets in order to fully guarantee the minimum value of the fund. The guaranteed value is ensured by a combination of an investment in risk-free assets such as bank deposits, and a lowest possible value of the shareholding based on the strike price of the put options.

In the case of options funds created using the protective put approach, since the guaranteed minimum value is provided from two sources – the investment in risk-free assets and a shareholding combined with put options – it is necessary to use simultaneous equations to calculate the amounts of the constituent components. If M is the guaranteed minimum value, X is the amount to be invested in risk-free assets, K is the option strike price, r is the interest rate on risk-free assets, T is the maturity of the fund, and N is the number of put options (which matches the amount of stock purchased), then:

$$M = X(1 + r)^T + NK$$

i.e. the guaranteed minimum fund value equals the maturity value of the investment in risk-free assets plus the minimum value of the shareholding guaranteed by the put options.

The value of N can be calculated as:

$$N = (V - X)/(S + P)$$

where V is the initial value of the fund, S is the value of stock covered by one option, and P is the price of a put option. N is thus the number of combinations of stock and put option that can be purchased after X has been allocated to investment in risk-free assets. The portfolio of shares purchased would be the stock index portfolio, which is the portfolio of shares comprising all the shares in the index in proportions that correspond to their weightings in the index. The stock index would be that upon which the options are based: for example, the FTSE 100 Index and FTSE 100 options.

The two equations can be simultaneously solved for X and N. In this way, the amount to be invested in risk-free assets can be ascertained together with the number of matched combinations of stock and put option.

EXERCISE 34.2

A fund manager wants to construct an options fund. The value of the portfolio is £10 million and the fund has an investment horizon of one year. The FTSE 100 stands at 4,000, and the 12-month interest rate is 5% p.a. The prices of FTSE 100 options with one year to expiry and a strike price of 4,000 are 250 index points for calls and 200 for puts.

On the basis of the guaranteed minimum value for the fund being £10 million, show how the fiduciary call and protective put approaches can be used to structure the fund. In each case indicate the proportion of any rise in the FTSE 100 that would be received. What are the relative merits of the two approaches?

Answer

At an interest rate of 5% p.a., a deposit of £9,523,809 (£10,000,000/1.05) would provide £10,000,000 at the end of the year. So £9,523,809 is deposited to provide the guaranteed return of capital. This leaves £10,000,000 − £9,523,809 = £476,190 available for the purchase of call options. At £10 per index point each call option costs £2,500. The number of call options that can be bought is £476,190/£2,500 = 190.48. Since option contracts are indivisible (only whole numbers can be bought), the number purchased would be 190. The value of stock to which 190 contracts relates is 4,000 × £10 × 190 = £7,600,000. So the proportion of any increase in the FTSE 100, above 4,000, obtained by the fund would be £7,600,000/£10,000,000 = 0.76, i.e. 76%.

The use of the protective put approach involves the solution of the following simultaneous equations:

$$M = X(1 + r)^T + NK \qquad (1)$$

$$N = (V − X)/(S + P) \qquad (2)$$

$$£10,000,000 = X(1.05)^1 + (N × £40,000) \qquad (1a)$$

$$N = (£10,000,000 − X)/(£40,000 + £2,000) \qquad (2a)$$

Substituting for N in equation (1a) gives:

$$£10,000,000 = X(1.05) + [(£10,000,000 − X)/(£40,000 + £2,000)] × £40,000$$

$$£10,000,000 = X(1.05) + [£10,000,000 × (£40,000/£42,000)] − £40,000X/£42,000$$

£10,000,000 = X(1.05) + £9,523,800 − 0.95238X

£10,000,000 − £9,523,800 = (1.05 − 0.95238)X

£476,200 = 0.09762X

X = £476,200/0.09762 = £4,878,098.80

£4,878,098.80 is put on deposit. The sum available for expenditure on stocks and options is:

V − X = £10,000,000 − £4,878,098.80 = £5,121,901.2.

N = (V − X)/(S + P)   (2)

N = £5,121,901.2/(£40,000 + £2,000)

N = 121.95

Since option contracts are indivisible 122 put option contracts, and £40,000 × 122 = £4,880,000 of stock are purchased. The fund will receive £4,880,000/£10,000,000 = 0.488, i.e. 48.8%, of any rise in the FTSE 100 above 4,000 (the stocks purchased would be the FTSE 100 portfolio).

The fiduciary call approach realises a higher proportion of any rise in the FTSE 100, but the protective put structure benefits from receipt of the dividends on the shares held (whereas the fiduciary call fund entails no receipt of dividends).

EXERCISE 34.3

A fund manager has £20 million for an options fund. The FTSE 100 Index stands at 4,500 points. Five-year European-style at-the-money call options are priced at 700 index points. The five-year risk-free interest rate is 6% p.a.

(a) Construct a fiduciary call options fund (guaranteed investment fund) that guarantees the return of the initial £20 million at the end of a five-year period while providing upside exposure to the FTSE 100 Index. What proportion of the increase in the FTSE 100 would be obtained?

(b) If the objective is to obtain exactly 100% of the increase in the FTSE 100, what return can be guaranteed from the guaranteed investment fund?

Answers

(a) The sum that needs to be deposited now in order to guarantee the return of £20,000,000 in five years is:

£20,000,000/(1.06)^5 = £14,945,163.

The sum available for the purchase of call options is:

£20,000,000 − £14,945,163 = £5,054,837.

The price of a call option contract is:

700 × £10 = £7,000.

The number of call option contracts that can be bought is:

£5,054,837/£7,000 = 722 (rounding down to the nearest whole number).

Each contract would provide a return of £10 from a 1 point rise in the index, so 722 contracts would provide £7,220. A £20,000,000 fund invested wholly in shares (the FTSE 100 portfolio) would provide a percentage increase of:

$$[(4501/4500) - 1] \times 100\% = 0.02222\%.$$

In money terms this amounts to £20,000,000 × 0.0002222 = £4,444.44. So the proportion of the increase in the FTSE 100 is £7,220/£4,444.44 = 1.6245 (i.e. 162.45%).

(b) The closest to obtaining 100% of the rise in the index would come from 444 option contracts. A 1-point rise in the index provides £10 per contract on 444 contracts, which is £4,440.

£4,440/£4,444.44 = 0.999 (i.e. 99.9% of a rise in the index is obtained).

444 call option contracts would cost 444 × 700 × £10 = £3,108,000. This leaves £20,000,000 − £3,108,000 = £16,892,000 available to be deposited to produce the guaranteed sum. The sum guaranteed at the end of five years is:

$$£16,892,000 \times (1.06)^5 = £22,605,306$$

which as an annual rate of return is:

$$(£22,605,306/£20,000,000)^{0.2} - 1 = 0.0248 \text{, i.e. } 2.48\% \text{ p.a.}$$

A return of 2.48% p.a. can be guaranteed.

Since 2003 a new product has become available: Constant Protection Portfolio Insurance (CPPI) funds. These link to a stock index and the investors' money is split between shares and cash. As markets fall shares are sold in order to reduce exposure to the stock market. The reverse happens when markets rise. It is possible to obtain the stock market exposure by using stock index futures rather than shares. One disadvantage is that shares are sold as markets fall, and bought when they rise, with the result that the fund sells at low prices and buys at high prices. Buying high and selling low is a strategy that loses money. However this may be seen as an acceptable cost of obtaining protection against the worst effects of market falls. (In fact the strategy amounts to simulating the purchase of a put option to obtain insurance against a falling market. The buy high/sell low losses are the counterpart of paying an option premium.) There is also the risk that markets may fall so rapidly that there is no opportunity to sell the shares in time to obtain protection. For example during the stock market crash of October 1987 most of the losses occurred in one day so there was little time to unwind shareholdings (and there were few buyers so selling was difficult). In fact this portfolio insurance strategy was suggested as one of the causes of the crash since it entailed selling into a falling market, thereby adding to the downward pressure on share prices.

Break-Even Points

The break-even point of an options fund is the index value that must be reached for the return on the fund to match the return on a risk-free investment (such as a fixed-rate bank deposit). Suppose that the current index value is 5,000, that the fixed five-year interest rate available is 4% p.a., and that the fund guarantees the return of the original sum (without interest). Over five years a sum of £1,000 deposited at 4% p.a. would grow to £1,000 $\times$ $(1.04)^5$ = £1,216.65 (i.e. there is a 21.665% increase). If a fund provides 100% of the increase in the stock index then the break-even index, at the end of five years, is equal to X in the following equation:

X/5,000 = £1,216.65/£1,000

So X is (£1,216.65/£1,000) $\times$ 5,000 = 6,083.25

In other words, a 21.665% increase in the index is required.

If the fund provides less than 100% of the increase in the index, the break-even index is correspondingly higher. If, in the previous example, the fund offered 80% (0.8) of the increase in the index then the break-even point is equal to Y in the following equation:

Y = 5,000 + (6,083.25 − 5,000)/0.8 = 6,354.06

In other words, the index should rise by 21.665/0.8 = 27.081%.

EXERCISE 34.4

A fund manager has £100 million for an options fund. The FTSE 100 Index stands at 5000 points. Five-year European-style at-the-money call options are priced at 500 index points. The five-year risk-free interest rate is 5% p.a.

(a) Use the fiduciary call approach to construct an options fund (guaranteed equity fund) that guarantees the return of the initial £100 million at the end of a five-year period while providing upside exposure to the FTSE 100 Index. What proportion of the increase in the FTSE 100 would be obtained?

(b) What is the break-even point?

(c) If the fund manager aimed to provide a return of 100% of the rise in the FTSE 100, what rate of interest could be guaranteed in addition to matching rises in the index?

(d) How would the answers to (a), (b), and (c) change if the option price were 1,200 index points?

(e) If the FTSE 100 rises to 7,000 over the five years, how do the returns on the options funds compare with investing the £100 million in an index tracker fund (which aims to match movements in the FTSE 100).

Answers

(a) The sum that needs to be deposited now in order to guarantee the return of £100,000,000 in five years is:

£100,000,000/$(1.05)^5$ = £78,352,617.

The sum available for the purchase of call options is:

£100,000,000 − £78,352,617 = £21,647,383.

The price of a call option contract is:

500 × £10 = £5,000.

The number of call option contracts that can be bought is:

£21,647,383 / £5,000 = 4,329 (rounding down to the nearest whole number).

Each option contract would provide a return of £10 from a 1-point rise in the index, so 4,329 contracts would provide £43,290. A £100,000,000 fund invested wholly in shares (the FTSE 100 portfolio) would provide a percentage increase of $[(5,001/5,000) - 1] \times 100\% = 0.02\%$ from a 1-point rise in the index. In money terms this amounts to £100,000,000 × 0.0002 = £20,000. So the proportion of the increase in the FTSE 100 is £43,290/ £20,000 = 2.1645 (i.e. 216.45%).

(b) At 5% p.a. over five years £100,000,000 would grow to:

£100,000,000 × $(1.05)^5$ = £127,628,156

(£127,628,156/£100,000,000) × 5,000 = 1.2762816 × 5,000 = 6,381.408

5,000 + (6381.408 − 5,000)/2.1645 = 5,638 (to the nearest whole number)

(2.1645 is the decimal of 216.45%)

Alternatively

A pay-off of £27,628,156 from 4,329 call option contracts requires an increase in the index of:

£27,628,156/£43,290 = 638 points.

The break-even index is 5,000 + 638 = 5,638 points.

(c) For a fund invested wholly in shares, a 1-point rise in the index returns £20,000. Each option contract returns £10 for a 1-point rise in the index. Matching the rise in the share portfolio requires £20,000/£10 = 2,000 option contracts. The cost of 2,000 contracts is 2,000 × £5,000 = £10,000,000. This leaves £100,000,000 − £10,000,000 = £90,000,000 from the original fund. A deposit of £90,000,000 at 5% p.a. for five years produces £90,000,000 × $(1.05)^5$ = £114,865,340. This is equivalent to a rate of return of:

$(1.1486534)^{0.2} - 1 = 0.0281057$ i.e. 2.81% p.a.

The fund manager could guarantee an interest rate of 2.81% p.a. in addition to matching the rise in the FTSE 100 Index.

(d) The price of a call option contract is:

1,200 × £10 = £12,000

The number of call option contracts that can be bought is:

£21,647,383 / £12,000 = 1,803 (rounding down to the nearest whole number).

The return from a 1-point rise in the index arising from options is £18,030. So the proportion of the return on the FTSE 100 is £18,030 / £20,000 = 90.15%. The options fund receives 90.15% of any rise in the FTSE 100.

The break-even index would be based on an increase in the index of £27,628,156 / £18,030 = 1,532 points (to the nearest whole number). So the break-even point is 5,000 + 1,532 = 6,532.

Since the fund manager cannot provide a return of 100% of the rise in the FTSE 100, there is no possibility of an interest return in addition to matching the rise in the index.

(e) In the case in which 4,329 call option contracts are bought the total return from the options, when the index rises from 5,000 to 7,000, would be 4,329 × £10 × 2,000 = £86,580,000.

In the case in which 1,803 call option contracts are bought, the total return from the options would be 1,803 × £10 × 2,000 = £36,060,000.

If the £100,000,000 were invested in an index tracker fund, the return from share price rises would be $[(7,000-5,000)/5,000] \times £100,000,000 = £40,000,000$. To obtain the total return, dividends should be added. For example if the dividend yield were 3% p.a., the additional return over five years would be $(1.03)^5 - 1 = 0.1593$ i.e. 15.93% (£15,930,000). If the dividends were reinvested in shares, this additional return would be further boosted by the share price rises. The options funds would not provide the additional returns from dividends.

EXHIBIT 34.1

CLOSE UK ESCALATOR 100 FUND (31 AUGUST 2007)

Fund objective:

The Close Escalator 100 Fund is a protected unit trust which has been designed to provide returns linked to stockmarket growth with 100% capital protection in the event of a fall. It is a lower risk investment, suitable for investors tempted by stockmarket returns, but who are unwilling to risk loss of capital should the stockmarket fall.

The 100% capital protection was on a quarterly basis with the quarter dates being the third Fridays of March, June, September, and December. There was also instant access to funds, without penalty.

Charges: Initial   3%
                 Annual   1%
Benchmark: FTSE 100 Index
Fund size: £136.4 million

CLOSE UK ESCALATOR 95 FUND (31 AUGUST 2007)

Fund objective:

The Close Escalator 95 Fund is a protected unit trust which has been designed to provide returns linked to the growth of the FTSE 100 Share Index. With 95% protection from falls, the fund is suitable for investors tempted by stockmarket returns, but who are unwilling to risk an unspecified amount should the stockmarket fall.

The 95% capital protection was on a quarterly basis with the quarter dates being the third Fridays of March, June, September, and December. There was also instant access to funds, without penalty.

Charges: Initial   5%
                 Annual   1%

Benchmark: FTSE 100 Index

Fund size: £46.9 million

Source: Close Fund Management Limited.

With reference to Exhibit 34.1, it would appear that in the case of the Escalator 100 the investor could not lose money and that the gain made during a quarter became guaranteed in subsequent quarters. The guaranteed fund value in a quarter would be the value reached at the end of the previous quarter. The initial investment and the subsequent quarterly gains were guaranteed.

In the case of the Escalator 95 it was possible to lose 5% of the investment in a quarter, so that in a worst case scenario the value of the investment could fall by 5% in each of successive quarters. However in the event of market rises, the higher values become those to be protected in subsequent quarters.

The cost of protection (presumably using options) would be much less in the case of the Escalator 95 than for the Escalator 100. This may explain why the recorded actual performance over the previous eight quarters was 10.3% for the Escalator 100 but 25.7% for the Escalator 95.

If protection had been obtained by buying put options, the out-of-the-money options used for the Escalator 95 would have been cheaper than the at-the-money options bought for the Escalator 100 fund.

If protection had been obtained by combining money market investments with call options, the need to deposit enough to guarantee 95%, rather than 100%, of the fund would release much more cash for the purchase of options. Since more money would have been available for the purchase of call options, the profit prospects of the Escalator 95 would have been enhanced.

Options Funds as Disaster Insurance

Retail investors do not normally have access to long-term options. Options funds provide indirect access to long-term options. In the case of the fiduciary call approach, the investor buys a long-term call option combined with a money market investment (e.g. bank deposit). In the case of the protective put approach, the investor buys a long-term put option combined with part of a portfolio of shares.

Another possibility might be a long-term put option combined with a money market investment. In this case profits would arise from market falls rather than from rises. Such a structure could be attractive to investors who seek protection from an extreme fall in the stock market; in other words, disaster insurance. Since retail investors are not normally able to acquire long-term options directly, this structured product would provide indirect access to long-term put options. Exercise 34.5 illustrates the use of such a structured product for disaster insurance.

EXERCISE 34.5

The FTSE All-Share Index is currently 2,800 points. Five-year put options with a strike price of 2,100 are available for 101 index points. The five-year interest rate is 5% p.a.

(a) If a fund manager wanted to create an options fund that provides profits in the event of a fall in the index below 2,100, how could the fund be structured so that the initial investment is guaranteed to be returned after five years?

(b) What proportion of the fall below 2,100 would be realised as profit?

(c) If an investor spends £1,000 on the fund, what would be the sum returned to the investor after five years if the index value falls to 1,400 points?

(d) What would be the sum returned if the index fell to 700 points?

(e) Why might an institutional fund manager want to construct such a fund?

Answers

(a) Consider an investment of £28,000. If £28,000 is to be guaranteed for five years hence, the sum to be deposited at 5% p.a. is:

$£28,000/(1.05)^5 = £21,938.7$
£21,938.7 invested at 5% p.a. realises £28,000 at the end of five years.

The sum available for expenditure on options is:

$£28,000 - £21,938.7 = £6,061.3$

At £10 per index point each option contract costs $101 \times £10 = £1,010.$

So $£6,061.3/£1,010 = 6$ (to the nearest whole number) options can be bought.

(b) Since six options are bought, the proportion of any fall below 2,100 received as gains is 600%.

(c) There would be a pay-off from each option of 700 $(2,100 - 1,400)$ index points. The pay-off from six options would be $6 \times 700 = 4,200$ index points. In addition, the original 2,800 is guaranteed by the deposit. So the investor would receive:

$[(4,200 + 2,800) / 2,800] \times £1,000 = [7,000 / 2,800] \times £1,000 = £2,500.$

(d) There would be a pay-off from each option of 1,400 (2,100 − 700) index points. The pay-off from six options would be 6 × 1400 = 8,400 index points. In addition, the original 2,800 is guaranteed by the deposit. So the investor would receive:

[(8,400 + 2,800)] / 2,800] × £1,000 = [11,200 / 2,800] × £1,000 = £4,000.

(e) An institutional investor might create, and market, such an options fund as a form of disaster insurance. Retail investors might buy such an investment as a means of obtaining protection against extreme falls in the stock market. Effectively the price paid for the insurance, by the retail investor, is the interest that would otherwise have been obtained on the sum invested in the fund.

USE OF EXOTIC OPTIONS AND OPTION COMBINATIONS

The examples above used simple options. However the options used in options funds could be exotic options. In particular investors might be offered protection from a sharp fall in the index towards the end of the investment period. For example a five-year guaranteed equity bond may be on course to provide a good return when, a few months before maturity, a stock market crash wipes out all of the gain in the stock index.

Three possibilities would be Asian options, cliquet options, and ladder options. In the case of an Asian option the return is based on an average of experienced stock indices rather than the index at the end of the investment period. For example when using the fiduciary call approach, the average of the stock indices at the end of each of the five years could be used as the basis for assessing the final value of a five-year bond.

A cliquet option is effectively a series of options. In the case of a five-year bond, which uses the fiduciary call approach, there could be a new option for each of the five years. At the end of each year any profits from that year's option is added to the sum that is guaranteed. A new option, with a strike price matching the new level of the index, would then become operational. The investor is protected against a substantial fall in the stock market to the extent that the option profits from previous years would have been added to the guaranteed sum.

A ladder option would lock in profits when the stock index reaches pre-specified levels. For example the fund may be created when the stock index is 5,000, using call options with a strike price of 5,000. It may be pre-specified that, if the index reaches 6,000, profits from the first option will be added to the guaranteed sum. New call options with a strike price of 6,000 would then become operational. The addition of the profits from the first option to the guaranteed sum provides investors with some protection against a substantial fall in the stock market.

EXERCISE 34.6

An investment, described as a Capital Guaranteed Bond, is offered to retail investors. The bond has an initial maturity of three years, and no money may be withdrawn during that period. For every

£1,000 invested the bond would return £1,000 if the FTSE 100 is below its initial value at the end of the three years or £1,250 if the FTSE 100 equals, or exceeds, its initial value at the end of the three years. When the bond is issued the three-year interest rate is 5% p.a.

(a) How can the provider structure the bond?

(b) Is it a good investment?

(c) In what ways is the pay-off dependent on the rise in the FTSE 100?

Answers

(a) The bond could be structured by depositing £1,000/$(1.05)^3$ = £863.84 per £1,000 invested. This guarantees that £1,000 will be available after three years. In addition a FTSE 100 binary call option would be bought. The binary option is an all-or-nothing option, which pays a fixed sum of money in the event of the FTSE 100 exceeding a particular value. In the present case the binary option pays £250, at the end of three years, so long as the FTSE 100 at least equals its initial value.

(b) The return on the bond, in the event of £1,250 being received, is equivalent to $(1.25)^{1/3} - 1$ = 0.0772, i.e. 7.72% p.a. From the perspective of statistical expectation, this is superior to the 5% p.a. available on three-year deposits if the probability of the FTSE 100 falling over a three-year period is less than $(7.72 - 5.0)/7.72 = 0.3523$, i.e. 35.23%. Historically three-year declines in the FTSE 100 have been less frequent than 35.23%. If the investor is not too concerned about the risk of receiving a return of 0% p.a., the bond appears to be a good investment.

(c) The pay-off is not dependent upon a rise in the FTSE 100, but it is dependent on the FTSE 100 not falling. The £250 return is based on the expectations, of the seller of the binary option, concerning the statistical distribution of future values of the FTSE 100. The bond converts the expectations of the seller of the option, concerning the distribution of the future FTSE 100, into a distribution of interest rates (the distribution comprising the values of 0% p.a. and 7.72% p.a.)

In Chapter 33 on hedging with options, a form of option combination, often referred to as a cylinder option, was described. Option cylinders provide insurance against adverse price movements at the cost of foregoing the benefits of advantageous price movements. Figure 34.1 illustrates a short cylinder.

The purchase of a 5,875 put option might be financed by the sale of a 6,625 call option (the sale receipts may not necessarily equal the purchase cost). The result is a cylinder option, which provides protection against a fall in the index below 5,875 at the cost of foregoing gains from a rise in the index above 6,625. The options may subsequently be replaced by options with different strike prices so that the strike prices continue to be on either side of the spot index. For example in the event of the index rising above 6,625, the put option may be replaced by one with a strike price of 6,250 and the call option replaced by one with a strike price of 7,000.

Figure 34.1

EXHIBIT 34.2   FAMILY SAFETY NET STOCKMARKET UNIT TRUST (30 JUNE 2007)

INVESTMENT OBJECTIVE

To provide long-term capital growth. It is the Manager's policy to achieve that objective by selecting a diversified portfolio of shares of companies being primarily those included in the FTSE 100 Index. The Manager will enter into appropriate derivative transactions so as to enable the Trust to have the benefit of continuous downside protection.

Benchmark: FTSE 100
Fund size: £10.7 million

Initial charge: 5.54%
Annual management charge: 1.5%

ACTIVITY

The Trust's portfolio of equities is designed to closely mirror the return of the FTSE 100 Index, with a derivative overlay to protect the portfolio when equity markets fall. The effect of this overlay is to also cap the potential for gain during periods of rising markets. In January the Trust rolled over its derivative exposure into higher strike price puts and calls to lock in the gains in the index during 2006. At the same time the equity holdings in the portfolio were rebalanced to more closely match the constituents of the FTSE 100 Index.

Table 34.A

Major holdings (percentages of the fund)	
HSBC Holdings	7.06
BP	6.24
Vodafone Group	5.58
GlaxoSmithKline	4.90
Royal Dutch Shell 'A'	4.68

DERIVATIVE DISCLOSURE (ABRIDGED)

The Trust has purchased a put option, this means that the Trust's capital exposure is restricted. Should the index of leading shares as measured by the FTSE 100 Index fall beneath 5,897.51 the Trust's capital losses resulting from this fall will be matched by gains from the put option. Similarly the Trust's gains are limited through it writing a call option. This means that should the FTSE 100 Index rise above 6,605.21 the Trust's gains will be restricted due to losses on the call option.

Source: Family Investment Management Limited.

HIGH YIELD FUNDS (COVERED CALL FUNDS/PRECIPICE BONDS/SCARPS)

Another use of options, in the structuring of funds, is their use in enhancing income. In some high yield funds, options are written and the premiums received are used to enhance the income paid to investors. This is likely to be at the cost of the capital value of the funds. Such funds are illustrated in exercises 34.7, 34.8, and 34.9. At the time of writing, options that enhance income by writing call options are being marketed as a 'new' form of investment and are being called 'covered call funds' (Richards 2007). In some cases the writing of call options is accompanied by buying out-of-the-money put options in order to give some protection against share price falls. It is often the case with structured products that 'new' investment ideas are really repackaged old ones.

The CBOE (Chicago Board Options Exchange) publishes an index based on a covered call strategy. The strategy writes S&P 500 call options against the S&P 500 stock index and the index is called the CBOE S&P 500 Buy-Write (BXM) index. Feldman and Roy (2005) found that this index outperformed the S&P 500 index and suggested that this could be because option prices were higher than might be expected on the basis of option pricing models (in other words there appeared to be unjustifiably high implied volatility). They suggested that call option buyers may be systematically overestimating the value of call options and that such overestimation is consistent with behavioural finance biases such as overconfidence. Buyers of call options are likely to be more confident than other investors; a level of confidence evidenced by a desire to take geared (leveraged) positions. If this behavioural explanation for high option prices is correct, the additional return from the BXM buy-write strategy could be seen as a monetisation of the overconfidence bias.

When a high yield fund writes stock index put options, a decline in the relevant stock index below the strike price can cause a dramatic fall in capital value. The loss from the written put options adds to the loss on the portfolio. In consequence, high yield funds that write put options are often referred to as precipice bonds (the value of the investment can fall off a precipice).

EXERCISE 34.7

A high yield fund has £10,000,000 in a balanced portfolio of FTSE 100 shares. The dividend yield of 3% p.a. is added to by way of the premium receipts from writing options. The FTSE 100 stands at 5,000 and the investment horizon is one year. The fund manager writes European-style options that expire in one year. FTSE 100 option prices are shown in the table.

Table 34.B

Strike price	Calls	Puts
4,900	315	205
5,000	250	240
5,100	215	305

What would the income yield be if the equity exposure were matched by written:

(a) out-of the-money call options,

(b) at-the-money call and put options,

(c) out-of-the-money call and put options?

(d) What are the risks to investors in these three cases?

Answers

(a) 215/5,000 = 4.3. The total income yield becomes 3% + 4.3% = 7.3% (dividends plus option premium receipts).

(b) (250+240)/5,000 = 9.8. The total income yield becomes 3% + 9.8% = 12.8%.

(c) (215+205)/5,000 = 8.4. The total income yield becomes 3% + 8.4% = 11.4%.

(d) In the case of (a) the investor risks losing part of any increase in share prices so that long-term capital growth is reduced. In the case of (b) upside potential is lost and downside risk is increased. In the case of (c), upward movements are restricted and downward movements may be exaggerated. In all three cases, the increased income yield could be at the expense of the capital value of the fund.

EXERCISE 34.8

The FTSE 100 stands at 4,375. FTSE 100 option prices, with a year to maturity, are as shown in the table.

Table 34.C

Strike price	Calls	Puts
4,225	270	60
4,525	80	180

(a) If the holder of a balanced portfolio of FTSE 100 shares takes the view that 4,525 is a satisfactory selling price, and 4,225 a suitable buying price, what strategy might be undertaken?

(b) If the option contracts match the value of the stock portfolio, what is the enhancement to the rate of yield on the portfolio provided by the use of this strategy?

Answers

(a) A short strangle could be used. The investor might write puts with a strike price of 4,225, and would buy stocks at that level if the index falls below it and the puts are exercised. Calls are written with a strike price of 4,525. The investor would then sell at 4,525 in the event of the options being exercised.

(b) The options provide a total of $80 + 60 = 140$ index points of income. This amounts to a rate of return of $140/4,375 = 0.032$ i.e. 3.2%. This is the enhancement to the rate of return otherwise obtained on the portfolio of shares.

EXERCISE 34.9

The FTSE All-Share Index is currently 2,800 points. Five-year put options with a strike price of 2,100 are available for 90 index points. Five-year put options with a strike price of 2,800 are available for 320 index points. A fund manager decides to write put options in order to enhance portfolio returns. If the number of options written matches the size of the portfolio, what is the enhancement to portfolio returns in the cases of using (a) the 2,100 strike price options, and (b) the 2,800 strike price options? (c) Compare the risks of the two cases.

Answers

(a) Writing the 2,100 strike price options provides an addition to the portfolio return of $90/2,800 = 0.0321$ (i.e. 3.21%). This relates to a five-year period. The annual enhancement to return is:

$$(1.0321)^{0.2} - 1 = 0.0063 \text{ (i.e. } 0.63\% \text{ p.a.)}$$

(b) Writing the 2,800 strike price options provides an addition to the portfolio return of $320/2,800 = 0.1143$ (i.e. 11.43%). This relates to a five-year period. The annualised enhancement to return is:

$$(1.1143)^{0.2} - 1 = 0.0219 \text{ (i.e. 2.19\% p.a.)}$$

(c) In the case of writing the 2,100 strike price put options, there would be a loss from the options if there were a substantial fall in the stock market. Any fall below 2,100 would entail an option loss, which is additional to the loss on the portfolio of stocks. A 50% fall in the market to 1,400 would entail a loss on the written put options of 700 index points ($2,100 - 1,400$), which would take the total loss to 2,100 index points ($1,400 + 700$). In total 75% of the original investment would be lost (this ignores the premium receipts).

In the case of writing the 2,800 strike price put options, any fall in the stock market below the current 2,800 index points would entail a loss on the options that adds to the loss on the portfolio. If the portfolio falls in line with the stock index, the options would double the portfolio loss. If the stock market fell by 50%, the original investment fund would be reduced to zero (this ignores the premium receipts).

Between March 2000 and March 2003 the UK stock market approximately halved in value and many investors in high yield (precipice) bonds lost the whole of their investments.

The Financial Services Authority has given precipice bonds the alternative name of scarps (structured capital-at-risk products). There is a common characteristic amongst them of written options, particularly put options. They may vary as to whether the rest of the investment is in shares or cash. It may be that the put options are deeply out-of-the-money. This means that stock prices (and stock indices) have to fall substantially before losses arise from the written options. In the past this feature seems to have led some financial advisers to sell scarps as low risk products, on the grounds that such large falls in the stock market were unlikely. Unfortunately the heavy fall of the period 2000–3 (from peak to trough the FTSE 100 lost more than half its value) brought about losses from written put options that completely wiped out the value of some funds. So funds sold as low risk turned out to be very high risk.

A variation on the high yield theme takes the form of catastrophe bonds, which are used as insurance against natural disasters such as hurricanes and earthquakes (Vaugirard 2003). Buyers of the bonds invest money, which the intermediary uses to acquire government bonds. Organisations seeking insurance against disaster pay annual premiums, which the intermediary also uses to buy government bonds. At the end of the period of insurance, if no natural disaster has occurred, the bondholders receive all the proceeds of the investments. These comprise both the accumulated investment value of the initial investment, and the accumulated value from investing the insurance premiums. The bondholders obtain an investment return, which is enhanced by investing insurance receipts. In the event of the disaster occurring, the proceeds of the investments accrue to the organisation buying insurance. In effect the buyers of catastrophe bonds are writing options on the occurrence of natural disasters, and payment for the options is received in the form of an enhancement to the accumulated final investment value.

BONDS WITH VARIABLE PRINCIPALS (STRUCTURED NOTES)

A broad category of structured products comprises bonds with derivative features, which are based on other asset classes. These products are similar to other bonds except that instead of the principal sum to be repaid upon redemption being a fixed sum of money, the sum to be repaid is linked to an asset or commodity price.

The principal may be linked to a currency price, an oil price, the gold price, a stock index, an index of house prices, or one of a number of other prices or indices. The link could be through a forward contract, an option, or a more complex derivative position such as an option spread.

A bond could be issued with fixed annual coupon payments, and with a specified maturity date, but with a principal repayment that is linked to a house price index. Such a bond may be attractive to an investor who wants exposure to the UK property market without actually owning a property (perhaps an expatriate worker who intends to return to the UK in the future). One problem for the issuer of such a bond is the inability to hedge the inherent risk. If house prices rise more strongly than expected, the issuer of the bond would need to meet high redemption payments. The issuer could address this matter by issuing both bull and bear bonds. There is not only an issue of bonds that provide gains from rises in house prices (bull bonds), but also an issue that provides gains from price falls (bear bonds). The bear bonds would have principal repayments that are inversely related to house price movements (these may be attractive to investors who feel that they are overexposed to the housing market). The issue of both bull and bear bonds leaves the issuer with no net exposure to the housing market.

Where an asset or commodity has a derivatives market, the bond issuer has less need to simultaneously issue bull and bear bonds. For example an issuer could sell bonds with principal repayments linked to an oil price, and hedge the resulting exposure to the oil price by taking offsetting positions in oil forwards or futures.

The principal repayment could be linked to a price, or index, whilst guaranteeing that the principal repayment would not fall below a specified sum of money. In that case the principal repayment would entail an option. Effectively the bondholder would have a bond plus an option. At redemption the investor would receive a predetermined fixed sum of money plus a sum based on, for example, the increase in an index of share prices. The issuer might hedge its risk by buying call options. The cost of these options would be passed on to the bond investors. The investors might pay for the options by way of accepting reduced coupon receipts.

The attraction of variable principal bonds to investors would include the ability to gain exposure to a market, where such exposure may be difficult by other means. Such bonds could, alternatively, provide convenient means of hedging existing exposures. The attraction to the issuer would be the ability to borrow at favourable rates. If the issuer caters for the needs of investors, the investors would be willing to lend at lower coupon rates.

Structured funds can be constructed without the use of options. Consider the example in Exercise 34.10.

EXERCISE 34.10

A fund manager offers a structured retail investment with the following characteristics. The investment is for five years, there is a guaranteed 6.25% on half the investment, the other half is paid a return equal to half the increase in the FTSE 100, and there is a guarantee that the payment at the end of the five years cannot be less than the initial investment.

The fund manager can invest in a five-year bond at 5.25% p.a., and the expected rate of dividend yield on the FTSE 100 is 3% p.a.

(a) How can the fund manager construct the fund?

(b) What is the expected profit for the fund manager, and the expected cost to the retail investor?

(c) What is the retail investor paying for?

Answers

(a) The investment pays half the increase in the FTSE 100 on half the value of the fund. This is the same as paying the whole of the increase in the FTSE 100 on a quarter of the fund. This can be provided by investing a quarter of the fund in an index tracker. The remaining three-quarters can be invested in the bond at 5.25% p.a. So for every £1,000 made available to the fund manager, bonds to the value of £750 can be bought. The remaining £250 is invested in the index tracker fund.

(b) By the end of the five years the value of the investment in bonds would be £750 × $(1.0525)^5$ = £750 × 1.29155 = £968.66. The £250 invested in an index tracker fund is expected to provide a dividend yield of 3% p.a. in addition to the capital gain from the increase in the FTSE 100. The dividend yield is expected to provide £250 × 0.15 = £37.5, which would also attract interest. If interest rates were 5% p.a., the interest accruing would be a little over £2. The value of the fund, excluding the index tracker, would be (a little over):

£968.66 + £37.5 + £2 = £1,008.16.

So there is no need to buy an option to guarantee the return of the £1,000 invested. The value of the fund, inclusive of the index tracker, would be:

£1,008.16 + £250 + the capital gain from £250 invested in the index tracker fund
= £1,258.16 + the capital gain from £250 invested in the index tracker fund.

The retail investor is due to receive 6.25% p.a. on £500 (for every £1,000 invested). This amounts to:

£500 × $(1.0625)^5$ = £500 × 1.35408 = £677.04.

In addition there would be half the rate of rise in the FTSE 100 on £500. This amounts to returning £500 plus the capital gain on the £250 invested in the index tracker fund. So the total accruing to the retail investor is:

£677.04 + £500 + the capital gain from £250 invested in the index tracker fund
= £1,177.04 + the capital gain from £250 invested in the index tracker fund.

The expected profit for the fund manager is:

£1,258.16 + the capital gain from £250 invested in the index tracker fund
minus £1,177.04 + the capital gain from £250 invested in the index tracker fund.

= £1,258.16 − £1,177.04 = £81.12.

So for every £1,000 invested the expected profit for the fund manager is £81.12. The present value of £81.12 should be compared with the investment of £1,000 so that they both relate to the same point in time. Using the bond yield as the rate of discount, the present value of £81.12 is:

£81.12/$(1.0525)^5$ = £62.81.

This is both the profit to the fund manager and the cost to the investor (note that the profit to the fund manager will be reduced to the extent that commission is paid to financial advisers who sell the fund to their clients).

(c) The retail investor is paying £62.81 (for each £1,000 invested) for the expertise of the fund manager in the construction of the structured fund, in addition to paying for the underlying investments.

COLLATERALISED DEBT OBLIGATIONS AND THE SUB-PRIME MORTGAGE CRISIS

A mortgage lender could package a number of mortgages together and sell the package to a bank or institutional investor. If a bank were to buy the portfolio of mortgages, it might split the portfolio into tranches. For example there could be four tranches of equal size. Each tranche might receive an equal proportion of interest receipts but get a different priority as to order of receipt of capital repayments. Tranche A might receive all capital repayments by the borrowers until it is fully repaid. Next the capital repayments are paid to the holders of tranche B, and so on. Effectively tranche A is a short maturity asset, and subsequent tranches have progressively longer maturities. Tranche D, which is the final tranche to be retired, has the longest maturity. Tranche D is also the most subject to default risk. To the extent that some mortgage borrowers fail to repay the capital, the holders of tranche D are most at risk. If a quarter of borrowers were to default on their mortgages, the holders of tranche D could lose all of their investment. It could be the case that some of the mortgage loans were to sub-prime borrowers, who are borrowers with poor credit ratings. Such sub-prime borrowers are the most likely to default. If the portfolio of mortgages includes some sub-prime mortgages, holders of tranche D have very risky assets.

The sub-prime mortgage crisis of summer 2007 entailed such Collateralised Debt Obligation (CDO) structures. Defaults on sub-prime mortgages led to losses for the holders of the risky tranches of CDOs. Since banks did not know which other banks and institutional investors held risky CDOs, they became reluctant to lend to any financial organisation. That was a credit crunch. The credit crunch was worsened by the inability of mortgage lenders to sell their packages of mortgage debts. Sales of such packages funded further mortgage lending. Buyers of the packages became reluctant to buy because of the risks of default. When the mortgage lenders were unable to sell the packages, they were restricted in their ability to make new mortgage loans.

Some hedge funds had borrowed in order to buy the risky tranches of CDOs. This leveraged buying yielded high returns because the interest on the risky CDOs was much higher than the interest on the money borrowed to buy them. When mortgage defaults removed value from the CDOs, the hedge funds made losses. The banks, which had lent to the hedge funds, demanded repayment of their loans. The hedge funds sold assets, such as shares, in order to repay the loans. In consequence stock markets fell. A number of hedge funds found that their liabilities exceeded their assets and hence failed with the effect that the investors in those hedge funds lost all of their investments.

A number of banks and hedge funds had increased the risks by using carry trades. That involved borrowing in a low interest rate currency, typically the Japanese yen, in order to fund the purchase of high-yielding US dollar CDOs. When problems emerged with CDOs attempts were made to unwind the carry trades. Unwinding the carry trades required the purchase of Japanese yen in order to repay the loans denominated in Japanese yen. The increased demand for the yen caused the value of the yen to rise against the US dollar. So the problems faced by banks and hedge funds were worsened by the rise in the value of their liabilities (yen debts) relative to the value of their assets (dollar CDOs) associated with the adverse changes in the yen/dollar exchange rate.

CONCLUSION

Options provide the means to structure investment packages tailored to the specific needs of investors. Options funds, which provide gains from rising stock markets whilst protecting against losses, could suit loss-averse investors. Prospect theory indicates that many investors are loss-averse, such that they are prepared to forego some potential gains in order to avoid losses.

High yield funds use the receipts from the sale of options to enhance the income available to investors, albeit at the possible cost of capital value. Such funds could appeal to investors who require a high income whilst exhibiting mental accounting between capital and income. The mental accounting results in a 'never touch the capital' attitude based on the perception that erosion of the capital reduces future income potential.

Structured products are widely offered by institutional investors to retail consumers. They have a very wide variety of forms. Most make use of options in order to achieve risk-return characteristics that would be impossible without options.

Chapter 35

Warrants, convertibles, and split-caps

OBJECTIVE

The objective of this chapter is to provide knowledge of:

1. Warrants.
2. Convertible bonds (convertibles).
3. Split-capital investment trusts.

WARRANTS

Warrants are long-term options. They may have expiry dates that lie as much as five years or more in the future (in contrast to stock options which often have a maximum life of nine months). Most warrants are issued by the company upon whose shares they are based. If they are exercised, the company will issue new shares. So, unlike options, warrants are usually used as a means of raising corporate finance. The issuing company receives the money from the sale of the warrants and subsequently receives the money paid upon exercise. In contrast to options, warrants entail the expansion of the number of shares in issue. This can be to the disadvantage of existing shareholders in that future profits are divided among a larger number of shares (this is known as dilution); in consequence dividends per share may be reduced.

Warrants are often attached to newly issued corporate bonds when the warrants are issued. The presence of the warrants renders the bonds more attractive to investors, and hence the issuing company can raise money on more advantageous terms in that it needs to pay a lower rate of interest (a lower coupon rate) than would otherwise be the case. In most instances, the warrant is detachable from the host bond and can be traded in its own right. Some warrants are issued naked, that is without the presence of corporate bonds. Since warrants pay no dividend or coupon, they provide an issuing company with a source of finance that involves no servicing costs. Servicing costs (dividend payments) do not arise until the warrants are exercised.

Covered Warrants

Covered warrants (sometimes called third-party warrants) might be written without any involvement of the company on whose stock the warrants are based. They do not entail the issue of new shares upon exercise. Covered warrants may be either calls or puts, whereas other warrants tend to be calls. Many covered warrants are written on stock indices or foreign currencies.

The Capital Fulcrum Point

The capital fulcrum point is the minimum annual percentage increase in the share price that makes it worthwhile to hold a warrant on a share rather than the share itself; it is the rate at which percentage returns on the warrant overtake the percentage returns on the share. Share price rises greater than the capital fulcrum point render the warrants preferable to the shares. The rate of share price rise up to the warrant expiry date is the relevant rate.

The existence of a capital fulcrum point arises from two factors: (1) the existence of time value and (2) the effect of gearing. The increase in intrinsic value, caused by the share price rise, must exceed the loss in time value resulting from the passage of time. So the share price must rise at a particular rate simply for the holder of the warrant to break even. There would be a further rise in the share price required for the gain on the warrant to catch up with the gain on the share. This catching up is possible because of the gearing offered by the warrant.

The formula for the capital fulcrum point is:

$$\text{CFP} = \{[k/(s - w)]^{1/t} - 1\} \times 100\%$$

where CFP is the capital fulcrum point, k is the strike price of the warrant, s is the share price, w is the price of the warrant, and t is the number of years to the expiry date of the warrant.

For example suppose that the strike price is 100, the current share price is 145, the price of the warrant is 80, and expiry is in five years. Application of the formula provides a capital fulcrum point of 9% p.a. If the share price rises at a faster rate, the warrant is the better investment. If the share price increases at a slower rate, the share provides the higher percentage rate of return.

CONVERTIBLES

A convertible might be looked upon as a corporate bond with an attached warrant (which cannot be detached from the bond). Convertibles are often referred to as convertible bonds (or convertible unsecured loan stock, since most are unsecured) and involve the right to convert the bonds into shares at specified rates and points in time. The investor pays nothing to convert apart from surrendering the convertible bond. The period prior to the first possible date for conversion is known as the rest period.

The usual arrangement is for conversion into the shares of the company, which issues the convertible bond. Occasionally the conversion is into the shares of a different company, in which case the instrument is called an exchangeable bond. Some convertibles provide the right to convert to other bonds rather than shares. Convertible preference shares are preference shares with the right to convert to ordinary shares.

The number of shares for which the convertible bond can be exchanged is referred to as the conversion rate. So, for example, the convertible may allow the conversion of £100 par (nominal) value of loan stock into 20 shares. Multiplication of the conversion rate by the share price provides the conversion value. A share price of £6 would imply a conversion value of £120. In some cases the conversion rate declines over the life of the convertible bond. A convertible bond would also exhibit an investment, or straight bond, value. This is the value of the bond in the absence of the right to convert. The investment value is the price of a corresponding straight bond.

The market value (price) of a convertible would normally be higher than the greater of the conversion and investment values. The excess of the market value over the greater of the conversion or investment value is often referred to as the premium. Figure 35.1 illustrates the relationship between the conversion, investment, and market values of a convertible. It is assumed that the conversion rate is 20 and that the investment value is £90 per £100 par value. The market value (price) of the convertible is shown as the broken line.

The investment value, and hence the strike price of the implicit option, is not immutable. A rise in interest rates would lower the investment value and strike price. Similar effects would arise from a decline in the credit standing of the company. Such a decline in credit standing requires a higher rate of return which, given a constant coupon, implies a fall in the price of the straight bond. (It would also be expected that the investment value line would cease to be a horizontal straight line as the share price approaches zero. The investment value would be expected to fall as the stock price declines towards zero since the risk of default increases.)

Convertibles are hybrids in that they constitute a compromise between bonds and shares. They provide more upside exposure to share price movements than bonds, but less than ordinary shares. They provide less downside protection than bonds, but more than shares. The percentage rate of dividend or coupon yield would be less than that of a straight bond (because the market value exceeds the investment value), but probably more than that of the ordinary share (a rate of dividend

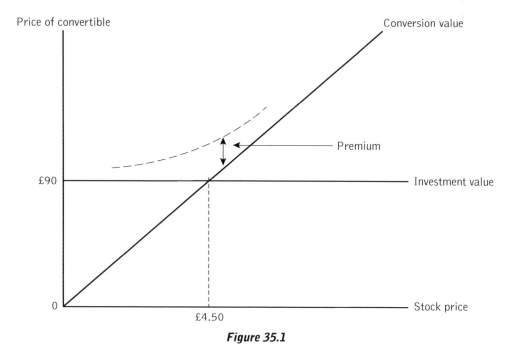

Figure 35.1

671

yield on the share that exceeds the rate of coupon yield on the convertible would probably induce conversion of the convertible into the share).

The fact that a convertible involves a lower rate of coupon yield than a straight bond renders it attractive to the issuer. The attached warrant causes the investor to require a lower coupon yield. Convertibles thus provide a cheaper source of finance than bonds or preference shares. Their advantage over ordinary shares, from the point of view of the issuer, is that they constitute a form of deferred equity. In particular, voting rights do not accrue to the holder until conversion takes place.

Holders of a convertible have the right to convert during a conversion period. If conversion does not take place during that period, the convertible simply becomes a bond. So, for example, a convertible might offer the right to convert on 1 June of the sixth, seventh, eighth, ninth, or tenth year of its life. If conversion does not take place on any of those dates it then becomes a bond maturing at the end of a life of a further ten years, at which point it would be redeemed at par. The period between the last possible conversion date and the maturity date of the bond is known as the stub (it is possible for the maturity date to coincide with the last possible conversion date).

The conversion rate would normally imply a high purchase price of the share (if acquired through conversion) on the issue date of the convertible so that a significant share price advance would be necessary for conversion to become worthwhile. The conversion price is the market value of the convertible divided by the number of shares obtained upon conversion; but sometimes it is defined as the par (nominal) value divided by the number of shares. At the time that the convertible is issued, the conversion price will be greater than the share price.

The question arises as to why the holder of a convertible would exercise the right to convert, since it might be expected that the market value would exceed the conversion value so that the sale of the convertible appears to be preferable to conversion. The circumstances in which conversion would take place are (1) call by the issuing corporation, (2) the existence of a final conversion date, or (3) the dividend yield of the share rising above the coupon yield of the convertible.

Sometimes the issuer of the convertible has the right to call it. This means that the holder must either accept redemption of the convertible (probably at the par value of the bond) or convert it into shares. If the latter provides the greater value, conversion will take place. When the final conversion date passes, the implicit option disappears, leaving only the investment value of the convertible. If the conversion value exceeds the investment value on the final conversion date, it would be rational to exercise the right to convert.

The excess of the conversion price over the share price, when expressed as a percentage of the share price, is known as the conversion premium:

Conversion price = Market value of convertible / Number of shares on conversion
Conversion premium (%) = {(Conversion price − Share price) / Share price} × 100

In most circumstances the conversion premium would be positive. However, a time may come when the dividend on the share exceeds the coupon on the convertible (the coupon is fixed, whereas the dividend is likely to rise over time). If conversion dates are at distant intervals (such as a year apart), the prospect of a lower rate of yield on the convertible than on the share could render it less valuable than the shares into which it might be converted. So a share dividend above the coupon of the convertible, together with a long time before the next conversion date, could entail a negative conversion premium. The prospect of a negative conversion premium subsequent to a conversion date could lead to conversion on that date.

EXERCISE 35.1

A convertible bond has a maturity of ten years and a conversion rate of 100. The current share price is £1.10p. Conversion can take place on 1 June of the fifth, sixth, seventh, and eighth years.

(a) Calculate the conversion value.

(b) What would be the significance for the market value of the convertible if conversion could take place in year five only, rather than in any of the four years?

Answers

(a) Conversion value = 100 × £1.10 = £110

(b) The ability to convert in year five only would reduce the time to expiry of the implicit option and hence would reduce its time value. So the convertible should have a lower market value (price).

SPLIT-CAPITAL INVESTMENT TRUSTS

Closed-end funds, such as investment trusts, have become the source of various financially engineered investments. One approach has been to divide funds into income shares and capital shares. Buyers of income shares receive all of the dividends from the fund but are entitled to only a pre-set amount of capital, which could be the initial share price, when the fund is wound up. The holders of the capital shares of such a split-capital investment trust receive all or most of the capital growth from the fund.

Such a split-capital investment trust has a predetermined date (maturity date) on which the assets of the fund are sold and the proceeds returned to investors in the fund. In other words, a split-capital investment trust has a maturity date on which it is wound up.

Another way in which a closed-end fund (investment trust) might take a split-capital form is through division into geared ordinary shares and zero dividend preference shares (sometimes referred to simply as zeros). Money raised from the issue of zero dividend preference shares is used to fund additional investment by the investment trust. The fund is thus geared (i.e. partly financed by borrowing) and in consequence the ordinary shares of the fund can be regarded as being geared. A geared ordinary share might be looked upon as an ordinary share partly financed through borrowing by means of the issue of zero dividend preference shares. Geared ordinary shares receive all of the dividends and some of the capital growth. (Strictly speaking, the sale of preference shares is an issue of equity rather than borrowing. However the effect is the same as borrowing by means of selling bonds. The issue of preference shares is equivalent to borrowing.)

The zero dividend preference shares would have redemption values above their initial issue price. The difference between the redemption value and the issue price of the zero dividend preference shares provides the investment return to their holders. If fund growth were more than what is required to meet the redemption value, the surplus growth would accrue to the holders of the geared ordinary shares.

673

EXERCISE 35.2

An investment trust has 100% gearing (the principal investment has been matched by borrowing so as to double the size of the shareholding). If the money were borrowed at 6% p.a., what would be the return on the principal investment in the event of stock returns of (a) 0%, (b) 3%, (c) 8%, and (d) 15% p.a.?

In the event of a sudden (e) halving, and (f) doubling, of the value of the shares held by the investment trust, what would happen to the net asset value (NAV) of the investment trust? In the cases in which share prices halve or double, what would be the outcome if the investment trust had invested (entirely) in other investment trusts with 100% gearing?

Answers

(a) If the portfolio return is 0% p.a. but 6% must be paid on a sum equal to the principal investment, the rate of return on the principal investment would be −6% p.a.

(b) If the total portfolio return is 3% p.a., this is equivalent to 6% p.a. on the principal investment since the total portfolio is double the principal investment. There is 6% p.a. interest on a sum equal to the principal investment. So the net return is 6% − 6% = 0% p.a.

(c) If the total portfolio return is 8% p.a., this is equivalent to 16% p.a. on the principal investment since the total portfolio is double the principal investment. There is 6% p.a. interest on a sum equal to the principal investment. So the net return is 16% − 6% = 10% p.a.

(d) If the total portfolio return is 15% p.a., this is equivalent to 30% p.a. on the principal investment. So the net return on the principal investment is 30% − 6% = 24% p.a.

(e) If the value of the shares held by the investment trust suddenly halved in value, there would be a loss equal to the principal investment (the value of the total portfolio was double the value of the principal investment). The assets would now be matched by liabilities (investments matched by debts) meaning that the investors have lost all their money but the debt can be repaid.

If the investments had been in investment trusts with 100% gearing, the investments would now be worth nothing. There would be liabilities but no assets. The investment trust defaults on its debts. (This type of situation faced investors in UK split-capital investment trusts in the early 2000s, when the holders of preference shares – effectively lenders to the investment trusts – lost their investments along with the other investors in the investment trusts.)

(f) If the value of the shares had suddenly doubled, the value of the shareholding would be four times the original principal investment. Net of the debt, the investment trust (its NAV) would be three times the value of the original principal investment. Investors would have tripled their wealth as a result of the doubling of share prices (ignoring any changes in discounts/premiums).

If the investments had been in investment trusts with 100% gearing, the total investment portfolio would have tripled in value (since each investment trust would be worth three times its original principal investment). Investments would then be six times the original principal value; and after subtracting the debt, investors would have seen their wealth increase five-fold.

In cases (e) and (f) if the portfolio of the investment trust were invested in geared investment trusts which also invested in geared investment trusts, the upward and downward effects would be intensified. In the UK in the early 2000s there was a 'magic circle' of split-capital investment trusts, which were geared and invested in one another. The fall in the stock market between 2000 and 2003 wiped out the value of many individuals' investments in the split-capital investment trusts. When an investment trust is geared and invests in other geared investment trusts (which in their turn might invest in geared investment trusts) the result is a hugely exaggerated effect of stock market movements.

During the 1990s in the UK, many investment trust issues combined both aspects of splitting. Those split-capital investment trusts had a predetermined maturity date on which the fund would be wound up and the capital of the fund distributed to shareholders. Typically they had dividend (income) shares, which paid out all of the dividends from the fund plus a capped return of capital at maturity. The capped return of capital entailed an upper limit to the capital to be returned at maturity. In addition there were capital shares that paid out any residual capital value at maturity, but which paid no dividends. The third component was, typically, zero dividend preference shares. These are similar to zero coupon bonds in that they pay no coupons during the life of the share but pay a predetermined capital sum when the investment trust matures.

Effectively these split-capital investment trusts stripped portfolios of shares into component parts, and traded those components separately on the stock market. Some of the investment trusts also traded composite units, which combined the components into shares similar to the shares of conventional investment trusts. Example 35.1 shows the capital structure of a hypothetical split-capital investment trust.

EXAMPLE 35.1

Income (dividend) shares, which pay all of the dividends plus £1 at maturity.

25% of capital

Zero dividend preference shares, which pay £2 at maturity.

50% of capital

Capital shares, which pay the residual value of the fund at maturity.

25% of capital

Composite units, which comprise 1 income share, 1 capital share, and 2 zero dividend preference shares.

So if the investment trust in Example 35.1 raised £100 million at issue, £25 million would have been from the sale of income shares, £25 million from the sale of capital shares, and £50 million from the sale of zero dividend preference shares. Some of these may have been combined into composite units. The zero dividend preference shares are similar to zero coupon bonds and hence could be regarded as a form of debt finance. In other words, 50% of the funding is equity (income shares and capital shares) and 50% is from borrowing (zero coupon preference shares).

All of the dividends from the £100 million fund are paid to the investors who paid £25 million for the income (dividend) shares. Their dividend yield is thus quadrupled. For example, a 3% p.a. dividend yield on the whole fund becomes 12% p.a. for the holders of the dividend shares. There is a doubling of the dividend yield from the split into income and capital shares, and a further doubling from the sale of zero dividend preference shares.

The holders of the capital shares bear a high proportion of the risk. Suppose that all shares (income, capital, and zero dividend preference) were issued at £1 each. There are 25 million income shares, 25 million capital shares, and 50 million zero dividend preference shares. At maturity the holders of the income shares receive £25 million and the holders of the zero dividend preference shares receive £100 million (£2 × 50 million). Since the holders of the capital shares receive the residual value of the fund, the capital value of the fund must rise by at least 25% (to £125 million) before the holders of capital shares receive anything. It must rise by 50% (to £150 million) simply to pay back the initial investment into the capital shares. However since any excess above £150 million accrues entirely to the holders of capital shares, the holders of those shares could experience very high rates of return. The holders of the capital shares thus have high risk but also the potential for high rates of return. The investors in capital shares accept a disproportionate amount of the risk of the total fund. The investors in income and zero dividend preference shares have correspondingly lowered risks.

Split-capital investment trusts can be interpreted as option structures. Consider the case of a split-capital investment trust divided into income and capital shares but without zero dividend preference shares (or other debt). The holders of the capital shares of such a split-capital investment trust receive all or most of the capital growth from the fund. In effect they hold call options on the fund, with the capital returnable to holders of income shares constituting the strike price of the call options.

The holders of the income shares of a split-capital trust are effectively the sellers (writers) of put options, since there is a maximum return of capital but no minimum other than zero. If the fund becomes bankrupt, there will be no capital to be returned to investors.

The combined position of the holders of the income and capital shares is illustrated in Figure 35.2. Adding the values of the income and capital shares produces the value of an ordinary share (an ordinary share is equivalent to an income share plus a capital share). Figure 35.2 illustrates the case in which the capital returnable to holders of income shares equals the initial (issue) price of the ordinary shares.

Split-capital investment trusts that issue zero dividend preference shares (or borrow in another way) add a further option dimension. Borrowing to finance investment constitutes gearing. This is equivalent to the gearing provided by a call option. So the holders of capital shares of a split-capital investment trust, which has an issue of zero dividend preference shares in addition to the income/capital share split, effectively have a compound option (an option on an option).

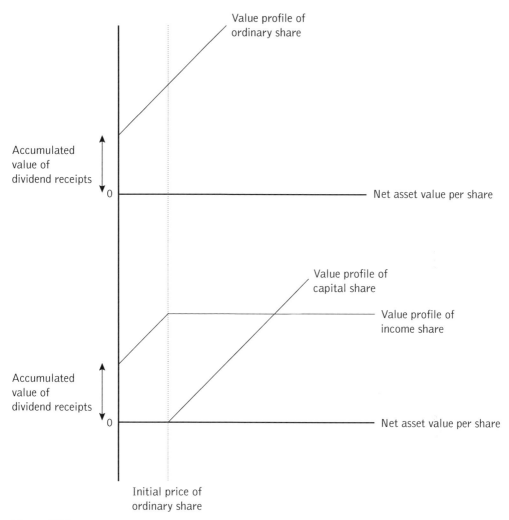

Figure 35.2   *The pay-offs of income and capital shares on the maturity (wind-up) date of a split-capital investment trust*

SHARES AND BONDS AS OPTIONS

The situations of shareholders and bondholders can be analysed by using option theory. Shares can be seen as call options, on the value of a company, with a strike price of zero. Bondholders can be seen as having written (sold) put options.

Figure 35.3 shows the value of the company shares (in total) as a function of the value of the company. The call options (shares) have no intrinsic value until the value of the company is greater than the value of its debt. It is here assumed that bonds are the only debt. The value of the bonds (in total) will be equal to B so long as the value of the company is at least equal to B. If the value of the company is less than B, the value of the bonds will equal the value of the company. If the company is liquidated when its value is below B, all the proceeds of liquidation will be paid to the

677

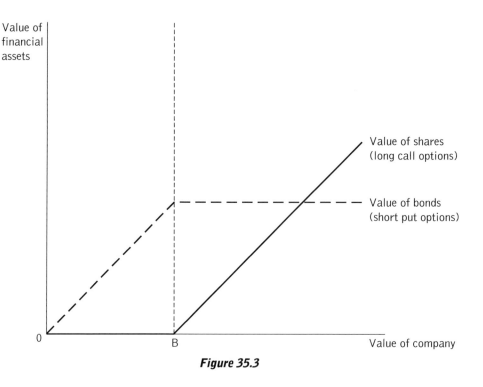

Figure 35.3

bondholders (and none would be available for shareholders). The value of the shares plus the value of the bonds equals the value of the company.

Figure 35.3 does not consider the time value of the options. When time value is included the call options (shares) increase in price if the expected volatility of the value of the company increases. In other words, increased risk increases share prices. This effect is magnified if the option loses intrinsic value; that is if the net value of the company approaches the strike price of zero. When the net value of the company is zero, shares can be seen as at-the-money options. Time value is at its highest when an option is at-the-money. High time value entails high sensitivity to changes in expected volatility of the value of the company. An increase in expected volatility can substantially increase the option time value, and hence the share price. A low net value of the company increases the desirability of accepting risk since the additional risk could considerably enhance the share price.

An increase in risk (expected volatility) worsens the position of option writers. An option is a liability to the writer and therefore an increase in risk, by increasing the value of that liability, works against option writers. So an increase in the expected volatility of the value of the company would worsen the position of bondholders; that is it would reduce the value of bonds. This effect would be particularly strong if the net value of the company (assets minus debts) is close to zero, since the put options would be close to their strike price. It follows that increased risk taking by the company, particularly when the company has little net value, can be expected to reduce bond prices whilst increasing share prices.

This analysis can be extended to the case of investment trusts that are geared as a result of issuing preference shares. After all, an investment trust is a company. In Figure 35.3 the strike price of the call option (geared ordinary share) would be at a net asset value of zero, and preference shares would replace bonds. The advantage of high risk taking for the shareholders might help to explain why so many split-capital investment trusts bought shares in other split-capital investment trusts (which were rendered high risk by their gearing). The disadvantage of high risk investing for the holders of the preference shares underlines the error made by marketing the zero dividend preference shares as low risk investments.

CONCLUSION

Some stock-exchange-traded investments have similarities to options. Warrants are long-term call options, normally on the shares of the company issuing the warrants. Convertibles are bonds with the right to exchange the bonds for shares of the company issuing the convertibles. They are somewhat similar to bonds with attached call options. Split-capital investment trusts are investment trusts, which are divided into income shares and capital shares. The income and capital shares could be interpreted as option positions. Even ordinary shares and bonds could be interpreted as option positions.

Convertibles could appeal to investors who are both loss-averse and prone to mental accounting. The bond dimension of a convertible gives protection against loss from stock price falls. The bond component also yields a greater income than the shares would. Convertibles could thus appeal to investors whose mental accounting leads them to take a 'never touch the capital approach' whilst requiring a relatively high flow of income from their investments.

Investment trusts can have a dual relationship to these option-like investments. The investment trust funds can invest in warrants, convertibles, and split-capital investment trusts. Also there can be warrants based on investment trusts, convertibles that convert into investment trusts, and investment trusts can have a split-capital structure. This means that very highly geared investments are available. For example a warrant on an investment trust, which invests in warrants, is a very highly geared investment. Small rises in the stock market can result in huge percentage gains, and small market falls can cause very large losses. In the early 2000s many split-capital investment trusts invested in other split-capital investment trusts. They provided extraordinarily high returns when the stock market was rising, but many investors found that their investments became worthless when the stock market fell.

Chapter 36

Option pricing and the Black-Scholes model

OBJECTIVE

The objective of this chapter is to provide knowledge of:

1. The determinants of option prices.
2. The Black-Scholes option pricing model.
3. The meaning and significance of early exercise.

OPTION PRICES AS THE COSTS OF REPLICATION

One way of looking at option prices is to see the option price as the expected cost of replicating the option. Option positions can be replicated by positions in the stock (or other underlying instrument). The positions in the stock should provide the same profit/loss outcome as the option being replicated. The amount of the stock should reflect the option delta. The delta is the change in the option price resulting from a 1p change in the stock price. For example, an option on £1 million of the stock with a delta of 0.7 would tend to give the same profit or loss as £700,000 of the stock.

Such replication will involve cash flows. Replicating long option positions (bought options) involves buying shares when the price of the stock rises and selling when it falls. This is because a rise in the price of the stock causes an increase in delta and hence the need to buy more of the stock. Conversely, a fall in price lowers delta and necessitates selling. Buying high and selling low entails a net cash outflow. The theoretical value of the option equals the expected losses from such transactions. So replicating long option positions results in losses that correspond to the value of the replicated option. Conversely, the replication of a short option position would be expected to provide profits that correspond to the value of the option. The cost of replicating an option is the basis for Black-Scholes option pricing.

THE DETERMINANTS OF OPTION PRICES

Probably the most popular way of calculating the 'fair price' of an option is by means of the Black-Scholes model. An intuitive feel for this model can be obtained by regarding it as equating the

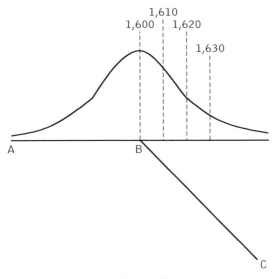

Figure 36.1

price (premium) with the expected pay-off from an option. Expected pay-off is used in the sense of possible pay-off outcomes weighted by their probabilities of occurrence (i.e. statistical expectation).

Figure 36.1 illustrates this with respect to options on the FTSE 100 stock index. The curve in the upper part of Figure 36.1 is a normal distribution curve and indicates the probabilities of the various possible outcomes. The profile ABC in the lower part shows the pay-off possibilities from buying a call option.

Suppose that the area under the normal distribution curve between 1,600 and 1,610, as a proportion of the total area under the curve, is 0.19. This means that there is a 19% chance that the index will fall between 1,600 and 1,610. If the area under the curve between 1,610 and 1,620 is 0.15 of the total area, there is a 15% probability of the index being between 1,610 and 1,620. The statistical expectation of the pay-off from the call option is given by the sum of the possible pay offs when each possible pay-off is weighted by its probability of occurrence. The calculation of this expected pay-off is illustrated by Table 36.1 in which, for the sake of simplification, the possible pay-offs are represented by the mid-points of the respective ranges. (Note that the probabilities are themselves expectations.)

Table 36.1 involves some simplifications that would be avoided in the actual calculation of expected pay-off. In particular, the mid-point of a range is not the best measure of the average possible outcome within the range. Nevertheless, the table serves to illustrate the principles behind the calculation of the fair price of an option using the Black-Scholes model. In the example shown the fair price of the option, expressed in index points, is 8.20. At £10 per index point, this would correspond to a money price of £82 per contract. (The FTSE 100 options traded on LIFFE are based on £10 per index point.) The option price estimated by means of the model is referred to as the fair (or theoretical) price. The fair price may differ from the option price observed in the market.

Intrinsic value is the pay-off from immediate exercise of an option. In the case of an in-the-money call option, intrinsic value is the stock price minus the strike price. Time value is the excess of the

Table 36.1

Range of index values	Range of pay-off possibilities	Probability of occurrence	Contribution to expected pay-off
1600–10	0–10	0.19	5 × 0.19 = 0.95
1610–20	10–20	0.15	15 × 0.15 = 2.25
1620–30	20–30	0.09	25 × 0.09 = 2.25
1630–40	30–40	0.05	35 × 0.05 = 1.75
1640–50	40–50	0.01	45 × 0.01 = 0.45
		.	.
		.	.
		.	.
		0.5	8.20

option price over the intrinsic value. Time value is at its greatest when the option is at-the-money (i.e. when the stock price equals the strike price) and declines as the option moves to being either in-the-money or out-of-the-money. This behaviour of time value can be explained intuitively.

An out-of-the-money option has to reach the at-the-money position before movements of the index can start generating opportunities for exercise. Thus, an option buyer would regard an out-of-the-money option as less valuable than an at-the-money option since some leeway has to be made up before it reaches the threshold of pay-offs from exercise, whereas an at-the-money option is already at this threshold. Consequently, the option buyer is prepared to pay less for an out-of-the-money option. Conversely, the option writer would accept a lower price because of the reduced chance of loss. (This line of reasoning also underlines the role of the market forces of demand and supply in the establishment of option prices. Black-Scholes calculations merely serve as guidelines to buyers and writers.)

The time value of an in-the-money option would be lower than if that option were at-the-money because of the possibility of erosion of the intrinsic value. In the case of a call option, a rise in the index would increase the intrinsic value of options that were either in-the-money or at-the-money prior to the rise in the index. However, a fall in the index would reduce the intrinsic value of an in-the-money option, whereas an at-the-money option has no intrinsic value to be eroded. This potential for loss of intrinsic value is reflected in a lower time value.

Another determinant of option prices is the expected volatility of the index. A high volatility would mean that the normal distribution of Figure 36.1 would spread out and flatten, indicating an increased chance of extreme values of the index. A calculation similar to that of Table 36.1 but with a normal distribution curve exhibiting a greater variance would produce a higher expected pay-off. Thus the fair price of the option rises as expected volatility increases, since the probability of high pay-offs is enhanced.

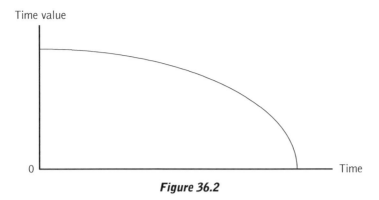

Time value

0

Time

Figure 36.2

The term 'volatility' can be seen as referring to the standard deviation of the distribution of possible spot prices at the end of a particular period of time. (More accurately, the distribution is log normal rather than normal.) This standard deviation depends upon the length of time involved. The standard deviation will increase as the period lengthens (graphically depicted by the normal distribution curve becoming wider and flatter), since the likelihood of substantial movements from the original price becomes greater.

The standard deviation is proportional to the square root of the period of time involved. So the volatility over t days is equal to the square root of t times the daily volatility.

This relationship between volatility and the square root of time explains the observed pattern of time value decline (decay). Time value is related to the square root of the amount of time remaining before expiry of the option. Time value decays at an accelerating rate as the expiry date is approached. This pattern of time value decay, which is slow when expiry is distant but becomes rapid close to expiry, is illustrated in Figure 36.2. Time value reaches zero on the expiry date of the option.

As an illustration, consider the decline in the period to expiry from 100 days to 81 days. The square root moves from 10 to 9. The passage of time from 4 days to 1 day to expiry moves the square root from 2 to 1. So the impact on volatility from the passage of 3 days, when expiry is close, is the same as the passage of 19 days (100−81) when expiry is distant. Volatility, and hence time value, declines more rapidly as expiry is approached.

From what has just been said, it is clear that time to expiry also influences the option price. Longer periods to expiry are associated with higher option prices. A long period to expiry provides more opportunity for the index to move sufficiently above a call option strike price (or below a put option strike price) to generate substantial intrinsic value. The enhanced likelihood of a substantial pay-off would tend to raise the price that a buyer is prepared to pay and that a writer would need to receive. (The point could alternatively be expressed in terms of a longer period leading to a greater variance of the (log) normal distribution curve.)

Interest rates also have an influence on option prices. The influence of interest rates can be understood by seeing options as a means of changing the timing of transactions in the underlying stock. An investor can buy call options with the intention of taking delivery of the corresponding shares when the option expires, and in the meantime can receive interest on the money that will be used. The attractiveness of this procedure relative to buying the shares immediately is improved by a rise in interest rates payable on the money held. It follows that when interest rates are high, the demand for call options will be somewhat greater, and option prices will be boosted by this additional demand.

Put options can be used to postpone the sale of shares. Instead of selling shares immediately, the investor might buy put options with the intention of selling shares in the future. Pending the sale of the shares, the investor would forgo interest on the money that would have been received from an immediate sale. Using puts in this way becomes less attractive as the interest receipts forgone rise. So investors are less likely to buy puts for this purpose when interest rates are high. High interest rates are therefore associated with a somewhat lower demand for put options and hence lower put option prices.

In the case of stock options, the prospect of an ex-dividend date can have an impact on the price of an option. When a stock goes ex-dividend its price falls by an amount approximately equal to the anticipated dividend. So an ex-dividend date can be seen as providing a price fall that is anticipated. The share price fall will cause a reduction in the prices of call options and an increase in those of put options. The option prices would normally discount the anticipated fall in the share price well before the ex-dividend date.

Two points are worth emphasising about the roles of volatility and time to expiry. The first is that whereas increases in these variables would increase potential losses as well as potential profits on the underlying instrument, for example a stock index or a stock, the asymmetrical nature of options means that potential profits are enhanced more than potential losses. This is because once the stock price is below the strike price of a call option (or above the strike price of a put option), any further stock price falls (increases) would not bring about increased losses in terms of intrinsic value. If an option is at-the-money or out-of-the-money, there is no potential for loss of intrinsic value.

The second point is that time value can be divided into two components. One might be regarded as the financing-cost component and corresponds to $K - K(1 + r)^{-t}$, where K is the strike price, r the interest rate, and t the time to expiry. This component is not affected by market expectations of volatility and is a linear function of time to expiry. It is the means whereby short-term interest rates have a direct impact on option prices.

The other component of time value might be termed volatility value. It is the part of the option price that is influenced by market expectations of volatility. It is also the component whose value tends to be (at least according to the Black-Scholes model) a function of the square root of time to expiry.

THE BLACK-SCHOLES OPTION PRICING MODEL

The Black-Scholes model, with its variants, is probably the most commonly used option pricing model. This is despite its shortcomings, in particular its inability to allow for exercise prior to expiry (this failure to allow for early exercise means that strictly it is applicable only to European-style options). One reason for its popularity is that it allows for an analytical solution; this means that there is a formula into which certain values are input and from which an option price is forthcoming. This formula, when programmed into a computer or calculator, can produce option prices within seconds.

The most basic Black-Scholes model (Black and Scholes 1973; Merton 1973) relates to non-dividend paying stocks. It can be expressed as follows:

$$C = SN(d_1) - Ke^{-rt}N(d_2)$$

$$d_1 = \frac{\ln(S/K) + rt}{\sigma\sqrt{t}} + 0.5\sigma\sqrt{t}$$

$$d_2 = \frac{\ln(S/K) + rt}{\sigma\sqrt{t}} - 0.5\sigma\sqrt{t}$$

where C is the call option price, S is the stock price, N( ) is the cumulative normal distribution function, K is the strike price, e is the exponential (which has the constant value of 2.7182818 and appears on most hand-held calculators), r is the risk-free (annualised continuous) interest rate (as a decimal), t is the time to expiry (in years), and σ (sigma) is the volatility (annualised standard deviation of stock returns) as a decimal. (It should be noted that, although this exposition focuses on call options, there are corresponding equations for put options.)

The expression e^{-rt} is a discount term similar to $1/(1 + r)^t$ and as such it determines the present value of a future sum of money. A distinctive feature of e^{-rt} is that it discounts on a continuous basis. Continuous discounting parallels continuous compounding. To appreciate the significance of continuous compounding, consider the alternatives of receiving 12% payable to an annual basis, 6% six-monthly, and 1% monthly. The annualised receipts are $1.12, (1.06)^2 = 1.1236$ and $(1.01)^{12} = 1.1268$ respectively, corresponding to annual interest rates of 12%, 12.36%, and 12.68%. The frequency of compounding affects the final outcome. The effective interest rate increases as the frequency of compounding rises. Continuous compounding is based on an infinite number of infinitely small periods (although it can normally be thought of as daily compounding). Likewise, the effect of discounting depends upon the time periods; for example annual discounting at 12% p.a. gives a discount term of $1/(1.12) = 0.8929$, whereas continuous discounting over a year at 12% p.a. provides a discount term equal to $e^{-0.12} = 0.8869$.

It is also necessary to be aware of the meaning of N(d), the cumulative normal distribution function. This is based on a standardised normal distribution. $N(d_1)$ is the area under the distribution to the left of d_1 and $N(d_2)$ is the area to the left of d_2. Standardised normal distributions have total areas of 1 so that $N(d_1)$ is the probability of d being d_1 or less (likewise for d_2). $N(d_1)$ can be interpreted as the probability of the call option being in-the-money at expiry. Areas under the standardised normal distribution to the left of particular values can be ascertained from tables (as illustrated by the ensuing exercises) or by means of computer or calculator programmes.

In the equations for d_1 and d_2, the term ln (S/K) appears. This is the natural logarithm of the price relative (ratio of stock price to strike price). The model uses a lognormal rather than a normal distribution. It is a normal distribution of logarithms. One reason for using a lognormal distribution is that the price relative can never be negative (since the stock price cannot be negative), and hence the price relatives cannot be normally distributed. The natural logarithm of the price relative can be negative and hence can be normally distributed.

Probably the best way to get a feel for the model is through worked exercises.

EXERCISE 36.1

The share price of Acme plc is 100p and no dividend is expected during the next six months. The six-month interest rate is 4% p.a. You expect the share price volatility to be 20% p.a. over the next six months. Estimate the price of a call option with a strike price of 100p and six months to expiry. Standard cumulative normal probabilities are shown in the table.

Table 36.A

X	N(X)
0.0	0.5000
0.1	0.5398
0.2	0.5793
0.3	0.6179
0.4	0.6554
0.5	0.6915

Answer

The Black-Scholes equations for a non-dividend paying stock are:

$$C = SN(d_1) - Ke^{-rt}N(d_2)$$

$$d_1 = \frac{\ln(S/K) + rt}{\sigma\sqrt{t}} + 0.5\sigma\sqrt{t}$$

$$d_2 = \frac{\ln(S/K) + rt}{\sigma\sqrt{t}} - 0.5\sigma\sqrt{t}$$

$$d_1 = \frac{\ln(100/100) + 0.04(0.5)}{0.2\sqrt{0.5}} + 0.5(0.2)\sqrt{0.5} = \frac{0.02}{0.2(0.7071)} + 0.1(0.7071) = 0.2121$$

$$d_2 = \frac{\ln(100/100) + 0.04(0.5)}{0.2\sqrt{0.5}} - 0.5(0.2)\sqrt{0.5} = \frac{0.02}{0.2(0.7071)} - 0.1(0.7071) = 0.0707$$

$N(d_1) = N(0.2121) = 0.5793 + 0.121(0.6179 - 0.5793) = 0.5840$

$N(d_2) = N(0.0707) = 0.5000 + 0.707(0.5398 - 0.5000) = 0.5281$

$C = 100(0.5840) - 100(0.9802)(0.5281)$ $[e^{-rt} = e^{-0.04.0.5} = e^{-0.02} = 0.9802]$

$C = 6.636$

The estimated fair price of a call option is 6.636p per share. So an option contract on 1000 shares should cost 6636p, i.e. £66.36p.

EXERCISE 36.2

Shares in Covuni plc are 105p. The six-month interest rate is 6% p.a. No dividends are expected during the next six months. Use the Black-Scholes option pricing model to estimate the fair price of a call option with six months to expiry and a strike price of 100p based on an expected annual volatility of 20%.

Standardised cumulative normal probabilities are shown in the table.

> ### Table 36.B
>
> | X | N(X) |
> |-----|--------|
> | 0.0 | 0.5000 |
> | 0.1 | 0.5398 |
> | 0.2 | 0.5793 |
> | 0.3 | 0.6179 |
> | 0.4 | 0.6554 |
> | 0.5 | 0.6915 |
> | 0.6 | 0.7257 |
> | 0.7 | 0.7580 |

Answer

$$C = S.N(d_1) - Ke^{-rt}.N(d_2)$$

$$d_1 = \frac{\ln(S/K) + rt}{\sigma\sqrt{t}} + 0.5\sigma\sqrt{t}$$

$$d_2 = \frac{\ln(S/K) + rt}{\sigma\sqrt{t}} - 0.5\sigma\sqrt{t}$$

$$d_1 = \frac{\ln(105/100) + (0.06 \times 0.5)}{0.2\sqrt{0.5}} + (0.5 \times 0.2)\sqrt{0.5}$$

$$d_2 = \frac{\ln(105/100) + (0.06 \times 0.5)}{0.2\sqrt{0.5}} - (0.5 \times 0.2)\sqrt{0.5}$$

$$d_1 = \frac{0.04879 + 0.03}{(0.2 \times 0.70711)} + (0.1 \times 0.70711)$$

$$= (0.07879/0.14142) + 0.07071$$
$$= 0.6278$$

$$d_2 = d_1 - 2(0.07071)$$
$$= d_1 - 0.14142 = 0.4864$$

$$N(d_1) = 0.7257 + [(0.7580 - 0.7257) \times 0.278]$$
$$= 0.7347$$

$$N(d_2) = 0.6554 + [(0.6915 - 0.6554) \times 0.864]$$
$$= 0.6866$$

$$C = (105 \times 0.7347) - (100e^{-0.06 \times 0.5} \times 0.6866)$$
$$= 77.1435 - 66.6308 = 10.5127$$

So the fair price of the call option is estimated to be 10.51p per share (to two decimal places). (10,510p, i.e. £105.10p for an option contract on 1,000 shares.)

EARLY EXERCISE

Early exercise refers to the exercise of an American-style option before the option expires (European-style options cannot be exercised before expiry). In the case of call options, it would never be rational to exercise an option on a non-dividend paying stock prior to expiry, since selling the option would always be preferable. By selling the option both the time and intrinsic values would be received, whereas exercise of the option would provide the intrinsic value only. It follows that American-style options on non-dividend paying stocks are equivalent to European-style options and can therefore be valued using the basic Black-Scholes model. The basic Black-Scholes model (described in this chapter) does not allow for the possibility of early exercise.

It may be rational to exercise a call option on a dividend paying stock before expiry. The optimum moment for such early exercise is just before the stock goes ex-dividend. (When a stock goes ex-dividend the existing holder becomes eligible for the next dividend even if the shares are subsequently sold before the dividend is paid; so a buyer foregoes the next dividend.) When the stock goes ex-dividend its price falls by the amount of dividend that had been expected. This reduction in the stock price entails a decline in the intrinsic value of a call option. If this potential loss of intrinsic value exceeds the time value that would exist subsequent to the ex-dividend date, it would be rational to exercise the option before it goes ex-dividend. In this case the intrinsic value just before the ex-dividend date exceeds the prospective total value just after it. Another way of looking at the point is in terms of dividend capture. By exercising before the ex-dividend date, the right to the dividend is ensured and, if the value of the expected dividend is greater than the prospective time value subsequent to (or on the) ex-dividend day, the option should be exercised. The optimum time for the early exercise is immediately before the stock goes ex-dividend, because such timing will minimise the financing costs of holding the stock.

In the case of American-style put options, early exercise may be rational whether or not the stock pays dividends. Consider the case in which a holder of stock has bought put options with a view to guaranteeing a minimum selling price. When the option is exercised the proceeds can be put on deposit to earn interest. Early exercise is rational when those prospective interest receipts exceed the time value of the option. Another way of seeing the same point is in terms of the prospective interest receipts exceeding the value of the possible increases in intrinsic value net of possible decreases (time value being the value of possible increases in intrinsic value net of the risk of losses in intrinsic value). Yet another way of interpreting the point is based on the minimum value of a European-style put being $K/(1 + rt) - S$, while that of the equivalent American-style put is $K - S$. If the difference, $K - K/(1 + rt)$, exceeds the time value (specifically volatility value), it would be possible to exercise an American-style put and use the proceeds to buy a European-style put while retaining part of the proceeds of exercise as cash. Again, this is based on a comparison of prospective interest receipts and time value.

In the case of put options on dividend paying stocks, it may be rational to delay exercise until after the stock has gone ex-dividend, particularly if the dividend is expected to be large. By such a delay the dividend is obtained and, since the receipt upon exercise (the strike price) is the same irrespective of whether the stock is cum- or ex-dividend, it makes sense to wait until the right to the dividend is secured before exercising the option. (A stock is cum-dividend before it goes ex-dividend.)

In the cases of both call and put options, at the time when it is rational to exercise early the price of the option should equal its intrinsic value. No one should pay more than the intrinsic value for an option that is about to be exercised. This prospective absence of time value should be reflected in the price of the option at earlier stages; in effect, the date on which early exercise is rational would be treated as the effective expiry date of the option when valuing it prior to that date.

CONCLUSION

Some future cash flows are contingent upon the occurrence of events or situations. An asset, or liability, that exhibits such contingent cash flows is an option. The Black-Scholes model provides a means of estimating fair prices for options. Discount models, together with a capital market theory such as the capital asset pricing model, can be used to estimate fair prices for investments with non-contingent cash flows and option pricing models, such as the Black-Scholes model, can be used to estimate fair prices for contingent cash flows. Option pricing models are thus of major importance to the theory and practice of valuing assets and liabilities that have future cash flows. The models are therefore central to finance since finance is concerned with pricing investments and debts that entail future cash flows. Unfortunately the basic Black-Scholes model is limited in its applicability, and for most uses it needs to be amended or replaced by other models.

Chapter 37

Variations on the basic Black-Scholes option pricing model

OBJECTIVE

The objective of this chapter is to provide knowledge of:

1. Variations on the basic Black-Scholes model.
2. Defects of Black-Scholes models in relation to pricing bond options.
3. Use of the put-call parity relationship to price put options.
4. The reliability of the Black-Scholes model.

EUROPEAN-STYLE CALL OPTIONS ON DIVIDEND PAYING STOCKS

To use the Black-Scholes model to value call options on dividend paying stocks, it is necessary to adjust the stock price by removing the present value of dividends receivable prior to expiry (more specifically, the dividends that relate to ex-dividend dates falling before expiry). Once the stock price is adjusted in this way, the Black-Scholes model (using the adjusted stock price) can be used in the usual way.

One means of understanding this adjustment process is in terms of the dividend discount model. According to the dividend discount model, the current stock price is the present (i.e. discounted) value of all future expected dividends. However, dividends accruing before the expiry date of the option will be incorporated into the current stock price, but not the stock price on the expiry date. Option pricing requires the use of the stock price on the one day (expiration day) on which exercise of the European-style option can occur. So the stock price used in the Black-Scholes model is the current stock price minus that part of the price that arises from dividends that will not be received by the holder of expiry-day stock. In other words, the present value of dividends expected prior to expiry needs to be subtracted from the current stock price in order to ascertain the stock price to be used in the Black-Scholes model.

EXERCISE 37.1

Shares in stock A are priced at 100p. The interest rate is 6% p.a. and a dividend of 2p is expected in two months. Expected share price volatility is 20% p.a. Using the Black-Scholes model estimate the price of a European-style call option with a strike price of 100p and three months to expiry.

Standardised cumulative normal probabilities are shown in the table.

Table 37.A

x	$N(x)$
0.0	0.5000
0.1	0.5398
0.2	0.5793
0.3	0.6179

Answer

For dividend paying stocks

$$C = S_p N(d_1) - Ke^{-rt}N(d_2)$$

$$S_p = S - De^{-rT}$$

where S_p is the adjusted stock price, t is the time (in years) to expiry of the option, T is the time to the receipt of the dividend, and D is the expected value of the dividend.

$$d_1 = \{ [\ln(S_p/K) + rt]/\sigma\sqrt{t} \} + 0.5\sigma\sqrt{t}$$

$$d_2 = \{ [\ln(S_p/K) + rt]/\sigma\sqrt{t} \} - 0.5\sigma\sqrt{t}$$

$$S_p = 100 - 2e^{-0.06.0.167}$$

$$= 100 - 2e^{-0.01}$$

$$= 100 - 2(0.99)$$

$$= 100 - 1.98 = 98.02$$

$$d_1 = \{ [\ln(98.02/100) + 0.06.0.25] / 0.2\sqrt{0.25} \} + (0.5 \times 0.2 \times \sqrt{0.25})$$

$$= [(\ln(0.9802) + 0.015)/0.1] + 0.05$$

$$= -0.2 + 0.15 + 0.05 = 0$$

$$d_2 = \{ [\ln(98.02/100) + 0.06.0.25] / 0.2\sqrt{0.25} \} - (0.5 \times 0.2 \times \sqrt{0.25})$$

$$= -0.2 + 0.15 - 0.05 = -0.1$$

$C = 98.02N(0) - 100e^{-0.06.0.25}N(-0.1)$

$C = (98.02 \times 0.5) - (100 \times e^{-0.015} \times 0.4602)$

$= 49.01 - 45.33$

$= 3.68p$ (to two decimal places)

The estimated option price is 3.68p per share i.e. £36.80 per contract (on 1,000 shares).

EXERCISE 37.2

Shares in Covuni plc are 100p and a 2p dividend is expected in three months. The three-month interest rate is 5% p.a. and the six-month interest rate is 6% p.a. Use a variation on the Black-Scholes option pricing model to estimate the fair price of an at-the-money call option with six months to expiry based on an expected volatility of 20% p.a.

Standardised cumulative normal probabilities are shown in the table.

Table 37.B

X	N(X)
0.0	0.5000
0.1	0.5398
0.2	0.5793
0.3	0.6179

Answer

The stock price to be used in the basic Black-Scholes model is $(100 - 2e^{-0.05.0.25}) = 98.025$.

$$C = 98.025 \, N(d_1) - 100e^{-0.06.0.5} \, N(d_2)$$

$$d_1 = \frac{\ln(98.025/100) + (0.06 \times 0.5) + (0.5 \times 0.2)\sqrt{0.5}}{0.2\sqrt{0.5}}$$

$$= \frac{-0.01995 + 0.03}{0.14142} + 0.07071$$

$$= 0.07108 + 0.07071 = 0.14179$$

$$d_2 = 0.07108 - 0.07071 = 0.00037$$

$$N(d_1) = 0.5398 + [(0.5793 - 0.5398) \times 0.4179] = 0.5563$$

$$N(d_2) = 0.5 + (0.0398 \times 0.0037) = 0.5001$$

$$C = (98.025 \times 0.5563) - (97.04 \times 0.5001)$$
$$= 54.5313 - 48.5297 = 6.0016p \text{ per share.}$$

It might be noted that different interest rates for three months and six months is inconsistent with the assumption of the Black-Scholes model that interest rates are constant and the same for all maturities. The expected volatility of 20% p.a. relates to the six months to expiry, and the Black-Scholes model assumes that volatility is expected to be constant during the period to expiry.

EXERCISE 37.3

It is 24 January and shares in the Burnham Bakery plc stand at 100p. The next option expiry date is 24 March and the next dividend is due in May. The two-month interest rate is 6% p.a. and you estimate the share price volatility to be 10% p.a. Use the Black-Scholes option pricing model to estimate fair prices for at-the-money American-style call options expiring in March. Why might the estimated fair prices for options expiring in September be less reliable?

Standardised cumulative normal probabilities are shown in the table.

Table 37.C

X	N(X)
0.0	0.5000
0.1	0.5398
0.2	0.5793
0.3	0.6179

Answer

The Black-Scholes equation for non-dividend paying stocks (no dividends before expiry) is

$$C = S.N(d_1) - Ke^{-rt}N(d_2)$$

$$d_1 = \frac{\ln(S/K) + rt + 0.5\sigma\sqrt{t}}{\sigma\sqrt{t}}$$

$$d_2 = \frac{\ln(S/K) + rt - 0.5\sigma\sqrt{t}}{\sigma\sqrt{t}}$$

So $d_1 = [(0.06 \times 0.167)/(0.1 \times 0.408)] + (0.5 \times 0.1 \times \sqrt{0.167}) = 0.2655$
    (NB $\ln(1) = 0$)

$d_2 = [0.06 \times 0.167)/(0.1 \times 0.408)] - (0.5 \times 0.1 \times \sqrt{0.167}) = 0.2247$

$C = 100N(0.2655) - Ke^{-0.06 \cdot 0.167}N(0.2247)$

$$C = (100 \times 0.6046) - (99 \times 0.5888)$$

$$C = 60.46 - 58.29 = 2.17$$

So the fair price of an at-the-money call option is 2.17p per share. (2170p, i.e. £21.70p, for an option contract on 1,000 shares.)

The estimated prices for options expiring in September may be less reliable because (1) there is a need to adjust the share price by the dividend expected in May, and that dividend may be uncertain, (2) there is a possibility of early exercise (exercise before expiry) and the basic Black-Scholes model does not allow for this, and (3) the assumptions of constancy of interest rates and volatility (two assumptions of the Black-Scholes model) are more likely to be violated over a long period than over a shorter period.

AMERICAN-STYLE CALL OPTIONS ON DIVIDEND PAYING STOCKS (BLACK'S APPROXIMATION)

Since the Black-Scholes model is strictly applicable only to European-style options, its use in valuing American-style options must be regarded as a relatively crude procedure that merely produces an approximate price. The use of Black's approximation makes the procedure less crude.

Black's approximation is based on the principle that the only time that it might be rational to exercise an American-style call option prior to expiry is just before an ex-dividend date. In the case of a stock with one ex-dividend date before the option expiry date, there would be two possible occasions on which a call option might be exercised, these being immediately before the ex-dividend date and on the expiry date. Effectively there are alternative expiry dates. Two option prices are calculated: one for each expiry date. The higher of the two prices is used as the estimate of the option price.

When using Black's approximation, the stock price is adjusted by removing the present value of dividends expected prior to expiry. In the case of a stock with just one ex-dividend date before the option expires, there would be no adjustment to the stock price when the day before the ex-dividend date is used as the expiry date, but an adjustment would be needed when the actual expiry date is used (note that when making such adjustments the expected dividends should be discounted from the prospective date of receipt and not from the ex-dividend date).

EXERCISE 37.4

On 1 January the price of a share, which pays a quarterly dividend of 50p and goes ex-dividend on 1 March and 1 June, is £40. The interest rate is 9% p.a. Outline a way of calculating the approximate value of a six-month American-style call option.

Answer

The option could be valued by means of Black's approximation. This approach values the European option expiring at the same time as the American and the European option that expires just before the last ex-dividend date. The higher of the two is used as an approximation to the value of the American option.

The present value of all dividends accruing before the exercise date (i.e. all dividends not receivable by the option holder) is subtracted from the current stock price and the resulting figure is used in the Black-Scholes formula. So the value used for the stock price when valuing an option expiring on 1 June would be:

$$£40 - £0.5e^{-0.09 \times 0.167} = £40 - £0.493 = £39.507$$

and the value used when valuing an option expiring on 1 July would be:

$$£40 - £0.50e^{-0.09 \times 0.167} - £0.50e^{-0.09 \times 0.417} = £40 - £0.493 - £0.482 = £39.025$$

It has been assumed that dividends are received on the ex-dividend dates (i.e. after 0.167 of a year and after 0.417 of a year) whereas the dividends would actually be received on a later date. The discounting should be based on the later date. The stock price adjustments, and Black's approximation, are used when the ex-dividend date falls before the expiry date but the discounting is from the date of receipt of the dividend.

EUROPEAN-STYLE CALL OPTIONS ON STOCK INDICES

Stock index portfolios can usually be treated as producing a continuous income stream, since the various component stocks would be paying dividends at different times. The adjustment that corresponds to subtracting the present value of expected dividends involves discounting the spot stock index by the expected rate of dividend yield. One way of looking at this is in terms of the potential reinvestment of dividends allowing a discounted amount in the present to correspond to the full amount at expiry, in much the same way as the future strike price is discounted to a present value. In the case of stocks with discrete dividend payments, the adjusted stock price is used in all three equations, including the equations for d_1 and d_2. In the case of stock index options, the corresponding amendment to the equations for d_1 and d_2 takes the form of subtracting the expected rate of dividend yield from the risk-free interest rate (i.e. from the discount rate applicable to the strike price). The equations, for valuing a European-style call option on a stock index, are thus:

$$C = Se^{-\delta t}N(d_1) - Ke^{-rt}N(d_2)$$

$$d_1 = \frac{\ln(S/K) + (r - \delta)t}{\sigma\sqrt{t}} + 0.5\sigma\sqrt{t}$$

$$d_2 = \frac{\ln(S/K) + (r - \delta)t}{\sigma\sqrt{t}} - 0.5\sigma\sqrt{t}$$

where C is the call option price, S is the spot stock index, e is the exponential (natural logarithm), δ is the expected rate of dividend yield (as a decimal), t is the time to expiry, N( ) is the cumulative normal distribution function, K is the strike price, r is the risk-free interest rate (as a decimal), and σ is the volatility (annualised standard deviation of returns, as a decimal).

EXERCISE 37.5

The FTSE 100 is 4,625, the three-month interest rate is 3% p.a., the expected rate of dividend yield is 3% p.a., and an investor expects price volatility to be 20% p.a. over the next three months.

(a) What is the fair price of a three-month European-style FTSE 100 call option with a strike price of 4,625?

(b) What would be the fair price if the index immediately rose by 1?

(c) What is the delta of the option?

Standardised cumulative normal probabilities are shown in the table.

Table 37.D

X	N(X)
0.0	0.5000
0.1	0.5398
0.2	0.5793
0.3	0.6179
0.4	0.6554
0.5	0.6915
0.6	0.7257
0.7	0.7580

Answers

The equations are:

$$C = Se^{-\delta t}N(d_1) - Ke^{-rt}N(d_2)$$

$$d_1 = \frac{\ln(S/K) + (r - \delta)t}{\sigma\sqrt{t}} + 0.5\sigma\sqrt{t}$$

$$d_2 = \frac{\ln(S/K) + (r - \delta)t}{\sigma\sqrt{t}} - 0.5\sigma\sqrt{t}$$

(a) $d_1 = \dfrac{\ln(4,625/4,625) + (0.03-0.03)0.25}{0.2\sqrt{0.25}} + 0.5 . 0.2\sqrt{0.25}$

$= 0.1\sqrt{0.25} = 0.1 \times 0.5 = 0.05$ [NB $\ln(4,625/4,625) = 0$]

$d_2 = \dfrac{\ln(4,625/4,625) + (0.03- 0.03)0.25}{0.2\sqrt{0.25}} - 0.5 . 0.2\sqrt{0.25}$

$$= -0.1\sqrt{0.25} = -0.05$$

$$C = 4{,}625e^{-0.03.0.25}N(0.05) - 4{,}625e^{-0.03.0.25}N(-0.05)$$

$$N(0.05) = 0.5000 + (0.5398 - 0.5000)/2 = 0.5199$$

$$N(-0.05) = 0.5000 + (0.5000 - 0.5398)/2 = 0.4801$$

$$C = (4{,}625e^{-0.03.0.25} \times 0.5199) - (4{,}625e^{-0.03.0.25} \times 0.4801)$$

$$= (4{,}590.4423 \times 0.5199) - (4{,}590.4423 \times 0.4801) = 2{,}386.5709 - 2{,}203.8713 = 182.6996$$

The fair price of the call option is 182.6996 index points (£1,827).

(b) $d_1 = \dfrac{\ln(4{,}626/4{,}625) + (0.03-0.03)0.25}{0.2\sqrt{0.25}} + 0.5.0.2\sqrt{0.25}$

$$= 0.0021619 + 0.1\sqrt{0.25} = 0.0521619$$

$d_2 = \dfrac{\ln(4{,}626/4{,}625) + (0.03-0.03)0.25}{0.2\sqrt{0.25}} - 0.5.0.2\sqrt{0.25}$

$$= 0.0021619 - 0.1\sqrt{0.25} = -0.047838$$

$$C = 4{,}626e^{-0.03.0.25}N(0.0521619) - 4{,}625e^{-0.03.0.25}N(-0.047838)$$

$$N(0.0522) = 0.5000 + [(0.5398 - 0.5000) \times 0.522] = 0.5207756$$

$$N(-0.0478) = 0.5000 + [(0.5000 - 0.5398) \times 0.478] = 0.4809756$$

$$C = (4{,}626e^{-0.03.0.25} \times 0.5208) - (4{,}625e^{-0.03.0.25} \times 0.4810)$$

$$= (4{,}591.4348 \times 0.5208) - (4{,}590.4423 \times 0.4810) = 2{,}391.2192 - 2{,}208.0027 = 183.2165$$

The fair price of the call option is 183.2165 index points (£1,832.17).

(c) The change in the option price is $183.2165 - 182.6996 = 0.5169$. The delta of the option is:
Change in option price/change in stock index $= 0.5169 / 1 = 0.5169$.

EXERCISE 37.6

The FTSE 100 is 4,625, the three-month interest rate is 3% p.a., the expected rate of dividend yield is 3% p.a., and an investor expects price volatility to be 20% p.a. over the next three months.

(a) What is the fair price of a three-month European-style FTSE 100 call option with a strike price of 4,625?

(b) What would be the fair price for an investor who expects volatility to be 21% p.a.?

(c) What is the vega (kappa) of the option?

Standardised cumulative normal probabilities are shown in the table.

Table 37.E

X	N(X)
0.0	0.5000
0.1	0.5398
0.2	0.5793
0.3	0.6179
0.4	0.6554
0.5	0.6915
0.6	0.7257
0.7	0.7580

Answers

The equations are:

$$C = Se^{-\delta t}N(d_1) - Ke^{-rt}N(d_2)$$

$$d_1 = \frac{\ln(S/K) + (r - \delta)t}{\sigma\sqrt{t}} + 0.5\sigma\sqrt{t}$$

$$d_2 = \frac{\ln(S/K) + (r - \delta)t}{\sigma\sqrt{t}} - 0.5\sigma\sqrt{t}$$

(a) $d_1 = \dfrac{\ln(4{,}625/4{,}625) + (0.03-0.03)0.25}{0.2\sqrt{0.25}} + 0.5.0.2\sqrt{0.25}$

$= 0.1\sqrt{0.25} = 0.1 \times 0.5 = 0.05$ [NB $\ln(4{,}625/4{,}625) = 0$]

$d_2 = \dfrac{\ln(4{,}625/4{,}625) + (0.03-0.03)0.25}{0.2\sqrt{0.25}} - 0.5.0.2\sqrt{0.25}$

$= -0.1\sqrt{0.25} = -0.05$

$C = 4{,}625e^{-0.03.0.25}N(0.05) - 4{,}625e^{-0.03.0.25}N(-0.05)$

$N(0.05) = 0.5000 + (0.5398 - 0.5000)/2 = 0.5199$

$N(-0.05) = 0.5000 + (0.5000 - 0.5398)/2 = 0.4801$

(This approach to obtaining the standardised cumulative normal probability from the above table is known as interpolation, and entails some approximation. A more precise number can be obtained using computer software.)

698

$$C = (4{,}625e^{-0.03.0.25} \times 0.5199) - (4{,}625e^{-0.03.0.25} \times 0.4801)$$

$$= (4{,}590.4423 \times 0.5199) - (4{,}590.4423 \times 0.4801) = 2{,}386.5709 - 2{,}203.8713 = 182.6996$$

The fair price of the call option is 182.6996 index points (£1,827).

(b) $d_1 = \dfrac{\ln(4{,}625/4{,}625) + (0.03-0.03)0.25}{0.21\sqrt{0.25}} + 0.5.0.21\sqrt{0.25}$

$\quad = 0.105\sqrt{0.25} = 0.105 \times 0.5 = 0.0525$

$\quad d_2 = \dfrac{\ln(4{,}625/4{,}625) + (0.03-0.03)0.25}{0.21\sqrt{0.25}} - 0.5.0.21\sqrt{0.25}$

$\quad = -0.105\sqrt{0.25} = -0.0525$

$\quad C = 4{,}625e^{-0.03.0.25}N(0.0525) - 4{,}625e^{-0.03.0.25}N(-0.0525)$

$\quad N(0.0525) = 0.5000 + [(0.5398 - 0.5000) \times 0.525] = 0.520895$

$\quad N(-0.0525) = 0.5000 + [(0.5398 - 0.5000) \times -0.525] = 0.479105$

$\quad C = (4{,}625e^{-0.03.0.25} \times 0.520895) - (4{,}625e^{-0.03.0.25} \times 0.479105)$

$\qquad = (4{,}590.4423 \times 0.520895) - (4{,}590.4423 \times 0.479105)$

$\qquad = 2{,}391.1384 - 2{,}199.3039 = 191.83454$

The fair price of the call option is 191.83454 index points (£1,918.35).

(c) The 1% p.a. rise in expected volatility has increased the option price by 191.83454 − 182.6996 = 9.1349419 index points. The vega (kappa) of the option is:
Change in option price/Change in volatility = 9.1349419/1 = 9.13 (to two decimal places).

THE GREEKS

Exercise 37.5 showed the estimation of delta, which is a measure of the sensitivity of the fair option price to changes in the stock index (or other underlying price). Exercise 37.6 illustrated vega (alternatively known as kappa), which is a measure of the sensitivity of the fair option price to variations in expected volatility. Delta and vega are members of a group of sensitivities collectively known as the 'Greeks' (notwithstanding that vega is not a Greek letter). Other Greeks include:

Gamma = Change in delta/Change in stock index

Theta = Change in option price/Change in time to expiry

Rho = Change in option price/Basis point change in short-term interest rates

699

EXERCISE 37.7

The FTSE 100 is 4,875, the three-month interest rate is 5% p.a., the expected rate of dividend yield is 3% p.a., and an investor expects price volatility to be 20% p.a. over the next three months.

(a) Using a Black-Scholes model estimate the fair price of a three-month European-style FTSE 100 call option with a strike price of 4,875.

(b) What would be the fair price of the option if the index immediately rose by 1 point?

(c) What is the delta of the option?

(d) What would be the fair price if the index immediately rose from 4,875 to 4,877?

(e) What is the gamma of the option?

Standardised cumulative normal probabilities are shown in the table.

Table 37.F

X	N(X)
0.0	0.5000
0.1	0.5398
0.2	0.5793
0.3	0.6179

Answers

The equations are:

$$C = Se^{-\delta t}N(d_1) - Ke^{-rt}N(d_2)$$

$$d_1 = \frac{\ln(S/K) + (r - \delta)t}{\sigma\sqrt{t}} + 0.5\sigma\sqrt{t}$$

$$d_2 = \frac{\ln(S/K) + (r - \delta)t}{\sigma\sqrt{t}} - 0.5\sigma\sqrt{t}$$

(a) $d_1 = \dfrac{\ln(4,875/4875) + (0.05-0.03)0.25}{0.2\sqrt{0.25}} + 0.5.0.2\sqrt{0.25}$

$= \dfrac{0.02.0.25}{0.2.0.5} + 0.5.0.2.0.5 = 0.05 + 0.05 = 0.1$ [NB $\ln(4875/4875) = 0$]

$d_2 = \dfrac{\ln(4,875/4,875) + (0.05-0.03)0.25}{0.2\sqrt{0.25}} - 0.5.0.2\sqrt{0.25}$

$= 0.05 - 0.05 = 0$

$$C = 4{,}875e^{-0.03.0.25}N(0.1) - 4{,}875e^{-0.05.0.25}N(0)$$

$$N(0.1) = 0.5398$$

$$N(0) = 0.5000$$

$$C = (4{,}875e^{-0.03.0.25} \times 0.5398) - (4{,}875e^{-0.05.0.25} \times 0.5)$$

$$= (4{,}838.5743 \times 0.5398) - (4{,}814.4418 \times 0.5) = 2{,}611.8624 - 2{,}407.2209 = 204.64151$$

The fair price of the call option is 204.64151 index points (£2,046).

(b) $d_1 = \dfrac{\ln(4{,}876/4{,}875) + (0.05-0.03)0.25}{0.2\sqrt{0.25}} + 0.5.0.2\sqrt{0.25}$

$$= \dfrac{0.0002051 + 0.005}{0.1} + 0.05 = 0.102051$$

$d_2 = \dfrac{\ln(4{,}876/4{,}875) + (0.05-0.03)0.25}{0.2\sqrt{0.25}} - 0.5.0.2\sqrt{0.25}$

$$= 0.002051$$

$$C = 4{,}876e^{-0.03.0.25}N(0.102051) - 4{,}875e^{-0.05.0.25}N(0.002051)$$

$$N(0.102051) = 0.5398 + [(0.5793 - 0.5398) \times 0.02051] = 0.5406$$

$$N(0.002051) = 0.5000 + [(0.5398 - 0.5000) \times 0.02051] = 0.5008$$

$$C = (4{,}876e^{-0.03.0.25} \times 0.5406) - (4{,}875e^{-0.05.0.25} \times 0.5008)$$

$$= (4{,}839.5668 \times 0.5406) - (4{,}814.4418 \times 0.5008) = 2{,}616.2698 - 2{,}411.0724 = 205.19735$$

The fair price of the call option is 205.19735 index points (£2,052).

(c) The change in the option price is $205.19735 - 204.64151 = 0.5558$. The delta of the option is:

Change in option price/change in index $= 0.5558 / 1 = 0.5558$.

(d) $d_1 = \dfrac{\ln(4{,}877/4{,}875) + (0.05-0.03)0.25}{0.2\sqrt{0.25}} + 0.5.0.2\sqrt{0.25}$

$$= \dfrac{0.0004102 + 0.005}{0.1} + 0.05 = 0.104102$$

$d_2 = \dfrac{\ln(4{,}877/4{,}875) + (0.05-0.03)0.25}{0.2\sqrt{0.25}} - 0.5.0.2\sqrt{0.25}$

$$= 0.004102$$

$$C = 4{,}877e^{-0.03.0.25}N(0.104102) - 4{,}875e^{-0.05.0.25}N(0.004102)$$

N(0.104102) = 0.5398 + [(0.5793 − 0.5398) × 0.04102] = 0.5414

N(0.004102) = 0.5000 + [(0.5398 − 0.5000) × 0.04102] = 0.5016

C = (4,877e$^{-0.03.0.25}$ × 0.5414) − (4,875e$^{-0.05.0.25}$ × 0.5016)

    = (4,840.5593 × 0.5414) − (4,814.4418 × 0.5016) = 2,620.6788 − 2,414.924 = 205.7548

The fair price of the call option is 205.7548 index points (£2,058).

(e) When the index is 4,876 the option price is 205.19735 and when the index is 4,877 the option price is 205.7548. Between 4,876 and 4,877 the option delta is 205.7548 − 205.19735 = 0.55745.

    Between the index levels of 4,875 and 4,876 the option delta was 0.5558.

    Gamma = Change in delta/change in index. When the initial index rises by 1 point, the option delta rises by 0.55745 − 0.5558 = 0.00165. The gamma of the option is 0.00165.

PRICING AMERICAN-STYLE OPTIONS

As for the valuation of American-style stock index options, the Black-Scholes model for European-style stock index call options is frequently used to value American-style stock index call options on the grounds that early exercise is unlikely. If an American-style option is unlikely to be exercised prior to expiry, then it may be a reasonable approximation to treat it as if it were European-style. (It is necessary to be wary of assuming that early exercise is unlikely in the case of put options. An American-style put option may be exercised prior to expiry if the time value is exceeded by the prospective interest returns, net of foregone dividend yield, on the funds receivable upon exercise.)

VALUING OPTIONS ON BONDS

There are particular problems that arise in relation to the use of the Black-Scholes model to value options on bonds, to the extent that the Black-Scholes model may be inapplicable to the pricing of such options. This is because bonds may seriously violate some of the assumptions underlying the Black-Scholes model.

First, the Black-Scholes model assumes that the price of the underlying asset follows a diffusion process (Brownian motion or Wiener process), which is a random walk process in which each period's price change is independent of the price changes of previous periods. The result is that the variance of possible prices increases over time. This generates a lognormal distribution of possible future prices with a standard deviation that increases over time (and is a function of the square root of time). Since the distribution is lognormal rather than normal, the possibility of negative values is allowed for.

Bonds usually have maturity dates on which their nominal, or par, values will be repaid. Since the bond will be valued at par on its maturity date, its price will tend towards the par value as maturity is approached. This is sometimes known as the pull to par. It implies that as maturity is approached the range, or variance, of possible bond prices decreases. This is in direct contradiction to the diffusion process assumed by the Black-Scholes model. However, if the bond has a very long period to maturity, the pull to par may not be too great a problem.

The diffusion process could also lead to bond prices so high that the redemption yields become negative (the prospective capital loss as the bond price is pulled to par exceeds the coupon yield on the bond). Since interest rates (redemption yields) cannot be negative, the diffusion model could generate an impossible situation.

Second, the Black-Scholes model assumes constant short-term interest rates (for the period to the expiry date of the option). Variations in bond prices arise from changes in long-term interest rates. Use of the Black-Scholes model for pricing bond options requires the assumption that short-term interest rates are constant, while long-term rates can vary. This is a difficult assumption to justify in the light of evidence that short-term interest rates tend to be more volatile than long-term rates.

Third, the Black-Scholes model assumes constant price volatility of the underlying asset for the period to the expiry date of the option. Quite apart from the evidence that volatility is itself volatile, bond price volatility is based on duration, which changes with the passage of time and with interest rate variations.

PUT-CALL PARITY AND THE PRICING OF PUT OPTIONS

Once the fair price of a call option has been estimated by an option pricing model, the fair price of the corresponding put option can be estimated by means of a put-call parity relationship. The basic put-call parity equation can be expressed as:

$$C - P + K/(1 + r)^t = S \text{ [equivalently } C - P = S - K/(1 + r)^t \text{]}$$

where C is the fair price of the call option, P is the fair price of the put option, K is the strike price of the options, r is the annualised interest rate, and t is the period to expiry in years. (The put-call parity equation is based on equality between the price of the stock, S, and the price of a synthetically created stock-equivalent, $C - P + K/(1 + r)^t$. By means of buying a call option and writing a put option, the purchase of the stock at the strike price is guaranteed. Depositing $K/(1 + r)^t$ provides the cash needed to buy the stock at the strike price. The resulting construction is equivalent to buying the stock.) So the equation for the fair price of a put option is:

$$P = K/(1 + r)^t - S + C$$

The formulation $C - P = S - K/(1 + r)^t$ is based on there being no dividend yield from the stock. If dividends were payable on a continuous basis, the put-call parity condition would become:

$$C - P = S/(1 + \delta)^t - K/(1 + r)^t$$

where δ is the annualised expected rate of dividend yield. (This can be understood in terms of the stock price having a present value based on discounting at the expected rate of dividend yield.)

For individual stocks the assumption of a continuous dividend yield is unrealistic. However, it is not too unrealistic for stock index portfolios that contain a large number of stocks paying dividends at different points in time. So the put-call parity formulation of $C - P = S/(1 + \delta)^t$

$- K/(1 + r)^t$ is a reasonably good approximation for stock index options. The equation for the fair price of a stock index put option is thus:

$$P = K/(1 + r)^t - S/(1 + \delta)^t + C$$

In the cases of individual stocks that pay dividends at discrete intervals (typically every six months) a different approach is required. This involves subtracting the present values of expected future dividends (those dividends relating to ex-dividend dates prior to the option expiry date) from the stock price. The reasoning is that part of the initial cost of the share can be met by borrowing on the basis of future dividend receipts (which would subsequently be used to repay the debt). If D represents the present value of expected future dividends, then put-call parity for an individual stock becomes:

$$C - P = S - D - K/(1 + r)^t$$

The fair price of a put option is estimated by the equation:

$$P = K/(1 + r)^t - S + C + D$$

EXERCISE 37.8

The FTSE 100 is 4,625, the three-month interest rate is 3% p.a., the expected rate of dividend yield is 3% p.a., and an investor expects price volatility to be 20% p.a. over the next three months.

(a) What is the fair price of a three-month European-style FTSE 100 call option with a strike price of 4,625?

(b) Using put-call parity estimate the fair price of a put option with a strike price of 4,625.

(c) What would be the fair prices of the call and put options for an investor who expects volatility to be 21% p.a.?

(d) What are the vegas (kappas) of the options?

Standardised cumulative normal probabilities are shown in the table.

Table 37.G

X	N(X)
0.0	0.5000
0.1	0.5398
0.2	0.5793
0.3	0.6179
0.4	0.6554
0.5	0.6915
0.6	0.7257
0.7	0.7580

Answers

The equations are:

$$C = Se^{-\delta t}N(d_1) - Ke^{-rt}N(d_2)$$

$$d_1 = \frac{\ln(S/K) + (r - \delta)t}{\sigma\sqrt{t}} + 0.5\sigma\sqrt{t}$$

$$d_2 = \frac{\ln(S/K) + (r - \delta)t}{\sigma\sqrt{t}} - 0.5\sigma\sqrt{t}$$

(a) $$d_1 = \frac{\ln(4{,}625/4{,}625) + (0.03-0.03)0.25}{0.2\sqrt{0.25}} + 0.5.0.2\sqrt{0.25}$$

$$= 0.1\sqrt{0.25} = 0.1 \times 0.5 = 0.05 \qquad\qquad \text{[NB } \ln(4{,}625/4{,}625) = 0]$$

$$d_2 = \frac{\ln(4{,}625/4{,}625) + (0.03-0.03)0.25}{0.2\sqrt{0.25}} - 0.5.0.2\sqrt{0.25}$$

$$= -0.1\sqrt{0.25} = -0.05$$

$$C = 4{,}625e^{-0.03.0.25}N(0.05) - 4{,}625e^{-0.03.0.25}N(-0.05)$$

$$N(0.05) = 0.5000 + (0.5398 - 0.5000)/2 = 0.5199$$

$$N(-0.05) = 0.5000 + (0.5000 - 0.5398)/2 = 0.4801$$

$$C = (4{,}625e^{-0.03.0.25} \times 0.5199) - (4{,}625e^{-0.03.0.25} \times 0.4801)$$

$$= (4{,}590.4423 \times 0.5199) - (4{,}590.4423 \times 0.4801) = 2{,}386.5709 - 2{,}203.8713 = 182.6996$$

The fair price of the call option is 182.6996 index points (£1,827).

(b) Put-call parity for European-style stock index options can be expressed as:

$$C - P = S/(1 + \delta)^t - K/(1 + r)^t$$

Inserting values gives:

$$C - P = 4{,}625/(1 + [0.03 \times 0.25]) - 4{,}625/(1 + [0.3 \times 0.25]) = 0$$

So: $P = C = 182.6996$ index points, i.e. £1,827.

When the options are at-the-money and the expected rate of dividend yield equals the risk-free interest rate, the fair price of the put option equals the fair price of the call option.

(c) $$d_1 = \frac{\ln(4{,}625/4{,}625) + (0.03-0.03)0.25}{0.21\sqrt{0.25}} + 0.5.0.21\sqrt{0.25}$$

$$= 0.105\sqrt{0.25} = 0.105 \times 0.5 = 0.0525$$

$$d_2 = \frac{\ln(4{,}625/4{,}625) + (0.03-0.03)0.25}{0.21\sqrt{0.25}} - 0.5.0.21\sqrt{0.25}$$

705

$$= -0.105\sqrt{0.25} = -0.0525$$

$$C = 4{,}625e^{-0.03.0.25}N(0.0525) - 4{,}625e^{-0.03.0.25}N(-0.0525)$$

$$N(0.0525) = 0.5000 + [(0.5398 - 0.5000) \times 0.525] = 0.520895$$

$$N(-0.0525) = 0.5000 + [(0.5398 - 0.5000) \times -0.525] = 0.479105$$

$$C = (4{,}625e^{-0.03.0.25} \times 0.520895) - (4{,}625e^{-0.03.0.25} \times 0.479105)$$

$$= (4{,}590.4423 \times 0.520895) - (4{,}590.4423 \times 0.479105)$$

$$= 2{,}391.1384 - 2{,}199.3039 = 191.83454$$

The fair price of the call option is 191.83454 index points (£1,918.35).

Since the options are at-the-money, and the expected rate of dividend yield equals the risk-free interest rate, the fair price of the put option is equal to the fair price of the call option.

(d) The 1% p.a. rise in expected volatility has increased the option prices by $191.83454 - 182.6996 = 9.1349419$ index points. The vegas (kappas) of the options are:

Change in option price/Change in volatility $= 9.1349419/1 = 9.13$ (to two decimal places).

Incidentally, the put-call parity equation can be used to demonstrate the equivalence of a shareholding plus a put option, on the one hand, to a call option plus a risk-free investment, on the other hand. For example the basic put-call parity equation:

$$C - P + K/(1 + r)^t = S$$

can be rewritten as:

$$S + P = C + K/(1 + r)^t$$

The shareholding, S, plus the put option, P, equals the call option, C, plus the risk-free investment, $K/(1 + r)^t$.

Implied Stock Prices, Observed Stock Prices, and Stock Price Bubbles

Expressions such as

$$C - P + K/(1 + r)^t$$

$$\text{and } C - P + D + K/(1 + r)^t$$

provide implied (synthetic) stock prices. Put-call parity suggests that those implied stock prices should equal observed stock prices. The chapters in Part 7 dealing with the efficient market hypothesis indicated situations in which apparently irrational trading could move stock prices away from their fundamental values (see especially Chapters 23 and 27 on weak form efficiency and on stock market bubbles and crashes, respectively). If there were rational traders who were aware of the mispricing, and prepared to profit from it, those traders might buy put options in the event of stocks being overpriced and call options if they were underpriced. If rational traders behaved in such a way, the implied stock prices might differ from observed stock prices. Overpricing of stocks would be accompanied by lower implied prices, and underpricing by higher synthetic prices. Battalio and Schultz (2006) investigated stock prices implied by option prices during the technology stock bubble of the late 1990s and found no evidence of a high demand for put options as would be indicated by relatively high put option prices and relatively low implied stock prices. There appeared to be no evidence that rational investors were offsetting the apparently irrational behaviour of the market (see Chapter 24 on noise traders and behavioural finance).

RELIABILITY OF THE BLACK-SCHOLES MODEL

It must always be remembered that the fair option prices produced by Black-Scholes models, together with the put-call parity relationship, are merely estimates of what the option prices should be. The reliability of the estimates depends upon whether:

- The Black-Scholes model is the appropriate model.
- The expectation of volatility is accurate.
- The expectation of dividend yield is accurate.
- Arbitrage maintains put-call parity.
- The assumptions made by the Black-Scholes model hold (the assumptions include constancy of interest rates, constancy of expected volatility, the absence of early exercise, a lognormal distribution of share prices, and the absence of share price jumps).

Implied Volatility

Implied volatility refers to the market expectations of share price volatility implied by observed option prices. Implied volatility is ascertained by reversing option pricing models. Instead of calculating the theoretical option price using the stock price, strike price, expected volatility, time to expiry, interest rate, and expected dividend yield, the observed option price becomes an input and the expected volatility the output. The method is to find the level of expected volatility that is consistent with an observed option price. The objective becomes one of finding the value of expected volatility that generates a theoretical option price equal to the observed option price.

Unfortunately, the Black-Scholes model cannot be rearranged to provide an analytical solution for expected share price volatility. Instead, a numerical method must be employed. This involves an iterative search process. This can be likened to a trial-and-error process in which various values of expected volatility are put into the model and the resulting theoretical option values are compared with the observed option price. Progressively the theoretical option price gets closer to the actual price. Eventually the theoretical price equals the observed option price, and the inputted value of expected volatility at that stage is the implied volatility.

For example it may be that the observed option price is 5. The first step might be to input an expected share price volatility value of 20% p.a. into the Black-Scholes model. If this gives a theoretical option price of less than 5, then a higher expected volatility is tried. It may be that a volatility of 25% produces a theoretical option price of 5.5. This tells us that the implied volatility lies between 20% and 25% p.a. The next step may be to take an intermediate value such as 22.5%. If this produces a fair option price less than 5, we then know that volatility lies between 22.5% and 25% p.a. Again, an intermediate value is taken (e.g. 23.75%) and the theoretical option price is calculated. If the fair option price is above 5, it follows that volatility lies between 22.5% and 23.75% p.a. This iterative process progressively narrows down the range of possible values of expected volatility and can be continued until implied volatility is estimated to the desired degree of accuracy.

A difficulty with the implied volatility approach is that different option series (different strike prices) may provide different implied volatilities, despite relating to the same share and having the same expiry date. The question arises as to which value of implied volatility to choose.

Volatility Smiles and Volatility Smirks

The variation of implied volatilities across different option series (strike prices) is not random. In particular, there is a relationship between implied volatility and the closeness of the option series to being at-the-money. At-the-money options tend to exhibit relatively low implied volatilities, whereas in-the-money and out-of-the-money options are prone to exhibit relatively high implied volatilities. This is known as the smile effect. However market expectations of share price volatility must be the same in all cases, since all of the option series relate to the same share and the same expiry date.

The smile effect may arise from a systematic tendency of the Black-Scholes option pricing model to misprice options. It seems to overprice at-the-money options and interprets the lower observed prices as indicative of low expected volatility. Conversely, it appears to underprice in-the-money and out-of-the-money options, and interprets the higher observed prices as being the result of high expected volatility.

The question arises as to why the Black-Scholes model may systematically misprice options. One explanation arises from the existence of leptokurtosis, better known as fat tails. Probabilities of extreme values are often greater than supposed by normal distributions, and probabilities of values near to the mean are often lower. There is general agreement that fat tails exist, but there is no such agreement as to why. One view is that the Black-Scholes assumption of a normal distribution is wrong and that fat-tailed distributions are more appropriate. In other words the Black-Scholes assumption of (log)normal distributions is at variance with reality; actual distributions of share prices show a greater tendency to extreme values than normal distributions.

Another explanation suggests that what is actually observed is a mixture of normal distributions with different variances. According to this view, the observed distribution consists of a sequence of normal distributions, each with a different variance. When combined, such distributions lead to fat tails. The Black-Scholes model assumes constant expected volatility of share prices. If this assumption is violated, fat-tailed distributions are observed.

A third explanation of fat tails lies in the possibility that while prices follow a smooth diffusion process most of the time, there is an occasional jump. In other words whereas share prices usually change by small amounts (such a smooth share price movement is assumed by the Black-Scholes model), there are occasional sudden and large share price movements (referred to as jumps).

These explanations suggest that at least one of the assumptions of the Black-Scholes model is violated. In consequence, just as the estimated values of implied volatility become unreliable, the fair option prices estimated by the Black-Scholes model may be unreliable.

Bollen and Whaley (2004) and Chan *et al.* (2004) found that out-of-the-money stock index put options appeared to be relatively expensive, and hence their prices reflected high levels of implied volatility. It was suggested that the effect arose as a result of net buying pressure from hedging by institutional investors. Foresi and Wu (2005) established the pervasive nature of a 'smirk' pattern wherein the smile effect is asymmetric. Their study indicated that implied volatility was higher for low strike price stock index put options than for high strike price options whose strike prices were of similar distance from the spot price. Their explanation was based on the idea of a 'crash-o-phobia' whereby investors buy deep out-of-the-money (very low strike price) stock index put options as insurance against stock market crashes. The high demand for such options raises their prices and hence their implied volatilities. The elevated prices are also supported by low supply of such options since option writers find it difficult to hedge the risk of a market crash. The observation of the smirk is a useful reminder that option prices are determined by the forces of demand and supply. Option pricing models inform buyers and sellers, but do not establish prices in the market.

One of the implications of prospect theory is that people overestimate extremely low probabilities (see Chapters 2 and 24 on the psychology of investment decisions and on noise trading and behavioural finance, respectively). Given the choice between £1 and a 0.1% chance of £1,000 most people choose the 0.1% chance of £1,000. This helps to explain why people buy lottery tickets and why demand for out-of-the-money call options, and hence their prices, may be high. Conversely given the choice between paying £1 and a 0.1% chance of losing £1,000 most people will pay the £1. This explains why people will buy insurance against long-shot possibilities and why demand for out-of-the-money put options, and hence their prices, may be high.

CONCLUSION

The basic Black-Scholes option pricing model provides estimates of fair prices for European-style call options on non-dividend paying stocks. However fair option prices are required for other instruments such as dividend paying stocks, stock indices, currencies, and futures. Fair option prices are also required for American-style options, and for put options.

The basic Black-Scholes model can be amended to produce a number of variations. Those variations can be used to estimate fair prices for options on a range of instruments, and to estimate the prices of American-style options. By adding the put-call parity condition, it is possible to estimate put option prices as well as call option prices.

The Black-Scholes model, despite the possibility of amendment, may not be suitable for a number of valuation purposes. In particular, it may be unsuitable for estimating fair prices for options on bonds and for estimating the fair prices of many exotic options. Other option pricing models, such as binomial models, often need to be used (see Chapter 38 on the binomial option pricing model).

The binomial option pricing model

OBJECTIVE

The objective of this chapter is to provide knowledge of:

1. The basic binomial model.
2. The role of the equivalent portfolio.
3. Simple applications of the binomial model.
4. How the binomial model avoids assumptions needed by the Black-Scholes model.
5. Real options and their significance.

The first major advance in option pricing was made by Black and Scholes (1973). Arguably the next was made by Cox *et al.* (1979), and takes the form of the binomial model. Black-Scholes models are, strictly speaking, applicable only to options that cannot be exercised before expiry (i.e. European-style options). Binomial models can deal with the possibility of early exercise, and hence can be used for the valuation of American-style options. Another advantage of binomial models, relative to Black-Scholes models, is that they are capable of allowing for variations in interest rates and volatility over time.

A major disadvantage of the binomial model is that it does not permit an analytical solution and must be solved numerically. This means that there is no formula that can be programmed into a computer or calculator; instead a computer must be programmed to ascertain the solution by an iterative process. This can take a considerable amount of computer time.

Binomial models use portfolios (consisting of shares and debt) that replicate the behaviour of options; such portfolios being referred to as equivalent portfolios. This is based on there being a portfolio of shares and debt that will behave in the same way as the option. Correspondingly the fair price of the option equals the value of the portfolio.

Although the exposition of the binomial model in this chapter will treat the time to expiry of an option as being one period, or divided into two periods, practical application of the binomial model requires the time to expiry to be divided into a much larger number of periods. Whereas some users consider as few as 15 periods to be sufficient, others regard 30 as the minimum number of periods.

THE ONE-PERIOD BINOMIAL MODEL

The basic principles of option pricing can be indicated by means of a simple binomial model. Although this simple form of the model is highly unrealistic, it nevertheless conveys the essence of the principles underlying more complex (and more realistic) option pricing models.

Suppose that a share, which is currently priced at 100p, can have one of two values one year hence. These two values are 150p and 50p. Further suppose that a call option has a strike price of 100p and an expiry date one year hence. Figure 38.1 shows binomial trees for the share and the option.

At the end of the year the share will be worth either 150p or 50p. The call option with a strike price of 100p will be worth either 50p (if the share price rises to 150p) or 0 (if the share price falls to 50p). Binomial option pricing looks for a share-based portfolio that has the same prospective pay-offs as the option. This share-based portfolio is referred to as the equivalent portfolio.

Suppose that it is possible to buy fractions of a share and that money can be borrowed at zero interest. The purchase of half a share for 50p, which is financed partly by borrowing 25p, will replicate the call option. The portfolio of 0.5 of a share plus a debt of 25p is equivalent to the call option in terms of prospective outcomes.

If the share price rises to 150p, the value of the portfolio will be 50p. This arises from a shareholding worth 75p and a debt of 25p. The value of the equivalent portfolio is therefore equal to the value of the option.

If the share price falls to 50p, the value of the portfolio will be 0. This is because the shareholding is worth 25p, and the debt is also 25p. Again the value of the portfolio is equal to the value of the call option.

Since the call option and the equivalent portfolio have identical pay-offs, they should have the same price. The construction of the portfolio involves a net cash outflow of 25p (50p for half a share minus 25p borrowed). It follows that the cash outflow for acquiring the option should also be 25p. In other words, the price of the option should be 25p.

MULTI-PERIOD MODELS

Figure 38.2 illustrates two-period binomial trees. The value at the end of a period is referred to as a node. Starting with just one node, the number of nodes increases with the passage of each period. The distance between the highest and lowest nodes also increases over time. The initial share price is S. In each period the share price may rise by U or fall by D.

Figure 38.1

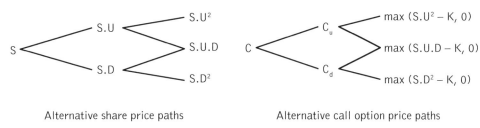

Alternative share price paths   Alternative call option price paths

Figure 38.2

At each node in a binomial tree for an option there is an option price. There will be two option prices in the next period arising from each node: one for the up-state and one for the down-state. At the end of the final period, the option would have no time value. Its price would equal its intrinsic value, which is the higher of zero or the share price minus the option strike price.

At each node in a binomial tree for an option (prior to expiry) it is possible to construct a portfolio that will behave in the same way as the option and exhibit the same end-of-period values. The portfolios for calls consist of shareholdings together with debt (i.e. each portfolio would be a margined shareholding, a shareholding partially financed by borrowing). The call option price should equal the value of the portfolio.

The quantities of shares and debt are ascertained by solving simultaneous equations. The number of shares corresponds to the option delta. The equivalent portfolio will be different at each node. The change in the portfolio from one node to the next (from one period to the next) will be self-financing. This self-financing condition means that the cash flows arising from the change in the quantity of stock are precisely matched by the change in the size of the debt. So as time passes there is no cash inflow to or outflow from the equivalent portfolio, and the proceeds from one period's portfolio will finance the next period's portfolio (both in the up-state and in the down-state).

At each node the theoretical call option price (which equals the value of the equivalent portfolio) is compared with the intrinsic value of the option. If the intrinsic value is the higher, it is assumed that the option would be exercised at that time and the intrinsic value (value upon exercise) is used as the option price at that node (instead of the value of the portfolio). In this way the binomial model can deal with the possibility of early exercise (and hence American-style options).

The call option price should equal the value of the equivalent portfolio otherwise there would be arbitrage opportunities. If their values differed, the cheaper would be bought and the more expensive sold, and this pursuit of arbitrage profits would tend to restore the equality of the two values.

The use of the binomial model is best illustrated by worked examples, and these follow. These illustrations are limited to two periods, but in reality the period to expiry should be divided into many more periods (normally at least 15). The division of a time period, such as a year, into a very large number of periods (and hence the use of short periods) generates greater accuracy but at the cost of more computer time.

Although the following illustrations use constant interest rates and volatility, it is possible to vary these from period to period (an advantage of the binomial model relative to the Black-Scholes model).

ILLUSTRATION OF THE APPLICATION OF THE ONE-PERIOD MODEL

The share price is 100p and the expected share price volatility is 0.2 (i.e. 20% p.a.) The risk-free interest rate is 6% p.a. Using a one-period binomial, estimate the fair price of a one-month call option with a strike price of (a) 100p and (b) 105p. (Assume that $D = 1/U$.)

Answer

If the annual volatility is 0.2, the monthly volatility is $0.2\sqrt{1/12}$ (volatility equals annual volatility multiplied by the square root of time to expiry in years). So U would be $e^{0.2\sqrt{(1/12)}} = 1.0594$ and D would be 0.9439 $(1/U)$. At the end of the month the share price would be 105.94p or 94.39p.

(a) The value of a 100p strike price call option at the end of the month would be 5.94p in the event of a share price rise and 0p in the event of a share price fall. These numbers are based on the higher of $(S - K)$ and 0. In the case of the up-state, this amounts to 105.94p − 100p = 5.94p. In the case of the down-state, 0 exceeds 94.39p − 100p.

The equivalent portfolio (margined shareholding) should consist of a long position in the share of Δ, and a cash borrowing with an end-of-month value of X, such that:

$$105.94\Delta - X = 5.94$$

and $\qquad 94.39\Delta - X = 0$

In other words the values of Δ and X should be such that the equivalent portfolio has the same pay-offs as the call option in the events of a rise and fall in the share price. It is possible to solve for Δ and X as follows:

$$105.94\Delta - X = 5.94$$

minus $\qquad (94.39\Delta - X = 0)$

gives $\qquad 11.55\Delta = 5.94$

so $\qquad \Delta = 5.94/11.55 = 0.514$

To solve for X:

$$(105.94 \times 0.514) - X = 5.94$$

$$54.483 - X = 5.94$$

$$54.483 - 5.94 = X$$

$$X = 48.543$$

So a portfolio equivalent to a call option comprises 0.514 shares and a borrowing equal to the present value of 48.543p. The present value of such a portfolio would be:

$(0.514 \times 100p) - (48.543/1.005) = 3.099 \qquad$ (1.005 is based on 6% p.a. for 1/12 year.)

So the fair price of the call option would be 3.10p (to two decimal places).

714

(b) The value of a 105p strike call option at the end of the month would be 0.94p (105.94p − 105p) in the event of a share price rise and 0p in the event of a share price fall. The equivalent portfolio (equivalent to the call option) should have values of Δ and X such that:

$$105.94\Delta − X = 0.94$$

and $\qquad 94.39\Delta − X = 0$

Solve for Δ

$$105.94\Delta − X = 0.94$$

minus $\qquad (94.39\Delta − X = 0)$

gives $\qquad 11.55\Delta = 0.94$

so $\qquad \Delta = 0.94/11.55 = 0.081$

Solve for X

$$(105.94 \times 0.081) − X = 0.94$$

$$8.622 − X = 0.94$$

$$8.622 − 0.94 = X$$

$$X = 7.682$$

The present cost of the equivalent portfolio would be $(0.081 \times 100) − (7.682/1.005) = 0.456p$. So the fair price of the call option is 0.46p (to two decimal places).

ILLUSTRATION OF THE APPLICATION OF THE TWO-PERIOD MODEL

The current share price is 100p and share price volatility is expected to be 0.2 (20% p.a.). The risk-free interest rate is 6% p.a. Using a two-period binomial, estimate the fair price of a two-month call option with a strike price of 100p. (Assume that D=1/U.)

Answer

If the annual volatility is 0.2, the monthly volatility is $0.2\sqrt{(1/12)}$. So U would be $e^{0.2\sqrt{(1/12)}} = 1.0594$ and D would be 0.9439. The possible stock prices after one and two months are shown by the lattice of Figure 38.3. The corresponding call option prices would be as shown by Figure 38.4.

To ascertain the one-month up-state call option price it is necessary to solve for Δ and X where:

$$112.23\Delta − X = 12.23$$

minus $\qquad (100\Delta − X = 0)$

gives $\qquad 12.23\Delta = 12.23$

so $\qquad \Delta = 1$

$$100\Delta − X = 0$$

715

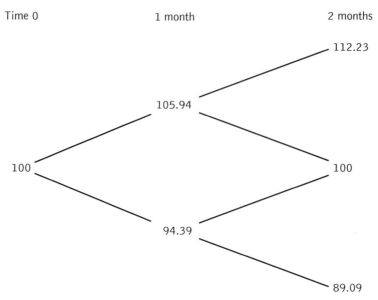

Figure 38.3 *Lattice of possible share prices*

$$100 - X = 0$$

therefore $\qquad X = 100$

So the equivalent portfolio after one month would consist of one share and a debt equal to the present value of 100p. At a share price of 105.94p such a portfolio would cost:

$$105.94 - 100/1.005 = 6.44\text{p (to two decimal places).}$$

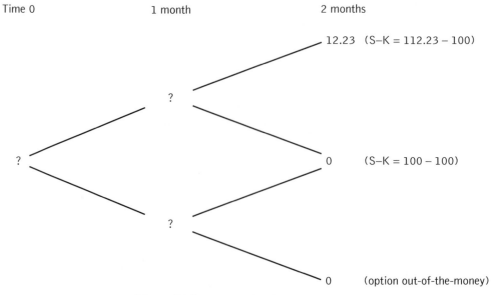

Figure 38.4 *Lattice of call option prices (1)*

(The share costs 105.94p and this is partly financed by borrowing 100/1.005 leaving the investor to pay a net 6.44p.)

The values of Δ and X for the one-month down-state call option are given by:

$$100\Delta - X = 0$$

minus $\quad (89.09\Delta - X = 0)$

gives $\quad\quad 10.91\Delta = 0$

so $\quad\quad\quad\quad \Delta = 0$

$$100\Delta - X = 0$$

therefore $\quad\quad 0 - X = 0$

so $\quad\quad\quad\quad\quad X = 0$

Solving for Δ and X yields values of zero for both. So the cost of the equivalent portfolio is zero. Figure 38.5 shows the lattice of call option prices.

To estimate the current call option price, it is necessary to find the cost of the portfolio that would have an up-state value of 6.44p and a down-state value of 0p:

$$105.94\Delta - X = 6.44$$

minus $\quad (94.39\Delta - X = 0)$

gives $\quad\quad 11.55\Delta = 6.44$

so $\quad\quad \Delta = 6.44/11.55 = 0.5576$

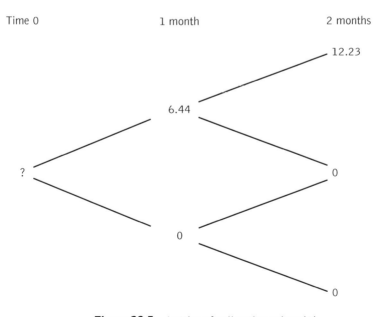

Figure 38.5   *Lattice of call option prices (2)*

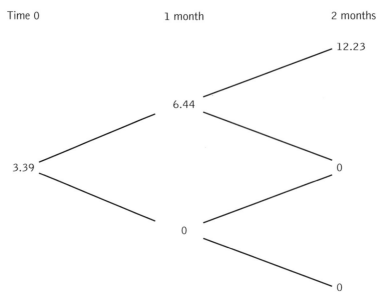

Time 0   1 month   2 months

12.23

6.44

3.39   0

0

0

Figure 38.6   *Lattice of call option prices (3)*

$$94.39\Delta - X = 0$$
$$(94.39 \times 0.5576) - X = 0$$
therefore $X = 94.39 \times 0.5576 = 52.63p$

So the time 0 cost of the equivalent portfolio is:

$$(100 \times 0.5576) - (52.63/1.005) = 55.76 - 52.37 = 3.39p$$

The lattice of call option prices becomes that of Figure 38.6.

The self-financing condition can be illustrated by this example. The time-zero portfolio comprises 0.5576 of a share and a debt of 52.37p. In the up-state this becomes worth:

$$(0.5576 \times 105.94) - 52.63 = 6.44p$$

which is the cost of the one-month up-state portfolio. The proceeds from the time-zero portfolio exactly equal the cost of the one-month portfolio.

ILLUSTRATION OF THE PRICING OF AN AMERICAN-STYLE OPTION

The current share price is 100p and share price volatility is expected to be 0.2 (20% p.a.). The share is expected to pay a dividend of 1p after one month (assume that the ex-dividend date and the dividend payment date are the same). The risk-free interest rate is 6% p.a. Using a two-period binomial, estimate the fair price of a two-month American-style call option with a strike price of 100p. (Assume that $D = 1/U$.)

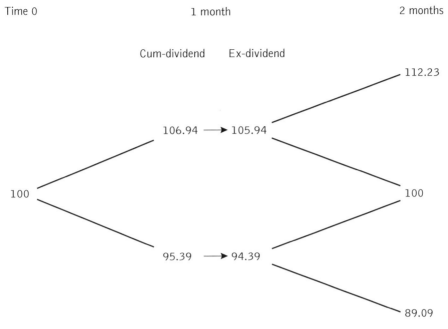

Figure 38.7   *Share price lattice with dividend payments*

Answer

If the annual volatility is 0.2, the monthly volatility is $0.2\sqrt{(1/12)}$. So U would be $e^{0.2\sqrt{(1/12)}} = 1.0594$ and D would be 0.9439. The lattice of Figure 38.7 shows the possible stock prices after 1 and 2 months. The corresponding call option prices would be as shown by Figure 38.8.

The lattice of Figure 38.7 reflects the expectation that the share price will fall, by the value of the expected dividend, when the dividend is paid. More specifically the share price is expected to fall when the share changes from being cum-dividend (the share price includes the dividend since a buyer would receive the dividend) to being ex-dividend (the share price no longer includes the dividend since a buyer would not receive the dividend). It is being assumed that this change occurs when the dividend is paid (in practice it normally occurs before the dividend payment date).

To ascertain the one-month up-state call option price it is necessary to solve for Δ and X:

$$112.23\Delta - X = 12.23$$

minus $(100\Delta - X = 0)$

gives $12.23\Delta = 12.23$

so $\Delta = 12.23/12.23 = 1$

$$100\Delta - X = 0$$

$$100\Delta = X$$

therefore $X = 100$

Time 0   1 month   2 months

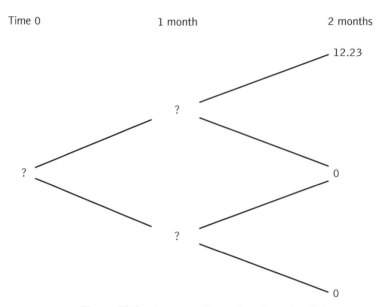

Figure 38.8   *Corresponding call option prices (1)*

So the equivalent portfolio after 1 month would consist of one share and a debt equal to the present value of 100p. When the share goes ex-dividend, the share price falls to 105.94p. At a share price of 105.94p the portfolio would cost:

$$105.94 - (100/1.005) = 6.44\text{p (to two decimal places).}$$

However, if the option were exercised cum-dividend, the intrinsic value realised would be 106.94p − 100p = 6.94p. So it would be rational to exercise the option to realise the intrinsic value of 6.94p in preference to holding the option and experiencing an ex-dividend value of 6.44p.

It can be seen that the binomial model allows for the possibility of early exercise (exercise before the expiry date of the option), and hence can be used to value American-style options. If exercise were rational it would occur immediately before the share goes ex-dividend. When the share goes ex-dividend its price falls by the amount of the expected dividend, and the intrinsic value of the call option falls by the same amount. Exercise avoids this loss of intrinsic value, but entails the loss of time value. If the time value remaining after the share goes ex-dividend is less than the intrinsic value lost, there would be a net gain from exercising and avoiding the loss of intrinsic value.

The values of Δ and X for the one-month down-state call option are given by:

$$100\Delta - X = 0$$

minus $(89.09\Delta - X) = 0$

gives $10.91\Delta = 0$

so $\Delta = 0$

$$100\Delta - X = 0$$

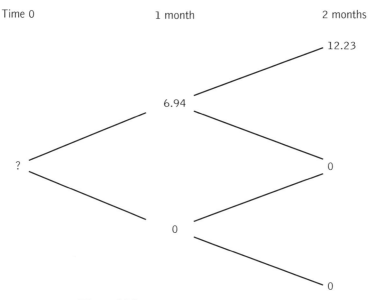

Figure 38.9 *Lattice of call option values (2)*

$$0 - X = 0$$

therefore $\quad X = 0$

Solving for Δ and X yields values of zero for both. So the cost of the equivalent portfolio is zero. The one-month down-state fair option price is thus zero. Figure 38.9 shows the lattice of call option values.

To estimate the time 0 call option price it is necessary to find the cost of the portfolio that would have an up-state value of 6.94p and a down-state value of 0p when the up-state stock price is 106.94p and the down-state stock price is 95.39p (shares held for the first month would receive the dividend and hence the dividend should be included in the 1 month stock valuation). The time 0 portfolio values of Δ and X are solved for as follows:

$$106.94\Delta - X = 6.94$$

minus $\quad (95.39\Delta - X) = 0$

gives $\quad\quad 11.55\Delta = 6.94$

$$\Delta = 6.94/11.55 = 0.6009$$

$$95.39\Delta - X = 0$$

therefore $\quad 95.39 \times 0.6009 = X = 57.3166$

So the time 0 cost of the equivalent portfolio is:

$$(100 \times 0.6009) - (57.3166/1.005) = 3.06p \text{ (to two decimal places).}$$

The lattice of the call option prices becomes that shown by Figure 38.10.

721

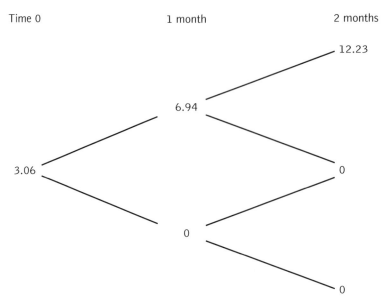

Figure 38.10 *Lattice of call option values (3)*

THE BINOMIAL MODEL AND THE ASSUMPTIONS OF THE BLACK-SCHOLES MODEL

The binomial option pricing model postulates that in any period of time the price of the underlying asset can either rise or fall (to an extent that reflects the price volatility of the asset). Over a number of periods this leads to a set of possible final prices. Corresponding to this set of final prices of the asset is a set of (at expiry) option prices. By working backwards from these potential future option prices it is possible to generate a (theoretical or fair) present option price based on a portfolio of shares and debt that gives the same outcomes as the option.

The binomial model avoids some of the restrictive assumptions of the Black-Scholes model. In particular it avoids the assumption that early exercise is impossible. The illustration of the pricing of an American-style option demonstrated that the binomial model can allow for early exercise, and hence can be used for pricing American-style options.

The binomial model also avoids the assumptions that the short-term interest rate is constant during the life of the option, and that volatility is constant during the life of the option. Within the binomial model it is possible to have a different interest rate and different volatility for each period. If the time to expiry of the option is divided into a large number of periods, considerable variation in interest rates and volatility can be allowed for. The binomial model does not need the assumption that the price of the asset follows a diffusion process that results in a lognormal distribution of possible values.

The absence of such restrictive assumptions can render the binomial model more attractive than the Black-Scholes model for the valuation of certain types of option, such as options on bonds. Unfortunately the iterative process required for the use of the binomial model can involve considerable computer time. Consequently option market participants who want option valuations quickly, or without resort to powerful computers, tend to prefer to use Black-Scholes models.

REAL OPTIONS AND COMPANY VALUATION

Real options assign a value to flexibility in production. For example an electricity generating company may invest in a power plant that is left idle during some periods but brought into production in other periods when electricity demand, and the price of electricity, is high. A gold mining company may have a mine that is not currently being used, but could be brought into production if gold prices rise above a particular level. To value such production facilities purely in terms of the net present value of their expected output would be to miss the benefit of flexibility. The flexibility in production levels constitutes real options. Flexibility has a value, which can be measured as the price of a real option. The flexibility can enhance the profitability of the company, and thereby expected earnings and dividends. So expectations of dividends and earnings should take account of real options. Recognition of real options would increase the estimated value of a company and the fair price of its shares. Company valuation and hence share valuation, which ignores real options (alternatively known as flexibility options), is likely to produce an underestimate of fundamental value.

The binomial model can be used to illustrate the valuation of real options. Consider a highly simplified example of an oil company with a two-year lease on an unused oil field capable of producing 10 million barrels of oil in a year. The cost of production of the oil is $50 per barrel (oil is conventionally priced in US dollars). The price of oil futures, with two-year maturity, is $50 per barrel. The expectation is that revenues would do no more than cover production costs. When the real option is ignored, the present value of the oil field lease is deemed to be zero. Valuation of the lease on the basis of the difference between expected revenues and costs ignores uncertainty and erroneously treats zero profit as certain.

Suppose that the price of one-year oil futures, one year hence, is expected to be either $60 or $40 per barrel. In the $60 case production could be carried out, during the second year, at a profit of ($60 − $50) × 10 million = $100 million. In the $40 case there would be no production, and hence zero profit. In terms of a one-period binomial, the up-state is $100 million and the down-state is 0.

It is possible to create an equivalent portfolio, comprising oil futures and risk-free assets (such as bank deposits or Treasury bills), with the same up-state and down-state pay-offs as the oil field. The composition of the equivalent portfolio can be found by solving the following simultaneous equations (which further simplify by ignoring discount rates):

$$(F \times \$10) + RFI = \$100,000,000 \tag{1}$$

$$(F \times -\$10) + RFI = 0 \tag{2}$$

where F is the quantity of oil covered by futures contracts, and RFI is the investment in risk-free assets.

Rewriting equation 2 as:

$$F = -RFI/-\$10 = RFI/\$10$$

and substituting into equation 1 gives:

$$([RFI/\$10] \times \$10) + RFI = \$100,000,000$$

RFI + RFI = $100,000,000

RFI = $50,000,000

$50 million is invested in risk-free assets. Substituting this value into equation 1 allows F to be ascertained.

(F × $10) + $50,000,000 = $100,000,000

F × $10 = $50,000,000

F = 5,000,000

The purchase of oil futures relates to 5 million barrels. Checking this value using equation 2 gives:

(5,000,000 × − $10) + $50,000,000 = 0

The value of the real option should equal the value of the equivalent portfolio. Since futures have a purchase price of zero, the cost of the equivalent portfolio equals the investment in risk-free assets. The value of the equivalent portfolio, and hence of the real option, is $50,000,000.

The lease on the oil field is worth $50,000,000 rather than the value of zero obtained by simply comparing expected revenues with costs of production. The value of the oil company includes the value of real options. Estimates of future earnings and dividends that ignore the flexibility provided by real options will be underestimates. (The comparison of expected revenues and costs indicates a certain profit of zero whereas consideration of the real option indicates that the profit would be either $100 million or zero.)

Chance and Peterson (2002) suggest that binomial option pricing is often more appropriate than Black-Scholes models because there may be multiple interacting options; a situation for which Black-Scholes models are inadequate. Also, the assumptions of Black-Scholes models are likely to be violated. The possible existence of multiple interacting options arises from the potential presence of various options relating to the same situation. For example options to expand, to contract, to abandon, and to defer may all be present simultaneously.

The data on which the pricing of financial options is based comes from observable prices since the shares or bonds (or other underlying instruments) are traded. The values to be used in the valuation of real options usually relate to assets that are not traded, and hence do not have observable prices. In the case of intellectual capital, such as that arising from research and development expenditure, measurement may be particularly difficult.

These considerations suggest that estimating the prices of real options is likely to be more difficult than estimating the prices of financial options. A survey of stock analysts by Glaum and Friedrich (2006) indicated that such analysts paid very little attention to real options.

CONCLUSION

The Black-Scholes option pricing model, and its variants, provides a convenient means of estimating the fair prices of options. The values of a number of variables are input into the formula and the fair option price is the output. However its applicability is limited.

There are a number of other approaches to estimating the fair prices of options. One approach is to use a binomial model. Binomial models are capable of substantial variation, and have wide applicability. However they are less convenient to use since it is not a matter of simply inputting values of variables into an equation; an iterative process is required. Since they are not dependent on the restrictive assumptions of the Black-Scholes model, such as the assumption of a lognormal distribution of returns, they are more generally applicable and their results can be used with a greater degree of confidence.

The flexibility of binomial models means that their use is not limited to financial options. In particular they can be used to estimate the fair values of real options. Real options can be useful for estimating the fair values of shares. In regards to the estimation of fair stock prices real options are particularly useful when other methods, such as dividend discount models, cannot be used (for example because of an absence of dividends).

Part 10

International Investing: Using Currency Derivatives

Chapter 39

Currency forwards, futures, swaps, and options

OBJECTIVE

The objective of this chapter is to provide knowledge of:

1. International money market investments.
2. Currency forwards and currency futures.
3. The role of arbitrage in the determination of forward and futures prices.
4. Hedging with currency futures.
5. Currency swaps.
6. Currency options as hedging instruments.
7. Zero-cost options.
8. Delta hedging with options.

INTERNATIONAL MONEY MARKET INVESTMENTS

When money is invested in foreign countries there are two elements to the return. There is the return in foreign currency terms, and the return from exchange rate movements (changes in the price of foreign currency in terms of the home currency). This might be expressed by equation 1.

$$(1 + r_D) = (1 + r_F)(E_1/E_0) \tag{1}$$

where r_D is the return in the investor's home (domestic) currency, r_F is the return in the foreign currency, E_1 is the currency price (exchange rate) at the end of the investment period, and E_0 is the currency price when the investment is made. The return in terms of the investor's own currency equals the foreign investment return (in foreign currency) multiplied by the return from the change in currency price (exchange rate movement).

It is possible to predetermine the currency price to be received at the end of the investment period by using currency forwards or futures. According to the principle of interest rate parity the change in the price of foreign currency, guaranteed by forwards or futures, exactly offsets the difference between the interest rates on the two currencies. The implication is that, when considering short-term risk-free investments such as bank deposits or Treasury bills, there is no difference in return between domestic and foreign investments when the currency price is guaranteed by forwards or futures. This arises from the way in which forward and futures prices are determined.

CURRENCY FORWARDS AND CURRENCY FUTURES

A forward contract removes exchange rate risk by guaranteeing a future exchange rate. The parties to the contract agree to exchange, on a future date, currencies at an exchange rate agreed in the present. Forward foreign exchange contracts are agreements between two parties (e.g. a bank and its client) for the exchange of two currencies on a future date at an exchange rate agreed in the present (the forward exchange rate).

A currency futures contract provides a notional commitment to buy or sell, on a specific future date (the maturity date of the futures contract), a standard amount of a particular currency at a price that is known at the time of entering the contract. Futures are tradable. A futures contract can be closed out (i.e. cancelled) by buying or selling an opposite contract. If a futures contract is bought, that contract can be closed out by means of selling a contract with the same maturity date. The two contracts cancel each other out.

It is desirable that the markets in futures contracts are liquid so as to ensure easy trading conditions (a liquid market is one in which there is a large volume of trading). Financial futures contracts are highly standardised so as to enhance the quantities of each contract and thereby generate market liquidity. The contracts traded on financial futures exchanges have a limited number of maturity dates each year. The contract sizes are also standard; for example for sterling currency contracts they are £62,500 on the Chicago Mercantile Exchange (CME). This standardisation limits the number of different contracts available and correspondingly increases the volume traded in each contract.

Comparing Currency Forwards and Currency Futures

Futures and forwards are similar instruments whose prices tend to be very close. There are, nonetheless, important differences. Forwards are actual commitments to future transactions, whereas futures are notional commitments. Forward contracts are used to effect the end transaction; the parties to the forward contract are the same as the parties to the subsequent exchange of currencies. Futures rarely go to the point of delivery of the currency and, if they do, the counterparties involved are not the same as the counterparties to the original futures deal. Futures are financial instruments that are independent of the underlying currency, albeit with prices that normally correlate with those of the underlying currency. Futures positions are normally closed out by taking an opposite futures position (e.g. someone who initially sells closes out the short position by buying an equal number of contracts of the same maturity as those sold). Most futures are closed out before they mature, and hence futures commitments are often referred to as 'notional' commitments to reflect the absence of actual exchanges of currencies.

Second, forwards are over-the-counter (OTC) instruments whereas futures are exchange-traded. OTC products take the form of an agreement between two parties (e.g. the client and a bank). This agreement is not visible to other parties - the market is not transparent. This lack of transparency means that it is not possible to know the prices at which others are transacting. Different clients may obtain different prices from the banks. Futures markets are transparent. Everyone can see the prices available. The most transparent markets are the face-to-face markets in which all transactors occupy the same trading area (known as a pit). Everyone can see what quantities are being traded and at what prices. Everyone can obtain the same prices: there is no discrimination between different transactors.

Third, forwards can be tailor-made to the specific requirements of a client. The client can specify dates and amounts to be transacted. Futures are highly standardised. Each futures contract relates to a standard quantity of a currency. Furthermore, only a limited number of maturity dates are available at any time. A high degree of standardisation is necessary for market liquidity, that is for ensuring that the volumes traded are sufficiently high for buyers and sellers to experience no difficulty in conducting their desired transactions. If the standardisation were less, for example through a greater number of maturity dates or a variety of contract sizes, the number of different contracts would be greater and each variety of contract might experience few and infrequent trades. Such inadequate liquidity could reduce the ability of users, such as hedgers, to establish and subsequently close out futures positions.

Fourth, the profit or loss from a forward contract is realised, in its entirety, when the contract matures. Profits and losses on a futures contract are realised on a daily basis in response to daily price movements (via a process known as marking to market).

In the case of currencies, successful forward and futures markets coexist. This coexistence is most marked in North America. Elsewhere, particularly in Europe, forward markets are predominant. A balanced coexistence might in time become the norm throughout the world since forwards and futures have their relative merits. Futures have a considerable advantage in that they allow flexibility as to the date of closing out (futures can be closed out on any trading day up to maturity), whereas forwards tend to involve a commitment to an exchange of currencies on a specific date. If there is doubt as to the timing of the cash flow being hedged, futures may be the more attractive hedging instrument.

On the other hand, futures can be more complex to administer because of the daily cash flows arising from marking to market. Typically a futures margin account would be held, possibly with a futures broker. Daily cash flows would move into and out of the account. The hedger would only be involved in making payments (or receiving money) if the balance in the margin account were to fall below (or exceed) a predetermined limit. Margin accounts do have the disadvantage of tying up liquidity.

When hedging with futures, the cash flows from the futures arise before the cash flows from the transaction being hedged. Losses may precede profits and there could be difficulty in financing those losses. There is a risk that losses from daily marking to market accumulate to a problematic extent and, although there would be offsetting future profits from the underlying transaction (the transaction being hedged), significant liquidity problems could arise prior to the date on which the cash flow from the underlying transaction takes place (Metalgesellschaft encountered this type of problem when using commodity derivatives).

Currency forwards and futures involve two simultaneous prices: the price of each currency in terms of the other. In the case of futures contracts possible confusion from this is reduced since the major contracts price currencies in US dollars, use US dollars for the daily marking to market cash flows, and stipulate contract sizes in amounts of the foreign (non-US dollar) currency, e.g. £62,500 is the size of the pound sterling futures contract.

PRICING CURRENCY FORWARDS AND FUTURES

To a large extent the determination of forward prices and of futures prices is similar in that they both reflect interest rate parity. Forward prices and futures prices should be very close. The mechanics of price determination may differ between the two markets in that currency forward prices are likely to be based on the costs of hedging the provision of forward contracts whereas futures prices are likely to be based on arbitrage.

Interest Rate Parity

The current price of a currency is referred to as the spot price. If the forward price of a currency exceeds the spot price, that currency is said to be at a premium. For example if the spot price of sterling in terms of US dollars is £1 = $1.50, while the six-month forward price is £1 = $1.55, then sterling is said to be at a premium against the dollar. Conversely, if the forward price is less than the spot price, the currency is said to be at a discount. With a spot exchange rate of £1 = $1.50, a forward price of £1 = $1.45 means that sterling is at a discount against the US dollar (correspondingly, the dollar is at a premium against sterling).

Interest rate parity describes a relationship between spot and forward (and futures) currency prices. One way of looking at this relationship is in terms of equality between the forward premium or discount on the one hand and the difference between the two interest rates on the other. The premium or discount offsets the difference in interest rates. For example if sterling yields the higher interest rate it would trade at a discount to the US dollar. This means that the forward (futures) price of sterling would be below the spot price so that, from the perspective of dollar-based traders, there would be a guaranteed capital loss from holding sterling that matched the additional interest from sterling deposits. Conversely if sterling interest rates were below US dollar rates, sterling should trade at a premium in the forward and futures markets, that is the forward (futures) price of sterling should be greater than the spot price so that there is a capital gain that compensates for the lower interest returns.

The interest rate parity relationship can be described by the following equation:

$$\frac{R_\$ - R_\pounds}{1 + R_\pounds} = \frac{F - S}{S}$$

where $R_\$$ is the (euro-)dollar interest rate for the period to the maturity of the forward or futures contract, $R_\pounds$ is the (euro-)sterling interest rate for the same period, F is the forward or futures price of sterling, and S is the spot price of sterling. (The prefix 'euro-' indicates that the interest rates are eurocurrency rates, i.e. interest rates for currency outside its country of origin, for example pounds sterling in Paris. This has nothing to do with the currency called the 'Euro'.)

Covered Interest Arbitrage

Arbitrage plays a crucial role in the determination of the prices of futures contracts on foreign exchange. The arbitrage is usually referred to as covered interest arbitrage. The arbitrage can be seen as being between the futures contract on the one hand and a synthetic forward contract on the other. The arbitrage involves buying the cheaper of the two and simultaneously selling the more expensive. The fair futures price is the futures price that provides no opportunity for arbitrage profits. The price of the futures should equal that of the synthetic forward.

To illustrate the general principle for the case of currencies, consider futures contracts on sterling using the US dollar as the base currency (the US dollar is normally the base currency in foreign exchange futures contracts). The synthetic long forward involves borrowing dollars and simultaneously buying spot sterling, which is put on deposit. There is no initial cash outlay but on the maturity date a sum of sterling is held and a dollar debt has to be repaid. So the transactions that occur on the maturity date are equivalent to those under a forward contract, dollars are paid and sterling is received.

If sterling futures are overpriced relative to the synthetic, an arbitrage profit can be made via a synthetic long forward position together with a short (sold) futures position. If the price of buying forward sterling by means of the synthetic is lower than the futures price of sterling, the dollar receipts from selling sterling via the (overpriced) futures will exceed the dollar debt to be repaid. The difference constitutes the arbitrage profit. This arbitrage is illustrated by Figure 39.1.

Conversely, a futures price below the synthetic price offers an arbitrage profit from buying the (underpriced) futures and simultaneously taking a short position in the synthetic.

The short synthetic position is established by means of borrowing sterling and using the proceeds to buy US dollars, which are then deposited. On the maturity date the sterling debt is repaid and the dollar deposit matures to provide US dollars (so on the maturity date there is an outflow of sterling and an inflow of dollars, just as in the case of a forward contract to sell sterling for US dollars). If the futures price is below the price provided by the synthetic, it would be possible for an arbitrager to construct the synthetic forward and use the dollar proceeds to buy sterling through the futures contract. The amount of sterling thereby obtained would exceed the sum needed to repay the sterling debt. The excess would be the arbitrage profit. This arbitrage is illustrated by Figure 39.2.

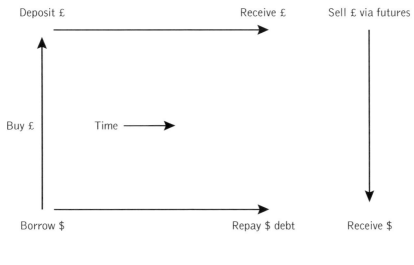

Synthetic long forward

Short futures

Figure 39.1

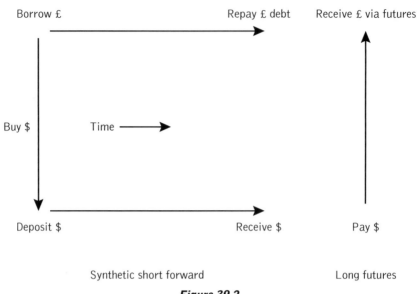

Figure 39.2

These arbitrage processes would tend to bring the futures price into line with the synthetic price. In the first case, the sale of futures would tend to reduce the futures price towards the price of the synthetic forward. Simultaneously, the purchase of spot sterling would tend to raise the spot price, with the consequence that more dollars need to be borrowed. So the ratio of dollars to be repaid to pounds received would rise; in other words, the forward price of sterling provided by the synthetic would rise. The actual futures price would fall and the synthetic forward price rise. Hence the two would move towards equality. When they are equal there would be no further arbitrage profits available (transaction costs may prevent complete equality, a point that will be returned to).

In the second case (underpriced futures and relatively overpriced synthetics), the opposite transactions would take place and tend to restore equality between the two prices. In particular the futures price would rise towards the price of the synthetic forward.

EXERCISE 39.1

The six-month US dollar interest rate is 5% p.a. and the six-month euro interest rate is 4% p.a. The price of the euro is currently $0.95. If the futures (with six months to maturity) price of the euro were $0.97, how might an arbitrage profit be made?

Answer

Using the interest rate parity equation to estimate the fair futures price (F):

$$(R_\$ - R\epsilon)/(1 + R\epsilon) = (F - S)/S$$

$$[(0.05/2) - (0.04/2)]/[1 + (0.04/2)] = (F - \$0.95)/\$0.95$$

$$(0.025 - 0.02)/1.02 = (F - \$0.95)/\$0.95$$

$$F = [(0.005/1.02) \times \$0.95] + \$0.95$$

$$= \$0.9547 \text{ (to four decimal places)}$$

The fair futures price is $0.9547.

If the futures price of the euro were $0.97, the futures would be overpriced. Covered interest arbitrage would entail selling the overpriced futures. The US dollar would be borrowed, the euro would be bought spot, euro futures would be sold, and the proceeds of the futures sale would be used to repay the dollar debt. The proceeds of the futures sale would exceed the amount required to repay the dollar debt. The excess is the arbitrage profit.

Synthetics and the Pricing of Forward Contracts

Such arbitrage operations may also help to determine forward currency prices. However the costs of synthetics may more directly affect forward prices. This is because banks offering forward contracts are likely to use the costs of synthetic forwards (and hence the interest rate parity equation) as the basis for pricing their forward contracts. They may even construct synthetic forwards in order to generate the cash flows to which the forward contracts commit them; this would be a means of hedging risks arising from the agreement to a forward exchange of currencies. For example a bank that provides a client with a short forward contract on sterling (the client sells sterling for dollars) will receive sterling and pay dollars on the maturity date of the forward contract. The bank may construct a synthetic short forward since such a structure requires sterling, and receives dollars, on the maturity date.

The Significance of Bid-Offer Spreads

The gross returns from arbitrage must exceed transaction costs, otherwise arbitrage would not occur. In ascertaining the synthetic forward price, account must be taken of the fact that currency is bought at an offer and sold at a bid price (and that the offer price is higher than the bid price). Likewise, money is borrowed at the offer (high) interest rate and deposited at the bid (low) rate. As a result, synthetic long and short positions have different prices. Specifically, synthetic purchases will be at a relatively high price and synthetic sales at a lower price. The difference between the prices will reflect the bid-offer spreads on currencies and interest rates (bid-offer spreads are the differences between bid and offer prices/rates). The following exercise illustrates covered interest arbitrage and the effects of bid-offer spreads.

EXERCISE 39.2

The spot £/$ exchange rate is £1 = $1.8000−1.7990. One-year interest rates are as shown in the table.

Table 39.A

£	$
5%−5.125%	3.875% − 4%

(a) Within what range should the prices of sterling futures, with one-year maturity, fall? What should be the offer (buy) and bid (sell) forward prices for delivery in one year?

(b) If a 1% rise in sterling interest rates causes a $0.1 rise in the spot price of the pound, what should happen to the futures and forward prices?

Answers

(a) Borrow $, buy £ with $ spot, deposit £, sell £ futures or forwards.

Using the interest rate parity equation:

$$\frac{R_\$ - R_£}{1 + R_£} = \frac{F - S}{S}$$

$$\frac{0.04 - 0.05}{1.05} = \frac{F - 1.8}{1.8}$$

(Note that money is borrowed at the offer (higher) interest rate and deposited at the bid (lower) interest rate. Currency is bought at the offer (higher) price.)

$$F = \frac{(0.04 - 0.05) \times 1.8}{1.05} + 1.8 = 1.7829$$

The offer (buy) price of one-year forward sterling should be £1 = $1.7829. This should be the upper limit of the futures no-arbitrage band.

It may be noted that forward/futures sterling trades at a discount to spot, which would be expected on the grounds that sterling interest rates are higher than dollar interest rates.

Borrow £, sell £ for $ spot, deposit $, buy £ futures or forwards.

$$\frac{0.03875 - 0.05125}{1.05125} = \frac{F - 1.799}{1.799}$$

(Note that currency is sold at the bid (lower) price.)

$$F = \frac{(0.03875 - 0.05125) \times 1.799}{1.05125} + 1.799 = 1.7776$$

The bid (sell) price of one-year forward sterling should be £1 = $1.7776. This should be the lower limit of the futures no-arbitrage band.

(b) The new £/$ exchange rate is £1 = $1.9000−1.8990. The new one-year interest rates are shown in the table.

Table 39.B

£	$
6%−6.125%	3.875% − 4%

Borrow $, buy £ with $ spot, deposit £, sell £ futures or forwards.

$$\frac{0.04 - 0.06}{1.06} = \frac{F - 1.9}{1.9}$$

$$F = \frac{(0.04 - 0.06) \times 1.9}{1.06} + 1.9 = 1.8642$$

The offer (buy) price of one-year forward sterling should be £1 = $1.8642. This should be the upper limit of the futures no-arbitrage band.

Borrow £, sell £ for $ spot, deposit $, buy £ futures or forwards.

$$\frac{0.03875 - 0.06125}{1.06125} = \frac{F - 1.899}{1.899}$$

$$F = \frac{(0.03875 - 0.06125) \times 1.899}{1.06125} + 1.899 = 1.8587$$

The bid (sell) price of one-year forward sterling should be £1 = $1.8587. This should be the lower limit of the futures no-arbitrage band.

EXERCISE 39.3

The spot $/£ exchange rate is £1 = $2.5000−2.4990 (buy £ at $2.5 and sell at $2.499). Six-month interest rates are as shown in the table.

Table 39.C

$	£
7 7/8 − 8% p.a.	5 7/8 − 6% p.a.

Borrowing is at the higher rate (the offer rate) and depositing is at the lower rate (the bid rate).

(a) What is the price of a six-month synthetic long forward (for the purchase of sterling)?

(b) What is the price of a six-month synthetic short forward (for the sale of sterling)?

(c) How could an arbitrage profit be made if a short forward (or futures) is available at $2.53/£?

Answers

(a) Borrow $, buy £, deposit £. At maturity £s are received and $s paid.

$$\frac{0.04 - 0.029375}{1.029375} = \frac{F - 2.5}{2.5}$$

(Since the period to maturity is six months, the annual interest rates are divided by 2.)

$$(0.010322 \times 2.5) + 2.5 = F = 2.5258$$

This is the price of a synthetic long forward. It could be seen as the fair price of a forward contract to buy £.

(b) Borrow £, buy $, deposit $. At maturity $s are received and £s paid.

$$\frac{0.039375 - 0.03}{1.03} = \frac{F - 2.499}{2.499}$$

$$(0.009102 \times 2.499) + 2.499 = F = 2.5217$$

This is the price of a synthetic short forward. It could be seen as the fair price of a forward contract to sell £.

Banks could create the synthetics as a means of providing the cash flows to meet the requirements of forward contracts.

(c) If a short forward (or futures) were available at $2.53/£ an arbitrage profit is available from a long synthetic. Forward sterling would be bought for $2.5258 by means of the synthetic and sold for $2.53.

A user of forward contracts can expect two different forward prices, one for forward purchases and one for sales. These prices should reflect the two prices of synthetic forwards. A user of futures will find that there is just one futures price (or at least a very small difference between buying and selling prices). For futures contracts the two prices implied by the synthetic forwards set upper and lower limits to the actual futures price. Arbitrage keeps the futures price within a range of values, the no-arbitrage band, with the two synthetic forward prices providing the upper and lower limits to the range. Within the no-arbitrage band, the actual futures price will be determined by the demand and supply arising from hedgers and speculators. The middle of this range of possible futures prices is known as the fair futures price, which is the futures price that arbitrage would tend to produce in the absence of transaction costs (transaction costs include bid-offer spreads).

HEDGING CURRENCY RISK WITH FUTURES

Hedgers using futures transfer their risks. If they buy futures, others must sell them, i.e. the notional commitment to buy currency on a specified date in the future at a price agreed upon in the present is matched by another user's notional commitment to sell the currency at that date and price. The seller of futures would be either a hedger wanting to avoid the opposite risk or a futures trader (speculator) willing to take on the risk in the expectation of making a profit.

In Example 39.1 it is assumed that a British exporter anticipates receipt of $1 million on 1 May. The sale of goods is agreed upon on 3 February and the exporter wants to hedge against the risk that the dollar will depreciate against the pound before 1 May, thus reducing the sterling value of the dollar receipts. The exporter might anticipate a fall in the dollar or might simply want to obtain protection against the possibility of a weakening of the dollar. In other words, the decision to hedge may be based on a forecast of an adverse exchange rate movement or on the risk that there would be an adverse change resulting from chance (unpredictable) currency movements. In either case the exporter could hedge by buying sterling currency futures.

EXAMPLE 39.1

3 February
An exporter anticipates receipt of $1 million on 1 May. The spot exchange rate is £1 = $1.50 ($1 million = £666,666).

The exporter buys ten sterling futures contracts, at £62,500 per contract, at an exchange rate of £1 = $1.50. The total face value of the futures is £625,000, notionally committing the exporter to a payment of $937,500 for £625,000 (625,000 × 1.50 = 937,500).

1 May
The dollar has fallen so that the exchange rate stands at £1 = $1.60. (A rise in the pound is a fall in the dollar.) The sterling value of the $1 million is now £625,000.

The exporter sells ten sterling futures contracts at £1 = $1.60. This gives the exporter the notional right to the receipt of $1,000,000 (625,000 × 1.60) in exchange for £625,000.

The currency loss is £666,666 − £625,000 = £41,666 (= $66,666).

The futures profit is $62,500 ($1,000,000 − $937,500, the futures selling price minus the futures buying price).

The loss in the currency market, arising from the weakening of the dollar, is largely offset by the profit in the futures market. The offset is not perfect since on 3 February the £666,666 in the currency market is coupled with only £625,000 in the futures market. Such a mismatch arises from the denomination of sterling futures contracts in units of £62,500; perfect matching is impossible. Fortunately the exchange rate in the futures market moves in line with that in the currency market, and is indeed equal to it.

The exchange rate for futures need not be equal to, nor move to the same extent as, the spot exchange rate. If the spot and futures rates change by different amounts, a degree of imperfection enters the hedge. This possibility is illustrated by Example 39.2, which differs from Example 39.1 only in the assumption that the rate of exchange for the sterling futures moves to £1 = $1.58 rather than £1 = $1.60. As a result the hedge is less successful.

EXAMPLE 39.2

3 February

The exporter anticipates receipt of $1 million on 1 May. The spot exchange rate is £1 = $1.50 ($1 million = £666,666).

The exporter buys ten sterling futures contracts at an exchange rate of £1 = $1.50. Notionally $937,500 is to be paid for £625,000.

1 May

The dollar has fallen so that the exchange rate stands at £1 = $1.60. The sterling value of the $1 million is now £625,000.

The exporter sells ten sterling futures contracts at £1 = $1.58. This is equivalent to sales proceeds of $987,500 (625,000 × 1.58) in exchange for £625,000.

The currency loss is £666,666 − £625,000 = £41,666 (= $66,666).

The futures profit is $50,000 ($987,500−$937,500).

EXERCISE 39.4

A UK institutional investor plans to invest £1,000,000 in US government bonds (Treasury bonds). The current $/£ exchange rate is $1.80/£ and the three-month forward (and futures) exchange rate is $1.7865. The investor takes the view that the US dollar is currently cheap but that US Treasury bonds are currently overpriced, and would prefer to delay the purchase by three months.

(a) How can the investor hedge the currency risk of the purchase of US bonds?

(b) How many dollars does the investor expect to have available for the purchase of bonds when hedging the currency risk?

(c) What is the forward (or futures) profit or loss after the three months if the exchange rate turns out to be (i) $1.60/£, and (ii) $2.00/£?

Answers

(a) The investor could sell £1,000,000 three month forward; or could sell 16 sterling futures contracts (£1,000,000/£62,500) using futures with a maturity of (or in excess of) three months.

(b) $1,786,500 (£1,000,000 × $1.7865/£).

(c) (i) The investor obtains $1,786,500 rather than $1,600,000 (£1,000,000 × $1.60/£) and hence profits by $186,500 ($1,786,500 − $1,600,000).

(ii) The investor obtains $1,786,500 rather than $2,000,000 (£1,000,000 × $2.00/£) and hence loses by $213,500 ($2,000,000 − $1,786,500).

In both case (i) and case (ii) the futures profit/loss will be increased by interest on variation margin payments.

EXERCISE 39.5

A UK investment company has a 'hedged' US equity fund that seeks to provide exposure to the US stock market whilst avoiding currency risk. The current exchange is $1.80/£ and the fund is worth $9,000,000.

(a) How can the currency risk be hedged?

(b) What practical difficulties are likely to be encountered?

Answers

(a) Sterling ($9,000,000/$1.80 = £5,000,000) could be bought forward, or 80 sterling futures purchased (£5,000,000/£62,500 = 80).

(b) One problem is that the currency exposure varies with movements in the US stock market. The size of the forward or futures position would need to be adjusted as the US dollar value of the fund changes. Since very frequent changes are costly in terms of transaction costs, it is not possible that the currency exposure will be perfectly covered at all times.

Forward and futures contracts would need to be renewed as they reach maturity. There would be corresponding transaction costs each time a maturity date is reached.

EXERCISE 39.6

A UK fund manager has £10 million for a US stock market fund. The S&P 500 stands at 2000 and S&P 500 futures trade at $250 per index point. The $/£ exchange rate is $2/£1. The size of the sterling currency futures contract is £62,500. The fund manager wishes the fund to be hedged against currency risk. Assume initial (and maintenance) margin of 5% for S&P 500 futures contracts, and ignore initial (and maintenance) margin on the currency futures.

(a) Show how a fund, hedged against currency risk, can be structured using US stocks and currency futures.

(b) Show how a fund, hedged against currency risk, can be structured using stock index futures (i.e. a futures fund) and currency futures.

(c) What hedge rebalancing may be required in (a) and (b)?

(d) What considerations would influence the choice between (a) and (b)?

Answers

(a) Sell the £10 million for $20 million. Use the $20 million to buy a portfolio of US stocks. Since the risk is that the dollar will fall against the pound, i.e. that the pound will rise against the dollar, it is necessary to buy sterling currency futures in order to hedge the fund. Initially the requisite number of sterling currency futures contracts would be:

£10,000,000/£62,500 = 160

(b) Each S&P 500 futures contract relates to $2,000 \times \$250 = \$500,000$ of stock. To match a balanced portfolio of $20 million of stock would require the purchase of:

$20,000,000/\$500,000 = 40$ S&P 500 futures contracts.

There would be a deposit of initial margin, which would need to be hedged against currency risk. If initial margin were to be 5%, $1,000,000 would need to be hedged. This is equivalent to hedging $1,000,000/\$2 = £500,000$. The number of sterling currency futures contracts to be bought is:

£500,000/£62,500 = 8

The remaining £9,500,000 could be held on deposit in sterling.

(c) In case (a), a rise in the S&P 500 would increase the exposure to the dollar. The sterling value of the capital gain would need to be hedged, so the number of futures contracts should be increased. The converse would apply to a fall in the S&P 500.

In case (b), movements in the S&P 500 futures price would cause changes in the level of maintenance margin. This would require changes in the number of sterling currency futures contracts. Variation margin cash flows could not be hedged with currency futures since variation margin cannot be forecast (because movements of the S&P 500 and its futures cannot be predicted).

(d) If there were a wish to actively manage the fund, the use of a futures fund would not be appropriate.

If there is a desire to have an index tracker fund, the choice between (a) and (b) would be influenced by factors such as relative transaction costs in stock and futures markets, relative liquidity in stock and futures markets, the proximity of futures prices to their fair prices, basis risk in futures markets, and the suitability of the S&P 500 as a stock index to be tracked.

There may be a case for combining approaches (a) and (b) when structuring an index tracker fund. The relative importance of the two approaches could be varied over time in the light of factors such as the relationship of the futures price to its fair price (futures priced below the fair price would be an attractive purchase). This would impart a form of active management to an index tracker fund.

The 'Guaranteed' Exchange Rate

When using currency futures for hedging, the user attempts to guarantee an exchange rate. The principles of futures pricing, in particular the interest rate parity relationship, have implications for the exchange rate that a hedger may hope to guarantee. The exchange rate that a hedger expects to obtain will lie between the spot rate and the futures rate, and will be dependent upon the timing of closing out.

If the futures position is closed out immediately after being opened, the exchange rate obtained will be the initial spot rate, e.g. £1 = $1.50. If the futures contract is held to maturity, the rate obtained will be the futures rate ruling on the date of entering the contract, e.g. £1 = $1.48. Closing out on an intermediate date would attain an exchange rate between these two extremes. The exchange rate expected is a function of time. So, for example, if the futures contract initially has six months to maturity and is closed out after three months, the exchange rate expected might be £1 = $1.49.

When a futures contract is held to maturity, currencies would be exchanged at the spot exchange rate on the futures maturity date. The original futures exchange rate is obtained by setting the futures profit/loss against the new currency price. Likewise the expected exchange rates on intermediate dates are based on the new currency prices being offset (or added to) by profits (or losses) from futures contracts.

The variation of the realised exchange rate with the passage of time can be explained in terms of changes in basis. Basis is initially $0.02 ($1.50 − $1.48), but after six months it will have eroded to zero: at maturity of a futures contract the futures and spot prices are identical. The difference between the spot and futures prices can be regarded as the rate of depreciation/appreciation required to offset the interest rate differential. As the time period shortens, the cash value of the interest rate differential falls and the corresponding depreciation/appreciation declines to match. So with just three months remaining to maturity the cash value of the interest rate differential is half its level when six months remained and, correspondingly, the depreciation prior to maturity is $0.01 rather than the original $0.02.

When closing out futures contracts prior to maturity there is no certainty that the anticipated exchange rate will be obtained. If interest rates change before maturity, the implied currency appreciation/depreciation will change, and with it the fair futures price. Furthermore the futures price can move within the no-arbitrage band with the effect that the exchange rate actually obtained using futures differs from the expected value.

EXERCISE 39.7

It is 1 December. A UK institutional investor is due to receive dividends of US$800,000 on 29 January. The Chicago Mercantile Exchange $/£ futures price for December maturity is $1.6012/£, and for March maturity it is $1.6020/£. The futures maturity dates are 15 December and 15 March.

(a) How can the investor hedge the currency risk with futures?

(b) What exchange rate can the investor expect to be guaranteed for 29 January?

(c) If on 29 January the March futures price is $1.6500/£, what is the profit or loss from the futures contracts?

Answers

(a) Based on an exchange rate of $1.6016/£, the expected $800,000 is equivalent to:

800,000/1.6016 = £499,500.5

At £62,500 per contract, this corresponds to 499,500.5/62,500 = 7.99 sterling futures contracts. The investor is most likely to hedge by buying eight futures contracts for March maturity.

(b) 29 January falls midway between 15 December and 15 March. The expected exchange rate therefore falls midway between the two futures prices, i.e. at $1.6016/£. (Assuming that the futures prices equal the fair futures prices.)

(c) The profit is $0.048 ($1.6500 − $1.6020) per £1 on £500,000. This amounts to $0.048 × 500,000 = $24,000.

CURRENCY SWAPS

Currency swaps can be used to convert an investment in one currency into one in another currency. Figure 39.3 illustrates a currency swap. Investor A has a US dollar bank deposit and wishes to swap the interest receipts for the interest on a bank deposit in euros. Investor B has a euro deposit and wants to exchange the interest receipts for those on a US dollar deposit. Investors A and B agree to exchange interest and principal on their respective investments. A effectively obtains a euro deposit and B simulates a dollar deposit.

The currency swap may be carried out by direct negotiation between the counterparties or by means of a bank acting as intermediary and effectively becoming the counterparty to both participants. Figure 39.4 illustrates the latter case. The bank operates as counterparty to both, and investors A and B need not know the other's identity.

The bank runs the risk of losses arising from default by one of the parties. If, for example, the dollar strengthens against the euro, the bank will be gaining from its transactions with A and losing

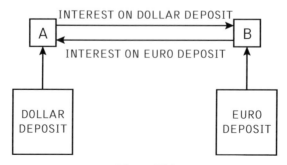

Figure 39.3

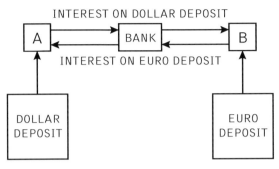

Figure 39.4

with respect to B. Normally these gains and losses would cancel each other out but if A were to renege on its obligations, the bank would be left with its loss-making commitments to B. The bank is committed to paying both interest and principal in the relatively strong dollar while receiving the same in the weakened euro.

CURRENCY OPTIONS AS HEDGING INSTRUMENTS

The ultimate economic function of financial derivatives (forwards, futures, swaps, and options) is to provide means of risk reduction. Someone who is at risk from a price change can use options to offset that risk. A call option gives the right to buy currency at a particular price, the strike price, and a put option gives the right to sell currency at the strike price. A call option can be seen as a means of ensuring an upper limit to the purchase price (if the market price exceeds the strike price, then the option may be exercised in order to buy at the strike price). A put option provides a lower limit to the selling price (exercise of the right to sell might occur in the event of the market price being below the strike price). So options can be regarded as means of insurance against adverse price movements.

A hedger needs to compare the use of options with at least two alternatives. Those alternatives are leaving the exposure unhedged and covering it with futures or forwards. Consider a hedger with a long position (such as a holder of a foreign currency investment) who seeks protection from a fall in the currency price. The protection can be obtained by buying a put option. The put option protects the hedger from a price fall since it allows the holder to sell the currency at the strike price, and hence prevents any lower price being suffered. However, the put option does not prevent gains being made from a rise in the currency price.

If the holder of a foreign currency investment is convinced that the currency price will not fall, he or she will not be prepared to pay a premium for a put option to protect the position from a price fall. At the other extreme, if the hedger feels certain that the price will fall, he or she would cover the currency exposure completely by an offsetting short position (in markets where futures or forwards are available, the short position can be achieved by selling futures contracts or selling forward). The exposure to the currency price movement is thereby eliminated completely. It follows that options will be used only when there is uncertainty as to the direction of price movement.

One difficulty when using currency options to hedge foreign currency investments is that the sum of foreign currency to be hedged is uncertain. The extent of the currency risk depends upon the performance of the foreign currency investment. If the investment is in a stock that performs very well, the currency exposure increases correspondingly. It is impossible to know how many currency options are required. One solution for an investor is to use a quanto option. A quanto option automatically adjusts the amount of currency being hedged to match changes in the foreign currency value of the investment.

ZERO-COST OPTIONS

Buying an option involves paying a premium, whereas selling an option gives rise to the receipt of a premium. Zero-cost options are instruments that can be broken down into constituent options. They consist of long option positions financed by the sale of other options.

One form of zero-cost option is known as a cylinder, or range forward. The constituent options have different strike prices. A price fall could be hedged against by buying a put option with a strike price below the currency price. The purchase of the put option could be financed by means of writing a call option, which has a strike price that is higher than the currency price. This has the advantage of allowing some profit from a rise in the currency price (up to the strike price of the call option), but at the cost of having no protection against a price fall until the currency price reaches the strike price of the put option. The other potential cost of this strategy is the loss of profit potential above the strike price of the written call option. If the currency price rises above the strike price of the call, the buyer of the option is likely to exercise the right to buy currency at the strike price. The writer of the call (the user of the zero-cost option) must sell currency at the strike price when the currency price is higher. There is thus a loss on the written call that offsets the gain that would otherwise have been made from a rise in the price of the currency.

DELTA HEDGING WITH OPTIONS

Matching the value to be hedged with the face value of options is known as fixed hedging. For example hedging a currency holding of €1,000,000 against a price fall might entail buying put options that give the right to sell €1,000,000. A fixed hedge will not provide full protection because the premium paid will tend to ensure that there is a net loss.

Delta hedging provides a means of obtaining full compensation for an adverse currency price movement. Delta hedging is alternatively known as dynamic hedging. Delta hedging provides a technique for maintaining the original value of the currency holding. In other words, it can ensure that the currency price plus profit on the options equals the original currency price. This is achieved by factoring up the number of option contracts purchased.

The delta of an option is the ratio of the change in the price of that option to the change in the price of the underlying currency. Delta hedging involves the face value of the options exceeding the amount of currency being hedged. If for example the delta were 0.5, the hedger would buy options with a face value twice that of the currency covered. When the option price changes by half as much as the currency price, twice as many options are bought. By using the appropriate ratio of options to currency, any loss on the currency can be exactly offset by a profit from the options.

The delta of an option is a measure of the responsiveness of the option price to movements in the underlying currency price. It is the change in the option price divided by the change in the currency price. Put options have negative deltas because they become more valuable as the currency price falls. Call options have positive deltas because they rise in price as the currency price increases.

An option buyer can be regarded as having acquired an asset. Delta hedging involves ensuring that increases in the value of one asset (the option) offset declines in the value of another asset (the currency holding).

A difficulty that arises with delta hedging is the tendency for the delta to change as the currency price moves. This suggests the need to adjust constantly the number of options held as the currency price moves. This is problematical not only because of the time and expense involved in constantly monitoring and adjusting option holdings, but also because option contracts are indivisible. Since fractions of contracts cannot be bought, precise cover cannot be achieved.

CONCLUSION

The universe of investments includes foreign investments as well as domestic investments. Investments in foreign countries tend to carry additional risks, when compared to domestic investments. One of those risks is currency risk (exchange rate risk). A fall in the value of the foreign currency relative to the domestic currency can severely damage the domestic currency value of a foreign investment. Exchange rates can experience large changes in short periods. From the perspective of a UK investor, a 50% rise in the value of a dollar-denominated asset would be cancelled by a change in the exchange rate from £1=$1.50 to £1=$2.25.

Derivatives are available for the management of currency risk; they include forwards, futures, options, and swaps. By using currency derivatives it is possible to remove the currency dimension of an investment, and hence the currency risk. For example, covering a $1,500,000 investment with £1,000,000 of sterling futures provides a cash flow of $750,000 if the exchange rate moves from £1=$1.50 to £1=$2.25. This amounts to £333,333 at the new exchange rate. This removes the currency loss on the original investment, but there remains a currency loss on the gain from the dollar asset. If the dollar investment produced a $450,000 gain, that gain would amount to £200,000 ($450,000/$2.25 = £200,000) at the new exchange rate rather than £300,000 ($450,000/$1.50 = £300,000).

Part 11

Bond and Interest Rate Analysis

Chapter 40

Bond prices and redemption yields

OBJECTIVE

The objective of this chapter is to provide knowledge of:

1. Estimation of the fair price of a bond.
2. Consols and Permanent Interest-Bearing Shares (PIBs).
3. The significance of bond price convexity.
4. Bond equivalent yields, effective annual yields, and realised compound yields.
5. Horizon returns.
6. Estimating the real redemption yield on index-linked gilts.

DISCOUNT MODELS

As with other financial investments, the fair prices of bonds are based on the present value of expected future cash flows. The general formula for estimating the fair price of a bond is:

$$P = C/(1+r) + C/(1+r)^2 + C/(1+r)^3 + \ldots + C/(1+r)^n + B/(1+r)^n \qquad (1)$$

$$\text{or } P = C \sum_{k=1}^{n} 1/(1+r)^k + B/(1+r)^n \qquad (2)$$

where P is the fair price of the bond (its dirty price, which includes accrued interest), C is the regular coupon payment each period, B is the money value to be paid to the bondholder at redemption, r is the rate of discount per period, and n is the number of periods remaining to redemption.

An important simplification that has been made in equations (1) and (2) is the use of the same rate of discount for all the future cash flows. This assumes that interest rates are the same irrespective of the term of the investment (i.e. that the yield curve is flat). When valuing a bond an investment analyst could use a different rate of discount for each cash flow in order to take account of the fact that there are different interest rates for different maturities. However, typically a single rate, the redemption yield or yield to maturity, is applied to all future cash flows. The redemption yield

(yield to maturity) of a bond could be looked upon as an average of discount rates applicable to the various future cash flows. The redemption yield indicates the average annual return to be received by an investor holding a bond to maturity.

Interest rates (in the sense of redemption yields on risk-free bonds) are not the only determinants of discount rates. Bonds with relatively high default risk need to yield a high expected rate of return to compensate for the risk. The rate of discount is the required rate of return from a bond. The required rate of return can be regarded as the sum of the yield on bonds that are free of default risk (government bonds) and a risk premium to reflect the default risk of the bond being valued. High default risk entails a high required rate of return and hence a high discount rate. It follows that, for any particular stream of future cash flows, high risk bonds would have higher rates of discount and hence lower fair prices than low risk bonds.

Two conclusions that can be drawn from this account of bond pricing are, first, that bond prices have an inverse relationship to interest rates, and second, that they have an inverse relationship to the risk of default. High interest rates and high risk are associated with low prices.

Discount models estimate the fair prices of bonds. The fair price of a bond is the price that an investment analyst believes to be justified. Market prices of bonds may differ from fair prices. This may be because market prices fail accurately to reflect all relevant information, or because the estimated fair prices are poor estimates. The use of a single discount rate, rather than a time-varying discount rate, on all future coupon and principal receipts is a potential source of error. Another source of error is the possibility of inaccurate estimates of discount rates.

The estimation of future discount rates requires an understanding of the factors that affect discount rates. This divides into understanding the determinants of risk-free rates (government bond rates) and the determinants of risk premiums (the additions to government bond rates required to compensate for the risk of default). If a single discount rate is to be used, the risk-free rate is the redemption yield on a government bond of similar maturity (more precisely, duration) to the bond being analysed. If a time-varying risk-free discount rate is to be used it may be necessary to produce estimates based on the factors that influence government bond redemption yields. Fleming and Remolona (1999), when investigating US government bonds, found that their prices (and, by extension, their redemption yields) were influenced by economic data. In particular data on employment, inflation, and short-term interest rates (central bank monetary policy) were found to be important determinants of redemption yields. Other relevant factors included retail sales and industrial production.

Ewing (2003) looked for factors that appeared to influence the default risk premiums to be added to government bond redemption yields when estimating discount rates for corporate bonds. Industrial production, inflation, and short-term interest rates (central bank monetary policy) were found to be important factors. These factors may affect the risk of default by impacting on the financial position of companies. Ewing acknowledged that other researchers had found overreaction to be a factor in the determination of risk premiums, which suggests that behavioural finance factors (such as representativeness, sentiment, and momentum) may be partly responsible for the size of risk premiums.

An important distinction to be made when considering bond prices is between the clean and dirty prices. When a bond is purchased, the buyer must include in the purchase price a sum corresponding to the seller's share of the next coupon. If the coupon is paid six-monthly, and the bond is sold three months after the last coupon payment date, the seller would require the price to include half the next coupon so that holding the bond for the previous three months provides an interest yield. The rights to the coupon accumulated by the seller are referred to as accrued interest. The clean price of a bond excludes accrued interest whereas the dirty price includes it. Quoted prices are usually clean prices whereas the price to be paid is the dirty price.

EXERCISE 40.1

A bond pays a coupon of £4 every six months, and £100 will be repaid at redemption. There are two years to redemption and the next coupon is due in six months. The redemption yield on similar bonds is 6% p.a. Estimate the fair price of the bond.

Answer

$$P = C/(1+r) + C/(1+r)^2 + C/(1+r)^3 + C/(1+r)^4 + 100/(1+r)^4$$

where P is the fair price of the bond, C is the periodic coupon, and r is the redemption yield on a six-month basis. Since coupons are paid every six months, the relevant period for discounting is six months. Two years to redemption amounts to four six-month periods to redemption. An interest rate of 6% p.a. indicates a rate of 3% per six-month period.

$$P = £4/(1.03) + £4/(1.03)^2 + £4/(1.03)^3 + £4/(1.03)^4 + £100/(1.03)^4$$

$$P = £3.88 + £3.77 + £3.66 + £3.55 + £88.85$$

$$P = £103.71$$

EXERCISE 40.2

(a) It is 22 November 1994. Treasury 10% 1996 matures on 21 November 1996. Calculate the fair price of this bond when the redemption yield is:

(i) 10% p.a. and (ii) 5% p.a.

(b) It is 22 November 1994. Treasury 5% 1996 matures on 21 November 1996. Calculate the fair price of this bond when the redemption yield is:

(i) 10% p.a. and (ii) 5% p.a.

(c) It is 22 November 1994. A zero-coupon bond matures on 21 November 1996. Calculate the fair price of this bond when the redemption yield is:

(i) 10% p.a. and (ii) 5% p.a.

Answers

(a) (i) Treasury 10% pays £10 per year, i.e. £5 every six months.

$£5/(1.05) + £5/(1.05)^2 + £5/(1.05)^3 + £105/(1.05)^4$

(Note that $£105/(1.05)^4$ is the same as $£5/(1.05)^4 + £100/(1.05)^4$)

$= £4.76 + £4.54 + £4.32 + £86.38 = £100$

(ii) $£5/(1.025) + £5/(1.025)^2 + £5/(1.025)^3 + £105/(1.025)^4$

$= £4.88 + £4.76 + £4.64 + £95.12 = £109.40$

(b) (i) Treasury 5% pays £5 per year, i.e. £2.50 every six months.

$£2.5/(1.05) + £2.5/(1.05)^2 + £2.5/(1.05)^3 + £102.5/(1.05)^4$

$= £2.38 + £2.27 + £2.16 + £84.33 = £91.14$

(ii) $£2.5/(1.025) + £2.5/(1.025)^2 + £2.5/(1.025)^3 + £102.5/(1.025)^4$

$= £2.44 + £2.38 + £2.32 + £92.86 = £100$

(c) (i) A zero coupon bond pays no coupons. The only cash flow receipt is the £100 at redemption.

$£100/(1.1)^2 = £82.64 \text{ or } £100/(1.05)^4 = £82.27$

(ii) $£100/(1.05)^2 = £90.70 \text{ or } £100/(1.025)^4 = £90.60$

It is to be noted that when the redemption yield equals the coupon rate the bond trades at par (i.e. its price equals its nominal value of £100). Also sensitivity to interest rate changes rises as the coupon rate falls. A fall in the interest rate from 10% p.a. to 5% p.a. causes a 9.4% rise in the price of the 10% coupon bond, a 9.72% $[(100-91.14)/91.14 = 0.0972]$ rise in the price of the 5% coupon bond, and a 9.75% rise in the price of the zero coupon bond using annual discounting or a 10.13% rise in the price of the zero coupon bond when six-monthly discounting is used.

It can thus be seen that, when the discounting is carried out in a consistent way (six-monthly) across the three cases, the relationship between coupon rate and sensitivity to interest rate changes is as shown in the table.

Table 40.A

Coupon rate	% Bond price change
10%	9.4%
5%	9.72%
0%	10.13%

Lower coupon bonds have the greater sensitivity to interest rate changes.

VALUING COUPON STREAMS AS ANNUITIES

An annuity is a stream of future payments, typically a fixed sum of money each period. The stream of coupon payments on a bond can be seen as equivalent to an annuity. Correspondingly the prospective series of coupon receipts can be valued as an annuity. The equation for valuing an annuity is:

$$AV = \{ C - [C/ (1 + r)^n] \}/ r \tag{3}$$

where AV is the value of the annuity (the present value of the expected coupons), C is the coupon, n is the number of periods for which the coupon will be paid (typically six-month periods), and r is the periodic interest rate (which is half the per annum rate in the case of six-monthly payments). The equation shown is applicable when the next coupon receipt is a full period away.

The value of the bond can be estimated as being equal to the value of the annuity plus the present value of the sum payable at maturity.

$$BV = AV + M/ (1 + r)^n \tag{4}$$

where BV is the estimated value (fair price) of the bond and M is the sum to be received by the bondholder at maturity. Despite the appearance of precision, this remains merely an estimate of the fair price. This is partly because r is a proxy for a series of separate interest rates, each applicable to a particular future cash flow.

EXERCISE 40.3

A corporate bond pays a six-monthly coupon of £5, has just paid a coupon, and matures in ten years. Ten-year government bond redemption yields are 5% p.a., and the corporate bond has a risk premium of 3% p.a. Treating the coupon stream as an annuity, estimate the fair price of the bond.

Answer

The equation for an annuity is:

$$AV = \{C - [C/(1 + r)^n]\} /r$$

The discount rate is 4% since the annual interest rate is 8% (5% + 3%), and the coupons are paid six-monthly. The number of six-month periods, n, is 20.

The present value of the future coupons (the value of the annuity) is therefore:

$$AV = \{5 - [5/(1.04)^{20}]\} /0.04$$
$$= \{5 - [5/2.1911]\} /0.04$$
$$= \{5 - 2.2819\} /0.04$$
$$= 2.7181/0.04 = £67.95$$

755

The annuity, in the form of the future coupon stream, has a value of £67.95.
The fair price of the bond is:

$$BV = AV + M/(1 + r)^n$$

$$BV = £67.95 + £100/(1.04)^{20}$$

$$= £67.95 + £100/2.1911$$

$$= £67.95 + £45.64 = £113.59$$

CONSOLS AND PIBs

Consols are undated government bonds; the government may choose to pay the fixed periodic coupon in perpetuity, there is no obligation to ever redeem the bond. PIBs (Permanent Interest-Bearing shares) are issued by building societies. Like consols, PIBs pay a fixed annual sum in perpetuity; the building society need never repay the original investment. Preference shares are issued by firms and (usually) pay a fixed annual dividend in perpetuity, with no obligation to repay the initial sum paid for the shares. The factor that consols, PIBs, and preference shares have in common is the perpetual nature of the coupon or dividend payments. When cash flows are perpetual equation (1) or (2) can be simplified to equation (5).

$$P = C/r \tag{5}$$

P is the fair price of the security, C is the periodic coupon, and r is the discount rate (required rate of return). It can be noted that equation (5) implies inverse proportionality between discount rates and asset prices. If the discount rate halves the fair price doubles, if the discount rate doubles the fair price halves. Since discount rates and interest rates are closely related this implies a relationship, between asset prices and interest rates, which is close to being inversely proportional.

ACCRUED INTEREST AND REBATE INTEREST

If an investor buys a bond between coupon payment dates, the investor receives the next coupon whereas the seller receives no coupon. This means that the seller receives no coupon return from holding the bond since the previous coupon payment. To deal with this, an adjustment is made. The buyer adds the value of accumulated coupon rights to the purchase price. This addition is known as accrued interest. Accrued interest ensures that the next coupon is shared between the buyer and seller in proportion to the amount of time (the time between coupon payments) each has held the bond. The price of the bond excluding accrued interest is the clean price, and the price inclusive of accrued interest is the dirty price. So the buyer receives the whole of the next coupon, but will have already paid part of it to the seller.

For a bond that makes coupon payments twice a year, the accrued interest if the settlement date (the date of sale/purchase) occurs on or before the ex-dividend date is:

$$(c/2) \times (t/s)$$

where c is the annual coupon, t is the number of days since the last coupon payment, and s is the number of days in the coupon period (period between the last and next coupon payment dates).

Most bonds have ex-dividend dates. After the ex-dividend date the next coupon, in its entirety, is paid to the seller. As an example, UK government bonds go ex-dividend seven days before the coupon payment date. Subsequent to the ex-dividend date there is negative accrued interest. The buyer pays a reduced price (a price below the clean price) to compensate for losing coupon returns for a few days. Negative accrued interest is called rebate interest.

For a bond that makes coupon payments twice a year, the rebate interest in the event of the settlement date occurring between the ex-dividend date and the coupon payment date is:

$$(c/2) \times (1 - [t/s])$$

BOND PRICE CONVEXITY

Bond prices are inversely related to interest rates, but the relationship is not symmetrical. A particular percentage point interest rate change will have asymmetric effects on the bond price dependent upon whether rates rise or fall. The proportionate fall in the bond price resulting from a rise in interest rates is less than the proportionate rise in the bond price caused by a fall when the percentage point change in interest rates is the same in the two cases.

This can be illustrated by reference to the case of an irredeemable bond (a bond with no maturity date such as a consol or PIB). The price of an irredeemable bond is given by equation 5.

$$P = C/r \tag{5}$$

where P represents the fair price of the bond, C the coupon, and r is the interest rate (required rate of return). Consider the case of a £5 annual coupon and an initial interest rate of 10% p.a. The fair price of the bond would be estimated as:

£5 / 0.1 = £50

If the interest rate falls by 2 percentage points to 8% p.a., the price of the bond is expected to rise to:

£5 / 0.08 = £62.50

If the interest rate rises by 2 percentage points to 12% p.a., the fair price of the bond falls to:

£5 / 0.12 = £41.67

Whereas the interest rate fall results in a 25% price rise, the equivalent interest rate increase causes a 16.67% price decline. This asymmetry of price response is referred to as convexity.

BOND EQUIVALENT YIELDS, EFFECTIVE ANNUAL YIELDS, AND REALISED COMPOUND YIELDS

Earlier in this chapter it was shown that the future cash flows from a bond, together with the required rate of return, could be used to estimate the fair price of the bond. An investor could estimate the fair price by using the required rate of return to discount the future cash flows. The process could be reversed in order to ascertain the redemption yield of the bond from knowledge of its current price and the future cash flows. For a bond that pays coupons annually, and has four years to redemption, the redemption yield (y) can be obtained by solving equation 6 for y.

$$P = C/(1 + y) + C/(1 + y)^2 + C/(1 + y)^3 + C/(1 + y)^4 + B/(1 + y)^4 \tag{6}$$

where P is the current market price of the bond, C is the annual coupon, B is the redemption value of the bond, and y is the redemption yield (yield to maturity).

Suppose that a bond has six years to maturity, pays an annual coupon of £6, and is trading at £104. From this information the redemption yield is found to be 5.21% p.a. (This can be calculated using computer software or a financial calculator.) This says that at the end of the six years, assuming that coupons are invested at 5.21% p.a., the value of the bond investment will be the same as the value of a deposit of £104 paying 5.21% p.a. accumulated over six years.

The redemption yield is less than the coupon rate of 6% because of the capital loss from the fall in price from £104 to the redemption value of £100 over the six years. (This fall in price to the par value of £100 is known as the pull to par.) A crude approximation can be obtained by dividing the price fall by the number of years (£4/6 = £0.67) in order to estimate the average price fall per year. This figure is then subtracted from the coupon (£6 − £0.67 = £5.33). The resulting figure is divided by the bond price in order to obtain a rate of return (£5.33/£104 = 5.13% p.a.). The result is known as the simple yield to maturity.

UK government bonds (gilts) typically pay coupons twice a year. In this case a semi-annual redemption yield can be computed. The semi-annual redemption yield is shown as w in equation 7.

$$P = (C/2)/(1 + w) + (C/2)/(1 + w)^2 + (C/2)/(1 + w)^3 + (C/2)/(1 + w)^4 + (C/2)/ (1 + w)^5 + (C/2)/(1 + w)^6 + (C/2)/(1 + w)^7 + (C/2)/(1 + w)^8 + B/(1 + w)^8 \tag{7}$$

The bond equivalent yield is obtained by doubling the semi-annual redemption yield. If the bond equivalent yield is denoted by z, then z = 2w. The bond equivalent yield ignores compounding when converting from a semi-annual yield to an annual yield.

The effective annual yield takes account of the compounding. The effective annual yield is given by:

$$(1 + w)^2 - 1$$

The realised compound yield is the average compound rate of return actually obtained from an investment. The realised compound yield is affected by the rate of yield on reinvested coupons. The above calculations of redemption yield assume that coupons are reinvested at the redemption yield. The realised compound yield equals the redemption yield if coupons are reinvested at the redemption yield and the bond is held to redemption. If the reinvestment rate for the coupons exceeds the redemption yield, the realised compound yield will exceed the redemption yield. If the reinvestment rate for the coupons is less than the redemption yield, the realised compound yield will be less than the redemption yield. So if an investor buys a bond (with a view to holding it to redemption) when the redemption yield is 5% p.a., and redemption yields on similar bonds subsequently rise above 5% p.a., the realised compound yield will exceed 5% p.a. If redemption yields fall below 5% p.a., the realised compound yield by the redemption date would be less than 5% p.a.

EXERCISE 40.4

A bond, which has recently paid a coupon, pays a coupon of £5 annually and has two years to redemption. The redemption yield on similar bonds is 5% p.a.

(a) What is the fair price of the bond?

(b) What is the realised compound yield if redemption yields remain at 5% p.a., and the bond is held to redemption?

(c) What is the realised compound yield if redemption yields are 8% p.a. at the time of the next coupon payment, and the bond is held to redemption?

(d) What is the realised compound yield if redemption yields are 2% p.a. at the time of the next coupon payment, and the bond is held to redemption?

Answers

(a) The fair price, P, is given by:

$$P = £5/(1.05) + £105/(1.05)^2 = £100$$

(The £105 comprises £5 coupon plus £100 redemption value.)

(b) Reinvesting coupons at 5% p.a. produces a final sum of:

£5 (1.05) + £105 = £110.25

The realised compound yield is $(1.1025)^{0.5} - 1 = 0.05$, i.e. 5% p.a.

So, when coupons are reinvested at the initial redemption yield, the realised compound yield equals the original redemption yield.

(c) Reinvesting coupons at 8% p.a. produces a final sum of:

£5 (1.08) + £105 = £110.4

The realised compound yield is $(1.104)^{0.5} - 1 = 0.0507$, i.e. 5.07% p.a.

So, when coupons are reinvested at a rate higher than the initial redemption yield, the realised compound yield exceeds the original redemption yield.

(d) Reinvesting coupons at 2% p.a. produces a final sum of:

£5 (1.02) + £105 = £110.1

The realised compound yield is $(1.101)^{0.5} - 1 = 0.0493$, i.e. 4.93% p.a.

So, when coupons are reinvested at a rate lower than the initial redemption yield, the realised compound yield is below the original redemption yield.

HORIZON RETURN (HOLDING-PERIOD RETURN)

The redemption yield can be decomposed into three components:

Redemption Yield = Coupons + Interest on Coupons + Pull to Par

The pull to par refers to the bond price change that results from the tendency of bond prices to move towards their par (i.e. nominal) values as they approach maturity. For example a bond bought for £90 would gain £10 by maturity as its price moves to £100, which is the bond value at redemption (maturity). The value at redemption is the par, or nominal, value.

Bonds are not always held to redemption. If a bond is sold before redemption, the realised return is unlikely to equal the redemption yield. In such a case any price change arising from interest rate movements (the yield change effect) must be taken into account. The total yield (horizon return) is now:

Horizon Return = Coupons + Interest on Coupons + Pull to Par + Yield Change Effect

The pull-to-par gain (or loss) will be related to the ratio between the time to sale of the bond and the time to redemption.

EXERCISE 40.5

Two years ago, an investor bought a five-year zero coupon bond with a par value of £100 when interest rates were 7% p.a. The investor sold it recently when interest rates were 5% p.a. Assume that the interest rate is the same (per annum) for all investment horizons.

What was the horizon return?

Answer

The price of the bond, two years ago, was $£100/[1.07]^5 = £71.30$.

The current fair price would be $£100/[1.05]^3 = £86.38$.

The realised compound yield was $[£86.38/£71.30]^{0.5} - 1 = 1.1007 - 1 = 0.1007$ i.e. 10.07% p.a.

If interest rates had remained at 7% p.a., the price would have been $£100/[1.07]^3 = £81.63$ after two years. There would have been a pull to par of $(£81.63 - £71.30)/£71.30 = 0.1449$, i.e. 14.49%. As a per annum rate this is $(1.1449)^{0.5} - 1 = 0.07$, i.e. 7% p.a. In addition to this pull to par there is a yield change effect of $(£86.38 - £81.63)/£81.63 = 0.0582$, i.e. 5.82%. As a per annum rate the yield change effect is $(1.0582)^{0.5} - 1 = 0.0287$, i.e. 2.87% p.a. Between them the pull to par and the yield change effect provide $(1.07 \times 1.0287) - 1 = 0.1007$, i.e. 10.07% p.a.

INDEX-LINKED GILT REDEMPTION YIELDS

Index-linked gilts adjust coupon and redemption payments so that they rise in line with inflation. Inflation is measured by means of the Retail Prices Index (RPI) and the RPI used to adjust a cash flow is the index eight months prior to the cash flow. To calculate a redemption yield for an index-linked gilt, it is necessary to assume a rate of inflation. A constant inflation rate is normally assumed for the period to redemption.

When a rate of inflation, for the period to redemption, is assumed it becomes possible to calculate the future cash flows in nominal (money) terms. The redemption yield (in nominal terms) can then be derived from the current gilt price, the future coupons, and the future redemption payment. It is then necessary to convert the nominal redemption yield to a real redemption yield. For a bond that pays coupons once a year the real redemption yield can be derived from equation 8.

$$1 + r = (1 + n)/1 + i \tag{8}$$

where r is the real redemption yield, n is the nominal redemption yield, and i is the assumed rate of inflation. Equation 8 can be readily amended to deal with gilts that pay their coupons twice yearly. In newspapers such as the *Financial Times* real redemption yields for index-linked gilts are shown based on the assumption of inflation rates of 3% p.a. and 5% p.a.

CONCLUSION

The word bond is used in many ways in the context of investments. Insurance companies and building societies often use the word to describe particular institutional investments. In this chapter, the word bond has been used to describe a class of assets that takes the form of debt. Bonds are debts of the governments, companies, and organisations that issue them.

One of the ways in which bonds differ from shares is in the relative certainty of future cash flows.

In the absence of default by the issuer, the future cash flows from a bond are typically known with certainty. This is in contrast to shares since shares typically have dividend payments, which are variable and uncertain. The relative certainty of bond cash flows renders the pricing and analysis of bonds more precise than the pricing and analysis of shares. Whereas dividend discount models are just one of many approaches to pricing shares, and do not provide absolutely reliable estimates of fair prices, a discount model is often all that is required for the reliable estimation of the fair price of a bond. The relative certainty of bond cash flows means that other characteristics, such as duration and convexity, can also be reliably estimated.

When including bonds in a portfolio, along with other asset classes such as shares, it is necessary to have estimates of future bond yields and of bond price volatility (risk). Expected return and risk are values required for each prospective investment to be included in a portfolio (see Chapter 13 on portfolio diversification). The present chapter has examined some measures of bond return (bond yield) and the next chapter examines measures of bond risk (bond duration).

Chapter 41

Duration and risk

OBJECTIVE

The objective of this chapter is to provide knowledge of:

1. Macaulay's duration.
2. Modified duration.
3. Money duration (price value of a basis point).
4. Immunisation of a bond portfolio against interest rate risk.
5. Bond index (tracker) funds.
6. Interest rate anticipation strategies.

There are two types of risk encountered by investors in bonds. There is price (or capital) risk, and reinvestment (or income) risk. Price risk is the risk that bond prices can change. For example a general rise in interest rates, or a fall in the credit rating of a particular bond, would reduce the price of a bond. A capital loss would result.

Reinvestment risk refers to the uncertainty as to the interest rate at which coupons and redemption sums can be invested. This causes uncertainty as to the final sum that will be available at the end of an investment horizon.

Capital risk is measured by duration. The duration measures are useful for the purposes of predicting the effects of interest rate changes, and protecting bond portfolios against the effects of such changes. Duration measures can also be used to design portfolios such that price risk and reinvestment risk tend to cancel each other out.

THE MEASUREMENT OF BOND PRICE VOLATILITY (DURATION)

Bond price volatility is measured by duration. The duration measures include Macaulay's duration, modified duration, and money duration. Macaulay's duration is the average period of time to the receipt of cash flows. Each time period (to the receipt of a cash flow) is weighted by the proportionate contribution of that cash flow to the fair price of the bond. Macaulay's duration is transformed into modified duration by means of dividing it by $(1+r/n)$ where r is the redemption yield (which approximates an interest rate) and n is the number of coupon payments per year.

Macaulay's duration has another meaning, it is the proportionate change in the bond price (fair price of the bond) arising from a unit proportional change in $(1+$redemption yield$)$. That is:

$$\text{Macaulay's duration} = \frac{\Delta P/P}{\Delta(1+r)/(1+r)} \qquad (1)$$

(The symbol Δ signifies 'change in', and P is the bond price.)
The corresponding interpretation of modified duration is:

$$\text{Modified duration} = \frac{\Delta P/P}{\Delta r} \qquad (2)$$

Equation (2) is derived from equation (1) by means of dividing by $(1+r)$ and observing that $\Delta(1+r) = \Delta r$.

Equations (1) and (2) assume annual coupon payments. When coupons are paid more frequently, r is replaced by r/n (the annual redemption yield divided by the number of coupon payments per year). This is consistent with treating the redemption yield as being on a per period basis. For example UK and US government bonds typically pay coupons six-monthly. In those cases $n = 2$, and $r/2$ is the redemption yield per six-month period.

The calculation of duration can be demonstrated by an example. Suppose that a bond has just paid a coupon, matures in two years, and pays a coupon of £6 six-monthly. The interest rate is 10% p.a. for all maturities. The fair price of the bond is:

$$P = £6/(1.05) + £6/(1.05)^2 + £6/(1.05)^3 + £106/(1.05)^4$$
$$= £5.71 + £5.44 + £5.18 + £87.21 = £103.54$$

(Note that an interest rate of 10% p.a. is 5% per six-month period.)

Macaulay's duration is calculated as the weighted average of the periods to the receipt of cash flows. The weighting is based on the contribution of the period's cash flow to the fair price of the bond. The periods are 0.5, 1, 1.5, and 2 years.

$$\text{Macaulay's duration} = (5.71/103.54)0.5 + (5.44/103.54)1.0 + (5.18/103.54)1.5 + (87.21/103.54)2.0$$
$$= 0.028 + 0.053 + 0.075 + 1.685 = 1.841 \text{ years}$$

Conversion of Macaulay's duration to modified duration entails division by $(1+r/n)$.

$$\text{Modified duration} = 1.841/(1 + 0.1/2) = 1.841/(1.05) = 1.753$$

EXERCISE 41.1

A corporate bond pays an annual coupon of £10 and has four years to maturity. It has just paid a coupon. As a result of a downgrading of its credit rating, its required rate of return rises from 8% p.a. to 12% p.a. What are the effects of this change on (a) the price, and (b) the Macaulay's duration, of the bond? (c) Discuss your results.

Answers

(a) The fair price of the bond, when the required rate of return is 8% p.a., is shown as P_1 in the following calculation.

$$P_1 = £10/(1.08) + £10/(1.08)^2 + £10/(1.08)^3 + £110/(1.08)^4$$

(The £110 equals the final coupon of £10 plus the redemption value of £100.)

$$P_1 = £9.26 + £8.57 + £7.94 + £80.85 = £106.62$$

The fair price of the bond, when the required rate of return is 12% p.a., is shown as P_2 in the following calculation.

$$P_2 = £10/1.12 + £10/(1.12)^2 + £10/(1.12)^3 + £110/(1.12)^4$$

$$P_2 = £8.93 + £7.97 + £7.12 + £69.91 = £93.93$$

(b) Macaulay's duration when the required rate of return is 8% p.a. is shown as D_1 in the following calculation.

$$D_1 = (9.26/106.62)1 + (8.57/106.62)2 + (7.94/106.62)3 + (80.85/106.62)4$$

$$D_1 = 0.087 + 0.161 + 0.223 + 3.033 = 3.50 \text{ years (to two decimal places).}$$

Macaulay's duration, when the required rate of return is 12% p.a., is shown as D_2 in the following calculation.

$$D_2 = (8.93/93.93)1 + (7.97/93.93)2 + (7.12/93.93)3 + (69.91/93.93)4$$

$$D_2 = 0.095 + 0.170 + 0.227 + 2.977 = 3.47 \text{ years (to two decimal places).}$$

(c) The calculations illustrate the inverse relationship between bond prices and interest rates.

The relationship between default risk and bond price is also illustrated. Higher default risk is associated with a higher required rate of return (and hence higher interest rate and discount rate). The higher required rate of return entails a lower fair price of the bond.

A higher discount rate is associated with lower duration because the high discount rate has a relatively large impact on the more distant cash flows, and hence the weighting of longer periods is reduced (in the calculation of duration).

The calculations also illustrate that discount rates above coupon rates are associated with bond prices below par, and vice versa for discount rates below coupon rates.

EXERCISE 41.2

Treasury 10% 1999, which pays coupons six-monthly, will reach maturity on 10 June 1999. It is now 11 June 1997. Interest rates for 0.5, 1, 1.5, and 2 years are all 7% p.a. Estimate the fair price, Macaulay's duration, and modified duration of the bond.

Answers

A 10% government bond pays coupons at £10 p.a. The £10 p.a. coupon is £5 six-monthly, and the 7% p.a. interest rate is 3.5% six-monthly.

Fair price = £5/1.035 + £5/(1.035)² + £5/ (1.035)³ + £105/(1.035)⁴ = £4.83 + £4.67
+ £4.51 + £91.50

= £105.51

Macaulay's duration = (4.83/105.51)0.5 + (4.67/105.51)1.0 + (4.51/105.51)
1.5 + (91.5/105.51)2.0

= 0.02 + 0.04 + 0.06 + 1.73 = 1.85 years

Modified duration = 1.85/(1.035) = 1.79

A Formula for Calculating Macaulay's Duration

An alternative means of calculating Macaulay's duration (when coupons are paid annually) is provided by the following formula:

$$D = \frac{1 + r}{r} - \frac{(1 + r) + T(C - r)}{C[(1 + r)^T - 1] + r}$$

where D is Macaulay's duration, r is the redemption yield of the bond, C is the coupon rate, and T is the term to maturity of the bond.

EXERCISE 41.3

A corporate bond pays an annual coupon of £10 and has four years to maturity. It has just paid a coupon. The redemption yield is 8% p.a. What is the Macaulay's duration of the bond?

Answer

$$D = \frac{1.08}{0.08} - \frac{(1.08) + 4(0.1 - 0.08)}{0.1[(1.08)^4 - 1] + 0.08}$$

D = 13.5 − 10 = 3.5 years

MONEY DURATION (PRICE VALUE OF A BASIS POINT)

Modified duration multiplied by the change in bond redemption yield (multiplied by -1) shows the approximate proportionate change in the bond price resulting from the yield change.

$$\Delta P/P = -MD \times \Delta r \qquad\qquad (3)$$

where $\Delta P/P$ is the proportionate change in the bond price, $-MD$ is the negative of modified duration, and Δr is the change in the redemption yield of the bond. (The redemption yield approximates the interest rate relating to the duration of the bond.)

Multiplying both sides of equation (3) by the initial bond price, P, gives equations (4) and (5).

$$\Delta P = (\Delta P/P) \times P = -MD \times \Delta r \times P \qquad\qquad (4)$$

$$\Delta P/\Delta r = -MD \times P \qquad\qquad (5)$$

The term $(MD \times P)$ might be called money duration. It shows the price change resulting from a yield change. It should be noted that yields are here expressed as decimals rather than percentages, so for example 1% would be expressed as 0.01 and a basis point (0.01%) as 0.0001. Alternative names for money duration are perturbation and, where the yield change is 0.01%, the price value of a basis point (PVBP).

For small changes in redemption yield (e.g. 0.1%), equation (4) provides a reasonably good approximation to the actual change in the bond price. However for large changes (e.g. 1%), the approximation is less satisfactory. As the size of the change in the yield (or interest rate) increases, equation (4) becomes less accurate as a means of estimating bond price movements. This is because of convexity. (Since MD and P change when r changes, the ratio $\Delta P/\Delta r$ changes when r changes. Equations (4) and (5) are based on a constant $MD \times P$.)

EXERCISE 41.4

A bond has just paid a six-monthly coupon of £5. There are four more coupons to be paid by its maturity. Current redemption yields on similar bonds are 3.5% p.a.

(a) Calculate the bond's money duration.

(b) Using money duration estimate the bond's sensitivity to a 0.1% p.a. decrease in the redemption yield.

(c) Using money duration estimate the bond's sensitivity to a 1% p.a. decrease in the redemption yield.

(d) Compute the fair price at the altered redemption yields referred to in (b) and (c) above using the discount model.

(e) Comment on any discrepancy between the results indicated using money duration and those found by means of the discount model.

Answers

(a) A redemption yield of 3.5% p.a. is 1.75% per six-month period.

The fair price of the bond is:

$$P = £5/1.0175 + £5/[1.0175]^2 + £5/[1.0175]^3 + £105/[1.0175]^4$$

$$= £4.91 + £4.83 + £4.75 + £97.96 = £112.45$$

Macaulay's duration is:

$$D = (4.91/112.45)0.5 + (4.83/112.45)1.0 + (4.75/112.45)1.5 + (97.96/112.45)2.0$$

$$= 0.0218 + 0.043 + 0.0634 + 1.7423 = 1.8705 \text{ years}$$

Modified duration is:

$$MD = 1.8705/1.0175 = 1.8383$$

Money duration is:

$$M = 1.8383 \times £112.45 = £206.72$$

(b) A 0.1% p.a. decrease in redemption yield should, using money duration, cause a:

$£206.72 \times 0.001 = £0.21$ increase in the bond price.

The new bond price should therefore be:

$£112.45 + £0.21 = £112.66$.

(c) A 1% p.a. decrease in redemption yield should, using money duration, cause a:

$£206.72 \times 0.01 = £2.07$ increase in the bond price.

Therefore the new bond price should be:

$£112.45 + £2.07 = £114.52$.

(d) Using the discount model, the fair price of the bond at a redemption yield of 3.4% p.a. $(3.5\% - 0.1\%)$ is:

$$P = £5/1.017 + £5/[1.017]^2 + £5/[1.017]^3 + £105/[1.017]^4$$

$$= £4.92 + £4.83 + £4.75 + £98.15 = £112.65$$

The fair price of the bond at a redemption yield of 2.5% p.a. $(3.5\% - 1\%)$ is:

$$P = £5/1.0125 + £5/[1.0125]^2 + £5/[1.0125]^3 + £105/[1.0125]^4$$

$$= £4.94 + £4.88 + £4.82 + £99.91 = £114.55$$

(e) With a 0.1% p.a. change in redemption yield there is virtually no difference between the bond price estimated using money duration, and that estimated using the discount model. In fact the small difference, of 0.01, partly arises from rounding to two decimal places (i.e. it would be less than 0.01 in the absence of the rounding).

With a 1% p.a. change in redemption yield the estimate using money duration is 0.03 lower than that from the discount model. This small error from the money duration approach arises from convexity. Money duration fails to reflect the convexity of the bond price-yield relationship and hence produces an erroneous estimate.

The estimate of the bond price change, using money duration, is more reliable when redemption yield (interest rate) changes are small than when they are large.

EXERCISE 41.5

An investor has two bonds. Bond A pays a £5 annual coupon and matures in five years. Bond B pays a £4 coupon semi-annually and matures in three years. The investor needs to sell one bond immediately and hold the other for two years. The current rate of interest, for all maturities up to five years, is 6% p.a.

Which bond would the investor sell if that investor expected interest rates to:

(a) increase, (b) decrease?

Answers

The fair price of bond A is:

$£5/(1.06) + £5/(1.06)^2 + £5/(1.06)^3 + £5/(1.06)^4 + £105/(1.06)^5$

$= £4.72 + £4.45 + £4.20 + £3.96 + £78.46 = £95.79$

The Macaulay's duration of bond A is:

$(£4.72/£95.79)1.0 + (£4.45/£95.79)2.0 + (£4.2/£95.79)3.0 + (£3.96/£95.79)4.0 +$
$(£78.46/£95.79)5.0$

$= 0.049 + 0.093 + 0.132 + 0.165 + 4.095 = 4.534$ years

Modified duration is:

$4.534/(1.06) = 4.277$

The fair price of bond B is:

$£4/(1.03) + £4/(1.03)^2 + £4/(1.03)^3 + £4/(1.03)^4 + £4/(1.03)^5 + £104/(1.03)^6 =$
$£3.88 + £3.77 + £3.66 + £3.55 + £3.45 + £87.10 = £105.41$

The Macaulay's duration of bond B is:

$(£3.88/£105.41)0.5 + (£3.77/£105.41)1.0 + (£3.66/£105.41)1.5 + (£3.55/£105.41)2.0$
$+ (£3.45/£105.41)2.5 + (£87.1/£105.41)3.0$

$= 0.018 + 0.036 + 0.052 + 0.067 + 0.082 + 2.479 = 2.734$ years

Modified duration is:

$2.734/(1.03) = 2.654$

(a) If the investor expects interest rates to increase, bond prices are expected to fall. The bond with the higher modified duration should show the greatest fall. The investor would therefore choose to sell bond A because it has the higher modified duration.

(b) If the investor expects interest rates to decrease, bond prices are expected to rise. The bond with the higher modified duration would show the greater price rise. The investor should choose to hold bond A and sell bond B since bond A has the higher modified duration.

THE BEHAVIOUR OF MACAULAY'S DURATION

The duration (Macaulay's duration) of a bond is systematically affected by certain characteristics of that bond. This can be summarised by a set of rules.

Rule 1: The duration of a zero coupon bond equals its time to maturity.

Since a zero coupon bond generates only one cash flow, the payment of principal at maturity, the average time to the receipt of cash flows equals the time to that payment.

Rule 2: Holding time to maturity and redemption yield (yield to maturity) constant, duration is inversely related to the coupon.

Duration is the weighted average time to the receipt of cash flows, and the weighting of each time period is related to the cash flow at the end of that time period. Low coupon bonds involve low weightings attached to time periods other than the period to final maturity. The period to the repayment of principal will dominate the earlier periods in the determination of duration. High coupon bonds give higher weightings to the earlier periods with the result that the average period (the duration) is shorter.

Rule 3: Holding the coupon rate constant, duration generally increases with time to maturity.

As maturity increases, the time periods to the receipt of cash flows will increase. This will tend to increase duration. However for bonds trading at a very deep discount (bonds whose coupon rates are far below their redemption yields) increases in maturity may eventually be associated with reductions in duration.

Duration increases by less than a year for each year that maturity increases (unless the bond has a zero coupon). Furthermore duration increases at a decreasing rate as time to maturity increases. Doubling the time to maturity tends to increase duration, but by less than double.

Rule 4: Holding coupon and maturity constant, duration is inversely related to redemption yield (yield to maturity).

Higher redemption yields imply higher discount rates. Higher discount rates reduce the relative importance of distant cash flows. Distant time periods receive lower weightings, and hence duration falls. This rule does not apply to zero coupon bonds.

Rule 5: The duration of an irredeemable bond is given by $(1 + r)/r$, where r is the redemption yield.

If a bond pays the same coupon each period forever without the principal ever being repaid, the duration equals $(1 + r)/r$. It is illustrative to consider some examples. Table 41.1 shows the duration relating to various redemption yields.

In the case of high redemption yields, the cash flows occurring early in the life of the bond dominate the calculation of duration. The distant cash flows are so heavily discounted that they provide

Table 41.1

Redemption yield (% p.a.)	Duration (in years)
21	5.76
16	7.25
11	10.09
6	17.67
1	101.00

very low weightings for the longer periods. Finally it might be noted that as the maturity of a bond increases, its duration will eventually converge towards that of an irredeemable bond.

EXERCISE 41.6

It is 27 January 1998. Treasury 15% 2000 pays coupons six-monthly and matures on 26 January 2000. The interest rate, for all maturities up to two years, is 6% p.a. In relation to this bond estimate the:

(a) Fair price.

(b) Macaulay's duration.

(c) Modified duration.

(d) A fund manager holds Treasury 15% 2000 and is considering replacing it with either three-month Treasury bills or Treasury 12% 2002. What should the fund manager do if he/she expects (i) a rise, and (ii) a fall, in interest rates? Explain your answer.

Answers

A 15% government bond pays coupons at £15 p.a., and hence £7.50 six-monthly. An interest rate of 6% p.a. is 3% six-monthly.

(a) Let P = fair price.

$$P = £7.50/(1.03) + £7.50/(1.03)^2 + £7.50/(1.03)^3 + £107.50/(1.03)^4$$
$$P = £7.28 + £7.07 + £6.86 + £95.51 = £116.72p$$

(b) Let D = Macaulay's duration.

$$D = (£7.28/£116.72)0.5 + (£7.07/£116.72)1.0 + (£6.86/£116.72)1.5$$
$$+ (£95.51/£116.72)2.0$$
$$D = 0.031 + 0.061 + 0.088 + 1.637 = 1.817 \text{ years}$$

(c) Modified duration $= D/(1 + r/n) = 1.817/(1.03) = 1.764$

(d) (i) If the fund manager expects a rise in interest rates, bond prices are expected to fall. The fund manager should shorten duration by replacing Treasury 15% 2000 with three-month Treasury bills. This will reduce the extent of the loss since Treasury bills, having lower duration, are less sensitive to interest rate changes than the bonds.

   (ii) If the fund manager expects interest rates to fall, the expectation is that bond prices will rise. Higher duration provides greater sensitivity to interest rate changes. By replacing Treasury 15% 2000 with Treasury 12% 2002, the fund manager raises duration and hence increases the profit to be made from a fall in interest rates. (Since duration increases with greater maturity and lower coupons, Treasury 12% 2002 will have a longer duration than Treasury 15% 2000.)

PORTFOLIO IMMUNISATION

A portfolio of bonds may be held with a view to the provision of a known flow of income in the future. The investor could be an individual or an institution such as an insurance company making annuity payments. Immunisation of a bond portfolio aims to protect the investor against the future cash flows falling below the levels required. Shortfalls could occur as a result of either capital losses or a decline in the interest rates at which proceeds can be reinvested.

One approach to portfolio immunisation is the construction of a dedicated portfolio. A dedicated portfolio entails future cash flow receipts, both of coupons and repayments of principal at redemption, that precisely match the cash flows required. For example the future payments to pensioners from an annuity fund might be synchronised with the coupon and redemption receipts from the bonds that comprise the fund. The matching of receipts with requirements must relate to both amount and timing. Although dedicated portfolios achieve immunisation they are very difficult to construct.

An alternative approach to immunisation is maturity matching. The required cash flows from the portfolio, in terms of both amount and timing, are used as the basis for choosing the bonds for the portfolio. By ensuring that bond maturities coincide with cash withdrawals from the portfolio, the risk of interest rate changes depressing the market values of bonds is avoided. In this way the portfolio manager would be sure of receiving the redemption value of a bond. One element of uncertainty does remain when such a strategy is used. Since interest rates vary over time, there is uncertainty as to the rate of return to be obtained from investing coupon receipts. This is reinvestment risk. Changes in the rates of return on reinvested income can have a substantial impact on subsequent values of the portfolio. This risk can be reduced by using duration matching instead of maturity matching.

The duration of a portfolio can be calculated as the weighted average of the durations of the bonds in the portfolio. The weighting is based on the market values of the various bond holdings (e.g. if a particular bond provides 25% of the value of the portfolio, its duration would get a 0.25 weighting when calculating the duration of the portfolio).

772

EXERCISE 41.7

A fund manager holds a £100-million bond portfolio comprising three bonds: A, B, and C. Bond A has a duration of four years and accounts for £25 million of the portfolio. Bond B has a duration of seven years and accounts for £25 million. Bond C, of which £50 million is held, has a duration of ten years. What is the duration of the portfolio?

Answer

$D_p = 0.25(4) + 0.25(7) + 0.5(10) = 1 + 1.75 + 5 = 7.75$ years

Duration matching involves matching the Macaulay's duration of the bond portfolio to the time at which the cash flow will be required. Bond price changes tend to offset variations in returns from reinvested coupons. The capital risk of bond price changes and the income risk from reinvestment of coupons tend to cancel each other out. Losses from bond price falls are offset by increased income from the reinvestment of coupons, and vice versa. Redemption yield rises that reduce bond prices raise the returns from reinvesting coupons. Conversely redemption yield falls raise bond prices but lower the rate of return on reinvested coupons.

EXERCISE 41.8

(a) Find the Macaulay's duration of a bond, with four years to maturity and a £6 annual coupon, using a redemption yield of 8% p.a. (The next coupon is a year hence.)

(b) Show numerically how this bond will be immune from interest rate risk if the holding period is equal to the duration of the bond. For the calculation assume that interest rates (and redemption yields) increase by 1% p.a. before the next coupon payment and remain at the new level.

Answers

(a) Denoting the fair price of the bond by P:

$P = £6/(1.08) + £6/(1.08)^2 + £6/(1.08)^3 + £106/(1.08)^4$

$P = £5.56 + £5.14 + £4.76 + £77.91 = £93.37.$

Macaulay's duration $= (5.56/93.37)1 + (5.14/93.37)2 + (4.76/93.37)3 + (77.91/93.37)4$

$= 0.06 + 0.11 + 0.15 + 3.34 = 3.66$ years

(b) The holding period is 3.66 years. At the end of the holding period, the Macaulay's duration of the bond will be 0.34 years (i.e. the remaining period to maturity).

Modified duration $= 0.34/1.08 = 0.315$

%ΔP = $-0.315 \times 1\%$ = -0.315% (-0.00315 as a decimal) where %ΔP is the percentage price change.

ΔP = £93.37 $\times$ -0.00315 = $-£0.294$ where ΔP is the price change.

The prospective capital loss is £0.294.

The next coupon can be invested for 2.66 years, the second for 1.66 years, and the third for 0.66 years.

$$£6[(1.01)^{2.66} + (1.01)^{1.66} + (1.01)^{0.66} - 3] = £0.300$$

The additional interest from the reinvestment of coupons is £0.300.

It can be seen that the capital loss from the 1% p.a. rise in interest rates is approximately matched by the increase in interest receipts.

Since there would normally be more than one cash outflow to be funded from a bond portfolio, duration matching becomes a matter of matching the Macaulay's duration of the portfolio with the Macaulay's duration of the cash outflows.

A bond portfolio immunised by duration matching will require frequent rebalancing in order to maintain the matching. In other words, it will be necessary to make frequent changes to the composition of the portfolio. This is because Macaulay's duration changes as a result of interest rate movements, and in consequence of the passage of time.

These factors are likely to affect the duration of the cash outflow commitments differently from the duration of the bond portfolio. In consequence, the composition of the portfolio would need to be changed in order to keep its duration in line with that of the cash outflow commitments.

Duration matching is probably the easiest means of immunising a portfolio because of the facility of using bond futures to achieve the requisite adjustments. Any discrepancy between the duration of the liabilities (prospective cash outflows) and the duration of the bond portfolio can be removed by taking an offsetting position in bond futures.

Bond futures are commitments to trade bonds during a future month at a price agreed when taking the futures position. Futures positions make profits and losses as bond prices change, and hence as redemption yields change. Futures thus have durations. Buying futures adds to a portfolio's duration, and selling futures reduces the portfolio's duration. Since futures positions cost nothing to establish (the only initial cash outlay is a returnable deposit known as initial margin), they provide an easy and cash efficient means of altering the duration of a portfolio.

One problem with using portfolio duration is that the interest rate (redemption yield) becomes ambiguous. Each bond in the portfolio will have its own redemption yield. Redemption yields do not move to equal extents. Two portfolios with the same duration may respond differently to a general change in interest rates because their redemption yields change to different degrees.

Short-term, medium-term, and long-term interest rates may change to different degrees. Portfolios with identical durations may be constructed in different ways. A portfolio could be structured entirely using bonds with a medium maturity (a bullet portfolio), or a portfolio might be constructed using a combination of bonds from two very different maturity ranges (this is known as a barbell portfolio and may combine very short maturity and very long maturity bonds), or a portfolio could be structured using maturities spread over a wide range (a ladder portfolio). Despite the identical durations, the values of these portfolios would respond very differently to a general change in interest rates if the interest rate change is not uniform along the maturity spectrum.

INVERSE FLOATERS AND FLOATING RATE NOTES

Financial engineering can create derivatives from a non-derivative investment. One example is the division of a conventional bond into an inverse floater and a floating rate note. An inverse floater is a bond whose interest rate is inversely related to a market rate. For example an inverse floater might pay a coupon rate of 10% p.a. minus LIBOR (LIBOR is a commonly used benchmark interest rate that reflects market rates). The price of an inverse floater is extremely sensitive to interest rate movements. Not only does the coupon rate fall when interest rates rise, but the rate at which the coupons and principal value are discounted also rises. There are two effects of interest rate rises that act to reduce the bond price. Conversely interest rate falls have two positive effects on the bond price; the higher coupons are accompanied by a lower discount rate. So inverse floaters are very sensitive to interest rate changes, in other words they have very long durations.

Inverse floaters are structured by dividing a conventional bond into an inverse floater and a floating rate note. A floating rate note is a bond whose coupon rate moves in line with market rates. For example the coupon rate on a floating rate note might be 2% p.a. plus LIBOR. Since the coupon rate moves in the same direction as the rate of discount, effects of interest rate changes tend to offset each other with the effect that there is little net effect on the bond price. Floating rate notes exhibit low price volatility and hence short durations.

Suppose that a conventional bond has a coupon rate of 6% p.a. and LIBOR is 4% p.a. A bank could buy £100 million of the conventional bond and divide it into £50 million of inverse floaters and £50 million of floating rate notes. The inverse floaters might pay a coupon rate of 10% p.a. minus LIBOR, whilst the floating rate notes pay 2% p.a. plus LIBOR. The annual coupon rates are shown in Table 41.2.

Table 41.2

LIBOR	Inverse floater	Floating rate note
0	10	2
1	9	3
2	8	4
3	7	5
4	6	6
5	5	7
6	4	8
7	3	9
8	2	10
9	1	11
10	0	12
11	0	12

It can be seen that the coupon rates always average 6% p.a., which is the coupon rate on the conventional bond from which the inverse floater and the floating rate note are derived. LIBOR interest rates above 10% p.a. are treated as if they were 10% p.a. since the coupon rate on the inverse floater is not allowed to fall below 0% p.a.

The high duration of inverse floaters renders them useful for hedging long-term liabilities. Falling interest rates increase the value of the liabilities, but that would be offset by the increase in the value of the inverse floaters. Inverse floaters might be attractive to institutions with long-term liabilities such as pension funds, annuity providers, and life assurance companies. Conversely floating rate notes could be attractive to institutions with short-term liabilities, such as banks and building societies.

BOND INDEX (TRACKER) FUNDS

Bond index funds attempt to construct portfolios that replicate the performance of a bond index. The argument for index funds is based on the view that fund managers are unable to consistently outperform indices. For example Blake *et al.* (1993) measured the performance of 223 bond funds over 1986-1991 and compared them with index tracking portfolios. Most of the 223 funds underperformed the index portfolios. The average amount of underperformance was slightly higher than the charges on the funds (i.e. charges accounted for most of the underperformance).

The performance to be tracked is total return; which comprises coupons, capital gains (or losses), and interest on reinvested coupons. Differences between the performance of an index and that of an index tracking portfolio are referred to as tracking error.

Tracking error has three sources. First there is tracking error resulting from a mismatch between the bonds in the portfolio and the bonds in the index. Second, there may be differences between the bond prices used for calculating an index and those available to a portfolio manager. Third, a portfolio manager faces transaction costs whereas the constructor of an index does not.

The first two sources of deviation can be either advantageous or disadvantageous to a portfolio manager. Transaction costs are always disadvantageous. There is a trade-off between tracking error arising from mismatches and the error from transaction costs. Attempts to replicate precisely the contents of an index may entail a large number of relatively small transactions. This is expensive in terms of transaction costs. On the other hand, use of a smaller sample of bonds to represent an index increases deviations arising from mismatches between the index and the index tracking portfolio. Use of a small number of bonds, with infrequent rebalancing, reduces transaction costs but the reduction in transaction costs incurs increased mismatch error.

Since it is unlikely that perfect replication of an index in terms of specific bonds and precise proportions is practical in terms of transaction costs, a representative sample of bonds would normally be used. One approach to obtaining a representative sample is the cell, or stratified sampling, approach. Each cell contains its own combination of characteristics, and the portfolio manager would ensure that all the important cells are reflected in the chosen sample.

For example the relevant characteristics might be duration (e.g. above five years versus below five years), coupon (e.g. above 5% versus below 5%), and sector (e.g. government versus corporate). This produces eight cells (one would be short duration, low coupon, government and another would be long duration, low coupon, corporate, and so on). The portfolio manager might attempt to hold at least one bond with the characteristics of each cell. The relative importance of each cell in the index would be reflected in the value of bonds allocated to the cell.

Bonds are removed from index calculations one year prior to maturity, since bonds with less than a year to maturity cease to be regarded as bonds. So as bonds approach maturity they drop out of bond indices. This entails the rebalancing of index tracking portfolios, and the associated transaction costs.

An alternative form of passive management of bond portfolios is the buy-and-hold strategy. The investor buys a portfolio of bonds that satisfy the investor's needs, and holds those bonds until they mature. Investors do not sell their bonds at any stage. An attraction of such a strategy is that the investor need not be concerned about the liquidity of the bonds held. Bonds that lack liquidity, that is bonds that may be difficult to sell, tend to have higher yields to compensate for the poor liquidity. This is one reason why corporate bonds have higher yields than government bonds. If an investor is not concerned about the poor liquidity, the additional yield is a free bonus. Another advantage of a buy-and-hold strategy is that it largely avoids transaction costs such as brokers' commissions. The only transaction costs are those of the initial purchases; the costs of subsequent selling and buying are avoided.

There are hybrid funds that have characteristics of both index funds and actively managed funds. Enhanced index funds allow limited deviation from the index in an attempt to outperform the index.

Closet trackers are actively managed funds that use part of the fund to track an index. Managers of closet trackers seek to avoid the risk of substantially underperforming the index, and of thereby being low in league tables of fund managers.

INTEREST RATE ANTICIPATION

If it were possible to forecast interest rates, active management of bond portfolios could be profitable. If interest rates were expected to fall, portfolio duration should be increased in order to enhance the gains from such a fall. If interest rates were expected to rise, portfolio duration should be reduced in order to reduce the prospective price falls. It needs to be remembered that the investor does not simply need to be able to forecast interest rates, but needs to forecast more accurately than other investors. Existing bond prices would reflect market expectations of future interest rates. The rates at which future cash flows are discounted to arrive at bond prices are based on market expectations of future interest rates. The success of active fund management based on forecasting depends upon accurately identifying circumstances in which the market forecasts are wrong (and upon being able to do better). Bond fund managers who adopt such a strategy would use highly liquid bonds, such as government bonds, so as to be able easily to undertake the buying and selling required to adjust portfolio duration quickly. Speed is important to such a strategy. Any superior forecasting ability needs to be acted upon before other investors correct their forecasts.

The question arises as to whether it is possible to forecast interest rates. The *Wall Street Journal* publishes the interest rate forecasts of prominent analysts. The surveys appear twice a year and are for six months ahead. Kolb and Stekler (1996) analysed 17 of the surveys. They found that there was usually a consensus amongst forecasters, but also found that the forecasts were not significantly better than a forecast of no change (i.e. using current rates as the forecast rates).

777

The conclusions of the Kolb and Stekler (1996) study, that professional forecasters do no better than someone who simply assumes that interest rates will remain unchanged, is probably representative of the research on the effectiveness of forecasting (Stephenson 1997). So there should be doubt about the value of interest rate anticipation as an investment strategy. If it is not possible to forecast interest rate changes, it is not possible to use forecasts to make profits from bond portfolio management.

CONCLUSION

The two characteristics of investments most frequently considered are expected return and risk. In the case of shares, beta is the most frequently used measure of risk. In the case of bonds, it is duration.

Bonds are used in institutional investment portfolios not only as means of accumulating wealth but also as means of funding annuity payments. Since it is possible to obtain reasonably reliable estimates of the duration of prospective annuity payment streams as well as the duration of bond portfolios, it is possible to match the duration of the bond portfolio with the duration of the annuity payments. Such duration matching, or immunisation, is very useful for annuity and pension providers since it provides a high degree of protection against interest rate risk.

Duration is important for the structuring of bond index tracker funds. If such a fund were to be constructed using stratified sampling based on a cell structure, one of the characteristics of a cell would be duration. Other characteristics might be redemption yield and credit rating. There would be a cell for each combination of characteristics (e.g. high duration, low redemption yield, high credit rating), and the portfolio would contain an appropriately weighted combination of cells.

Chapter 43 on bond futures explains how futures can be used for the management of portfolio duration. If an annuity fund, index tracker fund, or other bond fund exhibits a duration that differs from the optimum it is possible to use bond futures to adjust the portfolio duration to the desired value.

Chapter 42

Bond price convexity

OBJECTIVE

The objective of this chapter is to provide knowledge of:

1. The problem of convexity.
2. The value of convexity.
3. The construction of bond portfolios.
4. Callable bonds.

THE PROBLEM OF CONVEXITY

Money duration merely provides an approximation to the relationship between yield changes and bond price movements. This is illustrated by Figure 42.1. Figure 42.1 shows the price/yield relationship for a bond together with a straight line representing money duration (i.e. price value of a basis point, PVBP).

It can be seen from Figure 42.1 that for small changes in yield, such as R_0 to R_1 or R_0 to R_2, the price change indicated by money duration along the straight line is a fair approximation to the actual price change as shown by the curved price/yield relationship. However for large yield changes, such as R_0 to R_3 or R_0 to R_4, the money duration line provides a poor estimate of the actual price change. Money duration underestimates price rises and overestimates falls. In both cases the new bond price is underestimated. The inaccuracies arise because money duration fails to take account of the convexity (curvature) of the actual price/yield relationship of a bond.

EXERCISE 42.1

It is 24 November 1992. Treasury 12% 1994 (which has just paid a six-monthly coupon) has a maturity date of 23 May 1994. The interest rate is 8% p.a. for all maturities up to 1.5 years.

Estimate (a) the Macaulay's duration, and (b) the modified duration, of the gilt.

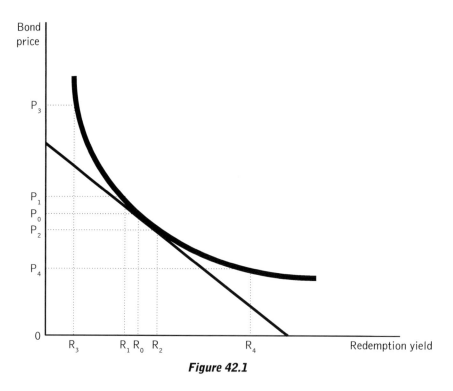

Figure 42.1

What capital gain or loss would arise from a holding of £1 million nominal of this gilt in the event of a $1/_4$% p.a. fall in interest rates? Comment on the accuracy of this estimate of capital gain or loss.

Answers

Treasury 12% would pay a coupon of £12 p.a., i.e. £6 six-monthly, and an 8% p.a. interest rate implies 4% per six-month period.

The fair price of the bond would be:

$$P = £6/(1.04) + £6/(1.04)^2 + £106/(1.04)^3$$

(The £106 comprises the final coupon of £6 and the redemption value of £100.)

$$P = £5.77 + £5.55 + £94.23 = £105.55$$

(a) The Macaulay's duration of the bond would be:

$$D = (£5.77/£105.55)\,0.5 + (£5.55/£105.55)\,1.0 + (£94.23/£105.55\,)1.5$$

$$= 0.0273 + 0.0526 + 1.3391 = 1.419$$

$$= 1.42 \text{ years (to two decimal places)}.$$

(b) The modified duration would be:

$$M = 1.419/1.04 = 1.3644$$

$$= 1.36 \text{ (to two decimal places)}.$$

780

The fair value of £1 million nominal of the gilt would be:

£1,000,000 × £105.55/£100 = £1,055,500

The capital gain would be estimated from:

% change in bond price = − modified duration × change in redemption yield

= −1.36 × −0.25 = 0.34%

So the capital gain would be 0.0034 × £1,055,500 = £3,588.7. Hence the new value of the bonds should be £1,055,500 + £3,588.7 = £1,059,088.7

It is to be noted that £6/(1.03875) + £6/(1.03875)^2 + £106/(1.03875)^3 = £5.7762 + £5.5607 + £94.5742 = £105.9111. (8% − 0.25% = 7.75%. 7.75/2 = 3.875%.) Hence, according to the discount model, the new value of the bonds should be £1,059,111. So the modified duration approach predicts the new value of the bonds quite accurately − the error is less than £23.

Modified duration does not provide a precisely accurate answer since it assumes a linear price-yield relationship, whereas the relationship is actually convex.

EXERCISE 42.2

A bond has just paid a six-monthly coupon of £4. There are four more coupons to be paid by maturity. How accurate is modified duration for the purpose of estimating the effect of a (a) 0.2% p.a., and (b) 1% p.a., decrease in the redemption yield on the bond price, when redemption yields are initially 2% p.a. Comment on the results of the calculations.

Answers

(a) With a redemption yield of 2% p.a., the fair price of the bond would be:

£4/(1.01) + £4/(1.01)^2 + £4/(1.01)^3 + £104/(1.01)^4 = £3.96 + £3.92 + £3.88 + £99.94 = £111.70

Macaulay's duration is:

(3.96/111.7)0.5 +(3.92/111.7)1.0 +(3.88/111.7)1.5 +(99.94/111.7)2.0
= 0.018+0.035+0.052+1.789 = 1.894 years

Modified duration is:

1.894/(1.01) = 1.875

A fall in the redemption yield of 0.2% implies a price rise of 0.375%. (%ΔP = −1.875 × −0.2% = 0.375%)

The new bond price is estimated to be £111.70 × 1.00375 = £112.12
The dividend discount model predicts a new price of:

£4/(1.009) + £4/(1.009)^2 + £4/(1.009)^3 + £104/(1.009)^4 = £3.96 + £3.93 + £3.89 + £100.34 = £112.12

(0.009 is based on a six-month interest rate of 2% − 0.2% = 1.8% p.a., i.e. 0.9% per six-month period.)

The estimate based on modified duration is accurate.

(b) A fall in the redemption yield of 1% implies an estimated price rise of:

− 1.875 × − 1% = 1.875%

Therefore modified duration indicates a new price of £111.70 × 1.01875 = £113.79. The dividend discount model shows a new price of:

£4/(1.005) + £4/(1.005)^2 + £4/(1.005)^3 + £104/(1.005)^4 = £3.98 + £3.96 + £3.94 + £101.95 = £113.83.

(0.005 is based on a six-month interest rate of 2% − 1% = 1% p.a., i.e. 0.5% per six-month period.)

Modified duration underestimates the extent of the bond price rise when the interest rate (redemption yield) change is large. This error arises because of convexity.

THE VALUE OF CONVEXITY

Two bonds with identical durations, prices, and yields may have different convexities. In Figure 42.2 the curve A shows the price/yield relationship for bond A, and curve B does so for bond B. It can be seen that bond B has greater convexity (curvature) than bond A. This gives bond B an advantage over bond A. Changes in yield from R_0, in either direction, raise the price of B relative to that of A. This renders B preferable to A, especially if high volatility is expected. This should entail

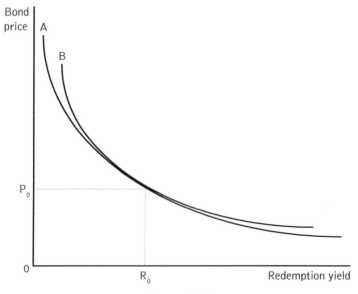

Figure 42.2

B selling at a higher price, and hence lower yield, compared with A. It is unlikely that a situation in which the bonds have identical prices and yields will persist.

CONSTRUCTION OF BOND PORTFOLIOS

The construction of a bond portfolio is frequently based on taking a view with respect to interest rates. If interest rates are expected to fall, so that bond prices are expected to rise, a portfolio with a relatively high duration would be constructed. Conversely, an expectation of a rise in interest rates would entail a portfolio with low duration so that potential losses are reduced.

It is not just duration that a bond portfolio manager needs to be concerned with. Convexity has value in that it leads to higher bond prices following interest rate movements, when compared with an investment with zero convexity. High convexity bonds provide this benefit to a greater extent than low convexity bonds. The benefits of convexity are greater when interest rate changes are relatively large. This implies that the portfolio manager needs to consider the prospective size of interest rate movement as well as the direction.

A bond with high convexity will tend to have a relatively low redemption yield. The advantage bestowed by high convexity would be offset by a lower prospective yield. If interest rate movements are small, the gains from convexity would not compensate for the low yield. So if a portfolio manager expects a small interest rate change, bonds with low convexity should be chosen. If the expectation is that there will be a substantial interest rate movement, high convexity bonds should be chosen.

Convexity is greatest for low coupon, long maturity, and low-redemption-yield bonds (i.e. high duration bonds). Convexity can be calculated and combined with measures of duration when evaluating the potential effects of interest rate changes on bond prices. Since measures of duration are accurate only for very small changes in interest rates, a convexity correction is required in the case of large interest rate movements. To estimate the effects of relatively large interest rate changes on bond prices, it is necessary to combine an estimate of convexity with an estimate of duration.

CALLABLE BONDS

Some corporate bonds are callable. This means that the issuer has the right to repurchase the bonds at a predetermined price (the issuer has a call option on the bonds). A rise in the bond price that renders the repurchase desirable would be brought about by a fall in market interest rates or an improvement in the credit rating of the bonds. Under these circumstances the issuer could repurchase the bonds and issue new bonds at a lower coupon rate. The issuer would choose to repurchase since that would allow for a reduction in financing costs. Bonds with a relatively high coupon could be repurchased with money raised from the sale of bonds with a lower coupon. The issuer thereby reduces coupon payments.

The predetermined price at which the issuer has the right to repurchase puts an upper limit on the value of the bonds. No one would pay a higher price knowing that that they could be forced to sell at the predetermined price. The price/yield relationship for a callable bond has an upper limit to the price, as shown in Figure 42.3. The maximum price is depicted as P_{max}.

An implication of the upper limit to the price is that, around point X, the convexity turns into concavity. Another implication is that the coupon rate on a callable bond will be higher than the

783

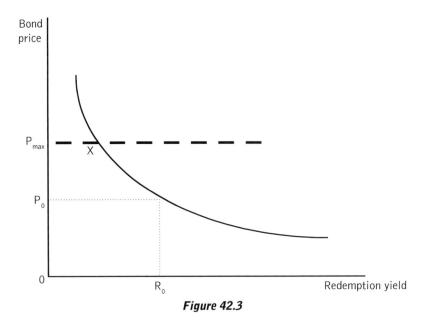

Figure 42.3

coupon rate on a bond without the call feature. If investors face a ceiling on their prospective capital gains, they would require an enhanced coupon yield in compensation. Effectively investors are providing the issuer with a call option. The investors would require payment for the call option. The payment to the investors takes the form of increased coupons.

CONCLUSION

The relative certainty of bond cash flows makes it worthwhile to make estimates that would be pointless in the case of shares, whose future cash flows are much less certain. One such estimate is duration, another is convexity.

Duration provides a relationship between redemption yields and bond prices; a relationship that permits estimates of the effects of redemption yield changes on bond prices. However the relationship provided by duration measures is a linear relationship whereas the actual relationship is a curve rather than a straight line. The straight line approximates the curve reasonably well when redemption yield changes are very small. For larger changes in redemption yield a reliable estimate of bond price change requires a measure of convexity to be combined with the measure of duration. The effect of a redemption yield change on a bond price is a combination of the effects that operate via duration with the effects that operate through convexity.

The degree of detail offered by convexity estimates may seem excessive. However an institutional investor might hold more than £100 million in a particular bond issue. Apparent details translate into substantial monetary values when investments are very large.

Chapter 43

Bond futures

OBJECTIVE

The objective of this chapter is to provide knowledge of:

1. The nature of government bond futures.
2. The use of government bond futures to hedge, or immunise, bond portfolios.
3. The role of arbitrage in the determination of bond futures prices.
4. Implied repos.
5. Basis risk as a source of hedge imperfection.
6. The use of bond futures to simulate (synthesise) bond portfolios.
7. Credit derivatives.

BONDS

Bonds are issued in a wide variety of forms. However, most government bonds conform to a conventional format. The conventional government bond (gilt in the UK):

1. pays a fixed coupon per period (usually 6 months);
2. has a definite redemption date;
3. has a market price expressed as a sum per £100 of nominal value.

A conventional gilt pays a fixed sum of money, known as the coupon, every six months. It has a definite redemption date on which the government is obliged to pay the nominal value of the bond to its owner. Its market price is expressed in relation to its nominal value, for example pounds per £100 nominal (so a market price of £96 means that £96 must be paid for every £100 to be repaid at redemption).

FUTURES CONTRACTS

Government bond futures are commitments to buy or sell government bonds during specified future months. A limited number of bonds are eligible for delivery in fulfilment of a futures contract, and the seller has the choice as to the specific bond to be delivered. Contracts are commonly not held until maturity but are closed out by means of the holder taking out an opposite contract; for example a buyer can close out by selling bond futures in an amount and for a delivery month corresponding to those of the contracts previously bought. Daily cash flows (by way of marking-to-market variation margin) reflect the change in futures prices between the dates of buying and selling.

HEDGING THE VALUE OF A PORTFOLIO

A portfolio manager may fear an increase in long-term interest rates, an occurrence that would reduce the prices of bonds held in a portfolio. The manager could attempt to avoid this effect on the value of the portfolio by taking a position in futures that would provide an offsetting gain from a fall in bond prices. To achieve this, futures contracts would be sold. A fall in bond prices should be accompanied by a fall in the prices of bond futures. If a loss were made from a decline in the value of bonds, the portfolio manager would be compensated with profits from the futures position. The fund manager would be able to close out by buying bond futures at a price lower than that at which they were sold.

This process is illustrated by Example 43.1, in which a fund manager hedges with futures. The Gilt futures contract has a nominal value of £100,000 and the prices of contracts are expressed as pounds per £100 nominal value. The portfolio manager has bonds worth £1,000,000 on 2 January and is anxious about the possibility that interest rates might rise thereby reducing the value of the bonds.

EXAMPLE 43.1

2 January
The long-term interest rate is 5% p.a. A £1,000,000 bond portfolio is vulnerable to an increase in long-term interest rates.

The fund manager sells ten Gilt futures contracts. The futures price is £115.

15 February
The long-term interest rate has risen to 6% p.a. Correspondingly, the value of the bond portfolio has fallen to £850,000.

The fund manager closes out by buying ten Gilt futures contracts. The price of the contracts has fallen to £100.

There is a loss of £150,000 in the value of the bond portfolio.

There is a profit of £150,000 from the futures position [(115−100) × £1,000 × 10 contracts].

In Example 43.1 the hedge was perfect. The profit on the futures exactly matched the loss on the portfolio. Perfect hedges are very unlikely. This is partly because spot and futures markets do not move perfectly in line with each other.

Some of the mismatch between portfolio and futures price movements can be removed by ascertaining the appropriate ratio of futures value to portfolio value. In Example 43.1, the ratio was treated as 1. This is not usually the case. The hedger would be able to ascertain the appropriate number of futures contracts required before selling the contracts. The ratio of the nominal value of futures contracts required to the nominal value of assets or liabilities to be hedged is known as the hedge ratio.

Even with the correct hedge ratio, hedging may not be perfect. Imperfections will still arise if the cash market and futures interest rates do not change to the same extent. However the difference between cash and futures interest rates fluctuates less than cash market rates and hence an imperfect hedge is better than no hedge. Also it is unlikely that a whole number of futures contracts will exactly match the exposure of the portfolio to be hedged (it is not possible to trade in fractions of contracts).

EXERCISE 43.1

(a) An institutional investor holds undated bonds with a value of £10,000,000 when long-term interest rates are 6% p.a. How can the investor use government bond futures to hedge against the possibility of a rise in interest rates (recall that there is an inverse relationship between bond prices and interest rates)?

(b) If long-term interest rates rise to 7.5% p.a., what happens to the value of the bonds? How much futures profit is needed to keep the value at £10,000,000?

(c) If the futures price is initially £100 and falls to £82, how effective is the hedge?

Answers

(a) If the value of the bond holding is to be maintained at £10,000,000, any fall in the value of the bonds must be matched by a profit on futures. A profit from futures, in the event of an interest rate rise, requires the sale of futures. An increase in interest rates will reduce bond prices and hence the prices of bond futures. A profit from a fall in the prices of bond futures requires the sale of futures contracts.

(b) If long-term interest rates rise to 7.5%, the value of the bonds would fall to £8,000,000. Since for undated bonds the fair price equals the coupon divided by the interest rate, a rise in interest rates from 6% p.a. to 7.5% p.a. entails a fall in value from £10,000,000 to £8,000,000; £10,000,000 × 0.06 = £8,000,000 × 0.075 = the unchanged value of coupons. A futures profit of £2,000,000 is required.

(c) If the futures price were initially £100 and falls to £82, and if the £10,000,000 were matched by futures contracts (i.e. futures with a nominal value of £10,000,000 were sold), the futures profit would be $[(100-82)/100] \times £10,000,000 = £1,800,000$. The hedge efficiency would be $£1,800,000/£2,000,000 = 0.9$, i.e. 90%.

EXERCISE 43.2

(a) An investment trust intends to issue long-term bonds in order to borrow £10,000,000 when long-term interest rates are 6% p.a. How can the investment trust use government bond futures to hedge against the possibility of a rise in interest rates before the bonds are issued?

(b) If long-term interest rates rise to 7.5% p.a., what happens to the borrowing cost of the debt of part (a)? How much futures profit is needed to keep the borrowing cost at £600,000 p.a.? What further advantage do the futures provide?

(c) If the futures price is initially £100 and falls to £82, how effective is the hedge?

Answers

(a) The expected borrowing cost is $£10,000,000 \times 0.06 = £600,000$. If the borrowing cost is to be maintained at £600,000, any increase in interest rates must be matched by a fall in the sum to be borrowed. The sum to be borrowed can be reduced by making profits on government bond futures. Profits from futures, in the event of an interest rate rise, require the sale of futures. An increase in interest rates will reduce bond prices and hence the prices of bond futures. The futures contracts are then closed out by buying futures. Since the futures buying price is less than the futures selling price, a profit is made from the futures.

(b) If long-term interest rates rise to 7.5%, the cost of borrowing £10,000,000 would rise to £750,000 p.a. A futures profit of £2,000,000 is required since this would reduce the sum to be borrowed to £8,000,000. The borrowing cost would then be returned to £600,000 p.a. ($£8,000,000 \times 0.075 = £600,000$).

The futures profit reduces the sum to be repaid from £10,000,000 to £8,000,000.

(c) If the futures price were initially £100 and falls to £82, and if futures with a nominal value of £10,000,000 were sold, the futures profit would be $[(100-82)/100] \times £10,000,000 = £1,800,000$. This could be used to reduce the borrowing requirement.

The borrowing requirement is reduced to $£10,000,000 - £1,800,000 = £8,200,000$. At an interest rate of 7.5% p.a., the annual borrowing cost becomes $£8,200,000 \times 0.075 = £615,000$. The hedge reduces the borrowing cost from £750,000 to £615,000, but does not completely reduce it to the original £600,000. The hedge efficiency is $(750,000 - 615,000)/(750,000 - 600,000) = 135/150 = 0.9$, i.e. 90%.

Delivery, Price Factors, Invoice Amounts, and the Cheapest-to-Deliver Bond

A futures contract will have a specific maturity month (alternatively known as the delivery month). Typically the months in which government bonds may be delivered in settlement of futures contracts are March, June, September, and December (i.e. traders choose between these maturity months when buying or selling futures contracts). If a futures contract were held until maturity, the seller chooses which bond to deliver. The seller also chooses the day of the month on which delivery takes place (although for some futures contracts there is no choice as to delivery date). The buyer must accept the bond and date chosen by the seller.

The coupon yield of a bond is the coupon (the total of the coupon payments during a year) divided by the bond price. If the rate of coupon yield on the bond exceeds the interest rate on funds borrowed to finance the purchase of the bond, the bond will be delivered at the end of the month so as to maximise the benefit from the relatively high coupon yield. If the coupon yield is less than the financing cost, the bond would be delivered at the beginning of the month so as to avoid the net cost of holding the bond during the month.

The futures exchange specifies which bonds are eligible for delivery. Every deliverable bond has a price factor. Price factors are of considerable significance for users of bond futures. UK gilt futures contracts each have a nominal value of £100,000. Likewise, the gilts delivered when a contract matures must amount to £100,000 in nominal value (the nominal value of a bond is the sum to be repaid at redemption). Gilts may, however, have differing market values despite identical nominal values. A £100,000 bond issued when the market rate was 12% p.a. would provide a coupon of £12,000 p.a., whereas a £100,000 bond issued at a rate of 5% p.a. would yield £5,000 p.a. The market value of bonds will vary according to the size of the coupon yield. A bond yielding £12,000 p.a. is worth more than one with a coupon of just £5,000 p.a. A seller delivering a high coupon gilt would expect to receive more money than if a lower coupon gilt were delivered. To ensure that this happens, price factors are used in the calculation of the sums for which buyers are invoiced.

The invoice amount is the sum that the buyer of a futures contract must pay to the seller if the contract is taken to delivery of the bond. The futures price upon which the invoice amount is based might be referred to as the settlement price, which is the market price of futures contracts at a specific point in time prior to delivery. The principal invoice amount is the settlement price multiplied by the price factor and by the nominal value of the futures contract (divided by 100 since the settlement price is quoted per £100 nominal value). The sum for which the buyer is invoiced is equal to the principal invoice amount plus accrued interest on the bond. The resulting invoice amounts would normally differ from the market values of the bonds.

The seller chooses which bond to deliver in fulfilment of the contract. It is in the interests of the seller to deliver the bond whose invoice amount exceeds the market price by the largest margin (or whose invoice amount falls short of the market price by the smallest margin). This is the cheapest-to-deliver (CTD) bond.

Hedge Ratios

The hedger must decide upon the number of contracts required to accomplish the desired hedge. This calculation is simplest when hedging the cheapest-to-deliver bond:

$$\text{Number of contracts} = \frac{\text{Nominal value of position}}{\text{Nominal value of a contract}} \times \text{Price factor}$$

The multiplication by the price factor is necessary to adjust for the price difference between the cheapest-to-deliver bond and the notional bond on which the futures is based. A high coupon yield bond has a higher value to be hedged than a low coupon yield bond and will require a correspondingly larger number of futures contracts for the hedging (this difference will be greater the more distant are the maturity dates of the bonds).

Suppose that for the December 2006 contract month the cheapest-to-deliver gilt was the Exchequer 12% 2024, whose price factor was 1.2. If the hedger wished to hedge £10,000,000 nominal of this gilt, the requisite number of contracts would have been calculated thus:

$$\text{Number of contracts} = \frac{£10,000,000}{£100,000} \times 1.2 = 120$$

The hedger would have used 120 gilt futures contracts to hedge the position.

When hedging bonds other than the cheapest-to-deliver, account must be taken of the relative volatility of the bonds. Volatility can be measured in terms of the money value of a (for example) 1% yield change per £100 nominal value. If the bond being hedged is more volatile than the cheapest-to-deliver, a correspondingly greater number of futures contracts would be required for the hedge (and vice versa for less volatile bonds). In this way, the larger price movements of relatively volatile bonds are covered. The formula is as follows:

$$\text{Number of contracts} = \frac{\text{Nominal value of position}}{\text{Nominal value of a contract}} \times \frac{\text{Price factor of}}{\text{cheapest-to-deliver}} \times \frac{\text{Relative}}{\text{volatility}}$$

Thus, if the money value of a 1% redemption yield change per £100 nominal were £5.00 for the gilt being hedged and £3.50 for the cheapest-to-deliver gilt, then the number of contracts necessary to hedge £10,000,000 nominal of the gilts, in an example parallel to the previous one, would be as follows:

$$\text{Number of contracts} = \frac{£10,000,000}{£100,000} \times 1.2 \times \frac{£5.00}{£3.50} = 171.43$$

The appropriate number of gilt futures contracts is 171. A large number of futures contracts are necessary so that the profits/losses on futures succeed in offsetting the relatively large losses/profits on the gilt being hedged. Without adjusting for relative volatility, only £3.50 of every £5 price change would be offset.

The definition of volatility used above is known as perturbation (or money duration). This uses the impact of a specific interest rate change (e.g. 1%) on the prices of the bond to be hedged and the cheapest-to-deliver. A frequently used interest rate (or redemption yield) change is the basis point (0.01%), in which case perturbation is alternatively referred to as the price value of a basis point (or PVBP). The measurement of volatility is illustrated in Chapter 41 on duration and risk.

Perturbation or PVBP is estimated as:

$$\frac{\text{Duration}}{1 + \text{Redemption Yield}} \times \text{Bond Price}$$

where duration is Macaulay's duration and the redemption yield is the redemption yield per coupon period (i.e. annual redemption yield divided by the number of coupons per year).

Relative volatility is:

$$\frac{D_A}{D_B} \times \frac{(1 + r_B/N)}{(1 + r_A/N)} \times \frac{P_A}{P_B}$$

where D_A is the duration of the hedged bond, D_B is the duration of the cheapest-to-deliver bond, r_A and r_B are the redemption yields, N is the number of coupon payments per year, P_A and P_B are the bond prices.

The hedge ratio is thus:

$$F_B \times \frac{D_A}{D_B} \times \frac{(1 + r_B/N)}{(1 + r_A/N)} \times \frac{P_A}{P_B}$$

where F_B is the price factor of the cheapest-to-deliver bond.

Fixed interest securities other than government bonds can be hedged with government bond futures; however, it must be borne in mind that the more dissimilar are the cheapest-to-deliver bond and the instrument being hedged, the less effective is the hedge likely to be. This is the problem of cross-hedging. Increasing difference between the instrument being hedged, and the instrument on which the futures are based, is associated with increasing imperfection of the hedge.

EXERCISE 43.3

A fund manager has a portfolio of gilts with a nominal value of £5 million. The average price of the gilts in the portfolio is £80. The duration of the portfolio is 12 years. The cheapest-to-deliver gilt has a price of £130, a price factor of 1.2, and a duration of 10 years. Ten- and 12-year redemption yields are both 8% p.a. How could the fund manager approximately halve the volatility of the portfolio of gilts?

Answer

To fully hedge the portfolio the number of gilt futures to be sold is given as:

Nominal Value of Portfolio/Size of a Futures Contract × Price Factor of CTD × Relative Volatility

$$\text{where Relative Volatility} = \frac{(\text{Duration of Portfolio})}{(\text{Duration of CTD})} \times \frac{(1 + \text{rctd})}{(1 + \text{rp})} \times \frac{(\text{Average Price of Gilts})}{(\text{Price of CTD})}$$

CTD is the cheapest-to-deliver gilt, rctd is the redemption yield of the cheapest-to-deliver gilt, and rp is the redemption yield of the portfolio.

$$\frac{£5m}{£0.1m} \times 1.2 \times \frac{12}{10} \times \frac{(1.08)}{(1.08)} \times \frac{£80}{£130} = 50 \times 1.2 \times 1.2 \times 1 \times 0.615 = 44.28$$

The volatility of the portfolio could be halved by selling $44.28 / 2 = 22.14$ gilt futures contracts. Since futures contracts are indivisible 22 would be sold.

Bond Portfolio Immunisation

Sometimes bond portfolios are held for the purpose of funding a known series of future cash flows. Interest rate risk on such bond portfolios may be reduced by the following means:

1. *Dedicated portfolios.* The prospective cash flows from the bonds held correspond to the future cash flow requirements in both amount and timing. For example the future payments to pensioners from an annuity fund might be synchronised with the coupon and redemption receipts from the bonds that constitute the fund. Such a dedicated portfolio is difficult to construct.

2. *Maturity matching.* The maturities of the bonds in the portfolio match the times at which cash flows will be required. This avoids the price risk from interest rate changes but is subject to reinvestment risk (the rate of interest on reinvested coupon receipts is uncertain).

3. *Duration matching.* The Macaulay's duration of the bonds matches the time at which a cash flow will be required. Bond price changes tend to offset variations in returns from reinvested coupons. So both the bond price risk of interest rate changes and the reinvestment risk are substantially reduced. Bond futures can be used to adjust portfolio duration to the desired level. Any discrepancy between the durations of the liabilities (prospective cash outflows) and the durations of the bonds can be removed by taking an offsetting position in bond futures. A difference between the average duration of the liabilities and the average duration of the bonds in the portfolio can be offset by government bond futures. Since government bond futures have durations, portfolio duration can be increased by buying futures or decreased by selling them.

A bond portfolio manager using duration-based immunisation needs to be aware of the need for frequent rebalancing (restructuring the portfolio). Frequent rebalancing is necessary first because duration declines more slowly than term to maturity. The passage of a year will reduce duration by less than a year. Duration would then exceed the investment horizon. Second, the price-yield relationship for bonds is convex. So duration changes as interest rates change. When portfolio duration is matched to the average duration of liabilities, rather than a single investment horizon, rebalancing remains necessary since the duration of the portfolio is unlikely to move precisely in line with the average duration of the liabilities.

Adjusting Portfolio Duration with Futures

The volatility of a bond portfolio may be measured as the change in portfolio value arising from a basis point, 0.01% p.a., change in yield (i.e. the price value of a basis point). Suppose that a portfolio of bonds has a Macaulay's duration of 15 years, a redemption yield of 4% p.a., a market value of £10,000,000, and that coupons are paid annually (and remembering that a basis point as a decimal is 0.0001). Portfolio volatility can be estimated as:

$$\frac{15}{1.04} \times £10,000,000 \times 0.0001 = £14,423$$

An interest rate change of 0.01% p.a. is expected to result in the value of the portfolio changing by £14,423. This calculation is based on:

Modified Duration $\times$ Bond Price $\times$ Interest Rate Change,

which comes from the equation for money duration (price value of a basis point) described in Chapter 41 on duration and risk.

If the portfolio manager seeks to reduce the portfolio duration to ten years, the desired volatility (i.e. the PVBP, price value of a basis point) is given by:

$$\frac{10}{1.04} \times £10,000,000 \times 0.0001 = £9,615$$

Portfolio volatility needs to be reduced by £14,423 − £9,615 = £4,808.

The next step is to measure the volatility of a futures contract. This entails calculating the volatility of the cheapest-to-deliver bond and then dividing by its price factor. Suppose that the cheapest-to-deliver bond has a Macaulay's duration of 12 years, a redemption yield of 4% p.a., a price of £110 (£110,000 per £100,000 nominal), and pays an annual coupon. The volatility of the cheapest-to-deliver bond is:

$$\frac{12}{1.04} \times £110,000 \times 0.0001 = £126.92$$

If the cheapest-to-deliver bond has a price factor of 0.9875, the volatility of a futures contract is estimated as £126.92/0.9875 = £128.52. In order to reduce the portfolio volatility by £4,808 it is necessary to sell £4,808/£128.52 = 37.4 futures contracts. Since futures contracts are indivisible, either 37 or 38 contracts would be sold.

DETERMINATION OF BOND FUTURES PRICES

Arbitrage Pricing

As with other assets that can be carried during the life of a futures contract, bond futures prices tend to be determined by cash-and-carry arbitrage. Long cash-and-carry involves buying bonds while simultaneously selling bond futures. Short cash-and-carry (in its pure form) involves borrowing bonds and selling them while buying futures. The futures price should be such that no profit is available from cash-and-carry arbitrage. The fair futures price is a price that precludes any profit from arbitrage.

When arbitrage involves buying bonds, pure arbitrage entails borrowing money in order to buy the bonds. Interest must be paid on the borrowed money, and this is referred to as the financing cost of holding the bonds. For no arbitrage profits to be available from long cash-and-carry, the financing cost of holding bonds should be matched by the returns from holding the bonds. The returns would be in the form of coupon receipts plus capital gains (or losses) guaranteed by the futures price relative to the spot price of the bonds. If the financing cost exceeds the coupon yield, there will be a net cost of holding the bonds. The absence of profit/loss requires a capital gain that matches this net cost. The capital gain comes from an excess of the futures price over the spot price (i.e. there should be a futures premium over spot). The futures price should guarantee a selling price of bonds that exceeds the buying price by the amount of capital gain required to match the net cost of holding the bonds (the net cost of carry). If the financing cost is less than the coupon receipts, a futures discount, providing a capital loss, should exist.

For long cash-and-carry, when there are no coupons before the futures delivery date:

$$S(1 + rt) = F$$

The interest rate is r and the time to the futures maturity (delivery) date in years is t. The cost of buying the bonds (S), plus the financing cost (S × rt), should equal the sum receivable from selling against the futures (F). If the futures price is higher, there is an arbitrage profit from buying bonds and simultaneously selling futures.

For long cash-and-carry, when there are coupons before the futures delivery date:

$$S(1 + rt) - D = F$$

The sum to be paid by the delivery date, S(1 + rt), minus what is received, D (the future value of the coupons), should match the sum receivable from selling against the futures. The future value of coupons equals the value of the coupons plus interest on that value between the coupon payment date and the futures delivery date.

By subtracting S from both sides it can be seen that the futures premium (or discount) relative to spot matches the difference between the financing cost and coupon yield. Thus:

$$F - S = S(1 + rt) - S - D$$
$$F - S = S + (S \times rt) - S - D$$
$$F - S = (S \times rt) - D$$

It has been implicitly assumed that the bond has a price factor of 1; if this is not the case (and it hardly ever will be), F in the equations needs to be divided by the price factor. More precisely, F net of accrued interest should be divided by the price factor of the bond in order to ascertain the futures price. Since S and F relate to sums actually paid and received, they must include accrued interest (the rights to coupon payment between the last coupon payment date and the date on which the bond is bought and sold). The price factor involved would be that of the bond used, which would normally be the cheapest-to-deliver. Since the bond normally used in cash-and-carry arbitrage would be the cheapest-to-deliver, the behaviour of the futures price would tend to relate closely to the behaviour of the price of the cheapest-to-deliver bond.

794

EXERCISE 43.4

It is 30 September 1997 and Exchequer 9% 2007 has just paid a coupon. The price of this gilt is £123 and its price factor is 1. The three-month interest rate is 7% p.a. If the December futures contract is held to maturity, what is the most likely date on which delivery into the futures contract would occur? What is the fair futures price on 30 September?

Answers

The current coupon yield on the gilt is $(9/123) \times 100 = 7.32\%$ p.a. So at current values the coupon yield exceeds the interest rate (financing cost) and so it seems likely that any delivery would be made at the end of December. (The seller of the futures chooses on which day of the maturity month to deliver the bond and there is a net gain to the seller from holding the bond during December.)

The cost of buying and holding the gilt until the end of December would be $[£123 \times (1.0175)]$ $= £125.15$, from which accrued interest should be subtracted. The net cost of buying and holding the gilt is thus $£125.15 - £2.25 = £122.9$, which is the fair futures price.

(The financing rate of 1.75% is based on $7\% \times 0.25$ where 30 September to 31 December is treated as 0.25 years. The accrued interest is based on $£9 \times 0.25$ since a 9% gilt pays coupons of £9 per year.)

EXERCISE 43.5

It is 30 June 1997 and Treasury 10% 2007 has just paid a coupon. The price of this gilt is £130 and its price factor is 1.06. The six-month interest rate is 7% p.a. If the December futures contract is held to maturity, what is the most likely date on which delivery into the futures contract would occur? What is the fair futures price on 30 June?

Answers

The current coupon yield on the gilt is $(10/130) \times 100 = 7.69\%$ p.a. So at current values the coupon yield exceeds the interest rate (financing cost) and so it seems likely that any delivery would be made at the end of December.

The cost of buying and holding the gilt until the end of December would be $[£130 \times (1.035)]$ $- £5 = £129.55$. (£5 is accrued interest, which in this case would be received as a coupon payment towards the end of December.)

£129.55 corresponds to a futures price of $£129.55/1.06 = £122.22$, which is the fair futures price.

Transaction costs have been ignored here. If bid-offer spreads are allowed for in both the bond market and the interest rates, the result is a no-arbitrage band of futures prices rather than the unique fair futures price (the fair futures price is the price that would prevail in the absence of transaction costs). The no-arbitrage band can be described by the expression:

$$S_B(1 + r_B t) - D \leq F \leq S_0(1 + r_0 t) - D$$

where S_B is the spot bid price (dirty price, i.e. inclusive of accrued interest), S_0 is the spot offer price (dirty price), r_B is the interest rate for period t (bid rate), r_0 is the interest rate for period t (offer rate), t is the time to maturity of the futures contract (in years), D is the future value of coupons (relating to ex-coupon dates prior to the futures maturity date), and F is the futures price (multiplied by the price factor and inclusive of accrued interest).

The left of the equation is based on short cash-and-carry arbitrage, which entails selling bonds (at the bid price) and depositing the proceeds (at the bid rate). The right of the equation is based on long cash-and-carry arbitrage, which involves buying bonds (at the offer price) with money borrowed at the offer rate.

Arbitrage should operate to keep the futures price within the no-arbitrage band. If the futures price rises above the band, long cash-and-carry arbitrage would tend to bring it back into the band. This would involve bonds being bought (the consequent upward pressure on bond prices will tend to raise the band) and futures being sold (thereby pushing futures prices down into the band). If the futures price falls below the band, the underpriced futures should be bought and the bonds sold; in other words, short cash-and-carry arbitrage should (at least in principle) take place. Short cash-and-carry arbitrage will tend to lower the no-arbitrage band (via reducing the spot bond price) and will raise the futures price until it is again within the band.

Futures prices do not slavishly follow spot prices. Within the no-arbitrage band futures prices can vary independently of spot prices. Hedging, and speculation based on expectations of movements in futures prices, can move the futures price within the no-arbitrage band.

Futures prices can lead spot prices via cash-and-carry transactions. Hedging and speculation, influenced by expectations, can push futures prices out of the no-arbitrage band. The resulting arbitrage moves spot prices. In this way trading in futures can cause changes in spot prices that are led by the changes in futures prices.

The Role of Implicit Options

The seller of bond futures contracts has choices relating to when to deliver during the delivery month and which bond to deliver. In effect this gives the futures seller options, and the futures buyer has provided them. The seller of futures must, in some way, pay for the options and the buyer be paid. This is accomplished by a reduction in the bond futures price below the level that would otherwise pertain. In this way, at delivery the futures seller receives a sum which is reduced by the value of the option premiums, while the futures buyer receives payment for the options in the form of having to pay less for the bonds when they are delivered upon maturity of the futures contract.

Implied Repos

Buying bonds and simultaneously selling futures constitutes an investment whose maturity is the same as that of the futures contract. The implied repo is the rate of return on that investment. The return comprises coupon receipts plus the capital gain (or loss) guaranteed by the futures price. The investment is equivalent to a bank deposit for the period to maturity of the futures in that there is an initial outflow of cash and a subsequent receipt of cash. The implied repo rate is effectively the interest rate.

Selling bonds and buying futures constitutes borrowing for the period to the futures maturity date, at the implied repo rate. (Repo is an abbreviation of sale and repurchase: selling bonds and buying futures is a form of sale and repurchase arrangement.) There is a source of risk, to the borrower, in the use of the construction for borrowing in that there is no certainty as to which bond will be delivered at maturity, and no certainty as to the date on which delivery will take place (these being at the discretion of the seller of futures contracts). The procedure is equivalent to borrowing since there is an initial receipt of cash and a subsequent payment of cash. The implied repo rate is effectively the interest rate. The provision of bonds gives the lender security (the bonds act as collateral) so the interest rate should be a risk-free rate.

EXERCISE 43.6

It is 31 March 1998. The cheapest-to-deliver bond is Treasury 2015 8%. Bond futures for June maturity are priced at £102. The price factor of Treasury 2015 8% is 0.89. Two- and three- month interest rates are 7.5% p.a. Treasury 2015 8% has just paid a coupon and is priced at £91.

(a) On what date is delivery into the futures contract likely to occur?

(b) What is the implied repo to that date?

(c) How could an arbitrage profit be made?

Answers

(a) The coupon yield on the bond is £8/£91 = 8.79% p.a. which exceeds the financing cost of 7.5% p.a. The bond will be delivered on the last business day in June since the seller can profit from holding the bond as long as possible.

(b) The implied repo is:

$$[\{(102 \times 0.89) + 2\} - 91]/91 = 0.01956 = 1.956\% \text{ for three months, } i.e.\ 7.824\% \text{ p.a.}$$

(The £2 is the accrued interest at the end of June.)

(c) Buy bonds and sell futures thereby investing at a risk-free 7.824% p.a. The bonds are bought with money borrowed at 7.5% p.a. There is an arbitrage profit of 7.824 − 7.5 = 0.324% p.a. (This is a long cash-and-carry arbitrage.)

BASIS RISK

Fair basis – the difference between the fair futures price and the adjusted spot price (clean spot price divided by the price factor) – reflects the financing cost (interest rate) relative to the coupon yield on the bond. A change in the interest rate on money borrowed to finance the purchase of a bond in cash-and-carry arbitrage would alter the fair basis. Such a change in basis introduces a degree of imperfection into a hedge. This possibility is known as basis risk. Fortunately, basis risk is likely to be low when the cheapest-to-deliver bond is being hedged.

As the characteristics of the bond being hedged diverge further and further from those of the cheapest-to-deliver bond, basis risk progressively increases. To the basis risk arising from the possibility of changes in financing costs must be added the basis risk from possible changes in the relative prices of the cheapest-to-deliver bond and the bond being hedged. The greater the difference between the cheapest-to-deliver bond and the bond being hedged, the greater the basis risk arising from this latter source. When basis risk is so large that there is not a close relationship between changes in the futures price and changes in the price of the bond being hedged, the futures contract does not provide a suitable means of hedging.

SYNTHETIC BOND PORTFOLIOS

Government bond futures, together with a corresponding sum in money market investments (e.g. bank deposits), can be used to create a portfolio with the same characteristics as a portfolio of government bonds. This could be particularly advantageous as a means of structuring a bond investment based on foreign currency bonds. An advantage arises from the avoidance of currency risk (the risk that losses could be experienced as a result of falls in the values of the currencies in which the bonds are priced). A portfolio of foreign currency bonds entails a currency exposure equal to the full value of the bonds held. A portfolio that uses bond futures rather than bonds will have a currency exposure that is limited to the sum held in margin accounts, which will be a small fraction of the value of the fund.

When replicating a bond portfolio with futures it is necessary to reproduce two characteristics of the portfolio being synthesised. One of these characteristics is the exposure to capital gain or loss from changes in interest rates. The other characteristic is the stream of income, which would take the form of a series of coupon payments in the case of the actual portfolio of bonds. This amounts to the creation of the risk and return characteristics of a bond portfolio. A futures position would provide both characteristics.

To replicate the exposure to capital gain or loss from changes in interest rates it is necessary to ascertain the volatility (i.e. the PVBP, price value of a basis point) of the bond portfolio and of a futures contract. Division of the PVBP of the replicated portfolio by the PVBP of a futures contract provides the number of futures contracts that should be bought in order to replicate the portfolio. (See earlier in this chapter the section on Adjusting Portfolio Duration with Futures.)

The creation of the stream of income equivalent to the coupon receipts from a portfolio of bonds involves two components. One component is the interest from the money market investments (e.g. interest on bank deposits). Since a futures contract costs nothing, the money that would otherwise have been used to buy bonds is available to invest in the money market (the part of the money that is held in margin accounts can also earn interest).

The other component of the cash flow arises from capital gains or losses guaranteed by the futures price. For no arbitrage profits to be available from long cash-and-carry, the financing cost of holding bonds (the interest rate) should be matched by the returns from holding the bonds in the form of coupon receipts, plus capital gains (or losses) guaranteed by the futures premium (or discount) relative to the spot price of the bonds.

This implies that the interest on a bank deposit, plus the gains (or losses) from futures, will tend to equal the coupon return on the bonds. If the interest rate is lower than the coupon yield, there will be a futures discount to spot. When the futures price rises relative to the spot bond price as the futures maturity date approaches, the holder of a futures contract will enjoy a capital gain. The converse occurs if the interest rate is higher than the coupon yield.

If the interest rate (financing cost) exceeds the coupon yield, cash-and-carry arbitrage requires an offsetting capital gain from futures. In cash-and-carry arbitrage the purchase of bonds is associated with a sale of futures. A sale of futures provides a profit from a fall in the futures price. Futures should trade at a premium to the spot price of bonds so that a profit is generated as the futures price converges on (falls towards) the spot price as the maturity date of the futures is approached.

An excess of the interest rate over the coupon yield implies that a futures fund provides a cash flow in excess of that of the corresponding bond fund. The futures fund should provide an offsetting capital loss in order to equalise the cash flows. The futures fund entails the purchase of futures with the effect that the fall in the futures price as it converges towards the bond price produces the capital loss required to offset the excess of the interest rate over the coupon yield.

EXERCISE 43.7

An investor holds £10,000,000 nominal of a government bond that is priced at £110, has a redemption yield of 5.2% p.a., pays coupons twice a year, and has a (Macaulay's) duration of 11 years. The cheapest-to-deliver government bond is priced at £105, has a redemption yield of 5% p.a., pays coupons twice a year, has a (Macaulay's) duration of 9 years, and has a price factor of 1.2.

(a) How many futures contracts are needed to hedge the government bond holding? Should the futures position be long or short?

(b) If the investor, rather than hedging the government bond holding, wanted to simulate a further £10,000,000 nominal of the bond, how could that be achieved?

(c) Why might the strategies of (a) and (b) prove to be imperfect?

(d) What additional problems would arise when attempting to simulate a holding of corporate bonds using government bond futures?

Answers

(a) If the bond to be hedged is denoted as bond A, and the cheapest-to-deliver as bond B, the hedge ratio is:

$$F_B \times \frac{D_A}{D_B} \times \frac{(1+r_B/_N)}{(1+r_A/_N)} \times \frac{P_A}{P_B}$$

where F = price factor, D = duration, r = redemption yield, N = number of coupon payments per year, P = price.

$$1.2 \times \frac{11}{9} \times \frac{(1.025)}{(1.026)} \times \frac{£110}{£105} = 1.53501$$

In the absence of a hedge ratio the number of futures contracts required would be:

£10,000,000/£100,000 = 100

where £100,000 is the (nominal) size of a futures contract. Taking account of the hedge ratio the required number of futures contracts is:

100 × 1.53501 = 153.501

The nearest whole number, rounding down, is 153 futures contracts. The futures should be sold, i.e. a short position in futures is required.

(b) To simulate a bond holding identical to the existing holding, the investor would undertake transactions opposite to those of the hedge. The investor would buy 153 futures contracts.

(c) Reasons for imperfect hedging and simulation could include:

(i) Changes in basis.
(ii) Bond price convexity (duration based hedge ratios are accurate only for small redemption yield changes).
(iii) The inability to trade the required number of contracts because of liquidity problems.
(iv) Changes in the cheapest-to-deliver bond, i.e. another bond could take over as the cheapest-to-deliver with the effect that the hedge ratio needs to be changed.
(v) The required hedge ratio could change as a result of changes in price factors, bond prices, durations, and redemption yields during the period of the hedge or simulation.
(vi) Indivisibility of contracts means that the precise number of required contracts cannot be achieved (the nearest whole number has to be used).

(d) An additional problem when simulating a holding of corporate bonds is the creation of the higher default risk, and corresponding risk premium. (The risk premium is the addition to expected return required to compensate for the default risk.) Also this risk, and risk premium, could change over time. These problems may be dealt with by using credit derivatives.

EXERCISE 43.8

A fund manager holds £100,000,000 nominal of a government bond that is priced at £105, has a redemption yield of 5% p.a., pays coupons twice a year, and has a (Macaulay's) duration of 10 years. The cheapest-to-deliver government bond is priced at £102, has a redemption yield of 4.8% p.a., pays coupons twice a year, has a (Macaulay's) duration of 8 years, and has a price factor of 1.1.

(a) How many futures contracts should be sold to reduce the duration of the bond holding (i) to zero, and (ii) to 5 years?

(b) How could an institutional investor structure a £100,000,000 bond futures fund?

Answers

(a) If the bond to be hedged is denoted as bond A, and the cheapest-to-deliver as bond B, the hedge ratio is:

$$F_B \times \frac{D_A}{D_B} \times \frac{(1+r_B/N)}{(1+r_A/N)} \times \frac{P_A}{P_B}$$

where F = price factor, D = duration, r = redemption yield, N = number of coupon payments per year, P = price.

$$1.1 \times \frac{10}{8} \times \frac{(1.024)}{(1.025)} \times \frac{£105}{£102} = 1.41406$$

In the absence of a hedge ratio the number of futures contracts required would be:

(i) £100,000,000/£100,000 = 1,000 (reducing duration to zero is the same as a full hedge)
(ii) 1,000/2 = 500 (reducing the duration from 10 to 5 years is the same as a 50% hedge)

where £100,000 is the (nominal) size of a futures contract. Taking account of the hedge ratio the required number of futures contracts is:

(i) 1,000 × 1.41406 = 1,414 contracts (rounding down to the nearest whole number).
(ii) 500 × 1.41406 = 707 contracts (rounding down to the nearest whole number).

(b) To construct a £100,000,000 futures fund, the investor would undertake transactions opposite to those of the full hedge. The investor would buy 1,414 futures contracts.

CREDIT DERIVATIVES

Credit derivatives are derivatives on credit risk and can be used to hedge credit risk on a specific bond. The pay-off from a credit derivative might be based on the relationship between the price of a corporate bond and the price of a risk-free (normally government) bond. Alternatively the pay-off may be based on the difference between the redemption yields. These relationships would be affected by credit events.

Credit events would include bankruptcy, insolvency, or payment default on the part of the issuer of the bond whose credit risk is being hedged. Other credit events could include rating changes for the hedged bond, or a substantial price decline on the part of the bond. A reference bond may be used for the derivatives rather than the actual bond being hedged.

A yield spread is the difference between the yields on two bonds. A forward contract might be based on a specified bond's yield spread over a benchmark asset (such as a government bond). At maturity of the forward contract a payment would be made based on the difference between the spread agreed in the contract and the spread at maturity.

Credit options take a number of different forms. A common form is the default put. If there is a credit event the writer (seller) of the option pays the buyer a sum of money. In this way the option buyer obtains protection from credit events. The credit event that triggers the payment could arise in relation either to the specific bond being hedged or to a reference bond. Whereas default puts pay a fixed sum of money when a credit event occurs, spread options pay a sum of money that varies according to the severity of the event. The severity of the event is measured by the change in yield spread. The option strike price would be a particular spread, and the option would provide a pay-off if the actual spread differed from the strike price spread. The pay-off would increase as the difference increased.

The purchase of a bond, together with appropriate derivative positions, can simulate a bond with different risk characteristics. For example the purchase of a UK government bond could be combined with a derivatives position based on the credit risk of a corporate bond. This combination simulates a holding of the corporate bond.

By combining credit derivatives with government bond derivatives, it is possible to simulate a portfolio of corporate bonds. The addition of currency derivatives could allow the currency of the simulated portfolio to be changed.

Credit derivatives allow the credit risk of an asset to be transferred to another party, thereby separating the credit risk from ownership of the asset. Batten and Hogan (2002) point out that most credit derivatives are created when an investor seeks to hedge a particular risk, which results in the credit derivative being specifically designed to meet that particular need. So the market for credit derivatives is one that provides a variety of unique derivatives, each designed for a particular situation. The lack of standardisation and uniformity, in the view of Batten and Hogan, has inhibited the development of exchange-traded credit derivatives.

Bomfim (2002) suggests that the determinants of the prices of credit derivatives include the credit risk of the bond issuer, the credit risk of the seller of the derivative, the likelihood of simultaneous default by those two parties, and the sum of money that might be recovered subsequent to a default.

Credit derivatives could be combined with government bond derivatives for the purpose of hedging corporate bonds. An alternative is to combine government bond derivatives with stock index derivatives. Clare et al. (2000) investigated the effectiveness of combining government bond futures with stock index futures for the purpose of hedging corporate bonds. Combining futures in this way is known as dual-asset hedging. They found that this dual-asset hedging was superior to the use of government bond futures alone in the cases of some low-grade bonds but that in most cases single-asset hedging with government bond futures was more effective.

CONCLUSION

Bond futures are used to manage bond risk. Bond risk can be seen either as bond price risk or as interest rate (bond redemption yield) risk because of the relationship between bond prices and interest rates. So bond futures can be seen as means of managing bond price risk, or as means of managing interest rate risk.

Institutional investors hold bond portfolios either as means of accumulating capital, or as means of funding cash flows (such as payments to annuity holders). Bond futures can be used to manipulate the duration of a bond portfolio. Reduction of the price risk of a bond portfolio (hedging against bond price falls) entails reducing the duration of the portfolio. A short bond futures position reduces the duration of a long position in bonds (holding bonds).

Reduction in the cash flow risk could be seen in isolation from any liabilities in the form of cash flow payment commitments, or in combination with any such liabilities. Reduction in cash flow risk may aim at guaranteeing a specific level of cash flows. Such a guarantee entails hedging bond price risk, which amounts to hedging interest rate risk. Reduction of the risk of cash flow variations relative to cash flow liabilities (variations of inflows relative to outflows) could be achieved by duration matching, which entails matching the duration of the bond portfolio with the duration of the liabilities.

It is possible to construct portfolios using bond and credit derivatives, and without any investment in bonds. However the accuracy of simulation of a bond portfolio can be compromised in a number of ways, which mirror the sources of hedge imperfection when using futures (see especially Part 8 on stock index futures). Sources of imperfection and inaccuracy include changes in basis within (fairly wide) no-arbitrage bands. These sources are in addition to the interest rate risk, which is the risk of a movement of the band. Movements within the band arise from the behaviour of hedgers and speculators. So the value of a synthetic bond portfolio could be substantially influenced by the behaviour of speculators, and in some cases their trading might be akin to noise trading (see Chapter 24 on noise trading and behavioural finance). Of course, such sources of uncertainty are also present when bond futures are used for risk management purposes.

Chapter 44

Yield curves and interest rate futures

OBJECTIVE

The objective of this chapter is to provide knowledge of:

1. Yield curves (the term structure of interest rates).
2. Bond portfolio construction.
3. The use of yield curves to estimate market expectations of future interest rates.
4. Forward yield curves.
5. Short-term interest rate futures.
6. Hedging the level, slope, and curvature of yield curves.

YIELD CURVES

A yield curve shows the relationship between the redemption yields of (interest rates on) bonds and the maturities of those bonds. Figure 44.1 illustrates three possible shapes of the yield curve. These are not the only possible shapes. The number of possible yield curve patterns (alternatively known as the term structure of interest rates) is infinite.

On the far left of the yield curve the investments are very short-term deposits that can be withdrawn without notice, or with just a few days notice. On the far right the investments have very distant maturities, for example 25-year government bonds.

The most common yield curve pattern is for yields (interest rates) to rise with increasing maturity but for the rate of increase to diminish. The diminishing rate of increase implies that, for distant maturities, increases in maturity entail little or no increment to yields. The yield curve labelled 'normal' illustrates this pattern.

The yield curve sometimes exhibits a downward slope, as illustrated by the curve labelled 'inverted'. The flat yield curve shows a situation in which interest rates are the same irrespective of the length of time for which money is invested; such a situation is extremely unusual.

Explanations of the term structure of interest rates, and hence the shape of the yield curve, can be divided into three theories. These three theories are pure expectations, expectations with risk premium, and market segmentation.

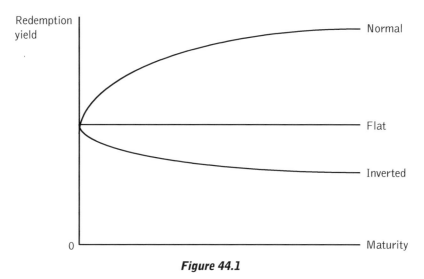

Figure 44.1

According to the pure expectations theory, long-term interest rates can be seen as averages (geometric means) of current and expected future short-term interest rates. So, for example, the 12-month interest rate would be an average of the current 3-month rate and the expected rates for each of the subsequent three 3-month periods. Likewise the 5-year interest rate would be an average of the current 1-year rate and the expected 1-year rates for each of the subsequent four years.

Suppose that the spot (current) 1-year interest rate is 10% p.a. and the expected rate for the following year is 12% p.a. The current 2-year interest rate should be the geometric mean of these two rates.

$$\sqrt{(1.1)(1.12)} = \sqrt{1.232} = 1.11 \tag{1}$$

The 2-year rate is $1.11 - 1 = 0.11$ as a decimal, which is 11% p.a. as a percentage. The 2-year rate is the rate which, when compounded over two years, gives the same final value as 10% in one year compounded with 12% in the following year. According to the pure expectations theory, investors should have no preference between the alternative of investing at 11% p.a. for two years and the other alternative of investing for one year at 10% p.a. whilst anticipating investment of the proceeds for a further year at 12% p.a.

EXERCISE 44.1

The current 3-month interest rate is 11% p.a. and market expectations of the next seven 3-month rates are 11%, 11%, 10%, 10%, 10%, 9%, and 9% p.a. What, according to the pure expectations theory, should the current 2-year rate be?

Answer

$$\sqrt{(1.0275)^3(1.025)^3(1.0225)^2} - 1 = \sqrt{1.22136} - 1 = 1.1052 - 1 = 0.1052$$

As a percentage this is 10.52% p.a.

Since the interest rates are 3-month rates, the annual rates need to be divided by four (3-months being treated as a quarter of a year). So, for example, 11% p.a. is 2.75% over three months. The eight 3-month returns are compounded on one another to obtain the value of the investment at the end of the two years, which is 1.22136. Since interest rates are always expressed on a per annum (per year) basis, the square root of the final sum is taken. The square root shows the per annum rate, which when compounded over two years, produces the final sum of 1.22136.

If the pure expectations theory is an accurate explanation of the level of long-term interest rates, it is possible to infer market expectations of future interest rates from the yield curve. The implied future interest rates are referred to as forward interest rates.

In the previous example, an investor knowing that the 1-year rate is 10% p.a. and the 2-year rate is 11% p.a. could deduce that the 1-year rate expected to be available one year from now is 12% p.a. In other words, the forward interest rate is 12% p.a. The forward interest rate is the rate which when compounded on the 1-year rate of 10% p.a. produces the same sum as 11% p.a. compounded over two years.

EXERCISE 44.2

If the 2-year interest rate is 10.5% p.a., and the 1-year rate is 9.5% p.a., what does the market expect the 1-year interest rate to be a year from now?

Answer

$(1.105)^2/1.095 = 1.1151$

$(1.1151 - 1) \times 100 = 11.51\%$ p.a.

This can be seen as 1.095 being invested, at the end of the first year, at 11.51% p.a. to yield $(1.105)^2$ at the end of the second year.

The pure expectations theory assumes that investors are indifferent between investing for a long period on the one hand and investing for a shorter period with a view to reinvesting the principal plus interest on the other hand. For example an investor would have no preference between making a 12-month deposit and making a 6-month deposit with a view to reinvesting the proceeds for a further six months so long as the expected interest receipts are the same. This is equivalent to saying that the pure expectations theory assumes that investors treat alternative maturities as perfect substitutes for one another.

The pure expectations theory assumes that investors are risk-neutral. A risk-neutral investor is not concerned about the possibility that interest rate expectations will prove to be incorrect, so long as potential favourable deviations from expectations are as likely as unfavourable ones. Risk is not regarded negatively.

Most people are not risk-neutral; they are risk-averse. They dislike risk. Risk-averse investors are prepared to forgo some investment return in order to achieve greater certainty in regard to the value of investments and the income from them. As a result of risk-aversion, investors may not be indifferent between alternative maturities. Attitudes to risk may generate preferences for either short or long maturities. If such is the case, the term structure of interest rates (the yield curve) would reflect risk premiums.

If an investment is close to maturity, there is little risk of capital loss arising from interest rate changes. A bond with a distant maturity (long duration) would suffer considerable capital loss in the event of a large rise in interest rates. The risk of such losses is known as capital risk. To compensate for the risk that capital losses might be realised on long-term investments, investors may require a risk premium on such investments. A risk premium is an addition to the interest or yield to compensate investors for accepting risk. This tends to impart an upward slope to a yield curve. This tendency towards an upward slope is likely to be reinforced by the preference of many borrowers to borrow for long periods (rather than borrowing for a succession of short periods). Such borrowers may be willing to pay an interest premium for the facility of borrowing long term.

There is a form of risk that would tend to have the opposite effect on the slope of a yield curve: this is known as income risk. Some investors may prefer long maturity investments because they provide greater certainty of income flows. For example a conventional UK government bond pays a constant coupon every six months until the bond reaches its redemption date. On the other hand, interest receipts from bank deposits can change frequently. Income flows from a bank deposit are very uncertain. This uncertainty is income risk.

If investors have a preference for predictability of interest receipts, they may require a higher rate of interest on short-term investments to compensate for income risk. This would tend to cause the yield curve to be inverted (downward sloping).

The effects on the slope of the yield curve from factors such as capital risk and income risk are in addition to the effect of expectations of future short-term interest rates. If money market participants expect short-term interest rates to rise, the yield curve would tend to be upward sloping. If the effect of capital risk were greater than the effect of income risk, the upward slope would be steeper as a result. If market expectations were that short-term interest rates would fall in the future, the yield curve would tend to be downward sloping. A dominance of capital-risk aversion over income-risk aversion would render the downward slope less steep (or possibly turn a downward slope into an upward slope).

Dimson *et al.* (2000) found that over the twentieth century, on average, long-term bonds showed a modest premium over short-term investments (Treasury bills). In the UK the long end of the maturity spectrum averaged a 0.3% premium over the short end. For a group of 12 countries the premium was 0.6% on average. King and Kurmann (2002) investigated US interest rates between 1951 and 2001 and found that the expectations theory provided a reasonable approximation to the observed term structure of interest rates. However they found that there were deviations from the term structure predicted by expectations, and that the deviations could be ascribed to risk premiums. They found that there was some tendency for the whole yield curve to move up and down, indicating that there were factors that affected both short- and long-term interest rates simultaneously. Not all studies have supported the expectations theory; for example a study by Sarno *et al.* (2007) rejected the expectations hypothesis in the sense of pure expectations plus a constant risk premium.

The third theory of the term structure of interest rates is the market segmentation approach. According to the market segmentation theory, interest rates for different maturities are determined independently of one another. The interest rate for short maturities is determined by the supply of and demand for short-term funds. Long-term interest rates are those that equate the sums that investors wish to lend long term with the amounts that borrowers are seeking on a long-term basis.

According to market segmentation theory, investors (and borrowers) do not consider successions of short-term investments (or borrowings) as substitutes for long-term ones. This lack of substitutability keeps interest rates of differing maturities independent of one another. If investors (or borrowers) considered alternative maturities as substitutes, they may switch between maturities. If investors (and borrowers) switch between maturities in response to interest rate changes, interest rates for different maturities would no longer be independent of each other. An interest rate change for one maturity would affect demand/supply, and hence interest rates, for other maturities.

A variation on the market segmentation theory is the preferred habitat hypothesis. The preferred habitat hypothesis is less extreme than the market segmentation theory since it allows for some substitutability between maturities. However the preferred habitat view sees substitutability as being less than perfect so that interest premiums are needed to entice investors from their preferred maturities to other maturities.

According to the market segmentation and preferred habitat explanations, government can have a direct impact on the yield curve. Governments borrow by selling bills and bonds of various maturities. If government borrows by selling long-term bonds, it will push up long-term interest rates (push down long-term bond prices) and cause the yield curve to be more upward sloping (or less downward sloping). If the borrowing were at the short maturity end, short-term interest rates would be pushed up.

CONSTRUCTION OF BOND PORTFOLIOS

A portfolio manager needs to take account of potential changes in the slope of the yield curve. If a portfolio manager expects the slope to change, the portfolio should be adjusted accordingly.

The effects of a change in slope can be seen by considering two possible portfolio constructions. These constructions are known as a bullet portfolio and a barbell portfolio. A bullet portfolio uses bonds of a single maturity, for example ten years. A barbell portfolio focuses on two maturities, for example five years and twenty years. The two portfolios may have identical durations but exhibit very different responses to a change in the slope of the yield curve. A steepening of the yield curve (long-term redemption yields rising relative to short-term redemption yields) would be to the disadvantage of the barbell portfolio relative to the bullet portfolio.

A steepening of the yield curve involves yields on distant maturity bonds rising relative to those on short-term bonds. For a barbell portfolio, the interest rate rise impacts (negatively) on the bonds that are most sensitive to interest rate changes whereas the interest rate fall (positively) affects the bonds that are less sensitive to interest rate movements. So a steepening of the yield curve tends to disadvantage barbell portfolios. Conversely a flattening of the yield curve (long-term yields falling and short-term yields rising) is to the advantage of a barbell portfolio.

A popular strategy among bond portfolio managers is known as 'riding the yield curve'. This strategy seeks to take advantage of risk (liquidity) premiums that cause longer-term redemption yields to exceed shorter-term yields. The process entails buying longer-term bonds, with the relatively high yields, and holding them until the yield declines as a result of the fall in risk premium (this fall is due to the bond acquiring a shorter maturity from the passage of time). The decline in yield would be associated with a rise in price (because of the inverse relationship between yields and prices). The procedure may, for example, entail buying a two-year bond and selling it when its maturity has fallen to one year. The decline in yield brings about a capital gain on the bond. The strategy depends on the yield curve having an upward slope.

One danger for the investor is that a general rise in yields could eliminate the gains from the fall in the relative yield. The decline in the risk premium could be overwhelmed by a rise in risk-free yields, in other words the strategy would entail interest rate risk. If riding the yield curve were seen as an alternative to holding a bond whose maturity matched the desired investment horizon, it would entail buying bonds with maturities exceeding the investment horizon and selling at the investment horizon. This would benefit from the decline in the risk premium but would be vulnerable to interest rate risk. Bieri and Chincarini (2005) suggest that this interest rate risk could be managed by the use of a barbell investment. The longer-term bond could be combined with a short-term investment such that the duration of the barbell matched the investment horizon. They found that riding the yield curve did provide higher returns than simply investing in a bond whose maturity matched the investment horizon. There were still excess returns when the barbell strategy was used.

FORWARD INTEREST RATES AND EXPECTED FUTURE INTEREST RATES

The manager of a portfolio of bonds may make changes to the portfolio in the light of that manager's expectations of future interest rates. The expectations that are relevant to investment decisions are expectations relative to market expectations. An active portfolio manager bases investment decisions on attempts to forecast interest rates more accurately than the average participant in the money market. For this reason the manager of an actively managed bond portfolio needs to be able to ascertain the market consensus forecast. Such market expectations can be deduced from forward interest rates.

Forward interest rates are rates for periods commencing at points of time in the future. They are implied by current rates for differing maturities. For example, the current 3-month interest rate and the current 6-month interest rate between them imply a rate for a 3-month period which runs from a point in time three months from the present until a point in time six months hence.

The forward 3-month rate for a period commencing three months from the present is the rate which, when compounded on the current 3-month rate, would yield the same return as the current 6-month rate. For example if the 3-month rate is 9% p.a. and the 6-month rate is 10% p.a., the forward rate is shown as x in equation (2).

$$(1.0225)(1 + x) = 1.05 \qquad (2)$$

0.0225 is the decimal rate for three months based on 9% p.a. (2.25% over a quarter of a year is obtained by taking a quarter of 9%) and 0.05 is the decimal rate for six months based on 10% p.a. The forward rate is calculated as:

$$x = (1.05/1.0225) - 1 = 0.0269$$

which is 2.69% over three months and hence 10.76% p.a. (multiplying 2.69% by four).

The forward rate can be interpreted as the market expectation of the future interest rate under specific circumstances. These circumstances are (1) the expectations theory of the yield curve is correct and (2) there is no risk premium. If the expectations theory is seen as a good model, but a risk premium is thought to be present, an adjustment is required to remove the effects of the risk premium before the result can be interpreted as the market forecast of the future interest rate. This is illustrated in Exercise 44.3.

EXERCISE 44.3

The one-year interest rate is 6.5% p.a. and the six-month interest rate is 6% p.a. What is the forward six-month interest rate for the period between six months and one year from now? Can this forward interest rate be taken to be the interest rate expected by money market participants?

Answers

Let x be the forward interest rate p.a. (so that the rate for six months is $x/2$).

$$(1.03)(1 + x/2) = 1.065$$
$$1 + x/2 = (1.065)/(1.03)$$
$$x/2 = [(1.065)/(1.03)] - 1$$
$$x = 2\{ [(1.065)/(1.03)] - 1\}$$

Therefore $x = 0.068$, i.e. 6.8% p.a.

The forward interest rate of 6.8% p.a. can be taken to be the market expectation if (1) the expectations theory of the yield curve is correct and (2) there is no risk premium. If the expectations theory is correct but there is a risk premium, the risk premium must be removed before carrying out the calculation. Suppose that the six-month rate contains no risk premium, but the one-year rate contains a risk premium of 0.1% p.a. The one-year interest rate, net of the risk premium, is 6.4% p.a. The new calculation would be as follows:

$$(1.03)(1 + x/2) = (1.064)$$
$$x = 2\{[(1.064)/(1.03)] - 1\}$$

Therefore $x = 0.066$, i.e. 6.6% p.a.

EXERCISE 44.4

Zero coupon bonds with maturities one, two, and three years from the present have prices of £95, £88, and £80 respectively.

(a) What are the spot one-, two-, and three-year interest rates?

(b) Draw the yield curve.

(c) What is the two-year forward interest rate for the period from one year hence to three years from the present?

Answers

(a) In the case of the one-year bond, an investment of £95 entails a receipt of £100 in one year.

£100/£95 = 1.0526 which implies a spot one-year interest rate of 5.26%.

In the case of the two-year bond, an investment of £88 yields a receipt of £100 after two years.

£100/£88 = 1.13636

$\sqrt{1.13636}$ = 1.0660 which implies a spot two-year interest rate of 6.60% p.a.

In the case of the three-year bond, an investment of £80 provides a receipt of £100 after three years.

£100/£80 = 1.25

$1.25^{0.33}$ = 1.0772 which implies a spot three-year interest rate of 7.72% p.a.

($1.25^{0.33}$ is the cube root of 1.25; the cube root converts the return over three years into a compound rate of return per year.)

(b)

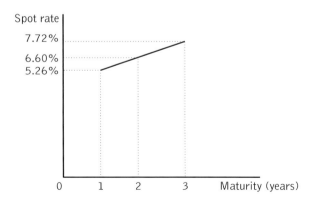

The yield curve based on zero coupon bonds is known as the spot yield curve. It is regarded as more informative than a yield curve that relates redemption yields to maturities of coupon-bearing bonds because it is unambiguous. Yield curves that relate redemption yields of coupon-bearing bonds to maturities involve ambiguities since each coupon represents a maturity. So the redemption date is not the only maturity date. Coupon-bearing bonds may have differing redemption yields, despite having common redemption dates, because of differences in the coupon payments. Yield curves based on coupon-bearing bonds may not provide a single redemption yield corresponding to a redemption (final maturity) date. As a result the relationship between redemption yield and maturity is ambiguous.

(c) $1.25/1.0526 = 1.18754$

(This is equivalent to investing £1.0526 and receiving £1.25 two years later.)

$\sqrt{1.18754} = 1.0897$

$1.0897 - 1 = 0.0897$ i.e. 8.97% p.a.

The two-year forward rate for the period beginning one year from the present is 8.97% p.a.

THE FORWARD YIELD CURVE

The forward yield curve relates forward interest rates to the points of time to which they relate. For example, rates of return on five-year bonds and rates on four-year bonds imply rates on one-year instruments to be entered into four years from the present. The implied forward rate can be calculated by means of the formula:

$$(1 + {}_4r_1) = (1 + r_5)^5 / (1 + r_4)^4$$

where r_5 is the five-year interest rate, r_4 is the four-year interest rate, and ${}_4r_1$ is the one-year rate expected in four years' time.

This formula arises from the relation:

$$(1 + r_5)^5 = (1 + r_4)^4 (1 + {}_4r_1)$$

which states that a five-year investment at the five-year interest rate should yield the same final sum as a four-year investment at the four-year rate with the proceeds reinvested for one year at the one-year rate expected to be available four years hence. The value of ${}_4r_1$ would be related to the point in time, of four years, on the yield curve.

Carrying out such a calculation for a succession of future periods produces a series of forward interest rates. When plotted against their respective dates, the series of forward rates produces a forward yield curve. An unambiguous forward yield curve requires the use of zero coupon bonds for the calculations.

SHORT-TERM INTEREST RATE FUTURES

Both borrowers and investors face interest rate risk. Borrowers lose from increasing interest rates, while investors lose in the event of declines. Short-term interest rate futures, which frequently take the form of three-month interest rate futures, are instruments suitable for the reduction of the risks of interest rate changes. Three-month interest rate futures are notional commitments to borrow or deposit for a three-month period that commences on the futures maturity date. They provide means whereby borrowers or investors can (at least approximately) predetermine interest rates for future periods.

Three-month interest rate futures have a limited number of maturity dates each year; typically one in each of March, June, September, and December. Buying a June three-month sterling interest rate futures contract notionally commits the buyer to the deposit of £500,000, for three months from the June maturity date, at an interest rate determined in the present. The seller is simultaneously notionally committed to borrowing for that period and is also guaranteed that interest rate.

Short-term interest rate futures contracts are quoted on an index basis. The index is equal to 100 minus the annualised futures interest rate. For example, a three-month interest rate of 3% giving an annualised rate of 12% p.a. implies that the contract would be priced at 88 (100 − 12). It is to be emphasised that such prices are merely indices that are used in ascertaining profits and losses from futures trading and do not represent money payable for contracts.

DETERMINATION OF FUTURES PRICES

The creation of a forward position in interest rates can be looked upon as a deferred deposit or borrowing. For example a potential investor who anticipates the receipt of money three months hence and intends to deposit it for three months can, in the present, borrow money for three months and deposit it for six months. When the cash is received, it is used to repay the three-month borrowing, leaving the six-month deposit intact for the remaining three months. So there is no net cash inflow or outflow in the present, but a cash outflow after three months (debt repayment) and a cash inflow after six months (maturity of the six-month deposit). These cash outflows and inflows are equivalent to a three-month deposit made three months hence. The advantage of the creation of a forward position is that it guarantees the intcrest rate for the future three-month period, this interest rate being implied by the spot three-month and six-month rates.

If the rates that can be guaranteed by such forward transactions differ from the rates that can be guaranteed using futures contracts, an arbitrage opportunity may exist. Arbitragers could borrow via the cheaper method and deposit through the approach yielding the higher interest rate. This pursuit of arbitrage profits would tend to cause both spot and futures rates to move so as to eliminate arbitrage possibilities (by moving the two deferred interest rates towards equality). For example if the futures interest rate is the lower one, arbitragers would sell futures (to guarantee being able to borrow at that lower rate), thereby causing the futures price to fall and hence the futures interest rate to rise until it has risen into line with the forward interest rate.

Arbitrage tends to ensure that the futures interest rate approximates closely to the forward interest rate. If the futures rate were significantly below the forward rate, arbitragers would lend long and borrow short, using the futures market to guarantee future short-term borrowing rates.

Lending for the longer term and financing the lending by short-term borrowing, whilst using futures to guarantee that the debt can be renewed at a low rate, provides a high future lending rate matched against a low future borrowing rate. This would involve selling futures (commitments to future borrowing) and the increased sales would push down their prices. The fall in futures prices corresponds to a rise in futures interest rates. This increase in futures interest rates will tend to eliminate the scope for further arbitrage profits.

EXERCISE 44.5

(a) If the three-month interest rate is 4.5% p.a. and the six-month interest rate is 5% p.a., what is the forward interest rate for the three-month period commencing three months from now?

(b) On the basis of the forward interest rate, what should be the price of the three-month interest rate futures contract maturing three months from now?

(c) If the futures price were 94.80, how could an arbitrage profit be made?

(d) What should be the effect of the arbitrage on the futures price and the futures interest rate?

Answers

(a) 5% p.a. is 2.5% over six months, and 4.5% p.a. is 1.125% over three months.

$(1.025)/(1.01125) = 1.013597$

$1.013597 - 1 = 0.013597$, i.e. 1.3597% for three months or 5.44% p.a. (to two decimal places).

The forward interest rate is 5.44% p.a.

(b) The price of the futures should be $100 - 5.44 = 94.56$.

(c) A futures price of 94.80 implies a futures interest rate of $100 - 94.80 = 5.20\%$ p.a. An arbitrage profit could be made by selling futures and structuring a long forward interest rate. A six-month deposit at 5% p.a. financed by borrowing for three months at 4.5% p.a. produces a three-month forward deposit at an interest rate of 5.44% p.a. By selling futures at 94.80 a future three-month borrowing rate of 5.20% p.a. is guaranteed. An arbitrage profit equivalent to $5.44\% - 5.20\% = 0.24\%$ p.a. is obtained.

(d) The sale of futures should reduce the futures price and raise the futures interest rate. The futures interest rate should rise towards the forward interest rate.

HEDGING THE YIELD CURVE WITH FUTURES

The basic principle of hedging with financial futures is that a futures position should be taken so that the feared interest rate change causes a profit on futures that compensates for the loss incurred on the assets or liabilities. If an investor expects interest rates to fall (i.e. the level of the yield curve to fall), short-term interest rate futures are bought. A decline in interest rates is associated with a rise in futures prices. Buying futures would profit from a price rise. So buying futures provides a profit that offsets the adverse effects of a fall in interest rates on the investor's returns.

Short-term interest rate futures prices are quoted on the basis of:

$$100 - \text{the interest rate}$$

For example a futures interest rate of 6% p.a. would be quoted as a futures price of 94 $(100 - 6)$. A fall in the futures interest rate causes a rise in the futures price, and vice versa.

A depositor (lender) would lose from a fall in interest rates and hence buys futures. A fall in interest rates would raise futures prices and hence provide a profit to the buyer of the futures. A borrower would lose from a rise in interest rates and hence sells futures in order to profit from a fall in the futures price (rise in the futures interest rate).

EXAMPLE 44.1   PERFECT HEDGE WITH SHORT-TERM INTEREST RATE FUTURES

2 January

A treasurer intends to borrow £1,000,000 on Feb 1st for 3 months. Fears that the interest rate will rise above the current 10% p.a.

Sells 20 futures contracts at a price of 90.

1 February

Borrows £10,000,000 at 12% p.a.

Buys 20 futures contracts at a price of 88.

Cash market loss is 2% on £10,000,000 for 3 months = £50,000.

Futures market profit = (90−88)% on (20 × £500,000) for 3 months = £50,000.

Example 44.1 illustrates a perfect hedge. Hedging is rarely, if ever, perfect. One reason is that the instrument underlying the futures contract is rarely identical to the instrument being hedged. In other words there may be an asset mismatch. In addition to asset mismatch, there are date and maturity mismatches. Futures have a limited number of maturity dates available, and it is unlikely that a futures maturity date coincides with a deposit or borrowing date. In addition, short-term interest rate futures are usually for three-month deposits and borrowings, whereas the hedged position may be for a different period of time. Date and maturity mismatches involve exposures to changes in the slope and curvature of the yield curve.

The objective of hedging is typically one of minimising, rather than eliminating, risk. When hedging is undertaken, some risk remains. Probably the most significant remaining risk is basis risk. Basis is the difference between the futures interest rate and the interest rate on the asset or liability being hedged. A change in basis renders a hedge imperfect. Basis risk arises from the tendency of futures interest rates to show movements that differ in unpredictable ways from the interest rate movements on the borrowing or investment being hedged. In other words, perfect hedging requires futures interest rates and cash market interest rates to move exactly in line with each other (or at least that any deviation should be predictable). Example 44.2 shows hedge imperfection arising from a change in basis.

> ## EXAMPLE 44.2   IMPERFECT HEDGE WITH SHORT-TERM INTEREST RATE FUTURES
>
> *2 January*
>
> A treasurer intends to borrow £10,000,000 on feb 1st for 3 months. Fears that the interest rate will rise above the current 10% p.a.
>
> Sells 20 futures contracts at a price of 90.
>
> *1 February*
>
> Borrows £10,000,000 at 12% p.a.
> Cash market loss is 2% on
> £10,000,000 for 3 months = £50,000.
>
> Buys 20 futures contracts at a price of 89.
> Futures market profit = (90−89)% on
> (20 × £500,000) for 3 months = £25,000.

One way of dealing with basis risk is based on the observation that basis risk largely arises from changes in the slope and curvature of the yield curve. One technique is the straddle, which involves purchases of contracts with one maturity date and simultaneous sales of contracts with another maturity date with a view to making profits from relative price movements. The straddle hedges against changes in the slope of the yield curve. This may be supported by the use of a futures butterfly, which hedges against changes in the curvature of the yield curve (Redhead 1997, 1999).

There are three dimensions of hedging yield curve risk. The first involves hedging against changes in the level of the yield curve. The second concerns hedging the risk that the slope of the curve may change. The third hedging dimension relates to possible changes in the curvature of the yield curve.

These are three ascending levels of sophistication. Ideally, all three dimensions should be hedged. Hedging the level of the yield curve is the basic hedge, but the effectiveness of the hedge could be undermined if the slope of the yield curve changed (thereby causing basis to change). An attempt to hedge against slope changes could be undermined by a change in curvature. So the most effective hedging strategy addresses all three dimensions.

Straddles

As the hedging strategy is developed through these three levels of refinement, it becomes increasingly complex. To deal with the risk of slope changes, a futures straddle (inter-delivery or time spread) should be added to the basic hedge. Hedging curvature risk would involve adding a futures butterfly (a straddle of straddles) to the previous two hedges. So the most complete hedge would add together a basic hedge, a straddle, and a butterfly. (Although the word 'most' has been used here, there is scope for even greater levels of refinement in hedging a yield curve.) If a borrower seeks protection from a rise in the slope of the yield curve, a futures straddle can be bought. Nearby futures contracts are bought and distant maturity contracts sold. A rise in the slope (steepening) of the forward yield curve raises distant forward interest rates relative to earlier forward rates. This lowers the price of the distant futures contracts relative to the nearby ones. Buying nearby contracts and selling distant ones generates profits in the event of the prices of distant contracts falling relative to nearby ones.

Futures straddles involve buying and selling equal numbers of futures contracts for different delivery months (e.g. buying five June and selling five September would constitute a long straddle). The objective is to make a profit from an otherwise unfavourable change in the gradient of the yield curve.

Butterfly Spreads

In the case of butterfly spreads, the view is on the relationship between two straddles. A butterfly is a spread of straddles.

Suppose that three-month sterling futures contracts have the prices shown in Table 44.1 for the next three maturity months. The value of a straddle is obtained by subtracting the farther futures price from the nearer futures price. Within the butterfly the nearby straddle is 150 basis points (92.00 − 90.50), while the deferred straddle is 50 basis points (90.50 − 90.00). The value of the butterfly spread is 100 basis points (150 − 50).

If the butterfly spread is expected to strengthen (more positive/less negative), the butterfly spread is bought (buy the nearby straddle and sell the distant one); in the opposite case, the butterfly is sold. A bought (long) butterfly profits from increased curvature of the yield curve.

For example the numbers in Table 44.1 imply forward interest rates of 8%, 9.50%, and 10%. If the December rate falls to 9%, the forward yield curve becomes more curved (curvature increases). In this case the December futures price rises to 91.00. This gives a profit from buying the butterfly since the long butterfly entails buying December futures contracts.

The addition of a straddle and a butterfly to a basic hedge does not necessarily lead to a large increase in the total number of futures contracts. Between the three strategies there would be some offsetting of long and short futures positions. The net number of futures bought, or sold, would match the size of the asset or liability being hedged. However if there is asset mismatch a further adjustment to the hedge is required, based on a generic hedge ratio.

Table 44.1

June	September	December
92.00	90.50	90.00

A GENERIC HEDGE RATIO

When the asset or liability being hedged differs in nature from the instrument on which the futures are based, a hedge ratio should be applied. This hedge ratio is generic in that it is applicable to all hedging with futures, irrespective of what is being hedged (interest rates, bond prices, stock indices, etc.). The generic hedge ratio is expressed as:

$$H = \rho \times (\sigma_S / \sigma_F)$$

where ρ is the coefficient of correlation between the cash market and the futures (e.g. between spot and futures interest rates), σ_S is the cash market standard deviation, and σ_F is the standard deviation of the futures.

FORWARD RATE AGREEMENTS

Forward Rate Agreements(FRAs) are often seen as OTC (over the counter) interest rate futures. A client and a bank agree on a target, or benchmark, future interest rate and if the actual interest rate differs from that target rate a compensatory cash flow will occur between the client and the bank.

The time periods used in FRAs correspond to the typical interest rate rollover periods in the money markets. These periods tend to be quarters and half-years. Typical FRAs are '3 against 6' and '6 against 12'. A '3 against 6' FRA entails a commitment to lend or borrow for a 3-month period starting three months from the present. A '6 against 12' FRA involves a commitment to lend or borrow for 6 months commencing six months from the present.

The target, or benchmark, interest rates are based on the forward interest rates derived from the yield curve. Consequently they are very close to futures interest rates. If the three rates were not very close there would be arbitrage opportunities, and the pursuit of those opportunities should bring the three rates together.

As with interest rate futures, FRAs can be used to hedge against unexpected changes in interest rates. An investor might want to hedge against a fall in interest rates. The investor would sell an FRA in order to guarantee the future interest rate (note that with futures the lender buys but with FRAs the lender sells). As with futures, FRAs entail accounting for differences. They do not entail lending or borrowing, they merely entail cash flows arising from differences between target and actual interest rates.

Suppose an investor sells an FRA with a target interest rate of 5% p.a. If the interest rate turns out to be less than 5% p.a., the investor will receive money from the bank to compensate for the reduced rate. If the interest rate turns out to be above 5% p.a., the investor pays the bank the monetary value of the difference between the interest rates. Either way the investor guarantees an interest rate of 5% p.a.

In the case of an FRA the cash flow occurs when the investment (or borrowing) is to be made. In the case of a '6 against 12' FRA, this would be six months after the FRA is sold (or bought). This contrasts with futures, which use marking to market. The marking to market of futures contracts entails daily cash flows that reflect daily changes in futures prices. Futures entail the accumulation of compensatory money flows over time, rather than the whole sum changing hands at one point in time.

As with other instruments, FRAs have bid-offer spreads. Borrowing rates exceed lending rates. The market for FRAs is very competitive and, in consequence, bid-offer spreads are small. Spreads of 4 basis points (0.04% p.a.) are common.

CONCLUSION

It is commonplace to talk about 'the' interest rate. In reality there are many interest rates. There is a different interest rate for each combination of maturity and credit risk. Yield curves indicate how interest rates vary with maturity. There would be a separate yield curve for each level of credit risk.

Market expectations of future interest rates can be estimated from observed yield curves. Such expectations are derived from the calculation of forward interest rates. Forward interest rates are the basis for pricing short-term interest rate futures.

Short-term interest rate futures can be used to hedge the level, slope, and curvature of a yield curve. They can be combined with bond futures to hedge longer-term interest rates (see Chapter 43 on bond futures). Short-term interest rate futures have low durations and their inclusion in a synthetic bond portfolio would help the manipulation of its duration.

Chapter 45

Interest rate swaps

OBJECTIVE

The objective of this chapter is to provide knowledge of:

1. The nature of interest rate swaps.
2. The use of interest rate swaps for hedging risk.
3. The warehousing of swaps by banks.
4. Floating rate notes (FRNs).
5. How swaps can be priced.
6. Credit default swaps.

The term 'swap' is most commonly used in the sense of an agreement to the future exchange of cash flows. The cash flows exchanged may have a wide variety of bases. In the case of interest rate swaps, the typical exchange is of cash flows arising from a fixed rate of interest (fixed for the period to the maturity of the swap) for cash flows arising from a floating interest rate (perhaps a rate changed every six months reflecting movements in a market rate such as LIBOR, the London Inter-Bank Offered Rate).

Most interest rate swaps involve cash flows in the same currency but on different interest bases. The 'plain vanilla' swap involves the exchange of fixed-rate interest flows for floating rate interest flows. One possible motivation is that of hedging.

Swaps are typically longer-term instruments than forwards, futures, and options. Periods in excess of ten years are not unusual. In many cases they are equivalent to a succession of forward contracts stretching into the future.

There are also swaptions. Swaptions are options on swaps. In return for the payment of a premium the buyer of a swaption obtains the right, but not the obligation, to enter a swap agreement in the future on terms agreed when buying the swaption.

HEDGING INTEREST RATE RISK

Floating rate deposits expose an investor to the risk of decreases in the interest rate. An investor may wish to avoid this risk by taking out a fixed-rate deposit but may be committed to a floating

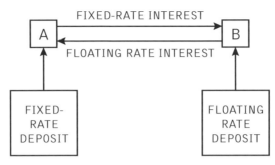

Figure 45.1

rate deposit. The investor could attempt to swap the floating rate asset for a fixed-rate asset, thereby obtaining a fixed-rate investment.

The swap may be carried out directly between two counterparties or may involve a bank as intermediary. In the latter case, the bank might take the role of counterparty to both of the participants, thereby bearing the risk of default by either party and eliminating the need for the participants to investigate the creditworthiness of the other. This has the additional advantage of allowing anonymity of the parties.

In Figure 45.1, investor A has a fixed-interest bank deposit and wishes to swap the interest receipts for the interest on a floating rate deposit. Investor B has a floating rate bank deposit and wants to exchange the interest receipts for those on a fixed-rate deposit. Investor A effectively converts to a floating rate whilst B simulates a fixed-rate investment.

Figure 45.1 depicts the situation in which the two investors negotiate a swap directly with each other. More usually a bank will be counterparty to both. This is illustrated by Figure 45.2.

When it acts as counterparty to both investors, the bank faces the risk that an investor could default. This leaves the bank exposed to an interest rate risk; the remaining customer may be receiving a high rate of interest and paying a low one. The original matching allowed losses from transactions with one customer to be offset by the corresponding gains from the deal with the other customer. Once one of the two counterparties defaults, the bank is exposed to the possibility of losses, and indeed the customer from whom the bank is making gains is the one most likely to renege on its agreement. The loss-making counterparty (the one paying more interest than it receives) is more likely to default than the profit-making counterparty.

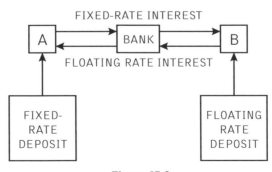

Figure 45.2

EXAMPLE 45.1

A building society raises £5 million by issuing a eurobond at a fixed interest rate of 6% p.a. over three years, payable annually, for the purpose of providing mortgages on a floating rate basis (with interest rates reassessed annually). It is exposed to the risk that interest rates might fall with the effect that interest receipts from the mortgages are inadequate to meet the interest payments on the eurobond. The building society could reduce its exposure by swapping its fixed-rate liability for one on a floating rate basis. It finds a bank prepared to enter a floating for fixed swap on the basis of receiving LIBOR + 0.75% p.a. in exchange for paying 6% p.a. Initially LIBOR stands at 5.25% p.a. Net interest payments to the bank under the swap arrangement, as shown in the table, are on an annual basis.

Table 45.A

Year	Floating rate interest payments	Fixed-rate interest payments	Cash flow from building society to bank
1	£300,000	£300,000	0
2	£325,000	£300,000	£25,000
3	£250,000	£300,000	−£50,000

LIBOR rises by 0.5% between the first and second years, with the result that the building society makes a net payment of £25,000 to the bank. LIBOR falls by 1.5% between years 2 and 3, with the result that the bank pays the building society £50,000.

This example illustrates the fact that a hedger could either gain or lose from the hedging instrument used. The essential point of hedging is that the gains/losses from the swap offset losses/gains on the position being hedged. In this case in year 2 the gain from higher mortgage receipts, arising from higher mortgage interest rates, is offset by a loss on the swap. If interest rates had fallen, thereby reducing mortgage interest receipts, there would have been an offsetting gain from the swap.

WAREHOUSING

Warehousing by a bank consists of doing a swap and hedging it. When a suitable swap counterparty appears, the hedge is undone. One way in which the hedging might be carried out is by the use of financial futures. For example a bank might agree to pay fixed against receiving floating and covers the risk of a fall in interest rates by buying financial futures.

By buying three-month interest rate futures contracts the bank can lock in interest rates. If interest rates fall the price of futures contracts will rise providing the bank with a gain that compensates for the interest rate fall.

The willingness to make a market in swaps has considerably increased the speed with which swaps are provided. Deals are available on demand without requiring simultaneous availability of a matching counterparty.

Indeed a bank is likely to have a large portfolio of swaps, many of which tend to offset one another. Only the net exposure needs to be hedged. The hedging may be undertaken with short-term interest rate futures, long-term interest rate (bond) futures, and bonds (it will be seen that swaps can be valued as the difference between two bond prices).

FLOATING RATE NOTES

Before turning to swap valuation it would be useful to examine floating rate notes (FRNs). A floating rate note is a bond whose coupons are not fixed but are varied at points in time, e.g. at six-month intervals. The coupon rate would be reassessed in the light of a reference interest rate. Such a bond might, for instance, pay 1% p.a. over LIBOR (the rate of interest at which major banks in London will lend to each other). Once determined, the rate would then be fixed for the appropriate time interval, e.g. six months.

In many ways, FRNs are similar to short-term money market instruments, such as bank deposits, in that the interest rate is variable. However, the rate is not quite as variable, because once determined it is fixed for a period. As a result of this incomplete variability, a small amount of capital risk persists (as opposed to bank deposits which exhibit no capital risk). If interest rates rise subsequent to a coupon fixing date, the fixed rate will seem unattractive and the bond price will fall below par. Conversely, a fall in interest rates would cause a small enhancement to the value of the FRN. This might be looked upon in terms of the next coupon being subject to discounting. Of course, the price variations would be much smaller than in the case of conventional fixed coupon bonds.

Since at each coupon adjustment date the rate of coupon yield would be equated to the required rate of return, and hence the rate of discount, the FRN will equal its par value on that date. As the value of an FRN will be equal to par on the coupon adjustment date, the valuation of an FRN can be carried out as if there were only two future cash flows. These cash flows are the next coupon payment and the par value on the coupon adjustment date. If the coupon payment date coincides with the coupon adjustment date, the equation for the value of an FRN would be:

$$P = C/(1+r)^T + B/(1+r)^T$$

where P is the price of the FRN, C is the next coupon, B is the par value of the FRN, r is the rate of discount, and T is the period in years (normally a fraction of a year) to the next coupon payment (and adjustment) date.

As the period for discounting (i.e. T) is short, normally less than six months, the price of a floating rate note will have only limited sensitivity to changes in the rate of discount, and hence to changes in the interest rate. This is in contrast to a conventional bond whose fixed coupons and repayment of principal involve long discount times and hence high sensitivity to interest rate movements.

SWAP PRICING

One way in which an interest rate (fixed for floating) swap can be valued is to treat the fixed rate payments as being equivalent to the cash flows on a conventional bond and the floating rate payments as being equivalent to a floating rate note (FRN). Although an interest rate swap does not entail an exchange of principal at maturity, the correspondence to a bond and FRN can be completed by evoking a hypothetical exchange of principal at maturity whereby the two counterparties give each other the same amount of money in the same currency.

The value of the swap could be expressed as the value of the bond minus the value of the FRN. That is:

$$V = B_1 - B_2 \tag{1}$$

where V is the value of the swap, B_1 is the value of the bond, and B_2 is the value of the floating rate note.

The value of the bond is given by:

$$B_1 = \sum_{i=1}^{n} ke^{-Ri.Ti} + Qe^{-Rn.Tn} \tag{2}$$

where k is the periodic fixed payment in the swap, Q is the principal sum, R the discount rates, and T the corresponding time periods to the cash flows. Equation (2) states that the value of the bond is the present value of the future fixed payment receipts plus the present value of the principal sum. The value of the bond is the discounted value of the future cash flows.

The value of the floating rate note is:

$$B_2 = k^*e^{-R1.T1} + Qe^{-R1.T1} \tag{3}$$

where k* is the next coupon payment and Q is the principal sum, while R1 and T1 are the (annualised) interest rate and length of time to the next coupon payment (next coupon reassessment date). Only the next coupon reassessment date is relevant for discounting purposes since FRNs tend to revert to their par values on the coupon reassessment dates. This is because coupon rates on FRNs are set equal to the required rates of return, which are the relevant discount rates. Equation (3) states that the value of the FRN is the discounted value of the next coupon payment plus the discounted value of the principal sum where there is just one period to the receipt of the cash flows.

CREDIT DEFAULT SWAPS

Interest rate risk is not the only risk involved when investing in bonds. There is also credit risk, which is the risk that the issuer of a bond will default on payments or that the bond will receive a downgrade in its credit rating. Credit default swaps allow an investor to transfer the credit risk to an insurer whilst continuing to hold the bonds.

Credit default swaps are a form of insurance against default. The bondholder pays a regular premium to the insurer for a specified period. If there is no default during that period, nothing more happens. If the bond does default (or receives a credit rating downgrade), the insurer buys the bond from the investor for a pre-agreed price. If the swap agreement lasts for the life of the bond, the pre-agreed purchase price is likely to be the nominal value of the bond.

The premium paid for this insurance will be equal to (or related to) the default premium component of the bond yield. Bonds, other than government bonds, will incorporate some compensation for default risk in their rates of yield. This is normally quoted as a yield spread relative to the yield on government bonds. It is this yield spread that determines the payments to be made by the investor to the insurer. Typically the payments equal the monetary value of the yield spread. If the bonds had a value of £10 million, and if the yield spread were 1.2% p.a. (i.e. 120 basis points), the payments would amount to £120,000 per year (£120,000 is 1.2% of £10 million).

Default, or credit downgrading, would normally lead to the insurer buying the bond at the agreed price. Alternatively the insurer pays the bondholder a sum of money that matches the loss, in value of the bond, resulting from the default or credit downgrade. In some cases the compensatory cash flows are not based on a particular bond, but are based on credit risk indices which indicate the average credit risk of a class of bonds. An index may, for example, be based on the credit risk of 100 bonds of a particular type. If there were a default of one out of the hundred, each insured investor would receive a payment of about 1% of the value insured (assuming an equally weighted index). This may be convenient for hedging the credit risk of bond portfolios.

CONCLUSION

Previous chapters looked at futures, forwards, and options as instruments for managing risk. This chapter has examined the other major form of derivative, the swap. Swaps are similar to a sequence of futures or forward contracts. Their relative advantage is that they typically cover risks further into the future than futures and forwards can. However they lack flexibility such that the commitments to future cash flows are difficult to cancel. Futures offer flexibility as to terminating (closing out) contracts and options provide flexibility as to whether cash flows will take place (but at the cost of premiums to be paid).

# Glossary

Acceptance By accepting a bill issued by a company a bank guarantees that it will be honoured.

Accrued interest The interest earned since the last payment on a bond. This amount is paid to a seller of a bond.

Accumulation phase The phase in the life cycle during which people in the early and middle years of their working lives save to accumulate assets.

Accumulation unit/share Units in a unit trust (or shares in an OEIC) where the income is automatically reinvested.

Active investment management Fund management that entails stock selection and/or market timing in an attempt to outperform the market.

Actuarial rate of return The discount rate used to ascertain the present value of the liabilities of a defined-benefit (final-salary) pension scheme, and thereby determine the required annual contributions to the scheme.

Additional voluntary contributions (AVCs) Pension contributions by an individual that are additional to the main scheme contributions.

ADR (American depository receipt) When dealing in many of the big UK shares, American investors need not deal in London. Instead shares are left with US banks, while investors trade in ADRs which effectively give them the right to those shares should they want them.

Advisory manager An investment manager who offers advice to a client and makes no investment transactions without the client's agreement.

Aggressive stocks High expected return/high risk stocks. They have betas greater than one.

AIM (Alternative Investment Market) The junior market of the London Stock Exchange. It is for small and young companies.

All-Share Index Also known as the FTSE Actuaries All-Share Index. A broad indicator of London share prices, it covers more than 700 shares.

American-style options Options that can be exercised prior to expiration.

Amortisation Depreciation of intangible assets.

Annual charge The annual management charge made by an investment manager.

Annuity A fund that provides an annual income, generally for retirement and most often for the life of the annuitant (the person who owns the annuity). Typically nothing accrues to the estate of the annuitant at death.

Arbitrage The exploitation of price anomalies for profit. For example if prices for the same item differ between locations, the item may be bought relatively cheaply and sold at a higher price. Pure arbitrage involves no risk and no use of the arbitrager's own capital.

Ask price The price at which an investor can buy. (Also known as offer price.)

Asset allocation The attempt to find a mix of asset classes (particularly equities, bonds, property, and money market investments) that best meets the needs of the investor.

Asset allocation fund A fund that allows the investment managers to vary the proportions of asset classes (such as equities, bonds, property, and money market investments).

Asset backing What a company would be worth if it became insolvent.

At best An order to a stockbroker to deal at the best possible price rather than at a limit, getting the highest selling price or finding the lowest buying price.

AVC *see* additional voluntary contributions.

Attainable set All possible portfolios that can be constructed from a given universe of securities.

Back-end load Also called a redemption charge, an exit fee, or deferred sales charge. Refers to a fee paid upon the redemption of unit trusts or OEICs.

Backtest Testing an investment strategy using past data.

Balance sheet The financial statement of what a company owns and what it owes at a particular date.

Balanced fund A fund that aims to achieve a balance of growth, income yield, and low risk.

Bank bill A bill of exchange accepted by a bank.

Barbell strategy A bond strategy in which holdings are concentrated at the extreme ends of a range of maturities.

Basic state pension The state pension in the UK which is based on the individual's national insurance contribution record subject to a maximum weekly payment.

Basic sum assured The minimum maturity value of a 'with-profits' policy which is guaranteed irrespective of investment returns.

Basis The difference between the spot price and the futures price.

Basis point 1/100th of 1%.

Basket trade The trade of an entire portfolio of securities at one time.

Bear Someone who expects a fall in the prices of instruments such as stocks and bonds.

Bearer bond A bond that is not registered in a name. The rights to coupons and principal accrue to the holder.

Bed and breakfast Market practice of selling securities and buying them back to establish a profit or loss for capital gains tax purposes.

Bed and spouse An alternative to *bed and breakfast* where one spouse repurchases shares sold by the other.

Behavioural finance The application of the psychology of decision-making to financial market behaviour.

Bellwether stock A stock that tends to lead the market.

Benchmark bonds Bonds used to price other bonds. They are normally liquid bonds with a coupon in line with the general level of interest rates.

Benchmark error A situation, in portfolio performance evaluation, in which portfolio performance is compared with the wrong benchmark.

Beta A measure of the responsiveness of the price of an individual stock, or portfolio, to movements in stock prices as a whole.

Bid/offer spread Also known as bid/ask spread. The difference between the selling and buying prices of an investment.

Bid price The price at which an investor can sell to a market-maker.

Bid rate The rate of interest at which an investor can deposit money.

Big Bang The deregulation of London capital markets in 1986 which, among other things, permitted foreign ownership of British brokerage firms.

Bill of Exchange A document which commits one company to pay a specific sum of money to another on a particular date.

Black Monday 19 October 1987: the date of the 1987 stock market crash.

Blue chip Blue chip companies are high quality, financially strong companies that are leaders in industries that have been viable over some years.

Bond A security sold in order to raise capital. Bonds normally provide the buyer with a fixed income flow plus the return of the initial capital on the maturity date of the bond. Bonds are debts of the issuer.

Bond rating A measure of the risk that the issuer of a bond will default on payments.

Bond swap An exchange of one bond for another within a portfolio.

Book value The part of a company's assets that belongs to its shareholders; known as shareholders' funds or net assets.

Bottom-up A portfolio construction strategy that focuses on share selection rather than allocation between sectors or asset classes.

Broker An intermediary that buys or sells on behalf of an investor.

Broker-dealer A broker that can deal on their own account as well as acting as an agent for clients.

Bull Someone who expects a rise in the price of an investment.

Bulldog bonds Sterling-denominated bonds issued in the United Kingdom by non-UK borrowers.

Bullet strategy A bond strategy that entails concentration on a narrow range of maturities.

Buy-and-hold strategy Purchase of a portfolio which is held unchanged for the full investment horizon.

Buyout cost The cost of purchasing annuities to meet a pension scheme's liabilities to its members.

CAC 40 The most widely quoted French stock index.

Call market A stock market in which trading takes place at points in time rather than on a continuous basis.

Call money A bank loan repayable on demand.

Call option The right to buy a financial instrument at a specific price during a period of time (or at a point in time).

Call provision A bond with a call provision allows the issuer to redeem the bond prior to maturity.

Capital gain (or loss) The change in value of an investment.

Capital gains tax Tax on the increase in the value of an investment.

Capital gains tax allowance The amount of capital gains that can be made in a tax year without incurring a capital gains tax liability.

Capital growth Increase in the value of an investment.

Capital market line The set of efficient portfolios arising from combinations of a risk-free asset with the market portfolio. It is a straight line, tangent to the efficiency frontier, starting from the risk-free rate of interest.

Capitalisation issue Also known as a scrip issue. A free issue of shares to shareholders in proportion to their existing holding. They should become no richer as a result, since the share price should fall proportionately.

Career averaged revalued earnings scheme (CARE) A defined-benefit pension scheme that links the pension to average earnings, during the whole period of employment, rather than final salary.

CAT-marked investment A regulated investment that must provide fair Charges, flexible Access, and reasonable Terms.

CD *see* Certificate of Deposit.

Certificate of Deposit (CD) A tradable instrument issued by a bank in return for a deposit. The maturity is normally short, for example three months.

Chartered financial analyst (CFA) A US professional qualification awarded by the Association for Investment Management and Research. It has international credibility.

Chartists Technical analysts who believe that they can predict future price movements by analysing trends in past movements, hence their reliance upon charts.

Chinese wall A figurative wall that aims to stop privileged information flowing between departments of a financial institution.

Circuit breaker A price change limit and trading halt aimed at curbing the extent of price fluctuation.

Clean price The price of a bond excluding accrued interest.

Clearing house An institution that settles mutual indebtedness between organisations and which records trades (in the case of futures and options the clearing house also becomes the counterparty to contract holders).

Closely held shares Insider-owned shares that are not likely to be sold.

Closet tracker An actively managed fund that limits deviations from a stock index.

Closing price The price at the close of the market.

Coincident indicators Economic variables whose values reach their peaks and troughs at about the same time as the aggregate economy.

Collateral Security for a loan. Assets that can be claimed by the lender in the event of default.

Commercial bill A bill issued by an organisation other than a government.

Commercial paper Unsecured bills or notes issued by companies for short-term borrowing.

Commission The fee charged by brokers, or financial advisers, for security transactions. Investors pay brokers' commissions directly, but normally pay financial advisers' commissions indirectly via the management fees charged by the investment management company.

Commutation Swapping pension for a cash lump sum in a company pension scheme.

Compound rate of return The average rate of return on an investment held for more than one period. It involves interest on interest. It is calculated as a geometric mean.

Concurrency Simultaneous membership of a company pension scheme and a stakeholder or personal pension plan.

Conflicts of interest The potential that actions taken on one's own behalf are at the expense of a customer, such as when an account executive owns a sizeable position in a particular security and issues an advisory to customers to buy that security.

830

Consolidation phase The phase in the life cycle during which individuals, who are typically past the mid-points of their careers, save for retirement.

Constant growth model Also known as the Gordon growth model. A special case of the dividend discount model in which expected growth in dividends is assumed to be constant.

Constant protection portfolio insurance product (CPPI) An investment based on a fund (possibly linked to a stock index) in which the investors' money is divided between the fund and cash. There is an automatic switch towards cash in falling markets, and a switch out of cash in rising markets. So exposure to the stock market is reduced during falling markets, and increased during rising markets.

Contrarian An approach to investing which is to buy into a market decline and sell into a market advance.

Conversion premium The price of a convertible security minus the conversion value. Frequently expressed as a percentage of the latter.

Conversion price The face value of a convertible security divided by the conversion ratio.

Conversion ratio The number of shares of stock for each convertible security.

Conversion value The value of a convertible security if converted now. The conversion value equals the conversion ratio times the market price of the stock (share price).

Convertible (bond) A bond that can be converted into a specified number of shares of stock at a point, or points, in time.

Convexity The difference between the actual percentage change in bond value due to a yield change and the approximate percentage change in bond value as measured by modified duration.

Core/satellite portfolios Investment management style in which most of the fund (the core) aims to approximately track the market whilst the remainder is in portfolios (satellites) that are more adventurous.

Corporate bond A bond issued by a company, rather than by a government.

Corporate governance The way in which companies are accountable to their stakeholders, particularly their shareholders.

Correlation The coefficient of correlation is a measure of the extent to which two values move in parallel. If the values tend to move in the same direction, correlation is positive. If they tend to move in opposite directions, correlation is negative. Correlation has a maximum of $+1$, and a minimum of -1.

Counterparty The party on the other side of a transaction.

Country risk The possibility of adverse change in the country where an investment is located.

Coupon An income payment on a bond or note.

Covered call Writing a call option on shares that are already held.

Covered warrant Alternatively known as a third-party warrant. The entity that issues the warrants is not the company whose shares underly the warrant.

Credit analysis The analysis of bonds and their issuers in order to assess the probability of default.

Crest An electronic means of settling share transactions and registering investors on companies' lists of shareholders.

Cross-hedging The use of a futures on one underlying as a 'near substitute' for the asset that one really wishes to hedge.

Cum Latin for 'with'. A share quoted as 'cum' something will carry with it the rights to the forth-coming dividend, scrip issue, rights issue, or whatever. If quoted 'ex' it will not carry those rights.

Cumulative performance Investment returns measured over a number of years. It evens out yearly variations in rates of return.

Cumulative preference shares Preference shares for which, if a dividend payment is missed, it must be made up before dividends may be paid to ordinary shareholders.

Currency account Bank account in a foreign currency.

Current account mortgage A combined account that covers both saving and borrowing, with an overall lending limit. Interest is charged on the net debt.

Custodian A custodian, which is frequently a bank, looks after the assets of a fund.

Cyclical stocks Shares of companies whose earnings fluctuate with the business cycle.

DAX The most frequently quoted index of German stocks.

Day order A limit order that is good only for the day on which it is placed.

Dead-cat bounce A small price rise that follows a sharp fall. The small rise is not part of a substantial recovery.

Debenture Bond issued by a UK company and secured against assets of the company.

Debt ratio The ratio of long-term debt to the total capital of a company.

Default/lifestyle DC investment A defined-contribution pension plan with predetermined asset allocation changes (e.g. from shares to bonds as retirement is approached).

Default risk The risk that the issuer of a bond will not make its fixed payments.

Defensive share A share with a beta less than 1. It may be the share of a defensive company, which is a company whose earnings fluctuate less than the aggregate economy.

Deferred pension A pension, usually from a previous employer, that will be paid when pension age is reached.

Defined benefit Also known as final salary. A pension scheme in which the pension is based on final salary and number of years worked.

Defined contribution Also known as money purchase. A pension scheme in which contributions are paid into a fund whose eventual value determines the amount of the pension paid.

Delta The change in the price of an option due to a one pence change in the price of the stock underlying the option.

Demutualisation The process by which a mutual life assurance company, or building society, becomes a proprietary company. Ownership passes from policyholders or members to shareholders, often by giving shares to the policyholders and members.

Deregulation Reduction in government control.

Derivatives E.g. options, futures, swaps. Instruments whose prices are based upon, or derived from, the prices of other instruments, such as stocks, stock indices, or bonds.

Diffusion index An indicator of the number of share prices rising, relative to the number declining, during a period.

Dilution The reduction in the interests of existing shareholders when new shares are issued.

Direct quotation Quotation of an exchange rate in terms of a number of units of the domestic currency per unit of the foreign currency.

Dirty price The total price of a bond, including accrued interest.

Discount Amount by which the current price falls below the redemption value of a security.

Discount rate The rate of interest used to convert a future value into a present value.

Discrete performance Investment returns measured year-on-year rather than on a cumulative basis.

Discretionary management An investment service where the client gives an investment manager control over the management of the client's portfolio.

Disintermediation Flows of funds between borrowers and lenders (e.g. by bond sales) that do not involve the money passing through financial intermediaries such as banks.

Diversifiable risk Non-market or non-systematic risk that can be reduced through portfolio diversification.

Dividend The six-monthly or annual distribution to shareholders of part of the company's profits.

Dividend cover The number of times that the dividend could have been paid from a company's profits (i.e. profits/dividends).

Dividend discount model (DDM) A share price valuation model in which the value of a share is estimated as the present value of the dividends that can be expected from the share over the share's lifetime or horizon, which may be assumed to be infinite.

Dividend payout ratio The dividend that a company pays as a fraction of its earnings (profits) per share.

Dividend yield The annual dividend divided by the current price of the stock.

DMO Debt Management Office. The department of the Treasury in the UK that issues and redeems government bonds (gilts).

Domestic bond A bond issued in the country in which the borrower is located, and in the currency of that country.

Dow Jones Industrial Average An American stock index covering 30 stocks.

Downside gearing When the index to which a precipice bond is linked falls below a certain level, the investors' capital is reduced (possibly more than proportionately to the index fall with the effect that the capital could be entirely lost without the index falling to zero).

Dow theory A theory, used by some technical analysts, suggesting that stock prices move in waves.

Drop-lock bond A floating rate bond which automatically becomes a fixed-rate bond in the event of interest rates falling below a particular level.

Dual-currency bonds Bonds that pay coupons in one currency and repay principal in another.

Dual-listed stocks Stocks listed on more than one stock exchange.

Duration Also known as Macaulay's duration. A measure of bond price volatility. Measured as the average time to the receipt of cash flows.

Dynamic portfolio insurance A strategy that attempts to protect the return on a portfolio by quickly pulling money out of asset markets that are performing poorly.

Earnings Net profit after tax due to holders of ordinary shares but not necessarily paid out to them. Earnings are usually expressed as so many pence per share.

Earnings cap A limit to the level of earnings on which pension contributions or benefits can be based.

Earnings momentum An investment strategy which favours firms whose earnings have been rising.

Earnings multiplier model Model for estimating the fair value of a share as a multiple of its earnings. The price-earnings ratio.

Earnings surprise Difference between reported earnings and analysts' prior expectations.

Earnings yield A company's annual earnings per share, expressed as a percentage of the share's market price.

Economic indicator Statistical information that provides a guide to the state of the economy.

Efficient frontier All Markowitz-efficient portfolios shown in expected return/risk space. It shows the greatest possible expected return for each level of risk.

Efficient market hypothesis (EMH) A view that asset prices respond quickly to new information and that all relevant information is incorporated into security prices by the time it reaches the investing public.

EIS *see* enterprise investment scheme.

Elliot wave theory A theory, used by some technical analysts, suggesting that stock markets move in cycles but with an upward tendency.

Emerging market Relatively new and immature stock market. Often the capital market of a developing country.

Empirical duration A measure of the sensitivity of a bond price to interest rate changes based on analysing past bond price and interest rate movements.

Ending-wealth value The total amount of money available from investing in a bond until maturity. It comprises principal, coupons, and income from reinvestment of coupons.

Enhanced rate annuity An annuity that pays a relatively high income because of a lifestyle feature, such as smoking or obesity, that lowers life expectancy.

Enterprise investment scheme (EIS) EISs offer a range of tax reliefs to investors in small, mainly unquoted, companies.

Enterprise value A firm's market capitalisation plus the value of its debt. The total value of the capital employed by the firm.

Equal-weighted index Another name for an unweighted stock index.

Equities Ordinary shares (common stock) whose owners take the main risks and who are entitled to those profits left over after all prior charges have been met. They represent part ownership of a company.

Equity Represents ownership in a business.

Equity release mortgage A mortgage taken out for the purpose of buying an annuity. It is a means of converting property value into income. The mortgage is repaid when the property is sold upon death.

ETF *see* exchange-traded fund.

Ethical investment Investment screened according to ethical criteria (e.g. eliminating investments in companies providing armaments/tobacco/alcohol/gambling, and/or companies with poor environmental or human rights records). Also known as socially responsible investment.

Eurobonds Bonds issued in countries other than the country whose currency is being borrowed.

Eurocurrency Deposits and loans denominated in a currency other than that of the country in which the deposit is held or loan made.

Eurodollars US dollars held on deposit in a bank or bank branch outside of the United States.

Euronext A combination of a number of European stock and derivatives exchanges.

European-style options Options that cannot be exercised prior to the expiration date.

Ex The opposite to cum, ex means 'without'. A price quoted 'ex dividend' will not carry the right to the next dividend. Similarly shares which are ex rights, or ex scrip, will exclude the rights to such distributions.

Excess return In some cases this refers to investment returns in excess of what would be expected on the basis of the systematic risk of the investment. In other cases it refers to investment returns in excess of a risk-free rate of interest.

Exchange rate risk Also known as currency risk. It is the risk associated with a foreign investment in that the exchange rate may move against the investor.

Exchange-traded funds (ETFs) Collective investments (usually index tracking) that trade on stock exchanges without the discounts and premiums of investment trusts.

Ex-dividend Any one who acquires an ex-dividend stock will not receive the declared dividend.

Execution The implementation of an order to purchase or sell a security.

Execution-only With this type of service a stockbroker simply buys or sells at the investor's request, without offering any advice.

Exercise price Also known as the strike or striking price. The price at which the holder of an option has the right to buy or sell stock.

Exit charge A charge made if an investor sells an investment before holding it for a specified period.

Expected rate of return Also known as the required rate of return. It is the rate of return on an asset expected or required by investors.

Expiry date The last day on which an option can be exercised.

Extendible bond A bond that may be extended for a longer period at the holder's option, possibly at a higher interest rate.

Fallen angel A previously strongly performing share that has subsequently fallen sharply.

Family income benefit (FIB) An insurance policy that provides an income for the beneficiaries in the event of the death of the policyholder.

Fed (Federal Reserve) The US government agency that controls monetary policy.

Fee-based adviser A financial adviser who does not receive commission, but charges the client a fee. Any commission is transferred to the client.

Fill-or-kill order A limit order for immediate execution. If it cannot be immediately executed, it is withdrawn.

Final-salary scheme Also known as defined-benefit scheme. A pension scheme that relates the pension received to the final salary and number of years worked for the employer providing the pension.

Financial future The notional right to buy or sell a standard quantity of a financial instrument on a specific future date at a price determined at the time of buying or selling the futures contract.

Financial planning certificate (FPC) The basic UK examination requirement for sellers of institutional investments, and other personal finance products, to retail customers. There are a number of more advanced qualifications.

Financial Services Authority (FSA) The main regulatory body for financial services in the UK.

Financial Services Compensation Scheme A UK scheme whereby compensation can be paid to a client when the offending organisation is no longer in business.

Fixed annuities Annuities that pay a constant amount of money each year and, as such, are subject to erosion by inflation.

Fixed income (or interest) investment An investment, such as a bond, that pays a stated amount of money per period.

Floating rate notes (FRNs) Relatively long-dated securities on which the coupon payment is determined periodically at a prevailing money market interest rate.

Flotation The issue of shares of stock in a company for the first time.

Foreign bond A bond issued by a foreign entity in the local country and currency, e.g. a US dollar bond issued in the US by a British issuer.

Forex Foreign exchange.

Formula maturity value An estimated value of a second-hand with-profits endowment policy.

Forward Agreement to exchange financial instruments on a future date at a price determined in the present, e.g. forward currency.

Forward-forward Agreement on the future exchange of financial instruments that will mature on a more distant date, e.g. forward-forward interest rates.

Forward rate agreement (FRA) Notional agreement to deposit or borrow on a specific future date at an interest rate determined in the present (a form of interest rate future).

FRA *see* forward rate agreement.

Free cash flow The cash generated by a company from its normal trading operations which is left over for the shareholders.

FRN *see* floating rate note.

Front-end load Also known as initial charge. A sales fee paid for the purchase of mutual fund shares (or unit trusts).

FSA *see* Financial Services Authority.

FTSE 100 Financial Times Stock Exchange 100. A value-weighted index of the top 100 UK stocks.

FTSE 250 Value-weighted index of 250 UK stocks (approximately the 101st to the 350th in terms of size).

FTSE 350 Financial Times Stock Exchange 350. A value-weighted index covering all the shares in both the FTSE 100 and the FTSE 250.

FTSE4Good A set of socially responsible (ethical) investment indices.

837

FTSE-A All-Share Index Value-weighted index of more than 700 stocks traded on the London Stock Exchange.

FTSE All-Small The Smallcap and Fledgling indices combined.

FTSE Eurotrack 100 Value-weighted index of 100 European stocks (excluding UK stocks).

FTSE Fledgling An index covering the shares, listed on the London Stock Exchange, that are too small for inclusion in the All-Share Index.

FTSE SmallCap An index covering the shares in companies that are too small for inclusion in the FTSE 350 but large enough for inclusion in the All-Share Index.

FTSE techMARK A UK index of technology stocks.

Fundamental analysis Ascertaining the appropriate prices of securities by analysing economic data.

Fund of funds A unit trust (or OEIC) that invests solely in other unit trusts (or OEICs).

Fund supermarket A facility offered by some investment management firms, and large financial advisers. They provide access to a wide range of funds from various fund managers.

Futures contract A notional obligation to buy or sell an investment or commodity at a given price on a specified future date.

Futures option An option on a futures contract.

Gearing Expressed as a percentage, gearing refers to the extent of a company's indebtedness, being the ratio of all its borrowings to its assets. A geared investment is one in which the exposure to the stock market exceeds the investor's money outlay; gearing can be obtained by using futures or options.

Geometric mean The *n*th root of the product of a series of numbers where *n* is the number of numbers. It is used to calculate the compound average rate of return of an investment.

Gilt Gilt-edged security. A British government bond.

Gilt–equity yield ratio Ratio of the yield on gilts to the yield on equities (shares).

Good-till-cancelled order An order to buy or sell shares that remains on the books until it is cancelled.

Grey market The trading that takes place between the launch of a new share issue and the receipt of allotment letters, which tell applicants how many shares they have received.

Growth company A company that consistently has opportunities to invest in projects providing rates of return that exceed the company's cost of capital. In consequence the company retains a high proportion of earnings for the purpose of financing investment, and its earnings grow faster than those of average companies.

Growth stocks Shares whose prices are expected to rise relatively rapidly. They tend to be characterised by high price-earnings ratios.

838

Guaranteed annuity rate (GAR) This guarantees defined-contribution pension investors that the annuity rate at retirement will not fall below the guaranteed level.

Guaranteed equity funds Funds that limit exposure to falls in the stock market whilst providing a proportion of the gains. They are usually constructed using options.

Guaranteed income bond (GIB) An investment bond that guarantees a fixed income over a specified period.

Hang Seng The most widely quoted stock index for Hong Kong.

Hard currency A currency that is fully convertible into major currencies such as the US dollar through the currency markets.

Head and shoulders A chart pattern widely used by technical analysts.

Hedge A transaction undertaken in order to reduce an existing risk.

Hedge funds Funds that use a broader range of investments and strategies than other mutual funds. Hedge funds often use short selling, arbitrage, and derivatives. They do not necessarily hedge.

Hoare Govett Smaller Companies Index (HGSCI) Stock index of the smallest 10% of companies on the London Stock Exchange.

Home income plan A form of equity release. An arrangement whereby a home is mortgaged and the mortgage proceeds used to buy an annuity. The mortgage, plus interest, is repaid at death out of the sale proceeds from the property.

Home reversion plan A form of equity release. The exchange of a percentage of the value, of a residential property, for an income for life.

Horizon premium The excess return that investors seek for holding long-term bonds as opposed to short-term bonds or money market investments. It can be used as a cheapness or expensiveness indicator for long-term bonds.

Horizon yield The total yield on a bond that is not held to redemption. Otherwise known as holding period return.

Immunisation The elimination of interest rate risk in a fixed income portfolio.

Impaired life annuity An annuity that pays at a relatively high rate because the annuitant has a relatively low life expectancy. Also known as an enhanced annuity.

Income drawdown As opposed to buying an annuity at retirement, income drawdown involves taking an income from the pension fund which otherwise remains intact.

Income protection insurance This pays an income in the event of the policyholder being unable to work because of illness.

Income unit Income units of a unit trust pay the dividends to the investor rather than automatically investing them.

Index arbitrage Arbitrage between a portfolio of stocks, on which a stock index is based, and derivatives based on that stock index.

Index funds Alternatively known as tracker funds. Portfolios constructed so that their returns mirror, as closely as possible, those of a stock index.

Index-linked gilts UK government bonds on which both the level of the coupon paid, and the final redemption payment, are linked to the Retail Price Index.

Index trackers Funds that aim to track a stock index, by replicating or simulating the index. The value of the fund should move in line with the index.

Indirect quotation Quotation of an exchange rate in terms of the number of units of foreign currency per unit of domestic currency.

Industry risk Stock price risk associated with a particular industry.

Inflation risk Also known as purchasing power risk. It is the risk that inflation will erode the value of an investment.

Information coefficient Correlation between forecasts and outcomes. It is a measure of the information content of forecasts.

Information risk The risk that other investors may not recognise an investment's true worth.

Information trade A trade based upon information concerning the security.

Initial charge The charge made by the investment manager when a unit trust or OEIC share is purchased.

Initial public offering The first time that shares in a company are offered for sale to the public.

Inside information Information about a company that is not available to the general public.

Insider trading Trading on inside information.

Institutional investor An institution that invests money on behalf of a number of smaller investors, e.g. pension fund, insurance fund, unit trust, OEIC, investment trust.

Intangible assets Assets without a physical form; examples include patents and copyrights.

Inter-bank market The market in which banks lend to, and borrow from, one another.

Interest rate parity The equilibrium relationship between the spot and forward exchange rates, and the interest rates associated with the two currencies.

Interest rate risk The risk of price change in fixed income investments due to changes in market interest rates.

Interim results Profit figures that precede the final figures issued by a company for a financial year. Interim results may be published halfway through the financial year.

Intermediary An institution that takes deposits and uses the receipts to make loans.

Internal rate of return The discount rate that equates the present value of expected future cash flows from an asset to the current price of the asset.

In-the-money Options that provide a pay-off from immediate exercise.

Intrinsic value The gross profit available from the immediate exercise of an option.

Investment horizon The length of time for which an investment is expected to be held.

Investment trust A quoted company whose business is to invest, mainly in other shares, for the benefit of its own shareholders. It differs from a unit trust in being a 'closed-end fund' and in having its own shares quoted on the Stock Exchange. (A type of mutual fund.)

Irredeemable bonds Bonds without maturity dates. The issuer has no obligation to redeem the bonds at any stage. Also known as perpetual or undated bonds.

ISA (Individual Savings Account) A tax-advantaged investment scheme that operates in the UK.

Japanese candlesticks A chart that shows the high, low, and closing price of a security.

Junk bond Corporate bond with high risk of default and corresponding high yield.

Kerb market Unofficial market, often operating outside the normal trading hours of the official market.

Laddered portfolio A strategy of spreading a bond portfolio evenly over a range of maturities.

Leading indicator Economic indicator that precedes movements in the business cycle.

Liability Something that is owed.

LIBOR (London Inter-Bank Offered Rate) The rate of interest at which major banks in London will lend to each other. (It is the borrowing rate as opposed to the deposit rate which is LIBID.)

LIFFE The London International Financial Futures and Options Exchange. The main derivatives exchange in the UK.

Life office A life assurance company authorised to sell life assurance products and pensions.

Lifetime allowance The maximum total pension fund that a person can accumulate in a tax-advantaged pension scheme.

Limit move The maximum price change allowed by an exchange during a single trading session.

Limit order An order to a stockbroker which only permits a deal to be done if it is possible to execute at a certain price or better.

Liquidation The sale of assets.

Liquidity Assets that are either in the form of money or can be easily converted into money.

Liquidity premium The additional return paid to investors for sacrificing the liquidity of their investments.

Liquidity risk The risk that an investment may not be easily convertible into cash at the full current market value.

Listed share A share that is authorised to be traded on a formal stock exchange.

Loan stock An unsecured bond issued by a UK company.

Loan-to-value ratio The ratio between a mortgage debt and the value of the property against which it is secured.

Long Someone holding shares is said to be long of them. A long position gains from price rises and loses from price falls.

LSE London Stock Exchange.

Manipulation The activity of a person or a pool of people that is designed to make the price of a security behave in a manner that is different from that caused by normal supply and demand forces.

Manipulation risk The risk that the price of an investment could be affected by manipulation.

Market capitalisation The total value of the shares issued by a company. The number of shares multiplied by the share price.

Market efficiency The tendency for security prices to reflect economic information fully.

Market-maker A dealer who publishes bid and offer prices on certain securities and is committed to trade at those prices. It is thus ensured that a market always exists in those securities.

Market model The relationship between the rate of return on a share (or portfolio) and the rate of return on the market. Alternatively known as the characteristic line.

Market order An order placed at the market price.

Market portfolio A portfolio of all securities in proportion to their relative market values.

Market price The price at which a security currently trades.

Market risk Non-diversifiable or systematic risk that affects the entire market.

Market timing Attempts to move capital in and out of various markets to maximise participation in bullish movements, and minimise exposure to bear markets.

Marking to market The realisation of profits and losses on a daily basis by means of daily cash flows.

Markowitz-efficient A portfolio that has the highest expected return for a particular level of risk.

Matched bargain A stock market trading system in which buy offers and sell offers are matched at a mutually agreed price.

Maturity Period to the redemption of a financial claim.

Mean reversion The tendency of a price to revert back towards its long-run average.

Mean-variance analysis Analysing portfolios in terms of their expected (*mean*) return and their risk (standard deviation or *variance*). Markowitz diversification and efficiency frontiers are examples of mean-variance analysis.

Mid-cap Companies with a middle-ranking market capitalisation. In the UK this usually refers to companies in the FTSE 250 index.

Momentum Of, for example, earnings, measures the 'growth in the growth rate' of earnings.

Momentum trading Buying shares that have recently been rising; or selling shares that have recently been falling.

Money broker As a broker in the inter-bank market, a money broker brings together banks wishing to lend and those wishing to borrow. There are also money brokers in currencies and eurobonds.

Money market fund A mutual fund that invests in short-term money market assets, such as bills and certificates of deposit.

Money purchase Also known as defined contribution. A pension scheme that accumulates a fund for the individual, with a view to using the fund to buy an annuity at retirement.

Morgan Stanley Capital International (MSCI) Indices Group of value-weighted stock indices for individual countries and groups of countries.

Mortality cross-subsidy The pooling mechanism for annuity holders by which the income of those who live longer is subsidised by those who die early.

Mortgage A legal agreement in which one party (the mortgagee) agrees to make a loan and the borrower (mortgagor) pledges specific assets (typically real estate property) as security against the loan.

Multi-manager funds Funds that invest in a set of sub-funds. The sub-funds are often run by specialist asset managers.

Mutual life office A life office that is formally owned by its policyholders, rather than by shareholders.

Naked position Options position without an offsetting position in stock, futures, or options.

NASDAQ An electronically operated stock market that focuses on technology stocks.

NAV *see* net asset value.

Negative equity A situation in which the value of a property is less than the mortgage on the property.

Negative Yield Curve Short-term interest rates higher than long-term ones.

Net asset value (NAV) The value of all assets held by an investment trust divided by the number of investment trust shares outstanding.

Net relevant earnings The earnings that can be taken into account for the calculation of the maximum payment into a defined-contribution pension scheme.

Net worth statement A personal balance sheet.

New York Stock Exchange The largest stock exchange in the world.

New York Stock Exchange (NYSE) composite index A value-weighted stock index based on all the stocks listed on the NYSE.

Nikkei 225 The most widely quoted stock index for the Tokyo Stock Exchange.

Noise trading The trading activity of those without sound fundamental information.

Nominal rate of return The rate of return that is not adjusted for inflation.

Nominal value The face value or par value of a security as opposed to its market value.

Nominee Shares can be registered in a nominee name, rather than the real one, if they are being managed on behalf of someone else (also known as street name).

Non-systematic risk Risk that is specific to individual shares rather than being common to all shares.

Normal distribution The distribution of the probabilities of alternative values of a variable (e.g. a price). It has a bell-shaped form indicating high probabilities of values near the average and low probability of extreme values.

Normal portfolio A customised benchmark for portfolio evaluation. It is a benchmark portfolio created for the purpose of evaluating portfolios, which are based on specialised investment styles or philosophies.

Note An instrument recording a promise to pay sums of money in the future. Similar to bonds but typically of shorter maturity.

Occupational pension scheme Pension scheme sponsored by an employer.

OEICs Open-ended investment companies. Similar to unit trusts but in the form of shares.

OFEX An over-the-counter stock market in London. It focuses on the shares of small companies.

Offer price The price at which an investor can buy.

Offer rate The rate of interest at which money can be borrowed.

Offset mortgage An arrangement where there are separate accounts for savings and a mortgage. The savings account earns no interest but its value is offset against the mortgage with the effect that the mortgage interest is charged on the reduced sum.

Offshore banking Banking facilities in locations that offer a very favourable tax environment. Typically the country in which the bank is registered is not that in which the actual banking operations are undertaken.

Offshore investment bonds Bonds registered in tax-advantaged locations. They include distribution bonds, which pay a regular income, and non-distribution bonds, whose returns are reinvested.

On-the-run issue The most recently issued government bond for a particular maturity range.

Open architecture This is the simultaneous offer of the provider's own funds and a selection of funds from other managers.

Open interest The number of outstanding contracts in a futures market.

Open market operations Dealings in the financial markets by a central bank (e.g. the Bank of England) for the purpose of influencing the liquidity of financial institutions and/or controlling interest rates.

Open market option The facility of using a pension fund accumulated with one provider to buy an annuity from a different provider.

Open outcry Face-to-face trading used on some derivatives exchanges, particularly in the United States.

Optimal portfolio The portfolio on the efficiency frontier that is best for an investor in the light of that investor's attitude to risk.

Option The right to buy or sell at a specific price during a time period (or at a point in time). Can also be a right to borrow or lend at a particular interest rate.

OTC *see* over the counter.

Out-of-the-money Options for which there is no pay-off from immediate exercise.

Over the counter (OTC) Tailor-made instruments, as opposed to the standardised exchange-traded ones.

Oversubscription An offer of shares or other securities to the investing public is oversubscribed when the number of shares applied for exceeds the number available. This can lead to the scaling down of applications, their placing in a ballot, or even their rejection.

Overweight A portfolio is overweight in a share, sector, or asset class if it holds a greater proportion than is indicated by a benchmark portfolio.

P/E (price/earnings) ratio The share price divided by the company's annual earnings per share.

Par value The value of a bond at maturity, also known as face value, or nominal value.

Partly paid Securities on which only part of the full cost has been paid, with a further call or calls due to be paid by holders at a future date.

Payback The time required for the added income from a convertible bond, relative to the income from the corresponding shares, to offset the conversion premium.

Pension unlocking The transfer from a defined-benefit pension scheme to a defined-contribution pension scheme in order to make an early withdrawal of the tax-free lump sum.

PEP *see* personal equity plan.

Personal equity plan (PEP) A tax-advantaged UK investment scheme that operated from 1987 to 1999 and was replaced by the Individual Savings Account (ISA).

Phased retirement A personal pension is gradually converted into an annuity over time. Each year part of the tax-free lump sum is released and used as pension income.

Plain vanilla A standard financial instrument without any unusual characteristics.

Political risk The risk associated with foreign investments due to political uncertainty in the country or region.

Portfolio An investor's collection of assets.

Portfolio insurance Strategies used to protect a portfolio in the event of a market downturn.

Portfolio rate of return Rate of return on an entire portfolio of investments.

Positive yield curve Long-term interest rates higher than short-term ones.

Pre-emption rights The rights of shareholders to maintain their proportionate ownership of a company, for example when new shares are issued.

Preference shares Shares on which a constant level of dividend is paid, providing the money is available. The dividends must be paid before holders of ordinary shares get any money.

Premium 1. Price of an option. 2. Amount by which the forward price of a currency exceeds its spot price. 3. Excess of a futures value over the spot value.

Price/earnings (P/E) ratio The ratio of the share price to the company's earnings (profits) per share.

Price continuity The tendency for successive price movements to be small. A characteristic of a liquid market with depth.

Primary market Market for newly raised capital.

Principal 1. Someone buying or selling on their own account rather than as an agent for a client. 2. The sum of money repayable at the maturity of a bond or other debt instrument.

Private placement The sale of an entire issue of securities to one or a few investors.

Privatisation Selling government assets to the private sector.

Programme trading Trading of entire portfolios or baskets of stock at one time, often in conjunction with derivatives.

Purchased life annuity A purchased life annuity is bought with funds other than those from a pension scheme. An annuity bought with a pension fund is known as a compulsory purchase annuity.

Purchasing power risk The risk that inflation may diminish the purchasing power of funds.

Put bonds Limit buyer risk by obligating the issuer to buy the bond if the price falls below a certain level.

Put option The right to sell an instrument at a particular price during a time period (or on a specific date).

Quality spread The difference between the yields of bonds of different credit ratings.

Quantitative management A statistical/mathematical approach to fund management.

Random walk hypothesis The theory that price changes will be random if they rationally reflect available economic information.

Rate of return The return on an investment stated as a percentage of the amount invested.

Realistic balance sheet A measure of a life assurance company's assets less liabilities. An alternative to the free asset ratio.

Real rate of return The inflation-adjusted rate of return.

Real-time information Continuously updated information.

Redemption date The date when fixed-interest stocks, such as gilts and debentures, are redeemed, usually at their nominal value.

Redemption yield The yield on a fixed-interest stock which takes into account the annual benefit to be gained as the stock climbs towards its redemption price. If the stock stands above its redemption price, the redemption yield will be lower than the coupon yield.

Reduction in yield (RIY) A measure of the costs of a collective fund (e.g. unit trust, pension fund, endowment fund). It shows the percentage reduction in the return or yield resulting from costs, where all costs are taken into account.

Refunding issue A bond issue that raises funds for the purpose of prematurely retiring another bond issue.

Regression analysis The use of statistical techniques to test the relationship between two or more variables in a mathematical model. The objective is to find past relationships that may continue into the future and hence provide a means of forecasting.

Regression to the mean The tendency of extreme values to move towards the average over time.

Reinvestment rate The rate of return on reinvested investment income.

Reinvestment risk The risk that proceeds (such as bond coupons) in the future will be reinvested at a low rate of return.

Relative strength The price performance of a share relative to a stock index.

Repo Sale and repurchase agreement. The sale of securities with a simultaneous commitment to buy them back at a later date. A means of short-term borrowing.

Repo rate The rate of interest paid in a repo transaction.

Retention ratio The percentage of profits retained rather than paid as dividends.

Retractable bonds Bonds that may be redeemed, at the holder's option, on a specified date prior to expiration.

Return on equity (ROE) Net income (earnings) divided by equity.

Return on investment (ROI) Net income divided by total capital, where total capital is debt plus equity.

Return to Volatility Ratio Also known as the Treynor measure. Measures the ratio of excess return to portfolio beta.

Reward to Variability Ratio Also known as the Sharpe measure. Measures the return to the investor above the riskless rate due to taking on the uncertainty of a portfolio of risky securities rather than T-bills. It is calculated as the ratio of excess return to portfolio standard deviation, where excess return is the difference between portfolio return and Treasury bill yields or riskless returns.

Rights issue An issue of new shares to shareholders, generally at a discount to the current market price, with the number of shares offered being in proportion to the shareholder's existing holding.

Risk Alternatively defined as uncertainty that can be quantified by a statistical distribution, or as uncertainty that matters.

Risk-adjusted return The return on an investment adjusted for its risk.

Risk arbitrage A strategy that aims to make an automatic profit if an event (e.g. a takeover bid) occurs. If the event does not take place there is no profit, hence the risk.

Risk-aversion The dislike of risk.

Risk-free investment An investment that is virtually free of risk, such as a short-term Treasury bill.

Risk-free rate of return The rate of return on a risk-free investment.

Risk management Controlling the level of financial risk to which an investment is exposed, e.g. by hedging.

Risk-return space A graph with risk and return on the two axes.

ROE *see* return on equity.

ROI *see* return on investment.

Round-trip commission Often used in commodities and futures, involves paying the purchase and sales commissions up front.

Rule of 72 Division of 72 by the rate of interest gives the approximate time required for an investment to double in value.

Running yield Alternatively known as the coupon yield, dividend yield, flat yield, interest yield, or current yield. The annual rate of return offered by the coupon or dividend on a bond or stock.

S&P 500 A widely quoted American stock index based on 500 large capitalisation stocks.

Samurai bonds Yen-denominated bonds issued in Japan by non-Japanese issuers.

Scheme-specific funding requirement The requirement that occupational pension schemes in the UK adopt a funding level that is appropriate to scheme liabilities.

Scrip issue The issue of free shares to investors in proportion to their existing shareholdings. There should be a proportionate fall in the share price leaving investors no better off.

SEATS PLUS Stock Exchange Alternative Trading Service. The computerised price information service used on the London Stock Exchange for many small company shares.

SEC *see* Securities and Exchange Commission.

Secondary market A market in which already existing securities are bought and sold. Distinct from the primary market in which newly issued securities are sold.

Securities and Exchange Commission (SEC) The main regulatory body for investment business in the United States.

Securitisation 1. The aggregation of existing assets such as mortgages so as to use them as backing for bond issues, effectively selling a bundle of existing assets. 2. Sale of bills or bonds as an alternative to borrowing from banks.

Security A medium of investment, e.g. stocks, bonds, bills.

Security market line (SML) Arising from the capital asset pricing model, it is a line relating the required rate of return on a stock to the beta of the stock.

Self-select ISA An Individual Savings Account that can be used to hold individual shares and bonds, as well as institutional investments.

Semi-strong form The form of the efficient market hypothesis that maintains that all publicly available information is reflected in share prices.

SETS Stock Exchange Electronic Trading Service. A London Stock Exchange share trading system that matches deals between buyers and sellers automatically.

Settlement The actual transfer of the security from seller to buyer.

Share Instrument denoting part ownership of the equity of a company. Alternatively known as a stock.

Short position A position that profits from price falls and loses from price rises. It entails a commitment to deliver a financial instrument.

Short selling Selling borrowed stock.

SICAV The French equivalent of an OEIC.

Signalling theory Says that companies may signal information through the use of dividends, etc. rather than announce it, partly because a signal has greater credibility.

Sinking fund Provisions in a bond's indenture that help to guarantee that the bond will be repaid at maturity. The indenture specifies that a certain amount of the firm's earnings are put aside each year to fund the repayment.

Single life policy An annuity, or life assurance policy, that runs only for the lifetime of one individual. This is opposed to a joint life policy, which runs until the second death.

Single premium A one-off or lump-sum payment into a pension or life assurance plan.

Sixtieth scheme A defined-benefit pension scheme where the pension accrual is one-sixtieth of salary (final or average) for each year of service.

Small cap Companies with a relatively small market capitalisation. In the UK they are usually seen as firms below the FTSE 350.

Small firm effect Findings that the shares of smaller capitalisation companies produce relatively strong performance.

Sovereign risk Risk that a government will default on its debt.

Specialist Market-maker on the New York Stock Exchange.

Specific risk Risk beyond market and industry risk that relates to the specific investment being undertaken.

Speculation Buying or selling with a view to making profits from price changes.

Speculative share A share that appears to be highly overpriced relative to its fundamental (intrinsic) value.

Split-capital trust An investment trust that splits its share capital into different types, for example income shares that receive the income and capital shares that benefit from any capital growth.

Spot price Current price as opposed to forward or futures price.

Spread The excess of the ask (offer) price or interest rate over the bid price or interest rate. It is the market-maker's or banker's margin.

SSAP Statement of Standard Accounting Practice. Accounting practice recommended by the Accounting Standards Committee in the UK.

Stag Someone who applies for a new issue of shares, intending to sell them almost immediately in order to make a quick profit.

Stamp duty A tax on the purchase of shares.

Standard deviation A measure of the extent to which a set of possible values (forming a normal distribution) are dispersed around their average (mean). Often used as a measure of price volatility or risk.

State second pension An earnings-related pension that is additional to the basic state pension.

Statistical expectation The mean (average) of the distribution of possible outcomes. The mean is calculated by weighting each possible value by its probability of occurrence.

Statistically significant A value is statistically significant when the probability (likelihood) of it occurring by chance is small.

Statutory money-purchase illustration The annual illustration of the retirement income, in today's prices, that a defined-contribution pension plan is projected to generate.

Stepped preference share A preference share that provides a dividend that rises at a predetermined rate. They have often been offered by split-capital investment trusts, in which case they provide a fixed redemption price to be paid when the investment trust is wound up.

Stock Most commonly used to denote shares representing ownership of the equity of a firm (common stock, ordinary shares). However, it is sometimes treated as synonymous with bonds.

Stockbroker An agent who buys and sells shares and bonds on behalf of clients.

Stock dividend A dividend paid in the form of shares.

Stock exchange Market for the trading of stocks and bonds.

Stock index A measure of the average value of stock prices at a point in time (e.g. S&P 500, FTSE 100, Nikkei 225, DAX, CAC 40, Hang Seng).

Stock split Similar to a scrip issue in that the shareholder is given a certain number of new shares for every share owned.

Stock dividends Extra shares of stock, based upon the number already owned.

Stop-loss order An order to sell shares once the price of the stock falls to a certain level.

Straddle The simultaneous long position of a put and call option on the same stock with the same expiry date and strike price. (A short straddle involves short positions in both put and call options).

Strangle A put and a call option on the same stock with different strike prices but the same expiry date (the options are either both long or both short).

Strap The purchase of two calls and a put option.

Street name Also known as a nominee account. The registration of customers' securities in the name of the brokerage firm.

Strike price Also known as exercise price. The stock price at which the holder of an option has the right to buy or sell shares.

Strips Separating out individual coupons, or the principal, from a bond in order to trade them as zero coupon bonds.

Strong form The form of the efficient market hypothesis that maintains that all information of any kind, including non-public inside information, is already reflected in security prices.

Sub-prime mortgage A mortgage loan made to a borrower with a low credit rating.

Swap 1. An agreement by two parties to exchange future cash flows on terms agreed in the present. 2. A simultaneous spot purchase (or sale) and forward sale (or purchase), i.e. buying for one point in time and selling for another.

Swap spread A measure of the risk premium for an interest rate swap. It is calculated as the difference between the agreement's fixed rate and the yield on a government bond with the same maturity.

SWOT analysis An analysis of a firm's Strengths, Weaknesses, Opportunities, and Threats.

Systematic risk The part of share price risk that arises from movements in the stock market as a whole.

Tactical asset allocation Varying the proportions of asset classes (e.g. shares, bonds, and cash) in a portfolio in the light of forecasts of relative returns of the asset classes. It is market timing in that the portfolio manager attempts to predict the time at which particular asset classes will begin to outperform or underperform.

Taper relief The decline in the rate of capital gains tax resulting from increases in the period for which an investment is held.

Tap stock Government securities of which only part of the issue has so far been sold to the public, the rest being let out on to the market as the government, through its agents, sees fit.

Tax rate risk The risk that tax rates may change, resulting in a loss of after-tax return.

Tax shelter An investment whose purposes include the reduction of taxes.

TechMARK A market for technology stocks within the London Stock Exchange.

Technical analysis Prediction of price movements based on the proposition that markets have their own internal momentum independent of economic events. Chartism is a form of technical analysis that uses charts and graphs of past price movements to forecast future price behaviour.

Tender An issue of securities in which investors must bid a maximum price at which they are willing to subscribe. When the striking price is fixed, all those tendering at that level or above will receive shares.

Term spread The difference in yield between bonds of different maturities, e.g. between two-year and ten-year bonds.

TESSA Tax-Exempt Special Savings Account. A tax-advantaged saving scheme in the UK. Largely replaced by ISAs.

Theta The change in the price of an option as a function of the passage of time (price change per unit of time).

Time value The amount by which the price of an option exceeds its intrinsic value.

Tombstone An advertisement for a public issue of bonds that contains the names of all the members of the selling syndicate.

Top-down An approach to fund management that begins with the allocation between asset classes and then considers the selection of shares and bonds within those classes.

TOPIX Tokyo stock Price Index. A broad based index of Tokyo stock prices.

Total expense ratio (TER) The annual management charge on a fund plus other costs such as audit fees, custody fees, and other administration charges.

Tracker fund Also known as index fund. The fund manager aims to mirror the performance of a stock index.

Traded endowment policy A second-hand endowment policy. Trading arises because the surrender value of a policy is often far below its value as an investment.

Trading turnover The value of shares traded during a period of time as a percentage of the total value of shares held.

Trail commission The annual commission paid by a financial product provider to the financial adviser who sold the investment. It would ultimately be paid out of the annual management charge on the fund.

Transaction costs The costs of trading shares and bonds. They include stockbrokers' commissions, taxes (stamp duty in the UK), and bid-offer spreads.

Transfer value The sum of money that is available to be taken from a pension scheme when moving to a new one.

Treasury bill A debt instrument issued by the central government for raising short-term finance. It is seen as a risk-free investment, and the return on it is regarded as being risk-free.

Treasury bond A debt instrument issued by the US government for raising long-term finance.

Triple witching Once every quarter in the United States, contracts in stock options, stock index options, and stock index futures all expire on the same day. This can cause frenetic trading in stocks.

Trough The lowest point of a bear market, after which share prices begin to rise.

Trust A legal structure that recognises two owners of an asset: the trustees, who have legal control of the asset, and the beneficiaries, who are entitled to the income and capital.

Trustee Legal owner of a fund. Looks after the assets of the fund on behalf of investors (beneficiaries).

Turnover In the brokerage business turnover is the volume of buying and selling.

Undated Government bonds which have no fixed date set for repayment.

Underfunded plan A defined-benefit pension plan in which the present value of the liabilities exceeds the present value of the assets.

Underweight A portfolio is underweight in an asset if it holds a lower proportion than indicated by a benchmark portfolio.

Underwriter Someone who undertakes to subscribe for all or part of an issue of securities if it is not wholly taken up by the public, in return for which an underwriting commission is paid. The underwriter will pass on this commitment to sub-underwriters such as banks, insurance companies, and pension funds, and they will also receive commission.

Unit trust A trust formed to manage a portfolio on behalf of the holders of its units. Each unitholder's stake in that trust is in direct proportion to the number of units he/she holds. The value of units depends upon the value of the portfolio. A unit trust is an open-ended mutual fund.

Unrealised capital gains Gains from the price appreciation of unsold investments.

Unsecured loan stock A bond issued by a company, but which is not secured by any of the company's assets.

Value stocks Shares that are believed to be underpriced. They tend to be characterised by low price-earnings ratios.

Value-weighted A stock index whose components are weighted by the market capitalisations of the companies.

Variable annuities Annuities that each year pay an amount of money that is determined by the market performance of funds invested.

Variance A statistical measure of the extent to which a series of numbers are dispersed around (vary from) their average. Standard deviation (risk) is the square root of variance.

VCTs *see* venture capital trusts.

Venture capital trusts (VCTs) Collective investments for shares in small and new enterprises.

Vesting The process of converting a pension fund into an income, usually by purchasing an annuity.

Volatility The degree of price, or return, fluctuation over time. It is often measured by standard deviation.

Warrant A long-term call option giving the holder the right to subscribe for a stock at a specific price during a period of time.

Weak form The form of the efficient market hypothesis according to which share prices fully reflect all information contained in past share prices.

Weighted average A measure of the average value of a set of numbers that, rather than giving each number an equal contribution to the measure, allows some numbers to affect the measure more than others.

White knight A friendly acquirer of a company faced with a hostile takeover.

White squires Prevent hostile takeovers by holding large blocks of a company's shares in their friendly hands.

Wholesale market The market for deposits and loans in which each transaction involves a large sum of money. It is largely an inter-bank market.

Wilshire 5000 A very broad US value-weighted stock index. It covers about 7,000 stocks including all stocks traded on the New York Stock Exchange and on the American Stock Exchange.

With-profits fund A form of investment fund for pensions and life assurance related investments. There is a guaranteed minimum sum payable at maturity. The minimum sum is added to each year by means of reversionary bonuses that cannot be taken away. At maturity a terminal bonus is added.

Wrap account An online facility that displays and aggregates an investor's portfolio.

Writer The seller of an option contract.

Yankee bond A dollar-denominated bond issued in the United States by a borrower outside of the United States.

Yield The annual return on an investment divided by its price, measured as a percentage.

Yield curve Relationship between the time to maturity of bonds (strictly speaking zero coupon bonds) and their redemption yields.

Yield gap The difference between the average coupon yield on long-dated gilts and the average dividend yield on equities.

Yield spread The difference in yield between bonds of similar coupon and term to maturity.

Yield to maturity Another name for redemption yield.

Zero coupon bond A bond that pays no coupon. The return to the holder arises from the bond being sold at a discount to its redemption value at maturity.

Zero dividend preference shares Sometimes called 'zeros', they are often sold by investment trusts. They pay no dividends but provide a capital sum to the investor when the investment trust is wound up.

References

Abarbanell, J. S. and B. J. Bushee (1997). 'Fundamental Analysis, Future Earnings, and Stock Prices', *Journal of Accounting Research*, 6.

Abarbanell, J. S. and B. J. Bushee (1998). 'Abnormal Returns to a Fundamental Analysis Strategy', *Accountancy Review*, 73.

Abolafia, M. Y. (1996). *Making Markets: Opportunism and Restraint on Wall Street*, Harvard University Press.

Aboody, D.; M. F. Barth, and R. Kasznik (1999). 'Revaluations of Fixed Assets and Future Firm Performance: Evidence from the UK', *Journal of Accounting and Economics*, 26.

Adair, A.; J. Berry, and S. McGreal (1996). 'Valuation of Residential Property: Analysis of Participant Behaviour', *Journal of Property Valuation and Investment*, 14.

Agnew, J. and L. R. Szykman (2004). 'Asset Allocation and Information Overload: The Influence of Information Display, Asset Choice and Investor Experience', Boston Center for Retirement Research Working Paper 2004–15.

Agyei-Ampomah, S. (2007). 'The Post-Cost Profitability of Momentum Trading Strategies: Further Evidence from the UK', *European Financial Management*, 13.

Aharony, J.; C. P. Jones, and I. Swary (1980). 'An Analysis of the Risk and Return Characteristics of Corporate Bankruptcy Using Capital Market Data', *Journal of Finance*, 35.

Ahmed, P. and S. Nanda (2001). 'Style Investing: Incorporating Growth Characteristics in Value Stocks', *Journal of Portfolio Management*, 27.

Ainsle, G. (1991). 'Derivation of "Rational" Economic Behavior from Hyperbolic Discount Curves', *American Economic Review*, 81.

Akerlof, G. (1970). 'The Market for "Lemons": Quality, Uncertainty and the Market Mechanism', *Quarterly Journal of Economics*, 84.

Akerlof, G. (1991). 'Procrastination and Obedience', *American Economic Review*, 81.

Al-Debie, M. and M. Walker (1999). 'Fundamental Information Analysis: An Extension and UK Evidence', *British Accounting Review*, 31.

Alexander, S. (1964). 'Price Movements in Speculative Markets: Trends or Random Walks, No. 2', in Paul Cootner (ed.) *The Random Character of Stock Market Prices*, MIT Press.

Alhakami, A. S. and P. Slovic (1994). 'A Psychological Study of the Inverse Relationship between Perceived Risk and Perceived Benefit', *Risk Analysis*, 14.

Ali, A.; L-S. Hwang, and M. A. Trombley (2003). 'Arbitrage Risk and the Book-to-Market Anomaly', *Journal of Financial Economics*, 69.

Allen, G. C. (2005). 'The Active Management Premium in Small-Cap U.S. Equities', *Journal of Portfolio Management*, 31.

Al-Loughani, N. and D. Chappell (1997). 'On the Validity of the Weak Form Efficient Market Hypothesis Applied to the London Stock Exchange', *Applied Financial Economics*, 7.

Altman, E. I. (1968). 'Financial Ratios, Discriminant Analysis and the Prediction of Corporate Bankruptcy', *Journal of Finance*, 23.

Altman, E. I. (1991). 'Defaults and Returns on High Yield Bonds through the First Half of 1991', *Financial Analysts Journal*, 47.

Altman, E. I.; R. Haldeman, and P. Narayanan (1977). 'ZETA Analysis: A New Model to Identify Bankruptcy Risk of Corporations', *Journal of Banking and Finance*, 1.

Ambachtsheer, K. (1974). 'Profit Potential in an "Almost Efficient" Market', *Journal of Portfolio Management*, 1.

Ambachtsheer, K. (2005). 'Beyond Portfolio Theory: The Next Frontier', *Financial Analysts Journal*, 61.

Ambachtsheer, K. (2007). 'Why We Need a Pension Revolution', *Financial Analysts Journal*, 63.

Ambachtsheer, K.; R. Capelle, and T. Scheibelhut (1998). 'Improving Pension Fund Performance', *Financial Analysts Journal*, 54.

Amenc, N.; L. Martellini, and M. Vaissie (2003). 'Benefits and Risks of Alternative Investment Strategies', *Journal of Asset Management*, 4.

Amenc, N.; J. R. Giraud, L. Martellini, and M. Vaissie (2004). 'Taking a Close Look at the European Fund of Hedge Funds Industry: Comparing and Contrasting Industry Practices and Academic Recommendations', *Journal of Alternative Investments*, 7.

Amihud, Y. and H. Mendelson (1991). 'Liquidity, Asset Prices, and Financial Policy', *Financial Analysts Journal*, 47.

Amin, G. S. and H. M. Kat (2003). 'Welcome to the Dark Side: Hedge Fund Attrition and Survivorship Bias over the Period 1994–2001', *Journal of Alternative Investments*, 6.

Amin, G. S. and H. M. Kat (2003a). 'Stocks, Bonds, and Hedge Funds', *Journal of Portfolio Management*, 29.

Ammann, M. and M. Verhofen (2007). 'Prior Performance and Risk-Taking of Mutual Fund Managers: A Dynamic Bayesian Network Approach', *Journal of Behavioral Finance*, 8.

Anderson, J. and G. Smith (2006). 'A Great Company Can Be a Great Investment', *Financial Analysts Journal*, 62.

Ang, A. and J. Chen (2001). 'Asymmetric Correlations of Equity Portfolios', *Journal of Financial Economics*, 52.

Ang, A.; G. Bekaert, and J. Liu (2005). 'Why Stocks May Disappoint', *Journal of Financial Economics*, 76.

Antoniou, A.; I. Garrett, and R. Priestley (1998). 'Macroeconomic Variables as Common Pervasive Risk Factors and the Empirical Content of the Arbitrage Pricing Theory', *Journal of Empirical Finance*, 5.

Antoniou, A.; E. C. Galariotis, and S. I. Spyrou (2005). 'Contrarian Profits and the Overreaction Hypothesis: The Case of the Athens Stock Exchange', *European Financial Management*, 11.

Antunovich, P. and D. S. Laster (2003). 'Are Good Companies Bad Investments?', *Journal of Investing*, 12.

Arbel, A. and P. J. Strebel (1983). 'Pay Attention to Neglected Firms', *Journal of Portfolio Management*, 9.

Arnott, R. (1979). 'Relative Strength Revisited', *Journal of Portfolio Management*, 5.

Arnott, R. D. and C. S. Asness (2003). 'Surprise! Higher Dividends = Higher Earnings Growth', *Financial Analysts Journal*, 59.

Asch, S. E. (1952). *Social Psychology*, Prentice Hall.

Asness, C. S. (2003). 'Fight the Fed Model', *Journal of Portfolio Management*, 29.

Asness, C. S. (2005). 'Rubble Logic: What Did We Learn from the Great Stock Market Bubble?', *Financial Analysts Journal*, 61.

Asness, C. S.; J. M. Liew, and R. L. Stevens (1997). 'Parallels between the Cross-Sectional Predictability of Stock and Country Returns', *Journal of Portfolio Management*, 23.

Atkinson, S. M. and R. R. Sturm (2003). 'All-Star Mutual Funds?', *Journal of Investing*, 12.

Attanasio, O. P. and S. Rohwedder (2004). 'Pension Wealth and Household Saving', *American Economic Review*, 93.

Azar, B. (2000). 'Blinded by Hindsight', *Monitor on Psychology*, 31.

Baker, H. K. and J. R. Nofsinger (2002). 'Psychological Biases of Investors', *Financial Services Review*, 11.

Baker, M. and J. Wurgler (2004). 'A Catering Theory of Dividends', *Journal of Finance*, 59.

Baker, M. and J. Wurgler (2006). 'Investor Sentiment and the Cross-Section of Stock Returns', *Journal of Finance*, 61.

Baker, W. (1984). 'The Social Structure of a National Securities Market', *American Journal of Sociology*, 89.

Bal, Y. and L. A. Leger (1996). 'The Performance of UK Investment Trusts', *Service Industries Journal*, 16.

Ball, R. and P. Brown (1968). 'An Empirical Evaluation of Accounting Income Numbers', *Journal of Accounting Research*, Autumn.

Band, R. E. (1989). *Contrary Investing for the '90s*, St Martin's Press.

Banks, J.; R. Blundell, and S. Tanner (1998). 'Is There a Retirement-Savings Puzzle?', *American Economic Review*, 88.

Banz, R. (1981). 'The Relation Between Return and Market Value of Common Stocks', *Journal of Financial Economics*, 9.

Baquero, G.; J. ter Horst, and M. Verbeck (2005). 'Survival, Look-Ahead Bias, and Persistence in Hedge Fund Performance', *Journal of Financial and Quantitative Analysis*, 40.

Barber, B. and T. Odean (1999). 'The Courage of Misguided Convictions', *Financial Analysts Journal*, 55.

Barber, B. and T. Odean (2000). 'Trading is Hazardous to Your Wealth: The Common Stock Investment Performance of Individual Investors', *Journal of Finance*, 55.

Barber, B. and T. Odean (2001). 'The Internet and the Investor', *Journal of Economic Perspectives*, 15.

Barber, B. and T. Odean (2001a). 'Boys Will Be Boys: Gender, Overconfidence, and Common Stock Investment', *Quarterly Journal of Economics*, 116.

Barber, B. and T. Odean (2002). 'Online Investors: Do the Slow Die First?', *Review of Financial Studies*, 15.

Barber, B.; R. Lehavey, M. McNichols, and B. Trueman (2001). 'Can Investors Profit from the Prophets? Security Analyst Recommendations and Stock Returns', *Journal of Finance*, 56.

Barber, B.; T. Odean, and L. Zheng (2005). 'Out of Sight, Out of Mind: The Effects of Expenses on Mutual Fund Flows', *Journal of Business*, 78.

Barber, B. M.; Y-T. Lee, Y-J. Liu, and T. Odean (2007). 'Is the Aggregate Investor Reluctant to Realise Losses? Evidence from Taiwan', *European Financial Management*, 13.

Barberis, N. and A. Shleifer (2001). 'Style Investing', University of Chicago Working Paper.

Barberis, N.; A. Shleifer, and R. Vishny (1998). 'A Model of Investor Sentiment', *Journal of Financial Economics*, 49.

Barberis, N.; M. Huang, and R. Thaler (2003). 'Individual Preferences, Monetary Gambles, and the Equity Premium', University of Chicago Working Paper, December.

Barclay, M.; C. Holderness, and J. Pontiff (1993). 'Private Benefits from Block Ownership and Discounts on Closed-End Funds', *Journal of Financial Economics*, 33.

Bargh, J. A. and T. L. Chartrand (1999). 'The Unbearable Automaticity of Being', *American Psychologist*, 54.

Barker, R. (2001). *Determining Value*, Financial Times/Prentice Hall.

Barry, C. B.; J. W. Peavy, and M. Rodriguez (1998). 'Performance Characteristics of Emerging Capital Markets', *Financial Analysts Journal*, 54.

Barnes, M. A.; A. Bercel, and S. H. Rothmann (2001). 'Global Equities: Do Countries Still Matter?', *Journal of Investing*, 10.

Basu, S. (1977). 'The Investment Performance of Common Stocks in Relation to their Price-Earnings Ratios: A Test of the Efficient Market Hypothesis', *Journal of Finance*, 32.

Batchelor, R. and R. Ramyar (2006). 'Magic Numbers in the Dow', Cass Business School, City University.

Bathala, C. T.; C. K. Ma, and R. P. Rao (2005). 'What Stocks Appeal to Institutional Investors?', *Journal of Investing*, 14.

Battalio, R. and P. Schultz (2006). 'Options and the Bubble', *Journal of Finance*, 6.

Batten, J. and W. Hogan (2002). 'A Perspective on Credit Derivatives', *International Review of Financial Analysis*, 11.

Beckett, A.; P. Hewer, and B. Howcroft (2000). 'An Exposition of Consumer Behaviour in the Financial Services Industry', *International Journal of Bank Marketing*, 18.

Benartzi, S. (2001). 'Excessive Extrapolation and the Allocation of 401(k) Accounts to Company Stock', *Journal of Finance*, 56.

Benartzi, S. and R. H. Thaler (1995). 'Myopic Loss Aversion and the Equity Premium Puzzle', *Quarterly Journal of Economics*, 110.

Benartzi, S. and R. H. Thaler (1999). 'Risk Aversion or Myopia? Choices in Repeated Gamble and Retirement Investments', *Management Science*, 45.

Benartzi, S. and R. H. Thaler (2001). 'Naïve Diversification Strategies in Defined Contribution Savings Plans', *American Economic Review*, 91.

Benartzi, S. and R. H. Thaler (2004). 'Save More Tomorrow: Using Behavioral Economics to Increase Employee Saving', *Journal of Political Economy*, 112.

Berk, J. B. (1995). 'A Critique of Size-Related Anomalies', *Review of Financial Studies*, 8.

Berk, J. B. (1997). 'Does Size Really Matter?', *Financial Analysts Journal*, 53.

Bernanke, B. S. and K. N. Kuttner (2005). 'What Explains the Stock Market's Reaction to Federal Reserve Policy?', *Journal of Finance*, 60.

Bessembinder, H. and K. Chan (1998). 'Market Efficiency and the Returns to Technical Analysis', *Financial Management*, 27.

Bessler, D. A. and J. Yang (2003). 'The Structure of Interdependence in International Stock Markets', *Journal of International Money and Finance*, 22.

Best, K. (2005). 'Celebrity.com: Internet Finance and Frenzy at the Millennium', *Consumption, Markets and Culture*, 8.

Biais, B. and M. Weber (2006). 'Hindsight Bias and Investment Performance', paper presented to the Behavioural Finance and Market Efficiency Workshop, University of Warwick, March.

Biddle, G. C.; R. M. Bowen, and J. S. Wallace (1997). 'Does EVA Beat Earnings? Evidence on Associations with Stock Returns and Firm Values', *Journal of Accounting and Economics*, 24.

Biddle, G. C.; R. M. Bowen, and J. S. Wallace (1999). 'Evidence on EVA', *Journal of Applied Corporate Finance*, 12.

Bieri, D. S. and L. B. Chincarini (2005). 'Riding the Yield Curve: A Variety of Strategies', *Journal of Fixed Income*, 15.

Bierman, H. (2002). 'The Price-Earnings Ratio', *Journal of Portfolio Management*, 28.

Bjerring, J. H., J. Lakonishok, and T. Vermaelen (1983). 'Stock Prices and Financial Analysts Recommendations', *Journal of Finance*, 48.

Black, F. (1986). 'Noise', *Journal of Finance*, 51.

Black, F. and M. Scholes. (1973). 'The Pricing of Options and Corporate Liabilities', *Journal of Political Economy*, 81.

Black, F.; M. C. Jensen, and M. S. Scholes (1972). 'The Capital Asset Pricing Model: Some Empirical Tests', in M. C. Jensen (ed.) *Studies in the Theory of Capital*, Praeger.

Black, K.; C. S. Ciccotello, and H. D. Skipper (2002). 'Issues in Comprehensive Personal Financial Planning', *Financial Services Review*, 11.

859

REFERENCES

Black, R. T. (1997). 'Expert Property Negotiators and Pricing Information, Revisited', *Journal of Property Valuation and Investment*, 15.

Black, R. T. and J. Diaz III (1996). 'The Use of Information Versus Asking Price in the Real Property Negotiation Process', *Journal of Property Research*, 13.

Blake, C.; E. Elton, and M. Gruber (1993). 'The Performance of Bond Mutual Funds', *Journal of Business*, 66.

Blake, D. and A. Timmermann (2005). 'Returns from Active Management in International Equity Markets: Evidence from a Panel of UK Pension Funds', *Journal of Asset Management*, 6.

Blake, D.; B. N. Lehmann, and A. Timmermann (1999). 'Asset Allocation Dynamics and Pension Fund Performance', *Journal of Business*, 72.

Bleiberg, S. (1989). 'How Little We Know – about P/Es, but Also Perhaps More Than We Think', *Journal of Portfolio Management*, 15.

Block, S. B. (1999). 'A Study of Financial Analysts: Practice and Theory', *Financial Analysts Journal*, 55.

Blume, M. E. (1971). 'On the Assessment of Risk', *Journal of Finance*, 36.

Boehm, E. A. and G. H. Moore (1991). 'Financial Market Forecasts and Rates of Return Based on Leading Index Signals', *International Journal of Forecasting*, 7.

Bogle, J. C. (1992). 'Selecting Equity Mutual Funds', *Journal of Portfolio Management*, 18.

Bogle, J. C. (1998). 'The Implications of Style Analysis for Mutual Fund Performance Evaluation', *Journal of Portfolio Management*, 24.

Bogle, J. C. (2002). 'An Index Fund Fundamentalist Goes Back to the Drawing Board', *Journal of Portfolio Management*, 28.

Bogle, J. C. (2005). 'The Mutual Fund Industry 60 Years Later: For Better or Worse?', *Financial Analysts Journal*, 61.

Bollen, N. P. B. and R. Whaley (2004). 'Does Net Buying Pressure Affect the Shape of Implied Volatility Functions?', *Journal of Finance*, 59.

Bomfim, A. N. (2002). 'Credit Derivatives and Their Potential to Synthesize Riskless Assets', *Journal of Fixed Income*, 12.

Booth, P. and G. E. Wood (2000). 'Interest Rates Are Low but Are Annuities Expensive?', *Economic Affairs*, 20.

Booth, P. and B. Rodney (2002). 'The Repayment of Mortgages by Endowment Assurances', *Journal of Property Investment & Finance*, 20.

Boswijk, H. P.; C. H. Hommes, and S. Manzan (2007). 'Behavioral Heterogeneity in Stock Prices', *Journal of Economic Dynamics and Control*, 31.

Boudoukh, J. and M. Richardson (1993). 'Stock Returns and Inflation: A Long-Horizon Effect', *American Economic Review*, 83.

Brav, A. and R. Lehavy (2001). 'An Empirical Analysis of Analysts' Target Prices', Working Paper.

Bremer, M. A. and R. J. Sweeney (1991). 'The Reversal of Large Stock Price Decreases', *Journal of Finance*, 46.

Breton, G. and R. J. Taffler (1995). 'Creative Accounting and Investment Analyst Response', *Accounting and Business Research*, 25.

Brinson, G.; B. Singer, and G. Beebower (1991). 'Determinants of Portfolio Performance', *Financial Analysts Journal*, 47.

Brock, W.; J. Lakonishok, and B. LeBaron (1992). 'Simple Technical Trading Rules and the Stochastic Properties of Stock Returns', *Journal of Finance*, 47.

Brown, G. W. (1999). 'Volatility, Sentiment, and Noise Traders', *Financial Analysts Journal*, 55.

Brown, G. W. and M. T. Cliff (2005). 'Investor Sentiment and Asset Valuation', *Journal of Business*, 78.

Brown, G.; P. Draper, and E. McKenzie (1997). 'Consistency of UK Pension Fund Investment Performance', *Journal of Business Finance and Accounting*, 24.

860

Brown, K. C. and W. V. Harlow (1988). 'Market Overreaction: Magnitude and Intensity', *Journal of Portfolio Management*, 7.

Brown, K. C.; W. V. Harlow, and L. Starks (1996). 'Of Tournaments and Temptations: An Analysis of Managerial Incentives in the Mutual Fund Industry', *Journal of Finance*, 51.

Brown, S.; K. Taylor, and S. W. Price (2005). 'Debt and Distress: Evaluating the Psychological Cost of Credit', *Journal of Economic Psychology*, 26.

Bruce, B. and A. Eisenberg (1992). 'Global Synthetic Index Funds', *Journal of Investing*, 1.

Brunel, J. (2003). 'Revisiting the Asset Allocation Challenge Through a Behavioral Finance Lens', *Journal of Wealth Management*, 6.

Bruner, R. F.; R. M. Conroy, W. Li, E. F. O'Halloran, and M. Palacios Lleras (2003). *Investing in Emerging Markets*, Research Foundation of AIMR Monograph.

Brush, J. S. (1986). 'Eight Relative Strength Models Compared', *Journal of Portfolio Management*, 5.

Budden, R. (2006). 'It Doesn't Pay to be Healthy and Wealthy', *Financial Times*, 11/12 November.

Burtless, G. (1999). 'An Economic View of Retirement', in H. J. Aaron (ed.) *Behavioral Dimensions of Retirement*, Brookings Institution Press.

Byrne, A. (2007). 'Employee Saving and Investment Decisions in Defined Contribution Pension Plans: Survey Evidence from the UK', *Financial Services Review*, 16.

Byrne, A.; D. Blake, A. Cairns, and K. Dowd (2006). 'There's No Time Like The Present: The Cost of Delaying Retirement Saving', *Financial Services Review*, 15.

Caginalp, G.; D. Porter, and V. Smith (2000). 'Overreaction, Momentum, Liquidity and Price Bubbles in Laboratory and Field Asset Markets', *Journal of Psychology and Financial Markets*, 1.

Callan, V. J. and M. Johnson (2002). 'Some Guidelines for Financial Planners in Measuring and Advising Clients About Their Levels of Risk Tolerance', *Journal of Personal Finance*, August.

Camerer, C. F. (1981). 'General Conditions for the Success of Bootstrapping Models', *Organizational Behavior and Human Performance*, 27.

Campbell, J. Y. and R. J. Shiller (1998). 'Valuation Ratios and the Long-Run Stock Market Outlook', *Journal of Portfolio Management*, 24.

Campbell, J. Y. and T. Vuolteenaho (2004). 'Bad Beta, Good Beta', *American Economic Review*, 94.

Campbell, J. Y. and T. Vuolteenaho (2004a). 'Inflation Illusion and Stock Prices', National Bureau of Economic Research (NBER) Working Paper 10263.

Campbell, J. Y.; A. W. Lo, and A. C. MacKinlay (1997). *The Econometrics of Financial Markets*, Princeton University Press.

Capaul, C.; I. Rowley, and W. F. Sharpe (1993). 'International Value and Growth Stock Returns', *Financial Analysts Journal*, 49.

Capon, N.; G. Fitzsimons, and R. Prince (1996). 'An Individual Level Analysis of the Mutual Fund Investment Decision', *Journal of Financial Services Research*, 10.

Carhart, M. (1997). 'On Persistence in Mutual Fund Performance', *Journal of Finance*, 52.

Carpenter, J. N. and A. W. Lynch (1999). 'Survivorship Bias and Attrition Effects in Measures of Performance Persistence', *Journal of Financial Economics*, 54.

Carroll, D.; S. Ebrahim, K. Tilling, J. Macleod, and G. Davey Smith (2002). 'Admissions for Myocardial Infarction and World Cup Football: Database Survey', *British Medical Journal*, 325.

Carvell, S. A. and P. J. Strebel (1987). 'Is There a Neglected Firm Effect?', *Journal of Business Finance and Accounting*, 14.

Cassidy, J. (2002). *dot.com: the Greatest Story Ever Told*, Penguin.

Cecchetti, S. G.; P. Lam, and N. Mark (1990). 'Mean Reversion in Equilibrium Asset Prices', *American Economic Review*, 80.

Chalk, A. J. and J. W. Peavy (1987). 'Initial Public Offerings: Daily Returns, Offering Types and the Price Effect', *Financial Analysts Journal*, 43.

REFERENCES

Chan, A. and A. P. L. Chui (1996). 'An Empirical Re-examination of the Cross-Section of Expected Returns: UK Evidence', *Journal of Business Finance and Accounting*, 23.

Chan, K.; A. Hameed, and W. Tong (2000). 'Profitability of Momentum Strategies in the International Equity Markets', *Journal of Financial and Quantitative Analysis*, 35.

Chan, K. C. and N. Chen (1991). 'Structural and Return Characteristics of Small and Large Firms', *Journal of Finance*, 46.

Chan, K. C.; N. Chen, and D. A. Hsieh (1985). 'An Exploratory Investigation of the Firm Size Effect', *Journal of Financial Economics*, 14.

Chan, K. C.; L. T. W. Cheng, and P. P. Lung (2004). 'Net Buying Pressure, Volatility Smile, and Abnormal Profit of Hang Seng Index Options', *Journal of Futures Markets*, 24.

Chan, L. K. C. and J. Lakonishok (1993). 'Are the Reports of Beta's Death Premature?', *Journal of Portfolio Management*, 19.

Chan, L. K. C.; N. Jegadeesh, and J. Lakonishok (1999). 'The Profitability of Momentum Strategies', *Financial Analysts Journal*, 55.

Chance, D. M. and P. P. Peterson (2002). *Real Options and Investment Valuation*, Research Foundation of AIMR Monograph.

Chang, E. C. and W. G. Lewellen (1984). 'Market Timing and Mutual Fund Investment Performance', *Journal of Business*, 57.

Chapman, G. B. and E. J. Johnson (2002). 'Incorporating the Irrelevant: Anchors in Judgments of Belief and Value', in T. Gilovich, D.W. Griffin, and D. Kahneman (eds) *The Psychology of Intuitive Judgment: Heuristics and Biases*, Cambridge University Press.

Chapman, J. (2006). 'Past Masters', *Money Management* (UK), July.

Chapman, J. (2006a). 'Single Pricing Shambles', *Money Management* (UK), November.

Chen, H.; G. Noronha, and V. Singal (2006). 'Index Changes and Losses to Index Fund Investors', *Financial Analysts Journal*, 62.

Chen, N. (1988). 'Equilibrium Asset Pricing Models and the Firm Size Effect', in E. Dimson (ed.) *Stock Market Anomalies*, Cambridge University Press.

Chen, N. F.; R. Roll, and S. Ross (1986). 'Economic Forces and the Stock Market', *Journal of Business*, 59.

Chen, P.; R. G. Ibbotson, M. A. Milevsky, and K. X. Zhu (2006). 'Human Capital, Asset Allocation, and Life Insurance', *Financial Analysts Journal*, 62.

Chen, S-S.; C-F. Lee, and K. Shrestha (2004). 'An Empirical Analysis of the Relationship Between the Hedge Ratio and Hedging Horizon: A Simultaneous Estimation of the Short- and Long-Run Hedge Ratios', *Journal of Futures Markets*, 24.

Cheng, L. T. W.; L. K. Pi, and D. Wort (1999). 'Are There Hot Hands Among Mutual Fund Houses in Hong Kong?', *Journal of Business Finance and Accounting*, 26.

Chhabra, A. B. (2005). 'Beyond Markowitz: A Comprehensive Wealth Allocation Framework for Individual Investors', *Journal of Wealth Management*, 7.

Choi, J.; D. Laibson, B. Madrian, and A. Metrick (2001). 'For Better or for Worse: Default Effects and 401(k) Savings Behavior', in D. Wise (ed.) *Frontiers in the Economics of Aging*, National Bureau of Economic Research.

Chopra, N.; J. Lakonishok, and J. R. Ritter (1992). 'Measuring Abnormal Performance: Do Stocks Overreact?', *Journal of Financial Economics*, 31.

Chowdhury, M; J. S. Howe, and J. Lin (1993). 'The Relationship between Aggregate Insider Transactions and Stock Market Returns', *Journal of Financial and Quantitative Analysis*, 28.

Chung, R.; M. Firth, and J-B. Kim (2002). 'Institutional Monitoring and Opportunistic Earnings Management', *Journal of Corporate Finance*, 8.

Citizens Advice (2003). 'In Too Deep: CAB Clients' Experience of Debt', Citizens Advice and Citizens Advice Scotland.

Clare, A.; S. Thomas, and M. Wickens (1994). 'Is the Gilt-Equity Yield Ratio Useful for Predicting UK Stock Returns?', *Economic Journal*, 104.

Clare, A.; R. Priestley, and S. Thomas (1997). 'Stock Return Predictability or Mismeasured Risk?', *Applied Financial Economics*, 7.

Clare, A.; R. Priestley, and S. Thomas (1997a). 'The Robustness of the APT to Alternative Estimators', *Journal of Business Finance and Accounting*, 24.

Clare, A.; R. Priestley, and S. Thomas (1998). 'Reports of Beta's Death are Premature: Evidence from the UK', *Journal of Banking and Finance*, 22.

Clare, A.; M. Ioannides, and F. S. Skinner (2000). 'Hedging Corporate Bonds with Stock Index Futures: A Word of Caution', *Journal of Fixed Income*, 10.

Clark, T. A. and M. I. Weinstein (1983). 'The Behaviour of the Common Stock of Bankrupt Firms', *Journal of Finance*, 38.

Clarke, R. G. and M. Statman (1998). 'Bullish or Bearish', *Financial Analysts Journal*, 54.

Clarke, R. G. and M. Statman (2000). 'The DJIA Crossed 652,230', *Journal of Portfolio Management*, 26.

Clarke, R. G.; S. Krase, and M. Statman (1994). 'Tracking Errors, Regret, and Tactical Asset Allocation', *Journal of Portfolio Management*, 20.

Cocco, J. F. and P. F. Volpin (2007). 'Corporate Governance of Pension Plans: The U.K. Evidence', *Financial Analysts Journal*, 63.

Cochrane, J. H. (1991). 'Volatility Tests and Efficient Markets: A Review Essay', *Journal of Monetary Economics*, 27.

Coggan, P. (2006). 'Darwinian Truth behind the Investment Struggle', *Financial Times*, 12 August.

Coggan, P. (2006a). 'The Lessons I've Learned in the Past 20 Years', *Financial Times*, 2/3 September.

Coggin, D. T.; F. J. Fabozzi, and S. Rahman (1993). 'The Investment Performance of US Equity Pension Fund Managers: An Empirical Investigation', *Journal of Finance*, 48.

Coggin, D. T. and J. E. Hunter (1983). 'Problems in Measuring the Quality of Investment Information: The Perils of the Information Coefficient', *Financial Analysts Journal*, 39.

Cohen, R. B.; C. Polk, and T. Vuolteenaho (2003). 'The Value Spread', *Journal of Finance*, 58.

Congdon, T. (2005). 'Money and Asset Prices in Boom and Bust', Hobart paper 152, Institute of Economic Affairs.

Congdon, T. (2006). 'Money, Asset Prices and the Boom-Bust Cycles in the UK: An Analysis of the Transmission Mechanism from Money to Macro-Economic Outcomes', in K. Matthews and P. Booth (eds) *Issues in Monetary Policy*, Wiley.

Conrad, J. and G. Kaul (1988). 'Time-Variation in Expected Returns', *Journal of Business*, 61.

Cooper, M.; I. Dimitrov, and R. Rau (2001). 'A Rose.com by Any Other Name', *Journal of Finance*, 56.

Cooper, M.; H. Gulen, and R. Rau (2005). 'Changing Names with Style: Mutual Fund Name Changes and Their Effects on Fund Flows', *Journal of Finance*, 60.

Cooper, M. J.; J. J. McConnell, and A. V. Ovtchinnikov (2006). 'The Other January Effect', *Journal of Financial Economics*, 82.

Cordell, D. M.; T. P. Langdon, and C. W. Lemoine (2006). 'Bridging the Gap: Academic Research That Is Relevant to Practitioners', *Journal of Financial Service Professionals*, 60.

Corhay, A.; G. Hawawini, and P. Michel (1988). 'The Pricing of Equity on the London Stock Exchange: Seasonality and Size Premium', in E. Dimson (ed.) *Stock Market Anomalies*, Cambridge University Press.

Cornell, B. (2000). 'Valuing Intel: A Strange Tale of Analysts and Announcements', UCLA Working Paper.

Cornell, B. (2001). 'Is the Response of Analysts to Information Consistent with Fundamental Valuation? The Case of Intel', *Financial Management*, 30.

Cornell, B. and R. Roll (1981). 'Strategies for Pairwise Competitions in Markets and Organizations', *Bell Journal of Economics*, 12.

Cornell, B. and Q. Liu (2001). 'The Parent Company Puzzle: When is the Whole Worth Less Than One of the Parts?', *Journal of Corporate Finance*, 7.

Cornett, M. M.; A. J. Marcus, A. Saunders, and H. Tehranian (2007). 'The Impact of Institutional Ownership on Corporate Operating Performance', *Journal of Banking and Finance*, 31.

Costanzo, L. A. and J. K. Ashton (2006). 'Product Innovation and Consumer Choice in the UK Financial Services Industry', *Journal of Financial Regulation and Compliance*, 14.

Coval, J. and T. Moskowitz (1999). 'Home Bias at Home: Local Equity Preference in Domestic Portfolios', *Journal of Finance*, 54.

Cowles, A. (1933). 'Can Stock Market Forecasters Forecast?', *Econometrica*, 1.

Cox, J. C.; S. A. Ross, and M. Rubinstein (1979). 'Option Pricing: A Simplified Approach', *Journal of Financial Economics*, 7.

Cremers, K. J. M. and V. B. Nair (2005). 'Governance Mechanisms and Equity Prices', *Journal of Finance*, 60.

Cross, F. (1973). 'The Behavior of Stock Prices on Fridays and Mondays', *Financial Analysts Journal*, 29.

Cyree, K. B.; D. L. Domian, D. A. Louton, and E. J. Yobaccio (1999). 'Evidence of Psychological Barriers in the Conditional Moments of Major World Stock Indices', *Review of Financial Economics*, 8.

Damodaran, A. (2001). *Corporate Finance: Theory and Practice*, Wiley.

Daniel, K. and S. Titman (1995). 'Evidence of the Characteristics of Cross Sectional Variation in Common Stock Returns', *Journal of Finance*, 50.

Daniel, K.; M. Grinblatt, S. Titman, and R. Wermers (1997). 'Measuring Mutual Fund Performance with Characteristic-Based Benchmarks', *Journal of Finance*, 52.

Daniel, K.; D. Hirschleifer, and A. Subrahmanyam (1999). 'Investor Psychology and Security Under- and Overreactions', *Journal of Finance*, 53.

Daniel, W. E. and H. D. Blank (2002). 'The Defensive Asset Class: A New Paradigm in Plan Diversification', *Journal of Investing*, 11.

D'Antonio, L.; T. Johnson, and B. Hutton (1997). 'Expanding Socially Screened Portfolios: An Attribution Analysis of Bond Portfolios', *Journal of Investing*, 6.

Davies, P. L. and M. Canes (1978). 'Stock Prices and the Publication of Second-Hand Information', *Journal of Business*, 51.

Davis, A. (2006). 'The Role of the Mass Media in Investor Relations', *Journal of Communication Management*, 10.

Day, T. E. and P. Wang (2002). 'Dividends, Nonsynchronous Prices, and the Returns from Trading the Dow Jones Industrial Average', *Journal of Empirical Finance*, 9.

DeBondt, W. F. M. (1993). 'Betting on Trends: Intuitive Forecasts of Financial Risk and Return', *International Journal of Forecasting*, 9.

DeBondt, W. F. M. (1998). 'A Portrait of the Individual Investor', *European Economic Review*, 42.

DeBondt, W. F. M. and R. Thaler (1985). 'Does the Stock Market Overreact?', *Journal of Finance*, 40.

DeBondt, W. F. M. and R. H. Thaler (1987). 'Further Evidence on Investor Overreaction and Stock Market Seasonality', *Journal of Finance*, 42.

DeBondt, W. F. M. and R. H. Thaler (1990). 'Do Security Analysts Overreact?', *American Economic Review*, 80.

Degeorge, F.; J. Patel, and R. J. Zeckhauser (1999). 'Earnings Management to Exceed Thresholds', *Journal of Business*, 72.

DeLong, J. B.; A. Shleifer, L. H. Summers, and R. J. Waldmann (1990). 'Noise Trader Risk in Financial Markets', *Journal of Political Economy*, 98.

DeMiguel, V.; L. Garlappi, and R. Uppal (2006). 'How Inefficient is the 1/N Asset-Allocation Strategy?', paper presented to the Behavioural Finance and Market Efficiency Workshop, University of Warwick, March.

Department for Work and Pensions (2003). 'British Household Panel Survey'.

Department for Work and Pensions (2005). 'Family Resources Survey: United Kingdom 2003–04'.

Department for Work and Pensions (2006). 'Security in Retirement: Towards a New Pensions System'.

Desai, H.; B. Liang, and A. K. Singh (2000). 'Do All-Stars Shine? Evaluation of Analyst Recommendations', *Financial Analysts Journal*, 56.

DeStefano, M. (2004). 'Stock Returns and the Business Cycle', *Financial Review*, 39.

Deutsch, M. and H. Gerard (1955). 'A Study of Normative and Informational Influence upon Individual Judgment', *Journal of Abnormal and Social Psychology*, 51.

Devaney, S. P.; S. L. Lee, and M. S. Young (2007). 'Serial Persistence in Individual Real Estate Returns in the UK', *Journal of Property Investment & Finance*, 25.

Dhakal, D.; M. Kandil, and S. C. Sharma (1993). 'Causality between the Money Supply and Share Prices: A VAR Investigation', *Quarterly Journal of Business and Economics*, 32.

Dhar, R. and A. Kumar (2001) 'A Non-Random Walk Down the Main Street: Impact of Price Trends on Trading Decisions of Individual Investors', Yale School of Management Working Paper.

Diacon, S. (2004). 'Investment Risk Perceptions. Do Consumers and Advisers Agree?', *International Journal of Bank Marketing*, 22.

Diacon, S. and J. Hasseldine (2007). 'Framing Effects and Risk Perception: The Effect of Prior Performance Presentation Format on Investment Fund Choice', *Journal of Economic Psychology*, 28.

Diamonte, R. L.; J. M. Liew, and R. L. Stevens (1996). 'Political Risk in Emerging and Developed Markets', *Financial Analysts Journal*, 52.

Diaz, J. III (1997). 'An Investigation into the Impact of Previous Expert Value Estimates on Appraisal Judgment', *Journal of Real Estate Research*, 13.

Diaz, J. III (1999). 'The First Decade of Behavioral Research in the Discipline of Property', *Journal of Property Investment & Finance*, 17.

Diaz, J. III and J. A. Hansz (1997). 'How Valuers Use the Value Opinions of Others', *Journal of Property Valuation and Investment*, 15.

Diaz, J. III and M. L. Wolverton (1998). 'A Longitudinal Examination of the Appraisal Smoothing Hypothesis', *Real Estate Economics*, 26.

Diaz, J. III; R. Zhao, and R. T. Black (1999). 'Does Contingent Reward Reduce Negotiation Anchoring?', *Journal of Property Investment & Finance*, 17.

DiFonzo, N. and P. Bordia (1997). 'Rumor and Prediction: Making Sense (but Losing Dollars) in the Stock Market', *Organizational Behavior and Human Decision Processes*, 71.

Diltz, J. D. (1995). 'The Private Cost of Socially Responsible Investing', *Applied Financial Economics*, 5.

Dimson, E. and P. Marsh (1984). 'An Analysis of Brokers' and Analysts' Unpublished Forecasts of UK Stock Returns', *Journal of Finance*, 39.

Dimson, E. and P. Marsh (2001). 'UK Financial Market Returns, 1955–2000', *Journal of Business*, 74.

Dimson, E.; P. Marsh, and M. Staunton (2000). *The Millennium Book: A Century of Investment Returns*, ABN Amro/London Business School.

Dimson, E.; P. Marsh, and M. Staunton (2004). 'Low-Cap and Low-Rated Companies', *Journal of Portfolio Management*, 30.

Distribution Technology (2005). 'Benchmarking UK Consumer Attitudes to Risk'.

Dodd, P. (1980). 'Merger Proposals, Management Discretion and Stockholder Wealth', *Journal of Financial Economics*, 8.

Dolvin, S. D. and W. K. Templeton (2006). 'Financial Education and Asset Allocation', *Financial Services Review*, 15.

Doukas, J. A. and P. J. McKnight (2005). 'European Momentum Strategies, Information Diffusion, and Investor Conservatism', *European Financial Management*, 11.

Doukas, J. A.; C. Kim, and C. Pantzalis (2005). 'The Two Faces of Analyst Coverage', *Financial Management*, 34.

Dowd, K. (2000). 'Adjusting for Risk: An Improved Sharpe Ratio', *International Review of Economics & Finance*, 9.

Dowen, R. J. and T. Mann (2004). 'Mutual Fund Performance, Management Behavior, and Investor Costs', *Financial Services Review*, 13.

Doyle, J. T.; R. J. Lundholm, and M. T. Soliman (2006). 'The Extreme Future Stock Returns Following I/B/E/S Earnings Surprises', *Journal of Accounting Research*, 44.

Dreman, D. (2001). 'The Role of Psychology in Analysts' Estimates', *Journal of Psychology and Financial Markets*, 2.

Dreman, D. (2004). 'The Influence of Affect on Investor Decision-Making', *Journal of Behavioral Finance*, 5.

Drew, M. E. and J. D. Stanford (2001). 'Asset Selection and Superannuation Fund Performance: A Note for Trustees', *Economic Papers*, 20.

Drew, M. E.; J. D. Stanford, and M. Veeraraghavan (2002). 'Selecting Australian Equity Superannuation Funds: A Retail Investor's Perspective', *Journal of Financial Services Marketing*, 7.

Drinkwater, M. and E. T. Sondergeld (2004). 'Perceptions of Mortality Risk: Implications for Annuities', in O. S. Mitchell and S. P. Utkus (eds) *Pension Design and Structure: New Lessons from Behavioral Finance*, Oxford University Press.

Driscoll, K.; M. Malcolm, M. Sirull, and P. Slotter (1995). '1995 Gallup Survey of Defined Contribution Plan Participants', John Hancock Financial Services.

Duflo, E. and E. Saez (2002). 'Participation and Investment Decisions in a Retirement Plan: The Influence of Colleagues' Choices', *Journal of Public Economics*, 85.

Dufwenberg, M.; T. Lindqvist, and E. Moore (2005). 'Bubbles and Experience: An Experiment', *American Economic Review*, 95.

Dukes, W. P.; Z. Peng, and P. C. English (2006). 'How Do Practitioners Value Common Stock?', *Journal of Investing*, 15.

Dunbar, N. (2000). *Inventing Money*, Wiley.

Dunn, J. R. and M. E. Schweitzer (2005). 'Feeling and Believing: The Influence of Emotions on Trust', *Journal of Personality and Social Psychology*, 88.

Dweck, C. S. and E. L. Leggett (1988). 'A Social-Cognitive Approach to Motivation and Personality', *Psychological Review*, 95.

Edelen, R. M. and J. B. Warner (2001). 'Aggregate Price Effects of Institutional Trading: A Study of Mutual Fund Flow and Market Returns', *Journal of Financial Economics*, 59.

Edmans, A.; D. Garcia, and O. Norli (2007). 'Sports Sentiment and Stock Returns', *Journal of Finance*, 62.

Ekerdt, D. J.; J. Hackney, K. Kosloski, and S. DeViney (2001). 'Eddies in the Stream: The Prevalence of Uncertain Plans for Retirement', *Journals of Gerontology Social Sciences*, 56B.

Ellison, G. and D. Fudenberg (1993). 'Rules of Thumb for Social Learning', *Journal of Political Economy*, 101.

Elmerick, S. A.; C. P. Montalto, and J. J. Fox (2002). 'Use of Financial Planners by US Households', *Financial Services Review*, 11.

Elton, E. J.; M. J. Gruber, and S. Grossman (1986). 'Discrete Expectational Data and Portfolio Performance', *Journal of Finance*, 41.

Elton, E. J.; M. J. Gruber, S. Das, and M. Hlavka (1993). 'Efficiency with Costly Information: A Reinterpretation of Evidence from Managed Portfolios', *Review of Financial Studies*, 6.

Elton, E. J.; M. J. Gruber, and C. R. Blake (1996). 'Survivorship Bias and Mutual Fund Performance', *Review of Financial Studies*, 9.

866

Elton, E. J.; M. J. Gruber, and C. R. Blake (1996a). 'The Persistence of Risk-Adjusted Mutual Fund Performance', *Journal of Business*, 69.

Elton, E. J.; M. J. Gruber, and C. R. Blake (2003). 'Incentive Fees and Mutual Funds', *Journal of Finance*, 58.

Elton, E. J.; M. J. Gruber, and J.A. Busse (2004). 'Are Investors Rational? Choices Among Index Funds', *Journal of Finance*, 59.

Emanuelli, J. F. and R. G. Pearson (1994). 'Using Earnings Estimates for Global Asset Allocation', *Financial Analysts Journal*, 50.

Enderle, F. J.; B. Pope, and L. B. Siegel (2003). 'Broad-Capitalization Indexes of the U.S. Equity Market', *Journal of Investing*, 12.

Erb, C.; C. Harvey, and T. Viskanta (1994). 'Forecasting International Equity Correlations', *Financial Analysts Journal*, 50.

Estelami, H. (1999). 'The Computational Effect of Price Endings in Multi-Dimensional Price Advertising', *Journal of Product & Brand Management*, 8.

Estrada, J.; M. Kritzman, S. Myrgren, and S. Page (2005). 'Countries versus Industries in Europe: A Normative Portfolio Approach', *Journal of Asset Management*, 6.

Ewing, B. T. (2003). 'The Response of the Default Risk Premium to Macroeconomic Shocks', *Quarterly Review of Economics and Finance*, 43.

Fair, R. (2002). 'Events that Shook the Market', *Journal of Business*, 75.

Fama, E. F. (1965). 'The Behavior of Stock Market Prices', *Journal of Business*, 38.

Fama, E. F. (1990). 'Stock Returns, Expected Returns, and Real Activity', *Journal of Finance*, 45.

Fama, E. F. (1991). 'Efficient Capital Markets II', *Journal of Finance*, 46.

Fama, E. F. (1998). 'Market Efficiency: Long-term Returns and Behavioral Finance', *Journal of Financial Economics*, 49.

Fama, E. F. and M. Blume (1966). 'Filter Rules and Stock Market Trading Profits', *Journal of Business*, 39.

Fama, E. F. and J. D. MacBeth (1973). 'Risk, Return and Equilibrium: Empirical Tests', *Journal of Political Economy*, 81.

Fama, E. F. and K. R. French (1988). 'Dividend Yields and Expected Stock Returns', *Journal of Financial Economics*, 22.

Fama, E. F. and K. R. French (1989). 'Business Conditions and Expected Returns on Stocks and Bonds', *Journal of Financial Economics*, 25.

Fama, E. F. and K. R. French (1992). 'The Cross Section of Expected Stock Returns', *Journal of Finance*, 47.

Fama, E. F. and K. R. French (1993). 'Common Risk Factors in the Returns on Stocks and Bonds', *Journal of Financial Economics*, 33.

Fama, E. F. and K. R. French (1996). 'Multifactor Explanations of Asset Pricing Anomalies', *Journal of Finance*, 47.

Fama, E. F. and K. R. French (2004). 'The Capital Asset Pricing Model: Theory and Evidence', *Journal of Economic Perspectives*, 18.

Fama, E. F. and K. R. French (2004a). 'Disagreement, Tastes, and Asset Prices', Working Paper No. 2004–03, Tuck Business School.

Fama, E. F. and K. R. French (2006). 'The Value Premium and the CAPM', *Journal of Finance*, 61.

Fama, E. F.; L. Fisher, M. Jensen, and R. Roll (1969). 'The Adjustment of Stock Prices to New Information', *International Economics Review*, 10.

Farrar, D. E. (1962). *The Investment Decision Under Uncertainty*, Prentice Hall.

Farrow, D. (2006). 'Managing Investor Behavior', *Advisor Today*, December.

Fehle, F.; S. Tsyplakov, and V. Zdorovtsov (2005). 'Can Companies Influence Investor Behaviour through Advertising? Super Bowl Commercials and Stock Returns', *European Financial Management*, 11.

Feinman, J. N. (2005). 'Inflation Illusion and the (Mis) Pricing of Assets and Liabilities', *Journal of Investing*, 14.

Feldman, B. and D. Roy (2005). 'Passive Options-Based Investment Strategies: The Case of the CBOE S&P 500 BuyWrite Index', *Journal of Investing*, 14.

Fenton-O'Creevy, M.; N. Nicholson, E. Soane, and P. Willman (2003). 'Trading on Illusions: Unrealistic Perceptions of Control and Trading Performance', *Journal of Occupational and Organisational Psychology*, 76.

Fenton-O'Creevy, M.; N. Nicholson, E. Soane, and P. Willman (2005). *Traders: Risks, Decisions, and Management in Financial Markets*, Oxford University Press.

Ferguson, R. and D. Leistikow (2001). 'Valuing Active Managers, Fees, and Fund Discounts', *Financial Analysts Journal*, 57.

Ferguson, R. and D. Leistikow (2004). 'Closed-End Fund Discounts and Expected Investment Performance', *Financial Review*, 39.

Ferris, S. P.; R. A. Haugen, and A. K. Makhija (1987). 'Predicting Contemporary Volume with Historic Volume at Differential Price Levels: Evidence Supporting the Disposition Effect', *Journal of Finance*, 43.

Fesenmaier, J. and G. Smith (2002). 'The Nifty-Fifty Re-Visited', *Journal of Investing*, 11.

Fidelity International (2005). 'Market Review'.

Fielding, D. and L. Stracca (2007). 'Myopic Loss Aversion, Disappointment Aversion, and the Equity Premium Puzzle', *Journal of Economic Behavior and Organization*, 64.

Filbeck, G.; P. Hatfield, and P. Horvath (2005). 'Risk Aversion and Personality Type', *Journal of Behavioral Finance*, 6.

Finnerty, J. E. (1976). 'Insiders and Market Efficiency,' *Journal of Finance*, 31.

Finnerty, J. E. (1976a). 'Insiders' Activity and Inside Information: A Multivariate Analysis', *Journal of Financial and Quantitative Analysis*, 11.

Firth, M. (1975). 'The Information Content of Large Investment Holdings', *Journal of Finance*, 30.

Firth, M. (1978). *Unit Trusts: Performance and Prospects*, MCB Publications.

Fischhoff, B. (1982). 'For Those Condemned to Study the Past: Heuristics and Biases in Hindsight', in D. Kahneman, P. Slovic, and A. Tversky (eds) *Judgment Under Uncertainty: Heuristics and Biases*, Cambridge University Press.

Fischhoff, B.; P. Slovic, and S. Lichtenstein (1977). 'Knowing with Certainty: The Appropriateness of Extreme Confidence', *Journal of Experimental Psychology, Human Precision and Performance*, 4.

Fisher, K. L. and M. Statman (1999). 'A Behavioral Framework for Time Diversification', *Financial Analysts Journal*, 55.

Fisher, K. L. and M. Statman (2000). 'Investor Sentiment and Stock Returns', *Financial Analysts Journal*, 56.

Fisher, K. L. and M. Statman (2002). 'Blowing Bubbles', *Journal of Psychology and Financial Markets*, 3.

Fisher, K. L. and M. Statman (2004). 'Sentiment, Value, and Market-Timing', *Journal of Investing*, 13.

Flanegin, F. R. and D. P. Rudd (2005). 'Should Investments Professors Join the "Crowd"', *Managerial Finance*, 31.

Flannery, M. J. and A. A. Protopapadakis (2002). 'Macroeconomic Factors *Do* Influence Aggregate Stock Returns', *Review of Financial Studies*, 15.

Fleming, M. J. and E. M. Remolona (1999). 'What Moves Bond Prices?', *Journal of Portfolio Management*, 25.

Fletcher, J. and J. Kihanda (2006). 'An Examination of Alternative CAPM-Based Models in UK Stock Returns', *Journal of Banking and Finance*, 29.

Foresi, S. and L. Wu (2005). 'Crash-O-Phobia: A Domestic Fear or a Worldwide Concern?', *Journal of Derivatives*, 13.

Forgas, J. P. (1995). 'Mood and Judgment: The Affect Infusion Model (AIM)', *Psychological Bulletin*, 117.

Forner, C. and J. Marhuenda (2003). 'Contrarian and Momentum Strategies in the Spanish Stock Market', *European Financial Management*, 9.

Fortuna, P. S. (2000). 'Old and New Perspectives on Equity Risk', AIMR Conference Proceedings.

Fortune, P. (1991). 'Stock Market Efficiency: An Autopsy?', *New England Economic Review*, March/April.

Foster, G. (1979). 'Briloff and the Capital Markets', *Journal of Accounting Research*, 17.

Francis, J.; Q. Chen, D. R. Philbrick, and R. H. Willis (2004). *Security Analyst Independence*, Research Foundation of CFA Institute Monograph.

Franzoni, F. and J. M. Marin (2006). 'Pension Plan Funding and Stock Market Efficiency', *Journal of Finance*, 61.

Fraser, S. P.; W. W. Jennings, and D. R. King (2000). 'Strategic Asset Allocation for Individual Investors: The Impact of the Present Value of Social Security Benefits', *Financial Services Review*, 9.

Fraser, W. D.; C. Leishman, and H. Tarbert (2002). 'The Long-Run Diversification Attributes of Commercial Property', *Journal of Property Investment & Finance*, 20.

Frazzini, A. (2006). 'The Disposition Effect and Under Reaction to News', *Journal of Finance*, 61.

Frederick, S. (2005). 'Cognitive Reflection and Decision Making', *Journal of Economic Perspectives*, 19.

French, K. (1980). 'Stock Returns and the Weekend Effect', *Journal of Financial Economics*, 8.

French, K. and J. Poterba (1991). 'Investor Diversification and International Equity Markets', *American Economic Review*, 81.

Friedland, N.; G. Keinan, and Y. Regev (1992). 'Controlling the Uncontrollable – Effects of Stress on Illusory Perceptions of Controllability', *Journal of Personality and Social Psycholgy*, 63.

Friedman, M. (1957). *A Theory of the Consumption Function*, Princeton University Press.

Friend, I.; F. Brown, E. Herman, and D. Vickers (1962). 'A Study of Mutual Funds', US Government Printing Office.

Friend, I.; R. Westerfield, and M. Granito (1978). 'New Evidence on the Capital Asset Pricing Model', *Journal of Finance*, 33.

Froot, K. and K. Rogoff (1995). 'Perspectives on PPP and Long-Run Real Exchange Rates', in G. M. Grossman and K. Rogoff (eds) *Handbook of International Economics*, Vol. 3, North-Holland.

Froot, K. and E. Dabora (1999). 'How Are Stock Prices Affected by the Location of Trade?', *Journal of Financial Economics*, 53.

Fuller, R. J. and G. W. Wong (1988). 'Traditional Versus Theoretical Risk Measures', *Financial Analysts Journal*, 44.

Fung, H-G.; X. E. Xu, and J. Yau (2004). 'Do Hedge Fund Managers Display Skill?', *Journal of Alernative Investments*, 6.

Fung, J. K. W. (2007). 'Order Imbalance and the Pricing of Index Futures', *Journal of Futures Markets*, 27.

Gadarowski, S. (2001). 'Financial Press Coverage and Stock Returns', Cornell University Working Paper.

Galbraith, J. K. (1988). *The Great Crash 1929*, Houghton Mifflin.

Gallimore, P. (1994). 'Aspects of Information Processing in Valuation Judgment and Choice', *Journal of Property Research*, 11.

Gallimore, P. (1996). 'Confirmation Bias in the Valuation Process: A Test for Corroborating Evidence', *Journal of Property Research*, 13.

Gallo, J. G. and L. J. Lockwood (1999). 'Fund Management Changes and Equity Style Shifts', *Financial Analysts Journal*, 55.

Garrett, I. and R. Priestley (1997). 'Do Assumptions about Factor Structure Matter in Empirical Tests of the APT?', *Journal of Business Finance and Accounting*, 24.

Gaspar, J-M.; M. Massa, and P. Matos (2006). 'Favoritism in Mutual Fund Families? Evidence on Strategic Cross-Fund Subsidization', *Journal of Finance*, 61.

Gemmill, G. (2006). 'Catering for Dividends by Stripping Mutual-Fund Portfolios: The Rise and Fall of Split-Capital Investment Trusts', paper presented to the Behavioural Finance and Market Efficiency Workshop, University of Warwick, March.

Gemmill, G. and D. C. Thomas (2006). 'The Impact of Corporate Governance on Closed-end Funds', *European Financial Management*, 12.

Genesove, D. and C. Mayer (2001). 'Loss Aversion and Seller Behaviour', *Quarterly Journal of Economics*, 116

Gibbons, M. and P. Hess (1983). 'Day of the Week Effects and Asset Returns', *Journal of Business*, 54.

Gibson, C. (2004). 'Why Analysts are Entangled in a Web of Influence', *Financial Times*, 24/25 January.

Gillan, S. and L. Starks (2000). 'Corporate Governance Proposals and Shareholder Activism: The Role of Institutional Investors', *Journal of Financial Economics*, 57.

Giuliodori, M. (2005). 'The Role of House Prices in the Monetary Transmission Mechanism across European Countries', *Scottish Journal of Political Economy*, 52.

Givoly, D. and J. Lakonishok (1979). 'The Information Content of Financial Analysts' Forecasts of Earnings: Some Evidence on Semi-Strong Inefficiency', *Journal of Accounting and Economics*, 1.

Glaum, M. and N. Friedrich (2006). 'After the "Bubble": Valuation of Telecommunications Companies by Financial Analysts', *Journal of International Financial Management & Accounting*, 17.

Glickstein, D. A. and R. E. Wubbels (1983). 'Dow Theory is Alive and Well', *Journal of Portfolio Management*, 9.

Goetzmann, W. and N. Peles (1997). 'Cognitive Dissonance and Mutual Fund Investors', *Journal of Financial Research*, 20.

Gollwitzer, P. M. and R. F. Kinney (1989). 'Effects of Deliberative and Implemental Mind-Sets on Illusion of Control', *Journal of Personality and Social Psychology*, 56.

Gooding, A. E. (1978). 'Perceived Risk and Capital Asset Pricing', *Journal of Finance*, 33.

Goyal, A. and P. Santa-Clara (2003). 'Idiosyncratic Risk Matters!', *Journal of Finance*, 58.

Grable, J. E. and S. Joo (1997). 'Determinants of Risk Preference: Implications for Family and Consumer Services Professionals', *Family Economics and Resource Management Biennial*, 2.

Grable, J. E. and R. H. Lytton (1997). 'Determinants of Retirement Savings Plan Participation: A Discriminant Analysis', *Personal Finances and Worker Productivity*, 1.

Grable, J.; R. Lytton, and B. O'Neill (2004). 'Projection Bias and Financial Risk Tolerance', *Journal of Behavioral Finance*, 5.

Grable, J.; R.H. Lytton, B. O'Neill, S-H. Joo, and D. Klock (2006). 'Risk Tolerance, Projection Bias, Vividness, and Equity Prices', *Journal of Investing*, 15.

Graff, R. A.; A. Harrington, and M. S. Young (1999). 'Serial Persistence in Disaggregated Australian Real Estate Returns', *Journal of Real Estate Portfolio Management*, 5.

Graham, J. R. and C. R. Harvey (1997). 'Grading the Performance of Market Timing Newsletters', *Financial Analysts Journal*, 53.

Gregoriou, G. N. (2002). 'Hedge Fund Survival Lifetimes', *Journal of Asset Management*, 3.

Gregory, A. and I. Tonks (2006). 'Performance of Personal Pension Schemes in the UK', Exeter University.

Gregory, A.; J. Matatko, I. Tonks, and R. Purkis (1994). 'UK Directors' Trading: the Impact of Dealings in Smaller Firms', *Economic Journal*, 100.

Griffiths, I. (1995). *New Creative Accounting: How To Make Your Profits What You Want Them To Be*, Macmillan.

Grinblatt, M. and S. Titman (1993). 'Performance Measurement without Benchmarks: An Examination of Mutual Fund Returns', *Journal of Business*, 66.

Grinblatt, M. and B. Han (2001). 'The Disposition Effect and Momentum', UCLA Working Paper.

Grinblatt, M. and M. Keloharju (2001). 'What Makes Investors Trade?', *Journal of Finance*, 56.

Groocock, J. (1998). 'Effective Quality Assurance in the Personal Investment Industry: Part 1 – An Impossible Task?', *Managing Service Quality*, 8.

Grossman, S. and J. Stiglitz (1980). 'On the Impossibility of Informationally Efficient Markets', *American Economic Review*, June.

Grundy, K. and B. G. Malkiel (1996). 'Reports of Beta's Death have been Greatly Exaggerated', *Journal of Portfolio Management*, 22.

Gu, A. Y. (2003). 'The Declining January Effect: Evidences from the U.S. Equity Markets', *Quarterly Review of Economics and Finance*, 43.

Gu, A. Y. (2004). 'The Reversing Weekend Effect', *Review of Quantitative Finance and Accounting*, 22.

Guerard, J. B. (1997). 'Is There a Cost to Being Socially Responsible in Investing: It Costs Nothing to Be Good?', *Journal of Investing*, 6.

Gultekin, M. N. and N. B. Gultekin (1983). 'Stock Market Seasonality: International Evidence', *Journal of Financial Economics*, 12.

Guyatt, D. (2005). 'Meeting Objectives and Resisting Conventions: A Focus on Institutional Investors and Long-Term Responsible Investing', *Corporate Governance*, 5.

Halifax Financial Services (2005). 'Savings Ratios over the Decades'.

Hallahan, T. A.; R. W. Faff, and M. D. McKenzie (2004). 'An Empirical Investigation of Personal Financial Risk Tolerance', *Financial Services Review*, 13.

Hanley, K. W. (1993). 'The Underpricing of Initial Public Offerings and the Partial Adjustment Phenomenon', *Journal of Financial Economics*, 34.

Harlow, W. V. and K. C. Brown (2006). 'The Right Answer to the Wrong Question: Identifying Superior Active Portfolio Management', *Journal of Investment Management*, 4.

Harmer, G. P. and D. Abbott (1999). 'Game Theory: Losing Strategies Can Win by Parrondo's Paradox', *Nature*, 402.

Harney, M. and E. Tower (2003). 'Predicting Equity Returns Using Tobin's q and Price-Earnings Ratios', *Journal of Investing*, 12.

Harris, D. (2007). 'The Products They Are A Changin'', *Money Management* (UK), single premium bonds supplement, June.

Harrison, D. (2005). *Personal Financial Planning*, FT Prentice Hall.

Harrison, T.; K. Waite, and P. White (2006). 'Analysis by Paralysis: The Pension Purchase Decision Process', *International Journal of Bank Marketing*, 24.

Hartzell, J. C. and L. T. Starks (2003). 'Institutional Investors and Executive Compensation', *Journal of Finance*, 58.

Hashemazadeh, N. and P. Taylor (1988). 'Stock Prices, Money Supply, and Interest Rates: The Question of Causality', *Applied Economics*, 20.

Hauser, T. and D. Vermeersch (2002). 'Is Country Diversification Still Better Than Sector Diversification?', *Financial Markets and Portfolio Management*, 16.

Heal, G. (2001). 'The Bottom Line to a Social Conscience', Financial Times (Mastering Investment Supplement, Part 8), 2 July. Reprinted in K. Redhead, *Introducing Investments: A Personal Finance Approach*, Financial Times Prentice Hall, 2003.

Heath, C.; S. Huddart, and M. Lang (1999). 'Psychological Factors and Stock Option Exercise', *Quarterly Journal of Economics*, 114.

Hedesstrom, T. M.; H. Svedsater, and T. Garling (2004). 'Identifying Heuristic Choice Rules in the Swedish Premium Pension Scheme', *Journal of Behavioral Finance*, 5.

Hedesstrom, T. M.; H. Svedsater, and T. Garling (2007). 'Determinants of the Use of Heuristic Choice Rules in the Swedish Premium Pension Scheme: An Internet-Based Survey', *Journal of Economic Psychology*, 28.

Hendricks, D.; J. Patel, and R. Zeckhauser (1993). 'Hot Hands in Mutual Funds: Short-Run Persistence of Relative Performance, 1974–1988', *Journal of Finance*, 48.

REFERENCES

Henriksson, R. D. (1984). 'Market Timing and Mutual Fund Performance: An Empirical Investigation', *Journal of Business*, 57.

Hershey, D. A. and J. C. Mowen (2000). 'Psychological Determinants of Financial Preparedness for Retirement', *The Gerontologist*, 40.

Herzberg, M. M. and S. Wang (2002). 'Identifying Lead Analysts for Stock Selection', *Journal of Investing*, 11.

Heston, S. L.; K. G. Rouwenhorst, and R. E. Wessels (1999). 'The Role of Beta and Size in the Cross-Section of European Stock Returns', *European Financial Management*, 5.

Hill, I. and S. Duffield (2000). 'Ownership of United Kingdom Quoted Companies at the End of 1998', *Economic Trends*, 557.

Hilton, D. J. (2001). 'The Psychology of Financial Decision-Making: Applications to Trading, Dealing, and Investment Analysis', *Journal of Psychology and Financial Markets*, 2.

Hirschey, M. and J. Nofsinger (2008). *Investments: Analysis and Behavior*, McGraw-Hill.

Hirshleifer, D. (2001). 'Investor Psychology and Asset Pricing', *Journal of Finance*, 56.

Hirshleifer, D. and T. Shumway (2003). 'Good Day Sunshine: Stock Returns and the Weather', *Journal of Finance*, 58.

HM Treasury (2002). 'Medium- and Long-Term Retail Savings in the UK: A Review' (Sandler Report), HM Treasury.

Hoch, S. and G. Loewenstein (1991). 'Time-Inconsistent Preferences and Consumer Self-Control', *Journal of Consumer Research*, 17.

Holmes, P. and M. Tomsett (2004). 'Information and Noise in U.K. Futures Markets', *Journal of Futures Markets*, 24.

Hong, H.; T. Lim, and J.C. Stein (2000). 'Bad News Travels Slowly: Size, Analyst Coverage, and the Profitability of Momentum Strategies', *Journal of Finance*, 55.

Hong, H.; K. D. Kubik, and J. C. Stein (2004). 'Social Interaction and Stock-Market Participation', *Journal of Finance*, 59.

Hong, H.; W. Torous, and R. Valkanov (2007). 'Do Industries Lead Stock Markets?', *Journal of Financial Economics*, 83.

House of Commons Treasury Committee (2004). 'Restoring Confidence in Long-Term Savings'.

Huang, L. and H. Liu (2007). 'Rational Inattention and Portfolio Selection', *Journal of Finance*, 62.

Huberman, G. (2001). 'Familiarity Breeds Investment', *Review of Financial Studies*, 14.

Huberman, G. and S. Kandel (1990). 'Market Efficiency and Value Line's Record', *Journal of Business*, 63.

Hudson, J. (2006). *The Social Responsibility of the Investment Profession*, Research Foundation of CFA Institute Monograph.

Hudson, R.; M. Dempsey, and K. Keasey (1996). 'A Note on the Weak Form Efficiency of Capital Markets: The Application of Simple Technical Trading Rules to UK Stock Prices – 1935 to 1994', *Journal of Banking and Finance*, 20.

Huhmann, B. A. and N. Bhattacharyya (2005). 'Does Mutual Fund Advertising Provide Necessary Investment Information?', *International Journal of Bank Marketing*, 23.

Hulbert, M. (1993). *The Hulbert Guide to Financial Newsletters*, Dearborn Financial.

Hunter, D. M. and D. P. Simon (2005). 'A Conditional Assessment of the Relationships between the Major World Bond Markets', *European Financial Management*, 11.

Hussein, K. and M. Omran (2005). 'Ethical Investment Revisited: Evidence from Dow Jones Islamic Indexes', *Journal of Investing*, 14.

Hwang, S. and M. Salmon (2006). 'Sentiment and Beta Herding', paper presented to the Behavioural Finance and Market Efficiency Workshop, University of Warwick, March.

Ibbotson, R. G. and G. P. Brinson (1993). *Global Investing*, McGraw-Hill.

Ibbotson, R.; J. Sindelar, and J. Ritter (1988). 'Initial Public Offerings', *Journal of Applied Corporate Finance*, 1.

Ibbotson, R.; G. Sindelar, and J. Ritter (1994). 'The Market Problem with the Pricing of Initial Public Offerings', *Journal of Applied Corporate Finance*, 7.

Indro, D. C. (2004). 'Does Mutual Fund Flow Reflect Investor Sentiment?', *Journal of Behavioral Finance*, 5.

Indro, D. C.; C. X. Jiang, M. Y. Hu, and W. Y. Lee (1999). 'Mutual Fund Performance: Does Fund Size Matter?', *Financial Analysts Journal*, 55.

Ippolito, R. A. (1989). 'Efficiency with Costly Information: A Study of Mutual Fund Performance, 1965–1984', *Quarterly Journal of Economics*, 104.

Isen, A. M. (1997). 'Positive Affect and Decision Making', in W. M. Goldstein and R. M. Hogarth (eds) *Research on Judgment and Decision Making*, Cambridge University Press.

Iyengar, S. S. and M. R. Lepper (2000). 'When Choice is Demotivating: Can One Desire Too Much of a Good Thing?', *Journal of Personality and Social Psychology*, 79.

Jacobs-Lawson, J. M. and D. A. Hershey (2005). 'Influence of Future Time Perspective, Financial Knowledge, and Financial Risk Tolerance on Retirement Saving Behaviors', *Financial Services Review*, 14.

Jacquier, E. and A. Marcus (2001). 'Asset Allocation Models and Market Volatility', *Financial Analysts Journal*, 57.

Jaffe, J. F. (1974). 'Special Information and Insider Trading', *Journal of Business*, 47.

Jaffe, J.; D. B. Keim, and R. Westerfield (1989). 'Earnings Yields, Market Values, and Stock Returns', *Journal of Finance*, 44.

Jagannathan, R. and Y. Wang (2007). 'Lazy Investors, Discretionary Consumption, and the Cross-Section of Stock Returns', *Journal of Finance*, 62.

Jain, P. C. (1988). 'Responses of Hourly Stock Prices and Trading Volume to Economic News', *Journal of Business*, 61.

Jain, P. C. and J. S. Wu (2000). 'Truth in Mutual Fund Advertising: Evidence on Future Performance and Fund Flows', *Journal of Finance*, 55.

Jan, Y-C. and M-W. Hung (2004). 'Short-Run and Long-Run Persistence in Mutual Funds', *Journal of Investing*, 13.

Jansen, W. J. and N. J. Nahius (2003). 'The Stock Market and Consumer Confidence: European Evidence', *Economic Letters*, 79.

Jegadeesh, N. (1990). 'Evidence of Predictable Behavior of Security Returns', *Journal of Finance*, 45.

Jegadeesh, N. and S. Titman (1993). 'Returns to Buying Winners and Selling Losers: Implications for Stock Market Efficiency', *Journal of Finance*, 48.

Jennergren, P. and P. Korsvold (1975). 'The Non-Random Character of Norwegian and Swedish Stock Market Prices', in E. J. Elton and M. J. Gruber (eds) *International Capital Markets*, North-Holland.

Jensen, G. R.; R. R. Johnson, and J. M. Mercer (1997). 'New Evidence on Size and Price-to-Book Effects in Stock Returns', *Financial Analysts Journal*, 53.

Jensen, M. C. (1968). 'The Performance of Mutual Funds in the Period 1945–1964', *Journal of Finance*, 23.

Jha, V.; D. Lichtblau, and H. Mozes (2003). 'The Usefulness of Analysts' Recommendations', *Journal of Investing*, 12.

Jia, J.; J. S. Dyer, and J. C. Butler (1999). 'Measures of Perceived Risk', *Management Science*, 45.

Johansen, A. and D. Sornette (1999). 'Modelling the Stock Market Prior to Large Crashes', *European Physics Journal*, 9.

Johansen, A. and D. Sornette (2001). 'Bubbles and Antibubbles in Latin American, Asian and Western Stock Markets: An Empirical Study', *International Journal of Theoretical and Applied Finance*, 4.

Jones, C. P.; R. J. Rendleman, and H. A. Latane (1984). 'Stock Returns and SUEs During the 1970s', *Journal of Portfolio Management*, 10.

Jordan, J. and K. P. Kaas (2002). 'Advertising in the Mutual Fund Business: The Role of Judgmental Heuristics in Private Investors' Evaluation of Risk and Return', *Journal of Financial Services Marketing*, 7.

Jung, J. and R. J. Shiller (2002). 'One Simple Test of Samuelson's Dictum for the Stock Market', NBER Working Paper 9348.

Kahn, R. N. and A. Rudd (1995). 'Does Historical Performance Predict Future Performance?', *Financial Analysts Journal*, 51.

Kahneman, D. and A. Tversky (1972). 'Subjective Probability: A Judgment of Representativeness', *Cognitive Psychology*, 3.

Kahneman, D. and A. Tversky (1973). 'On the Psychology of Prediction', *Psychology Review*, 80.

Kahneman, D. and A. Tversky (1979). 'Prospect Theory: An Analysis of Choice Under Risk', *Econometrica*, 47.

Kahneman, D. and A. Tversky (1982). 'The Psychology of Preferences', *Scientific American*, 246.

Kahneman, D. and A. Tversky (1983). 'Extensional Versus Intuitive Reasoning: The Conjunction Fallacy in Probability Judgement', *Psychological Review, 90.*

Kahneman, D. and M. W. Riepe (1998). 'Aspects of Investor Psychology', *Journal of Portfolio Management*, 24.

Kahneman, D.; J. L. Knetsch, and R. H.Thaler (1986). 'Fairness as a Constraint on Profit Seeking', *American Economic Review*, 76.

Kahneman, D.; J. L. Knetsch, and R. H. Thaler (1990). 'Experimental Tests of the Endowment Effect and the Coase Theorem', *Journal of Political Economy*, 98.

Kahneman, D.; J. L. Knetsch, and R. H. Thaler (1991). 'The Endowment Effect, Loss Aversion, and Status Quo Bias', *Journal of Economic Perspectives*, 5.

Kamstra, M.; L. Kramer, and M. Levi (2003). 'Winter Blues: A Sad Stock Market Cycle', *American Economic Review*, 93.

Kang, J. and R. Stulz (1997). 'Why Is There a Home Bias? An Analysis of Foreign Portfolio Equity Ownership in Japan', *Journal of Financial Economics*, 46.

Kanto, A. J.; H. A. Kahra, D. R. Blevins, and H. J. Schadewitz (1998). 'An Explanation of the Unusual Behavior of Some Market Model Residuals', *Finnish Journal of Business Economics*, 47.

Kaplan, R. S. and R. Roll (1972). 'Investor Evaluation of Accounting Information: Some Empirical Evidence', *Journal of Business*, 45.

Karapetrovic, S. and W. Willborn (1999). 'Quality Assurance in Investment Services', *Managing Service Quality*, 9.

Karceski, J. (2002). 'Returns-Chasing Behavior, Mutual Funds, and Beta's Death', *Journal of Financial and Quantitative Analysis*, 37.

Karpoff, J. M.; P. H. Malatesta, and R. A. Walkling (1996). 'Corporate Governance and Shareholder Initiatives: Empirical Evidence', *Journal of Financial Economics*, 42.

Kat, H. M. (2003). '10 Things That Investors Should Know about Hedge Funds', *Journal of Wealth Management*, 5.

Kat, H. M. (2004). 'Why Indexation Can Be a Dangerous Strategy', *Journal of Wealth Management*, 6.

Kat, H. M. (2005). 'Integrating Hedge Funds into the Traditional Portfolio', *Journal of Wealth Management*, 7.

Kat, H. M. and G. S. Amin (2001). 'Hedge Fund Performance 1990–2000: Do the Money Machines Really Add Value?', EFMA Lugano Meetings.

Kat, H. M. and H. P. Palaro (2006). 'Superstars or Average Joes? A Replication-Based Performance Evaluation of 1917 Individual Hedge Funds', Cass Business School, City University, Alternative Investments Research Centre Working Paper 30.

Kato, K. and J. Shallheim (1985). 'Seasonal and Size Anomalies in the Japanese Stock Market', *Journal of Financial and Quantitative Analysis*, 20.

Katona, G. (1975). *Psychological Economics*, Elsevier.

Katz, S.; S. Lilien, and B. Nelson (1985). 'Stock Market Behaviour around Bankruptcy Model Distress and Recovery Predictions', *Financial Analysts Journal*, 41.

Kavanagh, D. J.; J. Andrade, and J. May (2005). 'Imaginary Relish and Exquisite Torture: The Elaborated Intrusion Theory of Desire', *Psychological Review*, 112.

Keim, D. B. (1983). 'Size Related Anomalies and Stock Return Seasonality: Further Empirical Evidence', *Journal of Financial Economics*, 12.

Keim, D. B. and R. F. Stambaugh (1984). 'A Further Investigation of the Weekend Effect in Stock Returns', *Journal of Finance*, 39.

Keller, C. and M. Siegrist (2006). 'Money Attitude Typology and Stock Investment', *Journal of Behavioral Finance*, 7.

Kempf, A. and S. Ruenzi (2006). 'Status Quo Bias and the Number of Alternatives: An Empirical Illustration from the Mutual Fund Industry', *Journal of Behavioral Finance*, 7.

Kendall, M. (1953). 'The Analysis of Economic Time Series, Part I: Prices', *Journal of the Royal Statistical Society*, 96.

Keppler, M. and X. H. Xue (2003). 'The Seasonal Price Behavior of Global Equity Markets', *Journal of Investing*, 12.

Keynes, J. M. (1936). *The General Theory of Employment, Interest and Money*, Macmillan.

Kilka, M. and M. Weber (2000). 'Home Bias in International Stock Return Expectations', *Journal of Psychology and Financial Markets*, 1.

Kim, K. A. and J. R. Nofsinger (2004). *Corporate Governance*, Pearson Prentice Hall.

Kimmel, A. J. (2004). 'Rumors and the Financial Marketplace', *Journal of Behavioral Finance*, 5.

Kimmel, A. J. and A. F. Audrain (2002). 'Rumor Control Strategies within French Consumer Goods Firms', 110th American Psychological Association conference.

Kindleberger, C. P. (1989). *Manias, Panics, and Crashes: A History of Financial Crises*, Macmillan.

Kindleberger, C. P. and R. Z. Aliber (2005). *Manias, Panics, and Crashes: A History of Financial Crises*, 5th edn, Palgrave Macmillan.

King, R. G. and A. Kurmann (2002). 'Expectations and the Term Structure of Interest Rates: Evidence and Implications', *Economic Quarterly, Federal Reserve Bank of Richmond*, 88.

Kirman, A. P. (1991). 'Epidemics of Opinion and Speculative Bubbles in Financial Markets', in M. Taylor (ed.) *Money and Financial Markets*, Macmillan.

Kiymaz, H. (2002). 'The Stock Market Rumours and Stock Prices: A Test of Price Pressure and the Size Effect in an Emerging Market', *Applied Financial Economics*, 12.

Knight, R. (2005). 'Check Behind the Bond Wrapper', *Financial Times*, 16/17 July.

Ko, K. J. and Z. Huang (2007). 'Arrogance Can Be a Virtue: Overconfidence, Information Acquisition, and Market Efficiency', *Journal of Financial Economics*, 84.

Kohers, T. and G. Kohers (1995). 'The Impact of Firm Size Differences on the Day-of-the-Week Effect: A Comparison of Major Stock Markets', *Applied Financial Economics*, 5.

Kolb, R. A. and H. O. Stekler (1996). 'How Well do Analysts Forecast Interest Rates?', *Journal of Forecasting*, 15.

Kon, S. J. (1983). 'The Market-Timing Performance of Mutual Fund Managers', *Journal of Business*, 56.

Kosowski, R.; A. Timmermann, R. Wermers, and H. White (2006). 'Can Mutual Fund "Stars" Really Pick Stocks? New Evidence from a Bootstrap Analysis', *Journal of Finance*, 61.

Kothari, S. P. and J. Shanken (2002). *Anomalies and Efficient Portfolio Formation*, Research Foundation of AIMR Monograph.

Kothari, S. P.; J. Shanken, and R. G. Sloan (1995). 'Another Look at the Cross-Section of Expected Returns', *Journal of Finance*, 50.

Kraus, A. and H. R. Stoll (1972). 'Price Impacts of Block Trading on the New York Stock Exchange', *Journal of Finance*, 27.

875

Kyriazis, D. and C. Anastassis (2007). 'The Validity of the Economic Value Added Approach: An Empirical Application', *European Financial Management*, 13.

Laatsch, F. E. and D. P. Klein (2003). 'Nominal Rates, Real Rates, and Expected Inflation: Results from a Study of U.S. Treasury Inflation-Protected Securities', *Quarterly Review of Economics and Finance*, 43.

Lakonishok, J. and A. C. Shapiro (1984). 'Stock Returns, Beta, Variance and Size: An Empirical Analysis', *Financial Analysts Journal*, 40.

Lakonishok, J.; A. Shleifer, and R. W. Vishny (1992). 'The Structure and Performance of the Money Management Industry', *Brookings Papers on Economic Activity: Microeconomics*.

Lakonishok, J.; A. Shleifer, and R. W. Vishny (1994). 'Contrarian Investment, Extrapolation and Risk', *Journal of Finance*, 49.

Lamont, O. A. and R. H. Thaler (2003). 'Anomalies: The Law of One Price in Financial Markets', *Journal of Economic Perspectives*, 17.

Langer, E. J. (1975). 'The Illusion of Control', *Journal of Personality and Social Psychology*, 32.

La Porta, R. (1996). 'Expectations and the Cross Section of Stock Returns', *Journal of Finance*, 51.

La Porta, R.; F. Lopez-de-Silanes, A. Shleifer, and R. Vishny (2000). 'Investor Protection and Corporate Governance', *Journal of Financial Economics*, 58.

Latane, H. A. and C. P. Jones (1979). 'Standardized Unexpected Earnings: 1971–1977', *Journal of Finance*, 34.

Latzko, D. A. (1999). 'Economies of Scale in Mutual Fund Administration', *Journal of Financial Research*, 22.

Lee, C. (2003). 'Fusion Investing', paper presented to the Equity Valuation in a Global Context Conference, AIMR.

Lee, C.; A. Shleifer, and R. Thaler (1991). 'Investor Sentiment and the Closed-End Fund Puzzle', *Journal of Finance*, 46.

Lee, I. H. (1998). 'Market Crashes and Informational Avalanches', *Review of Economic Studies*, 65.

Lee, J. (2002). 'A Key to Marketing Financial Services: The Right Mix of Products, Services, Channels and Customers', *Journal of Services Marketing*, 16.

Lee, S. and S. Stevenson (2006). 'Real Estate in the Mixed-Asset Portfolio: The Question of Consistency', *Journal of Property Investment & Finance*, 24.

Lee, S. L. and C. W. R. Ward (2001). 'Persistence of UK Real Estate Returns: A Markov Chain Analysis', *Journal of Asset Management*, 1.

Lee, W. Y. and M. E. Solt (1986). 'Insider Trading: A Poor Guide to Market Timing', *Journal of Portfolio Management*, 12.

Lehmann, B. (1990). 'Fads, Martingales and Market Efficiency', *Quarterly Journal of Economics*, 105.

Leijonhufvud, A. (1968). *On Keynesian Economics and the Economics of Keynes*, Oxford University Press.

Leland, H. E. (1987). *On the Stock Market Crash and Portfolio Insurance*, University of California, Berkeley.

Lerner, J. S.; D. A. Small, and G. Loewenstein (2004). 'Heart Strings and Purse Strings: Carryover Effects of Emotions on Economic Decisions', *Psychological Science*, 15.

Lesmond, D. A.; M. J. Schill, and C. Zhou (2004). 'The Illusory Nature of Momentum Profits', *Journal of Financial Economics*, 71.

Lev, B. and S. R. Thiagarajan (1993). 'Fundamental Information Analysis', *Journal of Accounting Research*, 31.

Levin, E. J. and R. E. Wright (1998). 'The Information Content of the Gilt–Equity Yield Ratio', *Manchester School*, 66.

Levis, M. (1989). 'Stock Market Anomalies: A Re-Assessment Based on UK Evidence', *Journal of Banking and Finance*, 13.

876

Levy, H. and Z. Lerman (1985). 'Testing P/E Ratio Filters with Stochastic Dominance', *Journal of Portfolio Management*, 10.

Levy, H. and T. Post (2005). *Investments*, FT Prentice Hall.

Levy, R. (1966). 'Conceptual Foundations of Technical Analysis', *Financial Analysts Journal*, 22.

Lewellen, J. and S. Nagel (2006). 'The Conditional CAPM Does Not Explain Asset-Pricing Anomalies', *Journal of Financial Economics*, 82.

Lhabitant, F-S. and M. Learned (2002). 'Hedge Fund Diversification: How Much Is Enough?', *Journal of Alternative Investments*, 5.

Lichenstein, S. and B. Fischoff (1977). 'Do Those Who Know More Also Know More About How They Know? The Calibration of Probability Judgements', *Organizational Behavior and Human Performance*, 3.

Liden, E. R. (2006). 'Stock Recommendations in Swedish Printed Media: Leading or Misleading?', *European Journal of Finance*, 12.

Lim, S. S. (2006). 'Do Investors Integrate Losses and Segregate Gains? Mental Accounting and Investor Trading Decisions', *Journal of Business*, 79.

Lin, C-H.; S-C. Chuang, D. T. Kao, and C-Y. Kung (2006). 'The Role of Emotions in the Endowment Effect', *Journal of Economic Psychology*, 27.

Lin, C-H.; W-H. Huang, and M. Zeelenberg (2006a). 'Multiple Reference Points in Investor Regret', *Journal of Economic Psychology*, 27.

Liu, W. (2006). 'A Liquidity-Augmented Capital Asset Pricing Model', *Journal of Financial Economics*, 82.

Liu, W.; N. Strong, and X. Xu (2001). 'Post Earnings Announcement Drift in the UK', LUMS Working Paper.

Liu, W.; N. Strong, and X. Xu (2003). 'Post-Earnings-Announcement Drift in the UK', *European Financial Management*, 9.

Ljungqvist, A.; F. Marston, L. T. Starks, K. D. Wei, and H. Yan (2007). 'Conflicts of Interest in Sell-Side Research and the Moderating Role of Institutional Investors', *Journal of Financial Economics*, 85.

Lo, A. W. (2004). 'The Adaptive Markets Hypothesis: Market Efficiency from an Evolutionary Perspective', *Journal of Portfolio Management*, 30.

Lo, A. W.; H. Mamaysky, and J. Wang (2000). 'Foundations of Technical Analysis', *Journal of Finance*, 55.

Lo, W. and G. MacKinlay (1988). 'Stock Market Prices Do Not Follow Random Walks: Evidence from a Simple Specification Test', *Review of Financial Studies*, 1.

Locke, P. and S. Mann (1999). 'Do Professional Traders Exhibit Loss Aversion?' Working Paper.

Loewenstein, G. F.; E. U. Weber, C. K. Hsee, and N. Welch (2001). 'Risk as Feelings', *Psychological Bulletin*, 127.

Loewenstein, G.; T. O'Donoghue, and M. Rabin (2003). 'Projection Bias in Predicting Future Utility', *Quarterly Journal of Economics*, 118.

Lofthouse, S. (2001). *Investment Management*, 2nd edn, Wiley.

Longin, F. (2001). 'Portfolio Insurance and Market Crashes', *Journal of Asset Management*, 2.

Longin, F. and B. Solnik (1995). 'Is the Correlation in International Equity Returns Constant: 1960–1990?', *Journal of International Money and Finance*, 14.

Longin, F. and B. Solnik (2001). 'Extreme Correlation of International Equity Markets', *Journal of Finance*, 56.

Longstaff, F. (1992). 'Are Negative Option Prices Possible?', *Journal of Business*, 65.

Loughran, T. (1997). 'Book-to-Market Across Firm Size, Exchange, and Seasonality', *Journal of Financial and Quantitative Analysis*, 32.

Lovatt, D. and A. Parikh (2000). 'Stock Returns and Economic Activity: The UK Case', *European Journal of Finance*, 6.

Lovatt, D.; A. Boswell, and R. Noor (2007). 'A Note on the Predictability of UK Stock Returns', *European Journal of Finance*, 13.

Lovink, G. (2002). *Dark Fiber: Tracking Critical Internet Culture*, MIT Press.

Lusardi, A. (1999). 'Information, Expectations, and Savings for Retirement', in H. J. Aaron (ed.) *Behavioral Dimensions of Retirement*, Brookings Institution Press.

Lynch, A. (2001). 'Thought Contagions in the Stock Market', *Journal of Psychology and Financial Markets*, 1.

Lynch, W. A. and R. R. Mendenhall (1997). 'New Evidence on Stock Price Effects Associated with Changes in the S&P 500 Index', *Journal of Business*, 70.

McGreal, S.; A. Adair, J. N. Berry, and J. R. Webb (2006). 'Institutional Real Estate Portfolio Diversification in Ireland and the UK', *Journal of Property Investment & Finance*, 24.

MacGregor, D. G.; P. Slovic, D. Dreman, and M. Berry (2000). 'Imagery, Affect, and Financial Judgment', *Journal of Psychology and Financial Markets*, 1.

MacKay, C. (1852). 'Extraordinary Popular Delusions and the Madness of Crowds' (republished by Barnes & Noble, 1989).

McKenzie, M. D.; T. J. Brailsford, and R. W. Faff (2001). 'New Insights into the Impact of the Introduction of Futures Trading on Stock Price Volatility', *Journal of Futures Markets*, 21.

MacKillop, S. (2003). 'Confidence Builder', *Investment Advisor*, March.

McMillan, D. G. and A. E. H. Speight (2006). 'Nonlinear Dynamics and Competing Behavioral Interpretations: Evidence from Intra-Day FTSE-100 Index and Futures Data', *Journal of Futures Markets*, 26.

McRae, T. (1995). *Personal Financial Planning*, Chapman & Hall.

Madhavan, A. and K. Ming (2003). 'The Hidden Costs of Index Rebalancing', *Journal of Investing*, 12.

Madrian, B. C. and D. F. Shea (2000). 'The Power of Suggestion: Inertia in 401(k) Participation and Savings Behavior', *Social Science Research Network*, April.

Malkiel, B. G. (1988). 'Is the Stock Market Efficient?', Princeton University Financial Research Center, Memorandum 97.

Malkiel, B. G. (1995). 'Returns from Investing in Equity Mutual Funds', *Journal of Finance*, 50.

Malkiel, B. G. (2003). 'The Efficient Market Hypothesis and its Critics', *Journal of Economic Perspectives*, 17.

Malkiel, B. G. (2003a). 'Passive Investment Strategies and Efficient Markets', *European Financial Management*, 9.

Malkiel, B. G. and J. G. Cragg (1970). 'Expectations and the Structure of Share Prices', *American Economic Review*, 60.

Malkiel, B. G. and A. Radisich (2001). 'The Growth of Index Funds and the Pricing of Equity Securities', *Journal of Portfolio Management*, 26.

Malmendier, U. and D. Shanthikumar (2007). 'Are Small Investors Naïve About Incentives?', *Journal of Financial Economics*, 85.

Marais, D. (1982). 'Corporate Financial Strength', *Bank of England Quarterly Bulletin*, June.

Marcato, G. and T. Key (2005). 'Direct Investment in Real Estate: Momentum Profits and Their Robustness to Trading Costs', *Journal of Portfolio Management*, 32.

Marcus, A. J. (1990). 'The Magellan Fund and Market Efficiency', *Journal of Portfolio Management*, 17.

Markowitz, H. (1952). 'Portfolio Selection', *Journal of Finance*, 7.

Markowitz, H. (1959). *Portfolio Selection: Efficient Diversification of Investments*, Wiley.

Marshall, B. R.; M. R. Young, and L. C. Rose (2006). 'Candlestick Technical Trading Strategies: Can They Create Value for Investors?', *Journal of Banking and Finance*, 30.

Mehra, R. and R. Sah (2002). 'Mood Fluctuations, Projection Bias, and Volatility of Equity Prices', *Journal of Economic Dynamics and Control*, 26.

Mei, J. and L. Guo (2004). 'Political Uncertainty, Financial Crisis and Market Volatility', *European Financial Management*, 10.

Meric, I.; L. W. Coopersmith, D. Wise, and G. Meric (2002). 'Major Stock Market Linkages in the 2000–2001 Bear Market', *Journal of Investing*, 11.

Merton, R. C. (1973). 'Theory of Rational Option Pricing', *Bell Journal of Economics and Management Science*, 4.

Merton, R. C. (1980). 'On Estimating the Expected Return on the Market: An Exploratory Investigation', *Journal of Financial Economics*, 8.

Merton, R. C. (1987). 'A Simple Model of Capital Market Equilibrium with Incomplete Information', *Journal of Finance*, 42.

Michaely, R. and K. L. Womack (1999). 'Conflict of Interest and the Credibility of Underwriter Analyst Recommendations', *Review of Financial Studies*, 12.

Mikhail, M. B.; B. R. Walther, and R. H. Willis (2004). 'Do Security Analysts Exhibit Persistent Differences in Stock Picking Ability?', *Journal of Financial Economics*, 74.

Miles, D. and A. Timmermann (1996). 'Variations in Expected Stock Returns: Evidence on the Pricing of Equities from a Cross-Section of UK Companies', *Economica*, 63.

Miller, M. H. and F. Modigliani (1961). 'Dividend Policy, Growth, and the Valuation of Shares', *Journal of Business*, 34.

Miller, R. E. and F. K. Reilly (1987). 'Examination of Mispricing, Returns, and Uncertainty for Initial Public Offerings', *Financial Management*, 16.

Mills, T. C. (1997). 'Technical Analysis and the London Stock Exchange: Testing Trading Rules Using the FT30', *International Journal of Finance and Economics*, 2.

Minhas, R. S. and E. M. Jacobs (1996). 'Benefit Segmentation by Factor Analysis: An Improved Method of Targeting Customers for Financial Services', *International Journal of Bank Marketing*, 14.

Mitchell, O. S. and J. F. Moore (1998). 'Can Americans Afford to Retire? New Evidence on Retirement Savings Adequacy', *Journal of Risk Insurance*, 65.

Mitchell, O. S. and S. P. Utkus (2004). *Pension Design and Structure: New Lessons from Behavioral Finance*, Oxford University Press.

Mitchell, O. S. and S. P. Utkus (2006). 'How Behavioral Finance Can Inform Retirement Plan Design', *Journal of Applied Corporate Finance*, 18.

Modigliani, F. and R. Cohn (1979). 'Inflation, Rational Valuation, and the Market', *Financial Analysts Journal*, 35.

Modigliani, F. and L. Modigliani (1997). 'Risk-Adjusted Performance', *Journal of Portfolio Management*, 23.

Montezuma, J. (2004). 'Owner-Occupied Housing and Household Asset Allocation: A Review of the Issues', *Property Management*, 22.

Montier, J. (2002). *Behavioural Finance*, Wiley.

Montier, J. (2003/2004). 'Part Man, Part Monkey', *Professional Investor*, December/January.

Montier, J. (2007). *Behavioural Investing: A Practitioner's Guide to Applying Behavioural Finance*, Wiley.

Mookerjee, R. (1987). 'Monetary Policy and the Informational Efficiency of the Stock Market: The Evidence from Many Countries', *Applied Economics*, 19.

Moore, A. (1964). 'Some Characteristics of Changes in Common Stock Prices', in P. Cootner (ed.) *The Random Character of Stock Market Prices*, MIT Press.

Moore, D.; T. Kurtzberg, C. Fox, and M. Bazerman (1999). 'Positive Illusions and Forecasting Errors in Mutual Fund Investment Decisions', *Organizational Behavior and Human Decision Processes*, 79.

Moore, D. A.; P. E. Tetlock, L. Tanlu, and M. H. Bazeman (2006). 'Conflicts of Interest and the Case of Auditor Independence: Moral Seduction and Strategic Issue Cycling', *Academy of Management Review*, 31.

Moore, G. H. and J. P. Cullity (1988). 'Security Markets and Business Cycles', in S. N. Levine (ed.) *The Financial Analyst's Handbook*, 2nd edn, Dow Jones-Irwin.

Mosebach, M. and M. Najand (1999). 'Are the Structural Changes in Mutual Funds Investing Driving the U.S. Stock Market to Its Current Levels?', *Journal of Financial Research*, 22.

Muga, L. and R. Santamaria (2007). '"New Economy" Firms and Momentum', *Journal of Behavioral Finance*, 8.

Mukherji, S. (2002). 'Stocks, Bonds, Bills, Wealth, and Time Diversification', *Journal of Investing*, 11.

Murphy, R. J. (2002). 'Omega: A More Complete Picture of Investment Performance', *Journal of Wealth Management*, 5.

Mussweiler, T. and K. Schneller (2003). '"What Goes Up Must Come Down" – How Charts Influence Decisions to Buy and Sell Stocks', *Journal of Behavioral Finance*, 4.

Naranjo, A.; M. Nimalendran, and M. Ryngaert (1998). 'Stock Returns, Dividend Yields, and Taxes', *Journal of Finance*, 53.

Naser, K. and M. Pendelbury (1992). 'A Note on the Use of Creative Accounting', *British Accounting Review*, 24.

Neal, R. and S. M. Wheatley (1998). 'Do Measures of Investor Sentiment Predict Returns?', *Journal of Financial and Quantitative Analysis*, 33.

Nejat, H. and H. Seyhun (1986). 'Insiders' Profits, Costs of Trading, and Market Efficiency', *Journal of Financial Economics*, 51.

Neukam, K. A. and D. A. Hershey (2003). 'Financial Inhibition, Financial Activation, and Saving for Retirement', *Financial Services Review*, 12.

Nevins, D. (2004). 'Goals-Based Investing: Integrating Traditional and Behavioral Finance', *Journal of Wealth Management*, 6.

Newlands, C. (2007). 'The French State Pensions Reserve Fund Continues to Thrive, and Survived the Potentially Disruptive Stock Market Correction of Last Year', *European Pensions and Investment News*, 12 February.

Niarchos, N. A. and C. A. Alexakis (2003). 'Intraday Stock Price Patterns in the Greek Stock Exchange', *Applied Financial Economics*, 13.

Niederhoffer, F. M. and M. F. M. Osborne (1966). 'Market Making and Reversal on the Stock Exchange', *Journal of the American Statistical Association*, 61.

Nofsinger, J. R. (2001). 'The Impact of Public Information on Investors', *Journal of Banking and Finance*, 25.

Nofsinger, J. R. (2002). *The Psychology of Investing*, Pearson Education/Prentice Hall.

Nofsinger, J. R. (2002a). *Investment Blunders*, FT Prentice Hall.

Nofsinger, J. R. (2002b). 'Do Optimists Make the Best Investors?', *Corporate Finance Review*, 6.

Nofsinger, J. R. (2005). *The Psychology of Investing*, 2nd edn, Pearson Education/Prentice Hall.

Nofsinger, J. R. (2005a). 'Social Mood and Financial Economics', *Journal of Behavioral Finance*, 6.

Northcraft, G. and M. Neale (1987). 'Experts, Amateurs, and Real Estate: An Anchoring Perspective on Property Pricing Decisions', *Organizational Behavior and Human Decision Processes*, 39.

Nunn, K.; G. P. Madden, and M. Gombola (1983). 'Are Some Investors More "Inside" Than Others?', *Journal of Portfolio Management*, 9.

Nygren, T. E.; A. M. Isen, P. J. Taylor, and J. Dulin (1996). 'The Influence of Positive Affect on the Decision Rule in Risk Situations: Focus on Outcome (and Especially Avoidance of Loss) Rather Than Probability', *Organizational Behavior and Human Decision Processes*, 66.

O'Brien, C.; P. Fenn, and S. Diacon (2005). 'How Long Do People Expect to Live? Results and Implications', Nottingham University Centre for Risk and Insurance Studies Research Report 2005–1.

Odean, T. (1998). 'Are Investors Reluctant to Realize their Losses?', *Journal of Finance*, 53.

Odean, T. (1998a). 'Volume, Volatility, Price and Profit When All Traders are Above Average', *Journal of Finance*, 53.

Odean, T. (1999). 'Do Investors Trade Too Much?', *American Economic Review*, 89.

Odean, T. (2001). 'Behavior of Mutual Fund Investors', Working Paper.

Office for National Statistics (2006). *Consumer Price Indices: Technical Manual*, HMSO.

Ohlson, J. A. (1995). 'Earnings, Book Value and Dividends in Equity Valuation', *Contemporary Accounting Research*, 11.

Ojasalo, J. (2001). 'Managing Customer Expectations in Professional Services', *Managing Service Quality*, 11.

Olsen, R. A. (1997). 'Investment Risk: The Experts' Perspective', *Financial Analysts Journal*, 53.

Olsen, R. A. (1998). 'Behavioral Finance and its Implications for Stock-Price Volatility', *Financial Analysts Journal*, 54.

Olson, K. R. (2006). 'A Literature Review of Social Mood', *Journal of Behavioral Finance*, 7.

Osborne, M. F. M. (1959). 'Brownian Motion in the Stock Market', *Operations Research*, March–April.

Osler, C. L. (1998). 'Identifying Noise Traders: The Head-and-Shoulders Pattern in U.S. Equities', *Federal Reserve Bank of New York Staff Reports*, 42.

Ou, J. A. and S. H. Penman (1989). 'Financial Statement Analysis and the Prediction of Stock Returns', *Journal of Accounting and Economics*, 11.

Paas, L. J.; T. H. A. Bijmolt, and J. K. Vermunt (2007). 'Acquisitional Patterns of Financial Products: A Longitudinal Investigation', *Journal of Economic Psychology*, 28.

Palacios, R. and M. Pallares-Miralles (2000). *International Patterns of Pension Provision*, World Bank.

Panchenko, V. (2007). 'Impact of Analysts' Recommendations on Stock Performance', *European Journal of Finance*, 13.

Papke, L. E. (2003). 'Individual Financial Decisions in Retirement Plans: The Role of Participant Direction', *Journal of Public Economics*, 88.

Park, C-L. and S. H. Irwin (2004). 'The Profitability of Technical Analysis: A Review', AgMAS Project Research Report No. 2004–04.

Parrino, R.; R. W. Sias, and L. T. Starks (2003). 'Voting with Their Feet: Institutional Ownership Changes around Forced CEO Turnover', *Journal of Financial Economics*, 68.

Pastor, L. (2001). 'A Model Weighting Game in Estimating Expected Returns', *Financial Times*, Mastering Investment Supplement, 21 May.

Pastor, L. and R. Stambaugh (2001). 'Liquidity Risk and Expected Stock Returns', University of Chicago Working Paper.

Payne, J. (1973). 'Alternative Approaches to Decision Making Under Risk: Moments vs Risk Dimensions', *Psychological Bulletin*, 80.

Pearce, D. K. and V. V.Roley (1985). 'Stock Prices and Economic News', *Journal of Business*, 58.

Peers, A. (1992). 'Insiders Reap Big Gains from Big Trades', *Wall Street Journal*, 23 September.

Pepper, G. and M. J. Oliver (2006). *The Liquidity Theory of Asset Prices*, Wiley.

Pesaran, M. H. and A. Timmermann (1994). 'Forecasting Stock Returns: An Examination of Stock Market Trading in the Presence of Transaction Costs', *Journal of Forecasting*, 13.

Peters, E. E. (1991). *Chaos and Order in the Capital Markets*, Wiley.

Peters, E. E. (1994). *Fractal Market Analysis: Applying Chaos Theory to Investment and Economics*, Wiley.

Peterson, D. and G. Pitz (1988). 'Confidence, Uncertainty, and the Use of Information', *Journal of Experimental Psychology*, 14.

Pettit, R. R. (1972). 'Dividend Announcements, Security Performance and Capital Market Efficiency', *Journal of Finance*, 25.

Pilbeam, K. (2005). *Finance and Financial Markets*, 2nd edn, Palgrave Macmillan.

Plous, S. (1993). *The Psychology of Judgment and Decision Making*, McGraw-Hill.

Pontiff, J. (1996). 'Costly Arbitrage: Evidence from Closed-End Funds', *Quarterly Journal of Economics*, 111.

881

Pope, P. F.; R. C. Morris, and D. A. Peel (1990). 'Insider Trading: Some Evidence on Market Efficiency and Directors' Share Dealings in Great Britain', *Journal of Business Finance and Accounting*, 17.

Poterba, J. M. and L. H. Summers (1988). 'Mean Reversion in Stock Prices: Evidence and Implications', *Journal of Financial Economics*, 22.

Pratt, M. J. (1993). 'Using a Z Score: The Bank of England's Experience', *Economia Aziendale*, 12.

Prechter, R. R. (1999). *The Wave Principle of Human Social Behavior and the New Science of Socionomics*, New Classics Library.

Prechter, R. R. (2001). 'Unconscious Herding Behavior as the Psychological Basis of Financial Market Trends and Patterns', *Journal of Psychology and Financial Markets*, 2.

Prechter, R. R. and W. D. Parker (2007). 'The Financial/Economic Dichotomy in Social Behavioral Dynamics: The Socionomic Perspective', *Journal of Behavioral Finance*, 8.

Prelec, D. and G. Loewenstein (1998). 'The Red and the Black: Mental Accounting of Savings and Debt', *Marketing Science*, 17.

Presson, P. and V. Benassi (1996). 'Illusion of Control: A Meta-Analytic Review', *Journal of Social Behavior and Personality*, 11.

Prudential (2006). 'Principles & Practices of Financial Management', Prudential Assurance Company Limited.

Rabinovich, A. and P. Webley (2007). 'Filling the Gap Between Planning and Doing: Psychological Factors Involved in the Successful Implementation of Saving Intention', *Journal of Economic Psychology*, 28.

Rachev, S. T.; A. Weron, and R. Weron (1999). 'A DEC Model for Asset Returns and the Fractal Market Hypothesis', *Mathematical and Computer Modelling*, 29.

Rahman, S. (2001). 'The Introduction of Derivatives on the Dow Jones Industrial Average and Their Impact on the Volatility of Component Stocks', *Journal of Futures Markets*, 21.

Raines, J. P.; J. A. McLeod and C. G. Leathers (2007). 'Theories of Stock Prices and the Greenspan-Bernanke Doctrine on Stock Market Bubbles', *Journal of Post Keynesian Economics*, 29.

Ramachandran, A. (2006). 'Profiling Could Be a Risky Venture for Advisers', *Money Management* (Australia), 17 August.

Randall, M. R.; D. Y. Suk, and S. W. Tully (2003). 'Mutual Fund Cash Flows and Stock Market Performance', *Journal of Investing*, 12.

Rapson, D.; D. Shiers, C. Roberts, and M. Keeping (2007). 'Socially Responsible Property Investment (SRPI): An Analysis of the Relationship between Equities SRI and UK Property Investment Activities', *Journal of Property Investment & Finance*, 25.

Ray, R. (2006). 'Prediction Markets and the Financial "Wisdom of Crowds"', *Journal of Behavioral Finance*, 7.

Read, D.; G. Loewenstein, and M. Rabin (1999). 'Choice Bracketing', *Journal of Risk and Uncertainty*, 19.

Ready, M. J. (2002). 'Profits from Technical Trading Rules', *Financial Management*, 31.

Reber, R. and N. Schwartz (1999). 'Effects of Perceptual Fluency on Judgements of Truth', *Consciousness and Cognition*, 8.

Redhead, K. (1976). 'Stock Appreciation and the Definition of Profit – A Macroeconomic Perspective', *Journal of Business Finance and Accounting*, 3.

Redhead, K. (1981). 'On Keynesian Economics and the Economics of Keynes: A Suggested Interpretation', *Bulletin of Economic Research*, 33.

Redhead, K. (1994). 'Hedging – How Many Futures or Options Contracts?', *Treasury Management International*, May.

Redhead, K. (1995). 'Calculating Numbers of Futures and Options Contracts Required for Hedging', in P. Stonham and K. Redhead (eds) *European Casebook on Finance*, Prentice Hall.

Redhead, K. (1997). *Financial Derivatives*, Prentice Hall.

Redhead, K. (1999). *Risk Management with Futures and Options,* Prentice Hall.

Reichenstein, W. (1999). 'Bond Fund Returns and Expenses: A Study of Bond Market Efficiency', *Journal of Investing,* 8.

Reinganum, M. R. (1981). 'Misspecification of Capital Asset Pricing: Empirical Anomalies Based on Earnings Yield and Market Values', *Journal of Financial Economics,* 9.

Reinganum, M. R. (1999). 'The Significance of Market Capitalization in Portfolio Management over Time', *Journal of Portfolio Management,* 25.

Rhodes, M. (2000). 'Past Imperfect? The Performance of UK Equity Managed Funds', Financial Services Authority, Occasional Paper OP09.

Richards, A. J. (1997). 'Winner–Loser Reversals in National Stock Market Indices: Can They be Explained?', *Journal of Finance,* 52.

Richards, M. (2007). 'Derivatives Become More User-Friendly', *Financial Times (FTMoney),* 17/18 March.

Riess, M. and J. Taylor (1984). 'Ego-Involvement and Attributions for Success and Failure in a Field Setting', *Personality and Social Psychology Bulletin,* 10.

Ritter, J. R. (2005). 'Economic Growth and Equity Returns', *Pacific-Basin Finance Journal,* 13.

Roberts, H. (1959). 'Stock Market "Patterns" and Financial Analysis: Methodological Suggestions', *Journal of Finance,* 14.

Roberts, R. (2004). *The City: A Guide to London's Global Financial Centre,* The Economist/Profile Books.

Roll, R. (1977). 'A Critique of the Capital Asset Theory Tests: Part I: On Past and Potential Testability of the Theory', *Journal of Financial Economics,* 4.

Roll, R. (1988). 'The International Crash of October 1987', *Financial Analysts Journal,* 44.

Roll, R. (1988a). 'R^2', *Journal of Finance,* 43.

Roll, R. (1995). 'Style Return Differentials: Illusions, Risk Premiums, or Investment Opportunities', in T. D.Coggin and F. J. Fabozzi (eds) *The Handbook of Equity Style Investment,* Frank J. Fabozzi Associates.

Roll, R. and S. A. Ross (1980). 'An Empirical Investigation of the APT', *Journal of Finance,* 35.

Rosenberg, B. and J. Guy (1976). 'Prediction of Beta from Investment Fundamentals', *Financial Analysts Journal,* 32.

Rosenberg, B.; K. Reid, and R. Lanstein (1985). 'Persuasive Evidence of Market Inefficiency', *Journal of Portfolio Management,* 11.

Ross, S. A. (1976). 'The Arbitrage Theory of Capital Asset Pricing', *Journal of Economic Theory,* December.

Ross, S. A. (2002). 'Neoclassical Finance, Alternative Finance and the Closed End Fund Puzzle', *European Financial Management,* 8.

Rozeff, M. S. and W. R. Kinney (1976). 'Capital Market Seasonality: The Case of Stock Returns', *Journal of Financial Economics,* 3.

Rozeff, M. S. and M. A. Zaman (1988). 'Market Efficiency and Insider Trading: New Evidence', *Journal of Business,* 61.

Rudd, A. (1980). 'Optimal Selection of Passive Portfolios', *Financial Management,* 9.

Rutterford, J. (2007). 'Savings and Investments', in G. Callaghan; I. Fribbance, and M. Higginson (eds) *Personal Finance,* Wiley.

Ryan, P. and I. Overmeyer (2004). 'Profitability of Price Momentum Strategies: The DAX 100 Evidence', *Journal of Investing,* 13.

Samuelson, P. A. (1998). 'Summing Up On Business Cycles', in J. C. Fuhrer and S. Schuh (eds) *Beyond Shocks: What Causes Business Cycles,* Federal Reserve Bank of Boston.

Samuelson, W. and R. Zeckhauser (1988). 'Status Quo Bias in Decision Making', *Journal of Risk and Uncertainty,* 1.

883

REFERENCES

Sandelands, L. E.; J. Brockner, and M. A. Glynn (1988). 'If At First You Don't Succeed, Try, Try Again: Effects of Persistence Performance Contingencies, Ego Involvement, and Self-Esteem on Task Persistence', *Journal of Applied Psychology*, 73.

Sapp, T. and A. Tiwari (2005). 'Does Stock Return Momentum Explain the 'Smart Money' Effect?', *Journal of Finance*, 59.

Sapp, T. and A. Tiwari (2006). 'Stock Return Momentum and Investor Fund Choices', *Journal of Investment Management*, 4.

Sarno, L.; D. L. Thornton, and G. Valente (2007). 'The Empirical Failure of the Expectations Hypothesis of the Term Structure of Bond Yields', *Journal of Financial and Quantitative Analysis*, 42.

Schachter, S.; D. C. Hood, P. B. Andreassen, and W. Gerin (1986). 'Aggregate Variables in Psychology and Economics: Dependence and the Stock Market', in B. Gilad and S. Kaish (eds) *Handbook of Behavioral Economics*, Vol. B, JAI Press.

Scheicher, M. (2000). 'Time-Varying Risk in the German Stock Market', *European Journal of Finance*, 6.

Schiereck, D.; W. De Bondt, and M. Weber (1999). 'Contrarian and Momentum Strategies in Germany', *Financial Analysts Journal*, 55.

Schilit, H.M. (1993). *Financial Shenanigans: How to Detect Accounting Gimmicks and Fraud in Financial Reports*, McGraw-Hill.

Schlarbaum, G. G.; W. G. Lewellen, and R. C. Lease (1978). 'Realized Returns on Common Stock Investments: The Experience of Individual Investors', *Journal of Business*, 51.

Schwaiger, W. S. A. (1995). 'A Note on GARCH Predictable Variances and Stock Market Efficiency', *Journal of Banking and Finance*, 19.

Schwartz, R. A. (1988). *Equity Markets: Structure, Trading and Performance*, Harper Business. *European Journal of Social Psychology*, 17.

Schwarz, N.; F. Strack, D. Kommer, and D. Wagner (1987). 'Soccer, Rooms, and the Quality of Your Life: Mood Effects on Judgements of Satisfaction with Life in General and with Specific Domains',

Scott, J. and G. Stein (2004). 'The Impact of Advice on Employee Behavior and Retirement Prospects', in O. Mitchell and S. Utkus (eds) *Pension Design and Structure: New Lessons from Behavioral Finance*, Oxford University Press.

Scottish Widows (2005). 'A Major Assessment of Pension Savings Behaviour'.

Senior, C. (2007). '130/30 Band Wagon Powers into Europe', *Professional Wealth Management*, 1 September.

Sethi-Iyengar, S.; G. Huberman, and W. Jiang (2004). 'How Much Choice is Too Much? Contributions to 401(k) Retirement Plans', in O. Mitchell and S. Utkus (eds) *Pension Design and Structure: New Lessons from Behavioral Finance*, Oxford University Press.

Setiono, B. and N. Strong (1998). 'Predicting Stock Returns Using Financial Statement Information', *Journal of Business Finance and Accounting*, 25.

Seyhun, H. N. (1988). 'The Information Content of Aggregate Insider Trading', *Journal of Business*, 61.

Seyhun, H. N. (1992). 'Why Does Aggregate Insider Trading Predict Future Stock Returns?', *Quarterly Journal of Economics*, 107.

Shadwick, W. F. and C. Keating (2002). 'A Universal Performance Measure', *Journal of Performance Measurement*, 6.

Shafir, E.; P. Diamond, and A. Tversky (1997). 'Money Illusion', *Quarterly Journal of Economics*, 112.

Shalen, C. (1993). 'Volume, Volatility, and the Dispersion of Beliefs', *Review of Financial Studies*, 6.

Sharpe, W. F. (1966). 'Mutual Fund Performance', *Journal of Business*, 39.

Sharpe, W. F. (1992). 'Asset Allocation: Management Style and Performance Evaluation', *Journal of Portfolio Management*, 19.

Sharpe, W. F. and G. M. Cooper (1972). 'Risk-Return Classes of New York Stock Exchange Common Stocks 1931–1967', *Financial Analysts Journal*, 28.

Shefrin, H. (2000). *Beyond Fear and Greed: Understanding Behavioral Finance and the Psychology of Investing*, Harvard Business School Press.

Shefrin, H. (2001). 'Behavioral Corporate Finance', *Journal of Applied Corporate Finance*, 14.

Shefrin, H. and M. Statman (1984). 'The Disposition to Sell Winners Too Early and Ride Losers Too Long: Theory and Evidence', *Journal of Finance*, 40.

Shefrin, H. and M. Statman (1984a). 'Explaining Investor Preference for Cash Dividends', *Journal of Financial Economics*, 13.

Shefrin, H. and M. Statman (1994). 'Behavioral Capital Asset Pricing Theory', *Journal of Financial and Quantitative Analysis*, 29.

Shefrin, H. and M. Statman (1997). 'Comparing Expectations about Stock Returns to Realized Returns', Leavey School of Business, Santa Clara University.

Shefrin, H. and M. Statman (2000). 'Behavioral Portfolio Theory', *Journal of Financial and Quantitative Analysis*, 35.

Shefrin, H. and R. Thaler (1992). 'Mental Accounting, Saving, and Self-Control', in G. Loewenstein and J. Elster, (eds) *Choice Over Time*, Russell Sage Foundation.

Shiller, R. J. (1981). 'Do Stock Prices Move Too Much to be Justified by Subsequent Changes in Dividends?', *American Economic Review*, 71.

Shiller, R. J. (1984). 'Stock Prices and Social Dynamics', *Brookings Papers on Economic Activity*, 2.

Shiller, R. J. (1987). 'Investor Behavior in the October 1987 Stock Market Crash: Survey Evidence', National Bureau of Economic Research, Working Paper No. 2446.

Shiller, R. J. (1988). 'Fashions, Fads, and Bubbles in Financial Markets', in J. C. Coffee; L. Lowenstein, and S. Rose-Ackeman (eds) *Knights, Raiders and Targets*, Oxford University Press.

Shiller, R. J. (1989). *Market Volatility*, MIT Press.

Shiller, R. J. (2000). *Irrational Exuberance*, Princeton University Press.

Shiller, R. J. (2005). *Irrational Exuberance*, 2nd edn, Princeton University Press.

Shiller, R. J. and J. Pound (1989). 'Survey Evidence on Diffusion of Interest and Information Among Investors', *Journal of Economic Behavior and Organization*, 12.

Shiv, B. and A. Fedorikhin (1999). 'Heart and Mind in Conflict: Interplay of Affect and Cognition in Consumer Decision Making', *Journal of Consumer Research*, 26.

Shleifer, A. (2005). 'Understanding Regulation', *European Financial Management*, 11.

Shleifer, A. and L. H. Summers (1990). 'The Noise Trader Approach to Finance', *Journal of Economic Perspectives*, 4.

Shleifer, A. and R. Vishny (1997). 'Limits to Arbitrage', *Journal of Finance*, 52.

Shugan, S. M. (1980). 'The Cost of Thinking', *Journal of Consumer Research*, 7.

Shukla, R. (2004). 'The Value of Active Portfolio Management', *Journal of Economics and Business*, 56.

Siebenmorgen, N. and M. Weber (2003). 'A Behavioural Model for Asset Allocation', *Financial Markets and Portfolio Management*, 17.

Siegel, J. (1991). 'Does it Pay Stock Investors to Forecast the Business Cycle?', *Journal of Portfolio Management*, 18.

Siegel, J. (1998). *Stocks for the Long Run*, 2nd edn, McGraw-Hill.

Siegel, J. (2001). 'Markets and the Business Cycle', *Financial Times, Mastering Investment Supplement*, Part 2. Reprinted in K. Redhead, *Introducing Investments*, Financial Times/ Prentice Hall, 2003.

Simon, D. P. and R. A. Wiggins III (2001). 'S&P Futures Returns and Contrary Sentiment Indicators', *Journal of Futures Markets*, 21.

Simon, H. (1955). 'A Behavioral Model of Rational Choice', *Quarterly Journal of Economics*, 69.

Singh, R. A. (1993). 'Response of Stock Prices to Money Supply Announcements: Australian Evidence', *Accounting and Finance*, 33.

Sirri, E. and P. Tufano (1998). 'Costly Search and Mutual Funds Flows', *Journal of Finance*, 53.

Sjoberg, L. (2001). 'Limits of Knowledge and the Limited Importance of Trust', *Risk Analysis*, 21.

Slovic, P.; M. Finucane, E. Peters, and D. MacGregor (2002). 'The Affect Heuristic', in T Gilovich; D. Griffin, and D. Kahneman (eds) *Heuristics and Biases: The Psychology of Intuitive Judgment*, Cambridge University Press.

Smith, M. P. (1996). 'Shareholder Activism by Institutional Investors: Evidence from CalPERS', *Journal of Finance*, 51.

Smith, T. (1996). *Accounting for Growth: Stripping the Camouflage from Company Accounts*, 2nd edn, Century Business.

Smith, V. L. (1991). 'Rational Choice: The Contrast Between Economics and Psychology', *Journal of Political Economy*, 99.

Solt, M. and M. Statman (1989). 'Good Companies, Bad Stocks', *Journal of Portfolio Management*, 15.

Song, W-L.; S. H. Szewczyk, and A. Safieddine (2003). 'Does Coordinated Institutional Investor Activism Reverse the Fortunes of Underperforming Firms?', *Journal of Financial and Quantitative Analysis*, 38.

Spurgin, R. and M. Tamarkin (2005). 'Switching Investments Can Be a Bad Idea When Parrondo's Paradox Applies', *Journal of Behavioral Finance*, 6.

Stanley, K.; W. G. Lewellen, and G. G. Schlarbaum (1981). 'Further Evidence on the Value of Professional Investment Research', *Journal of Financial Research*, 4.

Statman, M. (1997). 'Behavioral Finance', *Contemporary Finance Digest*, 1.

Statman, M. (2005). 'The Religions of Social Responsibility', *Journal of Investing*, 14.

Statman, M.; S. Thorley, and K. Vorkink (2006). 'Investor Overconfidence and Trading Volume', *Review of Financial Studies*, 19.

Stephenson, K. (1997). 'Just How Bad are Economists at Predicting Interest Rates?', *Journal of Investing*, 6.

Stevenson, S. (2004). 'Testing the Statistical Significance of Real Estate in an International Mixed Asset Portfolio', *Journal of Property Investment & Finance*, 22.

Stewart, S. D. (1998). 'Is Consistency of Performance a Good Measure of Manager Skill?', *Journal of Portfolio Management*, 24.

Stickel, S. E. (1985). 'The Effect of Value Line Investment Survey Rank Changes on Common Stock Prices', *Journal of Financial Economics*, 14.

Stone, B. and R. V. Maury (2006). 'Indicators of Personal Financial Debt Using a Multi-Disciplinary Behavioral Model', *Journal of Economic Psychology*, 27.

Strong, N. and X. G. Xu (1997). 'Explaining the Cross-Section of UK Expected Stock Returns', *British Accounting Review*, 29.

Strong, N. and X. G. Xu (2003). 'Understanding the Equity Home Bias: Evidence from Survey Data', *Review of Economics and Statistics*, 85.

Stulz, R. (2001). 'Why Risk Management is Not Rocket Science', in J. Pickford (ed.) *Mastering Risk: Volume 1: Concepts*, Pearson Education.

Sullivan, R.; A. Timmermann, and H. White (1999). 'Data-Snooping, Technical Trading Rule Performance, and the Bootstrap', *Journal of Finance*, 54.

Summers, L. H. (1986). 'Do We Really Know that Financial Markets are Efficient?', in J. Edwards; J. Franks, C. Mayer, and S. Schaefer (eds) *Recent Developments in Corporate Finance*, Cambridge University Press.

Sunder, S. (1973). 'Relationship between Accounting Changes and Stock Prices: Problems of Measurement and Some Empirical Evidence', *Journal of Accounting Research*, 10, 'Empirical Research in Accounting: Selected Studies', supplement.

Swaminathan, B. and C. Lee (2000). 'Do Stock Prices Overreact to Earnings News?', Cornell University Working Paper.

Swank, P. B.; M. A. Rosen, and J. W. Goebel (2002). 'The Next Step: 100% Equity Allocation for Pension Plans', *Journal of Investing*, 11.

Sweeney, R. J. (1988). 'Some New Filter Rule Tests: Methods and Results', *Journal of Financial and Quantitative Analysis*, 23.

Sweeney, R. J. (1990). 'Evidence on Short-Term Trading Strategies', *Journal of Portfolio Management*, 16.

Swisher, P. and G. W. Kasten (2005). 'Post-Modern Portfolio Theory', *Journal of Financial Planning*, September.

Taffler, R. J. (1983). 'The Assessment of Company Solvency and Performance Using a Statistical Model', *Accounting and Business Research*, 15.

Taffler, R. J. (1997). 'Enhancing Equity Returns with Z-Scores', *Professional Investor*, 7.

Taffler, R. J. and D. A. Tuckett (2002). 'Anomalous Valuations of Internet Stocks: A Psychoanalytic Interpretation of dot.com Mania', Sixth Annual Financial Reporting and Business Communication Conference, Cardiff Business School.

Tang, L.; L. C. Thomas, S. Thomas, and J-F. Bozzetto (2007). 'It's the Economy Stupid: Modelling Financial Product Purchases', *International Journal of Bank Marketing*, 25.

Taylor, S. E. and D. A. Armor (1996). 'Positive Illusions and Coping with Adversity', *Journal of Personality*, 64.

Taylor, S. J. (2001). 'Stock Index and Price Dynamics in the UK and the US: New Evidence from a Trading Rule and Statistical Analysis', *European Journal of Finance*, 6.

Tetlock, P. C. (2007). 'Giving Content to Investor Sentiment: The Role of Media in the Stock Market', *Journal of Finance*, 62.

Thaler, R. (1980). 'Towards a Positive Theory of Consumer Choice', *Journal of Economic Behavior and Organization*, 1.

Thaler, R. (1985). 'Mental Accounting and Consumer Choice', *Marketing Science*, 4.

Thaler, R. (1994). 'Psychology and Savings Policies', *American Economic Review*, 84.

Thaler, R. and H. Shefrin (1981). 'An Economic Theory of Self-Control', *Journal of Political Economy*, 89.

Thaler, R. and E. Johnson (1990). 'Gambling with the House Money and Trying to Break Even: The Effects of Poor Outcomes on Risky Choice', *Management Science*, 36.

Thaler, R. and O. Lamont (2000). 'Can the Market Add and Subtract?', University of Chicago Working Paper.

Tice, D.; E. Bratslavsky, and R. Baumeister (2001). 'Emotional Distress Regulation Takes Precedence Over Impulse Control: If You Feel Bad, Do It!', *Journal of Personality and Social Psychology*, 80.

Tourani-Rad, A. and S. Kirkby (2005). 'Investigation of Investors' Overconfidence, Familiarity and Socialization', *Accounting and Finance*, 45.

Treynor, J. L. and K. Mazuy (1966). 'Can Mutual Funds Outguess the Market?', *Harvard Business Review*, 43.

Trumble, R. R. and F. Cavazotte (2000). 'The Role of Behavioral Finance and Retirement Education', *Journal of Compensation and Benefits*, 16.

Tumarkin, R. and R. F. Whitelaw (2001). 'News or Noise? Internet Postings and Stock Prices', *Financial Analysts Journal*, 57.

Tunbridge Wells Equitable (2006). 'The *Children's* Mutual – A Guide to our With-Profits Fund'.

Turner, J. (2004). 'Individual Accounts: Lessons from Sweden', *International Social Security Review*, 57.

Turner, J. (2006). 'Designing 401(k) Plans That Encourage Retirement Savings: Lessons from Behavioral Finance', *Benefits Quarterly*, 22.

Tversky, A. and D. Kahneman (1974). 'Judgement Under Uncertainty: Heuristics and Biases', *Science*, 185.

Tversky, A. and D. Kahneman (1982). 'Judgment Under Uncertainty: Heuristics and Biases', in D. Kahneman; P. Slovic, and A. Tversky (eds) *Judgment Under Uncertainty: Heuristics and Biases*, Cambridge University Press.

887

Tversky, A. and D. Kahneman (1982a). 'Belief in the Law of Small Numbers', in D. Kahneman; P. Slovic, and A. Tversky (eds) *Judgment Under Uncertainty: Heuristics and Biases*, Cambridge University Press.

Tversky, A. and D. Kahneman (1982b). 'Causal Schemas in Judgments Under Uncertainty', in D. Kahneman; P. Slovic, and A. Tversky (eds) *Judgment Under Uncertainty: Heuristics and Biases*, Cambridge University Press.

Tversky, A. and D. Kahneman (1982c). 'Evidential Impact of Base Rates', in D. Kahneman; P. Slovic, and A. Tversky (eds) *Judgment Under Uncertainty: Heuristics and Biases*, Cambridge University Press.

Tversky, A. and D. Kahneman (1982d). 'Availability: A Heuristic for Judging Frequency and Probability', in D. Kahneman; P. Slovic, and A. Tversky (eds) *Judgment Under Uncertainty: Heuristics and Biases*, Cambridge University Press.

Tversky, A. and E. Shafir (1992). 'Choice under Conflict: The Dynamics of Deferred Decision', *Psychological Science*, 3.

Valdez, S. (2007). *An Introduction to Global Financial Markets*, 5th edn, Palgrave Macmillan.

Van de Velde, E.; W. Vermeir, and F. Corten (2005). 'Corporate Social Responsibility and Financial Performance', *Corporate Governance*, 5.

Vandewalle, N.; M. Ausloos, P. Boveroux, and A. Minguet (1999). 'Visualizing the Log-Periodic Pattern before Crashes', *European Physics Journal*, 9.

Van Eaton, R. D. and J. Conover (2002). 'Equity Allocations and the Investment Horizon: A Total Portfolio Approach', *Financial Services Review*, 11.

Varki, S.; S. Sabherwal, A. D. Bitta, and K. M. Moore (2006). 'Price-End Biases in Financial Products', *Journal of Product & Brand Management*, 15.

Vaugirard, V. E. (2003). 'Pricing Catastrophe Bonds by an Arbitrage Approach', *Quarterly Review of Economics and Finance*, 43.

Veres, B. (2006). 'Beyond the Pyramid', *Financial Planning*, March.

Vergin, R. C. (1996). 'Market-Timing Strategies: Can You Get Rich?', *Journal of Investing*, 5.

Vespro, C. (2006). 'Stock Price and Volume Effects Associated with Compositional Changes in European Stock Indices', *European Financial Management*, 12.

Volkman, D. A. (1999). 'Market Volatility and Perverse Timing Performance of Mutual Fund Managers', *Journal of Financial Research*, 22.

Wadhwani, S. and M. Shah (1993). *Valuation Indicators and Stock Market Prediction: 1*, Goldman Sachs.

Walter, A. and F. M. Weber (2006). 'Herding in the German Mutual Fund Industry', *European Financial Management*, 12.

Warther, V. A. (1995). 'Aggregate Mutual Fund Flow and Security Returns', *Journal of Financial Economics*, 39.

Watson, J. J. (2003). 'The Relationship of Materialism to Spending Tendencies, Saving, and Debt', *Journal of Economic Psychology*, 24.

Weber, E. U.; N. Siebenmorgen, and M. Weber (2005). 'Communicating Asset Risk: How Name Recognition and the Format of Historic Volatility Information Affect Risk Perception and Investment Decisions', *Risk Analysis*, 25.

Weber, M. and F. Welfens (2006). 'The Disposition Effect, Individual Differences, Stability, and Learning: An Experimental Investigation', paper presented to the Behavioural Finance and Market Efficiency Workshop, University of Warwick, March.

Webley, P.; A. Lewis, and C. Mackenzie (2001). 'Commitment Among Ethical Investors: An Experimental Approach', *Journal of Economic Psychology*, 22.

Weidig, T.; A. Kemmerer, and B. Born (2005). 'The Risk Profile of Private Equity Funds of Funds', *Journal of Alternative Investments*, 7.

Weigand, R. A.; S. Belden, and T. J. Zwirlein (2004). 'Stock Selection Based on Mutual Fund Holdings: Evidence from Large-Cap Funds', *Financial Services Review*, 13.

Weigel, E. J. (1991). 'The Performance of Tactical Asset Allocation', *Financial Analysts Journal*, 47.

Welch, I. (2000). 'Herding among Security Analysts', *Journal of Financial Economics*, 58.

Wermers, R. (2000). 'Mutual Fund Performance: An Empirical Decomposition into Stock-Picking Talent, Style, Transactions Costs, and Expenses', *Journal of Finance*, 55.

Whitbeck, V. S. and M. Kisor (1963). 'A New Tool in Investment Decision-Making', *Financial Analysts Journal*, 19.

Williams, L. V. (1994). 'Market "Anomalies" as Evidence of Market "Inefficiency": The State of the Debate', Occasional Paper in Economics, Department of Economics and Public Administration, Nottingham Trent University.

Winnett, A. and A. Lewis (2000). '"You'd Have to Be Green to Invest in This": Popular Economic Models, Financial Journalism, and Ethical Investment', *Journal of Economic Psychology*, 21.

Witan Investment Trust PLC (2006). 'Report & Accounts 2005'.

Womack, K. (1996). 'Do Brokerage Analysts' Recommendations Have Investment Value?', *Journal of Finance*, 51.

Woolridge, J. R. (2004). 'Performance of Stocks Recommended by Brokerages', *Journal of Investing*, 13.

Wright, W. and G. Bower (1992). 'Mood Effects on Subjective Probability Assessment', *Organizational Behavior and Human Decision Processes*, 52.

Yao, R.; S. D. Hanna, and S. Lindamood (2004). 'Changes in Financial Risk Tolerance, 1983-2001', *Financial Services Review*, 13.

Yook, K. C. and R. Everett (2003). 'Assessing Risk Tolerance: Questioning the Questionnaire Method', *Journal of Financial Planning*, August.

Young, M. S. and R. A. Graff (1996). 'Systematic Behavior in Real Estate Investment Risk: Performance Persistence in NCREIF Returns', *Journal of Real Estate Research*, 12.

Young, M. S. and R. A. Graff (1997). 'Performance Persistence in Equity Real Estate Returns', *Real Estate Finance*, 14.

Yuen, K. S. L. and T. M. C. Lee (2003). 'Could Mood State Affect Risk-Taking Decisions?', *Journal of Affective Disorders*, 75.

Yuh, Y. and S. A. DeVaney (1996). 'Determinants of Couples' Defined Contribution Retirement Funds', *Financial Counseling and Planning*, 7.

Zavgren, C. V.; M. T. Dugan, and J. M. Reeve (1988). 'The Association between Probabilities of Bankruptcy and Market Responses – A Test of Market Anticipation', *Journal of Business Finance and Accounting*, 15.

Zielonka, P. (2004). 'Technical Analysis as the Representation of Typical Cognitive Biases', *International Review of Financial Analysis*, 13.

Zweig, M. E. (1986). *Martin Zweig's Winning on Wall Street*, Warner.

Zweig, M. E. (2000). 'You Get the Clients You Deserve', in *Ethical Issues for Today's Firm*, AIMR.

Index

909